KEY TO MAP PAGES II

ADMINISTRATIVE & POSTCODE BOUNDARIES IV

MAP SYMBOLS VI

STREET MAPS 1

KEY TO CENTRAL LONDON MAPS, SYMBOLS 77

CENTRAL LONDON ENLARGED MAPS 78

PHILIP'S STREET ATLAS OF LONDON

INDEX 174

LIST OF NUMBERED LOCATIONS 288

NOTES 304

CENTRAL LONDON THEATRES & CINEMAS 314

LONDON UNDERGROUND INSIDE BACK COVER

WWW.PHILIPS-MAPS.CO.UK

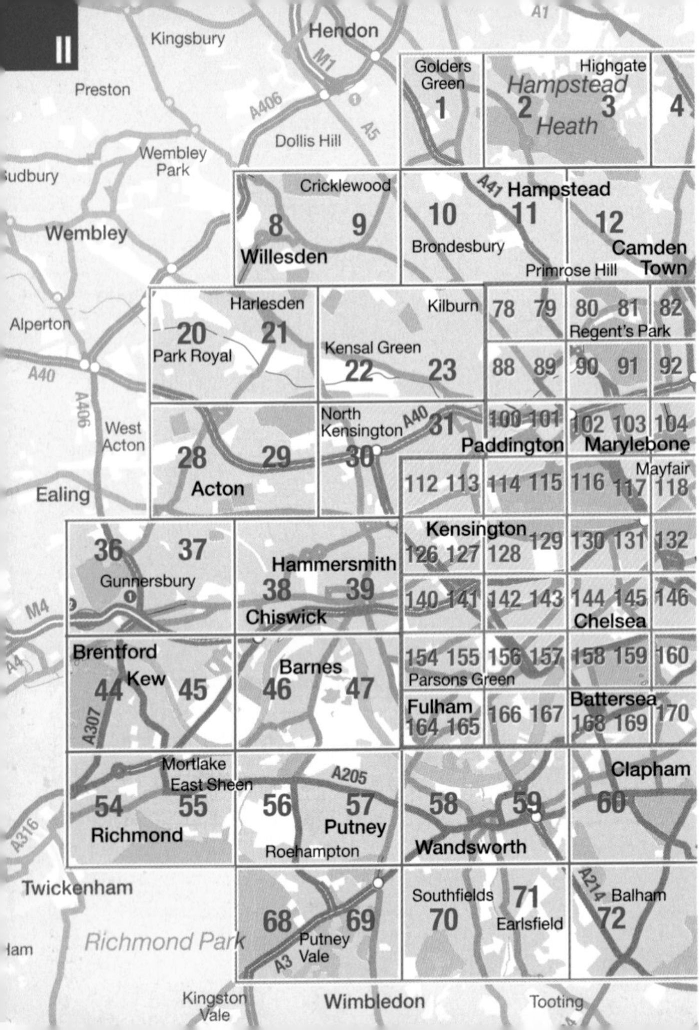
Kingsbury
Hendon
A1
M1
Preston
A406
A5
Dollis Hill
Golders Green
1
Highgate
Hampstead Heath
2
3
4
Wembley Park
Sudbury
Cricklewood
A41
Hampstead
10
11
12
8
9
Wembley
Willesden
Brondesbury
Camden Town
Primrose Hill
Harlesden
Kilburn
78
79
80
81
82
Regent's Park
Alperton
20
21
Park Royal
Kensal Green
22
23
88
89
90
91
92
A40
A406
West Acton
North Kensington
A40
31
100
101
102
103
104
Paddington
Marylebone
28
29
30
Acton
Ealing
Mayfair
112
113
114
115
116
117
118
Kensington
126
127
128
129
130
131
132
36
37
Gunnersbury
Hammersmith
38
39
Chiswick
M4
140
141
142
143
144
145
146
Chelsea
A4
Brentford
Kew
44
45
Barnes
46
47
154
155
156
157
158
159
160
Parsons Green
Fulham
164
165
166
167
Battersea
168
169
170
A307
Mortlake
East Sheen
A205
Clapham
54
55
56
57
58
59
60
Richmond
Putney
Roehampton
Wandsworth
A316
Twickenham
Southfields
71
70
Earlsfield
A214
Balham
72
68
69
Richmond Park
Putney Vale
A3
Kingston Vale
Wimbledon
Tooting

Key to map pages

Atlas pages at 3½ inches to 1 mile are shown in blue

Central London atlas pages at 7 inches to 1 mile are shown in red
(See page 77)

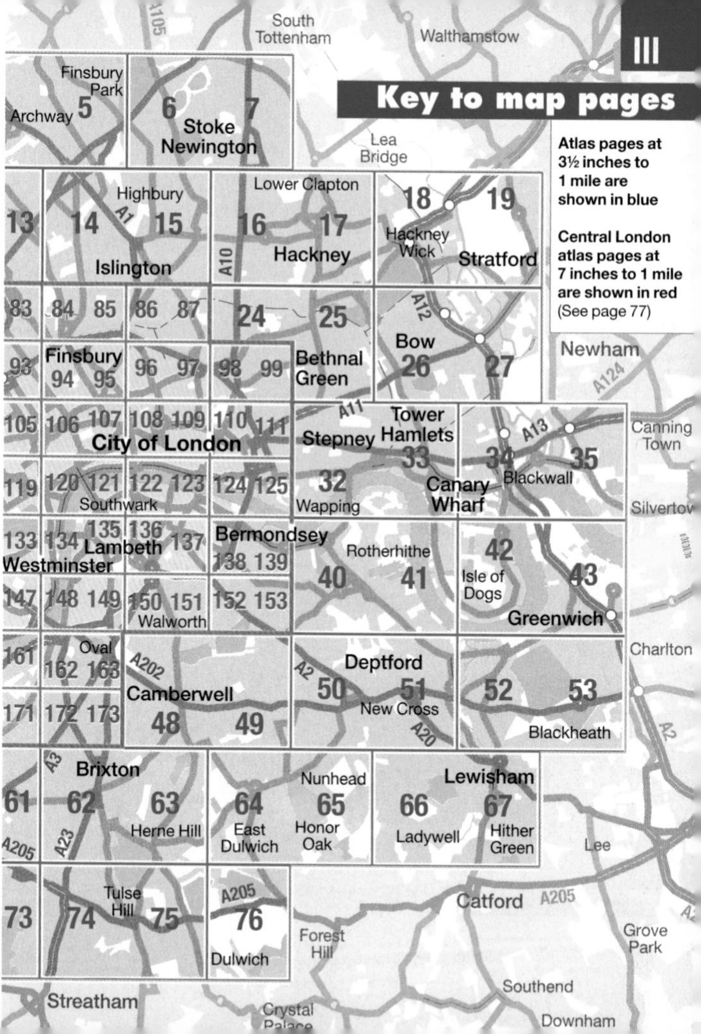

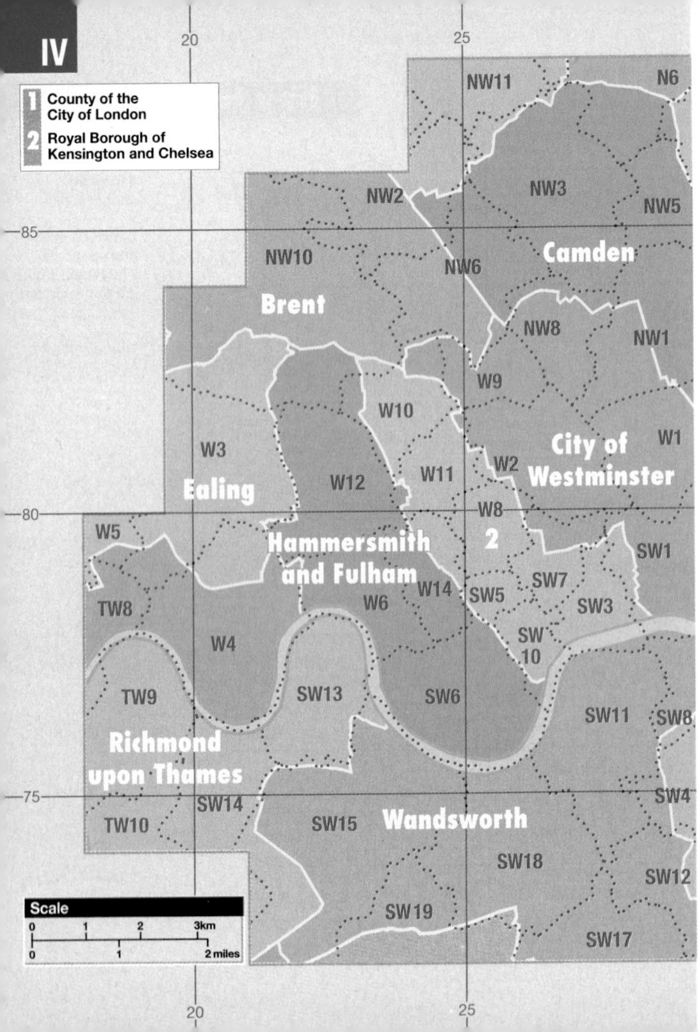
IV
1 County of the City of London
2 Royal Borough of Kensington and Chelsea
20
25
85
80
75
NW11
N6
NW2
NW3
NW5
NW10
NW6
Camden
Brent
NW8
NW1
W9
W10
W3
City of Westminster
W1
W2
Ealing
W12
W11
W8
W5
Hammersmith and Fulham
2
SW1
SW7
W14
SW5
SW3
TW8
W6
SW 10
W4
TW9
SW13
SW6
SW11
SW8
Richmond upon Thames
SW4
SW14
TW10
SW15
Wandsworth
SW18
SW12
SW19
SW17
Scale
0
1
2
3km
0
1
2 miles

Administrative and Postcode boundaries

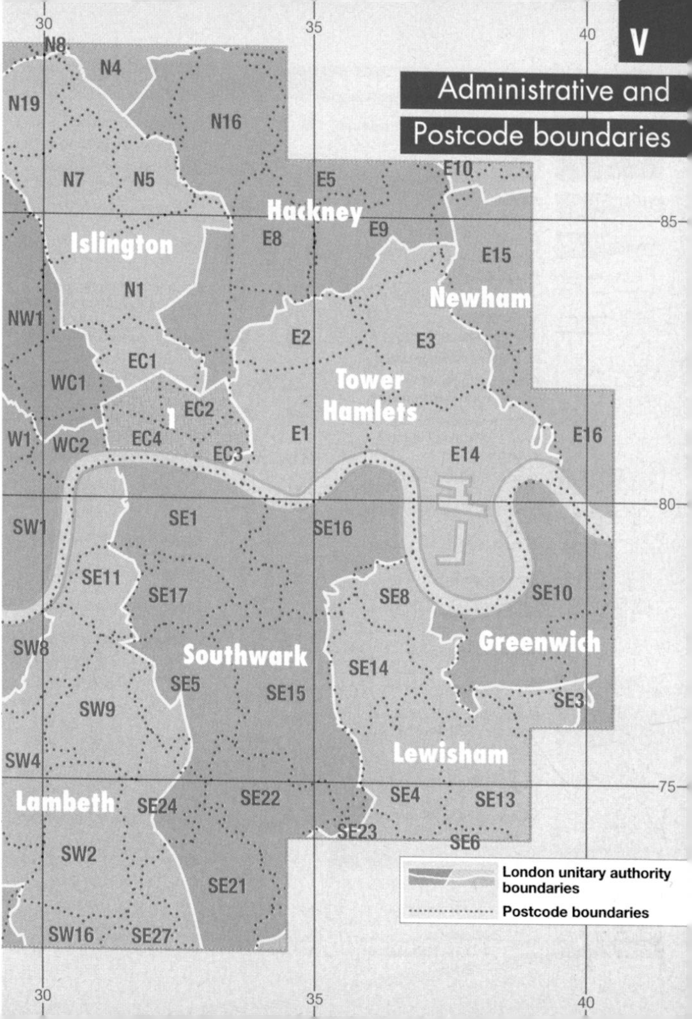

30
35
40
85
80
75
N8
N4
N19
N16
N7
N5
E10
E5
Hackney
E9
E8
Islington
E15
N1
Newham
NW1
E2
E3
EC1
WC1
Tower Hamlets
EC2
1
W1
WC2
EC4
EC3
E1
E16
E14
SW1
SE1
SE16
SE11
SE17
SE8
SE10
SW8
Southwark
Greenwich
SE14
SE5
SE15
SE3
SW9
Lewisham
SW4
Lambeth
SE24
SE22
SE4
SE13
SE23
SE6
SW2
SE21
SW16
SE27
London unitary authority boundaries
Postcode boundaries

Key to map symbols

- **Motorway** with junction number
- **Primary route** – single, dual carriageway
- **A road** – single, dual carriageway
- **B road** – single, dual carriageway
- **Through-route** – single, dual carriageway
- **Minor road** – single, dual carriageway
- **Road under construction**
- **Rural track, private road or narrow road in urban area**
- **Path, bridleway, byway open to all traffic, road used as public path**
- **Tunnel, covered road**
- **Speed camera** – single, multiple
- **Gate or barrier, car pound**
- **Parking, park and ride**
- **Junction name** (Three Legged Cross)
- **Pedestrianised area**
- **Restricted access area**
- **Congestion Charge Zone boundary** Roads within the zone are outlined in green
- **Houses, important buildings**
- **Woods, parkland/common**
- **Railway with station**
- **London Underground station**
- **Docklands Light Railway station**
- **Bus/coach station, tram stop**
- **Ambulance, police, fire station**
- **Hospital, accident and emergency entrance**
- **Market, public amenity site**
- **Sports stadium**
- **Information centre, post office**
- **Roman, non-Roman antiquity** (VILLA, House)
- **House number, spot height** – in metres (100, 304)
- **Christian place of worship**
- **Mosque, synagogue**
- **Other place of worship**
- **Adjoining page number** (65)
- **Postcode boundary** (NW6)
- **Unitary authority boundary** (City of Westminster)
- **Water, tidal water**
- **River or canal** – minor, major

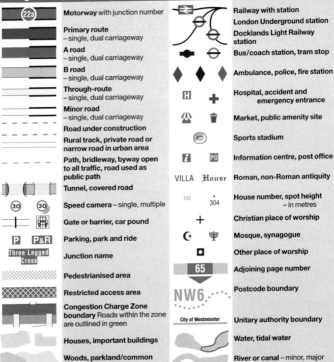

Scale

3½ inches to 1 mile 1:18103

0 220yds 440yds 660yds ½ mile

0 250m 500m 750m 1km

A502 Hendon
A598 Finchley
A41 Mill Hill, M1
1
88
87
86
4
3
2
1
A
B
C
24
25
10
Golders Green
Golders Hill Sch
Child's Hill
Jewish Cemy
Crem
Garden of Remembrance
Golders Green
Hippodrome
Depot
Mast
Basing Hill Park
Child's Hill Park
Wessex Gardens Prim Sch
Granville Ind Est
Allot Gdns
All Saints' CE Prim Sch
Child's Hill Prim Sch
St Agnes RC Sch
King's Coll London
St Margaret's Sch
Golders Park
NW3
GOLDERS GREEN RD
HENDON WAY
FINCHLEY RD
CRICKLEWOOD LA
NORTH END RD
WOODSTOCK AVE
ACCOMMODATION RD
GOLDERS WAY
HOOP LA
CORRINGHAM RD
ROTHERWICK RD
MIDDLETON RD
DUNSTAN RD
HODFORD RD
WEST HEATH RD
WEST HEATH DR
WEST HEATH AVE
RIDGE HILL
GRESHAM GDNS
ARMITAGE RD
BASING HILL
VALE RISE
HELENSLEA AVE
WYCOMBE GDNS
THE VALE
WAYSIDE
PENNINE DR
CHEVIOT GDNS
GRANVILLE RD
NANT RD
CREWYS RD
LLANVANOR RD
GARTH RD
CLOISTER RD
RIDGE RD
PROSPECT RD
CHURCH WLK
PATTISON RD
HERMITAGE LA
PLATT'S LA
HOLLYCROFT AVE
ROSECROFT AVE
FERNCROFT AVE
BRIARDALE GDNS
HOCROFT AVE
HOCROFT RD
SOMERTON RD
THORVERTON RD
GREENFIELD GDNS
DERSINGHAM RD
PURLEY AVE
SANDERSTEAD AVE
WOODVILLE RD
THE DRIVE
LIMES AVE
THE GROVE
GARRICK AVE
AMBROSE AVE
WENTWORTH RD
ST JOHN'S RD
ELMCROFT AVE
BEECHCROFT AVE
RAVENSCROFT AVE
THE RIDGEWAY
GOLDERS GDNS
GAINSBOROUGH GDNS
POWIS GDNS
WESSEX GDNS
MONTPELIER WAY
GRAMPIAN GDNS
COTSWOLD GATE
CLEVELAND GDNS
MALVERN GDNS
CHEVIOT GATE
CUMBRIAN GDNS
PENNINE PAR
PENNINE MANS
FORRES GDNS
DINGWALL GDNS
PORTSDOWN AVE
WILD HATCH
LINNELL DR
CORRINGWAY
KINGSCOTE
WHITE LO
GOLDERSLEA
FERNSIDE
CARLTON CL
EDEN CL
WESTOVER HILL
ELM WLK
BEECHWORTH CL
BEAUMONT GDNS
WEST HEATH CL
TELEGRAPH HILL
ELM TERR
DEVONSHIRE PL
LYNDALE AVE
LONGBERRYS
AVENUE CT
HARMAN DR
FARM AVE
GALSWORTHY RD
LICHFIELD RD
BESANT RD
Tenn Cts
Liby
Coll
Pav
Bwg Gn
L Ctr
Sch

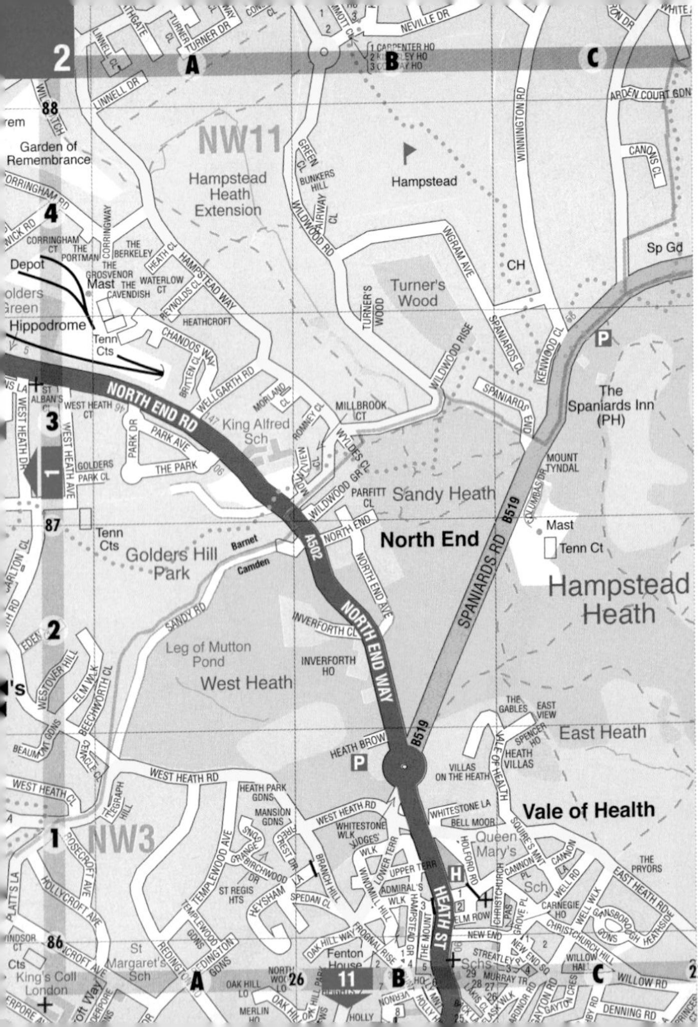
2
A
B
C
NW11
Hampstead Heath Extension
Hampstead
Garden of Remembrance
Golders Green Hippodrome
Depot
Mast
Tenn Cts
WINNINGTON RD
ARDEN COURT GDNS
CANONS CL
NEVILLE DR
1 CARPENTER HO
3 CONWAY HO
TURNER DR
LINNELL DR
LINNELL CL
CORRINGHAM RD
CORRINGHAM CT
CORRINGWAY
THE PORTMAN
THE BERKELEY
THE GROSVENOR
THE CAVENDISH
HEATH CL
HAMPSTEAD WAY
WATERLOW CT
REYNOLDS CL
HEATHCROFT
CHANDOS WAY
BRITTEN CL
WELLGARTH RD
GREEN CL
BUNKERS HILL
FAIRWAY CL
WILDWOOD RD
INGRAM AVE
Turner's Wood
TURNER'S WOOD
WILDWOOD RISE
SPANIARDS CL
KENWOOD CL
CH
Sp Gd
P
The Spaniards Inn (PH)
SPANIARDS END
MOUNT TYNDAL
COLUMBAS DR
B519
SPANIARDS RD
Mast
Tenn Ct
Hampstead Heath
North End
Sandy Heath
PARFITT CL
WILDWOOD GR
WYLDES CL
MILLBROOK CT
ROMNEY CL
MORLAND CL
King Alfred Sch
NORTH END RD
ST ALBAN'S CL
WEST HEATH CT
PARK DR
PARK AVE
THE PARK
GOLDERS PARK CL
WEST HEATH DR
WEST HEATH AVE
1
87
88
3
4
Tenn Cts
Golders Hill Park
Barnet
Camden
A502
NORTH END
NORTH END AVE
NORTH END WAY
INVERFORTH CL
INVERFORTH HO
SANDY RD
Leg of Mutton Pond
West Heath
EDEN CL
WESTOVER HILL
ELM WLK
BEECHWORTH CL
BEAUMONT GDNS
PINNACLE CL
WEST HEATH CL
TELEGRAPH HILL
WEST HEATH RD
HEATH BROW
P
THE GABLES
EAST VIEW
SPENCER HO
East Heath
VALE OF HEALTH
HEATH VILLAS
VILLAS ON THE HEATH
Vale of Health
WHITESTONE LA
BELL MOOR
Queen Mary's
H
HOLFORD RD
SQUIRE'S MT
CANNON LA
CANNON PL
Sch
WELL RD
THE PRYORS
EAST HEATH RD
NW3
ROSECROFT AVE
HOLLYCROFT AVE
PLATT'S LA
HEATH PARK GDNS
MANSION GDNS
WEST HEATH RD
WHITESTONE WLK
JUDGES' WLK
TEMPLEWOOD AVE
GRANGE GDNS
BIRCHWOOD DR
FIRECREST DR
BRANCH HILL
HEYSHAM LA
SPEDAN CL
ST REGIS HTS
TEMPLEWOOD GDNS
REDINGTON GDNS
St Margaret's Sch
King's Coll London
86
LOWER TERR
UPPER TERR
ADMIRAL'S WLK
WINDMILL HILL
HAMPSTEAD GR
THE MOUNT
HEATH ST
ELM ROW
CHRISTCHURCH PAS
GROVE PL
CARNEGIE HO
WELL WLK
GAINSBOROUGH GDNS
HEATHSIDE
CHRISTCHURCH HILL
NEW END
NEW END SQ
STREATLEY PL
WILLOW HALL
WILLOW RD
MURRAY TR
Schs
OAK HILL WAY
FROGNAL RISE
Fenton House
OAK HILL LO
NORTH WOOD LO
26
11
27
MERLIN HO
DENNING RD
GAYTON RD
GAYTON CRES
FLASK WLK
LAKIS CL
BACK LA

3
A
B
C
Highgate
CH
Allot Gdns
SHELDON AVE
DENEWOOD RD
VIEW RD
NORTH HILL
COURTENAY AVE
COMPTON AVE
STORMONT RD
Tenn Cts
BROADLANDS RD
BISHOPSWOOD RD
Highgate Sch
Pav
Highgate
St Michael's CE Prim Sch
Sp Gd
Sp Ctr
NORTH RD
SOUTHWOOD LA
CASTLE YD
KINGSLEY PL
CHOLMELEY CRES
Highgate Sch
HAMPSTEAD LA
PARK FLATS
Haringey
Camden
B519
B550
Athlone House
HIGHGATE HIGH ST
Kenwood House
Millfield La
THE GROVE
WEST HILL
SOUTH GR
BACON'S LA
FITZROY PK
HIGHFIELDS GR
THE HEXAGON
FITZROY CL
Allot Gdns
Tenn Cts
Bwg Gn
Open Air Stage
Ken Wood
N6
115
YH
Highgate Cemy
HOLLY TERR
HOLLY LODGE GDNS
MERTON LA
WESTHILL PK
HIGHGATE WEST HILL
ROBIN GR
OAKESHOTT AVE
HILLWAY
MAKEPEACE AVE
LANGBOURNE AVE
BROMWICH AVE
SWAIN'S LA
HOLLY LODGE MANS
MAKEPEACE MANS
LANGBOURNE MANS
MILLFIELD LA
MILLFIELD PL
Parliament Hill
Highgate Ponds
Brookfield Prim Sch
HOLLY VILLAGE
WEST HILL CT
BROOKFIELD
ST ANN'S CL
CHURCH WLK
ST ALBAN'S RD
BROOKFIELD PK
N6
HYLDA CT
COULTS CRES
ST ALBAN'S VILLAS
La Saint Union RC Sec Sch
Dartm Pa
Tenn Cts
Bwg Gn
William Ellis Sch
HIGHGATE RD
WOODSOME RD
Hampstead Ponds
NW3
SOUTH HILL PK GDNS
SOUTH HILL PK
TANZA RD
Parliament Hill Sch
Willow Road
27
12
28
88
87
86
Pav
Athletics Gd
Sw Pool
Hampstead Heath
NASSINGTON RD
PARLIAMENT HILL
LISSENDEN GDNS
GLENHURST AVE
GROVE TERR
GROVE END
1
2
3
4

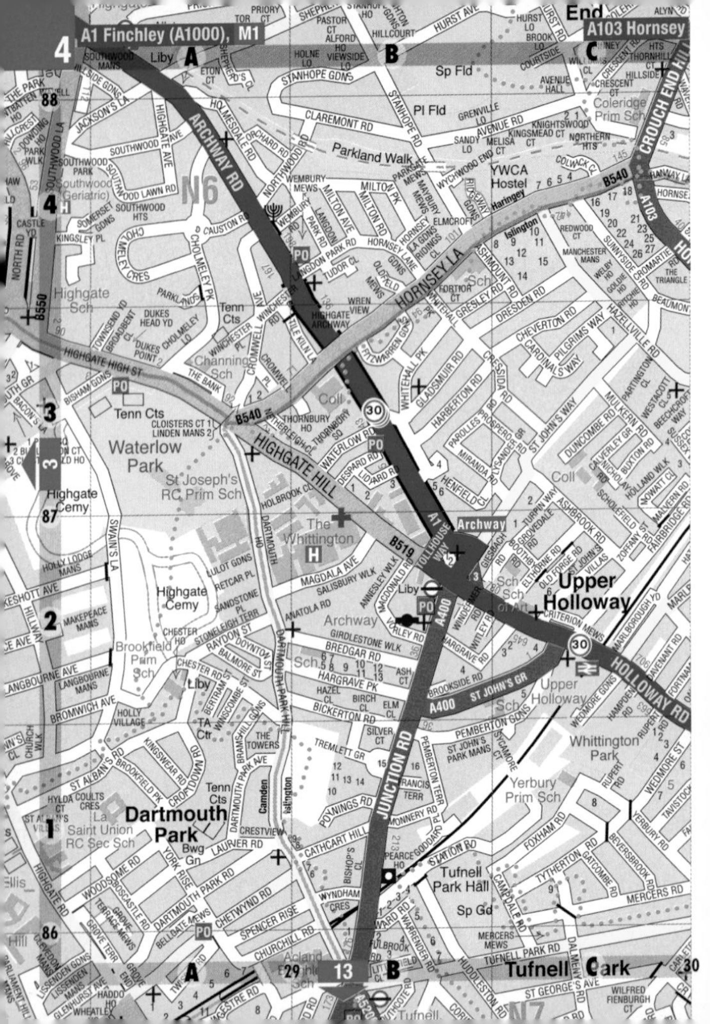
A1 Finchley (A1000), M1
A103 Hornsey
4
A
B
C
Highgate Sch
Tenn Cts
Channing Sch
Waterlow Park
St Joseph's RC Prim Sch
Highgate Cemy
The Whittington
Archway
Upper Holloway
Whittington Park
Yerbury Prim Sch
Tufnell Park Hall
Dartmouth Park
Saint Union RC Sec Sch
Brookfield Prim Sch
Holly Village
Coleridge Prim Sch
YWCA Hostel
Parkland Walk
Sp Fld
Pl Fld
N6
ARCHWAY RD
HORNSEY LA
HIGHGATE HILL
HIGHGATE HIGH ST
JUNCTION RD
HOLLOWAY RD
DARTMOUTH PARK HILL
CROUCH END HILL
ST JOHN'S GR
SWAIN'S LA
HIGHGATE RD
B540
B519
A400
A1
A103
Haringey
Islington
Camden
3
2
1
86
87
88
13
29
30
Tufnell Park

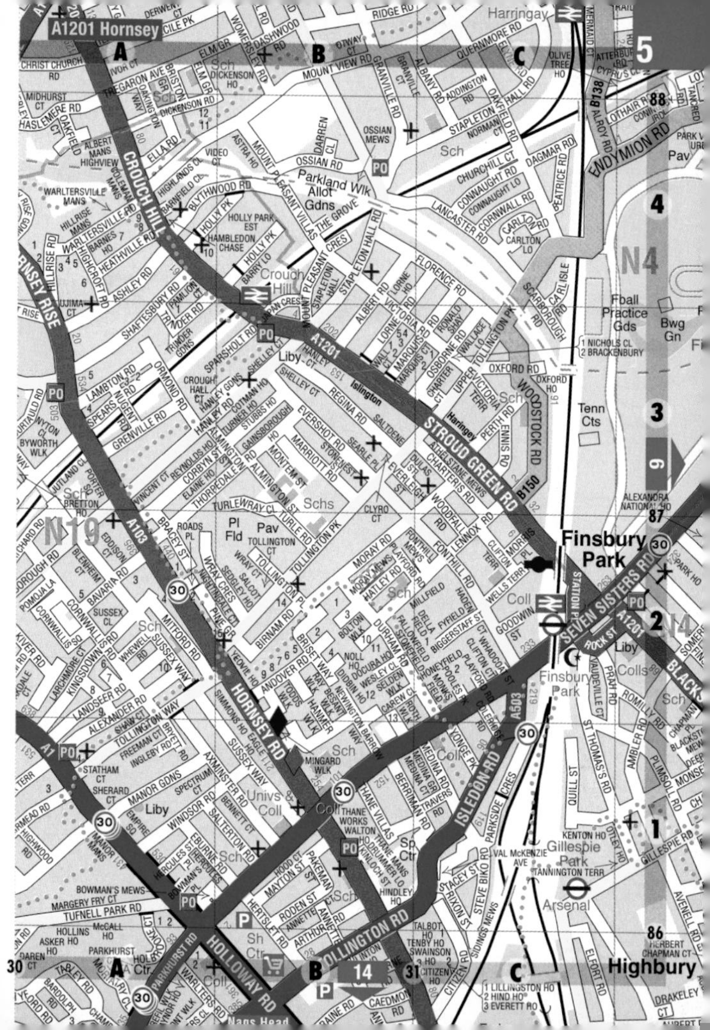

A1201 Hornsey
A
B
C
5
Harringay
RIDGE RD
DERWENT CT
CILE PK
CHRIST CHURCH RD
IVOR CT
ELM GR
WOMERSLEY RD
DASHWOOD RD
OTWAY CT
MOUNT VIEW RD
QUERNMORE RD
OLIVE TREE HO
MERMAID CT
ATTERBURY RD
CYPRUS CL
Sch
DICKENSON HO
DICKENSON RD
MIDHURST CT
HASLEMERE RD
TREGARON AVE
BRISTON GR
OAKINGTON WAY
ELM GR
GRANVILLE RD
GRANVILLE CT
ALBANY RD
ADDINGTON RD
OAKFIELD RD
HALL RD
STAPLETON
NORMAN CT
B138
ALROY RD
LOTHAIR RD
CONINGSBY RD
TANCRED RD
88
ENDYMION RD
PARK VIEW
Pav
OAKFIELD CT
ALBERT MANS
HIGHVIEW
ELLA RD
ASTRA HO
VIDEO CT
MOUNT PLEASANT RD
DARREN CL
OSSIAN MEWS
OSSIAN RD
PO
Sch
DAGMAR RD
CHURCHILL CT
CONNAUGHT RD
CONNAUGHT LO
BEATRICE RD
CORNWALL RD
LANCASTER RD
CARLTON RD
CARLTON LO
Parkland Wlk
Allot Gdns
THE GROVE
MOUNT PLEASANT VILLAS
CROUCH HILL
COLEMAN MANS
WALTERSVILLE MANS
HIGHLANDS CL
BARNFIELD CL
BLYTHWOOD RD
HOLLY PARK EST
HILLRISE MANS
WALTERSVILLE RD
HOLLY PK
HAMBLEDON CHASE
BARNES HO
HEATHVILLE RD
HILLRISE RD
HIGHCROFT RD
ASHLEY RD
BARRY LO
HOLLY LO
Crouch Hill
MOUNT PLEASANT CRES
STAPLETON HALL RD
STAPLETON HALL
4
N4
FLORENCE RD
SCARBOROUGH RD
CARLISLE RD
Fball Practice Gds
Bwg Gn
HORNSEY RISE
UJIMA CT
SHAFTESBURY RD
PAMLION CT
TRINDER RD
JAPAN CRES
ALBERT RD
LORNE HO
VICTORIA RD
RONALD SHAY
UPPER TOLLINGTON PK
WALLACE LO
1 NICHOLS CL
2 BRACKENBURY
TRINDER GDNS
SPARSHOLT RD
SHELLEY CT
PO
Liby
A1201
HANLEY CT
LORNE RD
MARQUIS RD
MARQUIS CT
OSBORNE RD
CHARTER CT
OXFORD RD
OXFORD HO
WOODSTOCK RD
Tenn Cts
3
LAMBTON RD
SPEARS RD
NUGENT RD
ORMOND RD
CROUCH HALL CT
HANLEY GDNS
COTMAN HO
TURNER HO
STUBBS HO
REGINA RD
Islington
Haringey
SALTDENE
STROUD GREEN RD
VICTORIA TERR
PERTH RD
ENNIS RD
PO
BYWORTH WLK
GRENVILLE RD
GAINSBOROUGH
EVERSHOT RD
MARRIOTT RD
STONENEST ST
SEARLE PL
EVERLEIGH ST
DULAS ST
ATHELSTANE MEWS
CHARTERIS RD
B150
9
ALEXANDRA NATIONAL HO
87
REYNOLDS HO
CORBYN ST
ALMINGTON ST
MONTEM ST
JUTLAND CL
PORTER SQ
BRETTON HO
Sch
VINCENT CT
ELAINE HO
THORPEDALE RD
Schs
TURLEWRAY CL
TURLE RD
CLYRO CT
WOODFALL RD
LENNOX RD
MORRIS PL
CLIFTON TERR
Finsbury Park
N19
EDDISON CT
A103
BRACEY ST
ROADS PL
Pl Fld
Pav
TOLLINGTON CT
TOLLINGTON PK
MORAY RD
FONTHILL MEWS
FONTHILL RD
PLAYFORD RD
30
PARK HO
BLENHEIM CT
BAVARIA RD
WRAY CRES
WRAY CT
SALCOT
SEDGLEY HO
NIGHTINGALE CT
TOLLINGTON PL
MORAY MEWS
HATLEY RD
Sch
MILLFIELD
HADEN CT
WELLS TERR
STATION PL
SEVEN SISTERS RD
POMOJA LA
CORNWALLIS CT
SUSSEX CL
30
PINE GR
BIRNAM RD
BOLTON WLK
DELLA FIELD
FYFIELD
BIGGERSTAFF ST
WHADCOAT ST
Coll
GOODWIN ST
PO
A1201
ROCK ST
Liby
2
CORNWALLIS SQ
KINGSDOWN RD
WHEWELL RD
SUSSEX WAY
MITFORD RD
YEOVIL HO
BRISET WAY
NOLL HO
DOCURA HO
DURHAM RD
FALLOWFIELD
STONEFIELD
HONEYFIELD
POOLES PK
CLIFTON CT
PLAYFORD RD
Finsbury Park
PRAH RD
VAUDEVILLE CT
Colls
BLACKSTOCK RD
SOMERFIELD RD
KIVER RD
LARCHMORE CT
LANDSEER RD
ALEXANDER RD
SHAW CT
TOLLINGTON WAY
FREEMAN CT
BRYETT RD
INGLEBY RD
HORNSEY RD
SIMMONS HO
ANDOVER RD
TODDS WLK
RAY WLK
BESANT WLK
HAMMER WLK
NEWINGTON BARROW WAY
DIDBIN HO
WESLEY CL
SELDEN WLK
CAREW CL
ROTH WLK
MONKS FIELD
COLERIDGE RD
A503
ROMILLY RD
AMBLER RD
CHAPMAN PL
BLACKSTOCK MEWS
A1
PO
STATHAM CT
SHERARD CT
MANOR GDNS
SPECTRUM CT
AXMINSTER RD
SUSSEX WAY
EAGLE HO
MINGARD WLK
Sch
MEDINA RD
MEDINA GR
MEDINA CT
BERRIMAN RD
Coll
YONGE PK
ISLEDON RD
CRES
ST THOMAS'S RD
QUILL ST
PLIMSOLL RD
MONSELL RD
Liby
EMPIRE SQ
WINDSOR RD
BENNETT CT
Univs & Coll
Coll
30
THANE WORKS
THANE VILLAS
WALTON HO
TRAVERS RD
Sp Ctr
PARKSIDE CT
1
MANOR MANS
HIGHWOOD RD
HERCULES ST
HERCULES PL
EBURNE RD
SALTERTON RD
Sch
PO
DRUMMER LO
THANE MANS
KINLOCH ST
HOOD CT
MAYTON ST
PAKEMAN ST
Sch
STACEY ST
RIXON ST
STEVE BIKO RD
VAL McKENZIE AVE
KENTON HO
Gillespie Park
TANNINGTON TERR
OTLEY HO
GILLESPIE RD
BOWMAN'S MEWS
BOWMAN'S PL
MARGERY FRY CT
TUFNELL PARK RD
PO
HINDLEY HO
Arsenal
AVENELL RD
SIDINGS MEWS
HOLLINS HO
McCALL HO
ASKER HO
DAREN CT
PARKHURST
HOLBROOKE CT
P
Sh Ctr
HERTSLET RD
RODEN ST
ANNETTE CT
ANNETTE RD
ARTHUR RD
HOLLOWAY RD
TOLLINGTON RD
TALBOT HO
TENBY HO
SWAINSON HO
CITIZEN HO
CITIZEN RD
86
HERBERT CHAPMAN CT
ELFORD RD
30
A
Ctr
PARKHURST RD
Coll
B
14
31
C
Highbury
TABLEY RD
BARDOLPH RD
MORAY RD
30
WALTERS HO
P
1 LILLINGSTON HO
2 HIND HO
3 EVERETT HO
CAEDMON RD
Nags Head
DRAKELEY CT

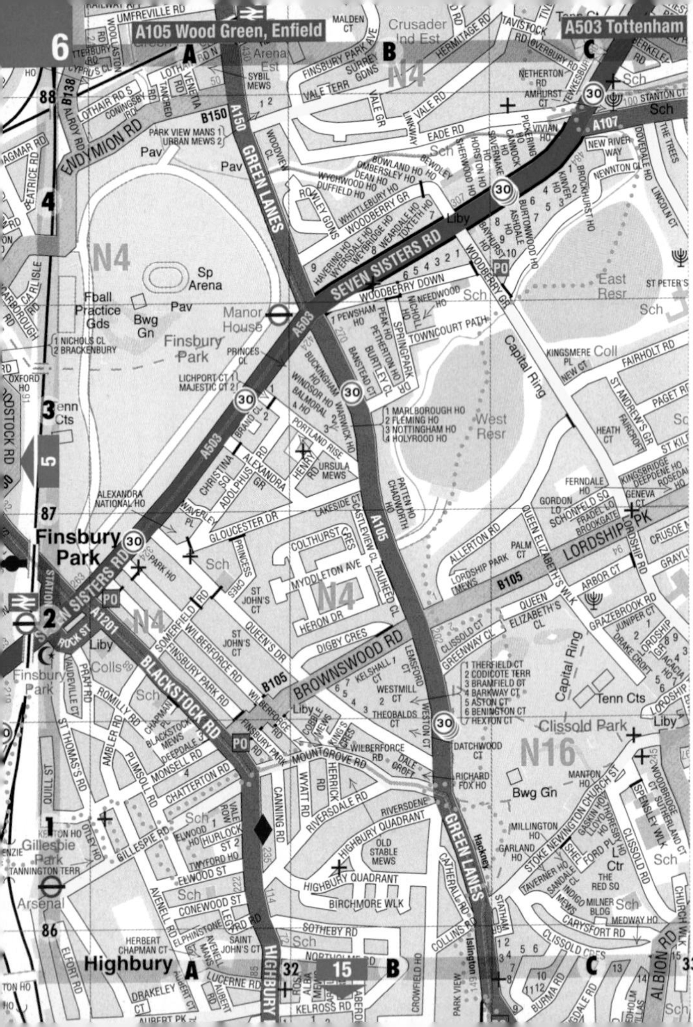
A105 Wood Green, Enfield
A503 Tottenham
A
B
C
N4
N16
UMFREVILLE RD
WOOLLASTON RD
CYPRUS CL
LOTHAIR RD S
CONINGSBY RD
TANCRED RD
VENETIA RD
SYBIL MEWS
MALDEN CT
Crusader Ind Est
HERMITAGE RD
TAVISTOCK RD
OVERBURY RD
NETHERTON RD
AMHURST CT
TEWKESBURY
STANTON CT
Sch
FINSBURY PARK AVE
SURREY GDNS
VALE TERR
VALE GR
VALE RD
LINKWAY
EADE RD
B138
ALROY RD
B150
ENDYMION RD
PARK VIEW MANS 1
URBAN MEWS 2
A150
GREEN LANES
WOODVIEW CL
Pav
ROWLEY GDNS
BOWLAND HO
OMBERSLEY HO
DEAN HO
WYCHWOOD HO
DUFFIELD HO
WHITTLEBURY HO
WOODBERRY GR
BEWDLEY
SHERWOOD HO
HORSTON HO
SAVERNAKE HO
CANNOCK HO
PICKERING HO
VIVIAN HO
A107
NEW RIVER WAY
NEWNTON CL
DOVEDALE HO
THE TREES
LINCOLN CT
BROCKHURST HO
KINVER HO
BURTONWOOD HO
ASHDALE HO
BAYHURST HO
Liby
SEVEN SISTERS RD
WEARDALE HO
TOXTETH HO
WEYBRIDGE HO
WYERSDALE HO
HAVERING HO
WOODBERRY DOWN
WOODBERRY GR
PO
East Resr
ST PETER'S
N4
Sp Arena
Fball Practice Gds
Bwg Gn
Finsbury Park
Manor House
A503
CARLISLE RD
SCARBOROUGH RD
1 NICHOLS CL
2 BRACKENBURY
OXFORD HO
PRINCES CL
LICHPORT CT 1
MAJESTIC CT 2
7 PEWSHAM HO
PEAK HO
PETHERTON HO
SPRINGPARK DR
NICHOLL HO
NEEDWOOD HO
TOWNCOURT PATH
Capital Ring
KINGSMERE PL
NEW CT
Coll
FAIRHOLT RD
PAGET RD
ST ANDREW'S GR
FAIRCROFT
HEATH CT
BUCKINGHAM HO
WINDSOR HO
BALMORAL HO
WARWICK HO
BANSTEAD CT
BURTLEY CL
1 MARLBOROUGH HO
2 FLEMING HO
3 NOTTINGHAM HO
4 HOLYROOD HO
West Resr
BRAND CL
PORTLAND RISE
HENRY RD
URSULA MEWS
CHRISTINA SQ
ALEXANDRA GR
ADOLPHUS RD
PATTEN HO
CHADWORTH HO
ALEXANDRA NATIONAL HO
WAVERLEY PL
GLOUCESTER DR
LAKESIDE CT
CASTLEVIEW CL
A105
FERNDALE HO
GORDON LO
SCHONFIELD SQ
FRADEL LO
BROOKGATE
KINGSBRIDGE
DEEPDENE HO
ROSEDALE HO
GENEVA CT
LORDSHIP PK
CRUSOE M
ALLERTON RD
PALM CT
QUEEN ELIZABETH'S WLK
LORDSHIP PARK MEWS
B105
ARBOR CT
LORDSHIP RD
GRAZEBROOK RD
JUNIPER CT
DRAKE CROFT
Finsbury Park
PARK HO
Sch
PRINCESS CRES
COLTHURST CRES
MYDDLETON AVE
TAUHEED CL
ST JOHN'S CT
HERON DR
STATION
SEVEN SISTERS RD
PO
A1201
ROCK ST
Liby
Colls
SOMERFIELD RD
WILBERFORCE RD
FINSBURY PARK RD
QUEEN'S DR
DIGBY CRES
BROWNSWOOD RD
CLISSOLD CT
GREENWAY CL
QUEEN ELIZABETH'S CL
Finsbury Park
BLACKSTOCK RD
VAUDEVILLE CT
PRAH RD
ROMILLY RD
CHAPMAN PL
BLACKSTOCK MEWS
DEEPDALE
KELSHALL CT
LEMSFORD CT
WESTMILL CT
THEOBALDS CT
WESTON CT
1 THERFIELD CT
2 CODICOTE TERR
3 BRAMFIELD CT
4 BARKWAY CT
5 ASTON CT
6 BENINGTON CT
7 HEXTON CT
Tenn Cts
Clissold Park
Liby
COBBLE MEWS
KING'S CRES
WILBERFORCE RD
DALE CROFT
DATCHWOOD CT
RICHARD FOX HO
MANTON HO
Bwg Gn
ST THOMAS'S RD
AMBLER RD
PLIMSOLL RD
MONSELL RD
CHATTERTON RD
MOUNTGROVE RD
CANNING RD
WYATT RD
HERRICK RD
RIVERSDALE RD
RIVERSDENE
HIGHBURY QUADRANT
OLD STABLE MEWS
GREEN LANES
Hackney
Islington
MILLINGTON HO
GARLAND HO
STOKE NEWINGTON CHURCH ST
GASKIN HO
LLOYD HO
THORESBY HO
SPENSLEY WLK
WOODBRIDGE CT
SUTHERLAND CT
CLISSOLD RD
FORD PL
Ctr
THE RED SQ
QUILL ST
Gillespie Park
TANNINGTON TERR
Arsenal
GILLESPIE RD
ELWOOD HO
HURLOCK ST
TWYFORD HO
ELWOOD ST
VALE ROW
CONEWOOD ST
HIGHBURY QUADRANT
BIRCHMORE WLK
CATHERALL RD
TAVERNER HO
SANDALE CL
INDIGO MEWS
MILNER BLDG
MEDWAY HO
CARYSFORT RD
CLISSOLD CRES
CHURCH WLK
ALBION RD
HERBERT CHAPMAN CT
ELPHINSTONE RD
AVENELL RD
AVENELL MANS
SAINT JOHN'S CT
SOTHEBY RD
NORTHOLME RD
HIGHBURY
COLLINS RD
CROWFIELD HO
STATHAM
BURMA RD
Highbury
DRAKELEY CT
AUBERT CT
AUBERT RD
LUCERNE RD
KELROSS RD
ELFORT RD
PARK VIEW
5
15
32
33
86
87
88

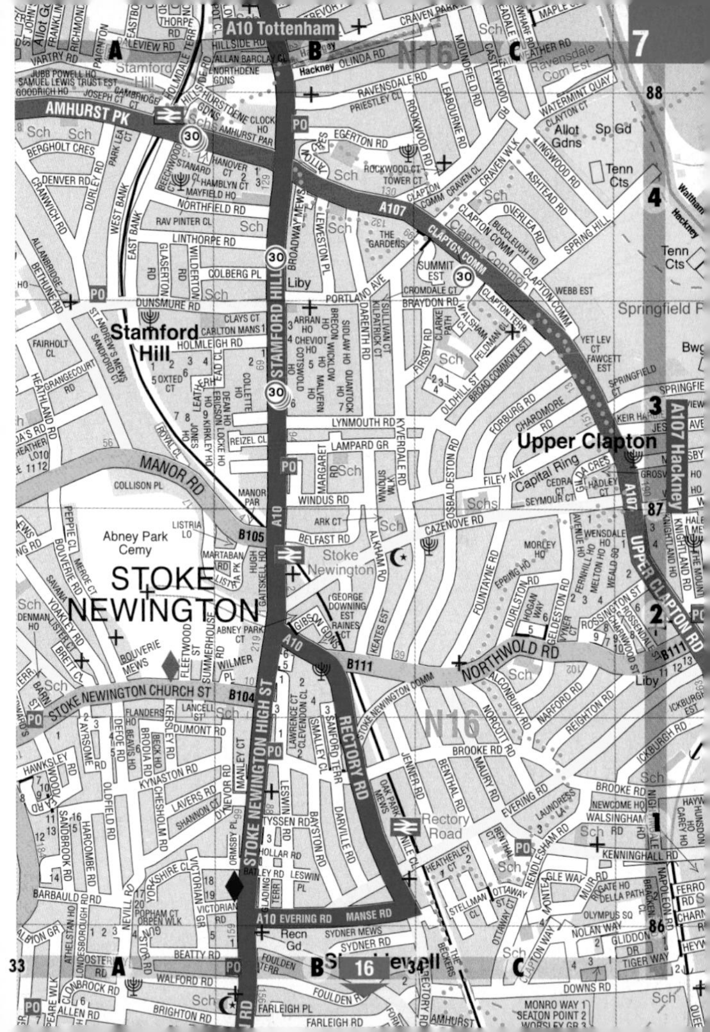
7
A10 Tottenham
A
B
C
N16
Stamford Hill
AMHURST PK
STAMFORD HILL
A107
CLAPTON COMM
Clapton Common
Upper Clapton
A107 Hackney
UPPER CLAPTON RD
Springfield
Stamford Hill
MANOR RD
Abney Park Cemy
STOKE NEWINGTON
Stoke Newington
B105
A10
B111
NORTHWOLD RD
STOKE NEWINGTON CHURCH ST
B104
STOKE NEWINGTON HIGH ST
RECTORY RD
Rectory Road
Capital Ring
N16
A10 EVERING RD
MANSE RD
Shacklewell
16
33
34
88
87
86
4
3
2
1
Waltham
Hackney
Allot Gdns
Sp Gd
Tenn Cts
Ravensdale Com Est
CLAPTON WAY
BROOKE RD
KENNINGHALL RD
NAPOLEON RD
FOULDEN RD
DOWNS RD
AMHURST RD
Recn Gd

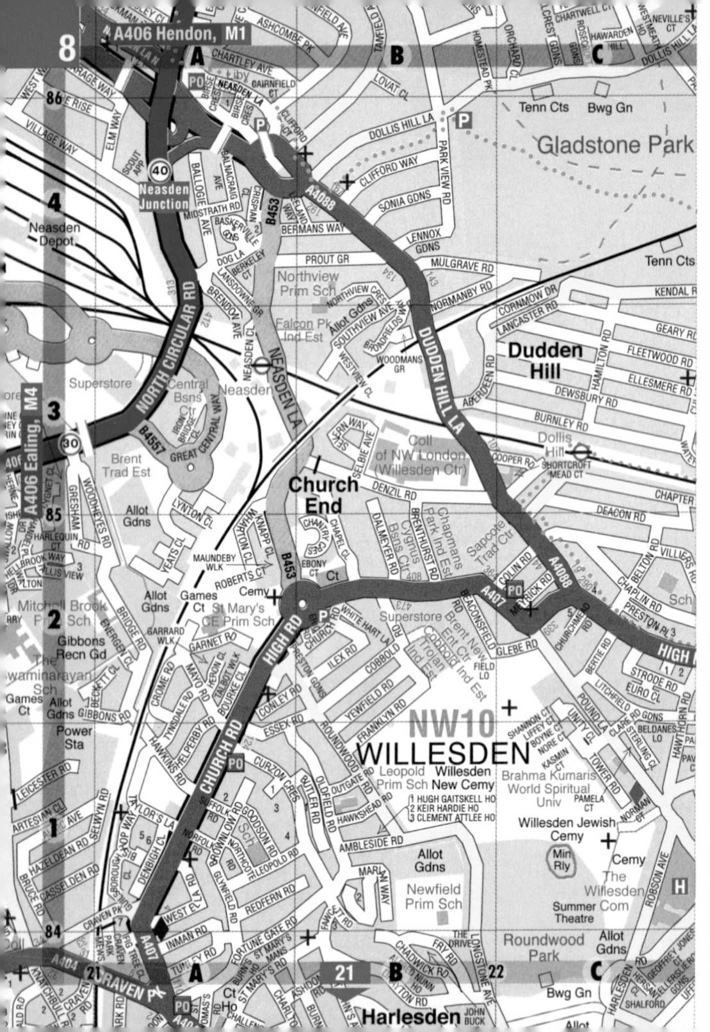

8
A406 Hendon, M1
A
B
C
ASHCOMBE PK
CHARTLEY AVE
NEASDEN LA
CAIRNFIELD CT
BIRSE CRES
CLIFFORD CT
TAMFIELD RD
LOVAT CL
DOLLIS HILL LA
PARK VIEW RD
HOMESTEAD PK
ORCHARD CL
HILLCREST GDNS
CHARTWELL CT
ROSECROFT GDNS
HAWARDEN HILL
WESTMEATH HO
NEVILLE'S CT
DOLLIS HILL LA
Tenn Cts
Bwg Gn
Gladstone Park
86
THE RISE
VILLAGE WAY
ELM WAY
SCOUT APP
40
Neasden Junction
BALLOGIE AVE
BALNACRAIG AVE
CRISPIAN CL
MIDSTRATH RD
BASKERVILLE GDNS
B453
LEELAND WAY
A4088
CLIFFORD WAY
SONIA GDNS
BERMANS WAY
LENNOX GDNS
4
Neasden Depot
DOG LA
BERKELEY CT
PROUT GR
MULGRAVE RD
Tenn Cts
Northview Prim Sch
NORTHVIEW CRES
NORMANBY RD
CORNMOW DR
LANCASTER RD
KENDAL RD
BRENDON AVE
LANSDOWNE GR
NORTH CIRCULAR RD
Falcon Pk Ind Est
Allot Gdns
SOUTHVIEW AVE
BROADFIELDS WAY
DUDDEN HILL LA
GEARY RD
Dudden Hill
HAMILTON RD
FLEETWOOD RD
NEASDEN CL
NEASDEN LA
WESTVIEW CL
WOODMANS GR
ELLESMERE RD
ABERDEEN RD
DEWSBURY RD
Superstore
Central Bsns Ctr
IRON BRIDGE CL
GREAT CENTRAL WAY
Neasden
BURNLEY RD
A406 Ealing, M4
3
30
B4557
SELKIRK WAY
SELBIE AVE
Coll of NW London (Willesden Ctr)
Dollis Hill
COOPER RD
SHORTCROFT MEAD CT
Brent Trad Est
Church End
DENZIL RD
CHAPTER RD
85
GRESHAM RD
WOODHEYES RD
Allot Gdns
LYNTON CL
WHARTON CL
KNAPP CL
CHANTRY CRES
CHAPEL CL
DALMEYER RD
BRENTHURST RD
Cygnus Bsns Ctr
Chapmans Park Ind Est
Sapcote Trad Ctr
DEACON RD
BELTON RD
VILLIERS RD
HARLEQUIN CT
HOLLIS VIEW
MAUNDEBY WLK
YEATS CL
B453
EBONY CT
ROBERTS CT
Cemy
COLIN RD
A4088
A407
MEYRICK RD
CHAPLIN RD
PRESTON PL
Mitchell Brook Prim Sch
2
Allot Gdns
Games Ct
St Mary's CE Prim Sch
HIGH RD
WHITE HART LA
Superstore
Brent New Ent Ctr
Cobbold Ind Est
Trojan Ind Est
BEACONSFIELD RD
GLEBE RD
CHURCHMEAD RD
BERTIE RD
HIGH RD
Gibbons Recn Gd
ENERGEN CL
BRIDGE RD
GARRARD WLK
GARNET RD
CHURCH RD
ILEX RD
COBBOLD RD
FIELD LO
STRODE RD
EURO CL
The Swaminarayan Sch
HERON CL
TALBOT WLK
BOURKE CL
PRESTON GDNS
LITCHFIELD GDNS
Games Ct
Allot Gdns
BECKETT CL
GIBBONS RD
CROME RD
MAYO RD
TYNSDALE RD
CONLEY RD
YEWFIELD RD
FRANKLYN RD
NW10
SHANNON CT
LIFFEY CT
BOYNE CT
NORE CT
UNITY CL
POUND LA
CLARE RD
BELDANES LO
HAWTHORN RD
Power Sta
HELPERBY RD
HAWKINS RD
ESSEX RD
ROUNDWOOD RD
WILLESDEN
KASMIN CT
STERLING CL
CHURCH RD
CURZON CRES
OLDFIELD RD
Leopold Prim Sch
Willesden New Cemy
Brahma Kumaris World Spiritual Univ
TOWER RD
LEICESTER RD
BUTLER RD
OUTGATE RD
HAWKSHEAD RD
1 HUGH GAITSKELL HO
2 KEIR HARDIE HO
3 CLEMENT ATTLEE HO
PAMELA CT
NORMAN CT
SELWYN RD
ARTESIAN CL
TAYLOR'S LA
SUFFOLK RD
GOODSON RD
Willesden Jewish Cemy
1
HAZELDEAN RD
HOP WAY
BROWNLOW RD
NORTHCOTE RD
LEOPOLD RD
AMBLESIDE RD
Allot Gdns
Min Rly
Cemy
ROBSON AVE
CASSELDEN RD
BRUCE RD
DENBIGH CL
NORFOLK RD
GLYNFIELD RD
MARLOW WAY
Newfield Prim Sch
The Willesden Com
Summer Theatre
WEST ELLA RD
REDFERN RD
H
84
CRAVEN PK
CRAVEN PARK MEWS
FIG TREE CL
A407
INMAN RD
FORTUNE GATE RD
ST MARY'S MANS
FAWCETT RD
THE DRIVE
FRY RD
LONGSTONE AVE
Roundwood Park
Allot Gdns
GEOFFREY JONES CT
A404
21
CRAVEN PK
TUNLEY RD
A
ST MARY'S RD
21
B
CHADWICK RD
ALDEN NUNN HO
DRAYTON RD
22
C
HARLESDEN RD
HERSANT CL
ELLERSLIE GDNS
Bwg Gn
SHALFORD
KNATCHBULL RD
CRAVEN RD
Ct Ho
CHALLENGE
CHARLTON
ASHDON
Harlesden
JOHN BUCK
Allot

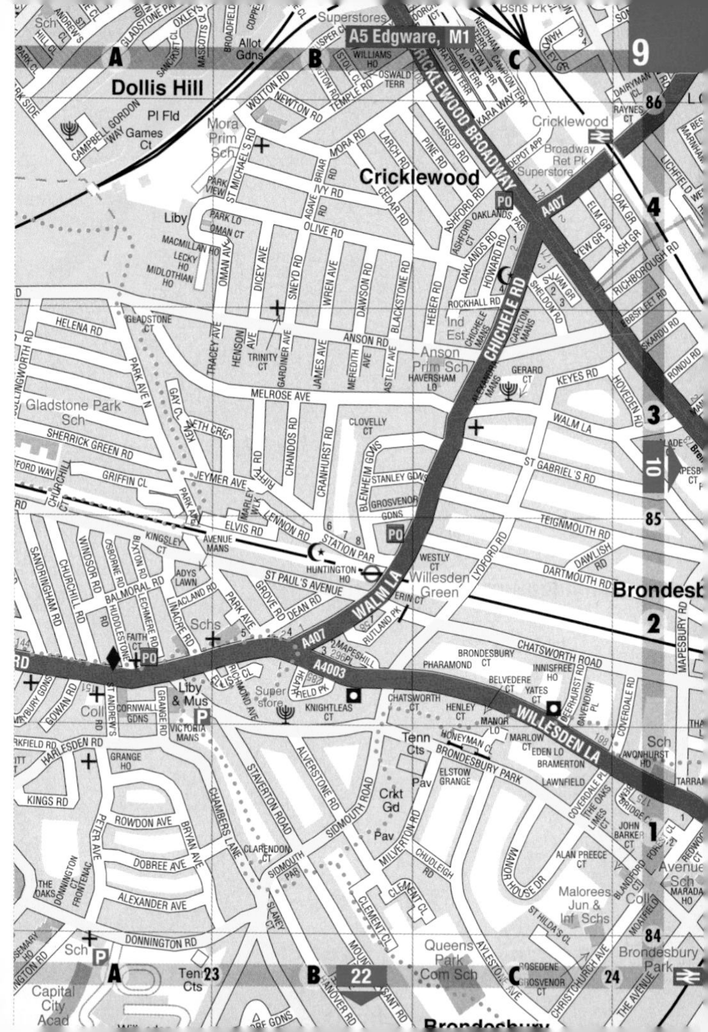
9
A5 Edgware, M1
A
B
C
Dollis Hill
Pl Fld
Games Ct
Allot Gdns
Superstores
Bsns Pk
Cricklewood
CRICKLEWOOD BROADWAY
Broadway Ret Pk
Superstore
Mora Prim Sch
Liby
86
4
3
2
1
85
84
10
22
23
24
Gladstone Park Sch
Anson Prim Sch
Ind Est
Willesden Green
Brondesbury
Schs
Liby & Mus
Coll
Super store
Tenn Cts
Crkt Gd
Pav
Queens Park Com Sch
Malorees Jun & Inf Schs
Avenue Sch
Brondesbury Park
Capital City Acad
Sch
A407
A4003
WALM LA
CHICHELE RD
WILLESDEN LA
GLADSTONE PARK
OXLEYS
CAMPBELL GORDON WAY
WOTTON RD
NEWTON RD
TEMPLE RD
WILLIAMS HO
OSWALD TERR
KARA WAY
MORA RD
LARCH RD
PINE RD
HASSOP RD
CEDAR RD
ASHFORD RD
OAKLANDS RD
DEPOT APP
ELM GR
OAK GR
YEW GR
ASH GR
RICHBOROUGH RD
PARK VIEW
ST MICHAEL'S RD
PARK LO
OMAN CT
OMAN AVE
IVY RD
OLIVE RD
AGAVE RD
BRIAR RD
MACMILLAN HO
LECKY HO
MIDLOTHIAN HO
DICEY AVE
SNEYD RD
WREN AVE
DAWSON RD
BLACKSTONE RD
HEBER RD
HOWARD RD
ROCKHALL RD
SYLVAN GR
SHELDON RD
EBBSFLEET RD
SKARDU RD
RONDU RD
HELENA RD
GLADSTONE CT
TRACEY AVE
HENSON AVE
TRINITY CT
GARDINER AVE
JAMES AVE
ANSON RD
MEREDITH AVE
ASTLEY AVE
HAVERSHAM LO
CHICHELE MANS
CARLTON MANS
ALEXANDRA MANS
GERARD CT
KEYES RD
HOVEDEN RD
PARK AVE N
MELROSE AVE
GAY CL
KENNETH CRES
CHANDOS RD
CRANHURST RD
CLOVELLY CT
WALM LA
SHERRICK GREEN RD
GRIFFIN CL
JEYMER AVE
RIFFEL RD
BLENHEIM GDNS
STANLEY GDNS
GROSVENOR GDNS
ST GABRIEL'S RD
CHURCHILL CT
PARK AVE
MARLEY WLK
LENNON RD
ELVIS RD
STATION PAR
TEIGNMOUTH RD
KINGSLEY CT
AVENUE MANS
HUNTINGTON HO
WESTLY CT
LYDFORD RD
DAWLISH RD
DARTMOUTH RD
SANDRINGHAM RD
CHURCHILL RD
WINDSOR RD
OSBORNE RD
BUXTON RD
BALMORAL RD
LECHMERE RD
ADYS LAWN
ACLAND RD
ST PAUL'S AVENUE
GROVE RD
DEAN RD
ERIN CT
RUTLAND PK
HUDDLESTONE RD
FAITH CT
LINACRE RD
CHATSWORTH ROAD
BRONDESBURY CT
PHARAMOND CT
INNISFREE HO
BELVEDERE CT
YATES CT
MAPESBURY RD
MAPESHILL PL
HEATHFIELD PK
RICHMOND AVE
ELLIS CL
GOWAN RD
CORNWALL GDNS
GRANGE RD
ST ANDREW'S RD
VICTORIA MANS
KNIGHTLEAS CT
CHATSWORTH CT
HENLEY CT
MANOR LO
MARLOW CT
EDEN LO
BRAMERTON
DEERHURST RD
CAVENDISH PL
COVERDALE RD
AVONHURST HO
HARLESDEN RD
GRANGE HO
KINGS RD
ROWDON AVE
BRYAN AVE
PETER AVE
DOBREE AVE
ALEXANDER AVE
FRONTENAC
DONNINGTON CT
THE OAKS
DONNINGTON RD
CHAMBERS LANE
STAVERTON ROAD
ALVERSTONE RD
SIDMOUTH ROAD
HONEYMAN CL
BRONDESBURY PARK
ELSTOW GRANGE
LAWNFIELD
COVERDALE PL
THE OAKS
LIMES CT
JOHN BARKER CT
ALAN PREECE CT
MANOR HOUSE DR
CLARENDON CT
SIDMOUTH PAR
MILVERTON RD
CHUDLEIGH RD
CLEMENT CL
ST HILDA'S CL
CHRISTCHURCH AVE
BLANDFORD CT
MOATFIELD
MARADA HO
REDWOOD CT
FOREST CL
ROSEDENE
GROSVENOR CT
AYLESTONE AVE
SLANEY CT
HANOVER RD
THE AVENUE

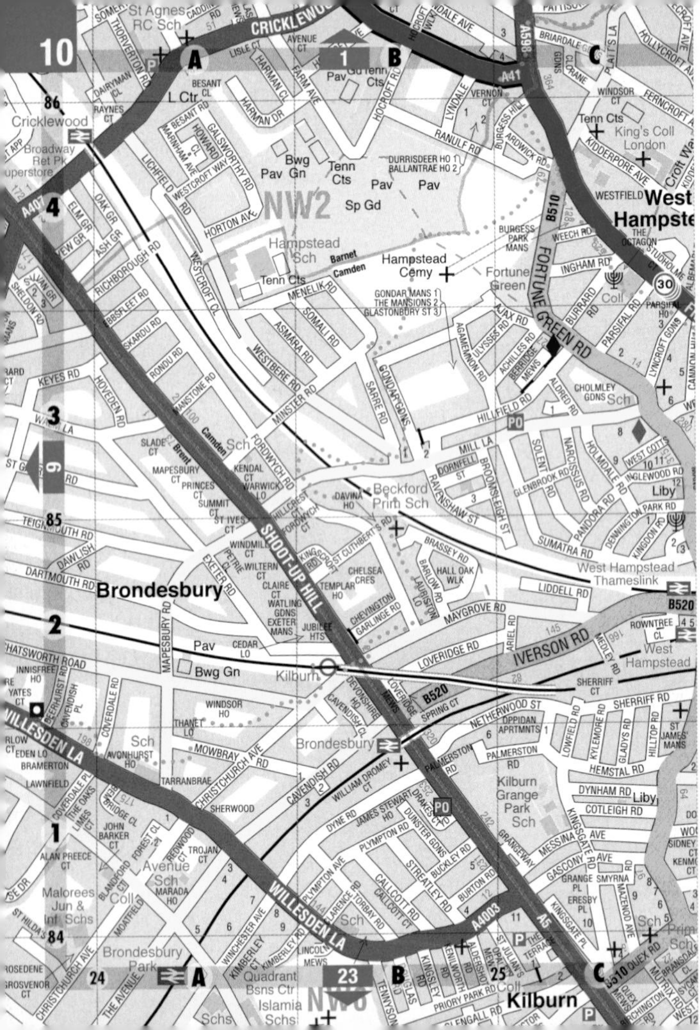
St Agnes RC Sch
CRICKLEWOOD
A
1
B
C
Cricklewood
Broadway Ret Pk
A407
4
3
2
1
86
85
84
9
NW2
Hampstead Sch
Tenn Cts
Barnet
Camden
Hampstead Cemy
Fortune Green
Bwg Gn
Pav
Sp Gd
West Hampstead
King's Coll London
Tenn Cts
FORTUNE GREEN RD
B510
A41
A598
Coll
30
Beckford Prim Sch
SHOOT-UP HILL
Brondesbury
Kilburn
Brondesbury
West Hampstead Thameslink
West Hampstead
IVERSON RD
B520
Kilburn Grange Park
Sch
Liby
PO
WILLESDEN LA
A4003
A5
Avenue Sch
Malorees Jun & Inf Schs
Coll
Brondesbury Park
Quadrant Bsns Ctr
Islamia Schs
24
A
23
B
25
C
NW6
Kilburn
CRICKLEWOOD LA
HOCROFT RD
RANULF RD
WESTCROFT WAY
HOWARD
GALSWORTHY RD
LICHFIELD RD
HORTON AVE
WESTCROFT CL
RICHBOROUGH RD
EBBSFLEET RD
SKARDU RD
RONDU RD
MANSTONE RD
MENELIK RD
SOMALI RD
ASMARA RD
WESTBERE RD
MINSTER RD
FORDWYCH RD
SARRE RD
GONDAR GDNS
AGAMEMNON RD
ULYSSES RD
AJAX RD
ACHILLES RD
BERRIDGE MEWS
HILLFIELD RD
MILL LA
SOLENT RD
NARCISSUS RD
HOLMDALE RD
GLENBROOK RD
PANDORA RD
SUMATRA RD
BURRARD RD
PARSIFAL RD
INGHAM RD
WEECH RD
KIDDERPORE AVE
BURGESS HILL
ARDWICK RD
KEYES RD
HOVEDEN RD
DAWLISH RD
DARTMOUTH RD
TEIGNMOUTH RD
MAPESBURY RD
CHATSWORTH ROAD
BRASSEY RD
BARLOW RD
HALL OAK WLK
MAYGROVE RD
LIDDELL RD
LOVERIDGE RD
ARIEL RD
MEDLEY RD
SHERRIFF RD
NETHERWOOD ST
PALMERSTON RD
HEMSTAL RD
DYNHAM RD
COTLEIGH RD
MESSINA AVE
GASCONY AVE
KINGSGATE RD
QUEX RD
CHRISTCHURCH AVE
MOWBRAY RD
CAVENDISH RD
WILLIAM DROMEY CT
DYNE RD
PLYMPTON RD
DUNSTER GDNS
BUCKLEY RD
STREATLEY RD
BURTON RD
CALLCOTT RD
TORBAY RD
KIMBERLEY RD
WINCHESTER AVE
PRIORY PARK RD
GLENGALL RD
THE AVENUE

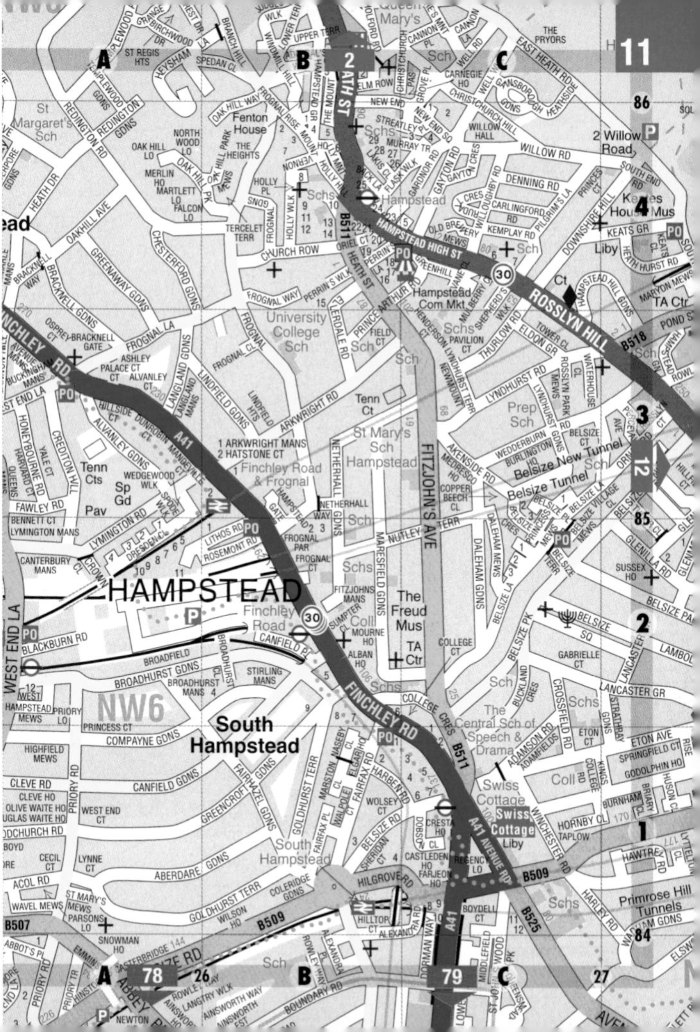
A
B
C
2
86
85
84
4
3
2
1
12
78
79
26
27
HAMPSTEAD
South Hampstead
NW6
Hampstead
ROSSLYN HILL
FINCHLEY RD
HEATH ST
HAMPSTEAD HIGH ST
FITZJOHN'S AVE
A41
B511
B518
B509
B507
B525
Fenton House
St Margaret's Sch
University College Sch
St Mary's Sch Hampstead
Finchley Road & Frognal
Finchley Road
Hampstead Com Mkt
The Freud Mus
TA Ctr
Tenn Ct
Tenn Cts
Sp Gd
Pav
Prep Sch
Belsize New Tunnel
Belsize Tunnel
2 Willow Road
Keats House Mus
Liby
Swiss Cottage
The Central Sch of Speech & Drama
Primrose Hill Tunnels
South Hampstead
Coll
Schs
Sch
PO
WEST END LA
FROGNAL
FROGNAL LA
CHURCH ROW
ARKWRIGHT RD
NUTLEY TERR
MARESFIELD GDNS
NETHERHALL GDNS
LINDFIELD GDNS
LANGLAND GDNS
CHESTERFORD GDNS
GREENAWAY GDNS
OAKHILL AVE
REDINGTON RD
REDINGTON GDNS
TEMPLEWOOD GDNS
HEATH DR
BRACKNELL GDNS
BRACKNELL WAY
HEYSHAM LA
BRANCH HILL
WINDMILL HILL
UPPER TERR
HOLFORD RD
CANNON PL
WELL RD
EAST HEATH RD
GAINSBOROUGH GDNS
WILLOW RD
DENNING RD
CARLINGFORD RD
KEMPLAY RD
DOWNSHIRE HILL
PILGRIM'S LA
KEATS GR
HEATH HURST RD
THURLOW RD
ELDON GR
LYNDHURST RD
LYNDHURST TERR
LYNDHURST GDNS
WEDDERBURN RD
AKENSIDE RD
BELSIZE LA
BELSIZE PK
BELSIZE SQ
BELSIZE PARK GDNS
BELSIZE VILLAGE
GLENILLA RD
LANCASTER GR
ETON AVE
ADAMSON RD
CROSSFIELD RD
WINCHESTER RD
COLLEGE CRES
DALEHAM GDNS
DALEHAM MEWS
BROADHURST GDNS
COMPAYNE GDNS
CANFIELD GDNS
GREENCROFT GDNS
FAIRHAZEL GDNS
GOLDHURST TERR
ABERDARE GDNS
PRIORY RD
CLEVE RD
BLACKBURN RD
BROADFIELD
CANFIELD PL
HILGROVE RD
BELSIZE RD
DORMAN WAY
BOUNDARY RD
AVENUE RD
HARLEY RD
WADHAM GDNS
HAWTREY RD
ALEXANDRA PL
ROWLEY WAY
LANGTRY WLK
AINSWORTH WAY
ABBEY RD
FAWLEY RD
LYMINGTON RD
HONEYBOURNE RD
CREDITON HILL
ALVANLEY GDNS
DRESDEN CL
CANTERBURY MANS
ROSEMONT RD
LITHOS RD
ACOL RD
WAVEL MEWS
MARSTON CL
NASEBY CL
FAIRFAX RD
HARBEN RD
SUMPTER CL
MOURNE HO
ALBAN HO
STIRLING MANS
WEST END CT
CASTLEDEN HO
FARJEON HO
BOYDELL CT
SNOWMAN HO
THE PRYORS
1 ARKWRIGHT MANS
2 HATSTONE CT

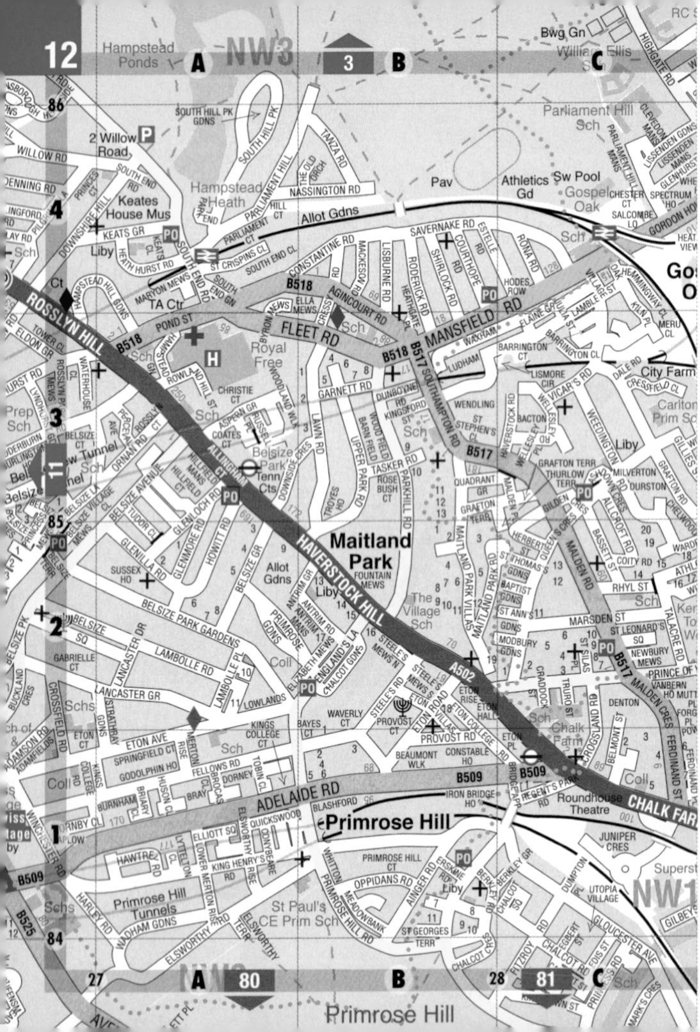
NW3
3
A
B
C
Hampstead Ponds
Bwg Gn
William Ellis Sch
RC
HIGHGATE RD
Parliament Hill Sch
SOUTH HILL PK GDNS
SOUTH HILL PK
TANZA RD
THE OLD ORCH
PARLIAMENT HILL
NASSINGTON RD
Hampstead Heath
Pav
Athletics Gd
Sw Pool
Gospel Oak
CHESTER CT
SALCOMBE LO
SPECTRUM HO
GORDON HO
CLEVEDON MANS
LISSENDEN GDNS
LISSENDEN MANS
GLENHURST
PARLIAMENT HILL MANS
2 Willow Road
WILLOW RD
DENNING RD
Keates House Mus
SOUTH END RD
KEATS GR
KEATS CL
Liby
HEATH HURST RD
DOWNSHIRE HILL
PRINCES CT
PILGRIM'S LA
Allot Gdns
PARLIAMENT CT
HILL CT
ST CRISPINS CL
SOUTH END CL
CONSTANTINE RD
MACKESON RD
LISBURNE RD
RODERICK RD
SHIRLOCK RD
COURTHOPE RD
SAVERNAKE RD
ESTELLE RD
RONA RD
HODES ROW
Sch
HEMMINGWAY CL
KILN PL
MERU CL
VILLAGE ST
LAMBLE ST
JULIA ST
OAK
Gospel Oak
86
4
3
2
1
11
85
84
MARYON MEWS
TA Ctr
SOUTH END GN
HAMPSTEAD HILL GDNS
Ct
ROSSLYN HILL
POND ST
B518
FLEET RD
AGINCOURT RD
ELLA MEWS
BYRON MEWS
CRESSY RD
HEATHGATE PL
MANSFIELD RD
WAXHAM
FLAINE GR
BARRINGTON CT
BARRINGTON CL
LUDHAM
LISMORE CIR
VICAR'S RD
DALE RD
City Farm
CRESSFIELD CL
Carlton Prim Sch
TOWER CL
ELDON GR
WATERHOUSE CL
Royal Free
H
ROWLAND HILL ST
CHRISTIE CT
WOODLAND WLK
GARNETT RD
DUNBOYNE RD
KINGSFORD ST
B517
SOUTHAMPTON RD
WENDLING
ST STEPHEN'S CL
HAVERSTOCK RD
BACTON
WELLESLEY RD
WELLESLEY PL
WEEDINGTON RD
GILLIES ST
LYNDHURST RD
ROSSLYN PK MEWS
Prep Sch
PERCEVAL AVE
ROSSLYN CT
ORNAN RD
ASPERN GR
RUSSELL PL
COATES CT
LAWN RD
UPPER PARK RD
BARN FIELD
WOOD FIELD
Sch
BELSIZE CT
Belsize Tunnel
Belsize Park
Tenn Cts
DOWNSIDE CRES
ALLINGHAM CT
HILLFIELD MANS
HILLFIELD CT
BELSIZE AVENUE
BELSIZE LA
BELSIZE VILLAGE
TASKER RD
ROSE BUSH CT
PARKHILL RD
TROYES HO
GRAFTON TERR
THURLOW TERR
MILVERTON
DURSTON
QUADRANT GR
GRAFTON TERR
ASHDOWN CRES
ALLCROFT RD
GRAFTON RD
CHELWOOD
GILDEN CRES
QUEEN'S CRES
MALDEN PL
TUDOR CL
GLENLOCH RD
GLENMORE RD
HOWITT RD
BELSIZE GR
HAVERSTOCK HILL
Maitland Park
FOUNTAIN MEWS
MAITLAND PARK VILLAS
MAITLAND PARK RD
HERBERT ST
ST THOMAS'S GDNS
BAPTIST GDNS
ST ANN'S GDNS
MALDEN RD
BASSETT ST
COITY RD
RHYL ST
WARDEN RD
ATHLONE
GLENILLA RD
SUSSEX HO
Allot Gdns
ANTRIM GR
ANTRIM RD
ANTRIM MANS
Liby
The Village Sch
MARSDEN ST
ST LEONARD'S SQ
NEWBURY MEWS
PRINCE OF WALES
TALACRE RD
BELSIZE PARK GARDENS
BELSIZE SQ
BELSIZE PK
GABRIELLE CT
LANCASTER DR
LAMBOLLE RD
LAMBOLLE PL
PRIMROSE GDNS
Coll
ELIZABETH MEWS
ENGLAND'S LA
CHALCOT GDNS
STEELE'S MEWS N
STEELE'S MEWS S
STEELE'S RD
A502
MODBURY GDNS
CRADDOCK ST
TRURO ST
ST SILAS PL
MALDEN CRES
FERDINAND ST
VANBERN HO
BUCKLAND CRES
LANCASTER GR
LOWLANDS
Schs
STRATHRAY GDNS
CROSSFIELD RD
MERTON RISE
WAVERLY CT
BAYES CT
KINGS COLLEGE CT
PROVOST CT
ETON ROAD
ETON VILLAS
ETON RISE
ETON HALL
ETON COLLEGE RD
PROVOST RD
Chalk Farm
CROGSLAND RD
DENTON
BELMONT ST
ADAMSON RD
ADAMFIELD
ETON CT
ETON AVE
SPRINGFIELD CT
GODOLPHIN HO
FELLOWS RD
BROCAS CL
DORNEY
TOBIN CL
BEAUMONT WLK
CONSTABLE HO
ETON PL
B509
KINGS COLLEGE RD
HUSON CL
BRAY
BRIARY CL
BURNHAM
ADELAIDE RD
BLASHFORD
IRON BRIDGE HO
BRIDGE APPR
REGENT'S PARK RD
Roundhouse Theatre
CHALK FARM
WINCHESTER RD
ORNBY CL
QUICKSWOOD
ELLIOTT SQ
ELSWORTHY RISE
Primrose Hill
JUNIPER CRES
HAWTREY RD
LYTTELTON CL
LOWER MERTON RISE
KING HENRY'S RD
CONYBEARE
WHITTON
PRIMROSE HILL CT
ERSKINE RD
BERKLEY GR
DUMPTON PL
Superstore
UTOPIA VILLAGE
NW1
GILBEYS
Primrose Hill Tunnels
Schs
HARLEY RD
WADHAM GDNS
ELSWORTHY RD
ELSWORTHY TERR
ELSWORTHY
St Paul's CE Prim Sch
PRIMROSE HILL RD
MEADOWBANK
OPPIDANS RD
AINGER RD
ST GEORGES TERR
CHALCOT CRES
BERKLEY RD
CHALCOT SQ
FITZROY RD
CHALCOT RD
EGBERT ST
EDIS ST
PRINCESS RD
GLOUCESTER AVE
ST MARK'S CRES
B525
27
28
80
81
Primrose Hill

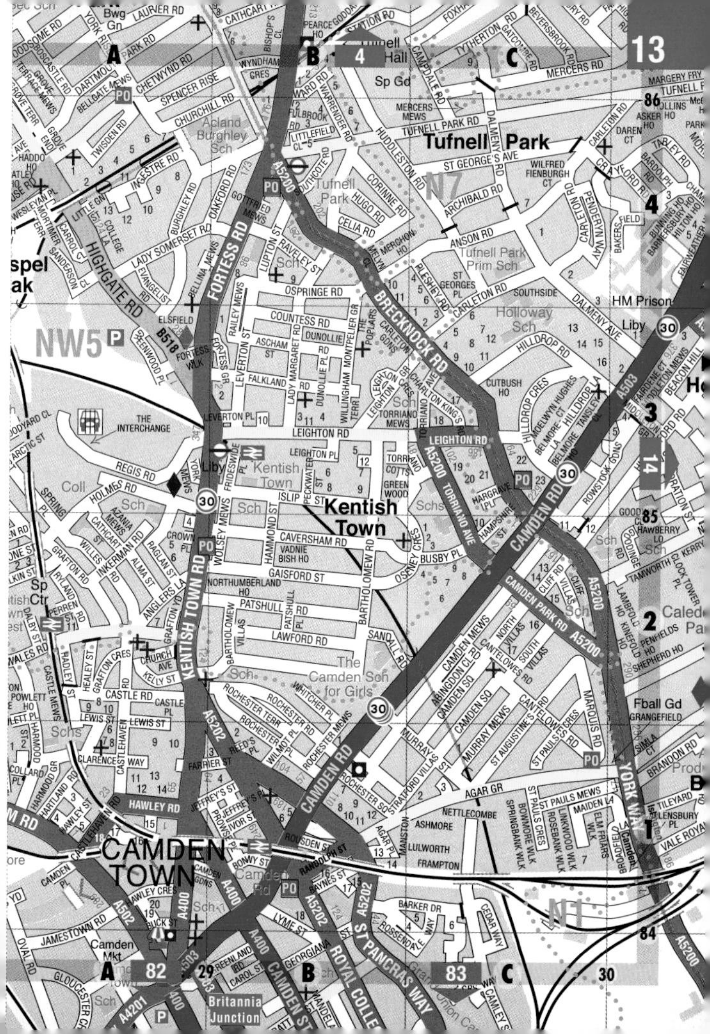
A
B
C
4
1
2
3
13
14
82
83
84
85
86
29
30
Tufnell Park
Kentish Town
CAMDEN TOWN
N7
NW5
N1
Tufnell Hall
Sp Gd
Acland Burghley Sch
Tufnell Park Prim Sch
Holloway Sch
HM Prison
The Interchange
The Camden Sch for Girls
Camden Mkt
Britannia Junction
Fball Gd
Sp Ctr
Coll
Sch
Schs
Liby
PO
LAURIER RD
CATHCART HILL
DARTMOUTH PARK RD
CHETWYND RD
SPENCER RISE
CHURCHILL RD
TWISDEN RD
INGESTRE RD
BURGHLEY RD
LADY SOMERSET RD
OAKFORD RD
FORTESS RD
HIGHGATE RD
B518
GOTTFRIED MEWS
LUPTON ST
RAVELEY ST
OSPRINGE RD
COUNTESS RD
DUNOLLIE RD
ASCHAM ST
FALKLAND RD
LEVERTON ST
LEVERTON PL
LEIGHTON RD
LEIGHTON PL
REGIS RD
HOLMES RD
KENTISH TOWN RD
ISLIP ST
CAVERSHAM RD
GAISFORD ST
PATSHULL RD
LAWFORD RD
BARTHOLOMEW RD
ROCHESTER RD
ROCHESTER TERR
CAMDEN RD
A5200
A5202
A503
A400
A502
BRECKNOCK RD
TORRIANO AVE
TUFNELL PARK RD
ST GEORGE'S AVE
ARCHIBALD RD
ANSON RD
CARLETON RD
DALMENY AVE
DALMENY RD
HUDDLESTON RD
CORINNE RD
HUGO RD
CELIA RD
HILLDROP CRES
HILLDROP RD
CAMDEN PARK RD
CAMDEN SQ
CAMDEN MEWS
MURRAY MEWS
ST AUGUSTINE'S RD
CANTELOWES RD
MARQUIS RD
YORK WAY
AGAR GR
ST PAULS MEWS
MAIDEN LA
HAWLEY RD
CASTLE RD
CLARENCE WAY
GRAFTON RD
INKERMAN RD
PRINCE OF WALES RD
RANDOLPH ST
ROYAL COLLEGE ST
ST PANCRAS WAY
CAMDEN ST
JAMESTOWN RD
GLOUCESTER CRES
MERCERS RD
TYTHERTON RD
BEVERSBROOK RD
MARGERY FRY CT
BRANDON RD
VALE ROYAL

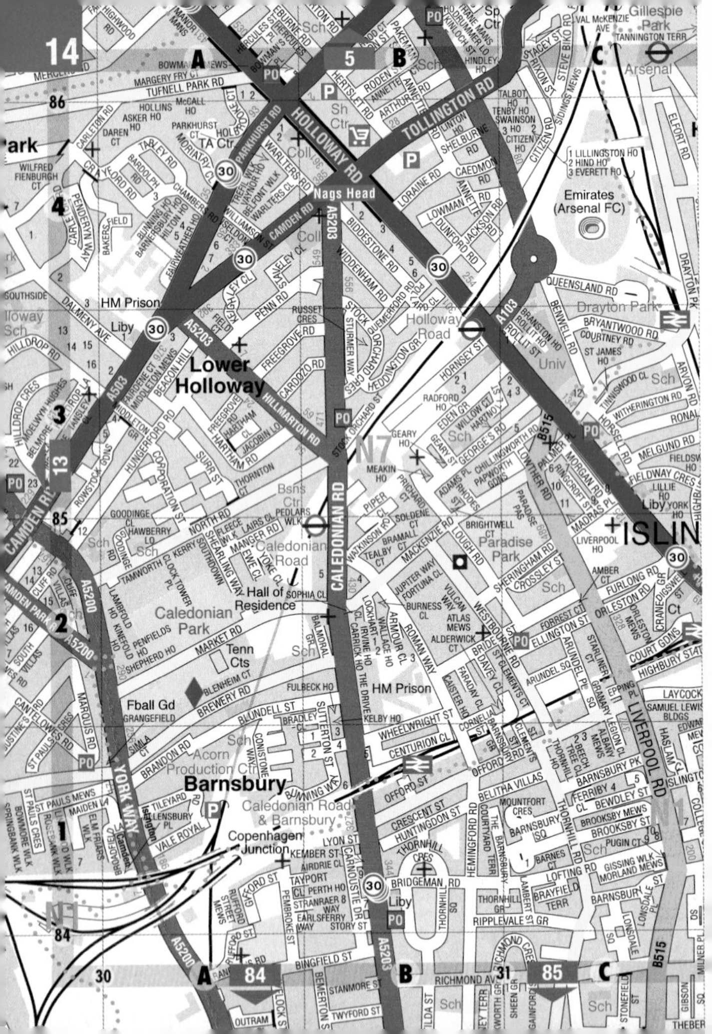
5
A
B
C
Holloway Rd
Tollington Rd
Nags Head
Camden Rd
Caledonian Rd
A5203
A503
A5200
A103
B515
Emirates (Arsenal FC)
Arsenal
Gillespie Park
Drayton Park
Holloway Road
HM Prison
Lower Holloway
Hillmarton Rd
N7
Caledonian Road
Caledonian Park
Hall of Residence
Paradise Park
Fball Gd
Tenn Cts
Acorn Production Ctr
Barnsbury
Caledonian Road & Barnsbury
Copenhagen Junction
York Way
Liverpool Rd
Islington
N1
Tufnell Park Rd
Parkhurst Rd
Hornsey St
Market Rd
Brewery Rd
Bridgeman Rd
Richmond Av
Hemingford Rd
Thornhill Rd
Offord Rd
Roman Way
Westbourne Rd
13
84
85
86
30

A
B
C
6
Highbury
HIGHBURY PK
HIGHBURY GR
HIGHBURY QUADRANT
BIRCHMORE WLK
SOTHEBY RD
NORTHOLME RD
KELROSS RD
HIGHBURY GRANGE
AUBERT PK
JACK WALKER CT
HAMILTON PK
MARTINEAU RD
FRAMFIELD RD
Recn Gd
Tenn Cts
N5
Frogmore Ind Est
ABERDEEN PK
NEWCOMBE HO
FAITHFULL HO
LYNTON LO
ABERDEEN LA
Aberdeen Ctr
SEAFORTH CRES
FRENSHAM CT
GROSVENOR AVE
HIGHBURY NEW PK
PARK VIEW
BELMONT CT
PETHERTON RD
NEW RIVER CT
CLISSOLD CRES
CLISSOLD RD
CARYSFORT RD
MILNER BLDG
ALBION RD
CHURCH WLK
SPRINGDALE RD
WINSTON RD
REEDHOLM VILLAS
LAVELL ST
PEGASUS CL
ADEN GR
BRIDGE GDNS
LIDFIELD RD
HOWARD RD
MATTHIAS RD
NEWINGTON GN
NEWINGTON GREEN RD
POET'S RD
FERNTOWER RD
PYRLAND RD
BERESFORD RD
LINDEN MEWS
MILDMAY GR N
MILDMAY GR S
MILDMAY PK
MILDMAY RD
MILDMAY AVE
MILDMAY ST
ALLEN RD
SHAKSPEARE WLK
ELTON PL
LANDOR WLK
SPENSER GR
COWPER RD
16
85
86
Highbury Fields
Highbury Pool
GTON
Highbury & Islington
Highbury Corner
Canonbury
ST PAUL'S RD
A1199
A1201
A104
A105
NORTHAMPTON GR
NORTHAMPTON PK
HOPE CL
BLAIR CL
WALLACE RD
BINGHAM ST
BALLS POND RD
CULFORD MEWS
DOVE RD
BAXTER RD
Kingsland
MITCHISON RD
OCKENDON RD
SOUTHGATE RD
B102
ARDLEIGH RD
CULFORD GR
CULFORD RD
CANONBURY RD
CANONBURY PK N
CANONBURY PK S
CANONBURY GR
CANONBURY PL
CANONBURY LA
CANONBURY SQ
CANONBURY ST
ALWYNE VILLAS
ALWYNE RD
ALWYNE PL
DOUGLAS RD
ESSEX RD
A1200
UPPER STREET
COMPTON AVE
COMPTON TERR
CROWLAND TERR
SWAN HO
OAKLEY RD
DE BEAUVOIR CT
NORTHCHURCH RD
ELMORE ST
N1
De Beauvoir Town
ENGLEFIELD RD
UFTON GR
UFTON RD
DEACON MEWS
SOUTHGATE GR
DOWNHAM RD
BENYON RD
BALMES RD
84
Liby
Essex Road
ROTHERFIELD ST
ECCLESBOURNE RD
ELIZABETH AVE
ALMORAH RD
CLEVELAND RD
RICHMOND GR
HALTON RD
SEBBON ST
FLORENCE ST
CROSS ST
GREENMAN ST
ISLINGTON EST
DIBDEN ST
POPHAM RD
POPHAM ST
QUEENSBURY ST
SHEPPERTON RD
CANAL WLK
WILTON SQ
86
32
87
33
Sch
Coll
PO
30

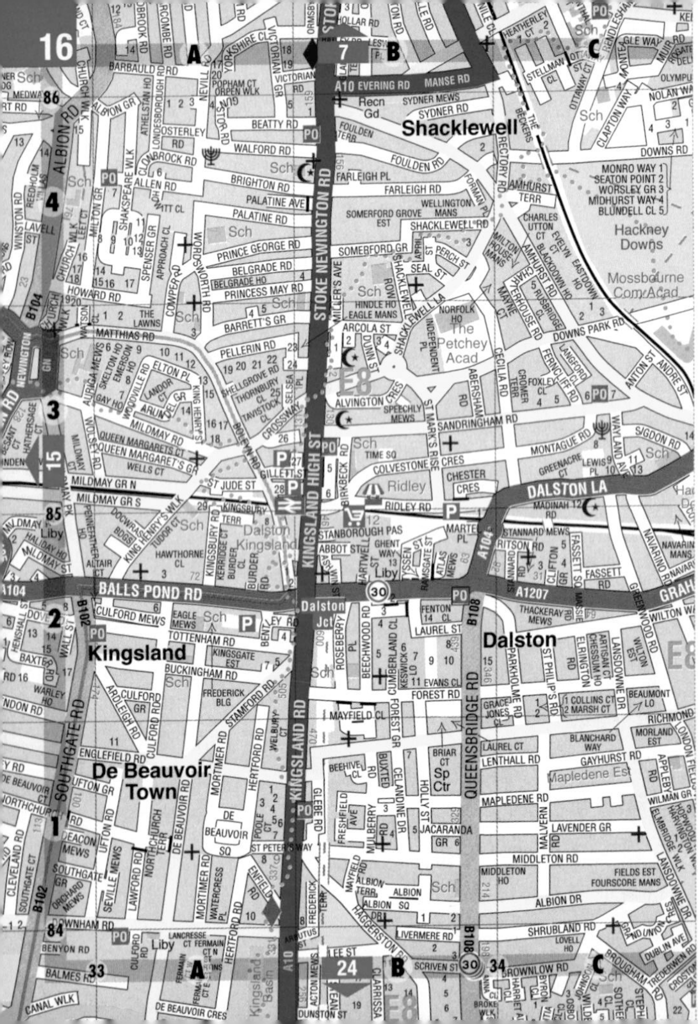
A
B
C
7
24
15
1
2
3
4
Shacklewell
Kingsland
Dalston
De Beauvoir Town
Hackney Downs
Mossbourne Com Acad
The Petchey Acad
Ridley
Dalston Kingsland
Dalston Jct
Kingsland Basin
E8
STOKE NEWINGTON RD
KINGSLAND HIGH ST
KINGSLAND RD
BALLS POND RD
DALSTON LA
QUEENSBRIDGE RD
SOUTHGATE RD
ALBION RD
EVERING RD
MANSE RD
A10
A104
A1207
B102
B104
B108
BARBAULD RD
YORKSHIRE CL
VICTORIAN GR
POPHAM CT
ORPEN WLK
BEATTY RD
WALFORD RD
BRIGHTON RD
PALATINE AVE
PALATINE RD
PRINCE GEORGE RD
BELGRADE RD
PRINCESS MAY RD
BARRETT'S GR
PELLERIN RD
SHELLGROVE RD
MATTHIAS RD
ELTON PL
MILDMAY RD
QUEEN MARGARET'S GR
WELLS CT
MILDMAY GR N
MILDMAY GR S
ST JUDE ST
HAWTHORNE CL
CULFORD MEWS
EAGLE MEWS
TOTTENHAM RD
KINGSGATE EST
BUCKINGHAM RD
CULFORD GR
FREDERICK BLG
STAMFORD RD
ENGLEFIELD RD
DE BEAUVOIR SQ
ST PETER'S WAY
DOWNHAM RD
BENYON RD
BALMES RD
CANAL WLK
DE BEAUVOIR CRES
DUNSTON ST
FOULDEN RD
FARLEIGH PL
FARLEIGH RD
SOMERFORD GROVE EST
SOMERFORD GR
SHACKLEWELL RD
SHACKLEWELL LA
SHACKLEWELL ROW
SEAL ST
PERCH ST
ARCOLA ST
DUNN ST
ALVINGTON CRES
SPEECHLY MEWS
ST MARK'S RISE
SANDRINGHAM RD
COLVESTONE CRES
CHESTER CRES
RIDLEY RD
STANBOROUGH PAS
ABBOT ST
GHENT WAY
MARTEL PL
SYDNER MEWS
SYDNER RD
RECTORY RD
AMHURST TERR
DOWNS PARK RD
DOWNS RD
MONRO WAY 1
SEATON POINT 2
WORSLEY GR 3
MIDHURST WAY 4
BLUNDELL CL 5
MONTAGUE RD
STANNARD MEWS
FASSETT RD
THACKERAY MEWS
FENTON CL
LAUREL ST
FOREST RD
EVANS CL
MAYFIELD CL
LAUREL CT
LENTHALL RD
GAYHURST RD
Mapledene Est
MAPLEDENE RD
LAVENDER GR
MIDDLETON RD
ALBION DR
SHRUBLAND RD
LIVERMERE RD
SCRIVEN ST
BROWNLOW RD
HAGGERSTON RD
ALBION SQ
JACARANDA GR
FOURSCORE MANS
RICHMOND RD
BLANCHARD WAY
WILTON WAY
NAVARINO RD
GREENWOOD RD
LANSDOWNE DR
Recn Gd
Sp Ctr
Liby
Sch
PO

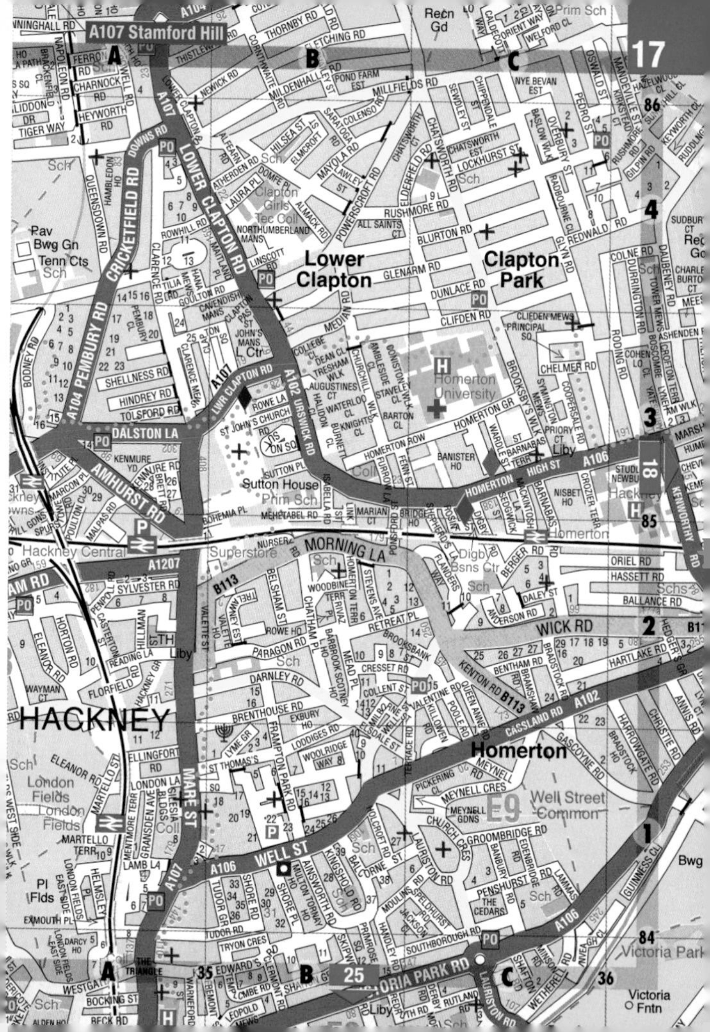

17
A107 Stamford Hill
A B C
A104 PEMBURY RD
CRICKETFIELD RD
LOWER CLAPTON RD
A107
A102 URSWICK RD
LWR CLAPTON RD
DALSTON LA
AMHURST RD
Lower Clapton
Clapton Park
Clapton Girls Tec Coll
Homerton University
HOMERTON HIGH ST
A106
HOMERTON ROW
MORNING LA
Hackney Central
Sutton House
Superstore
Digby Bsns Ctr
WICK RD
A1207
B113
CASSLAND RD
A102
HACKNEY
Homerton
E9
Well Street Common
London Fields
MARE ST
WELL ST
A106
VICTORIA PARK RD
Victoria Park
Victoria Fntn
Liby
Sch
PO
1 2 3 4
18
25
35
36
84
85
86

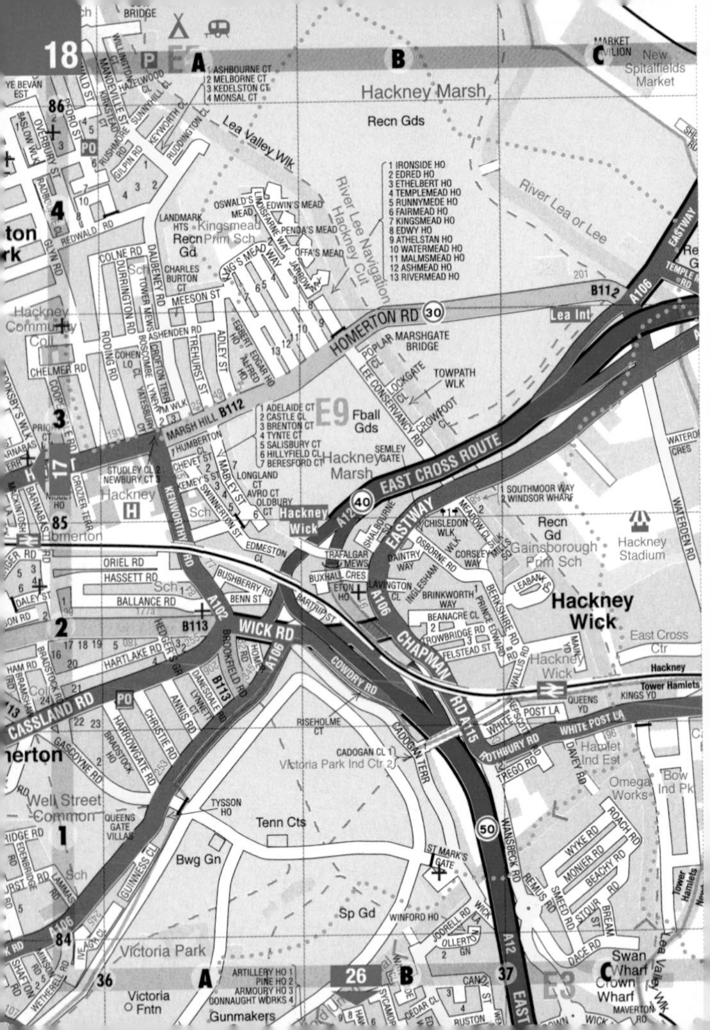
A
B
C
1 ASHBOURNE CT
2 MELBORNE CT
3 KEDELSTON CT
4 MONSAL CT
Hackney Marsh
Recn Gds
New Spitalfields Market
MARKET PAVILION
Lea Valley Wlk
River Lee Navigation Hackney Cut
River Lea or Lee
1 IRONSIDE HO
2 EDRED HO
3 ETHELBERT HO
4 TEMPLEMEAD HO
5 RUNNYMEDE HO
6 FAIRMEAD HO
7 KINGSMEAD HO
8 EDWY HO
9 ATHELSTAN HO
10 WATERMEAD HO
11 MALMSMEAD HO
12 ASHMEAD HO
13 RIVERMEAD HO
OSWALD'S MEAD
EDWIN'S MEAD
LINDISFARNE WAY
PENDA'S MEAD
OFFA'S MEAD
KING'S MEAD WAY
JARROW WAY
LANDMARK HTS
Kingsmead Prim Sch
Recn Gd
CHARLES BURTON CT
MEESON ST
COLNE RD
DURRINGTON RD
DAUBENEY RD
TOWER MEWS
REDWALD RD
GLYN RD
RUDDINGTON CL
KEYWORTH CL
SUNNYHILL CL
HAZELWOOD CL
MANDEVILLE ST
WILLINGTON CT
KIRKSTEAD CT
RUSHMORE RD
GILPIN RD
OVERBURY ST
BASLOW WLK
RADBOURNE CL
DEDRO ST
PO
86
4
Hackney Community Coll
CHELMER RD
RODING RD
COHEN LO
BOSCOMBE CL
ASHENDEN RD
CROFTON TERR
YATESBURY CT
LYNE WLK
TREHURST ST
ADLEY ST
EGBERT HO
EDGAR HO
ALFRED HO
HOMERTON RD
B112
Lea Int
EASTWAY
A106
TEMPLE MILL RD
POPLAR CL
MARSHGATE BRIDGE
LEE CONSERVANCY RD
LOCKGATE CL
TOWPATH WLK
CROWFOOT CL
1 ADELAIDE CT
2 CASTLE CL
3 BRENTON CT
4 TYNTE CT
5 SALISBURY CT
6 HILLYFIELD CL
7 BERESFORD CT
E9
Fball Gds
SEMLEY GATE
Hackney Marsh
MARSH HILL
3
HUMBERTON CL
CHEVET ST
KEMEY'S ST
MABLEY ST
SWINNERTON ST
LONGLAND CT
AVRO CT
OLDBURY CT
Hackney Wick
EAST CROSS ROUTE
A12
STUDLEY CL
NEWBURY CT
Hackney
KENWORTHY RD
CROZIER TERR
BARNABAS RD
MACKINTOSH LA
NISBET HO
85
Homerton
17
1 SOUTHMOOR WAY
2 WINDSOR WHARF
SHALBOURNE SQ
CHISLEDON WLK
MEADOW CL
SILK MILLS SQ
Recn Gd
Gainsborough Prim Sch
Hackney Stadium
WATERDEN RD
WATERDEN CRES
EDMESTON CL
TRAFALGAR MEWS
BUXHALL CRES
ETON HO
DAINTRY WAY
OSBORNE RD
CORSLEY WAY
INGLESHAM WLK
LAVINGTON CL
BRINKWORTH WAY
LEABANK SQ
Hackney Wick
ORIEL RD
HASSETT RD
BALLANCE RD
BUSHBERRY RD
BENN ST
BARTRIP ST
DALEY ST
B113
A102
WICK RD
BEANACRE CL
TROWBRIDGE RD
FELSTEAD ST
BERKSHIRE RD
PRINCE EDWARD RD
WALLIS RD
MAIN YD
East Cross Ctr
2
HEDGER'S GR
BROOKFIELD RD
HOMER RD
CHAPMAN RD
A115
COWDRY RD
HARTLAKE RD
BRADSTOCK RD
CASSLAND RD
PO
HARROWGATE RD
CHRISTIE RD
ANNIS RD
DANESDALE RD
LYNNETT CT
Hackney
Tower Hamlets
QUEENS YD
KINGS YD
HEPSCOTT RD
WHITE POST LA
ROTHBURY RD
TREGO RD
DAVEY RD
Hamlet Ind Est
Omega Works
Bow Ind Pk
RISEHOLME CT
CADOGAN CL 1
Victoria Park Ind Ctr 2
CADOGAN TERR
Homerton
GASCOYNE RD
BRADSTOCK HO
Well Street Common
TYSSON HO
QUEENS GATE VILLAS
Tenn Cts
1
Bwg Gn
GUINNESS CL
ST MARK'S GATE
WANSBECK RD
REMUS RD
SMEED RD
STOUR RD
BREAM ST
ROACH RD
WYKE RD
MONIER RD
BEACHY RD
DACE RD
Tower Hamlets
Sp Gd
WINFORD HO
JODRELL RD
OLLERTON GN
WICK LA
Lea Valley Wlk
EDENBRIDGE RD
LAMMAS RD
Sch
A106
84
IVE AGH CL
Victoria Park
WETHERELL RD
SHAFTON RD
36
ARTILLERY HO 1
PINE HO 2
ARMOURY HO 3
CONNAUGHT WORKS 4
26
37
E3
Swan Wharf
Crown Wharf
MAVERTON RD
Victoria Fntn
Gunmakers
CEDAR CL
RUSTON
EAST
50
40
30

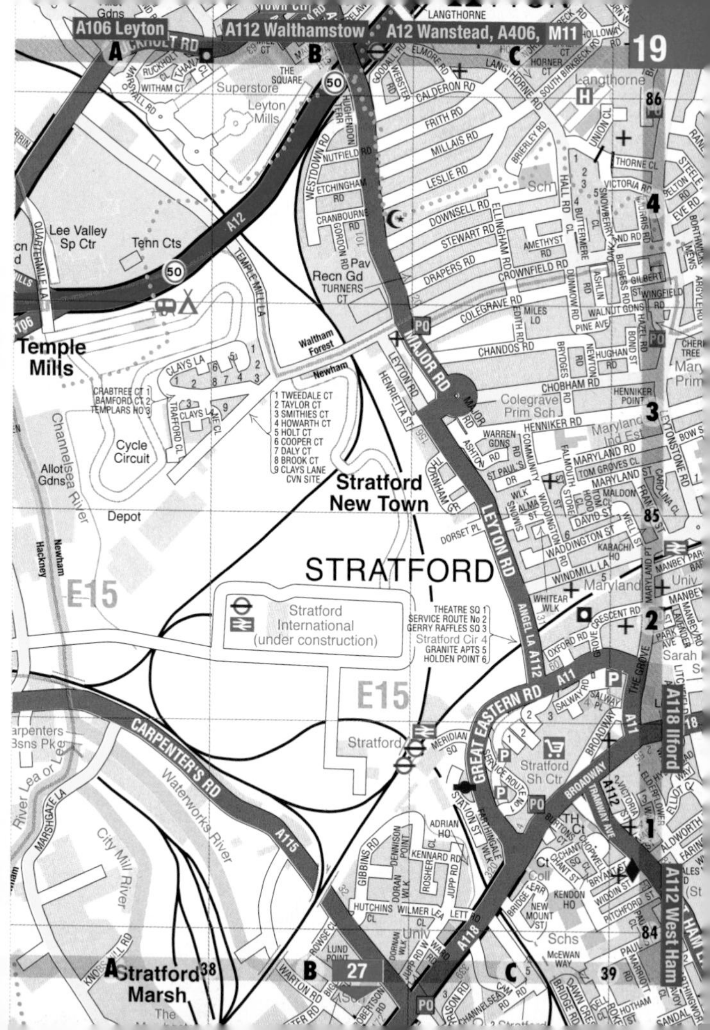
A106 Leyton
A112 Walthamstow
A12 Wanstead, A406, M11
A
B
C
Temple Mills
Lee Valley Sp Ctr
Tenn Cts
Leyton Mills
Superstore
The Square
A12
Langthorne
Calderon Rd
Frith Rd
Millais Rd
Leslie Rd
Downsell Rd
Stewart Rd
Drapers Rd
Colegrave Rd
Chandos Rd
Chobham Rd
Crownfield Rd
Ellingham Rd
Buttermere
Hall Rd
Westdown Rd
Nutfield Rd
Etchingham Rd
Cranbourne Rd
Gordon Rd
Hughendon Terr
Goodall Rd
Webster Rd
Elmore Rd
Langthorne Rd
South Birkbeck Rd
Horner Ct
Union Cl
Thorne Cl
Victoria Rd
Brierley Rd
Sch
Recn Gd
Pav
Turners Ct
Waltham Forest
Newham
Major Rd
Leyton Rd
Henrietta St
Colegrave Prim Sch
Maryland Ind Est
Henniker Rd
Henniker Point
Maryland Rd
Tom Groves Cl
Maryland St
Leytonstone Rd
Warren Gdns
St Paul's Dr
Community Rd
Falmouth St
Waddington St
Waddington Rd
David St
Karachi Ho
Windmill La
Whitear Wlk
Maryland
Gilbert St
Wingfield Rd
Walnut Gdns
Pine Ave
Hughan Rd
Brydges Rd
Edith Rd
Miles Lo
Dunmow Rd
Ashlin Rd
Burgess Rd
Bond St
Hazel Rd
Clays La
Trafford Cl
Crabtree Ct 1
Bamford Ct 2
Templars Ho 3
1 Tweedale Ct
2 Taylor Ct
3 Smithies Ct
4 Howarth Ct
5 Holt Ct
6 Cooper Ct
7 Daly Ct
8 Brook Ct
9 Clays Lane Cvn Site
Cycle Circuit
Allot Gdns
Channelsea River
Depot
Hackney
Newham
E15
Stratford New Town
STRATFORD
Stratford International (under construction)
Theatre Sq 1
Service Route No 2
Gerry Raffles Sq 3
Stratford Cir 4
Granite Apts 5
Holden Point 6
Angel La A112
Great Eastern Rd
A11
Oxford Rd
Grove Crescent Rd
The Grove
Salway Rd
Salway Pl
Broadway
Stratford Sh Ctr
Stratford
Meridian Sq
Station St
Farthingale Wlk
Carpenter's Rd
A115
Waterworks River
City Mill River
River Lea or Lee
Marshgate La
Carpenters Bsns Pk
Knobs Hill Rd
Stratford Marsh
Gibbins Rd
Dennison Point
Doran Wlk
Rosher Cl
Kennard Rd
Jupp Rd
Adrian Ho
Hutchins Cl
Wilmer Lea Cl
Lett Rd
Univ
Lund Point
Warton Rd
A118
Coll
Bridge Terr
New Mount St
Kendon Ho
Schs
McEwan Way
Chant St
Chant Sq
Chapel St
Bryant St
Widdin St
Pitchford St
Tramway Ave
Victoria St
Elderflower
A118 Ilford
A112 West Ham
Manbey Park
Lavender
Sarah
Aldworth
Hotham
Sandal
27
38
39
84
85
86
1
2
3
4

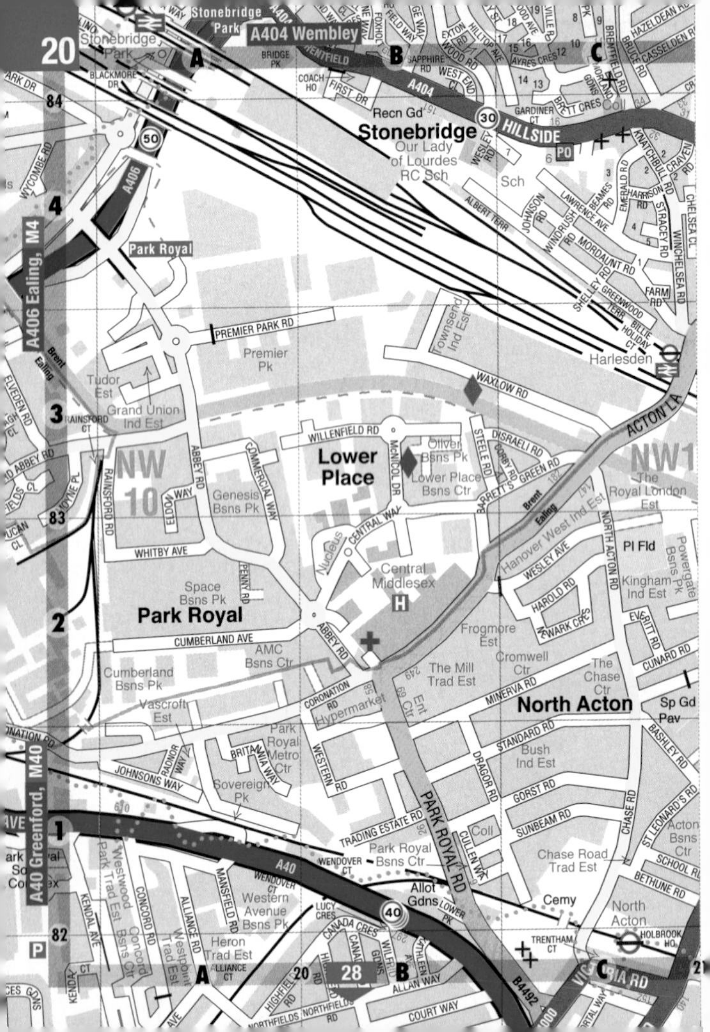
A404 Wembley
Stonebridge Park
Stonebridge
Recn Gd
Our Lady of Lourdes RC Sch
Sch
A404
HILLSIDE
PO
Coll
BRIDGE PK
COACH HO
FIRST DR
BLACKMORE DR
SAPPHIRE RD
WEST END CL
EXTON RD
HILLTOP AVE
AYRES CRES
GARDINER CT
BRETT CRES
WESLEY RD
BRENTFIELD RD
BRUCE RD
HAZELDEAN RD
CASSELDEN RD
KNATCHBULL RD
CRAVEN RD
EMERALD RD
HARRISON RD
STRACEY RD
CHELSEA CL
WINCHELSEA RD
JOHNSON RD
LAWRENCE AVE
BEAMES RD
WINDRUSH RD
MORDAUNT RD
ALBERT TERR
SHELLEY RD
GREENWOOD TERR
BILLIE HOLIDAY CT
FARM RD
Harlesden
ACTON LA
NW10
WYCOMBE RD
A406
Park Royal
PREMIER PARK RD
Premier Pk
Townsend Ind Est
WAXLOW RD
Tudor Est
Grand Union Ind Est
Brent
Ealing
A406 Ealing, M4
ELVEDEN RD
RAINSFORD CT
ABBEY RD
RAINSFORD RD
MOYNE PL
ELDON WAY
COMMERCIAL WAY
Genesis Bsns Pk
WHITBY AVE
WILLENFIELD RD
Lower Place
McNICOL DR
Oliver Bsns Pk
Lower Place Bsns Ctr
STEELE RD
DISRAELI RD
CORBY RD
BARRETT'S GREEN RD
The Royal London Est
Nucleus
CENTRAL WAY
Central Middlesex
H
Hanover West Ind Est
WESLEY AVE
HAROLD RD
NEWARK CRES
NORTH ACTON RD
Pl Fld
Powergate Bsns Pk
Kingham Ind Est
EVERITT RD
CUNARD RD
Space Bsns Pk
PENNY RD
Park Royal
CUMBERLAND AVE
AMC Bsns Ctr
Cumberland Bsns Pk
Frogmore Est
Cromwell Ctr
The Mill Trad Est
The Chase Ctr
Ent Ctr
MINERVA RD
North Acton
Sp Gd
Pav
Vascroft Est
CORONATION RD
Hypermarket
Park Royal Metro Ctr
BRITANNIA WAY
WESTERN RD
RADNOR WAY
JOHNSONS WAY
Sovereign Pk
STANDARD RD
Bush Ind Est
DRAGOR RD
GORST RD
SUNBEAM RD
BASHLEY RD
PARK ROYAL RD
CHASE RD
ST LEONARD'S RD
Acton Bsns Ctr
SCHOOL RD
BETHUNE RD
Chase Road Trad Est
Coll
CULLEN WAY
TRADING ESTATE RD
Park Royal Bsns Ctr
WENDOVER CT
A40
A40 Greenford, M40
Westwood Park Trad Est
Concord Bsns Ctr
CONCORD RD
ALLIANCE RD
MANSFIELD RD
Western Avenue Bsns Pk
Westpoint Trad Est
Heron Trad Est
ALLIANCE CT
KENDAL AVE
LUCY CRES
CANADA CRES
WILFRID GDNS
Allot Gdns
LOWER PK
Cemy
North Acton
TRENTHAM CT
HOLBROOK HO
B4492
ALLAN WAY
COURT WAY
NORTHFIELDS RD
HIGHFIELD RD
A
B
C
1
2
3
4
28
84
83
82
20

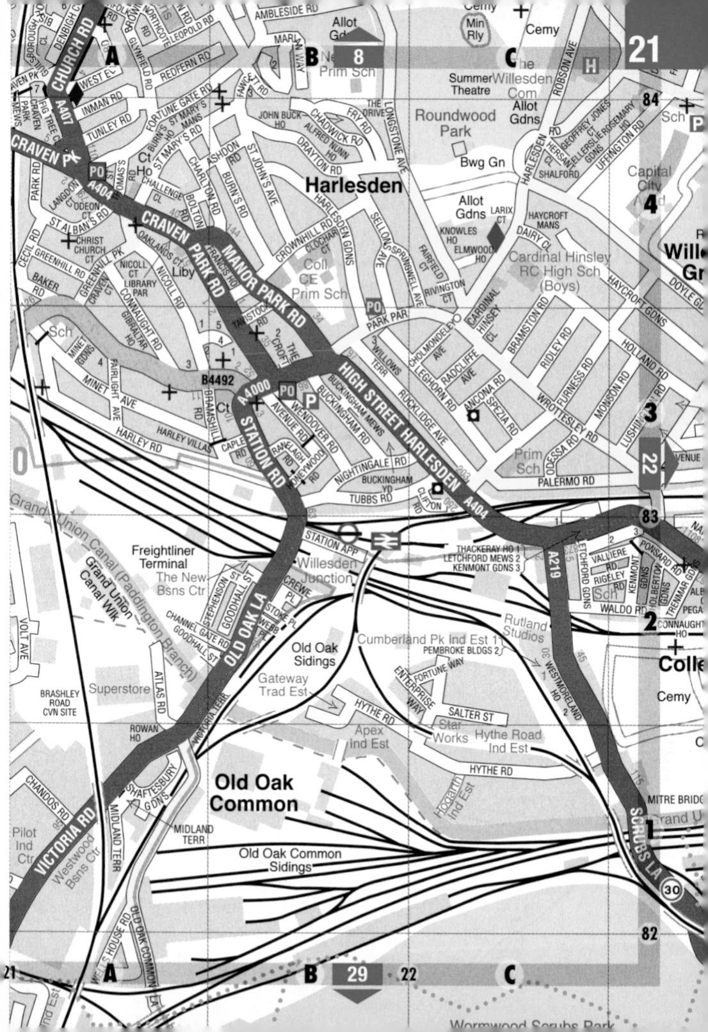
Harlesden
Old Oak Common
Old Oak Common Sidings
Old Oak Sidings
Freightliner Terminal
The New Bsns Ctr
Willesden Junction
Grand Union Canal (Paddington Branch)
Grand Union Canal Wlk
Roundwood Park
Bwg Gn
Summer Theatre
The Willesden Com
Allot Gdns
Cemy
Min Rly
Cardinal Hinsley RC High Sch (Boys)
Capital City Acad
Coll CE Prim Sch
Prim Sch
Sch
Liby
Superstore
BRASHLEY ROAD CVN SITE
Gateway Trad Est
Cumberland Pk Ind Est
Rutland Studios
Apex Ind Est
Star Works
Hythe Road Ind Est
Hogarth Ind Est
Pilot Ind Ctr
Westwood Bsns Ctr
Wormwood Scrubs Park
CRAVEN PK
CHURCH RD
CRAVEN PARK RD
MANOR PARK RD
HIGH STREET HARLESDEN
STATION RD
OLD OAK LA
VICTORIA RD
SCRUBS LA
A404
A407
A4000
A219
B4492
HARLESDEN RD
ROBSON AVE
HAYCROFT GDNS
HOLLAND RD
WROTTESLEY RD
FURNESS RD
RIDLEY RD
BRAMSTON RD
PALERMO RD
ODESSA RD
LEGHORN RD
RADCLIFFE AVE
CHOLMONDELEY AVE
RUCKLIDGE AVE
BUCKINGHAM RD
WENDOVER RD
AVENUE RD
TUBBS RD
NIGHTINGALE RD
MINET AVE
HARLEY RD
FAIRLIGHT AVE
CONNAUGHT RD
GREENHILL PK
ST ALBAN'S RD
CECIL RD
PARK RD
HYTHE RD
SALTER ST
FORTUNE WAY
ENTERPRISE WAY
WESTMORELAND HO
GOODHALL ST
STEPHENSON ST
CHANNEL GATE RD
ATLAS RD
VOLT AVE
CHANDOS RD
MIDLAND TERR
SHAFTESBURY GDNS
WELLS HOUSE RD
OLD OAK COMMON LA
MITRE BRIDGE
8
29
22
A
B
C
1
2
3
4
82
83
84

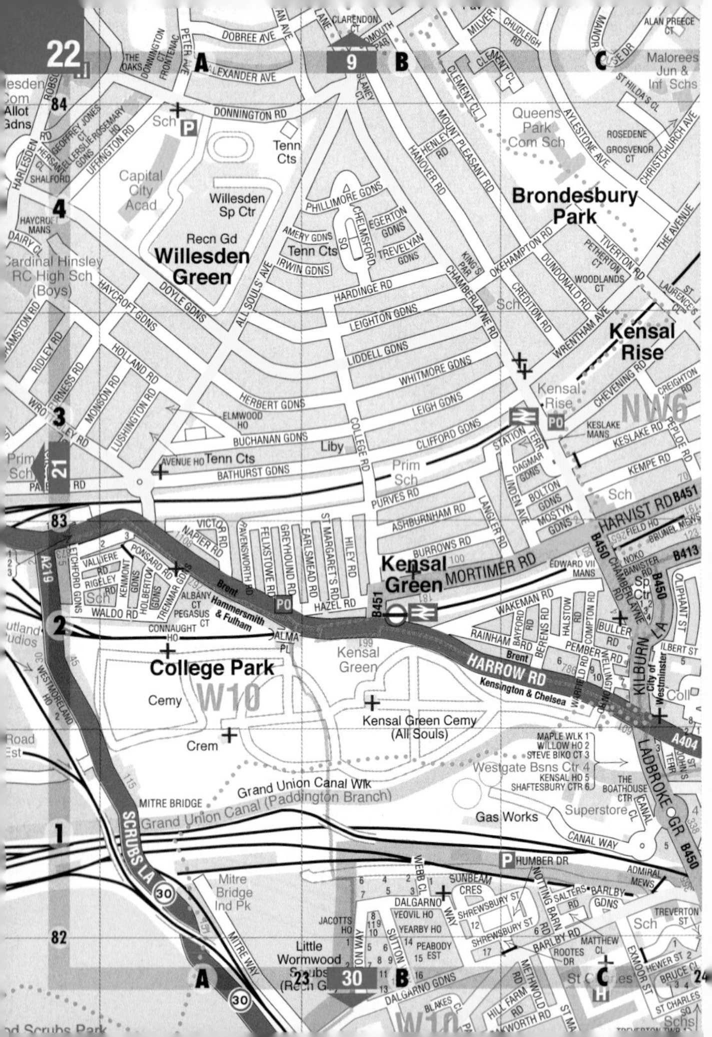

Willesden Green
Brondesbury Park
Kensal Rise
Kensal Green
College Park
NW6
W10
DOBREE AVE
ALEXANDER AVE
DONNINGTON RD
CLARENDON CT
PETER AVE
THE OAKS
DONNINGTON CT
FRONTENAC
9
A
B
C
CHUDLEIGH RD
MILVERTON
CLEMENT CL
ALAN PREECE CT
Malorees Jun & Inf Schs
ST HILDA'S CL
Queens Park Com Sch
AYLESTONE AVE
ROSEDENE
GROSVENOR CT
CHRISTCHURCH AVE
MOUNT PLEASANT RD
HENLEY RD
HANOVER RD
Tenn Cts
Sch
Capital City Acad
Willesden Sp Ctr
Recn Gd
PHILLIMORE GDNS
CHELMSFORD SQ
EGERTON GDNS
TREVELYAN GDNS
AMERY GDNS
IRWIN GDNS
HARDINGE RD
LEIGHTON GDNS
LIDDELL GDNS
WHITMORE GDNS
LEIGH GDNS
CLIFFORD GDNS
ALL SOULS' AVE
KING'S PAR
CHAMBERLAYNE RD
OKEHAMPTON RD
CREDITON RD
DUNDONALD RD
PETHERTON CT
TIVERTON RD
WOODLANDS CT
THE AVENUE
ST LAURENCE'S CL
WRENTHAM AVE
CHEVENING RD
CREIGHTON RD
Kensal Rise
PO
KESLAKE MANS
KESLAKE RD
PEPLOE RD
KEMPE RD
Sch
HARVIST RD
B451
FIELD HO
BRUNEL MEWS
B413
B450
84
Willesden Com Allot Gdns
HARLESDEN RD
ROBSON
GEOFFREY JONES CT
ELLERSLIE GDNS
ROSEMARY HO
UFFINGTON RD
HERSANT CL
SHALFORD
4
HAYCROFT MANS
DAIRY CL
Cardinal Hinsley RC High Sch (Boys)
HAYCROFT GDNS
DOYLE GDNS
HAMSTON RD
RIDLEY RD
FURNESS RD
HOLLAND RD
MONSON RD
LUSHINGTON RD
HERBERT GDNS
ELMWOOD HO
BUCHANAN GDNS
Liby
COLLEGE RD
3
WROTTESLEY RD
Prim Sch
21
AVENUE HO
Tenn Cts
BATHURST GDNS
Prim Sch
PURVES RD
ASHBURNHAM RD
BURROWS RD
STATION TERR
DAGMAR GDNS
LINDEN AVE
BOLTON GDNS
MOSTYN GDNS
LANGLER RD
83
A219
VICTOR RD
NAPIER RD
RAVENSWORTH RD
FELIXSTOWE RD
GREYHOUND RD
EARLSMEAD RD
ST MARGARET'S RD
HILEY RD
HAZEL RD
LETCHFORD GDNS
VALLIERE RD
RIGELEY RD
KENMONT GDNS
HOLBERTON GDNS
PONSARD RD
TRENMAR GDNS
ALBANY CT
PEGASUS CT
WALDO RD
Sch
CONNAUGHT HO
Brent
Hammersmith & Fulham
PO
ALMA PL
B451
MORTIMER RD
EDWARD VII MANS
WAKEMAN RD
RAINHAM RD
BAYFORD RD
BERENS RD
HALSTOW RD
COMPTON RD
PEMBER RD
WELLINGTON RD
WARFIELD RD
CHAMBERLAYNE RD
NOKO
BANISTER RD
Sp Ctr
BULLER RD
KILBURN LA
OLIPHANT ST
ILBERT ST
City of Westminster
Coll
2
Rutland Studios
WESTMORELAND HO
Cemy
Crem
Kensal Green
Kensal Green Cemy (All Souls)
HARROW RD
Brent
Kensington & Chelsea
A404
MAPLE WLK 1
WILLOW HO 2
STEVE BIKO CT 3
Westgate Bsns Ctr 4
KENSAL HO 5
SHAFTESBURY CTR 6
THE BOATHOUSE CTR
LADBROKE GR
ST JOHNS TERR
Road Est
MITRE BRIDGE
Grand Union Canal Wlk
Grand Union Canal (Paddington Branch)
Gas Works
Superstore
CANAL CL
CANAL WAY
1
SCRUBS LA
HUMBER DR
ADMIRAL MEWS
B450
NOTTING BARN RD
Mitre Bridge Ind Pk
WEBB CL
SUNBEAM CRES
DALGARNO WAY
SHREWSBURY ST
SALTERS RD
BARLBY GDNS
BARLBY RD
TREVERTON ST
Sch
JACOTTS HO
YEOVIL HO
YEARBY HO
PEABODY EST
SUTTON WAY
MATTHEW CL
ROOTES DR
EXMOOR ST
HEWER ST
BRUCE CL
82
MITRE WAY
Little Wormwood Scrubs (Recn Gd)
30
A
23
30
B
C
24
DALGARNO GDNS
BLAKES CL
HILL FARM RD
METHWOLD RD
St Charles
ST CHARLES SQ
Schs
Wormwood Scrubs Park

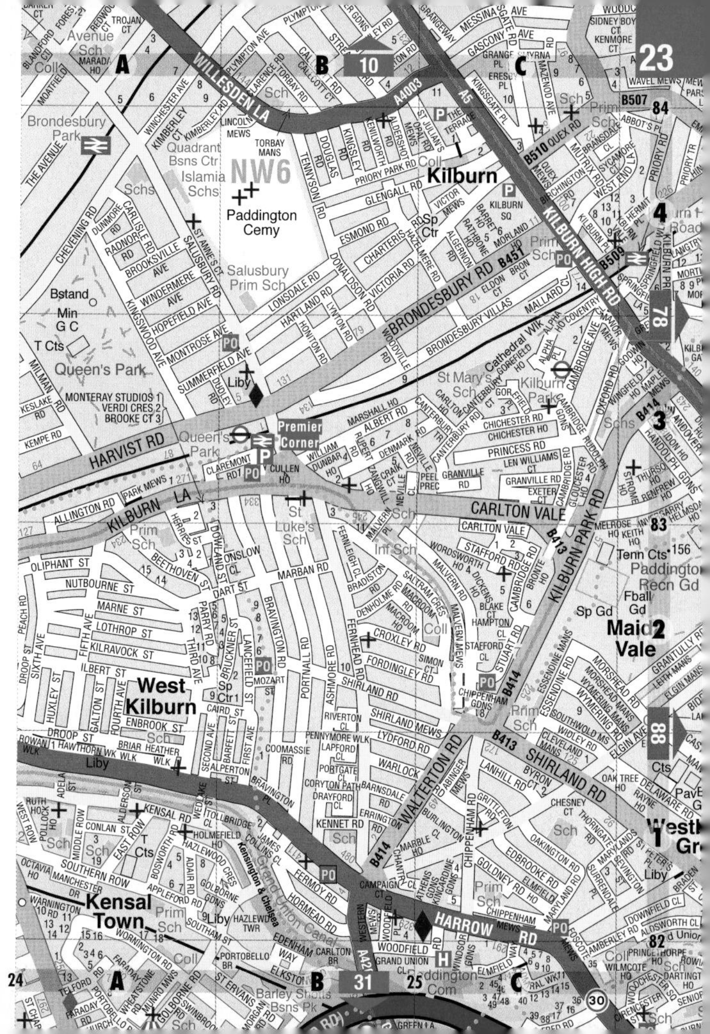
A
B
C
10
31
24
25
30
84
83
82
78
88
4
3
2
1
NW6
Kilburn
West Kilburn
Kensal Town
Maida Vale
Queen's Park
Brondesbury Park
Paddington Cemy
Paddington Recn Gd
Paddington Com
Premier Corner
Kensington & Chelsea
Grand Union Canal
WILLESDEN LA
A4003
A5
B507
B510
B509
B451
B414
B413
A404
KILBURN HIGH RD
KILBURN LA
HARVIST RD
BRONDESBURY RD
BRONDESBURY VILLAS
CARLTON VALE
KILBURN PARK RD
SHIRLAND RD
HARROW RD
WALTERTON RD
SALUSBURY RD
CHEVENING RD
KINGSWOOD AVE
WINCHESTER AVE
KIMBERLEY RD
THE AVENUE
TENNYSON RD
DOUGLAS RD
KINGSLEY RD
KENILWORTH RD
ALDERSHOT RD
PRIORY PARK RD
GLENGALL RD
ESMOND RD
CHARTERIS RD
VICTORIA RD
DONALDSON RD
LONSDALE RD
HARTLAND RD
HONITON RD
LYNTON RD
WOODVILLE RD
BROOKSVILLE AVE
WINDERMERE AVE
HOPEFIELD AVE
MONTROSE AVE
SUMMERFIELD AVE
DUDLEY RD
MILMAN RD
KESLAKE RD
KEMPE RD
ALLINGTON RD
CLAREMONT RD
CULLEN HO
ALBERT RD
DENMARK RD
CANTERBURY RD
CHICHESTER RD
PRINCESS RD
GRANVILLE RD
CAMBRIDGE AVE
CAMBRIDGE RD
OXFORD RD
RUDOLPH RD
MALVERN RD
STAFFORD RD
FERNHEAD RD
PORTNALL RD
ASHMORE RD
BRAVINGTON RD
LANCEFIELD ST
MARBAN RD
SHIRLAND MEWS
LYDFORD RD
WARLOCK RD
CROXLEY RD
FORDINGLEY RD
ESSENDINE RD
MORSHEAD RD
WYMERING RD
ELGIN AVE
LANHILL RD
OAKINGTON RD
EDBROOKE RD
GOLDNEY RD
ELMFIELD WAY
FERMOY RD
HORMEAD RD
PORTOBELLO RD
GOLBORNE RD
KENSAL RD
SOUTHERN ROW
MIDDLE ROW
ALDERSON ST
BOSWORTH RD
ADAIR RD
WEDLAKE ST
EDENHAM WAY
ELKSTONE RD
ST ERVANS RD
WHEATSTONE RD
FARADAY RD
TELFORD RD
WARNINGTON RD
OLIPHANT ST
NUTBOURNE ST
MARNE ST
LOTHROP ST
KILRAVOCK ST
ILBERT ST
ENBROOK ST
DROOP ST
HUXLEY ST
GALTON ST
FOURTH AVE
FIFTH AVE
SIXTH AVE
THIRD AVE
SECOND AVE
FIRST AVE
PEACH RD
BEETHOVEN ST
DART ST
Liby
Sch
Prim Sch
Coll
St Luke's Sch
St Mary's Sch
Salusbury Prim Sch
Islamia Schs
Quadrant Bsns Ctr
Barley Shotts Bsns Pk
Bstand
Min G C
T Cts
Tenn Cts
Sp Ctr
Sp Gd
Fball Gd
Kilburn Park
PO
MONTERAY STUDIOS 1
VERDI CRES 2
BROOKE CT 3

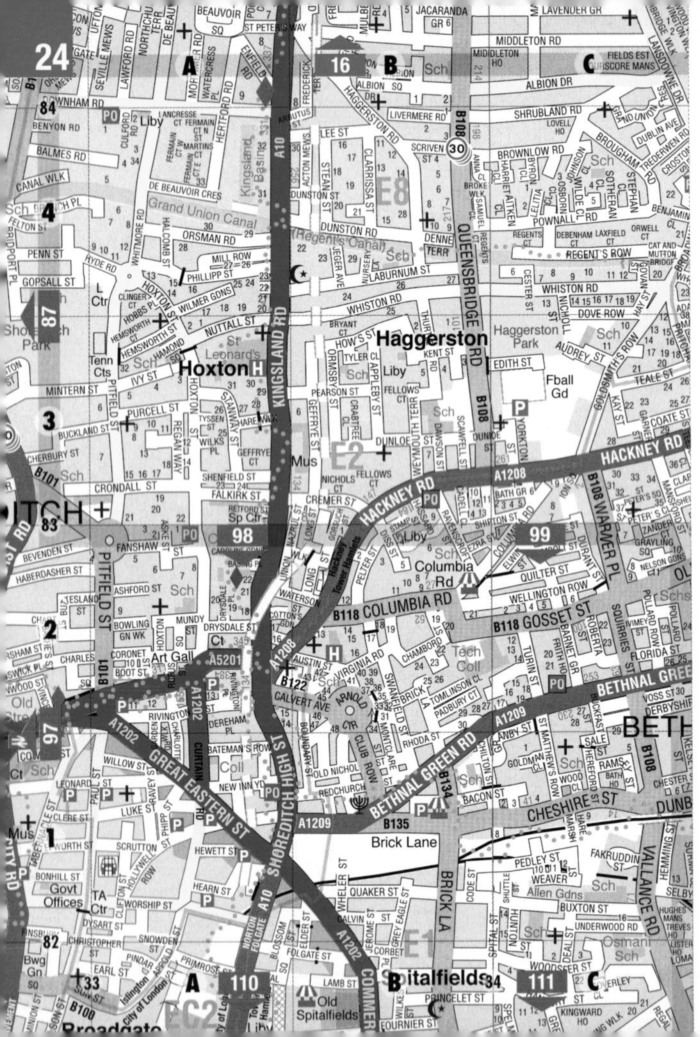
16
A
B
C
BEAUVOIR SQ
ST PETER'S WAY
JACARANDA GR
LAVENDER GR
MIDDLETON RD
MIDDLETON HO
FIELDS EST
ALBION DR
ALBION SQ
SHRUBLAND RD
LOVELL HO
LIVERMERE RD
HAGGERSTON RD
DOWNHAM RD
BENYON RD
BALMES RD
CANAL WLK
DE BEAUVOIR CRES
Grand Union Canal
(Regent's Canal)
Kingsland Basin
A10
KINGSLAND RD
LEE ST
ACTON MEWS
STEAN ST
CLARRISSA ST
E8
DUNSTON ST
DUNSTON RD
SCRIVEN ST
B108
QUEENSBRIDGE RD
BROWNLOW RD
BROUGHAM RD
DUBLIN AVE
POWNALL RD
BENJAMIN CL
REGENT'S ROW
LABURNUM ST
WHISTON RD
DOVE ROW
ORSMAN RD
MILL ROW
PHILLIPP ST
FELTON ST
PENN ST
HYDE RD
GOPSALL ST
WILMER GDNS
NUTTALL ST
HEMSWORTH ST
87
Haggerston
Haggerston Park
AUDREY ST
GOLDSMITH'S ROW
Hoxton
St Leonard's
IVY ST
MINTERN ST
PITFIELD ST
PURCELL ST
BUCKLAND ST
CHERBURY ST
HOXTON ST
STANWAY ST
GEFFRYE ST
E2
Mus
Fball Gd
YORKTON ST
HACKNEY RD
A1208
B108 WARNER PL
TEALE ST
COATE ST
CRONDALL ST
SHENFIELD ST
FALKIRK ST
83
98
99
FANSHAW ST
BEVENDEN ST
HABERDASHER ST
ASHFORD ST
CREMER ST
Columbia Rd
COLUMBIA RD
B118 COLUMBIA RD
B118 GOSSET ST
QUILTER ST
WELLINGTON ROW
DRYSDALE ST
Art Gall
A5201
A1202
CHARLES SQ
Tech Coll
BETHNAL GREEN RD
A1209
ARNOLD CIR
CALVERT AVE
B122
BOUNDARY ST
CLUB ROW
REDCHURCH ST
97
GREAT EASTERN ST
CURTAIN RD
RIVINGTON ST
OLD NICHOL ST
SHOREDITCH HIGH ST
LUKE ST
CHESHIRE ST
B135
Brick Lane
BRICK LA
B134
VALLANCE RD
FAKRUDDIN ST
WEAVER ST
Allen Gdns
BUXTON ST
QUAKER ST
WHELER ST
HEWETT ST
SCRUTTON ST
BONHILL ST
Govt Offices
WORSHIP ST
CHRISTOPHER ST
PRIMROSE ST
FOLGATE ST
LAMB ST
Old Spitalfields
E1
Spitalfields
Osmani Sch
WOODSEER ST
PRINCELET ST
FOURNIER ST
KINGWARD HO
110
111
82
33
34
EC2
Broadgate
B100
SUN ST

HACKNEY
South Hackney
Globe Town
NAL GREEN
Mile End
E8
E9
E2
VICTORIA PARK RD
A106 WELL ST
CAMBRIDGE HEATH RD
BETHNAL GREEN RD
BISHOP'S WAY
SEWARDSTONE RD
OLD FORD RD
ROMAN RD
MILE END RD
GROVE RD
LAURISTON RD
GLOBE RD
Regent's Canal
Royal Gate East
Royal Gate West
Gore Gate
Crown Gate East
Crown Gate West
Victoria Fntn
Bnstand
London Chest
Mus
Bethnal Green
Weavers Fields
Morpeth Sec Sch
Meath Gardens
The Royal London (Mile End)
Univ of London
Anchor Ret Pk
Stepney Green
Swanlea Sec Sch
Superstore
Cambridge Heath
Whitechapel
Wennington Green
Mile End Park
THREE COLTS LA
STEPNEY GN
17
32
26
84
83
82
36

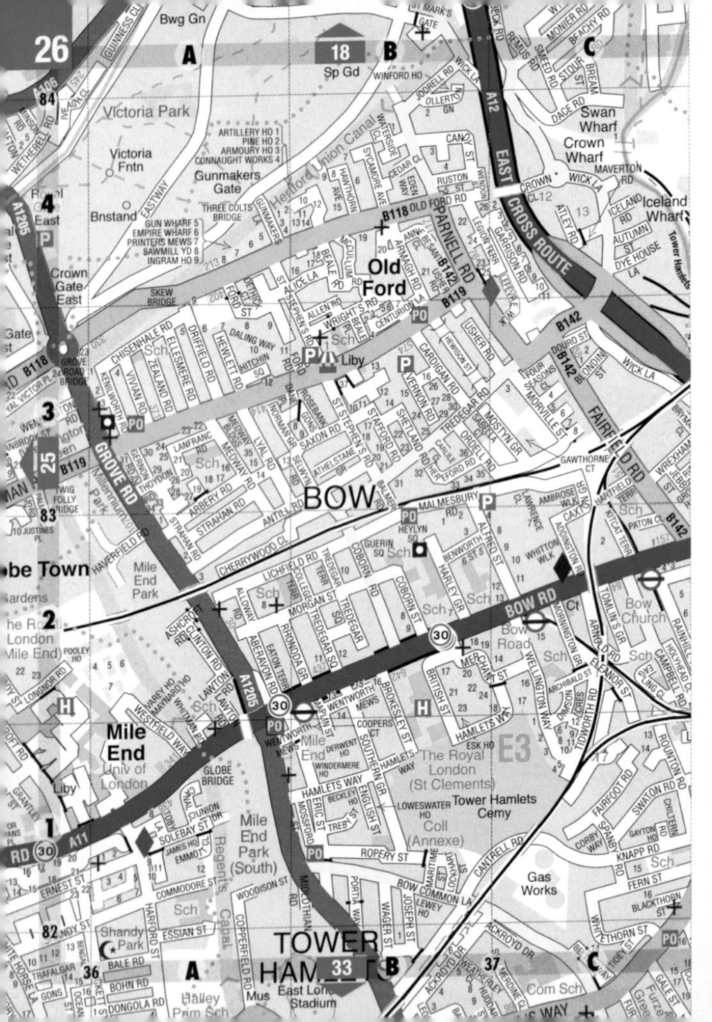

18
33
25
A
B
C
4
3
2
1
Victoria Park
Victoria Fntn
Gunmakers Gate
Bnstand
Royal Gate East
Crown Gate East
Hertford Union Canal
Old Ford
BOW
Bow Church
Bow Road
Mile End
Mile End Park
Mile End Park (South)
Univ of London
Millennium Park
Tower Hamlets Cemy
The Royal London (St Clements)
Coll (Annexe)
Gas Works
Swan Wharf
Crown Wharf
Iceland Wharf
TOWER HAMLETS
East London Stadium
Shandy Park
E3
GROVE RD
BOW RD
EAST CROSS ROUTE
FAIRFIELD RD
PARNELL RD
OLD FORD RD
A12
A11
A1205
B118
B119
B142
Regent's Canal

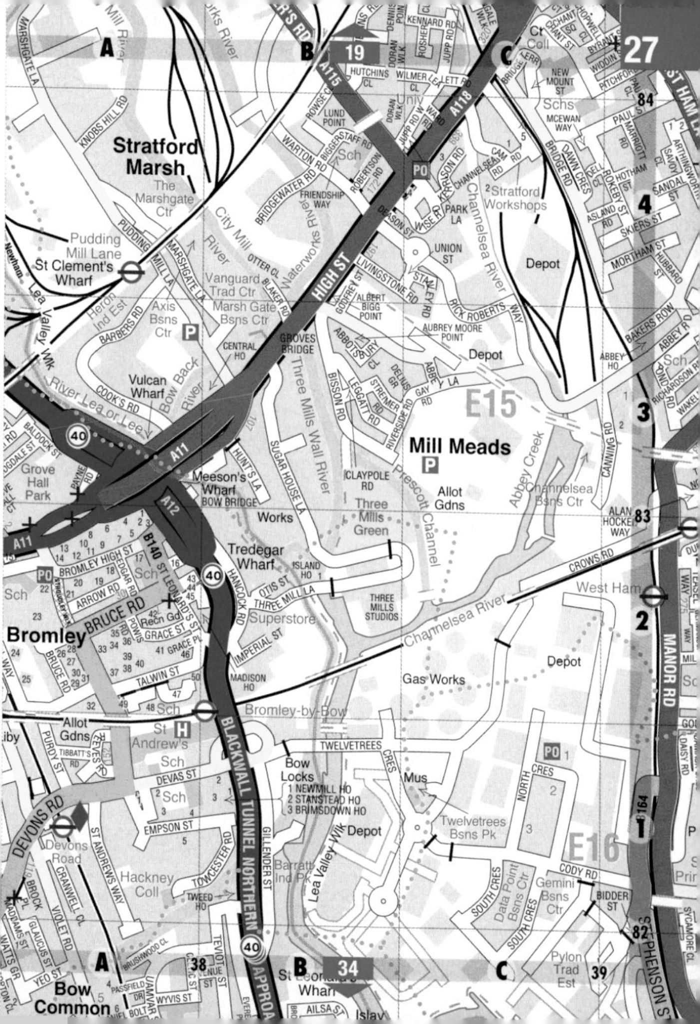
19
34
A
B
C
1
2
3
4
Stratford Marsh
The Marshgate Ctr
Pudding Mill Lane
St Clement's Wharf
Heron Ind Est
Axis Bsns Ctr
Vanguard Trad Ctr
Marsh Gate Bsns Ctr
City Mill River
Waterworks River
Bow Back River
River Lea or Lee
Lea Valley Wlk
Vulcan Wharf
Meeson's Wharf
Bow Bridge
Grove Hall Park
Tredegar Wharf
Works
Three Mills Wall River
Three Mills Green
Three Mills Studios
Prescott Channel
Channelsea River
Abbey Creek
Channelsea Bsns Ctr
Mill Meads
Allot Gdns
E15
E16
Stratford Workshops
Depot
Gas Works
West Ham
Bromley
Bromley-by-Bow
St Andrew's
Bow Locks
1 NEWMILL HO
2 STANSTEAD HO
3 BRIMSDOWN HO
Twelvetrees Bsns Pk
Mus
Gemini Bsns Ctr
Data Point Bsns Ctr
Pylon Trad Est
Barratt Ind Pk
Devons Road
Hackney Coll
Bow Common
St Leonard's Wharf
Superstore
HIGH ST
A11
A12
A115
A118
B140
B164
BLACKWALL TUNNEL NORTHERN APPROACH
MARSHGATE LA
KNOBS HILL RD
PUDDING MILL LA
BARBERS RD
COOK'S RD
HUNT'S LA
SUGAR HOUSE LA
BRIDGEWATER RD
WARTON RD
FRIENDSHIP WAY
ROBERTSON RD
LIVINGSTONE RD
ABBOTSBURY CL
RICK ROBERTS WAY
ABBEY LA
CLAYPOLE RD
RIVERSIDE RD
THREE MILL LA
CROWS RD
CANNING RD
BRIDGE RD
MANOR RD
ALAN HOCKEN WAY
TWELVETREES CRES
NORTH CRES
SOUTH CRES
CODY RD
BIDDER ST
STEPHENSON ST
DEVONS RD
BRUCE RD
BROMLEY HIGH ST
ST LEONARD'S ST
GRACE ST
TALWIN ST
DEVAS ST
EMPSON ST
ST ANDREWS WAY
GILLENDER ST
TOWCESTER RD
PURDY ST
CRANWELL CL
VIOLET RD
BROCK PL
WATTS GR
YEO ST
ARROW RD
HANCOCK RD
IMPERIAL ST
OTIS ST
SKIERS ST
MORTHAM ST
BAKERS ROW
ABBEY RD
PAUL ST
40

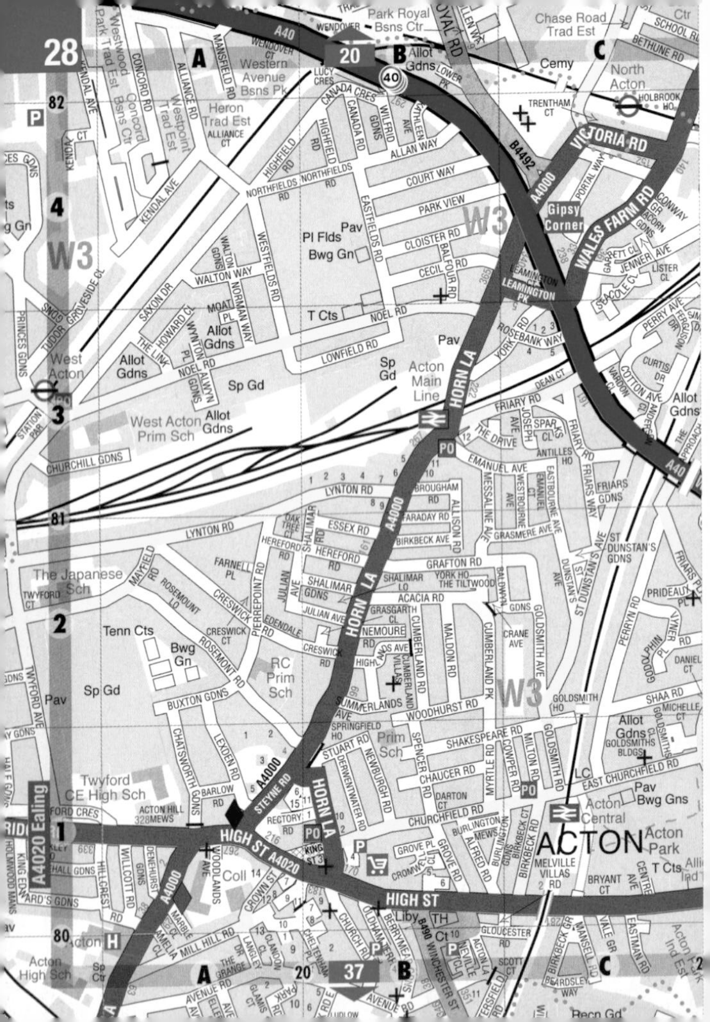

A40
20
37
A
B
C
82
81
80
1
2
3
4
W3
Park Royal Bsns Ctr
Chase Road Trad Est
Westwood Park Trad Est
Concord Bsns Ctr
Westpoint Trad Est
Western Avenue Bsns Pk
Heron Trad Est
ALLIANCE CT
WENDOVER
WENDOVER CT
MANSFIELD RD
ALLIANCE RD
CONCORD RD
KENDAL AVE
KENDAL CT
Allot Gdns
LOWER PK
Cemy
North Acton
HOLBROOK HO
TRENTHAM CT
SCHOOL RD
BETHUNE RD
LUCY CRES
CANADA CRES
CANADA RD
WILFRID GDNS
KATHLEEN AVE
ALLAN WAY
HIGHFIELD RD
NORTHFIELDS
NORTHFIELDS RD
COURT WAY
PARK VIEW
CLOISTER RD
CECIL RD
BALFOUR RD
EASTFIELDS RD
Pav
Pl Flds
Bwg Gn
B4492
A4000
VICTORIA RD
PORTAL WAY
Gipsy Corner
WALES FARM RD
CONWAY GR
ACORN GDNS
GARRETT CL
JENNER AVE
LISTER CL
LEAMINGTON CT
LEAMINGTON PK
SEACOLE CL
PERRY AVE
FERGUSON DR
CURTIS DR
VARDON CL
COTTON AVE
ANDERSON
Allot Gdns
THE APPROACH
WALTON GDNS
WALTON WAY
WESTFIELDS RD
NORMAN WAY
MOAT PL
T Cts
NOEL RD
LOWFIELD RD
SAXON DR
HOWARD CL
WYNTON PL
THE LINK
ALLWYN GDNS
Sp Gd
Acton Main Line
HORN LA
ROSEBANK WAY
YORK RD
DEAN CT
FRIARY RD
JOSEPH AVE
SPARKS CL
THE DRIVE
ANTILLES HO
FRIARY RD
FRIARS WAY
PO
West Acton
STATION PAR
West Acton Prim Sch
CHURCHILL GDNS
PRINCES GDNS
TUDOR GDNS
GROVESIDE CL
EMANUEL AVE
MESSALINE AVE
WESTBOURNE AVE
EMANUEL CT
EASTBOURNE AVE
FRIARS GDNS
LYNTON RD
BROUGHAM RD
FARADAY RD
ALLISON RD
OAK TREE CT
SHALIMAR RD
ESSEX RD
BIRKBECK AVE
GRASMERE AVE
ST DUNSTAN'S AVE
ST DUNSTAN'S GDNS
HEREFORD RD
GRAFTON RD
YORK HO
THE TILTWOOD
BALDWYN GDNS
FARNELL PL
MAYFIELD RD
ROSEMOUNT LO
PIERREPOINT RD
JULIAN AVE
SHALIMAR GDNS
SHALIMAR LO
ACACIA RD
The Japanese Sch
TWYFORD CT
CRESWICK RD
CRESWICK CT
EDENDALE
GRASGARTH CL
NEMOURE RD
CUMBERLAND RD
MALDON RD
CUMBERLAND PK
GOLDSMITH AVE
CRANE AVE
FRIARS PL
PRIDEAUX PL
VYNER RD
PERRYN RD
GODOLPHIN PL
DANIEL CT
Tenn Cts
Bwg Gn
ROSEMONT RD
RC Prim Sch
HIGH
CUMBERLAND VILLAS
Sp Gd
TWYFORD AVE
TWYFORD GDNS
Pav
BUXTON GDNS
SUMMERLANDS AVE
WOODHURST RD
GOLDSMITH HO
SHAA RD
MICHELLE CT
SPRINGFIELD HO
Prim Sch
SPENCER RD
SHAKESPEARE RD
MYRTLE RD
COWPER RD
MILTON RD
GOLDSMITH RD
Allot Gdns
GOLDSMITHS BLDGS
GOLDSMITHS CL
CHATSWORTH GDNS
LEXDEN RD
STUART RD
DERWENTWATER RD
NEWBURGH RD
CHAUCER RD
DARTON CT
EAST CHURCHFIELD RD
LC
Pav
Bwg Gns
Twyford CE High Sch
STEYNE RD
FORD CRES
BARLOW RD
ACTON HILL MEWS
RECTORY RD
CHURCHFIELD RD
BURLINGTON MEWS
BURLINGTON GDNS
BIRKBECK CT
BIRKBECK RD
Acton Central
ACTON
Acton Park
A4020 Ealing
HIGH ST A4020
KING ST
GROVE PL
CROMWELL PL
GROVE RD
ALFRED RD
MELVILLE VILLAS RD
BRYANT CT
CENTRE AVE
T Cts
HOLMWOOD MANS
KING EDWARD'S GDNS
HALL GDNS
HILLCREST RD
WILLCOTT RD
DENEHURST GDNS
WOODLANDS AVE
Coll
CROWN ST
HIGH ST
Liby
TH
Acton Park Ind Est
CHURCH RD
OLDHAM TERR
BERRYMEAD GDNS
B490 WINCHESTER ST
GLOUCESTER RD
BIRKBECK GR
MANSELL RD
VALE GR
EASTMAN RD
Acton H
Acton High Sch
Sp Ctr
MARBLE CL
AMELIA CL
MILL HILL RD
THE GRANGE
LANGLEY DR
CLANDON CL
CHELTENHAM PL
NEVILLE CL
ACTON LA
SCOTT CT
BEARDSLEY WAY
AVENUE RD
GLAMIS CT
PARK RD
AVENUE RD
LUDLOW
Recn Gd

Old Oak Common Sidings
A
B
21
C
82
Wormwood Scrubs Park
4
Old Oak Common
W12
The Lindford Christie Stadium
Tenn Cts
Pl Fld
Victoria Ind Est
WELLS HOUSE RD
OLD OAK COMMON LA
TELFORD WAY
BRUNEL RD
John Perryn Prim Sch
LONG DR
THE TEE
MASHIE RD
THE BYE
THE GREEN
DUNCAN GR
THE FAIRWAY
Allot Gdns
CARLISLE AVE
HOYLAKE RD
ELM GN
ST ANDREW'S RD
MUIRFIELD
OSMUND ST
BRAYBROOK ST
MELLITUS ST
Old Oak Prim Sch
WULFSTAN ST
HENCHMAN ST
ERCONWALD ST
STOKESLEY ST
East Acton
FITZNEAL ST
FOLIOT ST
WEEDON HO 1
GREY TURNER HO 2
HM Prison Wormwood Scrubs
ARTILLERY LA
Hammersmith
3
Queen Charlottes & Chelsea
WEST QUARTERS
DU CANE RD
30
BRASSIE AVE
TEMPLEMEAD CL
WESTERN AVE
KINGS DOWN AVE
SUNNINGDALE AVE
EAST ACTON ARC
CACTUS WLK
NORBROKE ST
HILARY RD
BEGONIA WLK
PRIMULA ST
ROSEWOOD SQ
HEATHSTAN RD
81
Savoy Circus
A40
WESTWAY
40
LILAC ST
VIOLA SQ
Liby
PEONY GDNS
CLEMATIS ST
THE CURVE
ORWELL HO
MILFOIL ST
1 WENGHAM HO
2 HAYTER HO
CREIGHTON CL
STRELLEY WAY
FOSTER RD
GIBBON RD
BOWES RD
GLENDUN RD
GLENDUN CT
Superstore
FOXGLOVE ST
HILARY RD
YEW TREE RD
HEMLOCK RD
TAMARISK SQ
DAFFODIL ST
SUNDEW AVE
ORCHID ST
T Cts
Phoenix High Sch
2
Allot Gdns
EAST ACTON CT
King Fahed Acad
BURGHLEY TWR
EAST ACTON LA
BEECHWOOD GR
TRINITY WAY
HADDON CT
WALLFLOWER ST
PANSY GDNS
ERICA ST
BRYONY RD
BLOEMFONTEIN RD
East Acton Prim Sch
T Cts
Bwg Gn
BROMYARD AVE
PERRYN HO
Recn Gd
BRAMBLE GDNS
OLD OAK RD
STEVENTON RD
GRAVESEND RD
Wormholt Park Prim Sch
Wormholt Park
East Acton
HOLSGROVE CT
CLEVERLY COTTS
CLEVERLY EST
SAWLEY RD
Tenn Cts
Sp Gd
ASHFIELD RD
Hammersmith & Fulham
Ealing
SEDGEFORD RD
DUNRAVEN RD
CANTERBURY CT
SIR ALEXANDER CL
ALEXANDER RD
BLAKENHAM CT
CLEVERLY COTTS
WORMHOLT RD
ORCHARD HO
COLLINGBOURNE RD
Pl Fld
Allot Gdns
1 PARKSIDE
2 GREENVIEW CL
SYCAMORE CL
SIR FIRST AVE
AYCLIFFE RD
GALLOWAY RD
THORPEBANK RD
WILLOW VALE
ADELAIDE GR
OAKLANDS GR
ORMISTON GR
HALSBURY RD
OAK WAY
THE VALE EST
MAPLE AVE
CHERRY CT
BROMYARD HO
ARMSTRONG RD
THIRD AVE
EASTVALE
SECOND AVE
VALE CT
ALDBOURNE RD
OLLGAR CL
ASKHAM RD
ASKHAM CT
MONK CT
1
LARCH AVE
BEECH AVE
SHILLAKER CT
THE VALE
A4020
TRILLINGTON HO
HANOVER CT
UXBRIDGE RD
ESSEX PARK MEWS
Ind Est
B408
CLIFTON AVE
ASKEW CRES
BECKLOW GDNS
WESTBRIDGE CL
CONINGHAM MEWS
ARCHDALE CT
80
STANLEY GDNS
DU CROS RD
CURRICLE ST
DORDRECHT RD
WESTVALE MEWS
AGNES RD
COWLEY RD
ELIZABETH GDNS
DAVIS RD
KEITH GR
BOSCOMBE RD
HETLEY RD
21
BRADFORD RD
ALLIED WAY
A
LARDEN RD
SWAINSON RD
B
38
22
BECKLOW RD
VESPAN RD
C
PERCY RD
FINDON RD
THE GLADE
OLD FORGE MEWS
VALETTA RD
HOLLEY RD
JEDDO MEWS
JEDDO RD
OLDFIELD RD
ROXWELL RD
HADYN PARK RD
WARPLE WAY

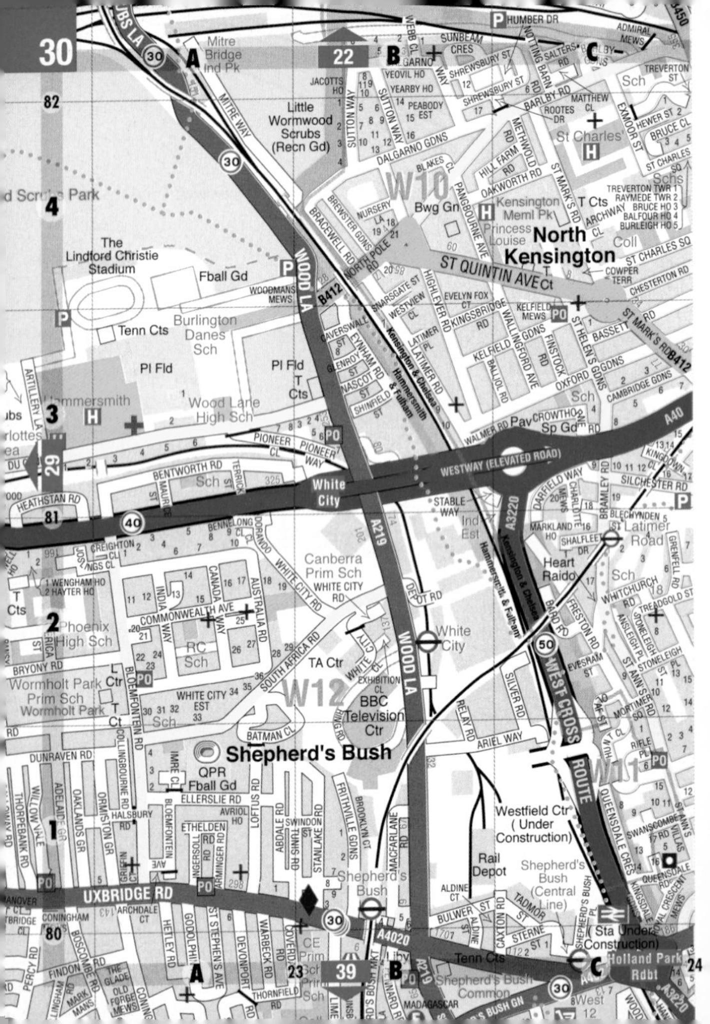
30
22
A
B
C
Mitre Bridge Ind Pk
Little Wormwood Scrubs (Recn Gd)
Wood Lane
Wood La
Mitre Way
Sutton Way
Dalgarno Gdns
Peabody Est
Sunbeam Cres
Humber Dr
Shrewsbury St
Notting Barn Rd
Barlby Rd
Rootes Dr
Matthew Cl
Exmoor St
St Charles'
Treverton St
Hewer St
Bruce Cl
St Charles Sq
W10
Blakes Cl
Hill Farm Rd
Methwold Rd
Oakworth Rd
St Mark's Rd
Kensington Meml Pk
Princess Louise
Bwg Gn
Pangbourne Ave
North Kensington
Coll
St Quintin Ave
Highlever Rd
North Pole Rd
Bracewell Rd
Brewster Gdns
Nursery La
Evelyn Fox Ct
Kingsbridge Rd
Wallingford Ave
Kelfield Gdns
Finstock Rd
St Helen's Gdns
Bassett Rd
Chesterton Rd
Oxford Gdns
Cambridge Gdns
B412
A40
Wormwood Scrubs Park
The Lindford Christie Stadium
Fball Gd
Woodmans Mews
Tenn Cts
Burlington Danes Sch
Pl Fld
Wood Lane High Sch
Hammersmith
Artillery La
Caverswall St
Eynham Rd
Glenroy St
Nascot St
Shinfield St
Latimer Rd
Latimer Pl
Kensington & Chelsea
Hammersmith & Fulham
Pioneer Cl
Pioneer Way
Walmer Rd
Crowthorne Rd
Sp Gd
Westway (Elevated Road)
White City
Bentworth Rd
Heathstan Rd
Terrick St
Mairi St
Kingsdown
Silchester Rd
Darfield Way
Stable Way
Ind Est
A3220
Bramley Rd
Blechynden St
Latimer Road
Markland Ho
Shalfleet Dr
Heart Raido
Grenfell Rd
Whitchurch Rd
Treadgold St
Ansleigh Pl
Stoneleigh St
Bennelong Cl
Dorando Cl
Creighton Cl
Canberra Prim Sch
White City Rd
A219
Depot Rd
1 Wengham Ho
2 Hayter Ho
Commonwealth Ave
India Way
Canada Way
Australia Rd
RC Sch
South Africa Rd
TA Ctr
White City Cl
Exhibition Cl
BBC Television Ctr
W12
Phoenix High Sch
Bryony Rd
Wormholt Park Prim Sch
Wormholt Park
Bloemfontein Rd
White City Est
Batman Cl
Wood La
Shepherd's Bush
Silver Rd
Relay Rd
Ariel Way
Freston Rd
Evesham St
West Cross Route
St Ann's Rd
Mortimer Sq
Rifle Pl
W11
Dunraven Rd
Collingbourne Rd
Imre Cl
QPR Fball Gd
Ellerslie Rd
Avriol Ho
Loftus Rd
Halsbury Rd
Ethelden Rd
Ingersoll Rd
Arminger Rd
Bloemfontein Ave
Adelaide Gr
Willow Vale
Thorpebank Rd
Oaklands Gr
Ormiston Gr
Abdale Rd
Swindon St
Tunis Rd
Stanlake Rd
Frithville Gdns
Brooklyn Ct
Macfarlane Rd
Westfield Ctr (Under Construction)
Rail Depot
Shepherd's Bush (Central Line)
Queensdale Cres
Swanscombe Rd
St Ann's Villas
Queensdale Rd
Royal Crescent Mews
Uxbridge Rd
Archdale Ct
Coningham Rd
Hetley Rd
Godolphin Rd
St Stephen's Ave
Devonport Rd
Warbeck Rd
Coverdale Rd
Shepherd's Bush
A4020
Aldine Ct
Bulwer St
Caxton Rd
Tadmor St
Sterne St
Shepherd's Bush Pl
(Sta Under Construction)
Holland Park Rdbt
A3220
Tenn Cts
Shepherd's Bush Common
Shepherd's Bush Gn
Liby
CE Prim Sch
Findon Rd
Boscombe Rd
Percy Rd
The Glade
Old Forge Mews
Thornfield Rd
Madagascar
39
23
24
29
80
81
82
West 12
PO
Sch
H

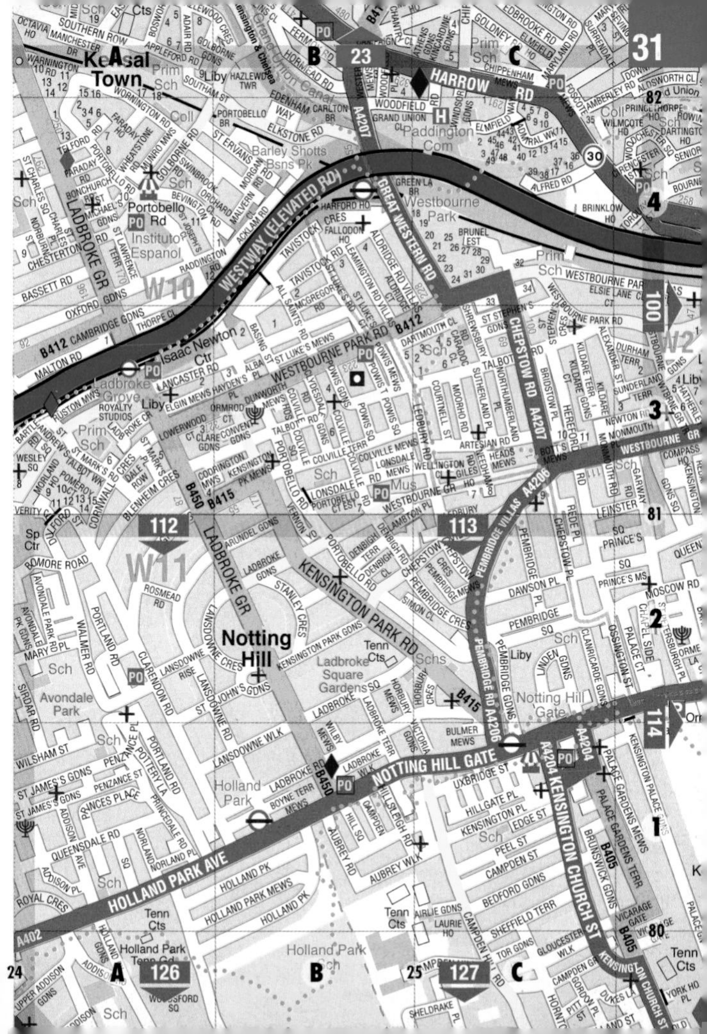
A
B
C
23
Kensal Town
Portobello Rd
Instituto Espanol
W10
Westway (Elevated Rd)
Harrow Rd
Grand Union Canal
Paddington Com
Barley Shotts Bsns Pk
Westbourne Park
Great Western Rd
Ladbroke Gr
Isaac Newton Ctr
Ladbroke Grove
Westbourne Park Rd
Chepstow Rd
A4207
B412
B450
B415
W2
100
112
113
W11
Kensington Park Rd
Notting Hill
Ladbroke Square Gardens
Pembridge Villas
Pembridge Rd
A4206
Notting Hill Gate
Kensington Church St
A4204
114
Holland Park
Holland Park Ave
A402
Avondale Park
Holland Park Sch
Holland Park Tenn Gd
126
127
24
25
80
81
82
1
2
3
4

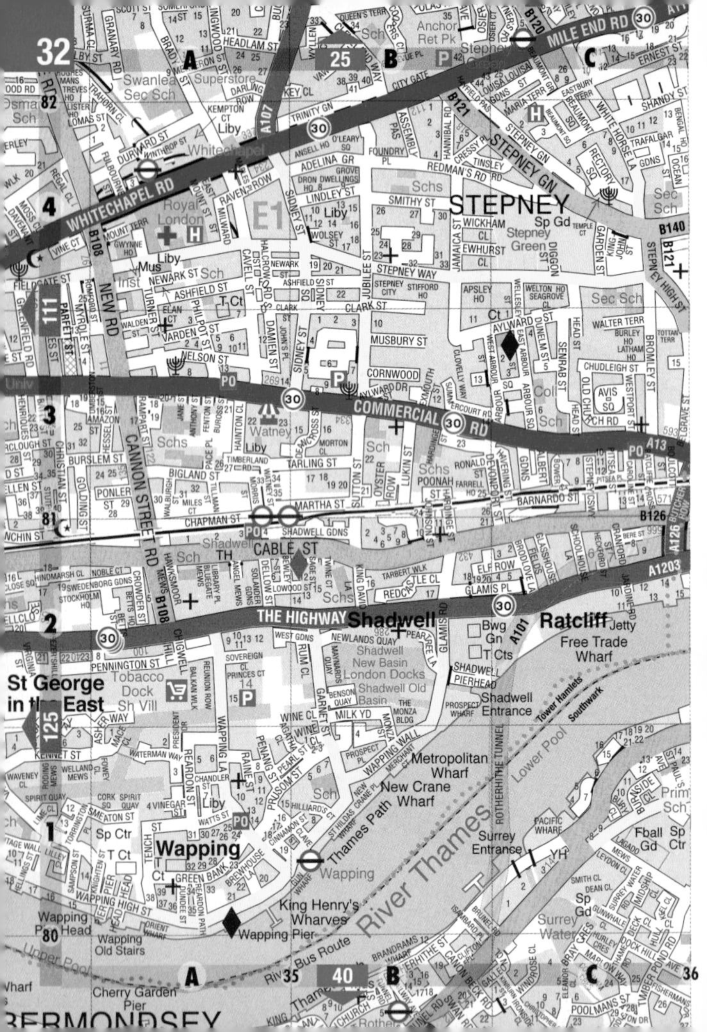
25
A
B
C
MILE END RD
Anchor Ret Pk
Stepney Green
ERNEST ST
HEADLAM ST
Swanlea Sec Sch
Superstore
CITY GATE
DARLING ROW
TRINITY GN
KEMPTON CT
Liby
Whitechapel
DURWARD ST
ADELINA GR
STEPNEY GN
REDMAN'S RD
WHITE HORSE LA
SHANDY ST
TRAFALGAR GDNS
RECTORY SQ
WHITECHAPEL RD
Royal London
E1
LINDLEY ST
SMITHY ST
STEPNEY
Sp Gd
WICKHAM CL
EWHURST CL
Stepney Green
Sec Sch
B140
NEW RD
STEPNEY WAY
Mus
Inst
NEWARK ST
ASHFIELD ST
FIELDGATE ST
111
CLARK ST
JUBILEE ST
APSLEY HO
AYLWARD ST
WALTER TERR
MUSBURY ST
CORNWOOD DR
CHUDLEIGH ST
NELSON ST
VARDEN ST
Univ
COMMERCIAL RD
Coll
Sch
AVIS SQ
Watney
Liby
TARLING ST
CANNON STREET RD
BURSLEM ST
BIGLAND ST
PONLER ST
POONAH ST
Schs
MARTHA ST
BARNARDO ST
A13
CHAPMAN ST
SHADWELL GDNS
CABLE ST
Shadwell
TH
B126
A126
A1203
NOBLE CT
SWEDENBORG GDNS
ELF ROW
GLAMIS PL
REDCASTLE CL
THE HIGHWAY
Shadwell
Ratcliff
Jetty
Free Trade Wharf
A101
Bwg Gn
T Cts
WEST GDNS
NEWLANDS QUAY
Shadwell New Basin
London Docks
Shadwell Old Basin
PENNINGTON ST
St George in the East
Tobacco Dock
Sh Vill
125
SHADWELL PIERHEAD
Shadwell Entrance
Tower Hamlets
Southwark
WINE CL
MILK YD
THE MONZA BLDG
PROSPECT WHARF
WAPPING WALL
Metropolitan Wharf
New Crane Wharf
ROTHERHITHE TUNNEL
Lower Pool
WAPPING LA
KENNET ST
WATERMAN WAY
CHANDLER ST
Sch
Liby
Thames Path
River Thames
Surrey Entrance
PACIFIC WHARF
YH
Sp Ctr
T Ct
Wapping
Wapping
King Henry's Wharves
Wapping Pier
WAPPING HIGH ST
Wapping Pier Head
Wapping Old Stairs
Fball Gd
Sp Ctr
Surrey Water
Sp Gd
Upper Pool
River Bus Route
BRANDRAMS WHARF
A
40
B
C
35
36
80
81
82
Cherry Garden Pier
Wharf
BERMONDSEY
POOLMANS ST
Rotherhithe

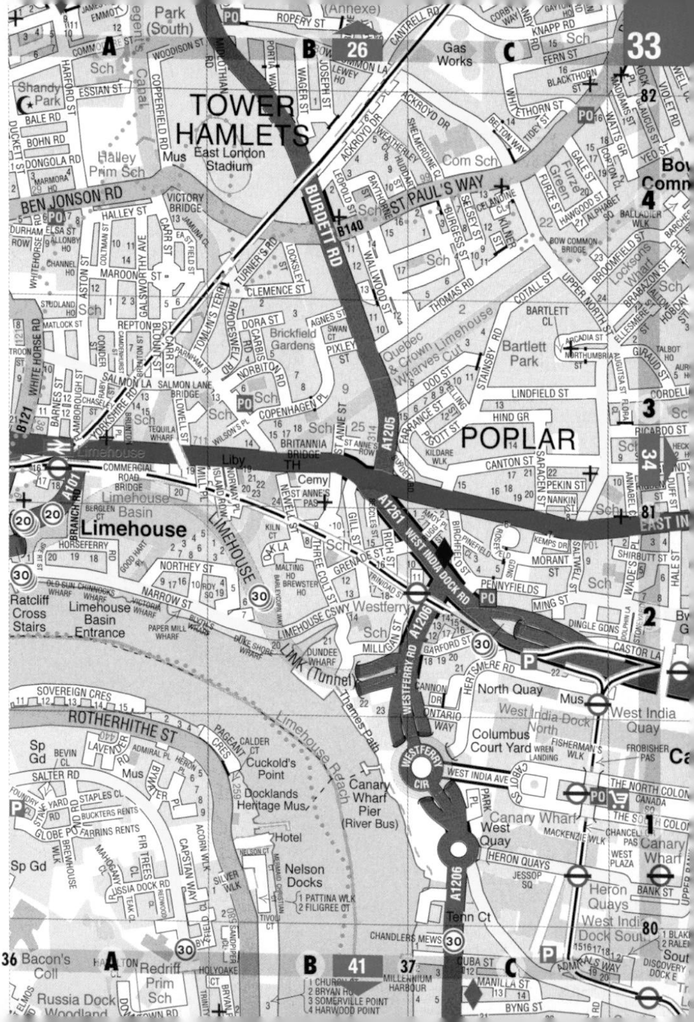
TOWER HAMLETS
East London Stadium
POPLAR
Limehouse
Limehouse Basin
Shandy Park
Halley Prim Sch
Brickfield Gardens
Bartlett Park
Quebec & Crown Wharves Limehouse Cut
Furze Green
Gas Works
Com Sch
BEN JONSON RD
BURDETT RD
ST PAUL'S WAY
COMMERCIAL ROAD
WEST INDIA DOCK RD
WESTFERRY RD
EAST INDIA DOCK RD
NARROW ST
LIMEHOUSE CSWY
ROTHERHITHE ST
LIMEHOUSE LINK (Tunnel)
Limehouse Reach
Thames Path
Ratcliff Cross Stairs
Limehouse Basin Entrance
Cuckold's Point
Docklands Heritage Mus
Canary Wharf Pier (River Bus)
Nelson Docks
Hotel
North Quay
West India Dock North
West India Quay
Columbus Court Yard
Canary Wharf
West Quay
Heron Quays
West India Dock South
Tenn Ct
Westferry
WESTFERRY CIR
Redriff Prim Sch
Russia Dock Woodland
Bacon's Coll
Sp Gd
A1205
A1261
A1206
A101
A13
B140
B121
26
34
41
36
37
82
81
80
A
B
C
1
2
3
4
1 CHURCH ST
2 BRYAN HO
3 SOMERVILLE POINT
4 HARWOOD POINT
1 PATTINA WLK
2 FILIGREE CT

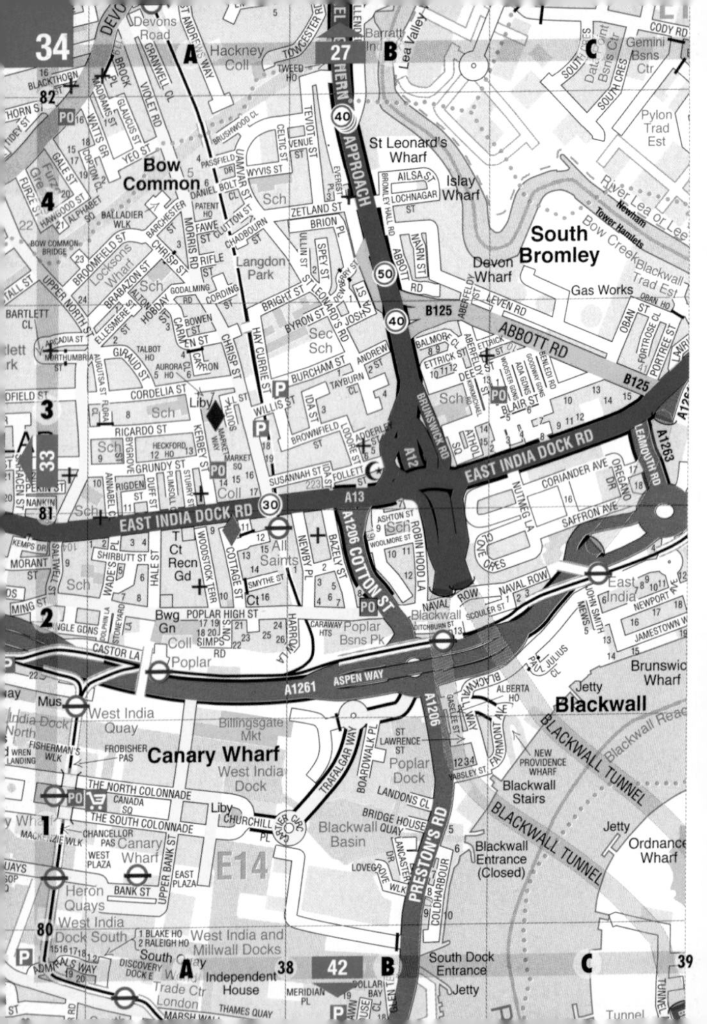
27
42
33
39
38
A
B
C
4
3
2
1
Devons Road
Hackney Coll
Barratt Ind
Lea Valley
Gemini Bsns Ctr
Data Point Bsns Ctr
SOUTH CRES
CODY RD
Pylon Trad Est
Bow Common
St Leonard's Wharf
Islay Wharf
River Lea or Lee
Bow Creek
Newham
Tower Hamlets
South Bromley
Devon Wharf
Blackwall Trad Est
Gas Works
Langdon Park
Sec Sch
Sch
Locksons Wharf
BOW COMMON BRIDGE
BOW COMMON LA
UPPER NORTH ST
BROOMFIELD ST
BRABAZON ST
ELLESMERE ST
HOBDAY ST
GODALMING RD
CORDING ST
BOWEN ST
CARMEN ST
CARRON
TALBOT HO
GIRAUD ST
AURORA HO
CORDELIA ST
RICARDO ST
HECKFORD HO
GRUNDY ST
BYGROVE ST
RIGDEN ST
ANNABEL CL
DUFF ST
PLIMSOLL CL
STURRY ST
KERBEY ST
MARKET SQ
CHRISP ST
HAY CURRIE ST
WILLIS ST
BRIGHT ST
BYRON ST
ST LEONARD'S RD
DEWBERRY ST
JOSHUA ST
BURCHAM ST
TAYBURN CL
ANDREW ST
IDA ST
BROWNFIELD ST
LODORE ST
ADDERLEY ST
SUSANNAH ST
FOLLETT ST
ZETLAND ST
BRION PL
SPEY ST
ULLIN ST
TEVIOT ST
CELTIC ST
VENUE ST
WYVIS ST
BRUSHWOOD CL
PASSFIELD DR
BOLT CL
LAMMAS ST
DANIEL BOLT CL
PATENT HO
FAWE ST
CLUTTON ST
CHADBOURN ST
RIFLE ST
MORRIS RD
BARCHESTER ST
BALLADIER WLK
ALPHABET SQ
HAWGOOD ST
FURZE ST
GALE ST
COPTON CL
WATTS GR
YEO ST
GLAUCUS ST
VIOLET RD
CRAMWELL CL
BROCK PL
BLACKTHORN ST
ST ANDREWS WAY
TOWCESTER RD
TWEED HO
APPROACH
BROMLEY HALL RD
AILSA ST
LOCHNAGAR ST
ABBOTT RD
NAIRN ST
ABERFELDY ST
LEVEN RD
B125
BALMORE CL
ETTRICK ST
DEE ST
BLAIR ST
ADA GDNS
BENLEDI RD
OBAN ST
OBAN HO
FORTROSE CL
PORTREE ST
BRUNSWICK RD
A12
A13
A1261
A1263
A1206
EAST INDIA DOCK RD
LEAMOUTH RD
CORIANDER AVE
OREGANO DR
SAFFRON AVE
NUTMEG LA
CLOVE CRES
ASHTON ST
WOOLMORE ST
ROBIN HOOD LA
COTTON ST
BAZELY ST
NEWBY PL
All Saints
SMYTHE ST
COTTAGE ST
WOODSTOCK TERR
HALE ST
WADE'S PL
SHIRBUTT ST
SALTWELL ST
MORANT ST
KEMPS DR
Recn Gd
Bwg Gn
POPLAR HIGH ST
SIMPSONS RD
HARROW LA
CARAWAY HTS
Poplar Bsns Pk
Poplar
Coll
CASTOR LA
STONEYARD LA
DOLPHIN LA
NAVAL ROW
East India
JOHN SMITH MEWS
NEWPORT AVE
JAMESTOWN WAY
Blackwall
DITCHBURN ST
SCOULER ST
PAUL JULIUS CL
Brunswick Wharf
Jetty
Blackwall
ALBERTA HO
BLACKWALL WAY
FAIRMONT AVE
GASELEE ST
NEW PROVIDENCE WHARF
Blackwall Stairs
BLACKWALL TUNNEL
Blackwall Entrance (Closed)
Ordnance Wharf
ASPEN WAY
Mus
West India Quay
Billingsgate Mkt
Canary Wharf
West India Dock
TRAFALGAR WAY
BOARDWALK PL
ST LAWRENCE ST
Poplar Dock
YABSLEY ST
LANDONS CL
BRIDGE HOUSE QUAY
Blackwall Basin
LANCASTER DR
LOVEGROVE WLK
PRESTON'S RD
COLDHARBOUR
FISHERMAN'S WLK
FROBISHER PAS
WREN LANDING
THE NORTH COLONNADE
CANADA SQ
THE SOUTH COLONNADE
CHURCHILL PL
CABOT SQ
CARTIER CIRC
CHANCELLOR PAS
MACKENZIE WLK
WEST PLAZA
Canary Wharf
UPPER BANK ST
EAST PLAZA
BANK ST
Heron Quays
E14
West India Dock South
1 BLAKE HO
2 RALEIGH HO
West India and Millwall Docks
South Quay
DISCOVERY DOCK E
ADMIRALS WAY
Independent House
Trade Ctr London
MERIDIAN PL
THAMES QUAY
MARSH WALL
South Dock Entrance
Jetty
Tunnel
TUNNEL

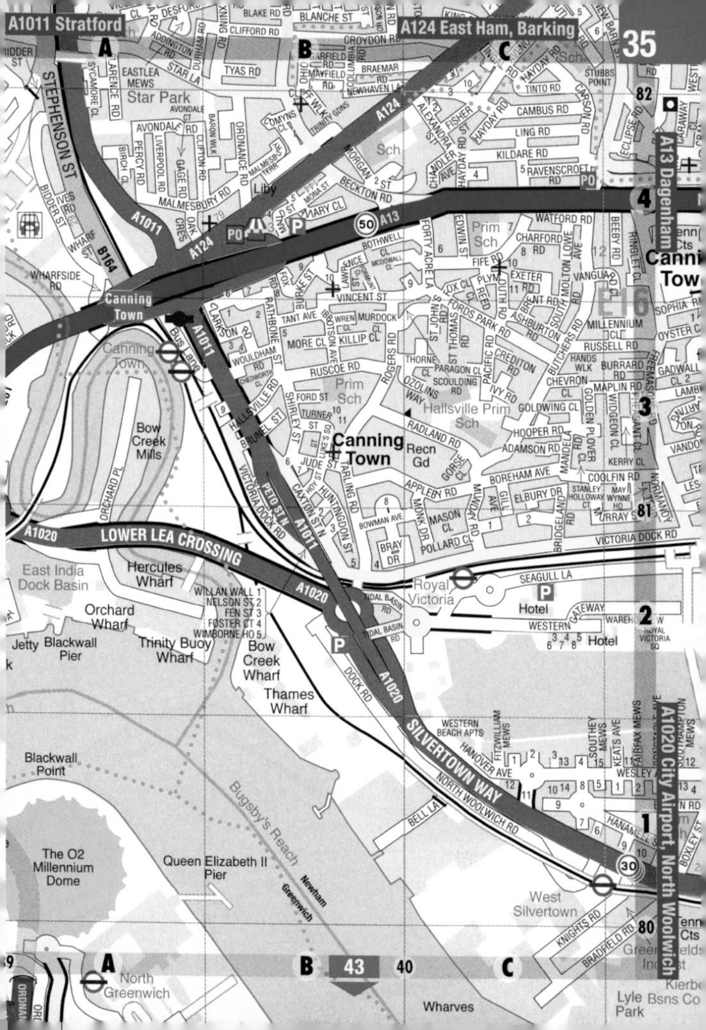
A1011 Stratford
A124 East Ham, Barking
A13 Dagenham
A1020 City Airport, North Woolwich
STEPHENSON ST
BIDDER ST
STAR LA
EASTLEA MEWS
Star Park
AVONDALE RD
TYAS RD
CLIFFORD RD
BLAKE RD
BLANCHE ST
CROYDON RD
BRAEMAR RD
NEWHAVEN LA
HAYDAY RD
TINTO RD
CAMBUS RD
LING RD
KILDARE RD
RAVENSCROFT RD
STUBBS POINT
MALMESBURY RD
ORDNANCE RD
BECKTON RD
Liby
Sch
Prim Sch
WATFORD RD
CHARFORD RD
EXETER RD
VANGUARD CL
FORTY ACRE LA
BOTHWELL CL
VINCENT ST
MURDOCK CL
KILLIP CL
RUSCOE RD
FORDS PARK RD
ASHBURTON RD
MILLENNIUM CL
RUSSELL RD
SOPHIA RD
OYSTER CL
E16
Canning Town
Canning Town
WHARFSIDE RD
Bus Lane
Bow Creek Mills
ORCHARD PL
HALLSVILLE RD
BRUNEL ST
ROGERS RD
Hallsville Prim Sch
RADLAND RD
Recn Gd
HOOPER RD
ADAMSON RD
BOREHAM AVE
COOLFIN RD
GOLDWING CL
MAPLIN RD
ELBURY DR
MURRAY SQ
VICTORIA DOCK RD
POLLARD CL
MASON CL
APPLEBY RD
BOWMAN AVE
BRAY DR
A1020
LOWER LEA CROSSING
East India Dock Basin
Hercules Wharf
Orchard Wharf
Jetty
Blackwall Pier
Trinity Buoy Wharf
WILLAN WALL 1
NELSON ST 2
FEN ST 3
FOSTER CT 4
WIMBORNE HO 5
Bow Creek Wharf
Thames Wharf
Royal Victoria
SEAGULL LA
Hotel
WESTERN GATEWAY
ROYAL VICTORIA SQ
TIDAL BASIN RD
DOCK RD
SILVERTOWN WAY
NORTH WOOLWICH RD
WESTERN BEACH APTS
HANOVER AVE
FITZWILLIAM MEWS
SOUTHEY MEWS
KEATS AVE
FAIRFAX MEWS
WESLEY AVE
HANAMEEL ST
BELL LA
Blackwall Point
Bugsby's Reach
Newham
Greenwich
The O2 Millennium Dome
Queen Elizabeth II Pier
West Silvertown
KNIGHTS RD
BRADFIELD RD
Lyle Park
Wharves
North Greenwich
43
40
80
81
82

A406 Ealing
A
B
C
W5
WARWICK RD
WARWICK DENE
ELM AVE
GUNNERSBURY MANOR
TRING AVE
WHITEHALL GDNS
KING EDWARD'S GDNS
KESWICK MEWS
KERRISON RD
WORTH RD
YMCA
80
WARWICK RD
SOANE CL
LIVERPOOL RD
MARLBOROUGH RD
BLANDFORD RD
RANELAGH RD
RANELAGH MEWS
RICHMOND RD
ELM GROVE RD
ELM CRES
HAZELWOOD CL
ASCOTT AVE
DELAMERE RD
ELGAR AVE
ST PAUL'S CL
Sch
EVELYN GR
STUART AVE
A406
Pav
Acton
Acton High Sch
VICTORIA CT
CLARIAT CT 1
RELTON CT 2
TIGNEL CT 3
COPPERFIELDS CT 4
KINGSBRIDGE AVE
Allot Gdns
CARBERY AVE
BODDINGTON GDNS
BROOK HO
4
Allot Gdns
1 ST MARY'S CT
2 CONINGSBY COTTS
3 ST MARY'S SQ
4 EALING COURT MAN
QUEEN ANNE'S GR
QUEEN ANNE'S GDNS
Pav
Pl Fld
North Korea
BLOSSOM CL
ASPEN CL
ROWAN CL
WILLOW RD
ELDERBERRY RD
GUNNERSBURY AVENUE
Tenn Cts
TUDOR WAY
TUDOR CT
LILLIAN AVE
GUNNERSBURY GDNS
GUNNERSBURY CRES
GUNNERSBURY
THE BROADWAY
Acton Town
Sch
LIMES WLK
CHESTNUT GR
CEDAR GR
PALM GR
BEECH GDNS
ASH GR
ALMOND AVE
SPRUCE CT
BAY CT
KNIGHT'S AVE
BARONSMEDE
Tenn Cts
Sp Gd
Bwg Gn
Tenn Cts
GUNNERSBURY DR
PARK PAR
PO
A4000
RIDGEWAY DR
THE RIDGEWAY
Bwg Gn
TRANCE WAY
PRINCES AVE
PRINCES WAY
MAPLE GR
LILAC GDNS
Rec Gd
ROSE GDNS
SYCAMORE AVE
OLIVE RD
BERRY WAY
POPE'S LA
Ealing
Hounslow
B4491
(NORTH CIRCULAR ROAD)
Gunnersbury Park
P
PARK DR
PARK PLACE DR
3
HAWTHORN GDNS
84
THE PAVEMENT
Bwg Gns
Gunnersbury Park Mus
B4491
NORTH RD
SOUTH RD
79
CHILTON AVE
South Ealing Cemy
Tenn Cts
Gunnersbury Park
PARK WAY
PARK PL
International Sch of London
40
MANOR GDNS
MANOR WAY
MANOR CT
OCCUPATION LA
2
CLAYPONDS GDNS
MONMOUTH GR
BRAMBER CT
STERLING PL
H
Claypones
LIONEL ROAD N
TW8
Gunnersbury Cemy
Lionel Road Prim Sch
CARVILLE CRES
BRENTWICK GDNS
CROWTHER AVE
CLAYPONDS AVE
GREENLAWN LA
APPLE GARTH
CHESTNUT AVE
CHERRY
SPRINGVALE AVE
Potomac
Superstore
POWER RD
Chiswick Rdbt
A4 Hounslow
Phoenix Trad Pk
Pav
GREAT WEST RD (UNDER)
A406
A315
M4 (ELEVATED)
2
40
Brentford Fountain L Ctr
CAPITAL INTERCHANGE WAY
1
M4 Heathrow Airport
1
1 PEGASUS CT
2 TITAN CT
3 TEMERAIRE PL
Kew Bridge Dist Ctr
Kew Bridge
CHISWICK HIGH RD
A205
CLARENCE RD
STONEHILL RD
PO
A3000
B455
Ealing Road Trad Est
CLAYPONDS LA
LIONEL ROAD S
GREEN DRAGON LA
Kew Bridge
STILE HALL GDNS
PINKHAM MANS
REGENT ST
BROOKS RD
EALING RD
BURFORD RD
PERRAN WLK
COATES WLK
CLAYPONDS
BOULTON HO
HARNAGE HO
MAUDSLEY HO
HARVEY HO
CORNISH HO
FRASER HO
WICKSTEAD HO
Mus
KEW BRIDGE RD
MALTINGS
SPRING GR
HEARNE RD
STRAND-ON-THE-GREEN
WALDECK RD
PYRMONT RD
MEADE CL
GERALDINE RD
BROOKS LA
78
Griffin Park Fball Gd
30
18
NETLEY RD
Sch
THAMES ROW
HOLLAND GDNS
Mus
REGATTA HO
Thameside Ctr
A205
19
Kew Pier
NORTH RD
44
HIGH ST
Brentford
KEW BRIDGE
Strand on the Green
B455
BRAEMAR RD
BROOK RD S
KINGSLEY
WALNUT
PO

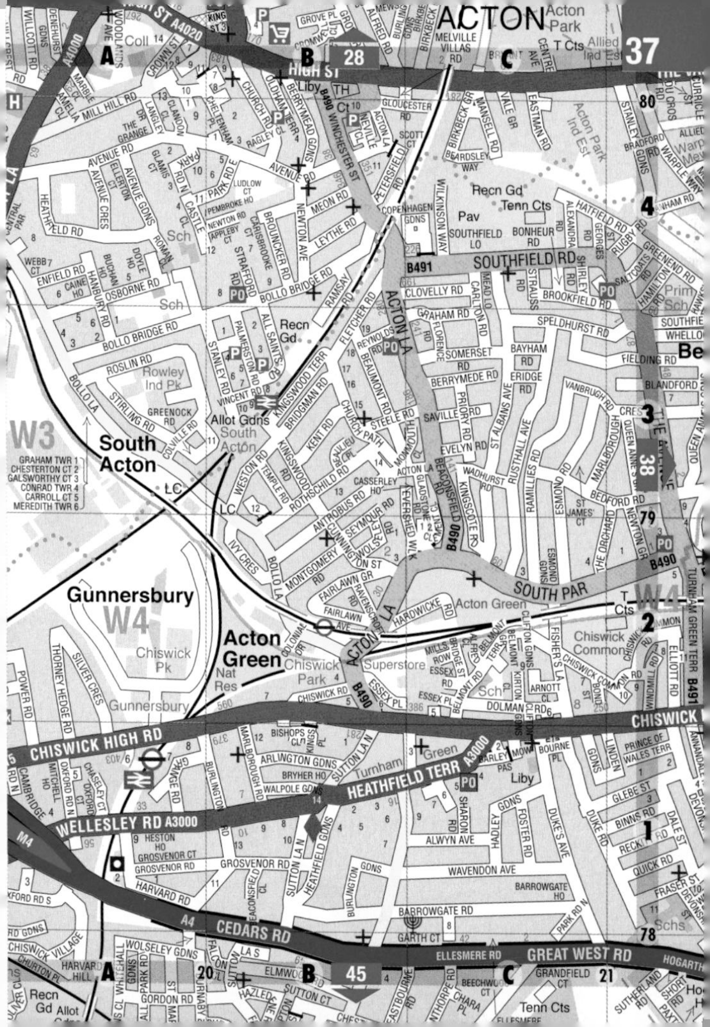
ACTON
Acton Park
South Acton
Gunnersbury
Acton Green
W3
W4
HIGH ST
CHISWICK HIGH RD
WELLESLEY RD A3000
HEATHFIELD TERR A3000
CEDARS RD
GREAT WEST RD
SOUTHFIELD RD
SOUTH PAR
ACTON LA
B490 WINCHESTER ST
BOLLO BRIDGE RD
BOLLO LA
AVENUE RD
Chiswick Pk
Chiswick Common
Chiswick Park
Acton Park Ind Est
Rowley Ind Pk
Recn Gd
Tenn Cts
Allot Gdns
Nat Res
Superstore
Turnham Green
GRAHAM TWR 1
CHESTERTON CT 2
GALSWORTHY CT 3
CONRAD TWR 4
CARROLL CT 5
MEREDITH TWR 6
A
B
C
1
2
3
4
28
38
45
20
21
78
79
80

Bedford Park
W12
W4
CHISWICK
THE VALE
A4020
TRILLINGTON HO
29
37
46
80
79
78
A
B
C
1
2
3
4
Allied Ind Est
Acton Park Ind Est
Warple Mews
ALLIED WAY
ESSEX PARK MEWS
BEECH AVE
THE VALE EST
SHILLAKER CT
OLLGAR CL
ASKHAM CT
HANOVER HO
WESTBRIDGE CL
CONINGHAM MEWS
KEITH GR
BOSCOMBE RD
FINDON RD
ROXWELL RD
VESPAN RD
BECKLOW RD
BECKLOW GDNS
ASKEW CRES
CLIFTON AVE
B408
ASKEW RD
HADYN PARK RD
BATSON ST
ELLINGHAM RD
MARK MANS
STARFIELD RD
CURWEN RD
DAVISVILLE RD
PERCY RD
WESTVILLE RD
LEFFERN RD
GREENSIDE RD
LEYSFIELD RD
ELGIN
GAYFORD RD
EDANS CT
COBBOLD RD
COBBOLD MEWS
JEDDO RD
JEDDO MEWS
VALETTA RD
SWAINSON RD
ELIZABETH GDNS
DAVIS RD
OLDFIELD RD
ST ELMO RD
COWLEY RD
AGNES RD
WESTVALE MEWS
DORDRECHT RD
LARDEN RD
HOLLEY RD
MAYFIELD RD
LEFROY RD
KINNEAR RD
STRONSA RD
COTTON HO
EVELYN HO
AYLMER RD
WENDELL RD
GRANSDEN RD
BASSEIN PARK RD
ASHCHURCH TERR
ASHCHURCH GR
ASHCHURCH PARK VILLAS
KELMSCOTT GDNS
BALMORAL MEWS
COSMUR CL
RYLETT CRES
RYLETT RD
BINDEN RD
JOHN BETTS HO
ST MARY'S CT
FLANCHFORD RD
HARTSWOOD RD
EMLYN RD
Tenn Cts
Allot Gdns
ABINGER RD
PALGRAVE RD
STAMFORD BROOK RD
B409
A402
GOLDHAWK RD
SEVEN STARS CNR
PADDENSWICK RD
Bndstd
Sch
Bwg Gn
Ravenscourt Park
RAVENSCOURT SQ
Stamford
STAMFORD CT
RAVENSCOURT GDNS
VERNEAD CL
PARK MANS
SOUTH SIDE
PLEYDELL AVE
PREBEND GDNS
STAMFORD BROOK AVE
WELSTEAD WAY
VAUGHAN AVE
BATH RD
GAINSBOROUGH RD
LONSDALE RD
ADDISON GR
RUPERT RD
FAIRFAX RD
PRIORY AVE
WOODSTOCK RD
BLENHEIM RD
QUEEN ANNE'S GDNS
THE AVENUE
FLANDERS RD
Turnham Green
SALISBURY CT
Stamford Brook
HAMLET GDNS
KINGS CT
Prep Sch
RAVENSCOURT AVE
KING ST
A315
ST PETER'S GR
STANDISH RD
AITEN PL
THERESA RD
BEAVOR LA
VENCOURT PL
WELTJE RD
ST PETER'S RD
ST PETER'S SQ
BLACK LION LA
BRITISH GR
NETHERAVON RD
PARR PL
AIREDALE AVE
MERTON AVE
CLEVELAND AVE
RAVENSMEDE WAY
THE POWER HO
ENNISMORE AVE
UPHAM PARK RD
THORNTON AVE
MAYFIELD AVE
ELLIOTT RD
WINDMILL RD
CHISWICK COMMON RD
Chiswick Common
TURNHAM GREEN TERR
B491
CHISWICK HIGH RD
A316
CHISWICK LA
HOMEFIELD RD
T Cts
BEVERLEY RD
VERONA CT
CRANBROOK RD
BRACKLEY RD
ANNANDALE RD
PRINCE OF WALES TERR
LINDEN GDNS
GLEBE ST
BINNS RD
RECKITT RD
QUICK RD
DALE ST
DEVONSHIRE RD
SWANSCOMBE RD
ALKERDEN RD
COOMBE RD
WILTON AVE
ASHBOURNE GR
BALFERN GR
CORNWALL GR
DORCHESTER GR
EASTBURY GR
BENNETT ST
FRASER ST
WOOD ST
Schs
GRIFFIN CT
AIREDALE AVE S
Recn Gd
A4
GREAT WEST RD
40
NETHERAVON RD S
EYOT GDNS
CHISWICK MALL
Thames Path
MULBERRY PL
SAMELS CT
OIL MILL LA
LORD NAPIER PL
MYLNE CL
River Thames
St Paul's Sch
Tenn Cts
Pl Flds
LONSDALE RD
HOGARTH
Hogarth's House
GRANDFIELD CT
SUTHERLAND RD
SHORT RD
MAWSON LA
CHURCH ST
CHISWICK LAS
Pl Fld
DUKE RD
DUKE'S AVE
FOSTER RD
BARROWGATE HO
BOURNE PL
Liby
CLIFTON GDNS
ARNOTT CL
FISHER'S LA
BOND ST
SOUTH PAR
B490
ESMOND GDNS
THE ORCHARD
NEWTON GR
BEDFORD RD
ST JAMES' CT
MARLBOROUGH CRES
QUEEN ANNE'S GR
VANBRUGH RD
BLANDFORD RD
FIELDING RD
SOUTHFIELD RD
WHELLOCK RD
SPELDHURST RD
BROOKFIELD RD
SOUTHFIELD RD
STRAUSS RD
SHIRLEY RD
BONHEUR RD
HATFIELD RD
GEORGES RD
RUGBY RD
GREENEND RD
SALTCOATS RD
HAMILTON RD
HAWKSHEAD RD
WORCESTER GDNS
CANHAM RD
MULTI WAY
WARPLE WAY
BRADFORD RD
STANLEY GDNS
EASTMAN RD
RAMILLIES RD
RUSTHALL AVE
BAYHAM RD
Prim Sch
Ealing
Hounslow
Gd
Tenn Cts
PO
H
P

UXBRIDGE RD
ARCHDALE CT
HETLEY RD
GODOLPHIN RD
ST STEPHEN'S AVE
DEVONPORT RD
WARBECK RD
COVERDALE RD
Shepherd's Bush
Rail Depot
Shepherd's Bush (Central Line)
BULWER ST
ALDINE ST
CAXTON RD
TADMOR ST
STERNE ST
Sta Under Construction
Holland Park Rdbt
QUEENSDALE RD
ROYAL CRESCENT MEWS
KINGSDALE GDNS
THE GLADE
OLD FORGE MEWS
CONINGHAM RD
MELINA RD
CATHNOR RD
MORLAND CT
STOWE RD
THORNFIELD RD
SCOTT'S RD
TITMUSS ST
CE Prim Sch
Prim Sch
Coll
LIME GR
GAINSBOROUGH CT
SHEPHERD'S BUSH MKT
MARKET LA
PENNARD RD
Liby
Tenn Cts
Shepherd's Bush Common
MADAGASCAR
SHEPHERD'S BUSH GN
MILLER'S WAY
West 12
CHARECROFT WAY
WOODSTOCK GR
HANSARD MEWS
UPPER ADDISON GDNS
ADDISON GDNS
SINCLAIR GDNS
SINCLAIR RD
MINFORD GDNS
ROCKLEY RD
RICHMOND WAY
WESTWICK GDNS
NETHERWOOD RD
LAKESIDE RD
ADDISON GDNS
BOLINGBROKE RD
FIELDING RD
Goldhawk Road
ELGIN CL
PARNELL CL
GOLDHAWK RD
AUGUSTUS CL
BRACKENBURY GDNS
SYCAMORE GDNS
UNDERWOOD
BENBOW CT
ASTROP TERR
ASTROP MEWS
RICHFORD ST
WELLS RD
RAILWAY COTTS
WOODGER RD
SULGRAVE RD
POPLAR GR
CROMWELL GR
MELROSE TERR
MELROSE GDNS
STANLEY RD
Ind Est
WINGATE RD
CRESSY CT
BENBOW RD
BEAUCLERC RD
GROVE MEWS
RICHFORD GATE
BATOUM GDNS
OSMAN RD
LORIS RD
LENA GDNS
SHEPHERD'S BUSH RD
W14
MILSON RD
IRVING RD
HOFLAND RD
REDAN ST
MASBRO' RD
BERGHEM MEWS
DEWHURST RD
BLYTHE RD
FAROE RD
CEYLON RD
COLERIDGE CT
GRATTON RD
HAZLITT RD
BRACKENBURY RD
CARTHEW VILLAS
CARTHEW RD
COULTER RD
DALLING RD
ROSEDALE TERR
NASMYTH ST
DORVILLE CRES
WELLESLEY AVE
CARDROSS ST
HEBRON RD
AGATE RD
AMOR RD
HAMMERSMITH GR
TRUSSLEY RD
OSRAM CT
BARB MEWS
DUNSANY RD
STERNDALE RD
AUGUSTINE RD
APPLEGARTH
CAITHNESS RD
TABOR RD
MARCO RD
ADIE RD
1 PORTLAND VILLAGE
2 ESSEX CT
IFFLEY RD
ALDENSLEY RD
FURBER ST
PERRERS RD
BRADMORE PARK RD
ST JOHN'S CT
Schs
SOUTHERTON RD
OVERSTONE RD
Cts
BROOK GN
AYNHOE RD
AYNHOE MANS
GIRDLERS RD
OXFORD GATE
BLYTHE RD
WINDSOR WAY
PLANETREE CT
RAVENSCOURT RD
ATWOOD RD
RAYNHAM RD
REDMORE RD
BANIM ST
KILMARSH RD
W6
MERCERS PL
LUXEMBURG GDNS
QUEEN'S MANS
Prep Sch
Brook Green
Girls' Sch
STUART HO
WINDSOR WAY
ST JOSEPH'S HO
TUDOR HO
HAMMERSMITH
Ravenscourt Park
DALLING RD
GLENTHORNE RD
GLENTHORNE MEWS
BEADON RD
Kings Mall
Hammersmith
BUTE GDNS
WOLVERTON GDNS
ROWAN TERR
ROWAN RD
TA Ctr
LATYMER CT
HAMMERSMITH RD
MORE CL
AURIOL RD
MUNDEN ST
RAVENSCOURT PL
STUDLAND ST
GALENA RD
CAMBRIDGE GR
ALBION PL
LEAMORE ST
ARGYLE PL
CHALK HILL RD
BUTTERWICK
Hammersmith Broadway
NAZARETH HO
SHORTLANDS
COLET GDNS
LILY CL
Coll
RIVERCOURT RD
CROMWELL AVE
NIGEL PLAYFAIR AVE
HOLCOMBE ST
MACBETH ST
RIVERSIDE GDNS
DOWN PL
BRIDGE AVE
ANGEL WLK
BLACK'S RD
GREAT WEST RD
TALGARTH RD
GREAT CHURCH LA
Hammersmith Flyover
LOWER MALL
RUTLAND GR
DIGBY MANS
WORLIDGE ST
QUEEN CAROLINE ST
THE SQUARE
GUINNESS TRUST BLDGS
YELDHAM HO
YELDHAM RD
MARGRAVINE GDNS
Barons Court
Cemy
PALLISER RD
Thames
Hammersmith & Fulham
Richmond upon Thames
Tenn Cts
HAMMERSMITH BRIDGE RD
RIVER TERR
CRISP RD
CHANCELLORS ST
ST JAMES ST
CHANCELLOR'S RD
DISTILLERY RD
DISTILLERY LA
PLAYFAIR ST
BISCAY RD
Acad
BERYL RD
ST DUNSTAN'S RD
1 WILSONS RD
2 LINACRE CT
3 WATERHOUSE CL
HAMMERSMITH BRIDGE
Charing Cross
MARGRAVINE RD
CLAXTON GR
CHELMSFORD CL
CASTLENAU MANS
ST HILDA'S RD
GLENTHAM RD
1 ST EDMUND'S SQ
2 RICHARD BURBIDGE MANS
3 CHARLES HARROD CT
4 WILLIAM HUNT MANS
5 WRENN HO
CASTLENAU
RIVERVIEW GDNS
CHALINE ST
KEIR HARDIE HO
PARFREY ST
FULHAM PALACE RD
WILLIAM MORRIS HO
CLAYBROOK
GASTEIN RD
GREYHOUND RD
KING HENRY'S
A4020
A219
A402
A3220
A315
A306
A4
B408
B350
30
47
126
140
23
24
78
79
80

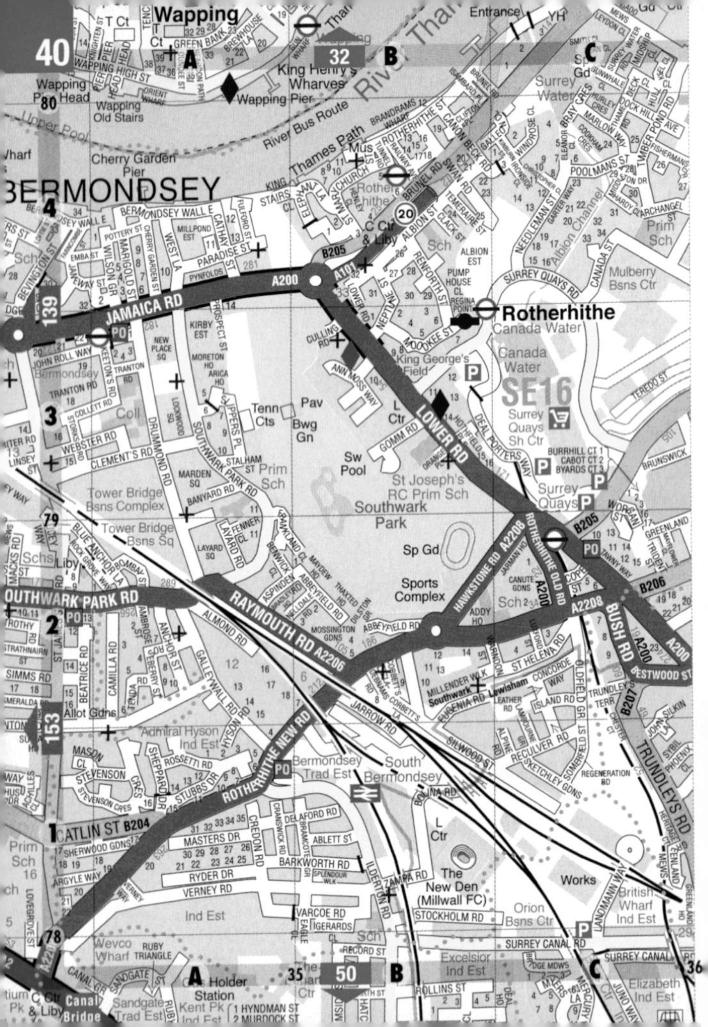
Wapping
32
A
B
C
King Henry's Wharves
Wapping Pier
Wapping High St
Wapping Pier Head
Wapping Old Stairs
80
Upper Pool
River Thames
River Bus Route
Thames Path
Cherry Garden Pier
BERMONDSEY
Bermondsey Wall E
Rotherhithe St
Brunel Rd
Rotherhithe
Mus
Surrey Water
Sp Gd
Dock Hill Ave
Timber Pond Rd
Poolmans St
Needleman St
Albion Channel
Prim Sch
Mulberry Bsns Ctr
Surrey Quays Rd
Canada St
Jamaica Rd
A200
A101
B205
Paradise St
Cathay St
West La
Marigold St
Wilson Gr
Cherry Garden St
Pumphouse
Albion Est
Lower Rd
Rotherhithe
Canada Water
SE16
Surrey Quays Sh Ctr
Deal Porters Way
King George's Field
Neptune St
Culling Rd
Ann Moss Way
L Ctr
Gomm Rd
Sw Pool
St Joseph's RC Prim Sch
Southwark Park
Tenn Cts
Pav
Bwg Gn
Sp Gd
Sports Complex
139
Bermondsey
John Roll Way
Keeton's Rd
Tranton Rd
Coll
Drummond Rd
Southwark Park Rd
Webster Rd
Clement's Rd
Stalham St
Prim Sch
Marden Sq
Banyard Rd
Tower Bridge Bsns Complex
Tower Bridge Bsns Sq
Layard Rd
Layard Sq
Fenner Cl
Blue Anchor La
79
Schs
Liby
Raymouth Rd A2206
Almond Rd
Galleywall Rd
Hawkstone Rd A2208
Rotherhithe Old Rd
Canute Gdns
Addy Ho
A2208
Bush Rd
A200
B206
Bestwood St
St Helena Rd
Oldfield Gr
Millender Wlk
Southwark
Lewisham
Concorde Way
Trundley's Terr
B207
Trundleys Rd
Eugenia Rd
Island Rd
Reculver Rd
Silwood St
Sketchley Gdns
Regeneration Rd
Jarrow Rd
Corbett's La
Rotherhithe New Rd
Bermondsey Trad Est
South Bermondsey
Bolina Rd
L Ctr
The New Den (Millwall FC)
Works
British Wharf Ind Est
Orion Bsns Ctr
Surrey Canal Rd
Excelsior Ind Est
Zampa Rd
Stockholm Rd
153
Allot Gdns
Admiral Hyson Ind Est
Mason Cl
Stevenson Cres
Rossetti Rd
Stubbs Dr
Catlin St B204
Masters Dr
Credon Rd
Delaford Rd
Ablett St
Barkworth Rd
Ryder Dr
Verney Rd
Varcoe Rd
Ilderton Rd
Ind Est
Prim Sch
Sherwood Gdns
Argyle Way
78
A2206
Wevco Wharf
Ruby Triangle
Sandgate St
Gas Holder Station
35
50
36
Kent Pk Ind Est
1 Hyndman St
2 Murdock St
C Ctr & Liby
Canal Bridge
Sandgate Trad Est
Rollins St
Mercury Way
Juno Way
Elizabeth Ind Est
1
2
3
4

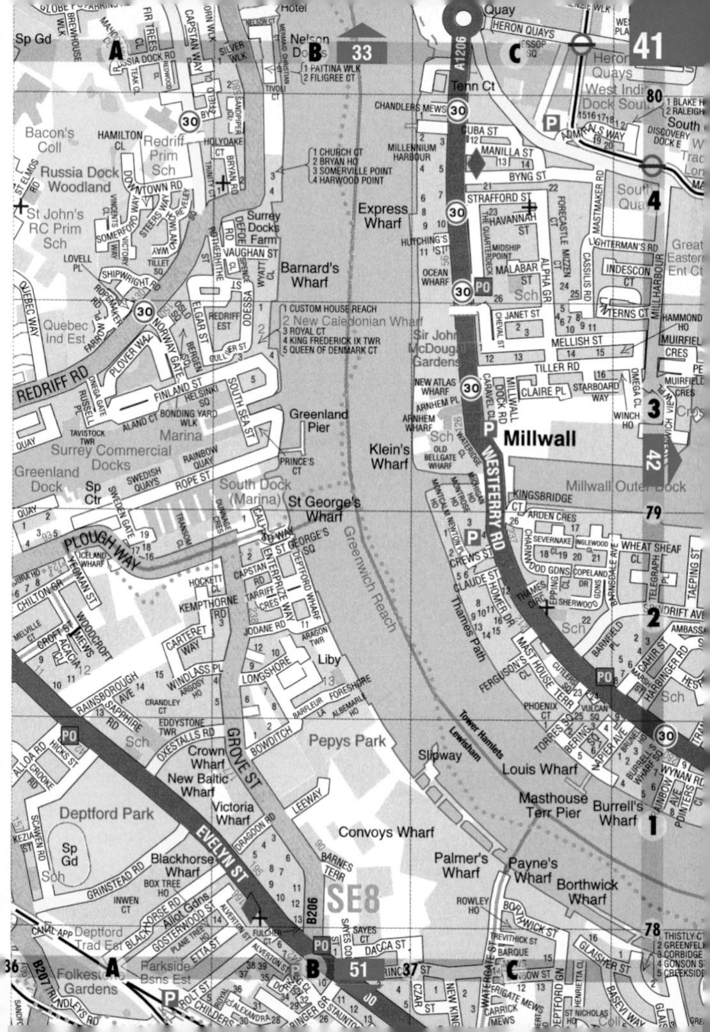
33
A
B
C
Sp Gd
Nelson Docks
Heron Quays
West India Dock South
South Quay
Russia Dock Woodland
St John's RC Prim Sch
Bacon's Coll
Redriff Prim Sch
Surrey Docks Farm
Barnard's Wharf
Express Wharf
Ocean Wharf
Millennium Harbour
Tenn Ct
Chandlers Mews
Cuba St
Manilla St
Byng St
Strafford St
Havannah St
Malabar St
Mellish St
Tiller Rd
Claire Pl
Starboard Way
Millharbour
Great Eastern Ent Ctr
Lightermans Rd
Indescon Ct
Lanterns Ct
Sir John McDougal Gardens
New Atlas Wharf
Arnhem Pl
Arnhem Wharf
Klein's Wharf
Old Bellgate Wharf
Millwall
Westferry Rd
Millwall Outer Dock
Kingsbridge Ct
Arden Cres
Severnake
Inglewood
Wheat Sheaf Cl
Telegraph Pl
Taeping St
Spindrift Ave
Crews St
Claude St
Homer Dr
Thames Path
Thames Circ
Fergusons Cl
Mast House Terr
Phoenix Ct
Torres Sq
Bering Sq
Napier Ave
Louis Wharf
Masthouse Terr Pier
Burrell's Wharf
Wynan Rd
Harbinger Rd
Greenwich Reach
Greenland Pier
South Dock (Marina)
St George's Wharf
Surrey Commercial Docks
Greenland Dock
Sp Ctr
Quebec Ind Est
Quebec Way
Redriff Rd
Plough Way
Rope St
Swedish Quays
Rainbow Quay
Finland St
Helsinki Sq
Bonding Yard Wlk
South Sea St
Norway Gate
Plover Way
Odessa St
Elgar St
Redriff Est
Rotherhithe St
Vaughan St
Defoe Rd
Salter Rd
Downtown Rd
Somerford Way
Holyoake Ct
Hamilton Cl
Lovell Pl
Shipwright Rd
Ropemaker Rd
Tavistock Twr
Iceland Wharf
Yeoman St
Chilton Gr
Woodcroft Mews
Croft St
Acacia Cl
Kempthorne Rd
Carteret Way
Windlass Pl
Rainsborough Ave
Sapphire Rd
Eddystone Twr
Oxestalls Rd
Grove St
Crown Wharf
New Baltic Wharf
Victoria Wharf
Capstan Rd
Enterprize Way
Deptford Wharf
Tarriff Cres
Jodane Rd
Aragon Twr
Longshore
Foreshore
Barfleur La
Albemarle Ho
Bowditch
Pepys Park
Liby
Slipway
Tower Hamlets
Lewisham
Leeway
Dragoon Rd
Convoys Wharf
Palmer's Wharf
Payne's Wharf
Borthwick Wharf
Borthwick St
Rowley Ho
Deptford Park
Alloa Rd
Hicks St
Crooke Rd
Scawen Rd
Grinstead Rd
Blackhorse Wharf
Box Tree Ho
Inwen Ct
Evelyn St
Allot Gdns
Gosterwood St
Etta St
Deptford Trad Est
Parkside Bsns Est
Folkestone Gardens
Canal App
Barnes Terr
Sayes Ct
Dacca St
Prince St
Czar St
Watergate St
Frigate Mews
Carrick Mews
Glaisher St
Basevi Way
SE8
B206
A1206
B207
42
51
79
78
80
PO
Sch
Coll

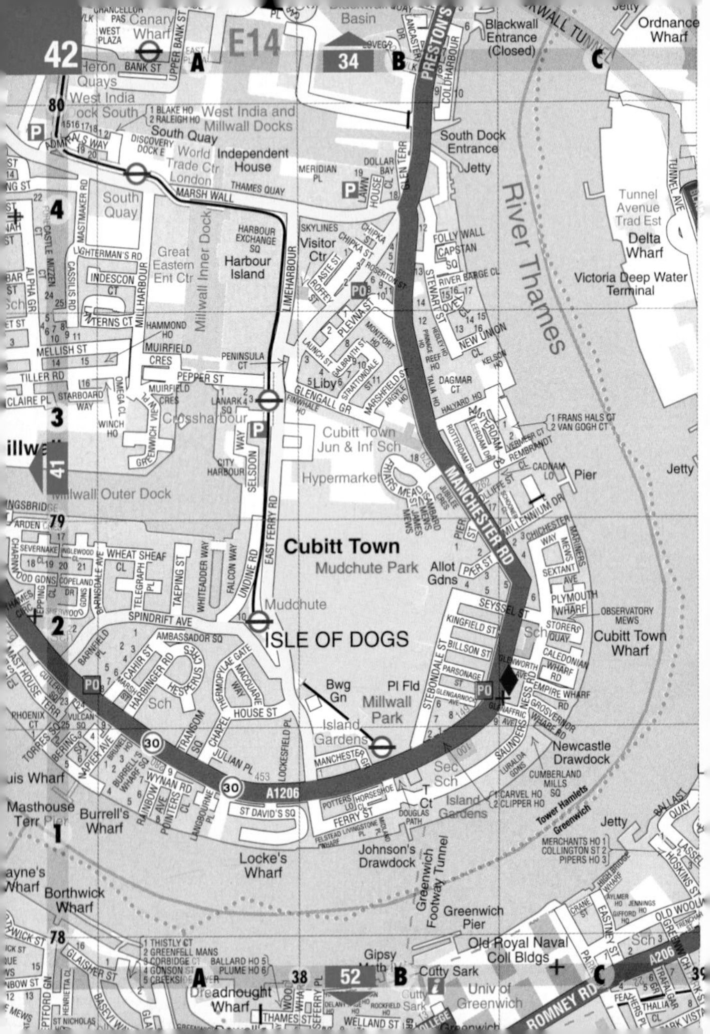
E14
Canary Wharf
Heron Quays
West India Dock South
West India and Millwall Docks
South Quay
Blackwall Basin
Blackwall Entrance (Closed)
Ordnance Wharf
34
A
B
C
PRESTON'S RD
COLDHARBOUR
BANK ST
UPPER BANK ST
1 BLAKE HO
2 RALEIGH HO
ADMIRALS WAY
DISCOVERY DOCK E
World Trade Ctr London
Independent House
MERIDIAN PL
DOLLAR BAY
LAWN HOUSE CL
GLEN TERR
South Dock Entrance
Jetty
River Thames
Tunnel Avenue Trad Est
TUNNEL AVE
Delta Wharf
Victoria Deep Water Terminal
MARSH WALL
THAMES QUAY
South Quay
Millwall Inner Dock
Great Eastern Ent Ctr
HARBOUR EXCHANGE SQ
Harbour Island
LIMEHARBOUR
SKYLINES
CHIPKA ST
Visitor Ctr
ASTE ST
ROFFEY ST
ROSERTON ST
PLEVNA ST
MONTFORT HO
LAUNCH ST
GALBRAITH ST
STRATTONDALE ST
MARSHFIELD ST
ARGYLE HO
Liby
FOLLY WALL
CAPSTAN SQ
RIVER BARGE CL
STEWART ST
HEDGER ST
LOVEX CL
NEW UNION CL
KELSON HO
PINNACE HO
REEF HO
TALIA HO
DAGMAR CT
HALYARD HO
AMSTERDAM RD
LEERDAM DR
ROTTERDAM DR
1 FRANS HALS CT
2 VAN GOGH CT
VERMEER CT
REMBRANDT CL
CADMAN LO
Pier
Jetty
MASTMAKER RD
LIGHTERMAN'S RD
CASTLE MIZZEN CT
ALPHA GR
CASSILIS RD
INDESCON CT
LANTERNS CT
MILLHARBOUR
HAMMOND HO
MUIRFIELD CRES
MELLISH ST
TILLER RD
PENINSULA CT
PEPPER ST
OMEGA CL
STARBOARD WAY
CLAIRE PL
WINCH HO
GREENWICH VIEW PL
LANARK SQ
GLENGALL GR
FINWHALE HO
Crossharbour
Cubitt Town Jun & Inf Sch
SELSDON WAY
CITY HARBOUR
Hypermarket
FRIARS MEAD
ST JAMES MEWS
ISAMBARD MEWS
JUBILEE CRES
MANCHESTER RD
CLIFFE ST
SCHOONER
MILLENNIUM DR
Millwall
41
Millwall Outer Dock
EAST FERRY RD
UNDINE RD
FALCON WAY
WHITEADDER WAY
TAEPING ST
TELEGRAPH PL
WHEAT SHEAF CL
BARNSDALE AVE
SEVERNAKE CL
INGLEWOOD CL
CHARNWOOD GDNS
COPELAND DR
THAMES CIRC
EPPING CL
SPINDRIFT AVE
Cubitt Town
Mudchute Park
Allot Gdns
PIER ST
CHICHESTER WAY
MARINERS MEWS
SEXTANT AVE
PLYMOUTH WHARF
OBSERVATORY MEWS
STORERS QUAY
Cubitt Town Wharf
CALEDONIAN WHARF RD
SEYSSEL ST
KINGFIELD ST
BILLSON ST
PARSONAGE ST
STEBONDALE ST
GLENGARNOCK AVE
GLENWORTH AVE
GLENAFFRIC AVE
NESS RD
EMPIRE WHARF RD
GROSVENOR WHARF RD
Mudchute
ISLE OF DOGS
AMBASSADOR SQ
BARNFIELD PL
CAHIR ST
HARBINGER RD
HESPERUS CRES
THERMOPYLAE GATE
MACQUARIE WAY
HOUSE ST
Bwg Gn
Pl Fld
Millwall Park
Island Gardens
MANCHESTER GR
LOCKESFIELD PL
CHAPEL
TRANSOM SQ
JULIAN PL
CUTLERS TERR
MAST HOUSE TERR
PHOENIX CT
VULCAN SQ
NAPIER AVE
BERING SQ
TORRES SQ
BRUNEL HO
BURRELL'S WHARF SQ
WYNAN RD
RAINBOW AVE
POINTERS CL
LANGBOURNE PL
30
A1206
ST DAVID'S SQ
POTTERS LO
HORSESHOE CL
FERRY ST
DOUGLAS PATH
FELSTEAD WHARF
LIVINGSTONE PL
MIDLAND PL
Sec Sch
Island Gardens
SAUNDERS NESS RD
LURALDA GDNS
CUMBERLAND MILLS SQ
1 CARVEL HO
2 CLIPPER HO
Newcastle Drawdock
Tower Hamlets
Greenwich
Jetty
BALLAST QUAY
MERCHANTS HO 1
COLLINGTON ST 2
PIPERS HO 3
Masthouse Terr Pier
Burrell's Wharf
Locke's Wharf
Johnson's Drawdock
Greenwich Footway Tunnel
Greenwich Pier
Old Royal Naval Coll Bldgs
Borthwick Wharf
Payne's Wharf
HIGH BRIDGE WHARF
CRANE ST
EASTNEY ST
PARK ST
OLD WOOLWICH RD
HOSKINS ST
LASSELL ST
A206
ROMNEY RD
1 THISTLY CT
2 GREENFELL MANS
3 CORBIDGE CT
4 GONSON ST
5 CREEKSIDE
BALLARD HO 5
PLUME HO 6
GLAISHER ST
HENRIETTA CL
SPITFORD GN
ST NICHOLAS
Gipsy Moth IV
Cutty Sark
Univ of Greenwich
Dreadnought Wharf
THAMES ST
WELLAND ST
ROCKFIELD HO
52
38
39
80
79
78
1
2
3
4

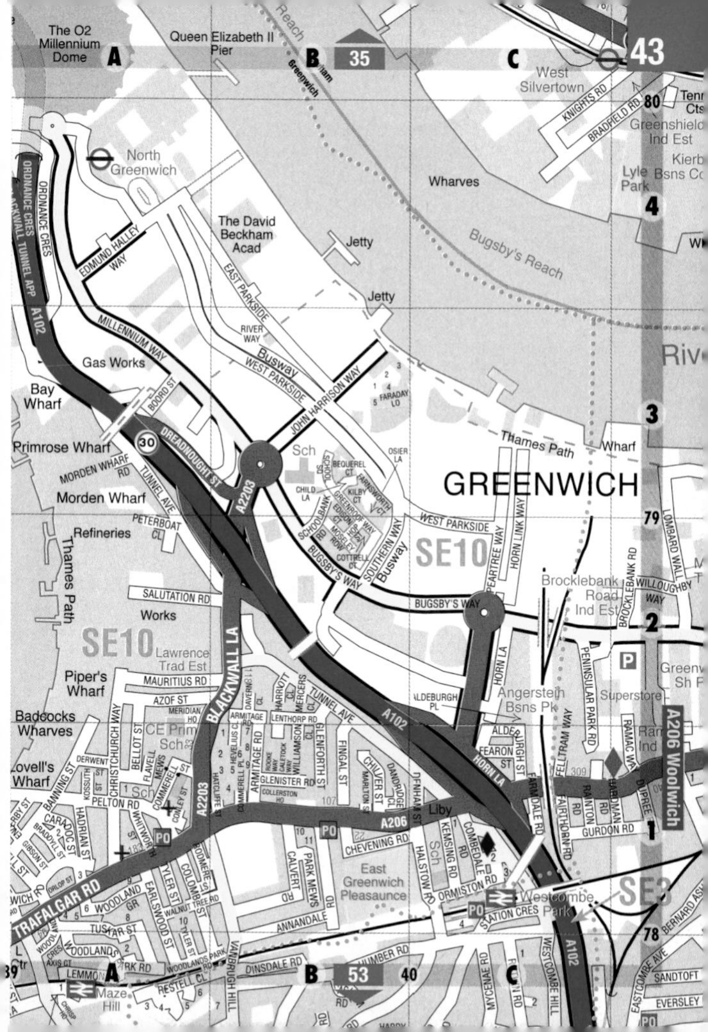
The O2 Millennium Dome
Queen Elizabeth II Pier
A
B
35
C
Greenwich Reach
West Silvertown
KNIGHTS RD
BRADFIELD RD
80
Greenshield Ind Est
Lyle Park
4
North Greenwich
Wharves
ORDNANCE CRES
BLACKWALL TUNNEL APP
ORDNANCE CRES
EDMUND HALLEY WAY
The David Beckham Acad
Jetty
Bugsby's Reach
EAST PARKSIDE
Jetty
A102
MILLENNIUM WAY
RIVER WAY
Busway
WEST PARKSIDE
JOHN HARRISON WAY
FARADAY LO
Gas Works
Bay Wharf
BOORD ST
3
Primrose Wharf
30
DREADNOUGHT ST
Sch
SCHOOL SQ
BEQUEREL CT
OSIER LA
Thames Path
Wharf
GREENWICH
MORDEN WHARF RD
TUNNEL AVE
A2203
CHILD LA
KILBY CT
FARNSWORTH CT
Morden Wharf
GREENROOF WAY
SCHOOLBANK RD
EDISON CT
WEST PARKSIDE
79
LOMBARD WALL
PETERBOAT CL
Refineries
MOSELEY ROW
SE10
PEARTREE WAY
HORN LINK WAY
Thames Path
BUGSBY'S WAY
COTTRELL CT
SOUTHERN WAY
Busway
Brocklebank Road Ind Est
BROCKLEBANK RD
WILLOUGHBY WAY
SALUTATION RD
BUGSBY'S WAY
2
Works
SE10
Lawrence Trad Est
BLACKWALL LA
P
PENINSULAR PARK RD
HORN LA
Piper's Wharf
MAURITIUS RD
Greenwich Sh Pk
AZOF ST
HARROTT CL
MERCERS CL
TUNNEL AVE
ALDEBURGH PL
Angerstein Bsns Pk
Superstore
Badcocks Wharves
MERIDIAN HO
ARMITAGE RD
LENTHORP RD
A102
FELLTRAM WAY
RAMAC WAY
A206 Woolwich
CE Prim Sch
ALDEBURGH ST
CHRISTCHURCH WAY
BELLOT ST
HEVELIUS CL
ARMITAGE RD
WILLIAMSON CL
GLENFORTH ST
FINGAL ST
FEARON ST
HORN LA
Lovell's Wharf
DERWENT
FLAVELL MEWS
COMMERELL ST
GLENISTER RD
CHILVER ST
DANDRIDGE CL
309
BANNING ST
KOSSUTH ST
COLLERSTON HO
MARLTON ST
HARDMAN RD
RAINTON RD
FARMDALE RD
FAIRTHORN RD
DUPREE RD
Sch
CONLEY ST
HATCLIFFE ST
COMMERELL PL
107
DENHAM ST
Liby
PELTON RD
CARADOC ST
HADRIAN ST
WHITWORTH ST
A2203
A206
KEMSING RD
COMBEDALE RD
GURDON RD
1
BRADDYLL ST
PO
PO
CHEVENING RD
Sch
GIBSON ST
TRAFALGAR RD
TYLER ST
COLOMB ST
BODMERE
CALVERT RD
PARK MEWS
East Greenwich Pleasaunce
HALSTOW RD
ORMISTON RD
Westcombe Park
SE3
ORLOP ST
WOODLAND GR
EARLSWOOD ST
WALNUT TREE RD
PO
STATION CRES
BERNARD ASHLEY
TUSKAR ST
ANNANDALE RD
78
WOODLANDS
PARK RD
WOODLANDS PARK RD
VANBRUGH HILL
HUMBER RD
EASTCOMBE AVE
LEMMON RD
A
DINSDALE RD
B
53
40
C
MYCENAE RD
WESTCOMBE HILL
A102
SANDTOFT
Maze Hill
RESTELL CL
EVERSLEY
39

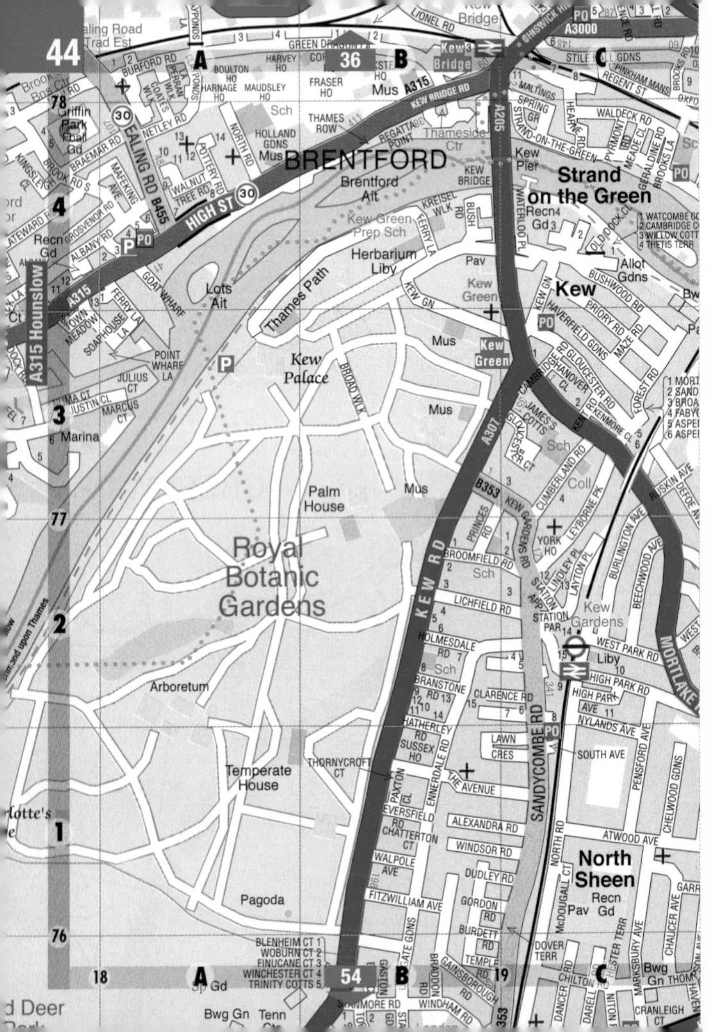

BRENTFORD
Strand on the Green
Kew
Royal Botanic Gardens
North Sheen
Kew Bridge
Kew Palace
Palm House
Temperate House
Pagoda
Arboretum
Brentford Ait
Lots Ait
Thames Path
Herbarium Liby
Kew Green
Kew Green Prep Sch
Kew Gardens
Kew Pier
Thameside Ctr
Griffin Park Fball Gd
Marina
A315 Hounslow
A315
A3000
A205
A307
B353
B455
HIGH ST
KEW BRIDGE RD
KEW RD
MORTLAKE RD
SANDYCOMBE RD
EALING RD
CHISWICK HIGH RD
GREEN DRAGON LA
STRAND-ON-THE-GREEN
KEW GN
BROAD WLK
LICHFIELD RD
BROOMFIELD RD
HOLMESDALE RD
WEST PARK RD
HIGH PARK RD
NYLANDS AVE
ATWOOD AVE
FITZWILLIAM AVE
BRANSTONE RD
ALEXANDRA RD
WINDSOR RD
DUDLEY RD
CLARENCE RD
LAWN CRES
SOUTH AVE
THE AVENUE
STATION PAR
STATION APP
CUMBERLAND RD
LEYBORNE PK
BURLINGTON AVE
BEECHWOOD AVE
PENSFORD AVE
CHELWOOD GDNS
HAVERFIELD GDNS
GLOUCESTER RD
KENT RD
BUSHWOOD RD
PRIORY RD
FOREST RD
WATERLOO PL
BUSH RD
FERRY LA
KREISEL WLK
NETLEY RD
BRAEMAR RD
ALBANY RD
GROSVENOR RD
BURFORD RD
NORTH RD
WALNUT TREE RD
POTTERY RD
GOAT WHARF
POINT WHARF LA
JULIUS CT
MARCUS CT
JUSTIN CL
HOLLAND GDNS
THAMES ROW
REGATTA POINT
BOULTON HO
HARNAGE HO
MAUDSLEY HO
HARVEY HO
FRASER HO
LIONEL RD
STILE HALL GDNS
REGENT ST
WALDECK RD
PYRMONT RD
MEADE CL
GERALDINE RD
BROOKS LA
HEARNE RD
MALTINGS
SPRING GR
OLD DOCK CL
1 WATCOMBE COTTS
2 CAMBRIDGE COTTS
3 WILLOW COTTS
4 THETIS TERR
Allot Gdns
Recn Gd
York Ho
Liby
Coll
Sch
Mus
Pav
PO
TEMPLE RD
BURDETT RD
GORDON RD
DOVER TERR
CHILTON RD
MARKSBURY AVE
CHAUCER AVE
McDOUGALL CT
WALPOLE AVE
CHATTERTON CT
EVERSFIELD RD
PAXTON CL
SUSSEX HO
HATHERLEY RD
ENNERDALE RD
THORNYCROFT CT
BLENHEIM CT 1
WOBURN CT 2
FINUCANE CT 3
WINCHESTER CT 4
TRINITY COTTS 5
GAINSBOROUGH RD
BRADDON RD
STANMORE RD
WINDHAM RD
CRANLEIGH CT
36
54
A B C
1 2 3 4
18 19 76 77 78

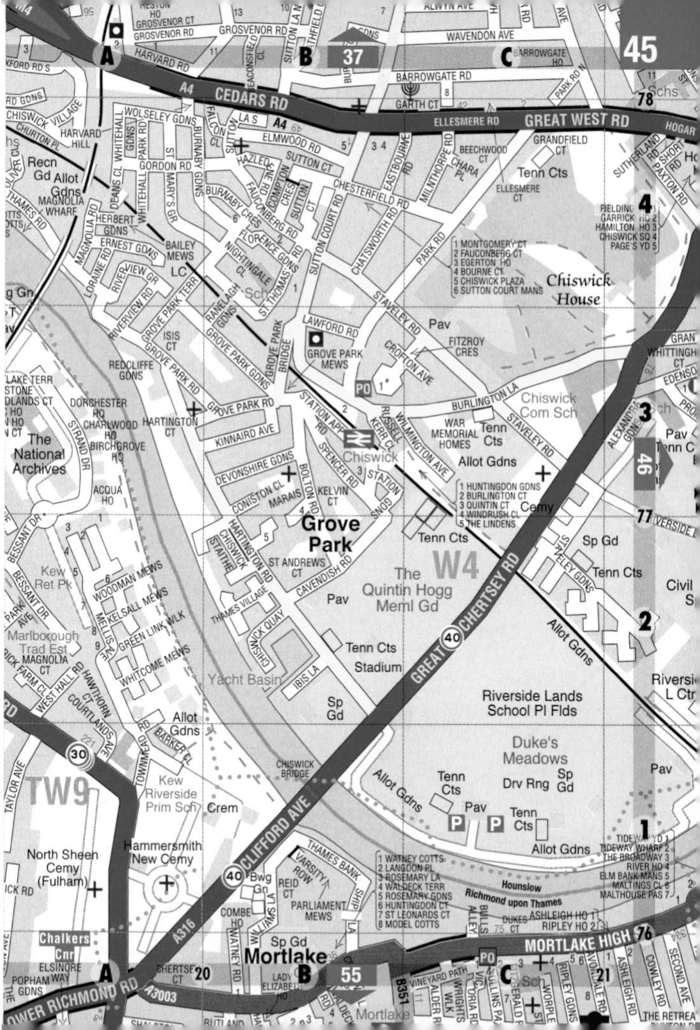
37
A
B
C
A4
CEDARS RD
GREAT WEST RD
ELLESMERE RD
GROSVENOR CT
GROSVENOR RD
HARVARD RD
WAVENDON AVE
BARROWGATE HO
BARROWGATE RD
GARTH CT
78
Schs
HOGARTH
CHISWICK VILLAGE
HARVARD HILL
CHURTON PL
WOLSELEY GDNS
BURNABY GDNS
ELMWOOD RD
SUTTON CT
GRANDFIELD CT
BEECHWOOD CT
Tenn Cts
ELLESMERE CT
SUTHERLAND RD
SHORT RD
PAXTON RD
Recn Gd
Allot Gdns
MAGNOLIA WHARF
THAMES RD
MAGNOLIA RD
HERBERT GDNS
ERNEST GDNS
BAILEY MEWS
LC
GORDON RD
ST MARY'S GR
BURNABY CRES
FAUCONBERG RD
FLORENCE GDNS
NIGHTINGALE CL
ST THOMAS' RD
SUTTON COURT RD
CHESTERFIELD RD
CHATSWORTH RD
EASTBOURNE RD
MILNTHORPE RD
CHARA PL
PARK RD
4
FIELDING HO 1
GARRICK HO 2
HAMILTON HO 3
CHISWICK SQ 4
PAGE'S YD 5
1 MONTGOMERY CT
2 FAUCONBERG CT
3 EGERTON HO
4 BOURNE CT
5 CHISWICK PLAZA
6 SUTTON COURT MANS
Chiswick House
LORAINE RD
RIVERVIEW GR
RIVERVIEW RD
GROVE PARK TERR
RANELAGH GDNS
GROVE PARK BRIDGE
LAWFORD RD
GROVE PARK MEWS
STAVELEY RD
CROFTON AVE
FITZROY CRES
Pav
ISIS CT
REDCLIFFE GDNS
GROVE PARK GDNS
GROVE PARK RD
PO
BURLINGTON LA
Chiswick Com Sch
WHITTINGHAM CT
EDENSOR
LAKE TERR
DORCHESTER HO
CHARLWOOD HO
BIRCHGROVE HO
HARTINGTON CT
KINNAIRD AVE
STATION APP
RUSSELL KERR CL
WILMINGTON AVE
WAR MEMORIAL HOMES
Tenn Cts
3
The National Archives
STRAND DR
DEVONSHIRE GDNS
SPENCER RD
Chiswick
STATION GDNS
Allot Gdns
ALEXANDRA GDNS
46
Pav
Tenn Cts
ACQUA HO
CONISTON CL
MARAIS
BOLTON RD
KELVIN CT
1 HUNTINGDON GDNS
2 BURLINGTON CT
3 QUINTIN CT
4 WINDRUSH CL
5 THE LINDENS
Cemy
77
RIVERSIDE DR
BESSANT DR
Grove Park
HARTINGTON RD
CHISWICK STAITHE
Tenn Cts
Sp Gd
W4
STAVELEY GDNS
Tenn Cts
Kew Ret Pk
ST ANDREWS CT
CAVENDISH RD
The Quintin Hogg Meml Gd
GREAT CHERTSEY RD
Civil S
WOODMAN MEWS
KELSALL MEWS
THAMES VILLAGE
Pav
40
2
Allot Gdns
PARK AVE
GREEN LINK WLK
MELLISS AVE
CHISWICK QUAY
Tenn Cts
Marlborough Trad Est
MAGNOLIA CT
WHITCOMBE MEWS
Stadium
Riverside L Ctr
RICK FARM CL
WEST HALL RD
HAWTHORN CT
Yacht Basin
IBIS LA
Sp Gd
Riverside Lands School Pl Flds
COURTLANDS AVE
Allot Gdns
BARKER CL
TOWNMEAD RD
Duke's Meadows
30
Pav
CHISWICK BRIDGE
Allot Gdns
Tenn Cts
Sp Gd
Drv Rng
TAYLOR AVE
TW9
Kew Riverside Prim Sch
Crem
CLIFFORD AVE
Pav
P
P
Tenn Cts
1
North Sheen Cemy (Fulham)
Hammersmith New Cemy
THAMES BANK
VARSITY ROW
Allot Gdns
TIDEWAY YD 1
TIDEWAY WHARF 2
THE BROADWAY 3
RIVER HO 4
ELM BANK MANS 5
MALTINGS CL 6
MALTHOUSE PAS 7
40
Bwg Gn
REID CT
1 WATNEY COTTS
2 LANGDON PL
3 ROSEMARY LA
4 WALDECK TERR
5 ROSEMARY GDNS
6 HUNTINGDON CT
7 ST LEONARDS CT
8 MODEL COTTS
Hounslow
Richmond upon Thames
PARLIAMENT MEWS
COMBE HO
BULLS ALLEY
DUKES CT
ASHLEIGH HO 1
RIPLEY HO 2
A316
WATNEY RD
WILLIAMS LA
SHIP LA
Sp Gd
MORTLAKE HIGH ST
76
Chalkers Cnr
Mortlake
PO
ELSINORE WAY
CHERTSEY CT
20
B
55
C
21
A
POPHAM GDNS
LOWER RICHMOND RD
A3003
LADY ELIZABETH HO
B351
VINEYARD PATH
ALDER RD
WRIGHTS WLK
VICTORIA RD
MULLINS PATH
FITZGERALD RD
WORPLE ST
RIPLEY GDNS
AVONDALE RD
ASHLEIGH RD
COWLEY RD
SECOND AVE
THE RETREAT
Mortlake

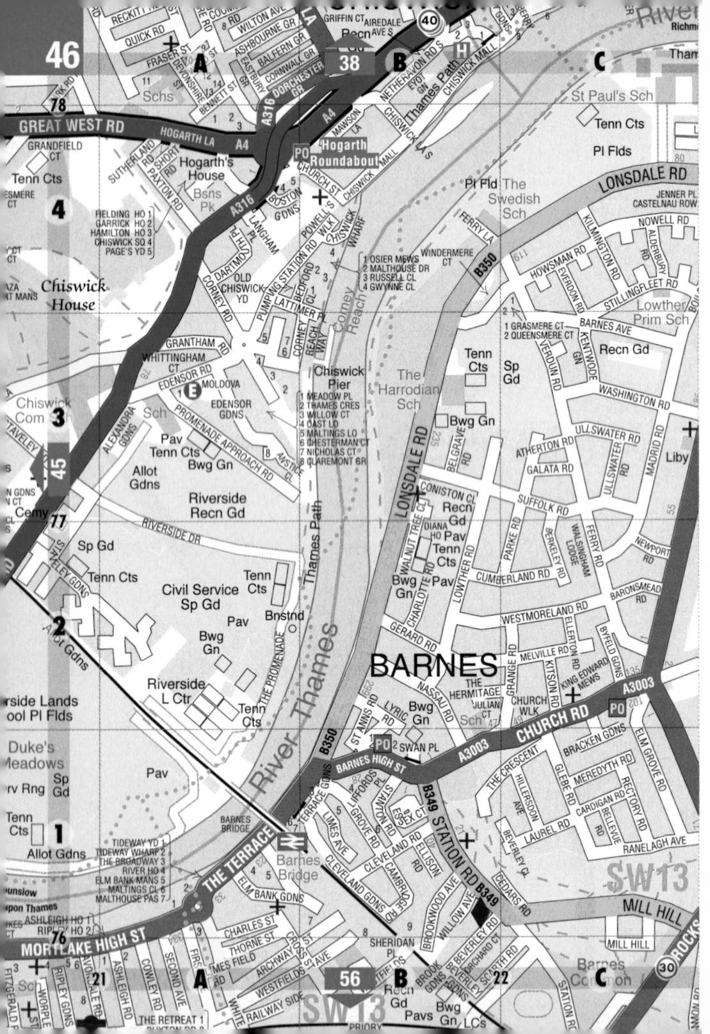
GREAT WEST RD
HOGARTH LA
A4
A316
Hogarth Roundabout
Hogarth's House
Bsns Pk
Chiswick House
GRANDFIELD CT
Tenn Cts
FIELDING HO 1
GARRICK HO 2
HAMILTON HO 3
CHISWICK SQ 4
PAGE'S YD 5
CHISWICK MALL
Thames Path
CHURCH ST
BOSTON GDNS
POWELL'S WLK
CHISWICK WHARF
PUMPING STATION RD
OLD CHISWICK YD
BEDFORD CL
LATTIMER PL
CORNEY RD
CORNEY REACH WAY
Corney Reach
1 OSIER MEWS
2 MALTHOUSE DR
3 RUSSELL CL
4 GWYNNE CL
GRANTHAM RD
WHITTINGHAM CT
EDENSOR RD
MOLDOVA
EDENSOR GDNS
Chiswick Pier
1 MEADOW PL
2 THAMES CRES
3 WILLOW CT
4 OAST LO
5 MALTINGS LO
6 CHESTERMAN CT
7 NICHOLAS CT
8 CLAREMONT GR
PROMENADE APPROACH RD
ALEXANDRA GDNS
Allot Gdns
Riverside Recn Gd
RIVERSIDE DR
Sp Gd
Civil Service Sp Gd
Riverside L Ctr
THE PROMENADE
River Thames
Duke's Meadows
TIDEWAY YD 1
TIDEWAY WHARF 2
THE BROADWAY 3
RIVER HO 4
ELM BANK MANS 5
MALTINGS CL 6
MALTHOUSE PAS 7
ASHLEIGH HO 1
RIPLEY HO 2
MORTLAKE HIGH ST
THE TERRACE
Barnes Bridge
St Paul's Sch
Pl Flds
LONSDALE RD
The Swedish Sch
FERRY LA
WINDERMERE CT
B350
The Harrodian Sch
HOWSMAN RD
KILMINGTON RD
NOWELL RD
STILLINGFLEET RD
Lowther Prim Sch
1 GRASMERE CT
2 QUEENSMERE CT
BARNES AVE
Recn Gd
WASHINGTON RD
ULLSWATER RD
ATHERTON RD
GALATA RD
SUFFOLK RD
CONISTON CL
CUMBERLAND RD
WESTMORELAND RD
MELVILLE RD
BARNES
THE HERMITAGE
CHURCH RD
A3003
BARNES HIGH ST
SWAN PL
B349
STATION RD
CLEVELAND RD
CLEVELAND GDNS
LIMES AVE
GROVE RD
TERRACE GDNS
ELM BANK GDNS
CHARLES ST
THORNE ST
ARCHWAY ST
CROSS ST
WESTFIELDS AVE
RAILWAY SIDE
SHERIDAN PL
BROOKWOOD AVE
WILLOW AVE
BEVERLEY RD
CEDARS RD
MILL HILL
Barnes Common
SW13
GLEBE RD
MEREDYTH RD
CARDIGAN RD
RECTORY RD
LAUREL RD
RANELAGH AVE
ELM GROVE RD
HILLERSDON AVE
THE CRESCENT
BRACKEN GDNS
FERRY RD
NEWPORT RD
BARONSMEAD RD
MADRID RD
Liby
38
56
45
40
30

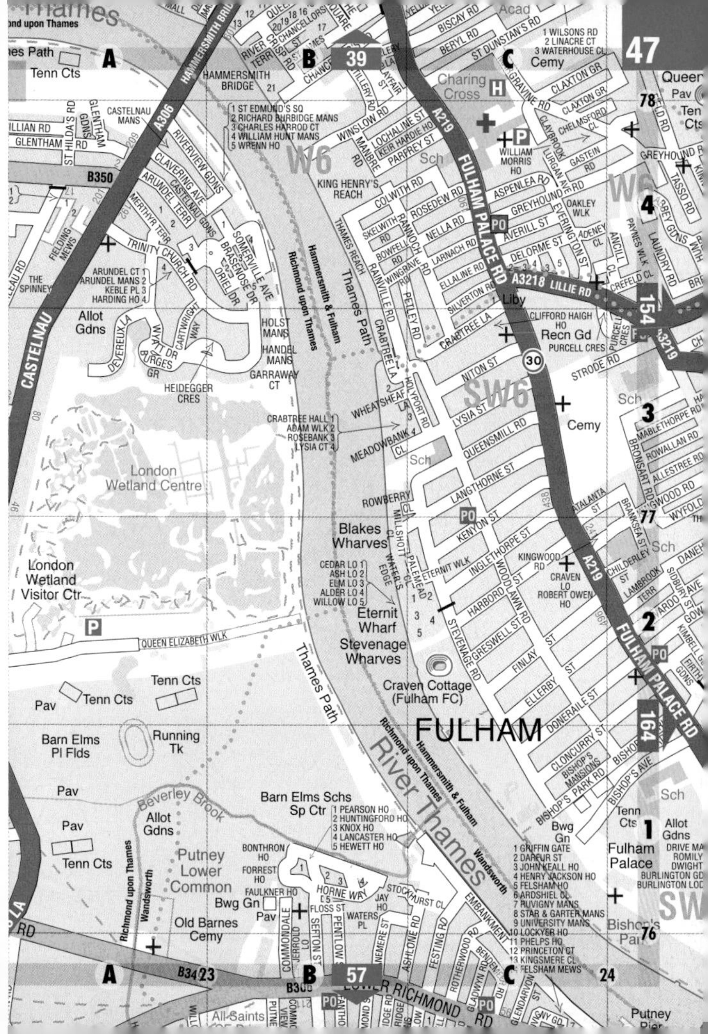
47
A
B
C
39
57
Tenn Cts
Hammersmith Bridge
Castelnau Mans
Glentham Rd
St Hilda's Rd
Glentham Gdns
B350
A306
Riverview Gdns
Clavering Ave
Castelnau Gdns
Arundel Terr
Merthyr Terr
Trinity Church Rd
Somerville Ave
Brasenose Dr
Oriel Dr
Fielding Mews
The Spinney
Arundel Ct 1
Arundel Mans 2
Keble Pl 3
Harding Ho 4
Allot Gdns
Castelnau
Devereux La
Wyatt Dr
Burges Gr
Cartwright Way
Heidegger Cres
Holst Mans
Handel Mans
Garraway Ct
London Wetland Centre
London Wetland Visitor Ctr
Queen Elizabeth Wlk
Tenn Cts
Pav
Barn Elms Pl Flds
Running Tk
Beverley Brook
Allot Gdns
Putney Lower Common
Old Barnes Cemy
Bwg Gn
Barn Elms Schs Sp Ctr
1 Pearson Ho
2 Huntingford Ho
3 Knox Ho
4 Lancaster Ho
5 Hewett Ho
Bonthron Ho
Forrest Ho
Faulkner Ho
Horne Way
Jay Ho
Floss St
Waters Pl
Stockhurst Cl
Commondale
Pentlow St
Sefton St
Ashlone Rd
Festing Rd
Rotherwood Rd
Glawyn Rd
Glendarvon St
Embankment
Lower Richmond Rd
B306
All Saints
Richmond upon Thames
Wandsworth
Hammersmith & Fulham
Thames Path
River Thames
1 St Edmund's Sq
2 Richard Burbidge Mans
3 Charles Harrod Ct
4 William Hunt Mans
5 Wrenn Ho
W6
King Henry's Reach
Thames Reach
Winslow Rd
Lochaline St
Keir Hardie Ho
Parfrey St
Manbre Rd
Colwith Rd
Rosedew Rd
Skelwith Rd
Rannoch Rd
Bowfell Rd
Wingrave Rd
Nella Rd
Larnach Rd
Ellaline Rd
Silverton Rd
Crabtree La
Pettley Rd
Rainville Rd
Wheatsheaf La
Holyport Rd
Crabtree Hall 1
Adam Wlk 2
Rosebank 3
Lysia Ct 4
Meadowbank Cl
Rowberry Cl
Millshott Cl
Waterside Edge
Palemead Cl
Blakes Wharves
Cedar Lo 1
Ash Lo 2
Elm Lo 3
Alder Lo 4
Willow Lo 5
Eternit Wharf
Stevenage Wharves
Craven Cottage (Fulham FC)
FULHAM
SW6
Niton St
Lysia St
Queensmill Rd
Langthorne St
Kenyon St
Inglethorpe St
Eternit Wlk
Woodlawn Rd
Harbord St
Greswell St
Stevenage Rd
Finlay St
Ellerby St
Doneraile St
Cloncurry St
Bishop's Mansions
Bishop's Park Rd
Bishop's Ave
1 Griffin Gate
2 Darfur St
3 John Keall Ho
4 Henry Jackson Ho
5 Felsham Ho
6 Ardshiel Cl
7 Ruvigny Mans
8 Star & Garter Mans
9 University Mans
10 Lockyer Ho
11 Phelps Ho
12 Princeton Ct
13 Kingsmere Cl
14 Felsham Mews
Bwg Gn
Tenn Cts
Fulham Palace
Bishop's Park
Allot Gdns
Sch
1
2
3
4
24
76
77
78
154
164
Fulham Palace Rd
A219
A3218
Lillie Rd
Liby
Clifford Haigh Ho
Recn Gd
Purcell Cres
Strode Rd
Cemy
Atalanta St
Kingwood Rd
Craven Lo
Robert Owen Ho
Branksea St
Childerley St
Lambrook Terr
Mablethorpe Rd
Bronsart Rd
Rowallan Rd
Allestree Rd
Ingwood Rd
Wyfold Rd
Sidbury St
Charing Cross
William Morris Ho
Biscay Rd
Beryl Rd
St Dunstan's Rd
1 Wilsons Rd
2 Linacre Ct
3 Waterhouse Cl
Cemy
Margravine Rd
Claxton Gr
Chelmsford Cl
Claybrook Rd
Lurgan Ave
Gastein Rd
Aspenlea Rd
Greyhound Rd
Oakley Wlk
Averill St
Everington St
Adeney Cl
Delorme St
Ancill Cl
Paynes Wlk
Laundry Rd
Tasso Rd
Crefeld Cl
Queen's Club
Pav
Tenn Cts

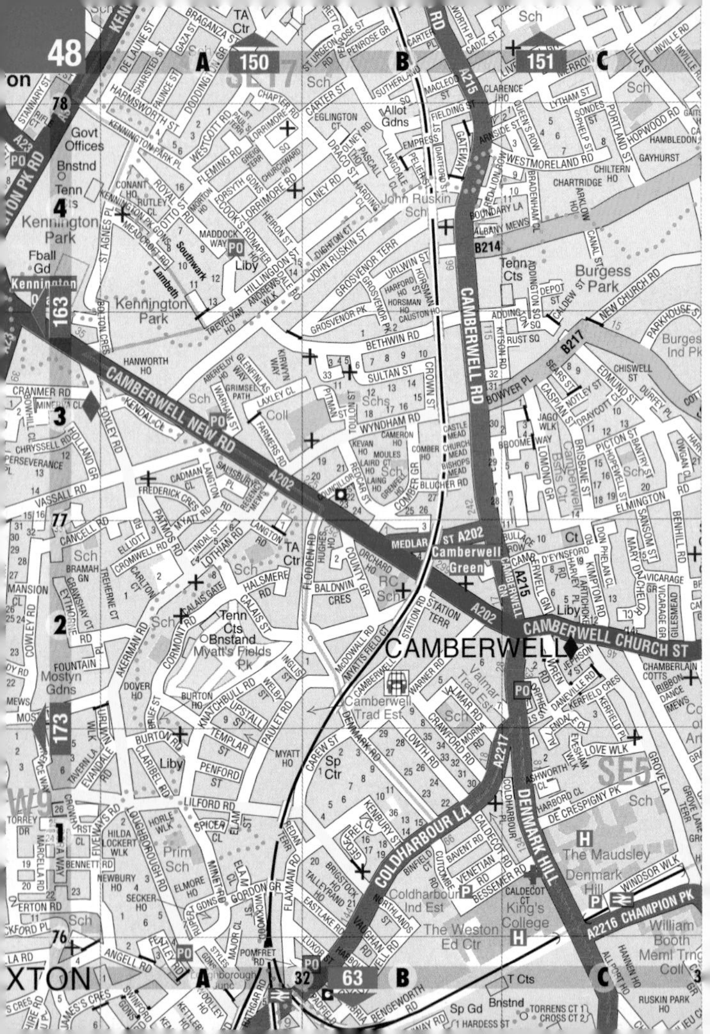
A
150
B
151
C
SE17
SE5
KENNINGTON PARK RD
Govt Offices
Kennington Park
Fball Gd
Kennington
163
173
CAMBERWELL NEW RD
A202
CAMBERWELL RD
A215
CAMBERWELL
Camberwell Green
CAMBERWELL CHURCH ST
Burgess Park
B214
B217
DENMARK HILL
COLDHARBOUR LA
A2217
A2216 CHAMPION PK
The Maudsley
Denmark Hill
King's College
The Weston Ed Ctr
Coldharbour Ind Est
Camberwell Trad Est
Valmar Trad Est
Myatt's Fields Pk
Mostyn Gdns
John Ruskin Sch
William Booth Meml Trng Coll
Loughborough Junc
XTON
63
32
76
77
78
W9
VASSALL RD
WYNDHAM RD
JOHN RUSKIN ST
WESTMORELAND RD
NEW CHURCH RD
ELMINGTON
BETHWIN RD
SULTAN ST
LOUGHBOROUGH RD
FLAXMAN RD
DENMARK RD
CAREW ST
BENGEWORTH RD

A
152
B
153
C
49
B215
A2
OLD KENT RD A2
A2208
B214
ALBANY RD
EMBERTON
DANESFIELD
BEACONSFIELD RD
CHUMLEIGH ST
CHUMLEIGH GDNS
Cobourg Prim Sch
COBOURG RD
CAMMINGTON RD
LONCROFT RD
Pl Fld
Pl Fld
Burgess Park
NEATE ST
WAITE ST
GLENGALL TERR
TRAFALGAR AVE
GLENGALL RD
OSSORY RD
Superstore
MALT ST
OLMAR ST
Cantium Ret Pk
Surrey Wharf
Nye's Wharf
Acorn Wharf
C Ctr & Liby
Canal Bridge
ST JAMES'S RD
CANAL GR
SANDGATE ST
Sandgate Trad Est
RUBY ST
Wevco Wharf
RUBY TRIANGLE
SHERWOOD
ARGYLE WAY
LOVEGROVE ST
Prim Sch
Sch
78
4
PO
Mus
OLD
SE15
ST GEORGE'S WAY
WELLS WAY
DRAGON RD
NEWENT CL
LONGHOPE CL
Gloucester Prim Sch
DANIEL GDNS
EBLEY CL
CATOR ST
DAVEY ST
ALDER HO
WILLOWBROOK RD
PENNACK RD
BRIDEALE CL
COLEGROVE RD
BIANCA RD
LATONA RD
HAYMERLE RD
UNWIN CL
REDDINS RD
Recn Gd
MAISMORE ST
PECKHAM PARK RD
B216
EDNAM HO
FRENSHAM ST
GREYSTOKE
LIVESEY PL
GREEN HUNDRED RD
ETHNARD RD
PENCRAIG WAY
BIRD IN BUSH RD
LYMPSTONE GDNS
FRIARY RD
LEDBURY ST
CARDINE MEWS
NAYLOR RD
COMMERCIAL WAY
HOLBECK ROW
FENHAM RD
PENNETHORNE RD
3
50
MEETING HOUSE
77
LYNBROOK GR
PECKHAM GR
BLAKE'S RD
INNES ST
SAMUEL ST
GARNIES CL
NUTT ST
SHURLAND GDNS
ROSEMARY RD
CARISBROOKE GDNS
JOWETT ST
Recn Gd
RADNOR RD
DOWLAS ST
RAINBOW ST
BONSOR ST
COLEMAN RD
PO
SOUTHAMPTON WAY
MELBURY DR
SEDGMOOR PL
STANSWOOD GDNS
CHANDLER WAY
PENTRIDGE ST
CRONIN ST
EAST SURREY GR
Coll
SUMNER RD
PECKHAM HILL ST
BULLER CL
LEONTINE CL
FURLEY RD
DIAMOND ST
BRANCH ST
COMMERCIAL WAY
COMPTON CL
STOPES ST
ASHMORE CL
GRENARD CL
BONAR RD
BUNBURY HO
EDWIN CL
WENTWORTH CRES
MARMONT RD
Prim Sch
ADA RD
REDBRIDGE GDNS
MUSCATEL PL
WODEHOUSE AVE
MOODY RD
KELLY AVE
WATTS ST
HASLAM ST
LISFORD ST
PIONEER ST
JOCELYN ST
WILMOT CL
NEVILLE CL
GOLDSMITH RD
STAFFORDSHIRE ST
ST GILES RD
GABLES CL
HAVIL ST
DALWOOD ST
FLORIAN
MARIE CURIE
GATONBY ST
BEATON CL
CORBDEN CL
Liby
MISSION PL
Sp Gd
Cts
St Giles
FONTENELLE
MISTRAL
Coll
Art Gall
Sch
B217
Sch
SUMNER AVE
MELON RD
Peckham
PECKHAM HIGH ST
PECKHAM RD
A202
KINGFISHER HO
GANNET HO
HERON HO
OSPREY HO
GRUMMANT RD
The Acad at Peckham
COLLYER PL
Bellenden Rd Ret Pk
RYE LA
BULL YD
Aylesham Sh Ctr
L Ctr
McKERRELL RD
A2215
HANOVER PK
CONSORT RD
2
Tuke Sch
WOOD'S RD
MORTLOCK CL
SUNWELL CL
WILSON RD
DAGMAR RD
MAUDE RD
VESTRY RD
Lucas Gdns
WELTON CT
SHENLEY RD
CROFTON RD
BUSHEY HILL RD
TALFOURD RD
TALFOURD PL
MANOR CT
LYNDHURST SQ
DENMAN RD
LYNDHURST WAY
OPHIR TERR
Sch
CERISE RD
RAUL RD
CICELY RD
CLAYTON RD
BISHOP WILFRED WOOD CL
HARDERS RD
GRACE'S RD
FEARNLEY HO
LINNELL RD
OSWYTH RD
CROSS RD
HIGHSHORE RD
OLIVER MEWS
MONCRIEFF ST
LETTSOM ST
PEMBURY HO
GAIRLOCH RD
GRANGE CT
ELM GR
HARDEN HO
LYNDHURST GR
Recn Gd
HOLLY GR
SE15
CAMBERWELL GR
MCNEIL RD
CACTUS CL
AINSWORTH CL
AZENBY RD
Bellendon Rd Bsns Ctr
Peckham Rye
BLENHEIM GR
CHURCHILL CT
BOURNEMOUTH RD
ALMOND CL
BIRCH CL
BOURNEMOUTH CL
COPELAND RD
BLACKPOOL RD
BRAYARDS RD
1
GROVELANDS CL
LINWOOD CL
Print Village Ind Est
GROVE PK
CHADWICK RD
BELLENDEN RD
CHOUMERT MEWS
CHOUMERT GR
RYE LA
PO
HAZEL CL
SANDLINGS CL
GODMAN RD
CONSORT RD
CANNING CROSS
THE BIRCHES
GROVE PK
QUEENS CT
PELHAM CL
THE LIMES
CHOUMERT RD
JOHN HARRIS HO
REEDHAM ST
COSTA ST
ALPHA ST
Sch
STERNHALL LA
HEATON RD
76
WILVENHOE CL
MANATON CL
GROVE LA
STORIES RD
GLEBELANDS CL
Allot Gdns
A
B
64
34
C
SANDISON ST
MCDERMOTT RD
NIGEL RD
HUGUENOT SQ
TROY TOWN FLATS
AUSTINS CT
PHILIP WLK
GROVE HILL RD
MALFORT RD
BROMAR RD
IVANHOE RD
AVONDALE RISE
WINGFIELD ST
WINGFIELD MEWS
HOWDEN ST
MAXTED RD
WAGHORN ST
ANSTEY RD
GALATEA SQ

40
49
65

The New Den (Millwall FC)
Orion Bsns Ctr
British Wharf Ind Est
STOCKHOLM RD
SURREY CANAL RD
Excelsior Ind Est
Lewisham Bsns Ctr
Elizabeth Ind Est
Juno Way Ind Est
Bridge House Meadows
OLD BLOW LA
SE14
DEPTFORD
Wevco Wharf
RUBY TRIANGLE
Gas Holder Station
Sandgate Trad Est
Kent Pk Ind Est
1 HYNDMAN ST
2 MURDOCK ST
3 SKENFRITH HO
4 SARNESFIELD HO
5 PETERCHURCH HO
The Penarth Ctr
Canal Bridge
OLD KENT RD
DEVONSHIRE GR
SE15
PECKHAM PARK RD
BIRD IN BUSH RD
COMMERCIAL WAY
Caroline Gardens
Recn Gd
CLIFTON CRES
Brimmington Park
New Cross
EDRIC RD
Monson Sch
Ecklington Gardens
Liby
BESSON ST A202
New Cross Gate
HATCHAM PARK RD
Hatcham Mews Bsns Ctr
PECKHAM HIGH ST
A2215
HANOVER PK
Queen's Road
QUEEN'S RD
A2214 LAUSANNE RD
Coll
New Cross Gate
SHERWIN RD
ARBUTHNOT RD
B2142 GELLATLY RD
DRAKEFELL RD
Telegraph Hill Park
Tenn Cts
EVELINA RD
Nunhead
KIMBERLEY AVE
RYE LA
SE15
BLACKPOOL RD
HUGUENOT SQ
PHILIP WLK
TROY TOWN FLATS
ST ASAPH RD
GREENSTREET HILL

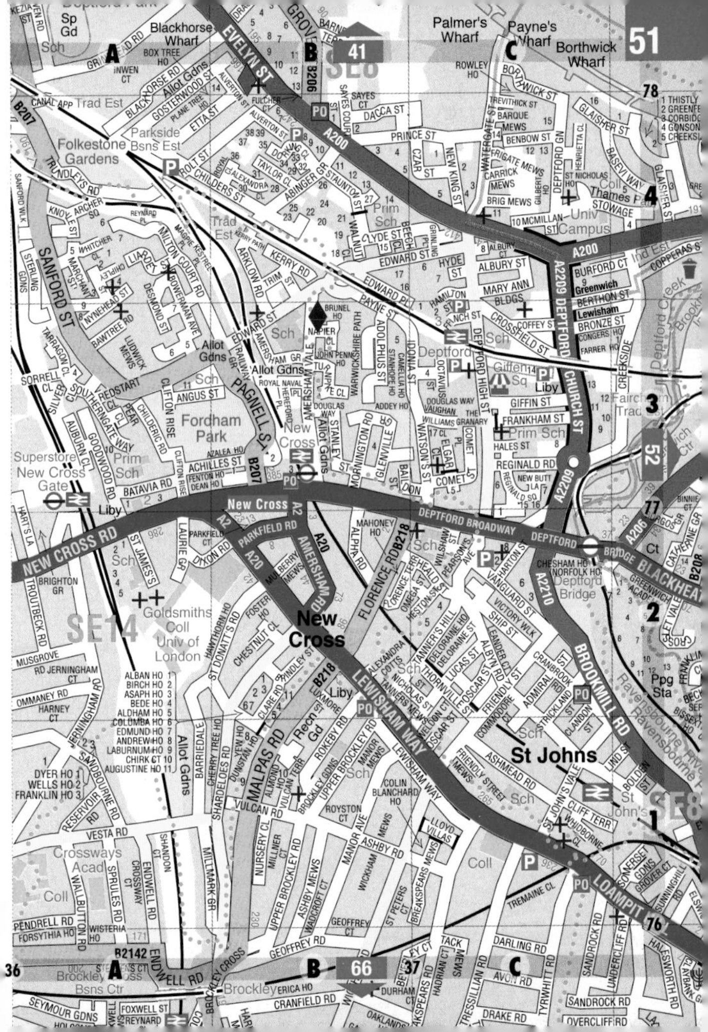
51
41
52
66
36
37
76
77
78
A
B
C
1
2
3
4
SE8
SE14
New Cross
St Johns
Deptford
Deptford Bridge
New Cross Gate
Brockley
Fordham Park
Folkestone Gardens
Goldsmiths Coll Univ of London
Crossways Acad
Blackhorse Wharf
Palmer's Wharf
Payne's Wharf
Borthwick Wharf
Parkside Bsns Est
Trad Est
Superstore
Brockley Cross Bsns Ctr
Thames Univ Campus
Giffen Sq
Ravensbourne
Deptford Creek
Fairchild Trad
EVELYN ST
A200
A2
A20
A2209 DEPTFORD CHURCH ST
A2210
BROOKMILL RD
NEW CROSS RD
DEPTFORD BROADWAY
LEWISHAM WAY
LOAMPIT VALE
DEPTFORD HIGH ST
AMERSHAM RD
AMERSHAM VALE
PARKFIELD RD
FLORENCE RD
MALPAS RD
PAGNELL ST
SANFORD ST
CLIFTON RISE
ACHILLES ST
BATAVIA RD
ENDWELL RD
MILLMARK GR
VESTA RD
JERNINGHAM RD
TROUTBECK RD
ST DONATT'S RD
SHARDELOES RD
UPPER BROCKLEY RD
BROCKLEY GDNS
VULCAN RD
ASHBY RD
MANOR AVE
ST JOHN'S VALE
FRIENDLY ST
ASHMEAD RD
ADMIRAL ST
TANNER'S HILL
VANGUARD ST
CRANBROOK RD
TYRWHITT RD
SANDROCK RD
UNDERCLIFF RD
DARLING RD
AVON RD
GEOFFREY RD
CRANFIELD RD
SEYMOUR GDNS
B207
B218
B206
B2142
B208
A206
BLACKHEATH

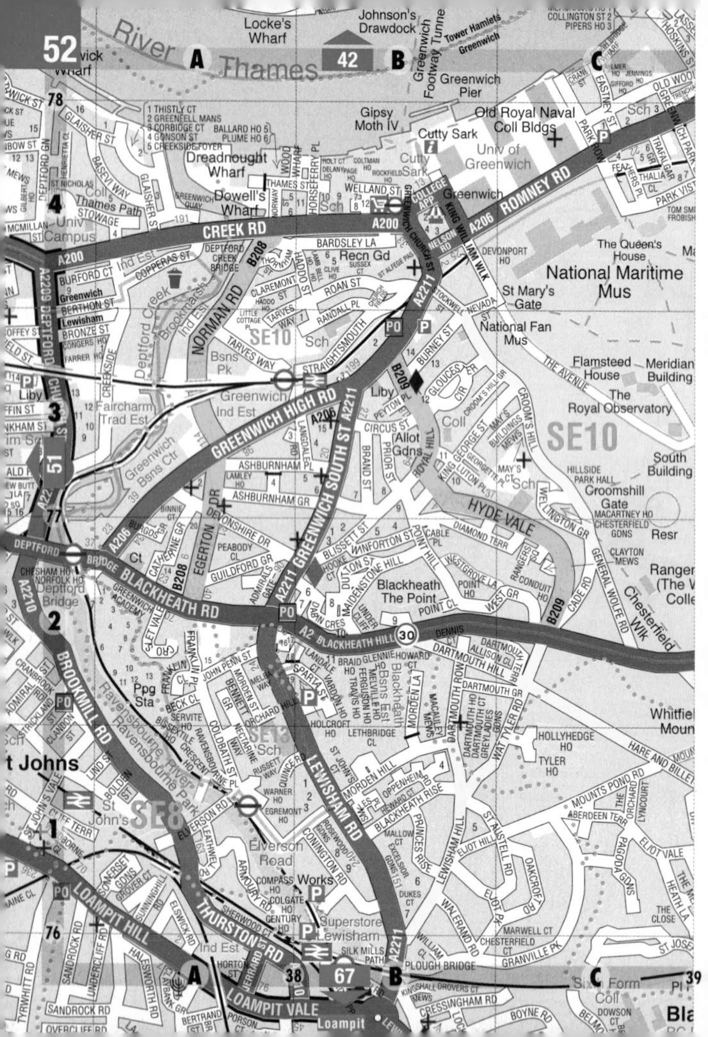
River Thames
Locke's Wharf
Johnson's Drawdock
Greenwich Footway Tunnel
Tower Hamlets
Greenwich
Greenwich Pier
Old Royal Naval Coll Bldgs
Gipsy Moth IV
Cutty Sark
Univ of Greenwich
Dreadnought Wharf
Dowell's Wharf
Thames Path
Univ Campus
CREEK RD
A200
ROMNEY RD
A206
KING WILLIAM WLK
GREENWICH CHURCH ST
COLLEGE APP
NELSON RD
BARDSLEY LA
Recn Gd
The Queen's House
National Maritime Mus
St Mary's Gate
National Fan Mus
Flamsteed House
Meridian Building
The Royal Observatory
SE10
South Building
Groomshill Gate
Resr
HYDE VALE
B209
ROYAL HILL
CROOM'S HILL
GREENWICH HIGH RD
GREENWICH SOUTH ST
A2211
NORMAN RD
B208
SE10
Greenwich Ind Est
Faircharm Trad Est
Greenwich Bsns Ctr
Deptford Creek
A2209 DEPTFORD CHURCH ST
DEPTFORD BRIDGE
Deptford Bridge
BLACKHEATH RD
A2 BLACKHEATH HILL
Blackheath The Point
DARTMOUTH HILL
DARTMOUTH ROW
WAT TYLER RD
Whitfield Mount
Chesterfield Wlk
GENERAL WOLFE RD
BROOKMILL RD
A2210
Ravensbourne Park
Ravensbourne River
Ppg Sta
St Johns
SE8
SE13
LEWISHAM RD
Elverson Road
Works
Superstore Lewisham
LOAMPIT HILL
LOAMPIT VALE
THURSTON RD
Loampit
PLOUGH BRIDGE
Sixth Form Coll
A
B
C
42
67
51
1
2
3
4
30
38
39
76
77
78

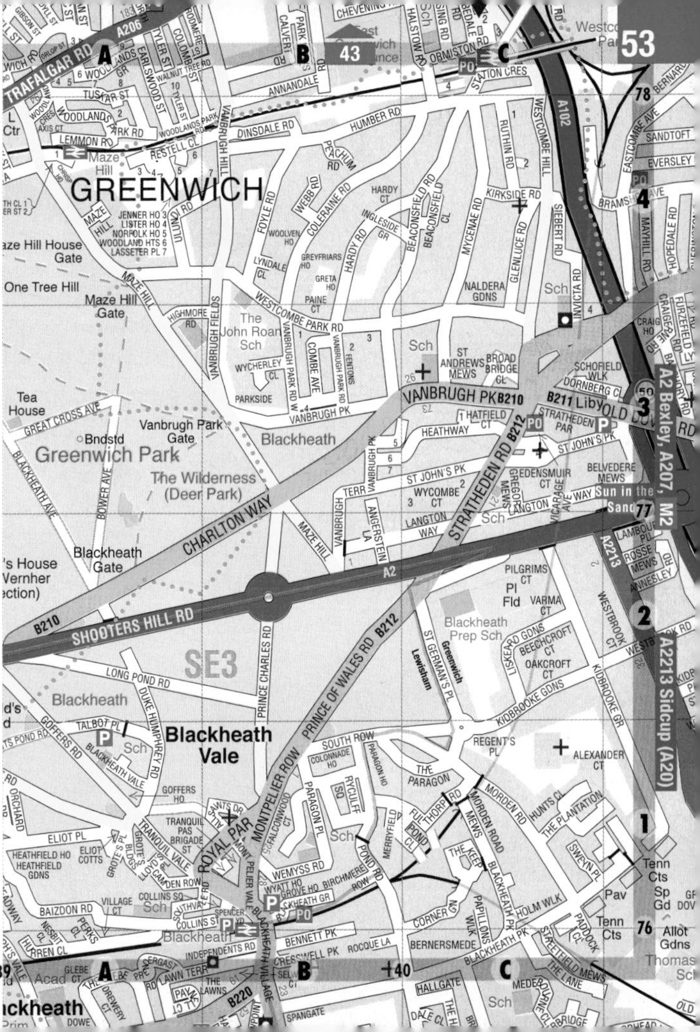
GREENWICH
TRAFALGAR RD
A206
WOODLANDS PARK RD
WOODLANDS GR
TUSKAR ST
EARLSWOOD ST
TYLER ST
COLOMB ST
WALNUT TREE RD
LEMMON RD
Maze Hill
RESTELL CL
VANBRUGH HILL
DINSDALE RD
HUMBER RD
PEACHUM RD
ANNANDALE RD
CALVERT RD
PARK
43
East Greenwich Pleasance
HALSTOW RD
ORMISTON RD
STATION CRES
A102
WESTCOMBE HILL
RUTHIN RD
KIRKSIDE RD
SIEBERT RD
GLENLUCE RD
MYCENAE RD
BEACONSFIELD RD
BEACONSFIELD CL
HARDY CT
INGLESIDE GR
HARDY RD
COLERAINE RD
WEBB RD
FOYLE RD
WOOLVEN HO
GREYFRIARS HO
GRETA HO
PAINE CT
LYNDALE CL
MAZE HILL
JENNER HO 3
LISTER HO 4
NORFOLK HO 5
WOODLAND HTS 6
LASSETER PL 7
ULUNDI RD
Maze Hill House Gate
One Tree Hill
Maze Hill Gate
HIGHMORE RD
VANBRUGH FIELDS
The John Roan Sch
WESTCOMBE PARK RD
VANBRUGH PARK RD W
VANBRUGH PARK RD
COMBE AVE
FENTONS
WYCHERLEY CL
PARKSIDE
VANBRUGH PK
Sch
ST ANDREWS MEWS
BROAD BRIDGE CL
NALDERA GDNS
INVICTA RD
SCHOFIELD WLK
DORNBERG CL
B210
B211
Liby
OLD DOVER RD
HATFIELD CT
STRATHEDEN PAR
STRATHEDEN RD
B212
HEATHWAY
ST JOHN'S PK
EDENSMUIR CT
GREGOR MEWS
BELVEDERE MEWS
VICARAGE AVE
WAY
Sun in the Sands
77
WYCOMBE CT
LANGTON WAY
VANBRUGH TERR
ANGERSTEIN LA
Tea House
GREAT CROSS AVE
Bndstd
Vanbrugh Park Gate
Blackheath
Greenwich Park
The Wilderness (Deer Park)
CHARLTON WAY
BLACKHEATH AVE
BOWER AVE
Blackheath Gate
A2
SHOOTERS HILL RD
PRINCE CHARLES RD
PRINCE OF WALES RD
SE3
PILGRIMS CT
Pl Fld
VARMA CT
Blackheath Prep Sch
ST GERMAN'S PL
Lewisham
Greenwich
LISKEARD GDNS
BEECHCROFT CT
OAKCROFT CT
KIDBROOKE GDNS
KIDBROOKE GR
WESTBROOK CT
WESTBROOK RD
A2213
LAMBOURN PL
ROSSE MEWS
ANNESLEY RD
A2 Bexley, A207, M2
A2213 Sidcup (A20)
EASTCOMBE AVE
SANDTOFT
EVERSLEY
BRAMSHOT AVE
MAYHILL RD
HOPEDALE RD
CRAIGERNE RD
FURZEFIELD RD
CRAIG HO
78
LONG POND RD
DUKE HUMPHREY RD
Blackheath Vale
TALBOT PL
GOFFERS RD
BLACKHEATH VALE
GOFFERS HO
ORCHARD
ELIOT PL
HEATHFIELD HO
HEATHFIELD GDNS
ELIOT COTTS
GROTE'S PL
GROTE'S BLDGS
TRANQUIL VALE
TRANQUIL PAS
BRIGADE ST
LLOYD PL
DEN ROW
COLLINS SQ
VILLAGE CT
BAIZDON RD
PERKS CL
HURREN CL
NESBIT CL
COLLINS ST
SPENCER YD
ALL SAINTS DR
ROYAL PAR
MONTPELIER ROW
MONTPELIER VALE
SOUTH ROW
COLONNADE HO
PARAGON HO
RYCULFF SQ
PARAGON PL
WEMYSS RD
WYATT HO
GROVE HO
BIRCHMERE ROW
BLACKHEATH GR
PONDRD
MERRYFIELD
THE PARAGON
REGENT'S PL
ALEXANDER CT
MORDEN RD
MORDEN ROAD MEWS
THORPE RD
FULTHORP RD
POND CL
THE KEEP
BLACKHEATH PK
PAPILLONS WLK
CORNER GN
HOLM WLK
HUNTS CL
THE PLANTATION
SWEYN PL
PADDOCK CL
STREETFIELD MEWS
Tenn Cts
Pav
Sp Gd
Allot Gdns
76
BENNETT PK
CRESSWELL PK
ROCQUE LA
BERNERSMEDE
INDEPENDENTS RD
BLACKHEATH VILLAGE
THE LANE
THE LAWNS
LAWN TERR
PAGET
DOWE
B220
SPANGATE
HALLGATE
MEDEBOURNE CL
40
39
A
B
C
1
2
3
4

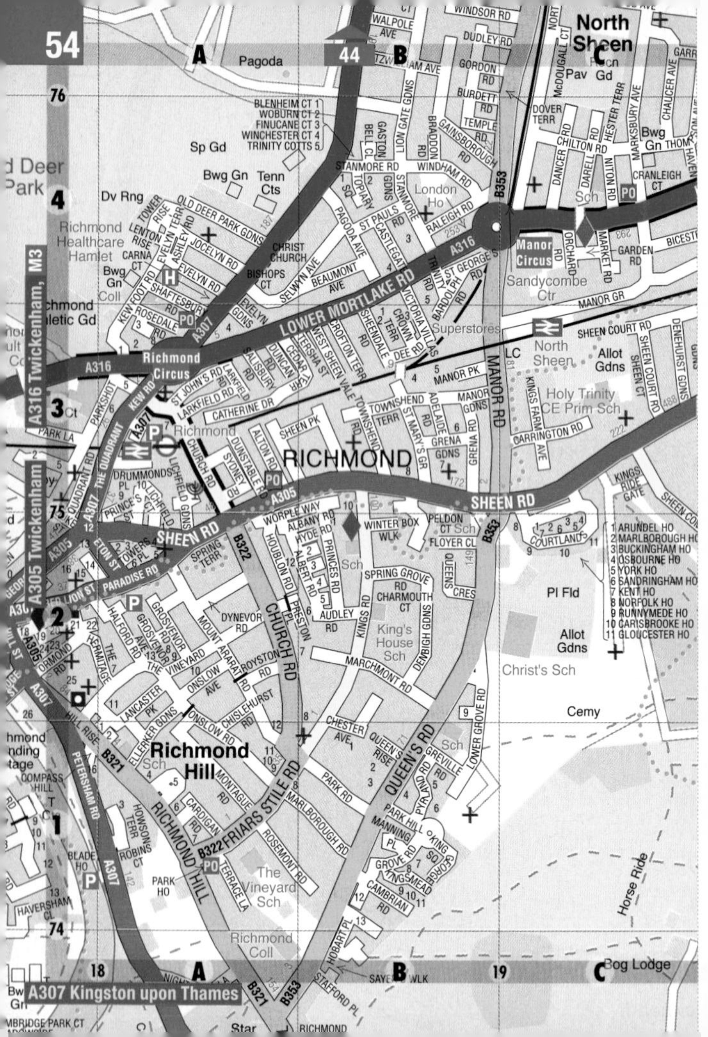
44
A
B
C
76
75
74
4
3
2
1
18
19
Pagoda
North Sheen
Recn Gd
Pav
Deer Park
Sp Gd
Bwg Gn
Tenn Cts
Dv Rng
Richmond Healthcare Hamlet
Richmond Athletic Gd
Coll
CHRIST CHURCH
London Ho
Manor Circus
Sandycombe Ctr
Superstores
North Sheen
Allot Gdns
Holy Trinity CE Prim Sch
Richmond Circus
Richmond
RICHMOND
Sch
King's House Sch
Pl Fld
Allot Gdns
Christ's Sch
Cemy
Richmond Hill
The Vineyard Sch
Richmond Coll
Horse Ride
Bog Lodge
PARK HO
BLADE HO
WINDSOR RD
WALPOLE AVE
DUDLEY RD
FITZWILLIAM AVE
GORDON RD
BURDETT RD
TEMPLE RD
DOVER TERR
McDOUGALL CT
HESTER TERR
MARKSBURY AVE
CHAUCER AVE
CHILTON RD
DANCER RD
DARELL RD
NITON RD
CRANLEIGH CT
THOMSON
HAVEN
BLENHEIM CT 1
WOBURN CT 2
FINUCANE CT 3
WINCHESTER CT 4
TRINITY COTTS 5
GASTON BELL CL
LION GATE GDNS
BRADDON RD
GAINSBOROUGH RD
STANMORE RD
WINDHAM RD
STANMORE GDNS
TOPIARY SQ
PAGODA AVE
ST PAULS CL
CASTLEGATE
STANMORE RD
RALEIGH RD
B353
A316
ORCHARD RD
MARKET RD
GARDEN RD
BICESTER
OLD DEER PARK GDNS
TOWER RISE
LENTON RISE
EVELYN TERR
ASHLEY RD
JOCELYN RD
EVELYN RD
CARNAC CT
KEW FOOT RD
SHAFTESBURY RD
ROSEDALE RD
BISHOPS CT
SELWYN AVE
BEAUMONT AVE
EVELYN GDNS
LOWER MORTLAKE RD
TRINITY RD
ST GEORGE'S RD
BARDOLPH RD
VICTORIA VILLAS
CROWN TERR
SHEENDALE RD
CROFTON TERR
WEST SHEEN VALE
DEE RD
MANOR GR
SHEEN COURT RD
DENEHURST GDNS
SHEEN COURT RD
SHEEN CT
KINGS FARM AVE
CARRINGTON RD
MANOR PK
MANOR GDNS
MANOR RD
ST JOHN'S RD
LARKFIELD RD
SALISBURY RD
DUNCAN RD
CEDAR TERR
HERSHA ST
CATHERINE DR
TOWNSHEND RD
TOWNSHEND TERR
ST MARY'S GR
ADELAIDE RD
GRENA RD
GRENA GDNS
A307
KEW RD
PARKSHOT
PARK LA
QUADRANT RD
THE QUADRANT
DRUMMONDS PL
LICHFIELD CT
LICHFIELD GDNS
CHURCH RD
SYDNEY RD
DUNSTABLE RD
ALTON RD
SHEEN PK
PRINCE'S ST
A305
SHEEN RD
WORPLE WAY
ALBANY RD
HYDE RD
PRINCES RD
WINTER BOX WLK
PELDON CT
FLOYER CL
QUEENS CRES
KINGS RIDE GATE
SHEEN COMMON
COURTLANDS
1 ARUNDEL HO
2 MARLBOROUGH HO
3 BUCKINGHAM HO
4 OSBOURNE HO
5 YORK HO
6 SANDRINGHAM HO
7 KENT HO
8 NORFOLK HO
9 RUNNYMEDE HO
10 CARISBROOKE HO
11 GLOUCESTER HO
ETON ST
TOWERS PL
SPRING TERR
PARADISE RD
LION ST
B322
HOUBLON RD
ALBERT RD
SPRING GROVE RD
CHARMOUTH CT
AUDLEY RD
KINGS RD
DENBIGH GDNS
PRESTON PL
DYNEVOR RD
MOUNT ARARAT RD
ROYSTON RD
MARCHMONT RD
HALFORD RD
GROSVENOR AVE
GROSVENOR RD
HERMITAGE
THE VINEYARD
ONSLOW AVE
ONSLOW RD
CHISLEHURST RD
LANCASTER PK
ELLERKER GDNS
ORMOND RD
HILL RISE
CHESTER AVE
QUEEN'S RISE
QUEEN'S RD
GREVILLE RD
LOWER GROVE RD
PYRLAND RD
PARK RD
B321
PETERSHAM RD
COMPASS HILL
MONTAGUE RD
CARDIGAN RD
FRIARS STILE RD
MARLBOROUGH RD
ROSEMONT RD
HOWSONS TERR
ROBINS CT
RICHMOND HILL
TERRACE LA
PARK HILL
MANNING PL
KING GEORGE SQ
GROVE RD
KINGSMEAD
CAMBRIAN RD
HOBART PL
SAYER'S WLK
STAFFORD PL
HAVERSHAM CL
A316 Twickenham, M3
A305 Twickenham
A307 Kingston upon Thames
RICHMOND
Star

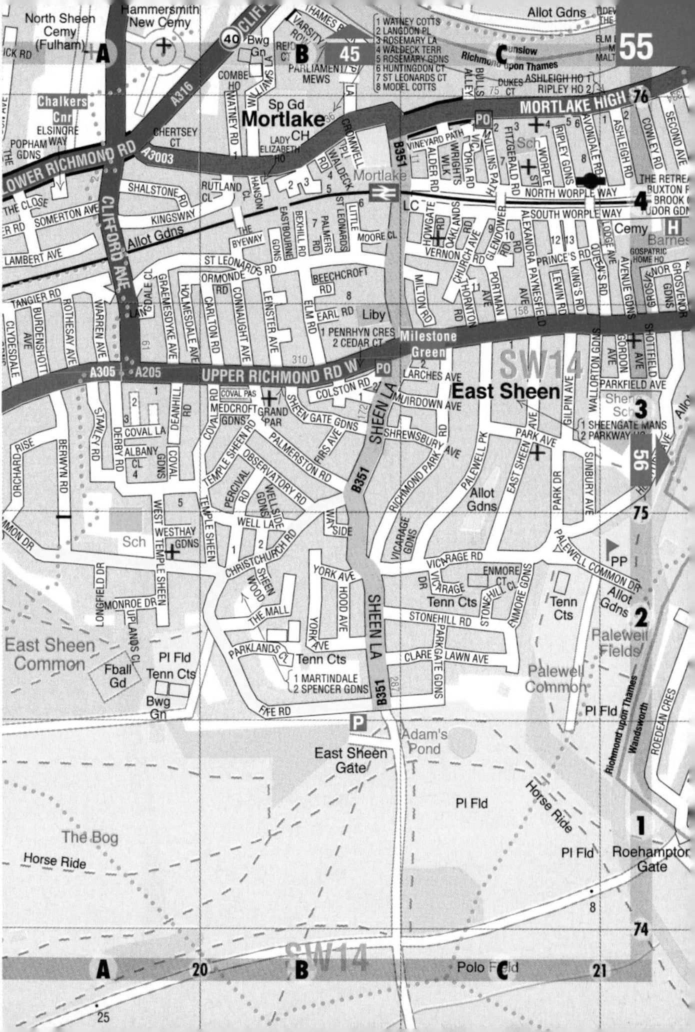
North Sheen Cemy (Fulham)
Hammersmith New Cemy
A
B
C
40
CLIFF
Bwg Gn
THAMES B
VARSITY ROW
REID CT
45
1 WATNEY COTTS
2 LANGDON PL
3 ROSEMARY LA
4 WALDECK TERR
5 ROSEMARY GDNS
6 HUNTINGDON CT
7 ST LEONARDS CT
8 MODEL COTTS
Allot Gdns
Hounslow
Richmond upon Thames
PARLIAMENT MEWS
COMBE HO
WATNEY RD
WILLIAMS LA
A316
Chalkers Cnr
ELSINORE WAY
POPHAM GDNS
CHERTSEY CT
Sp Gd
Mortlake
CH
LADY ELIZABETH HO
CROMWELL PL
BULLS ALLEY
DUKES CT
ASHLEIGH HO 1
RIPLEY HO 2
MORTLAKE HIGH
76
A3003
LOWER RICHMOND RD
B351
VINEYARD PATH
ALDER RD
WRIGHTS WLK
VICTORIA RD
MULLINS PATH
FITZGERALD RD
Sch
WORPLE ST
RIPLEY GDNS
AVONDALE RD
ASHLEIGH RD
COWLEY RD
SECOND AVE
PO
CLIFFORD AVE
SHALSTONE RD
RUTLAND CL
HANSON CL
WALDECK RD
Mortlake
NORTH WORPLE WAY
THE RETREAT
BUXTON RD
BROOK
TUDOR GDNS
4
THE CLOSE
SOMERTON AVE
KINGSWAY
THE BYEWAY
EASTBOURNE GDNS
BEXHILL RD
PALMERS RD
ST LEONARDS RD
LITTLE
LC
HOWGATE RD
OAKLANDS
SOUTH WORPLE WAY
Cemy
H
Barnes
GOSPATRIC HOME HO
Allot Gdns
LAMBERT AVE
MOORE CL
VERNON RD
CHURCH AVE
GLENDOWER RD
ALEXANDRA RD
PRINCE'S RD
LODGE AVE
AVENUE GDNS
GROSVENOR GDNS
GROSVENOR
ST LEONARDS RD
ORMONDE RD
BEECHCROFT RD
MILTON RD
THORNTON RD
PORTMAN AVE
PAYNESFIELD AVE
LEWIN RD
KING'S RD
QUEEN'S RD
TANGIER RD
BURDENSHOTT AVE
ROTHESAY AVE
WARREN AVE
LANSDALE CL
GRAEMESDYKE AVE
HOLMESDALE RD
CARLTON RD
CONNAUGHT AVE
LEINSTER AVE
ELM RD
EARL RD
Liby
1 PENRHYN CRES
2 CEDAR CT
Milestone Green
CLYDESDALE
SW14
WALLORTON GDNS
GORDON AVE
SHOTTFIELD AVE
A305
A205
UPPER RICHMOND RD W
PO
LARCHES AVE
East Sheen
GILPIN AVE
PARKFIELD AVE
Sheen Sch
COVAL PAS
MEDCROFT GDNS
GRAND PAR
COLSTON RD
SHEEN LA
MUIRDOWN AVE
3
DEANHILL RD
COVAL RD
SHEEN GATE GDNS
1 SHEENGATE MANS
2 PARKWAY
COVAL LA
ALBANY CL
COVAL GDNS
TEMPLE SHEEN RD
PALMERSTON RD
FIRS AVE
SHREWSBURY AVE
PARK AVE
EAST SHEEN AVE
Allot
ORCHARD RISE
BERWYN RD
STANLEY RD
DERBY RD
OBSERVATORY RD
RICHMOND PARK RD
PALEWELL PK
PARK DR
SUNBURY AVE
56
PERCIVAL RD
WELLSIDE GDNS
B351
Allot Gdns
75
COMMON DR
WEST TEMPLE SHEEN
WESTHAY GDNS
TEMPLE SHEEN
WELL LA
WAYSIDE
Sch
CHRISTCHURCH RD
VICARAGE GDNS
VICARAGE RD
PALEWELL COMMON DR
PP
LONGFIELD DR
SHEEN WOOD
YORK AVE
ENMORE CT
VICARAGE DR
HOOD AVE
Tenn Cts
STONEHILL CL
ENMORE GDNS
Tenn Cts
Allot Gdns
2
MONROE DR
UPLANDS CL
THE MALL
SHEEN LA
STONEHILL RD
Palewell Fields
East Sheen Common
YORK AVE
PARKGATE GDNS
Pl Fld
Fball Gd
Tenn Cts
PARKLANDS CL
Tenn Cts
CLARE LAWN AVE
Palewell Common
1 MARTINDALE
2 SPENCER GDNS
Bwg Gn
B351
FIFE RD
Pl Fld
Richmond upon Thames
Wandsworth
ROEDEAN CRES
P
Adam's Pond
East Sheen Gate
Pl Fld
Horse Ride
The Bog
1
Pl Fld
Roehampton Gate
Horse Ride
74
SW14
A
20
B
Polo Field
C
21
25

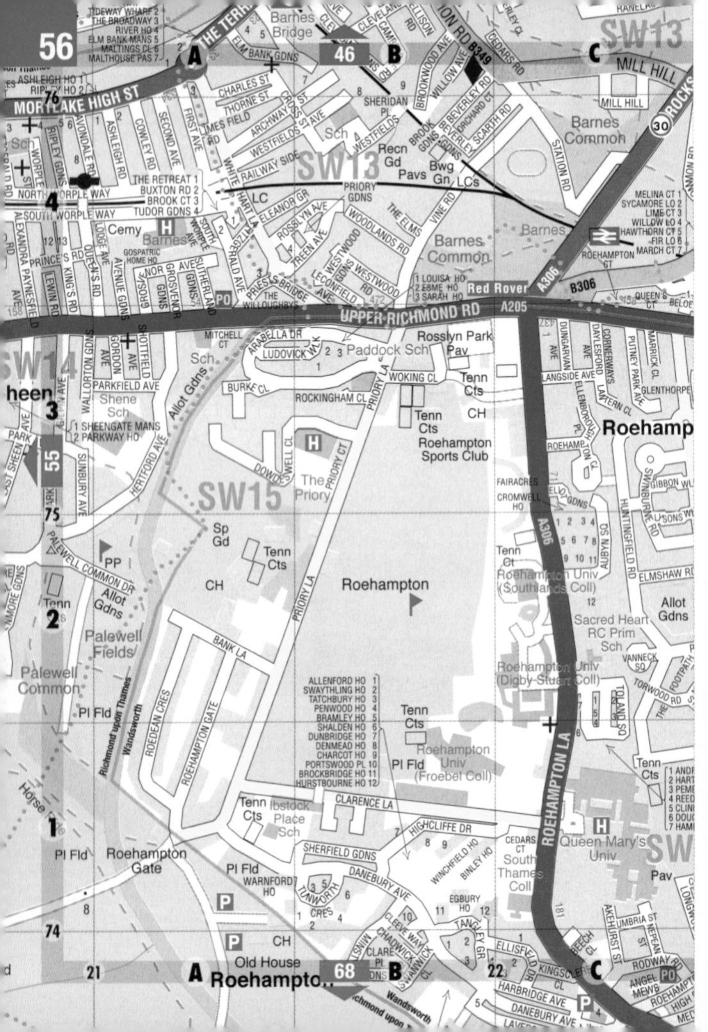
TIDEWAY WHARF 2
THE BROADWAY 3
RIVER HO 4
ELM BANK MANS 5
MALTINGS CL 6
MALTHOUSE PAS 7
Barnes Bridge
46
SW13
MILL HILL
MORTLAKE HIGH ST
ASHLEIGH HO 1
RIPLEY HO 2
ELM BANK GDNS
CHARLES ST
THORNE ST
CROSS ST
ARCHWAY ST
WESTFIELDS AVE
RAILWAY SIDE
LIMES FIELD RD
SHERIDAN PL
WESTFIELDS
BROOKWOOD AVE
WILLOW AVE
BEVERLEY RD
ORCHARD CT
SCARTH RD
BROOK GDNS
BEVERLEY GDNS
CEDARS RD
B349
MILL HILL
Barnes Common
STATION RD
Recn Gd
Bwg Gn
Pavs
LCs
WORPLE ST
RIPLEY GDNS
AVONDALE RD
ASHLEIGH RD
COWLEY RD
SECOND AVE
FIRST AVE
WHITE HART LA
NORTH WORPLE WAY
SOUTH WORPLE WAY
THE RETREAT 1
BUXTON RD 2
BROOK CT 3
TUDOR GDNS 4
PRIORY GDNS
LC
ELEANOR GR
ROSSLYN AVE
TREEN AVE
WOODLANDS RD
THE ELMS
VINE RD
Barnes
MELINA CT 1
SYCAMORE LO 2
LIME CT 3
WILLOW LO 4
HAWTHORN CT 5
FIR LO 6
MARCH CT 7
ROEHAMPTON CT
Cemy
Barnes
ALEXANDRA RD
PAYNESFIELD AVE
PRINCE'S RD
KING'S RD
QUEEN'S RD
LODGE AVE
AVENUE GDNS
GOSPATRIC HOME HO
NOR AVE
GROSVENOR GDNS
SUTHERLAND GDNS
SOUTH WORPLE AVE
FITZGERALD AVE
PRIEST'S BRIDGE
THE WILLOUGHBYS
WESTWOOD GDNS
WESTWOOD RD
LECONFIELD AVE
1 LOUISA HO
2 ESME HO
3 SARAH HO
Red Rover
A306
B306
QUEEN'S CT
LEWIN RD
PO
UPPER RICHMOND RD
A205
SW14
WALLORTON GDNS
GORDON AVE
SHOTTFIELD AVE
PARKFIELD AVE
MITCHELL CT
Sch
ARABELLA DR
LUDOVICK WLK
Paddock Sch
Rosslyn Park Pav
DUNGARVAN AVE
DAYLESFORD AVE
CORNERWAYS
PUTNEY PARK AVE
MARRICK CL
LANGSIDE AVE
GLENTHORPE
ELLENBOROUGH PL
LANTERN CL
Sheen
Shene Sch
Allot Gdns
BURKE CL
ROCKINGHAM CL
PRIORY LA
WOKING CL
Tenn Cts
CH
Roehampton Sports Club
Roehampton
1 SHEENGATE MANS
2 PARKWAY HO
HERTFORD AVE
SUNBURY AVE
55
DOWDESWELL CL
The Priory
PRIORY CT
SW15
ROEHAMPTON CL
FAIRACRES
CROMWELL HO
ELLOY GDNS
SWINBURNE RD
GIBBON WLK
HUNTINGFIELD RD
AUBYN SQ
Sp Gd
PALEWELL COMMON DR
PP
Tenn Ct
Roehampton Univ (Southlands Coll)
ELMSHAW RD
Allot Gdns
Sacred Heart RC Prim Sch
Palewell Fields
Palewell Common
BANK LA
VANNECK SQ
Roehampton Univ (Digby-Stuart Coll)
TORWOOD RD
TOLAND SQ
Pl Fld
Richmond upon Thames
Wandsworth
ROEDEAN CRES
ROEHAMPTON GATE
ALLENFORD HO 1
SWAYTHLING HO 2
TATCHBURY HO 3
PENWOOD HO 4
BRAMLEY HO 5
SHALDEN HO 6
DUNBRIDGE HO 7
DENMEAD HO 8
CHARCOT HO 9
PORTSWOOD PL 10
BROCKBRIDGE HO 11
HURSTBOURNE HO 12
Roehampton Univ (Froebel Coll)
ROEHAMPTON LA
1 ANDR
2 HART
3 PEME
4 REED
5 CLIN
6 DOUG
7 HAM
Horse Ride
Ibstock Place Sch
CLARENCE LA
HIGHCLIFFE DR
Queen Mary's Univ
Roehampton Gate
SHERFIELD GDNS
WINCHFIELD HO
BINLEY HO
CEDARS CT
South Thames Coll
WARNFORD HO
TUNWORTH CRES
DANEBURY AVE
EGBURY HO
Pav
CLEEVE WAY
CHADWICK CL
SWANWICK CL
MINSTEAD GDNS
CLARE PL
TANGLEY GR
ELLISFIELD DR
BEECH CL
AKEHURST ST
UMBRIA ST
NEPEAN ST
RODWAY RD
LONGWOOD
CH
Old House
Roehampton
68
KINGSCLERE CL
HARBRIDGE AVE
DANEBURY AVE
ANGEL MEWS
ROEHAMPTON HIGH ST
Wandsworth
Richmond upon Thames
76
75
74
21
22
A
B
C
4
3
2
1

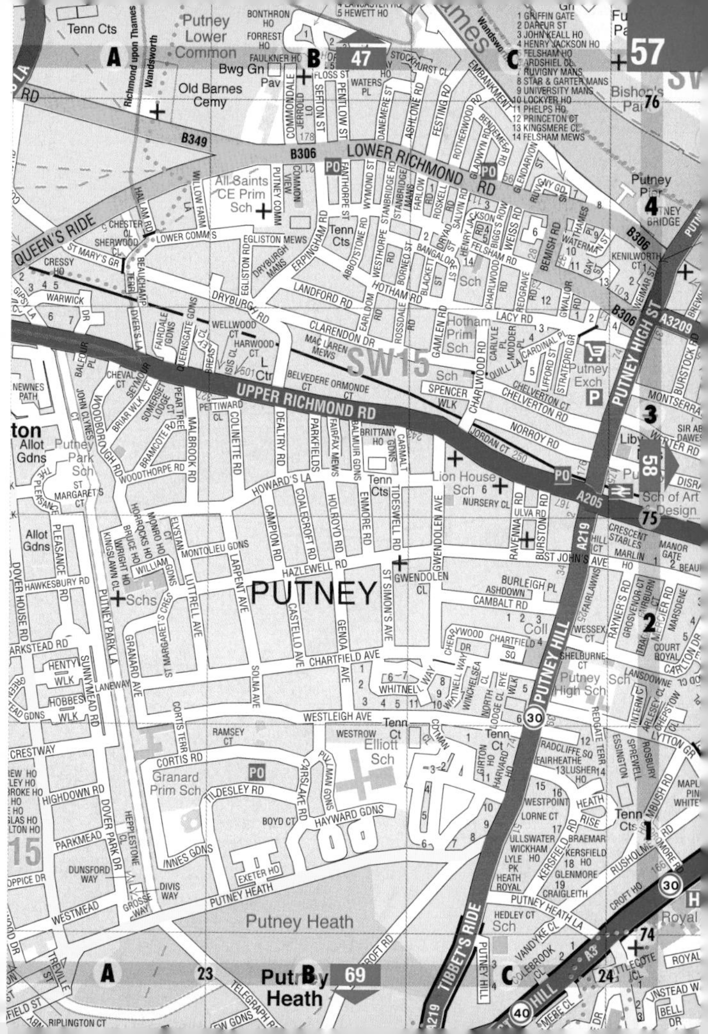
57
47
58
69
A
B
C
4
3
2
1
PUTNEY
SW15
Putney Lower Common
Tenn Cts
Bwg Gn
Pav
Old Barnes Cemy
Richmond upon Thames
Wandsworth
B349
B306
LOWER RICHMOND RD
QUEEN'S RIDE
UPPER RICHMOND RD
PUTNEY HIGH ST
PUTNEY HILL
TIBBET'S RIDE
A205
A219
A3209
A3
All Saints CE Prim Sch
Hotham Prim Sch
Putney Exch
Lion House Sch
Sch of Art & Design
Putney High Sch
Elliott Sch
Granard Prim Sch
Putney Park Sch
Allot Gdns
Putney Pier
PUTNEY BRIDGE
Bishop's Park
Putney Heath
1 GRIFFIN GATE
2 DARFUR ST
3 JOHN KEALL HO
4 HENRY JACKSON HO
5 FELSHAM HO
6 ARDSHIEL CL
7 RUVIGNY MANS
8 STAR & GARTER MANS
9 UNIVERSITY MANS
10 LOCKYER HO
11 PHELPS HO
12 PRINCETON CT
13 KINGSMERE CL
14 FELSHAM MEWS
4 LANCASTER HO
5 HEWETT HO
BONTHRON HO
FORREST HO
FAULKNER HO
FLOSS ST
WATERS PL
STOCKHURST CL
EMBANKMENT
COMMONDALE
JERROLD
SEFTON ST
PENITLOW ST
DANEMERE ST
ASHLONE RD
FESTING RD
ROTHERWOOD RD
BENDEMEER RD
GLADWYN RD
GLENDARVON ST
CHESTER CL
SHERWOOD CL
CRESSY HO
ST MARY'S GR
HALLAM RD
WILLOW FARM LA
LOWER COMMS
BEAUCHAMP TERR
EGLISTON MEWS
EGLISTON RD
DRYBURGH MANS
DRYBURGH RD
ERPINGHAM RD
ABBOTSTONE RD
WESTHORPE RD
LANDFORD RD
HOTHAM RD
BANGALORE ST
FELSHAM RD
BEMISH RD
WATERMAN ST
KENILWORTH CT
WEIMAR ST
GWALIOR RD
LACY RD
CLARENDON DR
MAC LAREN MEWS
WELLWOOD CT
HARWOOD CT
WARWICK DR
DYER'S LA
FAIRDALE GDNS
QUEENSGATE GDNS
BALFOUR PL
CHEVAL CT
SEYMOUR
BRIAR WLK
SOMERSET LODGE
PEAR TREE CT
PETTIWARD CL
COLINETTE RD
DEALTRY RD
PARKFIELDS
FAIRFAX MEWS
BALMUIR GDNS
BRITTANY HO
CARMALT GDNS
BELVEDERE CT
ORMONDE CT
SPENCER WLK
CHARLWOOD RD
QUILL LA
CARDINAL PL
STRATFORD GR
CHELVERTON CT
CHELVERTON RD
NORROY RD
JORDAN CT
MONTSERRAT
SIR ABRAHAM DAWES
WERTER RD
DISRAELI
BURSTOCK RD
NEWNES PATH
JOHN CLYNES CT
WOODBOROUGH RD
BRAMCOTE RD
MALBROOK RD
WOODTHORPE RD
HOWARD'S LA
CAMPION RD
COALECROFT RD
HOLROYD RD
ENMORE RD
TIDESWELL RD
GWENDOLEN AVE
NURSERY CL
RAVENNA RD
ULVA RD
BURSTON RD
CRESCENT STABLES
MARLIN HO
MANOR GATE
ST JOHN'S AVE
THE PLEASANCE
ST MARGARET'S CT
PLEASANCE RD
HORROCKS HO
MONRO HO
BRUCE HO
WRIGHT HO
KINGSLAWN CL
ELYSTAN CT
MONTOLIEU GDNS
WILLIAM GDNS
HAZLEWELL RD
LARPENT AVE
ST SIMON'S AVE
GWENDOLEN CL
BURLEIGH PL
ASHDOWN
CAMBALT RD
FAIRLAWNS
WESSEX CT
RAYNER'S RD
GROSVENOR CT
MERCIER RD
MARSDENE
DOVER HOUSE RD
HAWKESBURY RD
PUTNEY PARK LA
ST MARGARET'S CRES
LUTTRELL AVE
CASTELLO AVE
GENOA AVE
CHARTFIELD AVE
CHERRYWOOD DR
CHARTFIELD SQ
SHELBURNE CT
LANSDOWNE
COURT ROYAL
CARLTON DR
ARKSTEAD RD
HENTY WLK
HOBBES WLK
SUNNYMEAD RD
LANEWAY
GRANARD AVE
SOLNA AVE
WHITNELL WAY
WINCHELSEA CL
NORTH LODGE CL
RYE WLK
TINTERN CL
ARLESEY CL
CHEPSTOW CL
LYTTON GR
WESTLEIGH AVE
CORTIS TERR
RAMSEY CT
WESTROW
COTMAN CL
GIRTON HO
HARVARD HO
RADCLIFFE SQ
FAIRHEATHE
LUSHER HO
REDGATE TERR
ESSINGTON
SPREWELL
ROSBURY
CRESTWAY
CORTIS RD
PULLMAN GDNS
CARSLAKE RD
TILDESLEY RD
HIGHDOWN RD
DOVER PARK DR
HEPPLESTONE CL
BOYD CT
HAYWARD GDNS
WESTPOINT
HEATH RISE
LORNE CT
KERSFIELD RD
BRAEMAR
KERSFIELD HO
ULLSWATER
WICKHAM HO
LYLE PK
HEATH ROYAL
GLENMORE
CRAIGLEITH
RUSHOLME RD
AMBUSH RD
PARKMEAD
DUNSFORD WAY
INNES GDNS
EXETER HO
DIVIS WAY
GROSSE WAY
PUTNEY HEATH
PUTNEY HEATH LA
HEDLEY CT
VANDYKE CL
COLEBROOK CL
CROFT HO
LITTLECOTE CL
ROYAL CL
UNSTEAD WAY
BELL DR
WESTMEAD
OPPICE DR
TREVILLE ST
RIPLINGTON CT
TELEGRAPH RD
Putney Heath
Royal

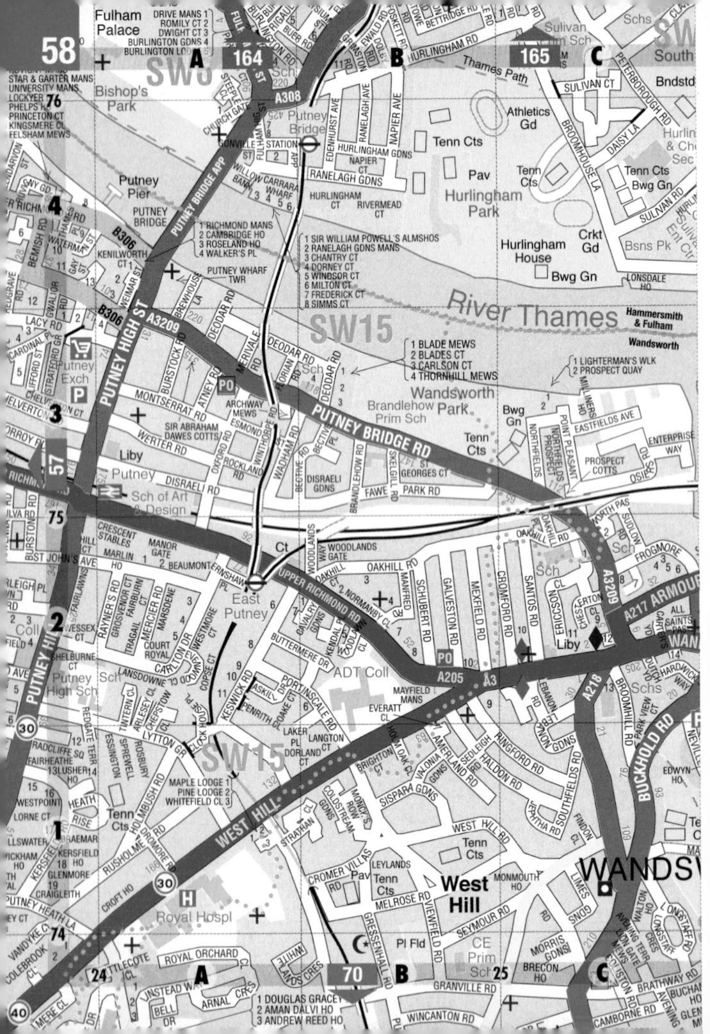

Fulham Palace
DRIVE MANS 1
ROMILY CT 2
DWIGHT CT 3
BURLINGTON GDNS 4
BURLINGTON LODGE
A
164
B
HURLINGHAM RD
165
C
SW6
Thames Path
Sulivan Sch
South
Bishop's Park
STAR & GARTER MANS
UNIVERSITY MANS
LOCKYER
PHELPS
76
PRINCETON CT
KINGSMERE CL
FELSHAM MEWS
A308
CHURCH GATE
Putney Bridge
STATION APP
EDENHURST AVE
RANELAGH AVE
NAPIER AVE
HURLINGHAM GDNS
NAPIER CT
RANELAGH GDNS
Athletics Gd
Tenn Cts
Pav
Hurlingham Park
SULIVAN CT
PETERBOROUGH RD
Bndstd
BROOMHOUSE LA
DAISY LA
SULIVAN RD
Tenn Cts
Bwg Gn
Putney Pier
PUTNEY BRIDGE APP
WILLOW BANK
CARRARA WHARF
HURLINGHAM CT
RIVERMEAD CT
PUTNEY BRIDGE
1 RICHMOND MANS
2 CAMBRIDGE HO
3 ROSELAND HO
4 WALKER'S PL
1 SIR WILLIAM POWELL'S ALMSHOS
2 RANELAGH GDNS MANS
3 CHANTRY CT
4 DORNEY CT
5 WINDSOR CT
6 MILTON CT
7 FREDERICK CT
8 SIMMS CT
Crkt Gd
Hurlingham House
Bsns Pk
Bwg Gn
LONSDALE HO
4
B306
KENILWORTH CT
PUTNEY WHARF TWR
BREWHOUSE LA
WEIMAR ST
BEMISH RD
WATERMAN ST
GAY ST
GWALIOR RD
LACY RD
River Thames
SW15
Hammersmith & Fulham
Wandsworth
PUTNEY HIGH ST
A3209
DEODAR RD
MERIVALE RD
BURSTOCK RD
CARDINAL PL
CLIFFORD ST
STRATFORD GR
Putney Exch
1 BLADE MEWS
2 BLADES CT
3 CARLSON CT
4 THORNHILL MEWS
1 LIGHTERMAN'S WLK
2 PROSPECT QUAY
ATNEY RD
PO
FLORIAN RD
Sch
Wandsworth Park
Brandlehow Prim Sch
MONTSERRAT RD
ARCHWAY MEWS
ESMOND RD
WINTHORPE RD
PUTNEY BRIDGE RD
Bwg Gn
Tenn Cts
NORTHFIELDS
POINT PLEASANT
MILLINERS HO
EASTFIELDS AVE
ENTERPRISE WAY
PROSPECT COTTS
OSIERS RD
CHELVERTON RD
3
SIR ABRAHAM DAWES COTTS
WERTER RD
OXFORD RD
ROCKLAND RD
WADHAM RD
BECTIVE RD
BECTIVE PL
BRANDLEHOW RD
SKELGILL RD
ST GEORGES CT
Liby
Putney
57
DISRAELI RD
DISRAELI GDNS
FAWE PARK RD
RICHMOND RD
Sch of Art & Design
75
BURSTON RD
CRESCENT STABLES
MANOR GATE
HILL CT
MARLIN HO
ST JOHN'S AVE
BEAUMONT
ERNSHAW PL
Ct
WOODLANDS WAY
WOODLANDS GATE
OAKHILL RD
OAKHILL CT
NORMANBY CL
MANFRED RD
SCHUBERT RD
GALVESTON RD
MEXFIELD RD
CROMFORD RD
SANTOS RD
ERICCSON CL
CHESTERTON CL
OAKHILL PL
WORTH PAS
SUDLOW RD
FROGMORE
Sch
A3209
A217 ARMOURY WAY
ALL SAINTS PAS
CARTER'S YD
Liby
FAIRLAWNS
RAYNER'S RD
GROSVENOR CT
FAIRBURN CT
MERCIER RD
MARSDENE
TRAGAIL
2
East Putney
UPPER RICHMOND RD
CAVALRY GDNS
KENDAL PL
WOODLAWN CL
BUTTERMERE DR
WESSEX CT
COURT ROYAL
CARLTON DR
WESTMORE CT
COPSE CT
PO
A205
A3
Coll
SHELBURNE CT
LANSDOWNE CL
Putney High Sch
KESWICK RD
PORTINSCALE RD
ADT Coll
MAYFIELD MANS
EVERATT CL
LEBANON RD
LEBANON GDNS
A218
BROOMHILL RD
PARK VIEW CT
Schs
HARDWICK WAY
DUTCH YD
TINTERN CL
ARLESEY CL
CHEPSTOW CL
CLOCK HOUSE PL
ASKILL DR
PENRITH CL
CLOAKE CT
LAKER PL
LANGTON CT
DORLAND CT
HOLM OAK CL
AMERLAND RD
SEDLEIGH RD
RINGFORD RD
HALDON RD
SOUTHFIELDS RD
BUCKHOLD RD
EDWYN HO
PUTNEY HILL
30
REDGATE TERR
ESSINGTON
SPREWELL
ROSBURY
LYTTON GR
SW15
BRIGHTON CT
VALONIA GDNS
RADCLIFFE SQ
FAIRHEATHE
13 LUSHER HO
HOLMBUSH RD
MAPLE LODGE 1
PINE LODGE 2
WHITEFIELD CL 3
SISPARA GDNS
JEPHTHA RD
FINDON CL
WESTPOINT
HEATH RISE
LORNE CT
Tenn Cts
WEST HILL
COLDSTREAM GDNS
MONCY'S ROW
STRATHAN CL
WEST HILL RD
Tenn Cts
1
ULLSWATER
BRAEMAR
WICKHAM HO
KERSFIELD RD
18 KERSFIELD HO
GLENMORE
19 CRAIGLEITH
DROMORE RD
RUSHOLME RD
30
CROMER VILLAS RD
Pav
LEYLANDS
Tenn Cts
West Hill
MONMOUTH HO
WANDSWORTH
LIMES GDNS
PUTNEY HEATH LA
CROFT HO
H
Royal Hospl
MELROSE RD
VIEWFIELD RD
SEYMOUR RD
GRESSENHALL RD
74
VANDYKE CL
COLEBROOK CL
WHITE LANDS CRES
Pl Fld
CE Prim Sch
MORRIS GDNS
AVENING TERR
LION GATE MEWS
WALTON HO
LONGSTAFF RD
LONGSTAFF CRES
ROYAL ORCHARD CL
24
TITTLECOTE
A
70
B
25
BRECON HO
C
BRATHWAY RD
GRANVILLE RD
UNSTEAD WAY
ARNAL CRES
BELL DR
1 DOUGLAS GRACEY
2 AMAN DALVI HO
3 ANDREW REED HO
WINCANTON RD
CAMBORNE RD
40

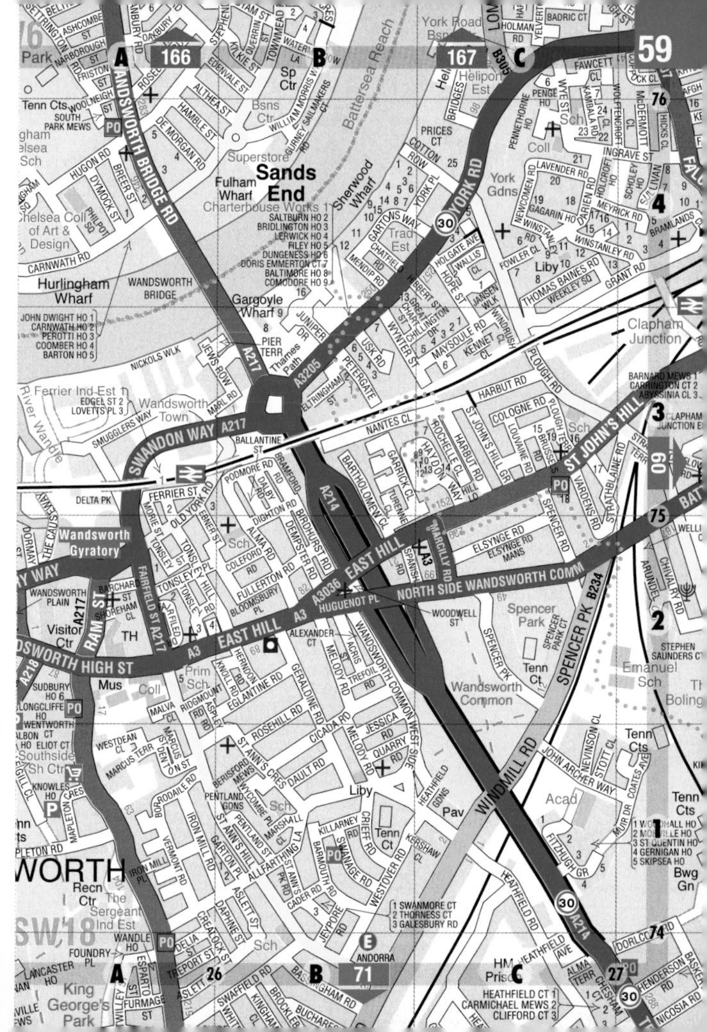
166
167
71
60
A
B
C
Sands End
Fulham Wharf
Charterhouse Works
Sherwood Wharf
Battersea Reach
York Road Bsns Ctr
Heliport Est
Superstore
Bsns Ctr
Sp Ctr
Hurlingham Wharf
WANDSWORTH BRIDGE
Gargoyle Wharf
Chelsea Coll of Art & Design
Ferrier Ind Est
Wandsworth Town
Wandsworth Gyratory
Visitor Ctr
Mus
Coll
Prim Sch
Liby
Trad Est
York Gdns
Clapham Junction
Spencer Park
Wandsworth Common
Emanuel Sch
Tenn Cts
Acad
Bwg Gn
Recn Ctr
The Sergeant Ind Est
SW18
King George's Park
HM Prison
ANDORRA
WANDSWORTH BRIDGE RD
YORK RD
SWANDON WAY A217
EAST HILL
WANDSWORTH HIGH ST
NORTH SIDE WANDSWORTH COMM
ST JOHN'S HILL
SPENCER PK B234
WINDMILL RD
WANDSWORTH COMMON WEST SIDE
FAIRFIELD ST A217
RAM ST
A3205
A214
A3036
A3
A217
A218
B305
CARNWATH RD
HUGON RD
DE MORGAN RD
ALTHEA ST
HAMBLE ST
EDENVALE ST
KILKIE ST
TOWNMEAD RD
WILLIAM MORRIS WAY
GURNEY SAILMAKERS CT
SALTBURN HO 2
BRIDLINGTON HO 3
LERWICK HO 4
FILEY HO 5
DUNGENESS HO 6
DORIS EMMERTON CT 7
BALTIMORE HO 8
COMODORE HO 9
JOHN DWIGHT HO 1
CARNWATH HO 2
PEROTTI HO 3
COOMBER HO 4
BARTON HO 5
EDGEL ST 2
LOVETTS PL 3
NICKOLS WLK
JEWS ROW
PIER TERR
Thames Path
JUNIPER DR
PETERGATE
USK RD
WYNTER ST
MAYSOULE RD
KENNET CL
HOLGATE AVE
WALLIS CL
HOPE ST
JANSEN WLK
WINDRUSH CL
FOWLER CL
THOMAS BAINES RD
WEEKLEY SQ
GRANT RD
WINSTANLEY RD
MEYRICK RD
LAVENDER RD
GAGARIN HO
INGRAVE ST
BRAMLANDS CL
FAWCETT CL
PENGE HO
PRICES CT
COTTON ROW
GARTONS WAY
CHATFIELD RD
MENDIP RD
HARBUT RD
COLOGNE RD
PLOUGH RD
NANTES CL
BALLANTINE ST
PODMORE RD
DALBY RD
BRAMFORD RD
BIRDHURST RD
DEMPSTER RD
ALMA RD
DIGHTON RD
COLEFORD RD
FULLERTON RD
BLOOMSBURY PL
HUGUENOT PL
BARTHOLOMEW CL
GARRICK CL
HAYDON WAY
ROCHELLE CL
ST JOHN'S HILL GR
LOUVAINE RD
ELSYNGE RD
ELSYNGE RD MANS
MARCILLY RD
SPANISH RD
VARDENS RD
STRATHBLAINE RD
BARNARD MEWS 1
CARRINGTON CT 2
ABYSSINIA CL 3
FERRIER ST
DELTA PK
OLD YORK RD
TONSLEY ST
TONSLEY HILL
MORIE ST
EBNER ST
BARCHARD ST
SHOREHAM CL
WANDSWORTH PLAIN
ALEXANDER CT
WOODWELL ST
ACRIS ST
TREFOIL RD
MELODY RD
GERALDINE RD
ROSEHILL RD
CICADA RD
JESSICA RD
QUARRY RD
HEATHFIELD GDNS
EGLANTINE RD
RIDGMOUNT RD
MALVA CL
WESTDEAN CL
MARCUS TERR
ST ANN'S CRES
DAULT RD
BERISFORD MEWS
PENTLAND GDNS
WYCOMBE PL
PENTLAND ST
ST ANN'S HILL
MARSHALL CL
ALLFARTHING LA
KILLARNEY RD
CRIEFF RD
SWANAGE RD
BARMOUTH RD
WESTOVER RD
KERSHAW CL
BORODAILE RD
IRON MILL RD
VERMONT RD
IRON MILL PL
GARTON PL
ASLETT ST
DAPHNE ST
CREATOCK ST
JEYPORE RD
CADER RD
1 SWANMORE CT
2 THORNESS CT
3 GALESBURY RD
HEATHFIELD RD
HEATHFIELD AVE
JOHN ARCHER WAY
NEVINSON CL
STOTT CL
COATES AVE
MUIR DR
FITZHUGH GR
1 WOODHALL HO
2 MORVILLE HO
3 ST QUENTIN HO
4 GERNIGAN HO
5 SKIPSEA HO
STEPHEN SAUNDERS CT
ARUNDEL
CHIVALRY RD
SPENCER PARK CT
SUDBURY HO
LONGCLIFFE HO
WENTWORTH CT
ELIOT CT
Southside Sh Ctr
KNOWLES HO
MAPLETON CRES
WANDLE HO
FOUNDRY PL
LANCASTER HO
DELIA ST
ESPARTO ST
TREPORT ST
FURMAGE ST
SWAFFIELD RD
BASSINGHAM RD
HEATHFIELD CT 1
CARMICHAEL MEWS 2
CLIFFORD CT 3
DORLCOTE RD
HENDERSON RD
NICOSIA RD
ALMA TERR
CHESHAM CT

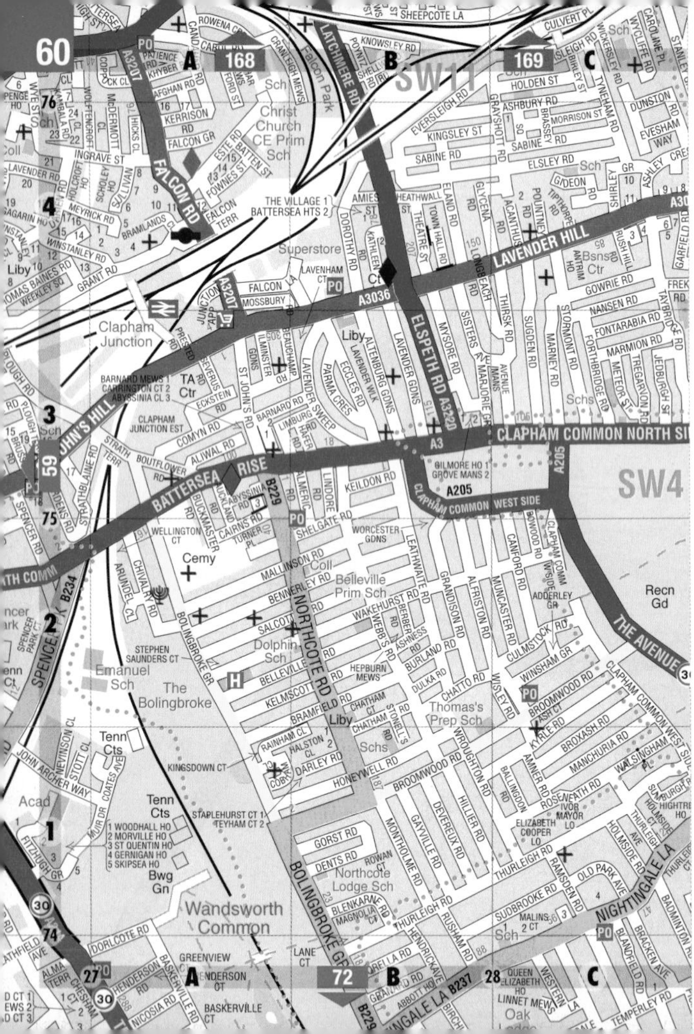
168
169
72
59
A
B
C
SW11
SW4
ROWENA CRES
CANDAHAR RD
CABUL RD
KNOWSLEY RD
SHEEPCOTE LA
CULVERT PL
CULVERT RD
LATCHMERE RD
CRANLEIGH MEWS
Falcon Park
POYNTZ RD
SHELLWOOD RD
PATIENCE RD
KHYBER RD
AFGHAN RD
KERRISON RD
FALCON GR
FALCON RD
A3207
COPPOCK CL
MCDERMOTT CL
WOLFTENCROFT CL
HICKS CL
WYE ST
PENGE HO
KIMBALA RD
INGRAVE ST
LAVENDER RD
Coll
Sch
Christ Church CE Prim Sch
ESTE RD
BATTEN ST
FOWNES ST
SCHOLEY HO
SULLIVAN
HOLCROFT HO
MEYRICK RD
SAGARIN HO
WINSTANLEY RD
BRAMLANDS CL
FALCON TERR
THE VILLAGE 1
BATTERSEA HTS 2
Superstore
Liby
THOMAS BAINES RD
WEEKLEY SQ
GRANT RD
FALCON LA
LAVENHAM CT
PO
MOSSBURY RD
JUNCTION APP
Clapham Junction
PRESTED RD
A3036
EVERSLEIGH RD
KINGSLEY ST
SABINE RD
GRAYSHOTT RD
HOLDEN ST
ASHBURY RD
MORRISON ST
BRASSEY SQ
ELSLEY RD
ASFLEIGH RD
WICKERSLEY RD
BIRLEY ST
TYNEHAM RD
CAROLINE PL
WYCLIFFE RD
DUNSTON RD
EVESHAM WAY
ASHLEY CRES
SHIRLEY GR
GIDEON RD
TIPTHORPE RD
POUNTNEY RD
ACANTHUS RD
GLYCENA RD
ELAND RD
AMIES ST
HEATHWALL ST
DOROTHY RD
KATHLEEN RD
THEATRE ST
TOWN HALL RD
LONGBEACH RD
LAVENDER HILL
Bsns Ctr
ANTRIM HO
RUSH HILL RD
GARFIELD RD
GOWRIE RD
NANSEN RD
FONTARABIA RD
MARMION RD
TAYBRIDGE RD
FREKE RD
ELSPETH RD
A3220
MYSORE RD
SISTERS AVE
THIRSK RD
SUGDEN RD
MARNEY RD
STORMONT RD
FORTHBRIDGE RD
METEOR ST
TREGARVON RD
JEDBURGH ST
MARJORIE GR
AVENUE MANS
Schs
ALTENBURG GDNS
LAVENDER GDNS
LAVENDER WLK
ECCLES RD
PARMA CRES
LAVENDER SWEEP
BEAUCHAMP RD
ILMINSTER GDNS
ST JOHN'S RD
SEVERUS RD
TA Ctr
BARNARD MEWS 1
CARRINGTON CT 2
ABYSSINIA CL 3
ECKSTEIN RD
CLAPHAM JUNCTION EST
COMYN RD
ALIWAL RD
BOUTFLOWER RD
BARNARD RD
LIMBURG RD
HAFER RD
ST JOHN'S HILL
PLOUGH TERR
STRATH TERR
STRATHBLAINE RD
CLAPHAM COMMON NORTH SIDE
A3
A205
GILMORE HO 1
GROVE MANS 2
CLAPHAM COMMON WEST SIDE
BATTERSEA RISE
B229
BUCKMASTER RD
AUCKLAND RD
ABYSSINIA RD
CAIRNS RD
TURNER PL
ALMERIC RD
LINDORE RD
KEILDON RD
SHELGATE RD
WORCESTER GDNS
LEATHWAITE RD
BOWOOD RD
CANFORD RD
SPENCER RD
WELLINGTON CT
Cemy
MALLINSON RD
Coll
Belleville Prim Sch
BENNERLEY RD
CHIVALRY RD
ARUNDEL CL
BOLINGBROKE GR
SALCOTT RD
NORTHCOTE RD
WAKEHURST RD
BERBER RD
WEBB'S RD
ASHNESS RD
BURLAND RD
GRANDISON RD
ALFRISTON RD
MUNCASTER RD
CLAPHAM COMM W SIDE
ADDERLEY GR
CULMSTOCK RD
Recn Gd
THE AVENUE
SPENCER PARK
B234
Spencer Park
SPENCER PARK CT
STEPHEN SAUNDERS CT
Dolphin Sch
Emanuel Sch
The Bolingbroke
BELLEVILLE RD
HEPBURN MEWS
DULKA RD
CHATTO RD
WISLEY RD
WINSHAM GR
BROOMWOOD RD
KELMSCOTT RD
BRAMFIELD RD
CHATHAM CT
CHATHAM RD
STONELL'S RD
Thomas's Prep Sch
ASH CT
KYRLE RD
BROXASH RD
MANCHURIA RD
WALSINGHAM PL
Liby
Schs
RAINHAM CL
HALSTON CL
DARLEY RD
COBHAM CL
HONEYWELL RD
BROOMWOOD RD
WROUGHTON RD
BALLINGDON RD
AMNER RD
ROSENEATH RD
IVOR MAYOR LO
ELIZABETH COOPER LO
HOLMSIDE RD
HIGHTREE HO
THURLEIGH AVE
SUNBURGH RD
Tenn Cts
NEVINSON CL
STOTT CL
COATES AVE
JOHN ARCHER WAY
KINGSDOWN CT
Acad
MUIR DR
1 WOODHALL HO
2 MORVILLE HO
3 ST QUENTIN HO
4 GERNIGAN HO
5 SKIPSEA HO
FITZHUGH GR
STAPLEHURST CT 1
TEYHAM CT 2
Tenn Cts
Bwg Gn
GORST RD
DENTS RD
ROWAN CT
Northcote Lodge Sch
MONTHOLME RD
GAYVILLE RD
DEVEREUX RD
HILLIER RD
THURLEIGH RD
RAMSDEN RD
OLD PARK AVE
NIGHTINGALE LA
BADMINTON RD
Wandsworth Common
BOLINGBROKE GR
BLENKARNE RD
MAGNOLIA CT
THURLEIGH RD
HENDRICK AVE
RUSHAM RD
SUDBROOKE RD
MALINS CT
Sch
BLANDFIELD RD
BRACKEN AVE
DORLCOTE RD
ALMA TERR
CHESHAM ST
HENDERSON RD
BASKERVILLE RD
GREENVIEW CL
HENDERSON CT
LANE CT
BASKERVILLE CT
NICOSIA RD
ORELLA RD
GRANARD RD
ABBOTT HO
NIGHTINGALE LA
B237
QUEEN ELIZABETH HO
LINNET MEWS
WESTERN LA
Oak Lodge
TEMPERLEY RD
30

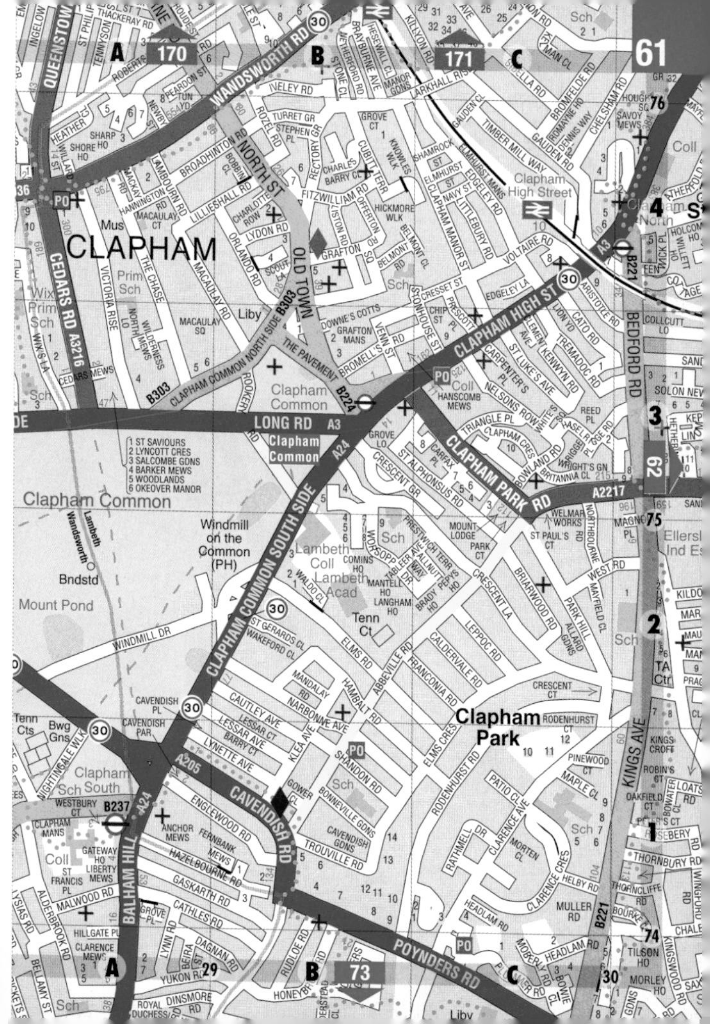
61
170
171
62
73
A
B
C
1
2
3
4
CLAPHAM
Clapham Common
Clapham Park
Clapham High Street
Clapham Common
Clapham South
Windmill on the Common (PH)
Mount Pond
Bndstd
Lambeth
Wandsworth
Lambeth Coll
Lambeth Acad
Tenn Ct
Liby
Mus
Prim Sch
Wix Prim Sch
Ellersl Ind Es
TA Ctr
1 ST SAVIOURS
2 LYNCOTT CRES
3 SALCOMBE GDNS
4 BARKER MEWS
5 WOODLANDS
6 OKEOVER MANOR
WANDSWORTH RD
QUEENSTOWN RD
CEDARS RD
A3216
NORTH ST
OLD TOWN
CLAPHAM HIGH ST
CLAPHAM PARK RD
A2217
LONG RD
A3
A24
A205
B303
B224
B221
B237
CLAPHAM COMMON NORTH SIDE
CLAPHAM COMMON SOUTH SIDE
THE PAVEMENT
BEDFORD RD
KINGS AVE
CAVENDISH RD
POYNDERS RD
BALHAM HILL
WINDMILL DR
ELMS RD
ABBEVILLE RD
FRANCONIA RD
CALDERVALE RD
LEPPOC RD
BRIAROOD RD
PARK HILL
CRESCENT LA
RODENHURST RD
CLARENCE AVE
CLARENCE CRES
HEADLAM RD
MULLER RD
VICTORIA RISE
MACAULAY RD
ROOKERY RD
VENN ST
STONHOUSE ST
CLAPHAM MANOR ST
EDGELEY RD
VOLTAIRE RD
ST LUKE'S AVE
NELSONS ROW
KENWYN RD
TREMADOC RD
LARKHALL RISE
TIMBER MILL WAY
GAUDEN RD
BROMFELDE RD
CHELSHAM RD
FITZWILLIAM RD
GRAFTON SQ
SHANDON RD
NARBONNE AVE
CAUTLEY AVE
LESSAR AVE
LYNETTE AVE
ENGLEWOOD RD
HAZELBOURNE RD
GASKARTH RD
CATHLES RD
MALWOOD RD
ALDERBROOK RD
NIGHTINGALE WLK
CAVENDISH PL
CAVENDISH PAR
TROUVILLE RD
BONNEVILLE GDNS
HAMBALT RD
KLEA AVE
ELMS CRES
CRESCENT GR
ST ALPHONSUS RD
PRESTWICH TERR
WORSOPP DR
TRIANGLE PL
BOWLAND RD
WEST RD
MAYFIELD CL
NORTHBOURNE RD
THORNBURY RD
ROSEBERY RD
KINGSWOOD RD
HONEYBROOK RD
RUDLOE RD
YUKON RD
DAGNAN RD
BELLAMY ST

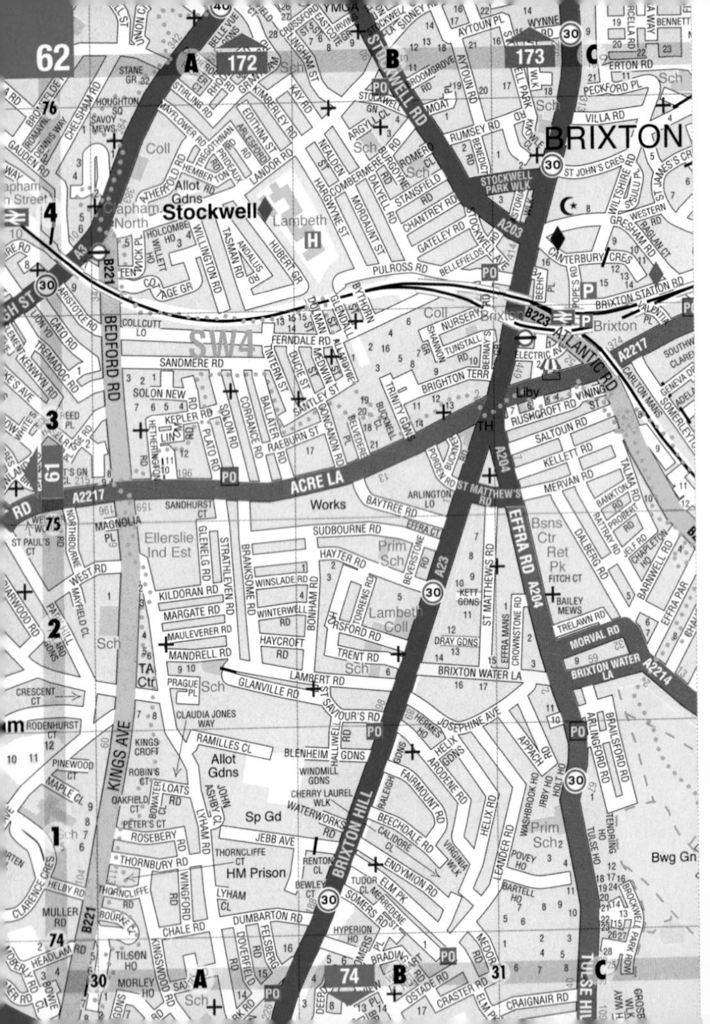
172
173
BRIXTON
Stockwell
Lambeth
Clapham North
Coll
Allot Gdns
SW4
ACRE LA
A2217
A3
A23
A203
A204
A2214
B221
B223
BEDFORD RD
KINGS AVE
BRIXTON HILL
EFFRA RD
STOCKWELL RD
ATLANTIC RD
STOCKWELL PARK WLK
Works
Ellerslie Ind Est
Bsns Ctr
Ret Pk
Lambeth Coll
HM Prison
Sp Gd
Bwg Gn
Liby
Prim Sch
TA Ctr
BRIXTON WATER LA
MORVAL RD
ST MATTHEW'S RD
ST JOHN'S CRES
CANTERBURY CRES
BRIXTON STATION RD
COLDHARBOUR LA
ELECTRIC AV
RUSHCROFT RD
SALTOUN RD
KELLETT RD
MERVAN RD
SUDBOURNE RD
HAYTER RD
BAYTREE RD
JOSEPHINE AVE
LAMBERT RD
GLANVILLE RD
ST SAVIOUR'S RD
BLENHEIM GDNS
JEBB AVE
THORNBURY RD
DUMBARTON RD
CHALE RD
ENDYMION RD
ELM PK
TULSE HILL
CRAIGNAIR RD
SANDMERE RD
FERNDALE RD
SANTLEY ST
SOLON RD
KEPLER RD
CLAPHAM RD
LANDOR RD
COMBERMERE RD
PULROSS RD
GATELEY RD
CHANTREY RD
STANSFIELD RD
VILLA RD
PECKFORD PL
RUMSEY RD
BRIGHTON TERR
NURSERY RD
TUNSTALL RD
ARLINGFORD RD
BRAILSFORD RD
HELIX RD
LEANDER RD
FAIRMOUNT RD
BEECHDALE RD
CALIDORE CL
VIRGINIA WLK
MARGATE RD
KILDORAN RD
MANDRELL RD
WESTRD
CRESCENT CT
KINGSWOOD RD
MORLEY HO
A
B
C
1
2
3
4
61
74
75
76

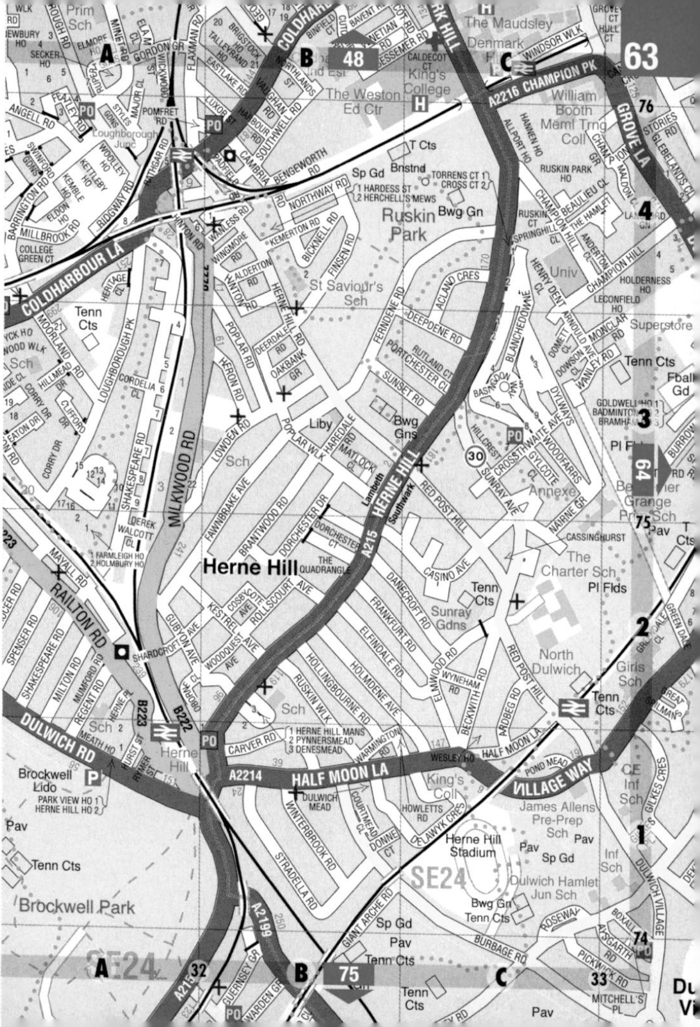
A
B
C
48
Prim Sch
The Maudsley
Denmark Hill
COLDHARBOUR LA
GORDON GR
CHAMPION PK
A2216
The Weston Ed Ctr
King's College
William Booth Meml Trng Coll
GROVE LA
Loughborough Junc
ANGELL RD
WOOLLEY HO
KETTLEBY HO
KEMBLE HO
RIDGWAY RD
MILLBROOK RD
BARRINGTON RD
COLLEGE GREEN CT
BENGEWORTH RD
CAMBRIA RD
SOUTHWELL RD
NORTHWAY RD
1 HARDESS ST
2 HERCHELL'S MEWS
TORRENS CT
CROSS CT
Ruskin Park
Bwg Gn
T Cts
Sp Gd
Bnstnd
RUSKIN PARK HO
CHAMPION HILL
ALLPORT HO
HAMMEN HO
4
WANLESS RD
KEMERTON RD
BICKNELL RD
FINSEN RD
WINGMORE RD
ALDERTON RD
HINTON RD
HERNE HILL RD
St Saviour's Sch
Univ
CHAMPION HILL
HOLDERNESS HO
LECONFIELD HO
Superstore
Tenn Cts
MOORLAND RD
LOUGHBOROUGH PK
HERITAGE CL
POPLAR RD
DEERDALE RD
OAKBANK GR
HERON RD
FERNDENE RD
DEEPDENE RD
ACLAND CRES
RUTLAND CT
PORTCHESTER CL
SUNSET RD
BASINGDON WAY
BLANCHEDOWNE
DYLWAYS
DOMETT CL
DOWSON CL
MONCLAR RD
WANLEY RD
Fball Gd
CORDELIA CL
HILLMEAD DR
CLIFFORD DR
CORRY DR
MILKWOOD RD
SHAKESPEARE RD
LOWDEN RD
Sch
Liby
POPLAR WLK
HAREDALE RD
MATLOCK CL
Bwg Gns
HERNE HILL
A215
RED POST HILL
HILLCREST
SUNRAY AVE
CROSSTHWAITE AVE
GYLCOTE CL
WOODFARRS
30
Annexe
NAIRNE GR
3
64
Pl Flds
Grange
Sch
75
Pav
DEREK WALCOTT CL
1 FARMLEIGH HO
2 HOLMBURY HO
FAWNBRAKE AVE
BRANTWOOD RD
DORCHESTER DR
DORCHESTER CT
Lambeth
Southwark
Herne Hill
THE QUADRANGLE
CASINO AVE
CASSINGHURST
The Charter Sch
Tenn Cts
Pl Flds
MAYALL RD
RAILTON RD
SPENSER RD
SHAKESPEARE RD
MILTON RD
MUMFORD RD
REGENT RD
B223
SHARDCROFT AVE
GUBYON AVE
KESTREL AVE
COSBYCOTE AVE
ROLLSCOURT AVE
WOODQUEST AVE
DANECROFT RD
FRANKFURT RD
ELFINDALE RD
HOLMDENE AVE
HOLLINGBOURNE RD
RUSKIN WLK
Sunray Gdns
ELMWOOD RD
WYNEHAM RD
BECKWITH RD
ARDBEG RD
North Dulwich
Girls Sch
2
GREEN DALE
GRENDALE
GREAT SPILMANS
DULWICH RD
HERNE PL
MEATH HO
HURST ST
RYMER ST
B222
Herne Hill
CARVER RD
1 HERNE HILL MANS
2 PYNNERSMEAD
3 DENESMEAD
WARMINGTON RD
WESLEY HO
HALF MOON LA
A2214
POND MEAD
VILLAGE WAY
CE Inf Sch
GILKES CRES
Brockwell Lido
PARK VIEW HO 1
HERNE HILL HO 2
DULWICH MEAD
COURTMEAD CL
King's Coll
HOWLETTS RD
DELAWYK CRES
DONNE CT
WINTERBROOK RD
James Allens Pre-Prep Sch
Herne Hill Stadium
Pav
Sp Gd
Inf Sch
1
DULWICH VILLAGE
Tenn Cts
Brockwell Park
STRADELLA RD
SE24
Dulwich Hamlet Jun Sch
Bwg Gn
Tenn Cts
ROSEWAY
BOXALL RD
AYSGARTH RD
GIANT ARCHE RD
BURBAGE RD
PICKWICK RD
74
A2199
Sp Gd
Pav
Tenn Cts
SE24
A215
32
B
75
C
33
GUERNSEY GR
WARDEN GR
MITCHELL'S PL
Tenn Cts
Pav

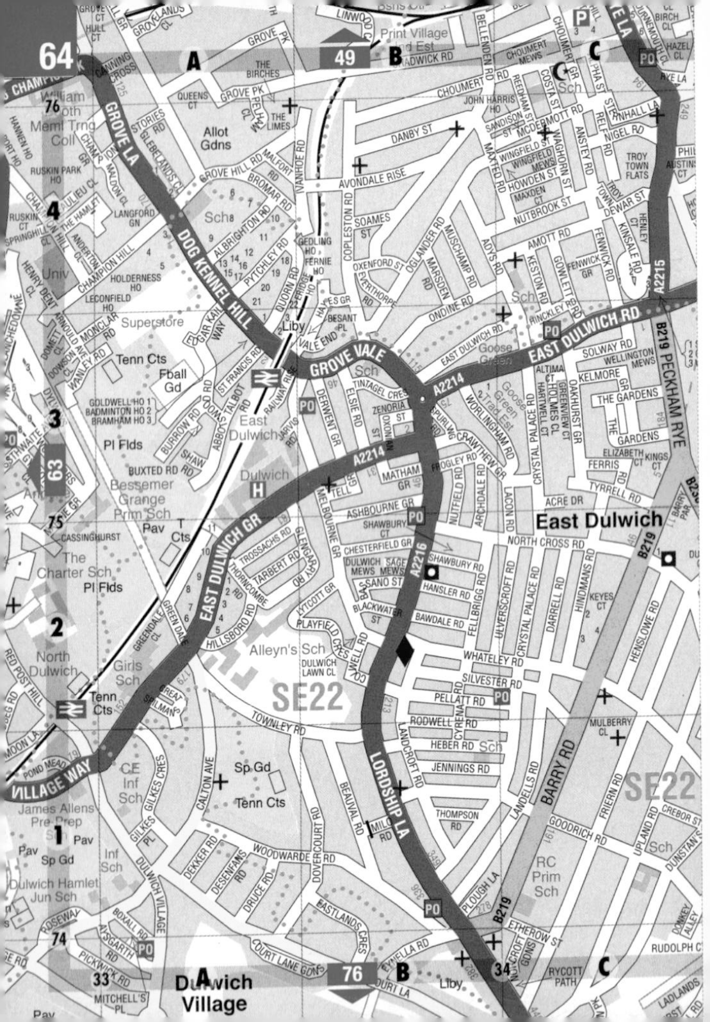

A
B
C
49
GROVE PK
THE BIRCHES
Print Village Ind Est
CHOUMERT RD
BELLENDEN RD
CHOUMERT MEWS
CHOUMERT GR
COSTA ST
RYE LA
QUEENS CT
THE LIMES
PELHAM CL
CANNING CROSS
CHAMPION PK
William Booth Meml Trng Coll
GROVE LA
STORIES RD
GLEBELANDS CL
Allot Gdns
JOHN HARRIS HO
REEDHAM ST
SANDISON ST
MCDERMOTT RD
DANBY ST
NIGEL RD
TROY TOWN FLATS
HANNEN HO
RUSKIN PARK HO
CHAMPION GR
MALDON CL
GROVE HILL RD
MALFORT RD
BROMAR RD
IVANHOE RD
AVONDALE RISE
WINGFIELD ST
WINGFIELD MEWS
HOWDEN ST
MAXDEN CT
WAGHORN ST
ANSTEY RD
NUTBROOK ST
DEWAR ST
4
RUSKIN CT
THE HAMLET
LANGFORD GN
Sch
DOG KENNEL HILL
ALBRIGHTON RD
SOAMES ST
COPLESTON RD
OGLANDER RD
MUSCHAMP RD
ADYS RD
AMOTT RD
KINSALE RD
HENLEY CT
CHAMPION HILL
HOLDERNESS HO
PYTCHLEY RD
GEDLING HO
FERNIE HO
OXENFORD ST
MARSDEN RD
KESTON RD
GOWLETT RD
FENWICK GR
FENWICK RD
A2215
Univ
LECONFIELD HO
QUORN RD
EVERTHORPE RD
HAYES GR
BESANT PL
ONDINE RD
RINCKLEY RD
Superstore
EDGAR KAIL WAY
Liby
VALE END
EAST DULWICH RD
SOLWAY RD
WELLINGTON MEWS
MONCLAR RD
DOWSON CL
WANLEY RD
Tenn Cts
Fball Gd
ST FRANCIS RD
GROVE VALE
Goose Green
A2214
ALTIMA CT
HOLMES CL
HARTWELL CT
GREENVIEW CT
OAKHURST GR
KELMORE GR
THE GARDENS
B219 PECKHAM RYE
3
GOLDWELL HO
BADMINTON HO
BRAMHAM HO
BURROW RD
ABBOTSWOOD RD
TALBOT RD
RAILWAY RISE
East Dulwich
PO
DERWENT GR
ELSIE RD
TINTAGEL CRES
ZENORIA ST
OXONIAN ST
SPURLING RD
WORLINGHAM RD
Goose Green Trad Est
CRYSTAL PALACE RD
Pl Flds
SHAW RD
JARVIS RD
63
BUXTED RD
Dulwich H
TELL GR
MATHAM GR
FROGLEY RD
NUTFIELD RD
ARCHDALE RD
CRAWTHEW GR
LACON RD
ELIZABETH CT
FERRIS RD
KINGS CT
TYRRELL RD
Bessemer Grange Prim Sch
MELBOURNE GR
ASHBOURNE GR
ACRE DR
BARRY PAR
75
CASSINGHURST
Pav
Cts
EAST DULWICH GR
TROSSACHS RD
SHAWBURY CT
CHESTERFIELD GR
East Dulwich
NORTH CROSS RD
The Charter Sch
Pl Flds
TARBERT RD
GLENGARRY RD
DULWICH MEWS
SAGE MEWS
SHAWBURY RD
A2216
ULVERSCROFT RD
DARRELL RD
HINDMANS RD
B219
THORNCOMBE RD
SANO ST
HANSLER RD
FELLBRIGG RD
KEYES CT
LYTCOTT GR
BLACKWATER ST
BAWDALE RD
2
HILLSBORO RD
PLAYFIELD CRES
HENSLOWE RD
GREENDALE CL
GREEN DALE
Alleyn's Sch
WHATELEY RD
DULWICH LAWN CL
COLWELL RD
North Dulwich
Girls Sch
SILVESTER RD
RED POST HILL
Tenn Cts
SE22
PELLATT RD
CYRENAIC RD
GREAT SPILMANS
TOWNLEY RD
RODWELL RD
MULBERRY CL
HEBER RD
POND MEAD
VILLAGE WAY
CE Inf Sch
GILKES CRES
CALTON AVE
Sp Gd
LORDSHIP LA
LANDCROFT RD
JENNINGS RD
BARRY RD
SE22
LANDELLS RD
FRIERN RD
James Allens Pre-Prep Sch
Tenn Cts
BEAUVAL RD
THOMPSON RD
CREBOR ST
1
Pav
Sp Gd
GILKES PL
DOVERCOURT RD
MILO RD
GOODRICH RD
UPLAND RD
Inf Sch
WOODWARDE RD
RC Prim Sch
Dulwich Hamlet Jun Sch
DULWICH VILLAGE
DEKKER RD
DESENFANS RD
DRUCE RD
PLOUGH LA
DUNSTAN'S
ROSEWAY
BOXALL RD
EASTLANDS CRES
ETHEROW ST
DONKEY ALLEY
74
AYSGARTH RD
COURT LANE GDNS
TYLNEY RD
NORCROFT GDNS
RUDOLPH CT
PICKWICK RD
76
RYCOTT PATH
33
Dulwich Village
MITCHELL'S PL
COURT LA
Liby
34
LADLANDS
Pav

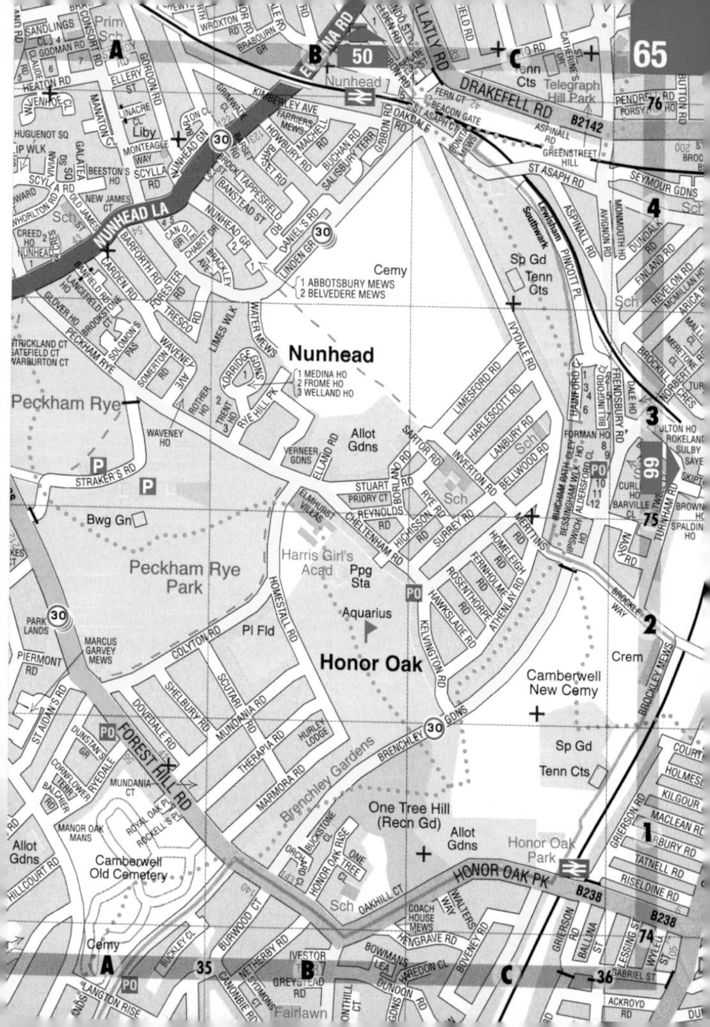
Nunhead
Honor Oak
Peckham Rye
Peckham Rye Park
Cemy
Allot Gdns
Harris Girl's Acad
Ppg Sta
Aquarius
Pl Fld
Bwg Gn
Camberwell New Cemy
Crem
Sp Gd
Tenn Cts
One Tree Hill (Recn Gd)
Honor Oak Park
Camberwell Old Cemetery
Brenchley Gardens
Telegraph Hill Park
Nunhead
NUNHEAD LA
DRAKEFELL RD
B2142
HONOR OAK PK
B238
FOREST HILL RD
PECKHAM RYE
EVELINA RD
LINDEN GR
IVYDALE RD
KELVINGTON RD
BRENCHLEY GDNS
COLYTON RD
HOMESTALL RD
CHELTENHAM RD
ST ASAPH RD
PINCOTT PL
BROCKLEY WAY
BROCKLEY MEWS
STRAKER'S RD
1 ABBOTSBURY MEWS
2 BELVEDERE MEWS
1 MEDINA HO
2 FROME HO
3 WELLAND HO
50
66
74
75
76
35
36

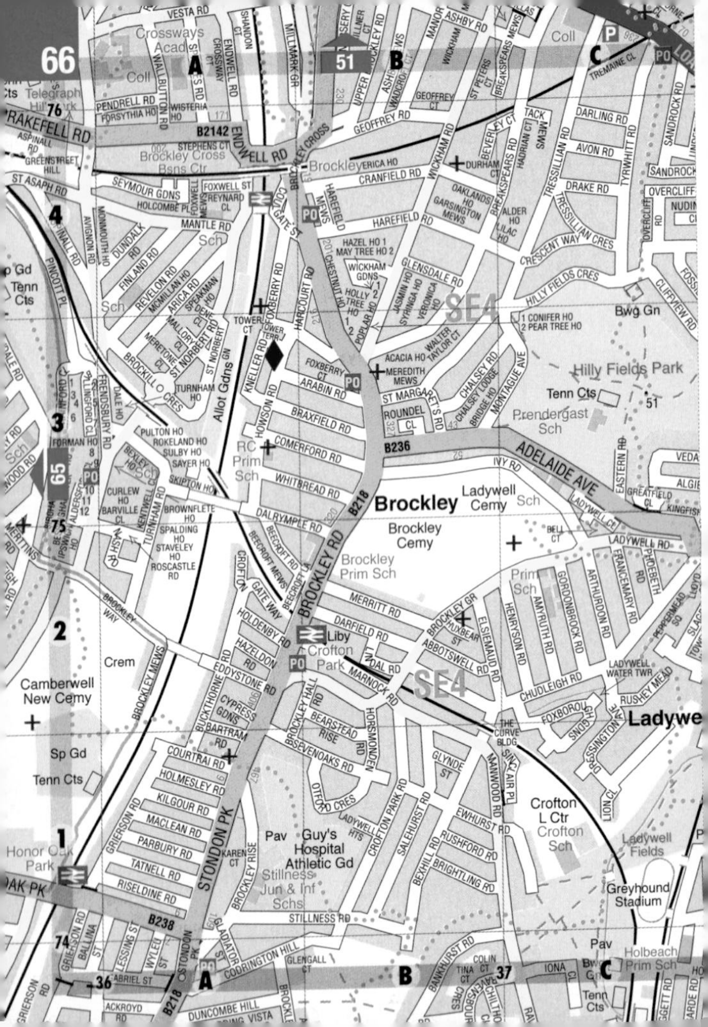
A
B
C
51
4
3
2
1
74
75
76
36
37
65
VESTA RD
Crossways Acad
Coll
Telegraph Hill Park
WALLBUTTON RD
SPARTA ST
SPARSHOLT RD
CROSSWAY CT
ENDWELL RD
SHANDON CT
MILLMARK GR
UPPER BROCKLEY RD
MILLNER CT
ASHBY MEWS
WADCROFT CT
MANOR
ASHBY RD
WICKHAM
GEOFFREY CT
ST PETERS CT
BREAKSPEARS MEWS
TREMAINE CL
PENDRELL RD
FORSYTHIA HO
WISTERIA HO
DRAKEFELL RD
B2142
ASPINALL RD
GREENSTREET HILL
STEPHENS CT
Brockley Cross Bsns Ctr
BROCKLEY CROSS
Brockley
ERICA HO
GEOFFREY RD
BEVERLEY CT
TACK MEWS
HADRIAN CT
BREAKSPEARS RD
TRESSILLIAN RD
DARLING RD
AVON RD
TYRWHITT RD
SANDROCK RD
DURHAM CT
CRANFIELD RD
WICKHAM RD
DRAKE RD
SANDROCK
OVERCLIFF
NUDIN
ST ASAPH RD
SEYMOUR GDNS
FOXWELL MEWS
FOXWELL ST
REYNARD CL
HOLCOMBE PL
MANTLE RD
COULGATE ST
HAREFIELD MEWS
HAREFIELD RD
OAKLANDS HO
GARSINGTON MEWS
ALDER HO
LILAC HO
TRESSILLIAN CRES
CRESCENT WAY
OVERCLIFF RD
AVIGNON RD
MONMOUTH RD
DUNDALK RD
FINLAND RD
Sch
CHESTNUT HO
HAZEL HO 1
MAY TREE HO 2
WICKHAM GDNS
HOLLY TREE HO
POPLAR HO
GLENSDALE RD
JASMIN HO
SYRINGA HO
VERONICA HO
HILLY FIELDS CRES
CLIFFVIEW RD
FOSS
Sp Gd
Tenn Cts
PINCOTT PL
REVELON RD
MCMILLAN HO
ARICA RD
SPEAKMAN HO
DENE CL
MALLORY CL
ST NORBERT RD
MERETONE CL
FOXBERRY RD
HARCOURT RD
TOWER CT
TOWER TERR
SE4
1 CONIFER HO
2 PEAR TREE HO
Bwg Gn
Hilly Fields Park
BROCKILL CRES
TURNHAM HO
ST NORBERT GN
Allot Gdns
KNELLER RD
FOXBERRY CT
ARABIN RD
ACACIA HO
WALTER TAYLOR CT
MEREDITH MEWS
ST MARGARET'S RD
CHALSEY RD
CHALSEY LODGE
BRIDGE HO
MONTAGUE AVE
Tenn Cts
Prendergast Sch
DALE RD
FRENDSBURY RD
DALE HO
LINGFORD CL
HOWSON RD
BRAXFIELD RD
ROUNDEL CL
FORMAN HO
PULTON HO
ROKELAND HO
SULBY HO
SAYER HO
RC Prim Sch
COMERFORD RD
B236
ADELAIDE AVE
IVY RD
EASTERN RD
VEDA
ALGIE
BEXLEY HO
CURLEW HO
BARVILLE CL
SKIPTON HO
BROWNFLETE HO
KENTWELL CL
TURNHAM RD
WHITBREAD RD
B218
Brockley
Ladywell Cemy
GREATFIELD CL
KINGFISH
LADYWELL CL
ALDERSFORD CL
IPSWICH HO
MERTINS RD
SPALDING HO
STAVELEY HO
ROSCASTLE RD
DALRYMPLE RD
BEECROFT RD
BEECROFT MEWS
Brockley Cemy
BELL CT
LADYWELL RD
FRANCEMARY RD
PHOEBETH RD
CROFTON GATE WAY
BEECROFT LA
BROCKLEY RD
Brockley Prim Sch
Prim Sch
BROCKLEY WAY
MERRITT RD
BROCKLEY GR
HUXBEAR ST
ELSIEMAUD RD
HENRYSON RD
AMYRUTH RD
GORDONBROCK RD
ARTHURDON RD
PEPPERMEAD SQ
LLOYD
HOLDENBY RD
Crem
BROCKLEY MEWS
DARFIELD RD
Liby
Crofton Park
ABBOTSWELL RD
HAZELDON RD
EDDYSTONE RD
LINDAL RD
MARNOCK RD
Camberwell New Cemy
LADYWELL WATER TWR
CHUDLEIGH RD
RUSHEY MEAD
FOXBOROUGH GDNS
DRESSINGTON AVE
Ladywe
BUCKTHORNE RD
CYPRESS GDNS
BARTRAM RD
BROCKLEY HALL RD
BEARSTEAD RISE
HORSMONDEN RD
THE CURVE BLDG
SINCLAIR PL
MANWOOD RD
COURTRAI RD
SEVENOAKS RD
GLYNDE ST
HOLMESLEY RD
KILGOUR RD
OTFORD CRES
EWHURST RD
Crofton L Ctr
Crofton Sch
LION CL
GRIERSON RD
MACLEAN RD
LADYWELL HTS
CROFTON PARK RD
SALEHURST RD
BEXHILL RD
RUSHFORD RD
PARBURY RD
STONDON PK
KAREN CT
Pav
Guy's Hospital Athletic Gd
Ladywell Fields
Honor Oak Park
TATNELL RD
BROCKLEY RISE
Stillness Jun & Inf Schs
BRIGHTLING RD
Greyhound Stadium
OAK PK
RISELDINE RD
B238
STILLNESS RD
GRIERSON RD
BALLINA ST
LESSING ST
WYLEU ST
STONDON PK
GLADIATOR ST
CODRINGTON HILL
GLENGALL CT
BANKHURST RD
TINA CT
COLIN CT
IONA CL
Pav
Holbeach Prim Sch
Bwg Gn
Tenn Cts
CABRIEL ST
ACKROYD RD
DUNCOMBE HILL
B218
RAVENSBOURNE
CHILTHORNE
Crem

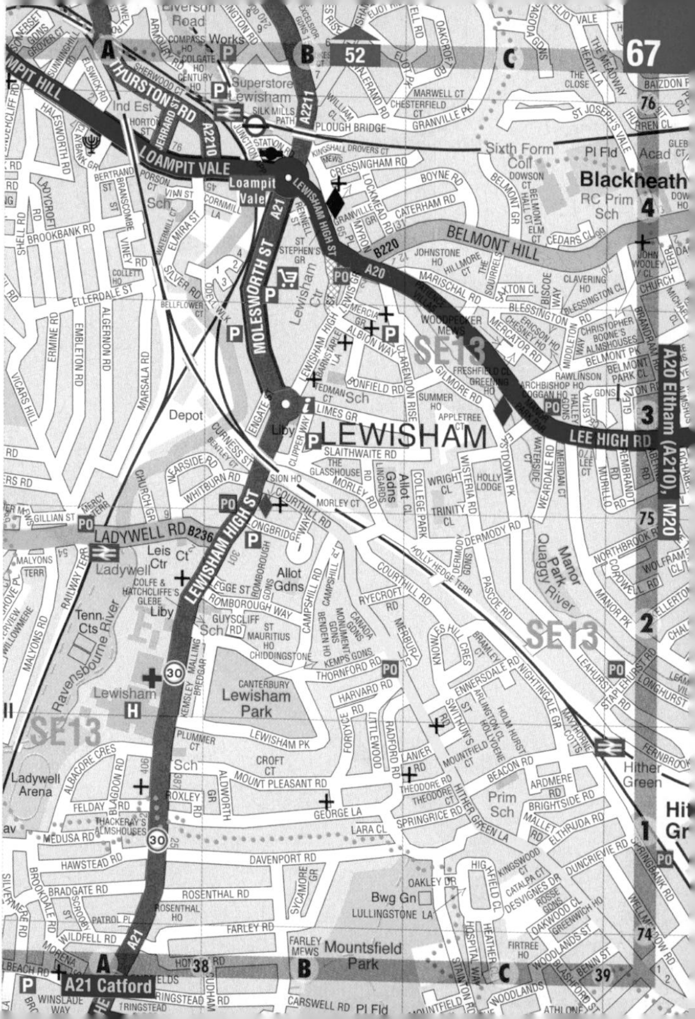
52
A
B
C
LOAMPIT HILL
THURSTON RD
LOAMPIT VALE
Loampit Vale
Lewisham
Superstore
Ind Est
JERRARD ST
A2210
A2211
PLOUGH BRIDGE
STATION RD
SILK MILLS PATH
JUNCTION APP
COMPASS HO
COLGATE HO
CENTURY HO
Works
Road
ARMOURY RD
SHERWOOD CT
HORTON ST
ELSWICK RD
SOMERSET GDNS
GROVER CT
SUNNINGHILL RD
HALESWORTH RD
CLAYBANK GR
LADYCROFT RD
BROOKBANK RD
SHELL RD
BERTRAND ST
BRANSCOMBE ST
PORSON CT
VIAN ST
Sch
CORNMILL LA
ELMIRA ST
WATERMILL CT
VINEY RD
COLLETT HO
ELLERDALE ST
SILVER RD
ODELL WLK
BELLFLOWER CT
ERMINE RD
EMBLETON RD
ALGERNON RD
MARSALA RD
VICARS HILL
Depot
MOLESWORTH ST
A21
RENNELL ST
ST STEPHEN'S GR
Lewisham Ctr
LEWISHAM HIGH ST
LEWIS GR
MERCIA GR
ALBION WAY
BARNSTAPLE LA
TEDMAN CT
Sch
BONFIELD RD
LIMES GR
ENGATE ST
Liby
CLIPPER WAY
LEWISHAM
SLAITHWAITE RD
THE GLASSHOUSE
MORLEY RD
LINGARDS RD
Allot Gdns
COLLEGE PARK CL
WRIGHT CL
TRINITY CL
WISTERIA RD
HOLLY LODGE
EASTDOWN PK
CURNESS ST
BENTLEY CT
WEARSIDE RD
WHITBURN RD
CHURCH GR
GILLIAN ST
MERCY TERR
LADYWELL RD
B236
PO
LEWISHAM HIGH ST
LONGBRIDGE WAY
COURTHILL RD
MORLEY CT
Leis Ctr
Ladywell
COLFE & HATCHCLIFFE'S GLEBE
Liby
MALYONS TERR
RAILWAY TERR
Tenn Cts
Ravensbourne River
LEGGE ST
ROMBOROUGH GDNS
ROMBOROUGH WAY
Allot Gdns
CAMPSHILL RD
CAMPSHILL PL
GUYSCLIFF RD
Sch
ST MAURITIUS HO
CHIDDINGSTONE
BENDEN HO
MONUMENT GDNS
CANADA GDNS
KEMPS GDNS
THORNFORD RD
CANTERBURY
Lewisham Park
KEMSLEY
MALLING
BREDGAR
Lewisham
H
SE13
MALYONS RD
WILLOWMERE
Ladywell Arena
ALBACORE CRES
BLAGDON RD
PLUMMER CT
LEWISHAM PK
Sch
CROFT CT
ROXLEY RD
ALDWORTH GR
MOUNT PLEASANT RD
FELDAY RD
THACKERAY'S ALMSHOUSES
GEORGE LA
LARA CL
MEDUSA RD
HAWSTEAD RD
DAVENPORT RD
SYCAMORE GR
BRADGATE RD
ROSENTHAL RD
ROSENTHAL HO
BROOKDALE RD
SILVERMERE RD
SCROOBY ST
PATROL PL
WILDFELL RD
FARLEY RD
MORENA ST
A21 Catford
BEACH RD
WINSLADE WAY
RINGSTEAD RD
38
FARLEY MEWS
Mountsfield Park
Bwg Gn
OAKLEY DR
LULLINGSTONE LA
CARSWELL RD
Pl Fld
HARVARD RD
FORDYCE RD
LITTLEWOOD
RADFORD RD
LANIER RD
THEODORE RD
THEODORE CT
SPRINGRICE RD
MERBURY CL
RYECROFT RD
KNOWLES HILL CRES
BRAMLEY CT
ENNERSDALE RD
ST SWITHUN'S RD
ARLINGTON CL
HOLLYDENE
HOLM HURST
NIGHTINGALE GR
MOUNTFIELD CT
BEACON RD
Prim Sch
HITHER GREEN LA
ARDMERE RD
BRIGHTSIDE RD
MALLET RD
ELTHRUDA RD
HIGHFIELD CL
KINGSWOOD CT
CATALPA CT
DESVIGNES DR
ROSSE GDNS
OAKWOOD CL
GREENWICH HO
HOSPITAL WAY
HEATHER RD
FIRTREE HO
WOODLANDS ST
BLASHFORD ST
BENIN ST
WOODLANDS
STAINTON RD
39
DUNCRIEVIE RD
SPRINGBANK RD
WELLMEADOW RD
74
MAYHORNE COTTS
Hither Green
FERNBROOK
HOLLY HEDGE TERR
COURTHILL RD
PASCOE RD
DERMODY RD
DERMODY GDNS
Manor Park
Quaggy River
SE13
LEAHURST RD
STAPLEHURST RD
LONGHURST
MANOR PK
NORTHBROOK RD
CORDWELL RD
WOLFRAM CL
ELLERTON
75
2
1
3
4
LEE HIGH RD
A20 Eltham (A210), M20
WEARDALE RD
MERIDIAN CT
WATERSIDE CT
MURILLO RD
REMBRANDT RD
LEE CT
HALLEY GDNS
GLENTON RD
RAWLINSON HO
ARCHBISHOP COGGAN HO
MANOR PARK PDE
FRESHFIELD CL
GREENING HO
GILMORE RD
SUMMER HO
APPLETREE CL
WOODPECKER MEWS
MERCATOR RD
ERICSON HO
CHESNEY HO
MIDDLETON WAY
BLESSINGTON RD
BLESSINGTON CL
CHRISTOPHER BOONE'S ALMSHOUSES
BELMONT PK
BELMONT PARK CL
MARISCHAL RD
PATIENCE VILLAS
JOHNSTONE HO
HILLMORE CT
THE SQUIRRELS
SAXTON CL
BISCOE WAY
CLAVERING HO
CHURCH
BRANDRAM RD
BELMONT HILL
B220
A20
CEDARS CL
BELMONT GR
DOWSON CT
BELMONT HALL CT
ELM CT
Sixth Form Coll
Blackheath RC Prim Sch
Pl Fld
Acad
JOHN WOOLEY CL
CARSWELL
GRANVILLE PK
GRANVILLE GR
MYRON PL
LOCKMEAD RD
CATERHAM RD
BOYNE RD
CRESSINGHAM RD
KINGSHALL MEWS
DROVERS CT
MARWELL CT
CHESTERFIELD CT
ELIOT PK
WILLIAM CL
OAKCROFT RD
PAGODA GDNS
ELIOT VALE
HEATH LA
THE MEADWAY
THE CLOSE
ST JOSEPH'S VALE
BAIZDON RD
76
Blackheath
EXCELSIOR GDNS
CLARENDON RISE
SION HO
SE13

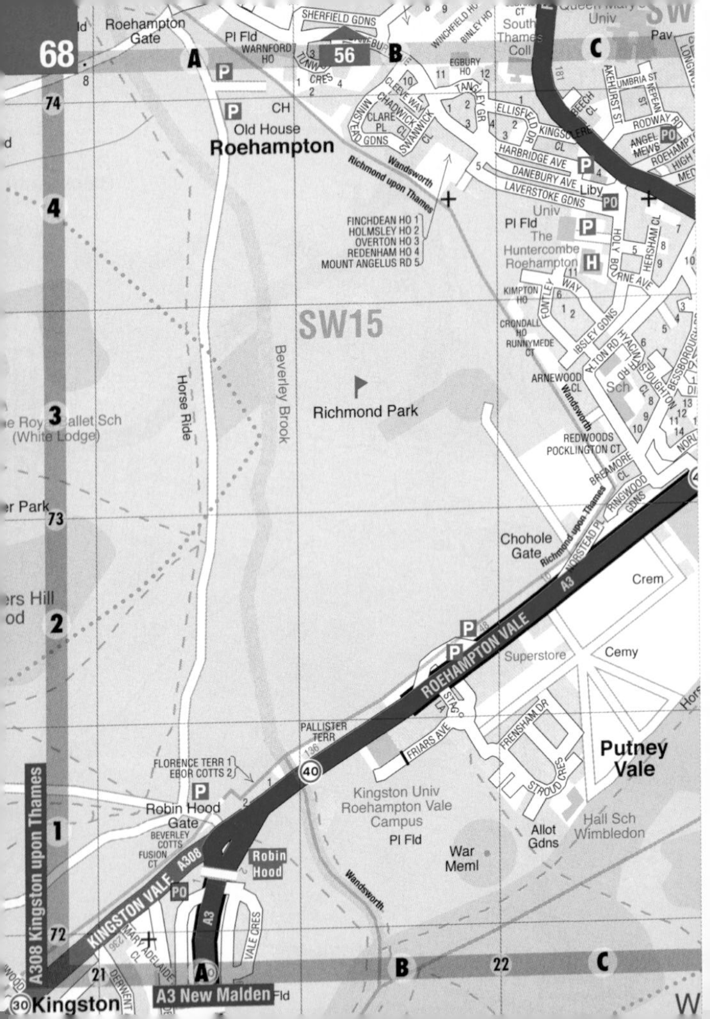
Roehampton Gate
Pl Fld
WARNFORD HO
SHERFIELD GDNS
56
A
B
C
WINCHFIELD HO
BINLEY HO
South Thames Coll
Queen Mary's Univ
Pav
SW
74
8
CRES
EGBURY HO
CH
Old House
Roehampton
CLEEVE WAY
CHADWICK PL
CLARE CL
MINSTEAD GDNS
SWANWICK CL
TANGLEY GR
ELLISFIELD DR
KINGSCLERE CL
BEECH CL
AKEHURST ST
UMBRIA ST
NEPEAN ST
RODWAY RD
ANGEL MEWS
ROEHAMPTON HIGH ST
PO
HARBRIDGE AVE
DANEBURY AVE
LAVERSTOKE GDNS
Liby
Wandsworth
Richmond upon Thames
Univ
Pl Fld
The Huntercombe Roehampton
H
HOLYBOURNE AVE
HERSHAM CL
FINCHDEAN HO 1
HOLMSLEY HO 2
OVERTON HO 3
REDENHAM HO 4
MOUNT ANGELUS RD 5
KIMPTON HO
FONTLEY WAY
CRONDALL HO
RUNNYMEDE CT
IBSLEY GDNS
ALTON RD
HYACINTH RD
STOUGHTON CL
BESSBOROUGH RD
ARNEWOOD CL
Sch
SW15
4
Beverley Brook
Horse Ride
Richmond Park
3
Royal Ballet Sch (White Lodge)
REDWOODS
POCKLINGTON CT
BREAMORE CL
RINGWOOD GDNS
Park
73
Chohole Gate
NORSTEAD PL
A3
Crem
ers Hill od
2
ROEHAMPTON VALE
Superstore
Cemy
STAG LA
FRENSHAM DR
PALLISTER TERR
FRIARS AVE
FLORENCE TERR 1
EBOR COTTS 2
136
40
STROUD CRES
Putney Vale
Kingston Univ Roehampton Vale Campus
Pl Fld
Robin Hood Gate
1
BEVERLEY COTTS
FUSION CT
A308
Robin Hood
War Meml
Allot Gdns
Hall Sch Wimbledon
Wandsworth
A308 Kingston upon Thames
KINGSTON VALE
72
MARY ADELAIDE CL
VALE CRES
21
22
DERWENT
A3 New Malden
30 Kingston
Fld

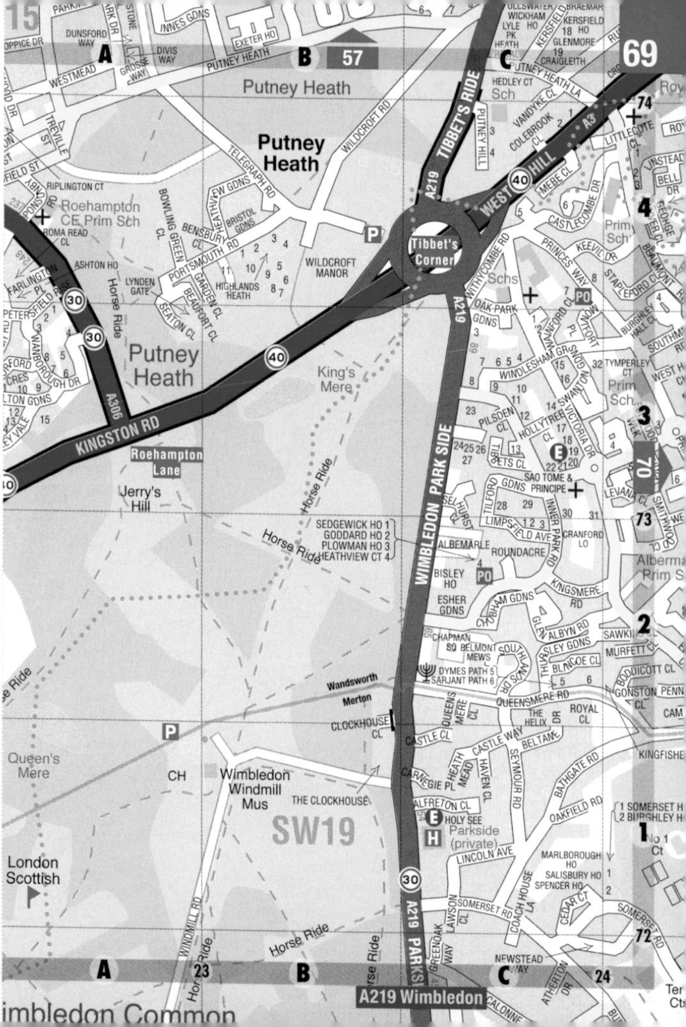

Putney Heath
Putney Heath
Putney Heath
Tibbet's Corner
TIBBET'S RIDE
WEST HILL
A3
A219
KINGSTON RD
A306
WIMBLEDON PARK SIDE
Roehampton CE Prim Sch
Roehampton Lane
Jerry's Hill
King's Mere
Horse Ride
WILDCROFT MANOR
WILDCROFT RD
TELEGRAPH RD
PORTSMOUTH RD
HIGHLANDS HEATH
BOWLING GREEN CL
LYNDEN GATE
SEATON CL
BEAUFORT CL
GARDEN CL
BENSBURY CL
BRISTOL GDNS
HEATHVIEW GDNS
RIPLINGTON CT
ROMA READ CL
ASHTON HO
FARLINGTON PL
PETERSFIELD RISE
WANBOROUGH DR
PUTNEY HEATH
PUTNEY HEATH LA
WESTMEAD
DUNSFORD WAY
GROSSE WAY
DIVIS WAY
INNES GDNS
EXETER HO
TREVILLE ST
HEDLEY CT
PUTNEY HILL
VANDYKE CL
COLEBROOK CL
LITTLECOTE CL
MERE CL
CASTLECOMBE DR
PRINCES WAY
KEEVIL DR
STAPLEFORD CL
WITHYCOMBE RD
OAK PARK GDNS
WAINFORD CL
WINDLESHAM GR
SWANTON GDNS
VICTORIA DR
HOLLYTREE CL
PILSDEN CL
TIBBETS CL
TILFORD GDNS
SAO TOME & PRINCIPE
INNER PARK RD
LIMPSFIELD AVE
CRANFORD LO
ALBEMARLE
ROUNDACRE
BISLEY HO
ESHER GDNS
KINGSMERE RD
CHOBHAM GDNS
GLEN ALBYN RD
THURSLEY GDNS
BLINCOE CL
SAWKINS CL
MURFETT CL
BODDICOTT CL
GONSTON CL
CHAPMAN SQ
BELMONT MEWS
SOUTHLANDS DR
DYMES PATH 5
SARJANT PATH 6
QUEENSMERE RD
QUEENS MERE CL
THE HELIX
ROYAL CL
CASTLE CL
CASTLE WAY
BELTANE DR
KINGFISHER
BATHGATE RD
HEATH MEAD
HAVEN CL
SEYMOUR RD
CARNEGIE PL
ALFRETON CL
HOLY SEE
Parkside (private)
OAKFIELD RD
1 SOMERSET H
2 BURGHLEY H
LINCOLN AVE
MARLBOROUGH HO
SALISBURY HO
SPENCER HO
CEDAR CT
SOMERSET RD
COACH HOUSE LA
LAWSON CL
GREENOAK WAY
NEWSTEAD WAY
ATHERTON DR
CALONNE
SEDGEWICK HO 1
GODDARD HO 2
PLOWMAN HO 3
HEATHVIEW CT 4
Wandsworth
Merton
CLOCKHOUSE CL
THE CLOCKHOUSE
Wimbledon Windmill Mus
CH
Queen's Mere
SW19
London Scottish
WINDMILL RD
A219 Wimbledon
Wimbledon Common
57
70

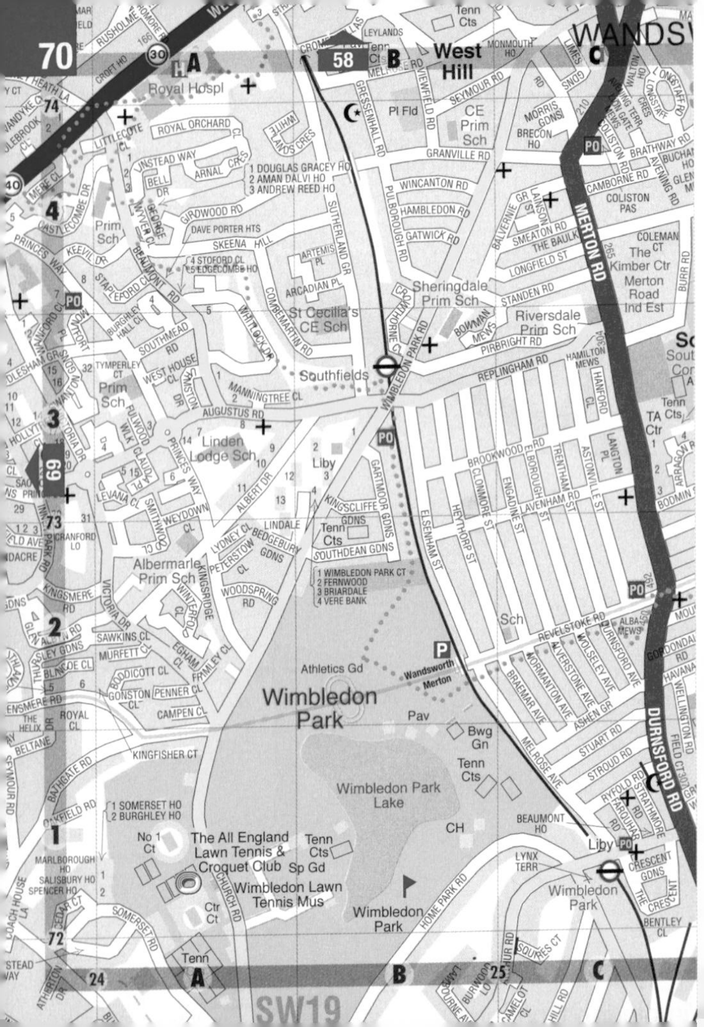
WANDSW
West Hill
58
69
A
B
C
1
2
3
4
Royal Hospl
ROYAL ORCHARD CL
LITTLECOTE CL
UNSTEAD WAY
BELL DR
ARNAL CRES
1 DOUGLAS GRACEY HO
2 AMAN DALVI HO
3 ANDREW REED HO
WHITELANDS CRES
GRESSENHALL RD
MELROSE RD
LEYLANDS
VIEWFIELD RD
SEYMOUR RD
Pl Fld
CE Prim Sch
MONMOUTH HO
LIMES GDNS
MORRIS GDNS
BRECON HO
GRANVILLE RD
WINCANTON RD
HAMBLEDON RD
GATWICK RD
PULBOROUGH RD
SUTHERLAND GR
GIRDWOOD RD
DAVE PORTER HTS
SKEENA HILL
ARTEMIS PL
ARCADIAN PL
4 STOFORD CL
5 EDGECOMBE HO
COMBEMARTIN RD
WHITLOCK DR
St Cecilia's CE Sch
CASTLECOMBE DR
PRINCES WAY
KEEVIL DR
STAPLEFORD CL
BEAUMONT RD
WYVERN CL
GEORGE
BURGHLEY HALL CL
SOUTHMEAD RD
WEST HOUSE CL
TYMPERLEY CT
Prim Sch
MANNINGTREE CL
AUGUSTUS RD
Southfields
WIMBLEDON PARK RD
Sheringdale Prim Sch
Riversdale Prim Sch
BOWMAN MEWS
PIRBRIGHT RD
STANDEN RD
LONGFIELD ST
THE BAULK
SMEATON RD
BALVERNIE GR
LAINSON ST
MERTON RD
The Kimber Ctr
Merton Road Ind Est
COLEMAN CT
BURR RD
COLISTON PAS
CAMBORNE RD
BRATHWAY RD
REPLINGHAM RD
HAMILTON MEWS
HANFORD CL
Tenn Cts
TA Ctr
Linden Lodge Sch
Liby
ALBERT DR
KINGSCLIFFE GDNS
GARTMOOR GDNS
BROOKWOOD RD
CLONMORE ST
ELBOROUGH ST
TRENTHAM ST
ENGADINE ST
ASTONVILLE ST
LANGTON PL
LAVENHAM RD
ELSENHAM ST
HEYTHORP ST
LINDALE
SOUTHDEAN GDNS
BEDGEBURY GDNS
LYDNEY CL
PETERSTOW CL
WOODSPRING RD
1 WIMBLEDON PARK CT
2 FERNWOOD
3 BRIARDALE
4 VERE BANK
Albermarle Prim Sch
KINGSRIDGE
WINTERFOLD CL
KINGSMERE RD
VICTORIA DR
WEYDOWN CL
SMITHWOOD CL
LEVANA CL
INNER PARK RD
CRANFORD LO
SAWKINS CL
MURFETT CL
EGHAM CL
FRIMLEY CL
BODDICOTT CL
GONSTON CL
PENNER CL
CAMPEN CL
ROYAL CL
THE HELIX
BELTANE DR
KINGFISHER CT
BATHGATE RD
OAKFIELD RD
1 SOMERSET HO
2 BURGHLEY HO
MARLBOROUGH HO
SALISBURY HO
SPENCER HO
CEDAR CT
SOMERSET RD
COACH HOUSE LA
ATHERTON DR
Athletics Gd
Wimbledon Park
Wandsworth
Merton
Pav
Bwg Gn
Sch
REVELSTOKE RD
ALBA MEWS
DURNSFORD AVE
WOLSELEY AVE
ALVERSTONE AVE
NORMANTON AVE
BRAEMAR AVE
ASHEN GR
STUART RD
STROUD RD
MELROSE AVE
RYFOLD RD
FARQUHAR RD
STRATHMORE RD
DURNSFORD RD
GORDONDALE RD
HAVANA RD
WELLINGTON RD
Wimbledon Park Lake
CH
BEAUMONT HO
LYNX TERR
CRESCENT GDNS
THE CRESCENT
BENTLEY CL
No 1 Ct
The All England Lawn Tennis & Croquet Club
Sp Gd
Wimbledon Lawn Tennis Mus
Ctr Ct
CHURCH RD
HOME PARK RD
ARTHUR RD
SQUIRES CT
BURWOOD LO
CAMELOT CL
HILL RD
24
25
72
73
74
SW19

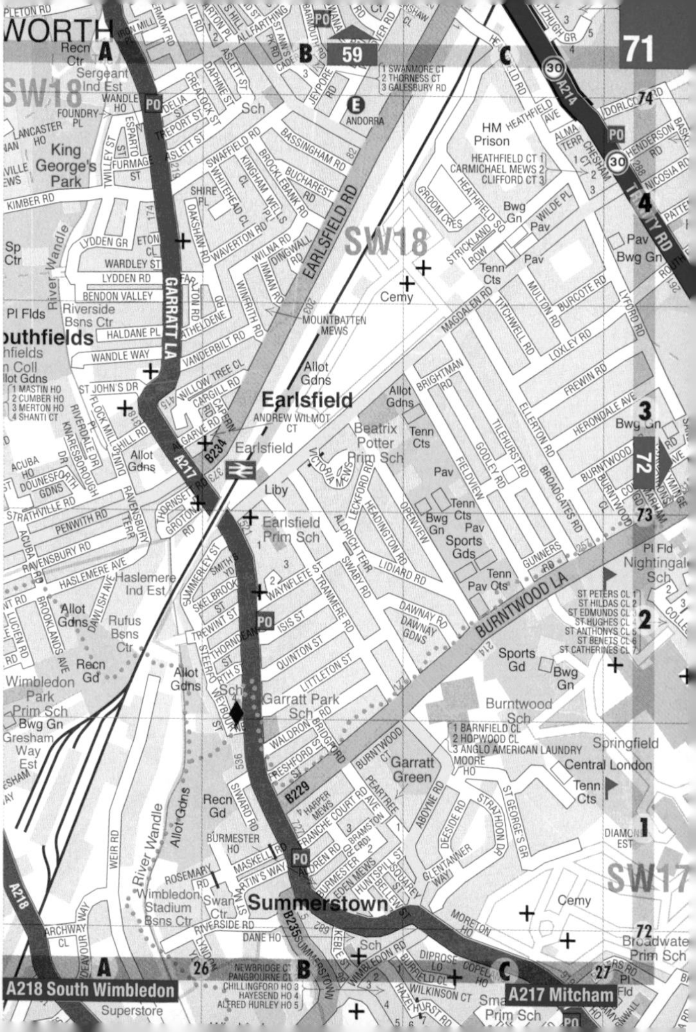

WORTH
SW18
King George's Park
Earlsfield
Southfields
Summerstown
GARRATT LA
EARLSFIELD RD
BURNTWOOD LA
HM Prison
Cemy
Beatrix Potter Prim Sch
Earlsfield Prim Sch
Garratt Park Sch
Burntwood Sch
Springfield
Garratt Green
Wimbledon Park Prim Sch
Wimbledon Stadium Bsns Ctr
River Wandle
SW17
A218 South Wimbledon
A217 Mitcham
59
72
26
27

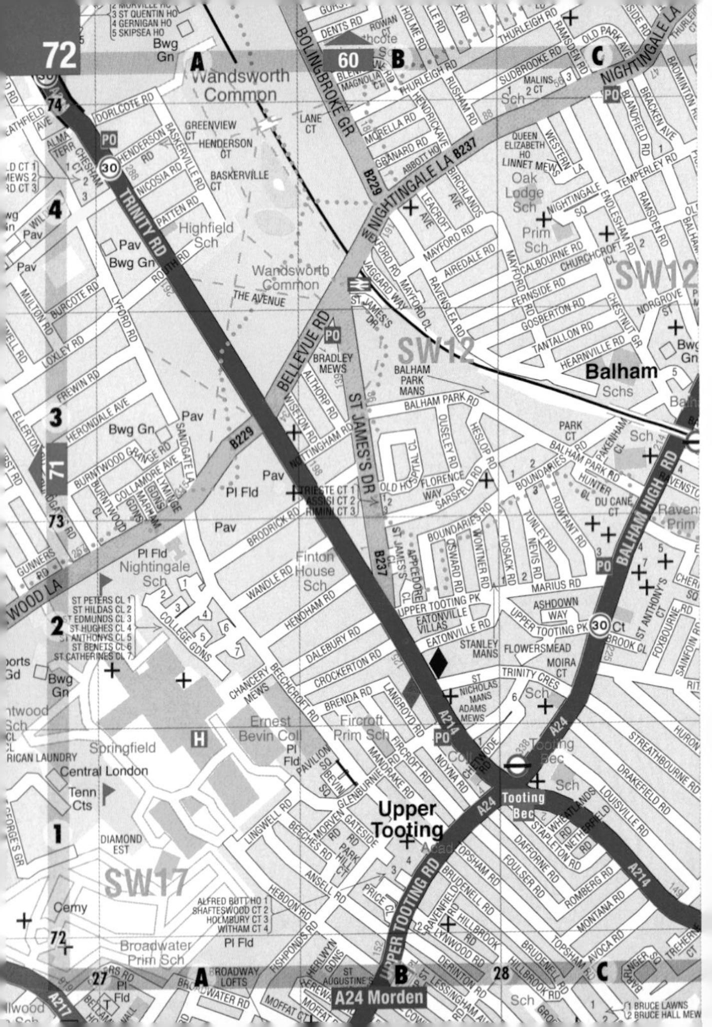

Wandsworth Common
BOLINGBROKE GR
60
NIGHTINGALE LA
TRINITY RD
BELLEVUE RD
ST JAMES'S DR
BALHAM HIGH RD
UPPER TOOTING RD
SW12
SW17
Balham
Upper Tooting
Tooting Bec
Springfield
Central London
Nightingale Sch
Highfield Sch
Oak Lodge Sch
Finton House Sch
Ernest Bevin Coll
Fircroft Prim Sch
Broadwater Prim Sch
Cemy
DIAMOND EST
71
A24 Morden
27
28
A
B
C
1
2
3
4

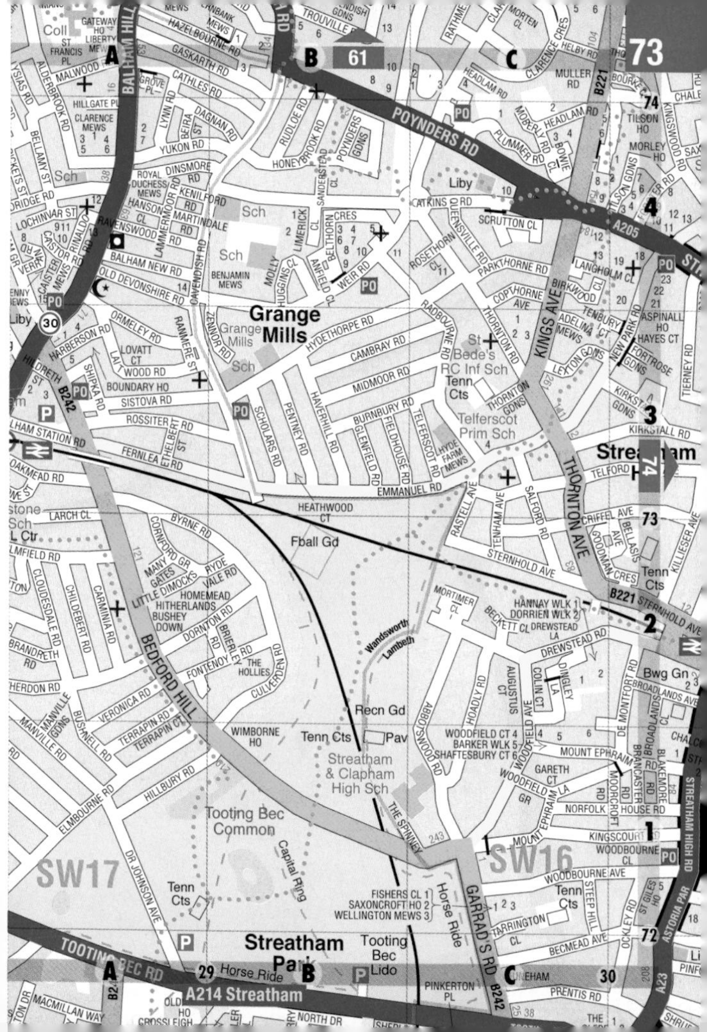
Grange Mills
Streatham
Streatham Park
Tooting Bec Common
SW17
SW16
Streatham & Clapham High Sch
Telferscot Prim Sch
St Bede's RC Inf Sch
Tooting Bec Lido
Capital Ring
Wandsworth
Lambeth
Horse Ride
Fball Gd
Recn Gd
Tenn Cts
Pav
Liby
Sch
PO
61
74
72
30
29
BALHAM HILL
POYNDERS RD
A205
KINGS AVE
THORNTON AVE
B221 STERNHOLD AVE
BEDFORD HILL
B242
GARRAD'S RD
TOOTING BEC RD
A214 Streatham
STREATHAM HIGH RD
A23
ASTORIA PAR
HAZELBOURNE RD
GASKARTH RD
CATHLES RD
DAGNAN RD
YUKON RD
LYNN RD
BEIRA ST
HILLGATE PL
CLARENCE MEWS
ALDERBROOK RD
MALWOOD RD
BELLAMY ST
ROYAL DUCHESS MEWS
DINSMORE RD
KENILFORD RD
HANSON CL
MARTINDALE RD
LAMMERMOOR RD
CAVENDISH RD
RAVENSWOOD RD
BALHAM NEW RD
OLD DEVONSHIRE RD
BENJAMIN MEWS
MOLLY HUGGINS CL
ANFIELD CL
WEIR RD
BELTHORN CRES
LIMERICK CL
SANDERSTEAD CL
HONEYBROOK RD
RUDLOE RD
POYNDERS GDNS
TROUVILLE RD
ATKINS RD
QUEENSVILLE RD
SCRUTTON CL
ROSETHORN CL
PARKTHORNE RD
COPTHORNE AVE
RADBOURNE RD
THORNTON RD
THORNTON GDNS
HEADLAM RD
MOBERLY RD
PLUMMER RD
BOWIE CL
CLARENCE CRES
HELBY RD
MULLER RD
TILSON HO
TILSON GDNS
MORLEY HO
KINGSWOOD RD
LANGHOLM CL
BIRKWOOD CL
ADELINA MEWS
TENBURY CT
LEYTON GDNS
NEW PARK RD
FORTROSE GDNS
ASPINALL HO
HAYES CT
TIERNEY RD
KIRKSTALL GDNS
KIRKSTALL RD
TELFORD RD
CRIFFEL AVE
BELLASIS AVE
GOODMAN CRES
KILLIESER AVE
HYDETHORPE RD
CAMBRAY RD
MIDMOOR RD
BURNBURY RD
TELFERSCOT RD
FIELDHOUSE RD
GLENFIELD RD
HYDE FARM MEWS
EMMANUEL RD
HEATHWOOD CT
SCHOLARS RD
PENTNEY RD
HAVERHILL RD
ZENNOR RD
RANMERE ST
ORMELEY RD
LOVATT CT
WOOD RD
HARBERSON RD
SHIPKA RD
BOUNDARY HO
SISTOVA RD
ROSSITER RD
ETHELBERT ST
FERNLEA RD
HILDRETH ST
BALHAM STATION RD
OAKMEAD RD
LARCH CL
ELMFIELD RD
BYRNE RD
CORNFORD GR
MANY GATES
LITTLE DIMOCKS
RYDE VALE RD
HOMEMEAD
HITHERLANDS
BUSHEY DOWN
DORNTON RD
BRIERLEY RD
FONTENOY RD
THE HOLLIES
CULVERDEN RD
CLOUDESDALE RD
CHILDEBERT RD
CARMINIA RD
BRANDRETH RD
VERONICA RD
TERRAPIN RD
TERRAPIN CT
MANVILLE GDNS
MANVILLE RD
BUSHNELL RD
HILLBURY RD
ELMBOURNE RD
WIMBORNE HO
DR JOHNSON AVE
RASTELL AVE
TENHAM AVE
SALFORD RD
STERNHOLD AVE
MORTIMER CL
BECKETT CL
HANNAY WLK 1
DORRIEN WLK 2
DREWSTEAD LA
DREWSTEAD RD
DINGLEY LA
COLIN CT
AUGUSTUS CT
HOADLY RD
ABBOTSWOOD RD
WOODFIELD AVE
WOODFIELD CT 4
BARKER WLK 5
SHAFTESBURY CT 6
GARETH CT
WOODFIELD GR
MOUNT EPHRAIM LA
MOUNT EPHRAIM RD
NORFOLK HOUSE RD
MOORCROFT RD
BRANCASTER RD
BLAKEMORE RD
BROADLANDS AVE
DE MONTFORT RD
Bwg Gn
KINGSCOURT RD
WOODBOURNE CL
WOODBOURNE AVE
STEEP HILL
OCKLEY RD
ST GILES HO
THE SPINNEY
FISHERS CL 1
SAXONCROFT HO 2
WELLINGTON MEWS 3
TARRINGTON CL
BECMEAD AVE
PINKERTON PL
PRENTIS RD
NORTH DR
MACMILLAN WAY
OLD HO

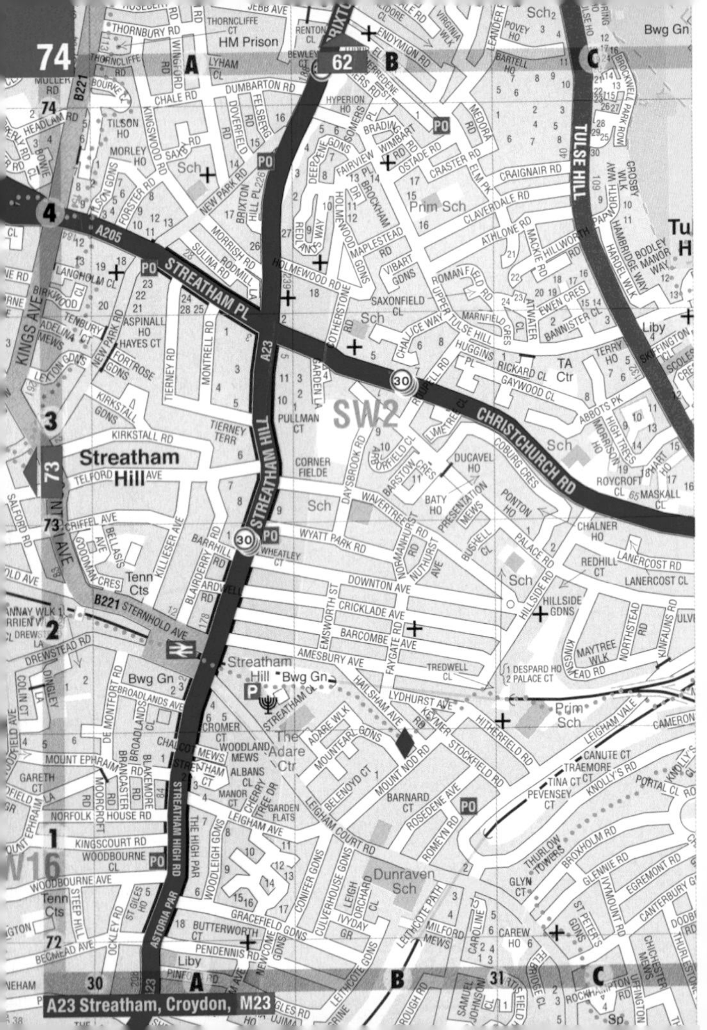

74
62
73
72
A
B
C
1
2
3
4
30
31
SW2
HM Prison
Streatham Hill
Streatham Hill
A23 Streatham, Croydon, M23
A205
A23
B221
STREATHAM PL
STREATHAM HILL
CHRISTCHURCH RD
TULSE HILL
STREATHAM HIGH RD
KINGS AVE
STERNHOLD AVE
THORNBURY RD
THORNCLIFFE CT
THORNCLIFFE RD
WINGFORD RD
LYHAM CL
RENTON CL
BEWLEY CT
ENDYMION RD
LEANDER RD
POVEY HO
BARTELL HO
Bwg Gn
MULLER RD
BOURKE CL
DUMBARTON RD
CHALE RD
FELSBERG RD
DOVERFIELD RD
HYPERION HO
BRADING RD
WIMBART RD
OSTADE RD
MEDORA RD
HEADLAM RD
TILSON HO
TILSON GDNS
MORLEY HO
KINGSWOOD RD
SAXBY RD
NEW PARK RD
BRIXTON HILL PL
DEEPDENE GDNS
FAIRVIEW PL
HOLMEWOOD RD
BROCKHAM DR
CRASTER RD
CRAIGNAIR RD
ELM PK
CLAVERDALE RD
Prim Sch
Sch
PO
FORSTER RD
MORRISH RD
SULINA RD
RODMILL LA
REDLANDS WAY
HOLMEWOOD GDNS
MAPLESTEAD RD
ATHLONE RD
MACKIE RD
HILLWORTH RD
PAPWORTH WAY
HAMBRIDGE WAY
HARDEL WLK
CROSBY WLK
BODLEY MANOR WAY
LANGHOLM CL
BIRKWOOD CL
TENBURY CT
ADELINA MEWS
ASPINALL HO
HAYES CT
NEW PARK RD
FORTROSE GDNS
LEXTON GDNS
VIBART GDNS
SAXONFIELD CL
ROMAN FIELD RD
UPPER TULSE HILL
MARNFIELD CRES
ATWATER CL
EWEN CRES
BANNISTER CL
CHALLICE WAY
HUGGINS PL
RICKARD CL
GAYWOOD CL
TA Ctr
Liby
TERRY HO
SKIFFINGTON CL
SCOLES CRES
ABBOTS PK
MORRISON HO
HIGH TREES
HART HO
ROYCROFT CL
MASKALL CL
TIERNEY RD
MONTRELL RD
COTHERSTONE RD
GARDEN LA
PULLMAN CT
CORNER FIELDE
DAYSBROOK RD
ARDFIELD CL
BARSTOW CRES
ELMTREE CL
DUCAVEL HO
COBURG CRES
PONTON HO
BATY HO
PRESENTATION MEWS
KIRKSTALL GDNS
KIRKSTALL RD
TIERNEY TERR
TELFORD AVE
CRIFFEL AVE
BELLASIS AVE
GOODMAN CRES
KILLIESER AVE
Tenn Cts
SALFORD RD
WAVERTREE RD
NORMANHURST RD
NUTHURST AVE
BUSHELL CL
PALACE RD
CHALNER HO
LANERCOST RD
LANERCOST CL
REDHILL CT
HILLSIDE RD
HILLSIDE GDNS
BARRHILL RD
BLAIRDERRY RD
ARDWELL RD
WYATT PARK RD
WHEATLEY CT
DOWNTON AVE
CRICKLADE AVE
BARCOMBE AVE
AMESBURY AVE
EMSWORTH ST
FAYGATE RD
TREDWELL CL
1 DESPARD HO
2 PALACE CT
KINGSMEAD RD
MAYTREE WLK
NORTHSTEAD RD
KINFAUNS RD
DREWSTEAD RD
DINGLEY LA
COLIN CT
DE MONTFORT RD
BROADLANDS AVE
BROADLANDS
HAILSHAM AVE
LYDHURST AVE
KEYMER RD
HITHERFIELD RD
LEIGHAM VALE
CAMERON
CROMER CT
CHALCOT MEWS
WOODLAND MEWS
STREATHAM CL
ADARE WLK
The Adare Ctr
MOUNTEARL GDNS
MOUNT EPHRAIM RD
GARETH CT
BRANCASTER RD
BLAKEMORE RD
MOORCROFT RD
STREATHAM CT
ALBANS CL
MANOR CT
CHERRY TREE DR
GARDEN FLATS
BELENOYD CT
MOUNT NOD RD
STOCKFIELD RD
BARNARD CT
CANUTE CT
TRAEMORE CT
TINA CT
PEVENSEY CT
KNOLLY'S RD
PORTAL CL
NORFOLK HOUSE RD
KINGSCOURT RD
WOODBOURNE CL
WOODBOURNE AVE
LEIGHAM AVE
LEIGHAM COURT RD
ROSEDENE AVE
ROMEYN RD
THURLOW TOWERS
BROXHOLM RD
GLENNIE RD
EGREMONT RD
CANTERBURY GROVE
THE HIGH PAR
WOODLEIGH GDNS
CONIFER GDNS
CULVERHOUSE GDNS
LEIGH ORCHARD CL
Dunraven Sch
LEITHCOTE PATH
CAROLINE CL
GLYN CT
ST PETER'S GDNS
AMMOUNT RD
CHICHESTER MEWS
THURLESTONE RD
STEEP HILL
OCKLEY RD
ST GILES HO
ASTORIA PAR
GRACEFIELD GDNS
IVYDAY GR
MILFORD MEWS
CAREW HO
FELBRIDGE CL
BUTTERWORTH CT
PENDENNIS RD
NEWCOME GDNS
LEITHCOTE GDNS
BECMEAD AVE
PINFOLD RD
SAMUEL JOHNSON CL
ROCKHAMPTON RD
UFFINGTON RD
Sp

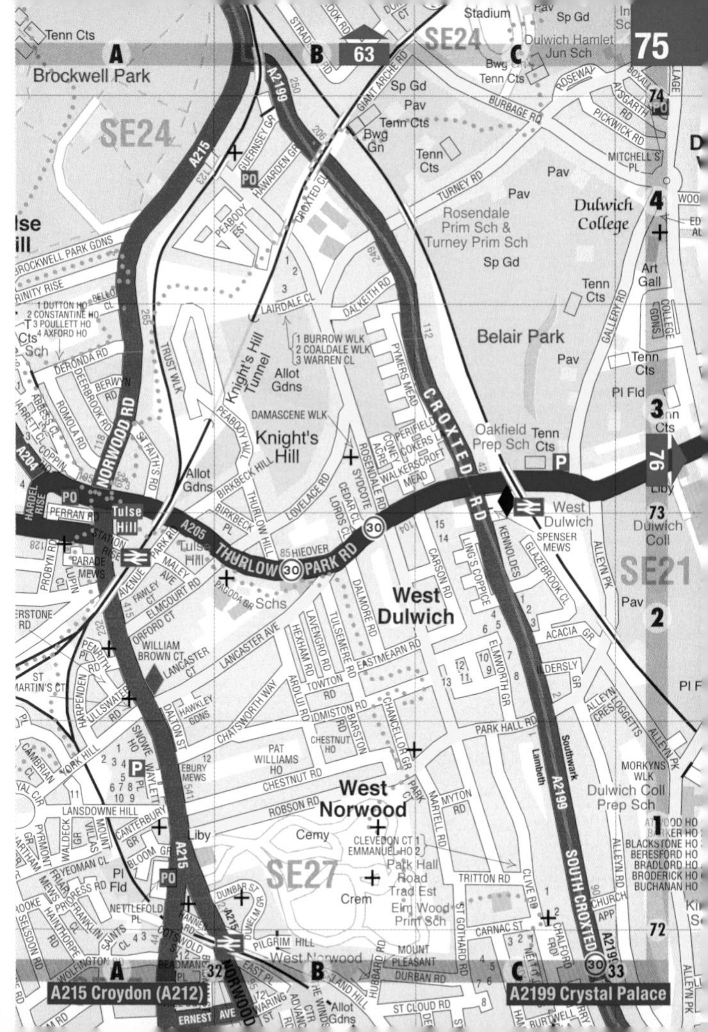
A
B
C
63
SE24
Tenn Cts
Brockwell Park
Stadium
Sp Gd
Dulwich Hamlet
Jun Sch
Bwg Gn
Tenn Cts
ROSEWAY
BOXALL RD
74
PO
AYSGARTH RD
PICKWICK RD
BURBAGE RD
GIANT ARCHE RD
Pav
Tenn Cts
Bwg Gn
Tenn Cts
MITCHELL'S PL
A215
A2199
GUERNSEY GR
HAWARDEN GR
CROXTED CL
PO
PEABODY EST
TURNEY RD
Pav
Pav
Dulwich College
4
Rosendale Prim Sch & Turney Prim Sch
Sp Gd
lse
ill
BROCKWELL PARK GDNS
TRINITY RISE
1 DUTTON HO
2 CONSTANTINE HO
3 POULLETT HO
4 AXFORD HO
BELLO CL
Cts
Sch
LAIRDALE CL
DALKEITH RD
Art Gall
Tenn Cts
GALLERY RD
COLLEGE GDNS
Belair Park
Pav
Tenn Cts
1 BURROW WLK
2 COALDALE WLK
3 WARREN CL
Knight's Hill Tunnel
Allot Gdns
DERONDA RD
DEERBROOK RD
BERWYN RD
ROMOLA RD
TRUST WLK
NORWOOD RD
PYMERS MEAD
CROXTED RD
Pl Fld
3
DAMASCENE WLK
Knight's Hill
PEABODY HILL
ST FAITH'S RD
COPPIN
A204
BIRKBECK HILL
Allot Gdns
SYDCOTE
ROSENDALE RD
CONEY ACRE
PERIFIELD
COKERS LA
WALKERSCROFT MEAD
Oakfield Prep Sch
Tenn Cts
P
76
Liby
HARDEL RISE
PO
PERRAN RD
Tulse Hill
A205
BIRKBECK PL
THURLOW HILL
LOVELACE RD
CEDAR CL
LORDS CL
30
West Dulwich
73
Dulwich Coll
STATION RISE
PARK RD
MALEY AVE
THURLOW PARK RD
HIEOVER
KENNOLDES
SPENSER MEWS
GLAZEBROOK CL
ALLEYN PK
SE21
PROBYN RD
LUPIN CL
PARADE MEWS
AVENUE
FAWLEY CT
ELMCOURT RD
PAGODA GR
Schs
CARSON RD
LING'S COPPICE
West Dulwich
Pav
2
ORFORD CT
WILLIAM BROWN CT
LANCASTER CT
LANCASTER AVE
HEXHAM RD
LAVENGRO RD
TULSEMERE RD
DALMORE RD
EASTMEARN RD
ACACIA GR
ST MARTIN'S CT
PENRITH PL
HARPENDEN RD
ULLSWATER RD
CHATSWORTH WAY
ARDLUI RD
TOWTON RD
ELMWORTH GR
ILDERSLY GR
ALLEYN CRES
LOGGETTS
Pl F
HAWKLEY GDNS
DALTON ST
IDMISTON RD
BARSTON RD
CHANCELLOR GR
PARK HALL RD
ALLEYN PK
CAMBRIAN CL
YORK HILL
P
SNOWE HO
WAYLETT PL
EBURY MEWS
PAT WILLIAMS HO
CHESTNUT HO
CHESTNUT RD
Lambeth
Southwark
MORKYNS WLK
Dulwich Coll Prep Sch
LANSDOWNE HILL
CANTERBURY GR
ROBSON RD
West Norwood
PARK CL
MARTELL RD
MYTON RD
1
ATWOOD HO
BARKER HO
BLACKSTONE HO
BERESFORD HO
BRADLORD HO
BRODERICK HO
BUCHANAN HO
WALDECK GR
VILLAS
MOUNT
YEOMAN CL
BLOOM GR
Liby
Cemy
CLEVEDON CT 1
EMMANUEL HO 2
SE27
Park Hall Road Trad Est
TRITTON RD
CLIVE RD
SOUTH CROXTED RD
ALLEYN RD
CHURCH APP
Pl Fld
PO
PRIORESS RD
FRIAR MEWS
DUNBAR ST
DUNELM GR
Crem
Elm Wood Prim Sch
ST GOTHARD RD
NETTLEFOLD PL
HANNEN RD
COTSWOLD ST
CARNAC ST
CHALFORD RD
72
SELSDON RD
HAINTHORPE RD
FRANKLIN CL
SAINTS CL
PILGRIM HILL
West Norwood
HUBBARD RD
MOUNT PLEASANT
DURBAN RD
BEADMANS PL
NORWOOD
EAST PL
32
33
A215 Croydon (A212)
A2199 Crystal Palace
ERNEST AVE
WARING ST
ST CLOUD RD
Allot Gdns
BURTWELL

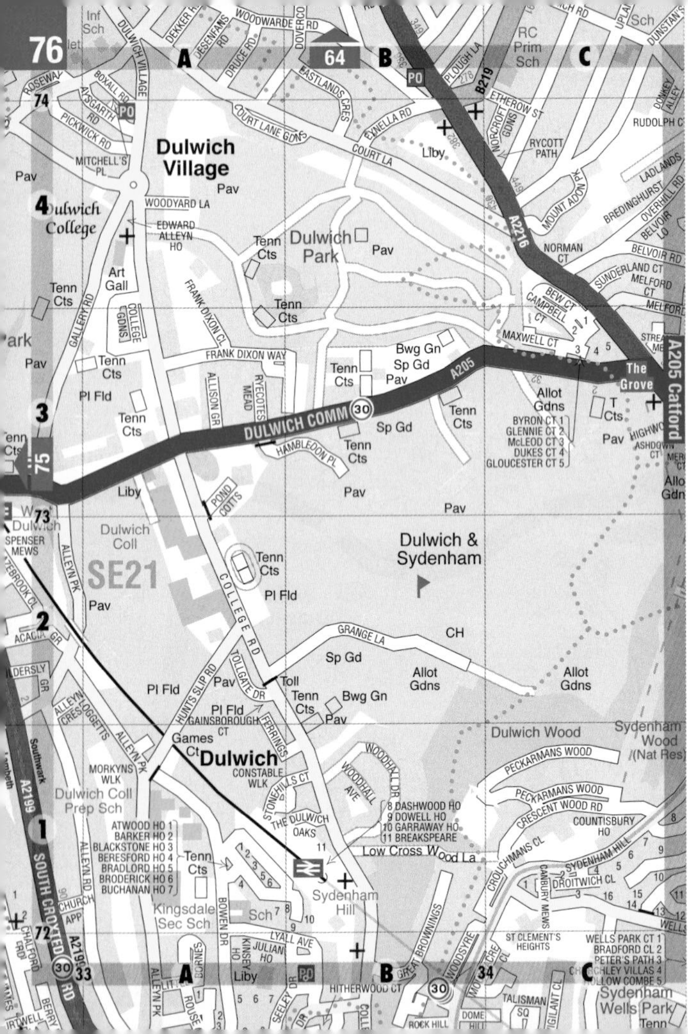

64
A
B
C
Dulwich Village
Dulwich College
Dulwich Park
Dulwich & Sydenham
SE21
Dulwich
Dulwich Wood
Sydenham Wood (Nat Res)
Sydenham Hill
Sydenham Wells Park
DULWICH COMM
A205
A205 Catford
A2216
B219
A2199
SOUTH CROXTED RD
COLLEGE RD
GRANGE LA
COURT LA
Low Cross Wood La
HUNTS SLIP RD
GALLERY RD
ALLEYN PK
ALLEYN RD
WOODWARDE RD
DEKKER RD
DESENFANS RD
DRUCE RD
DOVERCOURT RD
EASTLANDS CRES
COURT LANE GDNS
EYNELLA RD
PLOUGH LA
ETHEROW ST
NORCROFT GDNS
RYCOTT PATH
RUDOLPH CT
LADLANDS
BREDINGHURST
OVERHILL RD
BELVOIR LO
BELVOIR RD
MOUNT ADON PK
NORMAN CT
SUNDERLAND CT
MELFORD CT
BEW CT
CAMPBELL CT
MAXWELL CT
The Grove
BYRON CT 1
GLENNIE CT 2
McLEOD CT 3
DUKES CT 4
GLOUCESTER CT 5
HIGHWOOD
ASHDOWN CT
DULWICH VILLAGE
ROSEWAY
BOXALL RD
AYSGARTH RD
PICKWICK RD
MITCHELL'S PL
WOODYARD LA
EDWARD ALLEYN HO
COLLEGE GDNS
FRANK DIXON CL
FRANK DIXON WAY
ALLISON GR
RYECOTES MEAD
HAMBLEDON PL
POND COTTS
SPENSER MEWS
ACACIA GR
GREBROOK CL
ALLEYN CRES
LOGGETTS
TOLLGATE DR
GAINSBOROUGH CT
FERRINGS
CONSTABLE WLK
MORKYNS WLK
STONEHILLS CT
THE DULWICH OAKS
WOODHALL AVE
WOODHALL DR
8 DASHWOOD HO
9 DOWELL HO
10 GARRAWAY HO
11 BREAKSPEARE
ATWOOD HO 1
BARKER HO 2
BLACKSTONE HO 3
BERESFORD HO 4
BRADLORD HO 5
BRODERICK HO 6
BUCHANAN HO 7
PECKARMANS WOOD
CRESCENT WOOD RD
COUNTISBURY HO
CROUCHMANS CL
SYDENHAM HILL
CANBURY MEWS
DROITWICH CL
WELLS PARK CT 1
BRADFORD CL 2
PETER'S PATH 3
CHLEY VILLAS 4
LLOW COMBE 5
ST CLEMENT'S HEIGHTS
GREAT BROWNINGS
WOODSYRE
HITHERWOOD CT
LYALL AVE
JULIAN HO
KINSEY HO
BOWEN DR
BORNES
ROUSE
SEELEY DR
TALISMAN SQ
DOME HILL
ROCK HILL
GILANT CL
CHURCH APP
CHALFORD RD
BERRY
Kingsdale Sec Sch
Dulwich Coll Prep Sch
Dulwich Coll
Art Gall
RC Prim Sch
Inf Sch
Liby
PO
Pav
Tenn Cts
Pl Fld
Sp Gd
Bwg Gn
Allot Gdns
CH
Toll
Games Ct
Sch
75
73
74
72
33
34
30
1
2
3
4

Key to enlarged map pages

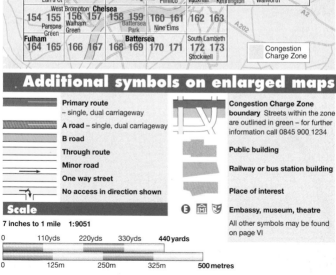

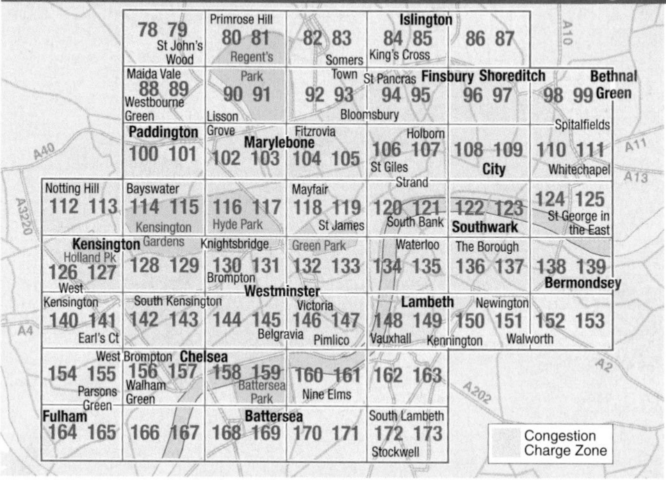

Additional symbols on enlarged maps

Primary route – single, dual carriageway

A road – single, dual carriageway

B road

Through route

Minor road

One way street

No access in direction shown

Congestion Charge Zone boundary Streets within the zone are outlined in green – for further information call 0845 900 1234

Public building

Railway or bus station building

Place of interest

Embassy, museum, theatre

All other symbols may be found on page VI

Scale

7 inches to 1 mile 1:9051

0 110yds 220yds 330yds **440 yards**

0 125m 250m 325m **500 metres**

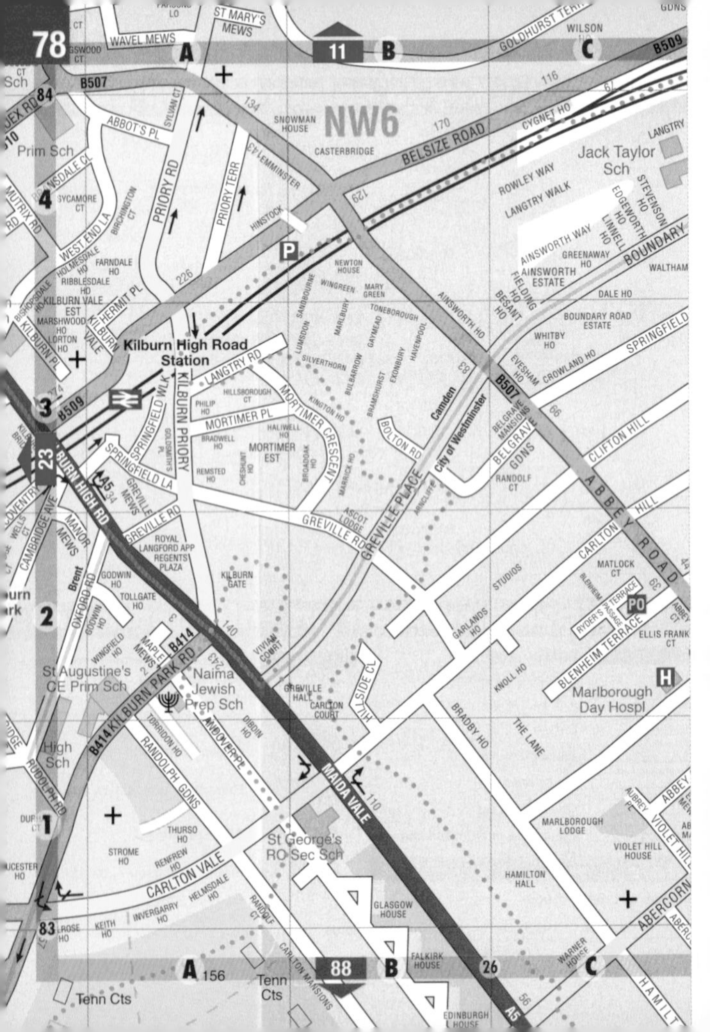
NW6
11
88
23
A
B
C
1
2
3
4
84
83
B507
B509
B414
A5
BELSIZE ROAD
GOLDHURST TERR
WILSON HO
WAVEL MEWS
ST MARY'S MEWS
ABBOT'S PL
SYLVAN CT
PRIORY RD
PRIORY TERR
LEMMINSTER
SNOWMAN HOUSE
CASTERBRIDGE
HINSTOCK
CYGNET HO
LANGTRY
Jack Taylor Sch
ROWLEY WAY
LANGTRY WALK
AINSWORTH WAY
AINSWORTH ESTATE
STEVENSON HO
EDGEWORTH HO
LINNELL HO
GREENAWAY HO
BOUNDARY
WALTHAM
FIELDING HO
BESANT HO
DALE HO
BOUNDARY ROAD ESTATE
WHITBY HO
SPRINGFIELD
CROWLAND HO
EVESHAM HO
AINSWORTH HO
Prim Sch
BRONSDALE CL
SYCAMORE CT
MUTRIX RD
WEST END LA
BIRCHINGTON CT
HOLMESDALE HO
FARNDALE HO
RIBBLESDALE HO
KILBURN VALE EST
HERMIT PL
BISHOPSDALE HO
MARSHWOOD HO
LORTON HO
KILBURN PL
KILBURN VALE
Kilburn High Road Station
NEWTON HOUSE
WINGREEN
MARY GREEN
TONEBOROUGH
SANDBOURNE
LUMSDON
MARLBURY
GAYMEAD
HAVENPOOL
EXONBURY
BULBARROW
BRAMSHURST
SILVERTHORN
LANGTRY RD
HILLSBOROUGH CT
PHILIP HO
MORTIMER PL
MORTIMER CRESCENT
KINGTON HO
HALIWELL HO
BRADWELL HO
MORTIMER EST
REMSTED HO
CHESHUNT HO
BROADOAK HO
MARRICK HO
BOLTON RD
Camden
City of Westminster
GREVILLE PLACE
ARNCLIFFE
BELGRAVE MANSIONS
BELGRAVE GDNS
RANDOLF CT
CLIFTON HILL
ABBEY ROAD
KILBURN PRIORY
SPRINGFIELD WLK
GOLDSMITH'S PL
SPRINGFIELD LA
GREVILLE MEWS
GREVILLE RD
ASCOT LODGE
KILBURN HIGH RD
COVENTRY CL
WELLS CT
CAMBRIDGE AVE
MANOR MEWS
ROYAL LANGFORD APP
REGENTS PLAZA
KILBURN GATE
CARLTON HILL
STUDIOS
MATLOCK CT
BLENHEIM PASSAGE
RYDER'S TERRACE
PO
ELLIS FRANK CT
BLENHEIM TERRACE
GARLANDS HO
Brent
OXFORD RD
GODWIN HO
TOLLGATE HO
WINGFIELD HO
MAPLE MEWS
KILBURN PARK RD
VIVIAN COURT
GREVILLE HALL
CARLTON COURT
HILLSIDE CL
KNOLL HO
Marlborough Day Hospl
St Augustine's CE Prim Sch
Naima Jewish Prep Sch
TORRIDON HO
ANDOVER PL
DIBDIN HO
BRADBY HO
THE LANE
High Sch
RUDOLPH RD
RANDOLPH GDNS
MAIDA VALE
THURSO HO
STROME HO
RENFREW HO
St George's RC Sec Sch
MARLBOROUGH LODGE
AUBREY PL
VIOLET HILL
VIOLET HILL HOUSE
HAMILTON HALL
ABERCORN
CARLTON VALE
HELMSDALE HO
INVERGARRY HO
KEITH HO
RANDOLF CT
GLASGOW HOUSE
FALKIRK HOUSE
WARNER HOUSE
CARLTON MANSIONS
EDINBURGH HOUSE
Tenn Cts
HAMILT
26
156
110
140
134
170
116
226
129
83
66

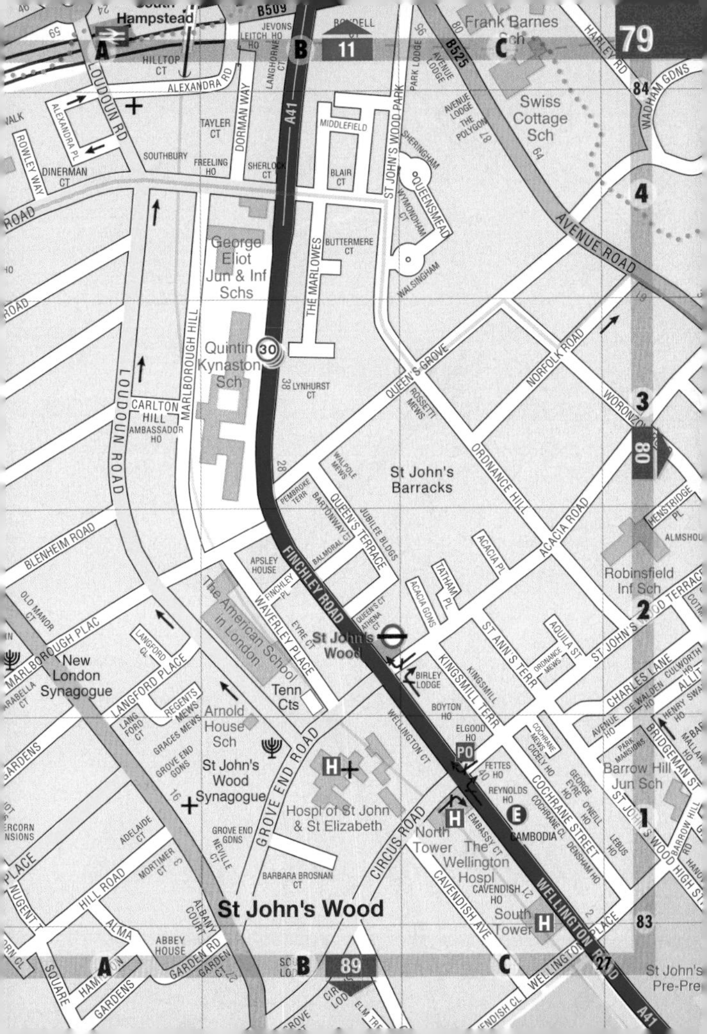
South Hampstead
B509
Jevons
Leitch Ho
Langhorne Ct
Rondell
11
Frank Barnes Sch
Harley Rd
84
Wadham Gdns
Hilltop Ct
Alexandra Rd
Loudoun Rd
Alexandra Pl
Dorman Way
Tayler Ct
A41
Middlefield
St John's Wood Park
Park Lodge
Avenue Lodge
B525
Avenue Lodge
The Polygon
Swiss Cottage Sch
Rowley Way
Dinerman Ct
Southbury
Freeling Ho
Sherlock Ct
Blair Ct
Sheringham
Queensmead
Wymondham Ct
4
Avenue Road
George Eliot Jun & Inf Schs
The Marlowes
Buttermere Ct
Walsingham
Marlborough Hill
Quintin Kynaston Sch
30
38
Lynhurst Ct
Queen's Grove
Rossetti Mews
Norfolk Road
Woronzow
3
80
Loudoun Road
Carlton Hill
Ambassador Ho
28
Walpole Mews
St John's Barracks
Ordnance Hill
Acacia Road
Henstridge Pl
Almshouses
Pembroke Terr
Bartonway Ct
Queen's Terrace
Jubilee Bldgs
Blenheim Road
Apsley House
Balmoral Ct
Acacia Pl
Tatham Pl
Acacia Gdns
Robinsfield Inf Sch
2
St John's Wood Terrace
Finchley Road
Finchley Pl
Waverley Place
Old Manor Ct
The American School in London
Eyre Ct
Queen's Ct
Athena Ct
St John's Wood
St Ann's Terr
Aquila St
Ordnance Mews
Kingsmill
Kingsmill Terr
Birley Lodge
Charles Lane
Culworth Ho
Marlborough Plac
Langford Cl
New London Synagogue
Langford Place
Arabella Ct
Tenn Cts
Avenue Ho
De Walden Ho
Regents Mews
Lang Ford Ct
Graces Mews
Arnold House Sch
Boyton Ho
Wellington Ct
Elgood Ho
Henry Ho
Park Mansions
Bridgeman St
Barrow Hill Jun Sch
Gardens
Grove End Gdns
St John's Wood Synagogue
Grove End Road
Hospl of St John & St Elizabeth
PO
40
Fettes Ho
Reynolds Ho
Cochrane Mews
Cicely Ho
George Eyre Ho
O'Neill Ho
Cochrane Street
Cochrane Cl
1
16
Adelaide Ct
Circus Road
North Tower
The Wellington Hospl
Embassy Ct
Cambodia
Densham Ho
Lebus Ho
Barrow Hill Rd
St John's Wood High St
Place
Hill Road
Mortimer Ct
Nevill Ct
Grove End Gdns
Barbara Brosnan Ct
Cavendish Ho
21
Cavendish Ave
Nugent T
Alma
Albany Court
St John's Wood
South Tower
Wellington Road
Wellington Place
83
Abbey House
Garden Rd
Garden Ct
A
B
89
C
Wellington
27
St John's Pre-Pre
Square
Hamilton
Gardens
Elm Tree
A41

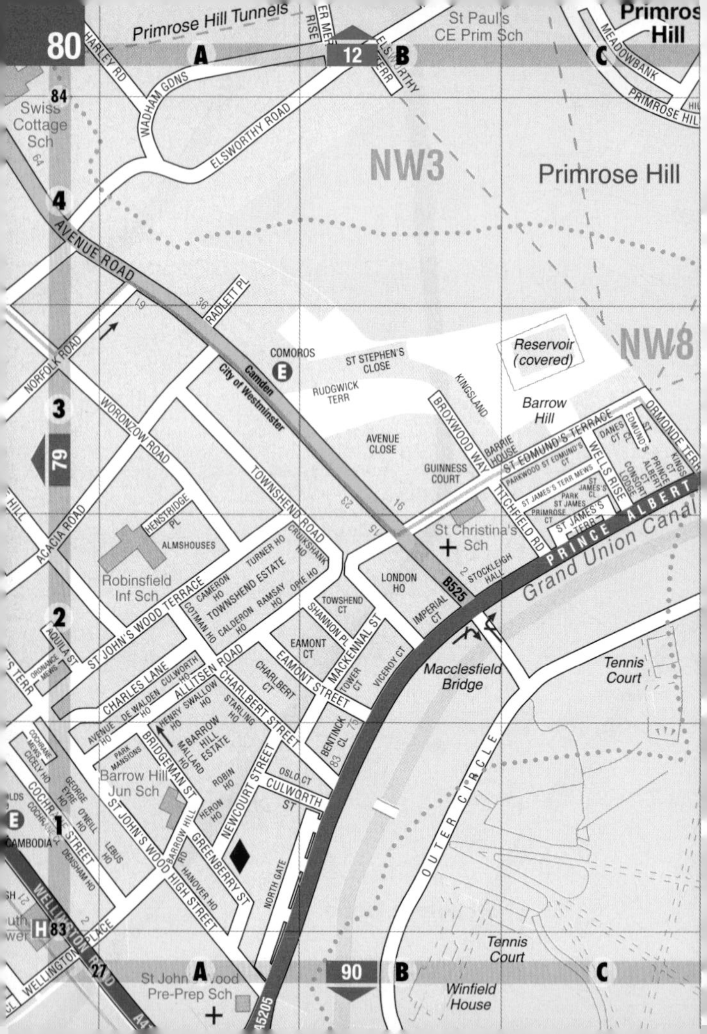
Primrose Hill Tunnels
St Paul's CE Prim Sch
Primrose Hill
12
A
B
C
HARLEY RD
WADHAM GDNS
ELSWORTHY ROAD
ELSWORTHY TERR
MEADOWBANK
PRIMROSE HILL
84
Swiss Cottage Sch
NW3
Primrose Hill
4
AVENUE ROAD
RADLETT PL
NORFOLK ROAD
WORONZOW ROAD
3
79
COMOROS
Camden
City of Westminster
ST STEPHEN'S CLOSE
RUDGWICK TERR
AVENUE CLOSE
BROXWOOD WAY
KINGSLAND
Reservoir (covered)
NW8
Barrow Hill
BARRIE HOUSE
ST EDMUND'S TERRACE
PARKWOOD ST EDMUND'S CT
GUINNESS COURT
ST JAMES'S TERR MEWS
WELLS RISE
DANES CT
EDMUND'S CL
ORMONDE TERR
KINGS CT
PRINCE ALBERT CT
CONSORT LODGE
ST JAMES'S CL
PARK ST JAMES
PRIMROSE CT
ST JAMES'S TERR
TITCHFIELD RD
PRINCE ALBERT
Grand Union Canal
St Christina's Sch
STOCKLEIGH HALL
TOWNSHEND ROAD
ACACIA ROAD
HENSTRIDGE PL
ALMSHOUSES
Robinsfield Inf Sch
CRUIKSHANK HO
TURNER HO
CAMERON HO
TOWNSHEND ESTATE
OPIE HO
RAMSAY HO
CALDERON HO
COTMAN HO
TOWSHEND CT
SHANNON PL
LONDON HO
IMPERIAL CT
B525
2
AQUILA ST
ST JOHN'S WOOD TERRACE
ORDNANCE MEWS
CHARLES LANE
CULWORTH HO
DE WALDEN HO
ALLITSEN ROAD
EAMONT CT
EAMONT STREET
MACKENNAL ST
CHARLBERT CT
TOWER CT
VICEROY CT
Macclesfield Bridge
Tennis Court
AVENUE HO
HENRY HO
SWALLOW HO
STARLING HO
CHARLBERT STREET
BENTINCK CL
BARROW HILL ESTATE
MALLARD HO
PARK MANSIONS
BRIDGEMAN ST
Barrow Hill Jun Sch
ROBIN HO
OSLO CT
CULWORTH ST
NEWCOURT STREET
OUTER CIRCLE
COCHRANE MEWS
CICELY HO
GEORGE EYRE HO
O'NEILL HO
COCHRANE STREET
DENSHAM HO
LEBUS HO
ST JOHN'S WOOD HIGH STREET
BARROW HILL RD
HERON HO
GREENBERRY ST
HANOVER HO
NORTH GATE
1
CAMBODIA
WELLINGTON ROAD
WELLINGTON PLACE
83
St John's Wood Pre-Prep Sch
90
Tennis Court
Winfield House
A5205
A41

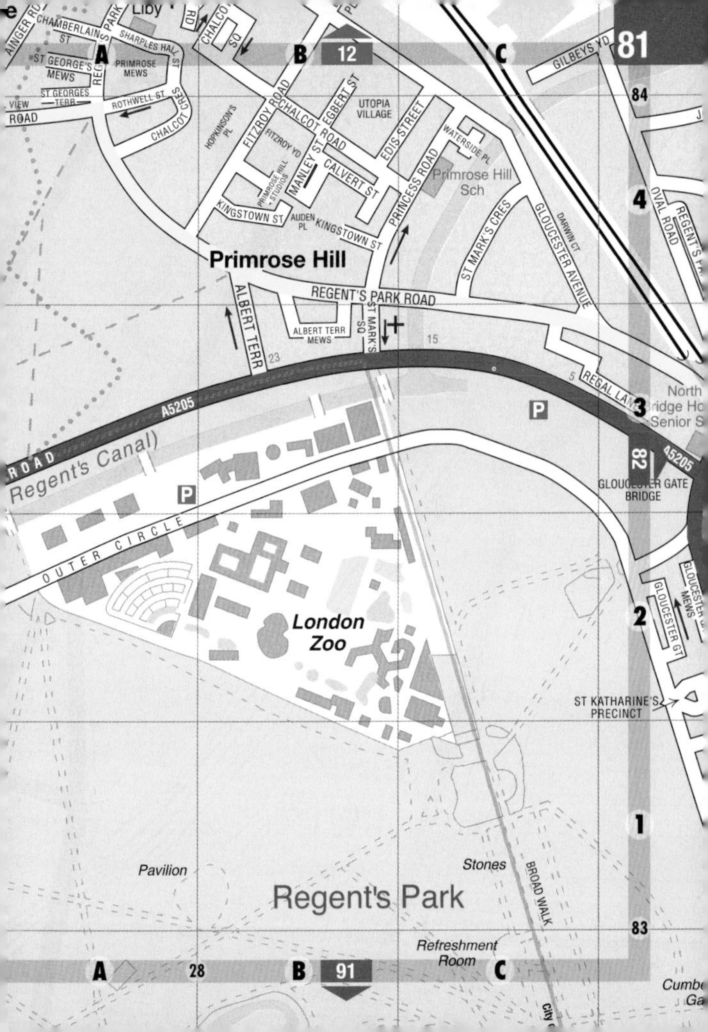
12
A
B
C
84
4
3
82
2
1
83
91
28
CHAMBERLAIN ST
SHARPLES HALL ST
ST GEORGE'S MEWS
PRIMROSE MEWS
ST GEORGES TERR
ROTHWELL ST
CHALCOT CRES
CHALCOT SQ
GILBEYS YD
HOPKINSON'S PL
FITZROY ROAD
CHALCOT ROAD
EGBERT ST
UTOPIA VILLAGE
EDIS STREET
FITZROY YD
MANLEY ST
PRIMROSE HILL STUDIOS
CALVERT ST
WATERSIDE PL
PRINCESS ROAD
Primrose Hill Sch
KINGSTOWN ST
AUDEN PL
ST MARK'S CRES
GLOUCESTER AVENUE
DARWIN CT
OVAL ROAD
Primrose Hill
REGENT'S PARK ROAD
ALBERT TERR
ALBERT TERR MEWS
ST MARK'S SQ
15
23
5
REGAL LANE
A5205
Regent's Canal
OUTER CIRCLE
London Zoo
GLOUCESTER GATE BRIDGE
GLOUCESTER GT
ST KATHARINE'S PRECINCT
Pavilion
Stones
BROAD WALK
Regent's Park
Refreshment Room

A
B
C
13
92
81
4
3
2
1
84
83
29
Hawley Cres
Hawley
Sch
Jamestown Rd
Camden Mkt
Early Mews
Buck St
Inverness Street
Camden Town
Camden High St
Kentish Town Rd
Camden Rd
Dewsbury Terr
Barnes Ho
Greenland Rd
Carol St
Lyme St
Prim Sch
Highstone Mans
Britannia Junc
Greenland Pl
Greenland St
St Martin's Almshouses
St Martin's Cl
Carpenters Court
Pratt
Warmsworth
Barnby
Mexborough
Billingley
Goldthorpe
Darfield
Conisbrough
Ravenscar
Thurnscoe
Brehon Ho
Pratt Mews
Bayham Street
King's Terrace
Gloucester Avenue
Darwin Ct
Oval Road
Regent's Park Terr
Gloucester Crescent
The Cavendish Sch
Stanmore Pl
Underhill Pas
Underhill St
Pleasant Row
Signmakers Yd
Arlington Road
Parkway
The Jewish Mus
Delancey Street
Delancey Pas
Mary Terrace
Fairfield
Foxfield
Brierfield
Delancey Studios
Albert Street
Latitude Ho
Regal Lane
North Bridge House Senior Sch
Gloucester Gate Bridge
Miller St
Symes Mews
Carlow St
Cobden House
Beatty St
Nelsons Yd
Mornington Street
Mornington Court
Mornington Crescent
Millbrook Pl
Hurdwick Pl
Hurdwick House
Harrington Sq
Gloucester Gate Mews
Gloucester Gt
Park Village West
St Katharine's Precinct
Mornington Terrace
Mornington Pl
Clarkson Row
Park Village East
Silsoe House
Regent's Park Barracks
Richmond House
NW1
Cumberland Terrace
Cumberland Terrace Mews
Outer Circle
Broad Walk
Camberley House
Edward Mews
Christ Church
Allot Gdns
Swinley House
Kendal
Ambleside
Tintern Ho
Augustus Ho
Augustus Street
Buttermere
Granby Terrace
Harrington St
Eskdale
Stalbridge House
Ainsdale
Silverdale
Langdale
Harrington
Coniston
Mackworth St
Stanhope Par
Harrington Ho
Dalehead
Gillfoot
Cumberland Gate
Chester Pl
Cmbrlnd Pl
Albany St
Redhill St
Ascot House
Hampstead Rd
A400
A503
A502
A4201
A5205
A4200
B511
PO
30

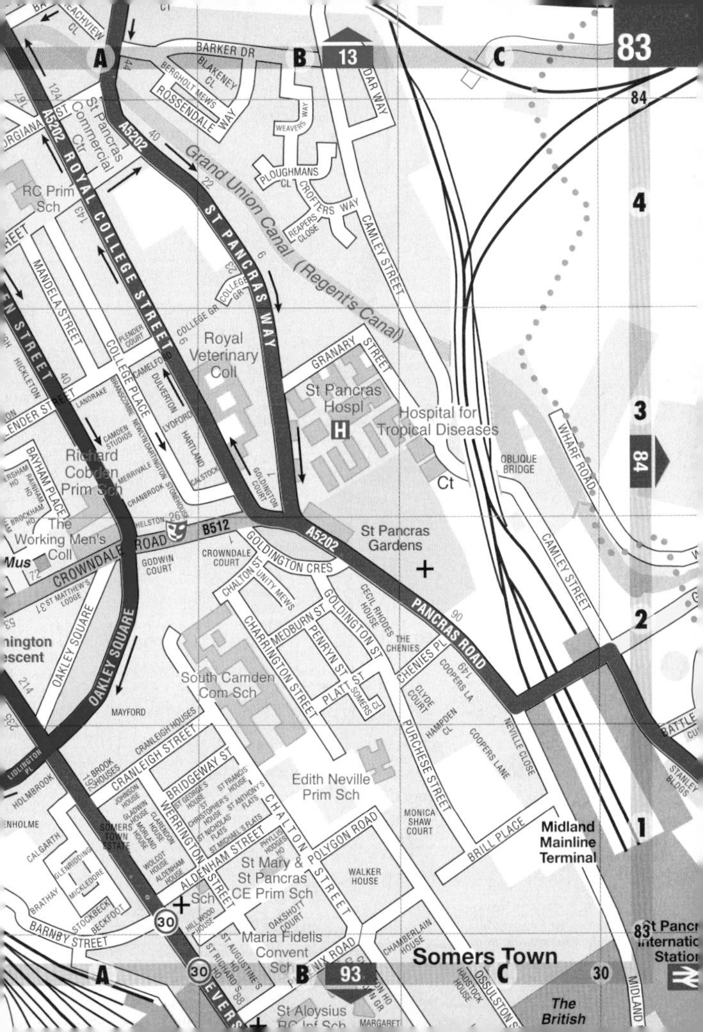
83
13
84
93
A
B
C
1
2
3
4
BEACHVIEW CL
BARKER DR
BLAKENEY CL
BERGHOLT MEWS
ROSSENDALE WAY
WEAVERS WAY
PLOUGHMANS CL
CROFTERS WAY
REAPERS CLOSE
CAMLEY STREET
A5202
ROYAL COLLEGE STREET
St Pancras Commercial Ctr
ST PANCRAS WAY
Grand Union Canal (Regent's Canal)
RC Prim Sch
MANDELA STREET
COLLEGE GR
PLENDER COURT
COLLEGE PLACE
CAMELFORD
DULVERTON
LYDFORD
HARTLAND
CALSTOCK
Royal Veterinary Coll
GRANARY STREET
St Pancras Hospl
H
Hospital for Tropical Diseases
Ct
OBLIQUE BRIDGE
WHARF ROAD
HICKLETON
LANDRAKE
BRANSCOMBE
NEWLYN
DARTINGTON
CAMDEN STUDIOS
MERRIVALE
CRANBROOK
STONEHOUSE
GOLDINGTON COURT
BAYHAM PLACE
RAINHAM HO
BROCKHAM HO
Richard Cobden Prim Sch
The Working Men's Coll
Mus
HELSTON
B512
CROWNDALE ROAD
GODWIN COURT
CROWNDALE COURT
GOLDINGTON CRES
St Pancras Gardens
PANCRAS ROAD
ST MATTHEW'S LODGE
OAKLEY SQUARE
CHALTON ST
UNITY MEWS
CHARRINGTON STREET
MEDBURN ST
PENRYN ST
GOLDINGTON ST
CECIL RHODES HOUSE
THE CHENIES
CHENIES PL
COOPERS LA
PLATT ST
SOMERS CL
CLYDE COURT
HAMPDEN CL
COOPERS LANE
NEVILLE CLOSE
South Camden Com Sch
MAYFORD
CRANLEIGH HOUSES
CRANLEIGH STREET
BROOK HOUSES
BRIDGEWAY ST
PURCHESE STREET
Edith Neville Prim Sch
MONICA SHAW COURT
BRILL PLACE
Midland Mainline Terminal
BATTLE
STANLEY BLDGS
LIDLINGTON PL
HOLMBROOK
CALGARTH
GLENRIDDING
MICKLEDORE
BRATHAY
STOCKBECK
BECKFOOT
BARNBY STREET
SOMERS TOWN ESTATE
JOHNSON HOUSE
GLADWIN HOUSE
MORLAND HOUSE
CLARENDON HOUSE
WOLCOT HOUSE
ALDENHAM HOUSE
WERRINGTON STREET
ST GEORGE'S HOUSE
ST CHRISTOPHER'S HOUSE
ST NICHOLAS' FLATS
ST MICHAEL'S FLATS
ST FRANCIS' HOUSE
ST ANTHONY'S FLATS
CHALTON STREET
ALDENHAM STREET
PHYLLIS HODGES HO
POLYGON ROAD
St Mary & St Pancras CE Prim Sch
WALKER HOUSE
Sch
HILLWOOD HOUSE
OAKSHOTT COURT
Maria Fidelis Convent Sch
CHAMBERLAIN HOUSE
Somers Town
ST AUGUSTINE'S HO
ST RICHARD'S HO
HADSTOCK HOUSE
OSSULSTON ST
St Pancras International Station
MIDLAND
The British
St Aloysius RC Inf Sch
MARGARET
30

14
A
B
C
84
4
3
2
1
83
A
B
C
94
83
30
PERTH HO
STRANRAER WAY
FREELING ST
Liby
PO
RUFFORD STREET MEWS
RUFFORD ST
Bingfield Park
PEMBROKE ST
EARLSFERRY WAY
CARNOUSTIE DR
STORY ST
A5200
A5203
SELKIRK HO
KINROSS HO
BINGFIELD STREET
RANDELL'S ROAD
178
BINGFIELD ST
PEMBROKE AVE
HAVELOCK STREET
BEMERTON STREET
COWDENBEATH PATH
FRANCIS WALK
STANMORE ST
WHEELER GDNS
OUTRAM PL
NAISH COURT
TWYFORD STREET
CAITHNESS HOUSE
ORKNEY HOUSE
VIBART WALK
CAMPBELL WALK
LAWRENCE PL
BRYDON WALK
JUBILEE CT
DELHI ST
CLAYTON CRES
Liby
166
DUNOON HOUSE
B514
COPENHAGEN STREET
B514
YORK WAY
YORK WAY COURT
TIBER GDNS
BOADICEA ST
JULIUS NYERERE CL
149
Blessed Sacrament RC Prim Sch
CALEDONIAN ROAD
EWEN HO
126
YORK WAY CT
TREATY STREET
Depot
Copenhagen Prim Sch
EDWARD SQ
159
RITSON HO
WHARF ROAD
MALDEN LANE BRIDGE
THORNHILL B W
BLIQUE RIDGE
WHARF ROAD
CAMLEY STREET
Islington
Camden
ICE WHARF
REGENTS WHARF
THORNHILL BRIDGE
Battlebridge Basin
GOODSWAY
London Canal Museum
NEW WHARF ROAD
LAVINA GR
ALL SAINTS ST
80
CRINAN ST
King's Cross
P
BATTLEBRIDGE CT
2
CALSHOT HO
GRIMALDI HO
PRIORY GN
A5203
WHARFDALE ROAD
FOLIOT HO
67
97
PO
SOUTHERN ST
BATTLE BRIDGE RD
CULROSS BLDGS
RAILWAY ST
BALFE STREET
P
Winton Prim Sch
TORNAY HO
PAVELEY HO
NEVILLE CLOSE
STANLEY BLDGS
ALBION YD
ALBION WLK
BONINGTON HO
KILLICK STREET
P
CALSHOT STREET
GRENDON HO
King's Cross Station
KEYSTONE CRES
NORTHDOWN STREET
COLLIER STREET
HENLEY PRIOR
Midland Mainline Terminal
CALEDONIA ST
STUART MILL HO
POLLARD HO
HALES PRIOR
PANCRAS ROAD
JOINERS YD
THE YARD
PROVIDENCE ROW
OMEGA PL
A5200
2
304
A5203
King's Cross
A501
YORK HO
223
LORENZO ST
DINWIDDY HO
188
St Pancras International Station
374
KING'S CROSS BRIDGE
B503
Town
A5202
King's Cross St Pancras
A5200
ST CHAD'S PL
FIELD ST
COBDEN BLDGS
King's Cross (Thameslink) Station
LEEKE STREET
The British
MIDLAND
PO
BIRKENHEAD ST
CHAD'S
BRITANNIA STREET

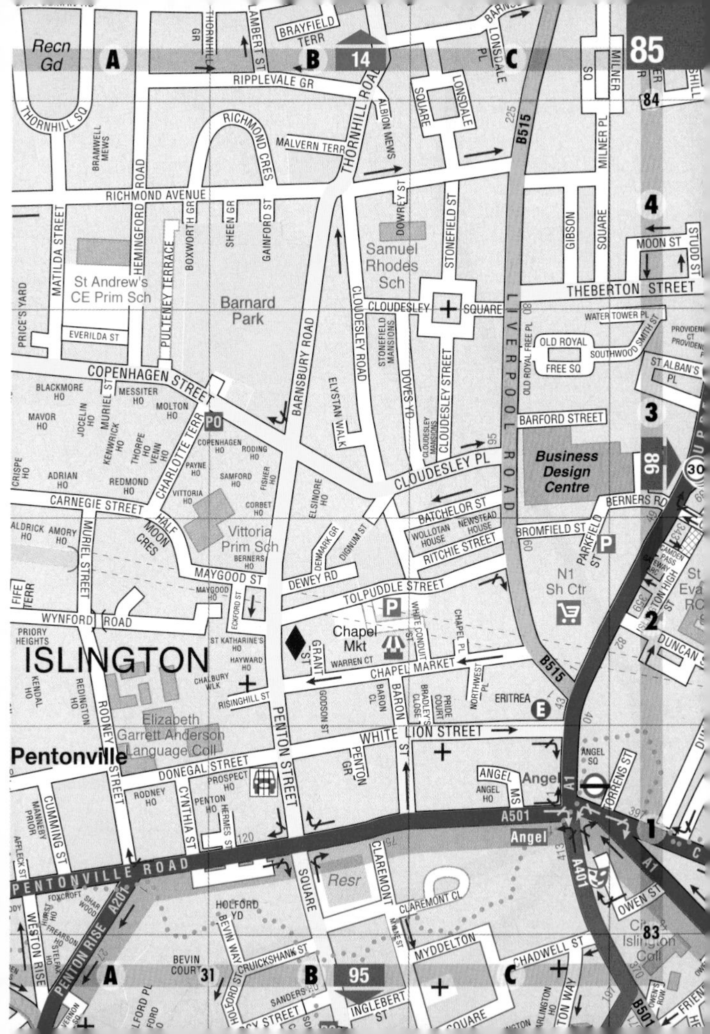
Recn Gd
THORNHILL SQ
THORNHILL GR
LAMBERT ST
BRAYFIELD TERR
RIPPLEVALE GR
THORNHILL ROAD
ALBION MEWS
LONSDALE PL
LONSDALE SQUARE
BARNSBURY
MILNER SQ
MILNER PL
BRAMWELL MEWS
RICHMOND CRES
MALVERN TERR
HEMINGFORD ROAD
RICHMOND AVENUE
MATILDA STREET
PULTENEY TERRACE
BOXWORTH GR
SHEEN GR
GAINFORD ST
DOWREY ST
STONEFIELD ST
GIBSON SQUARE
MOON ST
STUDD ST
St Andrew's CE Prim Sch
Barnard Park
Samuel Rhodes Sch
THEBERTON STREET
PRICE'S YARD
EVERILDA ST
BARNSBURY ROAD
CLOUDESLEY ROAD
CLOUDESLEY SQUARE
STONEFIELD MANSIONS
WATER TOWER PL
OLD ROYAL FREE SQ
OLD ROYAL FREE PL
SOUTHWOOD SMITH ST
PROVIDENCE CT
ST ALBAN'S PL
COPENHAGEN STREET
BLACKMORE HO
MESSITER HO
MOLTON HO
MURIEL ST
MAVOR HO
JOCELIN HO
KENWRICK HO
THORPE HO
VENN HO
ELYSTAN WALK
DOVES YD
CLOUDESLEY STREET
CLOUDESLEY MANSIONS
LIVERPOOL ROAD
BARFORD STREET
PO
CHARLOTTE TERR
COPENHAGEN HO
RODING HO
PAYNE HO
SAMFORD HO
FISHER HO
CRISPE HO
ADRIAN HO
REDMOND HO
VITTORIA HO
CLOUDESLEY PL
Business Design Centre
CARNEGIE STREET
CORBET HO
ELSINORE HO
BATCHELOR ST
BERNERS RD
HALF MOON CRES
Vittoria Prim Sch
WOLLOTAN HOUSE
NEWSTEAD HOUSE
BROMFIELD ST
ALDRICK HO
AMORY HO
MURIEL STREET
BERNERS HO
DENMARK GR
DIGNUM ST
RITCHIE STREET
PARKFIELD ST
CAMDEN PASSAGE
N1 Sh Ctr
MAYGOOD ST
DEWEY RD
TOLPUDDLE STREET
FIFE TERR
MAYGOOD HO
ECKFORD ST
WYNFORD ROAD
WHITE CONDUIT ST
CHAPEL PL
ISLINGTON HIGH ST
DUNCAN ST
PRIORY HEIGHTS
ST KATHARINE'S HO
GRANT ST
Chapel Mkt
WARREN CT
ISLINGTON
HAYWARD HO
CHAPEL MARKET
B515
KENDAL HO
REDINGTON HO
CHALBURY WLK
RISINGHILL ST
GODSON ST
BARON CL
BARON ST
BRADLEY'S CLOSE
PRIDE COURT
NORTHWEST PL
ERITREA
RODNEY STREET
Elizabeth Garrett Anderson Language Coll
PENTON STREET
WHITE LION STREET
ANGEL SQ
Pentonville
DONEGAL STREET
PENTON GR
ANGEL MS
Angel
TORRENS ST
PROSPECT HO
RODNEY HO
CYNTHIA ST
ANGEL HO
MANNEBY PRIOR
CUMMING ST
PENTON HO
HERMES ST
A501
A1
AFLECK ST
PENTONVILLE ROAD
CLAREMONT SQUARE
Resr
A401
OWEN ST
FOXCROFT
SHARWOOD
HOLFORD YD
CLAREMONT CL
WESTON RISE
HURST HO
FREARSON HO
STELFAX HO
BEVIN WAY
MYLNE ST
A201
PENTON RISE
CRUICKSHANK ST
MYDDELTON
CHADWELL ST
City & Islington Coll
BEVIN COURT
HOLFORD ST
SANDERS HO
INGLEBERT ST
ARLINGTON HO
OWEN'S ROW
VERNON SQ
SQUARE
B501
14
95
84
98
83
31
A
B
C
1
2
3
4

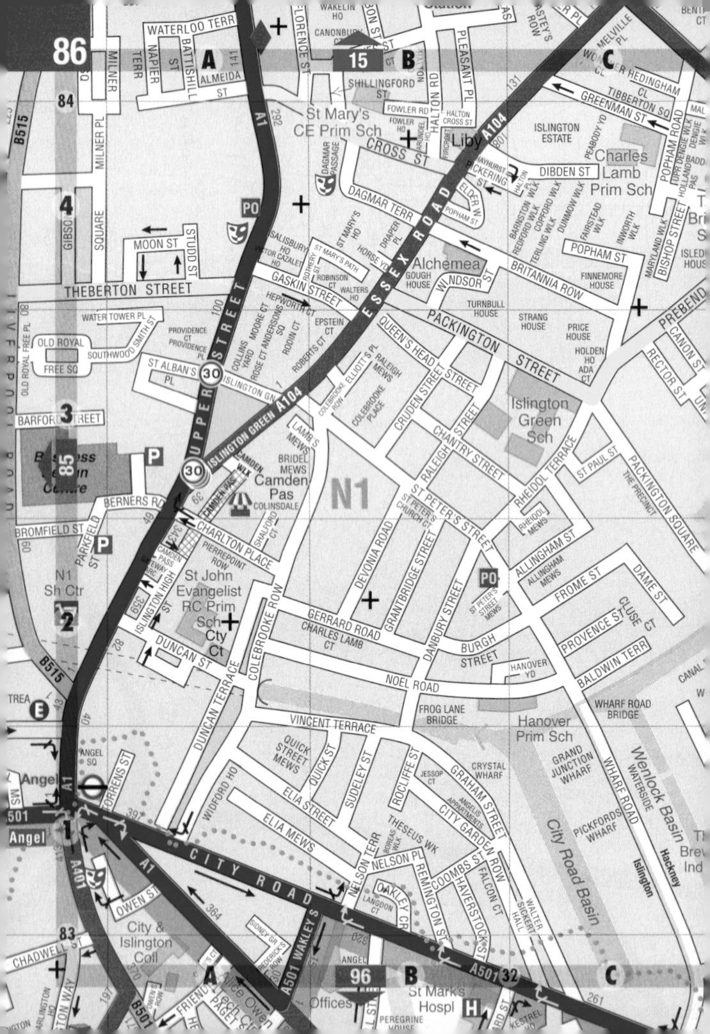

A
B
C
15
84
4
3
2
1
83
85
96
N1
A1
A104
A501
A401
B515
B501
WATERLOO TERR
NAPIER TERR
BATTISHILL ST
ALMEIDA ST
MILNER SQ
MILNER PL
GIBSON SQUARE
MOON ST
STUDD ST
THEBERTON STREET
WATER TOWER PL
OLD ROYAL FREE SQ
OLD ROYAL FREE PL
SOUTHWOOD SMITH ST
PROVIDENCE CT
ST ALBAN'S PL
BARFORD STREET
Business Design Centre
BERNERS RD
BROMFIELD ST
PARKFIELD ST
N1 Sh Ctr
LIVERPOOL ROAD
UPPER STREET
ISLINGTON GREEN
ISLINGTON HIGH ST
CAMDEN PAS
CAMDEN WLK
Camden Pas
COLINSDALE
CHARLTON PLACE
PIERREPOINT ROW
SHALFORD CT
St John Evangelist RC Prim Sch
Cty Ct
DUNCAN ST
DUNCAN TERRACE
COLEBROOKE ROW
BRIDEL MEWS
LAMB'S MEWS
FLORENCE ST
CANONBURY
SHILLINGFORD ST
FOWLER RD
HALTON RD
HALTON CROSS ST
PLEASANT PL
St Mary's CE Prim Sch
DAGMAR PASSAGE
CROSS ST
DAGMAR TERR
Liby
SALISBURY HO
VICTOR CAZALET HO
ST MARY'S PATH
ROBINSON CT
WALTERS HO
HORSE YD
DRAPER PL
GASKIN STREET
HEPWORTH CT
MOORE CT
ANDERSONS SQ
RODIN CT
COLLINS YARD
ROSE CT
EPSTEIN CT
ROBERTS CT
ESSEX ROAD
ELLIOTT'S PL
RALEIGH MEWS
COLEBROOKE PLACE
QUEEN'S HEAD STREET
CRUDEN STREET
RALEIGH STREET
CHANTRY STREET
ST PETER'S STREET
ST PETER'S CHURCH CT
DEVONIA ROAD
GRANTBRIDGE STREET
DANBURY STREET
GERRARD ROAD
CHARLES LAMB CT
BURGH STREET
NOEL ROAD
HANOVER YD
FROG LANE BRIDGE
VINCENT TERRACE
Alchemea
GOUGH HOUSE
WINDSOR ST
PACKINGTON STREET
TURNBULL HOUSE
STRANG HOUSE
PRICE HOUSE
HOLDEN HO
ADA CT
Islington Green Sch
RHEIDOL TERRACE
RHEIDOL MEWS
ALLINGHAM ST
ALLINGHAM MEWS
ST PETER'S STREET MEWS
ST PAUL ST
PACKINGTON SQUARE
THE PRECINCT
FROME ST
DAME ST
PROVENCE ST
CLUSE CT
BALDWIN TERR
WHARF ROAD BRIDGE
Hanover Prim Sch
GRAND JUNCTION WHARF
WHARF ROAD
WATERSIDE
Wenlock Basin
City Road Basin
PICKFORDS WHARF
CRYSTAL WHARF
GRAHAM STREET
JESSOP CT
ANGELIS APPARTMENTS
CITY GARDEN ROW
ROCLIFFE ST
THESEUS WK
BOREAS WLK
NELSON PL
NELSON TERR
REMINGTON ST
COOMBS ST
HAVERSTOCK ST
FALCON CT
WALTER SICKERT HALL
OAKLEY CR
LANGDON CT
QUICK STREET MEWS
QUICK ST
SUDELEY ST
ELIA STREET
ELIA MEWS
WIDFORD HO
CITY ROAD
TORRENS ST
ANGEL SQ
Angel
OWEN ST
City & Islington Coll
CHADWELL ST
SIDNEY GR
FREDERICK'S ROW
WAKLEY ST
Alice Owen
FRIEND ST
PAGET ST
St Mark's Hospl
PEREGRINE HOUSE
KESTREL HO
Offices
MELVILLE PL
HEDINGHAM CL
TIBBERTON SQ
GREENMAN ST
ISLINGTON ESTATE
PEABODY YD
POPHAM ROAD
DIBDEN ST
Charles Lamb Prim Sch
HAYHURST
PICKERING ST
ELDER WK
POPHAM ST
BARNSTON WLK
REDFORD WLK
COPFORD WLK
TERLING WLK
DUNMOW WLK
FAIRSTEAD WLK
INWORTH WLK
MARYLAND WLK
BISHOP STREET
BRITANNIA ROW
FINNEMORE HOUSE
PREBEND ST
CANON ST
RECTOR ST
Islington
Hackney

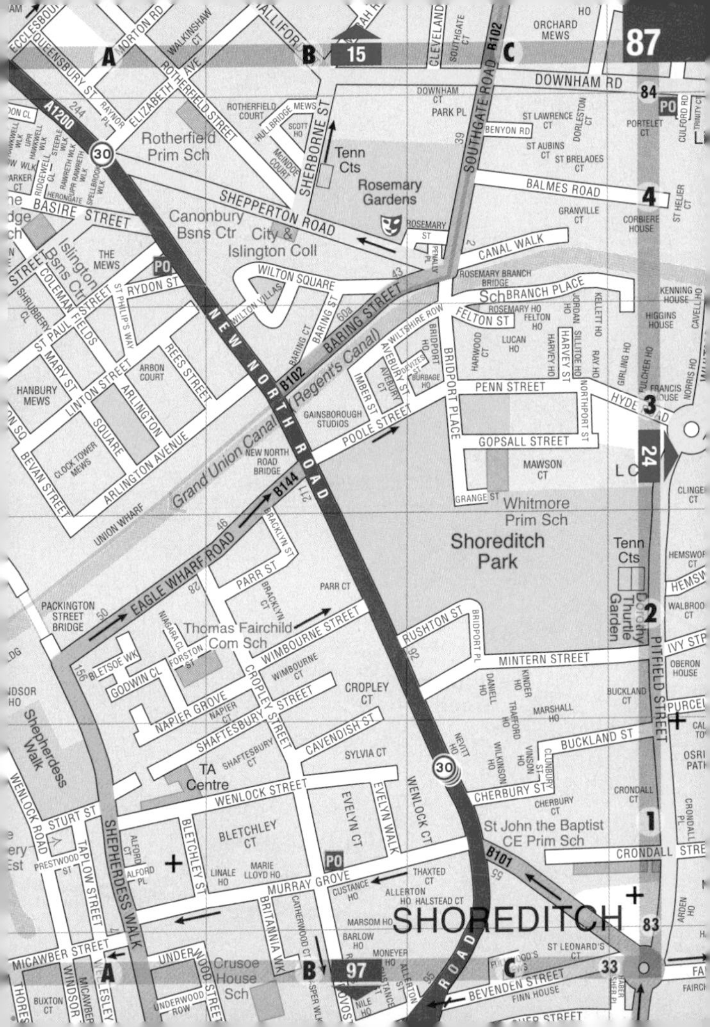

A
B
C
15
97
24
84
83
33
1
2
3
4
A1200
B102
B144
B101
30
NEW NORTH ROAD
SOUTHGATE ROAD
DOWNHAM RD
ORCHARD MEWS
ROTHERFIELD STREET
Rotherfield Prim Sch
SHEPPERTON ROAD
Canonbury Bsns Ctr
City & Islington Coll
Rosemary Gardens
Tenn Cts
SHERBORNE ST
BASIRE STREET
Islington Bsns Ctr
WILTON SQUARE
BARING STREET
CANAL WALK
BRANCH PLACE
FELTON ST
PENN STREET
HYDE ROAD
GOPSALL STREET
Regent's Canal
Grand Union Canal
POOLE STREET
NEW NORTH ROAD BRIDGE
EAGLE WHARF ROAD
PACKINGTON STREET BRIDGE
ARLINGTON AVENUE
ARLINGTON SQUARE
LINTON STREET
UNION WHARF
Whitmore Prim Sch
Shoreditch Park
Dorothy Thurtle Garden
PITFIELD STREET
MINTERN STREET
RUSHTON ST
WIMBOURNE STREET
Thomas Fairchild Com Sch
CROPLEY STREET
SHAFTESBURY STREET
NAPIER GROVE
CAVENDISH ST
TA Centre
WENLOCK STREET
WENLOCK ROAD
Shepherdess Walk
SHEPHERDESS WALK
BUCKLAND ST
CHERBURY ST
St John the Baptist CE Prim Sch
CRONDALL STREET
MURRAY GROVE
SHOREDITCH
Crusoe House Sch
MICAWBER STREET
BEVENDEN STREET

STROME HO
RENFREW HO
CARLTON VALE
RAMSDALE HO
St George's RC Sec Sch
78
A
B
C
LODGE
VIOLET HILL HOUSE
HAMILTON HALL
GLASGOW HOUSE
FALKIRK HOUSE
EDINBURGH HOUSE
ABERCORN
RANDOLF CT
INVERGARRY HO
KEITH HO
MELROSE HO
83
CARLTON MANSIONS
.156
Tenn Cts
Tenn Cts
WARNER HOUSE
HAMILTON
A5
56
4
Fball Gd
Paddington Recn Gd
Crkt Gd
Bwg Gn
ELGIN MEWS NORTH
Maida Vale
ELGIN MEWS SOUTH
HAMILTON CT
DUNDEE HO
WELLESLEY COURT
MARLBOROUGH
MAIDA VALE
Maida Vale
ASHWORTH MANSIONS
ELGIN AVENUE
VALE CL
30 VALE CT
BRAEMAR HO
ATHOLL HO
GRANTULLY RD
LEITH MANSIONS
ELGIN MANSIONS
BIDDULPH MANSIONS
BIDDULPH ROAD
ASHWORTH ROAD
RANDOLPH
LANARK ROAD
3
MORSHEAD RD
MORSHEAD MANSIONS
City of Westminster Coll
23
LAUDERDALE MANSIONS
LAUDERDALE MANSIONS
LAUDERDALE ROAD
LAUDERDALE MANSIONS
St Joseph's RC Prim Sch
LEONORA HOUSE
SUTHERLAND AVE
AVENUE
SOUTHWOLD MANSIONS
WIDLEY RD
CLEVELAND MANS
WESTSIDE CT
ELGIN CT
CASTELLAIN MANSIONS
CASTELLAIN MANSIONS
Tenn Cts
CASTELLAIN RD
2
CHESNEY CT
OAK TREE HO
RAYNE HO
DELAWARE RD
Pav
Bwg Gn
Tenn Cts
SUTHERLAND AVE
WARRINGTON CRESCENT
RANDOLPH CRESCENT
W9
Westbourne Green
B413 SHIRLAND RD
80
THORNGATE RD
MARYLANDS RD
SEVINGTON ST
ST PETER'S PL
Liby
Sch
SUTHERLAND CT
SURRENDALE PL
1
PINDOCK MEWS
PO
FORMOSA STREET
ELNATHAN MEWS
55
BRADEN ST
St Saviour's CE Prim Sch
CUMBERLAND HOUSE
CLIFTON GARDENS
WARRINGTON GDNS
MANOR HOUSE COURT
DOWNFIELD CL
ALDSWORTH CL
CHARFIELD COURT
CLEARWELL DRIVE
ELLWOOD CT
FORMOSA STREET
WARWICK AVENUE
B413
BRISTOL MEWS
Warwick Avenue
BARNWOOD CL
BRISTOL GDNS
CLIFTON VILLAS
FOSCOTE MEWS
82
AMBERLEY RD
Grand Union Canal (Paddington Br)
Coll
FB
100
26
PRINCETHORPE HO
St Mary Magdalene CE Prim Sch
ROWINGTON CL
WARWICK PLACE
WILMCOTE HO
CHESTER SQ
DARTINGTON
Grand

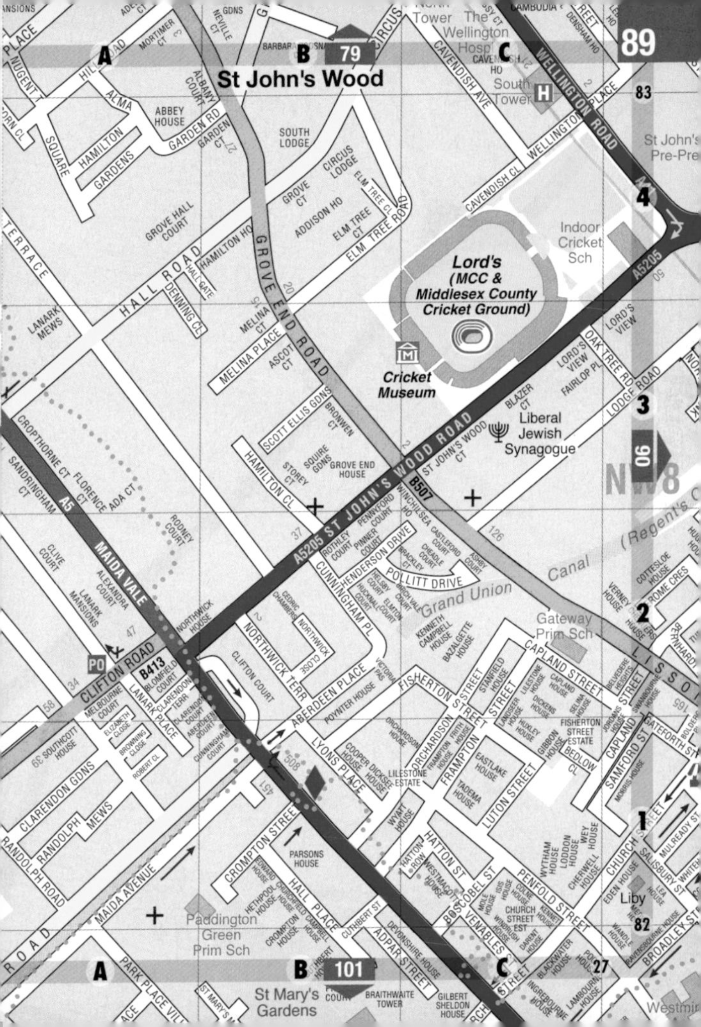
St John's Wood
79
A
B
C
83
St John's Pre-Prep
4
3
90
NW8
2
1
82
101
27
Lord's (MCC & Middlesex County Cricket Ground)
Cricket Museum
Indoor Cricket Sch
Liberal Jewish Synagogue
The Wellington Hosp
North Tower
South Tower
Gateway Prim Sch
Paddington Green Prim Sch
St Mary's Gardens
Liby
Westminster
Grand Union Canal (Regent's Canal)
WELLINGTON ROAD
WELLINGTON PLACE
A5205
A5205 ST JOHN'S WOOD ROAD
B507
GROVE END ROAD
HALL ROAD
ELM TREE ROAD
ELM TREE CL
ELM TREE CT
CIRCUS LODGE
GROVE CT
ADDISON HO
SOUTH LODGE
ABBEY HOUSE
GARDEN RD
GARDEN CT
ALBANY COURT
HILL ROAD
ALMA SQUARE
HAMILTON GARDENS
NUGENT TERRACE
GROVE HALL COURT
HAMILTON HO
HALL GATE
DENNING CL
LANARK MEWS
MELINA CT
MELINA PLACE
ASCOT CT
SCOTT ELLIS GDNS
BRONWEN CT
SQUIRE GDNS
GROVE END HOUSE
STOREY CT
HAMILTON CL
CAVENDISH AVE
CAVENDISH CL
LORD'S VIEW
OAK TREE RD
FAIRLOP PL
LODGE ROAD
BLAZER CT
ST JOHN'S WOOD CT
A5 MAIDA VALE
CROPTHORNE CT
FLORENCE CT
ADA CT
SANDRINGHAM CT
RODNEY COURT
CLIVE COURT
ALEXANDRA COURT
LANARK MANSIONS
NORTHWICK HOUSE
CLIFTON ROAD
B413
PO
BLOMFIELD COURT
LANARK PLACE
CLARENDON TERR
CLARENDON COURT
ABERDEEN COURT
CUNNINGHAM COURT
MELBOURNE COURT
ELIZABETH CLOSE
BROWNING CLOSE
ROBERT CL
SOUTHCOTT HOUSE
CLARENDON GDNS
RANDOLPH MEWS
RANDOLPH ROAD
MAIDA AVENUE
PARK PLACE VILLAS
ROTHLEY COURT
PENNYFORD COURT
PINNER COURT
WINCHILSEA HO
HENDERSON DRIVE
CASTLEFORD COURT
CHEADLE COURT
BRACKLEY CT
ASHBY COURT
POLLITT DRIVE
CUNNINGHAM PL
CEDRIC CHAMBERS
NORTHWICK CLOSE
NORTHWICK TERR
CLIFTON COURT
HELSBY COURT
BIRCH VALE COURT
HUCKNALL COURT
ELMTON COURT
KENNETH CAMPBELL HOUSE
BAZALGETTE HOUSE
ABERDEEN PLACE
POYNTER HOUSE
VICTORIA PAS
FISHERTON STREET
STANFIELD HOUSE
CAPLAND STREET
LILESTONE HOUSE
CAPLAND HOUSE
DICKENS HOUSE
SELINA HOUSE
LANDSEER HOUSE
HUXLEY HOUSE
GIBBON HOUSE
FISHERTON STREET ESTATE
BEDLOW CL
JORDANS HOUSE
BELVEDERE HEIGHTS
SWANBOURNE HOUSE
COTTESLOE HOUSE
VERNEY HOUSE
ROME CRES
LISSON
BERNHARDT
GATEFORTH ST
SAMFORD ST
MORRIS HOUSE
CAPLAND
LYONS PLACE
ORCHARDSON HOUSE
ORCHARDSON STREET
FRAMPTON HOUSE
FRITH HOUSE
FRAMPTON STREET
EASTLAKE HOUSE
TADEMA HOUSE
LUTON STREET
COOPER HOUSE
DICKSEE HOUSE
LILESTONE ESTATE
WYATT HOUSE
HATTON ROW
HATTON ST
WESTMACOTT HOUSE
BOSCOBEL ST
PENFOLD STREET
WYTHAM HOUSE
LODDON HOUSE
WEY HOUSE
CHERWELL HOUSE
MOLE HOUSE
ISIS HOUSE
COLNE HOUSE
KENNET HOUSE
CHURCH STREET EST
WINDRUSH HOUSE
DARENT HOUSE
CHURCH STREET
SALISBURY ST
MULREADY ST
EDEN HOUSE
LEA HOUSE
WANDLE HOUSE
RAVENSBOURNE HOUSE
BROADLEY ST
VENABLES STREET
BLACKWATER HOUSE
INGREBOURNE HOUSE
LAMBOURN HOUSE
CROMPTON STREET
PARSONS HOUSE
EDWARD HOUSE
HETHPOOL HOUSE
CHURCHFIELD HOUSE
CAMPBELL HOUSE
CROMPTON HOUSE
HALL PLACE
CUTHBERT ST
DEVONSHIRE HOUSE
ADPAR STREET
BRAITHWAITE TOWER
GILBERT SHELDON HOUSE
ST MARY'S MANSIONS

A
80
B
C
South Tower
83
WELLINGTON PLACE
WELLINGTON ROAD
St John's Wood Pre-Prep Sch
GREENBERRY ST
NORTH GATE
HIGH STREET
Tennis Court
Winfield House
4
Indoor Cricket Sch
A41
A5205
STRATHMORE CT
155
50
135
London Central Mosque
Boat Houses
FB
Jetty
LORD'S VIEW
OAK TREE RD
LODGE ROAD
NORTH BANK
REGENT CT
AIRLOP PL
BLAZER CT
3
Liberal Jewish Synagogue
89
NW8
GROVE GDNS
DURHAM HO
CROWN CT
MACMILLAN HO
PARK ROAD
Hanover Gate
ABBEY LODGE
HANOVER TERRACE
HANOVER TERR MEWS
KENT TERRACE
KENT PASSAGE
SUSSEX PLACE
LORNE CL
PARK LORNE
MONROE HO
ALPHA CL
MARY'S CT
ANNE'S CT
ALBERT'S CT
ELIZABETH CT
PALGRAVE GDNS
HANOVER GATE MANSIONS
Coll
98
London Business Sch
PO
ROSSMORE COURT
(Regent's Canal)
Canal
TICKFORD HO
SIMPSON HO
CASEY CL
PAVELEY STREET
SWAIN STREET
PADBURY HOUSE
OLNEY HOUSE
TRESHAM CRES
LINSLADE HOUSE
LAVENDON HOUSE
PAVELEY ST
HORWOOD HOUSE
HARDWICK HOUSE
KIMBLE HOUSE
COTTESLOE HOUSE
HUGHENDEN HOUSE
MISSENDEN HOUSE
CHETWODE HOUSE
JEROME CRES
VERNEY HOUSE
CHEQUERS HOUSE
TURVILLE HOUSE
GRENDON ST
WYCOMBE HOUSE
FINGEST HOUSE
DINTON HOUSE
LILESTONE STREET
GAYHURST HOUSE
MALLORY ST
RISBOROUGH HOUSE
PENN HOUSE
FULMAR HOUSE
BERNHARDT CRES
2
Gateway Prim Sch
CAPLAND STREET
LISSON GROVE
165
BELVEDERE HEIGHTS
SWANBOURNE HOUSE
ROSSMORE ROAD
TAUNTON PL
London Business Sch
IVOR CT
RADLEY HO
Francis Holland Sch
BOSTON HO
BALCOMBE HO
BRUNSWICK HO
HUNTSWORTH MEWS
LINHOPE STREET
IVOR PLACE
A41
207
MORDERN HOUSE
LASCELLES HOUSE
FARNHAM HOUSE
WIMBORNE HOUSE
BLANDFORD SQ
Marylebone Station
BOSTON PLACE
BALCOMBE STREET
170 CHAGFORD HOUSE
TAUNTON MEWS
147
DORSET
SQUARE
Marylebone
CAPLAND HOUSE
LILESTONE HOUSE
DICKENS HOUSE
SELINA HOUSE
FISHERTON STREET ESTATE
HUXLEY HOUSE
GIBBON HOUSE
BEDLOW CL
JORDANS HOUSE
CAPLAND ST
SAMFORD ST
MORRIS HOUSE
GATEFORTH ST
BOLDERO PL
Alfie's Antq Mkt
PLYMPTON PL
PLYMPTON ST
BROADLEY TERR
Sylvia Young Theatre Sch
PORTMAN GATE
110
St Edward's RC Prim Sch
1
WYTHAM HOUSE
LODDON HOUSE
WEY HOUSE
CHERWELL HOUSE
CHURCH STREET
MULREADY ST
ASHBRIDGE STREET
SALISBURY ST
WHITEHAVEN ST
COTES HOUSE
EDEN HOUSE
LEA HOUSE
Liby
PENFOLD STREET
CHURCH STREET EST
82
MEDWAY HOUSE
WANDLE HOUSE
RAVENSBOURNE HOUSE
BROADLEY STREET
LYON HOUSE
HUBERT HOUSE
SCOTT HOUSE
WHITFIELD HOUSE
EARL HOUSE
ALPHA HOUSE
Lisson Grove
HAYES PL
HAREWOOD AVENUE
Govt Offices
ASHMILL STREET
SHROTON STREET
COSWAY MANSIONS
PO
The Charter Nightingale Hosp
HAREWOOD ROW
BLACKWATER HOUSE
27
INGREBOURNE HOUSE
LAMBOURNE HOUSE
RANSTON ST
DAVENTRY ST
STALBRIDGE ST
102
BENDALL MEWS
Westminster
MELCOMBE PLACE
GT CENTRAL ST
DORSET
174
The Landmark

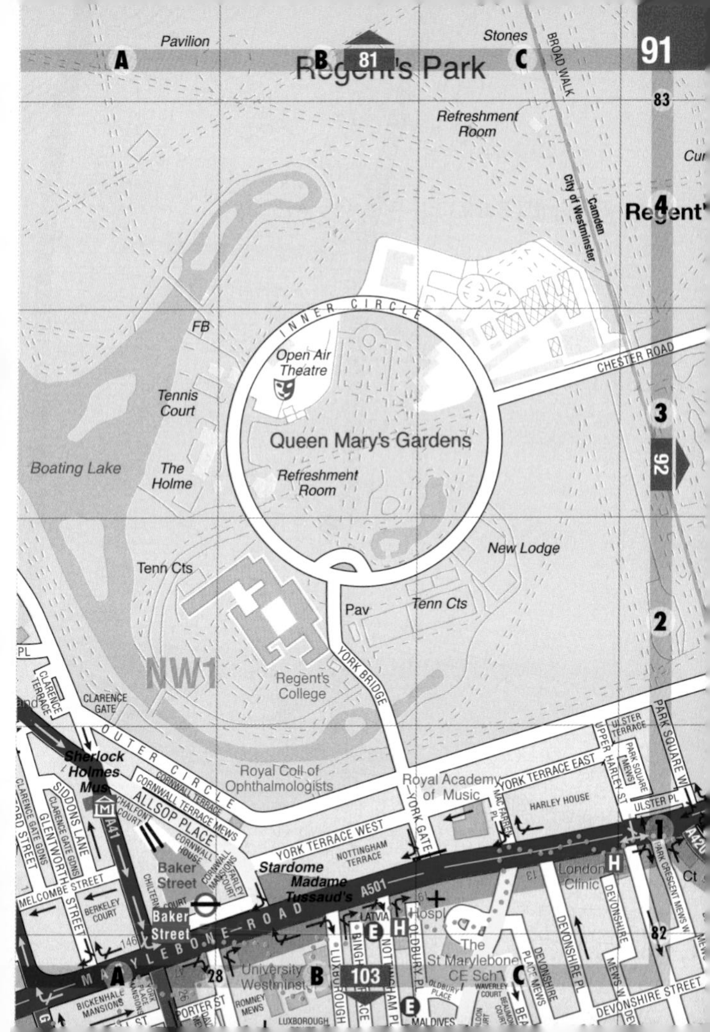
Regent's Park
Pavilion
Stones
A
B
C
81
BROAD WALK
83
Refreshment Room
City of Westminster
Camden
4
3
2
1
92
82
103
INNER CIRCLE
CHESTER ROAD
FB
Open Air Theatre
Tennis Court
Queen Mary's Gardens
Boating Lake
The Holme
Refreshment Room
New Lodge
Tenn Cts
Pav
Tenn Cts
NW1
YORK BRIDGE
Regent's College
CLARENCE TERRACE
CLARENCE GATE
OUTER CIRCLE
Sherlock Holmes Mus
Royal Coll of Ophthalmologists
Royal Academy of Music
YORK TERRACE EAST
ULSTER TERRACE
UPPER HARLEY ST
PARK SQUARE MEWS
PARK SQUARE W
HARLEY HOUSE
ULSTER PL
MACFARREN PL
YORK GATE
CORNWALL TERRACE
CORNWALL TERRACE MEWS
ALLSOP PLACE
CHALFONT COURT
CORNWALL HOUSE
CORNWALL MANSIONS
FARLEY COURT
YORK TERRACE WEST
NOTTINGHAM TERRACE
Stardome
Madame Tussaud's
A501
A41
Baker Street
London Clinic
DEVONSHIRE MEWS W
PARK CRESCENT MEWS W
A4201
Ct
SIDDONS LANE
CLARENCE GATE GDNS
GLENTWORTH STREET
MELCOMBE STREET
BERKELEY COURT
CHILTERN COURT
MARYLEBONE ROAD
LATVIA
Hospl
The St Marylebone CE Sch
DEVONSHIRE PL
DEVONSHIRE PLACE MEWS
DEVONSHIRE STREET
OLDBURY PL
OLDBURY PLACE
WAVERLEY COURT
LUXBOROUGH
NOTTINGHAM PL
University of Westminster
ROMNEY MEWS
PORTER ST
BICKENHALL MANSIONS
YORK PLACE MANSIONS
LUXBOROUGH
MALDIVES
28
146
13

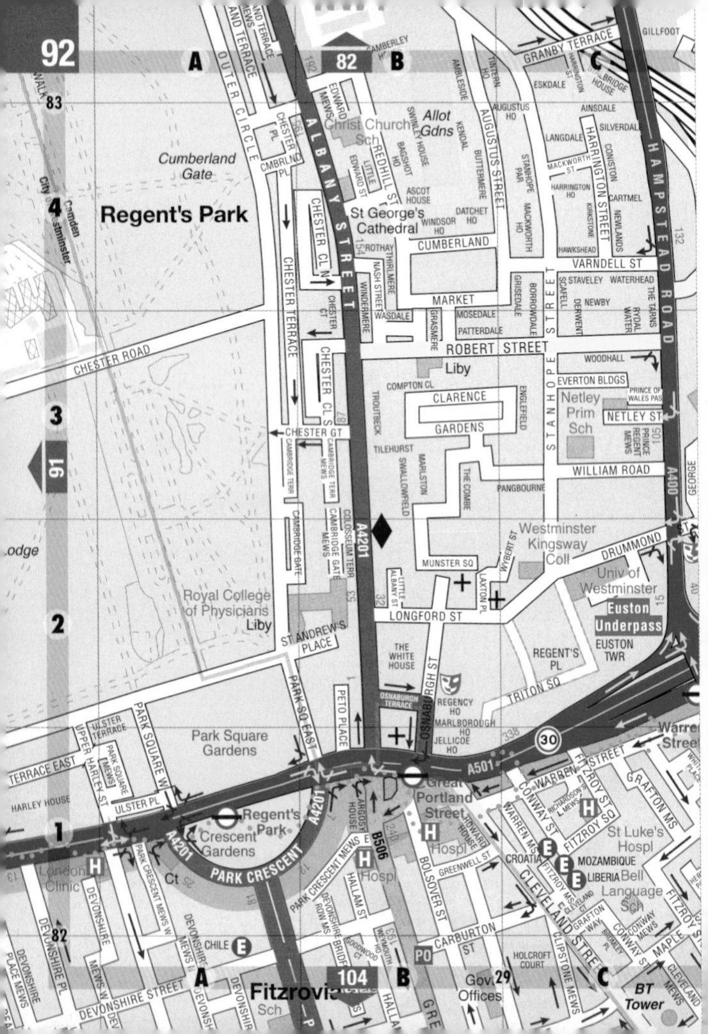
A
82
B
C
Regent's Park
Cumberland Gate
Royal College of Physicians
Liby
Park Square Gardens
Regent's Park
Crescent Gardens
London Clinic
Christ Church Sch
Allot Gdns
St George's Cathedral
Netley Prim Sch
Westminster Kingsway Coll
Univ of Westminster
Euston Underpass
EUSTON TWR
REGENT'S PL
TRITON SQ
Warren Street
Great Portland Street
Hospl
St Luke's Hospl
Bell Language Sch
Fitzrovia
Sch
Govt Offices
BT Tower
ALBANY STREET
A4201
HAMPSTEAD ROAD
A400
A501
B506
OUTER CIRCLE
CHESTER ROAD
CHESTER TERRACE
CHESTER GT
CAMBRIDGE TERR
CAMBRIDGE GATE
PARK SQ EAST
PARK SQUARE W
ULSTER TERRACE
ULSTER PL
UPPER HARLEY ST
PARK CRESCENT
PARK CRESCENT MEWS E
PARK CRESCENT MEWS W
DEVONSHIRE PL
DEVONSHIRE STREET
ROBERT STREET
LONGFORD ST
OSNABURGH ST
OSNABURGH TERRACE
PETO PLACE
ST ANDREW'S PLACE
MUNSTER SQ
CLARENCE GARDENS
WILLIAM ROAD
DRUMMOND
STANHOPE STREET
AUGUSTUS STREET
HARRINGTON STREET
GRANBY TERRACE
VARNDELL ST
NETLEY ST
CUMBERLAND
MARKET
WARREN STREET
CONWAY ST
FITZROY SQ
FITZROY ST
GRAFTON MS
CLEVELAND STREET
CARBURTON ST
BOLSOVER ST
HALLAM ST
GREENWELL ST
CLIPSTONE MEWS
MAPLE
CHILE
CROATIA
MOZAMBIQUE
LIBERIA
HOLCROFT COURT
PO
30
104
91
1
2
3
4

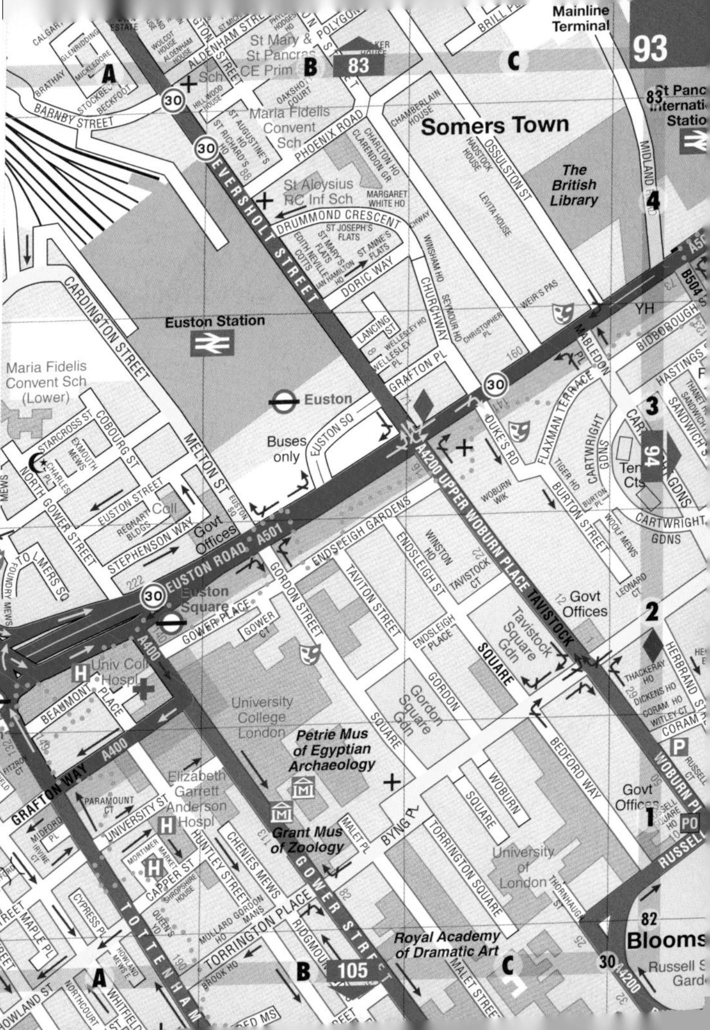
93
Mainline Terminal
A
B
C
83
Somers Town
St Mary & St Pancras CE Prim Sch
Maria Fidelis Convent Sch
St Aloysius RC Inf Sch
The British Library
St Pancras International Station
Euston Station
Euston
Buses only
Maria Fidelis Convent Sch (Lower)
Govt Offices
Coll
Euston Square
Univ Coll Hospl
University College London
Petrie Mus of Egyptian Archaeology
Grant Mus of Zoology
Elizabeth Garrett Anderson Hospl
Tavistock Square Gdn
Gordon Square Gdn
University of London
Royal Academy of Dramatic Art
Bloomsbury
Russell Square Gardens
YH
94
105
1
2
3
4
30
82
EVERSHOLT STREET
PHOENIX ROAD
DRUMMOND CRESCENT
DORIC WAY
OSSULSTON ST
MIDLAND ROAD
CHURCHWAY
CARDINGTON STREET
BARNBY STREET
ALDENHAM STREET
EUSTON ROAD
A501
UPPER WOBURN PLACE
A4200
TAVISTOCK SQUARE
ENDSLEIGH GARDENS
ENDSLEIGH ST
ENDSLEIGH PLACE
GORDON STREET
TAVITON STREET
GORDON SQUARE
WOBURN SQUARE
BEDFORD WAY
TORRINGTON SQUARE
TORRINGTON PLACE
GOWER STREET
GOWER PLACE
GOWER CT
MALET PL
MALET STREET
BYNG PL
CHENIES MEWS
HUNTLEY STREET
UNIVERSITY ST
GRAFTON WAY
A400
BEAUMONT PLACE
TOTTENHAM
NORTH GOWER STREET
EUSTON STREET
STEPHENSON WAY
MELTON ST
COBOURG ST
STARCROSS ST
DUKE'S RD
FLAXMAN TERRACE
BURTON STREET
CARTWRIGHT GDNS
MABLEDON PL
BIDBOROUGH ST
HASTINGS ST
HERBRAND ST
WOBURN PL
RUSSELL SQ
CORAM ST
THORNHAUGH ST
RIDGMOUNT
CAPPER ST
MAPLE PL
HOWLAND ST
WHITFIELD ST
CYPRESS PL
GRAFTON PL
EUSTON SQ
WOBURN WLK
LEONARD CT
WOOLF MEWS
TIGER HO
TOLMERS SQ
WEIR'S PAS
B504
PO
P

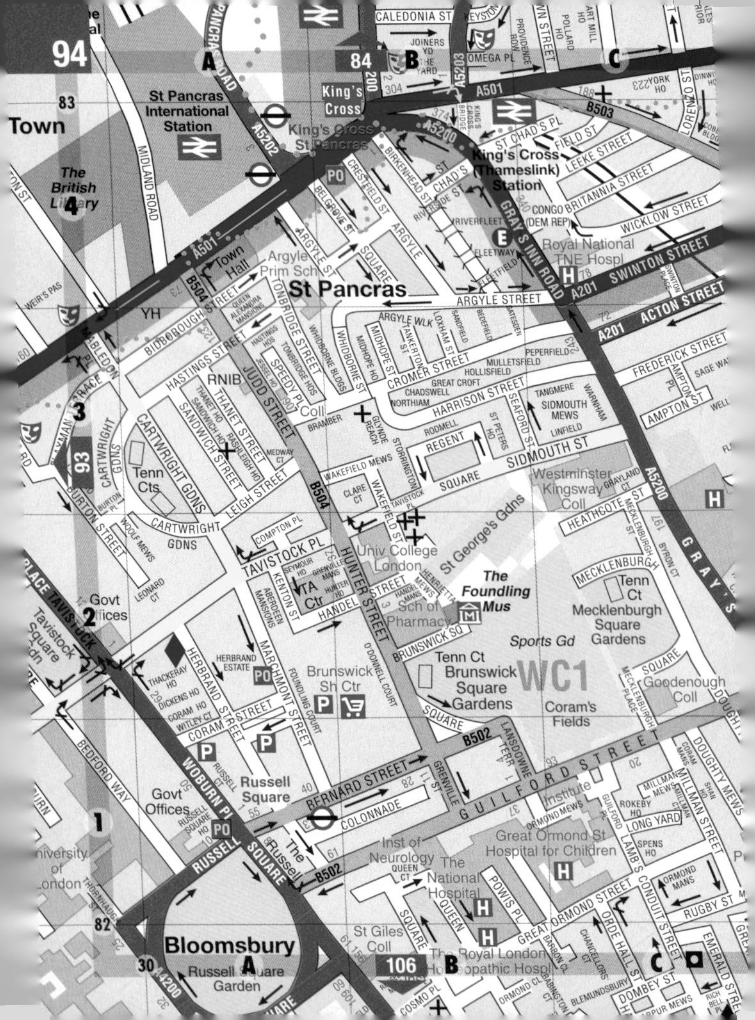
84
A
B
C
1
2
3
4
93
106
83
82
Town
St Pancras International Station
King's Cross
King's Cross St Pancras
The British Library
Midland Road
Pancras Road
A5202
A501
Caledonia St
Joiners Yd
The Yard
Omega Pl
Providence Row
Pollard Ho
York Ho
Lorenzo St
B503
A5203
A5200
King's Cross (Thameslink) Station
St Chad's Pl
Field St
Leeke Street
Britannia Street
Wicklow Street
Swinton Street
Acton Street
A201
Gray's Inn Road
Royal National TNE Hospl
Congo (Dem Rep)
Riverfleet
Fleetway
Fleetfield
Birkenhead St
St Chad's St
Crestfield St
Belgrove St
Argyle Square
Argyle St
Argyle Street
Argyle Wlk
Argyle Prim Sch
St Pancras
Town Hall
YH
Weir's Pas
Mabledon Pl
Bidborough Street
Queen Alexandra Mansions
Hastings Street
Hastings Hos
Tonbridge Street
Tonbridge Hos
Whidborne St
Whidborne Bldgs
Midhope St
Midhope Ho
Tankerton St
Loxham St
Sandfield
Bedefield
Cromer Street
Mulletsfield
Peperfield
Hollisfield
Great Croft
Chadswell
Northiam
Harrison Street
Frederick Street
Ampton Pl
Ampton St
Sage Way
Tangmere
Sidmouth Mews
Linfield
Warnham
Seaford St
St Peters Ho
Rodmell
Regent Square
Sidmouth St
Westminster Kingsway Coll
Grayland
Heathcote St
Mecklenburgh St
Byron Ct
Judd Street
B504
RNIB
Thanet St
Thanet Ho
Sandwich Ho
Sandwich Street
Rashleigh Ho
Speedy Pl
Coll
Bramber
Glynde Reach
Storrington
Medway Ct
Leigh Street
Cartwright Gdns
Tenn Cts
Burton Street
Burton Pl
Woolf Mews
Leonard Ct
Flaxman Terrace
Wakefield Mews
Wakefield St
Clare Ct
Tavistock Pl
Compton Pl
Tavistock Pl
Seymour Ho
Grenville Mans
Kenton St
Aberdeen Mansions
TA Ctr
Hunter Ho
Handel St
Hunter Street
Univ College London
St George's Gdns
Henrietta Mews
Handel Mans
Sch of Pharmacy
The Foundling Mus
Mecklenburgh
Tenn Ct
Mecklenburgh Square Gardens
Sports Gd
Brunswick Sq
Tenn Ct
Brunswick Square Gardens
WC1
Coram's Fields
Goodenough Coll
Mecklenburgh Place
Govt Offices
Tavistock Square Gdn
Tavistock Place
Herbrand Street
Herbrand Estate
Thackeray Ho
Dickens Ho
Goram Ho
Witley Ct
Coram Street
Marchmont Street
Foundling Court
Brunswick Sh Ctr
O'Donnell Court
Bedford Way
Woburn Pl
Russell Ct
Russell Square
Govt Offices
Russell Square Ho
Bernard Street
Colonnade
Grenville St
Lansdowne Terr
B502
Guilford Street
Institute
Ormond Mews
Guilford Pl
Coram Mans
Millman Mews
Millman Street
Doughty Mews
Rokeby Ho
Long Yard
Spens Ho
Lamb's Conduit Street
Great Ormond St Hospital for Children
Inst of Neurology
The National Hospital
Queen Ct
Queen Square
Powis Pl
Great Ormond Street
Ormond Mans
Rugby St
Orde Hall St
Chancellors Ct
Barbon Cl
Babington Ct
Emerald Street
Dombey St
Blemundsbury
Rich Bell
Harpur Mews
University of London
Thornhaugh St
Russell Square
The Russell
Bloomsbury
Russell Square Garden
A4200
St Giles Coll
The Royal London Homoeopathic Hospl
Ormond Cl
Cosmo Pl

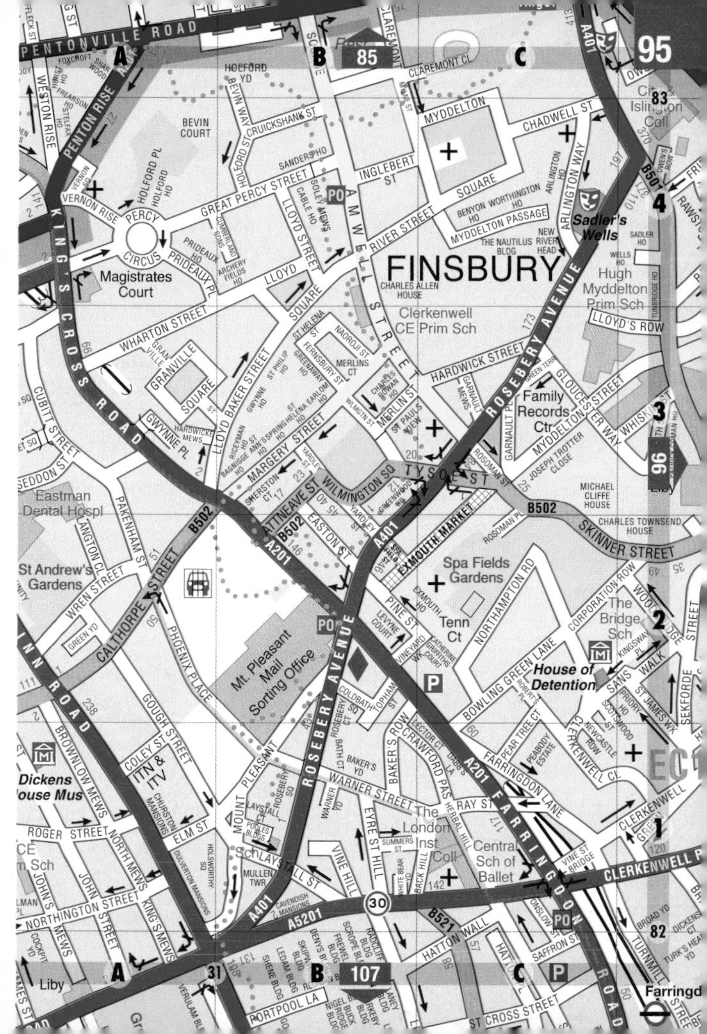
PENTONVILLE ROAD
A
B
85
C
PENTON RISE
WESTON RISE
FOXCROFT
HOLFORD YD
BEVIN WAY
CLAREMONT CL
MYDDELTON
CHADWELL ST
City & Islington Coll
83
BEVIN COURT
CRUICKSHANK ST
HOLFORD ST
HOLFORD PL
HOLFORD HO
SANDERS HO
INGLEBERT ST
SQUARE
VERNON SQ
VERNON RISE
GREAT PERCY STREET
SOLEY MEWS
CABLE HO
PO
AMWELL STREET
BENYON HO
WORTHINGTON HO
ARLINGTON HO
ARLINGTON WAY
B501
4
PERCY CIRCUS
LLOYD STREET
RIVER STREET
MYDDELTON PASSAGE
THE NAUTILUS BLDG
NEW RIVER HEAD
Sadler's Wells
SADLER HO
PRIDEAUX HO
PRIDEAUX PL
CUMBERLAND GDNS
ARCHERY FIELDS HO
WELLS HO
FINSBURY
Magistrates Court
LLOYD SQUARE
CHARLES ALLEN HOUSE
Hugh Myddelton Prim Sch
KING'S CROSS ROAD
WHARTON STREET
ST HELENA ST
NAOROJI ST
Clerkenwell CE Prim Sch
LLOYD'S ROW
TUNBRIDGE HO
GRANVILLE
GRANVILLE SQUARE
LLOYD BAKER STREET
ST PHILIP HO
FERNSBURY ST
GREENAWAY HO
MERLINS CT
HARDWICK STREET
GREEN TERR
GLOUCESTER WAY
CUBITT STREET
GWYNNE HO
ST HELENA HO
EARLOM HO
CHARLES BOWAN HO
MERLIN ST
GARNAULT MEWS
ROSEBERY AVENUE
Family Records Ctr
MYDDELTON ST
WHISKIN ST
3
GWYNNE PL
HARDWICKE MEWS
RICEYMAN HO
BAGNIGGE HO
ST ANN'S HO
SPRING HO
WILMGTN ST
ST PAULS VIEW
GARNAULT PL
JOSEPH TROTTER CLOSE
96
SEDDON ST
MARGERY STREET
YARDLEY ST
SHERSTON CT
WILMINGTON SQ
TYSOE ST
ROSOMAN ST
MICHAEL CLIFFE HOUSE
Eastman Dental Hospl
B502
PAKENHAM ST
ATTNEAVE ST
EASTON ST
GREENWOOD HO
EXMOUTH MARKET
ROSOMAN PL
SKINNER STREET
CHARLES TOWNSEND HOUSE
LANGTON CL
St Andrew's Gardens
WREN STREET
CALTHORPE STREET
A201
A401
SPA FIELD
Spa Fields Gardens
NORTHAMPTON RD
CORPORATION ROW
WOODBRIDGE STREET
The Bridge Sch
2
PHOENIX PLACE
Mt. Pleasant Mail Sorting Office
PINE ST
EXMOUTH HO
LEVYNE COURT
Tenn Ct
VINEYARD WK
CATHERINE GRIFFITHS COURT
BOWLING GREEN LANE
KINGSWAY PL
SANS WALK
GREEN YD
P
House of Detention
ROBERT'S PL
SEKFORDE STREET
GRAY'S INN ROAD
GOUGH STREET
COLDBATH SQ
TOPHAM ST
BAKER'S ROW
LECTOR CT
CRAWFORD PAS
DABB'S LA
PEAR TREE CT
PRIORY HO
SCOTSWOOD ST
ST JAMES WK
Dickens House Mus
BROWNLOW MEWS
COLEY ST
ITN & ITV
MOUNT PLEASANT
ROSEBERY CT
BATH CT
BAKER'S YD
FARRINGDON LANE
PEABODY ESTATE
NEWCASTLE ROW
CLERKENWELL CL
EC1
CHURSTON MANSIONS
ROSEBERY SQ
WARNER YD
WARNER STREET
RAY ST
FARRINGDON ROAD
CLERKENWELL GREEN
1
LAYSTALL CT
ROGER STREET
NORTH MEWS
ELM ST
POOLES BLDGS
EYRE ST HILL
The London Inst Coll
HERBAL HILL
Central Sch of Ballet
VINE ST BRIDGE
CLERKENWELL RD
JOHN'S MEWS
JOHN STREET
DULVERTON MANSIONS
HOLSWORTHY SQ
LAYSTALL ST
MULLEN TWR
VINE HILL
SUMMERS ST
WHITE BEAR YD
BACK HILL
NORTHINGTON STREET
KING'S MEWS
CAVENDISH MANSIONS
A5201
30
B521
HATTON WALL
ONSLOW ST
SAFFRON ST
BROAD YD
DICKENS CT
TURK'S HEAD YD
TURNMILL ST
82
COCKPIT YD
Liby
A
31
B
107
C
P
Farringdon
SKIPW BLDG
LEDAM BLDG
SHERIE BLDG
PORTPOOL LA
NIGEL BLDG
HATTON GDN
ST CROSS STREET

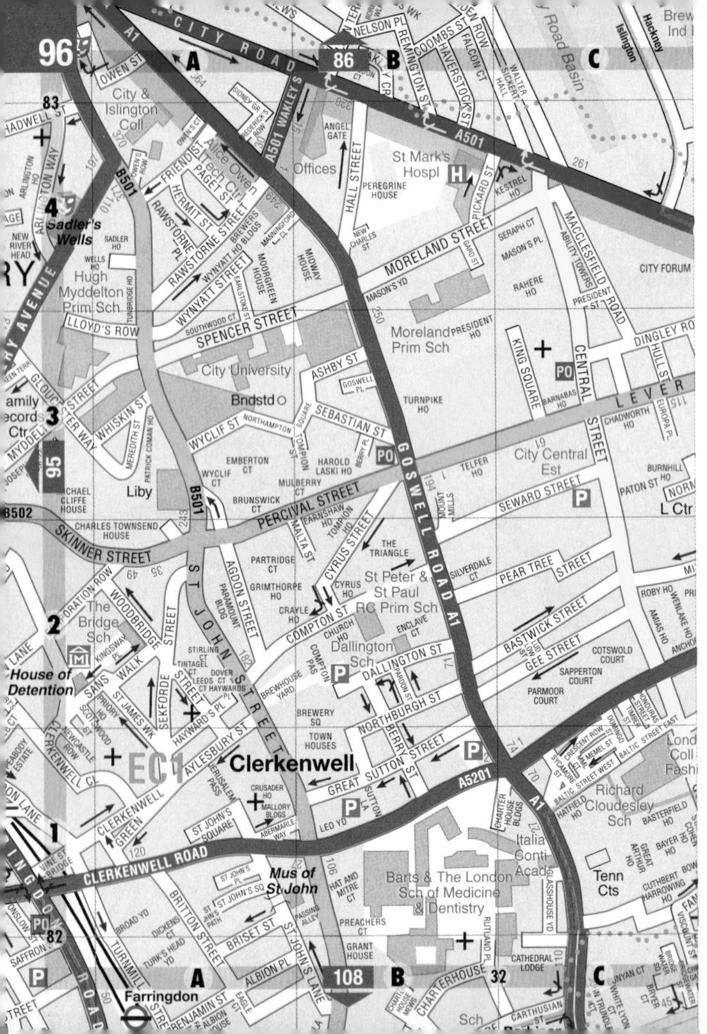
96
86
108
95
A
B
C
1
2
3
4
CITY ROAD
A1
A501
B501
A5201
B502
OWEN ST
City & Islington Coll
CHADWELL ST
ARLINGTON WAY
Sadler's Wells
NEW RIVER HEAD
Hugh Myddelton Prim Sch
LLOYD'S ROW
FRIEND ST
HERMIT ST
PAGET ST
Alice Owen Tech Ctr
RAWSTORNE ST
RAWSTORNE STREET
WYNYATT STREET
SPENCER STREET
City University
Bndstd
WAKLEY ST
ANGEL GATE
Offices
HALL STREET
St Mark's Hospl
PEREGRINE HOUSE
MORELAND STREET
Moreland Prim Sch
MACCLESFIELD ROAD
CITY FORUM
DINGLEY RD
KING SQUARE
CENTRAL STREET
LEVER STREET
City Central Est
SEWARD STREET
GOSWELL ROAD A1
ASHBY ST
SEBASTIAN ST
NORTHAMPTON SQUARE
WYCLIF ST
WHISKIN ST
GLOUCESTER WAY
MYDDELTON
Family Records Ctr
Liby
PERCIVAL STREET
SKINNER STREET
ST JOHN STREET
AGDON STREET
CYRUS STREET
PEAR TREE STREET
BASTWICK STREET
GEE STREET
St Peter & St Paul RC Prim Sch
COMPTON ST
Dallington Sch
DALLINGTON ST
NORTHBURGH ST
GREAT SUTTON STREET
BERRY ST
The Bridge Sch
WOODBRIDGE STREET
House of Detention
SANS WALK
SEKFORDE STREET
AYLESBURY ST
Clerkenwell
EC1
CLERKENWELL GREEN
CLERKENWELL CL
ST JOHN'S SQUARE
CLERKENWELL ROAD
Mus of St John
BRITTON STREET
TURNMILL
Farringdon
FARRINGDON ROAD
Barts & The London Sch of Medicine & Dentistry
CHARTERHOUSE
CATHEDRAL LODGE
Italia Conti Acad
Richard Cloudesley Sch
Tenn Cts
BALTIC STREET WEST
BALTIC STREET EAST
Lond Coll Fashi
City Road Basin
Islington
Hackney

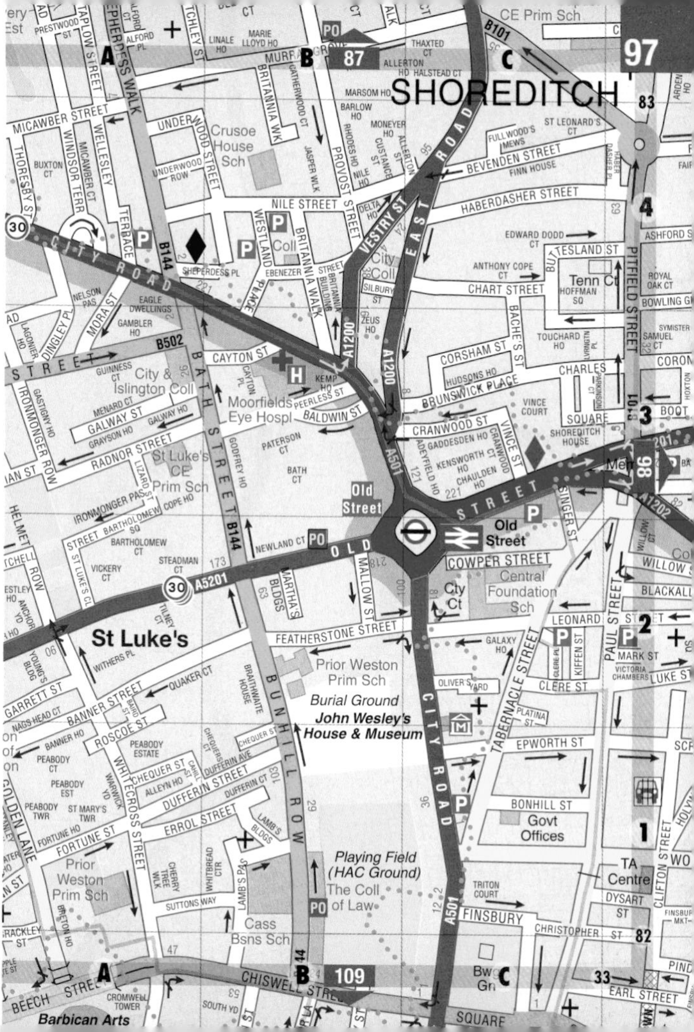
SHOREDITCH
St Luke's
A
B
C
87
109
98
97
83
82
4
3
2
1
CE Prim Sch
PRESTWOOD ST
TAPLOW STREET
SHEPHERDESS WALK
ALFORD PL
LINALE HO
MARIE LLOYD HO
MURRAY GROVE
PO
THAXTED CT
ALLERTON HO
HALSTEAD CT
B101
MARSOM HO
BARLOW HO
MONEYER HO
RHODES HO
NILE HO
CUSTANCE ST
ALLERTON ST
BRITANNIA WK
CATHERWOOD CT
JASPER WLK
PROVOST STREET
EAST ROAD
ST LEONARD'S CT
FULLWOOD'S MEWS
BEVENDEN STREET
FINN HOUSE
HABERDASHER PL
HABERDASHER STREET
MICAWBER STREET
WINDSOR TERR
MICAWBER CT
WELLESLEY TERRACE
THORESBY ST
BUXTON CT
UNDERWOOD STREET
UNDERWOOD ROW
Crusoe House Sch
NILE STREET
DELTA HO
VESTRY ST
WESTLAND PLACE
BRITANNIA WALK
P
Coll
City Coll
EDWARD DODD CT
BUTTESLAND ST
ANTHONY COPE CT
Tenn Ct
HOFFMAN SQ
CHART STREET
PITFIELD STREET
ASHFORD ST
ROYAL OAK CT
BOWLING GN
30
CITY ROAD
B144
SHEPHERDESS PL
EBENEZER ST
BRITANNIA BUILDING
SILBURY ST
221
NELSON PAS
EAGLE DWELLINGS
MORA ST
GAMBLER HO
DINGLEY PL
LAGONIER HO
ZEUS HO
A1200
BACHE'S ST
TOUCHARD HO
NUTTALL PL
SYMISTER
SAMUEL CT
CORONET
B502
STREET
GUINNESS CT
City & Islington Coll
BATH STREET
CAYTON ST
CAYTON PL
H
KEMP HO
PEERLESS ST
Moorfields Eye Hospl
BALDWIN ST
CORSHAM ST
HUDSONS HO
BRUNSWICK PLACE
VINCE COURT
CHARLES SQUARE
PARKINSON CT
HOXTON
BOOT
MENARD CT
GALWAY ST
GALWAY HO
GRAYSON HO
IRONMONGER ROW
GASTIGNY HO
RADNOR STREET
LIZARD ST
St Luke's CE Prim Sch
GODFREY HO
PATERSON CT
BATH CT
A501
CRANWOOD ST
GADDESDEN HO
ADEYFIELD HO
KENSWORTH CT
CRANWOOD
VINCE ST
CHAULDEN HO
SHOREDITCH HOUSE
OLD STREET
A1202
IRONMONGER PAS
COPE HO
Old Street
SINGER ST
BARTHOLOMEW SQ
BARTHOLOMEW CT
STEADMAN CT
VICKERY CT
ST LUKE'S CL
NEWLAND CT
B144
173
OLD
MALLOW ST
COWPER STREET
City Ct
Central Foundation Sch
WILLOW ST
BLACKALL
HELMET ROW
MITCHELL
A5201
TILNEY CT
MARTHA'S BLDGS
FEATHERSTONE STREET
LEONARD ST
PAUL STREET
WITHERS PL
YOUNG'S BLDG
ANCHOR YD
GALAXY HO
TABERNACLE STREET
CLERE PL
KIFFEN ST
MARK ST
VICTORIA CHAMBERS
LUKE ST
Prior Weston Prim Sch
Burial Ground
John Wesley's House & Museum
BRAITHWAITE HOUSE
BUNHILL ROW
OLIVER'S YARD
CLERE ST
PLATINA ST
GARRETT ST
NAGS HEAD CT
BANNER STREET
BAIRD ST
QUAKER CT
ROSCOE ST
BANNER HO
PEABODY CT
PEABODY ESTATE
CHEQUERS CT
CHEQUER ST
CAHILL ST
DUFFERIN AVE
DUFFERIN STREET
DUFFERIN CT
ALLEYN HO
EPWORTH ST
PEABODY EST
WARWICK YD
WHITECROSS STREET
PEABODY TWR
ST MARY'S TWR
FORTUNE HO
FORTUNE ST
ERROL STREET
LAMB'S BLDGS
GOLDEN LANE
BONHILL ST
Govt Offices
CLIFTON STREET
Playing Field (HAC Ground)
The Coll of Law
Prior Weston Prim Sch
CHERRY TREE WLK
WHITBREAD CTR
LAMB'S PAS
SUTTONS WAY
Cass Bsns Sch
TA Centre
DYSART ST
TRITON COURT
FINSBURY
CHRISTOPHER ST
FINSBURY MKT
BRETON HO
BRACKLEY ST
CHISWELL STREET
BEECH STREET
CROMWELL TOWER
Barbican Arts
SOUTH YD
Bwg Gn
EARL STREET
SQUARE
PIND
33

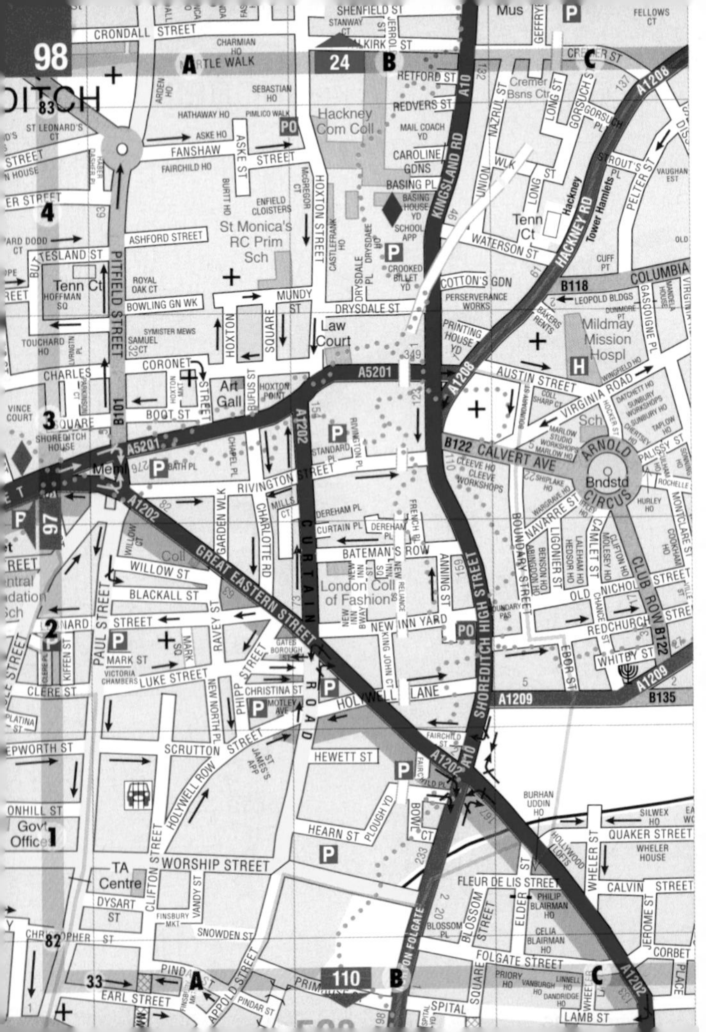
CRONDALL STREET
CHARMIAN HO
MYRTLE WALK
SHENFIELD ST
STANWAY CT
FALKIRK ST
JERROLD ST
24
RETFORD ST
REDVERS ST
MAIL COACH YD
CAROLINE GDNS
BASING PL
BASING HOUSE YD
SCHOOL APP
Hackney Com Coll
KINGSLAND RD
A10
Mus
GEFFRYE
FELLOWS CT
CREMER ST
Cremer Bsns Ctr
NAZRUL ST
LONG ST
GORSUCH ST
GORSUCH PL
A1208
UNION WLK
Tenn Ct
Hackney
Tower Hamlets
HACKNEY RD
STROUT'S PL
PELTER ST
VAUGHAN EST
WATERSON ST
CUFF PT
COLUMBIA RD
B118
LEOPOLD BLDGS
DUNMORE PT
GASCOIGNE PL
MANDELA HOUSE
BAKERS RENTS
Mildmay Mission Hospl
COTTON'S GDN
PERSERVERANCE WORKS
PRINTING HOUSE YD
SHOREDITCH
83
ST LEONARD'S CT
STREET
FANSHAW STREET
ASKE HO
ASKE ST
FAIRCHILD HO
HATHAWAY HO
PIMLICO WALK
SEBASTIAN HO
ARDEN HO
HABER DASHER PL
BURTT HO
ENFIELD CLOISTERS
McGREGOR CT
HOXTON STREET
CASTLEFRANK HO
DRYSDALE PL
DRYSDALE HO
CROOKED BILLET YD
St Monica's RC Prim Sch
ASHFORD STREET
ROYAL OAK CT
BOWLING GN WK
MUNDY ST
DRYSDALE ST
Law Court
PITFIELD STREET
ARD DODD CT
TESLAND ST
BUTTESLAND
Tenn Ct
HOFFMAN SQ
TOUCHARD HO
IVYINGTN PL
SYMISTER MEWS
SAMUEL CT
HOXTON SQUARE
CORONET ST
HOXTON MKT
Art Gall
RUFUS ST
HOXTON POINT
A5201
349
AUSTIN STREET
WINGFIELD HO
VIRGINIA ROAD
COLL SHARP CT
BOUNDARY ST
DATCHETT HO
SUNBURY WORKSHOPS
SUNBURY HO
TAPLOW HO
CHERTSEY HO
HOCKER ST
Sch
MARLOW STUDIO WORKSHOPS
MARLOW HO
CHARLES SQUARE
PARKINSON CT
BOOT ST
B101
VINCE COURT
SHOREDITCH HOUSE
A1202
STANDARD PL
RIVINGTON PL
123
B122 CALVERT AVE
CLEEVE HO
CLEEVE WORKSHOPS
SHIPLAKE HO
ARNOLD CIRCUS
Bndstd
PALISSY ST
ROCHELLE ST
HURLEY HO
A5201
Meml
BATH PL
CHAPEL PL
RIVINGTON STREET
MILLS CT
DEREHAM PL
CURTAIN PL
DEREHAM PL
FRENCH PL
WARGRAVE HO
NAVARRE ST
LIGONIER ST
BENSON HO
HEDSOR HO
LALEHAM HO
CAMLET ST
MOLESEY HO
CLIFTON HO
MONTCLARE ST
COOKHAM HO
CLUB ROW
97
WILLOW CT
Coll
GREAT EASTERN STREET
GARDEN WLK
CHARLOTTE RD
CURTAIN ROAD
BATEMAN'S ROW
ANNING ST
London Coll of Fashion
WILLOW ST
BLACKALL ST
NEW INN SQ
NEW INN ST
NEW INN BWAY
NEW RELIANCE ST
NEW INN YARD
SHOREDITCH HIGH STREET
BOUNDARY STREET
ABINGDON HO
BOUNDARY PAS
OLD NICHOL STREET
CHANCE ST
REDCHURCH ST
B122
LEONARD STREET
PAUL STREET
MARK ST
MARK SQ
RAVEY ST
GATES BOROUGH ST
PHIPP STREET
PO
EBOR ST
WHITBY ST
A1209
KIFFEN ST
CLERE PL
CLERE ST
VICTORIA CHAMBERS
LUKE STREET
CHRISTINA ST
MOTLEY AVE
KING JOHN CT
HOLYWELL LANE
A1209
B135
PLATINA ST
NEW NORTH PL
SCRUTTON STREET
ST JAMES'S APP
HEWETT ST
FAIRCHILD ST
FAIRCHILD PL
EPWORTH ST
HOLYWELL ROW
BURHAN UDDIN HO
SILWEX HO
QUAKER STREET
WHELER HOUSE
WHELER ST
HOLLYWOOD LOFTS
BONHILL ST
Govt Offices
HEARN ST
PLOUGH YD
BOWL CT
CLIFTON STREET
WORSHIP STREET
TA Centre
DYSART ST
VANDY ST
FINSBURY MKT
SNOWDEN ST
FLEUR DE LIS STREET
ELDER ST
PHILIP BLAIRMAN HO
CELIA BLAIRMAN HO
CALVIN STREET
JEROME ST
BLOSSOM PL
BLOSSOM STREET
CORBET PL
CHRISTOPHER ST
82
PINDAR ST
APPOLD STREET
110
PRIMROSE ST
FOLGATE STREET
PRIORY HO
VANBURGH HO
LINNELL HO
DANDRIDGE HO
33
EARL STREET
FINSBURY MKT
PINDAR ST
SPITAL YD
SPITAL SQUARE
NORTON FOLGATE
LAMB ST
A1202
A
B
C
1
2
3
4

24
25
111
A
B
C
4
3
2
1
BETHNAL GREEN
E2
Spitalfields
BETHNAL GREEN RD
A1209
B118
B108
B134
B135
OLD BETHNAL GREEN RD
WARNER PL
SQUIRRIES ST
VALLANCE RD
BRICK LANE
GOSSET ST
DUNBRIDGE ST
CHESHIRE ST
SCLATER STREET
Brick Lane
BUXTON STREET
WEAVER STREET
PEDLEY STREET
UNDERWOOD RD
WOODSEER ST
HANBURY
COVERLEY
LOMAS ST
SELBY ST
MANSFORD ST
POLLARD ROW
POLLARD ST
FLORIDA ST
VIVIMEY ST
VOSS ST
DERBYSHIRE ST
HAGUE ST
BUCKFAST ST
SALE ST
HEREFORD ST
RAMSEY ST
CHESTER ST
KELSEY ST
MAPE ST
WOOD CL
ST MATTHEW'S ROW
GOLDMAN CL
TURIN STREET
BARNET GROVE
ROBERTA ST
DURANT ST
WIMBOLT ST
BAXENDALE ST
QUILTER ST
WELLINGTON ROW
TILLET WAY
DELTA ST
ELWIN ST
COLUMBIA RD
EZRA ST
RAVENSCROFT ST
SHIPTON ST
CADELL CL
HORATIO ST
BATH GR
LONDON TERR
HASSARD ST
BARONESS RD
CHAMBORD STREET
TOMLINSON CL
PADBURY CT
SHACKLEWELL ST
GRANBY STREET
GRANBY ST
CHILTON ST
RHODA ST
SWANFIELD STREET
BACON ST
GRIMSBY STREET
FLEET STREET HILL
WEAVER ST
SHUTTLE ST
CODE ST
SPITAL STREET
DEAL ST
HUNTON ST
HEMMING ST
SURMA CL
GRANARY RD
FAKRUDDIN ST
ST PETER'S CL
ST PETER'S ST
NELSON GDNS
KITE PL
GREY EAGLE STREET
SHEBA PL
CYGNET ST
Ion Square Gdns
Jesus Green
Ravenscroft Park
Columbia Prim Sch
Columbia Road
Liby
Bethnal Green Tech Coll
Elizabeth Selby Inf Sch
Lawdale Jun Sch
Oaklands Sec Sch
Weavers Fields
Weaver's Field Sch
William Davis Prim Sch
St Matthias CE Prim Sch
Allen Gdns
Thomas Buxton Jun & Inf Sch
St Anne RC Prim Sch
Osmani Prim Sch
Vallance Road Gdns
Swanlea Sec Sch
PO

DOWNFIELD CL
ALDSWORTH CL
FOSCOTE MEWS
AMBERLEY RD
Coll
Grand Union Canal (Paddington Branch)
CLEARWELL DRIVE
CHARFIELD
ELLWOOD CT
BARNWOOD CL
88
CE Prim Sch
FORMOSA STREET
WARWICK AVENUE
B413
BRISTOL MEWS
BRISTOL GDNS
CLIFTON VILLAS
Warwick Avenue
FB
PRINCETHORPE HO
St Mary Magdalene CE Prim Sch
ROWINGTON CL
WILMCOTE HO
WOODCHESTER SQ
DARTINGTON HO
SENIOR ST
LORD HILLS RD
Grand Union Canal Wlk
DELAMERE TERRACE
WARWICK PLACE
BLOMFIELD RD
OLESWORTH HO
ALFRED RD
CIRENCESTER ST
Edward Wilson Prim Sch
DESBOROUGH CLOSE
ATHERSTONE CT
CHICHESTER RD
LAPWORTH COURT
WESTBOURNE TERRACE RD
Grand Union
WARWICK CRESCENT
A404
PO
Our Lady of Dolours RC Prim Sch
BOURNE TERRACE
GAYDON HO
BLOMFIELD VILLAS
DELAMERE STREET
STBOURNE GN P COMPLEX
BRINKLOW HO
TORQUAY ST
HARROW RD
A404
A40
WESTWAY (ELEVATED)
A40
PADDING
RANELAGH BRIDGE
WESTBOURNE BRIDGE
W2
B411
Royal Oak
31
WESTBOURNE PARK VILLAS
ELSIE LANE CT
CLIFFORD CT
CELBRIDGE MEWS
PORCHESTER ROAD
WESTBOURNE COURT
BREWERS COURT
TALBOT RD
WESTBOURNE PARK RD
VERA CT
PORCHESTER SQUARE
ORSETT MEWS
ORSETT TERRACE
BISHOP'S BRIDGE
DURHAM TERR
WESTBOURNE GDNS
PORCHESTER TERRACE
KILDARE TERR
ALEXANDER ST
ALEXANDER MEWS
Liby
Liby
PORCHESTER MEWS
PORCHESTER TERRACE N
GLOUCESTER GDNS
WESTBOURNE TERR MEWS
KILDARE CT
SUNDERLAND TERR
BURDETT MEWS
GREVILLE LO
BRIDGE FIELD HO
QUEENSWAY
RALPH COURT
PETERS COURT
BISHOPS COURT
CAERNARVON HOUSE
CLOVELLY HOUSE
GLOUCESTER
KILDARE GDNS
WESTBOURNE GROVE TERR
HATHERLEY GR
HATHERLEY CT
ARTHUR CT
PICKERING MEWS
B411
A4206
EXETER HOUSE
LYNTON HOUSE
BRIDGWATER HOUSE
BRECON HOUSE
GURNEY HO
NEWTON RD
NEWBURY HOUSE
MARLOW HOUSE
PEMBROKE HOUSE
PICKERING HOUSE
WORCESTER HOUSE
TENBY HOUSE
MONMOUTH PL
RIVEN CT
E
DOMINICAN REPUBLIC
WINCHESTER HOUSE
CLEVELAND GDNS
HEREFORD MEWS
MONMOUTH RD
A4206
WESTBOURNE GR
B411
INVER COURT
COMPASS HO
READING HOUSE
GARWAY RD
Whiteleys Ctr
Hallfield Jun & Inf Schs
TAUNTON HOUSE
CLEVELAND SQUARE
College Park Sch
GARDENS SQ
KENSINGTON
REDAN PLACE
CERVANTES COURT
PORCHESTER GDN MWS
LEINSTER PL
LEINSTER GARDENS
LEINSTER SQ
PO
PORCHESTER COURT
PORCHESTER
GARDENS
INVERNESS TERR
TENNIEL
QUEEN'S GARDENS
PRINCE'S SQ
114
QUEEN'S MEWS
SALEM RD
QUEENS
Bays
CHAPEL HILL GDNS
A
B
C
A
B
C
4
3
2
1
82
81
26
26

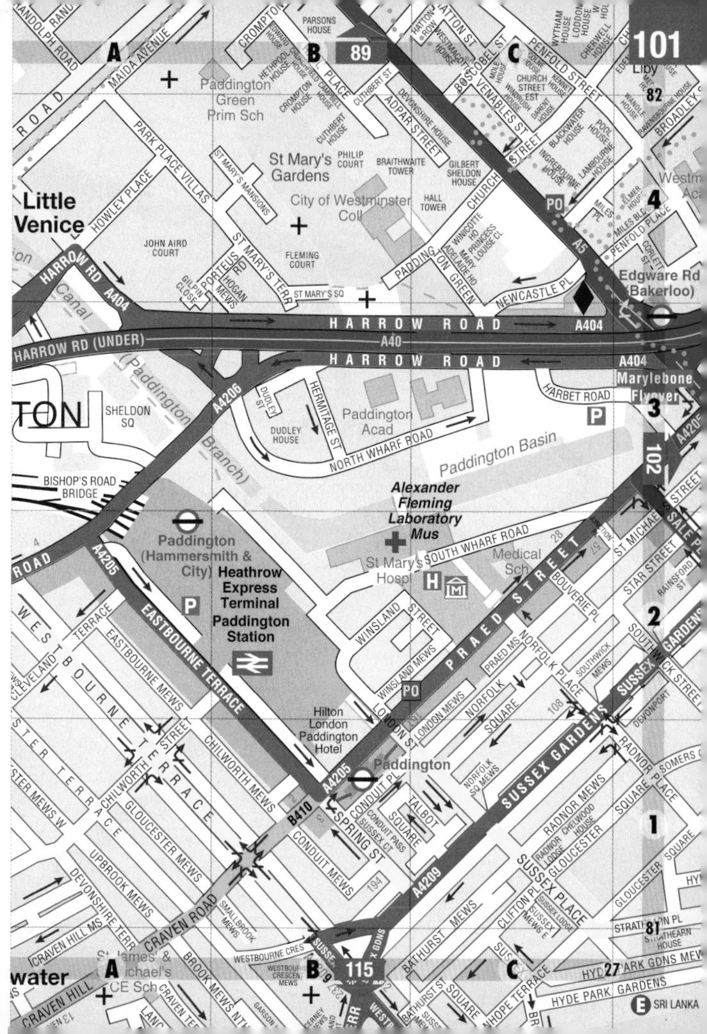
89
A
B
C
Maida Avenue
Randolph Road
Parsons House
Crompton St
Paddington Green Prim Sch
Hatton St
Westmacott House
Boscobel St
Penfold Street
Wytham House
Loddon House
Cherwell House
Liby
82
Church Street Est
Venables St
Cuthbert St
Devonshire House
Adpar Street
Braithwaite Tower
Gilbert Sheldon House
Hall Tower
Church Street
Blackwater House
Pool House
Lambourne House
Ingrebourne House
Broadley St
Park Place Villas
Howley Place
Little Venice
St Mary's Mansions
St Mary's Gardens
Philip Court
City of Westminster Coll
John Aird Court
St Mary's Terr
Fleming Court
Porteus Rd
Hogan Mews
Gilpin Close
St Mary's Sq
Paddington Green
Newcastle Pl
PO
A5
4
Miles Pl
Penfold Place
Corlett St
Edgware Rd (Bakerloo)
Harrow Rd
A404
Canal
Harrow Road
Harrow Rd (Under)
A40
Marylebone Flyover
Harbet Road
3
A4206
Sheldon Sq
(Paddington Branch)
Dudley St
Hermitage St
Dudley House
Paddington Acad
North Wharf Road
Paddington Basin
102
A4205
Bishop's Road Bridge
Paddington (Hammersmith & City)
Alexander Fleming Laboratory Mus
South Wharf Road
St Mary's Hospl
Medical Sch
Heathrow Express Terminal Paddington Station
Road
A4205
Eastbourne Terrace
Praed Street
Junction Pl
Bouverie Pl
St Michaels St
Star Street
Rainsford St
Sale Pl
2
Westbourne Terrace
Cleveland Terrace
Eastbourne Mews
Winsland Street
Winsland Mews
Praed Ms
Norfolk Place
Southwick Mews
Sussex Gardens
Southwick Street
PO
London Mews
Norfolk Square
London St
Devonport
Hilton London Paddington Hotel
Paddington
Norfolk Sq Mews
Radnor Place
Somers Cres
Chilworth Street
Chilworth Mews
Westbourne Terrace
Gloucester Mews
Conduit Pl
Talbot Square
Sussex Gardens
Radnor Mews
Chelwood House
Gloucester Square
1
B410
Spring St
Conduit Pass
Sussex Ct
Conduit Mews
Westbourne Terrace Mews
Upbrook Mews
Devonshire Terr
Craven Road
Craven Hill Ms
Smallbrook Mews
194
A4209
Radnor Lodge
Gloucester Square
Sussex Place
Clifton Pl
Sussex Mews E
Sussex Lodge
Strathearn Pl
81
Strathearn House
Bathurst Mews
Westbourne Cres
Westbourne Crescent Mews
115
Sussex Sq
Hyde Park Gdns Mews
27
St James' & St Michael's CE Sch
Craven Hill
Brook Mews Nth
Craven Terr
Bathurst St
Hyde Park Gardens
Stanhope Terrace
Sri Lanka
water

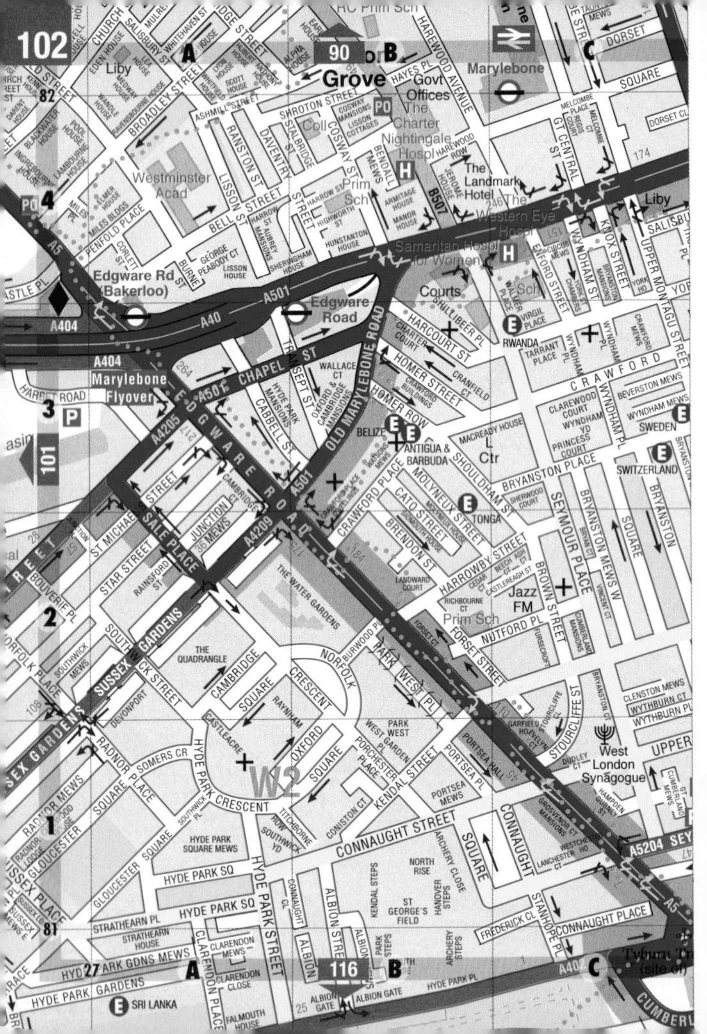
90
Grove
Marylebone
Govt Offices
The Charter Nightingale Hospl
The Landmark Hotel
The Western Eye Hospl
Samaritan Hospl for Women
Westminster Acad
Edgware Rd (Bakerloo)
Edgware Road
Courts
Marylebone Flyover
EDGWARE ROAD
OLD MARYLEBONE ROAD
CHAPEL ST
HAREWOOD AVENUE
DORSET SQUARE
BROADLEY STREET
LISSON ST
BELL ST
RANSTON ST
DAVENTRY ST
COSWAY ST
SHROTON STREET
ASHMILL STREET
PENFOLD PLACE
HARCOURT ST
HOMER STREET
HOMER ROW
CRAWFORD PLACE
CRAWFORD
MOLYNEUX STREET
CATO STREET
BRENDON ST
SHOULDHAM ST
HARROWBY STREET
BRYANSTON PLACE
SEYMOUR PLACE
BROWN STREET
BRYANSTON SQUARE
UPPER MONTAGU STREET
ENFORD STREET
WYNDHAM ST
KNOX STREET
CABBELL ST
TRANSEPT ST
SALE PLACE
STAR STREET
JUNCTION MEWS
SUSSEX GARDENS
SOUTHWICK STREET
CAMBRIDGE SQUARE
NORFOLK CRESCENT
OXFORD SQUARE
HYDE PARK CRESCENT
CONNAUGHT STREET
CONNAUGHT SQUARE
CONNAUGHT PLACE
KENDAL STREET
FORSET STREET
PARK WEST PL
HYDE PARK SQ
HYDE PARK STREET
HYDE PARK GARDENS
GLOUCESTER SQUARE
RADNOR PLACE
STRATHEARN PL
CLARENDON PLACE
THE WATER GARDENS
THE QUADRANGLE
Jazz FM
L Ctr
Prim Sch
West London Synagogue
Tyburn Tree (site of)
BELIZE
ANTIGUA & BARBUDA
TONGA
RWANDA
SWEDEN
SWITZERLAND
SRI LANKA
W2
A5
A40
A404
A501
A4205
A4209
A5204
A402
B507
116
101
A
B
C
1
2
3
4

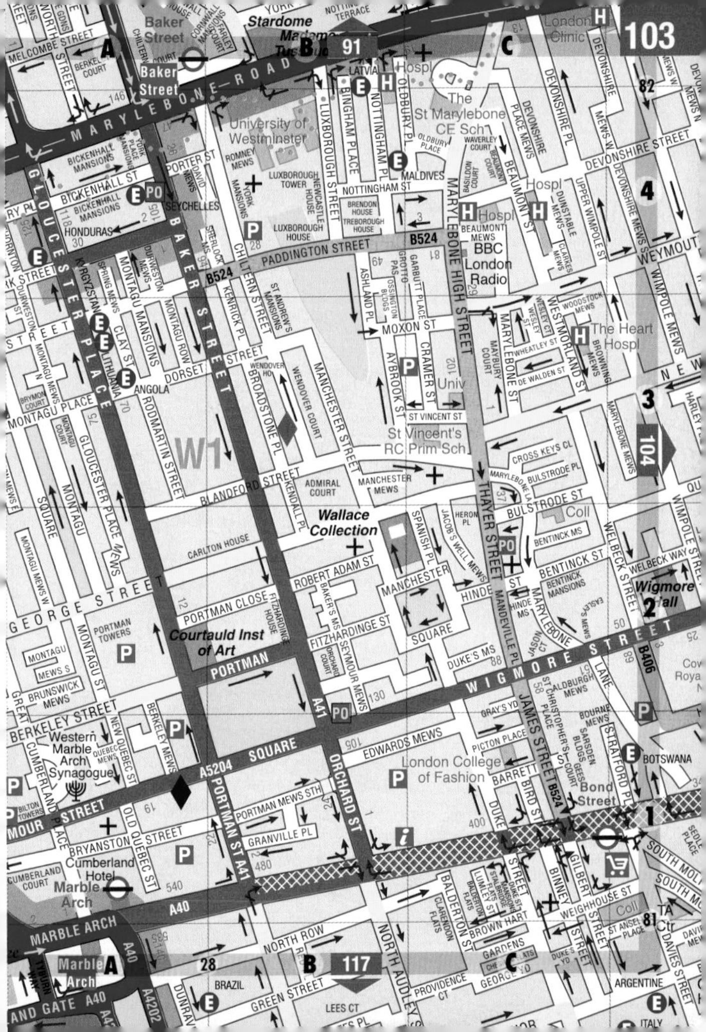
Baker Street
Stardome
Madame Tussauds
91
MELCOMBE STREET
BERKELEY COURT
MARYLEBONE ROAD
Hospl
The St Marylebone CE Sch
London Clinic
DEVONSHIRE PL
DEVONSHIRE PLACE MEWS
DEVONSHIRE MEWS W
DEVONSHIRE STREET
University of Westminster
BINGHAM PLACE
NOTTINGHAM PL
OLDBURY PL
OLDBURY PLACE
LUXBOROUGH STREET
LUXBOROUGH TOWER
LUXBOROUGH HOUSE
NEWCASTLE HOUSE
ROMNEY MEWS
YORK MANSIONS
PORTER ST
DAVID MEWS
BICKENHALL MANSIONS
BICKENHALL ST
SEYCHELLES
HONDURAS
MALDIVES
NOTTINGHAM ST
BRENDON HOUSE
TREBOROUGH HOUSE
WAVERLEY COURT
BEAUMONT COURT
BASILDON COURT
BEAUMONT ST
BEAUMONT MEWS
UPPER WIMPOLE ST
DUNSTABLE MEWS
CLARKES MEWS
WEYMOUTH
GLOUCESTER PLACE
BAKER STREET
SHERLOCK MS
CHILTERN STREET
PADDINGTON STREET
B524
GROTTO PAS
GARBUTT PLACE
ASHLAND PL
OSSINGTON BLDGS
MARYLEBONE HIGH STREET
BBC London Radio
WESTMORLAND ST
WOODSTOCK MEWS
WESLEY ST
WHEATLEY ST
DE WALDEN ST
The Heart Hospl
BROWNING MEWS
WIMPOLE MEWS
KYRGYZSTAN
SPRING MEWS
DURWESTON MEWS
CLAY ST
LITHUANIA
ANGOLA
MONTAGU MANSIONS
MONTAGU ROW
KENRICK PL
ST ANDREW'S MANSIONS
MOXON ST
AYBROOK ST
CRAMER ST
MAYBURY COURT
MARYLEBONE ST
DORSET STREET
WENDOVER HO
WENDOVER COURT
BROADSTONE PL
MANCHESTER STREET
Univ
ST VINCENT ST
St Vincent's RC Prim Sch
MONTAGU PLACE
BRYMON COURT
MONTAGU MEWS N
MONTAGU COURT
RODMARTIN STREET
W1
CROSS KEYS CL
MARYLEBONE LA
BULSTRODE PL
BULSTRODE ST
MARYLEBONE MEWS
104
MONTAGU SQUARE
BLANDFORD STREET
KENDALL PL
ADMIRAL COURT
MANCHESTER MEWS
THAYER STREET
HERON PL
Coll
WIMPOLE STREET
WELBECK STREET
WELBECK WAY
Wallace Collection
SPANISH PL
JACOB'S WELL MEWS
BENTINCK MS
BENTINCK ST
BENTINCK MANSIONS
CARLTON HOUSE
ROBERT ADAM ST
BAKER'S MS
MANCHESTER SQUARE
HINDE ST
HINDE MS
MARYLEBONE LANE
EASLEYS MEWS
Wigmore Hall
MONTAGU MEWS W
GEORGE STREET
PORTMAN CLOSE
FITZHARDINGE HOUSE
FITZHARDINGE ST
ORCHARD COURT
SEYMOUR MEWS
MANDEVILLE PL
JASON CT
PORTMAN TOWERS
Courtauld Inst of Art
PORTMAN
DUKE'S MS
WIGMORE STREET
B406
MONTAGU MEWS S
MONTAGU ST
ST CHRISTOPHER'S PLACE
ALDBURGH MEWS
BRUNSWICK MEWS
GREAT CUMBERLAND PLACE
BERKELEY STREET
BERKELEY MEWS
A41
PO
GRAY'S YD
BOURNE MEWS
SARSDEN BLDGS
STRATFORD PL
Western Marble Arch Synagogue
QUEBEC MEWS
NEW QUEBEC ST
SQUARE
EDWARDS MEWS
PICTON PLACE
JAMES STREET
GEES COURT
ST CHRISTOPHER'S COURT
BOTSWANA
BILTON TOWERS
SEYMOUR STREET
A5204
PORTMAN ST
ORCHARD ST
London College of Fashion
BARRETT ST
DUKE ST
BIRD ST
Bond Street
PORTMAN MEWS STH
OLD QUEBEC ST
BRYANSTON STREET
GRANVILLE PL
Cumberland Hotel
CUMBERLAND COURT
Marble Arch
A40
OXFORD STREET
BALDERTON ST
BALDERTON FLATS
LUMLEY ST
STAFFORD FLATS
DUKE ST MANSIONS
BINNEY ST
GILBERT STREET
WEIGHHOUSE ST
SOUTH MOLTON
SEDLEY PLACE
ST ANSELM PLACE
TA Ctr
DAVIES STREET
DAVIES MEWS
MARBLE ARCH
NORTH ROW
CLARENDON FLATS
BROWN HART GARDENS
DUKE'S YD
117
NORTH AUDLEY ST
TYBURN WAY
A4202
BRAZIL
GREEN STREET
LEES CT
PROVIDENCE CT
GEORGE YD
ARGENTINE
ITALY

Fitzrovia
MARYLEBONE
W1
PARK CRESCENT
PARK CRESCENT MEWS
DEVONSHIRE PL
DEVONSHIRE MEWS
DEVONSHIRE STREET
DEVONSHIRE CL
DEVONSHIRE MEWS N
DEVONSHIRE MEWS W
CHILE
CHINA
POLAND
KENYA
NAMIBIA
GRENADA
BOTSWANA
MEXICO
ARGENTINE
CROATIA
MOZAMBIQUE
LIBERIA
ELSALVADOR
PORTLAND PLACE
GREAT PORTLAND STREET
BOLSOVER ST
GREENWELL ST
CARBURTON ST
HALLAM STREET
HALLAM MEWS
BRIDFORD MEWS
GOODWOOD CT
Govt Offices
HOLCROFT COURT
CLIPSTONE STREET
CLIPSTONE MEWS
CLEVELAND STREET
CLEVELAND MEWS
CONWAY ST
CONWAY MEWS
GRAFTON WAY
BROMLEY PL
MAPLE ST
FITZROY ST
BT Tower
Univ of Westminster
COLLINGWOOD HOUSE
HANSON STREET
OGLE STREET
Blake Coll
FOLEY STREET
RIDING HOUSE STREET
NASSAU ST
BOURLET CL
WEST ONE HO
BYWELL PL
WEYMOUTH STREET
WEYMOUTH MEWS
UPPER WIMPOLE ST
WIMPOLE MEWS
WIMPOLE STREET
HARLEY STREET
HARLEY PL
NEW CAVENDISH STREET
CAVENDISH MEWS N
CAVENDISH MEWS S
DUCHESS MEWS
DUCHESS STREET
MANSFIELD MEWS
MANSFIELD ST
Portland Place Schs
BBC Broadcasting Ho
LANGHAM STREET
LANGHAM PL
GILDEA ST
GOSFIELD ST
GREAT TITCHFIELD ST
LITTLE TITCHFIELD ST
MIDDLETON PLACE
ALL SOULS PLACE
The Langham Hotel
Acad
B506
Law Ct
ST ANDREWS CHAMBERS
The Heart Hospl
WESTMORLAND ST
WOODSTOCK MEWS
WHEATLEY ST
DE WALDEN ST
BROWNING MEWS
MARYLEBONE MEWS
Queen's Coll
QUEEN ANNE STREET
QUEEN ANNE MEWS
CHANDOS ST
DEAN'S MEWS
BULSTRODE ST
BENTINCK MS
BENTINCK ST
BENTINCK MANSIONS
WELBECK STREET
WELBECK WAY
LISTER HOUSE
WIGMORE PL
Wigmore Hall
CAVENDISH PLACE
CAVENDISH SQUARE
A5204
LITTLE PORTLAND ST
MORLEY HOUSE
MARGARET STREET
MARGARET COURT
MARCOL HOUSE
MARKET PLACE
KENT HO
GT CASTLE ST
GREAT CASTLE STREET
JOHN PRINCE'S ST
HARCOURT HO
HOLLES ST
London Coll of Fashion
Cowdray Hall Royal College of Nursing
HENRIETTA PLACE
CHAPEL PLACE
OLD CAVENDISH ST
VERE ST
B406
WIGMORE STREET
MARYLEBONE LANE
JAMES STREET
ST CHRISTOPHER'S PLACE
ALDBURGH MEWS
BOURNE MEWS
SARSDEN BLDGS
GEES COURT
STRATFORD PL
Bond Street
OXFORD STREET
OXFORD CIRCUS
A40
Classic FM
SWALLOW PL
HAREWOOD PLACE
UNION YD
Radcliffe Coll
Oxford Circus
OXFORD CIRCUS AVE
HILLS PL
RAMILLIES PL
RAMILLIES ST
LITTLE ARGYLL STREET
ARGYLL ST
GREAT MARLBOROUGH
Carnaby
KINGLY STREET
FOUBERT'S PL
LOWNDES CT
LITTLE MARLBOROUGH ST
REGENT STREET
A4201
PRINCES ST
JERVIS CT
HANOVER SQUARE
HANOVER ST
TENTERDEN STREET
DERING ST
NEW BOND STREET
WOODSTOCK STREET
BLENHEIM STREET
SEDLEY PLACE
GLOBE YD
HAUNCH OF VENISON YD
SOUTH MOLTON STREET
SOUTH MOLTON LANE
GILBERT STREET
BINNEY
BROWN HART
ST ANSELM'S PLACE
DAVIES MEWS
DAVIES STREET
DUKE'S YD
TA Ctr
Claridge's Hotel
BROOK'S MEWS
BROOK STREET
AVERY ROW
WHITE LION YD
Handel House
POLLEN ST
MASON'S ARMS MEWS
ST GEORGE STREET
MADDOX STREET
NEW BURLINGTON PL
92
103
118
A
B
C
1
2
3
4

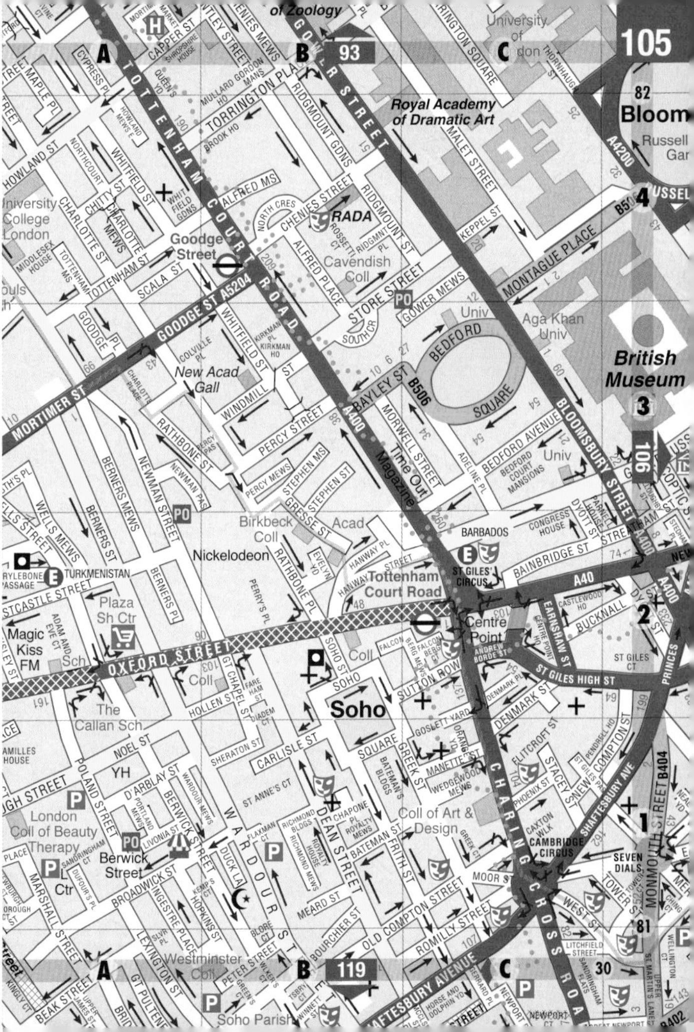
of Zoology
University of London
Royal Academy of Dramatic Art
Bloomsbury
Russell Gardens
University College London
Goodge Street
RADA
Cavendish Coll
Univ
Aga Khan Univ
British Museum
New Acad Gall
Time Out Magazine
Birkbeck Coll
Acad
Nickelodeon
BARBADOS
TURKMENISTAN
Plaza Sh Ctr
Tottenham Court Road
Centre Point
Magic Kiss FM
Sch
Coll
Soho
The Callan Sch
YH
London Coll of Beauty Therapy
Berwick Street
Coll of Art & Design
CAMBRIDGE CIRCUS
SEVEN DIALS
Westminster Coll
Soho Parish
TOTTENHAM COURT ROAD
GOWER STREET
BLOOMSBURY STREET
OXFORD STREET
CHARING CROSS ROAD
SHAFTESBURY AVENUE
MONMOUTH STREET
GOODGE ST A5204
MORTIMER ST
BEDFORD SQUARE
MONTAGUE PLACE
MALET STREET
TORRINGTON PLACE
RIDGMOUNT GDNS
CHENIES STREET
ALFRED PLACE
STORE STREET
WHITFIELD ST
CHARLOTTE ST
RATHBONE PL
SOHO SQUARE
DEAN STREET
WARDOUR STREET
FRITH ST
GREEK ST
OLD COMPTON STREET
ST GILES HIGH ST
NEW OXFORD STREET
BERNERS ST
NEWMAN STREET
WELLS STREET
POLAND STREET
BERWICK STREET
BROADWICK ST
MARSHALL STREET
LEXINGTON ST
BEAK STREET
A 93
B
C
A 119
B
C
106
1 2 3 4

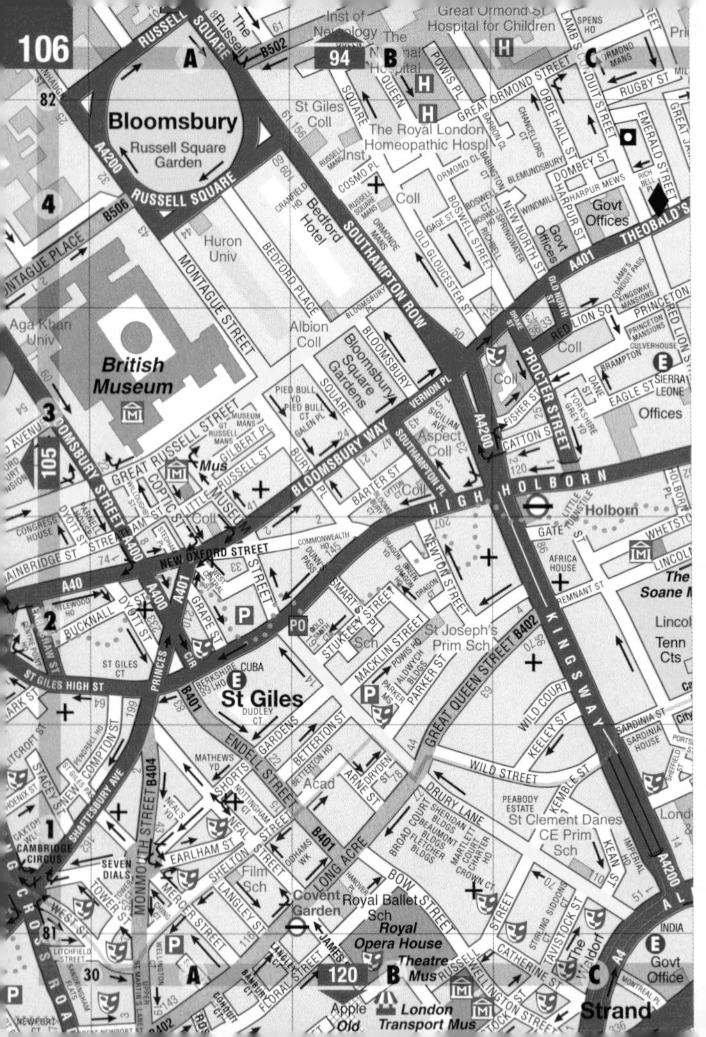
A
B
C
A
B
C
1
2
3
4
94
105
120
82
81
Bloomsbury
Russell Square Garden
RUSSELL SQUARE
A4200
B502
B506
The Russell
Inst of Neurology
The National Hospital
Great Ormond St Hospital for Children
SPENS HO
LAMB'S CONDUIT STREET
ORMOND MANS
RUGBY ST
GREAT ORMOND STREET
POWIS PL
QUEEN SQUARE
St Giles Coll
The Royal London Homeopathic Hospl
Inst
COSMO PL
Coll
ORMOND CL
BARBON CL
CHANCELLORS' CT
ORDE HALL ST
DOMBEY ST
HARPUR MEWS
HARPUR ST
EMERALD STREET
RICH BELL PL
Govt Offices
THEOBALD'S
BLEMUNDSBURY
WINDMILL
BOSWELL ST
BOSWELL STREET
RICHBELL
NEW NORTH ST
SPRINGWATER
Govt Offices
A401
OLD GLOUCESTER ST
GAGE ST
ORMONDE MANS
RUSSELL SQUARE MANS
RUSSELL MANS
SOUTHAMPTON ROW
Bedford Hotel
CRANFIELD HO
BEDFORD PLACE
Huron Univ
MONTAGUE STREET
MONTAGUE PLACE
Aga Khan Univ
British Museum
Albion Coll
BLOOMSBURY PL
Bloomsbury Square Gardens
BLOOMSBURY SQUARE
VERNON PL
LAMB'S CONDUIT PASS
KINGSWAY MANSIONS
PRINCETON ST
PRINCETON MANSIONS
RED LION SQ
RED LION ST
OLD NORTH ST
DRAKE ST
Coll
CULVERHOUSE
BRAMPTON
DANE ST
EAGLE ST
SIERRA LEONE Offices
PROCTER STREET
FISHER ST
YORKSHIRE GREY YD
CATTON ST
A4200
SICILIAN AVE
Aspect Coll
SOUTHAMPTON PL
BLOOMSBURY WAY
BARTER ST
LYTTON CT
BLOOMSBURY CT
Coll
HIGH HOLBORN
Holborn
LITTLE TURNSTILE
GATE ST
WHETSTONE
LINCOLN
The Soane M
AFRICA HOUSE
REMNANT ST
Lincol
Tenn Cts
MUSEUM MANS
GT RUSSELL MANS
GILBERT PL
PIED BULL YD
PIED BULL CT
GALEN PL
BURY PL
GREAT RUSSELL STREET
Mus
RUSSELL ST
MUSEUM ST
LITTLE
COPTIC ST
Coll
WILLOUGHBY ST
STREATHAM ST
STEDHAM PL
BLOOMSBURY STREET
A400
DYOTT ST
CONGRESS HOUSE
BAINBRIDGE ST
A40
NEW OXFORD STREET
COMMONWEALTH HO
DUNN'S PASS
WEST CENTRAL ST
DRAGON YD
GREEN DRAGON HO
DRAGON CT
NEWTON STREET
KINGSWAY
B402
GREAT QUEEN STREET
SMART'S PL
STUKELEY STREET
GOLDSMITH CT
PO
GRAPE ST
A401
CIR
PRINCES
ST GILES HIGH ST
ST GILES CT
BUCKNALL ST
DENMARK ST
CENTREPOINT HO
EARNSHAW ST
LITTLEWOOD HO
BERKSHIRE HO
CUBA
St Giles
DUDLEY CT
Sch
MACKLIN STREET
POWIS HO
ALDWYCH BLDGS
PARKER MS
PARKER ST
St Joseph's Prim Sch
WILD COURT
KEELEY ST
SARDINIA ST
SARDINIA HOUSE
PORTSMOUTH ST
SHEFFIELD ST
City
WILD STREET
KEMBLE ST
PEABODY ESTATE
St Clement Danes CE Prim Sch
Lond
KEAN ST
IMPERIAL HO
A4200
B401
ENDELL STREET
GARDENS
BETTERTON ST
BETTERTON HO
MATHEWS YD
SHORTS
NOTTINGHAM CT
Acad
ARNE ST
DRYDEN ST
DRURY LANE
BROAD COURT
SHERIDAN BLDGS
BEAUMONT BLDGS
FLETCHER BLDGS
MARTLETT COURT
CHARTER HO
CROWN CT
B404
MONMOUTH STREET
SHAFTESBURY AVE
NEW COMPTON ST
PENDRELL HO
ST GILES PAS
STACEY ST
PHOENIX ST
FLITCROFT ST
CAXTON WLK
CAMBRIDGE CIRCUS
SEVEN DIALS
NEAL'S YD
NEAL STREET
EARLHAM ST
SHELTON STREET
ODHAMS WK
LONG ACRE
Film Sch
HANOVER PL
BOW STREET
STREET
STIRLING SIDDONS CT
TAVISTOCK ST
The Waldorf
INDIA
Govt Office
A4
MONTREAL PL
Strand
CATHERINE ST
WELLINGTON STREET
RUSSELL
TOWER ST
WEST ST
MERCER STREET
LANGLEY ST
Covent Garden
Royal Ballet Sch
Royal Opera House
Theatre Mus
London Transport Mus
JAMES ST
LANGLEY CT
FLORAL STREET
BANBURY CT
CONDUIT CT
Apple Old
ST MARTIN'S LANE
UPPER
WELLINGTON
LITCHFIELD STREET
SANDRINGHAM FLATS
NEWPORT CT
CHARING CROSS ROAD
B402
P

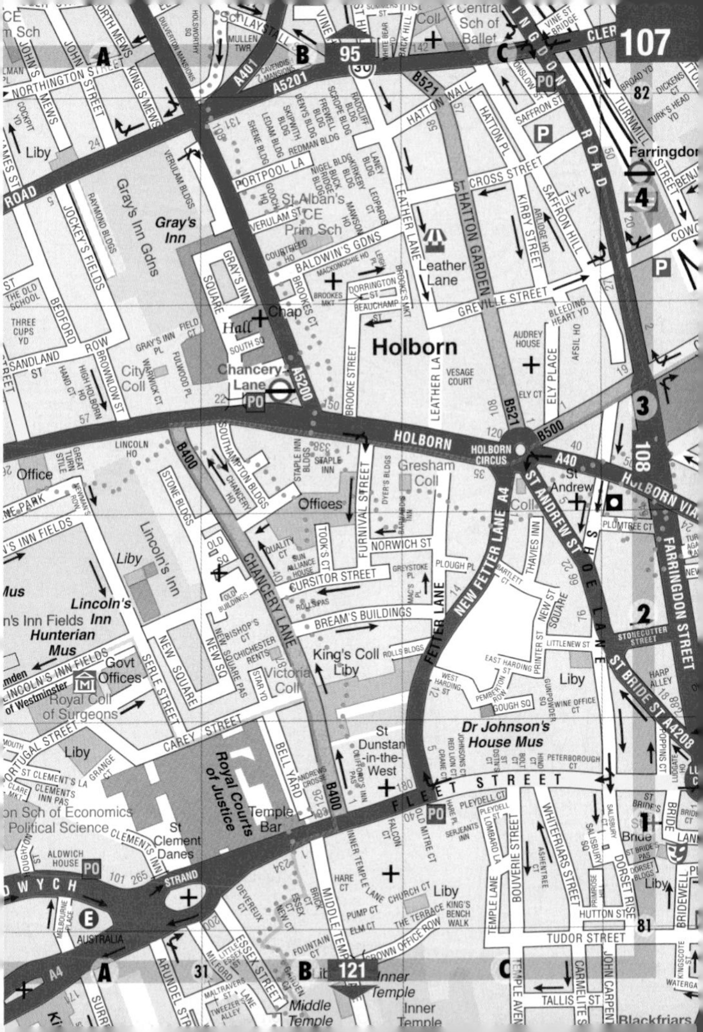

107
95
121
A
B
C
1
2
3
4
Holborn
Gray's Inn
Gray's Inn Gdns
Gray's Inn Square
Hall
Chap
South Sq
Chancery Lane
City Coll
Lincoln's Inn
Lincoln's Inn Fields
Lincoln's Inn Fields
Hunterian Mus
Govt Offices
Royal Coll of Surgeons
City of Westminster
Liby
Office
Offices
Gresham Coll
Coll
King's Coll Liby
Victoria Coll
Royal Courts of Justice
Temple Bar
St Clement Danes
St Dunstan-in-the-West
Dr Johnson's House Mus
St Andrew
St Bride
Inner Temple
Middle Temple
St Alban's CE Prim Sch
Leather Lane
Central Sch of Ballet
Farringdon
Blackfriars
Aldwich House
Australia
Holborn Circus
Holborn
Holborn Viaduct
Fleet Street
Strand
Aldwych
Chancery Lane
Fetter Lane
New Fetter Lane
Shoe Lane
St Andrew St
St Bride St
Farringdon Street
Farringdon Road
Clerkenwell Road
Theobalds Road
Gray's Inn Road
Hatton Garden
Hatton Wall
Hatton Pl
Leather Lane
Kirby Street
Saffron Hill
Saffron St
St Cross Street
Greville Street
Ely Place
Ely Ct
Brooke Street
Baldwin's Gdns
Portpool La
Verulam St
Northington Street
John Street
John's Mews
King's Mews
Jockey's Fields
Bedford Row
Sandland St
Brownlow St
Red Lion St
Lincoln Ho
Great Turnstile
Newman's Row
Serle Street
New Square
Portugal Street
Carey Street
Bell Yard
Cursitor Street
Bream's Buildings
Furnival Street
Norwich St
Took's Ct
Southampton Bldgs
Stone Bldgs
Plough Pl
Thavies Inn
New St Square
Little New St
Gunpowder Sq
Gough Sq
Wine Office Ct
Peterborough Ct
Stonecutter Street
Harp Alley
Plumtree Ct
Pleydell Ct
Whitefriars Street
Bouverie Street
Temple Lane
Dorset Rise
Salisbury Sq
Hutton St
Tudor Street
Carmelite St
John Carpenter St
Tallis St
Bride Lane
Bridewell Pl
Essex Street
Devereux Ct
Middle Temple La
Inner Temple Lane
Church Ct
King's Bench Walk
Crown Office Row
Arundel St
Milford Lane
Maltravers St
Melbourne Place
Clements Inn
St Clement's La
Grange Ct
Lon Sch of Economics & Political Science
A401
A5201
A5200
A40
A4
A4208
B521
B500
B400

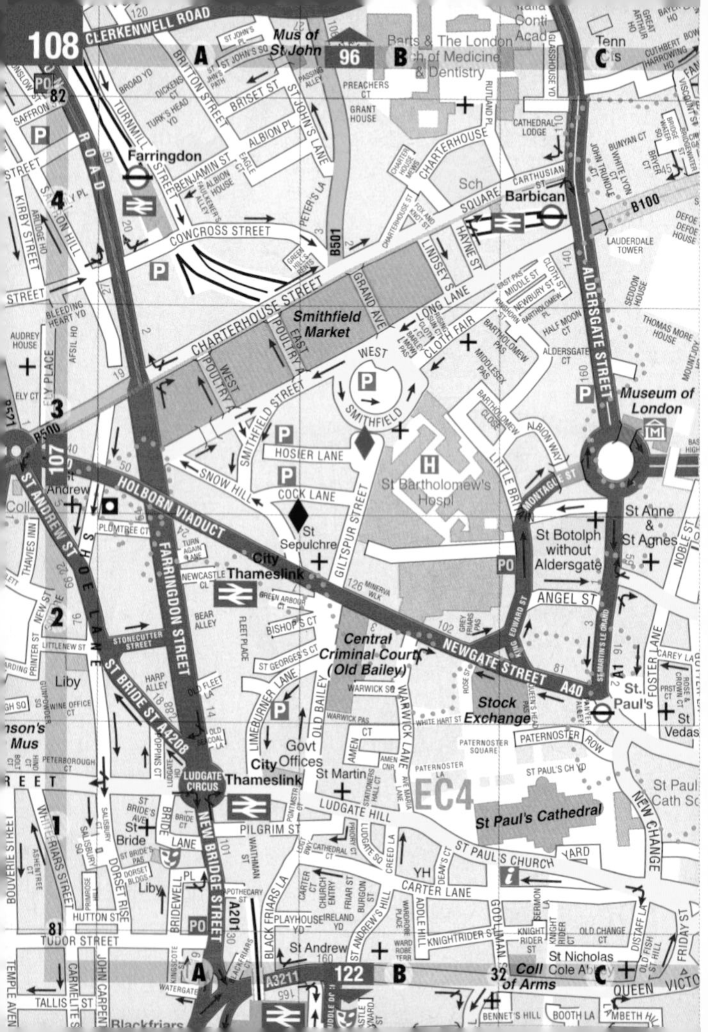
CLERKENWELL ROAD
A
B
C
96
Mus of St John
Barts & The London Sch of Medicine & Dentistry
ST JOHN'S SQ
BRITTON STREET
BRISET ST
ST JOHN'S LANE
ALBION PL
PREACHERS CT
GRANT HOUSE
CATHEDRAL LODGE
CHARTERHOUSE
CARTHUSIAN ST
Farringdon
TURNMILL STREET
BENJAMIN ST
COWCROSS STREET
FARRINGDON ROAD
SAFFRON HILL
KIRBY STREET
Sch
SQUARE
Barbican
B100
B501
LAUDERDALE TOWER
ALDERSGATE STREET
CHARTERHOUSE STREET
Smithfield Market
GRAND AVE
LONG LANE
CLOTH FAIR
EAST POULTRY AV
WEST POULTRY AV
WEST SMITHFIELD
SMITHFIELD STREET
BLEEDING HEART YD
AUDREY HOUSE
ELY PLACE
ELY CT
B500
107
ST ANDREW ST
HOLBORN VIADUCT
SNOW HILL
HOSIER LANE
COCK LANE
GILTSPUR STREET
St Bartholomew's Hospl
LITTLE BRITAIN
MONTAGUE ST
ALDERSGATE CT
Museum of London
St Anne & St Agnes
St Botolph without Aldersgate
PO
ANGEL ST
St Sepulchre
City Thameslink
SHOE LANE
FARRINGDON STREET
PLUMTREE CT
NEWCASTLE CL
BEAR ALLEY
FLEET PLACE
GREEN ARBOUR CT
BISHOP'S CT
MINERVA WLK
NEWGATE STREET
A40
KING EDWARD ST
ST MARTIN'S LE GRAND
A1
FOSTER LANE
St. Paul's
St Vedast
Central Criminal Court (Old Bailey)
ST GEORGE'S CT
LIMEBURNER LANE
OLD BAILEY
WARWICK SQ
WARWICK LANE
WARWICK PAS
WHITE HART ST
Stock Exchange
PATERNOSTER SQUARE
PATERNOSTER ROW
ST PAUL'S CH YD
STONECUTTER STREET
LITTLE NEW ST
PRINTER ST
Liby
ST BRIDE ST A4208
HARP ALLEY
OLD FLEET LA
OLD SEACOAL LA
WINE OFFICE CT
PETERBOROUGH CT
Govt Offices
City Thameslink
St Martin
LUDGATE CIRCUS
AMEN CT
AVE MARIA LANE
EC4
St Paul's Cathedral
St Paul's Cath Sch
NEW CHANGE
LUDGATE HILL
ST BRIDE'S AVE
St Bride
BRIDE LANE
NEW BRIDGE STREET
PILGRIM ST
WAITHMAN ST
CREED LA
YH
ST PAUL'S CHURCH YARD
CARTER LANE
WHITEFRIARS STREET
BOUVERIE STREET
DORSET RISE
HUTTON ST
TUDOR STREET
BRIDEWELL PL
PO
A201
APOTHECARY ST
BLACK FRIARS LA
PLAYHOUSE YD
IRELAND YD
ST ANDREW'S HILL
ADDLE HILL
KNIGHTRIDER ST
GODLIMAN ST
OLD CHANGE CT
DISTAFF LA
FRIDAY ST
St Andrew
St Nicholas Cole Abbey
Coll of Arms
A3211
122
QUEEN VICTORIA
TALLIS ST
CARMELITE ST
JOHN CARPENTER
TEMPLE AVEN
WATERGATE
Blackfriars
BENNET'S HILL
BOOTH LA
LAMBETH HILL

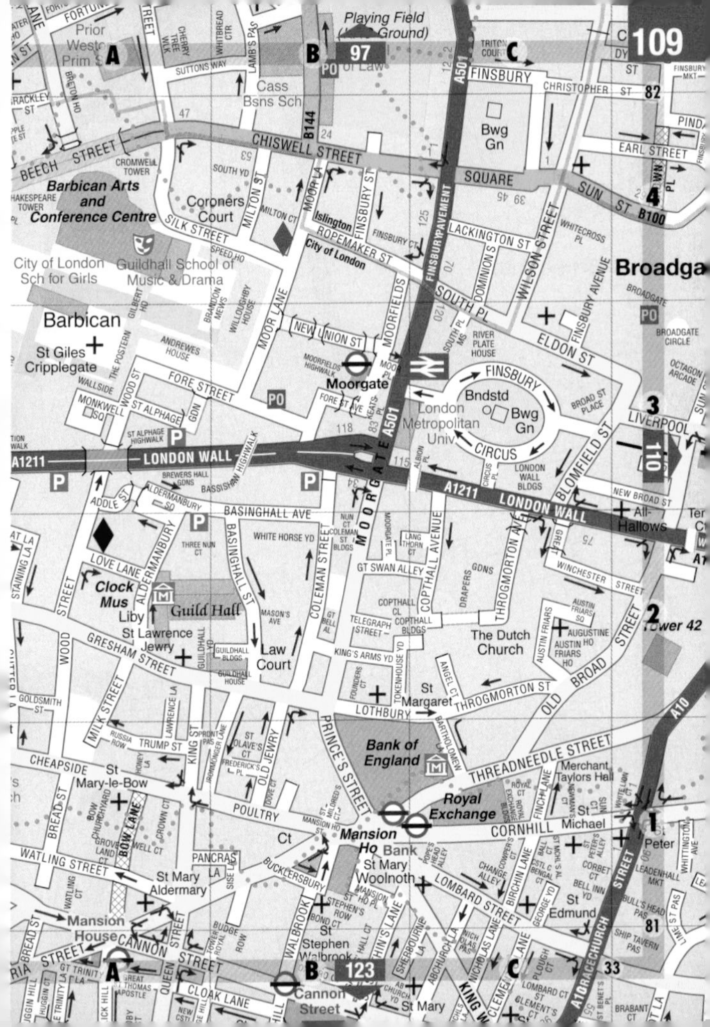
97
123
110
A
B
C
1
2
3
4
Playing Field
Prior Weston Prim Sch
Cass Bsns Sch
PO
FORTUNE ST
SUTTONS WAY
LAMB'S PAS
CHERRY TREE WLK
WHITBREAD CTR
BRETON HO
BRACKLEY ST
TRITON COURT
FINSBURY
CHRISTOPHER ST
FINSBURY MKT
82
PINDAR
EARL STREET
BEECH STREET
CHISWELL STREET
CROMWELL TOWER
B144
A501
Bwg Gn
SQUARE
SUN ST
B100
SHAKESPEARE TOWER
Barbican Arts and Conference Centre
SOUTH YD
Coroners Court
MILTON ST
MILTON CT
MOOR LA
FINSBURY ST
FINSBURY PAVEMENT
LACKINGTON ST
WILSON STREET
WHITECROSS PL
SILK STREET
Islington
City of London
ROPEMAKER ST
FINSBURY CT
SPEED HO
City of London Sch for Girls
Guildhall School of Music & Drama
DOMINION ST
Broadgate
BROADGATE
BROADGATE CIRCLE
FINSBURY AVENUE
SOUTH PL
SOUTH PL MS
RIVER PLATE HOUSE
ELDON ST
Barbican
GILBERT HO
BRANDON MEWS
WILLOUGHBY HOUSE
MOOR LANE
NEW UNION ST
MOORFIELDS
St Giles Cripplegate
THE POSTERN
ANDREWES HOUSE
MOORFIELDS HIGHWALK
Moorgate
MOOR PL
FINSBURY CIRCUS
OCTAGON ARCADE
WALLSIDE
WOOD ST
FORE STREET
FORE ST AVE
KEATS PL
Bndstd
London Metropolitan Univ
BROAD ST PLACE
MONKWELL SQ
ST ALPHAGE GDN
ST ALPHAGE HIGHWALK
LIVERPOOL
BLOMFIELD ST
A1211
LONDON WALL
BASSISHAW HIGHWALK
BREWERS HALL GDNS
ALBION PL
CIRCUS PL
LONDON WALL BLDGS
NEW BROAD ST
All-Hallows
ADDLE ST
ALDERMANBURY SQ
BASINGHALL AVE
NUN CT
COLEMAN ST BLDGS
MOORGATE
MOORGATE PL
LANGTHORN CT
COPTHALL AVENUE
THROGMORTON AVE
GREAT WINCHESTER ST
75
THREE NUN CT
WHITE HORSE YD
GT SWAN ALLEY
DRAPERS GDNS
WINCHESTER STREET
STAINING LA
LOVE LANE
ALDERMANBURY
BASINGHALL ST
COLEMAN STREET
COPTHALL CL
AUSTIN FRIARS SQ
Clock Mus
Liby
Guild Hall
MASON'S AVE
GT BELL AL
TELEGRAPH STREET
COPTHALL BLDGS
The Dutch Church
AUSTIN FRIARS
AUGUSTINE HO
AUSTIN FRIARS HO
Tower 42
WOOD STREET
St Lawrence Jewry
GRESHAM STREET
GUILDHALL YD
GUILDHALL BLDGS
GUILDHALL HOUSE
Law Court
KING'S ARMS YD
TOKENHOUSE YD
FOUNDERS CT
ANGEL CT
St Margaret
THROGMORTON ST
OLD BROAD STREET
GOLDSMITH ST
MILK STREET
LAWRENCE LA
LOTHBURY
A10
RUSSIA ROW
TRUMP ST
KING ST
IRONMONGER LANE
ST OLAVE'S CT
FREDERICK'S PL
OLD JEWRY
PRINCE'S STREET
Bank of England
BARTHOLOMEW LA
THREADNEEDLE STREET
Merchant Taylors Hall
CHEAPSIDE
St Mary-le-Bow
HONEY LA
BREAD ST
BOW CHURCHYARD
BOW LANE
CROWN CT
POULTRY
DOVE CT
ST MILDRED'S CT
Royal Exchange
ROYAL EXCHANGE BLDGS
FINCH LANE
St Michael
WHITE LION CT
CORNHILL
GROVELAND CT
WELL CT
Ct
MANSION HO ST
Mansion Ho
Bank
St Mary Woolnoth
POPE'S HEAD ALLEY
CHANGE ALLEY
COWPER'S CT
BIRCHIN LANE
BALL CT
ST MICHAEL'S AL
ST PETER'S ALLEY
St Peter
WHITTINGTON AVE
LEADENHALL MKT
WATLING STREET
PANCRAS LA
SISE LA
BUCKLERSBURY
St Mary Aldermary
LOMBARD STREET
CORBET CT
BELL INN YD
GEORGE YD
St Edmund
BULL'S HEAD PAS
GRACECHURCH STREET
LIME ST PAS
81
WATLING CT
Mansion House
CANNON STREET
QUEEN STREET
BUDGE ROW
WALBROOK
BOND CT
ST STEPHEN'S ROW
St Stephen Walbrook
MANSION HO PL
SHERBORNE LA
ABCHURCH LA
NICHOLAS LANE
NICHOLAS PAS
SHIP TAVERN PAS
GT TRINITY LA
GREAT ST THOMAS APOSTLE
CLOAK LANE
Cannon Street
ABCHURCH YD
St Mary
KING WILLIAM ST
CLEMENT'S LANE
PLOUGH CT
LOMBARD CT
ST CLEMENT'S CT
A1
33
BRABANT CT

A
B
C
98
WORSHIP STREET
TA Centre
DYSART ST
CLIFTON ST
FINSBURY MKT
SNOWDEN ST
CHRISTOPHER ST
82
PINDAR ST
EARL STREET
CROWN PL
APPOLD STREET
SUN ST
B100
4
WILSON STREET
WHITECROSS PL
Broadgate
BROADGATE
PO
BROADGATE CIRCLE
FINSBURY AVENUE
ELDON ST
OCTAGON ARCADE
SUN STREET PAS
3
Bwg Gn
109
LIVERPOOL STREET
BROAD ST AV
THE ARCADE
NEW BROAD ST
LONDON WALL
All-Hallows
Tenn Ct
St Botolph
BISHOPSGATE CHYD
WORMWOOD ST
A1211
WINCHESTER STREET
2
AUSTIN FRIARS
AUGUSTINE HO
Tower 42
OLD BROAD STREET
A10
NORTON FOLGATE
BLOSSOM ST
FLEUR DE LIS STREET
ELDER ST
FOLGATE STREET
PRIMROSE ST
PINDAR ST
EXCHANGE PL
EC2
City of London
Tower Hamlets
SPITAL SQUARE
STOTHARD PL
Stansted Express Terminal
EXCHANGE ARCADE
BROAD LA
Liverpool Street Station
BISHOPSGATE ARCADE
BISHOPS SQ
MARKET ST
Old Spitalfields
PRIORY HO
VANBURGH HO
LINNELL HO
DANDRIDGE HO
LAMB ST
CRISPIN PL
WHEELER LA
PHILIP BLAIRMAN HO
CELIA BLAIRMAN HO
CALVIN STREET
WHELER HOUSE
JEROME ST
CORBET PLACE
A1202
COMMERCIAL STREET
PUMA CT
BRUSHFIELD STREET
GUN ST
FORT ST
CRISPIN ST
Liby
ARTILLERY LANE
WHITE'S ROW
WIDEGATE ST
SANDY'S ROW
ARTILLERY PAS
FRYING PAN ALLEY
ESPIRIT CT
BRUNE STREET
CARTER HOUSE
BRUNE HOUSE
TOYNBEE ST
CATHERINE WHEEL ALLEY
VICTORIA AVE
ROSE ALLEY
NEW STREET
COCK HILL
MIDDLESEX STREET
STRYPE ST
LEYDEN ST
COBB ST
BELL LANE
Petticoat Lane
WENTWORTH
DEVONSHIRE ROW
DEVONSHIRE SQ
CUTLERS GDNS ARC
CUTLERS GDNS
HARROW PL
WENTWORTH DWELLINGS
NEW GOULSTON ST
GOULSTON STREET
JACOBSON HO
BISHOPSGATE
CAMOMILE ST
HOUNDSDITCH
BEVIS MARKS
CLARK'S PL
Liby
ST HELEN'S PL
St Helen
BURY CT
BURY ST
CUTLER ST
CLOTHIER ST
ARTIZAN ST
PETTICOAT SQ
WHITE KENNETT ST
PETTICOAT TWR
GRAVEL LANE
STONEY LA
PO
P
A11 ST BOTOLPH ST
Aldgate
ALDGATE HIGH ST
London Metropolitan Univ
ST MARY AXE
Swiss Re Building
HENEAGE LA
HENEAGE PL
CREECHURCH LA
DUKE'S PL
IRONGATE HO
UNDERSHAFT
CROSBY SQ
St Andrew Undershaft
BROWN'S BLDGS
BANKSIDE HOUSE
CUNARD PL
MITRE ST
MITRE SQ
Sir John Cass's Sch
LT SOMERSET
Whitechapel
THREADNEEDLE STREET
Merchant Taylors Hall
FINCH LANE
1
CORNHILL
St Michael
St Peter
LEADENHALL STREET
WHITTINGTON AVE
Lloyds Building
BILLITER ST
FENCHURCH BLDGS
HARTS HORN ALLEY
ALDGATE
LONDON METROPOLITAN UNIV
JEWRY ST
INDIA ST
ST CLARE ST
MINORIES
LEADENHALL MKT
LEADENHALL PL
LIME STREET
FENCHURCH AVE
CARLISLE AVE
NORTHUMBERLAND ALLEY
RANGOON ST
LLOYD'S AVE
VINE STREET
IVEAGH CT
HAYDON ST
GRACECHURCH STREET
St Edmund
81
BELL INN YD
GEORGE YD
BULL'S HEAD PAS
LIME ST PAS
SHIP TAVERN PAS
CULLUM ST
HOGARTH CT
FEN CT
FENCHURCH STREET
124
LONDON ST
KATHERINE'S ROW
Fenchurch Street Station
FRIARS
CROSSWALL
AMERICA SQ
PORTSOKEN
PLOUGH CT
LOMBARD CT
ST CLEMENT'S CT
A10
33
BRABANT CT
DUNSTER CT
EC3
GOODMAN

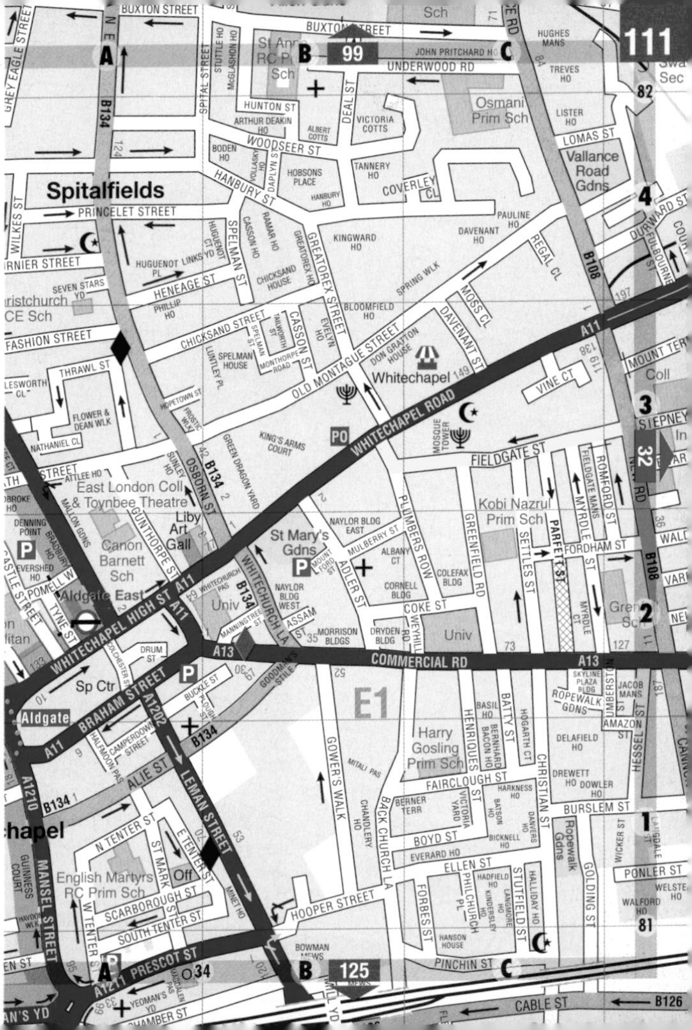
Spitalfields
Whitechapel
E1
BUXTON STREET
JOHN PRITCHARD HO
UNDERWOOD RD
99
125
32
A
B
C
1
2
3
4
St Anne's RC Prim Sch
Osmani Prim Sch
Vallance Road Gdns
HUNTON ST
ARTHUR DEAKIN HO
ALBERT COTTS
VICTORIA COTTS
WOODSEER ST
DEAL ST
STUTFIELD ST
McGLASHON HO
SPITAL STREET
HUGHES MANS
TREVES HO
LISTER HO
LOMAS ST
BODEN HO
VOLLASKY HO
DAPLYN ST
HOBSONS PLACE
TANNERY HO
COVERLEY CL
HANBURY ST
HANBURY HO
PRINCELET STREET
WILKES ST
FOURNIER STREET
HUGUENOT PL
HUGUENOT CT
LINKS YD
SPELMAN ST
CASSON HO
RAMAR HO
GREATOREX HO
GREATOREX STREET
KINGWARD HO
DAVENANT HO
PAULINE HO
REGAL CL
DURWARD ST
FULBOURNE ST
B108
B134
SEVEN STARS YD
HENEAGE ST
PHILLIP HO
Christchurch CE Sch
FASHION STREET
CHICKSAND HOUSE
CHICKSAND STREET
BLOOMFIELD HO
SPRING WLK
MOSS CL
DAVENANT ST
CASSON ST
EVELYN HO
TAILWORTH ST
SPELMAN ST
LUNTLEY PL
SPELMAN HOUSE
MONTHORPE ROAD
OLD MONTAGUE STREET
DON GRATTON HOUSE
Whitechapel
A11
VINE CT
MOUNT TER
Coll
STEPNEY
THRAWL ST
FLOWER & DEAN WLK
NATHANIEL CL
HOPETOWN ST
FROSTIC WLK
KING'S ARMS COURT
GREEN DRAGON YARD
WHITECHAPEL ROAD
MOSQUE TOWER
PO
FIELDGATE ST
ATTLEE HO
East London Coll & Toynbee Theatre
SUNLEY HO
OSBORN ST
MALLON GDNS
DENNING POINT
BRADBURY HO
EVERSHED HO
Canon Barnett Sch
GUNTHORPE ST
Liby Art Gall
NAYLOR BLDG EAST
MULBERRY ST
St Mary's Gdns
MOUNT FORD ST
ADLER ST
ALBANY CT
PLUMBERS ROW
GREENFIELD RD
Kobi Nazrul Prim Sch
SETTLES ST
PARFETT ST
MYRDLE ST
FIELDGATE MANS
ROMFORD ST
FORDHAM ST
WALDEN
VARDEN
NEW RD
COLEFAX BLDG
CORNELL BLDG
COKE ST
MYRDLE CT
Green Sch
CASTLE STREET
POMELL WAY
Aldgate East
TYNE ST
WHITECHAPEL HIGH ST
WHITECHURCH PAS
Univ
WHITECHURCH LA
NAYLOR BLDG WEST
ASSAM ST
MANNINGTREE ST
MORRISON BLDGS
DRYDEN BLDG
WEYHILL RD
A13
COMMERCIAL RD
DRUM ST
COLCHESTER ST
GOODMAN'S STILE
Sp Ctr
BRAHAM STREET
BUCKLE ST
PLOUGH ST
A1202
Aldgate
CAMPERDOWN STREET
HALFMOON PAS
ALIE ST
LEMAN STREET
GOWER'S WALK
MITALI PAS
CHANDLERY HO
BACK CHURCH LA
Harry Gosling Prim Sch
HENRIQUES ST
BASIL HO
BERNHARD BACON HO
BATTY ST
HOGARTH CT
CHRISTIAN ST
SKYLINE PLAZA BLDG
ROPEWALK GDNS
UMBERSTON ST
JACOB MANS
AMAZON ST
HESSEL ST
DELAFIELD HO
DREWETT HO
DOWLER HO
CANNON
A1210
B134
chapel
MANSEL STREET
GUINNESS COURT
N TENTER ST
ST MARK ST
E TENTER ST
English Martyrs RC Prim Sch
Off
SCARBOROUGH ST
SOUTH TENTER ST
W TENTER ST
HAYDON WLK
MINET HO
FAIRCLOUGH ST
BERNER TERR
VICTORIA YARD
HARKNESS HO
BATSON HO
DANVERS HO
BURSLEM ST
Ropewalk Gdns
WICKER ST
LANGDALE ST
BOYD ST
BICKNELL HO
EVERARD HO
ELLEN ST
HADFIELD HO
KINDERSLEY HO
LANGMORE HO
PHILCHURCH PL
STUTFIELD ST
HALLIDAY HO
GOLDING ST
PONLER ST
WELSTEAD HO
WALFORD HO
HOOPER STREET
FORBES ST
HANSON HOUSE
BOWMAN MEWS
PRESCOT ST
A1211
MAGDALEN PAS
YEOMAN'S YD
CHAMBER ST
PINCHIN ST
CABLE ST
B126
MILL YD
81
82

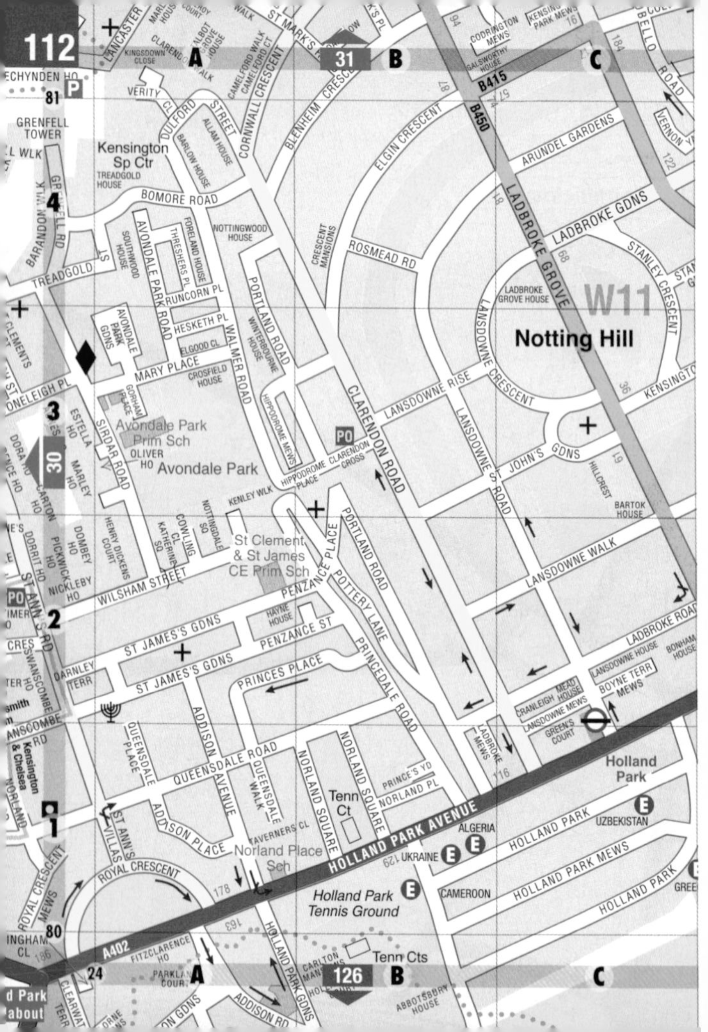
Notting Hill
W11
Kensington Sp Ctr
Avondale Park
Avondale Park Prim Sch
St Clement & St James CE Prim Sch
Norland Place Sch
Holland Park
Holland Park Tennis Ground
HOLLAND PARK AVENUE
A402
LADBROKE GROVE
B450
B415
CLARENDON ROAD
LANSDOWNE CRESCENT
LANSDOWNE RISE
LANSDOWNE ROAD
LANSDOWNE WALK
ST JOHN'S GDNS
LADBROKE GDNS
ELGIN CRESCENT
ARUNDEL GARDENS
ROSMEAD RD
STANLEY CRESCENT
BLENHEIM CRESCENT
PORTLAND ROAD
WALMER ROAD
BOMORE ROAD
AVONDALE PARK ROAD
MARY PLACE
WILSHAM STREET
PENZANCE PLACE
PENZANCE ST
ST JAMES'S GDNS
PRINCES PLACE
PRINCEDALE ROAD
POTTERY LANE
QUEENSDALE ROAD
ADDISON AVENUE
NORLAND SQUARE
ROYAL CRESCENT
ADDISON PLACE
HOLLAND PARK
HOLLAND PARK MEWS
HOLLAND PARK GDNS
ST ANN'S RD
SIRDAR ROAD
TREADGOLD ST
GRENFELL TOWER
31
30
126
A
B
C
1
2
3
4

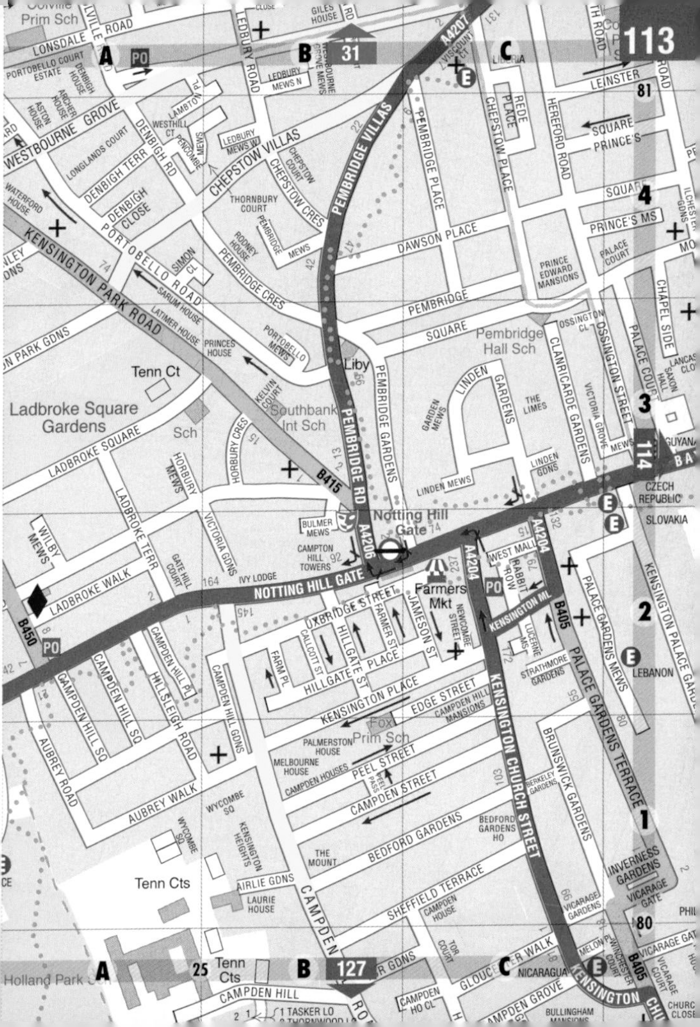
Prim Sch
LONSDALE ROAD
LEDBURY ROAD
GILES HOUSE
31
A
B
C
PO
PORTOBELLO COURT ESTATE
DENBIGH HOUSE
ARCHER HOUSE
ASTON HOUSE
LEDBURY MEWS N
WESTBOURNE GROVE MEWS
VISCOUNT CT
A4207
LIBERIA
LEINSTER
81
WESTBOURNE GROVE
LONGLANDS COURT
DENBIGH TERR
DENBIGH RD
LAMBTON PL
WESTHILL CT
PENCOMBE MEWS
LEDBURY MEWS W
CHEPSTOW VILLAS
PEMBRIDGE VILLAS
PEMBRIDGE PLACE
REDE PLACE
CHEPSTOW PLACE
HEREFORD ROAD
SQUARE
PRINCE'S
WATERFORD HOUSE
DENBIGH CLOSE
THORNBURY COURT
CHEPSTOW COURT
CHEPSTOW CRES
PRINCE'S MS
4
KENSINGTON PARK ROAD
PORTOBELLO ROAD
SIMON CL
RODNEY HOUSE
PEMBRIDGE MEWS
DAWSON PLACE
PRINCE EDWARD MANSIONS
PALACE COURT
PEMBRIDGE CRES
SARUM HOUSE
LATIMER HOUSE
PEMBRIDGE
SQUARE
Pembridge Hall Sch
OSSINGTON CL
OSSINGTON STREET
CHAPEL SIDE
PALACE COURT
PARK GDNS
PRINCES HOUSE
PORTOBELLO MEWS
Liby
Tenn Ct
KELVIN COURT
LINDEN GARDENS
CLANRICARDE GARDENS
VICTORIA GROVE
SAXON HALL
Ladbroke Square Gardens
Southbank Int Sch
PEMBRIDGE RD
PEMBRIDGE GARDENS
GARDEN MEWS
THE LIMES
3
Sch
HORBURY CRES
HORBURY MEWS
LADBROKE SQUARE
B415
LINDEN GDNS
LINDEN MEWS
MEWS
114
GUYANA
CZECH REPUBLIC
SLOVAKIA
WILBY MEWS
LADBROKE TERR
VICTORIA GDNS
BULMER MEWS
Notting Hill Gate
A4206
A4204
CAMPTON HILL TOWERS
WEST MALL
RABBIT ROW
KENSINGTON PALACE GARDENS
LADBROKE WALK
GATE HILL COURT
IVY LODGE
NOTTING HILL GATE
Farmers Mkt
PO
KENSINGTON MALL
B405
PALACE GARDENS MEWS
2
UXBRIDGE STREET
FARMER ST
JAMESON ST
NEWCOMBE STREET
B450
PO
CAMPDEN HILL PL
CALLCOTT ST
HILLGATE ST
FARM PL
HILLGATE PLACE
LUCERNE MS
STRATHMORE GARDENS
LEBANON
CAMPDEN HILL SQ
HILLSLEIGH ROAD
CAMPDEN HILL GDNS
KENSINGTON PLACE
EDGE STREET
CAMPDEN HILL MANSIONS
KENSINGTON CHURCH STREET
PALACE GARDENS TERRACE
AUBREY ROAD
Fox Prim Sch
PALMERSTON HOUSE
MELBOURNE HOUSE
CAMPDEN HOUSES
PEEL STREET
PEEL PASS
BRUNSWICK GARDENS
BERKELEY GARDENS
AUBREY WALK
WYCOMBE SQ
CAMPDEN STREET
1
KENSINGTON HEIGHTS
BEDFORD GARDENS
BEDFORD GARDENS HO
THE MOUNT
INVERNESS GARDENS
Tenn Cts
AIRLIE GDNS
LAURIE HOUSE
SHEFFIELD TERRACE
CAMPDEN HOUSE
VICARAGE GARDENS
VICARAGE GATE
80
CAMPDEN
TOR COURT
MELON PL
WINCHESTER COURT
VICARAGE GATE
Holland Park Sch
25
Tenn Cts
127
GDNS
GLOUCESTER WALK
NICARAGUA
KENSINGTON CHURCH
VICARAGE COURT
B405
CAMPDEN HILL
1 TASKER LO
CAMPDEN HO CL
CAMPDEN GROVE
BULLINGHAM MANSIONS
CHURCH CLOSE

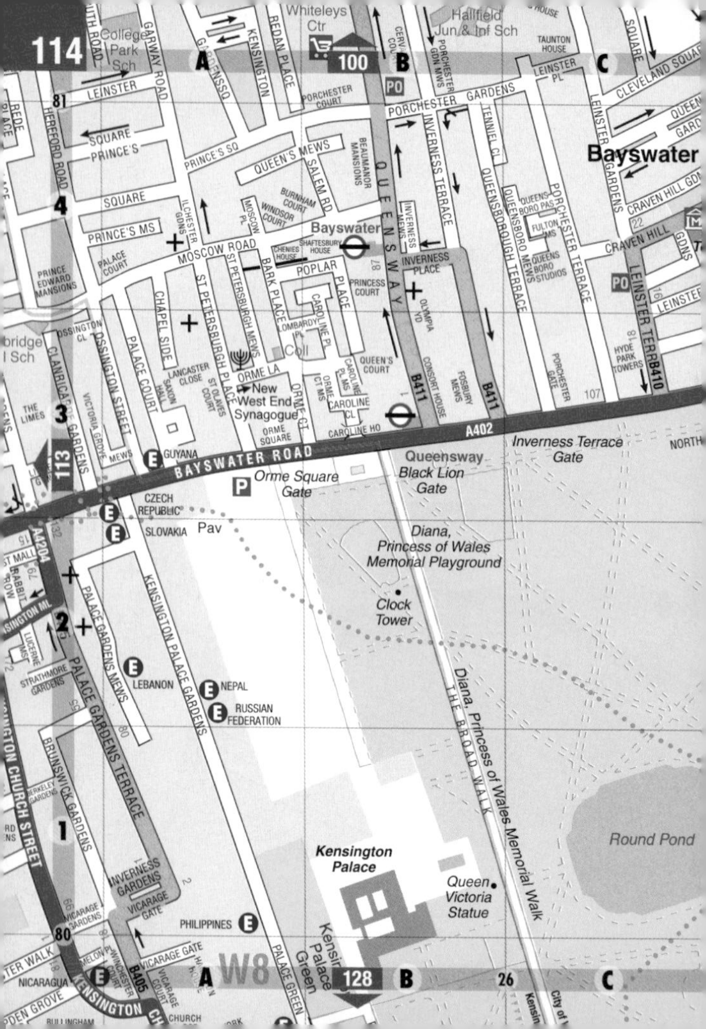
Whiteleys Ctr
100
Hallfield Jun & Inf Sch
College Park Sch
A
B
C
LEINSTER
GARWAY ROAD
KENSINGTON GARDENS SQ
REDAN PLACE
PORCHESTER COURT
PORCHESTER GARDENS
PORCHESTER GDN MWS
TAUNTON HOUSE
LEINSTER PL
CLEVELAND SQUARE
LEINSTER SQUARE
HEREFORD ROAD
PRINCE'S SQUARE
PRINCE'S SQ
QUEEN'S MEWS
BEAUMANOR MANSIONS
SALEM RD
QUEENSWAY
INVERNESS TERRACE
TENNIEL CL
Bayswater
LEINSTER GARDENS
CRAVEN HILL GDNS
CRAVEN HILL
QUEENSBOROUGH TERRACE
QUEENSBORO MEWS
QUEENSBORO PAS
FULTON MS
QUEENS BORO STUDIOS
PORCHESTER TERRACE
BURNHAM COURT
WINDSOR COURT
MOSCOW PL
ILCHESTER GDNS
PRINCE'S MS
MOSCOW ROAD
Bayswater
SHAFTESBURY HOUSE
CHENIES HOUSE
INVERNESS MEWS
INVERNESS PLACE
PALACE COURT
PRINCE EDWARD MANSIONS
ST PETERSBURGH PLACE
ST PETERSBURGH MEWS
BARK PLACE
POPLAR PLACE
PRINCESS COURT
OLYMPIA YD
CAROLINE PL
LOMBARDY PL
Coll
CHAPEL SIDE
OSSINGTON CL
OSSINGTON STREET
CLANRICARDE GARDENS
PALACE COURT
LANCASTER CLOSE
SAXON HALL
ST OLAVES COURT
ORME LA
New West End Synagogue
ORME CT
ORME CT MS
CAROLINE PL MS
QUEEN'S COURT
CONSORT HOUSE
FOSBURY MEWS
PORCHESTER GATE
HYDE PARK TOWERS
LEINSTER TERR
B410
B411
107
THE LIMES
VICTORIA GROVE MEWS
ORME SQUARE
CAROLINE CL
CAROLINE HO
A402
BAYSWATER ROAD
Inverness Terrace Gate
NORTH
GUYANA
Orme Square Gate
Queensway Black Lion Gate
113
CZECH REPUBLIC
SLOVAKIA
Pav
Diana, Princess of Wales Memorial Playground
A4204
KENSINGTON ML
LUCERNE MS
PALACE GARDENS MEWS
KENSINGTON PALACE GARDENS
Clock Tower
STRATHMORE GARDENS
LEBANON
NEPAL
RUSSIAN FEDERATION
PALACE GARDENS TERRACE
Diana, Princess of Wales Memorial Walk
THE BROAD WALK
KENSINGTON CHURCH STREET
BRUNSWICK GARDENS
BERKELEY GARDENS
Round Pond
Kensington Palace
INVERNESS GARDENS
VICARAGE GATE
Queen Victoria Statue
VICARAGE GARDENS
PHILIPPINES
Kensington Palace Green
80
MELON PL
WINCHESTER COURT
VICARAGE GATE
VICARAGE COURT
B405
W8
A
128
B
26
C
NICARAGUA
KENSINGTON
PALACE GREEN
CHURCH
City of

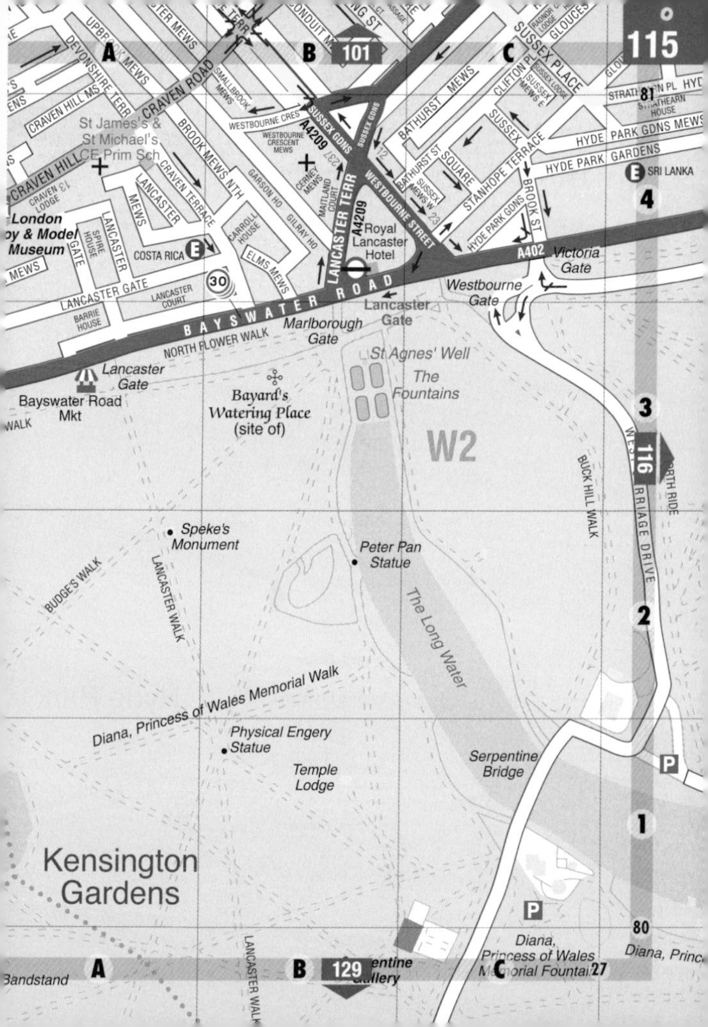

A
B
C
101
UPBROOK MEWS
DEVONSHIRE TERR
CRAVEN HILL MS
CRAVEN ROAD
SMALLBROOK MEWS
WESTBOURNE CRES
WESTBOURNE CRESCENT MEWS
SUSSEX GDNS
A4209
SUSSEX PLACE
RADNOR LODGE
CLIFTON PL
SUSSEX LODGE
SUSSEX MEWS E
BATHURST MEWS
STRATHEARN HOUSE
HYDE PARK GDNS MEWS
HYDE PARK GARDENS
SRI LANKA
St James's & St Michael's CE Prim Sch
CRAVEN HILL
CRAVEN LODGE
BROOK MEWS NTH
CRAVEN TERRACE
LANCASTER MEWS
GARSON HO
GILRAY HO
CERNEY MEWS
MAITLAND COURT
LANCASTER TERR
WESTBOURNE STREET
BATHURST ST
SUSSEX SQUARE
SUSSEX MEWS W
STANHOPE TERRACE
HYDE PARK GDNS
BROOK ST
London Toy & Model Museum
SPIRE HOUSE
LANCASTER GATE
COSTA RICA
CARROLL HOUSE
ELMS MEWS
Royal Lancaster Hotel
A402
Victoria Gate
Westbourne Gate
LANCASTER COURT
BARRIE HOUSE
BAYSWATER ROAD
Lancaster Gate
Marlborough Gate
NORTH FLOWER WALK
St Agnes' Well
The Fountains
Lancaster Gate
Bayswater Road Mkt
Bayard's Watering Place (site of)
W2
116
BUCK HILL WALK
WEST CARRIAGE DRIVE
NORTH RIDE
Speke's Monument
BUDGE'S WALK
LANCASTER WALK
Peter Pan Statue
The Long Water
Diana, Princess of Wales Memorial Walk
Physical Engery Statue
Temple Lodge
Serpentine Bridge
P
Kensington Gardens
Diana, Princess of Wales Memorial Fountain
Serpentine Gallery
Bandstand
129
LANCASTER WALK
Diana, Princ
4
3
2
1
80
81
27
30

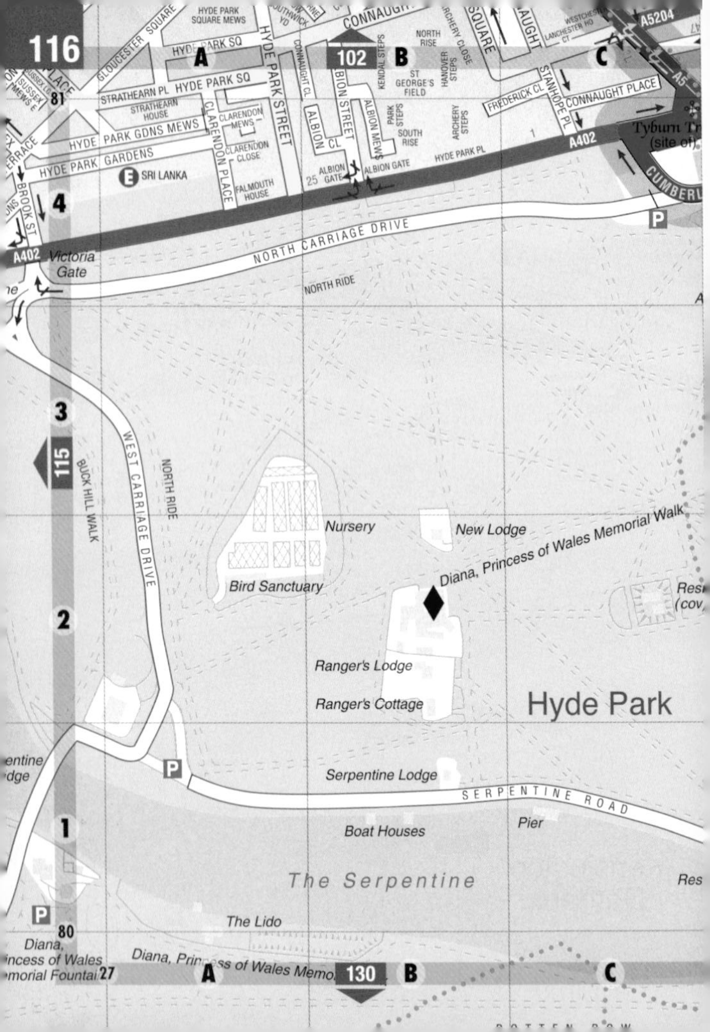

HYDE PARK SQUARE MEWS
GLOUCESTER SQUARE
CONNAUGHT
NORTH RISE
ARCHERY CLOSE
SQUARE
WESTCHESTER HO
LANCHESTER HO CT
A5204
A
102
B
C
HYDE PARK SQ
HYDE PARK STREET
CONNAUGHT CL
KENDAL STEPS
ST GEORGE'S FIELD
HANOVER STEPS
STANHOPE PL
FREDERICK CL
CONNAUGHT PLACE
A5
SUSSEX MEWS E
81
STRATHEARN PL
HYDE PARK SQ
STRATHEARN HOUSE
CLARENDON MEWS
ALBION STREET
ALBION CL
ALBION MEWS
PARK STEPS
SOUTH RISE
ARCHERY STEPS
1
A402
Tyburn Tr
(site of)
HYDE PARK GDNS MEWS
CLARENDON CLOSE
HYDE PARK GARDENS
CLARENDON PLACE
ALBION GATE
25
ALBION GATE
HYDE PARK PL
CUMBERL
E
SRI LANKA
FALMOUTH HOUSE
BROOK ST
4
P
A402
Victoria Gate
NORTH CARRIAGE DRIVE
NORTH RIDE
3
115
BUCK HILL WALK
WEST CARRIAGE DRIVE
NORTH RIDE
Nursery
New Lodge
Diana, Princess of Wales Memorial Walk
Bird Sanctuary
2
Ranger's Lodge
Ranger's Cottage
Hyde Park
P
Serpentine Lodge
SERPENTINE ROAD
1
Boat Houses
Pier
The Serpentine
P
The Lido
80
Diana, Princess of Wales Memorial Fountain
27
Diana, Princess of Wales Memo
A
130
B
C

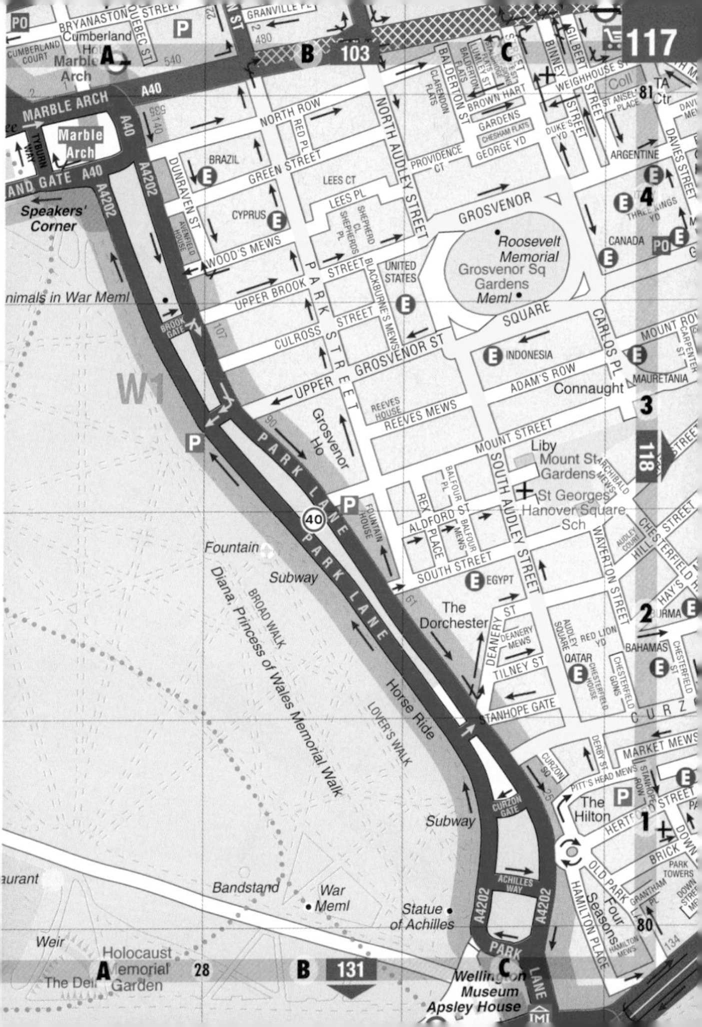

103
118
131
A
B
C
1
2
3
4
Marble Arch
Cumberland Hotel
Bryanaston Street
Quebec St
Granville Pl
Cumberland Court
Marble Arch
A40
A4202
Tyburn Way
North Row
Red Pl
Green Street
Brazil
Cyprus
Dunraven St
Avenfield House
Wood's Mews
Upper Brook Street
Brook Gate
Park Street
Lees Ct
Lees Pl
Shepherds Pl
Shepherd Cl
Blackburne's Mews
United States
Culross Street
Upper Grosvenor St
Reeves House
Reeves Mews
Grosvenor Ho
North Audley Street
Balderton St
Balderton Flats
Clarendon Flats
Lumley St
Lumley Flats
Brown Hart Gardens
Chesham Flats
George Yd
Providence Ct
Duke's Yd
Binney St
Gilbert Street
Weighhouse St
St Anselm Place
Coll
TA Ctr
Argentine
Davies Street
Three Kings Yd
Canada
PO
Grosvenor
Roosevelt Memorial
Grosvenor Sq Gardens
Meml
Square
Carlos Pl
Mount Row
Carpenter St
Indonesia
Adam's Row
Mauretania
Connaught
Mount Street
Liby
Mount St Gardens
Archibald Mews
St Georges Hanover Square Sch
Balfour Pl
Rex Place
Alford St
Balfour Mews
Fountain House
South Street
Egypt
South Audley Street
Waverton Street
Audley Court
Hill Street
Chesterfield Hill
Hay's
Burma
Bahamas
Chesterfield St
The Dorchester
Deanery St
Deanery Mews
Tilney St
Audley Square
Red Lion Yd
Qatar
Chesterfield House
Chesterfield Gdns
Stanhope Gate
Curzon
Derby St
Market Mews
Curzon Sq
Pitt's Head Mews
Stanhope Row
The Hilton
Hertford Street
Down
Brick
Park Towers
Old Park La
Grantham Pl
Hamilton Place
Four Seasons
Hamilton Mews
Speakers' Corner
Animals in War Meml
W1
Park Lane
40
Fountain
Subway
Broad Walk
Diana, Princess of Wales Memorial Walk
Lover's Walk
Horse Ride
Curzon Gate
Achilles Way
Subway
Restaurant
Bandstand
War Meml
Statue of Achilles
Weir
Holocaust Memorial Garden
The Dell
Wellington Museum
Apsley House
28
80
81

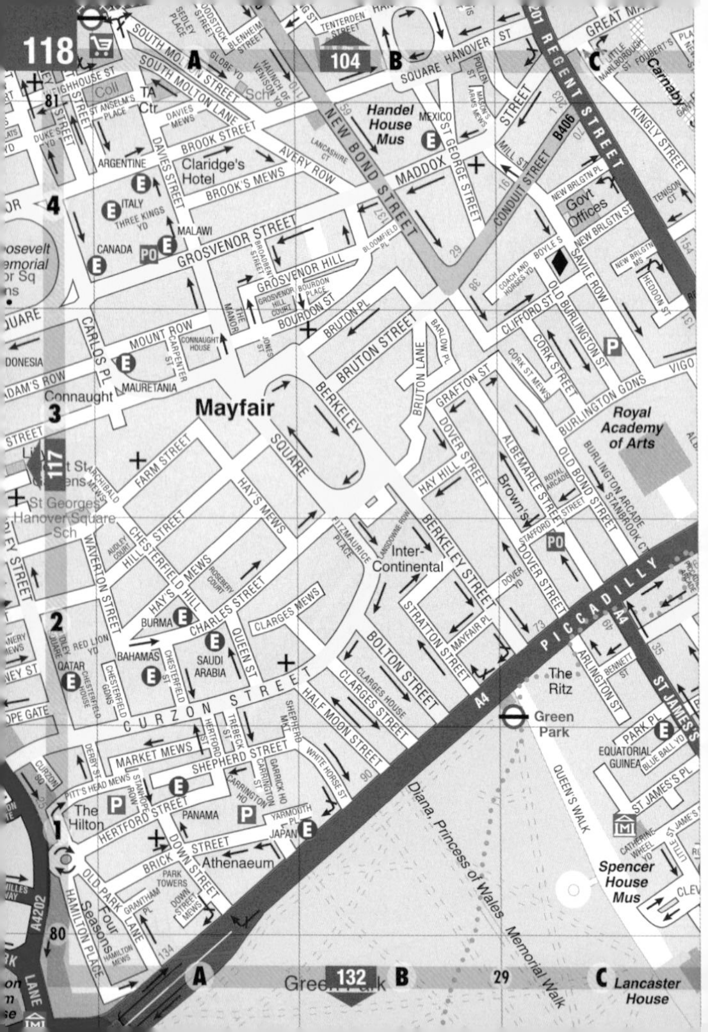
Mayfair
104
132
117
A
B
C
1
2
3
4
Green Park
SOUTH MOLTON STREET
SOUTH MOLTON LANE
BROOK STREET
Claridge's Hotel
BROOK'S MEWS
AVERY ROW
NEW BOND STREET
Handel House Mus
MEXICO
ST GEORGE STREET
MADDOX
HANOVER SQUARE
TENTERDEN STREET
BLENHEIM STREET
WOODSTOCK STREET
SEDLEY PLACE
GLOBE YD
HAUNCH OF VENISON YD
LANCASHIRE CT
POLLEN ST
MASON'S ARMS MEWS
MILL ST
CONDUIT STREET
REGENT STREET
B406
GREAT MARLBOROUGH ST
LITTLE MARLBOROUGH ST
FOUBERT'S PL
Carnaby
KINGLY STREET
NEW BRLGTN PL
NEW BRLGTN ST
NEW BRLGTN MS
Govt Offices
TENISON CT
HEDDON ST
SAVILE ROW
BOYLE S
COACH AND HORSES YD
CLIFFORD ST
OLD BURLINGTON ST
CORK STREET
CORK ST MEWS
VIGO
BURLINGTON GDNS
Royal Academy of Arts
BURLINGTON ARCADE
STANBROOK CT
OLD BOND STREET
ROYAL ARCADE
STAFFORD STREET
ALBEMARLE STREET
Brown's
DOVER STREET
DOVER YD
GRAFTON ST
HAY HILL
BRUTON LANE
BARLOW PL
BRUTON STREET
BRUTON PL
BERKELEY SQUARE
BERKELEY STREET
LANSDOWNE ROW
FITZMAURICE PLACE
Inter-Continental
STRATTON STREET
MAYFAIR PL
BOLTON STREET
CLARGES STREET
CLARGES HOUSE
CLARGES MEWS
HALF MOON STREET
PICCADILLY
A4
The Ritz
ARLINGTON ST
BENNETT ST
ST JAMES'S
PARK PL
BLUE BALL YD
EQUATORIAL GUINEA
ST JAMES'S PL
QUEEN'S WALK
CATHERINE WHEEL YD
LITTLE ST JAMES'S
Spencer House Mus
CLEV
Diana, Princess of Wales Memorial Walk
Lancaster House
GROSVENOR STREET
GROSVENOR HILL
GROSVENOR HILL COURT
BOURDON PLACE
BOURDON ST
BROADBENT STREET
BLOOMFIELD PL
THE MANOR
JONES ST
MOUNT ROW
CONNAUGHT HOUSE
CARPENTER ST
CARLOS PL
ADAM'S ROW
MAURETANIA
Connaught
DAVIES STREET
DAVIES MEWS
ARGENTINE
ITALY
THREE KINGS YD
MALAWI
CANADA
PO
WEIGHHOUSE ST
ST ANSELM'S PLACE
DUKE'S YD
Coll
TA Ctr
Sch
Roosevelt Memorial
SQUARE
INDONESIA
FARM STREET
ARCHIBALD MEWS
St Georges Hanover Square Sch
HAY'S MEWS
HILL STREET
CHESTERFIELD HILL
AUDLEY COURT
ROSEBERY COURT
HAY'S MEWS
CHARLES STREET
QUEEN ST
WAVERTON STREET
BURMA
SAUDI ARABIA
BAHAMAS
CHESTERFIELD ST
CHESTERFIELD GDNS
CHESTERFIELD HOUSE
RED LION YD
QATAR
TILNEY ST
CURZON STREET
MARKET MEWS
HERTFORD ST
TREBECK ST
SHEPHERD MKT
SHEPHERD STREET
WHITE HORSE ST
CARRINGTON ST
CARRINGTON HO
GARRICK HO
DERBY ST
PITT'S HEAD MEWS
STANHOPE ROW
HERTFORD STREET
PANAMA
YARMOUTH PL
JAPAN
The Hilton
BRICK STREET
DOWN STREET
Athenaeum
PARK TOWERS
DOWN STREET MEWS
OLD PARK LANE
GRANTHAM PL
HAMILTON PLACE
HAMILTON MEWS
Four Seasons
CURZON SQ
A4202
PARK LANE
HOPE GATE

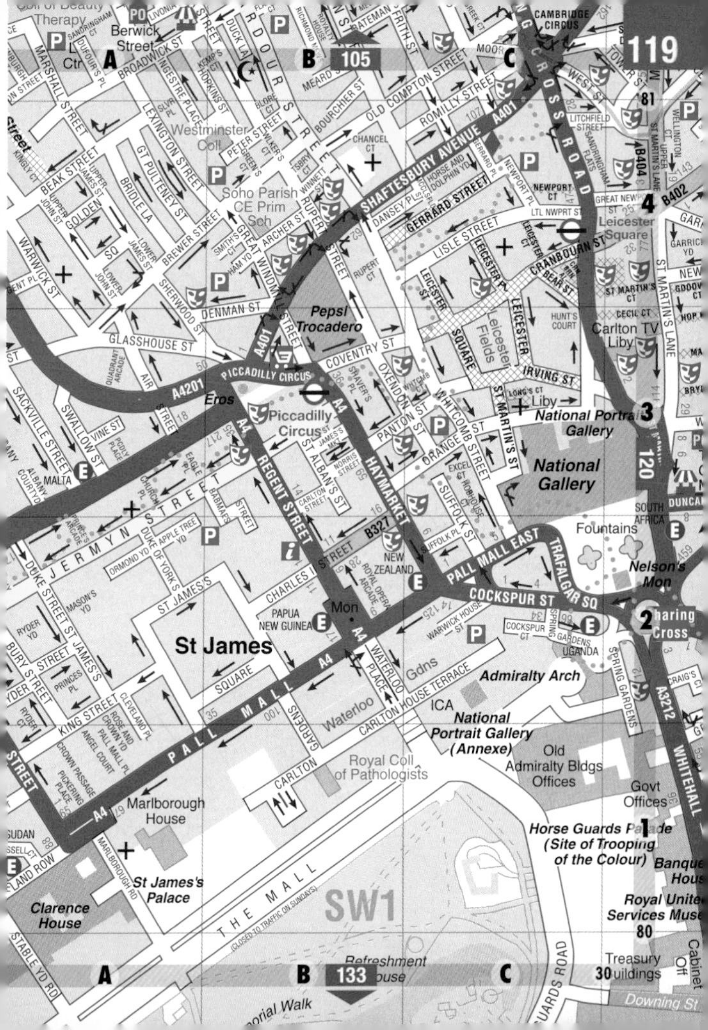
105
133
120
A
B
C
4
3
2
1
Berwick Street
Broadwick St
Marshall Street
Lexington Street
Ingestre Place
Wardour Street
Old Compton Street
Romilly Street
Frith St
Bateman St
Meard St
Bourchier St
Peter Street
Westminster Coll
Soho Parish CE Prim Sch
Cambridge Circus
Charing Cross Road
Shaftesbury Avenue
A401
West St
Litchfield Street
Gerrard Street
Lisle Street
Newport Ct
Cranbourn St
Leicester Square
Leicester Fields
Leicester St
Leicester Pl
Irving St
Hunt's Court
Carlton TV
Liby
St Martin's Lane
St Martin's Ct
Cecil Ct
B404
B402
Beak Street
Golden Sq
Bridle La
Gt Pulteney St
Brewer Street
Great Windmill St
Archer St
Rupert Street
Rupert Ct
Denman St
Sherwood St
Glasshouse St
Warwick St
Pepsi Trocadero
Coventry St
Piccadilly Circus
Eros
A4201
A4
Regent Street
Haymarket
Oxendon St
Whitcomb Street
Panton St
Orange St
Suffolk St
Suffolk Pl
St Martin's St
National Portrait Gallery
National Gallery
Fountains
Nelson's Mon
Charing Cross
South Africa
Trafalgar Sq
Pall Mall East
Cockspur St
Spring Gardens
Uganda
Admiralty Arch
New Zealand
B327
Charles II Street
St Alban's St
Norris St
Jermyn Street
Duke Of York's St
Ormond Yd
Apple Tree Yd
Babmaes Street
Eagle Pl
Church Pl
Vine St
Swallow St
Sackville Street
Air Street
Albany Courtyd
Malta
Duke Street St James's
Mason's Yd
Ryder Yd
Bury Street
Ryder Street
St James's Square
St James
King Street
Princes Pl
Crown Passage
Angel Court
Pickering Place
Pall Mall
Papua New Guinea
Mon
Waterloo Place
Waterloo Gdns
Carlton House Terrace
Carlton Gardens
ICA
National Portrait Gallery (Annexe)
Royal Coll of Pathologists
Old Admiralty Bldgs Offices
Govt Offices
Whitehall
A3212
Horse Guards Parade (Site of Trooping of the Colour)
Marlborough House
Marlborough Rd
St James's Palace
Clarence House
Sudan
Stable Yd Rd
The Mall
(Closed to traffic on Sundays)
SW1
Refreshment House
Horse Guards Road
Treasury Buildings
Cabinet Off
Downing St
Royal United Services Museum
Banqueting House
80
81
30

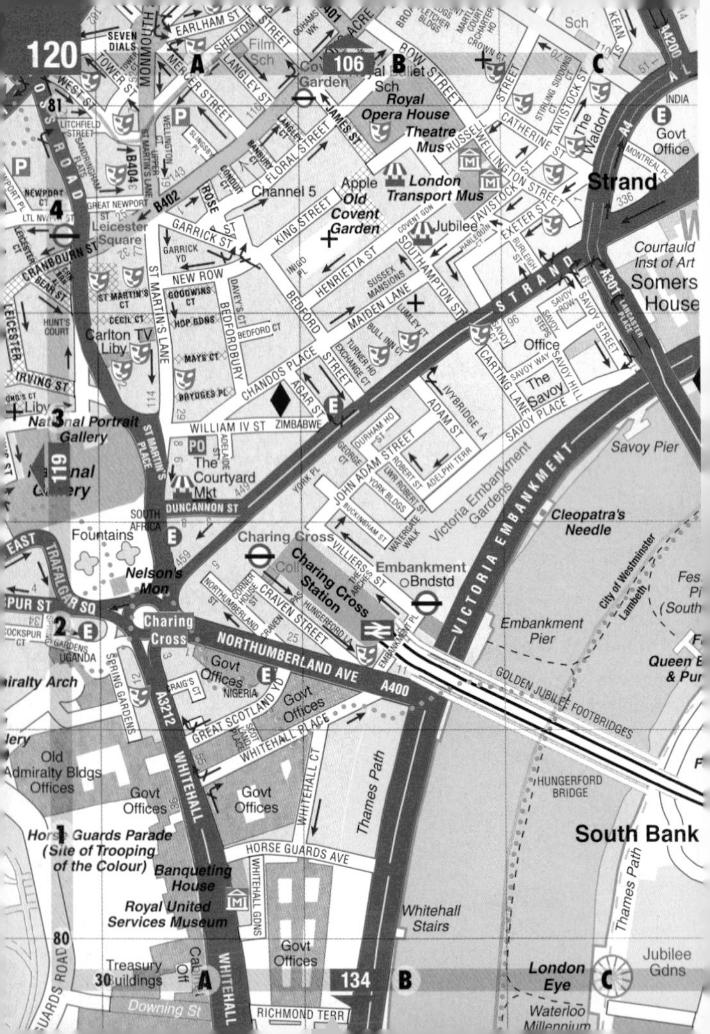
106
134
119
A
B
C
1
2
3
4
SEVEN DIALS
EARLHAM ST
SHELTON STREET
MONMOUTH
MERCER STREET
LANGLEY ST
TOWER ST
WEST ST
LITCHFIELD STREET
Film Sch
Covent Garden
Royal Ballet Sch
Royal Opera House
BOW STREET
Theatre Mus
RUSSELL
CATHERINE ST
WELLINGTON STREET
TAVISTOCK ST
The Waldorf
Govt Office
INDIA
Strand
Sch
FLORAL STREET
JAMES ST
Channel 5
Apple
Old Covent Garden
London Transport Mus
Jubilee
KING STREET
HENRIETTA ST
SOUTHAMPTON ST
EXETER ST
BURLEIGH ST
GARRICK ST
NEW ROW
ST MARTIN'S LANE
Leicester Square
CRANBOURN ST
GREAT NEWPORT ST
B402
B404
ROSE
BEDFORD
BEDFORDBURY
MAIDEN LANE
SUSSEX MANSIONS
STRAND
A301
LANCASTER PLACE
Courtauld Inst of Art
Somerset House
SAVOY STREET
SAVOY HILL
SAVOY PLACE
The Savoy
Office
SAVOY WAY
CARTING LANE
Carlton TV
Liby
IRVING ST
LEICESTER
HUNT'S COURT
CHANDOS PLACE
AGAR ST
WILLIAM IV ST
ZIMBABWE
National Portrait Gallery
National Gallery
ST MARTIN'S PLACE
PO
The Courtyard Mkt
DUNCANNON ST
SOUTH AFRICA
ADAM ST
IVYBRIDGE LA
JOHN ADAM STREET
ROBERT ST
ADELPHI TERR
YORK PL
Victoria Embankment Gardens
VICTORIA EMBANKMENT
Savoy Pier
Cleopatra's Needle
Charing Cross
Charing Cross Station
VILLIERS ST
Embankment
Bndstd
CRAVEN STREET
HUNGERFORD LA
NORTHUMBERLAND AVE
A400
Fountains
Nelson's Mon
TRAFALGAR SQ
SPUR ST
COCKSPUR CT
UGANDA
SPRING GARDENS
Admiralty Arch
A3212
Govt Offices
NIGERIA
GREAT SCOTLAND YD
WHITEHALL PLACE
WHITEHALL CT
Thames Path
Embankment Pier
GOLDEN JUBILEE FOOTBRIDGES
City of Westminster
Lambeth
Queen Elizabeth Hall & Purcell Room
HUNGERFORD BRIDGE
South Bank
Old Admiralty Bldgs Offices
WHITEHALL
Horse Guards Parade (Site of Trooping of the Colour)
Banqueting House
Royal United Services Museum
HORSE GUARDS AVE
WHITEHALL GDNS
Whitehall Stairs
Treasury Buildings
Cabinet Off
Downing St
RICHMOND TERR
HORSE GUARDS ROAD
London Eye
Jubilee Gdns
Waterloo Millennium

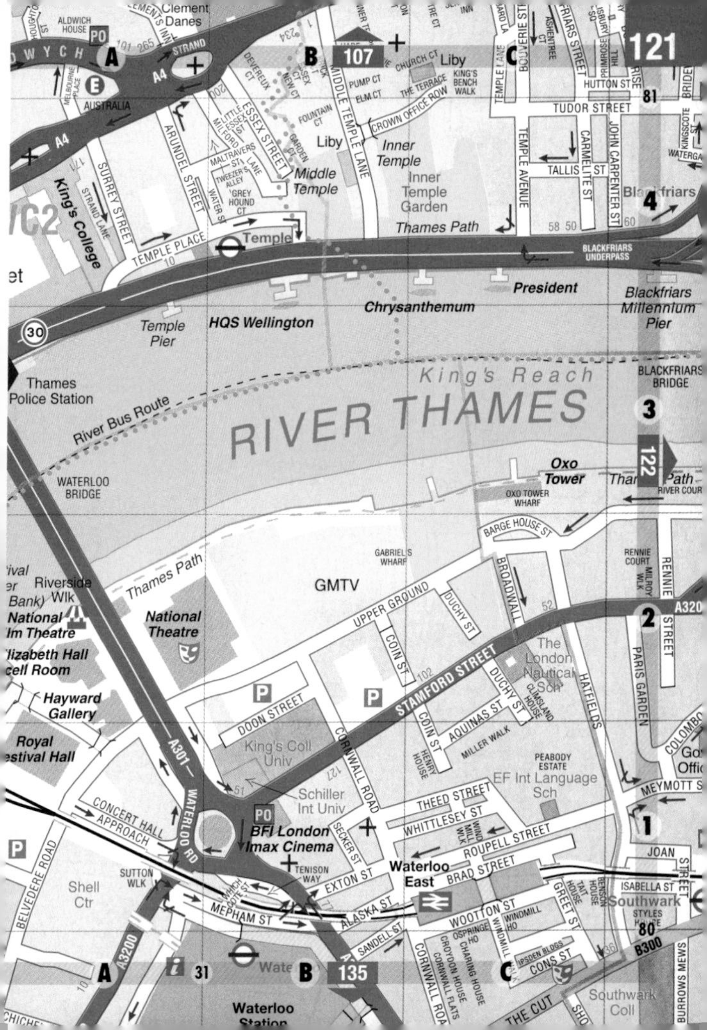

Clement Danes
ALDWICH HOUSE
PO
ALDWYCH
A
STRAND
A4
AUSTRALIA
MELBOURNE PLACE
B
107
C
Liby
CHURCH CT
KING'S BENCH WALK
THE TERRACE
CROWN OFFICE ROW
PUMP CT
ELM CT
MIDDLE TEMPLE LANE
DEVEREUX CT
ESSEX STREET
LITTLE ESSEX ST
MILFORD LANE
FOUNTAIN CT
GARDEN CT
MALTRAVERS ST
TWEEZER'S ALLEY
GREY HOUND CT
ARUNDEL STREET
WATER ST
SURREY STREET
STRAND LANE
King's College
WC2
Middle Temple
Inner Temple
Inner Temple Garden
Thames Path
Temple
TEMPLE PLACE
TEMPLE LANE
BOUVERIE ST
ASHENTREE CT
FRIARS STREET
PRIMROSE HILL
HUTTON ST
TUDOR STREET
81
TEMPLE AVENUE
CARMELITE ST
JOHN CARPENTER ST
TALLIS ST
KINGSCOTE ST
WATERGATE
Blackfriars
4
BLACKFRIARS UNDERPASS
President
Chrysanthemum
Blackfriars Millennium Pier
HQS Wellington
Temple Pier
30
Thames Police Station
King's Reach
RIVER THAMES
BLACKFRIARS BRIDGE
3
River Bus Route
WATERLOO BRIDGE
Oxo Tower
OXO TOWER WHARF
Thames Path
122
RIVER COURT
BARGE HOUSE ST
GABRIEL'S WHARF
GMTV
Riverside Wlk
Thames Path
National Film Theatre
National Theatre
Queen Elizabeth Hall
Purcell Room
Hayward Gallery
Royal Festival Hall
UPPER GROUND
DUCHY ST
BROADWALL
RENNIE COURT
MILROY WLK
RENNIE STREET
A3200
2
COIN ST
STAMFORD STREET
The London Nautical Sch
CLIMSLAND HOUSE
HATFIELDS
PARIS GARDEN
DOON STREET
King's Coll Univ
CORNWALL ROAD
AQUINAS ST
MILLER WALK
HENRY HOUSE
PEABODY ESTATE
EF Int Language Sch
COLOMBO
A301
WATERLOO RD
Schiller Int Univ
CONCERT HALL APPROACH
PO
BFI London Imax Cinema
SECKER ST
THEED STREET
WHITTLESEY ST
WINDMILL WLK
ROUPELL STREET
MEYMOTT ST
1
JOAN STREET
ISABELLA ST
Southwark
Waterloo East
BRAD STREET
TENISON WAY
EXTON ST
WHICHCOTE ST
ALASKA ST
SUTTON WLK
BELVEDERE ROAD
Shell Ctr
MEPHAM ST
SANDELL ST
WOOTTON ST
OSPRINGE HO
CROYDON HOUSE
CORNWALL FLATS
CHARING HOUSE
WINDMILL HO
GREET ST
TAIT HOUSE
BENSON HOUSE
STYLES HOUSE
80
B300
IPSDEN BLDGS
CONS ST
THE CUT
Southwark Coll
BURROWS MEWS
A
31
B
135
C
Waterloo Station

108
136
121
A
B
C
1
2
3
4
80
81
ST BRIDE'S PAS
DORSET BLDGS
DORSET RISE
PRIMROSE HILL
Liby
BRIDEWELL PL
BRIDGE STREET
A201
APOTHECARY ST
WATERMAN ST
BLACK FRIARS LA
PLAYHOUSE YD
IRELAND YD
CARTER CT
COBB'S CT
CREED LA
ST ANDREW'S HILL
WARDROBE PLACE
ADDLE HILL
YH
DEAN'S CT
ST PAUL'S CHURCH YARD
CARTER LANE
KNIGHTRIDER ST
GODLIMAN ST
SERMON LA
KNIGHT RIDER ST
KNIGHT RIDER CT
OLD CHANGE CT
DISTAFF LA
OLD FISH ST HILL
FRIDAY ST
HUTTON ST
TUDOR STREET
TEMPLE AVENUE
CARMELITE ST
JOHN CARPENTER ST
KINGSCOTE ST
WATERGATE
TALLIS ST
PO
St Andrew
WARD ROBE TERR
St Nicholas Cole Abbey
Coll of Arms
QUEEN VICTO
A3211
PUDDLE DOCK
CASTLE BAYNARD ST
Mermaid Theatre
BENNET'S HILL
BOOTH LA
LAMBETH HILL
CASTLE BAYNARD STREET
WHITE LION HILL
Blackfriars
BLKFRS PAS
Blackfriars Station
30
City of London Sch
TRIG LA
HIGH TIMBER ST
NORFOLK HO
BROKEN WF
GARDNERS LA
GLOBE VIEW
STEW LANE
BLACKFRIARS UNDERPASS
Thames Path
CITY OF LONDON
President
Blackfriars Millennium Pier
Queenhithe Stairs
City of London
Southwark
Reach
BLACKFRIARS BRIDGE
MILLENNIUM FOOTBRIDGE
Bankside Pier
Bankside Art Gal
FALCON POINT
Thames Path
RIVER COURT
OXO TOWER WHARF
Express Newspapers plc
BANKSIDE
CARDINAL CAP ALLEY
The Globe Theatre
HOUSE ST
HOPTON ST
Tate Modern
RENNIE COURT
MILROY WLK
RENNIE STREET
INVICTA PLAZA
HOPTON STREET
CASTLE YD
HOLLAND STREET
NEW GLOBE WLK
BEAR
A3200
BLACKFRIARS ROAD
HOPTON'S GARDENS
EMERSON ST
Bear Garden Mus
SUMNER STREET
The London Nautical Sch
PARIS GARDEN
HATFIELDS
CLIMSLAND HOUSE
BURRELL ST
CANVEY ST
ZOAR ST
SUMNER BLDGS
FALCON CL
FRIARS CLOSE
PRICE'S ST
BEAR LANE
GREAT GUILDFORD STREET
COLOMBO ST
Govt Office
CHANCEL STREET
TREVERIS ST
FARNHAM PL
SOUTHWARK STREET
PEABODY ESTATE
EDWARD EDWARD'S HOUSE
Int Language Sch
MEYMOTT ST
NICHOLSON ST
LAVINGTON STREET
Great Guildford Bsns Sq
Coll
BRINTON WLK
DOLBEN ST
Grand Vitesse Ind Est
EWER ST
KEPPEL RO
DOLBEN ST
ROTHERHAM WALK
WARDENS GR
AMERICA S
JOAN STREET
SCORESBY ST
GAMBIA ST
GREAT SUFFOLK ST
ISABELLA ST
Southwark
STYLES HOUSE
WINDMILL HO
GREET ST
TAIT HOUSE
BENSON HOUSE
UNION STREET
B300
RISBOROUGH ST
PEPPER ST
THOROLD HO
TRELAWNEY HO
FARNHAM HO
TOMLINE HO
BURROWS MEWS
ROWLAND HILL HO
NELSON SQUARE
VAUGHAN HO
APPLE
COPPERFIELD ST
DOYCE ST
A300
CONS ST
IPSDEN BLDGS
Southwark Coll
THE CUT
LOMAN STREET
Fire Brigade Mus
Crown Court
SAWYER
QUILP ST

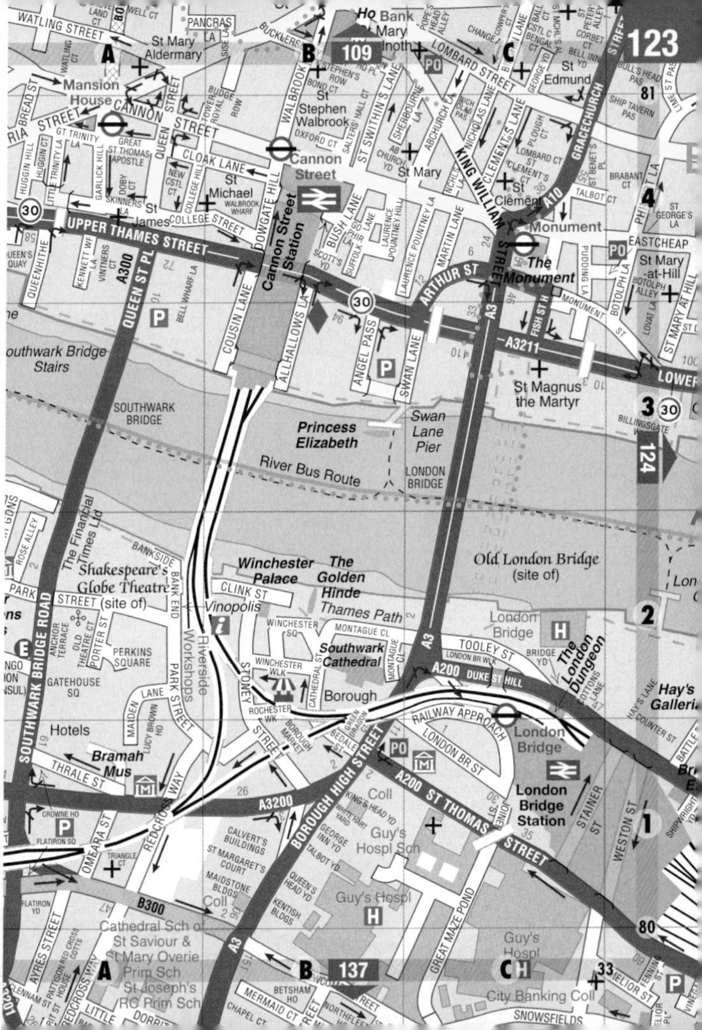

WATLING STREET
St Mary Aldermary
Mansion House
CANNON STREET
QUEEN STREET
BREAD ST
GT TRINITY LA
GREAT ST THOMAS APOSTLE
CLOAK LANE
St Michael
COLLEGE HILL
COLLEGE STREET
St James
GARLICK HILL
HUGGIN HILL
UPPER THAMES STREET
QUEENHITHE
VINTNERS CT
QUEEN ST PL
A300
BELL WHARF LA
DOWGATE HILL
WALBROOK
St Stephen Walbrook
Cannon Street
Cannon Street Station
OXFORD CT
BUCKLERSBURY
Bank
109
St Mary Woolnoth
LOMBARD STREET
PO
ST SWITHIN'S LANE
SALTERS' HALL CT
SHERBOURNE LA
ABCHURCH LA
St Mary
KING WILLIAM STREET
NICHOLAS LANE
CLEMENT'S LANE
St Clement
GRACECHURCH STREET
St Edmund
LOMBARD CT
PLOUGH CT
A10
Monument
The Monument
EASTCHEAP
St Mary-at-Hill
BOTOLPH LA
PUDDING LA
FISH ST H
MONUMENT ST
ST MARY AT HILL
LOVAT LA
BRABANT CT
TALBOT CT
PHILPOT LA
ST GEORGE'S LA
SHIP TAVERN PAS
BULL'S HEAD PAS
81
BUSH LANE
SUFFOLK LA
LAURENCE POUNTNEY HILL
LAURENCE POUNTNEY LA
MARTIN LANE
ARTHUR ST
A3
A3211
LOWER
30
ALLHALLOWS LA
ANGEL PASS
SWAN LANE
COUSIN LANE
P
St Magnus the Martyr
BILLINGSGATE WALK
Southwark Bridge Stairs
SOUTHWARK BRIDGE
Princess Elizabeth
Swan Lane Pier
LONDON BRIDGE
River Bus Route
124
Old London Bridge (site of)
The Financial Times Ltd
BANKSIDE
ROSE ALLEY
Shakespeare's Globe Theatre
PARK STREET (site of)
BANK END
Winchester Palace
The Golden Hinde
CLINK ST
Vinopolis
Thames Path
WINCHESTER SQ
MONTAGUE CL
Southwark Cathedral
WINCHESTER WLK
CATHEDRAL ST
Borough
ROCHESTER WK
STONEY STREET
Riverside Workshops
SOUTHWARK BRIDGE ROAD
ANCHOR TERRACE
OLD THEATRE CT
PORTER ST
PERKINS SQUARE
GATEHOUSE SQ
MAIDEN LANE
LUCY BROWN HO
PARK STREET
Hotels
Bramah Mus
THRALE ST
REDCROSS WAY
A3200
CROWNE HO
FLATIRON SQ
OMEARA ST
TRIANGLE CT
London Bridge
TOOLEY ST
BRIDGE YD
The London Dungeon
COTTONS LANE
A200 DUKE ST HILL
RAILWAY APPROACH
LONDON BR ST
London Bridge Station
STAINER ST
WESTON ST
Hay's Galleria
HAY'S LANE
COUNTER ST
BOROUGH HIGH STREET
BOROUGH MARKET
GREEN DRAGON CT
BEDALE ST
A200 ST THOMAS STREET
KING'S HEAD YD
WHITE HART YARD
GEORGE INN YD
TALBOT YD
Guy's Hospl Sch
CALVERT'S BUILDINGS
ST MARGARET'S COURT
MAIDSTONE BLDGS
Coll
QUEEN'S HEAD YD
KENTISH BLDGS
Guy's Hospl
JOINER ST
GREAT MAZE POND
B300
FLATIRON YD
AYRES STREET
PATTISON HOUSE
REDCROSS COTTS
REDCROSS WAY
Cathedral Sch of St Saviour & St Mary Overie Prim Sch
St Joseph's RC Prim Sch
LITTLE DORRIT
CHAPEL CT
MERMAID CT
BETSHAM HO
NORTHFLEET
137
Guy's Hospl
City Banking Coll
SNOWSFIELDS
80
33
A
B
C
E
1
2
3
4

A
B
C
110
138
123
4
3
2
1
EC3
Building
St Peter
Leadenhall Mkt
Fenchurch St
Lime Street
Gracechurch Street
St Edmund
Bull's Head Pas
Ship Tavern Pas
Lime St Pas
Cullum St
Fenchurch Street
Billiter Sq
Fen Ct
Hogarth Ct
London St
Fenchurch Pl
Katherine's Row
Fenchurch Street Station
Metropolitan Univ
Aldgate
Northumberland Alley
Carlisle Ave
Rangoon St
Jewry St
India St
Vine Street
St Clare St
Minories
Iveagh Ct
Haydon St
Portsoken
Goodman
Crosswall
America Sq
Lloyd's Ave
Friars
Plough Ct
Lombard Ct
St Benet's Pl
Brabant Ct
Philpot La
Talbot Ct
Rood La
St Margaret Pattens
St George's La
Plantation La
Mincing Lane
Dunster Ct
Star Alley
Minster Ct
Mark Lane
Hart St
New London St
Crutched
Pepys Street
St Olave's
Seething Lane
Savage Gardens
Cooper's Row
London Wall
Tower Hill
Crescent
Hammett St
Trinity Square
Trinity Pl
Univ
Monument
The Monument
PO
Eastcheap
Pudding La
Botolph La
St Mary-at-Hill
Botolph Alley
Lovat La
St Mary at Hill
Idol La
St Dunstan's Alley
St Dunstan's Hill
Pinnacle Ho
Great Tower Street
Monument St
Fish St H
St Dunstan's La
Cross La
Harp La
Bakers Hall Ct
Muscovy St
Trinity Sq Gdns
Byward St
Tower Hill A3211
A3211
All-Hallows
Lower Thames St
30
St Magnus the Martyr
Old Billingsgate Wlk
Custom House
Tower Pl W
Tower Pl E
Gloucester Ct
Tower Hill
Tenn Ct
St Peter ad Vincula
Royal Fusiliers Mus
The Tower
The Royal Armouries
St John's Chapel
Petty Wales
City of London
Tower Hamlets
Pontoon
River Thames
Tower Stairs
Tower Millennium Pier
Traitors Gate
Thames Path
London Bridge (site of)
London Bridge City Pier
River Bus Route
HMS Belfast
Tower Bridge
Tower Br Approach
Upper Pool
The London Dungeon
Bridge Yd
Cottons Lane
Hay's Lane
Hay's Galleria
Counter St
Battle Bridge Lane
English Grounds
Crown Court
London Bridge
London Bridge Station
Stainer St
Weston St
Britain at War Experience
Shipwright Yd
A2205
Tooley Street
Braidwood St
Abbots Lane
Oxford Dr
Bursar St
Magdalen St
Gibbon's Rents
Holyrood Street
Vine Lane
Weaver's Lane
Potters Fields
City Hall
London Bridge City Park
Lambeth Tertiary Coll (Tower Bridge Centre)
Horselydown
A100 Tower Bridge Rd
Horselydown Lane
Shand Street
Devon Mansions
Street
A200
A2207
St Olave's Estate
Guy's Hospl
Banking Coll
Snowsfields
Crucifix
Vinegar Yd
Fenning St
Great Yd
Ct
Queen Elizabeth St
Horselydown Mans
Jubilee
Brewery Square
Compass Court
Tower Br Piazza
Knot House
Eagle Wharf
Butler's Wharf
Shad Thames
Boiler
Malt Mill
Gainsford
Rayne Ct
Wheldon Ct
Admirals Ct
Candishe Ho
Knights Ho
Whitsters Ho
Cooperage Ct
80
33

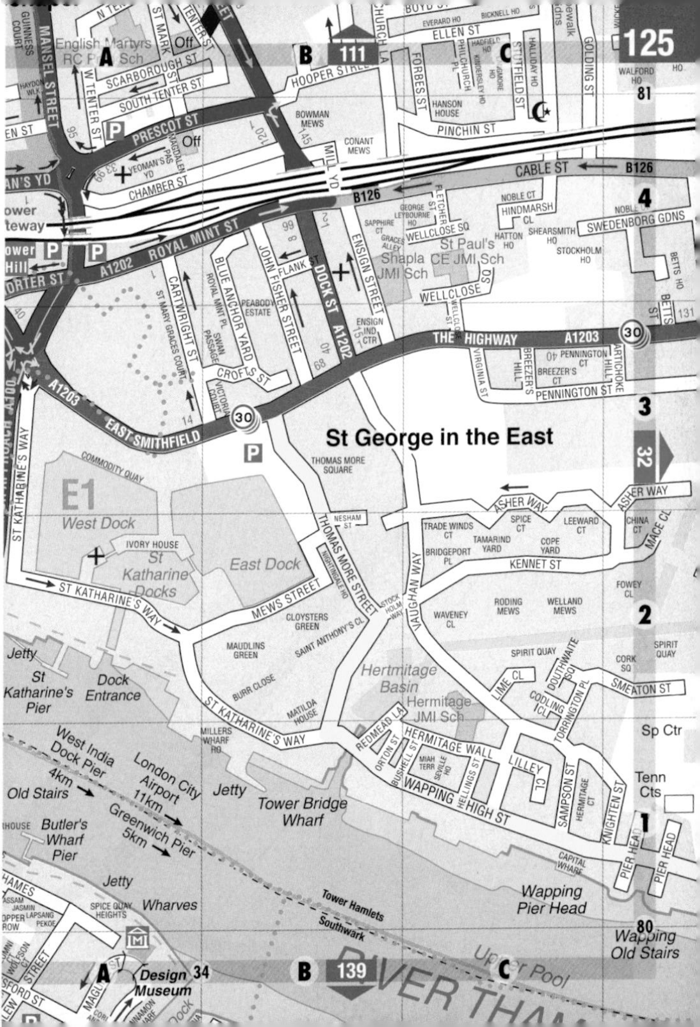
St George in the East
A
B
C
111
139
32
81
80
34
131
1
2
3
4
English Martyrs RC Prim Sch
Mansel Street
Guinness Court
Haydon Wlk
W Tenter St
St Mark St
Tenter St
Scarborough St
South Tenter St
Prescot St
Magdalen Pas
Yeoman's Yd
Chamber St
Hooper Street
Bowman Mews
Conant Mews
Mill Yd
Church La
Forbes St
Everard Ho
Ellen St
Bicknell Ho
Hadfield Ho
Philchurch Pl
Kindersley Ho
Stutfield St
Halliday Ho
Hanson House
Pinchin St
Golding St
Walford Ho
Cable St
B126
Fletcher St
George Leybourne Ho
Sapphire Ct
Graces Alley
Wellclose Sq
Noble Ct
Hindmarsh Cl
Hatton Ho
Shearsmith Ho
Stockholm Ho
Swedenborg Gdns
Betts Ho
Betts St
St Paul's Shapla CE JMI Sch
Shapla JMI Sch
Royal Mint St
A1202
Tower Hill
Tower Gateway
Cartwright St
St Mary Graces Court
Blue Anchor Yard
Royal Mint Pl
Swan Passage
Peabody Estate
John Fisher Street
Flank St
Dock St
Ensign Street
Ensign Ind Ctr
Crofts St
Victoria Court
The Highway
A1203
Virginia St
Breezer's Hill
Breezer's Ct
Pennington Ct
Artichoke Hill
Pennington St
East Smithfield
30
Thomas More Square
Commodity Quay
E1
West Dock
Ivory House
St Katharine Docks
East Dock
St Katharine's Way
Nesham St
Thomas More Street
Nightingale Ho
Mews Street
Asher Way
Trade Winds Ct
Tamarind Yard
Spice Ct
Cope Yard
Leeward Ct
China Ct
Mace Cl
Bridgeport Pl
Kennet St
Vaughan Way
Stockholm Way
Fowey Cl
Roding Mews
Welland Mews
Waveney Cl
Cloysters Green
Saint Anthony's Cl
Maudlins Green
Burr Close
Matilda House
Hermitage Basin
Hermitage JMI Sch
Spirit Quay
Cork Sq
Lime Cl
Douthwaite Sq
Codling Cl
Torrington Pl
Smeaton St
Sp Ctr
Redmead La
Orton St
Bushell St
Miah Terr
Seville Ho
Hermitage Wall
Hellings St
Lilley Cl
Wapping High St
Sampson St
Hermitage Ct
Knighten St
Tenn Cts
Pier Head
Capital Wharf
Wapping Pier Head
Wapping Old Stairs
Millers Wharf Ho
Jetty
St Katharine's Pier
Dock Entrance
West India Dock Pier 4km
Old Stairs
London City Airport 11km
Greenwich Pier 5km
Tower Bridge Wharf
Butler's Wharf Pier
Spice Quay Heights
Wharves
Tower Hamlets
Southwark
Upper Pool
River Thames
Design Museum
Jasmin
Lapsang
Pekoe
Assam
Wolfson Ct
Off
P

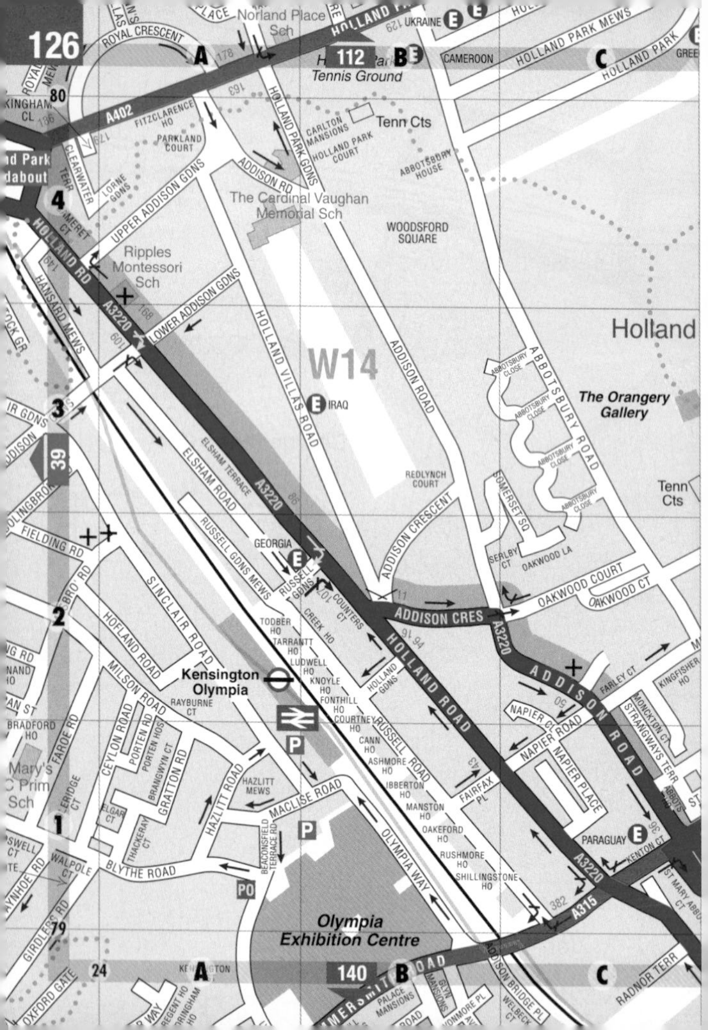
Norland Place Sch
HOLLAND PARK
UKRAINE
ROYAL CRESCENT
112
Holland Park Tennis Ground
CAMEROON
HOLLAND PARK MEWS
HOLLAND PARK
A
B
C
80
A402
FITZCLARENCE HO
PARKLAND COURT
CARLTON MANSIONS
HOLLAND PARK COURT
Tenn Cts
ABBOTSBURY HOUSE
HOLLAND PARK GDNS
CLEARWATER TERR
LORNE GDNS
UPPER ADDISON GDNS
ADDISON RD
The Cardinal Vaughan Memorial Sch
WOODSFORD SQUARE
4
Holland Park Roundabout
HOLLAND RD
Ripples Montessori Sch
LOWER ADDISON GDNS
HANSARD MEWS
A3220
HOLLAND VILLAS ROAD
W14
ADDISON ROAD
Holland
ABBOTSBURY CLOSE
ABBOTSBURY ROAD
The Orangery Gallery
3
IRAQ
39
ELSHAM TERRACE
ELSHAM ROAD
RUSSELL GDNS MEWS
REDLYNCH COURT
ADDISON CRESCENT
SOMERSET SQ
Tenn Cts
FIELDING RD
GEORGIA
RUSSELL GDNS
SERLBY CT
OAKWOOD LA
OAKWOOD COURT
OAKWOOD CT
COUNTERS CT
CREEK HO
ADDISON CRES
2
SINCLAIR ROAD
HOFLAND ROAD
TODBER HO
TARRANTT HO
LUDWELL HO
KNOYLE HO
FONTHILL HO
COURTNEY HO
CANN HO
ASHMORE HO
IBBERTON HO
MANSTON HO
OAKEFORD HO
RUSHMORE HO
SHILLINGSTONE HO
HOLLAND GDNS
HOLLAND ROAD
ADDISON ROAD
FARLEY CT
KINGFISHER HO
Kensington Olympia
MILSON ROAD
RAYBURNE CT
NAPIER CL
NAPIER ROAD
NAPIER PLACE
MONCKTON CT
STRANGWAYS TERR
BRADFORD HO
FAROE RD
CEYLON ROAD
PORTEN RD
PORTEN HOS
BRANGWYN CT
GRATTON RD
RUSSELL ROAD
FAIRFAX PL
Mary's C Prim Sch
HAZLITT ROAD
HAZLITT MEWS
MACLISE ROAD
1
ELGAR CT
THACKERAY CT
BEACONSFIELD TERRACE RD
OLYMPIA WAY
PARAGUAY
KENTON CT
WALPOLE CT
BLYTHE ROAD
PO
A315
ST MARY ABBOTS CT
GIRDLERS RD
79
Olympia Exhibition Centre
24
KENSINGTON
A
140
B
C
HAMMERSMITH ROAD
OXFORD GATE
PALACE MANSIONS
GLYN MANSIONS
ADDISON BRIDGE PL
WELBECK CT
RADNOR TERR

A
B
C
113
Tenn Cts
AIRLIE GDNS
LAURIE HOUSE
THE MOUNT
BEDFORD
SHEFFIELD TERRACE
CAMPDEN HOUSE
VICARAGE GARDENS
80
VICARAGE GATE
Holland Park Sch
Tenn Cts
CAMPDEN HILL
CAMPDEN HILL ROAD
TOR GDNS
TOR COURT
GLOUCESTER WALK
NICARAGUA
MELON PL
WINCHESTER COURT
B405
KENSINGTON CHURCH STREET
VICARAGE COURT
CHURCH CLOSE
1 TASKER LO
2 THORNWOOD LO
HOLLY LODGE
THORNWOOD GDNS
ATKINS LODGE
CAMPDEN HO CL
OBSERVATORY GDNS
CAMPDEN GROVE
HORNTON STREET
GORDON PLACE
BULLINGHAM MANSIONS
4
DUKES LANE
CARMEL CT
HOLLAND PL
W8
SHELDRAKE PLACE
DUCHESS OF BEDFORD HOUSE
ACADEMY GDNS
CAMPDEN HILL COURT
PITT ST
HOLLAND STREET
INGELOW HOUSE
GREGORY PL
KENSINGTON
CAMPDEN HILL GATE
DUCHESS OF BEDFORD'S WALK
Park
YH
TH
DRAYSON MEWS
St Mary Abbots CE Prim Sch
CHURCH
KENSINGTON CT
UPPER PHILLIMORE GARDENS
JORDAN
KENSINGTON
HOLLAND WLK
Liby
3
HORNTON PLACE
112
PHILLIMORE PLACE
ARGYLL ROAD
HORNTON COURT
128
Kensing
PHILLIMORE GARDENS
ESSEX VILLAS
STAFFORD TERRACE
PHILLIMORE WALK
PHILLIMORE COURT
KENSINGTON HIGH STREET
163
ILCHESTER PLACE
Tenn Cts
Commonwealth Institute
STAFFORD CT
160
IVERNA CT
WRIGHT'S LA
PHILLIMORE GDNS CL
ALLEN HO
EDEN CL
ADAM AND EVE MEWS
IVERNA GARDENS
PARK CLOSE
TROY CT
A315
PHILLIMORE TERR
WYNNSTAY GDNS
2
ARMENIA
KENSINGTON GARDENS
SCARSDALE PLACE
MELBURY ROAD
STAVORDALE LODGE
Leighton House (Art Gallery and Museum)
MELBURY COURT
240
PO
B316
249
ILCHESTER MANSIONS
ABINGDON MANSIONS
WARWICK CHAMBERS
ALLEN MANSIONS
CEDAR HO
ZETLAND HO
RUTLAND HO
FALKLAND HO
SUTHERLAND HO
HOLLAND PARK ROAD
KENBROOK HO
LEONARD CT
EDWARDES SQ
PATER ST
ABINGDON ROAD
VANTAGE PL
ABINGDON CT
ABINGDON VILLAS
ABINGDON GDNS
ALLEN STREET
MARY ABBOTS TERR
EARLS TERR
PEMBROKE PLACE
COPE PLACE
35
ST
EDWARDES PL
EDWARDES SQ
St Barnabas & St Philip CE Prim Sch
PEMBROKE MEWS
SCARSDALE VILLAS
1
SENEGAL
ST MARY ABBOTS PL
EDWARDES SQUARE
SOUTH EDWARDES SQ
EARLS WALK
INKERMAN TERR
STRATFORD STUDIOS
BLITHFIELD ST
MARLOES ROAD
PO
ALMA TERR
A3220
PEMBROKE STUDIOS
PEMBROKE GARDENS CLOSE
PEMBROKE SQ
PEMBROKE SQUARE
84
67
B316
SHAFTESBURY MEWS
STRATFORD ROAD
RADLEY MEWS
Tenn Ct
LEXHAM MEWS
SUNNINGDALE GDNS
79
LEXHAM GARDENS
PEMBROKE GDNS
PEMBROKE WLK
108
DURRELS HO
25
141
WARWICK GARDENS
160
185
PEMBROKE VILLAS
CHATSWORTH CT
SHERBOURNE CT
HUNTINGDON

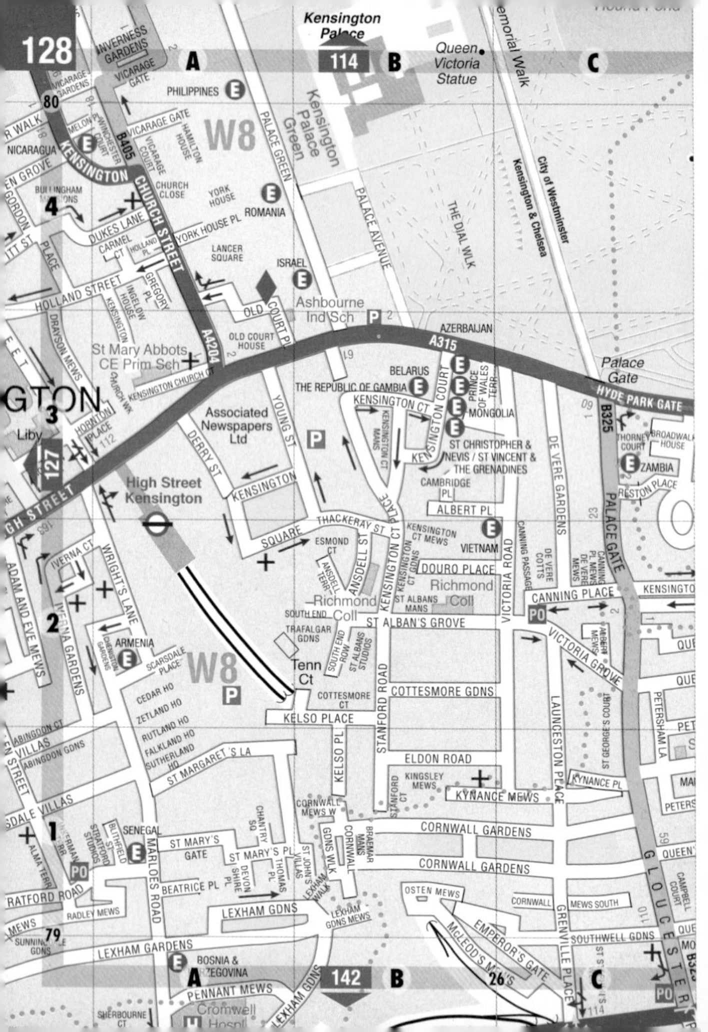

Kensington Palace
114
A
B
C
Queen Victoria Statue
Memorial Walk
INVERNESS GARDENS
VICARAGE GATE
VICARAGE GARDENS
PHILIPPINES
80
WINCHESTER COURT
MELON PL
VICARAGE GATE
HAMILTON HOUSE
W8
PALACE GREEN
Kensington Palace Green
NICARAGUA
KENSINGTON
B405
VICARAGE COURT
CHURCH CLOSE
BULLINGHAM MANSIONS
4
CHURCH STREET
YORK HOUSE
ROMANIA
PALACE AVENUE
THE DIAL WALK
Kensington & Chelsea
City of Westminster
DUKES LANE
CARMEL CT
HOLLAND PL
YORK HOUSE PL
LANCER SQUARE
ISRAEL
HOLLAND STREET
GREGORY PL
INGELOW HOUSE
KENSINGTON
OLD COURT PL
Ashbourne Ind Sch
DRAYSON MEWS
St Mary Abbots CE Prim Sch
A4204
OLD COURT HOUSE
AZERBAIJAN
A315
CHURCH WK
KENSINGTON CHURCH CT
BELARUS
PRINCE OF WALES TERR
Palace Gate
HYDE PARK GATE
GTON
3
Liby
127
HORNTON PLACE
112
Associated Newspapers Ltd
YOUNG ST
THE REPUBLIC OF GAMBIA
KENSINGTON CT
KENSINGTON COURT
MONGOLIA
KENSINGTON CT MANS
ST CHRISTOPHER & NEVIS / ST VINCENT & THE GRENADINES
DERRY ST
DE VERE GARDENS
B325
THORNEY COURT
BROADWALK HOUSE
ZAMBIA
RESTON PLACE
High Street Kensington
KENSINGTON
CAMBRIDGE PL
ALBERT PL
HIGH STREET
KENSINGTON CT PLACE
THACKERAY ST
SQUARE
ESMOND CT
KENSINGTON CT MEWS
VIETNAM
CANNING PASSAGE
DE VERE COTTS
CANNING PL MEWS
DE VERE MEWS
PALACE GATE
VICTORIA ROAD
IVERNA CT
WRIGHT'S LANE
ANSDELL ST
ANSDELL TERR
KENSINGTON CT GDNS
DOURO PLACE
Richmond Coll
ST ALBANS MANS
CANNING PLACE
KENSINGTON
ADAM AND EVE MEWS
2
IVERNA GARDENS
SOUTH END
TRAFALGAR GDNS
ST ALBAN'S GROVE
PO
VICTORIA GROVE
ALBERT MEWS
ARMENIA
CHENISTON GARDENS
SCARSDALE PLACE
SOUTH END ROW
ST ALBANS STUDIOS
Tenn Ct
STANFORD ROAD
W8
CEDAR HO
ZETLAND HO
RUTLAND HO
FALKLAND HO
SUTHERLAND HO
COTTESMORE CT
COTTESMORE GDNS
LAUNCESTON PLACE
ST GEORGE'S COURT
PETERSHAM LA
KELSO PLACE
ABINGDON CT
VILLAS
ABINGDON GDNS
ST MARGARET'S LA
KELSO PL
ELDON ROAD
KINGSLEY MEWS
STANFORD CT
KYNANCE MEWS
KYNANCE PL
SDALE VILLAS
CORNWALL MEWS W
CHANTRY SQ
1
SENEGAL
BLITHFIELD ST
STRATFORD STUDIOS
ALMA TERR
MARLOES ROAD
ST MARY'S GATE
ST MARY'S PL
DEVONSHIRE PL
THOMAS PL
ST JOHN'S VILLAS
GDNS WLK
CORNWALL
BRAEMAR MANS
CORNWALL GARDENS
CORNWALL GARDENS
GLOUCESTER
CAMPBELL COURT
PO
RATFORD ROAD
BEATRICE PL
LEXHAM WALK
OSTEN MEWS
CORNWALL MEWS SOUTH
RADLEY MEWS
LEXHAM GDNS
LEXHAM GDNS MEWS
EMPEROR'S GATE
GRENVILLE PLACE
MEWS
79
SUNNINGDALE GDNS
LEXHAM GARDENS
McLEOD'S MEWS
SOUTHWELL GDNS
BOSNIA & HERZEGOVINA
26
A
142
B
C
PENNANT MEWS
LEXHAM GDNS
SHERBOURNE CT
Cromwell Hospl
114

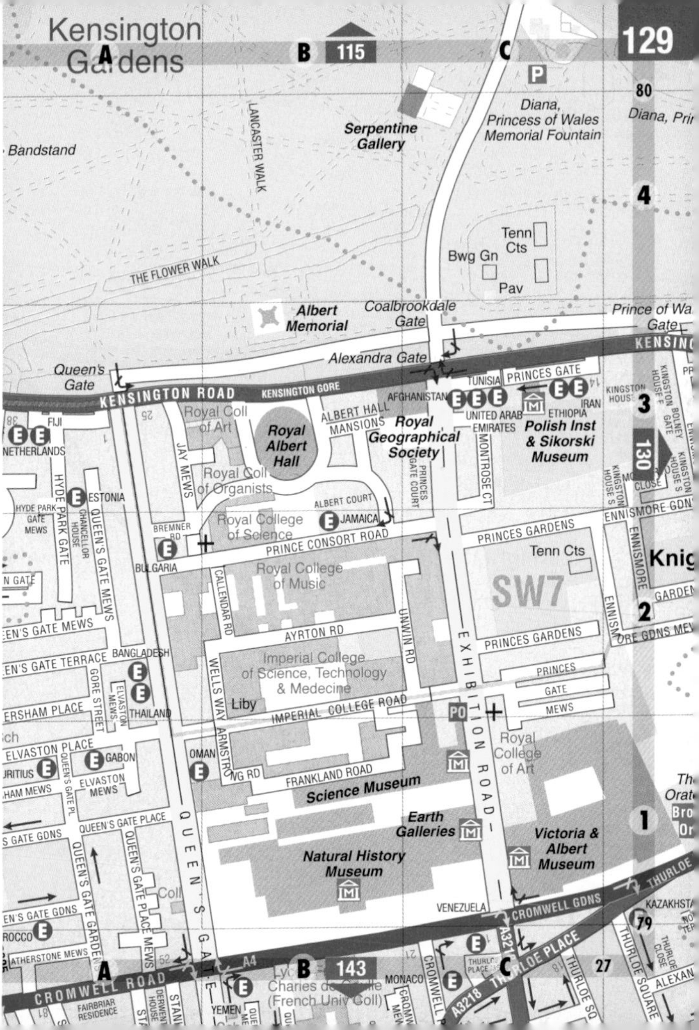
Kensington Gardens
A
B
115
C
P
80
Diana, Princess of Wales Memorial Fountain
Serpentine Gallery
Bandstand
LANCASTER WALK
4
Tenn Cts
Bwg Gn
Pav
THE FLOWER WALK
Albert Memorial
Coalbrookdale Gate
Prince of Wa
Gate
KENSING
Alexandra Gate
Queen's Gate
KENSINGTON ROAD
KENSINGTON GORE
TUNISIA
PRINCES GATE
AFGHANISTAN
IRAN
UNITED ARAB EMIRATES
ETHIOPIA
KINGSTON HOUSE
3
FIJI
NETHERLANDS
Royal Coll of Art
Royal Albert Hall
ALBERT HALL MANSIONS
Royal Geographical Society
Polish Inst & Sikorski Museum
130
JAY MEWS
Royal Coll of Organists
PRINCES GATE COURT
MONTROSE CT
HYDE PARK GATE
ESTONIA
HYDE PARK GATE MEWS
CHANCELLOR HOUSE
QUEEN'S GATE MEWS
ALBERT COURT
JAMAICA
BREMNER RD
Royal College of Science
PRINCE CONSORT ROAD
PRINCES GARDENS
ENNISMORE GDNS
Knig
Tenn Cts
BULGARIA
CALLENDAR RD
Royal College of Music
SW7
GARDEN
2
ENNISMORE GDNS MEWS
QUEEN'S GATE MEWS
AYRTON RD
UNWIN RD
EXHIBITION ROAD
PRINCES GARDENS
QUEEN'S GATE TERRACE
BANGLADESH
GORE STREET
ELVASTON MEWS
THAILAND
WELLS WAY
Imperial College of Science, Technology & Medecine
Liby
IMPERIAL COLLEGE ROAD
PRINCES GATE MEWS
PO
ELVASTON PLACE
GABON
OMAN
ARMSTRONG RD
Royal College of Art
MAURITIUS
QUEEN'S GATE PL
ELVASTON MEWS
FRANKLAND ROAD
Science Museum
Earth Galleries
Victoria & Albert Museum
1
QUEEN'S GATE PLACE
QUEEN'S GATE GDNS
QUEEN'S GATE GARDENS
QUEEN'S GATE PLACE MEWS
QUEEN'S GATE
Natural History Museum
THURLOE
CROMWELL GDNS
VENEZUELA
KAZAKHSTAN
79
MOROCCO
ATHERSTONE MEWS
A4
A3218
THURLOE PLACE
THURLOE SQ
THURLOE SQUARE
THURLOE CLOSE
27
A
B
143
C
CROMWELL ROAD
FAIRBRIAR RESIDENCE
YEMEN
Charles de Gaulle (French Univ Coll)
MONACO
CROMWELL PL
ALEXANDER

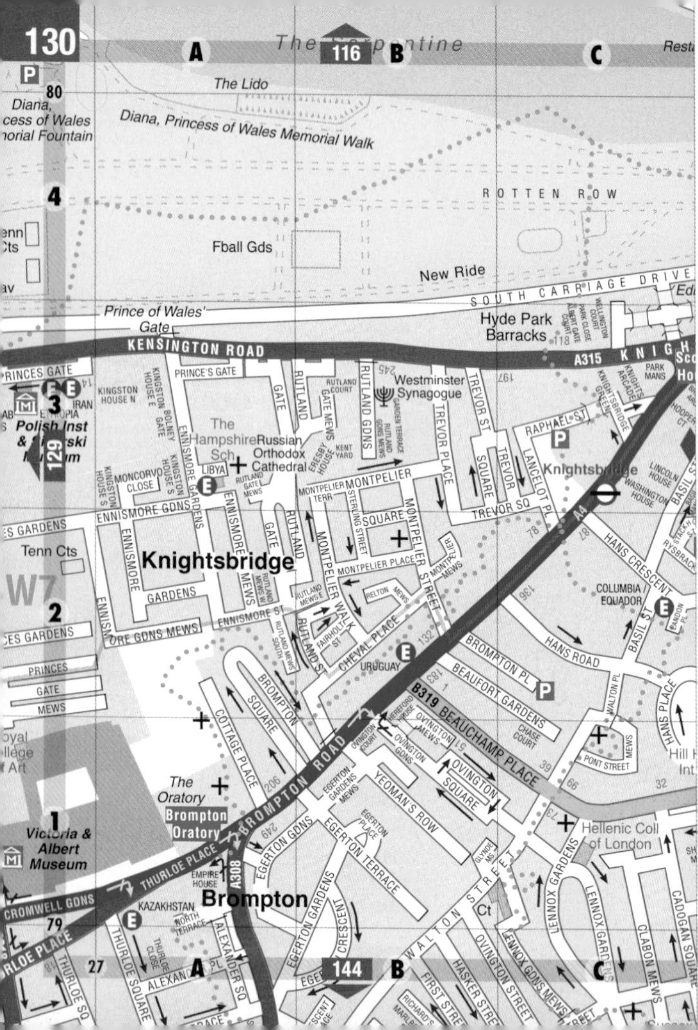
A
B
C
116
The Serpentine
The Lido
Diana, Princess of Wales Memorial Fountain
Diana, Princess of Wales Memorial Walk
4
ROTTEN ROW
Fball Gds
New Ride
SOUTH CARRIAGE DRIVE
Prince of Wales' Gate
Hyde Park Barracks
KENSINGTON ROAD
A315
KNIGHTSBRIDGE
PRINCES GATE
3
Polish Inst & Sikorski Museum
129
KINGSTON HOUSE N
PRINCE'S GATE
RUTLAND GATE
RUTLAND COURT
RUTLAND GDNS
Westminster Synagogue
TREVOR PLACE
TREVOR ST
TREVOR SQUARE
RAPHAEL ST
LANCELOT PL
KNIGHTSBRIDGE GREEN
KNIGHTS ARCADE
PARK MANS
The Hampshire Sch
Russian Orthodox Cathedral
LIBYA
IRAN
ETHIOPIA
MONCORVO CLOSE
ENNISMORE GARDENS
ENNISMORE GDNS
ENNISMORE MEWS
MONTPELIER SQUARE
MONTPELIER PLACE
MONTPELIER STREET
MONTPELIER WALK
MONTPELIER TERR
STERLING STREET
TREVOR SQ
Knightsbridge
LINCOLN HOUSE
WASHINGTON HOUSE
BASIL ST
HANS CRESCENT
Tenn Cts
Knightsbridge
W7
2
PRINCES GARDENS
PRINCES GATE MEWS
ENNISMORE ST
CHEVAL PLACE
FAIRHOLT ST
RELTON MEWS
URUGUAY
COLUMBIA / EQUADOR
HANS ROAD
BROMPTON PL
BEAUFORT GARDENS
A4
BROMPTON SQUARE
COTTAGE PLACE
BROMPTON ROAD
B319 BEAUCHAMP PLACE
OVINGTON SQUARE
OVINGTON GDNS
OVINGTON MEWS
CHASE COURT
WALTON PL
PONT STREET
HANS PLACE
Royal College of Art
1
The Oratory
Brompton Oratory
Victoria & Albert Museum
EGERTON GDNS
EGERTON GARDENS MEWS
EGERTON PLACE
EGERTON TERRACE
YEOMAN'S ROW
Hellenic Coll of London
LENNOX GARDENS
THURLOE PLACE
A308
EMPIRE HOUSE
Brompton
CROMWELL GDNS
KAZAKHSTAN
NORTH TERRACE
ALEXANDER SQ
EGERTON GARDENS
EGERTON CRESCENT
WALTON STREET
OVINGTON STREET
LENNOX GDNS MEWS
CLABON MEWS
CADOGAN SQUARE
THURLOE SQUARE
THURLOE CLOSE
144

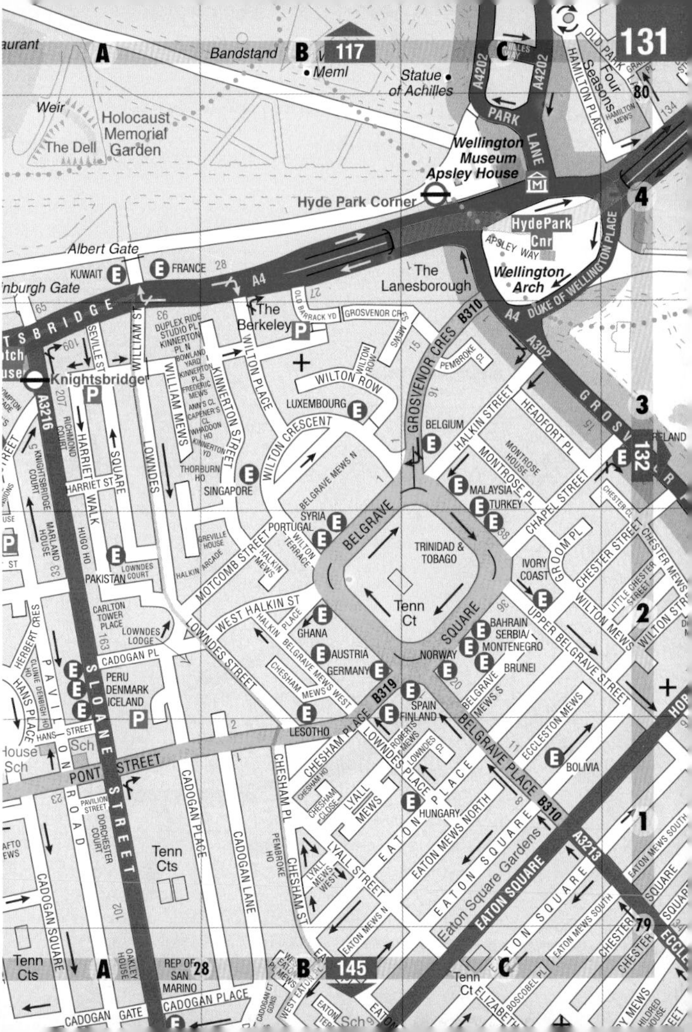
A
B
C
117
145
132
1
2
3
4
Bandstand
Meml
Statue of Achilles
Weir
Holocaust Memorial Garden
The Dell
Wellington Museum
Apsley House
Hyde Park Corner
Hyde Park Cnr
Apsley Way
Wellington Arch
Park Lane
A4202
Old Park Lane
Hamilton Place
Four Seasons
Hamilton Mews
Duke of Wellington Place
Albert Gate
Kuwait
France
Edinburgh Gate
A4
The Lanesborough
The Berkeley
Old Barrack Yd
Grosvenor Cres
Grosvenor Cres Mews
B310
A302
Grosvenor Place
Ireland
Knightsbridge
A3216
Seville St
William St
Duplex Ride
Studio Pl
Kinnerton Pl N
Bowland Yard
Kinnerton Pl S
Frederic Mews
Ann's Cl
Capener's Cl
Whaddon Ho
Kinnerton Yd
William Mews
Kinnerton Street
Wilton Place
Wilton Row
Pembroke Cl
Luxembourg
Wilton Crescent
Belgium
Halkin Street
Headfort Pl
Montrose House
Montrose Pl
Malaysia
Turkey
Chapel Street
Chester Cl
Chester Street
Chester Mews
Groom Pl
Little Chester Street
Wilton Mews
Wilton St
Richmond Court
Harriet Walk
Harriet St
Square
Lowndes
Knightsbridge Court
Marland House
Hugo Ho
Thorburn Ho
Singapore
Belgrave Mews N
Syria
Portugal
Wilton Terrace
Greville House
Halkin Arcade
Motcomb Street
Halkin Mews
Belgrave
Trinidad & Tobago
Tenn Ct
Ivory Coast
Pakistan
Lowndes Court
Carlton Tower Place
Lowndes Lodge
West Halkin St
Halkin Place
Ghana
Lowndes Street
Belgrave Mews West
Austria
Germany
Square
Bahrain
Serbia/Montenegro
Norway
Brunei
Upper Belgrave Street
Herbert Cres
Cadogan Pl
Peru
Denmark
Iceland
Chesham Mews
B319
Spain
Finland
Belgrave Mews S
Eccleston Mews
Bolivia
Hans Place
Clunie
Denbigh Ho
Hans Street
Sch
House Sch
Pavilion Road
Sloane Street
Pont Street
Lesotho
Chesham Place
Lowndes Place
Roberts Mews
Lowndes Cl
Belgrave Place
Hungary
Chesham Ho
Chesham Close
Lyall Mews
Eaton Place
Eaton Mews North
Eaton Square
Eaton Square Gardens
A3213
Eaton Mews South
Pavilion Street
Dorchester Court
Tenn Cts
Cadogan Place
Cadogan Lane
Chesham Pl
Pembroke Ho
Chesham St
Lyall Mews West
Lyall Street
Eaton Mews N
Cadogan Square
Oakley House
Rep of San Marino
Cadogan Gate
West Eaton Pl Mews
West Eaton Pl
Eaton Ter
Cadogan Ct Gdns
Boscobel Pl
Elizabeth
Chester Sq
Eccleston
Hildred House
Tenn Ct

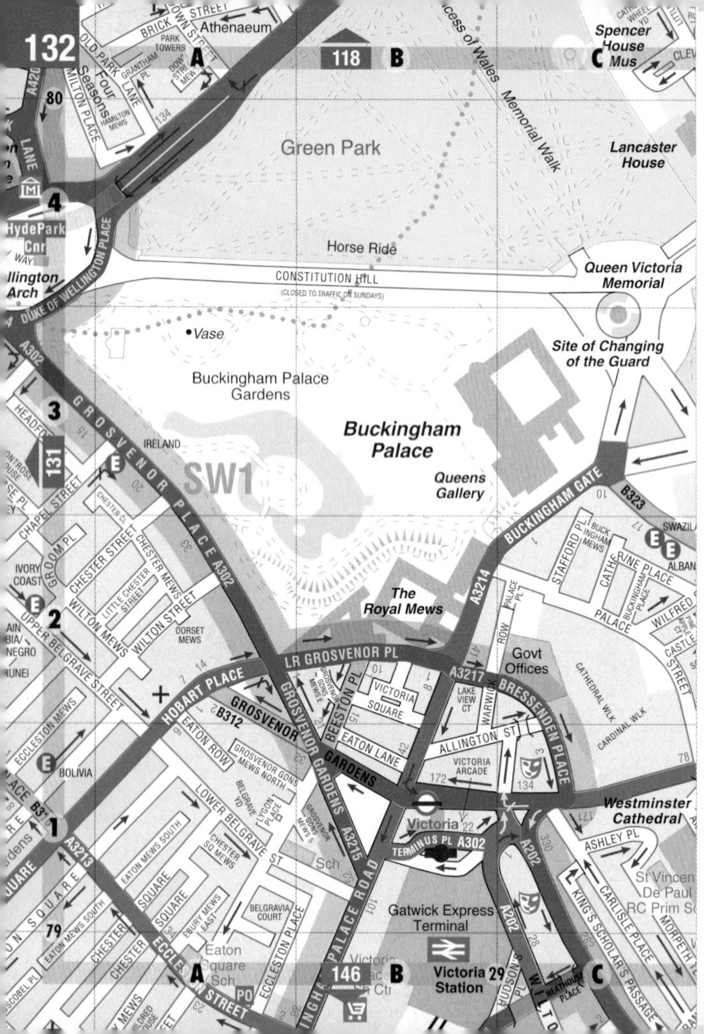
118
146
131
Athenaeum
Park Towers
Brick Street
Down Street
Old Park Lane
Grantham Pl
Four Seasons
Hamilton Place
Hamilton Mews
Down Street Mews
Spencer House Mus
Green Park
Princess of Wales Memorial Walk
Lancaster House
Horse Ride
Hyde Park Cnr
Wellington Arch
Duke of Wellington Place
Constitution Hill
(Closed to traffic on Sundays)
Queen Victoria Memorial
Site of Changing of the Guard
Vase
Buckingham Palace Gardens
Buckingham Palace
Queens Gallery
SW1
Ireland
Grosvenor Place A302
Headfort
Chapel Street
Groom Pl
Chester Cl
Chester Street
Chester Mews
Little Chester Street
Wilton Mews
Wilton Street
Dorset Mews
Ivory Coast
Upper Belgrave Street
Bolivia
Eccleston Mews
Buckingham Gate
B323
Stafford Pl
Buckingham Mews
Catherine Place
Buckingham Place
Palace Street
Wilfred St
Castle Street
Cathedral Wlk
Cardinal Wlk
The Royal Mews
A3214
Palace Pl
Govt Offices
Lr Grosvenor Pl
A3217
Bressenden Place
Warwick Row
Lake View Ct
Allington St
Victoria Arcade
Victoria Square
Beeston Pl
Eaton Lane
Grosvenor Gdns Mews E
Hobart Place
B312
Grosvenor Gardens
Eaton Row
Grosvenor Gdns Mews North
Belgrave Yd
Lygon Place
Grosvenor Gdns Mews S
Lower Belgrave St
Chester Sq Mews
Eaton Mews South
Eaton Square
Chester Square
Eaton Mews South
Ebury Mews East
Belgravia Court
Eccleston Place
Eccleston Street
A3213
A3215
Buckingham Palace Road
Victoria
Terminus Pl A302
Gatwick Express Terminal
Victoria Station
Victoria Place Shop Ctr
Eaton Square Sch
Sch
PO
A202
Hudson's Pl
Wilton Road
Neathouse Place
Westminster Cathedral
Ashley Pl
Carlisle Place
King's Scholar's Passage
Morpeth Ter
St Vincent De Paul RC Prim Sch
Swaziland
Albania
Escobel Pl
Wildred House

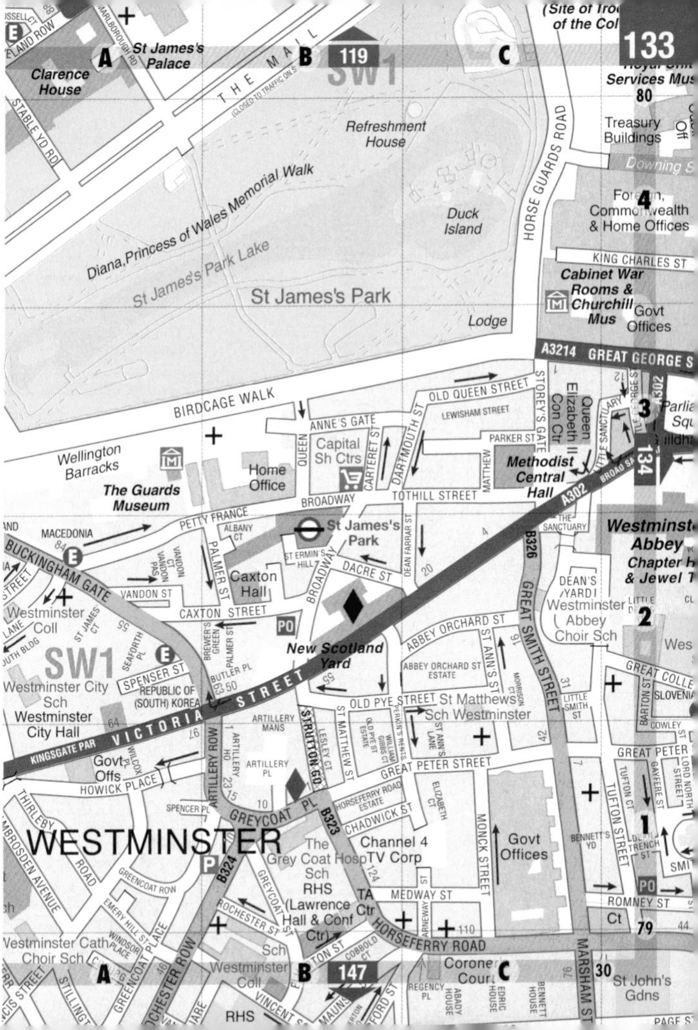
St James's Palace
Clarence House
THE MALL
(CLOSED TO TRAFFIC ON SUNDAYS)
119
SW1
A
B
C
STABLE YD RD
MARLBOROUGH RD
Refreshment House
Diana, Princess of Wales Memorial Walk
St James's Park Lake
St James's Park
Duck Island
Lodge
HORSE GUARDS ROAD
Treasury Buildings
Foreign, Commonwealth & Home Offices
KING CHARLES ST
Cabinet War Rooms & Churchill Mus
Govt Offices
A3214 GREAT GEORGE ST
BIRDCAGE WALK
Wellington Barracks
The Guards Museum
OLD QUEEN STREET
LEWISHAM STREET
ANNE'S GATE
QUEEN
Capital Sh Ctrs
Home Office
CARTERET ST
DARTMOUTH ST
PARKER ST
STOREY'S GATE
Queen Elizabeth II Con Ctr
MATTHEW
Methodist Central Hall
LITTLE SANCTUARY
134
BROADWAY
TOTHILL STREET
A302
BROAD SANCTUARY
PETTY FRANCE
MACEDONIA
ALBANY CT
St James's Park
THE SANCTUARY
Westminster Abbey
Chapter House & Jewel Tower
BUCKINGHAM GATE
VANDON CT
VANDON PAS
PALMER ST
ST ERMIN'S HILL
Caxton Hall
DACRE ST
DEAN FARRAR ST
B326
VANDON ST
CAXTON STREET
PO
DEAN'S YARD
Westminster Abbey Choir Sch
Westminster Coll
ST JAMES CT
SEAFORTH PL
BREWER'S GREEN
PALMER ST
New Scotland Yard
ABBEY ORCHARD ST
ST ANN'S ST
GREAT SMITH STREET
SW1
SPENSER ST
BUTLER PL
ABBEY ORCHARD ST ESTATE
GREAT COLLEGE ST
Westminster City Sch
REPUBLIC OF (SOUTH) KOREA
VICTORIA STREET
OLD PYE STREET
St Matthews Sch Westminster
MORRISON CT
LITTLE SMITH ST
BARTON ST
SLOVENIA
Westminster City Hall
ARTILLERY MANS
STRUTTON GD
LESLEY CT
ST MATTHEW ST
OLD PYE ST ESTATE
WILLIAM GIBBS CT
PERKIN'S RENTS
ST ANN'S LANE
COWLEY ST
KINGSGATE PAR
Govt Offs
WILCOX PL
ARTILLERY ROW
ARTILLERY HO
ARTILLERY PL
GREAT PETER STREET
GREAT PETER ST
TUFTON CT
GAYFERE ST
LORD NORTH STREET
HOWICK PLACE
HORSEFERRY ROAD ESTATE
ELIZABETH CT
TUFTON STREET
THIRLEBY ROAD
SPENCER PL
GREYCOAT PL
CHADWICK ST
MONCK STREET
Govt Offices
BENNETT'S YD
DEAN TRENCH ST
SMITH SQ
WESTMINSTER
AMBROSDEN AVENUE
B323
The Grey Coat Hosp Sch
Channel 4 TV Corp
P
B324
GREYCOAT ST
RHS (Lawrence Hall & Conf Ctr)
GREENCOAT ROW
EMERY HILL ST
MEDWAY ST
PO
ROMNEY ST
TA Ctr
ROCHESTER ST
HORSEFERRY ROAD
Ct
79
Westminster Cath Choir Sch
WINDSOR PLACE
GREENCOAT PLACE
ROCHESTER ROW
Sch
Westminster Coll
COBBOLD CT
MARSHAM ST
147
Coroner's Court
REGENCY PL
ABADY HOUSE
EDRIC HOUSE
BENNETT HOUSE
St John's Gdns
VINCENT SQ
RHS
PAGE ST
1
2
3
4

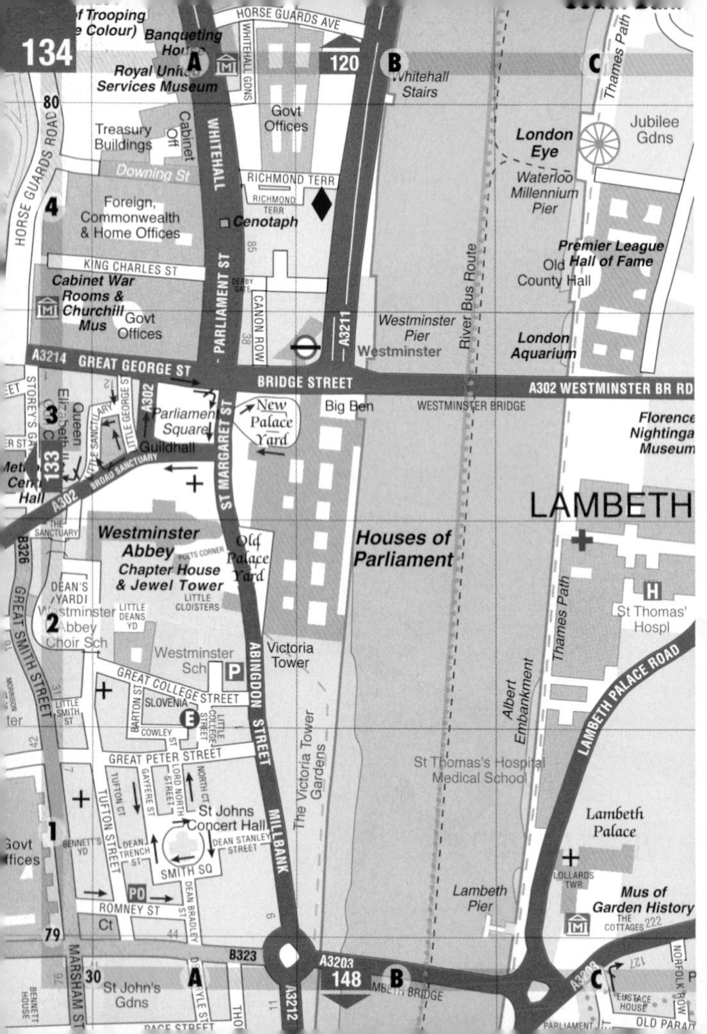

Banqueting House
Royal United Services Museum
HORSE GUARDS AVE
WHITEHALL GDNS
120
Whitehall Stairs
Thames Path
Treasury Buildings
Cabinet Off
WHITEHALL
Govt Offices
Jubilee Gdns
London Eye
HORSE GUARDS ROAD
Downing St
RICHMOND TERR
Waterloo Millennium Pier
Foreign, Commonwealth & Home Offices
Cenotaph
KING CHARLES ST
Premier League Hall of Fame
Old County Hall
Cabinet War Rooms & Churchill Mus
Govt Offices
PARLIAMENT ST
DERBY GATE
CANON ROW
A3211
Westminster Pier
Westminster
River Bus Route
London Aquarium
A3214 GREAT GEORGE ST
BRIDGE STREET
A302 WESTMINSTER BR RD
STOREY'S GATE
Queen Elizabeth II Centre
LITTLE SANCTUARY
LITTLE GEORGE ST
A302
Parliament Square
New Palace Yard
Big Ben
WESTMINSTER BRIDGE
Florence Nightingale Museum
Guildhall
ST MARGARET ST
133
BROAD SANCTUARY
A302
LAMBETH
THE SANCTUARY
B326
Westminster Abbey
POETS CORNER
Old Palace Yard
Houses of Parliament
Chapter House & Jewel Tower
LITTLE CLOISTERS
DEAN'S YARD
Westminster Abbey Choir Sch
LITTLE DEANS YD
Thames Path
St Thomas' Hospl
GREAT SMITH STREET
Westminster Sch
Victoria Tower
LAMBETH PALACE ROAD
GREAT COLLEGE STREET
SLOVENIA
BARTON ST
LITTLE COLLEGE STREET
LITTLE SMITH ST
COWLEY ST
ABINGDON STREET
Albert Embankment
GREAT PETER STREET
The Victoria Tower Gardens
St Thomas's Hospital Medical School
TUFTON CT
GAYFERE ST
LORD NORTH STREET
NORTH CT
St Johns Concert Hall
MILLBANK
Lambeth Palace
BENNETT'S YD
TUFTON STREET
DEAN TRENCH ST
DEAN STANLEY STREET
SMITH SQ
LOLLARDS TWR
Lambeth Pier
Mus of Garden History
DEAN BRADLEY ST
ROMNEY ST
THE COTTAGES
B323
A3203
148
LAMBETH BRIDGE
A3212
MARSHAM ST
St John's Gdns
BENNETT HOUSE
EUSTACE HOUSE
NORFOLK ROW
OLD PARADE

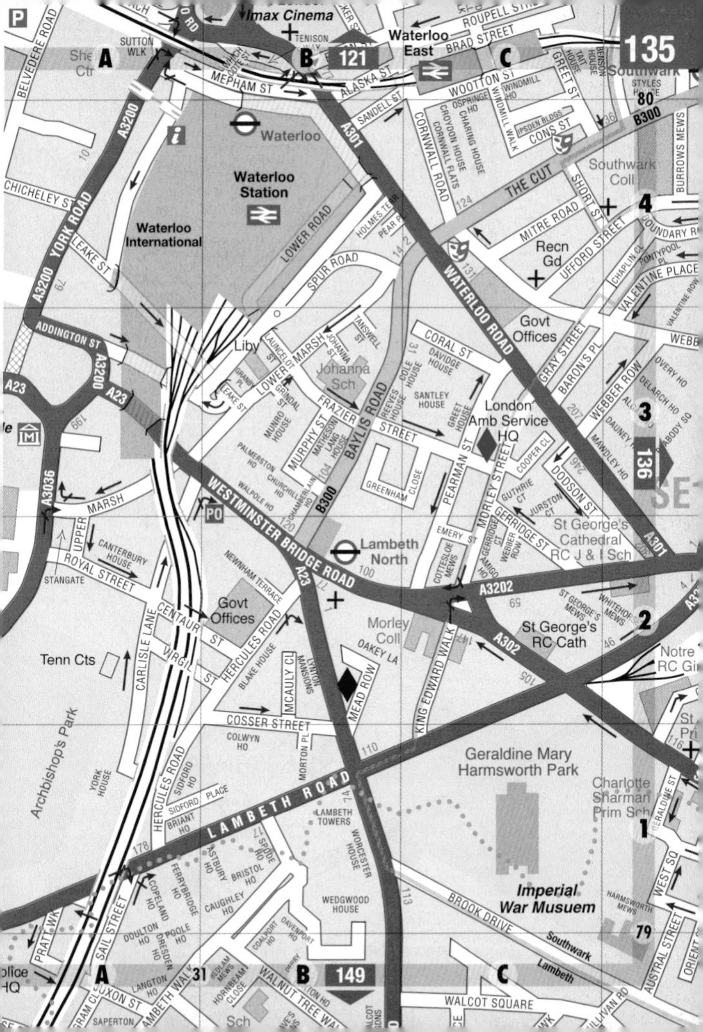

135
121
136
149
Waterloo Station
Waterloo International
Waterloo
Waterloo East
Imax Cinema
Lambeth North
Geraldine Mary Harmsworth Park
Imperial War Musuem
St George's RC Cath
St George's Cathedral RC J & I Sch
London Amb Service HQ
Govt Offices
Morley Coll
Johanna Sch
Southwark Coll
Recn Gd
Archbishop's Park
Charlotte Sharman Prim Sch
Tenn Cts
WESTMINSTER BRIDGE ROAD
LAMBETH ROAD
WATERLOO ROAD
BAYLIS ROAD
YORK ROAD
THE CUT
LOWER MARSH
HERCULES ROAD
KING EDWARD WALK
BROOK DRIVE
WALCOT SQUARE
ROYAL STREET
CARLISLE LANE
COSSER STREET
MEPHAM ST
ALASKA ST
ROUPELL STREET
BRAD STREET
CORNWALL ROAD
FRAZIER STREET
PEARMAN ST
MORLEY STREET
WEBBER ROW
VALENTINE PLACE
GERRIDGE ST
DODSON ST
SPUR ROAD
LOWER ROAD
ADDINGTON ST
LEAKE ST
CHICHELEY ST
BELVEDERE ROAD
MEAD ROW
OAKEY LA
Southwark
Lambeth

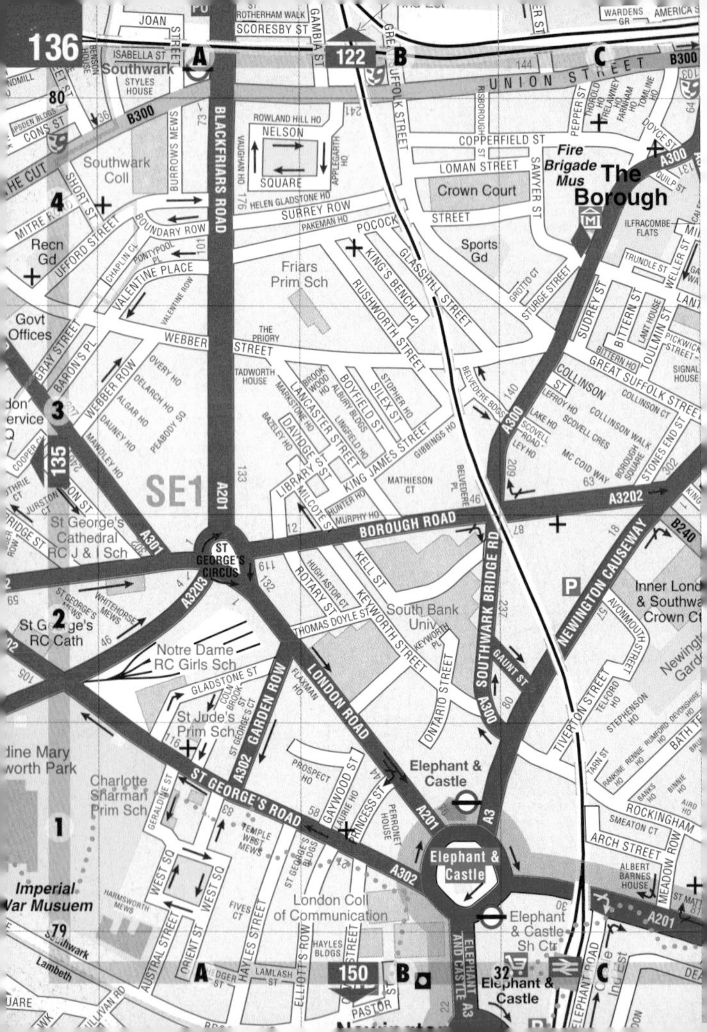
ROTHERHAM WALK
JOAN
SCORESBY ST
GAMBIA ST
ISABELLA ST
BENSON HOUSE
Southwark
STYLES HOUSE
A
122
B
C
UNION STREET
B300
144
80
CONS ST
B300
THE CUT
Southwark Coll
BURROWS MEWS
BLACKFRIARS ROAD
ROWLAND HILL HO
NELSON SQUARE
VAUGHAN HO
APPLEGARTH HO
SUFFOLK STREET
RISBOROUGH ST
COPPERFIELD ST
PEPPER ST
THOROLD HO
TRELAWNEY HO
FARNHAM HO
TOMLINE HO
DOYCE ST
LOMAN STREET
Crown Court
SAWYER ST
Fire Brigade Mus
The Borough
A300
QUILP ST
4
SHORT ST
MITRE RD
BOUNDARY ROW
HELEN GLADSTONE HO
SURREY ROW
PAKEMAN HO
POCOCK STREET
Sports Gd
ILFRACOMBE FLATS
Recn Gd
UFFORD STREET
CHAPLIN CL
PONTYPOOL PL
VALENTINE PLACE
VALENTINE ROW
Friars Prim Sch
KING'S BENCH ST
GLASSHILL STREET
RUSHWORTH STREET
GROTTO CT
STURGE STREET
SUDREY ST
TRUNDLE ST
WELLER ST
BITTERN ST
LANT HOUSE
TOULMIN ST
Govt Offices
GRAY STREET
BARON'S PL
WEBBER STREET
THE PRIORY
PICKWICK STREET
BITTERN HO
GREAT SUFFOLK STREET
SIGNAL HOUSE
WEBBER ROW
OVERY HO
DELARCH HO
ALGAR HO
DAUNEY HO
PEABODY SQ
TADWORTH HOUSE
BROOKWOOD HO
MARKSTONE HO
LANCASTER STREET
ALBURY BLDGS
BOYFIELD ST
SILEX ST
STOPHER HO
BELVEDERE BDGS
140
COLLINSON ST
LEFROY HO
LAKE HO
SCOVELL ROAD
SCOVELL CRES
COLLINSON WALK
COLLINSON CT
3
BAZELEY HO
DAVIDGE ST
LINGFIELD HO
KING JAMES STREET
GIBBINGS HO
LEY HO
MC COID WAY
BOROUGH SQUARE
STONES END ST
135
MANDLEY HO
COOPER CL
SE1
A201
133
LIBRARY ST
MILCOTE ST
HUNTER HO
MATHIESON CT
BELVEDERE PL
46
209
63
302
A3202
JURSTON CT
St George's Cathedral RC J & I Sch
A301
MURPHY HO
12
BOROUGH ROAD
87
B240
ST GEORGE'S CIRCUS
119
132
HUGH ASTOR CT
ROTARY ST
KELL ST
SOUTHWARK BRIDGE RD
NEWINGTON CAUSEWAY
P
Inner Lond & Southwa Crown Ct
2
St George's RC Cath
ST GEORGE'S MEWS
WHITEHORSE MEWS
A3203
46
THOMAS DOYLE ST
KEYWORTH STREET
South Bank Univ
KEYWORTH PL
237
GAUNT ST
AVONMOUTH STREET
57
Newingt Gard
Notre Dame RC Girls Sch
GLADSTONE ST
COLNBROOK ST
ST GEORGE'S CT
GARDEN ROW
FLAXMAN HO
LONDON ROAD
ONTARIO STREET
A300
80
TIVERTON STREET
TELFORD HO
STEPHENSON HO
DEVONSHIRE HO
BATH TE
St Jude's Prim Sch
116
A302
PROSPECT HO
GAYWOOD ST
44
Elephant & Castle
RUMFORD HO
TARN ST
RANKINE HO
RENNIE HO
BANKS HO
BINNIE HO
AIRD HO
Charlotte Sharman Prim Sch
GERALDINE ST
ST GEORGE'S ROAD
83
58
LAURIE HO
PRINCESS ST
PERRONET HOUSE
A201
A3
ROCKINGHAM
SMEATON CT
ARCH STREET
MEADOW ROW
ALBERT BARNES HOUSE
1
TEMPLE WEST MEWS
ST GEORGE'S BLDGS
A302
Elephant & Castle
Imperial War Museum
HARMSWORTH MEWS
WEST SQ
WEST SQ
FIVES CT
HAYLES STREET
London Coll of Communication
30
Elephant & Castle Sh Ctr
A201
79
Southwark
Lambeth
AUSTRAL STREET
ORIENT ST
A
HEDGER ST
LAMLASH ST
ELLIOTT'S ROW
HAYLES BLDGS
150
B
ELEPHANT AND CASTLE
A3
32
Elephant & Castle
ELEPHANT ROAD
C
Ind Est
PASTOR ST
SULLIVAN RD
22

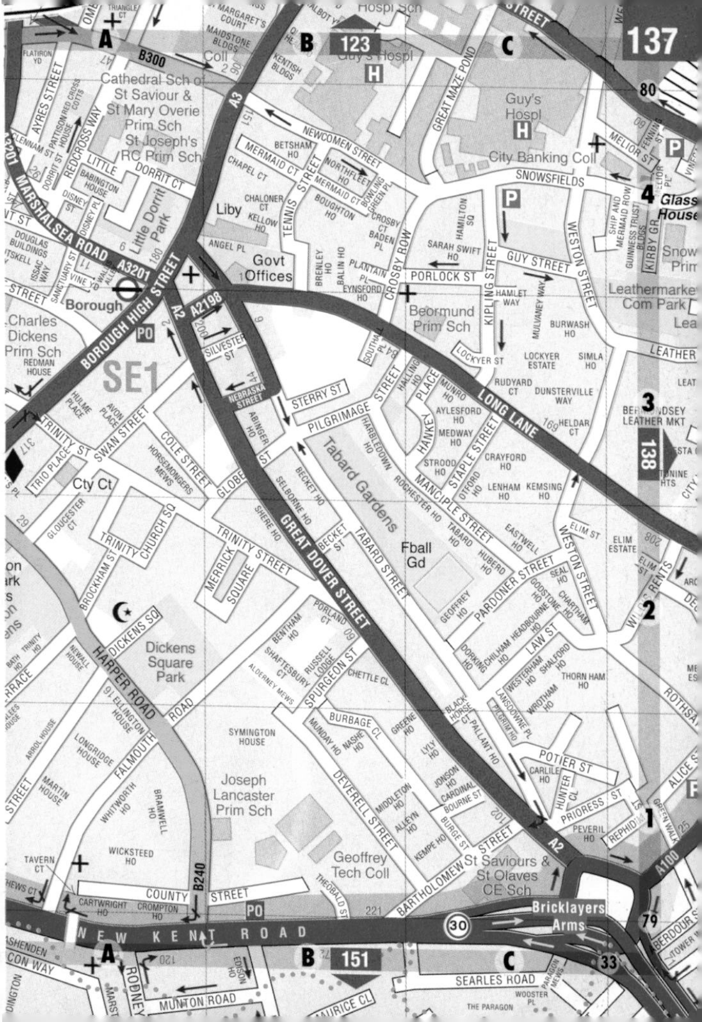
A
B
C
123
B300
A3
Cathedral Sch of St Saviour & St Mary Overie Prim Sch
St Joseph's RC Prim Sch
Guy's Hospl
Guy's Hospl
City Banking Coll
FLATIRON YD
AYRES STREET
PATTISON HOUSE
RED CROSS COTTS
REDCROSS WAY
LITTLE DORRIT CT
BABINGTON HOUSE
DISNEY ST
DISNEY PL
Little Dorrit Park
MARSHALSEA ROAD
A3201
DOUGLAS BUILDINGS
ISSAC WAY
SANCTUARY ST
VINE YD
Borough
BOROUGH HIGH STREET
A2
A2198
Charles Dickens Prim Sch
REDMAN HOUSE
SE1
PO
HULME PLACE
AVON PLACE
SWAN STREET
TRINITY ST
TRIO PLACE
Cty Ct
GLOUCESTER CT
TRINITY CHURCH SQ
BROCKHAM ST
HORSEMONGERS MEWS
COLE STREET
GLOBE ST
MERRICK SQUARE
TRINITY STREET
HARPER ROAD
DICKENS SQ
Dickens Square Park
NEWALL HOUSE
ELLINGTON HOUSE
LONGRIDGE HOUSE
FALMOUTH ROAD
ARROL HOUSE
MARTIN HOUSE
WHITWORTH HO
BRAMWELL HO
WICKSTEED HO
TAVERN CT
COUNTY STREET
B240
CARTWRIGHT HO
CROMPTON HO
NEW KENT ROAD
PO
221
30
Bricklayers Arms
33
79
A100
151
SEARLES ROAD
PARAGON MEWS
WOOSTER PL
THE PARAGON
MUNTON ROAD
RODNEY
EDSON HO
NEWCOMEN STREET
BETSHAM HO
MERMAID CT
CHAPEL CT
NORTHFLEET HO
MERMAID CT
BOWLING GREEN PL
TENNIS STREET
CHALONER CT
KELLOW HO
BOUGHTON HO
CROSBY CT
BADEN PL
Liby
ANGEL PL
Govt Offices
BRENLEY HO
BALIN HO
PLANTAIN PL
EYNSFORD HO
CROSBY ROW
SILVESTER ST
NEBRASKA STREET
STERRY ST
PILGRIMAGE STREET
ABINGER HO
SOUTHALL PL
HALLING HO
HANKEY PLACE
MUNRO HO
AYLESFORD HO
MEDWAY HO
STROOD HO
HARBLEDOWN HO
Tabard Gardens
BECKET HO
SELBORNE HO
SHERE HO
BECKET ST
TABARD STREET
ROCHESTER HO
MANCIPLE STREET
TABARD HO
Fball Gd
GREAT DOVER STREET
PORLAND CT
BENTHAM HO
SHAFTESBURY CT
RUSSELL LODGE
SPURGEON ST
ALDERNEY MEWS
CHETTLE CL
BURBAGE CL
MUNDAY HO
NASHE HO
GREENE HO
SYMINGTON HOUSE
Joseph Lancaster Prim Sch
DEVERELL STREET
LYLY HO
JONSON HO
MIDDLETON HO
ALLEYN HO
CARDINAL BOURNE ST
BURGE ST
KEMPE HO
Geoffrey Tech Coll
THEOBALD ST
BARTHOLOMEW STREET
St Saviours & St Olaves CE Sch
GREAT MAZE POND
SNOWSFIELDS
HAMILTON SQ
SARAH SWIFT HO
PORLOCK ST
KIPLING STREET
GUY STREET
HAMLET WAY
MULVANEY WAY
Beormund Prim Sch
LOCKYER ST
LOCKYER ESTATE
BURWASH HO
SIMLA HO
RUDYARD CT
DUNSTERVILLE WAY
LONG LANE
HELDAR CT
STAPLE STREET
CRAYFORD HO
OTFORD HO
LENHAM HO
KEMSING HO
EASTWELL HO
HUBERD HO
GEOFFREY HO
PARDONER STREET
SEAL HO
GODSTONE HO
CHARTHAM HO
WESTON STREET
DORKING HO
CHILHAM HO
HEADBOURNE HO
LAW ST
WESTERHAM HO
SHALFORD HO
THORN HAM HO
LANSDOWNE PL
PILGRIM HO
WROTHAM HO
BLACK HORSE CT
PALLANT HO
POTIER ST
CARLILE HO
HUNTER CL
PRIORESS ST
PEVERIL HO
REPHIDIM ST
102
MELIOR ST
FENNING ST
MELIOR PL
SHIP AND MERMAID ROW
GUINNESS TRUST BLDGS
KIRBY GR
Glass House
Snow Prim
Leathermarket Com Park
LEATHER
BERMONDSEY LEATHER MKT
138
ELIM ST
ELIM ESTATE
WILLOW RENTS
ROTHSAY
ALICE ST
GREEN WALK
1
2
3
4
80

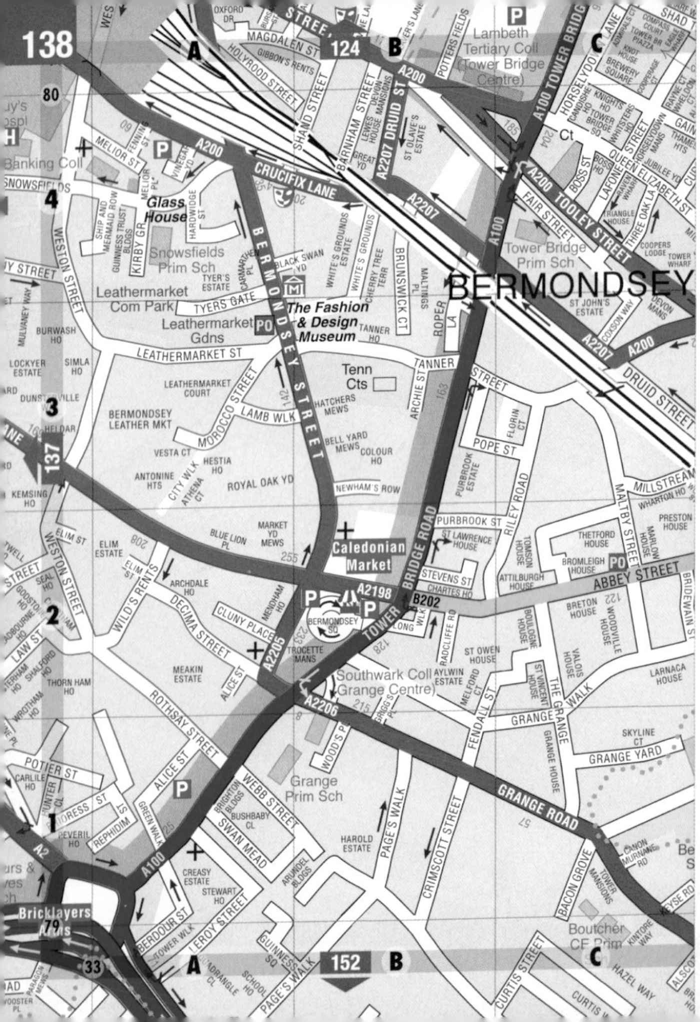
BERMONDSEY
A
B
C
124
152
137
79
33
80
4
3
2
1
Lambeth Tertiary Coll (Tower Bridge Centre)
Banking Coll
Glass House
Snowsfields Prim Sch
Leathermarket Com Park
Leathermarket Gdns
The Fashion & Design Museum
Tower Bridge Prim Sch
Caledonian Market
Bermondsey Sq
Southwark Coll Grange Centre
Grange Prim Sch
Boutcher CE Prim
Bricklayers Arms
Tenn Cts
A200
A2207
A100
A2198
A2205
A2206
B202
A2
MAGDALEN ST
HOLYROOD STREET
GIBBON'S RENTS
SHAND STREET
BARNHAM STREET
DRUID ST
POTTERS FIELDS
TOWER BRIDGE
HORSELYDOWN LANE
TOOLEY STREET
FAIR STREET
QUEEN ELIZABETH ST
CRUCIFIX LANE
SNOWSFIELDS
WESTON STREET
MELIOR ST
VINEGAR YD
KIRBY GR
HARDWIDGE ST
BERMONDSEY STREET
BLACK SWAN YD
TYERS GATE
WHITE'S GROUNDS
CHERRY TREE TERR
BRUNSWICK CT
MALTINGS PL
ROPER LA
TANNER ST
LEATHERMARKET ST
LEATHERMARKET COURT
BERMONDSEY LEATHER MKT
MOROCCO STREET
LAMB WLK
HATCHERS MEWS
ARCHIE ST
BELL YARD MEWS
COLOUR HO
POPE ST
FLORIN CT
PURBROOK ESTATE
MILLSTREAM
MALTBY STREET
RILEY ROAD
ROYAL OAK YD
NEWHAM'S ROW
HESTIA HO
VESTA CT
ANTONINE HTS
CITY WLK
PURBROOK ST
ST LAWRENCE HOUSE
TOWER BRIDGE ROAD
STEVENS ST
ABBEY STREET
THETFORD HOUSE
BROMLEIGH HOUSE
ATTILBURGH HOUSE
PRESTON HOUSE
MARLOW HOUSE
BRIDEWAIN ST
BRETON HOUSE
WOODVILLE HOUSE
BOULOGNE HOUSE
VALOIS HOUSE
LARNACA HOUSE
ELIM ESTATE
ELIM ST
WILD'S RENTS
ARCHDALE HO
DECIMA STREET
CLUNY PLACE
MENDHAM HO
MARKET YD MEWS
BLUE LION PL
TROCETTE MANS
LONG WLK
RADCLIFFE RD
ST OWEN HOUSE
AYLWIN ESTATE
MELFORD CT
FENDALL ST
GRANGE WALK
THE GRANGE
GRANGE HOUSE
GRANGE YARD
SKYLINE CT
GRANGE ROAD
MEAKIN ESTATE
ALICE ST
ROTHSAY STREET
WOOD'S PL
GREGG'S PL
THORN HAM HO
POTIER ST
CARLILE HO
HUNTER CL
PRIORESS ST
REPHIDIM ST
GREEN WALK
WEBB STREET
BRIGHTON BLDGS
BUSHBABY CL
SWAN MEAD
ARUNDEL BLDGS
HAROLD ESTATE
PAGE'S WALK
CRIMSCOTT STREET
BACON GROVE
TOWER MANSIONS
CANON MURNANE RD
KEYSE RD
KINTORE WAY
CREASY ESTATE
STEWART HO
LEROY STREET
ABERDOUR ST
TOWER WLK
QUADRANGLE CL
SCHOOL HO
GUINNESS SQ
CURTIS STREET
HAZEL WAY
BURWASH HO
LOCKYER ESTATE
SIMLA HO
DUNSTERVILLE
HELDAR
KEMSING HO
MULVANEY WAY
SEAL HO
LAW ST
WROTHAM HO
PEVERIL HO

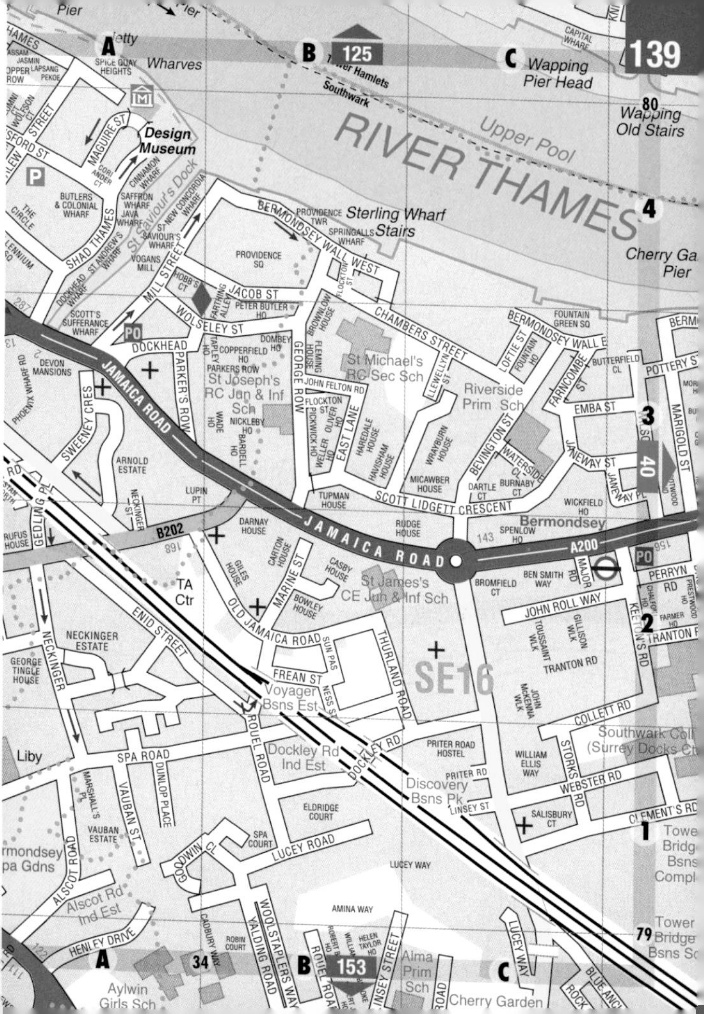
125
Tower Hamlets
Southwark
RIVER THAMES
Upper Pool
Wapping Pier Head
Wapping Old Stairs
80
Cherry Garden Pier
Spice Quay Heights
Wharves
Design Museum
Maguire St
Shad Thames
St Saviour's Dock
New Concordia Wharf
Butlers & Colonial Wharf
Saffron Wharf
Java Wharf
Cinnamon Wharf
Vogans Mill
Mill Street
Bermondsey Wall West
Providence Twr
Sterling Wharf Stairs
Springalls Wharf
Providence Sq
Jacob St
Peter Butler Ho
Farthing Alley
Wolseley St
Scott's Sufferance Wharf
Dockhead
Chambers Street
Fountain Green Sq
Bermondsey Wall E
Loftie St
Farncombe St
Butterfield Cl
Pottery St
Marigold St
Emba St
Janeway St
Janeway Pl
St Michael's RC Sec Sch
Riverside Prim Sch
Bevington St
Waterside Cl
Dartle Ct
Burnaby Ct
Wrayburn House
Micawber House
Scott Lidgett Crescent
Wickfield Ho
Spenlow Ho
Bermondsey
A200
Jamaica Road
Parker's Row
George Row
John Felton Rd
Flockton St
East Lane
Haredale House
Havisham House
Tupman House
Copperfield Ho
Parkers Row
St Joseph's RC Jun & Inf Sch
Nickleby Ho
Dombey Ho
Devon Mansions
Phoenix Wharf Rd
Sweeney Cres
Arnold Estate
Lupin Pt
Neckinger St
B202
Darnay House
Rudge House
Carton House
Giles House
Casby House
Marine St
St James's CE Jun & Inf Sch
Bowley House
Old Jamaica Road
Thurland Road
Sun Pas
Frean St
Ness St
Voyager Bsns Est
TA Ctr
Enid Street
Neckinger Estate
Neckinger
Gedling Pl
Rufus House
George Tingle House
SE16
Bromfield Ct
Ben Smith Way
Major Rd
John Roll Way
Perryn Rd
Keeton's Rd
Toussaint Wlk
Gillison Wlk
Tranton Rd
John McKenna Wlk
Collett Rd
Southwark Coll (Surrey Docks Ctr)
Storks Rd
Webster Rd
William Ellis Way
Priter Road Hostel
Priter Rd
Discovery Bsns Pk
Linsey St
Salisbury Ct
Clement's Rd
Tower Bridge Bsns Complex
Dockley Rd
Dockley Rd Ind Est
Rouel Road
Spa Road
Dunlop Place
Vauban St
Marshall's Pl
Vauban Estate
Liby
Alscot Road
Alscot Rd Ind Est
Bermondsey Spa Gdns
Eldridge Court
Spa Court
Lucey Road
Goodwin Cl
Lucey Way
Amina Way
Henley Drive
Aylwin Girls Sch
34
Cadbury Way
Robin Court
Woolstaplers Way
Yalding Road
153
Alma Prim Sch
Linsey Street
Cherry Garden
Tower Bridge Bsns Sq
79
Blue Anchor
40
143
156
PO

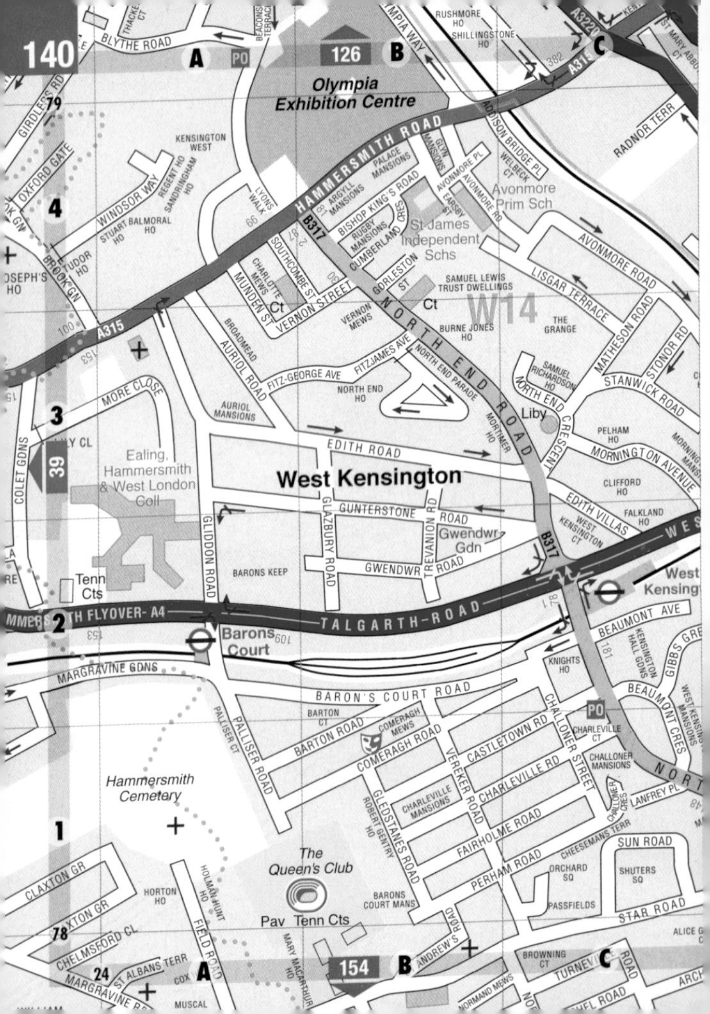
126
154
A
B
C
1
2
3
4
39
Olympia Exhibition Centre
West Kensington
W14
BLYTHE ROAD
HAMMERSMITH ROAD
A315
B317
NORTH END ROAD
TALGARTH ROAD
HAMMERSMITH FLYOVER- A4
EDITH ROAD
GUNTERSTONE ROAD
GWENDWR ROAD
Gwendwr Gdn
GLAZBURY ROAD
TREVANION RD
GLIDDON ROAD
BARONS KEEP
AURIOL ROAD
AURIOL MANSIONS
BROADMEAD
FITZ-GEORGE AVE
FITZJAMES AVE
NORTH END HO
NORTH END PARADE
VERNON STREET
VERNON MEWS
MUNDEN ST
CHARLOTTE MEWS
SOUTHCOMBE ST
GORLESTON ST
CUMBERLAND CRES
BISHOP KING'S ROAD
RUGBY MANSIONS
ARGYLL MANSIONS
PALACE MANSIONS
GLYN MANSIONS
AVONMORE PL
AVONMORE RD
EARSBY ST
St James Independent Schs
Avonmore Prim Sch
ADDISON BRIDGE PL
WELBECK CT
AVONMORE ROAD
LISGAR TERRACE
SAMUEL LEWIS TRUST DWELLINGS
BURNE JONES HO
THE GRANGE
MATHESON ROAD
STONOR RD
STANWICK ROAD
SAMUEL RICHARDSON HO
NORTH END CRESCENT
Liby
MORTIMER HO
PELHAM HO
MORNINGTON AVENUE
CLIFFORD HO
FALKLAND HO
EDITH VILLAS
WEST KENSINGTON CT
West Kensington
BEAUMONT AVE
KENSINGTON HALL GDNS
GIBBS GRN
BEAUMONT CRES
WEST KENSINGTON MANSIONS
KNIGHTS HO
RADNOR TERR
RUSHMORE HO
SHILLINGSTONE HO
OLYMPIA WAY
A3220
ST MARY ABBOTS CT
KENSINGTON WEST
WINDSOR WAY
REGENT HO
SANDRINGHAM HO
BALMORAL HO
STUART HO
TUDOR HO
BROOK GN
LYONS WALK
OXFORD GATE
GIRDLERS RD
THACKERAY CT
BEACONS TERRACE
MORE CLOSE
LILY CL
COLET GDNS
Ealing, Hammersmith & West London Coll
Tenn Cts
Barons Court
MARGRAVINE GDNS
BARON'S COURT ROAD
BARTON CT
BARTON ROAD
COMERAGH MEWS
COMERAGH ROAD
PALLISER CT
PALLISER ROAD
CASTLETOWN RD
CHALLONER STREET
CHARLEVILLE CT
CHALLONER MANSIONS
CHALLONER CRES
LANFREY PL
CHARLEVILLE RD
CHARLEVILLE MANSIONS
VEREKER ROAD
GLEDSTANES ROAD
ROBERT GENTRY HO
FAIRHOLME ROAD
PERHAM ROAD
CHEESEMANS TERR
SUN ROAD
ORCHARD SQ
SHUTERS SQ
PASSFIELDS
STAR ROAD
ALICE GILLIATT CT
BARONS COURT MANS
Hammersmith Cemetery
The Queen's Club
Pav
Tenn Cts
ST ANDREW'S ROAD
BROWNING CT
TURNEVILLE ROAD
NORMAND MEWS
CLAXTON GR
HORTON HO
HOLMAN HUNT HO
FIELD ROAD
CHELMSFORD CL
ST ALBANS TERR
MARGRAVINE RD
COX HO
MUSCAL
MARY MACARTHUR HO
PO

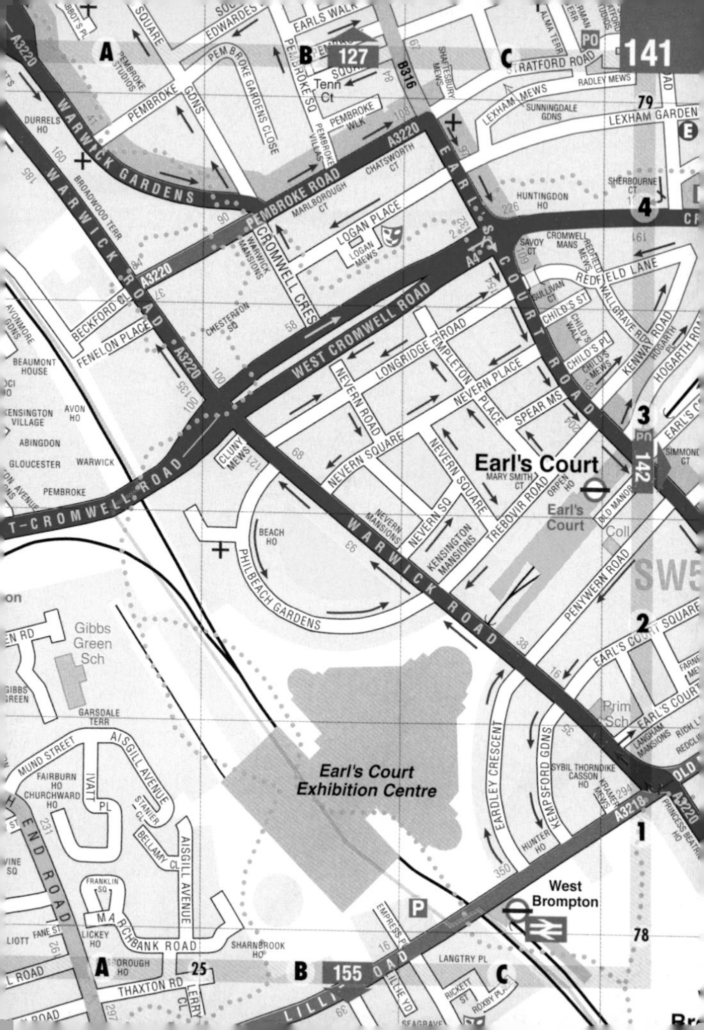

127
141
142
155
A
B
C
1
2
3
4
78
79
25
SW5
A3220
A3218
A4
B316
WARWICK GARDENS
WARWICK ROAD
PEMBROKE ROAD
PEMBROKE GDNS
PEMBROKE SQ
PEMBROKE GARDENS CLOSE
PEMBROKE STUDIOS
PEMBROKE VILLAS
PEMBROKE WLK
EDWARDES SQ
EARLS WALK
SQUARE
Tenn Ct
STRATFORD ROAD
RADLEY MEWS
LEXHAM MEWS
LEXHAM GARDENS
SUNNINGDALE GDNS
ALMA TERR
SHAFTESBURY MEWS
PO
DURRELS HO
BROADWOOD TERR
MARLBOROUGH CT
CHATSWORTH CT
LOGAN PLACE
LOGAN MEWS
WARWICK MANSIONS
CROMWELL CRES
HUNTINGDON HO
SHERBOURNE CT
EARL'S COURT ROAD
CROMWELL MANS
SAVOY CT
REDFIELD MEWS
REDFIELD LANE
WALLGRAVE RD
KENWAY ROAD
HOGARTH RD
HOGARTH PL
SULLIVAN CT
CHILD'S ST
CHILD'S WALK
CHILD'S PL
CHILD'S MEWS
BECKFORD CL
FENELON PLACE
CHESTERTON SQ
WEST CROMWELL ROAD
LONGRIDGE ROAD
TEMPLETON PLACE
NEVERN PLACE
NEVERN ROAD
NEVERN SQUARE
NEVERN SQ
NEVERN MANSIONS
SPEAR MS
AVONMORE GDNS
BEAUMONT HOUSE
KENSINGTON VILLAGE
AVON HO
ABINGDON
GLOUCESTER
WARWICK
PEMBROKE
CLUNY MEWS
Earl's Court
MARY SMITH CT
TREBOVIR ROAD
ORPEN HO
OLD MANOR
Coll
SIMMONDS CT
EARL'S CT
BEACH HO
PHILBEACH GARDENS
KENSINGTON MANSIONS
PENYWERN ROAD
EARL'S COURT SQUARE
Gibbs Green Sch
GIBBS GREEN
GARSDALE TERR
Earl's Court Exhibition Centre
EARDLEY CRESCENT
KEMPSFORD GDNS
Prim Sch
LANGHAM MANSIONS
SYBIL THORNDIKE CASSON HO
KRAMER MEWS
HUNTER HO
PRINCESS BEATRICE HO
West Brompton
MUND STREET
AISGILL AVENUE
FAIRBURN HO
CHURCHWARD HO
IVATT PL
STANIER CL
BELLAMY CL
FRANKLIN SQ
MARCHBANK ROAD
LICKEY HO
FANE ST
SHARNBROOK HO
THAXTON RD
LERRY CL
EMPRESS PL
LILLIE YD
LILLIE ROAD
LANGTRY PL
RICKETT ST
ROXBY PLACE
SEAGRAVE
P

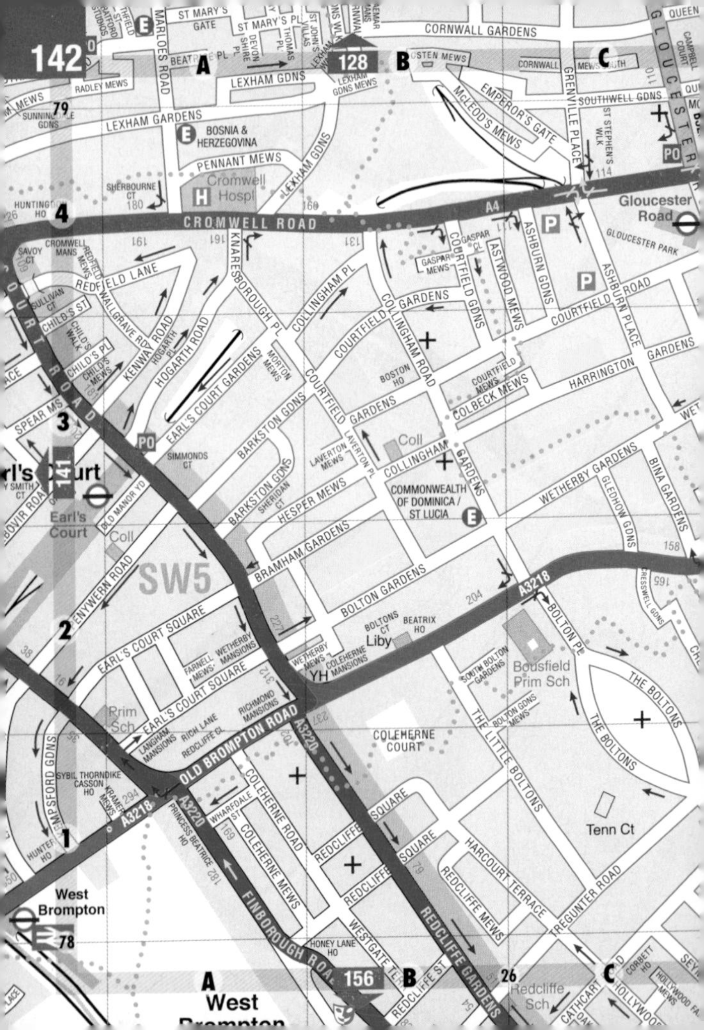
A
B
C
128
CORNWALL GARDENS
ST MARY'S GATE
ST MARY'S PL
DEVONSHIRE TCE
THOMAS PL
ST JOHN'S VILLAS
STRATFORD STUDIOS
MARLOES ROAD
BEATRICE PL
LEXHAM GDNS
LEXHAM GDNS MEWS
RADLEY MEWS
SUNNINGDALE GDNS
79
LEXHAM GARDENS
BOSNIA & HERZEGOVINA
PENNANT MEWS
Cromwell Hospl
SHERBOURNE CT
HUNTINGDON HO
4
CROMWELL ROAD
A4
CROMWELL MANS
REDFIELD MEWS
SAVOY CT
REDFIELD LANE
SULLIVAN CT
CHILD'S ST
CHILD'S WALK
CHILD'S PL
CHILD'S MEWS
WALLGRAVE RD
KENWAY ROAD
HOGARTH PL
HOGARTH ROAD
KNARESBOROUGH PL
EARL'S COURT GARDENS
MORTON MEWS
COLLINGHAM PL
COLLINGHAM ROAD
COURTFIELD GARDENS
COURTFIELD GDNS
GASPAR MEWS
GASPAR CL
ASTWOOD MEWS
ASHBURN GDNS
ASHBURN PLACE
COURTFIELD ROAD
GLOUCESTER PARK
Gloucester Road
McLEOD'S MEWS
EMPEROR'S GATE
GRENVILLE PLACE
SOUTHWELL GDNS
ST STEPHEN'S WLK
CORNWALL MEWS SOUTH
GLOUCESTER ROAD
CAMPBELL COURT
QUEEN
PO
EARL'S COURT ROAD
SPEAR MS
3
141
Earl's Court
BARKSTON GDNS
SIMMONDS CT
BOSTON HO
COURTFIELD MEWS
COLBECK MEWS
HARRINGTON GARDENS
LAVERTON MEWS
LAVERTON PL
COLLINGHAM GARDENS
Coll
COMMONWEALTH OF DOMINICA / ST LUCIA
WETHERBY GARDENS
GLEDHOW GDNS
BINA GARDENS
HESPER MEWS
SHERIDAN CT
OLD MANOR YD
BRAMHAM GARDENS
BOLTON GARDENS
SW5
PENYWERN ROAD
2
EARL'S COURT SQUARE
FARNELL MEWS
WETHERBY MANSIONS
WETHERBY MEWS
COLEHERNE MANSIONS
BOLTONS CT
BEATRIX HO
Liby
YH
A3218
BOLTON PL
SOUTH BOLTON GARDENS
Bousfield Prim Sch
BOLTON GDNS MEWS
THE BOLTONS
CRESSWELL GDNS
RICHMOND MANSIONS
LANGHAM MANSIONS
RICH LANE
REDCLIFFE CL
Prim Sch
OLD BROMPTON ROAD
A3220
COLEHERNE COURT
THE LITTLE BOLTONS
EMPSFORD GDNS
SYBIL THORNDIKE CASSON HO
KRAMER MEWS
1
HUNTER HO
WHARFDALE ST
COLEHERNE ROAD
COLEHERNE MEWS
PRINCESS BEATRICE HO
REDCLIFFE SQUARE
HARCOURT TERRACE
REDCLIFFE MEWS
Tenn Ct
TREGUNTER ROAD
West Brompton
78
FINBOROUGH ROAD
HONEY LANE HO
WESTGATE TER
156
REDCLIFFE ST
REDCLIFFE GARDENS
26
Redcliffe Sch
CATHCART ROAD
CORBETT HO
HOLLYWOOD MEWS
West Brompton

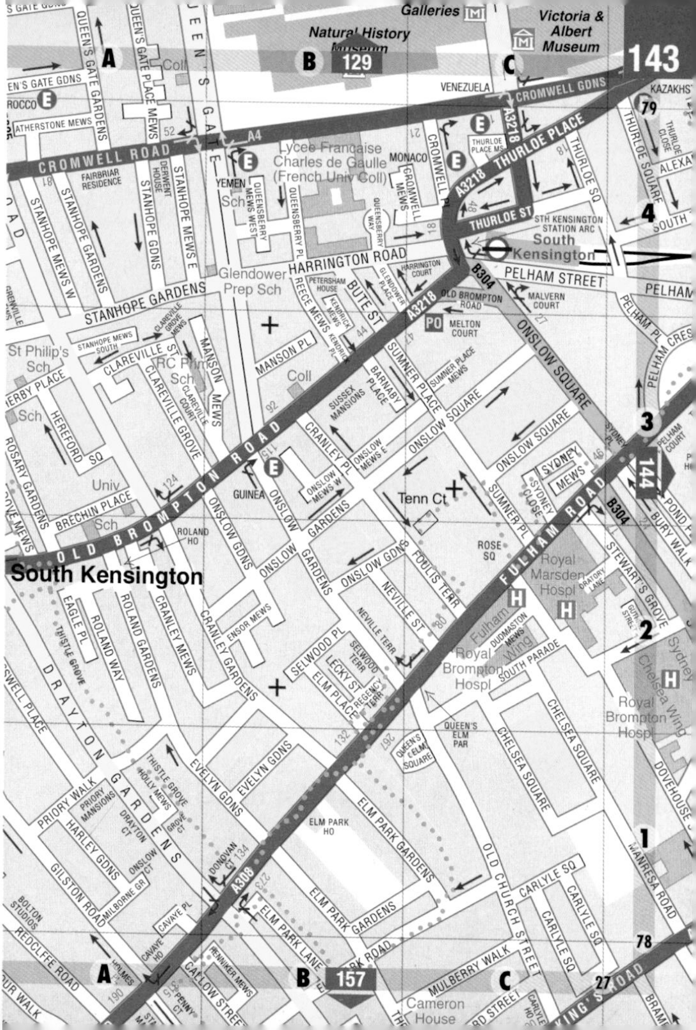

143
144
129
157
78
79
A
B
C
1
2
3
4
Natural History Museum
Galleries
Victoria & Albert Museum
VENEZUELA
KAZAKHSTAN
CROMWELL GDNS
CROMWELL ROAD
A4
A3218
THURLOE PLACE
THURLOE PLACE MS
THURLOE SQ
THURLOE SQUARE
THURLOE CLOSE
THURLOE ST
ALEXANDER
SOUTH TER
STH KENSINGTON STATION ARC
South Kensington
PELHAM STREET
PELHAM PL
PELHAM CRES
PELHAM COURT
MALVERN COURT
QUEEN'S GATE GARDENS
QUEEN'S GATE PLACE MEWS
QUEEN'S GATE
QUEEN'S GATE GDNS
ROCCO
ATHERSTONE MEWS
Coll
Lycee Francaise Charles de Gaulle (French Univ Coll)
MONACO
YEMEN
Sch
QUEENSBERRY MEWS WEST
QUEENSBERRY PL
QUEENSBERRY WAY
CROMWELL MEWS
CROMWELL PL
FAIRBRIAR RESIDENCE
DERWENT HOUSE
STANHOPE MEWS E
STANHOPE GDNS
STANHOPE GARDENS
STANHOPE MEWS W
STANHOPE MEWS SOUTH
HARRINGTON ROAD
HARRINGTON COURT
Glendower Prep Sch
GLENDOWER PLACE
PETERSHAM HOUSE
BUTE ST
REECE MEWS
KENDRICK MEWS
KENDRICK PL
OLD BROMPTON ROAD
B304
PO
MELTON COURT
ONSLOW SQUARE
CLAREVILLE GROVE MEWS
CLAREVILLE ST
CLAREVILLE GROVE
CLAREVILLE COURT
RC Prim Sch
MANSON MEWS
MANSON PL
St Philip's Sch
DERBY PLACE
HEREFORD SQ
ROSARY GARDENS
Univ
BRECHIN PLACE
SUMNER PLACE
SUMNER PLACE MEWS
BARNABY PLACE
SUSSEX MANSIONS
CRANLEY PL
ONSLOW MEWS E
ONSLOW MEWS W
ONSLOW GARDENS
ONSLOW GDNS
GUINEA
Tenn Ct
SYDNEY PL
SYDNEY MEWS
SYDNEY CLOSE
SUMNER PL
ROSE SQ
FULHAM ROAD
BURY WALK
POND PL
ROLAND HO
South Kensington
EAGLE PL
ROLAND WAY
ROLAND GARDENS
CRANLEY MEWS
CRANLEY GARDENS
ENSOR MEWS
FOULIS TERR
NEVILLE ST
NEVILLE TERR
Royal Marsden Hospl
ORATORY LANE
STEWART'S GROVE
GUTHRIE STREET
Fulham Wing
DUDMASTON MEWS
Royal Brompton Hospl
SOUTH PARADE
Sydney Wing
Chelsea Wing
SELWOOD PL
SELWOOD TERR
LECKY ST
ELM PLACE
REGENCY TERR
THISTLE GROVE
DRAYTON GARDENS
QUEEN'S ELM PAR
QUEEN'S ELM SQUARE
CHELSEA SQUARE
DOVEHOUSE ST
EVELYN GDNS
ELM PARK HO
ELM PARK GARDENS
PRIORY WALK
PRIORY MANSIONS
HOLLY MEWS
GROVE CT
DRAYTON CT
HARLEY GDNS
ONSLOW CT
MILBORNE GR
DONOVAN CT
A308
MANRESA ROAD
OLD CHURCH STREET
CARLYLE SQ
GILSTON ROAD
BOLTON STUDIOS
CAVAYE PL
CAVAYE HO
ELM PARK LANE
ELM PARK ROAD
HENNIKER MEWS
CALLOW STREET
REDCLIFFE ROAD
HOLMES PL
PENNY CT
MULBERRY WALK
Cameron House
KING'S ROAD

144
Oratory
THURLOE PLACE
A308
EGERTON GDNS
EGERTON TERRACE
130
A
B
C
Brompton
CROMWELL GDNS
79
KAZAKHSTAN
NORTH TERRACE
THURLOE SQUARE
THURLOE CLOSE
ALEXANDER PL
ALEXANDER SQ
SOUTH TERRACE
ST GEORGE'S COURT
THURLOE SQ
4
STH KENSINGTON STATION ARC
South Kensington
CROMPTON COURT
PELHAM STREET
MALVERN COURT
PELHAM PL
PELHAM CRESCENT
ONSLOW SQUARE
EGERTON GARDENS
EGERTON CRESCENT
CRESCENT PLACE
WALTON STREET
GLYNDE MS
LENNOX GARDENS
LENNOX GDNS MEWS
OVINGTON STREET
HASKER STREET
FIRST STREET
RICHARD'S PLACE
MARLBOROUGH FLATS
BULL'S GDNS
DONNE PLACE
IVES ST
MOSSOP STREET
LEVERETT STREET
DENYER STREET
MILNER STREET
ST CATHERINES MEWS
HALSEY STREET
MOORE STREET
CLABON MEWS
CADOGAN SQUARE
Sussex House Sch
RAWLINGS STREET
WILTSHIRE CLOSE
ROSEMOOR ST
DRAYCOTT AVENUE
St Thomas More Language Coll
St Joseph's RC Prim Sch
315
Marlborough Prim Sch
KEPPEL HOUSE
CURRAN HO
LUCAN PLACE
CHELSEA CLOISTERS
SLOANE AVENUE
NELL GWYNN HOUSE
MAKINS ST
COLEBROOK COURT
CADOGAN
BIDDESDEN HOUSE
GUINNESS COURT
GUINNESS TRUST BUILDINGS
CADOGAN COURT
DRAYCOTT HO
DRAYCOTT PLACE
3
143
SYDNEY PL
KIMBOLTON ROW
THURLOE COURT
PELHAM COURT
POND HOUSE
SAMUEL LEWIS TRUST DWELLINGS
IXWORTH PLACE
ELYSTAN STREET
CROWN LODGE
PETYWARD
CRANMER COURT
SLOANE AVENUE MANS
AVENUE COURT
WHITEHEAD'S GROVE
THE GATEWAYS
SPRIMONT PL
BRAY PLACE
LINCOLN
COULSON ST
SYDNEY CLOSE
FULHAM ROAD
B304
POND PLACE
BURY WALK
MARLBOROUGH ST
NETTLEDEN HO
OATWELL HO
MAYLANDS HOUSE
ALDBURY HO
MARLOWE CT
BYRON CT
LEVERSTOCK HO
SUTTON ESTATE
Oratory RC Prim Sch
ELYSTAN PLACE
THACKERAY CT
RANELAGH HO
MARKHAM PL
ANDERSON ST
TRYON ST
108
Royal Marsden Hospl
ORATORY LANE
STEWART'S GROVE
GUTHRIE STREET
2
CALE STREET
St Luke's Gardens
ST LUKE'S ST
DANUBE ST
ASTELL STREET
GODFREY STREET
WINDSOR CT
JUBILEE PLACE
ARUNDEL CT
JOUBERT MANSIONS
MARKHAM STREET
MARKHAM SQUARE
MARKHAM
BYWATER ST
Kings Wlk Sh Mall
ROYAL AVENUE
WELLINGTON SQ
Sydney Wing
Chelsea Wing
Royal Brompton Hospl
SYDNEY STREET
BRITTEN STREET
BRITTEN HOUSE
MERIDEN CT
DAVER CT
HEMUS PL
BURNSALL ST
KING'S ROAD
SW3
Capio
Chelsea Synagogue
SMITH STREET
WOODFALL ST
ST LEONARD'S
CHELSEA
CHARLES II PL
SMITH TERRACE
DURHAM PL
CHELSEA SQUARE
DOVEHOUSE STREET
Chelsea Antiques Mkt
PO
Chelsea Coll of Art & Design
CHELSEA MANOR STUDIOS
SHAWFIELD STREET
RADNOR WALK
TEDWORTH SQUARE
RALSTON ST
TEDWORTH GDNS
1
CARLYLE SQ
MANRESA ROAD
Liby
Sp Ctr
Offices
SWAN CT
KING'S COURT N
KING'S COURT S
CHELSEA MANOR GDNS
CHELSEA MANOR STREET
CHELSEA TOWERS
FLOOD WALK
CHELSEA MANOR CT
FLOOD STREET
REDESDALE ST
REDBURN STREET
CHRISTCHURCH STREET
CHRISTCHURCH TERR
CAVERSHAM ST
HAYDEN PIPER HO
CHEYNE PL
TITE
78
A3217
27
158
ALPHA PL

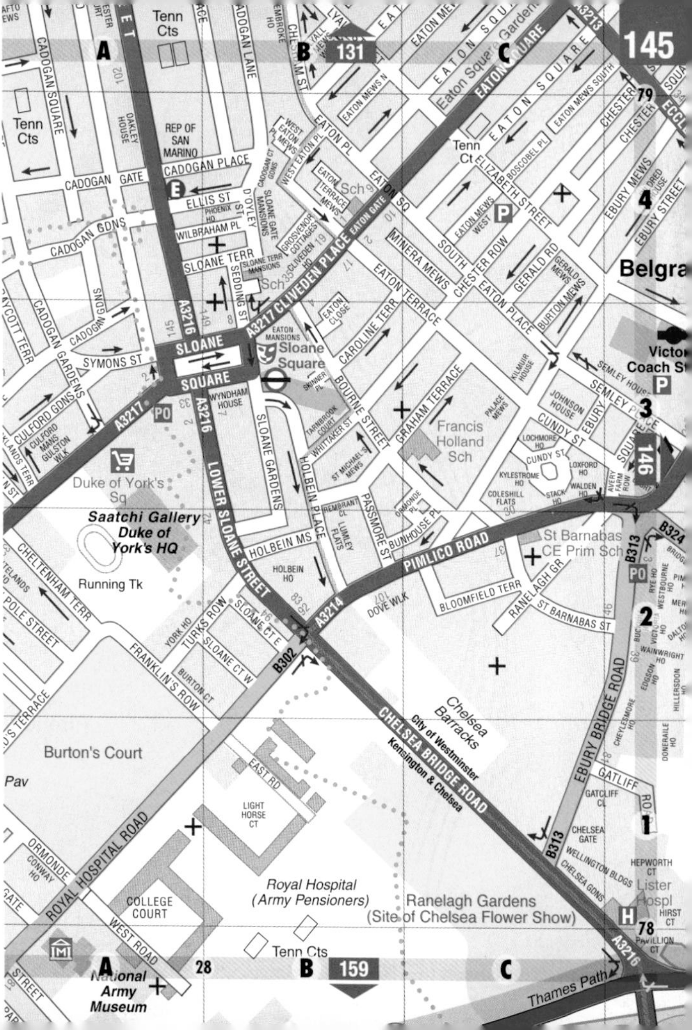

131
A
B
C
Tenn Cts
CADOGAN SQUARE
CADOGAN LANE
OAKLEY HOUSE
REP OF SAN MARINO
CADOGAN PLACE
CADOGAN GATE
ELLIS ST
WILBRAHAM PL
CADOGAN GDNS
SLOANE TERR
SEDDING ST
SLOANE GATE MANSIONS
D'OYLEY ST
GROSVENOR COTTAGES
CLIVEDEN HO
WEST EATON PL
EATON PL
EATON MEWS N
EATON SQUARE
Eaton Square Garden
EATON MEWS SOUTH
BOSCOBEL PL
ELIZABETH STREET
CHESTER ROW
CHESTER SQ
EBURY MEWS
EBURY STREET
Belgra
Victor
Coach St
EATON GATE
EATON TERRACE MEWS
Sch
A3217 CLIVEDEN PLACE
EATON TERRACE
MINERA MEWS
SOUTH EATON PLACE
GERALD RD
GERALD MEWS
BURTON MEWS
EATON MEWS WEST
EATON CLOSE
CAROLINE TERR
EATON MANSIONS
Sloane Square
SLOANE SQUARE
A3216
CADOGAN GARDENS
SYMONS ST
CULFORD GDNS
CULFORD MANS
GULSTON WLK
A3217
PO
WYNDHAM HOUSE
SKINNER PL
BOURNE STREET
GRAHAM TERRACE
KILMUIR HOUSE
PALACE MEWS
Francis Holland Sch
JOHNSON HOUSE
SEMLEY HOUSE
SEMLEY PLACE
EBURY SQUARE
CUNDY ST
LOCHMORE HO
LOXFORD HO
KYLESTROME HO
COLESHILL FLATS
STACK HO
WALDEN HO
AVERY FARM ROW
146
SLOANE GARDENS
HOLBEIN PLACE
TARNBROOK COURT
WHITTAKER ST
ST MICHAEL'S MEWS
REMBRANT CL
LUMLEY FLATS
PASSMORE ST
ORMONDE PL
BUNHOUSE PL
Duke of York's Sq
Saatchi Gallery
Duke of York's HQ
Running Tk
LOWER SLOANE STREET
HOLBEIN MS
HOLBEIN HO
PIMLICO ROAD
A3214
DOVE WLK
St Barnabas CE Prim Sch
RANELAGH GR
BLOOMFIELD TERR
ST BARNABAS ST
B313
B324
CHELTENHAM TERR
FRANKLIN'S ROW
YORK HO
TURKS ROW
SLOANE CT E
SLOANE CT W
BURTON CT
B302
CHELSEA BRIDGE ROAD
City of Westminster
Kensington & Chelsea
Chelsea Barracks
EBURY BRIDGE ROAD
WAINWRIGHT HO
EDGSON HO
HILLERSDON HO
CHEYLESMORE HO
DONERAILE HO
Burton's Court
Pav
EAST RD
LIGHT HORSE CT
GATLIFF ROAD
GATCLIFF CL
CHELSEA GATE
WELLINGTON BLDGS
CHELSEA GDNS
HEPWORTH CT
Lister Hospl
HIRST CT
PAVILLION CT
ROYAL HOSPITAL ROAD
ORMONDE
CONWAY HO
COLLEGE COURT
Royal Hospital (Army Pensioners)
Ranelagh Gardens (Site of Chelsea Flower Show)
WEST ROAD
Tenn Cts
National Army Museum
28
159
78
79
Thames Path

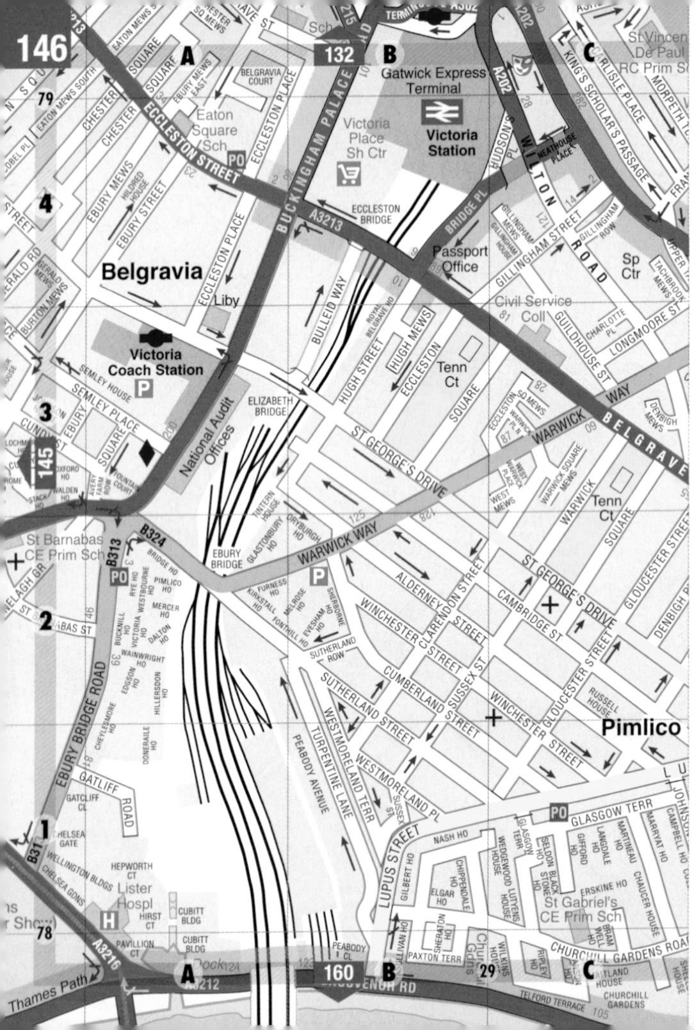
A
B
C
132
160
145
1
2
3
4
Belgravia
Pimlico
Victoria Station
Gatwick Express Terminal
Victoria Place Sh Ctr
Victoria Coach Station
National Audit Offices
Eaton Square Sch
Passport Office
Civil Service Coll
Liby
Sp Ctr
Tenn Ct
St Barnabas CE Prim Sch
St Vincent De Paul RC Prim Sch
St Gabriel's CE Prim Sch
Lister Hospl
Churchill Gdns
ECCLESTON STREET
ECCLESTON PLACE
ECCLESTON BRIDGE
ECCLESTON SQUARE
BUCKINGHAM PALACE RD
A3213
B324
B313
A202
A3216
A3212
BELGRAVE RD
WILTON ROAD
WARWICK WAY
ST GEORGE'S DRIVE
HUGH STREET
HUGH MEWS
BULLEID WAY
EBURY STREET
EBURY MEWS
EBURY SQUARE
EBURY BRIDGE
EBURY BRIDGE ROAD
ELIZABETH BRIDGE
CHESTER SQUARE
SEMLEY PLACE
SEMLEY HOUSE
GILLINGHAM STREET
GILLINGHAM MEWS
GILLINGHAM ROW
GUILDHOUSE ST
LONGMOORE ST
CHARLOTTE PL
BRIDGE PL
HUDSON'S PL
NEATHOUSE PLACE
CARLISLE PLACE
KING'S SCHOLAR'S PASSAGE
MORPETH TERR
TACHBROOK MEWS
DENBIGH MEWS
DENBIGH ST
WARWICK SQUARE
WARWICK SQUARE MEWS
WARWICK PL N
WEST WARWICK PLACE
WEST MEWS
ALDERNEY STREET
CLARENDON STREET
CAMBRIDGE ST
GLOUCESTER STREET
WINCHESTER STREET
CUMBERLAND STREET
SUSSEX ST
SUTHERLAND STREET
SUTHERLAND ROW
WESTMORELAND TERR
WESTMORELAND PL
TURPENTINE LANE
PEABODY AVENUE
LUPUS STREET
GLASGOW TERR
CHURCHILL GARDENS ROAD
TELFORD TERRACE
GROSVENOR RD
GATLIFF ROAD
ST BARNABAS ST
CHELSEA GATE
WELLINGTON BLDGS
CUBITT BLDG
PAXTON TERR
Thames Path
RUSSELL HOUSE

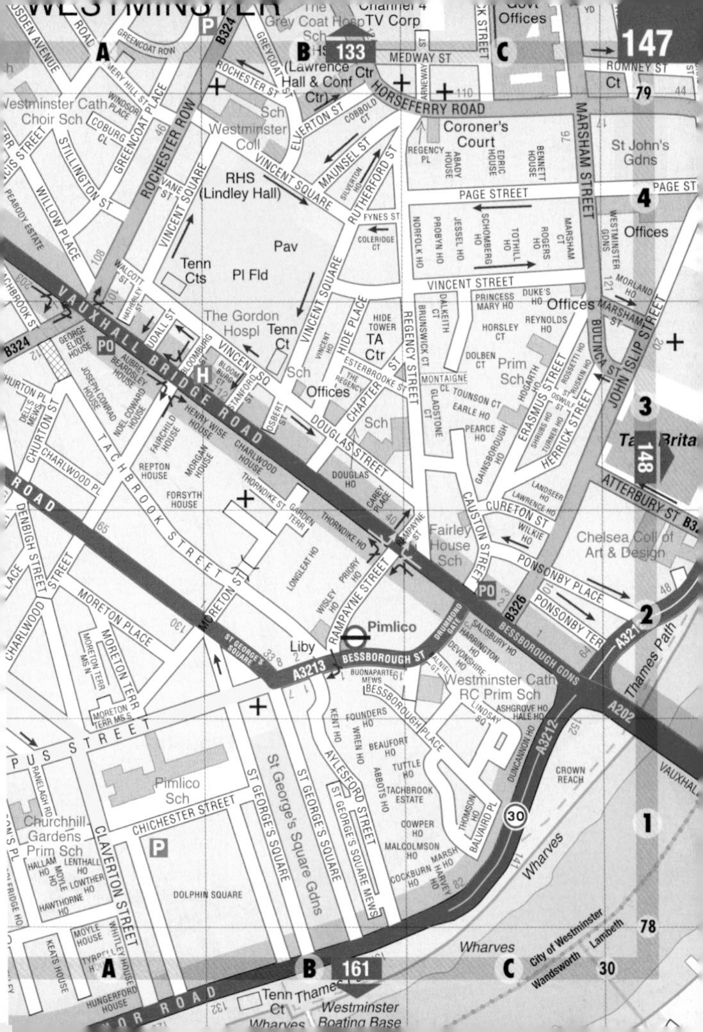
147
133
148
161
A
B
C
1
2
3
4
79
78
30
WESTMINSTER
Grey Coat Hosp Sch
Channel 4 TV Corp
Govt Offices
(Lawrence Hall & Conf Ctr)
Westminster Cath Choir Sch
Westminster Coll
Sch
RHS (Lindley Hall)
Pav
Tenn Cts
Pl Fld
The Gordon Hospl
Tenn Ct
Coroner's Court
St John's Gdns
Offices
TA Ctr
Prim Sch
Fairley House Sch
Tate Britain
Chelsea Coll of Art & Design
Pimlico
Liby
Westminster Cath RC Prim Sch
Pimlico Sch
Churchhill Gardens Prim Sch
St George's Square Gdns
Thames Path
Wharves
Crown Reach
City of Westminster
Lambeth
Wandsworth
Westminster Boating Base
Tenn Ct
HORSEFERRY ROAD
VAUXHALL BRIDGE ROAD
MARSHAM STREET
JOHN ISLIP STREET
ROCHESTER ROW
VINCENT SQUARE
VINCENT STREET
PAGE STREET
REGENCY STREET
DOUGLAS STREET
TACHBROOK STREET
BESSBOROUGH GDNS
BESSBOROUGH ST
BESSBOROUGH PLACE
ATTERBURY ST
PONSONBY PLACE
PONSONBY TER
CAUSTON STREET
ERASMUS STREET
HERRICK STREET
RAMPAYNE STREET
MORETON ST
MORETON PLACE
MORETON TERR
DENBIGH STREET
CLAVERTON STREET
CHICHESTER STREET
ST GEORGE'S SQUARE
AYLESFORD STREET
ST GEORGE'S SQUARE MEWS
LUPUS STREET
GROSVENOR ROAD
DOLPHIN SQUARE
MEDWAY ST
ROMNEY ST
GREENCOAT ROW
GREENCOAT PLACE
ROCHESTER ST
ELVERTON ST
MAUNSEL ST
RUTHERFORD ST
WILLOW PLACE
STILLINGTON ST
CHURTON ST
CHARLWOOD PL
CHARLWOOD
B324
B326
A3213
A3212
A202
A321
30

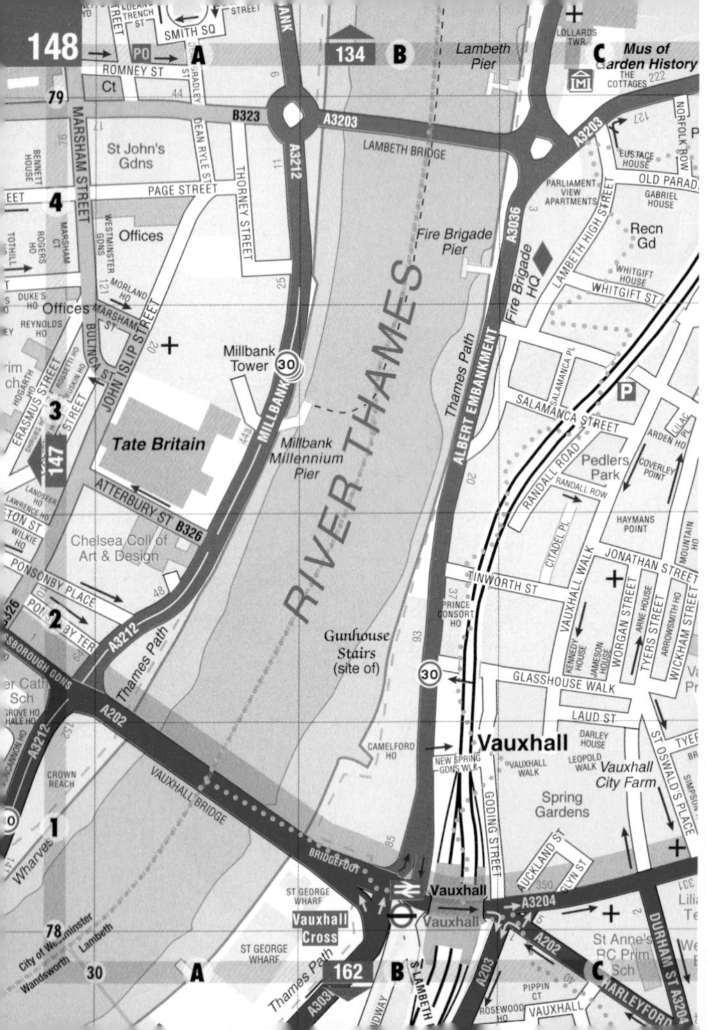

134
162
147
A
B
C
1
2
3
4
SMITH SQ
ROMNEY ST
PO
Ct
79
78
30
B323
A3203
A3212
A3036
A202
A203
A3204
B326
LAMBETH BRIDGE
Lambeth Pier
LOLLARDS TWR
Mus of Garden History
THE COTTAGES
EUSTACE HOUSE
NORFOLK ROW
OLD PARADE
PARLIAMENT VIEW APARTMENTS
GABRIEL HOUSE
LAMBETH HIGH STREET
Recn Gd
WHITGIFT HOUSE
WHITGIFT ST
Fire Brigade HQ
Fire Brigade Pier
MARSHAM STREET
St John's Gdns
DEAN RYLE ST
THORNEY STREET
PAGE STREET
BENNETT HOUSE
ROGERS HO
MARSHAM CT
TOTHILL
WESTMINSTER GDNS
Offices
MORLAND HO
DUKE'S HO
REYNOLDS HO
MARSHAM ST
BULINCA ST
JOHN ISLIP STREET
Millbank Tower
MILLBANK
RIVER THAMES
Thames Path
ALBERT EMBANKMENT
SALAMANCA PL
SALAMANCA STREET
P
HOGARTH HO
ERASMUS STREET
ROSSETTI HO
RUSKIN HO
SHRUBS HO
STREET
Tate Britain
Millbank Millennium Pier
ATTERBURY ST
RANDALL ROAD
RANDALL ROW
Pedlers Park
ARDEN HO
COVERLEY POINT
LILAC PL
HAYMANS POINT
MOUNTAIN
LANDSEER HO
LAWRENCE HO
TON ST
WILKIE HO
Chelsea Coll of Art & Design
PONSONBY PLACE
PONSONBY TER
CITADEL PL
VAUXHALL WALK
JONATHAN STREET
TINWORTH ST
PRINCE CONSORT HO
WORGAN STREET
ARNE HOUSE
TYERS STREET
ARROWSMITH HO
WICKHAM STREET
KENNEDY HOUSE
JAMESON HOUSE
Gunhouse Stairs (site of)
GLASSHOUSE WALK
LAUD ST
BOROUGH GDNS
Cath Sch
GROVE HO
HALE HO
CROWN REACH
VAUXHALL BRIDGE
CAMELFORD HO
Vauxhall
NEW SPRING GDNS WLK
VAUXHALL WALK
DARLEY HOUSE
LEOPOLD WALK
Vauxhall City Farm
ST OSWALD'S PLACE
Spring Gardens
GODING STREET
Wharves
BRIDGEFOOT
AUCKLAND ST
GLYN ST
ST GEORGE WHARF
Vauxhall Cross
Vauxhall
City of Westminster
Lambeth
Wandsworth
Thames Path
A3036
S LAMBETH
St Anne's RC Prim Sch
PIPPIN CT
ROSEWOOD HO
VAUXHALL
HARLEYFORD
DURHAM ST A3204

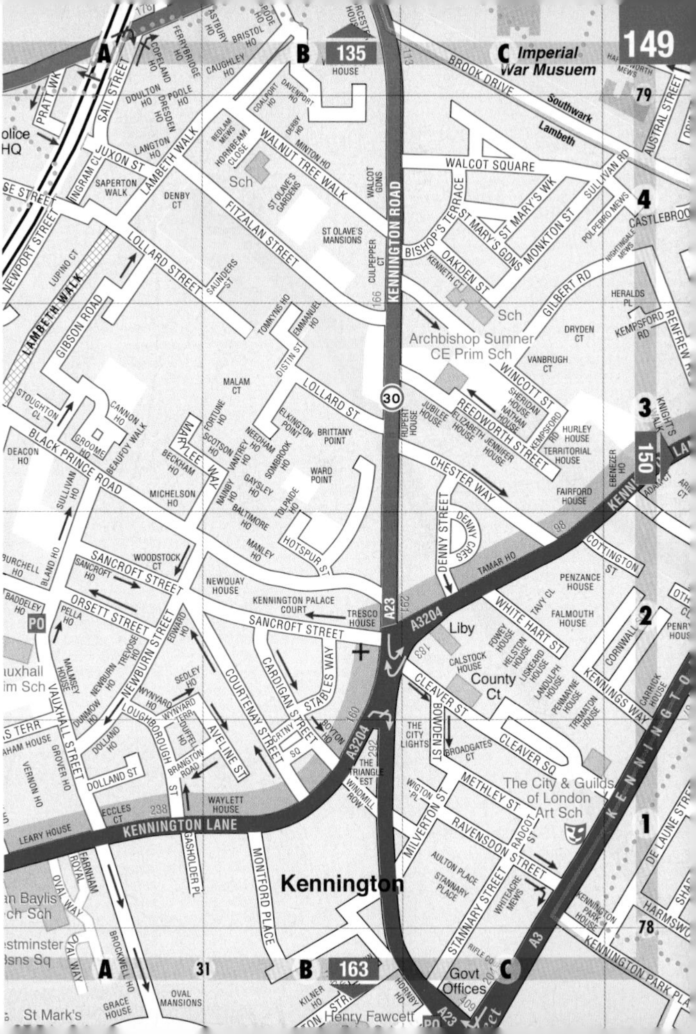
A
B
C
135
Imperial War Musuem
Brook Drive
Southwark
Lambeth
79
Austral Street
Harmsworth Mews
Pratt Wk
Sail Street
Copeland Ho
Ferrybridge Ho
Astbury Ho
Bristol Ho
Caughley Ho
Doulton Ho
Poole Ho
Dresden Ho
Coalport Ho
Davenport Ho
Derby Ho
Minton Ho
House
Police HQ
Juxon St
Langton Ho
Lambeth Walk
Bedlam Mews
Hornbeam Close
Walnut Tree Walk
Walcot Gdns
Kennington Road
Walcot Square
Sullivan Rd
Ingram Cl
Saperton Walk
Denby Ct
Sch
St Olave's Gardens
Fitzalan Street
St Olave's Mansions
Culpepper Ct
Bishop's Terrace
St Mary's Gdns
St Mary's Wk
Monkton St
Polperro Mews
Castlebrook
4
Newport Street
Lupino Ct
Lollard Street
Saunders St
Kenneth Ct
Oakden St
Nightingale Mews
Gilbert Rd
Heralds Pl
Kempsford Rd
Renfrew Rd
Lambeth Walk
Gibson Road
Tomkyns Ho
Emmanuel Ho
166
Sch
Dryden Ct
Archbishop Sumner CE Prim Sch
Vanbrugh Ct
Distin St
Malam Ct
Lollard St
30
Wincott St
Sheridan House
Nathan House
Kempsford Rd
Hurley House
Knight's Walk
3
150
Stoughton Cl
Cannon Ho
Groome Ho
Beaufoy Walk
Marylee Way
Fortune Ho
Scotson Ho
Elkington Point
Brittany Point
Needham Ho
Vantrey Ho
Sombrook Ho
Rupert House
Jubilee House
Elizabeth House
Reedworth Street
Jennifer House
Territorial House
Ebenezer Ho
Deacon Ho
Black Prince Road
Beckham Ho
Michelson Ho
Nainby Ho
Gaysley Ho
Ward Point
Tolpaide Ho
Chester Way
Fairford House
Adam Ct
Sullivan Ho
Baltimore Ho
Denny Street
Denny Cres
98
Manley Ho
Hotspur St
Tamar Ho
Cottington St
Burchell Ho
Bland Ho
Woodstock Ct
Sancroft Ho
Sancroft Street
Newquay House
Penzance House
Tavy Cl
Baddeley Ho
PO
Pella Ho
Orsett Street
Kennington Palace Court
Tresco House
Sancroft Street
A23
291
A3204
Liby
White Hart St
Falmouth House
2
Penry House
Edward Ho
Newburn Street
Trevose Ho
Cardigan Street
Stables Way
Courtenay Street
183
Calstock House
Fowey House
Helston House
Liskeard House
County Ct
Landulph House
Cornwall
Kennings Way
Vauxhall Prim Sch
Malmsey House
Newburn Ho
Sedley Ho
Wynyard Ho
Wynyard Terr
Dumow Ho
Loughborough
Duffell Ho
Aveline St
Crtny Sq
Boyton Ho
160
Cleaver St
Bowden St
The City Lights
Penmayne House
Trematon House
Carrick House
Vauxhall Street
Grover Ho
Vernon Ho
Dolland Ho
Dolland St
Brangton Road
St
A3204
292
The Triangle Est
Broadgates Ct
Cleaver Sq
Methley St
The City & Guilds of London Art Sch
Kennington
Windmill Row
Wigton Pl
Milverton St
Ravensdon Street
Radcot St
1
De Laune Street
Eccles Ct
238
Waylett House
Leary House
Kennington Lane
Gasholder Pl
Montford Place
Aulton Place
Stannary Place
Stannary Street
Whiteacre Mews
Kennington Park House
Harmsworth
78
Farnham Royal
Oval Way
Kennington
Brockwell Ho
A3
Kennington Park Place
31
163
Rifle Court
Govt Offices
Grace House
Oval Mansions
Kilner Ho
Hornby Ho
409
Henry Fawcett
A23
St Mark's
Westminster Bsns Sq

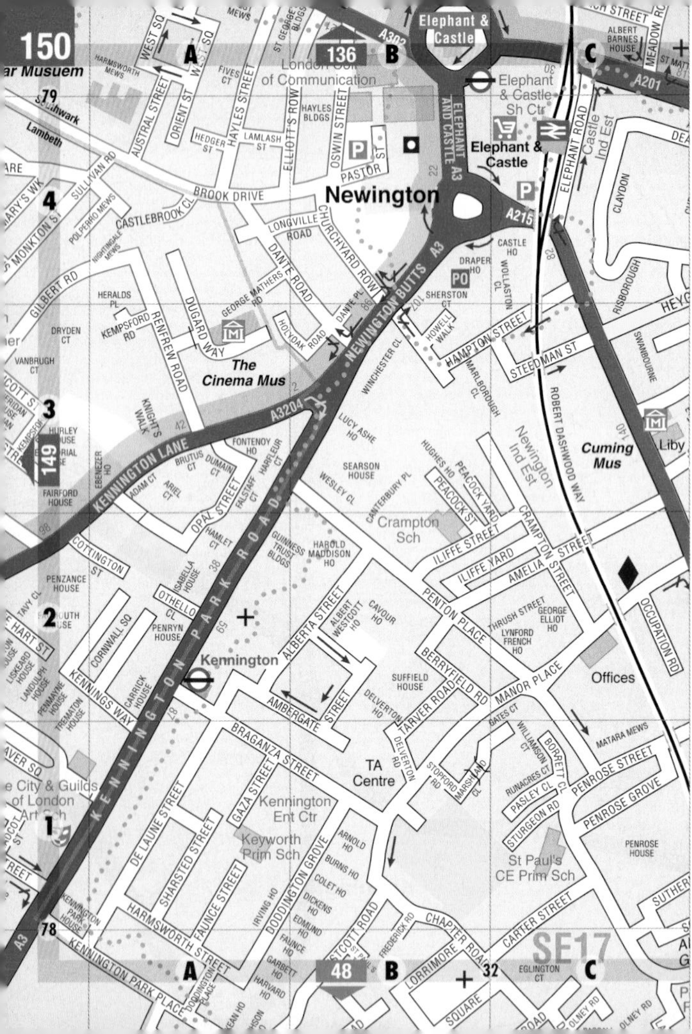

Elephant & Castle
136
A
B
C
A302
A201
A215
A3
A3204
Elephant & Castle Sh Ctr
Elephant & Castle
London Coll of Communication
Newington
The Cinema Mus
Cuming Mus
Liby
Kennington
Crampton Sch
Newington Ind Est
Offices
TA Centre
Kennington Ent Ctr
Keyworth Prim Sch
St Paul's CE Prim Sch
City & Guilds of London Art Sch
SE17
149
48
WEST SQ
MEWS
ST GEORGE'S BLDGS
ALBERT BARNES HOUSE
MEADOW RD
HARMSWORTH MEWS
FIVES CT
HAYLES STREET
ELLIOTT'S ROW
OSWIN STREET
HAYLES BLDGS
AUSTRAL STREET
ORIENT ST
HEDGER ST
LAMLASH ST
PASTOR ST
ELEPHANT AND CASTLE
ELEPHANT ROAD
Castle Ind Est
CLAYDON
BROOK DRIVE
SULLIVAN RD
POLPERRO MEWS
CASTLEBROOK CL
MONKTON ST
NIGHTINGALE MEWS
LONGVILLE ROAD
CHURCHYARD ROW
DANTE ROAD
DANTE PL
CASTLE HO
DRAPER HO
WOLLASTON CL
SHERSTON CT
GILBERT RD
HERALDS PL
KEMPSFORD RD
RENFREW ROAD
DUGARD WAY
GEORGE MATHERS RD
HOLYOAK ROAD
NEWINGTON BUTTS
HOWELL WALK
HAMPTON STREET
STEEDMAN ST
RISBOROUGH
SWANBOURNE
HEYG
DRYDEN CT
VANBRUGH CT
WINCHESTER CL
MARLBOROUGH CL
ROBERT DASHWOOD WAY
KNIGHT'S WALK
LUCY ASHE HO
HURLEY HOUSE
KENNINGTON LANE
FONTENOY HO
HARFLEUR CT
BRUTUS CT
DUMAIN CT
ADAM CT
ARIEL CT
OPAL STREET
FALSTAFF CT
SEARSON HOUSE
WESLEY CL
CANTERBURY PL
HUGHES HO
PEACOCK YARD
PEACOCK ST
EBENEZER HO
FAIRFORD HOUSE
COTTINGTON ST
HAMLET CT
GUINNESS TRUST BLDGS
HAROLD MADDISON HO
ILIFFE STREET
ILIFFE YARD
AMELIA STREET
CRAMPTON STREET
PENZANCE HOUSE
TAVY CL
ISABELLA HOUSE
OTHELLO CL
PENRYN HOUSE
KENNINGTON PARK ROAD
ALBERTA STREET
ALBERT WESTCOTT HO
CAVOUR HO
PENTON PLACE
THRUSH STREET
GEORGE ELLIOT HO
LYNFORD FRENCH HO
OCCUPATION RD
CORNWALL SQ
KENNINGS WAY
CARRICK HOUSE
LISKEARD HOUSE
LANDULPH HOUSE
PENMAYNE HOUSE
TREMATON HOUSE
AMBERGATE STREET
DELVERTON HO
SUFFIELD HOUSE
TARVER ROAD
BERRYFIELD RD
MANOR PLACE
GATES CT
WILLIAMSON CT
BORRETT CL
MATARA MEWS
BRAGANZA STREET
DELVERTON RD
STOPFORD RD
MARSHLAND CL
RUNACRES CT
PASLEY CL
PENROSE STREET
PENROSE GROVE
STURGEON RD
PENROSE HOUSE
DE LAUNE STREET
SHARSTED STREET
GAZA STREET
ARNOLD HO
BURNS HO
COLET HO
DICKENS HO
EDMUND HO
FAUNCE HO
GARBETT HO
HARVARD HO
IRVING HO
DODDINGTON GROVE
FAUNCE STREET
HARMSWORTH STREET
KENNINGTON PARK HOUSE
KENNINGTON PARK PLACE
DODDINGTON PLACE
FREDERICK RD
CHAPTER ROAD
CARTER STREET
SUTHERL
LORRIMORE SQUARE
EGLINTON CT
OLNEY RD
Southwark
Lambeth

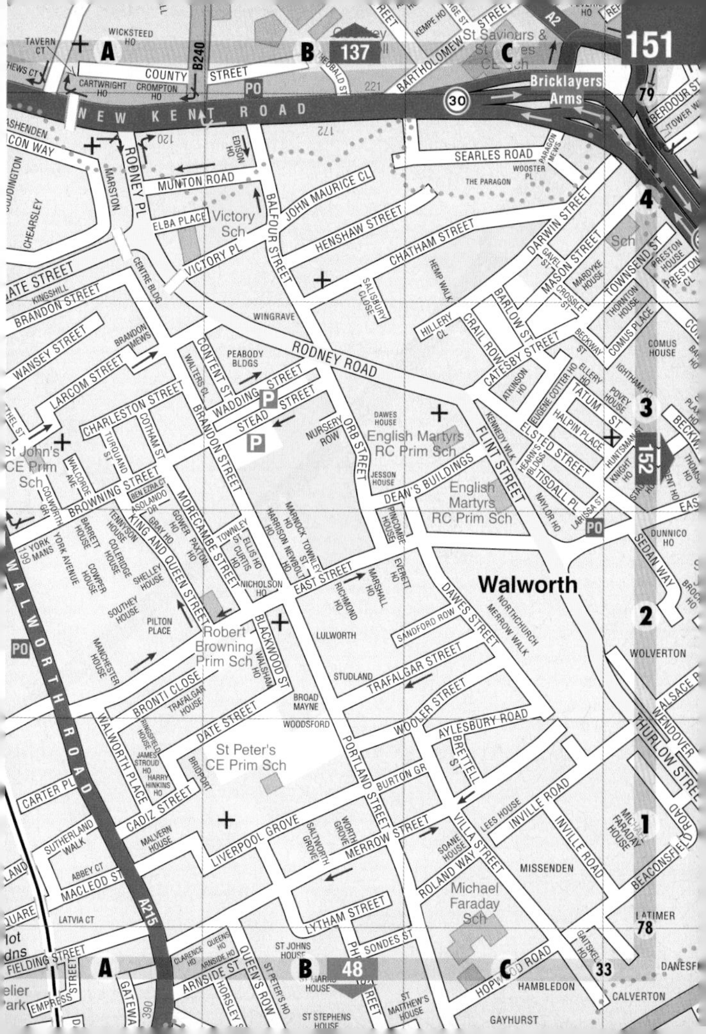
A
B
C
137
TAVERN CT
WICKSTEED HO
MEWS CT
CARTWRIGHT HO
CROMPTON HO
COUNTY STREET
B240
PO
THEOBALD ST
221
BARTHOLOMEW ST
KEMPE HO
St Saviours & St Johns CE Sch
A2
Bricklayers Arms
30
79
ABERDOUR ST
TOWER W
NEW KENT ROAD
172
120
ASHENDEN
DICKENS WAY
EDISON HO
MUNTON ROAD
RODNEY PL
MARSTON
CHEARSLEY
ELBA PLACE
Victory Sch
VICTORY PL
BALFOUR STREET
JOHN MAURICE CL
HENSHAW STREET
SEARLES ROAD
PARAGON MEWS
WOOSTER PL
THE PARAGON
CHATHAM STREET
DARWIN STREET
4
Sch
PRESTON HOUSE
PRESTON CL
TOWNSEND ST
MASON STREET
GAVEL ST
MARDYKE HOUSE
CROSSLET ST
THORNTON HOUSE
COMUS PLACE
COMUS HOUSE
HEMP WALK
SALISBURY CLOSE
CENTRE BLDG
GATE STREET
KINGSHILL
BRANDON STREET
WINGRAVE
RODNEY ROAD
HILLERY CL
CRAIL ROW
BARLOW ST
CATESBY STREET
BECKWAY ST
WANSEY STREET
BRANDON MEWS
LARCOM STREET
PEABODY BLDGS
CONTENT ST
WALTERS CL
WADDING STREET
STEAD STREET
P
ATKINSON HO
EUGENE COTTER HO
ELLERY HO
TATUM ST
POVEY HOUSE
3
CHARLESTON STREET
COTHAM ST
TURQUAND ST
BRANDON STREET
NURSERY ROW
ORB STREET
DAWES HOUSE
English Martyrs RC Prim Sch
KENNEDY WLK
FLINT STREET
ELSTED STREET
HALPIN PLACE
HUNTSMAN ST
152
KNIGHT HO
St John's CE Prim Sch
WALCORDE AVE
BROWNING STREET
BEN EZRA CT
ASOLANDO DR
MORECAMBE STREET
JESSON HOUSE
DEAN'S BUILDINGS
English Martyrs RC Prim Sch
HEARN'S BLDGS
TISDALL PL
LARISSA ST
NAYLOR HO
PO
DUNNICO HO
SEDAN WAY
COLWORTH GR
BARRETT HOUSE
TENNYSON HOUSE
KING AND QUEEN STREET
GRAY HO
GOWER HO
PAXTON HO
TOWNLEY ST
ELLIS HO
CURTIS HO
MARNOCK HO
HARRISON HO
NEWBOLT HO
TOWNLEY ST
PINCOMBE HOUSE
199
YORK MANS
YORK AVENUE
COLERIDGE HOUSE
COWPER HOUSE
SHELLEY HOUSE
NICHOLSON HO
EAST STREET
MARSHALL HO
EVERETT HO
RICHMOND HO
Walworth
DAWES STREET
NORTHCHURCH
MERROW WALK
SOUTHEY HOUSE
PILTON PLACE
Robert Browning Prim Sch
BLACKWOOD ST
WALSHAM HO
LULWORTH
SANDFORD ROW
2
PO
MANCHESTER HOUSE
WOLVERTON
BRONTI CLOSE
TRAFALGAR HOUSE
STUDLAND
TRAFALGAR STREET
ALSACE R
BROAD MAYNE
WOOLER STREET
WENDOVER
WALWORTH ROAD
WALWORTH PLACE
RINGSFIELD HOUSE
DATE STREET
WOODSFORD
AYLESBURY ROAD
THURLOW STREET
JAMES STROUD HO
St Peter's CE Prim Sch
BRETTELL ST
HARRY HINKINS HO
BRIDPORT
PORTLAND STREET
BURTON GR
CARTER PL
CADIZ STREET
LEES HOUSE
INVILLE ROAD
1
MICHAEL FARADAY HOUSE
BEACONSFIELD ROAD
SUTHERLAND WALK
MALVERN HOUSE
LIVERPOOL GROVE
SALTWORTH GROVE
WORTH GROVE
MERROW STREET
VILLA STREET
SOANE HOUSE
MISSENDEN
ABBEY CT
MACLEOD ST
ROLAND WAY
Michael Faraday Sch
A215
LATVIA CT
LYTHAM STREET
LATIMER
78
FIELDING STREET
CLARENCE HO
QUEENS HO
ARNSIDE HO
ST JOHNS HOUSE
SONDES ST
GAITSKELL HO
48
ARNSIDE ST
QUEEN'S ROW
ST PETER'S HO
HOPWOOD ROAD
33
DANESFI
EMPRESS STREET
GATEWAY
HORSLEY ST
390
ST MARKS HOUSE
ST MATTHEW'S HOUSE
HAMBLEDON
CALVERTON
ST STEPHENS HOUSE
GAYHURST

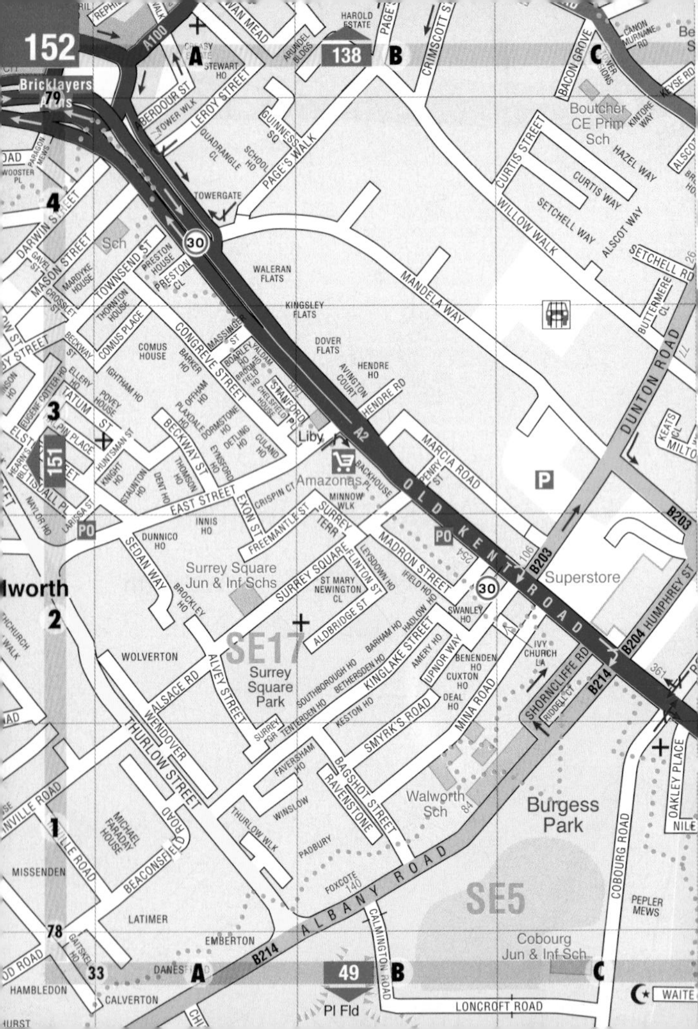

Bricklayers Arms
79
A100
REPHIDIM
CREASY ESTATE
STEWART HO
SWAN MEAD
ARUNDEL BLDGS
HAROLD ESTATE
138
PAGE'S WALK
CRIMSCOTT ST
CANON MURNANE RD
KEYSE RD
BACON GROVE
Boutcher CE Prim Sch
KINTORE WAY
HAZEL WAY
ALSCOT
CURTIS STREET
CURTIS WAY
SETCHELL WAY
ALSCOT WAY
WILLOW WALK
SETCHELL RD
26
BUTTERMERE CL
ABERDOUR ST
TOWER WLK
LEROY STREET
QUADRANGLE CL
SCHOOL HO
GUINNESS SQ
PAGE'S WALK
TOWERGATE
PARAGON MEWS
WOOSTER PL
4
DARWIN STREET
GAVEL ST
MASON STREET
Sch
TOWNSEND ST
PRESTON HOUSE
PRESTON CL
30
WALERAN FLATS
KINGSLEY FLATS
DOVER FLATS
MANDELA WAY
MARDYKE HOUSE
CROSSLET ST
THORNTON HOUSE
COMUS PLACE
COMUS HOUSE
MASSINGER ST
BEAKWAY ST
CONGREVE STREET
BARKER HO
BOARLEY HO
VALDAM HO
BROOMFIELD HO
AVINGTON COURT
HENDRE HO
HENDRE RD
DUNTON ROAD
77
ELLERY HO
EUGENE COTTER HO
IGHTHAM HO
TATUM ST
3
POVEY HOUSE
OFFHAM HO
PLAXDALE HO
DORMSTONE HO
CHELSFIELD HOUSE
STANFORD PL
Liby
A2
MARCIA ROAD
HENRY ST
KEATS CL
MILTON
ELSTED ST
ALPIN PLACE
HUNTSMAN ST
BECKWAY ST
DETLING HO
CULAND HO
EYNSFORD HO
THOMSON HO
KNIGHT HO
STAUNTON HO
DENT HO
151
BLOCK
HEARN'S BLDGS
BATISDALL PL
NAYLOR HO
LARISSA ST
PO
EAST STREET
EXON ST
CRISPIN CT
Amazonas
BACKHOUSE PL
MINNOW WLK
OLD KENT ROAD
P
B203
INNIS HO
DUNNICO HO
FREEMANTLE ST
SURREY TERR
MADRON STREET
PO
254
106
B203
Superstore
HUMPHREY ST
Walworth
SEDAN WAY
Surrey Square Jun & Inf Schs
SURREY SQUARE
FLINTON ST
LEYSDOWN HO
IFIELD HO
ST MARY NEWINGTON CL
SWANLEY HO
30
2
BROCKLEY HO
ALDBRIDGE ST
HADLOW HO
BARHAM HO
KINGLAKE STREET
AMERY HO
UPNOR WAY
BENENDEN HO
IVY CHURCH LA
B204
WOLVERTON
SE17
Surrey Square Park
SOUTHBOROUGH HO
BETHERSDEN HO
CUXTON HO
DEAL HO
SHORNCLIFFE RD
B214
361
ALSACE RD
ALVEY STREET
TENTERDEN HO
KESTON HO
SMYRK'S ROAD
MINA ROAD
RIDDELL CT
SURREY GR
WENDOVER
THURLOW STREET
FAVERSHAM HO
BAGSHOT STREET
RAVENSTONE
OAKLEY PLACE
1
Walworth Sch
84
Burgess Park
NILE
WINSLOW
THURLOW WLK
MICHAEL FARADAY HOUSE
BEACONSFIELD ROAD
PADBURY
FOXCOTE
140
ALBANY ROAD
COBOURG ROAD
MISSENDEN
PEPLER MEWS
SE5
LATIMER
78
GAITSKELL HO
EMBERTON
CALMINGTON ROAD
Cobourg Jun & Inf Sch
B214
33
DANESFIELD
A
49
B
C
HAMBLEDON
CALVERTON
LONCROFT ROAD
WAITE
Pl Fld

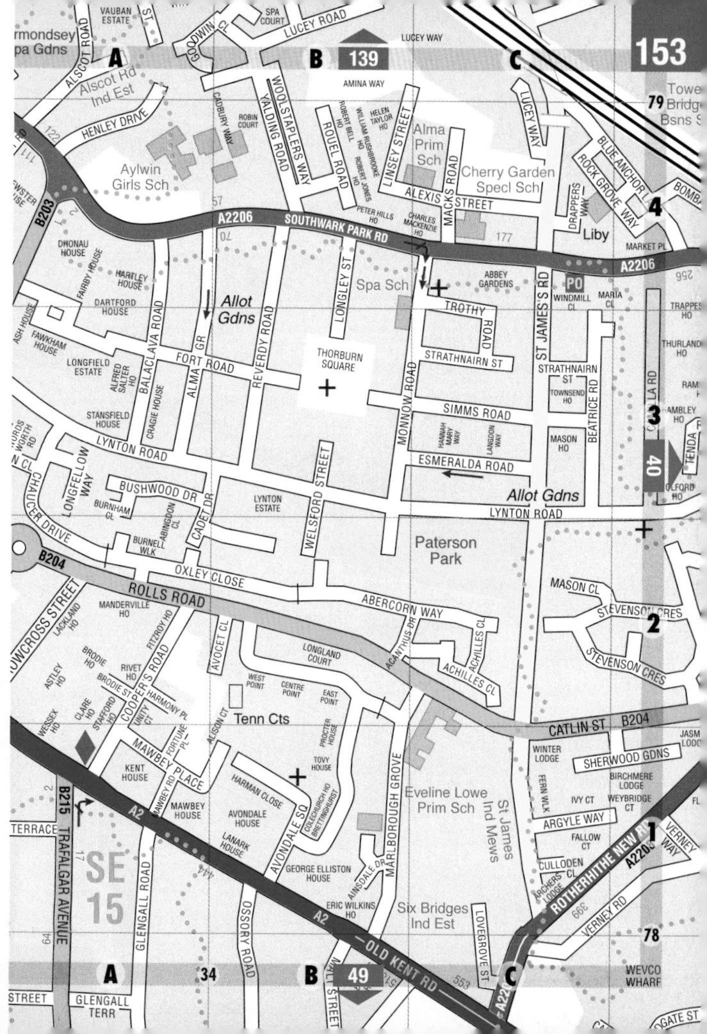
VAUBAN ESTATE
SPA COURT
LUCEY ROAD
LUCEY WAY
139
rmondsey Spa Gdns
ALSCOT ROAD
GOODWIN CL
A
B
C
Alscot Rd Ind Est
AMINA WAY
Towe Bridg Bsns S
79
HENLEY DRIVE
CADBURY WAY
ROBIN COURT
WOOLSTAPLERS WAY
YALDING ROAD
ROBERT BELL HO
WILLIAM RUSHBROOKE HO
HELEN TAYLOR HO
ROUEL ROAD
ROBERT JONES HO
LINSEY STREET
Alma Prim Sch
MACKS ROAD
Cherry Garden Specl Sch
LUCEY WAY
BLUE ANCHOR L
ROCK GROVE WAY
BOMB
Aylwin Girls Sch
ALEXIS STREET
DRAPPERS WAY
4
PETER HILLS HO
CHARLES MACKENZIE HO
Liby
B203
A2206
SOUTHWARK PARK RD
177
MARKET PL
DHONAU HOUSE
FAIRBY HOUSE
HARTLEY HOUSE
ABBEY GARDENS
PO
WINDMILL CL
MARIA CL
TRAPPES HO
Allot Gdns
Spa Sch
DARTFORD HOUSE
TROTHY ROAD
ST JAMES'S RD
ASH HOUSE
FAWKHAM HOUSE
BALACLAVA ROAD
ALMA GR
REVERDY ROAD
LONGLEY ST
THURLAND HO
LONGFIELD ESTATE
ALFRED SALTER HO
FORT ROAD
THORBURN SQUARE
STRATHNAIRN ST
STRATHNAIRN ST
TOWNSEND HO
CALLA RD
RAM
MONNOW ROAD
BEATRICE RD
STANSFIELD HOUSE
CRAGIE HOUSE
SIMMS ROAD
AMBLEY HO
3
HANNAH MARY WAY
LANGDON WAY
MASON HO
LYNTON ROAD
ESMERALDA ROAD
40
TENDA
LONGFELLOW WAY
CHAUCER DRIVE
BUSHWOOD DR
CADET DR
WELSFORD STREET
LYNTON ESTATE
Allot Gdns
OLFORD HO
BURNHAM CL
ABINGDON CL
LYNTON ROAD
BURNELL WLK
Paterson Park
B204
OXLEY CLOSE
ROLLS ROAD
MASON CL
ABERCORN WAY
STEVENSON CRES
2
MANDERVILLE HO
OWCROSS STREET
LACKLAND HO
FITZROY HO
AVOCET CL
ACANTHUS DR
ACHILLES CL
LONGLAND COURT
BRODIE HO
ASTLEY HO
RIVET HO
COOPER'S ROAD
STEVENSON CRES
ACHILLES CL
BRODIE ST
HARMONY PL
WEST POINT
CENTRE POINT
EAST POINT
WESSEX HO
CLARE HO
STAFFORD HO
UNITY CT
ALISON CT
Tenn Cts
PROCTER HOUSE
CATLIN ST
B204
JASM LODG
FORTUNE PL
MAWBEY PLACE
TOVY HOUSE
WINTER LODGE
SHERWOOD GDNS
KENT HOUSE
HARMAN CLOSE
COLECHURCH HO
BRETTINGHURST
MARLBOROUGH GROVE
Eveline Lowe Prim Sch
BIRCHMERE LODGE
B215
MAWBEY RD
MAWBEY HOUSE
AVONDALE HOUSE
AVONDALE SQ
St James Ind Mews
FERN WLK
IVY CT
WEYBRIDGE CT
A2
ARGYLE WAY
TERRACE
FALLOW CT
1
VERNEY WAY
SE 15
LANARK HOUSE
GEORGE ELLISTON HOUSE
AINSDALE DR
CULLODEN CL
ARCHERS LODGE
ROTHERHITHE NEW RD
A2206
TRAFALGAR AVENUE
GLENGALL ROAD
ERIC WILKINS HO
Six Bridges Ind Est
LOVEGROVE ST
VERNEY RD
78
OSSORY ROAD
A2
OLD KENT RD
34
49
WEVCO WHARF
STREET
GLENGALL TERR
MALT STREET
A2206
GATE ST

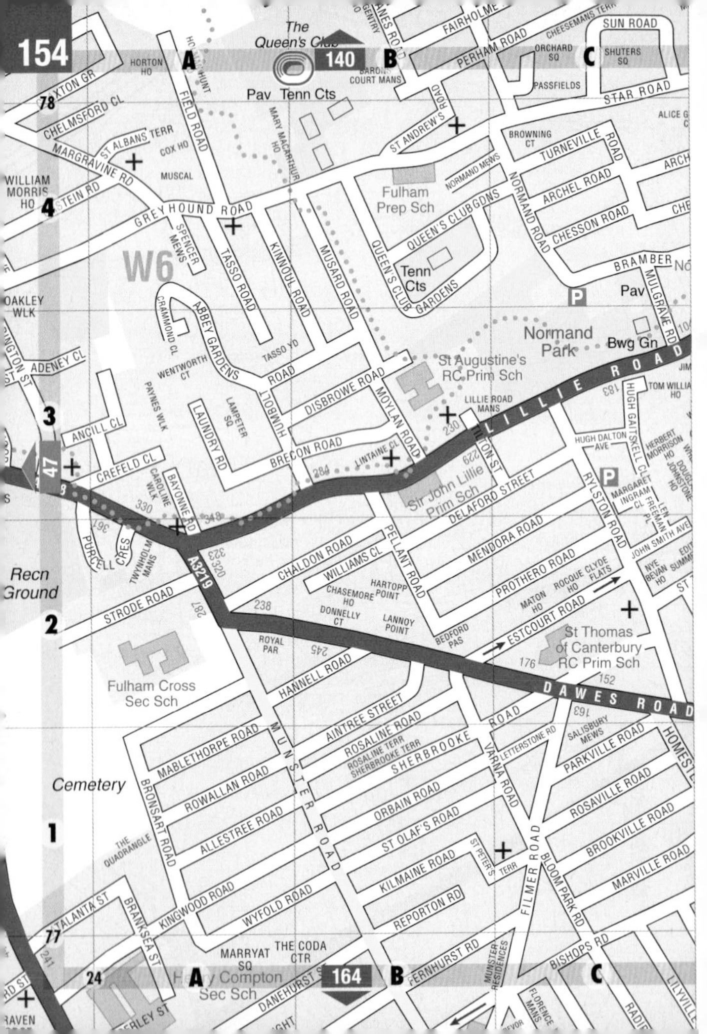
The Queen's Club
140
A
B
C
Pav
Tenn Cts
Horton Ho
Paxton Gr
78
Chelmsford Cl
Margravine Rd
St Albans Terr
Cox Ho
Muscal
William Morris Ho
Stein Rd
4
Greyhound Road
Spencer Mews
Field Road
Mary Macarthur Ho
Barons Court Mans
St Andrew's Road
Fairholme
Perham Road
Cheesemans Terr
Orchard Sq
Sun Road
Shuters Sq
Passfields
Star Road
Alice G
Browning Ct
Turneville Road
Normand Mews
Archel Road
Chesson Road
Bramber
Fulham Prep Sch
Queen's Club Gdns
Queen's Club Gardens
Tenn Cts
Normand Road
Mulgrave Rd
Pav
Normand Park
Bwg Gn
W6
Tasso Road
Kinnoul Road
Musard Road
Oakley Wlk
Crammond Cl
Abbey Gardens
Tasso Yd
Wentworth Ct
Adeney Cl
Paynes Wlk
Lampeter Sq
Humbolt Road
Disbrowe Road
Moylan Road
St Augustine's RC Prim Sch
Lillie Road Mans
Lillie Road
183
Tom Williams Ho
3
Ancill Cl
Laundry Rd
Brecon Road
Lintaine Cl
230
229
Tilton St
Hugh Dalton Ave
Hugh Gaitskell Cl
Herbert Morrison Ho
47
Crefeld Cl
Caroline Wlk
Bayonne Rd
330
348
284
Sir John Lillie Prim Sch
Delaford Street
Rylston Road
Margaret Ingram Cl
Freeman Pl
Len Johnstone Ho
361
Purcell Cres
Twynholm Mans
323
320
A3219
Chaldon Road
Williams Cl
Pellant Road
Mendora Road
John Smith Ave
Recn Ground
Hartopp Point
Chasemore Ho
Prothero Road
Rocque Ho
Clyde Flats
Nye Bevan Ho
2
Strode Road
287
238
Donnelly Ct
Lannoy Point
Maton Ho
Estcourt Road
Bedford Pas
Royal Par
245
St Thomas of Canterbury RC Prim Sch
176
152
Fulham Cross Sec Sch
Hannell Road
Dawes Road
163
Aintree Street
Rosaline Road
Rosaline Terr
Sherbrooke Terr
Sherbrooke Road
Letterstone Rd
Salisbury Mews
Parkville Road
Mablethorpe Road
Munster Road
Varna Road
Cemetery
Bronsart Road
Rowallan Road
Orbain Road
Rosaville Road
1
Allestree Road
St Olaf's Road
Brookville Road
The Quadrangle
St Peter's Terr
Filmer Road
Bloom Park Rd
Marville Road
Kilmaine Road
Kingwood Road
Wyfold Road
Reporton Rd
Atalanta St
Branksea St
77
241
Marryat Sq
The Coda Ctr
Fernhurst Rd
Munster Residences
Bishops Rd
24
Henry Compton Sec Sch
164
Danehurst St
Florence Mans
Raven
Radipole
Lillyville

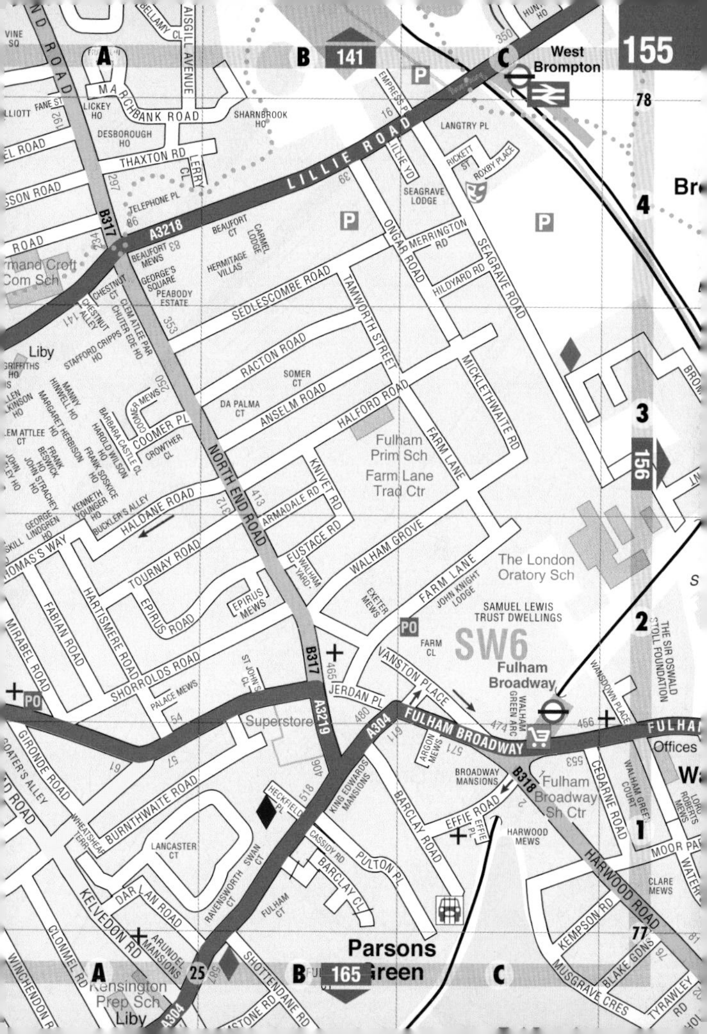

A
B
C
141
West Brompton
78
4
3
2
1
156
VINE SQ
ELLIOTT
FANE ST
LICKEY HO
MARCHBANK ROAD
BELLAMY CL
AISGILL AVENUE
SHARNBROOK HO
DESBOROUGH HO
THAXTON RD
LERRY CL
EMPRESS PL
LILLIE ROAD
LILLIE YD
LANGTRY PL
RICKETT ST
ROXBY PLACE
SEAGRAVE LODGE
TELEPHONE PL
A3218
B317
BEAUFORT CT
CARMEL LODGE
BEAUFORT MEWS
HERMITAGE VILLAS
GEORGE'S SQUARE
PEABODY ESTATE
Normand Croft Com Sch
CHESTNUT CT
CHESTNUT ALLEY
CLEM ATTLEE PAR
CHUTER EDE HO
STAFFORD CRIPPS HO
SEDLESCOMBE ROAD
TAMWORTH STREET
ONGAR ROAD
MERRINGTON RD
HILDYARD RD
SEAGRAVE ROAD
RACTON ROAD
SOMER CT
ANSELM ROAD
DA PALMA CT
HALFORD ROAD
MICKLETHWAITE RD
Liby
GRIFFITHS HO
MANNY HINWELL HO
MARGARET HERBISON HO
BARBARA CASTLE CL
HAROLD WILSON HO
FRANK SOSKICE HO
CLEM ATTLEE CT
FRANK BESWICK HO
JOHN STRACHEY HO
KENNETH YOUNGER HO
COOMER MEWS
COOMER PL
CROWTHER CL
NORTH END ROAD
Fulham Prim Sch
Farm Lane Trad Ctr
FARM LANE
KNIVET RD
ARMADALE RD
HALDANE ROAD
BUCKLER'S ALLEY
GEORGE LINDGREN HO
THOMAS'S WAY
EUSTACE RD
WALHAM YARD
WALHAM GROVE
TOURNAY ROAD
The London Oratory Sch
EPIRUS MEWS
EPIRUS ROAD
EXETER MEWS
JOHN KNIGHT LODGE
SAMUEL LEWIS TRUST DWELLINGS
FABIAN ROAD
HARTISMERE ROAD
MIRABEL ROAD
PO
FARM CL
SW6
Fulham Broadway
THE SIR OSWALD STOLL FOUNDATION
SHORROLDS ROAD
ST JOHN'S CL
JERDAN PL
VANSTON PLACE
WANSDOWN PLACE
PALACE MEWS
Superstore
A3219
WALHAM GREEN ARC
FULHAM BROADWAY
A304
ARGON MEWS
Offices
GIRONDE ROAD
COATER'S ALLEY
BURNTHWAITE ROAD
HECKFIELD PL
KING EDWARDS MANSIONS
BROADWAY MANSIONS
B318
Fulham Broadway Sh Ctr
CEDARNE ROAD
WALHAM GREEN COURT
ROBERTS MEWS
WHEATSHEAF TERR
LANCASTER CT
CASSIDY RD
PULTON PL
BARCLAY ROAD
EFFIE ROAD
EFFIE PL
HARWOOD MEWS
MOOR PARK
BARCLAY CL
HARWOOD ROAD
CLARE MEWS
DARLAN ROAD
SWAN CT
RAVENSWORTH CT
FULHAM CT
KEMPSON RD
KELVEDON RD
CLONMEL RD
ARUNDEL MANSIONS
Parsons Green
SHOTTENDANE RD
BLAKE GDNS
WINCHENDON RD
Kensington Prep Sch
165
MUSGRAVE CRES
TYRAWLEY RD

142
155
166
A
B
C
1
2
3
4
West Brompton
Brompton Cemetery
SW10
Stamford Bridge Stadium
(Chelsea F'ball Club)
Walham Green
Fulham Broadway
The London Oratory Sch
Redcliffe Sch
Servite RC Prim Sch
Kensington & Chelsea Coll
Westfield Park
Gas Works
FINBOROUGH ROAD
REDCLIFFE GARDENS
REDCLIFFE MEWS
HARCOURT TERRACE
TREGUNTER ROAD
WESTGATE TERR
REDCLIFFE ST
HONEY LANE HO
CATHCART ROAD
HOLLYWOOD ROAD
OAKFIELD ST
CLIFTON GATE
GUATEMALA
STREET
IFIELD ROAD
ADRIAN MEWS
WALNUT TREE HOUSE
FAWCETT
REDCLIFFE PL
BARKER STREET
A3220
A308
A304
GUNTER GROVE
FERNSHAW ROAD
GALLERY CT
HORTENSIA ROAD
COLLEGE PL
HUDSON HO
BROMPTON PARK CRESCENT
ST MARK'S GROVE
BILLING RD
BILLING PL
BILLING ST
HEREFORD HO
STAMFORD COTTS
BLORE HO
BENHAM HO
LUCAS HO
BAILEY HO
BREDIN HO
FRANCIS HO
MATHISON HO
COLERIDGE SQ
CLARK HO
WALSINGHAM MANSIONS
STAMFORD GATE HO
MOORE PARK 410 CT
KING CHARLES HO
HARRIET HO
WANDON RD
THE SIR OSWALD STOLL FOUNDATION
WANSDOWN PLACE
HILARY CL
FULHAM RD
Offices
TETCOTT RD
THORNDIKE CL
WESTFIELD CL
POOLES LANE
LOTS ROAD
HOLMEAD ROAD
RUMBOLD ROAD
REWELL ST
SANDFORD ST
MAYNARD CL
ASTOR CT
BURFORD WLK
CAMBRIA ST
GWYN CL
KING'S ROAD
SOTHERON PL
CEDARNE ROAD
WALHAM GREEN COURT
LORD ROBERTS MEWS
MOOR PARK ROAD
WATERFORD RD
BRITANNIA ROAD
DAN LENO WLK
GRANVILLE PLACE
MAXWELL ROAD
REGAL PL
BRITANNIA WAY
HARWOOD ROAD
HARWOOD MEWS
CLARE MEWS
KEMPSON RD
BLAKE GDNS
MUSGRAVE CRES
TYRAWLEY RD
B318
Fulham Broadway Sh Ctr
WALHAM GREEN ARC
PO
26

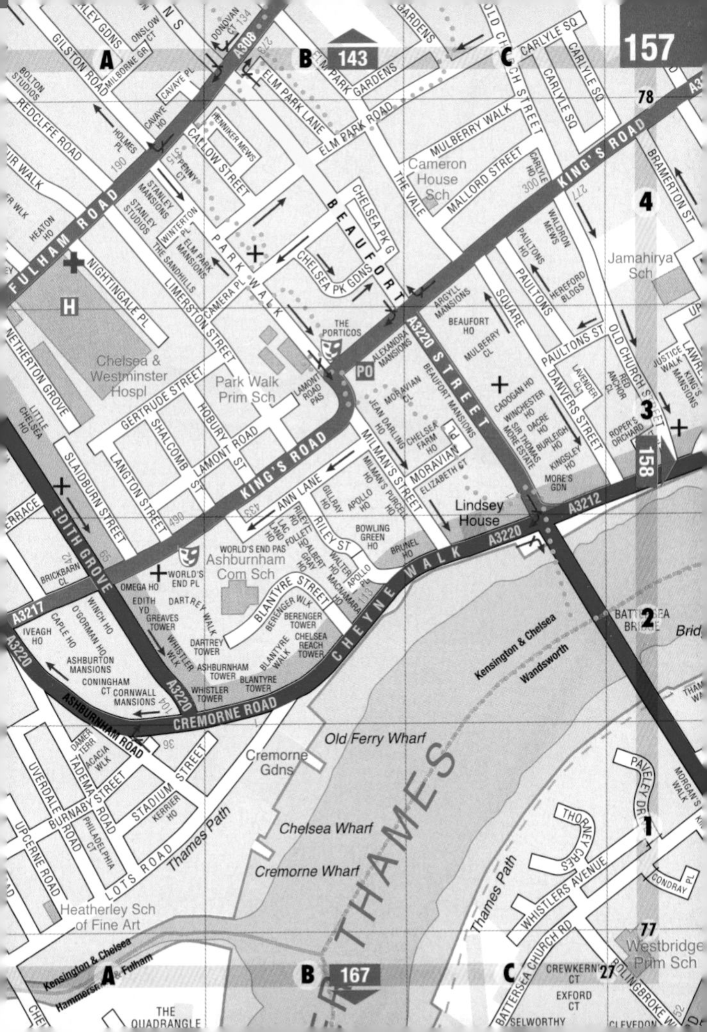
143
167
158
A
B
C
A
B
C
1
2
3
4
78
77
FULHAM ROAD
KING'S ROAD
GILSTON ROAD
REDCLIFFE ROAD
BOLTON STUDIOS
MILBORNE GR
ONSLOW CT
DONOVAN CT
CAVAYE PL
CAVAYE HO
HOLMES PL
A308
ELM PARK GARDENS
ELM PARK LANE
ELM PARK ROAD
OLD CHURCH STREET
CARLYLE SQ
MULBERRY WALK
MALLORD STREET
CARLYLE HO
Cameron House Sch
THE VALE
HENNIKER MEWS
CALLOW STREET
PENNY CT
STANLEY MANSIONS
STANLEY STUDIOS
WINTERTON PL
ELM PARK MANSIONS
THE SANDHILLS
LIMERSTON STREET
CAMERA PL
PARK WALK
BEAUFORT STREET
CHELSEA PK G
CHELSEA PK GDNS
THE PORTICOS
HEATON HO
NIGHTINGALE PL
H
Chelsea & Westminster Hospl
NETHERTON GROVE
LITTLE CHELSEA HO
GERTRUDE STREET
SHALCOMB ST
HOBURY ST
LAMONT ROAD
LAMONT ROAD PAS
Park Walk Prim Sch
PO
ALEXANDRA MANSIONS
ARGYLL MANSIONS
BEAUFORT HO
MULBERRY CL
A3220
PAULTONS HO
PAULTONS SQUARE
WALDRON MEWS
HEREFORD BLDGS
PAULTONS ST
DANVERS STREET
LAVENDER CL
RED ANCHOR CL
ROPER'S ORCHARD
JUSTICE WALK
KING'S MANSIONS
BRAMERTON ST
Jamahirya Sch
MORAVIAN CL
BEAUFORT MANSIONS
JEAN DARLING HO
CHELSEA FARM HO
MORAVIAN PL
ELIZABETH CT
CADOGAN HO
WINCHESTER HO
DACRE HO
SIR THOMAS MORE ESTATE
BURLEIGH HO
KINGSLEY HO
MORE'S GDN
Lindsey House
A3212
SLAIDBURN STREET
LANGTON STREET
EDITH GROVE
ANN LANE
MILMAN'S STREET
MILMAN'S HO
PURCELL HO
GILLRAY HO
APOLLO HO
RILEY ST
RILEY HO
LACLAND HO
FOLLETT HO
ALBERT GRAY HO
BOWLING GREEN HO
BRUNEL HO
WALTER HO
APOLLO PL
MACNAMARA HO
CHEYNE WALK
WORLD'S END PAS
Ashburnham Com Sch
WORLD'S END PL
OMEGA HO
EDITH YD
DARTREY WALK
GREAVES TOWER
BLANTYRE STREET
BERENGER WLK
BERENGER TOWER
CHELSEA REACH TOWER
BLANTYRE WALK
DARTREY TOWER
WHISTLER WLK
ASHBURNHAM TOWER
BLANTYRE TOWER
WHISTLER TOWER
BRICKBARN CL
A3217
IVEAGH HO
CAPLE HO
O'GORMAN HO
WINCH HO
ASHBURTON MANSIONS
CONINGHAM CT
CORNWALL MANSIONS
CREMORNE ROAD
ASHBURNHAM ROAD
BATTERSEA BRIDGE
Kensington & Chelsea
Wandsworth
Old Ferry Wharf
THAMES
Chelsea Wharf
Cremorne Wharf
Cremorne Gdns
DAMER TERR
ACACIA WLK
TADEMA ROAD
BURNABY STREET
STADIUM STREET
KERRIER HO
PHILADELPHIA CT
LOTS ROAD
Thames Path
UVERDALE ROAD
UPCERNE ROAD
Heatherley Sch of Fine Art
Kensington & Chelsea
Hammersmith & Fulham
THE QUADRANGLE
PAVELEY DR
MORGAN'S WALK
THORNEY CRES
WHISTLERS AVENUE
CONDRAY PL
BATTERSEA CHURCH RD
CREWKERNE CT
EXFORD CT
SELWORTHY
BOLINGBROKE WK
Westbridge Prim Sch
CLEVEDON

A
B
C
144
Offices
MANRESA ROAD
KING'S ROAD
A3217
B304
KING'S COURT N
KING'S COURT S
CHELSEA MANOR ST
CHELSEA TOWERS
SWAN CT
FLOOD WALK
MANOR STREET ESTATE
CHELSEA MANOR CT
FLOOD STREET
REDESDALE ST
REDBURN STREET
TEDWORTH GDNS
TEDWORTH SQUARE
RALSTON ST
CHRISTCHURCH STREET
CHRISTCHURCH TERR
CAVERSHAM ST
HAYDEN PIPER HO
CHEYNE PL
Christchurch CE Prim Sch
CARLYLE SQ
78
CARLYLE HO
BRAMERTON ST
GLEBE PLACE
MARGARETTA TERR
OAKLEY STREET
GROVE HO
OAKLEY GARDENS
ALPHA PL
ROSSETTI STUDIOS
CHESIL CT
ST LOO CT
ST LOO AVE
ROSSETTI GDNS MANSIONS
ROBINSON ST
CHEYNE CT
The English Gardening Sch
Chelsea Physic Garden
4
WALDRON MEWS
PAULTONS HO
PAULTONS
HEREFORD BLDGS
Jamahirya Sch
UPPER CHEYNE ROW
PHENE ST
ADAIR HO
HON CONSUL SURINAME
CHEYNE MEWS
CHEYNE GDNS
B302
Thames Path
CHELSEA
Carlyle's House
PAULTONS ST
OLD CHURCH STREET
JUSTICE WALK
LAWRENCE ST
KING'S MANSIONS
CHELSEA ESTATE LAWRENCE MANS
CHEYNE ROW
SHREWSBURY HO
PIER HO
E
LAVENDER CT
RED ANCHOR CL
LORDSHIP PLACE
CARLYLE MANS
CHEYNE WALK
A3031
3
DANVERS STREET
DACRE HO
ROPER'S ORCHARD
PETYT PLACE
Cadogan Pier
RIVER T
Chel
157
A3212
ALBERT BRIDGE (SUSPENSION)
Terrace Wa
Thames Path
2
BATTERSEA BRIDGE
BridgeWharf
Wandsworth
WATERSIDE POINT
RIVERSIDE
ALBION RIVERSIDE
THAMES WALK
RANSOMES MEWS
ANHALT ROAD
CRANBOURNE CT
CARRIAGE DRIVE NORTH
GREAT EASTERN WHARF
HESTER ROAD
Ransome's Dock
Pav
PAVELEY DRIVE
MORGAN'S WALK
RADSTOCK ST
ELCHO STREET
Bsns Ctr
PARKGATE ROAD
ST MARY-LE-PARK CT
ALBANY MANSIONS
ALBERT BRIDGE ROAD
Festival
Gard
P
1
THORNEY CRES
HOWIE ST
KINGSWATER PL
Royal Coll of Art Sculpture Sch
Govt Offices
WHISTLERS AVENUE
CONDRAY PL
PO
BATTERSEA BRIDGE ROAD
SEARLES CL
JUER STREET
WORFIELD ST
STAFFORD MANSIONS
CARRIAGE DRIVE WEST
77
B305
Westbridge Prim Sch
MUSGRAVE CT
HENTY CL
HERON HO
MASKELYNE CL
CREWKERNE CT
27
EXFORD CT
BOLINGBROKE
168
JAGGER HO
HYDE LA

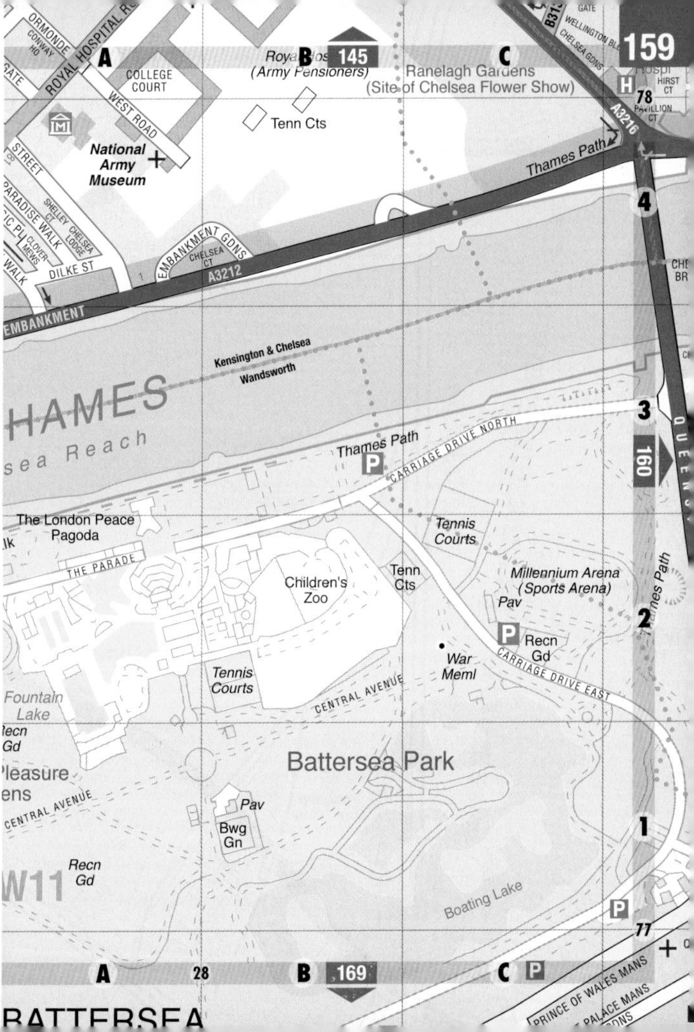
A
B
C
145
ORMONDE
CONWAY HO
ROYAL HOSPITAL RD
GATE
COLLEGE COURT
WEST ROAD
National Army Museum
STREET
PARADISE WALK
SHELLEY CT
CHELSEA LODGE
CLOVER MEWS
DILKE ST
WALK
EMBANKMENT
EMBANKMENT GDNS
CHELSEA CT
A3212
(Army Pensioners)
Tenn Cts
Ranelagh Gardens
(Site of Chelsea Flower Show)
WELLINGTON BLDGS
CHELSEA GDNS
HIRST CT
78
PAVILLION CT
A3216
Thames Path
4
Kensington & Chelsea
Wandsworth
THAMES
Reach
3
CARRIAGE DRIVE NORTH
Thames Path
160
The London Peace Pagoda
THE PARADE
Tennis Courts
Tenn Cts
Children's Zoo
Millennium Arena
(Sports Arena)
Pav
2
Recn Gd
War Meml
CARRIAGE DRIVE EAST
Tennis Courts
CENTRAL AVENUE
Fountain Lake
Recn Gd
Battersea Park
Pleasure
CENTRAL AVENUE
Pav
Bwg Gn
1
Recn Gd
W11
Boating Lake
77
28
169
PRINCE OF WALES MANS
PALACE MANS
BATTERSEA

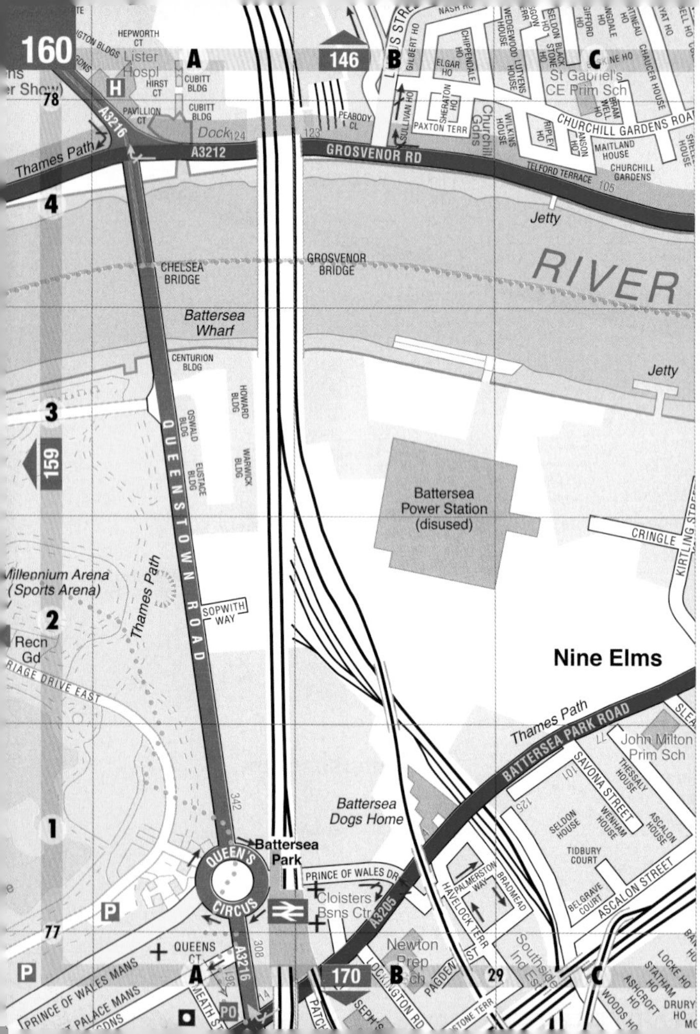
146
159
170
A
B
C
78
77
4
3
2
1
HEPWORTH CT
Lister Hospl
HIRST CT
CUBITT BLDG
CUBITT BLDG
PAVILLION CT
Dock
124
123
PEABODY CL
A3216
A3212
Thames Path
GROSVENOR RD
GILBERT HO
ELGAR HO
CHIPPENDALE HO
SHERATON HO
PAXTON TERR
SULLIVAN HO
Churchill Gdns
WEDGEWOOD HOUSE
LUTYENS HOUSE
WILKINS HOUSE
SELDON HO
BLACK STONE HO
GIFFORD HO
CHAUCER HOUSE
St Gabriel's CE Prim Sch
BRAMWELL HO
RIPLEY HO
ANSON HO
CHURCHILL GARDENS ROAD
MAITLAND HOUSE
CHURCHILL GARDENS
TELFORD TERRACE
105
Jetty
RIVER
CHELSEA BRIDGE
GROSVENOR BRIDGE
Battersea Wharf
CENTURION BLDG
HOWARD BLDG
OSWALD BLDG
EUSTACE BLDG
WARWICK BLDG
QUEENSTOWN ROAD
Jetty
Battersea Power Station (disused)
CRINGLE
KIRTLING STREET
Millennium Arena (Sports Arena)
Thames Path
SOPWITH WAY
Recn Gd
CARRIAGE DRIVE EAST
Nine Elms
Thames Path
BATTERSEA PARK ROAD
John Milton Prim Sch
SAVONA STREET
THESSALY HOUSE
101
125
SELDON HOUSE
WENHAM HOUSE
ASCALON HOUSE
TIDBURY COURT
BELGRAVE COURT
ASCALON STREET
Battersea Dogs Home
342
QUEEN'S CIRCUS
Battersea Park
PRINCE OF WALES DR
Cloisters Bsns Ctr
A3205
PALMERSTON WAY
BRADMEAD
HAVELOCK TERR
Southside Ind Est
Newton Prep Sch
PAGDEN ST
29
LOCKINGTON RD
QUEENS CT
308
A3216
PRINCE OF WALES MANS
PO
LOCKE HO
STATHAM HO
ASHCROFT HO
DRURY HO
WOODS HO

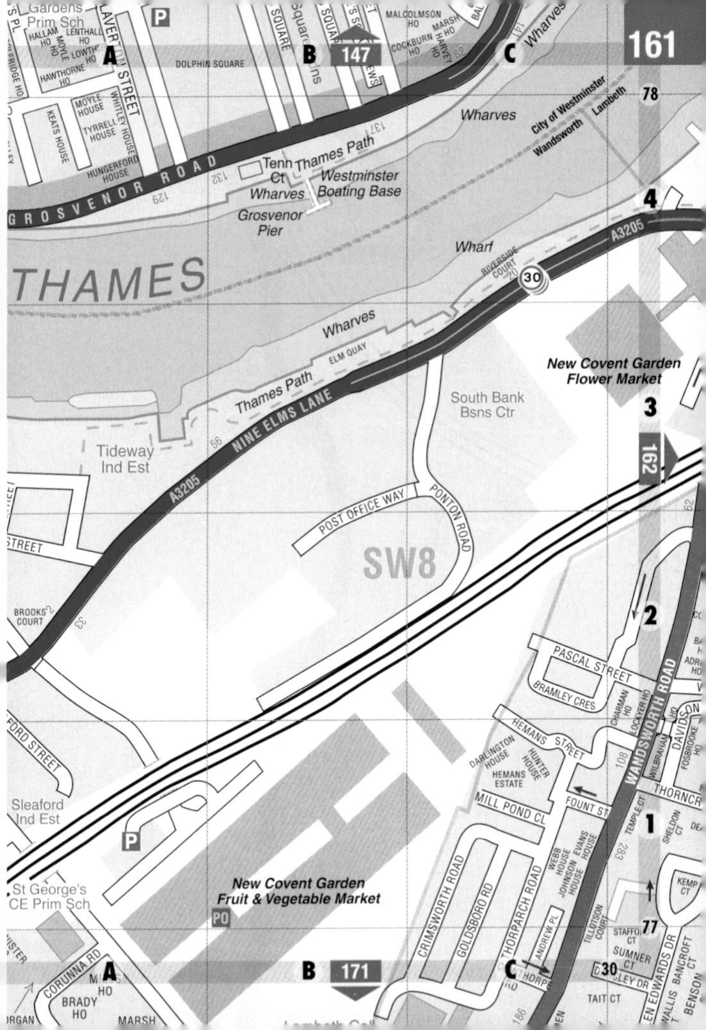
Gardens Prim Sch
HALLAM HO
LENTHALL HO
MOYLE HO
LOWTHER HO
HAWTHORNE HO
LAVERTON STREET
DOLPHIN SQUARE
MALCOLMSON HO
COCKBURN HO
MARSH HO
HARVEY HO
147
Wharves
City of Westminster
Wandsworth
Lambeth
78
MOYLE HOUSE
TYRRELL HOUSE
WHITLEY HOUSE
KEATS HOUSE
HUNGERFORD HOUSE
GROSVENOR ROAD
Tenn Ct
Thames Path
Westminster Boating Base
Wharves
Grosvenor Pier
4
THAMES
Wharf
A3205
RIVERSIDE COURT
30
Wharves
ELM QUAY
New Covent Garden Flower Market
Thames Path
NINE ELMS LANE
South Bank Bsns Ctr
3
Tideway Ind Est
162
A3205
POST OFFICE WAY
PONTON ROAD
STREET
SW8
BROOKS COURT
2
PASCAL STREET
BRAMLEY CRES
CHARMAN HO
LOCKYER HO
WANDSWORTH ROAD
DAVIDSON
HEMANS STREET
DARLINGTON HOUSE
HUNTER HOUSE
HEMANS ESTATE
WILBRAHAM HO
FOSBROOKE HO
THORNCR
MILL POND CL
FOUNT ST
TEMPLE CT
SHELDON CT
1
Sleaford Ind Est
WEBB HOUSE
JOHNSON HOUSE
EVANS HOUSE
KEMP CT
St George's CE Prim Sch
New Covent Garden Fruit & Vegetable Market
PO
CRIMSWORTH ROAD
GOLDSBORO RD
THORPARCH ROAD
ANDREW PL
TILLOTSON COURT
STAFFORD CT
77
SUMNER CT
EDWARDS DR
BANCROFT CT
WALLIS
BENSON
CORUNNA RD
BRADY HO
MARSH
171
30
TAIT CT

A
B
C
148
172
161
Vauxhall
Vauxhall Cross
ST GEORGE WHARF
Thames Path
City of Westminster
Lambeth
Wandsworth
A3036
A3205
A3204
A202
A203
PARRY ST
BONDWAY
S LAMBETH PL
AUCKLAND ST
GLYN ST
DURHAM ST A3204
HARLEYFORD ROAD
St Anne's RC Prim Sch
PIPPIN CT
ROSEWOOD HO
VAUXHALL GROVE
BONNINGTON SQUARE
LANGLEY MANSIONS
LANGLEY LANE
PARK MANSIONS
LAWN LANE
BANNERMAN HOUSE
EBBISHAM DRIVE
New Covent Garden Flower Market
MILES STREET
RUDOLF PL
WENDLE CT
Vauxhall Park
Tenn Cts
Bwg Gn
STANLEY CL
PO
TRENCHOLD ST
WYVIL ROAD
HANBURY HO
VAT HOUSE
REGENTS BRIDGE GDNS
BEAUFOY HO
RITA ROAD
MEADOW ROAD
FENTIMAN ROAD
QUINTON HO
FRANK HO
GILBERT HO
Wyvil Prim Sch
HENRY HO
EDGAR HO
DAVID HO
LUSCOMBE WAY
OLIVER HO
NORMAN HO
PETER HO
MARTIN HO
CONRAD HO
BASIL HO
ADRIAN HO
WHEATSHEAF LANE
SOUTH LAMBETH ROAD
OLD SOUTH LAMBETH ROAD
HEYFORD AVE
HEYFORD TERR
WALTON CL
KINGS HO
CASTLE HO
WILCOX CL
Liby
MEADOW PL
St Stephen's CE Prim Sch
BEAMINSTER HO
DORSET ROAD
HORTON HO
MELBURY HO
BLANDFORD HO
WAREHAM HO
CARROUN ROAD
IBBERTON HO
BRANKSOME HO
CHARMOUTH HO
ENSBURY HO
CORFE HO
LULWORTH HO
PASCAL STREET
BRAMLEY CRES
WILCOX ROAD
DAVIDSON GARDENS
CHARMAN HO
LOCKYER HO
WANDSWORTH ROAD
HEMANS STREET
HUNTER HOUSE
WILBRAHAM HO
FOSBROOKE HO
ALDWYN HO
COURTHOPE HO
DARYNGTON HO
EASTRY HO
LANG HO
BURDEN HO
Herbert Morrison Prim Sch
KENCHESTER CLOSE
ROSETTA CL
BROUGH CL
KINGSWOOD CL
PICKWORTH CL
BISHOPS HO
KNIGHTS HO
WALBERSWICK STREET
TRADESCANT RD
WEYMOUTH HO
ELY COTTS
BOLNEY ST
ST STEPHEN'S TERR
SHERBORNE HO
PURBECK HO
PULHAM HO
MELCOMBE HO
SWANAGE HO
KIBWORTH ST
WILKINSON STREET
CROZIER HO
MYTTON HO
ALBERT SQUARE
FOUNT ST
THORNCROFT ST
TEMPLE CT
SHELDON CT
DEAN CT
ABBOT CT
HARTINGTON ROAD
MAWBEY ST
THORNE ROAD
ALDEBERT TERRACE
WEBB HOUSE
JOHNSON HOUSE
EVANS HOUSE
KEMP CT
CAMELLIA ST
LANSCOMBE WLK
CAVENDISH HO
SELWAY HO
SADDLERS MEWS
SW8
TILLOTSON COURT
STAFFORD CT
SUMNER CT
EDWARDS DR
BANCROFT CT
BENSON CT
ANDREW PL
TAIT CT
VICEROY
KELVEDON HO
MONDRAGON HO
RUNDELL TOWER
30
77
78

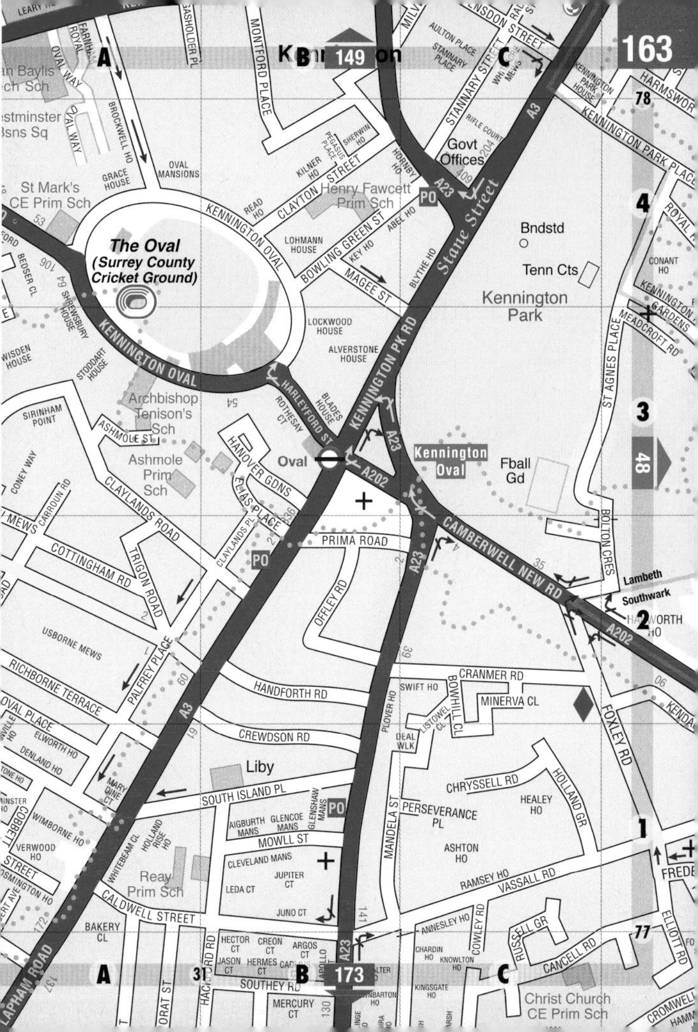
Kennington
149
173
48
A
B
C
1
2
3
4
The Oval
(Surrey County
Cricket Ground)
Oval
Kennington
Oval
Kennington
Park
Bndstd
Tenn Cts
Fball
Gd
Govt
Offices
Stane Street
A3
A23
A202
KENNINGTON OVAL
KENNINGTON PK RD
CAMBERWELL NEW RD
CLAPHAM ROAD
HARLEYFORD ST
BOWLING GREEN ST
CLAYTON STREET
MAGEE ST
MONTFORD PLACE
GASHOLDER PL
OVAL WAY
BROCKWELL HO
GRACE HOUSE
OVAL MANSIONS
St Mark's
CE Prim Sch
Henry Fawcett
Prim Sch
LOHMANN HOUSE
KILNER HO
PEGASUS PLACE
SHERWIN HO
READ HO
HORNBY HO
KEY HO
ABEL HO
BLYTHE HO
LOCKWOOD HOUSE
ALVERSTONE HOUSE
BLADES HOUSE
ROTHESAY CT
AULTON PLACE
STANNARY PLACE
STANNARY STREET
KENNINGTON PARK HOUSE
HARMSWORTH
KENNINGTON PARK PLACE
ROYAL
CONANT HO
KENNINGTON GARDENS
MEADCROFT RD
ST AGNES PLACE
BOLTON CRES
Lambeth
Southwark
HAYWORTH HO
RIFLE COURT
PO
BEDSER CL
SHREWSBURY HOUSE
WISDEN HOUSE
STODDART HOUSE
Archbishop
Tenison's
Sch
SIRINHAM POINT
ASHMOLE ST
Ashmole
Prim
Sch
CONEY WAY
CARROUN RD
CLAYLANDS ROAD
HANOVER GDNS
ELIAS PLACE
CLAYLANDS PL
PRIMA ROAD
OFFLEY RD
COTTINGHAM RD
TRIGON ROAD
USBORNE MEWS
RICHBORNE TERRACE
PALFREY PLACE
OVAL PLACE
ELWORTH HO
DENLAND HO
HANDFORTH RD
CREWDSON RD
CRANMER RD
SWIFT HO
BOWHILL CL
MINERVA CL
PLOVER HO
LISTOWEL CL
DEAL WLK
FOXLEY RD
KENDAL
Liby
SOUTH ISLAND PL
MARY DINE CT
WIMBORNE HO
VERWOOD HO
COBBETT STREET
OSMINGTON HO
WHITEBEAM CL
HOLLAND RISE HO
Reay
Prim Sch
CALDWELL STREET
BAKERY CL
AIGBURTH MANS
GLENCOE MANS
GLENSHAW MANS
MOWLL ST
CLEVELAND MANS
JUPITER CT
LEDA CT
JUNO CT
MANDELA ST
PERSEVERANCE PL
CHRYSSELL RD
HEALEY HO
HOLLAND GR
ASHTON HO
RAMSEY HO
VASSALL RD
ANNESLEY HO
COWLEY RD
RUSSELL GR
CANCELL RD
ELLIOTT RD
CHARDIN HO
KNOWLTON HO
KINGSGATE HO
HECTOR CT
CREON CT
ARGOS CT
JASON CT
HERMES CT
SOUTHEY RD
MERCURY CT
Christ Church
CE Prim Sch
CROMWELL
FREDE
78
77

FULHAM
SW6
SW6
A
B
C
154
58
47
1
2
3
4
76
77
24
A219
A304
A308
FULHAM PALACE RD
FULHAM RD
FULHAM HIGH ST
NEW KING'S RD
ATALANTA ST
BRANKSEA ST
KINGWOOD ROAD
WYFOLD ROAD
KILMAINE ROAD
REPORTON RD
FILMER RD
BLOOM PARK RD
MARVILLE ROAD
BISHOPS RD
FERNHURST RD
MUNSTER RESIDENCES
DANEHURST ST
CHILDERLEY ST
MARRYAT SQ
THE CODA CTR
Henry Compton Sec Sch
CONNAUGHT MANS
LAMBROOK TERR
SIDBURY ST
WARDO AVE
GOWAN AVE
St John's CE Prim Sch
ROSTREVOR MANS
PENHURST MANS
AVONDALE MANS
DEEPDENE MANS
FILMER HO
FILMER MEWS
FLORENCE MANS
HAZELWOOD MANSIONS
QUENINGTON MANSIONS
ROSTREVOR RD
CHESILTON RD
RADIPOLE RD
LILYVILLE
SWIFT ST
ROSTREVOR MEWS
FINLAY ST
ELLERBY ST
THE COURTYARD
VERA RD
PARK MANSIONS
KIMBELL GDNS
COLEHILL LA
HORDER RD
BURNFOOT AVE
FELDEN ST
MUNSTER RD
CROOKHAM
DANCER RD
PO
EDGARLEY TERR
FIRTH GDNS
ONERAILE ST
ELY COURT FLATS
RINGMER AVE
WALDEMAR AVENUE MANSIONS
COLEHILL GDNS
HESTERCOMBE AVE
DURRELL RD
WILSTON CT
ELMAR CT
CLARIDGE CT
WILLIAM BANFIELD HO
ARTHUR HENDERSON HOUSE
MUNSTER CT
CLONCURRY ST
BISHOP'S PARK RD
Tenn Cts
LALOR ST
WALDEMAR AVE
OXBERRY AVE
DORNCLIFFE RD
BISHOP'S MANSIONS
BISHOP'S AVE
Pav
The Moat Sch
Moat Gdn
ETHEL RANKIN CT
FULHAM PARK RD
New King's Prim Sch
LANDRIDGE RD
DRIVE MANS
ROMILY CT
FULHAM PARK GDNS
ELYSIUM GATE
Bwg Gn
DWIGHT CT
BURLINGTON PL
RIGAULT RD
ELYSIUM PL
Allot Gdns
ELYSIUM ST
BEAR CROFT HO
EWALD RD
Fulham Palace
PARKVIEW CT
BURLINGTON RD
BURLINGTON GDNS
BUER RD
GRIMSTON RD
DOLBY RD
MELBRAY MEWS
Fulham Prep Sch
Bishop's Park
RIVER THAMES
STEEPLE CL
SIR WILLIAM POWELL'S ALMSHOS
DENHURST AVE
RANELAGH AVE
Putney Bridge
STATION
GONVILLE
W15

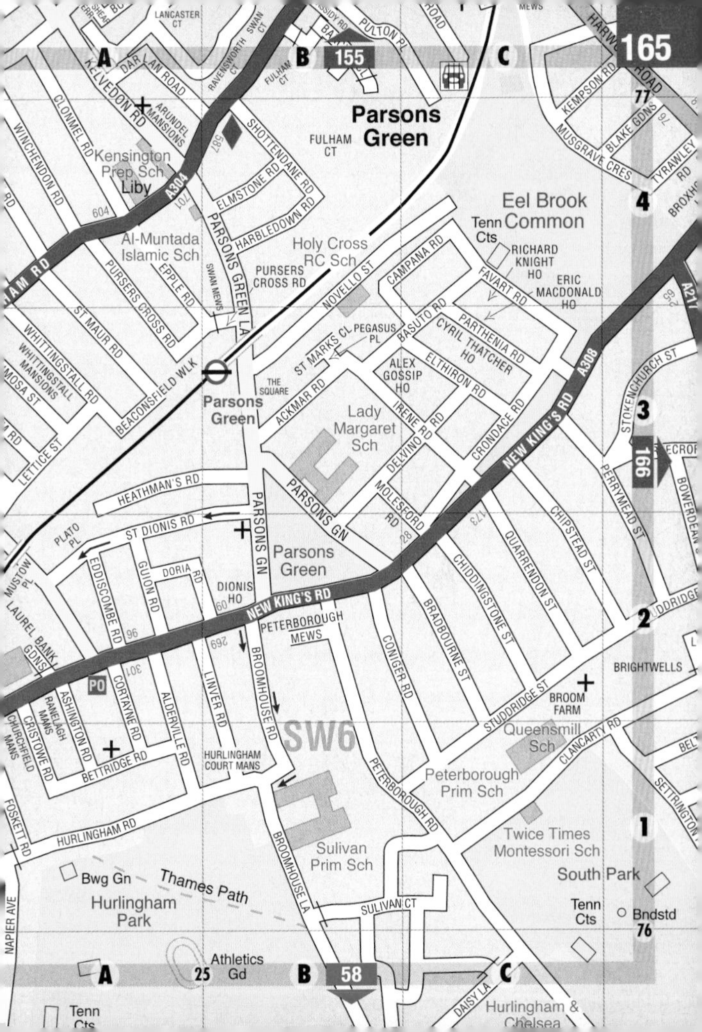

Parsons Green
Fulham Ct
Lancaster Ct
Swan Ravensworth Ct
Pulton Pl
Dar Lan Road
Kelvedon Rd
Arundel Mansions
Clonmel Rd
Winchendon Rd
Kensington Prep Sch
Liby
A304
Elmstone Rd
Shottendane Rd
Harbledown Rd
Parsons Green La
Swan Mews
Al-Muntada Islamic Sch
Holy Cross RC Sch
Pursers Cross Rd
Epple Rd
St Maur Rd
Whittingstall Rd
Whittingstall Mansions
Beaconsfield Wlk
Lettice St
Novello St
Campana Rd
Eel Brook Common
Tenn Cts
Richard Knight Ho
Eric Macdonald Ho
Favart Rd
Parthenia Rd
Cyril Thatcher Ho
Basuto Rd
Pegasus Pl
St Marks Cl
The Square
Ackmar Rd
Alex Gossip Ho
Elthiron Rd
Irene Rd
Delvino Rd
Crondace Rd
Lady Margaret Sch
New King's Rd
A308
Stokenchurch St
Perrymead St
Bowerdean St
Heathman's Rd
St Dionis Rd
Plato Pl
Parsons Gn
Molesford Rd
Chipstead St
Quarrendon St
Chiddingstone St
Bradbourne St
Mustow Pl
Eddiscombe Rd
Guion Rd
Doria Rd
Dionis Ho
Laurel Bank Gdns
Peterborough Mews
Broomhouse Rd
Coniger Rd
Studdridge St
Brightwells
Broom Farm
Queensmill Sch
Clancarty Rd
PO
Ashington Rd
Ranelagh Mans
Cortayne Rd
Alderville Rd
Linver Rd
Hurlingham Court Mans
SW6
Churchfield Mans
Cristowe Rd
Bettridge Rd
Peterborough Rd
Peterborough Prim Sch
Settrington Rd
Foskett Rd
Hurlingham Rd
Sulivan Prim Sch
Twice Times Montessori Sch
South Park
Bwg Gn
Thames Path
Hurlingham Park
Broomhouse La
Sulivan Ct
Bndstd
Napier Ave
Athletics Gd
Daisy La
Hurlingham & Chelsea
155
166
58

MOOR PARK RD
CLARE MEWS
HARWOOD ROAD
BRITANNIA ROAD
GRANVILLE PLACE
156
KING'S ROAD
CAMBRIA ST
MAYNARD CL
BURFORD WLK
ASTOR CT
GWYN CL
SOTHERON PL
KEMPSON RD
BLAKE GDNS
MUSGRAVE CRES
TYRAWLEY RD
BROXHOLME HO
B318
BRITANNIA WAY
EDITH ROW
MICHAEL RD
Gas Works
AVALON RD
SANDS END LA
Eel Brook Common
RICHARD KNIGHT HO
ERIC MACDONALD HO
PETERBOROUGH VILLAS
HARWOOD TERR
IMPERIAL SQ
EMDEN ST
CHERYLS CL
IMPERIAL RD
A217
A308
CRESFORD RD
MELDON CL
ACFOLD RD
BOVINGDON RD
MANOR CT
FULMEAD ST
MALTINGS PL
BAGLEY'S LA
TALINA CTR
THE BOULEVARD
STOKENCHURCH ST
NEW KING'S RD
165
RYECROFT ST
SANDILANDS RD
JEPSON HO
PEARSCROFT RD
PEARSCROFT CT
STANFORD CT
Chelsea Coll of Art & Design
WANDSWORTH BRIDGE RD
CHIPSTEAD ST
PERRYMEAD ST
BOWERDEAN ST
BULOW CT
BROUGHTON ROAD APP
Langford Prim Sch
STEPHENDALE RD
ELSWICK ST
ELBE ST
TOWNMEAD RD
QUARRENDON ST
LANGFORD RD
MARINEFIELD RD
ELIZABETH BARNES CT
GILSTEAD RD
TYNEMOUTH ST
Thames Path
STUDDRIDGE ST
Liby
PO
LOWLANDS
L'Ecole des Petits Sch
BROUGHTON RD
LINDROP ST
BRIGHTWELLS
FURNESS RD
GLENROSA ST
GREENSWARD HO
BROOM FARM
HAZLEBURY RD
Liby
Queensmill Sch
CLANCARTY RD
BELTRAN RD
SNOWBURY RD
BYAM ST
CHARLOW CL
POTTERS RD
ASHCOMBE ST
CRANBURY RD
STEPHENDALE RD
QUERRIN ST
TOWNMEAD RD
SETTRINGTON RD
OAKBURY RD
WATERMEADOW LA
Twice Times Montessori Sch
NARBOROUGH ST
KILKIE ST
ROSEBURY RD
EDENVALE ST
South Park
FRISTON ST
Sp Ctr
WILLIAM MORRIS WAY
Tenn Cts
Bndstd
ALTHEA ST
WOOLNEIGH ST
SOUTH PARK MEWS
HAMBLE ST
Townmead Bsns Ctr
SAILMAKERS CT
59
GURNEY RD
BARTON HO
DE MORGAN RD
Sands End
Hurlingham & Chelsea

A
B
C
157
Cremorne Wharf
Heatherley Sch of Fine Art
Kensington & Chelsea
Hammersmith & Fulham
CHELSEA HARBOUR DR
THE QUADRANGLE
THAMES AVE
ADMIRAL SQ
ADMIRAL CT
KING'S QUAY
THAMES QUAY
Chelsea Harbour Design Ctr
HARBOUR AVE
THE BELVEDERE
CHELSEA CRES
Chelsea Harbour Pier
Fulham Bsns Exchange
RIVER THAMES
Hammersmith & Fulham
Wandsworth
Thames Path
WHISTLERS AVENUE
BATTERSEA CHURCH RD
CREWKERNE CT
EXFORD CT
SELWORTHY HO
CHELWOOD CT
SPARKFORD HO
MISTERTON CT
SHEPTON CT
SUNBURY LA
CLEVEDON CT
DRAYCOTT CT
BOLINGBROKE WLK
Westbridge Prim Sch
WESTBRIDGE RD
77
4
OLD SWAN WHARF
VICARAGE WLK
BLOMFIELD CT 1
BOWSTEAD CT 2
VALIANT HO
BATTERSEA SQ
GRANFIELD ST
PRICHARD CT
BURNETT CT
COMPTON HO
WIGFORD CT
PARKHAM ST
THE RIVERAINS
VICARAGE CRES
COTSWOLD MEWS
ALTHORPE MEWS
HUMPHREY CT
LINDSAY CT
Salesian Coll
3
Royal Academy of Dance
Thomas's London Day Schs
CORBEL ST
168
EATON HO
HAYTHORN HO
ARCHER HO
WHITE HO
WINFIELD HO
RESTORATION SQ
POWRIE HO
BATTERSEA HIGH ST
COLES CT
TROTT ST
MEECHAM CT
B305
GROVESIDE CT
VICARAGE CRES
WINDSOR CT
MORGAN CT
Tenn Cts
Fred Wells Gdns
ORVILLE RD
McKIERNAN CT
GAITSKELL CT
WINDERS RD
2
Regent Wharf
LOMBARD RD
GWYNNE RD
HARROWAY RD
TOTTERIDGE HO
YELVERTON RD
BADRIC CT
HOLMAN RD
SIMPSON ST
BATTERSEA HIGH ST
A3205
A3207
1
York Rd Bsns Ctr
YORK RD
Heliport
The Heliport Est
BRIDGES CT
B305
A3205
FAWCETT CL
COPPOCK CL
FAIRCHILD CL
WYE ST
PENGE HO
MUSJID RD
KAMBALA RD
HEAVER RD
WOLFTONCROFT CL
76
McDERMOTT CL
Falconbrook Prim Sch
Battersea Reach
59
York Gdns
PENNETHORNE HO
MANTUA ST
JOHN KIRK HO
PRICES CT
27

158
60
167
A
B
C
1
2
3
4
Sculpture Sch
CONDRAY PL
PO
B305
BATTERSEA BRIDGE ROAD
HENTY CL
JUER STREET
WORFIELD ST
STAFFORD MANSIONS
BRIDGE ROAD
CARRIAGE DRIVE WEST
P
WHISTLER
BATTERSEA CHURCH
77
Westbridge Prim Sch
MUSGRAVE CT
HYDE LA
ETHELBURGA ST
HERON HO
MASKELYNE CL
JAGGER HO
ALBERT MANS
ALBERT STUDIOS
CREWKERNE CT
EXFORD CT
BOLINGBROKE WLK
RANDALL CL
VILLIERS CT
ETHELBURGA TOWER
SELWORTHY HO
WOOD CT
CLEVEDON CT
DRAYCOTT CT
SPARKFORD HO
MISTERTON CT
WHITGIFT HO
GARDINER HO
SANCROFT CT
WATFORD CL
PETWORTH ST
ROSENAU RD
SHEPTON CT
WESTBRIDGE RD
WIGRAM CT
FRASER CT
HARVEY CT
JACOBSON CT
MANSEL CT
BURNETT CT
COMPTON HO
CRANMER HO
MACEY HO
A3031
GRANFIELD ST
PARKHAM ST
SURREY LA
PRINCE OF WALES DR A3220
PRICHARD CT
ALTHORPE MEWS
HUMPHREY
Salesian Coll
Sch
CONNAUGHT MANS
ROSENAU CRES
PARK MANS
SOUDAN RD
LINDSAY CT
ORBEL ST
HENNING ST
EDNA ST
URSULA ST
OCTAVIA ST
BRIDGE LA
CAMBRIDGE MANS
CAMBRIDGE RD
FOXMORE ST
RESTORATION SQ
COLES CT
TROTT ST
McCARTHY CT
KERSLEY MEWS
POWRIE HO
MEECHAM CT
SHUTTLEWORTH RD
STANMER ST
BANBURY ST
KERSLEY ST
BATTERSEA HIGH ST
MORGAN CT
BALFERN ST
DOVEDALE COTTS
ROYDON CL
McKIERNAN CT
GOULDEN HO
BULLEN ST
INWORTH ST
COLESTOWN ST
A3220
WINDERS RD
BEAUFORT HO
GAITSKELL CT
HOME RD
BATTERSEA PARK RD
CROMBIE MEWS
FRERE ST
ATHERTON ST
LATCHMERE ST
HARLING CT
SOUTHSIDE QUARTER
BURNS RD
MATTHEWS ST
ABERCROMBIE ST
L Ctr
AMBROSE MEWS
STEVENSON HO
SIMPSON ST
ROWENA CRES
LATCHMERE RD
KNOWSLEY RD
A3205
CANDAHAR RD
CABUL RD
CRANLEIGH MEWS
POYNTZ RD
PATIENCE RD
FAWCETT CL
A3207
KHYBER RD
COPPOCK CL
FALCON RD
WAYFORD ST
TAKHAR MEWS
Sacred Heart Prim Sch, Battersea
SHELLWOOD RD
AFGHAN RD
NEPAUL RD
MUSJID RD
76
KAMBALA RD
HEAVER RD
HERTFORD CT
Falcon Park
Shillington Street Open Space
WOLFTON CROFT CL
McDERMOTT CL
KERRISON RD
ESTE RD
27
HICKS CL
MANTUA ST
JOHN KIRK HO
FALCON GR
Christ Church CE Prim Sch

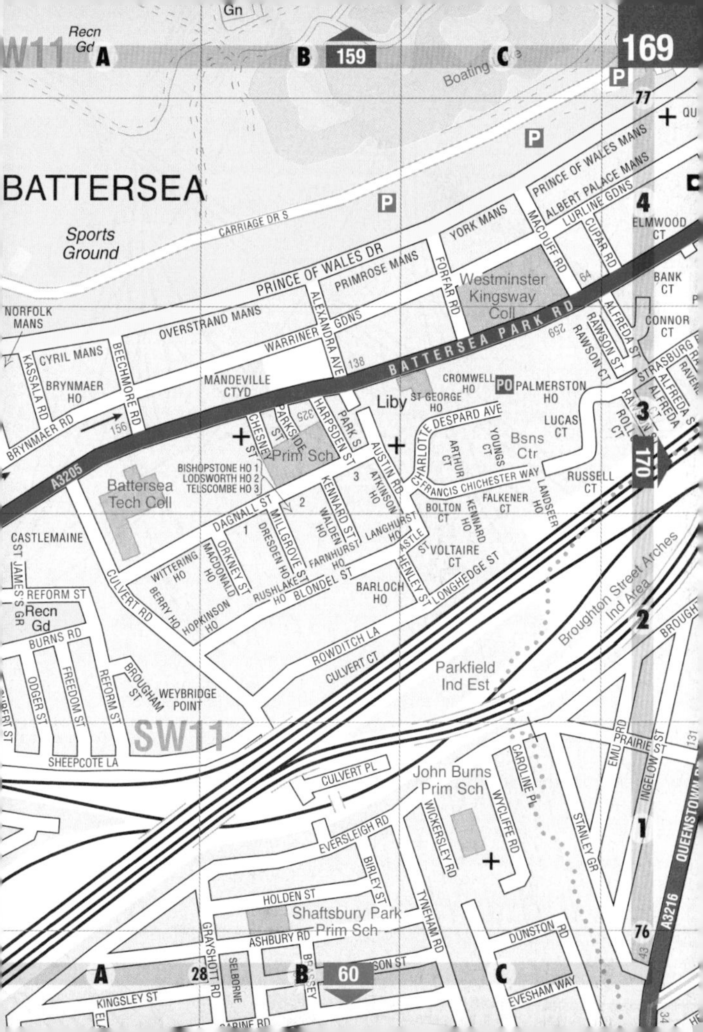
W11
Recn Gd
A
B
159
C
Gn
Boating Lake
77
BATTERSEA
Sports Ground
CARRIAGE DR S
PRINCE OF WALES DR
PRINCE OF WALES MANS
ALBERT PALACE MANS
LURLINE GDNS
4
ELMWOOD CT
YORK MANS
MACDUFF RD
CUPAR RD
PRIMROSE MANS
FORFAR RD
Westminster Kingsway Coll
64
BANK CT
ALFREDA ST
CONNOR CT
RAWSON ST
RAWSON CT
BATTERSEA PARK RD
259
NORFOLK MANS
OVERSTRAND MANS
ALEXANDRA AVE
WARRINER GDNS
138
CYRIL MANS
KASSALA RD
BRYNMAER HO
BEECHMORE RD
MANDEVILLE CTYD
CROMWELL HO
PO
PALMERSTON HO
STRASBURG RD
ALFREDA CT
Liby
ST GEORGE HO
CHARLOTTE DESPARD AVE
LUCAS CT
ROLL CT
3
BRYNMAER RD
156
CHESNEY ST
PARKSIDE ST
325
HARPSDEN ST
PARK S
Prim Sch
AUSTIN RD
ARTHUR CT
YOUNGS CT
Bsns Ctr
170
A3205
BISHOPSTONE HO 1
LODSWORTH HO 2
TELSCOMBE HO 3
Battersea Tech Coll
KENNARD ST
ATKINSON HO
FRANCIS CHICHESTER WAY
RUSSELL CT
DAGNALL ST
MILLGROVE ST
WALDEN HO
LANGHURST HO
BOLTON CT
KENNARD HO
FALKENER CT
LANDSEER HO
CASTLEMAINE
ORKNEY ST
DRESDEN HO
FARNHURST HO
ASTLE ST
VOLTAIRE CT
LONGHEDGE ST
WITTERING HO
MACDONALD HO
ST JAMES'S GR
REFORM ST
Recn Gd
BERRY HO
RUSHLAKE HO
BLONDEL ST
BARLOCH HO
HENLEY ST
Broughton Street Arches Ind Area
CULVERT RD
HOPKINSON HO
2
BROUGHTON
BURNS RD
ROWDITCH LA
Parkfield Ind Est
CULVERT CT
ODGER ST
FREEDOM ST
REFORM ST
BROUGHAM ST
WEYBRIDGE POINT
SW11
PRAIRIE ST
EMU RD
SHEEPCOTE LA
CULVERT PL
John Burns Prim Sch
CAROLINE PL
WYCLIFFE RD
INGELOW ST
131
QUEENSTOWN RD
STANLEY GR
1
WICKERSLEY RD
EVERSLEIGH RD
BIRLEY ST
HOLDEN ST
TYNEHAM RD
Shaftsbury Park Prim Sch
A3216
ASHBURY RD
DUNSTON RD
76
43
GRAYSHOTT RD
SELBORNE
BRASSEY
28
60
EVESHAM WAY
KINGSLEY ST
34

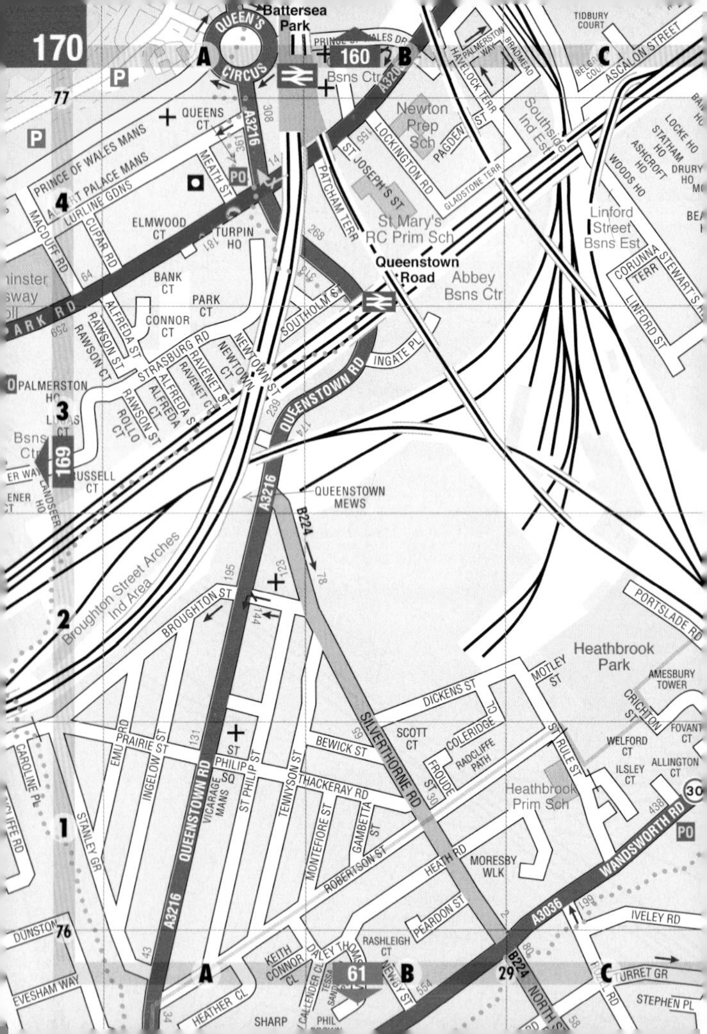

Battersea Park
QUEEN'S CIRCUS
PRINCE OF WALES DR
160
Bsns Ctr
A3205
A
B
C
TIDBURY COURT
ASCALON STREET
BELGRAVE COURT
PALMERSTON WAY
BRADMEAD
HAVELOCK TERR
Southside Ind Est
Newton Prep Sch
PAGDEN ST
LOCKINGTON RD
ST JOSEPH'S ST
GLADSTONE TERR
St Mary's RC Prim Sch
PATCHAM TERR
Queenstown Road
Abbey Bsns Ctr
LOCKE HO
STATHAM HO
ASHCROFT HO
WOODS HO
DRURY HO
Linford Street Bsns Est
CORUNNA TERR
STEWART'S RD
LINFORD ST
77
QUEENS CT
PRINCE OF WALES MANS
ALBERT PALACE MANS
LURLINE GDNS
MEATH ST
PO
A3216
308
361
4
MACDUFF RD
CUPAR RD
ELMWOOD CT
TURPIN HO
181
268
313
64
BANK CT
PARK CT
SOUTHOLM ST
PARK RD
259
ALFREDA ST
CONNOR CT
RAWSON ST
RAWSON CT
STRASBURG RD
RAVENET ST
NEWTOWN ST
NEWTOWN CT
INGATE PL
QUEENSTOWN RD
PALMERSTON HO
3
LUCAS CT
RAWSON ST
ROLLO CT
ALFREDA CT
ALFREDA ST
RAVENET CT
239
174
Bsns Ctr
169
RUSSELL CT
LANDSEER HO
QUEENSTOWN MEWS
B224
78
Broughton Street Arches Ind Area
195
BROUGHTON ST
123
144
2
PORTSLADE RD
Heathbrook Park
MOTLEY ST
AMESBURY TOWER
CRICHTON ST
DICKENS ST
COLERIDGE CL
SCOTT CT
FOVANT CT
WELFORD CT
ILSLEY CT
ALLINGTON CT
RADCLIFFE PATH
FROUDE ST
RULE ST
Heathbrook Prim Sch
30
438
WANDSWORTH RD
PO
SILVERTHORNE RD
65
BEWICK ST
THACKERAY RD
PRAIRIE ST
EMU RD
INGELOW RD
131
ST PHILIP ST
PHILIP SQ
VICARAGE MANS
TENNYSON ST
MONTEFIORE ST
GAMBETTA ST
ROBERTSON ST
HEATH RD
MORESBY WLK
PEARDON ST
CAROLINE PL
1
STANLEY GR
A3036
IVELEY RD
DUNSTON 76
43
RASHLEIGH CT
DALEY THOMPSON WAY
KEITH CONNOR CL
CALLENDER CL
TESSA SANDERSON PL
61
NEWBY ST
554
29
B224
NORTH ST
80
TURRET GR
STEPHEN PL
EVESHAM WAY
HEATHER CL
34
SHARP
PHIL BROWN
58

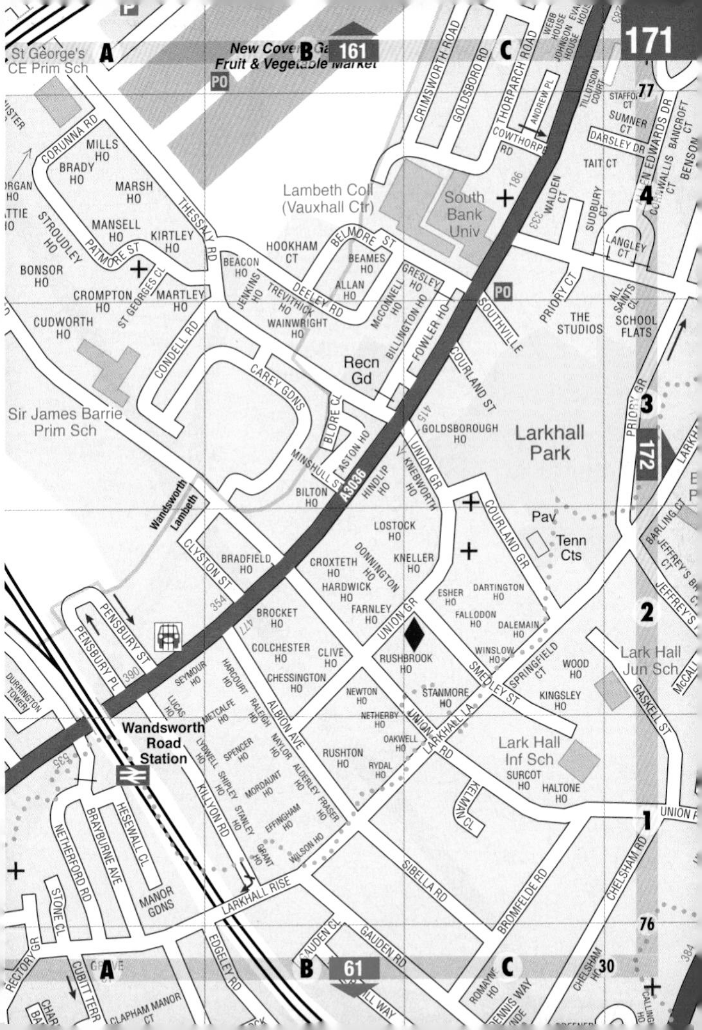

St George's CE Prim Sch
New Covent Garden Fruit & Vegetable Market
161
PO
CRIMSWORTH ROAD
GOLDSBORO RD
THORPARCH ROAD
ANDREW PL
COWTHORPE RD
WEBB HOUSE
JOHNSON HOUSE
TILLOTSON COURT
STAFFORD CT
77
SUMNER CT
DARSLEY DR
ALLEN EDWARDS DR
BANCROFT CT
BENSON
TAIT CT
CORNWALLIS CT
CORUNNA RD
MILLS HO
BRADY HO
MARSH HO
MORGAN HO
MANSELL HO
KIRTLEY HO
STROUDLEY HO
PATMORE ST
THESSALY RD
BONSOR HO
CROMPTON HO
ST GEORGES CL
MARTLEY HO
CUDWORTH HO
Lambeth Coll (Vauxhall Ctr)
South Bank Univ
186
333
WALDEN CT
SUDBURY CT
LANGLEY CT
4
BELMORE ST
HOOKHAM CT
BEAMES HO
BEACON HO
JENKINS HO
TREVITHICK HO
DEELEY RD
ALLAN HO
WAINWRIGHT HO
McCONNELL HO
GRESLEY HO
BILLINGTON HO
FOWLER HO
SOUTHVILLE
PRIORY CT
THE STUDIOS
ALL SAINTS CL
SCHOOL FLATS
CONDELL RD
CAREY GDNS
Recn Gd
COURLAND ST
Sir James Barrie Prim Sch
BLORE CL
415
GOLDSBOROUGH HO
Larkhall Park
PRIORY GR
3
172
LARKHALL
MINSHULL ST
ASTON HO
A3036
HINDLIP HO
KNEBWORTH HO
UNION GR
BILTON HO
Wandsworth
Lambeth
LOSTOCK HO
COURLAND GR
Pav
Tenn Cts
BARLING CT
JEFFREY'S PL
JEFFREY'S RD
CLYSTON ST
BRADFIELD HO
DONNINGTON HO
CROXTETH HO
KNELLER HO
HARDWICK HO
ESHER HO
DARTINGTON HO
FALLODON HO
DALEMAIN HO
FARNLEY HO
354
BROCKET HO
PENSBURY ST
PENSBURY PL
477
COLCHESTER HO
CLIVE HO
RUSHBROOK HO
WINSLOW HO
SPRINGFIELD CT
WOOD HO
2
Lark Hall Jun Sch
SEYMOUR HO
HARCOURT HO
CHESSINGTON HO
SMEDLEY ST
KINGSLEY HO
GASKELL ST
McCALL
390
DURRINGTON TOWER
LUCAS HO
METCALFE HO
RALEIGH HO
ALBION AVE
NEWTON HO
STANMORE HO
NETHERBY HO
LARKHALL LA
Wandsworth Road Station
LYDWELL HO
SPENCER HO
NAYLOR HO
OAKWELL HO
UNION RD
Lark Hall Inf Sch
335
RUSHTON HO
RYDAL HO
SURCOT HO
HALTONE HO
KILLYON RD
SHIPLEY HO
MORDAUNT HO
ALDERLEY HO
FRASER HO
KELMAN CL
HESEWALL CL
BRAYBURNE AVE
NETHERFORD RD
STANLEY HO
EFFINGHAM HO
UNION RD
1
GRANT HO
WILSON HO
SIBELLA RD
CHELSHAM RD
STONE CL
MANOR GDNS
LARKHALL RISE
BROMFELDE RD
76
GAUDEN CL
GAUDEN RD
RECTORY GR
CUBITT TERR
EDGELEY RD
A
B
C
61
ROMAYNE HO
DENNIS WAY
CHELSHAM HO
30
384
CLAPHAM MANOR CT

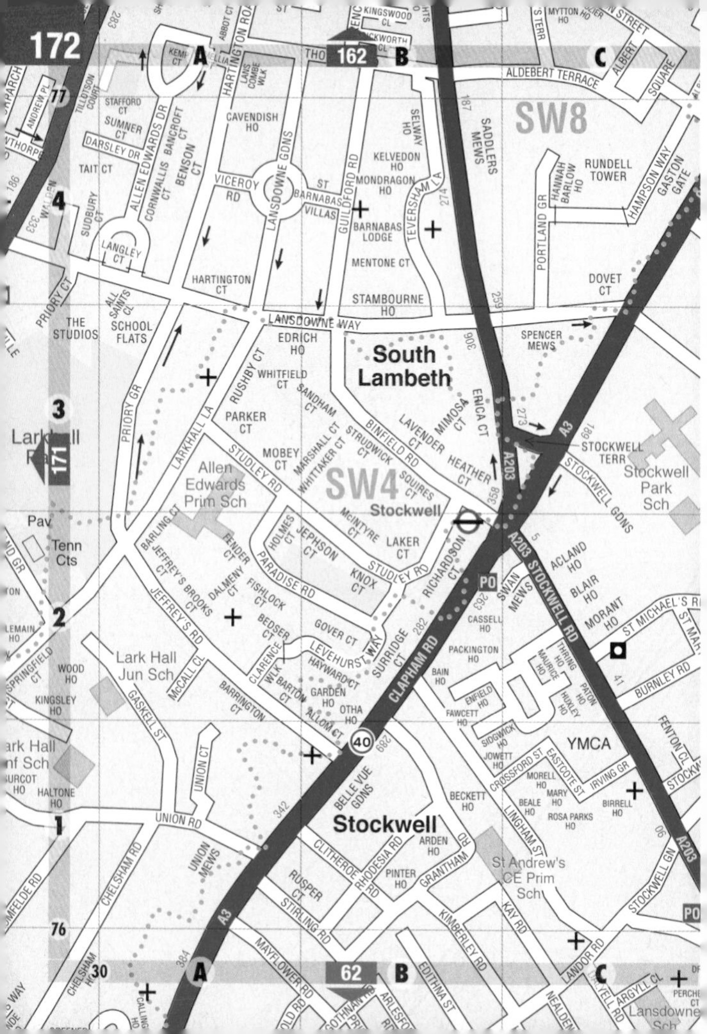

162
62
171
SW8
SW4
South Lambeth
Stockwell
A3
A203
CLAPHAM RD
STOCKWELL RD
LANSDOWNE WAY
ALDEBERT TERRACE
LARKHALL LA
PRIORY GR
GUILDFORD RD
LANSDOWNE GDNS
HARTINGTON RD
VICEROY RD
ST BARNABAS VILLAS
TEVERSHAM LA
SADDLERS MEWS
BINFIELD RD
STUDLEY RD
PARADISE RD
UNION RD
UNION MEWS
CHELSHAM RD
GASKELL ST
McCALL CL
JEFFREY'S RD
LEVEHURST WAY
SURRIDGE CT
CLITHEROE RD
RHODESIA RD
GRANTHAM RD
STIRLING RD
MAYFLOWER RD
KIMBERLEY RD
EDITHNA ST
LINGHAM ST
CROSSFORD ST
EASTCOTE ST
IRVING GR
BURNLEY RD
ST MICHAEL'S RD
STOCKWELL GDNS
STOCKWELL TERR
STOCKWELL GN
PORTLAND GR
HAMPSON WAY
GASTON GATE
ALLEN EDWARDS DR
DARSLEY DR
LANDOR RD
KAY RD
CAVENDISH HO
KELVEDON HO
MONDRAGON HO
BARNABAS LODGE
MENTONE CT
STAMBOURNE HO
HARTINGTON CT
EDRICH HO
WHITFIELD CT
PARKER CT
MOBEY CT
RUNDELL TOWER
DOVET CT
SPENCER MEWS
Allen Edwards Prim Sch
Lark Hall Jun Sch
Stockwell Park Sch
St Andrew's CE Prim Sch
YMCA
THE STUDIOS
SCHOOL FLATS
Tenn Cts
Pav
PO
A
B
C
1
2
3
4

163
62
48
A
B
C
4
3
2
1
SW9
BRIXTON
VERWOOD HO
STREET
OSMINGTON HO
Reay Prim Sch
CLEVELAND MANS
JUPITER CT
LEDA CT
JUNO CT
ASHTON HO
RAMSEY HO
ASSALL RD
CALDWELL STREET
BAKERY CL
CLAPHAM ROAD
HECTOR CT
CREON CT
ARGOS CT
JASON CT
HERMES CT
CADMUS CT
APOLLO CT
HACKFORD RD
SOUTHEY RD
MERCURY CT
ELM CT
COUNTY HO
MORAT ST
LIBERTY ST
CRANWORTH GDNS
ISABEL ST
Durand Prim Sch
DURAND GDNS
HILLYARD ST
PEMBRY CL
WILLOW CT
JOHNSTON CL
VINCENT CT
HACKFORD WLK
A23
ANNESLEY HO
CHARDIN HO
KNOWLTON HO
SEASALTER HO
DOWNBARTON HO
KINGSGATE HO
GARLINGE HO
MOIRA HO
REDLYNCH HO
STODMARSH HO
WOODCHURCH HO
ALVANLEY HO
HALLAM HO
GOSLING WAY
MANSION CL
BRICKWORTH HO
HANWAY HO
SACKETTS HO
DURLOCK HO
WHITENESS HO
BROMSTONE HO
PENELOPE HO
CLIFFSEND HO
NORMANDY RD
MELBOURNE MEWS
MELBOURNE SQ
THE CLOISTERS
COWLEY RD
RUSSELL GR
CANCELL RD
ELLIOTT RD
Christ Church CE Prim Sch
BRAMAH GN
CRAWSHAY CT
TREHERNE CT
EYTHORNE RD
FAIRBAIRN GN
CROMWELL
CARLTON CT
FOUNTAIN PL
Mostyn Gdns
AKERMAN RD
SHERIDAN CT
GROVEWAY
STOCKWELL PARK RD
Allot Gdns
MOSTYN RD
EAMANN CASEY HO
URLWIN WLK
LORN RD
LORN CT
BRIXTON RD
EVESHAM WLK
NORVAL GN
HILDA TERR
ST LAWRENCE WAY
CHURCH GN
LORD HOLLAND LA
BURTON LA
BURTON RD
STOCKWELL PARK CRES
Slade Gdns
INGLETON ST
INGLEBOROUGH ST
SORRELL CL
TAVERN LA
EVANDALE RD
LOUGHBOROUGH RD
PARK VIEW MEWS
ROBSART ST
THORNTON ST
CROWHURST CL
FIVEWAYS RD
REDMAYNE HO
CUMNOR CL
WAYLAND HO
LIDCOTE GDNS
DUDLEY HO
HOLLES HO
IVEAGH HO
SIDNEY RD
NORTON HO
DENCHWORTH HO
HAMPDEN HO
MARSTON HO
AYTOUN CT
AYTOUN PL
FITZGERALD HO
LEYS CT
MARCELLA RD
GOFFTON HO
ADDINGTON HO
LAMBERT HO
WYNNE RD
FERREY MEWS
NEWBURY HO
EDGEHILL HO
THORNICROFT HO
COLWALL HO
CROWHURST HO
STOCKWELL PARK RD
WINANS WLK
Max Roach Park
SERENADERS RD
IRETON HO
WALTHAM HO
BURFORD HO
BROOMGROVE RD
BURROW HO
AYTOUN RD
WARWICK HO
OVERTON RD
FAIRFAX HO
St John's Angell Town CE Prim Sch
LANGPORT HO
ASHBY HO
STOCKWELL RD
WYNTER HO
CHUTE HO
BEDWELL HO
PECKFORD PL
AMBERLEY CT
MOAT PL
TURBERVILLE
COMBERMERE RD
VILLA RD
WILTSHIRE RD
ANGELL PARK GDNS
ANGELL RD
MALLAMS MEWS
RUMSEY RD
BUCKMASTER CL
KNOWLE CL
THRAYLE
ROMERO
BEGBIE HO
BURTON RD
LILFORD
IVEAGH HO

Index

Church Rd **6** Beckenham BR2..........**53** C6 **228** C6

Place name	Location number	Locality, town or village	Postcode district	Standard scale reference	Enlarged scale reference
May be abbreviated on the map	Present when a number indicates the place's position in a crowded area of mapping	Shown when more than one place (outside London postal districts) has the same name	District for the indexed place	Page number and grid reference for the standard mapping	Page number and grid reference for the central London enlarged mapping, underlined in red

Public and commercial buildings are highlighted in magenta
Places of interest are highlighted in blue with a star*
Cities, towns and villages are listed in CAPITAL LETTERS

Abbreviations used in the index

Acad	**Academy**	Ct	**Court**	Int	**International**	Prom	**Promenade**
App	**Approach**	Ctr	**Centre**	Intc	**Interchange**	RC	**Roman Catholic**
Arc	**Arcade**	Crkt	**Cricket**	Jun	**Junior**	Rd	**Road**
Art Gall	**Art Gallery**	Ctry Pk	**Country Park**	Junc	**Junction**	Rdbt	**Roundabout**
Ave	**Avenue**	Cty	**County**	La	**Lane**	Ret Pk	**Retail Park**
Bglws	**Bungalows**	Ctyd	**Courtyard**	L Ctr	**Leisure Centre**	Sch	**School**
Bldgs	**Buildings**	Dr	**Drive**	Liby	**Library**	Sec	**Secondary**
Bsns Ctr	**Business Centre**	Ent Ctr	**Enterprise Centre**	Mans	**Mansions**	Sh Ctr	**Shopping Centre**
Bsns Pk	**Business Park**	Ent Pk	**Enterprise Park**	Mdw/s	**Meadow/s**	Sp	**Sports**
Bvd	**Boulevard**	Est	**Estate**	Meml	**Memorial**	Specl	**Special**
Cath	**Cathedral, Catholic**	Ex Ctr	**Exhibition Centre**	Mid	**Middle**	Sports Ctr	**Sports Centre**
CE	**Church of England**	Ex Hall	**Exhibition Hall**	Mix	**Mixed**	Sq	**Square**
Cemy	**Cemetery**	Fst	**First**	Mkt	**Market**	St	**Street, Saint**
Cir	**Circus**	Gdn	**Garden**	Mon	**Monument**	Sta	**Station**
Circ	**Circle**	Gdns	**Gardens**	Mus	**Museum**	Stad	**Stadium**
Cl	**Close**	Gn	**Green**	Obsy	**Observatory**	Tech	**Technical Technology**
Cnr	**Corner**	Gr	**Grove**	Orch	**Orchard**		
Coll	**College**	Gram	**Grammar**	Par	**Parade**	Terr	**Terrace**
Com	**Community**	Her Ctr	**Heritage Centre**	Pas	**Passage**	Trad Est	**Trading Estate**
Comm	**Common**	Ho	**House**	Pav	**Pavilion**	Twr/s	**Tower/s**
Comp	**Comprehensive**	Hospl	**Hospital**	Pk	**Park**	Univ	**University**
Con Ctr	**Conference Centre**	Hts	**Heights**	Pl	**Place**	Wlk	**Walk**
Cotts	**Cottages**	Ind Est	**Industrial Estate**	Prec	**Precinct**	Yd	**Yard**
Cres	**Crescent**	Inf	**Infant**	Prep	**Preparatory**		
Cswy	**Causeway**	Inst	**Institute**	Prim	**Primary**		

A

Abady Ho SW1 ... 147 C4
Abberley Mews 9 SW8 ... 61 A4
Abbess Cl SW2 ... 75 A3
Abbeville Mews 3 SW4 ... 61 C3
Abbeville Rd SW4 ... 61 B2
Abbey Bsns Ctr SW8 ... 170 B4
Abbey Ct
6 Bedford Pk W12 ... 38 A3
Camberwell SE17 ... 151 A1
St John's Wood NW8 ... 78 C2
Abbeyfield Rd SE16 ... 40 B2
Abbey Gdns
Bermondsey SE16 ... 153 C4
St John's Wood NW8 ... 79 A1
West Kensington W6 ... 154 A3
Abbey Ho NW8 ... 89 A4
Abbey La E15 ... 27 C3
Abbey Lo NW8 ... 90 B3
Abbey Orchard St SW1 ... 133 C2
Abbey Orchard Street Est SW1 ... 133 C2
Abbey Rd
St John's Wood NW8 ... 78 C2
Wembley NW10 ... 20 A3
Abbey Rd Motorist Ctr NW6 ... 78 A4
Abbey St SE1 ... 138 C2
Abbot Ct SW8 ... 162 A1
Abbot Ho 14 E14 ... 34 A2
Abbotsbury Cl
Kensington W14 ... 126 C3
Mill Meads E15 ... 27 B3
Abbotsbury Ho W14 ... 126 B4
Abbotsbury Mews SE15 ... 65 B4
Abbotsbury Rd W14 ... 126 C3
Abbotshade Rd 15 SE16 ... 32 C1
Abbots Ho
Kensington W14 ... 126 C1
Pimlico SW1 ... 147 B1
Abbots La SE1 ... 124 B1
Abbots Pk SW2 ... 74 C3
Abbot's Pl NW6 ... 78 A4
Abbot St E8 ... 16 B2
Abbotstone Ho 4 E5 ... 7 C2
Abbotstone Rd SW15 ... 57 B4
Abbotswell Rd SE4 ... 66 B2
Abbotswood Rd
London SE22 ... 64 A3
Streatham SW16 ... 73 C1
Abbott Ho SW12 ... 72 B4
Abbott Rd E14 ... 34 C3
Abbotts Cl N1 ... 15 B2
Abbotts Wharf 4 E14 ... 33 C3
Abchurch La EC2, EC4 ... 123 C4
Abchurch Yd EC4 ... 123 B4
Abdale Rd W12 ... 30 A1
Abel Ho SE11 ... 163 B4
Aberavon Rd E3 ... 26 A2
Abercorn Cl NW8 ... 88 C4
Abercorn Mans NW8 ... 79 A1
Abercorn Mews 10 TW10 ... 54 B3
Abercorn Pl NW8 ... 78 C1
Abercorn Way SE1 ... 153 B2
Abercrombie Ho 1 W12 ... 30 A2
Abercrombie St SW11 ... 168 B2
Aberdale Ct 22 SE16 ... 40 C4
Aberdare Gdns NW6 ... 11 A1
Aberdeen Ct
Canonbury N5 ... 15 B3
Paddington W2 ... 89 B1
Aberdeen Ctr N5 ... 15 B3
Aberdeen La N5 ... 15 B3
Aberdeen Mans WC1 ... 94 A2
Aberdeen Pk N5 ... 15 B3
Aberdeen Pl NW8 ... 89 B2
Aberdeen Rd
Canonbury N5 ... 15 B4
Dudden Hill NW10 ... 8 B3
Aberdeen Terr SE3 ... 52 C1
Aberdour St SE1 ... 152 A4
Aberfeldy Ho SE5 ... 48 A3
Aberfeldy St E14 ... 34 B3
Abersham Rd E8 ... 16 B3
Ability Plaza 8 E8 ... 16 B1
Ability Twrs EC1 ... 96 C4
Abingdon W14 ... 141 A3
Abingdon Cl
Fulham SE1 ... 153 A2
Kentish Town NW1 ... 13 C2
Abingdon Ct W8 ... 127 C1
Abingdon Gdns W8 ... 127 C1
Abingdon Ho E2 ... 24 B1 98 C2
Abingdon Mans W8 ... 127 B2
Abingdon Rd W8 ... 127 C1
Abingdon St SW1 ... 134 A2
Abingdon Villas W8 ... 127 C1
Abinger Gr SE8 ... 51 B4
Abinger Ho SE1 ... 137 B3
Abinger Mews W9 ... 23 C1
Abinger Rd W4 ... 38 A3
Ablett St SE16 ... 40 B1
Abney Gdns 5 N16 ... 7 B2
Abney Park Cemetery* N16 ... 7 A2
Abney Park Ct N16 ... 7 B2
Aborfield 6 NW5 ... 13 B3
Aboyne Rd SW17 ... 71 C1
Abyssinia Cl SW11 ... 60 A3
Abyssinia Rd SW11 ... 60 A3
Acacia Cl SE8 ... 41 A2
Acacia Gdns NW8 ... 79 C2
Acacia Gr SE21 ... 75 C2
Acacia Ho
Brockley SE4 ... 66 B3
Stoke Newington N16 ... 6 C2
Acacia Pl NW8 ... 79 C2
Acacia Rd
Acton W3 ... 28 B2
St John's Wood NW8 ... 79 C2
Acacia Wlk SW10 ... 157 A1
Acad at Peckham The SE15 ... 49 B2
Academy Ct 13 E2 ... 25 B2
Academy Gdns W8 ... 127 B4
Academy Sch The NW3 ... 11 C4
Academy The 2 N19 ... 4 B3
Acad of Live & Recorded Arts The SW18 ... 59 C1
Acanthus Dr SE1 ... 153 B2
Acanthus Rd SW11 ... 60 C4
Accommodation Rd NW11 ... 1 B3
Acer Ct 2 NW2 ... 9 C4
Acfold Rd SW6 ... 166 A3
Achilles Cl SE1 ... 153 C2
Achilles Ho 16 E2 ... 25 A3
Achilles Rd NW6 ... 10 C3
Achilles St SE14 ... 51 A3
Achilles Way W1 ... 117 C1
Acklam Rd W10 ... 31 B4
Ackmar Rd SW6 ... 165 B3
Ackroyd Dr E3 ... 33 C4
Acland Burghley Sch NW5 ... 13 A4
Acland Cres SE5 ... 63 C4
Acland Ho SW9 ... 172 C2
Acland Rd NW2 ... 9 A2
Acol Ct 3 NW6 ... 10 C1
Acol Rd NW6 ... 11 A1
Acorn Ct 5 E3 ... 26 C3
Acorn Gdns W3 ... 28 C4
Acorn Par 7 SE15 ... 50 A3
Acorn Production Ctr N7 ... 14 A1
Acorns The 21 SW19 ... 69 C3
Acorn Wharf SE15 ... 49 C4
Acorn Wlk SE16 ... 33 A1
Acqua Ho TW9 ... 45 A3
Acre Dr SE22 ... 64 C3
Acre La SW2 ... 62 B3
Acris St SW18 ... 59 B2
ACTON ... 28 C1
Acton Bsns Ctr NW10 ... 20 C1
Acton Central Ind Est 4 W3 ... 28 A1
Acton Central Sta W3 ... 28 C1
ACTON GREEN ... 37 B2
Acton High Sch W3 ... 36 C4
Acton Hill Mews W3 ... 28 A1
Acton Ho
5 Acton W3 ... 28 B3
16 Haggerston E8 ... 24 B4
Acton Hospl W3 ... 36 C4
Acton La
Acton Green W4 ... 37 B2
Acton W3 ... 37 B4
Harlesden NW10 ... 20 C3
Acton Main Line Sta W3 ... 28 B3
Acton Mews E8 ... 24 B4
Acton Park Ind Est W3 ... 37 C4
Acton St WC1 ... 94 C3
Acton Town Sta W3 ... 36 C4
Acton Vale Ind Pk W3 ... 29 B1
Acuba Ho SW18 ... 71 A3
Acuba Rd SW18 ... 71 A2
Ada Ct Islington N1 ... 86 C3
St John's Wood W9 ... 89 A3
Ada Gdns E14 ... 34 C3
Ada Ho 23 E2 ... 24 C4
Adair Ho SW3 ... 158 B4
Adair Rd W10 ... 23 A1
Adair Twr 7 W10 ... 23 A1
Ada Kennedy Ct 6 SE10 ... 52 B3
Adam Ct SE11 ... 150 A3
Adam & Eve Ct W1 ... 105 A2
Adam & Eve Mews W8 ... 127 C2
Adamfields NW3 ... 11 C1
Adams Gardens Est 5 SE16 ... 40 B4
Adams Ho 3 E14 ... 34 C3
Adams Mews SW17 ... 72 B2
Adamson Rd
Hampstead NW3 ... 11 C1
Newham E16 ... 35 C3
Adams Pl N7 ... 14 B3
Adam's Row W1 ... 117 C3
Adam St WC2 ... 120 B3
Adam Wlk SW6 ... 47 B3
Ada Pl E2 ... 24 C4
Ada Rd SE5 ... 49 A3
Adare Ctr The SW16 ... 74 A1
Adare Wlk SW16, SW2 ... 74 B2
Ada St E8 ... 25 A4
Adderley Gr SW11 ... 60 C2
Adderley St E14 ... 34 B3
Addey Ho SE8 ... 51 B3
Addey & Stanhope Sch SE14 ... 51 C2
Addington Ct 7 SW14 ... 55 C4
Addington Ho SW9 ... 173 A1
Addington Rd E3 ... 26 C2
Addington Sq SE5 ... 48 C3
Addington St SE1 ... 135 A3
Addis Ho 13 E1 ... 32 B4
Addison Ave W11 ... 31 A1 112 A1
Addison Bridge Pl W14 ... 140 C4
Addison Cres W14 ... 126 B2
Addison Gdns W14 ... 39 C3
Addison Gr W4 ... 38 A3
Addison Ho NW8 ... 89 B4
Addison Park Mans 12 W14 ... 39 C4
Addison Pl W11 ... 31 A1 112 A1
Addison Prim Sch W14 ... 39 C3
Addison Rd W14 ... 126 C2
Addle Hill EC4 ... 108 B1
Addle St EC2 ... 109 A3
Addlestone Ho 4 W10 ... 30 B4
Addy Ho SE16 ... 40 B2
Adela Ho 9 W6 ... 39 B1
Adelaide Ave SE4 ... 66 C3
Adelaide Cl SW9 ... 62 C3
Adelaide Ct
Hackney E5 ... 18 A3
St John's Wood NW8 ... 79 A1
Adelaide Gr W12 ... 29 C1
Adelaide Rd
Primrose Hill NW3 ... 12 A1
Richmond TW9 ... 54 B3
2 Wandsworth SW18 ... 58 C2
Adelaide St WC2 ... 120 A3
Adela St W10 ... 23 A1
Adelina Gr E1 ... 32 B4
Adelina Mews SW12 ... 73 C3
Adeline Pl WC1 ... 105 C3
Adelphi Ct 20 SE16 ... 40 C4
Adelphi Terr WC2 ... 120 B3
Adeney Cl W6 ... 47 C4
Aden Gr N16 ... 15 C4
Aden Ho 15 E1 ... 32 C4
Aden Lo N16 ... 15 C4
Adeyfield Ho EC1 ... 97 C3
Adie Rd W6 ... 39 B3
Adisham Ho 4 E5 ... 17 A3
Adler St E1 ... 111 B2
Adley St E5 ... 18 A3
Admiral Ct
Chelsea SW10 ... 167 A4
Marylebone W1 ... 103 B3
Admiral Hyson Ind Est SE16 ... 40 A1
Admiral Mews W10 ... 22 C1
Admiral Pl SE16 ... 33 A1
Admirals Ct
Bermondsey SE1 ... 124 C1
32 Putney SW19 ... 69 C3
Admirals Gate SE10 ... 52 A2
Admiral Sq SW10 ... 167 A4
Admiral St SE8 ... 51 C2
Admirals Way E14 ... 41 C4
Admiral's Wlk NW3 ... 2 B1
Admiralty Arch* SW1 ... 119 C2
Admiralty Cl 1 SE8 ... 51 C2
Admiral Wlk W9 ... 31 C4
Adolphus Rd N4 ... 6 A3
Adolphus St SE8 ... 51 B3
Adpar St W2 ... 101 B4
Adrian Bolt Ho 2 E2 ... 25 A2
Adrian Ho
Islington N1 ... 85 A3
South Lambeth SW8 ... 162 A2
Stratford E15 ... 19 C1
Adrian Mews SW10 ... 156 B4
Adriatic Bldg 18 E14 ... 33 A2
Adriatic Ho 18 E1 ... 25 C1
Adron Ho 13 SE16 ... 40 B2
Adstock Ho 5 N1 ... 15 A1
ADT Coll SW15 ... 58 B2
Adventurers Ct 17 E14 ... 34 C2
Adys Lawn NW2 ... 9 A2

Adys Rd SE15 64 B4
Aegean Apts 7 E16 35 C2
Aegon Ho 3 E14 42 A3
Affleck St N1 85 A1
Afghan Rd SW11 168 A1
Africa Ho WC2 106 C2
Afsil Ho EC1 107 C3
Aga Khan Univ WC1 105 C3
Agamemnon Rd NW6 10 B3
Agar Gr NW1 13 C1
Agar Pl NW1 13 B1
Agar St WC2 120 B3
Agate Rd W6 39 B3
Agatha Cl E1 32 B1
Agave Rd NW2 9 B4
Agdon St EC1 96 A2
Agincourt Rd NW3 12 B4
Agnes Ct 11 SW18 59 C3
Agnes Ho 13 W11 30 C2
Agnes Rd W3 38 B4
Agnes St E14 33 B3
Aigburth Mans SW9 163 B1
Ailsa St E14 34 B4
Ainger Rd NW3 12 B1
Ainsdale NW1 92 C4
Ainsdale Dr SE1 153 B1
Ainsley St E2 25 A2
Ainslie Wlk 8 SW12 73 A4
Ainsty St 20 SE16 40 B4
Ainsworth Cl SE5 49 A1
Ainsworth Est NW8 78 C4
Ainsworth Ho NW8 78 B3
Ainsworth Rd E9 17 B1
Ainsworth Way NW8 78 C4
Aintree St SW6 154 B2
Aird Ho SE1 136 C1
Airdrie Cl N1 14 B1
Airedale Ave W4 38 B1
Airedale Ave S W4 38 B1
Airedale Rd SW12 72 B4
Airlie Gdns W8 31 C1 113 B1
Air St W1 119 A3
Aisgill Ave SW5 141 A1
Aiten Pl W6 38 C2
Aithan Ho 15 E14 33 B3
Aitken Cl E8 24 C4
Ajax Ho 16 E2 25 A3
Ajax Rd NW6 10 C3
Akbar Ho 7 E14 42 A2
Akehurst St SW15 68 C4
Akenside Ct 3 NW3 11 C3
Akenside Rd NW3 11 C3
Akerman Rd SW9 48 A2
Akintaro Ho 7 SE8 51 B4
Alamaro Lo 5 SE10 43 B3
Aland Ct SE16 41 A3
Alan Preece Ct NW6 9 C1
Alaska Bldg 12 SE13 52 A2
Alaska St SE1 121 B1
Alastor Ho 10 E14 42 B3
Albacore Cres SE13 67 A1
Alba Mews SW18, SW19 70 C2
Alban Ho
Hampstead NW3 11 B2
New Cross SE14 51 B2
Albans Cl SW16 74 A1
Albany W1 118 C3
Albany Cl SW14 55 A3
Albany Ct
College Pk NW10 22 A2
NW8 79 B1
Westminster SW1 133 B2
Whitechapel E1 111 B2
Albany Ctyd W1 119 A3
Albany Ho 6 TW8 44 A4
Albany Mans SW11 158 B1
Albany Mews
Camberwell SE5 48 B4
Islington N1 14 C1
Albany Par 4 TW8 44 A4
Albany Pas 12 TW10 54 A2
Albany Rd
Camberwell SE5 49 A4
Richmond TW10 54 A2
Albany St NW1 92 B4
Albany Terr 6 TW10 54 B2
Alba Pl W11 31 B3
Albemarle SW19 69 C2
Albemarle Ho
2 Brixton SW9 62 C4
Rotherhithe SE8 41 B2
Albemarle Mans NW3 11 A4
Albemarle Prim Sch SW19 70 A2
Albemarle St W1 118 C3
Albemarle Way EC1 96 A1
Alberta Ct 1 TW10 54 B2
Alberta Ho E14 34 B1
Alberta St SE17 150 B2
Albert Ave SW8 162 C1
Albert Barnes Ho SE1 136 C1
Albert Bigg Point E15 27 B4
Albert Bridge Rd SW11 158 C1
Albert Cl 11 E9 25 A4
Albert Cotts E1 111 B4
Albert Ct
Knightsbridge SW7 129 B3
9 Putney SW19 70 A3
Albert Dr SW19 70 A3
Albert Emb SE1 148 B3
Albert Gate Ct SW1 130 C3
Albert Gdns E1 32 C3
Albert Gray Ho SW10 157 B2
Albert Hall Mans SW7 129 B3
Albert Mans
Battersea SW11 168 C4
Hornsey N8 5 A4
Albert Meml* SW7 129 B3
Albert Mews W8 128 C2
Albert Palace Mans SW11 169 C4
Albert Pl W8 128 B3
Albert Rd
Finsbury Pk N4 5 B4
Kilburn NW6 23 B3
Richmond TW10 54 B2
Albert's Ct NW1 90 B2
Albert Sq SW8 162 C1
Albert St NW1 82 B3
Albert Starr Ho 7 SE8 40 C2
Albert Studios SW11 168 C4
Albert Terr
Camden Town NW1 81 B3
Stonebridge NW10 20 B4
Albert Terr Mews NW1 81 B3
Albert Way SE15 50 A3
Albert Westcott Ho SE17 150 B2
Albion Ave SW8 171 B1
Albion Cl W2 116 B4
Albion Coll WC1 106 B3
Albion Ct 7 W6 39 A2
Albion Dr E8 16 C1
Albion Est SE16 40 B4
Albion Gate W2 116 B4
Albion Gdns 1 W6 39 A2
Albion Gr N16 16 A4
Albion Ho
17 Deptford SE8 51 C3
EC1 108 A4
Albion Mews
Bayswater W2 116 B4
6 Hammersmith W6 39 A2
Islington N1 85 B4
Albion Pl
Broadgate EC2 109 C3
Clerkenwell EC1 108 A4
Hammersmith W6 39 A2
Albion Prim Sch SE16 40 B4
Albion Rd N16 15 C4
Albion Riverside SW11 158 A2
Albion Sq E8 16 B1
Albion St
Bayswater W2 116 B4
Rotherhithe SE16 40 B4
Albion Terr E8 16 B1
Albion Way
Barbican EC1 108 C3
Lewisham SE13 67 B3
Albion Wlk N1 84 B1
Albion Works Studios 14 E8 16 C3
Albion Yd N1 84 B1
Albon Ho SW18 59 A1
Albrighton Rd SE5, SE22 64 A4
Albury Bldgs SE1 136 B3
Albury Ct SE8 51 C4
Albury Lo 7 SW2 74 B4
Albury St SE8 51 C4
Albyn Rd SE8 51 C2
Alchemea Coll of Audio Engineering N1 86 B4
Alconbury Rd E5 7 C2
Aldbourne Rd W12 29 C1
Aldbridge St SE17 152 B2
Aldburgh Mews W1 103 C2
Aldbury Ho SW3 144 A3
Aldebert Terr SW8 162 C1
Aldeburgh Pl SE10 43 C2
Aldeburgh St SE10 43 C1
Aldenham Ho NW1 83 A1
Aldenham St NW1 83 B1
Alden Ho E8 25 A4
Aldensley Rd W6 39 A3
Alderbrook Prim Sch SW12 73 A4
Alderbrook Rd SW12 61 A1
Alderbury Rd SW13 46 C4
Aldergrove Ho 3 E5 7 C2
Alder Ho
Camberwell SE15 49 B4
1 Maitland Pk NW3 12 B2
St Johns SE4 66 C4
Alderley Ho SW8 171 B1
Alder Lo SW6 47 C2
Aldermanbury EC2 109 A2
Aldermanbury Sq EC2 109 A3
Alderman's Wlk EC2 110 A3
Alder Mews 12 N19 4 B2
Alderney Ho 20 N1 15 B2
Alderney Mews SE1 137 B2
Alderney Rd E1 25 C1
Alderney St SW1 146 B2
Alder Rd SW14 55 C4
Aldersford Cl SE4 65 C3
Aldersgate Ct EC1 108 C3
Aldersgate St EC1 108 C3
Aldershot Rd NW6 23 B4
Alderson St W10 23 A1
Alderton Rd SE24 63 B4
Alderville Rd SW6 165 A2
Alderwick Ct N7 14 B2
Aldford St W1 117 C2
Aldgate EC3 110 B1
Aldgate East Sta E1 111 A2
Aldgate High St EC3 110 C1
Aldgate Sta EC3 110 C1
Aldham Ho SE4 51 B2
Aldine Ct W12 30 B1
Aldine St W12 39 B4
Aldington Ct 1 E8 16 C1
Aldred Rd NW6 10 C3
Aldren Rd SW17 71 B1
Aldrich Terr SW18 71 B2
Aldrick Ho N1 85 A2
Aldridge Ct W11 31 B4
Aldridge Rd Villas W11 31 B4
Aldsworth Cl W9 88 A1
Aldwich Ho WC2 107 A1
Aldworth Gr SE13 67 B1
Aldwych WC2 107 A1
Aldwych Bldgs WC2 106 B2
Aldwyn Ho SW8 162 A1
Alexander Ave NW10 9 A1
Alexander Ct SW18 59 B2
Alexander Fleming Laboratory Mus* W2 101 C2
Alexander Ho 15 E14 41 C3
Alexander Mews W2 100 A2
Alexander Pl SW7 144 A4
Alexander Rd N19 5 A2
Alexander Sq SW3 144 A4
Alexander St W2 31 C3
Alexandra Ave SW11 169 B3
Alexandra Cl SE8 51 B4
Alexandra Cotts SE14 51 B2
Alexandra Ct
Paddington W9 89 A2
4 Shacklewell N16 16 B4
5 Shepherd's Bush W12 38 C4
Alexandra Gdns W4 46 A3
Alexandra Gr N4 6 A3
Alexandra Ho 13 W6 39 B1
Alexandra Mans
Chelsea SW3 157 B3
Cricklewood NW2 9 C3
6 Hampstead NW6 10 C3
9 Shepherd's Bush W12 30 B1
Alexandra National Ho N4 6 A2
Alexandra Pl NW8 79 A4
Alexandra Rd
Acton W4 37 C4
Hampstead NW8 11 C1
Mortlake SW14 55 C4
Richmond TW9 44 B1
Alexandra St
5 Deptford SE14 51 A3
Newham E16 35 C4
Alex Gossip Ho SW6 165 B3
Alexis St SE16 153 C4
Alfearn Rd E5 17 B4
Alford Ct N1 87 A1
Alford Pl N1 87 A1
Alfreda Ct SW11 170 A3
Alfreda St SW11 170 A3
Alfred Butt Ho SW17 72 B1
Alfred Cl W4 37 C2
Alfred Ho E9 18 A3
Alfred Mews W1, WC1 105 B4
Alfred Nunn Ho NW10 21 B4
Alfred Pl WC1 105 B4
Alfred Rd
Acton W3 28 B1
Paddington W2 31 C4
Alfred Salter Ho SE1 153 A3

Alfred Salter Prim Sch SE16 40 C4
Alfred St E3 26 B2
Alfreton Cl SW19 69 C1
Alfriston Rd SW11 60 B2
Algar Ho SE1 136 A3
Algarve Rd SW18 71 A3
Algernon Rd
Kilburn NW6 23 C4
Lewisham SE13 67 A3
Algiers Rd SE13 66 C3
Alice Gilliott Ct W14 155 A4
Alice La E3 26 B4
Alice Owen Tech Ctr EC1 96 A4
Alice Shepherd Ho 12 E14 42 B4
Alice St SE1 138 A1
Alice Walker Cl 8 SE24 63 A3
Alie St E1 111 A1
Aliwal Rd SW11 60 A3
Alkerden Rd W4 38 A1
Alkham Rd N16 7 B2
Allam Ho W11 31 A2 112 A4
Allanbridge N16 7 A4
Allan Ho SW8 171 B4
Allan Way W3 28 B4
Allard Gdns SW4 61 C2
Allardyce St SW4, SW9 62 B3
Allbrook Ho 4 SW15 68 C4
Allcroft Rd NW5 12 C2
Allendale Cl SE5 48 C2
Allen Edwards Dr SW8 172 A4
Allen Edwards Prim Sch SW4 172 A3
Allenford Ho SW15 56 B1
All England Lawn Tennis & Croquet Club The SW19 70 A1
Allen Ho W8 127 C2
Allen Mans W8 127 C2
Allen Rd
Old Ford E3 26 B3
Stoke Newington N16 16 A4
Allensbury Pl
7 Camden Town NW1 13 C1
Camden Town NW1 14 A1
Allen St W8 127 C1
Allenswood 12 SW19 70 A3
Allerdale Ho 7 N4 6 C4
Allerton Ho N1 87 C1
Allerton Rd N16 6 B2
Allerton St N1 97 C4
Allerton Wlk 11 N7 5 B2
Allestree Rd SW6 154 A1
Alleyn Cres SE21 75 C2
Alleyn Ho
Bermondsey SE1 137 B1
St Luke's EC1 97 A1
Alleyn Pk SE21 76 A1
Alleyn Rd SE21 76 A1
Alleyn's Sch SE22 64 A2
Allfarthing La SW18 59 B1
Allfarthing Prim Sch SW18 59 B1
Allgood St 10 E2 24 B3
Allhallows La EC4 123 B3
Alliance Ct W3 28 A4
Alliance Rd W3 20 A1
Allied Ind Est W3 29 A1
Allied Way W3 38 A4
Allingham Ct NW3 12 A3
Allingham Mews N1 86 C2
Allingham St N1 86 C2
Allington Ct SW8 170 C1
Allington Rd W10 23 A3
Allington St SW1 132 B1
Allison Cl SE10 52 B2
Allison Gr SE21 76 A3
Allison Rd W3 28 B2
Alliston Ho E2 24 B2 99 A3
Allitsen Rd NW8 80 A2
All Nations Ho 10 E8 17 A1
Allnutt Way SW4 61 C2
Allom Ct SW4 172 B1
Allonby Ho E14 33 A4
Alloway Rd E3 26 A2
Allport Ho SE5 63 C4
Allport Mews 44 E1 25 B1
All Saints CE Prim Sch SW15 57 B4
All Saints' CE Prim Sch
Blackheath Vale SE3 53 A1
Child's Hill NW2 1 B1
All Saints Church 9 N19 4 C1
All Saints Ct
Lower Clapton E5 17 B4
10 Shadwell E1 32 B2
All Saints Dr SE3 53 B1
All Saints Ho 2 W11 31 B4
All Saints Pas SW18 58 C2
All Saints Rd W11 31 B3
All Saints' Rd W3 37 B3
All Saints St N1 84 C2
All Saints Sta E14 34 A2
Allsop Pl NW1 91 A1
All Souls' Ave NW10 22 A4
All Souls CE Prim Sch W1 104 C4
All Souls Pl W1 104 B3
Alma Birk Ho 1 NW6 10 B1
Almack Rd E5 17 B4
Alma Gr SE1 153 A3
Alma Ho 7 TW8 44 A4
Alma Pl NW10 22 A2
Alma Prim Sch SE16 153 C4
Alma Rd SW18 59 B2
Alma Sq NW8 89 A4
Alma St
Camden Town NW5 13 A2
Stratford New Town E15 19 C2
Alma Terr
Earl's Ct W8 127 C1
Wandsworth SW18 71 C4
Almeida St 10 N1 15 A1
Almeric Rd SW11 60 B3
Almington St N4 5 B3
Almond Ave W5 36 A3
Almond Cl SE15 49 C1
Almond Ho SE4 51 B1
Almond Rd SE16 40 A2
Almorah Rd N1 15 C1
Al-Muntada Islamic Sch SW6 165 A4
Alperton St W10 23 B1
Alphabet Sq E3 33 C4
Alpha Cl NW8 90 B3
Alpha Ct 6 NW5 13 A2
Alpha Gr E14 41 C4
Alpha Ho
19 Brixton SW4 62 B3
Kilburn NW6 23 C3
Lisson Gr NW8 90 B1
Alpha Pl
Chelsea SW3 158 B4
Kilburn NW6 23 C3
Alpha Rd SE14 51 B2
Alpha St SE15 49 C1
Alpine Gr 37 E9 17 B1
Alpine Rd SE16 40 C1
Alroy Rd N4 5 C4
Alsace Rd SE17 152 A2
Al Sadiq & Al Zahra Schs NW6 23 A4
Alscot Rd SE1 139 A1
Alscot Road Ind Est SE1 139 A1
Alscot Way SE1 152 C4
Altair Ct N1 15 C2
Altenburg Gdns SW11 60 B3
Althea St SW6 59 A4
Althorpe Mews SW11 167 C3
Althorp Rd SW17 72 B3
Altima Ct SE22 64 C3
Alton Ho 3 E3 27 A2
Alton Rd
Richmond TW10, TW9 54 A3
Roehampton SW15 68 C3
Alton St E14 34 A4
Alumni Ct SE1 139 A4
Alvanley Ct NW3 11 A3
Alvanley Gdns NW6 11 A3
Alvanley Ho SW9 173 B4
Alverstone Ave SW18, SW19 70 C2
Alverstone Ho SE11 163 B3
Alverstone Rd NW2 9 B1
Alverton St SE8 51 B4
Alvey St SE17 152 A2
Alvington Cres E8 16 B3
Alwyn Ave W4 37 C1
Alwyne La N1 15 A1
Alwyne Pl N1 15 B1
Alwyne Rd N1 15 B1
Alwyne Sq N1 15 B2
Alwyne Villas N1 15 A1
Alwyn Gdns W3 28 A3
Alzette Ho 11 E2 25 C3
Aman Dalvi Ho SW18 70 A4
Amazonas SE1 152 B3
Amazon St E1 32 A3
Ambassador Ct 9 NW6 10 C3
Ambassador Ho NW8 79 A3
Ambassador Sq E14 42 A2
Amber Ct N7 14 C2
Ambergate St SE17 150 B2
Amberley Ct 2 SW9 63 A4
Amberley Rd W9 31 C4
Amber Wharf 29 E2 24 B4
Ambler Prim Sch N4 6 A2
Ambler Rd N4 6 A1
Ambleside
13 Putney SW19 70 A3
Regent's Pk NW1 82 B1
Ambleside Cl E9 17 B3
Ambleside Point 1 SE15 50 B3
Ambleside Rd NW10 8 B1
Ambrosden Ave SW1 133 A1
Ambrose Ho 9 E14 33 C4
Ambrose Mews SW11 168 C2
Ambrose St SE16 40 A2
Ambrose Wlk E3 26 C3
AMC Bsns Ctr NW10 20 A2
Amelia Cl W3 37 A4
Amelia Ho 5 W6 39 B1
Amelia St SE17 150 C2
Amen Cnr EC4 108 B1
Amen Ct EC4 108 B1
American Intercontinental Univ W1 103 C3
American Sch in London The NW8 79 B2
American Univ in London The N7 5 B1
America Sq EC3 124 C4
America St SE1 122 C1
Amerland Rd SW18 58 B1
Amersham Gr SE14 51 B3
Amersham Rd SE14 51 B2
Amersham Vale SE14, SE8 51 B3
Amery Gdns NW10 22 A4
Amery Ho SE17 152 B2
Amesbury Ave SW2 74 B2
Amesbury Twr SW8 170 C2
Ames Cotts 12 E3 33 A4
Ames Ho 10 E2 25 C3
Amethyst Rd E15 19 C4
Amhurst Ct N4 6 C4
Amhurst Par N16 7 B4
Amhurst Pk N4, N16 7 A4
Amhurst Rd E8, N16 16 C4
Amhurst Terr E8 16 C4
Amias Ho EC1 96 C2
Amiel St 15 E1 25 B1
Amies St SW11 60 B4
Amigo Ho SE1 135 C2
Amina Way SE16 139 B1
Amner Rd SW11 60 C1
Amor Rd W6 39 B3
Amory Ho N1 85 A2
Amott Rd SE15 64 C4
Amoy Pl E14 33 C2
Ampton Pl WC1 94 C3
Ampton St WC1 94 C3
Amstel Ct 12 SE15 49 B3
Amsterdam Rd E14 42 B3
Amundsen Ct 7 E14 41 C1
Amwell St EC1 95 B4
Amyruth Rd SE4 66 C2
Anatola Rd N19 4 B2
Anchorage Point 1 E14 41 C4
Anchor Ho EC1 96 C2
Anchor Mews SW12 61 A1
Anchor Ret Pk E1 25 B1
Anchor St SE16 40 A2
Anchor Terr SE1 123 A2
Anchor Yd EC1 97 A2
Ancill Cl W6 154 A3
Ancona Rd NW10 21 C3
Andalus Rd SW9 62 A4
Andaman Ho 3 E1 33 A4
Andersens Wharf 9 E14 33 B3
Anderson Cl W3 28 C3
Anderson Ho 10 E14 34 B2
Anderson Rd E9 17 C2
Andersons Sq N1 86 A3
Anderson St SW3 144 C2
Anderton Cl SE5 63 C4
Andover Ho 5 N7 5 B2
Andover Pl NW6 78 A1
Andover Rd N7 5 B2
Andoversford Ct 2 SE15 49 A4
Andre St E8 16 C3
Andrew Borde St WC2 105 C2
Andrewes Ho EC2 109 A3
Andrew Ho
New Cross SE4 51 B1
Putney SW15 56 C2
Andrew Logan's Glass Ho* SE1 138 A4
Andrew Marvell Ho 12 N16 16 A4
Andrew Pl SW8 171 C4
Andrew Reed Ho SW18 70 A4
Andrews Crosse WC2 107 B1
Andrew's Rd E8 25 A4
Andrew St E14 34 B3
Andrews Wharf 14 E8 25 A4
Andrews Wlk SE17 48 A4
Andrew Wilmot Ct SW18 71 B3
Anfield Cl SW12 73 B4
Angel EC1 86 B1
Angela Davis Ind Est 20 SW9 63 A3
Angel Ct
Broadgate EC2 109 C2
St James SW1 119 A1
5 Willesden NW2 8 C2
Angel Gate EC1 96 B4
Angel Ho N1 85 C1
Angelina Ho 2 SE15 49 C2

Angelis Appartments N1 . . . 86 B1
Angel La E15 . . . 19 C2
Angell Park Gdns 4 SW9 . . . 62 C4
Angell Rd SW9 . . . 63 A4
Angel Mews
Finsbury N1 . . . 85 C1
Putney SW15 . . . 68 C4
Stepney E1 . . . 32 A2
Angel Pas EC4 . . . 123 B3
Angel Pl SE1 . . . 137 B4
Angel Sq N1 . . . 85 C1
Angel St EC1 . . . 108 C2
Angel Sta EC1 . . . 85 C1
Angel Wlk W6 . . . 39 B2
Angerstein Bsns Pk SE10 . . . 43 C2
Angerstein La SE3 . . . 53 B2
Anglebury 5 W2 . . . 31 C3
Anglers La NW5 . . . 13 A2
Anglesey Ho 13 E14 . . . 33 C3
Anglia Ho 13 E14 . . . 33 A3
Anglo American Laundry SW17 . . . 71 B1
Anglo Rd 16 E3 . . . 26 B3
Angrave Ct 4 E8 . . . 24 B4
Angrave Pas 5 E8 . . . 24 B4
Angus Ho 12 SW12 . . . 73 C4
Angus St SE14 . . . 51 A3
Anhalt Rd SW11 . . . 158 B2
Animals in War Meml* W1 . . . 117 A4
Anley Rd W14 . . . 39 C4
Annabel Cl E14 . . . 34 A3
Anna Cl E8 . . . 24 B4
Annandale Rd
Chiswick W4 . . . 38 A1
Greenwich SE10 . . . 43 B1
Anne Goodman Ho 3 E1 . . . 32 B3
Anne Kerr Ct 18 SW15 . . . 57 C1
Anne's Ct NW8 . . . 90 B2
Annesley Ho SW9 . . . 173 B4
Annesley Wlk N19 . . . 4 B2
Annette Cres 16 N1 . . . 15 B1
Annette Ct N7 . . . 5 B1
Annette Rd N7 . . . 14 B4
Annie Besant Cl E3 . . . 26 B4
Anning St E2 . . . 24 A1 98 B2
Annis Rd E9 . . . 18 A2
Ann La SW10 . . . 157 B3
Ann Moss Way SE16 . . . 40 B3
Ann's Cl SW1 . . . 131 B3
Ann's Pl E1 . . . 110 C3
Ansdell Rd SE15 . . . 50 B1
Ansdell St W8 . . . 128 B2
Ansdell Terr W8 . . . 128 B2
Ansell Ho E1 . . . 32 B4
Ansell Rd SW17 . . . 72 B1
Anselm Rd SW6 . . . 155 B3
Ansleigh Pl W11 . . . 30 C2
Anson Ho
Pimlico SW1 . . . 160 C4
6 Tower Hamlets E1 . . . 26 A1
Anson Prim Sch NW2 . . . 9 C3
Anson Rd
Cricklewood NW2 . . . 9 B3
Tufnell Pk N7 . . . 13 C4
Anstey Ct 6 W3 . . . 37 A4
Anstey Ho 7 E9 . . . 25 B4
Anstey Rd SE15 . . . 64 C4
Anstice Cl W4 . . . 46 A3
Antenor Ho 11 E2 . . . 25 A3
Anthony Cope Ct N1 . . . 97 C4
Anthony Ho NW8 . . . 90 A1
Anthony St E1 . . . 32 A3
Antilles Bay 10 E14 . . . 42 B4
Antilles Ho W3 . . . 28 C3
Antill Rd E3 . . . 26 A2
Antill Terr 5 E1 . . . 32 C3
Antonine Hts SE1 . . . 138 A3
Anton St E8 . . . 16 C3
Antony Ho
4 Deptford SE14 . . . 50 C3
2 Rotherhithe SE16 . . . 40 B2
Antrim Gr NW3 . . . 12 B2
Antrim Ho SW11 . . . 60 C4
Antrim Mans NW3 . . . 12 B2
Antrim Rd NW3 . . . 12 B2
Antrobus Rd W4 . . . 37 B3
Apex Ind Est NW10 . . . 21 B1
Aphrodite Ct 11 E14 . . . 41 C2
Apollo Bldg 2 E14 . . . 41 C2
Apollo Ho
Chelsea SW10 . . . 157 B3
32 Hackney E2 . . . 25 A3
Highgate N6 . . . 3 B4
Apollo Ind Bsns Ctr 29 SE8 . . . 50 C4
Apollo Pl SW10 . . . 157 B2
Apollo Studios 18 NW5 . . . 13 C3
Apothecary St EC4 . . . 108 A1
Appach Rd SW2 . . . 62 C1
Appleby Ct W3 . . . 37 B4
Appleby Rd
Hackney E8 . . . 16 C1
Newham E16 . . . 35 C3
Appleby St E2 . . . 24 B3
Appledore Cl SW12, SW17 . . . 72 B2
Appleford 8 NW5 . . . 13 B3
Appleford Ho 6 W10 . . . 23 A1
Appleford Rd W10 . . . 23 A1
Applegarth Ho
Borough The SE1 . . . 136 B4
9 Camberwell SE15 . . . 49 C3
Applegarth Rd W14 . . . 39 C3
Apple Mkt WC2 . . . 120 B4
Appleshaw Ho 4 SE5 . . . 64 A4
Appleton Ct 30 E8 . . . 17 A3
Appletree Ct SE13 . . . 67 C3
Apple Tree Yd SW1 . . . 119 A2
Appold St EC2 . . . 110 A4
Appollo Ct SW9 . . . 173 B4
Apprentice Way 5 E5 . . . 17 A4
Approach Cl N16 . . . 16 A4
Approach Rd E2 . . . 25 B3
Approach The W3 . . . 28 C3
April Ct 20 E2 . . . 24 C3
April St E8 . . . 16 B4
Apsley Ho
Stepney E1 . . . 32 B4
St John's Wood NW8 . . . 79 B2
Apsley Way W1 . . . 131 C4
Aquila St NW8 . . . 79 C2
Aquinas St SE1 . . . 121 C1
Arabella Ct NW8 . . . 79 A2
Arabella Dr SW15 . . . 56 A3
Arabian Ho 3 E1 . . . 26 A1
Arabin Rd SE4 . . . 66 B3
Aragon Twr SE8 . . . 41 B2
Arakan Ho 4 N16 . . . 15 C4
Aral Ho 14 E1 . . . 25 C1
Arapiles Ho 6 E14 . . . 34 C3
Arbery Rd E3 . . . 26 A3
Arbon Ct N1 . . . 87 A3
Arbor Ct N16 . . . 6 C2
Arborfield Cl SW2 . . . 74 B3
Arborfield Ho 7 E14 . . . 33 C2
Arbour Ho 3 E1 . . . 32 C3
Arbour Sq E1 . . . 32 C3
Arbuthnot Rd SE14 . . . 50 C1
Arbutus St E8 . . . 24 B4
Arcade The
Broadgate EC2 . . . 110 A3
1 Tufnell Pk N7 . . . 14 A4
Arcadian Ho SW6 . . . 167 A1
Arcadian Pl SW18 . . . 70 B4
Arcadia St E14 . . . 33 C3
Archangel St SE16 . . . 40 C4
Archbishop Coggan Ho SE13 . . . 67 C3
Archbishop Michael Ramsey Tech Coll SE5 . . . 48 A3
Archbishop's Pl 1 SW2 . . . 74 B4
Archbishop Sumner CE Prim Sch SE11 . . . 149 C3
Archbishop Tenison's Sch SE11 . . . 163 A3
Archdale Ct W12 . . . 30 A1
Archdale Ho SE1 . . . 138 A2
Archdale Rd SE22 . . . 64 B3
Archel Rd W14 . . . 154 C4
Archer Ho
Battersea SW11 . . . 167 C2
24 Hoxton N1 . . . 24 A4
1 New Cross SE14 . . . 51 A2
Notting Hill W11 . . . 31 B2 113 A4
Archers Lo SE16 . . . 153 C1
Archer Sq SE14 . . . 51 A4
Archer St W1 . . . 119 B4
Archery Cl W2 . . . 102 B1
Archery Fields Ho WC1 . . . 95 B4
Archery Stps W2 . . . 116 B4
Arches The WC2 . . . 120 B2
Archibald Mews W1 . . . 118 A3
Archibald Rd N7 . . . 13 C4
Archibald St E3 . . . 26 C2
Archie St SE1 . . . 138 B3
Arch St SE1 . . . 136 C1
Archway N19 . . . 4 B2
Archway Bsns Ctr 5 N19 . . . 4 C1
Archway Cl
North Kensington W10 . . . 30 C4
2 Upper Holloway N19 . . . 4 B2
Archway Hts 5 N19 . . . 4 B3
Archway Mews SW15 . . . 58 A3
Archway Rd N6 . . . 4 A4
Archway St SW13, SW14 . . . 56 A4
Archway Sta N19 . . . 4 B2
Arcola St E8 . . . 16 B3
Arctic St NW5 . . . 13 A3
Ardbeg Rd SE24 . . . 63 C2
Arden 17 SW19 . . . 69 C3
Arden Cres E14 . . . 41 C2
Arden Ho
21 Hoxton N1 . . . 24 A3
Stockwell SW9 . . . 172 B1
Vauxhall SE11 . . . 148 C3
Ardent Ho 30 E3 . . . 26 A3
Ardilaun Rd N5 . . . 15 B4
Ardleigh Rd N1 . . . 16 A2
Ardlui Rd SE27 . . . 75 B2
Ardmere Rd SE13 . . . 67 C1
Ardshiel Cl SW15 . . . 57 C4
Ardwell Rd SW2 . . . 74 A2
Ardwick Rd NW2 . . . 10 C4
Ares Ct 16 E14 . . . 41 C2
Arethusa Ho 8 E14 . . . 42 A2
Argo Bsns Ctr 7 NW6 . . . 23 C2
Argon Mews SW6 . . . 155 C1
Argos Ct SW9 . . . 173 B4
Argos Ho 8 E2 . . . 25 A3
Argosy Ho
Fitzrovia W1 . . . 92 B1
Rotherhithe SE8 . . . 41 A2
Argyle Ho E14 . . . 42 B3
Argyle Mans 4 NW2 . . . 9 C4
Argyle Pl W6 . . . 39 A2
Argyle Prim Sch WC1 . . . 94 A4
Argyle Rd E1 . . . 25 C1
Argyle Sq WC1 . . . 94 B4
Argyle St WC1 . . . 94 B4
Argyle Way SE16 . . . 153 C1
Argyle Wlk WC1 . . . 94 B3
Argyll Cl SW9 . . . 62 B4
Argyll Ct 15 SW2 . . . 74 A4
Argyll Mans
Chelsea SW3 . . . 157 C4
West Kensington W14 . . . 140 B4
Argyll Rd W8 . . . 127 C3
Argyll St W1 . . . 104 C1
Arica Ho SE16 . . . 40 A3
Arica Rd SE4 . . . 66 A4
Ariel Ct
5 Hammersmith W12 . . . 38 C3
Newington SE11 . . . 150 A3
Ariel Rd NW6 . . . 10 C2
Ariel Way W12 . . . 30 B1
Aristotle Rd SW4 . . . 61 C4
Arizona Bldg 10 SE13 . . . 52 A2
Arkansas Ho 21 N19 . . . 4 C4
Ark Ct N16 . . . 7 B2
Arklow Ho SE17 . . . 48 C4
Arklow Rd SE14 . . . 51 B4
Arklow Road Trad Est SE14 . . . 51 B4
Arkwright Ho 23 SW2 . . . 74 A4
Arkwright Mans NW3 . . . 11 B3
Arkwright Rd NW3 . . . 11 B3
Arlesey Cl SW15 . . . 58 A2
Arlesford Rd SW9 . . . 62 A4
Arlidge Ho EC1 . . . 107 C4
Arlingford Rd SW2 . . . 62 C1
Arlington Ave N1 . . . 87 A3
Arlington Cl SE13 . . . 67 C2
Arlington Ct 13 W3 . . . 28 A1
Arlington Gdns W4 . . . 37 B1
Arlington Ho
3 Deptford SE8 . . . 51 B4
Finsbury EC1 . . . 95 C4
1 Shepherd's Bush W12 . . . 30 A1
Arlington Lo SW2 . . . 62 B3
Arlington Park Mans 1 W4 . . . 37 B1
Arlington Pl 7 SE10 . . . 52 B3
Arlington Rd NW1 . . . 82 B3
Arlington Sq N1 . . . 87 A3
Arlington St SW1 . . . 118 C2
Arlington Way EC1 . . . 95 C4
Armada Ct 11 SE8 . . . 51 C4
Armadale Rd SW6 . . . 155 B3
Armada St 10 SE8 . . . 51 C4
Armagh Rd E3 . . . 26 B4
Arminger Rd W12 . . . 30 A1
Armitage Ho NW1 . . . 102 B4
Armitage Rd
Golders Green NW11 . . . 1 B3
Greenwich SE10 . . . 43 B1
Armour Cl N7 . . . 14 B2
Armoury Ho E3 . . . 26 A4
Armoury Rd SE8 . . . 52 A1
Armoury Way SW18 . . . 58 C2
Armsby Ho 17 E1 . . . 32 B4
Armstrong Ho 8 SW15 . . . 57 C1
Armstrong Rd
East Acton W3 . . . 29 B1
Knightsbridge SW7 . . . 129 B1
Arnal Cres SW18 . . . 70 A4
Arncliffe NW6 . . . 78 B3
Arndale Wlk 6 SW18 . . . 59 A2
Arne Ho SE11 . . . 148 C2
Arne St WC2 . . . 106 B1
Arneway St SW1 . . . 133 C1
Arnewood Cl SW15 . . . 68 C3
Arnhem Pl E14 . . . 41 C3
Arnhem Way 3 SE22 . . . 64 A2
Arnhem Wharf E14 . . . 41 C3
Arnhem Wharf Prim Sch E14 . . . 41 C3
Arnold Cir E2 . . . 24 B2 98 C3
Arnold Est SE1 . . . 139 A3
Arnold Ho
Newington SE17 . . . 150 B1

Arnold Ho *continued*
9 Stoke Newington N16 ... 7 A1
Arnold House Sch NW8 ... 79 B1
Arnold Rd E3 ... 26 C2
Arnot Ho 27 SE5 ... 48 B3
Arnott Cl W4 ... 37 C2
Arnould Ave SE5 ... 63 C3
Arnside Ho 2 SE17 ... 48 C4
Arnside St SE17 ... 48 B4
Arodene Rd SW2 ... 62 B1
Arragon Rd SW18 ... 70 C3
Arran Ho
5 Canary Wharf E14 ... 34 B1
Stoke Newington N16 ... 7 B3
Arran Wlk N1 ... 15 B1
Arrol Ho SE1 ... 137 A1
Arrowe Ct 6 E5 ... 17 A4
Arrow Ho 23 N1 ... 24 A4
Arrow Rd E3 ... 27 A2
Arrowsmith Ho SE11 ... 148 C2
Arsenal Sta N5 ... 5 C1
Arta Ho 26 E1 ... 32 B3
Artemis Ct 14 E14 ... 41 C2
Artemis Pl SW18 ... 70 B4
Artesian Rd W2 ... 31 C3
Arthur Ct
Battersea SW11 ... 169 C3
10 North Kensington W10 ... 30 C3
Paddington W2 ... 100 A2
Arthur Deakin Ho E1 ... 111 B4
Arthurdon Rd SE4 ... 66 C2
Arthur Henderson Ho
9 Crouch End N19 ... 4 C4
Fulham SW6 ... 164 C2
Arthur Newton Ho 20 SW11 ... 59 C4
Arthur Rd N7 ... 14 B4
Arthur St EC4 ... 123 C4
Arthur Wade Ho E2 ... 24 B2 99 A4
Artichoke Hill 8 E1 ... 32 A2
Artichoke Mews 5 SE5 ... 48 C2
Artichoke Pl SE5 ... 48 C2
Artillery Ho
Bow E3 ... 26 A4
Westminster SW1 ... 133 B1
Artillery La
Broadgate E1 ... 110 B3
North Kensington W12 ... 29 C3
Artillery Pas E1 ... 110 B3
Artillery Pl SW1 ... 133 B1
Artillery Row SW1 ... 133 B1
Artisan Ct E8 ... 16 C2
Artisan Mews 9 NW10 ... 22 C2
Artisan Quarter 10 NW10 ... 22 C2
Artizan St E1 ... 110 B2
Arton Wilson Ho 12 SW15 ... 56 C2
Arts Educational Sch The W4 ... 38 A2
Arundel Bldgs SE1 ... 138 B1
Arundel Cl SW11 ... 60 A2
Arundel Ct
Barnes SW13 ... 47 A4
Chelsea SW3 ... 144 B2
Putney SW15 ... 57 C2
Arundel Gdns W11 ... 31 B2 112 C4
Arundel Gr N16 ... 16 A3
Arundel Ho
Islington N1 ... 86 B4
Richmond TW10 ... 54 C2
3 South Acton W3 ... 37 A4
Arundel Lo 9 N19 ... 5 A2
Arundel Mans
Barnes SW13 ... 47 A4
Fulham SW6 ... 165 A4
Arundel Pl N1, N7 ... 14 C2
Arundel Sq N7 ... 14 C2
Arundel St WC2 ... 121 A4
Arundel Terr SW13 ... 47 A4
Arvon Rd N5 ... 14 C3
Asaph Ho SE14 ... 51 B2
Ascalon Ct 16 SW2 ... 74 B4
Ascalon Ho SW8 ... 160 C1
Ascalon St SW8 ... 160 C1
Ascham St NW5 ... 13 B3
Ascot Ct
8 Brixton SW4 ... 62 A3
St John's Wood NW8 ... 89 B3
Ascot Ho
6 Acton Green W4 ... 37 B1
1 Paddington W9 ... 31 C4
Regent's Pk NW1 ... 92 B4
Ascot Lo NW6 ... 78 B2
Ascot Par 9 SW4 ... 62 A3
Ascott Ave W5 ... 36 A4
Ashbourne Ct E5 ... 18 A4
Ashbourne Gr
Chiswick W4 ... 38 A1
East Dulwich SE22 ... 64 B3
Ashbourne Ind Sch W8 ... 128 A3
Ashbridge Ct 3 W6 ... 39 A3
Ashbridge St NW8 ... 90 A1
Ashbrook Rd N19 ... 4 C2
Ashburn Gdns SW7 ... 142 C4
Ashburnham Com Sch SW10 ... 157 B2
Ashburnham Gr SE10 ... 52 A3
Ashburnham Pl SE10 ... 52 A3
Ashburnham Rd
Chelsea SW10 ... 157 A1
Kensal Rise NW10 ... 22 B3
Ashburnham Retreat 4 SE10 ... 52 A3
Ashburnham Twr SW10 ... 157 B2
Ashburn Pl SW7 ... 142 C3
Ashburton Mans SW10 ... 157 A2
Ashburton Rd E16 ... 35 C3
Ashbury Rd SW11 ... 60 C4
Ashby Ct NW8 ... 89 C2
Ashby Gr N1 ... 15 B1
Ashby Ho
6 Brixton SW9 ... 48 A1
17 Islington N1 ... 15 B1
Ashby Mews
10 Clapham Pk SW2 ... 62 A2
Ashby Mews *continued*
New Cross SE4 ... 51 B1
Ashby Rd SE4 ... 51 B1
Ashby St EC1 ... 96 B3
Ashchurch Ct 2 W12 ... 38 C3
Ashchurch Gr W12 ... 38 C3
Ashchurch Park Villas W12 ... 38 C3
Ashchurch Terr W12 ... 38 C3
Ashcombe Ct 4 SW15 ... 58 A2
Ashcombe Ho 39 E3 ... 27 A2
Ashcombe St SW6 ... 166 A1
Ashcroft Ho SW8 ... 170 C4
Ashcroft Rd E3 ... 26 A2
Ashcroft Sq 8 W6 ... 39 B2
Ash Ct
Clapham SW11 ... 60 C2
Marylebone W1 ... 102 C2
6 Rotherhithe SE16 ... 33 A1
Upper Holloway N19 ... 4 B2
Ashdale Ho N4 ... 6 C4
Ashdene 6 SE15 ... 50 A3
Ashdon Rd NW10 ... 21 B4
Ashdown SW15 ... 57 C2
Ashdown Cres NW5 ... 12 C3
Ashdown Ct SE22 ... 76 C3
Ashdown Ho 7 E5 ... 7 C2
Ashdown Way SW17 ... 72 C2
Ashdown Wlk 20 E14 ... 41 C2
Ashenden SE17 ... 151 A4
Ashenden Rd E5 ... 18 A3
Ashen Gr SW19 ... 70 C2
Ashentree Ct EC4 ... 107 C1
Asher Way E1 ... 125 C3
Ashfield Ho 5 N5 ... 15 B3
Ashfield Rd W3 ... 29 B1
Ashfield St E1 ... 32 B4
Ashfield Yd 21 E1 ... 32 B4
Ashford Ct NW2 ... 9 C4
Ashford Ho
14 Brixton SW9 ... 63 A3
11 Deptford SE8 ... 51 B4
Ashford Rd NW2 ... 9 C4
Ashford St N1 ... 24 A2 98 A4
Ash Gr
Cricklewood NW2 ... 10 A4
Ealing W5 ... 36 A3
Hackney E8 ... 25 A4
Ashgrove Ct 2 W9 ... 31 C4
Ashgrove Ho SW1 ... 147 C2
Ash Ho
3 Canary Wharf E14 ... 42 B4
Fulham SE1 ... 153 A3
Ashington 1 NW5 ... 13 A2
Ashington Ho 16 E1 ... 25 A1
Ashington Rd SW6 ... 165 A1
Ashland Pl W1 ... 103 B4
Ashleigh Ho SW14 ... 56 A4
Ashleigh Rd SW14 ... 56 A4
Ashley Cres SW11 ... 60 C4
Ashley Ct
Hampstead NW3 ... 11 A3
19 Kingsland N16 ... 16 A3
Ashley Pl SW1 ... 132 C1
Ashley Rd
Hornsey N19 ... 5 A4
Richmond TW9 ... 54 A4
Ashlin Rd E15 ... 19 C4
Ash Lo SW6 ... 47 C2
Ashlone Rd SW15 ... 57 C4
Ashmead Bsns Ctr 2 E16 ... 27 C1
Ashmead Ho E9 ... 18 A3
Ashmead Prim Sch SE8 ... 51 C1
Ashmead Rd SE8 ... 51 C1
Ashmere Gr 11 SW2, SW4 ... 62 A3
Ashmere Ho 10 SW2 ... 62 A3
Ashmill St NW8 ... 102 A4
Ashmole Prim Sch SW8 ... 163 A3
Ashmole St SW8 ... 163 A3
Ashmore NW1 ... 13 C1
Ashmore Cl SE15 ... 49 B3
Ashmore Ho W14 ... 126 B1
Ashmore Rd W9 ... 23 B2
Ashmount Prim Sch N19 ... 4 B4
Ashmount Rd N19 ... 4 C4
Ashness Rd SW11 ... 60 B2
Ashpark Ho 4 E14 ... 33 B3
Ashtead Ct 15 SW19 ... 69 C3
Ashtead Rd E5 ... 7 C4
Ashton Ho
Kennington SW9 ... 163 C1
Roehampton SW15 ... 69 A4
Ashton Rd E15 ... 19 C3
Ashton St E14 ... 34 B2
Ashurst Lo 4 N5 ... 15 A3
Ashwin St E8 ... 16 B2
Ashworth Cl SE5 ... 48 C1
Ashworth Mans W9 ... 88 B3
Ashworth Rd W9 ... 88 B3
Aske Ho N1 ... 24 A2 98 A4
Asker Ho N7 ... 14 A4
Aske St N1 ... 24 A2 98 A4
Askew Cres W12 ... 38 C4
Askew Mans 14 W12 ... 38 C4
Askew Rd W12 ... 38 C4
Askham Ct W12 ... 29 C1
Askham Rd W12 ... 29 C1
Askill Dr SW15 ... 58 A2
Asland Rd E15 ... 27 C4
Aslett St SW18 ... 71 B4
Asmara Rd NW2 ... 10 A3
Asolando Dr SE17 ... 151 A3
Aspect Coll WC1 ... 106 B3
Aspect Ho 7 E14 ... 42 B4
Aspen Cl Ealing W5 ... 36 B4
13 Upper Holloway N19 ... 4 B2
Aspen Ct
10 Acton W3 ... 28 B3
12 Hackney E8 ... 16 C3
Richmond TW9 ... 44 C3
Aspen Gdns 2 W6 ... 39 A1
Aspen Ho
8 Deptford SE15 ... 50 B4
4 Maitland Pk NW3 ... 12 B2
Aspen Ho *continued*
Richmond TW9 ... 44 C3
Aspenlea Rd W6 ... 47 C4
Aspen Way E14 ... 34 B2
Aspern Gr NW3 ... 12 A3
Aspinall Ho SW12 ... 74 A3
Aspinall Rd SE4 ... 65 C4
Aspinden Rd SE16 ... 40 A2
Aspire Bld 10 SW15 ... 58 B2
Aspley Rd SW18 ... 59 A2
Assam SE1 ... 125 A1
Assam St E1 ... 111 B2
Assata Mews N1 ... 15 A2
Assembly Pas E1 ... 32 B4
Assisi Ct SW12 ... 72 B3
Astbury Bsns Pk 5 SE15 ... 50 B2
Astbury Ho SE11 ... 135 B1
Astbury Rd SE15 ... 50 B2
Astell St SW3 ... 144 B2
Aster Ho 3 SE13 ... 52 B1
Aste St E14 ... 42 B4
Astey's Row 1 N1 ... 15 B1
Astle St SW11 ... 169 C2
Astley Ave NW2 ... 9 B3
Astley Ho
Fulham SE1 ... 153 A2
39 Paddington W2 ... 31 C4
Aston Ct N4 ... 6 B2
Aston Ho
Notting Hill W11 ... 31 B2 113 A4
South Lambeth SW8 ... 171 B3
Aston St E14 ... 33 A4
Astonville St SW18 ... 70 C3
Astor Ct SW6 ... 156 C1
Astoria Mans 18 SW16 ... 74 A1
Astoria Par SW16 ... 74 A1
Astoria Wlk SW9 ... 62 C4
Astra Ho
4 Bow E3 ... 26 B2
Hornsey N4 ... 5 B4
Astrop Mews W6 ... 39 B3
Astrop Terr W6 ... 39 B4
Astwood Mews SW7 ... 142 C4
Asylum Rd SE15 ... 50 A3
Atalanta St SW6 ... 47 C3 154 A1
Atheldene Rd SW18 ... 71 B3
Athelstane Gr E3 ... 26 B3
Athelstane Mews N4 ... 5 C3
Athelstan Gdns 8 NW6 ... 10 A1
Athelstan Ho
Hackney Wick E9 ... 18 B3
Stoke Newington N16 ... 16 A4
Athena Ct
Bermondsey SE1 ... 138 A3
St John's Wood NW8 ... 79 B2
Athenia Ho 7 E14 ... 34 C3
Athenlay Rd SE15 ... 65 C2
Athenoeum Ct N5 ... 15 B4
Athens Gdns W9 ... 23 C1
Atherden Rd E5 ... 17 B4
Atherfield Ct SW18 ... 59 A1

Atherfold Rd SW9 62 A4
Atherstone Ct W2 100 B4
Atherstone Mews SW7 143 A4
Atherton Rd SW13 46 C3
Atherton St SW11 168 B2
Athlone Cl 24 E5 17 A3
Athlone Ho
16 Camden Town NW5 12 C2
9 Stepney E1 32 B3
Athlone House N6 3 B3
Athlone Rd SW2 74 C4
Athlone St NW5 12 C2
Athol Ct 15 N4 5 B2
Atholl Ho W9 88 C3
Athol Sq E14 34 B3
Atkins Ct 13 E3 26 B4
Atkins Lo W8 127 B4
Atkinson Ho
Battersea SW11 169 B3
15 Hackney E2 24 C3
Walworth SE17 151 C3
Atkins Rd SW4, SW12 73 C4
Atlanta Bldg 8 SE13 52 A2
Atlantic Ct 10 E14 34 C2
Atlantic Ho
5 Putney SW15 58 B2
4 Tower Hamlets E1 33 A4
Atlantic Rd SW2, SW9, SE24 62 C3
Atlas Mews
Dalston E8 16 B2
Islington N7 14 B2
Atlas Rd NW10 21 A2
Atley Rd E3 26 C4
Atney Rd SW15 58 A3
Atterbury St SW1 148 A3
Attilburgh Ho SE1 138 C2
Attlee Ho E1 111 A3
Attneave St WC1 95 B3
Atwater Cl SW2 74 C3
Atwell Rd 6 SE15 49 C1
Atwood Ave TW9 44 C1
Atwood Ho SE21 76 A1
Atwood Rd W6 39 A2
Aubert Ct N5 15 A4
Aubert Pk N5 15 A4
Aubert Rd N5 15 A4
Aubrey Beardsley Ho SW1 147 A3
Aubrey Mans NW1 102 A4
Aubrey Moore Point E15 27 B3
Aubrey Pl NW8 78 C1
Aubrey Rd W14 31 B1 113 A1
Aubrey Wlk W14 31 B1 113 A1
Auburn Cl SE14 51 A3
Aubyn Sq SW15 56 C2
Auckland Ho 11 W12 30 A2
Auckland Rd SW11 60 A3
Auckland St SE11 148 C1
Auden Pl NW1 81 B4
Audley Cl 8 SW11 60 C4
Audley Ct W1 118 A2
Audley Rd TW10 54 B2
Audley Sq W1 117 C2
Audrey Ho EC1 107 C3
Audrey St E2 24 C3
Augusta St E14 34 A3
Augustine Ho
Broadgate EC2 109 C2
New Cross SE4 51 B2
Augustine Rd W14 39 C3
Augustines Ct E9 17 B3
Augustus Cl W12 39 A3
Augustus Ct
8 Putney SW19 70 A3
Streatham SW16 73 C2
Augustus Ho NW1 92 C4
Augustus Rd SW19 70 A3
Augustus St NW1 92 B4
Aulton Pl SE11 149 C1
Aura Ho 3 TW9 45 A2
Auriga Mews N1 15 C3
Auriol Mans W14 140 A3
Auriol Rd W14 140 A3
Aurora Bldg 4 E14 34 B1
Aurora Ho E14 34 A3
Austen Ho 5 NW6 23 C2
Austin Friars EC2 109 C2
Austin Friars Ho EC2 109 C2
Austin Friars Sq EC2 109 C2
Austin Ho
6 Brixton SW2 62 B2
1 New Cross SE14 51 B3
Austin Rd SW11 169 B3
Austins Ct SE15 64 C4
Austin St E2 24 B2 98 C3
Australia Rd W12 30 A2
Austral St SE11 150 A4
Autumn Rise 9 W4 37 C1
Autumn St E3 26 C4
Avalon Rd SW6 166 A4
Avebury Ct N1 87 B3
Avebury St N1 87 B3
Aveline St SE11 149 B1
Aveling Ho 12 N19 4 B1
Ave Maria La EC4 108 B1
Avenell Mans N5 15 A4
Avenell Rd N5 6 A1
Avenfield Ho W1 117 A4
Avening Rd SW18 70 C4
Avening Terr SW18 70 C4
Avenue Cl NW8 80 B3
Avenue Cres W3 37 A4
Avenue Ct
Chelsea SW3 144 C3
Cricklewood NW2 1 A1
Avenue Gdns
Mortlake SW14 56 A4
South Acton W3 37 A4
Avenue Ho
St John's Wood NW8 80 A1
Upper Clapton N16 7 C2
Willesden Green NW10 22 A3
Avenue Lo 12 NW8 11 C1
Avenue Mans
Clapham SW11 60 C3
Hampstead NW3 11 A3
Avenue Mans *continued*
Willesden NW2 9 A2
Avenue Park Rd SE21, SE27 75 A2
Avenue Rd
Crouch End N6 4 C4
Harlesden NW10 21 B3
Primrose Hill NW8 80 A4
South Acton W3 37 A4
Avenue Sch The NW6 10 A1
Avenue The
Bedford Pk W4 38 A3
Brondesbury Pk NW6 23 A4
Clapham SW4 60 C2
Greenwich SE10 52 C3
Richmond TW9 44 B1
Wandsworth SW18, SW12 72 A4
Averill St W6 47 C4
Avery Farm Row SW1 146 A3
Avery Hill Coll (Mile End Annexe) E3 26 B1
Avery Row W1 118 B4
Aviary Cl E16 35 B4
Avignon Rd SE4 65 C4
Avingdor Ct 10 W3 28 B1
Avington Ct SE1 152 B3
Avis Sq E1 32 C3
Avocet Cl SE1 153 B2
Avon Ct
1 Acton W3 28 B3
11 Putney SW15 58 A2
Avondale Ct E16 35 A4
Avondale Ho
Bermondsey SE1 153 B1
6 Mortlake SW14 55 C4
Avondale Mans SW6 164 C4
Avondale Park Gdns W11 31 A2 112 A3
Avondale Park Prim Sch W11 31 A2 112 A3
Avondale Park Rd W11 31 A2 112 A4
Avondale Rd
Mortlake SW14 55 C4
Newham E16 35 A4
Avondale Rise SE15 64 B4
Avondale Sq SE1 153 B1
Avon Ho
2 Islington N1 14 C1
14 Stoke Newington N16 15 C4
West Kensington W14 141 A3
Avonhurst Ho NW6 10 A1
Avonley Rd SE14 50 B3
Avonmore Gdns W14 141 A3
Avonmore Pl W14 140 B4
Avonmore Prim Sch W14 140 B4
Avonmore Rd W14 140 C4
Avonmouth St SE1 136 C2
Avon Pl SE1 137 A3
Avon Rd SE4 66 C4
Avriol Ho W12 30 A1
Avro Ct E9 18 A3
Axford Ho SW2 75 A3
Axis Bsns Ctr E15 27 A4
Axis Ct SE10 53 A4
Axminster Rd N7 5 B1
Aybrook St W1 103 B3
Aycliffe Rd W12 29 C1
Aylesbury Ho 13 SE15 49 C4
Aylesbury Rd SE17 151 C1
Aylesbury St EC1 96 A1
Aylesford Ho SE1 137 C3
Aylesford St SW1 147 B1
Aylesham Sh Ctr SE15 49 C2
Aylestone Ave NW6 22 C4
Aylmer Ho SE10 42 C1
Aylmer Rd W12 38 B4
Aylton Est 28 SE16 40 B4
Aylward St E1 32 C3
Aylwin Est SE1 138 B2
Aylwin Girls Sch SE1 153 A4
Aynhoe Mans W14 39 C2
Aynhoe Rd W14 39 C3
Ayres St SE1 137 A4
Ayrsome Rd N16 7 A1
Ayrton Gould Ho 9 E2 25 C2
Ayrton Rd SW7 129 B2
Aysgarth Rd SE21 76 A4
Ayshford Ho E1 25 A2
Ayston Ho 19 SE8 40 C2
Aytoun Ct SW9 173 A1
Aytoun Pl SW9 173 A1
Aytoun Rd SW9 173 A1
Azalea Ho SE14 51 B3
Azania Mews NW5 13 A2
Azenby Rd SE15 49 B1
Azof St SE10 43 A2
Azov Ho 10 E1 26 A1
Aztec Ct 8 N16 16 A2
Azure Ho E2 24 C2 99 B3

B

Baalbec Rd N5 15 A3
Babington Ct WC1 106 B4
Babington Ho SE1 137 A4
Babmaes St SW1 119 B3
Bacchus Wlk 12 N1 24 A3
Bache's St N1 97 C3
Back Church La E1 111 B1
Back Hill EC1 95 C1
Backhouse Pl SE1 152 B3
Back La NW3 11 B4
Bacon Gr SE1 138 C1
Bacon's Coll SE16 41 A4
Bacon's La N6 3 C3
Bacon St E2 24 B1 99 A2
Bacton NW5 12 C3
Bacton St E2 25 B2
Baddeley Ho SE11 149 A2
Baddow Wlk N1 86 C4
Baden Pl SE1 137 B4
Badminton Ct 9 N4 6 B4
Badminton Ho SE22 64 A3
Badminton Mews 9 E16 35 C1
Badminton Rd SW12 60 C1
Badric Ct SW11 167 C1
Badsworth Rd 3 SE5 48 B2
Bagley's La SW6 166 B3
Bagnigge Ho WC1 95 B3
Bagshot Ho NW1 92 B4
Bagshot St SE17 152 B1
Baildon 27 E2 25 B3
Baildon St SE8 51 B3
Bailey Ct 9 W12 38 C4
Bailey Ho SW10 156 B2
Bailey Mews
Brixton SW2 62 C2
Chiswick W4 45 A4
Bainbridge St WC1 105 C2
Bain Ho SW9 172 B2
Baird Ho 29 W12 30 A2
Baird St EC1 97 A2
Baizdon Rd SE3 53 A1
Baker Ho 12 E3 27 A2
Baker Rd NW10 21 A4
Bakers Field N7 14 A4
Bakers Hall Ct EC3 124 B3
Baker's Mews W1 103 B2
Bakers Pas 22 NW3 11 B4
Bakers Rents E2 24 B2 98 C3
Baker's Row EC1 95 B1
Baker St W1 103 A4
Baker Street W1 103 A4
Baker Street Sta NW1 91 A1
Baker's Yd EC1 95 B1
Bakery Cl SW9 163 A1
Balaclava Rd SE1 153 A3
Balchier Rd SE22 65 A1
Balcombe Ho
Lisson Gr NW1 90 C2
3 Streatham SW2 74 B3
Balcombe St NW1 90 C1
Balcorne St E9 17 B1
Balderton Flats W1 103 C1
Balderton St W1 103 C1
Baldock Ho 31 SE5 48 B1
Baldock St E3 27 A3
Baldrey Ho 1 SE10 43 B1
Baldwin Cres SE5 48 B2
Baldwin Ho 15 SW2 74 C3
Baldwin's Gdns EC1 107 B4
Baldwin St EC1 97 B3
Baldwin Terr N1 86 C2
Baldwyn Gdns W3 28 C2
Balearic Apts 3 E16 35 C2
Bale Rd E1 33 A4
Bales Coll W10 22 C2
Balfern Gr W4 38 A1
Balfern St SW11 168 B2
Balfe St N1 84 B1
Balfour Ho W10 30 C4
Balfour Mews W1 117 C2

Balfour Pl
  Mayfair W1 117 C3
  Putney SW15 57 A3
Balfour Rd
  Highbury N5 15 B4
  North Acton W3 28 B4
Balfour St SE17 151 B4
Balfron Twr 4 E14 34 B3
BALHAM 72 C3
Balham Gr SW12 72 C4
Balham High Rd SW12, SW17 72 C3
Balham Hill SW12 61 A1
Balham New Rd SW12 73 A4
Balham Park Mans SW12 72 B3
Balham Park Rd SW12, SW17 72 C3
Balham Sta SW12 73 A3
Balham Station Rd SW12 73 A3
Balin Ho SE1 137 B4
Balkan Wlk E1 32 A2
Balladier Wlk E14 34 A4
Ballance Rd E9 18 A2
Ballantine St SW18 59 B3
Ballantrae Ho NW2 10 B4
Ballard Ho SE10 52 A4
Ballast Quay SE10 42 C1
Ballater Rd SW2, SW4 62 A3
Ball Ct EC3 109 C1
Ballin Ct 14 E14 42 B4
Ballingdon Rd SW11 60 C1
Ballinger Point 18 E3 27 A2
Balliol Ho 11 SW15 57 C1
Balliol Rd W10 30 C3
Ballogie Ave NW10 8 A4
Ballow Cl 15 SE5 49 A3
Ball's Pond Pl 3 N1 15 C2
Ball's Pond Rd N1 16 A2
Balman Ho 3 SE16 40 C2
Balmer Rd E3 26 B3
Balmes Rd N1 87 C4
Balmoral Cl 1 SW15 57 C1
Balmoral Ct
  21 Rotherhithe SE16 32 C1
  St John's Wood NW8 79 B2
Balmoral Gr N7 14 B2
Balmoral Ho
  2 Isle Of Dogs E14 42 A3
  Stoke Newington N4 6 B3
  West Kensington W14 140 A4
Balmoral Mews W12 38 B3
Balmoral Rd NW2 9 A2
Balmore Cl E14 34 B3
Balmore St N19 4 A2
Balmuir Gdns SW15 57 B3
Balnacraig Ave NW10 8 A4
Balniel Gate SW1 147 C2
Balsam Ho 9 E14 34 A2
Baltic Apts 5 E16 35 C2
Baltic Ho 7 SE5 48 B1
Baltic St E EC1 96 C1
Baltic St W EC1 96 C1
Baltimore Ho
  Clapham SW18 59 B3
  Kennington SE11 149 B2
Balvaird Pl SW1 147 C1
Balvernie Gr SW18 70 C4
Bamber Rd 5 SE15 49 B2
Bamborough Gdns 12 W12 39 B4
Bamford Ct E15 19 A3
Banbury Ct WC2 120 A4
Banbury Ho 5 E9 17 C1
Banbury Rd E9 17 C1
Banbury St SW11 168 B2
Bancroft Ct SW8 172 A4
Bancroft Ho 11 E1 25 B1
Bancroft Rd E1 25 C1
Banff Ho 1 NW3 12 A2
Banfield Rd SE15 65 A4
Bangabandhu Prim Sch E2 25 B2
Bangalore St SW15 57 C4
Banim St W6 39 A2
Banister Ho
  Hackney E9 17 C3
  Nine Elms SW8 171 A4
  9 West Kilburn W10 23 A2
Banister Rd W10 22 C2
Bank Ct SW11 170 A4
Bank End SE1 123 A2
Bank La SW15 56 A2
Bank of England★ EC2 109 B1
Bank of England Mus★ EC2 109 B1
Banks Ho SE1 136 C1
Bankside
  Borough The SE1 122 C3
  Borough The SE1 123 A2
Bankside Art Gal★ SE1 122 B3
Bankside Ave 1 SE13 67 B4
Bankside Ho EC3 110 B1
Bankside Pier SE1 122 C3
Bank St E14 34 A1
Bank Sta EC3 109 C1
Bank The N6 4 A3
Bankton Rd SW2 62 C3
Banner Ct 5 SE16 40 B2
Banner Ho EC1 97 A1
Bannerman Ho SW8 162 C3
Banner St EC1 97 A2
Banning Ho 4 SW19 69 C3
Banning St SE10 43 A1
Bannister Cl SW2 74 C3
Bannister Ho 28 SE14 50 C4
Banqueting Ho★ SW1 120 A1
Banstead Ct N4 6 B3
Banstead St SE15 65 B4
Bantock Ho 8 W10 23 A2
Bantry Ho 13 E1 25 C1
Bantry St SE5 48 C3
Banville Ho SW8 163 A1
Banyan Ho 8 NW3 11 A2
Banyard Rd SE16 40 A3
Baptist Gdns NW5 12 C2
Barandon Wlk 6 W11 30 C2
Barbanel Ho 26 E1 25 B1
Barbara Brosnan Ct NW8 79 B1
Barbara Castle Cl SW6 155 A3
Barbara Rudolph Ct 5 N19 5 A4
Barbauld Rd N16 7 A1
Barber Beaumont Ho 21 E1 25 C2
Barbers Rd E15 27 A3
BARBICAN 109 A3
Barbican★ EC2 109 A3
Barbican Arts & Con Ctr★ EC2 109 A4
Barbican Sta EC1 108 C4
Barb Mews W6 39 B3
Barbon Cl WC1 106 C4
Barbrook Ho E9 17 B2
Barchard St SW18 59 A2
Barchester St E14 34 A4
Barclay Cl SW6 155 B1
Barclay Ho 21 E9 17 B1
Barclay Rd SW6 155 C1
Barcombe Ave SW2 74 B2
Bardell Ho SE1 139 B3
Bardolph Rd
  Richmond TW9 54 B4
  Tufnell Pk N7 14 A4
Bard Rd W10 30 C2
Bardsey Pl 41 E1 25 B1
Bardsey Wlk 5 N1 15 B2
Bardsley Ho 6 SE10 52 B4
Bardsley La SE10 52 B4
Barents Ho 10 E1 25 C1
Barfett St W10 23 B1
Barfleur La SE8 41 B2
Barford Ho 23 E3 26 B3
Barford St N1 85 C3
Barforth Rd SE15 65 A4
Barge House St SE1 121 C2
Barge La 10 E3 26 B4
Barham Ho SE17 152 B2
Baring Ct N1 87 B3
Baring Ho 15 E14 33 C3
Baring St N1 87 B3
Barker Cl TW9 45 A1
Barker Dr NW1 13 C1
Barker Ho
  Dulwich SE21 76 A1
  Walworth SE17 152 A3
Barker Mews SW4 61 A3
Barker St SW10 156 C4
Barker Wlk SW16 73 C1
Bark Pl W2 114 A4
Barkston Gdns SW5 142 A3
Barkway Ct N4 6 B2
Barkwith Ho 27 SE14 50 C4
Barkworth Rd SE16 40 B1
Barlborough St SE14 50 C3
Barlby Gdns W10 22 C1
Barlby Prim Sch W10 22 C1
Barlby Rd W10 30 C4
Barleycorn Way E14 33 B2
Barley Mow Pas
  Chiswick W4 37 C1
  Clerkenwell EC1 108 B3
Barley Shotts Bsns Pk W10 31 B4
Barling 6 NW1 13 A1
Barling Ct SW4 172 A2
Barlings Ho 2 SE4 65 C3
Barloch Ho SW11 169 B2
Barlow Ho
  14 Bermondsey SE16 40 A2
  Notting Hill W11 31 A2 112 A4
  Shoreditch N1 97 B4
Barlow Pl W1 118 B3
Barlow Rd
  Acton W3 28 A1
  Brondesbury NW6 10 B2
Barlow St SE17 151 C3
Barmouth Ho 6 N7 5 B2
Barmouth Rd SW18 59 B1
Barnabas Ho EC1 96 C3
Barnabas Lo SW8 172 B4
Barnabas Rd E9 17 C3
Barnaby Pl SW7 143 B3
Barnard Ct SW16 74 B1
Barnard Ho 17 E2 25 A2
Barnard Lo 10 W9 31 C4
Barnard Mews SW11 60 A3
Barnardo Gdns 1 E1 32 C2
Barnardo St E1 32 C3
Barnard Rd SW11 60 A3
Barnard's Inn EC4 107 C2
Barnbrough NW1 82 C3
Barnby St NW1 93 A4
Barn Cl 19 NW5 13 C3
Barnersbury Ho N7 14 A4
BARNES 46 B2
Barnes Ave SW13 46 C3
Barnes Bridge Sta SW13 46 A1
Barnes Common★ SW13 56 C4
Barnes Ct N1 14 C1
Barnes High St SW13 46 B1
Barnes Ho
  14 Bethnal Green E2 25 B3
  Camden Town NW1 82 B4
  26 Deptford SE14 50 C4
  Hornsey N19 5 A4
Barnes Hospl SW14 56 A4
Barnes Prim Sch SW13 56 B4
Barnes St E14 33 A3
Barnes Sta SW13 56 C4
Barnes Terr SE8 41 B1
Barnet Gr E2 24 C2 99 B3
Barnet Ho 35 SE5 48 B1
Barnett Ho E1 110 C3
Barnett St 18 E1 32 A3
Barn Field NW3 12 B3
Barnfield Cl
  London N4 5 A4
  Wandsworth SW17 71 B1
Barnfield Pl E14 41 C2
Barnham St SE1 138 B4
BARNSBURY 14 A1
Barnsbury Gr N7 14 B1
Barnsbury Ho 12 SW4 61 C1
Barnsbury Pk N1 14 C1
Barnsbury Rd N1 85 B3
Barnsbury Sq N1 14 C1
Barnsbury St N1 14 C1
Barnsbury Terr N1 14 B1
Barnsdale Ave E14 41 C2
Barnsdale Rd W9 23 B1
Barnsley St E1 25 A1
Barn St N16 7 A2
Barnstaple La SE13 67 B3
Barnston Wlk N1 86 C4
Barnwell Ho 1 SE5 49 A2
Barnwell Rd SW2 62 C2
Barnwood Cl W9 88 B1
Baron Cl N1 85 B2
Baroness Rd E2 24 B2 99 A4
Barons Court Mans W14 140 B1
Baron's Court Rd W14 140 B2
Barons Court Sta W14 140 A2
Barons Gate 13 W4 37 B3
Barons Keep W14 140 A2
Barons Lo 9 E14 42 B2
Baronsmead Rd SW13 46 C2
Baronsmede W5 36 B4
Baron's Pl SE1 135 C3
Baron St N1 85 B2
Baron Wlk E16 35 B4
Barque Mews SE8 51 C4
Barradell Ho 15 W14 39 C3
Barratt Ho 15 N1 15 A1
Barratt Ind Pk E3 27 B1
Barret Ho NW6 23 C4
Barrett Ct 2 NW10 21 A3
Barrett's Gr N16 16 A3
Barrett's Green Rd NW10 20 C3
Barrett St W1 103 C1
Barrhill Rd SW2 74 A2
Barriedale SE14 51 A1
Barrie Ho
  Acton W3 37 B4
  Bayswater W2 115 A3
  Primrose Hill NW8 80 B3
  8 Stoke Newington N16 7 A1
Barrington Cl NW5 12 C3
Barrington Ct
  9 Acton W3 37 A4
  Kentish Town NW5 12 C3
  South Lambeth SW9 172 B1

Barrington Rd SW9 . . . . 63 A4
Barrowgate Ho W4 . . . . 37 C1
Barrowgate Rd W4 . . . . 37 C1
Barrow Hill Est NW8 . . . . 80 A1
Barrow Hill Jun Sch NW8 . . . . 80 A1
Barrow Hill Rd NW8 . . . . 80 A1
Barry Ct SW4 . . . . 61 B1
Barry Ho 4 SE16 . . . . 40 A1
Barry Lo N4 . . . . 5 B4
Barry Par SE22 . . . . 64 C3
Barry Rd SE22 . . . . 64 C2
Barset Rd SE15 . . . . 65 B4
Barston Rd SE27 . . . . 75 B1
Barstow Cres SW2 . . . . 74 B3
Bartell Ho SW2 . . . . 62 C1
Barter St WC1 . . . . 106 B3
Bartholomew Cl
Barbican EC1 . . . . 108 C3
Wandsworth SW18 . . . . 59 B3
Bartholomew Ct
16 Blackwall E14 . . . . 34 C2
St Luke's EC1 . . . . 97 A2
Bartholomew Ho 22 SE5 . . . . 48 B1
Bartholomew La EC2 . . . . 109 C1
Bartholomew Pas EC1 . . . . 108 B3
Bartholomew Pl EC1 . . . . 108 C3
Bartholomew Rd NW5 . . . . 13 B2
Bartholomew Sq
18 Bethnal Green E1 . . . . 25 A1
St Luke's EC1 . . . . 97 A2
Bartholomew St SE1 . . . . 137 C1
Bartholomew Villas NW5 . . . . 13 B2
Bartle Rd W11 . . . . 31 A3
Bartlett Cl E14 . . . . 33 C3
Bartlett Ct EC4 . . . . 107 C2
Bartok Ho W11 . . . . 31 B2 112 C3
Barton Cl
Hackney E9 . . . . 17 B3
Peckham SE15 . . . . 65 A4
Barton Ct
South Lambeth SW4 . . . . 172 A2
West Kensington W14 . . . . 140 B2
Barton Ho
8 Bromley E3 . . . . 27 A2
Islington N1 . . . . 15 A1
Sands End SW6 . . . . 59 A4
Barton Rd W14 . . . . 140 B1
Barton St SW1 . . . . 134 A2
Bartonway NW8 . . . . 79 B2
Bartram Rd SE4 . . . . 66 A1
Bartrip St E9 . . . . 18 B2
Barts & The London Sch of Medicine & Dentistry EC1 . . . . 96 B1
Barville Cl SE4 . . . . 66 A3
Barwell Ho E2 . . . . 24 C1 99 C2
Barwick Ho 7 W3 . . . . 37 B4
Bascome St 13 SW2 . . . . 62 C1
Base Apartments 8 N1 . . . . 15 B1
Baseline Business Studios 18 W11 . . . . 30 C2
Basevi Way SE8 . . . . 52 A4
Bashley Rd NW10 . . . . 20 C1
Basildon Ct W1 . . . . 103 C4
Basil Ho
South Lambeth SW8 . . . . 162 A2
Whitechapel E1 . . . . 111 C2
Basil Mans SW1 . . . . 130 C3
Basil St
Knightsbridge SW1 . . . . 130 C3
Knightsbridge SW1, SW3 . . . . 130 C2
Basin App 20 E14 . . . . 33 A3
Basing Ct 13 SE15 . . . . 49 B2
Basingdon Way SE5 . . . . 63 C3
Basinghall Ave EC2 . . . . 109 B2
Basinghall St EC2 . . . . 109 B2
Basing Hill NW11 . . . . 1 B3
Basing House Yd E2 . . . . 24 A2 98 B4
Basing Pl E2 . . . . 24 A2 98 B4
Basing St W11 . . . . 31 B3
Basire St N1 . . . . 87 A4
Baskerville Ct SW18 . . . . 72 A4
Baskerville Gdns NW10 . . . . 8 A4
Baskerville Rd SW18 . . . . 72 A4
Baslow Wlk E5 . . . . 17 C4
Basnett Rd 9 SW11 . . . . 60 C4
Basque Ct 21 SE16 . . . . 40 C4
Bassano St SE22 . . . . 64 B2
Bassein Park Rd W12 . . . . 38 B4
Bassett Rd W10 . . . . 30 C3
Bassett St NW5 . . . . 12 C2
Bassingbourn Ho 3 N1 . . . . 15 A1
Bassingham Rd SW18 . . . . 71 B4
Bassishaw Highwalk EC2 . . . . 109 B3
Basswood Cl 5 SE15 . . . . 65 A4
Basterfield Ho EC1 . . . . 96 C1
Bastion Highwalk EC2 . . . . 108 C3
Bastwick St EC1 . . . . 96 C2
Basuto Rd SW6 . . . . 165 C3
Batavia Ho 1 SE14 . . . . 51 A3
Batavia Mews 3 SE14 . . . . 51 A3
Batavia Rd SE14 . . . . 51 A3
Batchelor St N1 . . . . 85 C3
Bateman Ho 8 SE17 . . . . 48 A4
Bateman's Bldgs W1 . . . . 105 B1
Bateman's Row EC2 . . . . 24 A1 98 B2
Bateman St W1 . . . . 105 B1
Bate St 10 E14 . . . . 33 B2
Bath Cl SE15 . . . . 50 A3
Bath Ct
Finsbury EC1 . . . . 97 B3
3 Forest Hill SE26 . . . . 76 C1
Holborn EC1 . . . . 95 B1
Bathgate Ho 8 SW9 . . . . 48 A2
Bathgate Rd SW19 . . . . 69 C1
Bath Gr E2 . . . . 24 C3
Bath Ho
Bethnal Green E2 . . . . 24 C1 99 C2
Borough The SE1 . . . . 137 A2
Bath Pl
14 Hammersmith W6 . . . . 39 B1
Shoreditch EC2 . . . . 24 A2 98 A3
Bath Rd W4 . . . . 38 A2
Bath St EC1 . . . . 97 B3
Bath Terr SE1 . . . . 136 C2
Bathurst Gdns NW10 . . . . 22 A3
Bathurst Ho 2 W12 . . . . 30 A2
Bathurst Mews W2 . . . . 115 C4
Bathurst St W2 . . . . 115 C4
Batley Pl 3 N16 . . . . 7 B1
Batley Rd N16 . . . . 7 B1
Batman Cl W12 . . . . 30 A1
Batoum Gdns W6 . . . . 39 B3
Batson Ho E1 . . . . 111 C1
Batson St W12 . . . . 38 C4
Batten Ho
7 London SW4 . . . . 61 B2
10 West Kilburn W10 . . . . 23 A2
Batten St SW11 . . . . 60 A4
BATTERSEA 169 A4
Battersea Bridge Rd SW11 . . . . 158 A1
Battersea Bsns Ctr SW11 . . . . 60 C4
Battersea Church Rd SW11 . . . . 167 C4
Battersea Dogs Home SW8 . . . . 160 B1
Battersea High St SW11 . . . . 167 B1
Battersea Hts SW11 . . . . 60 B4
Battersea Park* SW11 . . . . 159 B1
Battersea Park Rd SW11, SW8 . . . . 169 A3
Battersea Park Sta SW8 . . . . 160 A1
Battersea Power Station(dis) SW8 . . . . 160 B4
Battersea Rise SW11 . . . . 60 A3
Battersea Sq SW11 . . . . 167 C3
Battishill St 9 N1 . . . . 15 A1
Battlebridge Ct NW1 . . . . 84 B2
Battle Bridge La SE1 . . . . 124 A1
Battle Bridge Rd NW1 . . . . 84 A2
Battledean Rd N5 . . . . 15 A3
Battle Ho 8 SE15 . . . . 49 C4
Batty St E1 . . . . 111 C2
Baty Ho SW2 . . . . 74 B3
Baulk The SW18 . . . . 70 C4
Bavaria Rd N19 . . . . 5 A2
Bavent Rd SE5 . . . . 48 B1
Bawdale Rd SE22 . . . . 64 B2
Bawtree Rd SE14 . . . . 51 A3
Baxendale St E2 . . . . 24 C2 99 B4
Baxter Ho 11 E3 . . . . 27 A2
Baxter Rd N1 . . . . 15 C2
Baycliffe Ho 8 E9 . . . . 17 C2
Bay Ct
Ealing W5 . . . . 36 A3
7 Stepney E1 . . . . 25 C1
Bayer Ho EC1 . . . . 96 C1
Bayes Ct NW3 . . . . 12 B1
Bayfield Ho 3 SE4 . . . . 65 C3
Bayford Rd NW10 . . . . 22 C2
Bayford St Ind Ctr 4 E8 . . . . 17 A1
Bayford St 5 E8 . . . . 17 A1
Bayham Pl NW1 . . . . 83 A3
Bayham Rd W4 . . . . 37 C3
Bayham St NW1 . . . . 82 C3
Bayhurst Ho N4 . . . . 6 B4
Bayley St WC1 . . . . 105 B3
Baylis Rd SE1 . . . . 135 B3
Baynes Mews 2 NW3 . . . . 11 C2
Baynes St NW1 . . . . 13 B1
Bayon Ho 27 N19 . . . . 4 C4
Bayonne Rd W6 . . . . 154 A3
Bayston Rd N16 . . . . 7 B1
BAYSWATER 114 C4
Bayswater Rd W2 . . . . 115 B3
Bayswater Sta W2 . . . . 114 B4
Bayton Ct 2 E8 . . . . 16 C1
Baytree Rd SW2 . . . . 62 B3
Bazalgette Ho NW8 . . . . 89 C2
Bazeley Ho SE1 . . . . 136 A3
Bazely St E14 . . . . 34 B2
BBC Television Ctr W12 . . . . 30 B1
Beach Ho SW5 . . . . 141 B2
Beachy Rd E3 . . . . 18 C1
Beaconfield Terrace Rd W14 . . . . 126 A1
Beacon Gate SE14 . . . . 65 C4
Beacon Hill N7 . . . . 14 A3
Beacon Ho
11 Camberwell SE5 . . . . 49 A3
7 Isle Of Dogs E14 . . . . 42 A1
South Lambeth SW8 . . . . 171 B4
Beacon Rd SE13 . . . . 67 C1
Beaconsfield Cl
Acton Green W4 . . . . 37 B1
Greenwich SE3 . . . . 53 C4
Beaconsfield Rd
Acton W4 . . . . 37 C3
Greenwich SE3 . . . . 53 C3
Walworth SE17 . . . . 152 A1
Willesden NW10 . . . . 8 B2
Beaconsfield Wlk SW6 . . . . 165 A3
Beadon Rd W6 . . . . 39 B2
Beak St W1 . . . . 119 A4
Beale Ho SW9 . . . . 172 C1
Beale Pl E3 . . . . 26 B3
Beale Rd E3 . . . . 26 B4
Beames Ho SW8 . . . . 171 B4
Beames Rd NW10 . . . . 20 C4
Beaminster Ho SW8 . . . . 162 C2
Beamish Ho 7 SE16 . . . . 40 B2
Beanacre Cl E9 . . . . 18 B2
Bear Alley EC4 . . . . 108 A2
Bear Croft Ho SW6 . . . . 164 C1
Beardsley Way W3 . . . . 37 C4
Bear Gardens Mus* SE1 . . . . 122 C2
Bear Gdns SE1 . . . . 122 C2
Bear La SE1 . . . . 122 B1
Bear St WC2 . . . . 119 C4
Bearstead Rise SE4 . . . . 66 B2
Beaton Cl SE15 . . . . 49 B2
Beatrice Ho
1 Brixton SW2 . . . . 62 B2
4 Hammersmith W6 . . . . 39 B1
2 Stepney E1 . . . . 32 C4
Beatrice Pl W8 . . . . 128 A1
Beatrice Rd
Bermondsey SE1 . . . . 153 C3
Finsbury Pk N4 . . . . 5 C4
2 Richmond TW10 . . . . 54 B2
Beatrice Tate Sch E2 . . . . 25 A2
Beatrice Webb Ho 4 E3 . . . . 26 A3
Beatrix Ho SW5 . . . . 142 B2
Beatrix Potter Prim Sch SW18 . . . . 71 B3
Beatson Wlk 23 SE16 . . . . 32 C1
Beattie Ho SW8 . . . . 171 A4
Beatty Ho 16 E14 . . . . 41 C4
Beatty Rd N16 . . . . 16 A4
Beatty St NW1 . . . . 82 C2
Beauchamp Cl 17 W4 . . . . 37 B3
Beauchamp Pl SW3 . . . . 130 B1
Beauchamp Rd SW11 . . . . 60 B3
Beauchamp St EC1 . . . . 107 B3
Beauchamp Terr SW15 . . . . 57 A4
Beauclerc Rd W6 . . . . 39 A3
Beauclerk Ho 10 SW16 . . . . 74 A1
Beaufort Cl SW19 . . . . 69 A4
Beaufort Ct SW6 . . . . 155 B4
Beaufort Gdns SW3 . . . . 130 B2
Beaufort Ho
Battersea SW11 . . . . 168 A2
Chelsea SW3 . . . . 157 C3
20 Millwall E14 . . . . 41 C4
Pimlico SW1 . . . . 147 B1
Beaufort Mans SW3 . . . . 157 C3
Beaufort Mews SW6 . . . . 155 A4
Beaufort St SW3 . . . . 157 B4
Beaufoy Ho
South Lambeth SW8 . . . . 162 C2
3 West Norwood SE27 . . . . 75 A1
Beaufoy Rd 11 SW8 . . . . 61 A4
Beaufoy Wlk SE11 . . . . 149 A3
Beaulieu Cl SE5 . . . . 63 C4
Beaulieu Pl W4 . . . . 37 B3
Beaumanor Mans W2 . . . . 114 B4

Beaumaris Twr 2 W3 37 A4
Beaumont SW15 58 A2
Beaumont Ave
Richmond TW9 54 B4
West Kensington W14 140 C2
Beaumont Bldgs WC2 106 B1
Beaumont Cres W14 140 C1
Beaumont Ct
10 Acton Green W4 37 B1
Marylebone W1 103 C4
7 Mile End E1 26 A2
Beaumont Gdns NW3 1 C1
Beaumont Gr E1 25 C1
Beaumont Ho
1 Streatham SW2 74 A3
West Kensington W14 141 A3
Wimbledon SW19 70 C1
Beaumont Lo E8 16 C2
Beaumont Pl NW1, WC1, W1 93 A2
Beaumont Rd
Putney SW15, SW19 70 A4
South Acton W4 37 B3
Beaumont Rise N19 4 C3
Beaumont Sq E1 32 C4
Beaumont St W1 103 C4
Beaumont Wlk NW3 12 B1
Beauvale 6 NW1 12 C1
Beauval Rd SE22 64 B1
Beavis Ho N16 7 A1
Beavor La W6 38 C1
Beccles St E14 33 B2
Beck Cl SE13 52 A2
Beckers The N16 16 C4
Becket Ho SE1 137 B3
Becket St SE1 137 B2
Beckett Cl
Streatham SW16 73 C2
Willesden NW10 8 A2
Beckett Ho
London SW9 172 B1
15 Stepney E1 32 B4
Beckfoot NW1 83 A1
Beckford Cl W14 141 A3
Beckford Ho 18 N16 16 A3
Beckford Prim Sch NW6 10 B3
Beckham Ho SE11 149 A3
Beck Ho N16 7 A1
Beckington 18 NW5 12 C2
Beckley Ho E3 26 B1
Becklow Gdns
Chiswick W12 38 B4
1 Shepherd's Bush W12 38 C4
Becklow Mews 7 W12 38 C4
Becklow Rd W12 38 C4
Beck Rd E8 25 A4
Beckton Rd E16 35 B4
Beckway St SE17 152 A3
Beckwith Ho 22 E2 25 A3
Beckwith Rd SE24 63 C2
Bective Pl SW15 58 B3
Bective Rd SW15 58 B3
Bedale St SE1 123 B1
Bedefield WC1 94 B3
Bede Ho
London SE14 51 B2
5 Putney SW15 57 C1
Bedford Ave WC1 105 C3
Bedfordbury WC2 120 A3
Bedford Cl W4 46 B4
Bedford Cnr 3 W4 38 A2
Bedford Court Mans WC1 105 C3
Bedford Ct
6 Richmond TW9 54 B3
St James WC2 120 A3
Bedford Gardens Ho W8 31 C1 113 C1
Bedford Gdns W8 31 C1 113 C1
Bedford Hill SW12 73 A2
Bedford Ho
2 Acton W4 38 A2
7 Stockwell SW4 62 A3
BEDFORD PARK 38 A3
Bedford Park Cnr 5 W4 38 A2
Bedford Park Mans 4 W4 37 C2
Bedford Pas SW6 154 B2
Bedford Pl WC1 106 A4
Bedford Rd
Acton W4 38 A3
Stockwell SW2, SW4 62 A3
Bedford Row WC1 107 A3
Bedford Sq WC1 105 C3
Bedford St WC2 120 B3
Bedford Way WC1 93 C1
Bedgebury Gdns SW19 70 A2
Bedlam Mews SE11 149 B4
Bedlow Cl NW8 89 C1
Bedser Cl SE11 163 A4
Bedser Ct SW4 172 A2
Bedwell Ho SW9 173 B1
Beech Ave W3 29 A1
Beech Cl
Deptford SE8 51 B4
Putney SW15 68 C4
Beechcroft Ave NW11 1 B4
Beechcroft Ct
3 Golders Green NW11 1 B4
Greenwich SE3 53 C2
Beech Croft Ct N5 15 A4
Beechcroft Rd
Mortlake SW14 55 B4
Upper Tooting SW17 72 A2
Beechcroft Way N19 4 C3
Beech Ct
Child's Hill NW2 1 B2
Marylebone W1 102 C2
43 Notting Hill W2 31 C4
7 Rotherhithe SE16 33 A1
Beechdale Rd SW2 62 B1
Beechdene 4 SE15 50 A2
Beeches Rd SW17 72 B1
Beeches The 1 N19 5 A3
Beechey Ho 30 E1 32 A1
Beech Gdns W5 36 A3
Beech Ho
6 Maitland Pk NW3 12 B2
22 Rotherhithe SE16 40 B4
5 Stoke Newington N16 6 C2
Beechmore Rd SW11 169 A3
Beech St EC2 109 A4
Beech Tree Cl N1 14 C1
Beechwood Ave TW9 44 C2
Beechwood Ct
Chiswick W4 45 C4
Stamford Hill N16 7 A4
Beechwood Gr W3 29 A2
Beechwood Ho 23 E2 24 C3
Beechwood Rd E8 16 B2
Beechworth Cl NW3 1 C2
Beecroft La SE4 66 A2
Beecroft Mews SE4 66 A2
Beecroft Rd SE4 66 A2
Beehive Cl E8 16 B1
Beehive Pl SW9 62 C4
Beemans Row 1 SW18 71 B2
Beeston Cl 5 E8 16 C3
Beeston Pl SW1 132 B2
Beeston's Ho SE15 65 A4
Beethoven St W10 23 A2
Begbie Ho SW9 173 A2
Begonia Wlk W12 29 B3
Beira St SW12 73 A4
Beis Chinuch Lebonos Girls Sch N4 6 B4
Beis Rochel d'Satmar Girls Sch N16 7 A4
Bekesbourne St 17 E14 33 A3
Beldanes Lo NW10 8 C1
Belenoyd Ct SW16 74 B1
Belfast Rd N16 7 B2
Belfont Wlk N7 14 A4
Belford Ho 7 E8 24 B4
Belfort Rd SE15 50 B1
Belfry Cl 33 SE16 40 A1
Belgrade Ho N16 16 A4
Belgrade Rd N16 16 A4
Belgrave Cl 1 W3 37 B4
Belgrave Ct
8 Acton Green W4 37 B1
22 Limehouse E14 33 B2
Nine Elms SW8 160 C1
Belgrave Gdns
Kilburn NW8 78 C3
St John's Wood NW8 78 C3
Belgrave Mans NW8 78 C3
Belgrave Mews N SW1 131 B3
Belgrave Mews S SW1 131 C2
Belgrave Mews W SW1 131 B2
Belgrave Pl SW1 131 C1
Belgrave Rd
Barnes SW13 46 B3
Westminster SW1 146 C3
Belgrave Sq SW1 131 B2
Belgrave St E1 32 C3
Belgrave Yd SW1 132 A1
BELGRAVIA 146 A4
Belgravia Ct SW1 132 A1
Belgravia Ho 11 SW4 61 C1
Belgrove St WC1 94 B4
Belham Wlk 13 SE5 48 C2
Belinda Rd 8 SW9 63 A4
Belitha Villas N1 14 C1
Bellamy Cl
13 Millwall E14 41 C4
West Kensington SW5 141 A1
Bellamy's Ct 16 SE16 32 C1
Bellamy St SW12 73 A4
Bellasis Ave SW2 74 A2
Bell Ct SE13 66 C2
Bell Dr SW18 70 A4
Bellefields Rd SW9 62 B4
Bellenden Prim Sch SE15 49 C1
Bellenden Rd SE15 49 B1
Bellenden Rd Ret Pk SE15 49 C2
Bellendon Road Bsns Ctr SE15 49 B1
Bellerbys Coll SE8 51 C4
Belleville Prim Sch SW11 60 B2
Belleville Rd SW11 60 B2
Belle Vue Gdns SW9 172 B1
Bellevue Pl E1 25 B1
Bellevue Rd
Barnes SW13 46 C1
Upper Tooting SW17 72 B3
Bellew St SW17 71 B1
Bell Flats 4 NW2 8 C2
Bellflower Ct SE13 67 A3
Bellgate Mews NW5 4 A1
Bellgrave Lo 9 W4 37 A1
Bell Ho
Greenwich SE10 52 B4
15 Streatham SW2 74 C4
Bellina Mews NW5 13 B4
Bell Ind Est 2 W4 37 B2
Bell Inn Yd EC3 109 C1
Bell La
Newham E16 35 C1
Spitalfields E1 110 C3
Bell Language Sch W1 92 C1
Bellmaker Ct 13 E3 33 C4
Bell Moor NW3 2 B1
Bello Cl SE24, SW2 75 A3
Bellot Gdns 1 SE10 43 A1
Bellot St SE10 43 A1
Bell St NW1 102 A4
Bell Wharf La EC4 123 A4
Bellwood Rd SE15 65 C3
Bell Yard Mews SE1 138 B3
Bell Yd WC2 107 B1
Belmont Cl SW4 61 B4
Belmont Ct
Highbury N5 15 B4
6 Stamford Hill N16 7 A3
Belmont Gr
Chiswick W4 37 C2
Lewisham SE13 67 C4
Belmont Hall Ct SE13 67 C4
Belmont Hill SE13 67 C4
Belmont Mews SW19 69 C2
Belmont Prim Sch W4 37 C2
Belmont Rd
Clapham SW4 61 B4
London W4 37 C2
Belmont St NW1 12 C1
Belmont Terr W4 37 C2
Belmore Ho N7 13 C3
Belmore La N7 13 C3
Belmore St SW8 171 B4
Beloe Cl SW15 56 C3
Belper Ct 11 E5 17 C4
Belsham St E9 17 B2
Belsize Ave NW3 12 A3
Belsize Court Garages 1 NW3 11 C3
Belsize Cres NW3 11 C2
Belsize Ct NW3 11 C3
Belsize Gr NW3 12 A2
Belsize La NW3 11 C3
Belsize Mews NW3 11 C2
Belsize Park Gdns NW3 12 A2
Belsize Park Mews 1 NW3 11 C2
Belsize Park Sta NW3 12 A3
Belsize Pk NW3 11 C2
Belsize Pl NW3 11 C3
Belsize Rd NW6 78 B4
Belsize Sq NW3 11 C2
Belsize Terr NW3 11 C2
Beltane Dr SW19 69 C1
Belthorn Cres SW12 73 B4
Belton Rd NW2 8 C2
Belton Way E3 33 C4
Beltran Rd SW6 166 A1
Belvedere Bldgs SE1 136 B3
Belvedere Ct
Brondesbury NW2 9 C2
7 Clapham Pk SW4 61 C1
Putney SW15 57 B3
33 Shoreditch N1 24 A4
Belvedere Htss NW8 90 A2
Belvedere Mews SE15 65 B4
Belvedere Pl
Brixton SW2 62 B3
Lambeth SE1 136 B3
Belvedere Rd SE1 121 A1
Belvedere The SW10 167 A3

Belvoir Lo SE22 ... 76 C4
Belvoir Rd SE22 ... 76 C4
Bembridge Cl NW6 ... 10 A1
Bembridge Ho
[9] Deptford SE8 ... 41 B2
Wandsworth SW18 ... 59 A1
Bemerton St N1 ... 84 C4
Bemish Rd SW15 ... 57 C4
Benabo Ct [6] E8 ... 16 C3
Benbow Ct W6 ... 39 A3
Benbow Ho [12] SE8 ... 51 C4
Benbow Rd W6 ... 39 A3
Benbow St SE8 ... 51 C4
Bence Ho [13] SE8 ... 41 A2
Bendall Mews NW1 ... 102 B4
Bendemeer Rd SW15 ... 57 C4
Benden Ho SE13 ... 67 B2
Bendon Valley SW18 ... 71 A4
Benedict Rd SW9 ... 62 B4
Benenden Ho SE17 ... 152 B2
Ben Ezra Ct SE17 ... 151 A3
Benfleet Ct [6] E8 ... 24 B4
Bengal Ct EC3 ... 109 C1
Bengal Ho E1 ... 32 C4
Bengeworth Rd SE5 ... 63 B4
Benham Cl [1] SW11 ... 59 C4
Benham Ho SW10 ... 156 B2
Benham's Pl [11] NW3 ... 11 B4
Benhill Rd SE5 ... 48 C2
Benington Ct N4 ... 6 B2
Benjamin Cl E8 ... 24 C4
Benjamin Ho [12] W3 ... 28 A1
Benjamin Mews SW12 ... 73 B4
Benjamin St EC1 ... 108 A4
Ben Jonson Ct [30] N1 ... 24 A3
Ben Jonson Prim Sch E1 ... 26 A1
Ben Jonson Rd E1 ... 33 A4
Benledi Rd E14 ... 34 C3
Bennelong Cl W12 ... 30 A3
Bennerley Rd SW11 ... 60 B2
Bennet's Hill EC4 ... 122 B4
Bennett Ct
Hampstead NW6 ... 11 A2
Lower Holloway N7 ... 5 B1
[7] South Acton W3 ... 37 A4
Bennett Gr SE13 ... 52 A2
Bennett Ho
[2] Streatham SW4 ... 73 C4
Westminster SW1 ... 147 C4
Bennett St
Chiswick W4 ... 38 A1
St James SW1 ... 118 C2
Bennett's Yd SW1 ... 133 C1
Benn Ho E2 ... 24 C2 99 B3
Benn St E9 ... 18 A2
Benns Wlk [8] TW9 ... 54 A3
Bensbury Cl SW15 ... 69 B4
Ben Smith Way SE16 ... 139 C2
Benson Ct
South Lambeth SW8 ... 172 A4
[1] Tufnell Pk N19 ... 13 B4
Benson Ho
Lambeth SE1 ... 121 C1
Shoreditch E2 ... 24 B1 98 C2
Benson Quay E1 ... 32 B2
Benthal Ct N16 ... 7 C1
Benthal Prim Sch N16 ... 7 C1
Benthal Rd N16 ... 7 C1
Bentham Ct [11] N1 ... 15 B1
Bentham Ho SE1 ... 137 B2
Bentham Rd E9 ... 17 C2
Bentinck Cl NW8 ... 80 B1
Bentinck Ho [4] W12 ... 30 A2
Bentinck Mans W1 ... 103 C2
Bentinck Mews W1 ... 103 C2
Bentinck St W1 ... 103 C2
Bentley Cl SW19 ... 70 C1
Bentley Ct SE13 ... 67 B3
Bentley Ho
[6] Bow E3 ... 26 C1
[4] Camberwell SE5 ... 49 A2
Bentley Rd N1 ... 16 A2
Bentworth Ct E2 ... 24 C1 99 B2
Bentworth Prim Sch W12 ... 30 A3
Bentworth Rd W12 ... 30 A3
Benwell Rd N7 ... 14 C3
Benwick Cl SE16 ... 40 A2
Benworth St E3 ... 26 B2
Benyon Ho EC1 ... 95 C4
Benyon Rd N1 ... 87 C4
Benyon Wharf [31] E8 ... 24 A4
Beormund Prim Sch SE1 ... 137 C3
Bequerel Ct SE10 ... 43 B3
Berberis Ho [17] E3 ... 33 C4
Berber Pl [2] E14 ... 33 C2
Berber Rd SW11 ... 60 B2
Berebinder Ho [21] E3 ... 26 B3
Berenger Twr SW10 ... 157 B2
Berenger Wlk SW10 ... 157 B2
Berens Rd NW10 ... 22 C2
Beresford Ct E9 ... 18 A3
Beresford Ho
Dulwich SE21 ... 76 A1
[15] Stockwell SW4 ... 62 A3
Beresford Lo N4 ... 15 C3
Beresford Rd N5 ... 15 C3
Beresford Terr [3] N5 ... 15 B3
Bere St E1 ... 32 C2
Berestede Rd [4] W6 ... 38 B1
Bergen Ho [1] SE5 ... 48 B1
Bergen Sq SE16 ... 41 A3
Berger Prim Sch E9 ... 17 C2
Berger Rd E9 ... 17 C2
Berghem Mews W14 ... 39 C3
Bergholt Cres N16 ... 7 A4
Bergholt Mews [4] NW1 ... 13 C1
Berglen Ct E14 ... 33 A2
Bering Sq E14 ... 41 C1
Berisford Mews SW18 ... 59 B1
Berkeley Ct
[1] Golders Green NW11 ... 1 B4
Marylebone NW1 ... 91 A1
Willesden NW10 ... 8 A4
Berkeley Gdns W8 ... 31 C1 113 C1
Berkeley Ho
[17] Bow E3 ... 26 C2
[8] Deptford SE8 ... 41 B1
Berkeley Mews W1 ... 103 A1
Berkeley Rd SW13 ... 46 C2
Berkeley Sq W1 ... 118 B3
Berkeley St W1 ... 118 B2
Berkeley The NW11 ... 2 A4
Berkeley Wlk [1] N7 ... 5 B2
Berkley Gr NW1 ... 12 C1
Berkley Rd NW1 ... 12 B1
Berkshire Ho WC2 ... 106 A2
Berkshire Rd E9 ... 18 B2
Bermans Way NW10 ... 8 B4
BERMONDSEY ... 40 A4
Bermondsey Leather Mkt SE1 ... 138 A3
Bermondsey Mkt* SE1 ... 138 B2
Bermondsey Sq SE1 ... 138 B2
Bermondsey St SE1 ... 138 A3
Bermondsey Trad Est SE16 ... 40 B1
Bermondsey Wall E SE16 ... 40 A4
Bermondsey Wall W SE1, SE16 ... 139 B4
Bernard Angell Ho [4] SE10 ... 52 C4
Bernard Cassidy St [2] E16 ... 35 B4
Bernard Ho E1 ... 110 C3
Bernard Shaw Ct [5] NW1 ... 13 B1
Bernard Shaw Ho [2] NW10 ... 20 C4
Bernard St WC1 ... 94 B1
Bernay's Gr SW9 ... 62 B3
Berners Ho N1 ... 85 B2
Berners Mews W1 ... 105 A3
Berners Pl W1 ... 105 A2
Berners Rd N1 ... 86 A3
Berners St W1 ... 105 A2
Berner Terr E1 ... 111 C1
Bernhard Baron Ho E1 ... 111 C1
Bernhardt Cres NW8 ... 90 A2
Bernie Grant Ho [40] E9 ... 17 B1
Bernwood Ho [6] N4 ... 6 C4
Berridge Mews NW6 ... 10 C3
Berriman Rd N7 ... 5 B1
Berry Cotts [2] E14 ... 33 A3
Berryfield Rd SE17 ... 150 B2
Berry Ho
Battersea SW11 ... 169 A2
[25] Bethnal Green E1 ... 25 A1
Berrymead Gdns W3 ... 37 B4
Berrymede Inf Sch W3 ... 37 A4
Berrymede Jun Sch W3 ... 37 A4
Berrymede Rd W4 ... 37 C3
Berry Pl EC1 ... 96 B3
Berry St EC1 ... 96 B1
Berry Way W5 ... 36 A3
Bertha Neubergh Ho [1] SE5 ... 48 B2
Berthon St SE8 ... 51 C4
Bertie Rd NW10 ... 8 C2
Bertram St N19 ... 4 A2
Bertrand Ho [11] SW16 ... 74 A1
Bertrand St SE13 ... 67 A4
Bertrum House Sch SW17 ... 72 C2
Berwick St W1 ... 105 A1
Berwyn Ho [3] N16 ... 7 B3
Berwyn Rd
Mortlake SW14, TW10 ... 55 A3
Streatham SE24 ... 75 A3
Beryl Rd W6 ... 39 C1
Besant Cl NW2 ... 1 A1
Besant Ct N1 ... 15 C3
Besant Ho NW8 ... 78 C3
Besant Pl SE22 ... 64 B3
Besant Rd NW2 ... 10 A4
Besant Wlk N7 ... 5 B2
Besford Ho [26] E2 ... 24 C3
Bessant Dr TW9 ... 45 A2
Bessborough Gdns SW1 ... 147 C2
Bessborough Pl SW1 ... 147 C2
Bessborough Rd SW15 ... 68 C3
Bessborough St SW1 ... 147 B2
Bessemer Ct [7] NW1 ... 13 B1
Bessemer Grange Prim Sch SE5 ... 64 A3
Bessemer Park Ind Est [3] SE24 ... 63 A3
Bessemer Rd SE5 ... 48 B1
Bessingham Wlk SE4 ... 65 C2
Besson St SE14 ... 50 C2
Bessy St E2 ... 25 B2
Bestwood St SE8 ... 40 C2
Beswick Mews [1] NW6 ... 11 A2
Beta Pl [20] SW4 ... 62 B3
Betchworth Ho [8] N7 ... 13 C3
Bethersden Ho SE17 ... 152 B2
Bethlehem Ho [13] E14 ... 33 B2
BETHNAL GREEN ... 25 A2
Bethnal Green Rd
Bethnal Green E2 ... 24 C2 99 B3
Shoreditch E1, E2 ... 24 B1 99 A2
Bethnal Green Sta
Bethnal Green E1 ... 25 A1
Bethnal Green E2 ... 25 B2
Bethnal Green Tech Coll E2 ... 24 B2 99 A3
Bethune Rd
North Acton NW10 ... 20 C1
Stamford Hill N16 ... 7 A4
Bethwin Rd SE5 ... 48 B3
Betsham Ho SE1 ... 137 B4
Betterton Ho WC2 ... 106 B1
Betterton St WC2 ... 106 B1
Bettridge Rd SW6 ... 165 A1
Betts Ho E1 ... 32 A2
Betts St E1 ... 32 A2
Betty Layward Prim Sch N16 ... 6 C1
Betty May Gray Ho [2] E14 ... 42 B2
Bevan St N1 ... 87 A3
Bev Callender Cl [4] SW8 ... 61 A4
Bevenden St N1 ... 97 C4
Beveridge Rd [1] NW10 ... 8 A1
Beverley Cl
Barnes SW13 ... 46 C1
[6] Wandsworth SW11 ... 59 C3
Beverley Cotts SW15 ... 68 A1
Beverley Ct
[9] Acton Green W4 ... 37 B1
[5] Acton W12 ... 38 A4
Brockley SE4 ... 66 B4
Islington N5 ... 15 A2
Beverley Gdns
Barnes SW13 ... 56 B4
Hendon NW11 ... 1 A4
Beverley Lo [6] TW10 ... 54 A2
Beverley Path [9] SW13 ... 46 B1
Beverley Rd
Barnes SW13 ... 56 B4
Chiswick W4 ... 38 B1
Beversbrook Rd N19 ... 4 C1
Beverstone Rd SW2 ... 62 B2
Beverston Mews NW1 ... 102 C3
Bevin Cl SE16 ... 33 A1
Bevin Ct WC1 ... 95 A4
Bevington Prim Sch W10 ... 31 A4
Bevington Rd W10 ... 31 A4
Bevington St SE16 ... 139 C3
Bevin Ho
[35] Bethnal Green E2 ... 25 B2
[8] Bow E3 ... 26 C2
Bevin Sq SW17 ... 72 B1
Bevin Way WC1 ... 95 B4
Bevis Marks EC3 ... 110 B2
Bew Ct SE21 ... 76 C4
Bewdley Ho N4 ... 6 B4
Bewdley St N1 ... 14 C1
Bewick Mews SE15 ... 50 A3
Bewick St SW8 ... 170 B1
Bewley Ct SW2 ... 62 B1

Bewley Ho 7 E1 . . . 32 A2
Bewley St E1 . . . . . . 32 A2
Bexhill Rd
Catford SE4 . . . . 66 B1
Mortlake SW14 . . . . . 55 B4
Bexley Ho SE4 . . . . . . 66 A3
BFI London Imax
Cinema SE1 . . . . . 121 B1
Bianca Rd SE1,
SE15 . . . . 49 C4
Bicester Rd TW9 . . . 55 A4
Bickenhall Mans
W1 . . . . 103 A4
Bickenhall St W1 103 A4
Bickerton Rd N19 . . . 4 B2
Bicknell Ho E1 . . . 111 C1
Bicknell Rd SE5 . . . . 63 B4
Bicknor Ho 2 E5 . . . 17 A3
Bidborough St N1,
WC1 . . . . 94 A3
Biddenham Ho 18
SE16 . . . . 40 C2
Bidder St E16 . . . . . . 35 A4
Biddesden Ho
SW3 . . . . 144 C3
Biddestone Rd N7 . . 14 B4
Biddulph Mans
W9 . . . . 88 B3
Biddulph Rd W9 . . 88 B3
Bidwell St SE15 . . . . 50 A2
Big Ben★ SW1 . . . . 134 B3
Biggerstaff Rd
E15 . . . . 27 B4
Biggerstaff St N4 . . . 5 C2
Bigg's Row SW15 . . . 57 C4
Bigland Green Prim
Sch E1 . . . . 32 A3
Bigland St E1 . . . . . . 32 A3
Bilberry Ho 18 E3 . . 33 C4
Billie Holiday Ct
NW10 . . . . 20 C3
Billingford Cl SE4 . . 65 C3
Billing Ho 7 E1 . . . . 32 C3
Billingley NW1 . . . . 82 C3
Billing Pl SW10 . . . 156 B2
Billing Rd SW10 . . . 156 B2
Billingsgate Mkt
E14 . . . . 34 A1
Billing St SW10 . . . 156 B2
Billington Ho
SW8 . . . . 171 C3
Billington Rd
SE14 . . . . 50 C3
Billiter Sq EC3 . . . 110 B1
Billiter St EC3 . . . . 110 B1
Billson St E14 . . . . . 42 B2
Bilton Ho SW8 . . . 171 B3
Bilton Twrs W1 . . . 103 A1
Bina Gdns SW5 . . . 142 C3
Binbrook Ho 13
W10 . . . . 30 B4
Binden Rd W12 . . . . 38 B3
Binfield Ct SE5 . . . . . 48 B1
Binfield Rd SW4 . . 172 B3
Bingfield St N1 . . . . 84 C4
Bingham Pl W1 . . 103 B4
Bingham St N1 . . . . . 15 C2
Binley Ho SW15 . . . . 56 B1
Binney St W1 . . . . 103 C1
Binnie Ct SE10 . . . . . 52 A3
Binnie Ho SE1 . . . . 136 C1
Binns Rd W4 . . . . 38 A1
Binns Terr 3 W4 . . . 38 A1
Binstead Ho SW18 . . 59 A1
Binyon Ho 8 N16 . . 16 A4
Birbeck Ho 4 N19 . . 4 C3
Bircham Path SE4 . . 65 C3
Birch Cl
Newham E16 . . . . 35 A4
Peckham SE15 . . . . . . 49 C1
Upper Holloway N19 . . 4 B2
Birchdown Ho 32
E3 . . . . 27 A2
Birches The SE5 . . . . 49 A1
Birchfield Ho 3
E14 . . . . 33 C2
Birchfield St E14 . . . 33 C2
Birchgrove Ho
TW9 . . . . 45 A3
Birch Ho
New Cross Gate
SE14 . . . . 51 B2
8 Tulse Hill SW2 . . . . 62 C1
Birchington Ct
NW6 . . . . 78 A4
Birchington Ho 1
E5 . . . . 17 A3
Birchington Rd
NW6 . . . . 23 C4
Birchin La EC3 . . . 109 C1
Birchlands Ave
SW12 . . . . 72 B4
Birchmere Lo 18
SE16 . . . . 40 A1
Birchmere Row
SE3 . . . . 53 B1
Birchmore Wlk N5 . . 6 B1
Birch Vale Ct NW8 . 89 C2
Birchwood Dr NW3 . . 2 A1
Birdcage Wlk
SW1 . . . . 133 B3
Birdhurst Rd
SW18 . . . . 59 B2
Bird In Bush Rd
SE15 . . . . 49 C3
Bird In Hand Yd 24
NW3 . . . . 11 B4
Birdsall Ho 5 SE5 . . 64 A4
Birdsfield La 12
E3 . . . . 26 B4
Bird St W1 . . . . 103 C1
Birkbeck Ave W3 . . . 28 B2
Birkbeck Coll W1 105 B2
Birkbeck Ct W3 . . . . 28 C1
Birkbeck Gr W3 . . . . 37 C4
Birkbeck Hill SE21 . . 75 A3
Birkbeck Mews 5
E8 . . . . 16 B3
Birkbeck Pl SE21 . . . 75 B2
Birkbeck Rd
Acton W3 . . . . 28 C1
Dalston E8 . . . . 16 B3
Birkbeck St E2 . . . . . 25 A2
Birkdale Cl 30
SE16 . . . . 40 A1
Birkenhead Ho 11
N7 . . . . 14 C3
Birkenhead St
WC1 . . . . 94 B4
Birkwood Cl SW12 . . 73 C4
Birley Lo NW8 . . . . . 79 C2
Birley St SW11 . . . 169 B1
Birnam Rd N4 . . . . 5 B2
Birrell Ho SW9 . . . 172 C1
Birse Cres NW10 . . . . 8 A4
Birtwhistle Ho 5
E3 . . . . 26 B4
Biscay Ho 11 E1 . . . . 25 C1
Biscay Rd W6 . . . . . . 39 C1
Biscoe Way SE13 . . . 67 C4
Biscott Ho 3 E3 . . . 27 A1
Bisham Gdns N6 . . . . 3 C3
Bishop Challoner
Collegiate Sch
E1 . . . . 32 B3
Bishop Ct 20 SW2 . . 62 C1
Bishop Duppa's
Almshouses 7
TW10 . . . . 54 A2
Bishop King's Rd
W14 . . . . 140 B4
Bishop's Ave SW6 164 A2
Bishop's Bridge Rd
W2 . . . . 100 C2
Bishops Cl W4 . . . . . 37 B1
Bishop's Cl N19 . . . . . 4 B1
Bishops Ct
Bayswater W2 . . . . 100 B2
Richmond TW9 . . . . . . 54 A4
Bishop's Ct
Holborn EC4 . . . . . . 108 A2
Holborn WC2 . . . . . 107 B2
Bishopsdale Ho 8
NW6 . . . . 23 C4
Bishopsgate EC2 . 110 A2
Bishopsgate Arc
E1 . . . . 110 B3
Bishopsgate
Churchyard EC2 110 A2
Bishops Ho SW8 . 162 B1
Bishop's Mans
SW6 . . . . 47 C1
Bishops Mead SE5 . 48 B3
Bishop's Park Rd
SW6 . . . . 47 C1
Bishops Rd SW6 . . 164 C4
Bishops Sq E1 . . . 110 B4
Bishop St N1 . . . . . . 86 C4
Bishop's Terr
SE11 . . . . 149 C4
Bishopstone Ho
SW11 . . . . 169 B2
Bishop's Way E2 . . . 25 B3
Bishopswood Rd
N6 . . . . 3 B4
Bishop Way NW10 . . . 8 A1
Bishop Wilfred Wood
Cl SE15 . . . . 49 C1
Bisley Ho SW19 . . . . 69 C2
Bissextile Ho SE13 . 52 A1
Bisson Rd E15 . . . . . . 27 B3
Bittern Ct 7 SE8 . . . 51 C4
Bittern Ho SE1 . . . 136 C3
Bittern St SE1 . . . . 136 C3
Blackall St
EC2 . . . . 24 A1 98 A2
Blackburn Ct 21
SW2 . . . . 62 C1
Blackburne's Mews
W1 . . . . 117 B3
Blackburn Rd
NW6 . . . . 11 A2
Blackdown Ho E8 . . 16 C4
Blackett St SW15 . . . 57 C4
Blackfriars Bridge
EC4 . . . . 122 A3
Blackfriars Ct
EC4 . . . . 122 A4
Black Friars La
EC4 . . . . 108 A1
Blackfriars Pas
EC4 . . . . 122 A4
Blackfriars Pier
EC4 . . . . 122 A4
Blackfriars Rd
SE1 . . . . 122 A1
Blackfriars Sta
EC4 . . . . 122 A4
Blackfriars Underpass
EC4 . . . . 121 C4
Blackheath★ SE3 . . 53 A2
Blackheath Ave
SE3 . . . . 53 A3
Blackheath Bsns Est
SE10 . . . . 52 B2
Blackheath Gr
SE3 . . . . 53 B1
Blackheath High Sch
Blackheath SE3 . . . . . 53 B1
Greenwich SE3 . . . . . . 53 C3
Blackheath Hill
SE10 . . . . 52 B2
Blackheath Prep Sch
SE3 . . . . 53 C2
Blackheath Rd
SE10 . . . . 52 A2
Blackheath Rise
SE13 . . . . 52 B1
BLACKHEATH VALE
. . . . 53 B1
Blackheath Vale
SE3 . . . . 53 A1
Blackheath Village
SE3 . . . . 53 B1
Black Horse Ct
SE1 . . . . 137 C2
Blackhorse Rd
SE8 . . . . 51 A4
Blacklands Terr
SW3 . . . . 145 A3
Black Lion La W6 . . 38 C2
Black Lion Mews 4
W6 . . . . 38 C2
Blackmore Ho
Islington N1 . . . . 85 A3
2 Wandsworth
SW18 . . . . 59 A2
Blackmore Twr 1
W3 . . . . 37 B3
Blackpool Rd
SE15 . . . . 50 A1
Black Prince Rd SE1,
SE11 . . . . 149 A3
Black Roof Ho 9
SE5 . . . . 48 A2
Black's Rd W6 . . . . . 39 B2
Blackstock Ho 2
N5 . . . . 6 A1
Blackstock Mews
N4 . . . . 6 A1
Blackstock Rd N4,
N5 . . . . 6 A2
Blackstone Ho
Dulwich SE21 . . . . . . 76 A1
Pimlico SW1 . . . . . . 146 C1
Blackstone Rd NW2 . 9 B4
Black Swan Yd
SE1 . . . . 138 A4
Blackthorn Ct
20 Camberwell
SE15 . . . . 49 B3
4 Leyton E15 . . . . . . 19 C4
Blackthorn St E3 . . . 26 C1
Blacktree Mews 11
SW9 . . . . 62 C4
BLACKWALL 34 C2
Blackwall Sta E14 . . 34 B2
Blackwall Trad Est
E14 . . . . 34 C4
Blackwall Tunnel E14,
SE10 . . . . 34 C1
Blackwall Tunnel App
SE10 . . . . 43 A4
Blackwall Tunnel
Northern Approach
E14, E3 . . . . 27 B1
Blackwall Way
E14 . . . . 34 B2
Blackwater Ho
NW8 . . . . 101 C4
Blackwater St
SE22 . . . . 64 B2
Blackwell Cl 10
E5 . . . . 17 C4
Blackwell Ho 3
SW4 . . . . 61 C1
Blackwood Ho 11
E1 . . . . 25 A1
Blackwood St
SE17 . . . . 151 B2
Blade Mews SW15 . . 58 B3
Bladen Ho 4 E1 . . . 32 C3
Blades Ct
4 Hammersmith
W6 . . . . 39 A1
Putney SW15 . . . . 58 B3
Blades Ho SE11 . . 163 B3
Blades Lo 16 SW2 . . 62 C1
Blagdon Rd SE13 . . . 67 A1
Blagrove Rd 1
W10 . . . . 31 B4
Blair Cl N1 . . . . 15 B2
Blair Ct NW8 . . . . . . 79 B4
Blairderry Rd
SW2 . . . . 74 A2
Blairgowrie Ct 13
E14 . . . . 34 C3
Blair Ho SW9 . . . . 172 C2
Blair St E14 . . . . 34 C3
Blake Coll W1 . . . . 104 C4
Blake Ct
8 Bermondsey
SE16 . . . . 40 A1
Kilburn NW6 . . . . 23 C2
Blake Gdns SW6 . . 166 A4
Blake Ho
2 Deptford SE8 . . . . 51 C4
Isle Of Dogs E14 . . . . 42 A4
1 Kentish Town
N19 . . . . 13 C3
Lambeth SE1 . . . . . 135 B2
14 Stoke Newington
N16 . . . . 16 A4
Blake Mews 15
TW9 . . . . 44 C2
Blakemore Rd
SW16 . . . . 74 A1
Blakeney Cl
5 Camden Town
NW1 . . . . 13 C1
4 Dalston E8 . . . . . . 16 C3
Blakenham Ct
W12 . . . . 29 C1
Blaker Rd E15 . . . . . . 27 B4
Blakes Cl W10 . . . . . . 30 B4
Blake's Rd SE15 . . . . 49 A3
Blanca Ho 16 N1 . . . 24 A3
Blanchard Way
E8 . . . . 16 C2
Blanch Cl SE15 . . . . . 50 B3
Blanchedowne
SE5 . . . . 63 C3
Blandfield Rd
SW12 . . . . 72 C4
Blandford Ct
Brondesbury Pk
NW6 . . . . 10 A1

Blandford Ct *continued*
6 De Beauvoir Town N1 16 A1
Blandford Ho SW8 162 C2
Blandford Rd W4 38 A3
Blandford Sq NW1 90 B1
Blandford St W1 103 B3
Bland Ho SE11 149 A2
Blantyre St SW10 157 B2
Blantyre Twr SW10 157 B2
Blantyre Wlk SW10 157 B2
Blashford NW3 12 B1
Blasker Wlk 8 E14 42 A1
Blaxland Ho 12 W12 30 A2
Blazer Ct NW8 89 C3
Blechynden Ho 17 W10 30 C3
Blechynden St W10 30 C2
Bleeding Heart Yd EC1 107 C3
Blemundsbury WC1 106 C4
Blendworth Point 4 SW15 69 A3
Blenheim 26 SW19 69 C3
Blenheim Cres
Notting Hill W11 31 A3
Notting Hill W11 31 A2 112 B4
Blenheim Ct
Barnsbury N7 14 A2
Richmond TW9 54 B4
17 Rotherhithe SE16 32 C1
Upper Holloway N19 5 A2
Blenheim Gdns
Clapham Pk SW2 62 B1
Dollis Hill NW2 9 B3
Blenheim Gr SE15 49 C1
Blenheim Pas NW8 78 C2
Blenheim Rd
Acton W4 38 A3
St John's Wood NW8 79 A2
Blenheim St W1 104 A1
Blenheim Terr NW8 78 C2
Blenkarne Rd SW11 60 B1
Blessed Sacrament RC Prim Sch N1 84 C3
Blessington Cl SE13 67 C4
Blessington Rd SE13 67 C3
Bletchley Ct N1 87 B1
Bletchley St N1 87 A1
Bletsoe Wlk N1 87 A2
Blick Ho 1 SE16 40 B3
Blincoe Cl SW19 69 C2
Blissett St SE10 52 B2
Bliss Mews 14 W10 23 A2
Blisworth Ho 12 E2 24 C4
Blithfield St W8 128 A1
Bloemfontein Ave W12 30 A1
Bloemfontein Rd W12 30 A2
Blomfield Ct
Battersea SW11 167 C4
Paddington W9 89 A2
Blomfield Ho 4 E14 34 A2
Blomfield Mans 3 W12 30 B1
Blomfield Rd W9 100 C4
Blomfield St EC2 109 C3
Blomfield Villas W9 100 C4
Blondel St SW11 169 B2
Blondin St E3 26 C3
Bloomburg St SW1 147 A3
Bloomfield Ho E1 111 B3
Bloomfield Pl W1 118 B4
Bloomfield Terr SW1 145 C2
Bloom Gr SE27 75 A1
Bloom Park Rd SW6 154 C1
BLOOMSBURY 106 A4
Bloomsbury Ct WC1 106 B3
Bloomsbury Ho 10 SW4 61 C1
Bloomsbury Pl
London SW18 59 B2
St Giles WC1 106 B3
Bloomsbury Sq WC1 106 B3
Bloomsbury St WC1 105 C3
Bloomsbury Way WC1 106 B3
Blore Cl SW8 171 B3
Blore Ct W1 119 B4
Blore Ho SW10 156 B2
Blossom Cl W5 36 A4
Blossom Pl E1 24 A1 98 B1
Blossom St E1 24 A1 98 B1
Blount St E14 33 A3
Blucher Rd SE5 48 B3
Blue Anchor Alley 4 TW9 54 A3
Blue Anchor La SE16 40 A2
Blue Anchor Yd E1 125 B4
Blue Ball Yd SW1 118 C1
Bluebell Cl 10 E9 25 B4
Blue Gate Fields Jun & Inf Schs E1 32 B2
Bluegate Mews E1 32 A2
Blue Lion Pl SE1 138 A2
Blueprint Apartments 15 SW12 73 A4
Blundell Cl E8 16 C4
Blundell St N7 14 A2
Blurton Rd E5 17 C4
Blyth Cl 4 E14 42 C2
Blythe Ho SE11 163 C4
Blythe Mews 2 W14 39 C3
Blythendale Ho 34 E2 24 C3
Blythe Rd W14 126 A1
Blythe St E2 25 A2
Blyth's Wharf E14 33 A2
Blythwood Rd N4 5 A4
Bnois Jerusalem Sch N16 6 C4
Boades Mews 3 NW3 11 C4
Boadicea St N1 84 C3
Boardwalk Pl E14 34 B1
Boarley Ho SE17 152 A3
Boathouse Ctr The W10 22 C1
Boathouse Wlk 24 SE15 49 B3
Boat Lifter Way 19 SE16 41 A2
Bobbin Cl SW4 61 B4
Bob Marley Way 11 SE24 62 C3
Bocking St E8 25 A4
Boddicott Cl SW19 70 A2
Boddington Gdns W3 36 C4
Boddington Ho 2 SE14 50 B2
Bodeney Ho 10 SE5 49 A2
Boden Ho E1 111 B4
Bodington Ct 2 W12 39 C4
Bodley Manor Way SE24 74 C4
Bodmin St SW18 70 C3
Bodney Rd E5, E8 17 A3
Bogart Ct 13 E14 33 C2
Bohemia Pl 1 E8 17 A2
Bohn Rd E1 33 A4
Boileau Rd SW13 47 A4
Boilerhouse SE1 124 C1
Boisseau Ho 31 E1 32 B4
Bolden St SE8 52 A1
Boldero Pl NW8 90 A1
Boleyn Rd N16 16 A3
Bolina Rd SE16 40 B1
Bolingbroke Gr SW11 60 B1
Bolingbroke Hospl The SW11 60 A2
Bolingbroke Rd W14 39 C3
Bolingbroke Wlk SW11 168 A4
Bollo Bridge Rd W3 37 B4
Bollo Ct 2 W3 37 B3
Bollo La W3 37 A3
Bolney Gate SW7 130 A3
Bolney St SW8 162 C1
Bolsover St W1 92 B1
Bolt Ct EC4 107 C1
Bolton Cres SE5 48 A3
Bolton Ct SW11 169 C3
Bolton Gdns
Kensal Rise NW10 22 C3
South Kensington SW5 142 B2
Bolton Gdns Mews SW10 142 C2
Bolton Ho 4 SE10 43 A1
Bolton Pl SW5 142 C2
Bolton Rd
Chiswick W4 45 B3
Harlesden NW10 21 A4
Kilburn NW8 78 B3
Boltons Ct SW5 142 B2
Bolton St W1 118 B2
Boltons The SW10 142 C2
Bolton Studios SW10 143 A1
Bolton Wlk N7 5 B2
Bombay Ct 8 SE16 40 B4
Bombay St SE16 40 A2
Bomore Rd W11 31 A2 112 A4
Bonar Rd SE15 49 C3
Bonchurch Rd W10 31 A4
Bond Ct EC4 109 B1
Bond Ho 4 NW6 23 B3
Bonding Yard Wlk SE16 41 A3
Bond St W4 37 C2
Bond Street Sta W1 103 C1
Bondway SW8 162 B4
Bonfield Rd SE13 67 B3
Bonham Ho W11 31 B1 112 C2
Bonham Rd SW2 62 B2
Bonheur Rd W4 37 C4
Bonhill St EC2 97 C1
Bonington Ho N1 84 C1
Bonita Mews SE15 65 C4
Bonner Ho 3 SW15 56 C2
Bonner Prim Sch E2 25 B2
Bonner Rd E2 25 B3
Bonner St E2 25 B3
Bonneville Gdns SW4 61 B1
Bonneville Prim Sch SW4 61 B1
Bonnington Sq SW8 162 C4
Bonny St NW1 13 B1
Bonsor Ho SW8 171 A4
Bonsor St SE5 49 A3
Bonthron Ho SW15 47 B1
Booker Cl 11 E3 33 B4
Boord St SE10 43 A3
Boothby Rd N19 4 C2
Booth Cl 10 E9 25 A4
Booth Ho 2 SW2 74 C4
Booth La EC4 122 C4
Booth's Pl W1 105 A3
Boot St N1 24 A2 98 A3
Bordon Wlk 5 SW15 68 C4
Boreas Wlk N1 86 B1
Boreham Ave E16 35 C3
Boreman Ho 11 SE10 52 B4
Borland Rd SE15 65 B3
Borneo St SW15 57 B4
Borough High St SE1 123 B2
Borough Mkt* SE1 123 B1
Borough Rd SE1 136 B2
Borough Sq SE1 136 C3
Borough Sta SE1 137 A3
BOROUGH THE 136 C4
Borrett Cl SE17 150 C1
Borrodaile Rd SW18 59 A1
Borrowdale NW1 92 C3
Borthwick St SE8 41 C1
Boscastle Rd NW5 4 A1
Boscobel Ho 4 E8 17 A2
Boscobel Pl SW1 145 C4
Boscobel St NW8 89 C1
Boscombe Cl E5 18 A3
Boscombe Rd W12 38 C4
Boss Ho SE1 138 C4
Boss St SE1 138 C4
Boston Gdns W4 46 A4
Boston Ho
24 Camberwell SE5 48 B1
Earl's Ct SW5 142 B3
Lisson Gr NW1 90 C2
Boston Pl NW1 90 C1
Bosun Cl 22 E14 41 C4
Boswell Ct
Bloomsbury WC1 106 B4
9 Hammersmith W14 39 C3
Boswell Ho WC1 106 B4
Boswell St WC1 106 B4
Bosworth Ho 4 W10 23 A1
Bosworth Rd W10 23 A1
Bothwell Cl E16 35 B4
Bothwell St 4 W6 47 C4
Botolph Alley EC3 124 A4
Botolph La EC3 124 A4
Bott's Mews W2 31 C3
Boughton Ho SE1 137 B4
Boulcott St E1 32 C3
Boulevard The
Chelsea SW6 167 A3
4 Upper Tooting SW17 72 C2
Boulogne Ho SE1 138 C2
Boulter Ho 4 SE14 50 B2
Boulton Ho TW8 36 A1
Boundaries Mans 3 SW12 72 C3
Boundaries Rd SW12 72 C3
Boundary Ho
Balham SW12 73 A3
1 Camberwell SE5 48 B3
15 Notting Hill W11 30 C1
Boundary La SE17 48 B4
Boundary Pas E2 24 B1 98 C2
Boundary Rd NW8 79 A4
Boundary Road Est NW8 78 C3
Boundary Row SE1 136 A4
Boundary St E2 24 B1 98 C2
Bourchier St W1 119 B4
Bourdon Pl W1 118 B4
Bourdon St W1 118 B3
Bourke Cl
London SW4 62 A1
Willesden NW10 8 A2
Bourlet Cl W1 104 C3
Bourne Ct W4 45 B4
Bourne Ho 5 SW4 61 B3
Bourne Mews W1 103 C
Bournemouth Cl SE15 49 C
Bournemouth Rd SE15 49 C

Bourne Pl W4 37 C1
Bourne St SW1 145 B3
Bourne Terr W2 100 B4
Bousfield Prim Sch SW10 142 C2
Bousfield Rd SE14 50 C1
Boutcher CE Prim Sch SE1 152 C4
Boutflower Rd SW11 60 A3
Bouverie Mews N16 7 A2
Bouverie Pl W2 101 C2
Bouverie Rd N16 7 A2
Bouverie St EC4 107 C1
Bovingdon Cl 4 N19 4 B2
Bovingdon Rd SW6 166 B3
BOW 26 B3
Bowater Cl SW2 62 A1
Bowater Ho EC1 97 A1
Bow Brook The 20 E2 25 C3
Bow Church Sta E3 26 C2
BOW COMMON 34 A4
Bow Common La E3 26 B1
Bowden Ho 29 E3 27 A2
Bowden St SE11 149 C1
Bowditch SE8 41 B1
Bowen Ct 2 N5 15 A4
Bowen Dr SE21 76 A1
Bowen St E14 34 A3
Bower Ave SE3 53 A3
Bowerdean St SW6 166 A2
Bower Ho SE14 50 C2
Bowerman Ave SE14 51 A4
Bowerman Ct 1 N19 4 C2
Bower St E1 32 C3
Bowes-Lyon Hall 13 E16 35 C1
Bowes Rd W3 29 A2
Bowfell Rd W6 47 B4
Bowhill Cl SW9 163 C2
Bow Ho 1 E3 26 C2
Bowie Cl SW4 73 C4
Bow Ind Pk E15 18 C1
Bow La EC2, EC4 109 A1
Bowland Ho N4 6 B4
Bowland Rd SW4 61 C3
Bowland Yd SW1 131 A3
Bowl Ct EC2 24 A1 98 B1
Bowles Rd 1 SE1 49 C4
Bowley Ho SE16 139 B2
Bowling Green Cl SW19 69 A4
Bowling Green Ho SW10 157 B2
Bowling Green La EC1 95 C2
Bowling Green Pl SE1 137 B4
Bowling Green St SE11 163 B4
Bowling Green Wlk N1 24 A2 98 A4
Bowman Ave E16 35 B2
Bowman Mews
St George in t East E1 125 B4
Wandsworth SW18 70 B3
Bowman's Mews N7 5 A1
Bowman's Pl N7 5 A1
Bowmore Wlk NW1 13 C1
Bowness Cl 5 E8 16 B2
Bowness Ho SE15 50 B3
Bowood Rd SW11 60 C2
Bow Rd E3 26 C2
Bow Road Sta E3 26 C2
Bowry Ho 14 E14 33 B4
Bow Sch E3 26 C2
Bowsprit Point 1 E14 41 C3
Bow St WC2 106 B1
Bowstead Ct SW11 167 C3
Bow Triangle Bsns Ctr 17 E3 26 C1
Bowyer Ho
27 Shoreditch N1 24 A4
Wandsworth SW18 59 A1
Bowyer Pl SE5 48 B3
Bowyer St 15 SE5 48 B3
Boxall Rd SE21 64 A1
Boxley Ho 3 E5 17 A3
Boxmoor Ho
16 Hackney E2 24 C4
9 Shepherd's Bush W11 30 C1
Box Tree Ho SE8 41 A1
Boxworth Gr N1 85 A4
Boyce Ho 1 W10 23 B2
Boyd Ct SW15 57 B1
Boydell Ct NW8 11 C1
Boyd St E1 111 C1
Boyfield St SE1 136 B3
Boyle St W1 118 C4
Boyne Ct NW10 8 C1
Boyne Rd SE13 67 C4
Boyne Terr Mews W11 31 B1 112 C2
Boyson Rd 10 SE17 48 C4
Boyton Cl E1 25 C1
Boyton Ho
Kennington SE11 149 B1
St John's Wood NW8 79 C2
Brabant Ct EC3 124 A4
Brabazon St E14 34 A4
Brabner Ho E2 24 C2 99 B4
Brabourn Gr SE15 50 B1
Bracer Ho 1 N1 24 A3
Bracewell Rd W10 30 B4
Bracey Mews 1 N4 5 A2
Bracey St N4 5 A2
Bracken Ave SW12 72 C4
Brackenbury N4 5 B3
Brackenbury Gdns W6 39 A3
Brackenbury Prim Sch W6 39 A3
Brackenbury Rd W6 39 A3
Bracken Gdns SW13 46 C1
Bracken Ho 15 E3 33 C4
Brackley Ave SE15 65 B4
Brackley Ct NW8 89 C2
Brackley Rd W4 38 A1
Brackley St EC1 109 A4
Brackley Terr 6 W4 38 A1
Bracklyn Ct N1 87 B2
Bracklyn St N1 87 B2
Bracknell Gate NW3 11 A3
Bracknell Gdns NW3 11 A4
Bracknell Way NW3 11 A4
Bradbeer Ho 24 E2 25 B2
Bradbourne St SW6 165 C2
Bradbury Ct 2 SE3 53 C3
Bradbury Ho E1 111 A2
Bradbury St 28 N16 16 A3
Bradby Ho NW8 78 B1
Braddon Rd TW9 54 B4
Braddyll St SE10 43 A1
Bradenham 11 SE17 48 C4
Bradenham Cl SE17 48 C4
Braden St W9 88 A1
Bradfield Ct 14 NW1 13 A1
Bradfield Ho SW8 171 B2
Bradford Ho 4 W14 39 C3
Bradford Rd W3 38 A4
Bradgate Rd SE6 67 A1
Brading Rd SW2 74 B4
Brading Terr W12 38 C3
Bradiston Rd W9 23 B2
Bradley Cl N7 14 B2
Bradley Ho
Bermondsey SE16 40 A2
1 Bromley E3 27 A2
Bradley Mews SW12 72 B3
Bradley's Cl N1 85 C2
Bradlord Ho SE21 76 A1
Bradmead SW8 160 C1
Bradmore Park Rd W6 39 A2
Brad St SE1 121 C1
Bradstock Ho E9 18 A1
Bradstock Rd E9 17 C2
Bradwell Ho NW6 78 A3
Brady Ho
London SW4 61 C2
South Lambeth SW8 171 A4
Brady St E1 25 A1
Braefoot Ct SW15 57 C2
Braemar SW15 57 C1
Braemar Ave SW18, SW19 70 C2
Braemar Ho W9 88 C3
Braemar Mans W8 128 B1
Braes St N1 15 A1
Braganza St SE17 150 A1
Braham Ho SE11 149 A1
Braham St E1 111 A2
Brahma Kumaris World Spiritual Univ NW10 8 C1
Braid Ave W3 29 A3
Braid Ho SE10 52 B2
Braidwood St SE1 124 A1
Brailsford Rd SW2 62 C1
Braintree Ho 6 E1 25 B1
Braintree St E2 25 B2
Braithwaite Ho EC1 97 B2
Braithwaite Twr W2 101 B4
Bramah Gn SW9 173 C4
Bramah Mus of Tea & Coffee* SE1 123 A1
Bramall Ct N7 14 B2
Bramber WC1 94 A3
Bramber Ct TW8 36 A2
Bramber Rd W14 154 C4
Brambledown 8 N4 5 A4
Bramble Gdns W12 29 B2
Bramble Ho 16 E3 33 C4
Brambling Ct 25 SE8 51 B4
Bramcote Gr SE16 40 B1
Bramcote Rd SW15 57 A3
Bramerton NW6 9 C1
Bramerton St SW3 158 A4
Bramfield Ct N4 6 B2
Bramfield Rd SW11 60 B2
Bramford Rd SW18 59 B3
Bramham Gdns SW5 142 B2
Bramham Ho SE22 64 A3
Bramlands Cl SW11 60 A4
Bramley Cres SW8 161 C2
Bramley Ct SE13 67 C2
Bramley Ho
19 North Kensington W10 30 C3
Roehampton SW15 56 B1
Bramley Rd W10 30 C3
Brampton WC1 106 C3
Bramshaw Rd E9 17 C2
Bramshill Gdns NW5 4 A1
Bramshill Rd NW10 21 B3
Bramshurst NW8 78 B3
Bramston Rd
Harlesden NW10 21 C3
Wandsworth SW17 71 B1
Bramwell Ho
Borough The SE1 137 A1
Chelsea SW1 160 C4
Bramwell Mews N1 85 A4
Brancaster Ho
22 Globe Town E1 25 C2
Islington N5 15 A3
Brancaster Rd SW16 74 A1
Branch Hill NW3 2 B1
Branch Pl N1 87 C4
Branch Rd E14 33 A2
Branch St SE15 49 A3
Brand Cl N4 6 A3
Branden Lo 13 W4 37 B1
Brandlehow Rd SW15 58 B3
Brandon Mews
Barbican EC2 109 B4
Walworth SE17 151 A3
Brandon Rd N7 14 A1
Brandon St SE17 151 A3
Brandrams Wharf SE16 40 B4
Brandreth Rd SW17 73 A2
Brand St SE10 52 B3
Brangton Rd SE11 149 A1
Brangwyn Ct W14 126 A1
Branksea St SW6 154 A1
Branksome Ho SW8 162 C2
Branksome Rd SW2 62 A2
Bransby Ct 4 N16 16 A4
Branscombe NW1 83 A3
Branscombe St SE13 67 A4
Bransdale Cl NW6 23 C4
Branstone Ct 9 TW9 44 B2
Branstone Rd TW9 44 B2
Branston Ho N7 14 C3
Brantwood Ho 9 SE5 48 B3
Brantwood Rd SE24 63 B2
Brasenose Dr SW13 47 B4
Brashley Road Cvn Site NW10 21 A2
Brassey Ho 1 E14 42 A2
Brassey Rd NW6 10 B2
Brassey Sq SW11 60 C4
Brassie Ave W3 29 A3
Brass Talley Alley 31 SE16 40 C4
Brathay NW1 83 A1
Brathway Rd SW18 70 C4
Bratley St E1 24 C1 99 B1
Bravington Pl W9 23 B1
Bravington Rd W9 23 B2
Brawne Ho 12 SE17 48 A4
Braxfield Rd SE4 66 B3
Bray NW3 12 A1
Brayard's Rd SE15 50 A1
Braybrook St W12 29 B3
Brayburne Ave SW4 171 A1
Bray Cres SE16 40 C4
Braydon Rd N16 7 C3
Bray Dr E16 35 B2
Brayfield Terr N1 14 C1
Brayford Sq 12 E1 32 B3
Bray Pl SW3 144 C3
Bread St EC2, EC4 109 A1
Breakspeare SE21 76 B1
Breakspears Mews SE4 51 C1
Breakspears Rd SE4 66 C4
Breakwell Ct 16 W10 23 A1
Breamore Cl SW15 68 C3
Breamore Ho 21 SE15 49 C3
Bream's Bldgs EC4 107 B2
Bream St E3 18 C1
Breasley Cl SW15 57 A3

Brechin Pl SW7 143 A3
Brecknock Prim Sch N7 13 C2
Brecknock Rd N19 13 C3
Brecon Ho
Stamford Hill N16 7 B3
Wandsworth SW18 70 C4
Brecon Rd W6 154 B3
Bredel Ho 1 E14 33 C4
Bredgar SE13 67 A2
Bredgar Rd N19 4 B2
Bredinghurst SE22 76 C4
Bredinghurst Sch SE15 65 C3
Bredin Ho SW10 156 B2
Breer St SW6 59 A4
Breezer's Ct E1 125 C3
Breezer's Hill E1 125 C3
Brehon Ho NW1 82 C3
Bremner Rd SW7 129 A2
Brenchley Gdns SE15, SE22, SE23 65 C1
Brenda Rd SW17 72 B2
Brendon Ave NW10 8 A4
Brendon Ho W1 103 B4
Brendon St W1 102 B2
Brenley Ho SE1 137 B4
Brennands Ct 14 N19 4 B1
Brent Adult Comm Education Service Coll NW10 20 C4
Brent Ct 5 W12 38 A3
Brentford Fountain L Ctr W4 36 C1
Brent Ho 16 E9 17 B2
Brenthouse Rd E9 17 B2
Brenthurst Rd NW10 8 B2
Brent Mus★ NW10 9 A2
Brent New Ent Ctr NW10 8 B2
Brenton Ct E9 18 A3
Brenton St E14 33 A3
Brent Rd E16 35 C4
Brent Trad Est NW10 8 A3
Brentwick Gdns TW8 36 A2
Brereton Ho 4 SW2 74 C4
Bressenden Pl SW1 132 C2
Breton Ho
Bermondsey SE1 138 C2
St Luke's EC2 97 A1
Brett Cl N16 7 A2
Brett Cres NW10 20 C4
Brettell St SE17 151 C1
Brett Ho 1 SW15 69 C4
Brett House Cl 2 SW15 69 C4
Brettinghurst SE1 153 B1
Bretton Ho N19 5 A3
Brett Pas 28 E8 17 A3
Brett Rd E8 17 A3
Brewers Bldgs EC1 96 A4
Brewers Ct W2 100 C2
Brewer's Gn SW1 133 B2
Brewers Hall Gdns EC2 109 A3
Brewer St W1 119 A4
Brewery Ind Est The N1 87 A1
Brewery Rd N7 14 A2
Brewery Sq
Bermondsey SE1 124 C1
Clerkenwell EC1 96 B2
Brewhouse La
Putney SW15 58 A4
Wapping E1 32 A1
Brewhouse Wlk SE16 33 A1
Brewhouse Yd EC1 96 A2
Brewster Gdns W10 30 B4
Brewster Ho
Bermondsey SE1 153 A4
Poplar E14 33 B2
Briant Ho SE1 135 A1
Briant St SE14 50 C3
Briar Ct 7 Bow E3 26 C3
Dalston E8 16 B1
Briardale SW19 70 B3
Briardale Gdns NW3 1 C1
Briardale Ho 12 N16 7 A3
Briar Rd NW2 9 B4
Briar Wlk
Putney SW15 57 A3
West Kilburn W10 23 A1
Briarwood Rd SW4 61 C2
Briary Cl NW3 12 A1
Briary Ct 10 E16 35 B3
Brickbarn Cl SW10 157 A2
Brick Ct EC4 107 B1
Brick Farm Cl TW9 45 A2
Brick La
Shoreditch E2 24 B2 99 A3
Spitalfields E1 24 B1 99 A1
Bricklayers Arms SE1 137 C1
Brick St W1 118 A1
Brickworth Ho SW9 173 C4
Brideale Cl SE15 49 B4
Bride Ct EC4 108 A1
Bride La EC4 108 A1
Bridel Mews N1 86 A3
Bride St N7 14 B2
Bridewain St SE1 138 C2
Bridewell Pl
Holborn EC4 108 A1
20 Wapping E1 32 A1
Bridford Mews W1 104 B4
Bridge App NW3 12 C1
Bridge Ave W6 39 B1
Bridge Avenue Mans 1 W6 39 B1
Bridge Cl 13 W10 30 C3
Bridge Ct
9 Blackwall E14 34 C2
7 Willesden NW10 8 A1
Bridge Field Ho W2 100 A2
Bridgefoot SE1 148 B1
Bridge Gdns N16 15 C4
Bridge Ho
Brockley SE4 66 B3
1 Camden Town NW1 12 C1
Bridge Ho *continued*
Homerton E9 17 C3
Bridge House Quay E14 34 B1
Bridge La SW11 168 B3
Bridgeland Rd E16 35 C2
Bridgeman Ho 19 E9 17 B1
Bridgeman Rd N1 14 B1
Bridgeman St NW8 80 A1
Bridge Meadows SE14 50 C4
Bridgend Rd SW18 59 B3
Bridgen Ho 9 E1 32 A3
Bridge Pk 7 SW18 58 C2
Bridge Pl SW1 146 B4
Bridgeport Pl E1 125 C2
Bridge Rd
Stratford Marsh E15 27 C4
Willesden NW10 8 A2
Bridge Sch The
Clerkenwell EC1 96 A2
Shoreditch N1 87 A4
Bridges Ct SW11 167 B1
Bridges Ho 15 SE5 48 C3
Bridge St
Chiswick W4 37 C2
Westminster SW1 134 B3
Bridge Terr E15 19 C1
Bridgeview 2 W6 39 B1
Bridgewater Rd E15 27 B4
Bridgewater Sq EC2 108 C4
Bridgewater St EC2 108 C4
Bridgeway St NW1 83 A1
Bridge Wharf 18 E2 25 C3
Bridge Yd SE1 123 C2
Bridgford St SW17, SW18 71 B1
Bridgman Rd W4 37 B3
Bridgnorth Ho 10 SE15 49 C4
Bridgwater Ho W2 100 C2
Bridle La W1 119 A4
Bridlington Ho SW18 59 B3
Bridport SE17 151 A1
Bridport Ho N1 87 C3
Bridport Pl N1 87 C3
Bridstow Pl W2 31 C3
Brief St SE5 48 A2
Brierfield NW1 82 C3
Brierley Rd
Leyton E11 19 C4
Upper Tooting SW12 73 B2
Brierly Gdns E2 25 B3
Brigade St SE3 53 B1
Briggeford Cl 5 E5 7 C2
Briggs Ho E2 24 B2 99 A4
Brightling Rd SE4 66 B1
Brightlingsea Pl 5 E14 33 B2
Brightman Rd SW18 71 C3
Brighton Bldgs SE1 138 A1
Brighton Ct SW15 58 B1
Brighton Gr SE14 51 A2
Brighton Ho 7 SE5 48 C2
Brighton Rd N16 16 A4
Brighton Terr SW9 62 B3
Brightside Rd SE13 67 C1
Bright St E14 34 A4
Brightwell Ct N7 14 B3
Brightwells SW6 166 A2
Brig Mews SE8 51 C4
Brigstock Ho SE5 48 B1
Brill Pl NW1 83 C1
Brimsdown Ho E3 27 B1
Brindley Ho
37 Notting Hill W2 31 C4
22 Streatham SW12 74 A4
Brindley St SE14 51 B2
Brine Ho 11 E3 26 A3
Brinklow Ho W2 100 A3
Brinkworth Way E9 18 B2
Brinsley Ho 17 E1 32 B3
Brinsley St 35 E1 32 A3
Brinton Wlk SE1 122 A1
Brion Pl E14 34 B4
Brisbane Ho 3 W12 30 A2
Brisbane St SE5 48 C3
Briset St EC1 96 A1
Briset Way N7 5 B2
Bristol Gdns
Putney SW15 69 B4
Westbourne Green W9 88 B1
Bristol Ho SE11 135 B1
Bristol Mews W9 88 B1
Bristowe Cl 24 SW2 62 C1
Britain at War Experience★ SE1 124 A1
Britannia Building N1 97 B4
Britannia Cl SW4 61 C3
Britannia Gate 11 E16 35 C1
Britannia Junc NW1 82 B4
Britannia Rd
23 Millwall E14 41 C2
Walham Green SW6 156 A1
Britannia Row N1 86 C4
Britannia St WC1 94 C4
Britannia Way NW10 20 A1
Britannia Wlk N1 97 B4
British Coll of Osteopathic Medicine NW3 11 B2
British Gr W4 38 B1
British Grove Pas 2 W4 38 B1
British Grove S 3 W4 38 B1
British Library The★ WC1 93 C4
British Mus★ WC1 106 A3
British St E3 26 B2
British Wharf Ind Est SE14 50 C4
Britley Ho 16 E14 33 B3
Brittany Ho SW15 57 B3
Brittany Point SE11 149 B3
Britten Cl NW11 2 A3
Britten Ho SW3 144 B2
Britten St SW3 144 A2
Britton St EC1 96 A1
BRIXTON 62 C4
Brixton Day Coll SW9 62 A4
Brixton Hill SW2 62 B1
Brixton Hill Ct 5 SW2 62 B2
Brixton Hill Pl SW2 74 A4
Brixton Mkt SW9 62 C3
Brixton Oval 7 SW2 62 C3
Brixton Rd SW9 173 B2
Brixton Sta SW9 62 C3
Brixton Station Rd SW9 62 C4
Brixton Water La SW2 62 B2
Broadbent Cl N6 4 A3
Broadbent St W1 118 A4
Broadbridge Cl SE3 53 C3
Broad Common Est N16 7 C3
Broad Ct WC2 106 B1
Broadfield NW6 11 A2
Broadfield La NW1 14 A1
Broadfields Way NW10 8 B3
Broadford Ho 12 E1 26 A1
BROADGATE 110 A4
Broadgate EC2 110 A4
Broadgate Circ EC2 110 A3
Broadgates Ct SE11 149 C1
Broadgates Rd SW18 71 C3
Broadhinton Rd SW4 61 B4
Broadhurst Cl
Hampstead NW6 11 B2
9 Richmond TW10 54 B2
Broadhurst Gdns NW6 11 A2
Broadhurst Mans NW6 11 A2
Broad La EC2 110 A4
Broadlands N6 3 C4
Broadlands Ave SW16 74 A2
Broadlands Cl
Highgate N6 3 C4
Streatham SW16 74 A2
Broadlands Ct TW9 44 C3
Broadlands Lo N6 3 B4
Broadlands Mans 2 SW16 74 A2
Broadlands Rd N6 3 B4
Broadley St NW8 102 A4
Broadley Terr NW1 90 B1
Broadmayne SE17 151 B2
Broadmead W14 140 A3

Broadoak Ct 8 SW9 62 C4
Broadoak Ho NW6. 78 B3
Broad St Ave EC2 110 A3
Broad Sanctuary SW1 134 A3
Broadstone Ho SW8 162 C1
Broadstone Pl W1 103 B3
Broad Street Pl EC2 109 C3
Broadwalk Ho SW7 128 C3
Broadwalk La NW11 1 B4
Broadwall SE1 121 C2
Broadway
Stratford E15 19 C1
Westminster SW1 133 B2
Broadway Arc 3 W6 39 B2
Broadway Ctr The 6 W6 39 B2
Broadway Ho 2 E8 25 A4
Broadway Mans SW6 155 C1
Broadway Market E8 25 A4
Broadway Market Mews 21 E8 24 C4
Broadway Mews E5 7 B4
Broadway Ret Pk NW2 9 C4
Broadway The
Barnes SW13 46 A1
South Acton W3 36 C4
Broadway Wlk 4 E14 41 C3
Broadwick St W1 105 A1
Broad Wlk
Mayfair W1 117 B2
Regent's Pk NW1 81 C1
Richmond TW9 44 B3
Broad Wlk The W8 114 B1
Broadwood Terr W14 141 A4
Broad Yd EC1 96 A1
Brocas Cl NW3 12 A1
Brockbridge Ho SW15 56 B1
Brocket Ho SW8 171 B2
Brockham Dr SW2 74 B4
Brockham Ho
Camden Town NW1 83 A3
11 Streatham SW2 74 B4
Brockham St SE1 137 A2
Brockhurst Ho N4 6 C4
Brockill Cres SE4 66 A3
Brocklebank Rd SW18 71 B4
Brocklebank Road Ind Est SE7 43 C2
Brocklehurst St SE14 50 C3
BROCKLEY 66 B3
Brockley Cross SE4 66 B4
Brockley Cross Bsns Ctr SE4 66 A4
Brockley Gdns SE4 51 B1
Brockley Gr SE4 66 B2
Brockley Hall Rd SE4 66 A2
Brockley Ho SE17 152 A2
Brockley Mews SE4 66 A2
Brockley Prim Sch SE4 66 B2
Brockley Rd SE4 66 B2
Brockley Sta SE4 66 A4
Brockley Way SE4 66 A2
Brockmer Ho 5 E1 32 A2
Brock Pl E3 27 A1
Brock St SE15 65 B4
Brockweir 28 E2 25 B3
Brockwell Ct 2 SW2 62 C2
Brockwell Ho SE11 163 A4
Brockwell Park* SE24 63 A1
Brockwell Park Gdns SE24 75 A4
Brockwell Park Row SW2 62 C1
Broderick Ho SE21 76 A1
Brodia Rd N16 7 A1
Brodick Ho 12 E3 26 B3
Brodie Ho SE1 153 A2
Brodie St SE1 153 A2
Brodlove La E1 32 C2
Brodrick Rd SW17 72 A2
Brody Ho E1 110 C3
Broken Wharf EC4 122 C4
Brokesley St E3 26 B2
Broke Wlk
Hackney E8 24 B4
1 Hackney E8 24 C4
Bromar Rd SE5 64 A4
Bromehead St 8 E1 32 B3
Bromell's Rd SW4 61 B3
Bromfelde Rd SW4 171 C1
Bromfield Ct SE16 139 C2
Bromfield St N1 85 C2
Bromleigh Ho SE1 138 C2
BROMLEY 27 A2
Bromley-by-Bow Sta E3 98 A4
Bromley Hall Rd E14 34 B4
Bromley High St E3 27 A2
Bromley Lo 2 W3 28 B3
Bromley Pl W1 104 C4
Bromley St E1 32 C3
BROMPTON 130 A1
Brompton Arc SW1 131 A3
Brompton Oratory SW3 130 A1
Brompton Park Cres SW6 156 A3
Brompton Pl SW3 130 B2
Brompton Rd SW3 130 A1
Brompton Sq SW3 130 A2
Bromstone Ho SW9 173 B3
Bromwich Ave N6 3 C2
Bromwich Ho 3 TW10 54 A1
Bromyard Ave W3 29 A2
Bromyard Ho
Acton W3 29 A1
3 Peckham SE15 50 A3
Bron Ct NW6 23 C4
BRONDESBURY 10 A2
Brondesbury Coll for Boys NW6 10 A1
Brondesbury Ct NW2 9 C2
Brondesbury Mews 11 NW6 10 C1
BRONDESBURY PARK 22 C4
Brondesbury Park Sta NW6 23 A4
Brondesbury Pk NW2 9 C1
Brondesbury Rd NW6 23 C3
Brondesbury Sta NW6 10 B1
Brondesbury Villas NW6 23 C3
Bronsart Rd SW6 154 A1
Bronte Ct 8 W14 39 C3
Bronte Ho
Kilburn NW6 23 C2
6 Stoke Newington N16 16 A3
Bronti Cl SE17 151 A2
Bronwen Ct NW8 89 B3
Bronze St SE8 51 C3
Brookbank Rd SE13 67 A4
Brook Cl SW17 72 C2
Brook Com Prim Sch E8 16 C3
Brook Ct
Mortlake SW14 56 A4
Stratford New Town E15 19 B3
Brookdale Rd SE6 67 A1
Brook Dr SE11 150 A4
Brooke Ct W10 23 A3
Brooke Ho 4 SE14 51 A2
Brooke Rd E5, N16 7 C1
Brookes Ct EC1 107 B4
Brooke's Mkt EC1 107 C4
Brooke St EC1 107 B3
Brookfield
Dartmouth Pk N6 3 C1
1 Finsbury Pk N4 5 C2
Brookfield Ho 23 E2 25 A3
Brookfield Pk NW5 4 A1
Brookfield Prim Sch N19 4 A2
Brookfield Rd
Acton W4 37 C4
Homerton E9 18 A2
Brookgate N16 6 C2
Brook Gate W1 117 A3
Brook Gdns SW13 56 B4
Brook Gn W6 39 C2
BROOK GREEN 39 C2
Brook Green Flats 11 W14 39 C3
Brook Ho
3 Clapham Pk SW4 61 B2
Ealing W3 36 C4
4 Hammersmith W6 39 B2
Brook Ho *continued*
Marylebone WC1 105 B4
Brook Hos NW1 83 A1
Brooklands Ave SW18 71 A2
Brooklands Court Apartments 3 NW6 10 B1
Brooklands Ct 2 NW6 10 B1
Brooklyn Ct W12 30 B1
Brookmarsh Ind Est SE10 52 A3
Brook Mews N W2 115 A4
Brookmill Rd SE8 51 C2
Brooksbank Ho 7 E9 17 B2
Brooksbank St 9 E9 17 B2
Brooksby Ho 9 N1 14 C1
Brooksby Mews N1 14 C1
Brooksby St N1 14 C1
Brooksby's Wlk E9 17 C3
Brooks Ct
London SW4 172 A2
Nine Elms SW8 161 A2
Brooks Ho 6 SW2 74 C3
Brookside Rd N19 4 B2
Brooks La W4 44 C4
Brook's Mews W1 118 A4
Brooks Rd W4 36 C1
Brook St
Bayswater W2 115 C4
Mayfair W1 118 A4
Brookstone Ct SE15 65 A3
Brooksville Ave NW6 23 A4
Brookville Rd SW6 154 C1
Brookwood Ave SW13 46 B1
Brookwood Ho SE1 136 B3
Brookwood Rd SW18 70 C3
Broome Ct 3 TW9 44 C2
Broome Ho 7 E5 17 A3
Broome Way SE5 48 C3
Broom Farm SW6 165 C2
Broomfield 7 NW1 12 C1
Broomfield Ho SE17 152 A3
Broomfield House Sch TW9 44 B2
Broomfield Rd TW9 44 B2
Broomfield St E14 34 A4
Broomgrove Rd SW9 173 A1
Broomhill Rd SW18 58 C2
Broomhouse La SW6 58 C4
Broomhouse Rd SW6 165 B2
Broomsleigh St NW6 10 B3
Broomwood Hall Sch SW12 72 C4
Broomwood Rd SW11 60 C2
Brougham Rd
Acton W3 28 B3
Hackney E8 24 C4
Brougham St SW11 169 A2
Brough Cl SW8 162 B1
Broughton Dr 19 SW9 63 A3
Broughton Rd SW6 166 B2
Broughton Road App SW6 166 A2
Broughton St SW8 170 A2
Brouncker Rd W3 37 B4
Browne Ho 13 SE8 51 C3
Brownfield St E14 34 B3
Brownflete Ho SE4 66 A3
Brown Hart Gdns W1 117 C4
Browning Cl W9 89 A1
Browning Ct W14 154 C4
Browning Ho
2 London SE14 51 A2
7 Shepherd's Bush W12 30 B3
10 Stoke Newington N16 16 A4
Browning Mews W1 103 C3
Browning St SE17 151 A3
Brownlow Ho SE16 139 B3
Brownlow Mews WC1 95 A1
Brownlow Rd
Hackney E8 24 C4
Willesden NW10 8 A1
Brownlow St WC1 107 A3
Brown's Bldgs EC3 110 B1
Brown St W1 102 C2
Brownswood Rd N4 6 B2
Broxash Rd SW11 60 C1
Broxbourne Ho 1 E3 27 A1
Broxholme Ho SW6 166 A4
Broxholm Rd SE27, SW16 74 C1
Broxwood Way NW8 80 B3
Bruce Cl W10 30 C4
Bruce Glasier Ho 13 N19 4 C4
Bruce Ho
4 Clapham Pk SW4 61 C1
North Kensington W10 30 C4
Putney SW15 57 A2
Bruce Rd E3 27 A2
Bruckner St W10 23 B2
Bruges Pl 16 NW1 13 B1
Brune Ho E1 110 C3
Brunel Ct 8 SW13 46 B1

Brunel Engine House Rotherhithe★ SE16 40 B4
Brunel Est W2 31 C4
Brunel Ho
Chelsea SW10 157 C2
[4] Gospel Oak NW5 13 A4
Millwall E14 42 A1
New Cross SE8 51 B3
[25] Streatham SW2 74 A4
Brunel Mews NW10 22 C2
Brunel Rd
Acton W3 29 A4
Wapping SE16 32 B1
Brunel St E16 35 B3
Brune St E1 110 C3
Brunlees Ho SE1 137 A1
Bruno Ct [5] E8 16 C2
Brunswick Ct
Bermondsey SE1 138 B4
Finsbury EC1 96 A3
Westminster SW1 147 C3
Brunswick Gdns W8 31 C1 113 C1
Brunswick Ho
[4] Haggerston E2 24 B3
Lisson Gr NW1 90 C2
Brunswick Mews W1 103 A2
Brunswick Park Prim Sch SE5 48 C3
Brunswick Pk SE5 49 A2
Brunswick Pl N1 97 C3
Brunswick Quay SE16 40 C3
Brunswick Rd E14 34 B3
Brunswick Sh Ctr WC1 94 B2
Brunswick Sq WC1 94 B2
Brunswick Villas [2] SE5 49 A2
Brunton Pl E14 33 A3
Brushfield St E1 110 C4
Brussels Rd SW11 59 C3
Bruton La W1 118 B3
Bruton Pl W1 118 B3
Bruton St W1 118 B3
Brutus Ct SE11 150 A3
Bryan Ave NW10 9 A1
Bryan Ct W1 102 C2
Bryan Ho SE16 41 B4
Bryan Rd SE16 41 B4
Bryanston Ct W1 102 C2
Bryanston Ho [12] SE15 49 B2
Bryanston Mans W1 102 C4
Bryanston Mews E W1 102 C3
Bryanston Mews W W1 102 C2
Bryanston Pl W1 102 C3
Bryanston Sq W1 102 C2
Bryanston St W1 103 A1
Bryant Ct
Acton W3 28 C1
Haggerston E2 24 B3
Bryantwood Rd N5, N7 14 C3
Bryce Ho [25] SE14 50 C4
Brydale Ho [2] SE16 40 C2
Brydges Pl WC2 120 A3
Brydges Rd E15 19 C3
Brydon Wlk N1 84 B4
Bryer Ct EC2 108 C4
Bryett Rd N7 5 A1
Bryher Ho W4 37 B1
Brymay Cl E3 26 C3
Brymon Ct W1 103 A3
Brynmaer Ho SW11 169 A3
Brynmaer Rd SW11 169 A3
Bryony Rd W12 29 C2
BT Telecom Twr★ W1 104 C4
Buccleuch Ho E5 7 C4
Buchanan Ct [16] SE16 40 C2
Buchanan Gdns NW10 22 A3
Buchanan Ho
Dulwich SE21 76 A1
Wandsworth SW18 70 C4
Buchan Ho W3 37 A4
Buchan Rd SE15 65 B4
Bucharest Rd SW18 71 B4
Buckfast St E2 24 C2 99 C3
Buck Hill Wlk W2 115 C3
Buckhold Rd SW18 58 C1
Buckhurst Ho [15] N7 13 C3
Buckhurst St E1 25 A1
Buckingham Gate SW1 133 A2
Buckingham Ho
Finsbury Pk N4 6 B3
Richmond TW10 54 C2
Buckingham Mans NW6 11 A3
Buckingham Mews
Harlesden NW10 21 B3
[7] Kingsland N1 16 A2
Westminster SW1 132 C2
Buckingham Pal★ SW1 132 C3
Buckingham Palace Rd SW1 146 B4
Buckingham Pl SW1 132 C2
Buckingham Rd
Harlesden NW10 21 B3
Kingsland N1 16 A2
Buckingham St WC2 120 B3
Buckingham Yd NW10 21 B3
Buckland Cres NW3 11 C2
Buckland Ct [6] N1 24 A3
Buckland Ho [3] N1 14 C1
Buckland St N1 87 C1
Buckland Wlk [2] W3 37 B4
Buckler's Alley SW6 155 A2
Bucklersbury EC2, EC4 109 B1
Buckle St
Whitechapel E1 111 A2
Whitechapel E1 111 B2
Buckley Ct [5] NW6 10 B1
Buckley Rd NW6 10 B1
Buckmaster Cl [1] SW9 62 C4
Buckmaster Ho [1] N7 14 B4
Buckmaster Rd SW11 60 A3
Bucknall St WC1 106 A2
Bucknell Cl SW2 62 B3
Buckner Rd SW2 62 B3
Buckridge Bldg EC1 107 B4
Buckshead Ho [19] W2 31 C4
Buck St NW1 13 A1
Buckstone Cl SE23 65 B1
Buckters Rents SE16 33 A1
Buckthorne Rd SE4 66 A2
Budge Row EC4 109 B1
Budge's Wlk W2 115 A2
Budleigh Ho [19] SE15 49 C3
Buer Rd SW6 164 B1
Bugsby's Way SE10 43 B2
Buick Ho [4] E3 26 C1
Bulbarrow NW8 78 B3
Bulinca St SW1 147 C3
Bullace Row SE5 48 C2
Bullards Pl [13] E2 25 C2
Bulleid Way SW1 146 B3
Bullen Ho [13] E1 25 A1
Bullen St SW11 168 B2
Buller Cl SE15 49 C3
Buller Rd NW10 22 C2
Bullfinch Ct [4] SE21 75 C2
Bullingham Mans W8 127 C4
Bull Inn Ct WC2 120 B3
Bullivant St [9] E14 34 B2
Bulls Alley SW14 45 C1
Bull's Gdns SW3 144 B4
Bulls Head Pas EC3 110 A1
Bull Yd SE15 49 C2
Bulmer Mews W11 31 C1 113 B2
Bulow Ct SW6 166 B2
Bulstrode Pl W1 103 C3
Bulstrode St W1 103 C2
Bulwer St W12 30 B1
Bunbury Ho SE15 49 C3
Bunhill Row EC1 97 B1
Bunhouse Pl SW1 145 C2
Bunkers Hill NW11 2 B4
Bunning Ho N7 14 A4
Bunning Way N7 14 B1
Bunsen Ho [2] E3 26 A3
Bunsen St [3] E3 26 A3
Bunyan Ct EC2 108 C4
Buonaparte Mews SW1 147 B2
Burbage Cl SE1 137 B1
Burbage Ho
[16] Deptford SE14 50 C4
Shoreditch N1 87 C3
Burbage Rd SE21, SE24 75 C4
Burbage Sch N1 24 A3
Burcham St E14 34 B3
Burchell Ho SE11 149 A2
Burchell Rd SE15 50 A2
Burcher Gale Gr [5] SE15 49 B3
Burcote Rd SW18 71 C4
Burden Ho SW8 162 A1
Burdenshott Ave TW10 55 A3
Burder Cl N1 16 A2
Burder Rd N1 16 A2
Burdett Coutts & Townshend CE Prim Sch SW1 147 C3
Burdett Mews W2 100 A2
Burdett Rd
Richmond TW9 54 B4
Tower Hamlets E3 33 B4
Burdon Ct [3] E8 16 C2
Burford Ct SE8 51 C4
Burford Ho
[1] Brentford TW8 36 A1
South Lambeth SW9 173 A1
Burford Rd
Brentford TW8 36 A1
[5] Stratford Marsh E15 27 C4
Burford Wlk SW6 156 B1
Burgate Ct [9] SW9 62 C4
Burges Gr SW13 47 A3
Burgess Hill NW2 10 C4
Burgess Ho [3] SE5 48 B3
Burgess Ind Pk SE5 48 C3
Burgess Park Mans NW6 10 C4
Burgess St E14 33 C4
Burge St SE1 137 C1
Burghley Hall Cl SW19 70 A3
Burghley Ho SW19 70 A1
Burghley Rd NW5 13 A4
Burghley Twr W3 29 B2
Burgh St N1 86 B2
Burgon St EC4 108 B1
Burgos Gr SE10 52 A2
Burgoyne Rd SW9 62 B4
Burhan Uddin Ho E1 24 B1 98 C1
Buriton Ho [9] SW15 69 A3
Burke Cl SW15 56 A3
Burke Ho [1] SW11 59 C3
Burke St E16 35 B4
Burland Rd SW11 60 B2
Burleigh Ho
Chelsea SW3 157 C3
North Kensington W10 30 C4
Burleigh Pl SW15 57 C2
Burleigh St WC2 120 C4
Burley Ho E1 32 C3
Burlington Arc W1 118 C3
Burlington Ave TW9 44 C2
Burlington Cl W9 23 C1
Burlington Ct
Chiswick W4 45 B3
Highgate N6 3 C3
Burlington Danes Sch W12 30 A3
Burlington Gdns
Acton Green W4 37 B1
Acton W3 28 B1
Burlington Gdns *continued*
Fulham SW6 164 B1
Marylebone W1 118 C3
Burlington Ho NW3 11 C3
Burlington La W4 45 C3
Burlington Mews
Acton W3 28 B1
[2] Putney SW15 58 B2
Burlington Pl SW6 164 B1
Burlington Rd
Acton Green W4 37 B1
Fulham SW6 164 B1
Burma Rd N16 15 C4
Burmarsh [6] NW5 12 C2
Burmester Ho SW17 71 B1
Burmester Rd SW17 71 B1
Burnaby Cres W4 45 B4
Burnaby Ct SE16 139 C3
Burnaby Gdns W4 45 A4
Burnaby St SW10 157 A1
Burnand Ho [3] W14 39 C3
Burnbury Rd SW12 73 B3
Burne Jones Ho W14 140 B3
Burnell Ho [18] SW2 74 C3
Burnell Wlk SE1 153 A2
Burness Cl N7 14 B2
Burne St NW1 102 A4
Burnett Cl E9 17 B3
Burnett Ct SW11 168 A3
Burnett Ho [6] SE13 52 B1
Burney St SE10 52 B3
Burnfoot Ave SW6 164 B3
Burnham NW3 12 A1
Burnham Cl SE1 153 A3
Burnham Ct W2 114 B4
Burnham Est [8] E2 25 B2
Burnham St E2 25 B2
Burnhill Ho EC1 96 C3
Burnley Rd
London SW9 172 C2
Willesden NW10 8 C3
Burnsall St SW3 144 B2
Burns Ho
[18] Bethnal Green E2 25 B2
[1] Islington N7 14 B2
Kennington SE17 150 B1
[11] Stoke Newington N16 16 A4
Burn's Ho NW10 21 A4
Burnside Cl SE16 32 C1
Burns Rd SW11 168 C2
Burn's Rd NW10 21 B4
Burnthwaite Rd SW6 155 A1
Burntwood Cl SW18 72 A3
Burntwood Ct SW17 71 B1
Burntwood Grange Rd SW18 72 A3
Burntwood La SW17 71 C2
Burntwood Sch SW17 71 C2

Buross St E1 .... 32 A3
Burrage Ct 17 SE16 .... 40 C2
Burrard Ho 11 E2 .... 25 B3
Burrard Rd NW6 .... 10 C4
Burr Cl E1 .... 125 B2
Burrell St SE1 .... 122 A2
Burrell's Wharf Sq E14 .... 42 A1
Burrhill Ct SE16 .... 40 C3
Burrow Ho SW9 .... 173 A1
Burrow Rd SE22 .... 64 A3
Burrows Mews SE1 .... 136 A4
Burrows Rd NW10 .... 22 B2
Burrow Wlk SE21 .... 75 B4
Burr Rd SW18 .... 70 C4
Bursar St SE1 .... 124 A1
Burslem St E1 .... 111 C1
Burstock Rd SW15 .... 58 A3
Burston Rd SW15 .... 57 C2
Burtley Cl N4 .... 6 B3
Burton Bank N1 .... 15 C1
Burton Ct SW3 .... 145 A2
Burton Gr SE17 .... 151 B1
Burton Ho
8 Bermondsey SE16 .... 40 A4
Brixton SE5 .... 48 A2
Burton Lo 6 SW15 .... 58 B2
Burton Mews SW1 .... 145 C3
Burton Pl WC1 .... 93 C3
Burton Rd
Brixton SW9 .... 48 A1
Brixton SW9 .... 173 B2
Brondesbury NW6 .... 10 B1
Burtons Ct E15 .... 19 C1
Burton St WC1 .... 93 C2
Burtonwood Ho N4 .... 6 C4
Burtt Ho N1 .... 24 A2 98 A4
Burwash Ho SE1 .... 137 C3
Burwell Cl 27 E1 .... 32 A3
Burwell Wlk 14 E3 .... 26 C1
Burwood Ho 11 SW9 .... 63 A3
Burwood Pl W2 .... 102 B2
Bury Cl SE16 .... 32 C1
Bury Ct EC3 .... 110 B2
Buryfield Ct 23 SE8 .... 40 C2
Bury Pl WC1 .... 106 B3
Bury St
St James SW1 .... 119 A2
Whitechapel EC3 .... 110 B2
Bury Wlk SW3 .... 144 A2
Busbridge Ho 24 E14 .... 33 C4
Busby Mews 5 NW1 .... 13 C2
Busby Pl NW5 .... 13 C2
Bushbaby Cl SE1 .... 138 A1
Bushberry Rd E9 .... 18 A2
Bush Cotts 12 SW18 .... 58 C2
Bush Ct 7 W12 .... 39 C4
Bushell Cl SW2 .... 74 B2
Bushey Down SW12 .... 73 A2
Bushey Hall SE5 .... 49 B2
Bushey Hill Rd SE5 .... 49 B2
Bushfield Ho N5 .... 15 B3
Bush Ind Est NW10 .... 20 C1
Bush La EC4 .... 123 B4
Bushnell Rd SW17 .... 73 A1
Bush Rd
Bermondsey SE8 .... 40 B2
Hackney E8 .... 25 A4
Richmond TW9 .... 44 B4
Bushwood Dr SE1 .... 153 A3
Bushwood Rd TW9 .... 44 C4
Business Design Ctr* N1 .... 85 C3
Buspace Studios 3 W10 .... 23 A1
Butcher Row E1 .... 32 C3
Butchers Rd E16 .... 35 C3
Bute Gdns W6 .... 39 C2
Bute House Prep Sch W6 .... 39 C2
Bute St SW7 .... 143 B4
Bute Wlk 18 N1 .... 15 C2
Butfield Ho 6 E9 .... 17 B2
Butler Ho
32 Bethnal Green E2 .... 25 B2
5 Brixton SW9 .... 48 A2
11 Poplar E14 .... 33 B3
Butler Pl SW1 .... 133 B2
Butler Rd NW10 .... 8 B1
Butlers & Colonial Wharf SE1 .... 139 A4
Butler St 33 E2 .... 25 B2
Butler's Wharf W SE1 .... 124 C1
Butley Ct 8 E3 .... 26 A3
Butterfield Cl 1 SE16 .... 40 A4
Butterfly Wlk 2 SE5 .... 48 C2
Buttermere NW1 .... 92 B4
Buttermere Cl
Bermondsey SE1 .... 152 C3
Leyton E11 .... 19 C4
Buttermere Ct NW8 .... 79 B4
Buttermere Dr SW15 .... 58 A2
Buttermere Ho 13 E3 .... 26 B2
Buttermere Wlk 9 E8 .... 16 B2
Butterwick W6 .... 39 B2
Butterworth Ct SW16 .... 74 A1
Buttesland St N1 .... 97 C4
Buxhall Cres E9 .... 18 B2
Buxted Rd
Camberwell SE22 .... 64 A3
Dalston E8 .... 16 B1
Buxton Ct N1 .... 97 A4
Buxton Gdns W3 .... 28 A2
Buxton Ho 3 SW11 .... 59 C3
Buxton Rd
Mortlake SW14 .... 56 A4
Upper Holloway N19 .... 4 C3
Willesden NW2 .... 9 A2
Buxton St E1 .... 24 B1 99 A1
Byam Shaw Sch of Art N19 .... 4 C2
Byam St SW6 .... 166 C1
Byards Ct SE16 .... 40 C3
Byas Ho 6 E3 .... 26 B2
Byefield Cl SE16 .... 41 A4
Byelands Cl 12 SE16 .... 32 C1
Bye The W3 .... 29 A3
Byeway The SW14 .... 55 B4
Byfeld Gdns SW13 .... 46 C2
Bygrove Prim Sch E14 .... 34 A3
Bygrove St E14 .... 34 A3
Byng Pl WC1 .... 93 B1
Byng St E14 .... 41 C4
Byrne Ho 11 SW2 .... 62 B2
Byrne Rd SW12 .... 73 A2
Byron Cl E8 .... 24 C4
Byron Ct
Chelsea SW3 .... 144 B3
Dulwich SE21 .... 76 C3
3 Hampstead NW6 .... 11 B1
Paddington W9 .... 23 C1
St Pancras WC1 .... 94 C2
Byron Mews
Hampstead NW3 .... 12 A4
2 Maida Vale W9 .... 23 C1
Byron St E14 .... 34 B3
Bythorn St SW9 .... 62 B3
Byward St EC3 .... 124 B3
Bywater Pl SE16 .... 33 A1
Bywater St SW3 .... 144 C2
Bywell Pl W1 .... 104 C3
Byworth Wlk N19 .... 5 A3

C

Cabbell St NW1 .... 102 A3
Cabinet Off SW1 .... 134 A4
Cabinet War Rooms & Churchill Mus* SW1 .... 133 C4
Cable Ho WC1 .... 95 B4
Cable Pl SE10 .... 52 B2
Cable St E1 .... 32 A2
Cabot Ct SE16 .... 40 C3
Cabot Sq E14 .... 33 C1
Cabul Rd SW11 .... 168 B1
Cactus Cl SE5 .... 49 A1
Cactus Wlk W12 .... 29 B3
Cadbury Way SE16 .... 153 B4
Caddington Rd NW2 .... 1 A1
Cadell Cl E2 .... 24 B3
Cadell Ho 12 E2 .... 24 B3
Cade Rd SE10 .... 52 C2
Cader Rd SW18 .... 59 B1
Cadet Dr SE1 .... 153 A2
Cade Tyler Ho 10 SE10 .... 52 B2
Cadiz St SE17 .... 151 A1
Cadman Cl SW9 .... 48 A3
Cadmore Ho 4 N1 .... 15 A1
Cadmus Cl 9 SW4 .... 61 C4
Cadmus Ct SW9 .... 173 B4
Cadnam Lo E14 .... 42 C3
Cadnam Point 15 SW15 .... 69 A3
Cadogan Cl E9 .... 18 B1
Cadogan Ct SW3 .... 144 C3
Cadogan Ct Gdns SW1 .... 145 B4
Cadogan Gate SW1 .... 145 A4
Cadogan Gdns SW3 .... 145 A3
Cadogan Ho SW3 .... 157 C3
Cadogan La SW1 .... 131 B1
Cadogan Pl SW1 .... 131 A1
Cadogan Sq SW1 .... 131 A1
Cadogan St SW3 .... 144 C3
Cadogan Terr E9 .... 18 B1
Caedmon Rd N7 .... 14 B4
Caernarvon Ho W2 .... 100 C2
Caesar Ct 25 E2 .... 25 C3
Cahill St EC1 .... 97 A1
Cahir St E14 .... 42 A2
Caine Ho W3 .... 37 A4
Caird St W10 .... 23 B2
Cairns Ho 3 N7 .... 14 B4
Cairns Rd SW11 .... 60 A2
Caister Ho N7 .... 14 B2
Caistor Ho 10 SW12 .... 73 A4
Caistor Mews SW12 .... 73 A4
Caistor Rd SW12 .... 73 A4
Caithness Ho N1 .... 84 C4
Caithness Rd W14 .... 39 C3
Calabria Rd N5 .... 15 A3
Calais Gate SE5 .... 48 A2
Calais St SE5 .... 48 A2
Calbourne Rd SW12 .... 72 C4
Calcraft Ho 10 E2 .... 25 B3
Caldecot Ct SE5 .... 48 B1
Caldecot Rd SE5 .... 48 B1
Calder Ct SE16 .... 33 B1
Calderon Ho NW8 .... 80 A2
Calderon Pl 20 W10 .... 30 B4
Caldervale Rd SW4 .... 61 C2
Caldew St SE5 .... 48 C3
Caldwell St SW9 .... 163 A1
Caldy Wlk 19 N1 .... 15 B2
Caleb St SE1 .... 137 A4
Caledonia Ho 15 E14 .... 33 A3
Caledonian Market SE1 .... 138 B2
Caledonian Rd
Islington N1 .... 84 C3
Lower Holloway N7 .... 14 B2
Caledonian Road & Barnsbury Sta N7 .... 14 B1
Caledonian Road Sta N7 .... 14 B2
Caledonian Sq 6 NW1 .... 13 C2
Caledonian Wharf Rd E14 .... 42 C2
Caledonia St N1 .... 84 B1
Cale St SW3 .... 144 A2
Caletock Way SE10 .... 43 B1
Calgarth NW1 .... 83 A1
Calgary Ct 30 SE16 .... 40 B4
Caliban Twr 9 N1 .... 24 A3
Calico Ho 4 SW11 .... 59 B4
Calico Row 5 SW11 .... 59 B4
Calidore Cl SW2 .... 62 B1
California Bldg 2 SE13 .... 52 A2
Callaby Terr 11 N1 .... 15 C2
Callahan Cotts 8 E1 .... 32 B4
Callan Sch The W1 .... 105 A2
Callcott Ct NW6 .... 10 B1
Callcott Rd NW6 .... 10 B1
Callcott St W8 .... 31 C1 113 B2
Callendar Rd SW7 .... 129 B2
Callingham Cl 13 E14 .... 33 B4
Callingham Ho 1 SW4 .... 62 A4
Callow St SW3 .... 157 B4
Calmington Rd SE5 .... 49 A4
Calshot Ho N1 .... 84 C2
Calshot St N1 .... 84 C1
Calstock NW1 .... 83 B3
Calstock Ho SE11 .... 149 C2
Calthorpe St WC1 .... 95 A2
Calton Ave SE21 .... 64 A1
Calver 13 NW5 .... 13 A4
Calverley Gr N19 .... 4 C3
Calvert Ave E2 .... 24 B2 98 C3
Calvert Ct
1 London N19 .... 4 B3
5 Richmond TW9 .... 54 B3
Calvert Ho 9 W12 .... 30 A2
Calverton SE5 .... 49 A4
Calvert Rd SE10 .... 43 B1
Calvert's Bldgs SE1 .... 123 B1
Calvert St NW1 .... 81 B4
Calvin St E1 .... 24 B1 98 C1
Calypso Cres 6 SE15 .... 49 B3
Calypso Way SE8, SE16 .... 41 B2
Cambalt Ho 3 SW15 .... 57 C2
Cambalt Rd SW15 .... 57 C2
Cambay Ho 7 E1 .... 26 A1
Camber Ho 4 SE15 .... 50 B4
Camberley Ho NW1 .... 82 B1
CAMBERWELL 48 B2
Camberwell Bsns Ctr SE5 .... 48 C3
Camberwell Church St SE5 .... 48 C2
Camberwell Coll of Arts
Camberwell SE5 .... 49 A2
Camberwell SE15 .... 49 B3
Camberwell Glebe SE5 .... 49 A2
Camberwell Gn SE5 .... 48 C2
Camberwell Gr SE5 .... 49 A1
Camberwell Green SE5 .... 48 B2
Camberwell New Rd SW9 .... 48 A3
Camberwell Rd SE5 .... 48 B3
Camberwell Station Rd SE5 .... 48 B2
Camberwell Trad Est SE5 .... 48 B2
Camborne Rd SW18 .... 70 C4
Cambourne Mews 6 W11 .... 31 A3
Cambray Rd SW12 .... 73 B3

Cambria Ho [14] E14 ... 33 A3
Cambria Lo [3] SW15 ... 58 B2
Cambrian Cl SE27 .. 75 A1
Cambrian Rd TW10 ... 54 B1
Cambria Rd SE5 ... 63 B4
Cambria St SW6 .. 156 B1
Cambridge Ave NW6 ... 23 C3
Cambridge Cir WC2 ... 105 C1
Cambridge Cotts TW9 ... 44 C4
Cambridge Cres [20] E2 ... 25 A3
Cambridge Ct
[26] Bethnal Green E2 ... 25 A3
[7] Hammersmith W6 ... 39 B2
[2] Kilburn NW6 ... 23 C3
Marylebone W2 ... 102 A3
Stamford Hill N16 ... 7 A4
Cambridge Gate NW1 ... 92 A2
Cambridge Gate Mews NW1 ... 92 B2
Cambridge Gdns
Kilburn NW6 ... 23 C3
North Kensington W10 ... 31 A3
Cambridge Gr W6 .. 39 A2
Cambridge Heath Rd E1, E2 ... 25 A2
Cambridge Heath Sta E2 ... 25 A3
Cambridge Ho SW6 ... 58 A4
Cambridge Mans SW11 ... 168 C3
Cambridge Pas [9] E9 ... 17 B1
Cambridge Pl W8 128 B3
Cambridge Rd
Barnes SW13 ... 46 B1
Battersea SW11 ... 168 C3
Kilburn NW6 ... 23 C2
Kilburn NW6 ... 23 C3
Richmond TW9 ... 44 C3
Cambridge Rd N W4 ... 37 A1
Cambridge Rd S [3] W4 ... 37 A1
Cambridge Sch W6 ... 39 A2
Cambridge Sq W2 ... 102 A2
Cambridge St SW1 ... 146 C2
Cambridge Terr NW1 ... 92 A3
Cambridge Terr Mews NW1 ... 92 B3
Cambus Rd E16 ... 35 C4
Cam Ct [2] SE15 ... 49 B4
Camden Coll of English NW1 ... 12 C1
Camden Gdns NW1 ... 13 A1
Camden High St NW1 ... 82 C3
Camden Ho [6] SE8 ... 41 B1
Camdenhurst St E14 ... 33 A3
Camden Lock Pl NW1 ... 13 A1
Camden Mews NW1 ... 13 C2
Camden Mkt* NW1 ... 82 B4
Camden Park Rd NW1 ... 13 C2
Camden Pas N1 ... 86 A3
Camden Rd NW1 ... 82 B4
Camden Road Sta NW1 ... 13 B1
Camden Row SE3 .. 53 A1
Camden Sch for Girls The NW5 ... 13 B2
Camden Sq NW1 ... 13 C2
Camden St NW1 ... 83 A3
Camden Studios NW1 ... 83 A3
Camden Terr [17] NW1 ... 13 C2
CAMDEN TOWN ... 13 A1
Camden Town Sta NW1 ... 82 B4
Camden Wlk N1 ... 86 A3
Cameford Ct [20] SW12 ... 74 A4
Camelford NW1 ... 83 A3
Camelford Ct [15] W11 ... 31 A3
Camelford Ho SE1 ... 148 B1
Camelford Wlk [13] W11 ... 31 A3
Camellia Ho SE8 ... 51 B3
Camellia St SW8 . 162 A1
Camelot Ho [15] NW1 ... 13 C2
Camelot Prim Sch SE15 ... 50 A4
Camera Pl SW10 . 157 B4
Cameret Ct [6] W11 ... 39 C4
Cameron Ct [3] SW19 ... 70 A3
Cameron Ho
Camberwell SE5 ... 48 B3
St John's Wood NW8 ... 80 A2
Cameron House Sch SW10 ... 157 C4
Cameron Pl SW16 .. 74 C2
Camerton Cl [8] E8 ... 16 B2
Camilla Rd SE16 ... 40 A2
Camlet St E2 ... 24 B1 98 C2
Camley St NW1 ... 83 C2
Camomile St EC3 . 110 B2
Campaign Ct W9 ... 23 B1
Campana Rd SW6 165 C4
Campbell Ct
Dulwich SE21 ... 76 C3
South Kensington SW7 ... 128 C1
Campbell Gordon Way NW2 ... 9 A4
Campbell Ho
Paddington W2 ... 89 B1
Pimlico SW1 ... 146 C1
[30] Shepherd's Bush W12 ... 30 A2
Campbell Rd E3 ... 26 C2
Campbell Wlk N1 . 84 B4
Campdale Rd N7 ... 4 C1
Campden Gr W8 . 127 C4
Campden Hill W8 127 B4
Campden Hill Ct W8 ... 127 C4
Campden Hill Gate W8 ... 127 B4
Campden Hill Gdns W8 ... 31 C1 113 B2
Campden Hill Mans W8 ... 31 C1 113 C2
Campden Hill Pl W14 ... 31 B1 113 A2
Campden Hill Rd W8 ... 127 B4
Campden Hill Sq W14 ... 31 B1 113 A2
Campden Ho [4] NW6 ... 11 C1
Campden Hos W8 ... 31 C1 113 B1
Campden House Cl W8 ... 127 C4
Campden St W8 ... 31 C1 113 B1
Campen Cl SW19 ... 70 A2
Camperdown St E1 ... 111 A1
Campion Ho [15] N16 ... 16 A3
Campion Rd SW15 .57 B2
Camplin St SE14 ... 50 C3
Campshill Pl SE13 .. 67 B2
Campshill Rd SE13 ... 67 B2
Campton Hill Twrs W8 ... 31 C1 113 B2
Cam Rd E15 ... 27 C4
Camsey Ho [8] SW2 ... 62 B2
Canada Cres W3 ... 20 B1
Canada Gdns SE13 .67 B2
Canada Rd W3 ... 28 B4
Canada Sq E14 ... 34 A1
Canada St SE16 ... 40 C4
Canada Water Sta SE16 ... 40 C3
Canada Way W12 ... 30 A2
Canal App SE8 ... 51 A4
Canal Bldg N1 ... 86 C2
Canal Bridge SE15 .49 C4
Canal Bvd [7] NW1 .. 13 C2
Canal Cl
Mile End E1 ... 26 A1
North Kensington W10 ... 22 C1
Canal Gr SE15 ... 50 A4
Canal Head Public Sq [1] SE15 ... 49 C2
Canal Path [22] E2 ... 24 B4
Canalside Studios [29] N1 ... 24 A4
Canal St SE5 ... 48 C4
Canal Way W10 ... 22 C1
Canal Wlk N1 ... 87 C4
CANARY WHARF .. 34 A1
Canary Wharf* E14 ... 34 A1
Canary Wharf Pier (River Bus) E14 ... 33 B1
Canary Wharf Sta E14 ... 34 A1
Canary Wharf Sta (DLR) E14 ... 33 C1
Canberra Prim Sch W12 ... 30 A2
Canbury Mews SE26 ... 76 C1
Cancell Rd SW9 .. 173 C4
Candahar Rd SW11 ... 168 B1
Candida Ct [9] NW1 ... 13 A1
Candishe Ho SE1 138 C4
Candle Gr SE15 ... 65 A4
Candlemakers [25] SW11 ... 59 C4
Candover St W1 .. 104 C3
Candy St E3 ... 26 B4
Canfield Gdns NW6 ... 11 A1
Canfield Pl NW6 ... 11 B2
Canford Rd SW11 ... 60 C2
Canham Rd W3 ... 38 A4
Cann Ho W14 ... 126 B1
Canning Cross SE5 ... 49 A1
Canning Ho [23] W12 ... 30 A2
Canning Pas W8 . 128 C2
Canning Pl W8 ... 128 C2
Canning Pl Mews W8 ... 128 C2
Canning Rd N5 ... 6 A1
Cannington [14] NW5 ... 12 C2
CANNING TOWN .. 35 B3
Canning Town E16 ... 35 A3
Canning Town Sta E16 ... 35 A3
Cannock Ho N4 ... 6 C4
Cannon Dr [21] E14 .. 33 C2
Cannon Hill NW6 ... 10 C3
Cannon Ho SE11 . 149 A3
Cannon La NW3 ... 2 C1
Cannon Pl NW3 ... 2 C1
Cannon St EC4 ... 123 A4
Cannon Street Rd E1 ... 32 A3
Cannon Street Sta EC4 ... 123 B4
Cannon Wharf Bsns Ctr [12] SE8 ... 41 A2
Canon Barnett Prim Sch E1 ... 111 A2
Canon Beck Rd SE16 ... 40 B4
CANONBURY ... 15 B2
Canonbury Bsns Ctr N1 ... 87 A4
Canonbury Cres N1 ... 15 B1
Canonbury Ct [21] N1 ... 15 A1
Canonbury Gr N1 .. 15 B1
Canonbury Hts [6] N1 ... 15 C2
Canonbury La N1 ... 15 A1
Canonbury Pk N N1 ... 15 B2
Canonbury Pk S N1 ... 15 B2
Canonbury Pl N1 ... 15 A2
Canonbury Prim Sch N1 ... 15 A2
Canonbury Rd N1 .. 15 A1
Canonbury Sq N1 .. 15 A1
Canonbury St N1 .. 15 B1
Canonbury Sta N1, N5 ... 15 B3
Canonbury Villas N1 ... 15 A1
Canon Murnane Rd SE1 ... 138 C1
Canon Row SW1 . 134 A3
Canons Cl N2 ... 2 C4
Canon St N1 ... 86 C3
Canrobert St E2 ... 25 A2
Cantelowes Rd NW1 ... 13 C2
Canterbury SE13 ... 67 B2
Canterbury Cl [16] SE5 ... 48 B1
Canterbury Cres SW9 ... 62 C4
Canterbury Ct
Acton W3 ... 29 A1
Kilburn NW6 ... 23 C3
Canterbury Gr SE27, SW16 ... 74 C1
Canterbury Ho
[6] Bromley E3 ... 27 A2
Lambeth SE1 ... 135 A2
Canterbury Ind Pk [15] SE15 ... 50 B4
Canterbury Mans NW6 ... 11 A2
Canterbury Pl SE17 ... 150 B3
Canterbury Rd NW6 ... 23 C3
Canterbury Terr NW6 ... 23 C3
Cantium Ret Pk SE1 ... 49 C4
Canton St E14 ... 33 C3
Cantrell Rd E3 ... 26 C1
Canute Ct SW16 ... 74 C1
Canute Gdns SE16 .. 40 C2
Canvey St SE1 ... 122 C2
Cape Henry Ct [15] E14 ... 34 C2
Capel Ho [17] E9 ... 17 B1
Capel Lo
[5] Richmond TW9 ... 44 B2
[12] Streatham SW2 .. 74 B4
Capener's Cl SW1 131 B3
Capern Rd SW18 ... 71 B3
Capio Nightingale Hospl SW3 ... 144 B1
Capital City Acad NW10 ... 22 A4
Capital East Apts [8] E16 ... 35 C2
Capital Interchange Way TW8 ... 36 C1
Capital Sh Ctrs SW1 ... 133 B3
Capital Wharf E1 125 C1
Capland Ho NW8 .. 89 C2
Capland St NW8 ... 89 C2
Caple Ho SW10 ... 157 A2
Caple Rd NW10 ... 21 B3
Capper St WC1 ... 93 A1
Capstan Ho [6] E14 ... 42 B2
Capstan Rd SE8 ... 41 B2
Capstan Sq E14 ... 42 B4
Capstan Way SE16 .. 33 A1
Capulet Mews [1] E16 ... 35 C1
Caradoc Cl W2 ... 31 C3
Caradoc St SE10 ... 43 A1
Cara Ho [10] N1 ... 14 C1
Caranday Villas [5] W11 ... 30 C1
Caravel Cl E14 ... 41 C3
Caravel Mews [14] SE8 ... 51 C4
Caraway Hts E14 ... 34 B2
Carbery Ave W3 ... 36 B4

Carbis Rd E14 ... 33 B3
Carbroke Ho 9 E9 ... 25 B4
Carburton St W1 ... 92 B1
Cardale St 1 E14 ... 42 B3
Carden Rd SE15 ... 65 A4
Cardiff Ho 9 SE15 ... 49 C4
Cardigan Rd
Barnes SW13 ... 46 C1
Bow E3 ... 26 B3
Richmond TW10 ... 54 A1
Cardigan St SE11 ... 149 B2
Cardigan Wlk 19 N1 ... 15 B1
Cardinal Bourne St SE1 ... 137 C1
Cardinal Cap Alley SE1 ... 122 C3
Cardinal Hinsey Cl NW10 ... 21 C3
Cardinal Hinsley RC High Sch (Boys) NW10 ... 21 C4
Cardinal Pl SW15 ... 57 C3
Cardinal Pole RC Sch
London E9 ... 17 C1
London E9 ... 18 A3
Cardinals Way N19 ... 4 C3
Cardinal Vaughan Meml Sch The W14 ... 126 A4
Cardinal Wlk SW1 ... 132 C1
Cardine Mews SE15 ... 50 A3
Cardington St NW1 ... 93 A3
Cardozo Rd N7 ... 14 A3
Cardross St W6 ... 39 A3
Cardwell Rd 3 N7 ... 14 A4
Career Ct 11 SE16 ... 40 C4
Carew Cl N7 ... 5 B2
Carew Ct 15 SE14 ... 50 C4
Carew Ho SW16 ... 74 C1
Carew St SE5 ... 48 B1
Carey Ct 20 SE5 ... 48 B3
Carey Gdns SW8 ... 171 B3
Carey La EC2 ... 108 C2
Carey Pl SW1 ... 147 B3
Carey St WC2 ... 107 A1
Carfax Pl SW4 ... 61 C3
Carfree Cl 5 N1 ... 14 C1
Cargill Rd SW18 ... 71 B3
Carinthia Ct 5 SE8 ... 41 A2
Carisbrooke Ct
Acton W3 ... 37 B4
1 Streatham SW16 ... 74 B1
Carisbrooke Gdns SE15 ... 49 B3
Carisbrooke Ho TW10 ... 54 C2
Carleton Gdns N19 ... 13 B3
Carleton Rd N7 ... 13 C4
Carlile Cl E3 ... 26 B3
Carlile Ho SE1 ... 137 C1
Carlingford Rd NW3 ... 11 C4
Carlisle Ave
Acton W3 ... 29 A3
Whitechapel EC3 ... 110 C1
Carlisle Ho 6 NW5 ... 4 B1
Carlisle La SE1 ... 135 A2
Carlisle Pl SW1 ... 132 C1
Carlisle Rd
Finsbury Pk N4 ... 5 C4
Kilburn NW6 ... 23 A4
Carlisle St W1 ... 105 B1
Carlisle Wlk 6 E8 ... 16 B2
Carlos Pl W1 ... 118 A3
Carlow St NW1 ... 82 C2
Carlson Ct SW15 ... 58 B3
Carlton Cl NW3 ... 1 C2
Carlton Ct
Brixton SW9 ... 48 A2
Kilburn NW6 ... 78 B2
8 Willesden NW2 ... 9 B2
Carlton Dr SW15 ... 58 A2
Carlton Gdns SW1 ... 119 B1
Carlton Gr SE15 ... 50 A2
Carlton Hill NW8 ... 78 C2
Carlton Ho
8 Kilburn NW6 ... 23 B3
Kilburn NW6 ... 23 C3
Marylebone W1 ... 103 A2
Carlton House Terr SW1 ... 119 C2
Carlton Lo N4 ... 5 C4
Carlton Mans
Brixton SW9 ... 62 C3
Cricklewood NW2 ... 9 C3
Kensington W14 ... 126 B4
Maida Vale W9 ... 88 B4
7 South Hampstead NW6 ... 10 C1
Stamford Hill N16 ... 7 B3
Carlton Prim Sch NW5 ... 12 C3
Carlton Rd
Acton W4 ... 37 C4
Finsbury Pk N4 ... 5 C4
Mortlake SW14 ... 55 B3
Carlton Sq E1 ... 25 C1
Carlton St SW1 ... 119 B3
Carltons The 5 SW15 ... 58 A2
Carlton Tower Pl SW1 ... 131 A2
Carlton Vale NW6 ... 23 C3
Carlton Vale Inf Sch NW6 ... 23 B2
Carlyle Ho
4 Camberwell SE5 ... 48 B3
Chelsea SW3 ... 157 C4
12 Stoke Newington N16 ... 7 A1
Carlyle Mans SW3 ... 158 A3
Carlyle Mews 24 E1 ... 25 C1
Carlyle Pl SW15 ... 57 C3
Carlyle Rd 1 NW10 ... 20 C4
Carlyle's Ho★ SW3 ... 158 A3
Carlyle Sq SW3 ... 143 C1
Carmalt Gdns SW15 ... 57 B3
Carmarthen Ho 8 SW15 ... 69 B4
Carmarthen Pl SE1 ... 138 A4
Carmel Ct W8 ... 128 A4
Carmelite St EC4 ... 121 C4
Carmel Lo SW6 ... 155 B4
Carmen St E14 ... 34 A3
Carmichael Cl 9 SW11 ... 59 C4
Carmichael Ct 5 SW13 ... 46 B1
Carmichael Ho 6 E14 ... 34 B2
Carmichael Mews SW18 ... 71 C4
Carminia Rd SW17 ... 73 A2
Carnaby St★ W1 ... 104 C1
Carnac St SE21, SE27 ... 75 C1
Carna Ct TW9 ... 54 A4
Carnegie Ho NW3 ... 2 C1
Carnegie Pl SW19 ... 69 C1
Carnegie St N1 ... 85 A3
Carnicot Ho 9 SE15 ... 50 A2
Carnoustie Dr N1 ... 14 B1
Carnwath Ho SW6 ... 59 A4
Carnwath Rd SW6 ... 59 A4
Caroline Cl
Bayswater W2 ... 114 B3
Streatham SW16 ... 74 B1
Caroline Gdns E2 ... 24 A2 98 B4
Caroline Ho
Bayswater W2 ... 114 B3
20 Hammersmith W6 ... 39 B1
Caroline Martyn Ho 8 N19 ... 4 C4
Caroline Pl
Bayswater W2 ... 114 B3
Clapham SW11 ... 169 C1
Caroline Pl Mews W2 ... 114 B3
Caroline St E1 ... 32 C3
Caroline Terr SW1 ... 145 B3
Caroline Wlk W6 ... 154 A3
Carol St NW1 ... 82 C4
Caronia Ct 4 SE16 ... 41 A2
Carpenter Ho
11 Tower Hamlets E14 ... 33 C4
5 Tufnell Pk N19 ... 13 C4
Carpenters Bsns Pk E15 ... 19 A1
Carpenters Ct NW1 ... 82 C4
Carpenter's Pl SW4 ... 61 C3
Carpenters Prim Sch E15 ... 27 B4
Carpenter's Rd E15 ... 19 A1
Carpenter St W1 ... 118 A3
Carradale Ho 2 E14 ... 34 B3
Carrara Cl 18 SW9 ... 63 A3
Carrara Wharf SW6 ... 58 A4
Carriage Dr E SW11 ... 159 C2
Carriage Drive E SW11 ... 159 C2
Carriage Drive N SW11, SW8 ... 159 C3
Carriage Dr N
Battersea SW8, SW11 ... 158 C2
Battersea SW8, SW11 ... 159 C3
Carriage Dr S SW11 ... 169 B4
Carriage Dr W SW11 ... 158 C1
Carrick Ho
Islington N7 ... 14 B2
Kennington SE11 ... 150 A2
Carrick Mews SE8 ... 51 C4
Carrington Ct SW11 ... 60 A3
Carrington Ho W1 ... 118 A1
Carrington Lo 3 TW10 ... 54 A2
Carrington Rd TW10 ... 54 C3
Carrington St W1 ... 118 A1
Carrol Cl NW5 ... 13 A4
Carroll Ct
Acton W3 ... 37 A3
4 Shacklewell E5 ... 7 C1
Carroll Ho W2 ... 115 B4
Carron Cl E14 ... 34 A3
Carroun Rd SW8 ... 162 C2
Carr St 5 E14 ... 33 A3
Carslake Rd SW15 ... 57 B1
Carson Rd
Dulwich SE21 ... 75 C2
Newham E16 ... 35 C4
Carter Ct EC4 ... 108 B1
Carteret Ho 8 W12 ... 30 A2
Carteret St SW1 ... 133 B3
Carteret Way SE8 ... 41 A2
Carter Ho
11 London SW2 ... 62 C2
Spitalfields E1 ... 110 C3
Carter La EC4 ... 108 B1
Carter Pl SE17 ... 151 A1
Carters Cl 10 NW5 ... 13 C2
Carter St SE17 ... 150 C1
Carter's Yd SW18 ... 58 C2
Carthew Rd W6 ... 39 A3
Carthew Villas W6 ... 39 A3
Carthusian St EC1 ... 108 C4
Cartier Circ E14 ... 34 B1
Carting La WC2 ... 120 B3
Cartmel NW1 ... 92 C4
Carton Ho
Bermondsey SE16 ... 139 B2
12 Shepherd's Bush W11 ... 30 C2
Cartoon Mus The★ WC1 ... 106 A3
Cartwright Gdns WC1 ... 94 A3
Cartwright Ho SE1 ... 137 A1
Cartwright St E1 ... 125 A3
Cartwright Way SW13 ... 47 A3
Carvel Ho E14 ... 42 B1
Carver Cl 15 W4 ... 37 B3
Carver Rd SE24 ... 63 B1
Carville Cres TW8 ... 36 A2
Caryl Ho 6 SW19 ... 69 C3
Carysfort Rd N16 ... 15 C4
Casby Ho SE16 ... 139 B2
Casella Rd SE14 ... 50 C3
Casey Cl NW8 ... 90 B3
Casino Ave SE24 ... 63 C2
Caspian Ho 10 E1 ... 32 C4
Caspian St SE5 ... 48 C3
Cassandra Ct 7 NW2 ... 9 B2
Cass Bsns Sch EC1 ... 97 B1
Cassell Ho SW9 ... 172 B2
Casserley Ho W4 ... 37 C3
Cass Ho 23 E9 ... 17 C2
Cassidy Rd SW6 ... 155 B1
Cassilis Rd E14 ... 41 C4
Cassinghurst SE24 ... 63 C2
Cassland Rd E9 ... 17 C2
Casson Ho E1 ... 111 B4
Casson St E1 ... 111 B3
Castalia Sq 6 E14 ... 42 B4
Castellain Mans W9 ... 88 A2
Castellain Rd W9 ... 88 B2
Castell Ho 11 SE8 ... 51 C3
Castello Ave SW15 ... 57 B2
Castelnau SW13 ... 47 A3
Castelnau Gdns SW13 ... 47 A4
Castelnau Mans SW13 ... 47 A4
Castelnau Row SW13 ... 47 A4
Casterbridge
Kilburn NW6 ... 78 B4
3 Notting Hill W11 ... 31 C3
Casterton St E8 ... 17 A2
Castleacre W2 ... 102 A1
Castle Baynard St EC4 ... 122 C4
Castlebrook Cl SE11 ... 150 A4
Castle Cl
12 Acton W3 ... 37 B4
Homerton E9 ... 18 A3
South Acton W3 ... 37 A4
Wimbledon SW19 ... 69 C1
Castlecombe Dr SW19 ... 69 C4
Castle Ct EC3 ... 109 C1
Castleden Ho NW6 ... 11 C1
Castleford Ct NW8 ... 89 C2
Castlefrank Ho N1 ... 24 A2 98 B4
Castlegate TW9 ... 54 B4
Castlehaven Rd NW1 ... 13 A1
Castle Ho
Newington SE1 ... 150 C4
South Lambeth SW8 ... 162 B2
Castle Ind Est SE17 ... 150 C4
Castle La SW1 ... 132 C2
Castlemaine SW11 ... 169 A2
Castlemaine St 2 E1 ... 32 A4
Castle Mead SE5 ... 48 B3
Castle Mews NW1 ... 13 A2
Castle Pl
8 Acton W4 ... 38 A2
Camden Town NW1 ... 13 A2
Castle Rd NW1 ... 13 A2
Castlereagh St W1 ... 102 C2
Castleton Ho 3 E14 ... 42 B2
Castletown Rd W14 ... 140 B1
Castleview Cl N4 ... 6 B2
Castle Way SW19 ... 69 C1
Castlewood Ho WC1 ... 105 C2
Castle Yd
Highgate N6 ... 3 C4

Castle Yd *continued*
Lambeth SE1 . . . . . 122 B2
Castor La E14 . . . . . . 34 A2
Catalpa Ct SE13 . . . . 67 C1
Caterham Rd
SE13 . . . . 67 C4
Catesby Ho 25 E9 . . 17 B1
Catesby St SE17 . . 151 C3
Cathay Ho SE16 . . . . 40 A4
Cathay St 12 SE16 . . 40 A4
Cathcart Hill N19. . . . 4 B1
Cathcart Rd
SW10 . . . . 156 C4
Cathcart St NW5 . . . 13 A2
Cathedral Ct EC4. 108 B1
Cathedral Lo EC1 108 C4
Cathedral Sch of St Saviour & St Mary Overie Prim Sch
SE1 . . . . 137 A4
Cathedral St SE1 . 123 B2
Cathedral Wlk
SW1 . . . . 132 C2
Catherall Rd N5,
N16. . . . . 6 B1
Catherine Baird Ct 12
SW12 . . . . 73 A4
Catherine Dr TW9 . . 54 A3
Catherine Gr SE10. . 52 A2
Catherine Griffiths Ct
EC1 . . . . 95 C2
Catherine Ho 16
N1. . . . . 24 A4
Catherine Pl SW1 132 C2
Catherine St WC2 120 C4
Catherine Wheel Alley
E1 . . . . 110 B3
Catherine Wheel Yd
SW1 . . . . 118 C1
Catherwood Ct N1 87 B1
Cathles Rd SW12 . . . 61 A1
Cathnor Rd W12 . . . 39 A4
Catlin St SE16 . . . . . . 40 A1
Catman Ho N4 . . . . . . 5 B3
Cato Rd SW4 . . . . 61 C3
Cator St
Camberwell SE15 . . . . 49 B3
Camberwell SE15 . . . . 49 B4
Cato St W1 . . . . . . 102 B2
Catton St WC1 . . . 106 C3
Caughley Ho
SE11 . . . . 135 B1
Caulfield Ct 15
NW1 . . . . 13 B1
Caulfield Rd SE15 . . 50 A1
Causeway The
SW18 . . . . 59 A2
Causton Cotts 3
E14 . . . . 33 A3
Causton Ho SE5 . . . . 48 B3
Causton Rd N6. . . . . . 4 A4
Causton St SW1. . 147 C2
Cautley Ave SW4 . . . 61 B2
Cavalry Gdns
SW15 . . . . 58 B2
Cavaye Ho SW10 . 157 A4
Cavaye Pl SW10. . 143 A1
Cavell Ct 5 N19. . . . . 4 B2
Cavell Ho 8 N1 . . . . 24 A4
Cavell St E1. . . . . 32 A4
Cavendish Ave
NW8 . . . . 79 C1
Cavendish Cl
Brondesbury NW6 . . . 10 B2
3 Putney SW15 . . . . 58 A2
Cavendish Cl *continued*
St John's Wood
NW8 . . . . 89 C4
Cavendish Coll
WC1 . . . . 105 B4
Cavendish Ct EC2 110 B2
Cavendish Gdns
SW4 . . . . 61 B1
Cavendish Ho
South Lambeth
SW8 . . . . 172 A4
St John's Wood
NW8 . . . . 79 C1
Cavendish Mans
2 Clapham Pk
SW12 . . . . 61 B1
Hackney E5. . . . . 17 B3
Holborn EC1 . . . . 95 B1
8 West Hampstead
NW6 . . . . 10 C3
Cavendish Mews N
W1 . . . . 104 B4
Cavendish Mews S
W1 . . . . 104 B3
Cavendish Par
SW12 . . . . 61 A1
Cavendish Pl
Balham SW4. . . . . 61 A1
Brondesbury NW2 . . . . 9 C2
Marylebone W1 . . . 104 B2
Cavendish Prim Sch
W4 . . . . 46 A3
Cavendish Rd
Brondesbury NW6 . . . 10 B1
Chiswick W4. . . . . 45 B2
Clapham Pk SW12 . . . 61 B1
Cavendish Sch The
NW1 . . . . 82 B4
Cavendish Sq W1 104 B2
Cavendish St N1 . . 87 B1
Cavendish Terr 11
E3 . . . . 26 B2
Cavendish The
NW11 . . . . 2 A4
Caversham Ho 7
SE15 . . . . 49 C4
Caversham Rd
NW5 . . . . 13 B2
Caversham St
SW3 . . . . 158 C4
Caverswall St
W12 . . . . 30 B3
Cavour Ho SE17 . . 150 B2
Caxton Gr E3. . . . . . . 26 C2
Caxton Hall*
SW1 . . . . 133 B2
Caxton Rd W12. . . . . 39 C4
Caxton St N E16. . . . 35 B3
Caxton St SW1 . . . 133 B2
Caxton Wlk WC2 . 105 C1
Cayford Ho 1
NW3 . . . . 12 B3
Cayley Prim Sch
E14 . . . . 33 A3
Cayton Pl EC1 . . . . . 97 B3
Cayton St EC1. . . . . 97 B3
Cazenove Mans 1
N16. . . . . 7 C2
Cazenove Rd N16 . . . 7 C2
Cecil Ct
Chelsea SW10 . . . . 156 C4
South Hampstead
NW6 . . . . 11 A1
St James WC2 . . . . 120 A3
Cecilia Rd E8 . . . . . . 16 C3
Cecil Mans 2
SW17 . . . . 72 C2
Cecil Rd Acton W3 . . 28 B4
Harlesden NW10 . . . . 21 A4
Cecil Rhodes Ho
NW1 . . . . 83 B2
Cedar Cl
Old Ford E3. . . . . 26 B4
West Norwood
SE21 . . . . 75 B2
Cedar Ct
Islington N1 . . . . 15 B1
Marylebone W1 . . . 102 B2
Mortlake SW14 . . . . . 55 B3
Wimbledon SW19. . . . 69 C1
Cedar Gr W5. . . . . . . 36 A3
Cedar Ho
5 Cubitt Town
E14 . . . . 42 B4
Kensington W8. . . . 128 A2
New Cross Gate
SE14 . . . . 50 C2
5 Richmond TW9 . . . 45 A2
16 Rotherhithe
SE16 . . . . 40 C4
Cedar Lo
Brondesbury NW2 . . . 10 B2
Fulham SW6. . . . . 47 C2
Cedarne Rd SW6 . 156 A1
Cedar Rd NW2 . . . . . . 9 B4
Cedars Cl SE13 . . . . . 67 C4
Cedars Ct SW15 . . . . 56 C1
Cedars Ho 21 SW2. . 62 B3
Cedars Mews
SW4 . . . . 61 A3
Cedars Rd
Barnes SW13 . . . . 46 C1
Clapham SW4. . . . . . . 61 A3
Cedars The E9 . . . . . 17 C1
Cedar Terr TW9 . . . . 54 A3
Cedar Way NW1. . . 83 B4
Cedra Ct N16. . . . . . . 7 C3
Cedric Chambers
NW8 . . . . 89 B2
Celandine Cl E3,
E14 . . . . 33 C4
Celandine Dr E8 . . . 16 B1
Celbridge Mews
W2 . . . . 100 B2
Celestial Gdns
SE13 . . . . 67 C3
Celia Blairman Ho
E1 . . . . 110 C4
Celia Ct 7 TW9 . . . . 44 B2
Celia Ho 10 N1 . . . . . 24 A3
Celia Rd N19 . . . . 13 B4
Celtic St E14 . . . . 34 A4
Cenacle Cl NW3. . . . . 1 C1
Cenotaph* SW1 . 134 A4
Centaur Ct 3
TW8 . . . . 36 A1
Centaur St SE1. . . 135 A2
Central Ave SW11 159 A1
Central Bsns Ctr
NW10 . . . . 8 A3
Central Criminal Court (Old Bailey)*
EC4 . . . . 108 B2
Central Foundation Boys' Sch EC2. . . . 97 C2
Central Foundation Lower Girls Sch The
E3 . . . . 26 A2
Central Foundation Upper Girls Sch The
E3 . . . . 26 B2
Central Ho E15 . . . . 27 B3
Central Middlesex Hospl NW10. . . . . . . 20 B2
Central Par W3 . . . . 37 A4
Central St Martins Coll EC1 . . . . 95 C1
Central St Martin's Coll of Art & Design
W1 . . . . 105 C1
Central St Martins Coll of Art & Design (The London Inst)
WC1 . . . . 106 C3
Central Sch of Ballet
EC1 . . . . 95 C1
Central Sch of Speech & Drama The
NW3 . . . . 11 C1
Central St EC1 . . . . 96 C3
Central Way
NW10 . . . . 20 B2
Centre Ave W3 . . . . . 28 C1
Centre Bldg SE17 151 A4
Centre Hts 5
NW3 . . . . 11 C1
Centre Point SE1. 153 B2
Centre Point Ho
WC2 . . . . 105 C2
Centre St E2 . . . . 25 A3
Centurion Bldg
SW8 . . . . 160 A3
Centurion Cl N7. . . . 14 B1
Centurion La E3. . . . 26 B3
Century Ho SE13 . . . 52 A1
Cephas Ave E1 . . . . . 25 B1
Cephas Ho 9 E1 . . . 25 B1
Cephas St E1 . . . . . . 25 B1
Cerise Rd SE15. . . . . 49 C2
Cerney Mews W2 115 B4
Cervantes Ct W2 . 100 B1
Cester St E2 . . . . 24 C4
Ceylon Rd
6 Hammersmith
W14 . . . . 39 C3
Kensington W14. . . 126 A1
Chabot Dr SE15 . . . . 65 A4
Chadacre Ho 10
SW9 . . . . 63 A3
Chadbourn St E14. . 34 A4
Chadston Ho 17
N1. . . . . 15 A1
Chadswell WC1 . . . 94 B3
Chadwell St EC1 . . 95 C4
Chadwick Cl
SW15 . . . . 68 B4
Chadwick Rd
Harlesden NW10 . . . . 21 B4
Peckham SE15 . . . . . . 49 B1
Chadwick St SW1 133 B1
Chadworth Ho
Finsbury EC1 . . . . . . 96 C3
Finsbury Pk N4. . . . . . 6 B3
Chagford Ho
38 Bromley E3 . . . . . 27 A2
Marylebone NW1 . . . 90 C1
Chagford St NW1. . 91 A1
Chalbury Ho 8
SW9 . . . . 62 B3
Chalbury Wlk N1. . 85 B2
Chalcot Cres NW1. 81 A4
Chalcot Gdns
NW3 . . . . 12 B2
Chalcot Mews
SW16 . . . . 74 A1
Chalcot Rd NW1. . . 81 B4
Chalcot Sch NW1. . . 13 A1
Chalcot Sq NW1. . . . 12 C1
Chaldon Rd SW6 . 154 B2
Chale Rd SW2. . . . . . 62 A1
Chalfont Ct NW1 . . 91 A1
Chalfont Ho 2
SE16 . . . . 40 A3
Chalford 7 NW3 . . . 11 B2
Chalford Ct 15
SW15 . . . . 57 C1
Chalkers Cnr TW9 . . 55 A4
Chalk Farm Sta
NW3 . . . . 12 C1
Chalk Hill Rd W6. . . 39 C2
Chalkwell Ho 10
E1 . . . . 32 C3
Challenge Cl
NW10 . . . . 21 A4
Challenger Ho 7
E14 . . . . 33 A2
Challice Way SW2 . . 74 B3
Challoner Cres
W14 . . . . 140 C1
Challoner Mans
W14 . . . . 140 C1
Challoner St W14 140 C1
Chalmers Ho 13
SW11 . . . . 59 B4
Chalmer's Wlk 14
SE17 . . . . 48 A4
Chalner Ho SW2 . . . 74 C3
Chaloner Ct SE1. . 137 B4
Chalsey Lodge
SE4 . . . . 66 B3
Chalsey Rd SE4 . . . . 66 B3
Chalton St NW1 . . . 83 B1
Chamberlain Cotts
SE5 . . . . 48 C2
Chamberlain Ho 6
E1 . . . . 32 B2
Chamberlain St 7
NW1 . . . . 12 B1
Chamberlayne Mans
3 NW10 . . . . 22 C2
Chamberlayne Rd
NW10 . . . . 22 B4
Chambers La NW10 . 9 B1
Chambers Rd N7. . . 14 A4
Chambers St
SE16 . . . . 139 C3
Chamber St E1. . . 125 A4
Chambon Pl 7
W6 . . . . 38 C2
Chambord Ho
E2 . . . . 24 B2 99 A3
Chambord St
E2 . . . . 24 B2 99 A3
Champion Gr SE5 . . 63 C4
Champion Hill
SE5 . . . . 63 C4
Champion Pk SE5 . . 48 C1
Champlain Ho 26
W12 . . . . 30 A2
Chancel Ct W1 . . . 119 B4
Chancellor Gr
SE21 . . . . 75 B1
Chancellor Ho
South Kensington
SW7 . . . . 129 A2
29 Wapping E1. . . . . 32 A1
Chancellor Pas
E14 . . . . 33 C1
Chancellors' Ct
WC1 . . . . 106 C4
Chancellor's Rd
W6 . . . . 39 B1
Chancellors St
W6 . . . . 39 B1
Chancellors Wharf 21
W6 . . . . 39 B1
Chancel St SE1. . . 122 A1

Chancery Bldgs 14 E1 ...32 B2
Chancery Ho WC2 ...107 B3
Chancery La EC4 ...107 B2
Chancery Lane Sta WC1 ...107 B3
Chancery Mews SW17 ...72 A2
Chance St E2 ...24 B1 98 C2
Chandler Ave E16 ...35 C4
Chandlers Mews E14 ...41 C4
Chandler St E1 ...32 A1
Chandlers Way 11 SE24 ...74 C4
Chandler Way SE15 ...49 B3
Chandlery Ho E1 ...111 B1
Chandos Pl WC2 ...120 A3
Chandos Rd
Cricklewood NW2 ...9 B3
Old Oak Comm NW10 ...21 A1
Stratford New Town E15 ...19 C3
Chandos St W1 ...104 B3
Chandos Way NW11 ...2 A3
Change Alley EC3 109 C1
Channel Gate Rd NW10 ...21 A2
Channel Ho E14 ...33 A4
Channelsea Bsns Ctr E15 ...27 C3
Channelsea Rd E15 ...27 C4
Channing Sch N6 ...4 A3
Chantrey Rd SW9 ...62 B4
Chantry Cl W9 ...23 B1
Chantry Cres NW10 ...8 B2
Chantry Ct SW6 ...58 A4
Chantry Sq W8 ...128 A1
Chantry St N1 ...86 B3
Chant Sq E15 ...19 C1
Chant St E15 ...19 C1
Chapel Cl NW10 ...8 B2
Chapel Ct SE1 ...137 B4
Chapel House St E14 ...42 A2
Chapel Market N1 ...85 B2
Chapel Pl
Islington N1 ...85 C2
Marylebone W1 ...104 A1
Shoreditch EC2 ...24 A2 98 A3
Chapel Side W2 ...114 A3
Chapel St
Paddington NW1 ...102 A3
Westminster SW1 ...131 C3
Chapleton Ho SW2 ...62 C2
Chaplin Cl SE1 ...136 A4
Chaplin Ho 6 SW9 ...62 C3
Chaplin Rd NW2 ...8 C2
Chaplow Cl SW6 ...166 C1
Chapman Ho
26 Stepney E1 ...32 A3
2 West Norwood SE27 ...75 A1
Chapman Rd E9 ...18 B2
Chapmans Park Ind Est NW10 ...8 B2
Chapman Sq SW19 ...69 C2
Chapman St E1 ...32 A2
Chapone Pl W1 ...105 B1
Chapter Cl 16 W4 ...37 B3
Chapter House & Jewel Twr* SW1 ...134 A2
Chapter Rd
Kennington SE17 ...150 B1
Willesden NW2 ...8 C3
Chapter St SW1 ...147 B3
Chara Pl W4 ...45 C4
Charcot Ho SW15 ...56 B1
Charcroft Ct 11 W14 ...39 C4
Chard Ho 7 N7 ...5 B2
Chardin Ho SW9 ...173 C4
Chardin Rd 11 W4 ...38 A2
Chardmore Rd N16 ...7 C3
Charecroft Way W12 ...39 C4
Charfield Ct W9 ...88 B1
Charford Rd E16 ...35 C4
Chargrove Cl 24 SE16 ...40 C4
Charing Cross SW1 ...120 A2
Charing Cross Hospl W6 ...39 C1
Charing Cross Rd WC2 ...105 C1
Charing Cross Sta WC2 ...120 B2
Charing Ho SE1 ...135 C4
Chariot Cl 3 E3 ...26 C4
Charlbert Ct NW8 ...80 A2
Charlbert St NW8 ...80 A2
Charles Allen Ho EC1 ...95 B4
Charles Auffray Ho 30 E1 ...32 B4
Charles Barry Cl SW4 ...61 B4
Charles Burton Ct E5 ...18 A4
Charles Coveney Rd 4 SE15 ...49 B2
Charles Darwin Ho 8 E2 ...25 A2
Charles Dickens Ho 1 E2 ...25 A2
Charles Dickens Prim Sch SE1 ...136 C3
Charles Edward Brooke Sch SW9 ...48 A2
Charles Edward Brooke Sch (Dennen Site) SE5 ...48 A2
Charles Flemwell Mews 7 E16 ...35 C1
Charles Haller St 25 SW2 ...74 C4
Charles Harrod Ct SW13 ...47 B4
Charles Hobson Ho 4 NW10 ...8 A1
Charles Hocking Ho 8 W3 ...37 B4
Charles II Pl SW3 144 C1
Charles II St SW1 ...119 B2
Charles La NW8 ...80 A2
Charles Lamb Ct N1 ...86 B2
Charles Lamb Prim Sch N1 ...86 C4
Charles Mackenzie Ho SE16 ...153 C4
Charles Pl NW1 ...93 A3
Charles Rowan Ho WC1 ...95 B3
Charles Sq N1 ...97 C3
Charles St
Barnes SW13 ...46 A1
Mayfair W1 ...118 A2
Charleston St SE17 ...151 A3
Charles Townsend Ho EC1 ...96 A2
Charles Utton Ct E8 ...16 C4
Charlesworth Ho 6 E14 ...33 C3
Charleville Ct SW5 ...140 C1
Charleville Mans W14 ...140 B1
Charleville Rd W14 ...140 C1
Charlotte Ct 10 W6 ...38 C2
Charlotte Despard Ave SW11 ...169 C3
Charlotte Ho 12 W6 ...39 B1
Charlotte Mews
Marylebone W1 ...105 A4
North Kensington W10 ...30 C3
West Kensington W14 ...140 A4
Charlotte Pl
Marylebone W1 ...105 A3
Westminster SW1 ...146 C3
Charlotte Rd
Barnes SW13 ...46 B2
Shoreditch EC2 ...24 A1 98 A2
Charlotte Row SW4 ...61 B4
Charlotte Sharman Prim Sch SE11 ...136 A1
Charlotte Sq 5 TW10 ...54 B1
Charlotte St W1 ...105 A4
Charlotte Terr N1 ...85 A3
Charlton Ct
25 Hackney E2 ...24 B4
17 Kentish Town N7 ...13 C3
Charlton Ho
5 Brentford TW8 ...44 A4
Somers Town NW1 ...93 B4
Charlton King's Rd NW5 ...13 C3
Charlton Pl N1 ...86 A2
Charlton Rd NW10 ...21 A4
Charlton Way SE10, SE3 ...53 A2
Charlwood Ho
Richmond TW9 ...45 A3
1 Streatham SW2 ...74 B3
Westminster SW1 ...147 B3
Charlwood Pl SW1 ...147 A3
Charlwood Rd SW15 ...57 C3
Charlwood St SW1 ...147 A2
Charlwood Terr 5 SW15 ...57 C3
Charman Ho
18 London SW2 ...62 C1
South Lambeth SW8 ...162 A2
Charmian Ho 19 N1 ...24 A3
Charmouth Ct TW10 ...54 B2
Charmouth Ho SW8 ...162 C2
Charnock Ho 22 W12 ...30 A2
Charnwood Gdns E14 ...41 C2
Charrington Ho 42 E1 ...25 B1
Charrington St NW1 ...83 B2
Charter Bldgs 14 SE10 ...52 A2
Charter Ct
Finsbury Pk N4 ...5 C3
Marylebone W1 ...102 B3
Charter Ho WC2 ...106 B1
Charterhouse Bldgs EC1 ...96 C1
Charterhouse Mews EC1 ...108 B4
Charterhouse Rd E8 ...16 C3
Charterhouse Sq EC1 ...108 B4
Charterhouse Square Sch EC1 ...108 B4
Charterhouse St EC1 ...108 A3
Charterhouse Works SW18 ...59 B3
Charteris Rd
Finsbury Pk N4 ...5 C3
Kilburn NW6 ...23 B4
Charter Nightingale Hospl The NW1 ...102 B4
Charter Sch The SE24 ...63 C2
Chartes Ho SE1 ...138 B2
Chartfield Ave SW15 ...57 B2
Chartfield Sch SW15 ...57 A2
Chartfield Sq SW15 ...57 C2
Chartham Ct 12 SW9 ...62 C4
Chartham Gr SE27 ...75 A1
Chartham Ho SE1 137 C2
Chart House The 5 E14 ...42 A1
Chartridge SE17 ...48 C4
Chart St N1 ...97 C4
Chartwell 25 SW19 ...69 C3
Chase Ct SW3 ...130 C1
Chase Ctr The NW10 ...20 C2
Chaseley Ct W4 ...37 A1
Chaseley St E14 ...33 A3
Chasemore Ho SW6 ...154 B2
Chase Rd NW10 ...20 C1
Chase Road Trad Est NW10 ...20 C1
Chase The SW4 ...61 A4
Chater Ho 6 E2 ...25 C2
Chatfield Rd SW11 ...59 B4
Chatham Ct SW11 ...60 B2
Chatham Ho 7 SE5 ...49 A1
Chatham Pl E9 ...17 B2
Chatham Rd SW11 ...60 B2
Chatham St SE17 151 C4
Chatsworth Ct
Brondesbury NW2 ...9 C2
Clapton Pk E5 ...17 C4
Earl's Ct W8 ...141 B4
Chatsworth Est E5 ...17 C4
Chatsworth Gdns W3 ...28 A1
Chatsworth Lo 1 W4 ...37 C1
Chatsworth Rd
Brondesbury NW2 ...9 C2
Chiswick W4 ...45 B4
Clapton Pk E5 ...17 C4
Chatsworth Way SE27 ...75 B1
Chattenden Ho 8 N4 ...6 C4
Chatterton Ct TW9 ...44 B1
Chatterton Rd N4 ...6 A1
Chatto Rd SW11 ...60 B2
Chaucer Ave TW9 ...44 C1
Chaucer Ct 17 N16 ...16 A4
Chaucer Dr SE1 ...153 A3
Chaucer Ho SW1 146 C1
Chaucer Rd
Acton W3 ...28 B1
Herne Hill SE24 ...63 A2
Chaulden Ho EC1 ...97 C3
Cheadle Ct NW8 ...89 C2
Cheadle Ho 17 E14 ...33 B3
Cheam St 6 SE15 ...65 A4
Cheapside EC2 ...109 A1
Chearsley SE17 ...151 A4
Cheddington Ho 9 E2 ...24 C4
Chedworth Cl E16 ...35 B3
Chedworth Ho 2 E5 ...7 C2
Cheesemans Terr W14 ...140 C1
Chelmer Rd E9 ...17 C3
Chelmsford Cl W6 ...47 C4
Chelmsford Ho 5 N7 ...14 B4
Chelmsford Sq NW10 ...22 B4
CHELSEA ...144 B1
Chelsea Barracks* SW1 ...145 C1
Chelsea Bridge SW1 ...160 A4
Chelsea Bridge Rd SW1 ...145 C1
Chelsea Cl NW10 ...20 C4
Chelsea Cloisters SW3 ...144 B3
Chelsea Coll of Art & Design
Chelsea SW3 ...144 A1
Pimlico SW1 ...148 A2
Chelsea Cres
Brondesbury NW2 ...10 B2
Chelsea SW10 ...167 A3
Chelsea Ct SW3 ...159 B4
Chelsea Emb SW3 ...158 C3
Chelsea Est SW3 ...158 A3
Chelsea Farm Ho SW10 ...157 C3

Chelsea Gate SW1 145 C1
Chelsea Gdns SW1 145 C1
Chelsea Harbour Design Ctr SW10 167 A4
Chelsea Harbour Dr SW10 167 A4
Chelsea Harbour Pier SW10 167 B3
Chelsea Lo SW3 159 A4
Chelsea Manor Ct SW3 158 B4
Chelsea Manor Gdns SW3 144 B1
Chelsea Manor St SW3 144 B1
Chelsea Manor Studios SW3 144 B1
Chelsea Park Gdns SW3 157 B4
Chelsea Physic Gdn★ SW1 158 C4
Chelsea Reach Twr SW10 157 B2
Chelsea Sq SW3 143 C1
Chelsea Twrs SW3 158 B4
Chelsea & Westminster Hospl SW10 157 A3
Chelsfield Ho SE17 152 A3
Chelsfield Point [3] E9 17 C1
Chelsham Ho [1] SW4 61 C4
Chelsham Rd SW4 61 C4
Cheltenham Pl
[10] Acton W3 28 A1
Acton W3 37 B4
[1] South Acton W3 37 A4
Cheltenham Rd SE15 65 B2
Cheltenham Terr SW3 145 A2
Chelverton Ct SW15 57 C3
Chelverton Rd SW15 57 C3
Chelwood NW5 12 C3
Chelwood Ct SW11 167 C4
Chelwood Gdns TW9 44 C1
Chelwood Ho W2 101 C1
Chenies Ho W2 114 A4
Chenies Mews WC1 93 B1
Chenies Pl NW1 83 C2
Chenies St WC1 105 B4
Chenies The NW1 83 C2
Cheniston Gdns W8 128 A2
Chepstow Cl SW15 58 A2
Chepstow Cres W11 31 C2 113 B4
Chepstow Ct W11 31 C2 113 B4
Chepstow Pl W2 31 C2 113 C4
Chepstow Rd W2 31 C3
Chepstow Villas W11 31 C2 113 B4
Chequers Ct EC1 97 B1
Chequers Ho NW8 90 A2
Chequer St EC1 97 A1
Cherbury Ct N1 87 C1
Cherbury St N1 87 C1
Cheriton Ho [9] E5 17 A3
Cheriton Sq SW17 72 C2
Cherry Cl [7] SW2 74 C4
Cherry Ct
Acton W3 29 A1
[5] Rotherhithe SE16 33 A1
Cherry Garden Ho [7] SE16 40 A4
Cherry Garden Sch SE16 153 C4
Cherry Garden St SE16 40 A4
Cherry Laurel Wlk SW2 62 B1
Cherry Tree Cl [11] E9 25 B4
Cherry Tree Ct
[1] Camden Town NW1 13 B1
[11] Peckham SE15 50 A2
Cherry Tree Dr SW16 74 A1
Cherrytree Ho [8] W10 22 C2
Cherry Tree Ho SE14 51 B1
Cherry Trees Sch The E3 26 C2
Cherry Tree Terr SE1 138 B4
Cherry Tree Wlk EC1 97 A1
Cherrywood Cl E3 26 A2
Cherrywood Dr SW15 57 C2
Chertsey Ct SW14 55 A4
Chertsey Ho E2 24 B2 98 C3
Cherwell Ho NW8 89 C1
Cheryls Cl SW6 166 B4
Chesham Cl SW1 131 B1
Chesham Ct SW18 71 C4
Chesham Flats W1 117 C4
Chesham Ho SW1 131 B1
Chesham Mews SW1 131 B2
Chesham Pl SW1 131 B1
Chesham St SW1 131 B1
Cheshire St E2 24 B1 99 A2
Chesholm Rd N16 7 A1
Cheshunt Ho NW6 78 A3
Chesil Ct
[17] Bethnal Green E2 25 B3
Chelsea SW3 158 B4
Chesilton Rd SW6 164 C4
Chesney Ct W9 23 C1
Chesney Ho SE13 67 C3
Chesney St SW11 169 B3
Chessington Ho SW8 171 B2
Chesson Rd W14 155 A4
Chessum Ho E8 16 C2
Chester Ave TW10 54 B1
Chester Cl
Barnes SW13 57 A4
Knightsbridge SW1 132 A3
Chester Cl *continued*
[1] Richmond TW10 54 B1
Chester Close N NW1 92 B4
Chester Close S NW1 92 B3
Chester Cres E8 16 B3
Chester Ct
Bermondsey SE8 40 C1
[4] Camberwell SE5 48 C3
Gospel Oak NW5 12 C4
Regent's Pk NW1 92 B3
Chesterfield Ct SE13 67 B4
Chesterfield Gdns
Greenwich SE10 52 C3
Mayfair W1 118 A2
Chesterfield Gr SE22 64 B2
Chesterfield Hill W1 118 A2
Chesterfield Ho
Highgate N6 3 C3
Mayfair W1 117 C2
Chesterfield Rd W4 45 B4
Chesterfield St W1 118 A2
Chesterfield Way SE15 50 B3
Chesterford Gdns NW3 11 A4
Chester Gate NW1 92 B3
Chester Ho
Dartmouth Pk N19 4 A2
[1] Deptford SE8 51 B4
Chesterman Ct W4 46 A3
Chester Mews SW1 132 A2
Chester Pl NW1 92 A4
Chester Rd
Dartmouth Pk N19 4 A2
Regent's Pk NW1 92 A4
Chester Row SW1 145 C4
Chester Sq SW1 146 A4
Chester Sq Mews SW1 132 A1
Chester St
Bethnal Green E2 24 C1 99 C2
Westminster SW1 131 C2
Chester Terr NW1 92 A4
Chesterton Cl SW18 58 C2
Chesterton Ct W3 37 A3
Chesterton Ho
[21] Battersea SW11 59 C4
[3] Kensal Town W10 31 A4
Chesterton Prim Sch SW11 169 B3
Chesterton Rd W10 31 A4
Chesterton Sq W8 141 B3
Chester Way SE11 149 C3
Chestnut Alley SW6 155 A3
Chestnut Ave [11] SW14 55 C4
Chestnut Cl
New Cross Gate SE14 51 B2
Chestnut Cl *continued*
[1] Stoke Newington N16 6 C2
Chestnut Ct SW6 155 A4
Chestnut Gr SW12 72 C3
Chestnut Grove Sch SW12 72 C3
Chestnut Ho
[1] Acton W4 38 A2
Brockley SE4 66 B4
[7] Maitland Pk NW3 12 B2
West Norwood SE27 75 B1
Chestnut Rd SE21, SE27 75 B1
Chestnuts The [1] N5 15 A4
Chettle Cl SE1 137 B2
Chetwode Ho NW8 90 A2
Chetwode Rd SW17 72 B1
Chetwynd Rd NW5 4 A1
Cheval Ct SW15 57 A3
Cheval Pl SW7 130 B2
Cheval St E14 41 C3
Chevening Rd
Cubitt Town SE10 43 B1
Kilburn NW6 23 A4
Cheverell Ho [25] E2 24 C3
Cheverton Rd N19 4 C3
Chevet St E9 18 A3
Chevington NW2 10 B2
Cheviot Ct [16] SE14 50 B3
Cheviot Gate NW2 1 A2
Cheviot Gdns NW2 1 A2
Cheviot Ho N16 7 B3
Chevron Cl E16 35 C3
Cheylesmore Ho SW1 146 A2
Cheyne Ct SW3 158 C4
Cheyne Gdns SW3 158 B3
Cheyne Mews SW3 158 B3
Cheyne Pl SW3 158 C4
Cheyne Row SW3 158 A3
Cheyne Wlk SW10 157 B2
Cheyney Ho [2] E9 17 C2
Chichele Mans NW2 9 C3
Chichele Rd NW2 9 C3
Chicheley St SE1 135 A4
Chichester Ct [2] NW1 13 B1
Chichester Ho NW6 23 C3
Chichester Rd
Bayswater W2 100 B4
Kilburn NW6 23 C3
Chichester Rents WC2 107 B2
Chichester St SW1 147 A1
Chichester Way E14 42 C2
Chicksand Ho E1 111 B4
Chicksand St E1 111 A3
Chicksand Street E1 111 B3
Chiddingstone SE13 67 B2
Chiddingstone St SW6 165 C2
Chigwell Ct [1] E9 18 A2
Chigwell Hill E1 32 A2
Chiham Ho [5] SE15 50 B4
Chilcombe Ho [6] SW15 68 C4
Chilcot Cl [13] E14 34 A3
Childebert Rd SW17 73 A2
Childeric Prim Sch SE14 51 A3
Childeric Rd SE14 51 A3
Childerley St SW6 164 A4
Childers St SE8 51 B4
Child La SE10 43 B3
CHILD'S HILL 1 C2
Child's Hill Prim Sch NW2 1 A1
Child's Mews SW5 141 C3
Child's Pl SW5 141 C3
Child's St SW5 141 C3
Child's Wlk SW5 141 C3
Chilham Ct [13] SW9 62 C4
Chilham Ho SE1 137 C2
Chillington Dr SW11 59 C3
Chillingworth Rd N7 14 C3
Chiltern Ct
[15] Deptford SE14 50 B3
Marylebone NW1 91 A1
Chiltern Ho
Camberwell SE17 48 C4
[4] Kensal Town W10 31 A4
[5] Stamford Hill N16 7 B3
Chiltern Rd E3 26 C1
Chiltern St W1 103 B4
Chilton Gr SE8 41 A2
Chilton Rd TW9 54 C4
Chilton St E2 24 B1 99 A2
Chilver St SE10 43 B1
Chilworth Ct [8] SW19 69 C3
Chilworth Mews W2 101 B1
Chilworth St W2 101 A1
Chimney Ct [23] E1 32 A1
China Ct [1] E1 32 A1
China Hall Mews [16] SE16 40 B3
China Mews [17] SW2 74 B4
Chindit Ho [11] N16 15 C4
Ching Ct WC2 106 A1
Chinnocks Wharf E14 33 A2
Chipka St E14 42 B4
Chipley St SE14 51 A4
Chippendale Ho SW1 146 B1
Chippenham Gdns NW6 23 C2
Chippenham Mews W9 23 C1
Chippenham Rd W9 23 C1
Chip St SW4 61 C3
Chipstead Ho [4] SW2 74 A3

Chipstead St SW6 165 C2
Chirk Ct SE4 51 B1
Chisenhale Prim Sch E3 26 A3
Chisenhale Rd E3 26 A3
Chisholm Ct 1 W6 38 C1
Chisholm Rd 13 TW10 54 B1
Chisledon Wlk E9 18 B2
Chislehurst Rd TW10 54 A2
Chislet 5 NW5 12 C2
Chiswell St
Barbican EC1 109 B4
Camberwell SE5 48 C3
CHISWICK 38 B1
Chiswick & Bedford Park Prep Sch W4 38 A2
Chiswick Common Rd W4 37 C2
Chiswick Com Sch W4 45 C3
Chiswick Green Studios 1 W4 37 B2
Chiswick High Rd W4 38 A2
Chiswick High Road (North Circular Rd) W4 36 C1
Chiswick Ho★ W4 45 C4
Chiswick La W4 38 A1
Chiswick La S W4 46 B4
Chiswick Mall W4 38 B1
Chiswick Maternity Hospl W4 38 B1
Chiswick Park Sta W4 37 B2
Chiswick Pier W4 46 B3
Chiswick Pk W4 37 A2
Chiswick Plaza W4 45 B4
Chiswick Quay W4 45 B2
Chiswick Rd W4 37 B2
Chiswick Rdbt W4 36 C1
Chiswick Sq W4 46 A4
Chiswick Sta W4 45 B3
Chiswick Staithe W4 45 B2
Chiswick Terr 6 W4 37 B2
Chiswick Village W4 45 A4
Chiswick Wharf W4 46 B4
Chitty St W1 105 A4
Chivalry Rd SW11 60 A2
Chivelston 27 SW19 69 C3
Chobham Gdns SW19 69 C2
Chobham Rd E15 19 C3
Cholmeley Cres N6 4 A4
Cholmeley Lo N6 4 A3
Cholmeley Pk N6 4 A4
Cholmley Gdns NW6 10 C3
Cholmondeley Ave NW10 21 C3
Chopin's Ct 13 E1 32 A1
Chopwell Cl E15 19 C1
Choumert Gr SE15 49 C1
Choumert Mews SE15 49 C1
Choumert Rd SE15 49 B1
Choumert Sq 4 SE15 49 C1
Chow Sq 2 E8 16 B3
Chrisp Ho SE10 53 A4
Chrisp St E14 34 A3
Christ Church TW9 54 A4
Christchurch Ave NW6 10 A1
Christ Church Bentinck CE Prim Sch NW1 102 B4
Christchurch CE Prim Sch SW3 158 C4
Christ Church CE Prim Sch
Battersea SW11 60 A4
Brondesbury NW6 10 B1
Cubitt Town SE10 43 A1
Christchurch CE Sch E1 111 A3
Christ Church Ct
1 Brondesbury Pk NW6 10 A1
Harlesden NW10 21 A4
Christchurch Hill NW3 11 C4
Christchurch Ho 2 SW2 74 A3
Christchurch Pas NW3 2 B1
Christ Church Prim Sch, Hampstead NW3 2 C1
Christchurch Rd
Mortlake SW14 55 B2
Streatham SW2 74 C3
Christ Church Sch NW1 92 B4
Christchurch Sq 2 E9 25 B4
Christchurch St SW3 158 C4
Christ Church Streatham CE Prim Sch SW2 74 B3
Christchurch Terr SW3 158 C4
Christchurch Way SE10 43 A1
Christian Ct SE16 33 B1
Christian St E1 111 C1
Christie Ct
Maitland Pk NW3 12 A3
2 Upper Holloway N19 5 A2
Christie Ho 2 SE10 43 B1
Christie Rd E9 18 A2
Christina Sq N4 6 A3
Christina St EC2 24 A1 98 A2
Christopher Boone's Almshouses SE13 67 C3
Christopher Cl SE16 40 C4
Christopher France Ho 6 E1 26 A2
Christopher Hatton Prim Sch EC1 95 B1
Christopher Lo 2 N6 4 C4
Christopher Pl NW1 93 C3
Christopher St EC2 97 C1
Christ's Sch TW10 54 C2
Christ the King RC Prim Sch N4 5 B2
Christ the King Sixth Form Coll SE13 67 C4
Chryssell Rd SW9 163 C1
Chubworthy St 5 SE14 51 A4
Chudleigh Rd
Hampstead NW6 9 C1
London SE4 66 C2
Chudleigh St E1 32 C3
Chumleigh Gdns SE5 49 A4
Chumleigh St SE5 49 A4
Church App SE21 75 C1
Church Ave
Camden Town NW1 13 A2
Mortlake SW14 55 C4
Church Cl W8 128 A4
Church Cres E9 17 C1
Churchcroft Cl SW12 72 C4
Church Ct
Holborn EC4 107 C1
Rotherhithe SE16 41 B4
Churchdale Ct 1 W4 37 A1
CHURCH END 8 B3
Church Entry EC4 108 B1
Church Estate Almshouses 8 TW9 54 B3
Churchfield Ho W2 89 B1
Churchfield Mans SW6 165 A1
Churchfield Rd W3 28 B1
Churchfields SE10 52 B4
Church Garth 4 N19 4 C2
Church Gate SW6 58 A4
Church Gn SW9 173 C2
Church Gr SE13 67 A2
Churchhill Gardens Prim Sch SW1 147 A1
Church Ho EC1 96 B2
Churchill Ct
Finsbury Pk N4 5 C4
Peckham SE15 49 C1
Willesden NW2 9 A3
Churchill Gdns SW1 160 C4
Churchill Gdns Rd SW1 160 C4
Churchill Pl E14 34 A1
Churchill Rd
Gospel Oak NW5 13 A4
Willesden NW2 9 A2
Churchill Wlk E9 17 B3
Church Mead SE5 48 B3
Churchmead Rd NW10 8 C2
Church Path W4 37 B3
Church Pl SW1 119 A3
Church Rd
Acton W3 37 B4
Barnes SW13 46 C2
24 Canonbury N1 15 B2
Richmond TW10, TW9 54 A2
Church Rd *continued*
Willesden NW10 8 A1
Church Row NW3 11 B4
Church St
Chiswick W4 46 B4
Lisson Gr NW8 90 A1
Church Street Est NW8 89 C1
Church Studios 16 NW1 13 C2
Churchward Ho
Camberwell SE17 48 A4
West Kensington SW5 141 A1
Churchway NW1 93 C4
Church Wlk
Barnes SW13 46 C2
Canonbury N16 15 C4
Child's Hill NW2 1 B1
Dartmouth Pk N6 3 C1
Churchyard Row SE11 150 B4
Churnfield 2 N4 5 C2
Churston Cl 16 SW2 74 C3
Churston Mans WC1 95 A1
Churton Pl
Brentford W4 45 A4
Pimlico SW1 147 A3
Churton St SW1 147 A3
Chute Ho SW9 173 B1
Chuter Ede Ho SW6 155 A3
Cicada Rd SW18 59 B2
Cicely Ho NW8 79 C1
Cicely Rd SE15 49 C2
Cinema Mus The★ SE11 150 A3
Cinnabar Wharf Central E1 125 C2
Cinnabar Wharf East E1 125 C2
Cinnabar Wharf West E1 125 C2
Cinnamon Cl 8 SE15 49 B3
Cinnamon Row 3 SW11 59 B4
Cinnamon St E1 32 A1
Cinnamon Wharf SE1 139 A4
Circle Ho 14 E14 34 C3
Circle The SE1 139 A4
Circus Lo NW8 89 B4
Circus Mews W1 102 C4
Circus Pl EC2 109 C3
Circus Rd NW8 79 B1
Circus St SE10 52 B3
Cirencester St W2 100 A4
Cissbury Ho 6 SE26 76 C1
Citadel Pl SE11 148 C2
Citizen Ho N7 14 C4
Citizen Rd N7 14 C4
Citron Terr 4 SE15 65 A4
Citrus Ho 14 SE8 41 B1
City Banking Coll SE1 137 C4
City Bsns Ctr 33 SE16 40 B4
City Central Est EC1 96 C3
City Coll N1 97 B4
City Coll of London The WC1 107 A3
City Forum EC1 96 C4
City Garden Row N1 86 B1
City Gate E1 25 B1
City & Guilds of London Art Sch The SE11 149 C1
City Harbour E14 42 A3
City & Islington 6th Form Coll EC1 96 A4
City & Islington Coll
Finsbury Pk N4 6 A2
Lower Holloway N7 14 A4
Lower Holloway N7 14 B4
Shoreditch EC1 97 A3
Shoreditch N1 87 B4
City Lights The SE11 149 C1
CITY OF LONDON 122 B4
City of London Sch EC4 122 C4
City of London Sch for Girls EC2 109 A4
City of Westminster Coll
Paddington NW1 102 B4
Paddington W2 101 B4
City of Westminster Coll, Maida Vale Ctr W9 88 A3
City of Westminster Coll, Queens Park Ctr W9 23 C2
City Rd EC1 97 A4
City Thameslink Sta EC4 108 A1
City University EC1 96 A3
City Wlk SE1 138 A3
Civil Service Coll SW1 146 C3
Clabon Mews SW1 144 C4
Clack St SE16 40 B4
Claire Ct NW2 10 A2
Claire Pl E14 41 C3
Clancarty Rd SW6 165 C1
Clandon Cl W3 37 A4
Clandon St SE8 51 C1
Clanfield Ho 12 SW15 68 C3
Clanricarde Gdns W2 31 C2 113 C3
CLAPHAM 61 A4
Clapham Common★ SW4 61 A3
Clapham Common North Side SW4 60 C3
Clapham Common South Side SW4 61 B2
Clapham Common Sta SW4 61 B3
Clapham Common West Side
Clapham SW4, SW11 60 B3
Clapham SW11 60 C2

Clapham Computer & Secretarial Coll SW11 60 B2
Clapham Court Terr 2 SW4 62 A2
Clapham Cres SW4 61 C3
Clapham Ct 3 SW4 62 A2
Clapham High St SW4 61 C3
Clapham High Street Sta SW4 61 C4
Clapham Junction Est SW11 60 A3
Clapham Junction Sta SW11 60 A3
Clapham Manor Ct 1 SW4 61 B4
Clapham Manor Prim Sch SW4 61 B4
Clapham Manor St SW4 61 C4
Clapham Mans SW4 61 A1
Clapham North Bsns Ctr 10 SW4 61 C4
Clapham North Sta SW4 62 A4
CLAPHAM PARK 61 C2
Clapham Park Rd SW4 61 C3
Clapham Park Terr 4 SW2 62 A2
Clapham Rd SW9 163 A2
Clapham South Sta SW4 61 A1
Clapton Comm E5 7 C4
Clapton Girls Tec Coll E5 17 B4
CLAPTON PARK 17 C4
Clapton Pas E5 17 B3
Clapton Sq E5 17 B3
Clapton Terr E5 7 C3
Clapton Way E5 16 C4
Clara Grant Ho 10 E14 41 C3
Clara Grant Prim Sch The E3 26 C1
Clare Ct WC1 94 B3
Claredale Ho 3 E2 25 A3
Claredale St E2 24 C3
Clare Gdns W11 31 A3
Clare Ho
Bermondsey SE1 153 A2
6 Old Ford E3 26 B4
Clare La N1 15 B1
Clare Lawn Ave SW14 55 C2
Clare Mews SW6 156 A1
Clare Mkt WC2 107 A1
Claremont 1 SW15 58 A2
Claremont Cl
Finsbury N1 85 C1
4 Streatham SW2 74 B3
Claremont Ct 1 W9 23 B3
Claremont Gr W4 46 A3
Claremont Rd
Highgate N6 4 B4
West Kilburn W9 23 B3
Claremont Sq N1 85 B1
Claremont St SE10 52 A4
Clarence Ave SW4 61 C1
Clarence Cres SW4 61 C1
Clarence Ct 10 W6 39 A2
Clarence Gate NW1 91 A2
Clarence Gate Gdns NW1 91 A1
Clarence Gdns NW1 92 B3
Clarence Ho SE17 48 B4
Clarence Ho* SW1 119 A1
Clarence La SW15 56 B1
Clarence Mews
Balham SW12 73 A4
Hackney E5 17 A3
1 Rotherhithe SE16 32 C1
Clarence Pl 25 E5 17 A3
Clarence Rd
Brentford W4 36 C1
Brondesbury NW6 10 B1
Lower Clapton E5 17 A4
Richmond TW9 44 C2
Clarence St 5 TW9 54 A3
Clarence Terr NW1 91 A2
Clarence Way NW1 13 A1
Clarence Wlk SW4 172 A2
Clarendon Cl
Bayswater W2 116 A4
38 Hackney E9 17 B1
Clarendon Cross W11 31 A2 112 B3
Clarendon Ct
Paddington W9 89 A2
1 Richmond TW9 44 C2
Willesden NW2 9 B1
Clarendon Dr SW15 57 B3
Clarendon Flats W1 103 C1
Clarendon Gdns W9 89 A1
Clarendon Gr NW1 93 B4
Clarendon Ho NW1 83 A1
Clarendon Mews W2 116 A4
Clarendon Pl W2 116 A4
Clarendon Rd W11 31 A2 112 B3
Clarendon Rise SE13 67 B3
Clarendon St SW1 146 B2
Clarendon Terr W9 89 A2
Clarendon Wlk 11 W11 31 A3
Clare Pl SW15 68 B4
Clare Rd
New Cross Gate SE14 51 B2
Willesden NW10 8 C1
Clare St E2 25 A3
Clareville Ct SW7 143 A3
Clareville Gr SW7 143 A3
Clareville Grove Mews SW7 143 A3
Clareville St SW7 143 A3
Clarewood Ct W1 102 C3
Clarewood Wlk SW9 62 C3
Clarges Ho W1 118 B2
Clarges Mews W1 118 A2
Clarges St W1 118 B2
Clariat Ct W3 36 C4
Claribel Rd SW9 48 A1
Claridge Ct SW6 164 C3
Clarissa Ho 7 E14 34 A3
Clarissa St E8 24 B4
Clarke Ho 2 SW4 61 B4
Clarke Path N16 7 C3
Clarkes Mews W1 103 C4
Clark Ho SW10 156 C2
Clark Lawrence Ct 11 SW11 59 C4
Clarkson Rd E16 35 B3
Clarkson Row NW1 82 C1
Clarkson St E2 25 A2
Clark's Pl EC2 110 A2
Clark St E1 32 B4
Classic Mans 33 E9 17 B1
Classinghall Ho 14 SW15 57 C1
Claude Rd SE15 50 A1
Claude St E14 41 C2
Claudia Jones Way SW2 62 A1
Claudia Pl SW19 70 A3
Clavell St 8 SE10 52 B4
Claverdale Rd SW2 74 C4
Clavering Ave SW13 47 A4
Clavering Ho SE13 67 C3
Claverton St SW1 147 A1
Clave St E1 32 B1
Claxton Gr W6 39 C1 140 A1
Claybank Gr SE13 67 A4
Claybrook Rd W6 47 C4
Claydon SE17 150 C4
Clayhall Ct 20 E3 26 B3
Claylands Pl SW8 163 B2
Claylands Rd SW8 163 A3
Claypole Rd E15 27 B3
Clayponds Ave TW8 36 A2
Clayponds Hospl & Day Treatment Ctr TW8 36 A2
Clayponds La TW8 36 A1
Clays Ct N16 7 B3
Clays La E15 19 A3
Clays Lane Cl E15 19 A3
Clays Lane Cvn Site E15 19 B3
Clay St W1 103 A3
Clayton Cres N1 84 C3
Clayton Ct N16 7 C4
Clayton Ho 22 E9 17 B1
Clayton Mews SE10 52 C2
Clayton Rd SE15 49 C2
Clayton St SE11 163 B4
Clearbrook Way 13 E1 32 B3
Clear Water Ho 9 TW10 54 A2
Clearwater Terr 4 W11 39 C4
Clearwell Dr W9 88 B1
Cleaver Ho 6 NW3 12 B1
Cleaver Sq SE11 149 C1
Cleaver St SE11 149 C2
Cleeve Ho E2 24 A2 98 B3
Cleeve Way SW15 68 B4
Cleeve Workshops E2 24 A2 98 B3
Clegg St 16 E1 32 A1
Cleland Ho 19 E2 25 B3
Clematis St W12 29 C2
Clem Atlee Par SW6 155 A3
Clem Attlee Ct SW6 155 A3
Clemence St E14 33 B4
Clement Attlee Ho NW10 8 B1
Clement Ave SW4 61 C3
Clement Cl
Acton W4 37 C2
Hampstead NW6 9 B1
Clement Danes Ho 2 W12 30 A3
Clement Ho
14 Deptford SE8 41 A2
17 North Kensington W10 30 B4
Clements Ave 1 E16 35 C2
Clements Inn WC2 107 A1
Clements Inn Pas WC2 107 A1
Clement's La EC2, EC4 123 C4
Clement's Rd SE16 40 A3
Clemson Ho 9 E8 24 B4
Clennam St SE1 137 A4
Clenston Mews W1 102 C2
Clent Ho 4 N16 7 B3
Cleopatra's Needle* WC2 120 C3
Clephane Rd 13 N1 15 B2
Clephane Rd N N1 15 B2
Clephane Rd S N1 15 C2
Clere Pl EC2 97 C2
Clere St EC2 97 C2
CLERKENWELL 96 A1
Clerkenwell Cl EC1 95 C1
Clerkenwell Gn EC1 96 A1
Clerkenwell Parochial CE Prim Sch EC1 95 B3
Clerkenwell Rd EC1 96 A1
Clermont Rd E9 25 B4
Clevedon Ct
Battersea SW11 168 A4
Dulwich SE21 75 C1
Clevedon Mans NW5 12 C4
Cleve Ho NW6 11 A1
Cleveland Ave W4 38 B2
Cleveland Ct W1 93 A1
Cleveland Gdns
Barnes SW13 46 B1
Paddington W2 100 C1
Cleveland Gr 39 E1 25 B1
Cleveland Mans
Brixton SW9 163 B1
4 Brondesbury NW6 10 B1
Paddington W9 23 C1
Cleveland Mews W1 104 C4
Cleveland Pl SW1 119 A2
Cleveland Rd
Barnes SW13 46 B1
Islington N1 15 C1
14 South Acton W4 37 B3
Cleveland Row SW1 119 A1
Cleveland Sq W2 100 C1
Cleveland St W1 92 C1
Cleveland Terr W2 101 A2
Cleveland Way E1 25 B1
Clevendon Cl N16 7 B1
Cleve Rd NW6 11 A1
Cleverly Cotts W12 29 B1
Cleverly Est W12 29 C2
Cley Ho SE4 65 C3
Clichy Ho 32 E1 32 B4
Clifden Mews E5 17 C3
Clifden Rd E5 17 C3
Cliff Ct 14 NW1 13 C2
Cliffe Ho 4 SE10 43 B1
Clifford Ave
Mortlake SW14 45 B1
Mortlake SW14, TW9 55 A4
Clifford Ct
Bayswater W2 100 A3
Wandsworth SW18 71 C4
Willesden NW10 8 A4
Clifford Dr SW9 63 A3
Clifford Gdns NW10 22 B3
Clifford Haigh Ho SW6 47 C3
Clifford Ho W14 140 C3
Clifford's Inn Pas EC4 107 B1
Clifford St W1 118 C3
Clifford Way NW10 8 B4
Cliff Rd NW1 13 C2
Cliff Road Studios 13 NW1 13 C2
Cliffsend Ho SW9 173 C3
Cliff Terr SE8 51 C1
Cliffview Rd SE13 66 C4
Cliff Villas NW1 13 C2
Cliff Wlk E16 35 B4
Clifton Ave W12 29 B1
Clifton Cres SE15 50 A3
Clifton Ct
Finsbury Pk N4 5 C2
Paddington NW8 89 B2
Peckham SE15 50 A3
Putney SW15 57 C2
Clifton Gate SW10 156 C4
Clifton Gdns
Chiswick W4 37 C2
Paddington W9 88 C1
Clifton Gr E8 16 C2
Clifton Hill NW8 78 C3
Clifton Ho E2 24 B1 98 C2
Clifton Mans 4 SW9 62 C3

Clifton Pl
Paddington W2 101 C1
Rotherhithe SE16 40 B4
Clifton Rd
Harlesden NW10 21 C3
Newham E16 35 A4
Paddington W9 89 A2
Clifton Rise SE14 51 A3
Clifton St
EC2 24 A1 98 A1
Clifton Terr N4 5 C2
Clifton Villas W9 100 C4
Clifton Way SE15 50 B3
Climsland Ho SE1 121 C2
Clinch Ct 11 E16 35 C4
Cline Ho SW15 56 C2
Clinger Ct N1 24 A4
Clink St SE1 123 B2
Clinton Rd E3 26 A2
Clipper Appts 12
SE10 52 B4
Clipper Cl 3 SE16 40 C4
Clipper Ho E14 42 B1
Clipper Way SE13 67 B3
Clipstone Ho 10
SW15 56 C2
Clipstone Mews
W1 104 C4
Clipstone St W1 104 C4
Clissold Cres N16 15 C4
Clissold Ct N4 6 B2
Clissold Ho 4 N16 6 C2
Clissold Rd N16 6 C1
Clitheroe Rd SW9 172 B1
Clive Ct W9 89 A2
Cliveden Ho SW1 145 B4
Cliveden Pl SW1 145 B4
Clive Ho
Clapham SW8 171 B2
Greenwich SE10 52 B4
Clive Rd SE21,
SE27 75 C1
Cloak La EC4 123 B4
Clochar Ct NW10 21 B4
Clock Ho N16 7 B4
Clockhouse Cl
SW19 69 B2
Clockhouse Pl
SW15 58 A1
Clockhouse The
SW19 69 B1
Clock Mus* EC2 109 A2
Clock Tower Mews
N1 87 A3
Clock Tower Pl
N7 14 A2
Cloister Rd
Acton W3 28 B4
Child's Hill NW2 1 B2
Cloisters Ct N6 4 A3
Cloisters The
SW9 173 C3
Clonbrock Rd N16 16 A4
Cloncurry St SW6 47 C1
Clone Ct 4 W12 38 A3
Clonmel Rd SW6 165 A4
Clonmore St
SW18 70 B3
Clorane Gdns NW3 1 C1
Close The
Lewisham SE3 52 C1
Mortlake TW9 55 A4
Cloth Ct EC1 108 B3
Cloth Fair EC1 108 B3
Clothier St EC3 110 B2
Cloth St EC1 108 C4

Cloudesdale Rd
SW17 73 A2
Cloudesley Mans
N1 85 C3
Cloudesley Pl N1 85 C3
Cloudesley Rd N1 85 B3
Cloudesley Sq N1 85 C4
Cloudesley St N1 85 C3
Clove Cres E14 34 C2
Clovelly Ct NW2 9 B3
Clovelly Ho W2 100 C2
Clovelly Rd W4 37 C4
Clovelly Way E1 32 B3
Clover Mews
SW3 159 A4
Clowes Ho 3
SW4 62 A3
Cloysters Gn E1 125 B2
Club Row
E2 24 B1 98 C2
Clunbury St N1 87 C1
Clunie Ho SW1 131 A2
Cluny Mews SW5 141 B3
Cluny Pl SE1 138 A2
Cluse Ct N1 86 C2
Clutton St E14 34 A4
Clyde Ct NW1 83 C2
Clyde Flats SW6 154 C2
Clydesdale Gdns
TW10 55 A3
Clydesdale Ho 4
W11 31 B3
Clydesdale Rd
W11 31 B3
Clyde St SE8 51 B4
Clynes Ho 3 E2 25 C2
Clyro Ct N4 5 B3
Clyston St SW8 171 A2
Coach & Horses Yd
W1 118 C4
Coach House La
Highbury N5 15 A4
Wimbledon SW19 69 C1
Coach House Mews
SE23 65 C1
Coach House Yd 5
NW3 11 C4
Coachmaker Mews 5
SW9 62 A4
Coalbrook Mans 3
SW12 73 A3
Coaldale Wlk
SE21 75 B4
Coalecroft Rd
SW15 57 B2
Coalport Ho SE11 149 B4
Coatbridge Ho 8
N1 14 B1
Coates Ave SW18 60 A1
Coates Ct NW3 12 A3
Coate St E2 24 C3
Coates Wlk TW8 36 A1
Cobbett St SW8 163 A1
Cobble La N1 15 A1
Cobble Mews N4,
N5 6 B1
Cobbold Ct SW1 147 B4
Cobbold Ind Est
NW10 8 B2
Cobbold Mews
W12 38 B4
Cobbold Rd
Bedford Pk W12 38 B4
Willesden NW10 8 B2
Cobb's Hall 1
SW6 47 C4
Cobb St E1 110 C3

Cobden Bldgs
WC1 94 C4
Cobden Ho
Bethnal Green
E2 24 C2 99 C4
Regent's Pk NW1 82 C2
Cobham Cl SW11 60 A1
Cobham Mews 3
NW1 13 C1
Coborn Mews 9
E3 26 B2
Coborn Rd E3 26 B2
Coborn St E3 26 B2
Cobourg Prim Sch
SE5 49 B4
Cobourg Rd SE5 49 B4
Cobourg St NW1 93 A3
Coburg Cl SW1 147 A4
Coburg Cres SW2 74 C3
Coburg Dwellings 11
E1 32 B2
Cochrane Cl NW8 79 C1
Cochrane Ho 15
E14 41 C4
Cochrane Mews
NW8 79 C1
Cochrane St NW8 79 C1
Coci Ho W14 141 A3
Cockburn Ho
SW1 147 C1
Cock Hill E1 110 B3
Cock La EC1 108 B3
Cockpit Yd WC1 107 A4
Cockspur Ct SW1 119 C2
Cockspur St SW1 119 C2
Coda Ctr The
SW6 164 B4
Code St E1 24 B1 99 A1
Codicote Ho 22
SE8 40 C2
Codicote Terr N4 6 B2
Codling Cl E1 125 C2
Codrington Ct 3
SE16 33 A1
Codrington Ho 7
E1 25 A1
Codrington Mews
W11 31 A3
Cody Rd E16 27 C1
Coffey St SE8 51 C3
Cohen Lo E5 18 A3
Coin St SE1 121 B2
Coity Rd NW5 12 C2
Cokers La SE21 75 C3
Coke St E1 111 C2
Colas Mews 7
NW6 23 C4
Colbeck Mews
SW5 142 B3
Colberg Pl N16 7 B4
Colbert 1 SE5 49 B2
Colborne Ho 8
E14 33 C2
Colchester Ho
SW8 171 B2
Colchester St E1 111 A2
Coldbath Sq EC1 95 B2
Coldbath St SE13 52 A1
Cold Blow La
SE14 50 C4
Coldharbour E14 34 B1
Coldharbour Ind Est
SE5 48 B1
Coldharbour La
SW9 63 A4
Coldharbour Pl
SE5 48 C1

Coldstream Gdns
SW18 58 B1
Colebeck Mews
N1 15 A2
Colebert Ave E1 25 B1
Colebert Ho 21 E1 25 B1
Colebrook Cl
SW19 69 C4
Colebrook Ct
SW3 144 B3
Colebrooke Pl N1 86 B3
Colebrooke Row
Islington N1 86 B3
Islington N1 86 A2
Colebrook Ho 1
E14 34 A3
Coleby Path 21
SE5 48 C3
Colechurch Ho
SE1 153 B1
Colefax Bldg E1 111 C2
Coleford Rd SW18 59 B2
Colegrave Prim Sch
E15 19 C3
Colegrave Rd E15 19 C3
Colegrove Rd
SE15 49 B4
Coleherne Ct
SW10 142 B1
Coleherne Mans
SW5 142 B2
Coleherne Mews
SW10 142 A1
Coleherne Rd
SW10 142 A1
Colehill Gdns
SW6 164 A3
Colehill La SW6 164 B3
Cole Ho SE1 135 C3
Coleman Ct SW18 70 C4
Coleman Fields
N1 87 A4
Coleman Mans N19 5 A4
Coleman Rd SE5 49 A3
Coleman St EC2 109 B2
Coleman Street Bldgs
EC2 109 B2
Colenso Rd E5 17 B4
Coleraine Rd SE3 53 B4
Coleridge Cl SW8 170 B1
Coleridge Ct W14 39 C3
Coleridge Gdns
NW6 11 B1
Coleridge Ho
Pimlico SW1 147 A1
Walworth SE17 151 A2
Coleridge Prim Sch
N8 4 C4
Coleridge Rd N4,
N7 5 C2
Coleridge Sq
SW10 156 C2
Coles Ct SW11 167 C3
Coleshill Flats
SW1 145 C3
Cole St SE1 137 A3
Colestown St
SW11 168 B2
Colet Gdns W14 39 C2
Colet Ho SE17 150 B1
Colette Ct 5 SE16 40 C4
Coley St WC1 95 A1
Colfe & Hatchcliffe's
Glebe SE13 67 A2
Colgate Ho SE13 52 A1
Colin Blanchard Ho
SE4 51 C1

Colin Ct SW16 73 C2
Colinette Rd
SW15 57 B3
Colin Rd NW10 8 C2
Colinsdale N1 86 A3
Colin Winter Ho 45
E1 25 B1
Coliston Pas
SW18 70 C4
Coliston Rd SW18 70 C4
Collamore Ave
SW18 72 A3
Collard Pl NW1 13 A1
Collcutt Lo SW4 62 A3
College App SE10 52 B4
College Cl E5 17 B3
College Cres NW3 11 C2
College Cross N1 14 C1
College Ct
Chelsea SW3 145 A1
3 Hammersmith
W6 39 B1
Hampstead NW3 11 C2
College Gdns
Dulwich SE21 76 A3
Upper Tooting
SW17 72 A2
College Gr NW1 83 B4
College Green Ct
SW9 63 A4
College Hill EC4 123 A4
College La NW5 13 A4
College Mews 5
SW18 59 A2
COLLEGE PARK 22 A2
College Park Cl
SE13 67 C3
College Park Sch
W2 100 A1
College Pl
Camden Town
NW1 83 A3
Chelsea SW10 156 C2
College Rd
Dulwich SE19,
SE21 76 A2
Kensal Green NW10 22 B3
College St EC4 123 A4
College Terr E3 26 B2
Collent Ho 12 E9 17 B2
Collent St E9 17 B2
Collerston Ho
SE10 43 B1
Collette Ho N16 7 B3
Collett Ho SE13 67 A4
Collett Rd SE16 139 C2
Colley Ho 12 N7 13 C3
Collier St N1 84 C1
Collingbourne Rd
W12 30 A1
Collingham Gdns
SW5 142 B3
Collingham Pl
SW5 142 B4
Collingham Rd
SW5 142 B3
Collingham Sixth
Form Coll SW5 142 B3
Collington St
SE10 42 C1
Collingwood Ho
27 Bethnal Green
E1 25 A1
Marylebone W1 104 C4

Collingwood St
E1 ... 25 A1
Collins Ct E8 ... 16 C2
Collins Ho
6 Cubitt Town SE10 ... 43 B1
4 Poplar E14 ... 34 B2
Collinson Ct SE1 ... 136 C3
Collinson Ho 14
SE15 ... 49 C3
Collinson St SE1 ... 136 C3
Collinson Wlk
SE1 ... 136 C3
Collins Rd N5, N16 ... 15 B4
Collins Sq SE3 ... 53 B1
Collins St SE3 ... 53 A1
Collins Yd N1 ... 86 A3
Collison Pl N16 ... 7 A3
Coll of Arms★
EC4 ... 122 C4
Coll of Central London The
EC2 ... 24 A1 98 A2
Coll of Law The
EC1 ... 97 B1
Coll of NW London
NW6 ... 23 C4
Coll of NW London (Willesden Centre)
NW10 ... 8 B3
Coll of Optometrists
The SW1 ... 120 A2
Coll Sharp Ct
E2 ... 24 B2 98 C3
Coll's Rd SE15 ... 50 B2
Collyer Pl SE15 ... 49 C2
Colmans Wharf 5
E14 ... 34 A4
Colmar Cl 3 E1 ... 25 C1
Colmore Mews
SE15 ... 50 A2
Colnbrook St SE1 ... 136 A2
Colne Ho NW8 ... 89 C1
Colne Rd E5 ... 18 A4
Cologne Rd SW11 ... 59 C3
Colombo St SE1 ... 122 A1
Colomb St SE10 ... 43 A1
Colonades The 4
SE5 ... 48 C2
Colonial Dr W4 ... 37 B2
Colonnade WC1 ... 94 B1
Colonnade Ho
SE3 ... 53 B1
Colonnades The 6
E8 ... 17 A2
Colonnade The 12
SE8 ... 41 B2
Colorado Bldg 9
SE13 ... 52 A2
Colosseum Terr
NW1 ... 92 B2
Colour Ho SE1 ... 138 B3
Colstead Ho 22 E1 ... 32 A3
Colston Rd SW14 ... 55 B3
Colthurst Cres N4 ... 6 B2
Coltman Ho SE10 ... 52 B4
Coltman St E14 ... 33 A4
Columba Ho SE14 ... 51 B2
Columbas Dr NW3 ... 2 C3
Columbia Ho 18
E3 ... 26 C2
Columbia Point 7
SE16 ... 40 B3
Columbia Prim Sch
E2 ... 24 B2 99 A4
Columbia Rd
9 Hackney E2 ... 24 C3
Shoreditch E2 ... 24 B2 98 C4
Columbia Road Mkt
E2 ... 24 B2 99 A4
Colverson Ho 14
E1 ... 32 B4
Colvestone Cres
E8 ... 16 B3
Colvestone Prim Sch
E8 ... 16 B3
Colville Gdns W11 ... 31 B3
Colville Ho
32 Bethnal Green E2 ... 25 B3
Notting Hill W11 ... 31 B3
Colville Mews
W11 ... 31 B3
Colville Pl W1 ... 105 A3
Colville Prim Sch
W11 ... 31 B3
Colville Rd
Notting Hill W11 ... 31 B3
South Acton W3 ... 37 A3
Colville Sq W11 ... 31 B3
Colville Terr W11 ... 31 B3
Colwall Ho SW9 ... 173 A1
Colwell Rd SE22 ... 64 B2
Colwick Cl N6 ... 4 C4
Colwith Rd W6 ... 47 B4
Colworth Gr SE17 ... 151 A3
Colwyn Ho SE1 ... 135 B1
Colyton Rd SE22 ... 65 A2
Combe Ave SE3 ... 53 B3
Combedale Rd
SE10 ... 43 C1
Combe Ho
Mortlake SW14 ... 45 B1
20 Paddington W2 ... 31 C4
Combemartin Rd
SW18 ... 70 A3
Combe Mews 4
SE3 ... 53 B3
Comber Gr SE5 ... 48 B3
Comber Grove Prim Sch SE5 ... 48 B3
Comber Ho SE5 ... 48 B3
Combermere Rd
SW9 ... 62 B4
Combe The NW1 ... 92 B3
Com Coll Hackney
The E8 ... 25 A4
Comeragh Mews
W14 ... 140 B1
Comeragh Rd
W14 ... 140 B1
Comerford Rd SE4 ... 66 B3
Comet Pl SE8 ... 51 C3
Comet St SE8 ... 51 C3
Comins Ho SW4 ... 61 B2
Commercial Rd
Stepney E1 ... 32 B3
Whitechapel E1 ... 111 C2
Commercial St
E1 ... 110 C4
Commercial Way
Peckham SE15 ... 49 C3
Wembley NW10 ... 20 A3
Commerell Pl
SE10 ... 43 B1
Commerell St
SE10 ... 43 A1
Commodity Quay
E1 ... 125 A3
Commodore Ct
SE8 ... 51 C2
Commodore Ho 7
E14 ... 34 B2
Commodore St E1 ... 26 A1
Commondale
SW15 ... 57 B4
Common Rd
SW13 ... 56 C4
Common View
SW15 ... 57 B4
Commonwealth Ave
21 Shepherd's Bush W12 ... 30 A2
25 Shepherd's Bush W12 ... 30 A2
Commonwealth Ho
WC1 ... 106 B2
Community Rd
E15 ... 19 C3
Comodore Ho
SW18 ... 59 B3
Compania Bldg 12
E1 ... 32 C2
Compass Ct SE1 ... 124 C1
Compass Ho
Bayswater W2 ... 100 A1
London SE8 ... 52 A1
Compass Point 10
E14 ... 33 C2
Compayne Gdns
NW6 ... 11 A1
Compton Ave
Islington N1 ... 15 A2
London N6 ... 3 A4
Compton Cl
Camberwell SE15 ... 49 B3
Regent's Pk NW1 ... 92 B3
Compton Cres W4 ... 45 B4
Compton Ho
SW11 ... 168 A4
Compton Pas EC1 ... 96 B2
Compton Pl WC1 ... 94 A2
Compton Rd
Islington N1 ... 15 A2
Kensal Green NW10 ... 22 C2
Compton St EC1 ... 96 B2
Compton Terr N1 ... 15 A2
Comus Ho SE17 ... 152 A3
Comus Pl SE17 ... 152 A3
Comyn Rd SW11 ... 60 A3
Comyns Cl E16 ... 35 B4
Conant Ho SE11 ... 48 A4
Conant Mews E1 ... 125 B4
Concanon Rd SW2, SW4 ... 62 B3
Concert Hall App
SE1 ... 121 A1
Concord Bsns Ctr
W3 ... 28 A4
Concorde Way
SE16 ... 40 C2
Concordia Wharf 10
E14 ... 34 B1
Concord Rd W3 ... 20 A1
Condell Rd SW8 ... 171 A3
Conder St E14 ... 33 A3
Condray Pl SW11 ... 158 A1
Conduit Ct WC2 ... 120 A4
Conduit Ho SE10 ... 52 C2
Conduit Mews
W2 ... 101 B1
Conduit Pas W2 ... 101 B1
Conduit Pl W2 ... 101 B1
Conduit St W1 ... 118 C4
Conewood St N5 ... 6 A1
Coney Acre SE21 ... 75 B3
Coney Way SW8 ... 163 A3
Congers Ho SE8 ... 51 C3
Congress Ho
WC1 ... 105 C2
Congreve Ho 10
N16 ... 16 A3
Congreve St SE17 ... 152 A3
Conifer Ct 23
SW19 ... 69 C3
Conifer Gdns
SW16 ... 74 B1
Conifer Ho SE4 ... 66 B3
Coniger Rd SW6 ... 165 B2
Coningham Ct
SW10 ... 157 A2
Coningham Mews
W12 ... 29 C1
Coningham Rd
W12 ... 39 A4
Coningsby Rd N4 ... 6 A4
Conington Rd
SE13 ... 52 B1
Conisbrough NW1 ... 82 C3
Coniston NW1 ... 92 C4
Coniston Cl
Barnes SW13 ... 46 B3
Chiswick W4 ... 45 B3
Coniston Ct
Marylebone W2 ... 102 B1
6 Rotherhithe SE16 ... 40 C4
Conistone Way
N7 ... 14 A1
Coniston Ho
14 Bow E3 ... 26 B2
18 Camberwell SE5 ... 48 B3
Coniston Wlk E9 ... 17 B3
Conlan St W10 ... 23 A1
Conley Rd NW10 ... 8 A2
Conley St SE10 ... 43 A1
Connaught Ave
SW14 ... 55 B3
Connaught Cl W2 ... 102 B1
Connaught Ho
College Pk NW10 ... 22 A2
Mayfair W1 ... 118 A3
Connaught Lo N4 ... 5 C4
Connaught Mans
Battersea SW11 ... 168 B3
3 Brixton SW9 ... 62 C3
15 Canonbury N16 ... 15 C4
Fulham SW6 ... 164 A4
Connaught Pl W2 ... 102 C1
Connaught Rd
Finsbury Pk N4 ... 5 C4
Harlesden NW10 ... 21 A3
5 Richmond TW10 ... 54 B2
Connaught Sq
W2 ... 102 C1
Connaught St W2 ... 102 B1
Connaught Works
E3 ... 26 A4
Connell Ct 6
SE14 ... 50 C4
Connor Ct SW11 ... 170 A3
Connor St E9 ... 25 C4
Conrad Ho
8 Limehouse SE16 ... 33 A2
South Lambeth SW8 ... 162 A2
12 Stoke Newington N16 ... 16 A3
Conrad Twr W3 ... 37 A3
Consort Ho W2 ... 114 B3
Consort Lo NW8 ... 80 C3
Consort Rd SE15 ... 50 A1
Cons St SE1 ... 135 C4
Constable Ct 11
SE16 ... 40 A1
Constable Ho
25 Millwall E14 ... 41 C4
Primrose Hill NW3 ... 12 B1
Constable Wlk
SE21 ... 76 A1
Constant Ho 26
E14 ... 34 A2
Constantine Ho
SW2 ... 75 A3
Constantine Rd
NW3 ... 12 A4
Constitution Hill SW1, W1 ... 132 B4
Consul Ho 5 E3 ... 26 C1
Content St SE17 ... 151 B3
Convent Gdns
W11 ... 31 B3
Convent of Jesus & Mary Language Coll
NW10 ... 21 B4
Convent of Jesus & Mary RC Inf Sch
NW2 ... 9 B2
Conway Gr W3 ... 28 C4
Conway Ho
Chelsea SW3 ... 145 A1
5 Millwall E14 ... 42 A2
6 Streatham SW2 ... 74 A3
Conway Mews W1 ... 92 C1
Conway St W1 ... 92 C1
Conybeare NW3 ... 12 A1
Conyer St 21 E3 ... 26 A3
Cookham Cres
SE16 ... 40 C4
Cookham Ho
E2 ... 24 B1 98 C2
Cook's Rd
Camberwell SE17 ... 48 A4
Stratford Marsh E15 ... 27 A3
Coomassie Rd W9 ... 23 B1
Coombe Ho 13 N7 ... 13 C3
Coombe Rd W4 ... 38 A1
Coomber Ho SW6 ... 59 A4
Coombs St N1 ... 86 B1
Coomer Mews
SW6 ... 155 A3
Coomer Pl SW6 ... 155 A3
Cooperage The
SE1 ... 124 C1
Cooper Cl SE1 ... 135 C3
Cooper Ct E15 ... 19 B3
Cooper Ho NW8 ... 89 B1
Cooper Rd NW10 ... 8 C3
Coopersale Rd E9 ... 17 C3
Coopers Cl E1 ... 25 B1
Coopers Ct
9 Acton W3 ... 28 B1
Tower Hamlets E3 ... 26 B1
Coopers La NW1 ... 83 C1
Coopers Lo SE1 ... 138 C4
Cooper's Rd SE1 ... 153 A2
Cooper's Row
EC3 ... 124 C4
Cooper St 10 E16 ... 35 B4
Coopers Yd N1 ... 15 A1
Cope Ho EC1 ... 97 A3
Copeland Dr E14 ... 41 C2
Copeland Ho
SE11 ... 135 A1
Copeland Rd SE15 ... 50 A1
Copenhagen Gdns
W4 ... 37 C4
Copenhagen Ho
N1 ... 85 B3

Copenhagen Pl E14 . . . 33 B3
Copenhagen Prim Sch N1 . . . 84 C3
Copenhagen St N1 . . . 84 C3
Cope Pl W8 . . . 127 B1
Cope St SE16 . . . 40 C2
Copford Wlk N1 . . . 86 C4
Copleston Rd SE15 . . . 64 B4
Copley Cl 15 SE17 . . 48 A4
Coppedhall 2 SE21 . . . 75 C2
Copperas St SE8 . . . 52 A4
Copper Beech N6 . . . 3 C4
Copperbeech Cl NW3 . . . 11 C3
Copperfield Ho SE1 . . . 139 B3
Copperfield Rd E3 . . . 33 A4
Copperfields Ct W3 . . . 36 C4
Copperfield St SE1 . . . 136 C4
Copper Mews 19 W4 . . . 37 B3
Copper Row SE1 . . 124 C1
Coppice Dr SW15 . . . 57 A1
Coppin Ho SW2 . . . 75 A3
Coppock Cl SW11 168 A1
Copse Ct SW15 . . . 58 A2
Copthall Ave EC2 109 C2
Copthall Bldgs EC2 . . . 109 C2
Copthall Cl EC2 . . 109 B2
Copthorne Ave SW12 . . . 73 C4
Coptic St WC1 . . . 106 A3
Copton Cl E3 . . . 33 C4
Coral Apts 6 E16 . . 35 C2
Coral Ho 5 E1 . . . 26 A1
Coral Row 14 SW11 . . . 59 B4
Coral St SE1 . . . 135 C3
Coram Ho
Bloomsbury WC1 . . . 94 A2
9 Chiswick W4 . . . 38 A1
Coram Mans WC1 . 94 C1
Coram St WC1 . . . 94 A1
Corbden Cl SE15 . . . 49 B2
Corbet Ct EC3 . . . 109 C1
Corbet Ho N1 . . . 85 B3
Corbet Pl E1 . . . 110 C4
Corbett Ho SW10 156 C4
Corbett's La SE16 . . 40 B2
Corbetts Pas 8 SE16 . . . 40 B2
Corbidge Ct SE8 . . . 52 A4
Corbiere Ho 5 N1 . . . 24 A4
Corbin Ho 7 E3 . . . 27 A2
Corbridge Cres E2 . . . 25 A3
Corbyn St N4, N19 . . . 5 A3
Corby Rd NW10 . . . 20 C3
Corby Way E3 . . . 26 C1
Cordelia Cl SE24 . . . 63 A3
Cordelia Ho 26 N1 . . 24 A3
Cordelia St E14 . . . 34 A3
Cording St E14 . . . 34 A4
Cordwainers Ct 18 E9 . . . 17 B1
Corfe Ho SW8 . . . 162 C2
Corfe Lodge 15 SE21 . . . 75 C2
Corfe Twr 6 W3 . . . 37 B4
Corfield St E2 . . . 25 A2
Coriander Ave E14 . . . 34 C3
Coriander Ct SE1 139 A4
Corinne Rd N19 . . . 13 B4
Cork St Mews W1 . . . 118 C3
Cork Sq E1 . . . 32 A1
Cork St W1 . . . 118 C3
Corlett St NW1 . . . 102 A4
Cormont Rd SE5 . . . 48 A2
Cormorant Ct
36 Deptford SE8 . . . 51 B4
13 Dulwich SE21 . . . 75 C2
Cornbury Ho 5 SE8 . . . 51 B4
Cornelia St N7 . . . 14 B2
Cornell Bldg E1 . . 111 B2
Corner Fielde SW2 . . . 74 B3
Corner Gn SE3 . . . 53 C1
Corner House St WC2 . . . 120 A2
Cornerstone Ct E1 . . . 24 C1 99 C1
Cornerways SW15 . . 56 C3
Corney Rd W4 . . . 46 A4
Corney Reach Way W4 . . . 46 A3
Cornflower Terr SE22 . . . 65 A1
Cornford Gr SW12 . . 73 A2
Cornhill EC3 . . . 109 C1
Cornick Ho 7 SE16 . . . 40 A3
Cornish Ho
Brentford TW8 . . . 36 B1
7 Camberwell SE17 . . . 48 A4
Cornmill La SE13 . . . 67 B4
Cornmow Dr NW10 . . 8 C3
Cornwall Ave E2 . . . 25 B2
Cornwall Cres W11 . . . 31 A3
Cornwall Flats SE1 . . . 135 C4
Cornwall Gdns
Kensington SW7 . . . 128 B1
Willesden NW10 . . . 9 A2
Cornwall Gdns Wlk SW7 . . . 128 B1
Cornwall Gr W4 . . . 38 A1
Cornwall Ho
Marylebone NW1 . . . 91 A1
3 Putney SW15 . . . 69 B4
Cornwallis Ct SW8 . . . 172 A4
Cornwallis Ho 24 W12 . . . 30 A2
Cornwallis Rd N19 . . 5 A2
Cornwallis Sq N19 . . . 5 A2
Cornwall Mans
Chelsea SW10 . . . 157 A2
Marylebone NW1 . . . 91 A1
Cornwall Mews S SW7 . . . 128 C1
Cornwall Mews W SW7 . . . 128 B1
Cornwall Rd
Finsbury Pk N4 . . . 5 C4
Lambeth SE1 . . . 135 C4
Cornwall Sq SE11 150 A2
Cornwall St 4 E1 . . 32 A2
Cornwall Terr NW1 . . . 91 A1
Cornwall Terrace Mews NW1 . . . 91 A1
Cornwood Dr E1 . . . 32 B3
Coronation Ave 1 N16 . . . 16 B4
Coronation Ct 19 W10 . . . 30 B4
Coronet St N1 . . . 24 A2 98 A3
Corporation Row EC1 . . . 95 C2
Corporation St N7 . . 14 A3
Corpus Christi RC Prim Sch SW2 . . . 62 B2
Corrance Rd SW2, SW4 . . . 62 A3
Corringham Ct NW11 . . . 1 C4
Corringham Ho 11 E1 . . . 32 C3
Corringham Rd NW11 . . . 1 C4
Corringway NW11 . . . 2 A4
Corry Dr SW9 . . . 63 A3
Corry Ho 2 E14 . . . 34 A2
Corsham St N1 . . . 97 C3
Corsica St N5 . . . 15 A2
Corsley Way E9 . . . 18 B2
Cortayne Rd SW6 165 A2
Cortis Rd SW15 . . . 57 A1
Cortis Terr SW15 . . . 57 A1
Corunna Rd SW8 171 A4
Corunna Terr SW8 . . . 170 C4
Corvette Sq 5 SE10 . . . 52 C4
Coryton Path W9 . . . 23 B1
Cosbycote Ave SE24 . . . 63 B2
Cosgrove Ho 11 E2 . . . 24 C4
Cosmo Pl WC1 . . . 106 B4
Cosmur Cl W12 . . . 38 B3
Cossall Wlk SE15 . . . 50 A2
Cossar Mews 10 SW2 . . . 62 C2
Cosser St SE1 . . . 135 B2
Costa St SE15 . . . 49 C1
Coston Wlk 4 SE4 . . . 65 C3
Cosway Mans NW1 . . . 102 B4
Cosway St NW1 . . 102 B4
Cotall St E14 . . . 33 C4
Cotes Ho NW8 . . . 90 A1
Cotham St SE17 . . 151 A3
Cotherstone Rd SW2 . . . 74 B3
Cotleigh Rd NW6 . . . 10 C1
Cotman Cl SW15 . . . 57 C2
Cotman Ho NW8 . . . 80 A2
Cotrill Gdns E8 . . . 17 A2
Cotswold Ct EC1 . . 96 C2
Cotswold Gate NW2 . . . 1 A3
Cotswold Ho N16 . . . 7 B3
Cotswold Mews SW11 . . . 167 C3
Cottage Gn SE5 . . . 48 C3
Cottage Gr SW9 . . . 62 A4
Cottage Pl SW3 . . 130 A1
Cottage St E14 . . . 34 A2
Cottages The SE1 134 C1
Cottage Wlk 2 N16 . 7 B1
Cottenham Ho 5 N19 . . . 5 A2
Cottesbrook St 9 SE14 . . . 51 A3
Cottesloe Ho NW8 . 90 A2
Cottesloe Mews SE1 . . . 135 C2
Cottesmore Ct W8 . . . 128 B2
Cottesmore Gdns W8 . . . 128 B2
Cottingham Rd SW8 . . . 163 A2
Cottington St SE11 . . . 150 A2
Cotton Ave W3 . . . 28 C3
Cotton Ho
Bedford Pk W12 . . . 38 B4
18 Streatham SW12 . . . 74 A4
Cotton Row SW11 . . 59 C4
Cotton's Gdns E2 . . . 24 A2 98 B4
Cottons La SE1 . . . 123 C2
Cotton St E14 . . . 34 B2
Cottrell Ct SE10 . . . 43 B2
Couchman Ho 8 SW4 . . . 61 B1
Coulgate St SE4 . . . 66 A4
Coulsdon Ho 5 SW2 . . . 74 A3
Coulson St SW3 . . 144 C2
Coulter Rd W6 . . . 39 A3
Coults Cres NW5 . . . 3 C1
Councillor St SE5 . . 48 B3
Counters Ct W14 . 126 B2
Counter St SE1 . . . 124 A1
Countess Rd NW5 . . 13 B3
Countisbury Ho SE26 . . . 76 C1
County Gr SE5 . . . 48 B2
County Ho
22 Herne Hill SE24 . . 63 A3
South Lambeth SW9 . . . 173 B4
County St SE1 . . . 137 A1
Courier Ho 17 SW2 . . . 74 C4
Courland Gr SW8 171 C3
Courland St SW8 171 C3
Courtauld Ho 12 E2 . . . 24 C3
Courtauld Inst of Art★
Marylebone W1 . . . 103 A2
Strand WC2 . . . 120 C4
Courtauld Rd N19 . . . 5 A3
Courtenay Ave N6 . . . 3 A4
Courtenay Sq SE11 . . . 149 B1
Courtenay St SE11 . . . 149 B2
Courtfield Gdns SW5 . . . 142 B3
Courtfield Ho EC1 . . . 107 B4
Courtfield Mews SW7 . . . 142 B3
Courtfield Rd SW7 . . . 142 C3
Court Gdns N7 . . . 14 C2
Courthill Rd SE13 . . 67 B3
Courthope Ho
14 Rotherhithe SE16 . . . 40 B3
South Lambeth SW8 . . . 162 A1
Courthope Rd NW3 . . . 12 B4
Court La SE21 . . . 76 B4
Courtlands TW10 . . . 54 C2
Courtlands Ave TW9 . . . 45 A1
Court Lane Gdns SE21 . . . 76 A4
Court Mans 8 W6 . . . 38 C2
Courtmead Cl SE24 . . . 63 B1
Courtnell St W2 . . . 31 C3
Courtney Ct N7 . . . 14 C3
Courtney Ho W14 126 B2
Courtney Rd N7 . . . 14 C3
Courtrai Rd SE23 . . . 66 A1
Court Royal SW15 . . 58 A2
Court St 3 E1 . . . 32 A4
Courtville Ho 12 W10 . . . 23 A2
Court Way W3 . . . 28 B4
Courtyard The
Fulham SW6 . . . 164 A3
Islington N1 . . . 14 B1
13 Wandsworth SW18 . . . 59 C3
Cousin La EC4 . . . 123 B3
Couzens Ho 8 E3 . . 33 B4
Coval Gdns SW14 . . . 55 A3
Coval La SW14 . . . 55 A3
Coval Pas SW14 . . . 55 B3
Coval Rd SW14 . . . 55 B3
Covell Ct 16 SE8 . . . 51 C3
Covent Garden Sta WC2 . . . 106 B1
Covent Gdn★ WC2 . . . 120 B4
Coventry Cl NW6 . . . 23 C4
Coventry Rd E1 . . . 25 A1
Coventry St W1 . . 119 B3
Coverdale Rd
Brondesbury NW2 . . . 10 A2
Hammersmith W12 . . 39 A4
Hampstead NW6 . . . 9 C1
Coverham Ho 5 SE4 . . . 65 C3
Coverley Cl E1 . . . 111 C4
Coverley Point SE11 . . . 148 C3
Cowcross St EC1 . 108 A4
Cowdenbeath Path N1 . . . 84 C4
Cowdray Hall Royal Coll of Nursing W1 . . . 104 A2
Cowdray Ho 22 SE22 . . . 64 A4
Cowdry Rd E9 . . . 18 B2
Cowley Rd
Brixton SW9 . . . 173 C4
East Acton W3 . . . 29 B1
Mortlake SW14 . . . 56 A4
Cowley St SW1 . . . 134 A1
Cowling Cl W11 . . . 31 A1 112 A2
Cowper Ho
Pimlico SW1 . . . 147 C1
Walworth SE17 . . . 151 A2
Cowper Rd
Acton W3 . . . 28 C1
Stoke Newington N16 . . . 16 A4
Cowper's Ct EC3 . 109 C1

Cowper St EC1, EC2 97 C2
Cowper Terr W10 30 C4
Cowthorpe Rd SW8 171 C4
Cox Ho W6 154 A4
Coxson Way SE1 138 C3
Coysh Ct 8 SW15 58 A2
Crabtree Cl E2 24 B3
Crabtree Ct E15 19 A3
Crabtree Hall SW6 47 B3
Crabtree La SW6 47 C3
Craddock St NW5 12 C2
Cragie Ho SE1 153 A3
Craigleith SW15 57 C1
Craignair Rd SW2 74 C4
Craig's Ct SW1 120 A2
Craik Ct NW6 23 B3
Crail Row SE17 151 C3
Cramer St W1 103 C3
Crammond Cl W6 154 A3
Crampton Sch SE17 150 B2
Crampton St SE17 150 C2
Cranbourn Alley WC2 119 C4
Cranbourne Ct SW11 158 B2
Cranbourne Rd E15 19 B4
Cranbourn Ho 6 SE16 40 A4
Cranbourn Pas 5 SE16 40 A4
Cranbourn St WC2 119 C4
Cranbrook NW1 83 A3
Cranbrook Ho 5 E5 17 A3
Cranbrook Rd
Chiswick W4 38 A1
St Johns SE8 51 C2
Cranbrook St E2 25 C3
Cranbury Rd SW6 166 B1
Crandale Ho 8 E5 17 A3
Crandley Ct SE8 41 A2
Crane Ave W3 28 B2
Crane Ct
7 Acton W12 38 A4
Holborn EC4 107 C1
Crane Gr N7 14 C2
Crane Ho
24 Bow E3 26 A3
10 Peckham SE15 49 B2
Crane Mead SE16 40 C2
Crane St
Greenwich SE10 42 C1
6 Peckham SE15 49 B2
Cranfield Ct NW1 102 B3
Cranfield Ho WC1 106 B4
Cranfield Rd SE4 66 B4
Cranford Cotts 8 E1 32 C2
Cranford Lo SW19 69 C2
Cranford St E1 32 C2
Cranhurst Rd NW2 9 B3
Cranleigh W11 31 B1 112 C2
Cranleigh Ct
Richmond TW9 54 C4
4 Stamford Hill N16 7 A3
Cranleigh Hos NW1 83 A1
Cranleigh Mews SW11 168 C1
Cranleigh St NW1 83 A1
Cranley Gdns SW7 143 B2
Cranley Mews SW7 143 A2
Cranley Pl SW7 143 B3
Cranmer Ct SW3 144 B3
Cranmer Ho SW11 168 A4
Cranmer Rd SW9 163 C2
Cranswick Rd SE16 40 A1
Cranwell Cl E3 27 A1
Cranwich Rd N16 7 A4
Cranwood Ct EC1 97 C3
Cranwood St EC1 97 C3
Cranworth Gdns SW9 173 B4
Cranworth Ho 6 N7 14 B4
Craster Rd SW2 74 B4
Craston Ho 2 SE5 49 A1
Craven Cl N16 7 C4
Craven Cottage (Fulham FC) SW6 47 C2
Craven Ct NW10 21 A4
Craven Hill W2 115 A4
Craven Hill Gdns W2 114 C4
Craven Hill Mews W2 115 A4
Craven Ho 2 SW14 55 C4
Craven Lo
Bayswater W2 115 A4
Fulham SW6 47 C2
Craven Mews 6 SW11 60 C4
Craven Park Mews NW10 21 A4
Craven Park Rd NW10 21 A4
Craven Pas WC2 120 A2
Craven Pk NW10 21 A4
Craven Rd
Paddington W2 101 A1
Stonebridge NW10 20 C4
Craven St WC2 120 A2
Craven Terr W2 115 A4
Craven Wlk E5, N16 7 C4
Crawford Bldgs NW1 102 B3
Crawford Mews W1 102 C3
Crawford Pas EC1 95 C1
Crawford Pl W1 102 B3
Crawford Place Dwellings NW1 102 B3
Crawford Point 4 E16 35 B3
Crawford Prim Sch SE5 48 B2
Crawford Rd SE5 48 B1
Crawford St W1 102 C3
Crawshay Ct SW9 173 C4
Crawshay Ho 13 N16 15 C4
Crawthew Gr SE22 64 B3
Crayford Ho
Bermondsey SE1 137 C3
Crayford Ho *continued*
5 Lower Holloway N7 14 A4
Crayford Rd N7 14 A4
Crayle Ho EC1 96 B2
Crealock St SW18 59 A1
Creasy Est SE1 138 A1
Crebor St SE22 64 C1
Credenhill Ho 2 SE15 50 A3
Crediton Hill NW6 11 A3
Crediton Rd
Brondesbury Pk NW10 22 C4
Newham E16 35 C3
Credon Rd SE16 40 A1
Creechurch La EC3 110 B1
Creechurch Pl EC3 110 B1
Creed Ct 5 E1 26 A2
Creed Ho SE15 65 A4
Creed La EC4 108 B1
Creek Ho W14 126 B2
Creek Rd SE10, SE8 52 A4
Creek Road Ind Est SE8 52 A4
Creekside SE8 52 A3
Creekside Foyer SE8 52 A4
Crefeld Cl W6 154 A3
Creighton Cl W12 30 A2
Creighton Rd NW6 22 C3
Cremer Bsns Ctr 13 E2 24 B3
Cremer Ho 9 SE8 51 C3
Cremer St E2 24 B3
Cremorne Rd SW10 157 B2
Creon Ct SW9 173 B4
Crescent EC3 124 C4
Crescent Arc 1 SE10 52 B4
Crescent Court Bsns Ctr 1 E16 27 C1
Crescent Ct SW4 61 C2
Crescent Gdns SW19 70 C1
Crescent Gr SW4 61 B3
Crescent Ho SE13 52 A1
Crescent La SW4 61 C2
Crescent Mans
Islington N5 15 A3
Notting Hill W11 31 A2 112 B4
Crescent Pl SW3 144 B4
Crescent Row EC1 96 C1
Crescent St N1 14 B1
Crescent Stables SW15 58 A2
Crescent The
Acton W3 29 A3
Barnes SW13 46 C1
Wimbledon SW19 70 C1
Crescent Way SE4 66 C4
Crescent Wood Rd SE21, SE26 76 C1
Cresford Rd SW6 166 A3
Cressage Ho 9 TW8 44 A4
Cressall Ho 14 E14 41 C3
Cresset Ho 8 E9 17 B2
Cresset Rd E9 17 B2
Cresset St SW4 61 C4
Cressfield Cl NW5 12 C3
Cressida Rd N19 4 C3
Cressingham Rd SE13 67 B4
Cressington Cl 4 N16 16 A3
Cresswell Gdns SW5 142 C2
Cresswell Pl SW10 143 A2
Cressy Ct
Hammersmith W6 39 A3
6 Stepney E1 32 B4
Cressy Ho SW13 57 A4
Cressy Hos 7 E1 32 B4
Cressy Pl E1 32 B4
Cressy Rd NW3 12 B4
Cresta Ho
7 Bow E3 26 C1
Hampstead NW6 11 C1
Crestfield St N1, WC1 94 B4
Crestview NW5 4 A1
Crestway SW15 57 A1
Creswick Ct W3 28 A2
Creswick Rd W3 28 A2
Creswick Wlk 7 E3 26 C2
Crewdson Rd SW9 163 B1
Crewe Pl NW10 21 B2
Crewkerne Ct SW11 167 C4
Crews St E14 41 C2
Crewys Rd
Child's Hill NW2 1 B2
London SE15 50 A1
Crichton St SW8 170 C2
Cricketers Mews 4 SW18 59 A2
Cricketfield Rd E5 17 A4
Cricklade Ave SW2 74 B2
CRICKLEWOOD 9 B4
Cricklewood Broadway NW2 9 C4
Cricklewood La NW2 1 B1
Cricklewood Sta NW2 9 C4
Crieff Rd SW18 59 B1
Criffel Ave SW2 73 C3
Crimscott St SE1 138 B1
Crimsworth Rd SW8 161 C1
Crinan St N1 84 B2
Cringle St SW8 160 C2
Cripplegate St EC1 109 A4
Crispe Ho N1 85 A3
Crispian Cl NW10 8 A4
Crispin Ct SE17 152 A3
Crispin Pl E1 110 C4
Crispin St E1 110 C3
Crisp Rd W6 39 B1
Cristowe Rd SW6 165 A1
Criterion Mews N19 4 C2
Crockerton Rd SW17 72 B2
Croft Ct SE13 67 B1
Croftdown Rd NW5 4 A1
Crofters Ct 9 SE8 41 A2
Crofters Way NW1 83 B4
Croft Ho
Putney SW15 58 A1
Croft Ho *continued*
11 West Kilburn W10 23 A2
Crofton Ave W4 45 C3
Crofton Gate Way SE4 66 A2
Crofton L Ctr SE4 66 C1
Crofton Park Rd SE4 66 B1
Crofton Park Sta SE4 66 A2
Crofton Rd SE5 49 A1
Crofton Sch SE4 66 C1
Crofton Terr
Homerton E5 18 A3
Richmond TW9 54 B3
Crofts Ho 21 E2 24 C3
Crofts St E1 125 B3
Croft St SE8 41 A2
Croft The NW10 21 B3
Crogsland Rd NW1 12 C1
Cromartie Rd N19 4 C4
Cromarty Ho 8 E1 33 A4
Crombie Mews SW11 168 B2
Cromdale Ct N16 7 B4
Cromer Ct
Streatham SW16 74 A1
Wandsworth SW18 58 B1
Crome Rd NW10 8 A2
Cromer St WC1 94 B3
Cromer Terr E8 16 C3
Cromer Villas Rd SW18 58 B1
Cromford Path 1 E5 17 C4
Cromford Rd SW18 58 C2
Crompton Ct SW3 144 A4
Crompton Ho
Borough The SE1 137 A1
Paddington W2 89 B1
South Lambeth SW8 171 A3
Crompton St W2 89 B1
Cromwell Ave
Hammersmith W6 39 A2
Highgate N6 4 A3
Cromwell Cl
Acton W3 28 B
2 Gunnersbury W4 37 A1
Cromwell Cres SW5 141 B4
Cromwell Ctr NW10 20 C2
Cromwell Gdns SW7 129 C1
Cromwell Gr W6 39 B3
Cromwell Ho
Battersea SW11 169 C3
Putney SW15 56 C3
Cromwell Hospl SW5 142 A4
Cromwell Lo 40 E1 25 B
Cromwell Mans SW5 141 C4
Cromwell Mews SW7 143 C4
Cromwell Pl
5 Acton W3 28 B
Highgate N6 4 A
Mortlake SW14 55 B4

Cromwell Pl *continued*
South Kensington SW7 143 C4
Cromwell Rd
Brixton SW9 48 A2
South Kensington SW7 143 A4
Cromwell Twr EC2 109 A4
Crondace Rd SW6 165 C3
Crondall Ct 7 N1 24 A3
Crondall Ho SW15 68 C3
Crondall Pl 15 N1 24 A3
Crondall St N1 24 A3
Crone Ct 5 NW6 23 B3
Cronin St SE15 49 B3
Crooked Billet Yd E2 24 A2 98 B4
Crooke Rd SE8 41 A1
Crookham Rd SW6 164 C3
Croom's Hill SE10 52 C3
Croom's Hill Gr SE10 52 B3
Cropley Ct N1 87 B2
Cropley St N1 87 B2
Cropthorne Ct W9 89 A3
Crosby Ct SE1 137 B4
Crosby Ho 18 E14 42 B3
Crosby Row SE1 137 B4
Crosby Sq EC3 110 A2
Crosby Wlk
3 Dalston E8 16 B2
Streatham SE24 74 C4
Crosfield Ct 3 W10 30 C3
Crosfield Ho W11 31 A2 112 A3
Crosland Pl 5 SW11 60 C4
Crossbow Ho 15 N1 24 A4
Cross Cl SE15 50 A1
Cross Ct SE5 63 C4
Crossfield Rd NW3 11 C2
Crossfield St SE8 51 C3
Crossford St SW9 172 C1
Crossharbour Sta E14 42 A3
Cross Keys Cl W1 103 C3
Cross La EC3 124 A3
Crossleigh Ct 3 SE14 51 B3
Crosslet St SE17 151 C4
Crosslet Vale SE10 52 A2
Crossley St N7 14 C2
Crossman Hos 19 SW12 74 A4
Crossmount Ho 13 SE5 48 B3
Cross Rd SE5 49 A1
Cross St
Islington N1 86 B4
Mortlake SW13 56 A4
Crossthwaite Ave SE5, SE24 63 C3
Crosstrees Ho 7 E14 41 C3
Crosswall EC3 124 C4
Crossway E8, N16 16 A3
Crossway Ct SE4 51 A1
Crossways Acad SE4 51 A1
Croston St E8 24 C4
Crouch End Hill N8 4 C4
Crouch Hall Ct N19 5 A3
Crouch Hill N4, N8, N19 5 A4
Crouch Hill Sta N4 5 B4
Crouchmans Cl SE21, SE26 76 C1
Crowder St E1 32 A2
Crowfield Ho N5 15 B4
Crowfoot Cl E9 18 B3
Crowhurst Cl SW9 173 C2
Crowhurst Ho SW9 173 A1
Crowland Ho NW8 78 C3
Crowland Terr N1 15 C1
Crowline Wlk 1 N1 15 B2
Crown Cl Bow E3 26 C4
Hampstead NW6 11 A2
Crown Close Bsns Ctr 12 E3 26 C4
Crown Ct
City of London EC4 109 A1
4 Putney SW15 57 C3
St Giles WC2 106 B1
St John's Wood NW8 90 B3
Crowndale Ct NW1 83 B2
Crowndale Rd NW1 83 A2
Crowne Ho SE1 123 A1
Crownfield Rd E15 19 C4
Crowngate Ho 33 E3 26 B3
Crownhill Rd NW10 21 B4
Crownleigh Ct SW2 62 C2
Crown Lo SW3 144 B3
Crown Mews 9 E1 32 C4
Crown Office Row EC4 121 B4
Crown Pas SW1 119 A1
Crown Pl
Broadgate EC2 110 A4
Kentish Town NW5 13 A2
Crown Reach SW1 147 C1
Crown St
Acton W3 28 A1
Camberwell SE5 48 B3
Crownstone Ct 1 SW2 62 C2
Crownstone Rd SW2 62 C2
Crown Terr TW9 54 B3
Crows Rd E15 27 C2
Crowther Ave TW8 36 A2
Crowther Cl SW6 155 A3
Crowthorne Cl SW18 70 B3
Crowthorne Rd W10 30 C3
Croxley Rd W9 23 B2
Croxted Cl SE21 75 B4
Croxted Rd SE21, SE24 75 C3
Croxteth Ho SW8 171 B2
Croydon Ho SE1 135 C4
Crozier Ho SW8 162 C1
Crozier Terr E9 17 C3
Crucifix La SE1 138 A4
Cruden Ho
15 Bow E3 26 B3
11 Camberwell SE17 48 A4
Cruden St N1 86 B3
Cruickshank St WC1 95 B4
Cruikshank Ho NW8 80 B2
Crusader Ho EC1 96 A1
Crusoe House Sch N1 97 B4
Crusoe Mews N16 6 C2
Crutched Friars EC3 124 B4
Crystal Palace Rd SE22 64 C2
Crystal Wharf N1 86 B1
Cuba St E14 41 C4
Cubitt Bldg SW1 146 A1
Cubitt Ho 4 SW4 61 B1
Cubitt St WC1 95 A3
Cubitt Terr SW4 61 B4
CUBITT TOWN 42 B2
Cubitt Town Jun & Inf Sch E14 42 B3
Cuddington SE17 151 A4
Cudworth Ho SW8 171 A3
Cudworth St E1 25 A1
Cuffley Ho 3 W10 30 B4
Cuff Point E2 24 B2 98 C4
Culand Ho SE17 152 A3
Culford Gdns SW3 145 A3
Culford Gr N1 16 A2
Culford Mans SW3 145 A3
Culford Mews N1 16 A2
Culford Rd
Kingsland N1 16 A2
Shoreditch N1 24 A4
Culham Ho
21 Paddington W2 31 C4
Shoreditch E2 24 B2 98 C3
Cullen Ho W9 23 B3
Cullen Way NW10 20 B1
Culling Rd SE16 40 B3
Cullingworth Rd NW10 9 A3
Culloden Cl SE16 153 C1
Culloden Prim Sch E14 34 B3
Cullum St EC3 124 A4
Culmore Rd SE15 50 B3
Culmstock Rd SW11 60 C2
Culpepper Ct SE11 149 B4
Culross Bldgs NW1 84 A2
Culross St W1 117 B3
Culver Ct SW18 59 A1
Culverden Rd SW12 73 B2
Culverhouse WC1 106 C3
Culverhouse Gdns SW16 74 B1
Culverin Ct 1 N7 14 B3
Culvert Ct SW11 169 B2
Culvert Pl SW11 169 B1
Culvert Rd SW11 169 A2
Culworth Ho NW8 80 A2
Culworth St NW8 80 A1
Cumber Ho SW18 70 C3
Cumberland Ave NW10 20 A2
Cumberland Bsns Pk NW10 20 A2
Cumberland Cl E8 16 B2
Cumberland Cres W14 140 B4
Cumberland Ct W1 103 A1
Cumberland Gate W1 117 A4
Cumberland Gdns WC1 95 B4
Cumberland Ho
Paddington W9 88 C1
1 Putney SW15 69 B4
Cumberland Mans
Marylebone W1 102 C2
7 West Hampstead NW6 10 C3
Cumberland Market NW1 92 B4
Cumberland Mills Sq E14 42 C1
Cumberland Park Ind Est NW10 21 C2
Cumberland Pk W3 28 B2
Cumberland Pl NW1 92 A4
Cumberland Rd
Acton W3 28 B2
Barnes SW13 46 C2
Richmond TW9 44 C3
Cumberland St SW1 146 B2
Cumberland Terr NW1 82 A1
Cumberland Terrace Mews NW1 82 A1
Cumberland Villas W3 28 B2
Cumberland Wharf 12 SE16 40 B4
Cumbrian Gdns NW2 1 A2
Cuming Mus★ SE17 150 C3
Cumming St N1 85 A1
Cumnor Cl SW9 173 A2
Cunard Pl EC3 110 B1
Cunard Rd NW10 20 C2
Cunard Wlk 3 SE16 41 A2
Cundy St SW1 145 C3
Cunningham Ct W2 89 B1
Cunningham Ho 16 SE5 48 C3
Cunningham Pl NW8 89 B2
Cunnington St W4 37 B2
Cupar Rd SW11 169 C4
Cureton St SW1 147 C3
Curlew Ho
Brockley SE4 66 A3
7 Peckham SE15 49 B2
Curlew St SE1 139 A4
Curness St SE13 67 B3
Curran Ho SW3 144 A3
Curricle St W3 29 A1
Currie Ho 13 SW12 73 C4
Cursitor St EC4 107 B2
Curtain Pl EC2 24 A1 98 B2
Curtain Rd EC2 24 A1 98 B2
Curtis Dr W3 28 C3
Curtis Ho SE17 151 B2
Curtis St SE1 152 C4
Curtis Way SE1 152 C4
Curve Bldg The SE4 66 B2
Curve The W12 29 C2
Curwen & New Acad Gall★ W1 105 B3
Curwen Rd W12 38 C4
Curzon Cres NW10 8 A1
Curzon Gate W1 117 C1
Curzon Sq W1 117 C1
Curzon St W1 118 A2
Custance Ho N1 87 B1
Custance St N1 97 B4
Custom House EC3 124 A3
Custom House Reach SE16 41 B3
Cutbush Ho N7 13 C3
Cutcombe Rd SE5 48 B1
Cuthbert Harrowing Ho EC1 96 C1
Cuthbert Ho W2 101 B4
Cuthbert St W2 89 B1
Cuthill Wlk 3 SE5 48 C2
Cutlers Gdns EC2 110 B2
Cutlers Gdns Arc EC2 110 B2
Cutlers Sq E14 41 C2
Cutler St EC2 110 B2
Cut The SE1 135 C4
Cutty Sark★ SE10 52 B4
Cutty Sark Ho 10 E14 42 A2
Cutty Sark Ret Development SE10 52 B4
Cutty Sark Sta SE10 52 B4
Cuxton Ho SE17 152 B2
Cyclops Mews 12 E14 41 C2
Cygnet Ho NW8 78 C4
Cygnet House N 18 E14 34 A3
Cygnet House S 19 E14 34 A3
Cygnet St E1 24 B1 99 A2
Cygnus Bsns Ctr NW10 8 B2
Cynthia St N1 85 A1
Cyntra Pl 8 E8 17 A1
Cypress Cl 9 E5 7 C2
Cypress Ct 5 E11 19 C4
Cypress Gdns SE4 66 A2
Cypress Ho SE14 50 C2
Cypress Pl W1 93 A1
Cyprus Pl 23 E2 25 B3
Cyprus St E2 25 B3
Cyrena Rd SE22 64 B2
Cyril Jackson Prim Sch (North Bldg) E14 33 B2
Cyril Jackson Prim Sch (South Bldg) E14 33 B2
Cyril Mans SW11 169 A3
Cyril Thatcher Ho SW6 165 C3
Cyrus Ho EC1 96 B2

Cyrus St EC1 96 B2
Czar St SE8 51 C4

D

Dabb's La EC1 95 C1
Dabin Cres SE10 52 B2
Dacca St SE8 51 B4
Dace Rd E3 26 C4
Dacre Ho SW3 157 C3
Dacre St SW1 133 B2
Daffodil St W12 29 B2
Dafforne Rd SW17 72 C1
Dagmar Ct E14 42 B3
Dagmar Gdns NW10 22 C3
Dagmar Pas N1 86 B4
Dagmar Rd
  Camberwell SE5 49 A2
  Finsbury Pk N4 5 C4
Dagmar Terr N1 86 B4
Dagnall St SW11 169 B3
Dagnan Rd SW12 73 B4
Dagobert Ho 27 E1 32 B4
Daimler Ho 8 E3 26 C1
Dainton Ho 22 W2 31 C4
Daintry Way E9 18 B2
Dairy Cl NW10 21 C4
Dairyman Cl NW2 1 A1
Daisy Dormer Ct 11 SW9 62 B3
Daisy La SW6 58 C4
Dakin Pl 9 E1 33 A4
Dakota bldg 6 SE13 52 A2
Dalberg Rd SW2 62 C2
Dalbury Ho 6 SW9 62 B3
Dalby Rd SW18 59 B3
Dalby St NW5 13 A2
Dalebury Rd SW17 72 B2
Dale Croft N4 6 B1
Dalehaed NW1 82 C1
Daleham Gdns NW3 11 C2
Daleham Mews NW3 11 C2
Dale Ho
  London SE4 66 A3
  St John's Wood NW8 78 C4
Dalemain Ho SW8 171 C2
Dalemain Mews 12 E16 35 C1
Dale Rd
  Camberwell SE17 48 A4
  Gospel Oak NW5 12 C3
Dale Row W11 31 A3
Dale St W4 38 A1
Daley Ho 6 W12 30 A3
Daley St E9 17 C2
Daley Thompson Way 7 SW8 61 A4
Dalgarno Gdns W10 30 B4
Dalgarno Way W10 22 B1
Daling Way E3 26 A3
Dalkeith Ct SW1 147 C3
Dalkeith Ho 6 SW9 48 A2
Dalkeith Rd SE21 75 B4
Dalling Rd W6 39 A2
Dallington Sch EC1 96 B2
Dallington St EC1 96 B2
Dalmeny Ave N7 13 C4
Dalmeny Avenue Est 3 N7 13 C4
Dalmeny Ct SW4 172 A2
Dalmeny Rd N7 13 C4
Dalmeyer Rd NW10 8 B2
Dalmore Rd SE21 75 B2
Dalrymple Rd SE4 66 A3
DALSTON 16 C2
Dalston Jct E8 16 B2
Dalston Kingsland Sta E8 16 B3
Dalston La E8 16 C3
Dalton Ho
  7 Balham SW12 73 A4
  10 Bow E3 26 A3
  19 Deptford SE14 50 C4
Dalton St SE27 75 A1
Dalwood St SE5 49 A2
Daly Ct E15 19 B3
Dalyell Rd SW9 62 B4
Damascene Wlk SE21 75 B3
Damer Ho 9 TW10 54 B1
Damer Terr SW10 157 A1
Dame St N1 86 C2
Damien Ct 12 E1 32 A3
Damien St E1 32 A3
Damory Ho 1 SE16 40 B2
Dan Bryant Ho 5 SW12 73 B4
Danbury St N1 86 B2
Danby Ho
  23 Hackney E9 17 B1
  3 West Kilburn W10 23 B2
Danby St SE15 64 B4
Dancer Rd
  Fulham SW6 164 C3
  Richmond TW9 54 C4
Dandridge Cl SE10 43 B1
Dandridge Ho E1 110 C4
Danebury 18 W10 30 B4
Danebury Ave SW15 56 B1
Danecroft Rd SE24 63 C2
Dane Ho 15 SE5 48 B1
Danehurst St SW6 164 A4
Danemere St SW15 57 B4
Dane Pl E3 26 B3
Danes Ct NW8 80 C3
Danesdale Rd E9 18 A2
Danesfield SE5 49 A4
Danes Ho 10 W10 30 B4
Dane St WC1 106 C3
Daneville Rd SE5 48 C2
Daniel Bolt Cl E14 34 A4
Daniel Ct W3 29 A2
Daniel Gdns SE15 49 B3
Daniell Ho N1 87 C2
Daniel's Rd SE15 65 B4
Dan Leno Wlk SW6 156 A1
Dansey Pl W1 119 B4
Dante Pl SE11 150 B3
Dante Rd SE11 150 A4
Danube Ct 13 SE15 49 B3
Danube St SW3 144 B2
Danvers Ho E1 111 C1
Danvers St SW3 157 C3
Da Palma Ct SW6 155 B3
Daphne St SW18 59 B1
Daplyn St E1 111 B4
D'arblay St W1 105 A1
Darcy Ho E8 25 A4
Darell Prim Sch TW9 54 C4
Darell Rd TW9 54 C4
Daren Ct N7 14 A4
Darent Ho NW8 101 C4
Darenth Rd N16 7 B3
Darfield NW1 82 C3
Darfield Rd SE4 66 B2
Darfield Way W10 30 C3
Darfur St SW15 57 C4
Darien Ho
  17 London SW11 59 C4
  11 Stepney E1 32 C4
Darien Rd SW11 59 C4
Daring Ho 23 E3 26 A3
Darlan Rd SW6 155 A1
Darley Ho SE11 148 C1
Darley Rd SW11 60 B1
Darling Rd SE4 66 C4
Darling Row E1 25 A1
Darlington Ho SW8 161 C1
Darnall Ho 4 SE10 52 B2
Darnay Ho SE16 139 B2
Darnell Ho 9 SE10 52 B3
Darnley Ho 7 E14 33 A3
Darnley Rd E9 17 B2
Darnley Terr 12 W11 30 C1
Darrell Rd SE22 64 C2
Darren Cl N4 5 B4
Darsley Dr SW8 172 A4
Dartford Ho SE1 153 A4
Dartford St SE17 48 B4
Dartington NW1 83 A3
Dartington Ho
  Bayswater W2 100 A4
  London SW8 171 C2
Dartle Ct SE16 139 C3
Dartmoor Wlk 18 E14 41 C2
Dartmouth Cl W11 31 C3
Dartmouth Ct SE10 52 B2
Dartmouth Gr SE10 52 B2
Dartmouth Hill SE10 52 B2
Dartmouth Ho
  Dartmouth Pk N19 4 A2
  Lewisham SE10 52 B1
DARTMOUTH PARK 4 A1
Dartmouth Park Ave NW5 4 A1
Dartmouth Park Hill N19 4 A2
Dartmouth Park Rd NW5 4 A1
Dartmouth Pl W4 46 A4
Dartmouth Rd NW2 9 C2
Dartmouth Row SE10 52 B2
Dartmouth St SW1 133 C3
Dartmouth Terr SE10 52 C2
Darton Ct W3 28 B1
Dartrey Twr SW10 157 B2
Dartrey Wlk SW10 157 A2
Dart St W10 23 B2
Darville Rd N16 7 B1
Darwen Pl E2 25 A4
Darwin Ct NW1 81 C4
Darwin Ho 8 SE13 52 B1
Darwin St SE17 151 C4
Daryngton Ho SW8 162 A1
Dashwood Ho SE21 76 B1
Data Point Bsns Ctr E16 27 C1
Datchelor Pl 14 SE5 48 C2
Datchet Ho NW1 92 B4
Datchett Ho E2 24 B2 98 C3
Datchwood Ct N4 6 B1
Datchworth Ho 8 N1 15 A1
Date St SE17 151 B1
Daubeney Prim Sch E5 18 A4
Daubeney Rd E5 18 A4
Daubeney Twr 2 SE8 41 B1
Dault Rd SW18 59 B1
Dauney Ho SE1 136 A3
Dave Adams Ho 8 E3 26 B3
Davenant Ho E1 111 C4
Davenant Rd N19 4 C2
Davenant St E1 111 C3
Davenport Ho SE11 135 B1
Davenport Mews 6 W12 30 A1
Davenport Rd SE6 67 B1
Daventry St NW1 102 A4
Dave Porter Hts SW19 70 A4
Daver Ct SW3 144 B1
Davern Cl SE10 43 B2
Davey Cl N7 14 B2
Davey Rd E9 18 C1
Davey's Ct WC2 120 A4
Davey St SE15 49 B4
David Beckham Acad The SE10 43 B4
David Devine Ho 7 E8 16 C3
David Game Coll SW7 143 B3
Davidge Ho SE1 135 C3
Davidge St SE1 136 B3
David Hewitt Ho 2 E3 34 A4
David Ho
  8 Putney SW15 56 C2
  South Lambeth SW8 162 A2
David Mews W1 103 A4
Davidson Gdns SW8 162 A2
Davidson Ho 7 N19 13 B4
David St E15 19 C3
Davies Laing & Dick Coll W1 103 C2
Davies Mews W1 118 A4
Davies St W1 118 A4
Davina Ho
  Brondesbury NW2 10 B2
  14 Hackney E5 17 A3
Da Vinci Ct 12 SE16 40 A1
Davis Ho 35 W12 30 A2
Davis Rd W3 38 B4
Davisville Rd W12 38 C4
Dawes Ho SE17 151 B3
Dawes Rd SW6 154 C2
Dawes St SE17 151 C2
Dawlish Ave SW18 71 A2
Dawlish Rd NW2 9 C2
Dawnay Gdns SW18 71 C2
Dawnay Rd SW17, SW18 71 C2
Dawn Cres E15 27 C4
Dawson Ho
  23 Bethnal Green E2 25 B2
  5 Camberwell SE5 49 A2
Dawson Pl W2 31 C2 113 C4
Dawson Rd NW2 9 B4
Dawson St E2 24 B3
Day Ho 2 SE5 48 B3
Daylesford Ave SW15 56 C3
Daynor Ho 4 NW6 23 C
Daysbrook Rd SW2 74 B3
Dayton Gr SE15 50 B2
Deacon Ho SE11 149 A3
Deacon Mews N1 15 C3
Deacon Rd NW2 8 C
Deacon Way SE17 151 A
Deal Ho
  Deptford SE15 50 C
  Walworth SE17 152 B
Deal Porters Way SE16 40 C
Deal St E1 111 B
Dealtry Rd SW15 57 B
Deal Wlk SW9 163 C
Dean Bradley St SW1 134 A
Dean Cl
  Hackney E9 17 B
  Rotherhithe SE16 32 C
Dean Coll of London N7 5 B
Deancross St E1 32 B
Dean Ct Acton W3 28 C
  South Lambeth SW8 162 A
Deanery Mews W1 117 C
Deanery St W1 117 C
Dean Farrar St SW1 133 C
Deanhill Ct 2 SW14 55 A
Deanhill Rd SW14 55 A
Dean Ho London N4 6 B
  New Cross SE14 51 B
  Stamford Hill N16 7 B
  18 Stepney E1 32 B
Dean Rd NW2 9 B
Dean Ryle St SW1 148 A

Dean's Bldgs SE17 151 C3
Deans Cl W4 45 A4
Dean's Ct EC4 108 B1
Deanshanger Ho [21] SE8 40 C2
Dean's Mews W1 104 B2
Dean St W1 105 B1
Dean Stanley St SW1 134 A1
Dean's Yd SW1 133 C2
Dean Trench St SW1 134 A1
Dearmer Ho [6] SW2 74 C4
Deason St E15 27 B4
Deauville Ct
[14] London SW4 61 B1
[4] Rotherhithe SE16 40 C4
Deauville Mans [13] SW4 61 B1
De Barowe Mews [1] N5 15 A3
Debdale Ho [20] E2 24 C4
De Beauvoir Cres N1 24 A4
De Beauvoir Ct N1 15 C1
De Beauvoir Pl [5] N1 16 A2
De Beauvoir Prim Sch N1 16 A2
De Beauvoir Rd N1 16 A1
De Beauvoir Sq N1 16 A1
DE BEAUVOIR TOWN 16 A1
Debenham Ct E8 24 C4
Debnams Rd SE16 40 B2
Decima St SE1 138 A2
Deck Cl SE16 32 C1
De Crespigny Pk SE5 48 C1
Deeley Rd SW8 171 B4
Deepdale N4 6 A1
Deepdene Gdns SW2 74 B4
Deepdene Ho N16 6 C3
Deepdene Lo [5] SW2 74 B4
Deepdene Mans SW6 164 C4
Deepdene Rd SE5, SE24 63 C3
Deerbrook Rd SE24, SW2 75 A3
Dee Rd TW9 54 B3
Deerdale Rd SE24 63 B3
Deerhurst Ho [6] SE15 49 C4
Deerhurst Rd NW2 9 C2
Deer Lo SW6 58 A4
Deeside Rd SW17 71 C1
Dee St E14 34 B3
Defoe Ave TW9 44 C3
Defoe Ho
Barbican EC2 108 C4
[5] Stoke Newington N16 7 A1
Defoe Pl EC2 108 C4
Defoe Rd
Rotherhithe SE16 41 B4
Stoke Newington N16 7 A1
De Gama Pl [3] E14 41 C1
Dekker Ho [19] SE5 48 C3
Dekker Rd SE21 64 A1
Delafield Ho E1 111 C1
Delaford Rd SE16 40 A1
Delaford St SW6 154 B3
Delamere Ho [4] N4 6 C4
Delamere Rd W5 36 A4
Delamere St W2 100 C3
Delamere Terr W2 100 B4
Delancey Pas NW1 82 B3
Delancey St NW1 82 B3
Delancey Studios NW1 82 B3
Delany Ho SE10 52 B4
Delarch Ho SE1 136 A3
De Laune St SE17 150 A1
Delaware Rd W9 88 A2
Delawyk Cres SE24 63 C1
Delft Way [2] SE22 64 A2
Delhi St N1 84 B3
Delia St SW18 71 A4
Delius Gr E15 27 B3
Dellafield N4 5 C2
Dell Cl E15 27 C4
Dellow Ho [6] E1 32 A2
Dellow St E1 32 A2
Dell's Mews SW1 147 A3
Deloraine Ho SE8 51 C2
Deloraine St SE8 51 C2
Delorme St W6 47 C4
Delta Bldg [7] E14 34 B3
Delta Ho N1 97 B4
Delta Pk SW18 59 A3
Delta Point E2 24 C2 99 B4
Delta St E2 24 C2 99 B4
Delverton Ho SE17 150 B2
Delverton Rd SE17 150 B1
Delvino Rd SW6 165 C3
De Montfort Ct [1] SW16 74 A1
De Montfort Rd SW16 74 A2
De Morgan Rd SW6 59 A4
Dempster Rd SW18 59 B2
Denbigh Cl
Notting Hill W11 31 B2 113 A4
Willesden NW10 8 A1
Denbigh Gdns TW10 54 B2
Denbigh Ho
Knightsbridge SW1 131 A2
[7] Notting Hill W11 31 B3
Notting Hill W11 31 B2 113 A4
Denbigh Mews SW1 146 C3
Denbigh Pl SW1 146 C2
Denbigh Rd W11 31 B2 113 A4
Denbigh St SW1 147 A2
Denbigh Terr W11 31 B2 113 A4
Denbury Ho [48] E3 27 A2
Denby Ct SE11 149 A4
Dence Ho E2 24 C2 99 B3
Denchworth Ho SW9 173 B1
Dene Cl SE4 66 A3
Denehurst Gdns
Acton W3 28 A1
Richmond TW10 54 C3
Dene Mans [1] NW6 10 C2
Denesmead SE24 63 B2
Denewood Rd N6 3 B4
Dengie Wlk N1 86 C4
Denham Ho [32] W12 30 A2
Denham St SE10 43 C1
Denholme Rd W9 23 B2
Denland Ho SW8 163 A1
Denman Ho N16 7 A2
Denman Rd SE15 49 B1
Denman St W1 119 B3
Denmark Gr N1 85 B2
Denmark Hill SE5 48 C1
Denmark Hill Sta SE5 48 C1
Denmark Mans [14] SE5 48 B1
Denmark Pl
[2] Bromley E3 26 C2
Soho WC2 105 C2
Denmark Rd
Camberwell SE5 48 B1
Kilburn NW6 23 B3
Denmark St WC2 105 C2
Denmead Ho SW15 56 B1
Denne Terr E8 24 B4
Dennett's Gr SE14 50 C1
Dennett's Rd SE14 50 B2
Denning Cl NW8 89 A3
Denning Point E1 111 A2
Denning Rd NW3 11 C4
Dennington Park Mansions [12] NW6 10 C3
Dennington Park Rd NW6 10 C2
Dennis Ct SE10 52 B2
Dennis Ho [4] E3 26 B3
Dennison Point E15 19 B1
Dennis Way SW4 61 C4
Denny Cres SE11 149 C2
Denny St SE11 149 C2
Densham Ho NW8 79 C1
Denstone Ho [5] SE15 49 C4
Dent Ho SE17 152 A3
Denton NW1 12 C2
Denton Ho N1 15 A1
Denton St SW18 59 A1
Dents Rd SW11 60 B1
Denver Rd N16 7 A4
Denyer Ho [1] NW5 13 A4
Denyer St SW3 144 B4
Denys Bldg EC1 107 B4
Denzil Rd NW10 8 B3
Deodar Rd SW15 58 A3
Depot App NW2 9 C4
Depot Rd W12 30 B2
Depot St SE5 48 C4
DEPTFORD 50 C3
Deptford Bridge SE8 51 C2
Deptford Bridge Sta SE8 51 C2
Deptford Broadway SE8, SE14 51 C2
Deptford Church St SE8 51 C3
Deptford Ferry Rd [24] E14 41 C2
Deptford Gn SE8 51 C4
Deptford Green Sch SE14 51 B3
Deptford Green Sch (Annex) SE14 51 A3
Deptford High St SE8 51 C3
Deptford Park Prim Sch SE8 41 A1
Deptford Sta SE8 51 C3
Deptford Trad Est SE8 51 A4
Deptford Wharf SE8 41 B2
Dept of Transport & Environment SW1 133 C1
De Quincey Mews [3] E16 35 C1
Derby Ct [8] E5 17 C4
Derby Gate SW1 134 A4
Derby Ho SE11 149 B4
Derby Rd
Mortlake SW14 55 A3
South Hackney E9 25 C4
Derbyshire St E2 24 C2 99 C3
Derby St W1 117 C1
Dereham Ho [7] SE4 65 C3
Dereham Pl EC2 24 A1 98 B2
Derek Walcott Cl SE24 63 A2
Dericote St E8 25 A4
Dering St W1 104 B1
Dermody Gdns SE13 67 C2
Dermody Rd SE13 67 C2
Deronda Rd SE24, SW2 75 A3
Derrick Ho [13] SW2 74 C3
Derrycombe Ho [18] W2 31 C4
Derry St W8 128 A3
Dersingham Rd NW2 1 A1
Derwent NW1 92 C3
Derwent Ct
[2] Hammersmith W6 38 C2
[8] Rotherhithe SE16 40 C4
Derwent Gr SE22 64 B3
Derwent Ho
South Kensington SW7 143 A4
Tower Hamlets E3 26 B1
Derwent St SE10 43 A1
Derwentwater Mans [2] W3 28 B1
Derwentwater Prim Sch W3 28 B1
Derwentwater Rd W3 28 B1
Desborough Cl W2 100 B4
Desborough Ho W14 155 A4
Desenfans Rd SE21 64 A1
Desmond St SE14 51 A4
Despard Ho SW2 74 C2
Despard Rd N19 4 B3
Desvignes Dr SE13 67 C1
Dethick Ct E3 26 A4
Detling Ho SE17 152 A3
Devas St E3 27 A1
Deventer Cres [8] SE22 64 A2
De Vere Cotts W8 128 C2
De Vere Gdns W8 128 C3
Deverell St SE1 137 B1
De Vere Mews W8 128 C2
Devereux Ct WC2 107 B1
Devereux Ho [7] SW15 56 C2
Devereux La SW13 47 A3
Devereux Rd SW11 60 B1
Devitt Ho [5] E14 34 A2
Devizes St N1 87 C3
Devonhurst Pl [4] W4 37 C1
Devonia Rd N1 86 B2
Devon Mans SE1 138 B4
Devonport W2 102 A2
Devonport Ho
Greenwich SE10 52 B4
[23] Paddington W2 31 C4
Devonport Rd W12 39 A4
Devonport St E1 32 C3
Devonshire Cl W1 104 A4
Devonshire Ct
[14] Balham SW12 73 A4
[6] Richmond TW9 44 B2
Devonshire Dr SE10 52 A2
Devonshire Gdns W4 45 B3
Devonshire Gr SE15 50 A4
Devonshire Hall [15] E9 17 B2
Devonshire Ho
Brondesbury NW6 10 B2
Newington SE1 136 C2
Paddington W2 101 C4
[2] Putney SW15 69 B4
Westminster SW1 147 C2
Devonshire Hospl W1 103 C4
Devonshire House Prep Sch NW3 11 C3
Devonshire House Sch NW3 11 B3
Devonshire Mews [2] W4 38 A1
Devonshire Mews N W1 104 A4
Devonshire Mews S W1 104 A4
Devonshire Mews W W1 103 C4
Devonshire Pl
Child's Hill NW2 1 C1
Kensington W8 128 A1
Marylebone W1 103 C4
Devonshire Place Mews W1 103 C4
Devonshire Rd W4 38 A1

Devonshire Row EC2 110 B3
Devonshire Row Mews W1 92 B1
Devonshire Sq EC2 110 B2
Devonshire St
Chiswick W4 38 A1
Marylebone W1 104 A4
Devonshire Terr W2 101 A1
Devons Rd E3 27 A1
Devons Road Sta E3 27 A1
Devon St SE15 50 A4
De Walden Ho NW8 80 A2
De Walden St W1 103 C3
Dewar St SE15 64 C4
Dewberry St E14 34 B4
Dewey Rd N1 85 B2
Dewhurst Rd W14 39 C3
Dewsbury Ct 5 W4 37 B2
Dewsbury Rd NW10 8 C3
Dewsbury Terr NW1 82 B4
D'eynsford Rd SE5 48 C2
Dhonau Ho SE16 153 A4
Diadem Ct W1 105 B2
Dial Wlk The W8 128 B4
Diamond Est SW17 72 A1
Diamond Ho 22 E3 26 A3
Diamond St SE15 49 A3
Diamond Terr SE10 52 B2
Diana Cl 27 SE8 51 B4
Diana Ho
Barnes SW13 46 B2
4 Brixton SW2 62 B2
Diana, Princess of Wales Mml Wlk W2 114 C1
Dibden Ho 8 SE5 49 A3
Dibden St N1 86 C4
Dibdin Ho W9 78 A1
Dicey Ave NW2 9 B4
Dickens Ct EC1 96 A1
Dickens Ho
Bloomsbury WC1 94 A2
Kennington SE17 150 B1
Kilburn NW6 23 C2
Paddington NW8 89 C2
Dickens House Mus* WC1 95 A1
Dickenson Rd N8 5 A4
Dickens Sq SE1 137 A2
Dickens St SW8 170 B2
Dickinson Ho E2 24 C2 99 B3
Dicksee Ho NW8 89 B1
Dick Shepherd Ct 17 SW2 62 C1
Dickson Ho 4 E1 32 A3
Didbin Ho N7 5 B2
Digby Bsns Ctr E9 17 C2
Digby Cres N4 6 B2
Digby Mans W6 39 B1
Digby Rd E9 17 C2
Digby St E2 25 B2
Diggon St E1 32 C4
Dighton Ct SE17 48 B4
Dighton Rd SW18 59 B3
Dignum St N1 85 B2
Digswell St N7 14 C2
Dilke St SW3 159 A4
Dilston Gr SE16 40 B2
Dilton Gdns SW15 69 A3
Dimes Pl 9 W6 39 A2
Dimson Cres E3 26 C2
Dinerman Ct NW8 79 A4
Dingle Gdns E14 33 C2
Dingley La SW16 73 C2
Dingley Pl EC1 97 A3
Dingley Rd EC1 96 C3
Dingwall Rd SW18 71 B4
Dinmont Ho 27 E2 24 C3
Dinmont St 1 E2 25 A3
Dinmore Ho 6 E9 25 B4
Dinnington Ho 17 E1 25 A1
Dinsdale Rd SE3 53 B4
Dinsmore Rd SW12 73 A4
Dinton Ho NW8 90 A2
Dinwiddy Ho N1 84 C1
Dionis Ho SW6 165 B2
Disbrowe Rd W6 154 B3
Discovery Bsns Pk SE16 139 C1
Discovery Dock E E14 42 A4
Discovery Ho 1 E14 34 B2
Disney Pl SE1 137 A4
Disney St SE1 137 A4
Disraeli Cl 1 W4 37 C2
Disraeli Gdns SW15 58 B3
Disraeli Rd
Acton NW10 20 C3
Putney SW15 58 A3
Diss St E2 24 B2 98 C4
Distaff La EC4 122 C4
Distillery La W6 39 B1
Distillery Rd W6 39 B1
Distillery Wlk 14 TW8 44 A4
Distin St SE11 149 B3
Ditchburn St E14 34 B2
Ditton Ho 10 E5 17 A3
Divis Way SW15 57 A1
Dixon Clark Ct N1 15 A2
Dixon Ho 20 NW10 30 C3
Dixon Rd SE14 51 A2
Dixon's Alley 10 SE16 40 A4
Dobree Ave NW10 9 A1
Dobson Cl NW6 11 C1
Dobson Ho 18 SE14 50 C4
Doby Ct EC4 123 A4
Dockers Tanner Rd 26 E14 41 C2
Dockhead SE1 139 A3
Dockhead Wharf SE1 139 A4
Dock Hill Ave SE16 40 C4
Docklands Ct 20 E14 33 B3
Docklands Heritage Mus* SE16 33 B1
Dockley Rd SE16 139 B1
Dockley Road Ind Est SE16 139 B1
Dock Offices 12 SE16 40 B3
Dock Rd E16 35 B2
Dock St E1 125 B4
Doctor Spurstowe Almshouses 9 E8 17 A2
Docura Ho N7 5 B2
Docwras Bldgs N1 16 A2
Dodbrooke Rd SE27 75 A1
Dodd Ho 18 SE16 40 A2
Doddington Gr SE17 150 B1
Doddington Pl 4 SE17 48 A4
Dodson St SE1 135 C3
Dod St E14 33 C3
Dog Kennel Hill SE22 64 A4
Dog Kennel Hill Sch SE22 64 A4
Dog La NW10 8 A4
Dolben Ct SW1 147 C3
Dolben St SE1 122 B1
Dolby Rd SW6 164 C1
Doleman Ho 19 SE10 52 A2
Dolland Ho SE11 149 A1
Dolland St SE11 149 A1
Dollar Bay E14 42 B4
DOLLIS HILL 9 A4
Dollis Hill Sta NW2 8 C3
Dolman Rd W4 37 C2
Dolman St SW4 62 B3
Dolphin Cl 2 SE16 40 C4
Dolphin Ct N7 13 C4
Dolphin La E14 34 A2
Dolphin Sch SW11 60 B2
Dolphin Sq SW1 147 A1
Dolphin Twr 21 SE8 51 B4
Dombey Ho
Bermondsey SE1 139 B3
4 Shepherd's Bush W11 30 C1
Dombey St WC1 106 C4
Domelton Ho SW18 59 A1
Domett Cl SE5 63 C3
Domfe Pl E5 17 B4
Domingo St EC1 96 C1
Dominion St EC2 109 C4
Donaghue Cotts 11 E14 33 A4
Donaldson Rd NW6 23 B4
Donegal Ho 2 E1 25 B1
Donegal St N1 85 A1
Doneraile Ho SW1 146 A1
Doneraile St SW6 47 C2
Dongola Rd E1 33 A4
Don Gratton Ho E1 111 B3
Donkey Alley SE22 64 C1
Donkin Ho 15 SE16 40 A2
Donne Ct SE24 63 B1
Donne Ho
18 Canonbury N16 15 C4
14 Deptford SE14 50 C4
11 Poplar E14 33 C3
Donnelly Ct SW6 154 B2
Donne Pl SW3 144 B4
Donnington Ct
11 Camden Town NW1 13 A1
Donnington Ct continued
Willesden NW10 9 A1
Donnington Ho SW8 171 B2
Donnington Prim Sch NW10 22 A4
Donnington Rd NW10 22 A4
Donovan Ct SW7 143 B1
Donovan Ho 4 E1 32 B2
Don Phelan Cl SE5 48 C2
Doon St SE1 121 B2
Doradus Ct 20 SW19 69 C3
Dora Ho
11 Shepherd's Bush W11 30 C2
1 Tower Hamlets E14 33 B3
Dorando Cl W12 30 A2
Doran Wlk
Stratford E15 19 B1
Stratford Marsh E15 27 B4
Dora St E14 33 B3
Dorcas Ct 9 SW18 59 C3
Dorchester Ct
1 De Beauvoir Town N1 16 A1
Herne Hill SE24 63 B2
Knightsbridge SW1 131 A1
6 Streatham SW16 74 A2
Dorchester Dr SE24 63 B2
Dorchester Gr W4 38 B1
Dorchester Ho TW9 45 A3
Dordrecht Rd W3 29 A1
Doria Rd SW6 165 A2
Doric Ho 7 E2 25 C3
Doric Way NW1 93 B4
Doris Emmerton Ct SW18 59 B3
Dorking Cl SE8 51 B4
Dorking Ho SE1 137 C2
Dorland Ct SW15 58 B1
Dorlcote Rd SW18 72 A4
Dorleston Ct N1 87 C4
Dorman Way NW8 79 B4
Dormay St SW18 59 A2
Dormstone Ho SE17 152 A3
Dornberg Cl SE3 53 C3
Dorncliffe Rd SW6 164 B2
Dorney NW3 12 A1
Dorney Ct SW6 58 A4
Dornfell St NW6 10 B3
Dornoch Ho 26 E3 26 B3
Dornton Rd SW12, SW17 73 B2
Dorothy Charrington Ho 1 SE22 64 C2
Dorothy Rd SW11 60 B4
Dorrien Wlk SW16 73 C2
Dorrington Point 20 E3 27 A2
Dorrington St EC1 107 B4
Dorrit Ho 2 W11 30 C1
Dorrit St SE1 137 A4
Dorset Bldgs EC4 108 A1
Dorset Cl NW1 102 C4
Dorset Ct 3 N1 16 A1
Dorset Mans 2 W6 47 C4
Dorset Mews SW1 132 A2
Dorset Pl E15 19 C2
Dorset Rd SW8 162 C2
Dorset Rise EC4 108 A1
Dorset Sq NW1 90 C1
Dorset St W1 103 A3
Dorton Cl 6 SE15 49 A3
Dorville Cres W6 39 A3
Doughty Ct 11 E1 32 A1
Doughty Mews WC1 94 C1
Doughty St WC1 94 C1
Douglas Bldgs SE1 137 A4
Douglas Ct 5 NW6 10 C1
Douglas Gracey Ho SW18 70 A4
Douglas Ho
Putney SW15 56 C1
Westminster SW1 147 B3
Douglas Johnstone Ho SW6 154 C3
Douglas Mews NW2 1 A1
Douglas Path E14 42 B1
Douglas Rd
Islington N1 15 B1
Kilburn NW6 23 B4
5 Newham E16 35 C4
Douglas Rd N N1 15 B2
Douglas Rd S N1 15 B2
Douglas St SW1 147 B3
Douglas Waite Ho NW6 11 A1
Douglas Way SE8 51 B3
Doulton Ho SE11 149 A4
Doulton Mews 4 NW6 11 A
Dounesforth Gdns SW18 71 A
Douro Pl W8 128 B
Douro St E3 26 C
Douthwaite Sq E1 125 C
Dovecote Gdns 8 SW14 55 C
Dove Ct EC2 109 B
Dovedale Cotts SW11 168 C
Dovedale Ho N16 6 C
Dovedale Rd SE22 65 A
Dovehouse St SW3 144 A
Dove Mews SW7 143 A
Dovercourt Rd SE22 64 B
Dover Ct
Clerkenwell EC1 96 A
17 Greenwich SE10 52 A
Dove Rd N1 15 C
Doverfield Rd SW2 74 A
Dover Flats SE1 152 B
Dover Ho
Brixton SE5 48 A
11 Deptford SE15 50 B
Dover House Rd SW15 57 A
Dover Mans 16 SW9 62 C
Dove Row E2 24 C
Dover Park Dr SW15 57 A

Dover St W1 118 C2
Dover Terr TW9 44 C1
Dover Yd W1 118 C2
Doves Yd N1 85 B3
Dovet Ct SW8 172 C4
Doveton Ho 7 E1 25 B1
Doveton St 8 E1 25 B1
Dove Wlk SW1 145 B2
Dovey Lo 4 N1 14 C1
Dowdeny Cl 12 NW5 13 B3
Dowdeswell Cl SW15 56 A3
Dowding Ho N6 3 C4
Dowell Ho SE21 76 B1
Dowes Ho 13 SW16 74 A1
Dowgate Hill EC4 123 B4
Dowland St W10 23 A2
Dowlas St SE5 49 A3
Dowlen Ct 14 E14 41 C4
Dowler Ho E1 111 C1
Downbarton Ho SW9 173 B4
Downbury Mews 13 SW18 58 C2
Downend Ct 1 SE15 49 A4
Downer's Cotts SW4 61 B3
Downey Ho 6 E1 25 C1
Downfield Cl W9 88 A1
Downham Ct 1 N1 15 C1
Downham Rd N1 15 C1
Downing Ho
2 North Kensington W10 30 C3
4 Putney SW15 56 C2
Downing St* SW1 134 A4
Down Pl W6 39 A1
Down St Mews W1 118 A1
Downs Ct 16 E8 17 A3
Downsell Prim Sch E15 19 C4
Downsell Rd E15 19 C4
Downshire Hill NW3 11 C4
Downside 2 SW15 58 A2
Downside Cres NW3 12 A3
Downs La 2 E5 17 A4
Downs Park Rd E5, E8 16 C3
Downs Rd E5, N16 16 C4
Down St W1 118 A1
Downsview Sch E5 17 A4
Downton Ave SW2 74 B2
Downtown Rd SE16 41 A4
Dowrey St N1 85 B4
Dowson Cl SE5 63 C3
Dowson Ct SE13 67 C4
Dowson Ho 8 E1 32 C3
Doyce St SE1 136 C4
Doyle Gdns NW10 22 A4
Doyle Ho W3 37 A4
D'Oyley St SW1 145 B4
Doynton St N19 4 A2
Draco St SE17 48 B4
Dragon Ct WC2 106 B2
Dragon Rd SE15 49 A4
Dragon Yd WC1 106 B2
Dragoon Rd SE8 41 B1
Dragor Rd NW10 20 B1
Drake Cl 30 SE16 40 C4
Drake Croft N16 6 C2
Drake Ct 5 W12 39 A4
Drakefell Rd SE4, SE14 65 C4
Drakefield Rd SW17 72 C1
Drake Ho
2 Limehouse E14 33 A2
20 Stepney E1 32 B4
Drakeley Ct N5 15 A4
Drake Rd SE4 66 C4
Drakes Ctyd NW6 10 B1
Drake St WC1 106 C3
Draper Ho SE1 150 B4
Draper Pl N1 86 B4
Drapers Almhouses 5 E3 26 C2
Drapers Gdns EC2 109 C2
Drapers Rd E15 19 C4
Drappers Way SE16 153 C4
Draycott Ave SW3 144 B3
Draycott Cl SE5 48 C3
Draycott Ct SW11 168 A4
Draycott Ho SW3 144 C3
Draycott Pl SW3 144 C3
Draycott Terr SW3 145 A3
Drayford Cl W9 23 B1
Dray Gdns SW2 62 B2
Draymans Ct 4 SW9 62 B4
Drayson Mews W8 127 C3
Drayton Ct SW10 143 A1
Drayton Gdns SW10 143 A1
Drayton Ho 14 SE5 48 C3
Drayton Park Mews 12 N5 14 C3
Drayton Park Prim Sch N5 14 C3
Drayton Park Sta N5 14 C3
Drayton Pk N5, N7 14 C4
Drayton Rd NW10 21 B4
Dreadnought St SE10 43 A3
Dresden Cl NW6 11 A2
Dresden Ho
Clapham SW11 169 B2
Lambeth SE11 149 A4
Dresden Rd N19 4 C3
Dressington Ave SE4 66 C1
Drewett Ho E1 111 C1
Drew Ho 12 SW16 74 A1
Drewstead La SW16 73 C2
Drewstead Rd SW16 73 C2
Driffield Rd E3 26 A3
Driftway Ho 19 E3 26 B3
Drinkwater Ho 11 SE5 48 C3
Drive Mans SW6 164 B2
Drive The
Acton W3 28 B3
Harlesden NW10 21 B4
Hendon NW11 1 A4
Islington N7 14 B2
Dr Johnson Ave SW17 73 A1
Dr Johnson's House Mus* EC4 107 C1
Droitwich Cl SE26 76 C1
Dromore Rd SW15 58 A1
Dron Ho E1 32 B4
Droop St W10 23 A1
Drovers Ct SE13 67 B4
Drovers Pl SE15 50 A3
Druce Rd SE21 64 A1
Druid St SE1 138 C3
Drummer Lo N7 5 B1
Drummond Cres NW1 93 B4
Drummond Gate SW1 147 C2
Drummond Ho 13 E2 24 C3
Drummond Rd SE16 40 A3
Drummonds Pl TW9 54 A3
Drummond St NW1 92 C2
Drum St E1 111 A2
Drury Ho SW8 170 C4
Drury La WC2 106 B1
Dryad St SW15 57 C4
Dryburgh Ho SW1 146 B2
Dryburgh Mans SW15 57 B4
Dryburgh Rd SW15 57 B4
Dryden Bldg E1 111 B2
Dryden Ct SE11 149 C3
Dryden Ho
6 Camberwell SE5 49 A2
16 Stoke Newington N16 7 A1
Dryden St WC2 106 B1
Dryfield Wlk 1 SE8 51 C4
Drysdale Flats 3 E8 16 B3
Drysdale Ho E2 24 A2 98 B4
Drysdale Pl N1 24 A2 98 B4
Drysdale St N1 24 A2 98 B4
Dublin Ave E8 24 C4
Ducal St E2 24 B2 99 A3
Ducane Cl 6 W12 30 B3
Du Cane Ct SW12 72 C3
Du Cane Rd W12 29 C3
Ducavel Ho SW2 74 B3
Duchess Mews W1 104 B3
Duchess of Bedford Ho W8 127 B4
Duchess of Bedford's Wlk W8 127 B3
Duchess St W1 104 B3
Duchy St SE1 121 C2
Ducie Ho 2 SW15 57 B2
Ducie St SW4 62 B3
Duckett St E1 33 A4
Duck La W1 105 B1
Du Cros Rd W3 29 A1
DUDDEN HILL 8 C3
Dudden Hill La NW10 8 B3
Dudley Ct
Marylebone W1 102 C1
Dudley Ct *continued*
St Giles WC2 106 A2
Dudley Ho
Brixton SW9 173 B2
Paddington W2 101 B3
Dudley Mews 14 SW2 62 C1
Dudley Rd
Kilburn NW6 23 B3
Richmond TW9 44 B1
Dudley St W2 101 B3
Dudmaston Mews SW3 143 C2
Duffell Ho SE11 149 A1
Dufferin Ave EC1 97 B1
Dufferin Ct EC1 97 B1
Dufferin St EC1 97 A1
Duffield Ho N4 6 B4
Duff St E14 34 A3
Dufour's Pl W1 105 A1
Dugard Way SE11 150 A3
Dugdale Ho 10 N7 13 C3
Duke Humphrey Rd SE3 53 A1
Duke of Wellington Pl SW1, W1 131 C4
Duke of York's Sq SW3 145 A3
Duke of York St SW1 119 A2
Duke Rd W4 37 C1
Duke St Hill SE1 123 C2
Duke St St James's SW1 119 A2
Duke's Ave W4 37 C1
Dukes Ct
Dulwich SE22 76 C3
East Dulwich SE22 65 A2
Lewisham SE13 52 B1
Mortlake SW14 45 C1
Dukes Gate 4 W4 37 B2
Dukes Head Yd N6 4 A3
Duke's Ho SW1 147 C4
Duke Shore Wharf E14 33 B2
Dukes La W8 128 A4
Duke's Mews W1 103 C2
Duke's Pl EC3 110 B1
Dukes Point N6 4 A3
Duke's Rd WC1 93 C3
Duke St W1 103 C1
Duke Street Mans W1 103 C1
Duke's Yd W1 117 C4
Dulas St N4 5 B3
Dulford St W11 31 A2 112 A4
Dulka Rd SW11 60 B2
Dulverton NW1 83 A3
Dulverton Mans WC1 95 A1
DULWICH 76 A1
Dulwich Coll SE21 76 A2
Dulwich Coll Picture Gall* SE21 76 A4
Dulwich Coll Prep Sch SE21 76 A1
Dulwich Comm SE21 76 A3
Dulwich Hamlet Jun Sch SE21 63 C1
Dulwich Hospl SE22 64 A3
Dulwich Lawn Cl SE22 64 B2
Dulwich Mead SE24 63 B1
Dulwich Mews
East Dulwich SE22 64 B2
1 East Dulwich SE22 64 B3
Dulwich Oaks The SE21 76 B1
Dulwich Rd SE24 63 A1
DULWICH VILLAGE 76 A4
Dulwich Village SE21 64 A1
Dulwich Village CE Inf Sch SE21 64 A1
Dumain Ct SE11 150 A3
Du Maurier Ho 2 NW3 12 B3
Dumbarton Ct 16 SW2 74 A4
Dumbarton Rd SW2 62 A1
Dumont Rd N16 7 A1
Dumphreys Ho 5 SW4 73 C4
Dumpton Pl NW1 12 C1
Dunbar St SE27 75 B1
Dunbar Wharf 20 E14 33 B2
Dunboyne Rd NW3 12 B3
Dunbridge Ho SW15 56 B1
Dunbridge St
Bethnal Green E2 25 A1
Bethnal Green E2 24 C1 99 C2
Duncan Ct 3 E14 34 B4
Duncan Gr W3 29 A3
Duncan Ho 3 NW3 12 B1
Duncannon Ho SW1 147 C1
Duncannon St WC2 120 A3
Duncan Rd
Hackney E8 25 A4
Richmond TW9 54 A3
Duncan St N1 86 A2
Duncan Terr N1 86 A2
Dunch St 33 E1 32 A3
Duncombe Ho 7 SW19 69 C3
Duncombe Prim Sch N19 5 A3
Duncombe Rd N19 4 C3
Duncrievie Rd SE13 67 C1
Dundalk Ho 2 E1 32 B3
Dundalk Rd SE4 66 A4
Dundas Ho 12 E2 25 B3
Dundas Rd SE15 50 B1
Dundee Ct 36 E1 32 A1
Dundee Ho W9 88 C4
Dundee St E1 32 A1
Dundee Wharf E14 33 B2
Dundonald Rd NW10 22 C4
Dundry Ho 8 SE26 76 C1
Dunelm Gr SE27 75 B1
Dunelm St E1 32 C3
Dunford Rd N7 14 B4
Dungarvan Ave SW15 56 C3

Dungeness Ho SW18 ... 59 B3
Dunhill Point 12 SW15 ... 69 A3
Dunkeld Ho 15 E14 ... 34 C3
Dunlace Rd E5 ... 17 C4
Dunlin Ct 12 SE21 ... 75 C2
Dunlin Ho 13 SE16 ... 40 C2
Dunloe Ct 7 E2 ... 24 B3
Dunloe St E2 ... 24 B3
Dunlop Pl SE16 ... 139 A1
Dunmore Point E2 ... 24 B2 98 C3
Dunmore Rd NW6 ... 23 A4
Dunmow Ho SE11 149 A2
Dunmow Rd E15 ... 19 C4
Dunmow Wlk N1 ... 86 C4
Dunnage Cres SE16 ... 41 A2
Dunne Mews 11 NW5 ... 13 B3
Dunnet Ho 27 E3 ... 26 B3
Dunnico Ho SE17 152 A2
Dunnock Ct 11 SE21 ... 75 C2
Dunn's Pas WC1 . 106 B2
Dunn St E8 ... 16 B3
Dunollie Pl NW5 ... 13 B3
Dunollie Rd NW5 ... 13 B3
Dunoon Ho N1 ... 84 C3
Dunraven Ho 12 TW9 ... 44 B2
Dunraven Rd W12 ... 29 C1
Dunraven Sch SW16 ... 74 B1
Dunraven St W1 . 117 A4
Dunrobin Ct NW3 ... 11 A3
Dunsany Rd W14 ... 39 C3
Dunsfold Ho 4 SW2 ... 74 B4
Dunsford Way SW15 ... 57 A1
Dunsmure Rd N16 ... 7 A3
Dunstable Ct 3 SE3 ... 53 C3
Dunstable Mews W1 ... 103 C4
Dunstable Rd TW10, TW9 ... 54 A3
Dunstall Ho 9 SE15 ... 49 C2
Dunstan Ho SE4 ... 51 B1
Dunstan Hos 5 E1 ... 32 B4
Dunstan Rd NW11 ... 1 C3
Dunstan's Gr SE22 ... 65 A1
Dunstan's Rd SE22 . 64 C1
Dunster Ct EC3 ... 124 B4
Dunster Gdns NW6 ... 10 B1
Dunsterville Way SE1 ... 137 C3
Dunston Rd
Clapham SW11 ... 169 C1
Hackney E8 ... 24 B4
Dunston St E8 ... 24 B4
Dunton Ho 14 SW16 ... 74 A1
Dunton Rd SE1 ... 152 C3
Duntshill Rd SW18 ... 71 A3
Dunworth Mews W11 ... 31 B3
Duplex Ride SW1 131 A3
Durand Gdns SW9 ... 173 A3
Durand Prim Sch SW9 ... 173 A4
Durant St E2 ... 24 C2 99 B4
Durban Ho 28 W12 ... 30 A2
Durdans Ho 3 NW1 ... 13 B1
Durfey Pl SE5 ... 48 C3
Durford Cres SW15 ... 69 A3
Durham Ct
Brockley SE4 ... 66 C4
4 Kilburn NW6 ... 23 C3
Durham Ho
7 Dartmouth Pk NW5 ... 4 B1
Lisson Gr NW8 ... 90 B3
Durham House St WC2 ... 120 B3
Durham Pl SW3 ... 144 C1
Durham Rd N4, N7 ... 5 B2
Durham Row E1 ... 33 A4
Durham St SE11 ... 162 C4
Durham Terr W2 . 100 A2
Durley Rd N16 ... 7 A4
Durlock Ho SW9 . 173 B4
Durlston Rd E5 ... 7 C2
Durnford St 4 SE10 ... 52 B4
Durnsford Ave SW18, SW19 ... 70 C2
Durnsford Rd SW18, SW19 ... 70 C1
Durrell Rd SW6 ... 164 C3
Durrels Ho W14 ... 141 A4
Durrington Rd E5 ... 18 A4
Durrington Twr SW8 ... 171 A2
Durrisdeer Ho NW2 ... 10 B4
Durston NW5 ... 12 C3
Durward St E1 ... 32 A4
Durweston Mews W1 ... 103 A4
Durweston St W1 103 A3
Dutch Yd SW18 ... 58 C2
Dutton Ho SW2 ... 75 A3
Dutton St SE10 ... 52 B2
Dwight Ct SW6 ... 164 B2
Dycer Ho 19 E9 ... 17 C2
Dye House La E3 ... 26 C4
Dyer Ho SE4 ... 51 A1
Dyer's Bldgs EC1 . 107 B3
Dyer's La SW15 ... 57 A3
Dykes Ct 11 SW2 ... 74 B3
Dylan Rd 2 SE24 ... 63 A3
Dylways SE5 ... 63 C3
Dymchurch Ho 12 E5 ... 17 A3
Dymes Path SW19 ... 69 C2
Dymock St SW6 ... 59 A4
Dyne Rd NW6 ... 10 B1
Dynevor Rd
Richmond TW10 ... 54 A2
Shacklewell N16 ... 7 B1
Dynham Rd NW6 ... 10 C1
Dyott St
Soho WC1 ... 105 C2
St Giles WC1, WC2 106 A2
Dysart St EC2 ... 24 A1 98 A1
Dyson Ho 3 SE10 ... 43 B1

E

Eade Rd N4 ... 6 B4
Eagle Cl SE16 ... 40 B1
Eagle Ct
10 Dulwich SE21 ... 75 C2
Holborn EC1 ... 108 A4
Eagle Dwellings EC1 ... 97 A4
Eagle Ho
22 Bethnal Green E1 ... 25 A1
Finsbury Pk N7 ... 5 B1
Eagle Hts 10 SW11 ... 60 A4
Eagle Lo NW11 ... 1 B4
Eagle Mans N16 ... 16 B3
Eagle Mews N1 ... 16 A2
Eagle Pl
South Kensington SW7 ... 143 A2
St James SW1 ... 119 A3
Eagle St WC1 ... 106 C3
Eagle Wharf SE1 . 124 C1
Eagle Wharf Rd N1 ... 87 A2
Eagle Works E1 ... 24 B1 99 A1
Eagling Cl E3 ... 26 C2
Ealing, Hammersmith & West London Coll W14 ... 140 A2
Ealing Tertiary Coll W3 ... 28 A1
Eamann Casey Ho SW9 ... 173 C3
Eamont Ct NW8 ... 80 B2
Eamont St NW8 ... 80 B2
Eardley Cres SW5 141 C1
Earldom Rd SW15 ... 57 B3
Earle Ho SW1 ... 147 C3
Earlham St WC2 ... 106 A1
Earl Ho NW1 ... 90 B1
Earlom Ho WC1 ... 95 B3
Earl Rd SW14 ... 55 B3
EARL'S COURT ... 141 C3
Earl's Court Ex Ctr★ SW5 ... 141 B1
Earl's Court Gdns SW5 ... 142 A3
Earl's Court Rd SW5, W8 ... 141 C4
Earl's Court Sq SW5 ... 142 A2
Earl's Court Sta SW5 ... 141 C3
Earlsferry Way N1 ... 14 A1
EARLSFIELD ... 71 B3
Earlsfield Prim Sch SW18 ... 71 B2
Earlsfield Rd SW18 ... 71 B4
Earlsfield Sta SW18 ... 71 B3
Earlsmead Rd NW10 ... 22 B2
Earl St EC2 ... 110 A4
Earls Terr W8 ... 127 A1
Earlsthorpe Mews 3 SW12 ... 60 C1
Earlstoke St EC1 ... 96 A4
Earlston Gr E9 ... 25 A4
Earls Wlk W8 ... 127 B1
Earlswood Cl 10 SE10 ... 43 A1
Earlswood Ho 2 SW2 ... 74 B3
Earlswood St SE10 ... 43 A1
Early Mews NW1 ... 82 B4
Earnshaw Ho EC1 . 96 B3
Earnshaw St WC1, WC2 ... 105 C2
Earsby St W14 ... 140 B4
Earth Galleries★ SW7 ... 129 C1
Eashing Point 5 SW15 ... 69 A3
Easleys Mews W1 ... 103 C2
EAST ACTON ... 29 A1
East Acton Arc W3 ... 29 B3
East Acton Ct W3 ... 29 A2
East Acton La W3 ... 29 A2
East Acton Prim Sch W3 ... 29 A2
East Acton Sta W12 ... 29 B3
East Arbour St E1 ... 32 C3
East Bank N16 ... 7 A4
East Block 5 E1 ... 32 C2
Eastbourne Ave W3 ... 28 C3
Eastbourne Gdns SW14 ... 55 B4
Eastbourne Mews W2 ... 101 A2
Eastbourne Rd W4 ... 45 B4
Eastbourne Terr W2 ... 101 A2
Eastbury Gr W4 ... 38 A1
Eastbury Terr E1 ... 25 C1
Eastcastle St W1 105 A2
Eastcheap EC3 ... 124 A4
East Churchfield Rd W3 ... 28 C1
Eastcote St SW9 . 172 C1
East Cross Ctr E15 ... 18 C2
East Cross Route
Bow E3 ... 26 C4
Hackney Wick E9 ... 18 B3
Eastdown Ho E8 ... 16 C4
Eastdown Pk SE13 ... 67 C3
EAST DULWICH ... 64 C2
East Dulwich Gr SE22 ... 64 A2
East Dulwich Rd SE15, SE22 ... 64 C3
East Dulwich Sta SE22 ... 64 A3
Eastern Rd SE4 ... 66 C3
East Ferry Rd E14 ... 42 A2
Eastfields Ave SW18 ... 58 C3
Eastfields Rd W3 ... 28 B4
Eastfield St E14 ... 33 A4
East Harding St EC4 ... 107 C2
East Heath Rd NW3 . 2 C1
East Hill SW18 ... 59 B2
East India Bldgs 9 E14 ... 33 C2
East India Ct 7 SE16 ... 40 B4
East India Dock Basin★ E14 ... 35 A2
East India Dock Rd E14 ... 34 A2
East India Dock Road Tunnel 18 E14 ... 34 C3
East India Sta E14 ... 34 C2
East La SE16 ... 139 B3
Eastlake Ho NW8 ... 89 C1
Eastlake Rd SE5 ... 48 B1
Eastlands Cres SE21 ... 64 B1
Eastleigh Wlk 9 SW15 ... 68 C4
East London Coll & Toynbee Theatre E1 ... 111 A3
East London Stad E3 ... 33 B4
Eastman Dental Hospl WC1 ... 94 C2
Eastman Ho 7 SW4 ... 61 B1
Eastman Rd W3 ... 37 C4
Eastmearn Rd SE21, SE27 ... 75 B2
East Mount St E1 ... 32 A4
Eastney St SE10 ... 42 C1
Easton Ho 4 SE27 ... 75 A1
Easton St WC1 ... 95 B2
East Parkside SE10 ... 43 B4
East Pas EC1 ... 108 C4
East Plaza E14 ... 34 A1
East Point SE1 ... 153 B2
East Poultry Ave EC1 ... 108 A3
East Putney Sta SW15 ... 58 A2
East Rd
Chelsea SW1 ... 145 B1
Shoreditch N1 ... 97 C4
East Row W10 ... 23 A1
Eastry Ho SW8 ... 162 A1
EAST SHEEN ... 55 C3
East Sheen Ave SW14 ... 55 C3
East Sheen Prim Sch SW14 ... 56 A3
East Smithfield E1 ... 125 A3
East St SE17 ... 151 B2
East Surrey Gr SE15 ... 49 B3
East Tenter St E1 111 A1
Eastvale W3 ... 29 B1
East View NW3 ... 2 C2
Eastway
South Hackney E3, E9 ... 26 A4
Temple Mills E9, E10 ... 18 C4
Eastwell Ho SE1 ... 137 C2
Eastwick Ct 2 SW19 ... 69 C3
Eastwood Cl 2 N7 ... 14 C3
Eaton Cl SW1 ... 145 B3
Eaton Dr SW9 ... 63 A3
Eaton Gate SW1 ... 145 B4
Eaton Ho
Battersea SW11 ... 167 C3
23 Limehouse E14 ... 33 B2
Eaton House Sch SW1 ... 145 B4
Eaton House The Manor Sch SW4 ... 61 A3
Eaton La SW1 ... 132 B1
Eaton Mans SW1 . 145 B3

Eaton Mews N SW1 131 C1
Eaton Mews S SW1 132 A1
Eaton Mews W SW1 145 C4
Eaton Pl SW1 131 C1
Eaton Row SW1 132 A1
Eaton Sq SW1 131 C1
Eaton Square Sch SW1 146 A4
Eaton Terr
Belgravia SW1 145 C4
Bow E3 26 A2
Eaton Terr Mews SW1 145 B4
Eatonville Rd SW17 72 B2
Eatonville Villas SW17 72 B2
Ebbisham Dr SW8 162 C3
Ebbsfleet Rd NW2 10 A4
Ebenezer Ho SE11 150 A3
Ebenezer Mussel Ho 5 E2 25 B3
Ebenezer St N1 97 B4
Ebley Cl SE15 49 B4
Ebner St SW18 59 A2
Ebony Ct NW10 8 B2
Ebony Ho
Bethnal Green E2 24 C2 99 B3
10 West Hampstead NW3 11 A2
Ebor Cotts SW15 68 A1
Ebor St E1, E2 24 B1 98 C2
Eburne Rd N7 5 A1
Ebury Bridge Rd SW1 145 C1
Ebury Mews
Belgravia SW1 146 A4
West Norwood SE27 75 A1
Ebury Mews E SW1 132 A1
Ebury Sq SW1 145 C3
Ebury St SW1 146 A4
Ecclesbourne Rd N1 15 B1
Eccles Ct SE11 149 A1
Eccles Rd SW11 60 B3
Eccleston Ho 1 SW2 62 C1
Eccleston Mews SW1 131 C1
Eccleston Pl SW1 146 A4
Eccleston Sq SW1 146 B3
Eccleston Sq Mews SW1 146 C3
Eccleston St SW1 146 A4
Eckford St N1 85 B2
Eckstein Rd SW11 60 A3
Edans Ct W12 38 B4
Edbrooke Rd W9 23 C1
Eddisbury Ho 7 SE26 76 C1
Eddiscombe Rd SW6 165 A2
Eddison Ct N19 5 A2
Eddystone Rd SE4 66 A2
Eddystone Twr SE8 41 A1
Edenbridge Cl 29 SE16 40 A1
Edenbridge Rd E9 17 C1
Eden Cl
Child's Hill NW3 1 C2
Kensington W8 127 C2
Edendale W3 28 A2
Eden Gr N7 14 B3
Edenham Way W10 31 B4
Eden Ho
15 Battersea SW11 60 A4
Lisson Gr NW8 90 A1
Edenhurst Ave SW6 58 B4
Eden Lodge NW6 9 C1
Eden Mews SW17 71 B1
Edensmuir Ct SE3 53 C3
Edensor Gdns W4 46 A3
Edensor Rd W4 46 A3
Edenvale St SW6 166 C1
Eden Way E3 26 B4
Edgar Ho
Homerton E9 18 A3
South Lambeth SW8 162 A2
Edgar Kail Way SE22 64 A3
Edgarley Terr SW6 164 A3
Edgar Rd E3 27 A2
Edgar Wallace Cl 4 SE15 49 A3
Edgcott Ho 2 W10 30 B4
Edgecombe Ho
4 London SE5 49 A1
Putney SW19 70 A4
Edgecote Cl 7 W3 28 B1
Edgehill Ho 4 SW9 48 A1
Edgeley La SW4 61 C4
Edgeley Rd SW4 61 C4
Edgel St SW18 59 A3
Edge St W8 31 C1 113 C2
Edgeworth Ho NW8 78 C4
Edgson Ho SW1 146 A2
Edgware Acad WC2 106 B1
Edgware Rd W1, W2, NW1, NW8 102 A3
Edgware Road Sta (Bakerloo) NW1 102 A3
Edgware Road Sta (Met, Distr, Circle) NW1 102 B3
Edinburgh Cl 7 E2 25 B3
Edinburgh Ct 10 SE16 32 C1
Edinburgh Ho
3 Acton W3 28 C3
Maida Vale W9 88 B4
Edington 20 NW5 12 C2
Edison Bldg 7 E14 41 C4
Edison Ct SE10 43 B3
Edison Ho SE1 151 B4
Edis St NW1 81 C4
Editha Mans SW10 156 C3
Edith Cavell Cl 2 N19 5 A4
Edith Gr SW10 157 A2
Edith Ho 6 W6 39 B1
Edithna St SW9 62 A4
Edith Neville Cotts NW1 93 B4
Edith Neville Prim Sch NW1 83 B1
Edith Ramsay Ho 2 E1 33 A4
Edith Rd
Stratford New Town E15 19 C3
West Kensington W14 140 B3
Edith Row SW6 166 B4
Edith St E2 24 C3
Edith Summerskill Ho SW6 154 C2
Edith Terr SW10 156 C2
Edith Villas W14 140 C2
Edith Yd SW10 157 A2
Edmeston Cl E9 18 A2
Edmond Ct SE14 50 B2
Edmonton Ct 5 SE16 40 B3
Edmund Halley Way SE10 43 A4
Edmund Ho
Kennington SE17 150 B1
New Cross Gate SE14 51 B2
Edmundsbury Ct Est 16 SW9 62 B3
Edmund St SE5 48 C3
Edmund Waller Prim Sch SE14 50 C1
Ednam Ho SE15 49 C4
Edna St SW11 168 A3
Edred Ho E9 18 A4
Edrich Ho SW4 172 A3
Edric Ho SW1 147 C4
Edric Rd SE14 50 C3
Edridge Ho 9 SE27 75 A1
Edward Alleyn Ho SE21 76 A4
Edward Ct 2 E16 35 C4
Edward Dodd Ct N1 97 C4
Edward Edward's Ho SE1 122 A1
Edwardes Pl W8 127 A1
Edwardes Sq W8 127 A1
Edward Friend Ho 6 N16 7 A1
Edward Ho
Paddington W2 89 B1
Vauxhall SE11 149 A2
Edward Kennedy Ho 18 W10 23 A1
Edward Mann Cl 13 E1 32 C3
Edward Mews NW1 82 B1
Edward Pl SE8 51 B4
Edward Robinson Ho 3 SE14 50 C3
Edward's Cotts 11 N1 15 A1
Edward's La N16 7 A2
Edwards Mews
Islington N1 14 C1
Marylebone W1 103 B1
Edward Sq
Islington N1 84 C3
1 Rotherhithe SE16 33 A1
Edward St SE14 51 B3
Edward VII Mans NW10 22 C2
Edward Wilson Prim Sch W2 100 A4
Edwin Ho SE15 49 C3
Edwin's Mead E9 18 A4
Edwin St
Bethnal Green E1 25 B1
Newham E16 35 C4
Edwy Ho E9 18 B4
Edwyn Ho SW18 59 A1
Effie Pl SW6 155 C1
Effie Rd SW6 155 C1
Effingham Ho SW8 171 B1
Effra Ct SW2 62 B2
Effra Mans SW2 62 C2
Effra Par SW2 62 C2
Effra Rd SW2 62 C2
Effra Road Ret Pk SW2 62 C2
EF International Language Sch SE1 121 C1
Egbert Ho E9 18 A3
Egbert St NW1 81 B4
Egbury Ho SW15 56 B1
Egerton Cres SW3 144 B4
Egerton Ct 5 TW10 54 A2
Egerton Dr SE10 52 A2
Egerton Gdns
Knightsbridge SW3 130 A1
Willesden NW10 22 B4
Egerton Gdns Mews SW3 130 B1
Egerton Ho W4 45 B4
Egerton Pl SW3 130 B1
Egerton Rd N16 7 B4
Egerton Terr SW3 130 B1
Egham Cl SW19 70 A2
Eglantine Rd SW18 59 B2
Eglington Ct SE17 48 B4
Egliston Mews SW15 57 B4
Egliston Rd SW15 57 B4
Egmont St SE14 50 C3
Egremont Ho SE13 52 A1
Egremont Rd SE27 74 C1
Egret Ho 11 SE16 40 C2
Eider Ct 33 SE8 51 B4
Elaine Ct 13 NW3 12 B2
Elaine Gr NW5 12 C3
Elaine Ho N4 5 A3
Elam Cl SE5 48 A1
Elam St SE5 48 A1
Elan Ct E1 32 A4
Eland Rd SW11 60 B4
Elba Pl SE17 151 A4
Elbe St SW6 166 C2
Elborough St SW18 70 C3
Elbury Dr E16 35 C3
Elcho St SW11 158 B1
Elcot Ave SE15 50 A3
Elderberry Rd W5 36 A4
Elderfield Ho 4 E14 33 C2
Elderfield Rd E5 17 B4
Elder St E1 24 B1 98 C1
Elder Wlk
Islington N1 86 B4
2 Lewisham SE13 67 B4
Eldon Ct NW6 23 C4
Eldon Gr NW3 11 C3
Eldon Ho SW9 63 A4
Eldon Rd W8 128 B1
Eldon St EC2 109 C3
Eldon Way NW10 20 A3
Eldridge Ct SE16 139 B1
Eleanor Cl SE16 40 C4
Eleanor Ct 13 E2 24 C4
Eleanor Gr SW13 56 A4
Eleanor Ho
18 Hammersmith W6 39 B1
1 Kentish Town NW5 13 B3
Eleanor Palmer Prim Sch NW5 13 B4
Eleanor Rathbone Ho 1 N6 4 C4
Eleanor Rd E8 17 A1
Eleanor St E3 26 C2
Electra Ct 6 NW2 9 B2
Electric Ave SW9 62 C3
Electric Ho 13 E3 26 C2
Electric La 2 SW9 62 C3
Electric Mans 1 SW9 62 C3
Elephant & Castle
Newington SE1 150 B4
Newington SE1 136 B1
Elephant & Castle Sh Ctr SE1 150 C4
Elephant & Castle Sta
Lambeth SE1 136 B1
Newington SE17 150 C4
Elephant La SE16 40 B4
Elephant Rd SE17 150 C4
Elfindale Rd SE24 63 B2
Elfort Rd N5 14 C4
Elf Row E1 32 B2
Elgar Ave W5 36 A4
Elgar Cl SE8 51 C3
Elgar Ct W14 126 A1
Elgar Ho
Pimlico SW1 146 B1
South Hampstead NW6 11 B1
Elgar St SE16 41 A3
Elgin Ave
Hammersmith W12 39 A3
Westbourne Green W9 88 B4
Elgin Cl W12 39 A4
Elgin Cres W11 31 A2 112 B4
Elgin Ct W9 88 A2
Elgin Ho 8 E14 34 A3
Elgin Mans W9 88 A3
Elgin Mews W11 31 A3
Elgin Mews N W9 88 B4
Elgin Mews S W9 88 B4
Elgood Cl W11 31 A1 112 A1
Elgood Ho NW8 79 C1
Elham Ho 13 E5 17 A3
Elia Mews N1 86 A1
Elias Pl SW8 163 B3
Elia St N1 86 A1
Elim Est SE1 138 A2

Elim St SE1 ... 138 A2
Eliot Cotts SE3 ... 53 A1
Eliot Ct SW18 ... 59 A1
Eliot Gdns SW15 ... 56 C3
Eliot Hill SE13 ... 52 B1
Eliot Ho [10] TW10 ... 54 B1
Eliot Mews NW8 ... 78 C1
Eliot Pk SE13 ... 52 B1
Eliot Pl SE3 ... 53 A1
Eliot Vale SE3 ... 52 C1
Elizabeth Ave
Islington N1 ... 15 C1
Shoreditch N1 ... 87 A4
Elizabeth Barnes Ct SW6 ... 166 B2
Elizabeth Blount Ct [4] E14 ... 33 A3
Elizabeth Cl
Paddington W9 ... 89 A1
[12] Poplar E14 ... 34 A3
Elizabeth Cooper Lo SW12 ... 60 C1
Elizabeth Cotts [5] TW9 ... 44 C2
Elizabeth Ct
Chelsea SW10 ... 157 C3
East Dulwich SE22 ... 64 C3
Marylebone NW8 ... 90 B2
Westminster SW1 ... 133 C1
Elizabeth Finn Ho [1] W12 ... 38 C3
Elizabeth Garrett Anderson Hospl NW1 ... 93 A1
Elizabeth Garrett Anderson Language Coll N1 ... 85 A1
Elizabeth Gdns W3 ... 29 B1
Elizabeth Ho
[15] Hammersmith W6 ... 39 B1
Lambeth SE11 ... 149 C3
Elizabeth Ind Est SE14 ... 50 C4
Elizabeth Kenny Ho N1 ... 15 B2
Elizabeth Mews
[28] Hackney E2 ... 24 C3
Maitland Pk NW3 ... 12 B2
Elizabeth Selby Inf Sch E2 ... 24 C2 99 C4
Elizabeth Sq [13] SE16 ... 33 A2
Elizabeth St SW1 ... 145 C4
Elkington Point SE11 ... 149 B3
Elkstone Rd W10 ... 31 B4
Ellacombe Ho [1] SW2 ... 74 C4
Ellaline Rd W6 ... 47 C4
Ella Mews NW3 ... 12 B4
Elland Ho [18] E14 ... 33 B3
Elland Rd SE15 ... 65 B3
Ella Rd N4, N8 ... 5 A4
Ellenborough Ho [5] W12 ... 30 A2
Ellenborough Pl SW15 ... 56 C3
Ellen St E1 ... 111 C1
Ellen Wilkinson Ho
[7] Globe Town E2 ... 25 C2
West Brompton SW6 ... 155 A3
Ellerby St SW6 ... 47 C2
Ellerdale Cl [15] NW3 ... 11 B4
Ellerdale Rd NW3 ... 11 B3
Ellerdale St SE13 ... 67 A4
Ellerker Gdns TW10 ... 54 A1
Ellerslie Gdns NW10 ... 21 C4
Ellerslie Ind Est SW2 ... 62 A2
Ellerslie Rd W12 ... 30 A1
Ellerton Ct W3 ... 37 A4
Ellerton Rd
Barnes SW13 ... 46 C2
Wandsworth SW17, SW18 ... 71 C3
Ellery Cl [5] NW10 ... 21 B3
Ellery Ho SE17 ... 151 C3
Ellery St SE15 ... 50 A1
Ellesmere Ct W4 ... 45 C4
Ellesmere Rd
Bow E3 ... 26 A3
Chiswick W4 ... 45 C4
Willesden NW10 ... 8 C3
Ellesmere St E14 ... 34 A3
Ellingfort Rd E8 ... 17 A1
Ellingham Rd
Leyton E15 ... 19 C4
Shepherd's Bush W12 ... 38 C4
Ellington Ho SE1 ... 137 A1
Ellington St N7 ... 14 C2
Elliott Rd
Acton W4 ... 38 A2
Brixton SW9 ... 48 A2
Camberwell SW9 ... 48 A2
Elliott Sch SW15 ... 57 B1
Elliott's Pl N1 ... 86 B3
Elliott Sq NW3 ... 12 A1
Elliott's Row SE11 ... 150 B4
Ellis Cl NW10 ... 9 B2
Ellisfield Dr SW15 ... 68 C4
Ellis Franklin Ct NW8 ... 78 C2
Ellis Ho SE17 ... 151 B2
Ellison Ho [1] SE13 ... 52 B1
Ellison Rd SW13 ... 46 B1
Ellis St SW1 ... 145 B4
Ellsworth St E2 ... 25 A2
Ellwood Ct W9 ... 88 B1
Elmar Ct SW6 ... 164 B2
Elm Bank Gdns SW13 ... 46 A1
Elm Bank Mans SW13 ... 46 A1
Elmbourne Rd SW17 ... 73 A1
Elmbridge Wlk E8 ... 16 C1
Elm Cl N19 ... 4 B2
Elmcourt Rd SE21, SE27 ... 75 A2
Elm Court Sch SE27 ... 75 B2
Elm Cres W5 ... 36 A4
Elmcroft N6 ... 4 B4
Elmcroft Ave NW11 ... 1 B4
Elmcroft Cres NW11 ... 1 A4
Elmcroft St E5 ... 17 B4
Elm Ct
Brixton SW9 ... 173 B4
Lewisham SE13 ... 67 C4
[42] Notting Hill W2 ... 31 C4
Strand EC4 ... 121 B4
Elmer Ho NW1 ... 102 A4
Elmfield Ho
[6] Canonbury N5 ... 15 B3
Elmfield Ho *continued*
Paddington W9 ... 23 C1
Elmfield Mans [5] SW17 ... 72 C2
Elmfield Rd SW17 ... 73 A2
Elmfield Way W9 ... 31 C4
Elm Friars Wlk NW1 ... 13 C1
Elm Gn W3 ... 29 A3
Elm Gr
Cricklewood NW2 ... 9 C4
Peckham SE15 ... 49 C1
Elm Grove Rd
Barnes SW13 ... 46 C1
Ealing W5 ... 36 A4
Elm Ho [4] E14 ... 42 B4
Elmhurst Mans SW4 ... 61 C4
Elmhurst St SW4 ... 61 C4
Elmhurst Villas SE15 ... 65 B3
Elmington Rd SE5 ... 48 C3
Elmira St SE13 ... 67 A4
Elm Lo SW6 ... 47 C2
Elmore Ho SW9 ... 48 A1
Elmore St N1 ... 15 C1
Elm Park Gdns SW10 ... 143 B1
Elm Park Ho SW10 ... 143 B1
Elm Park La SW3 ... 143 B1
Elm Park Mans SW10 ... 157 A4
Elm Park Rd SW3 ... 157 B4
Elm Pk SW2 ... 74 B4
Elm Pl SW7 ... 143 B2
Elm Quay SW8 ... 161 B3
Elm Rd SW14 ... 55 B3
Elm Row NW3 ... 2 B1
Elms Cres SW4 ... 61 C1
Elmshaw Rd SW15 ... 56 C2
Elmslie Point [2] E3 ... 33 B4
Elms Mews W2 ... 115 B4
Elms Rd SW4 ... 61 B2
Elm St WC1 ... 95 A1
Elms The
Barnes SW13 ... 56 B4
[3] Harlesden NW10 ... 21 A3
Elmstone Rd SW6 ... 165 B4
Elm Terr NW2 ... 1 C1
Elmton Ct NW8 ... 89 B2
Elm Tree Cl NW8 ... 89 B4
Elm Tree Ct
[5] Camberwell SE5 ... 48 B2
St John's Wood NW8 ... 89 B4
Elm Tree Rd NW8 ... 89 B4
Elm Way NW10 ... 8 A4
Elm Wlk NW3 ... 1 C2
Elmwood Ct SW11 ... 170 A4
Elm Wood Prim Sch SE27 ... 75 C1
Elmwood Rd
Chiswick W4 ... 45 B4
Herne Hill SE24 ... 63 C2
Elmworth Gr SE21 ... 75 C2
Elnathan Mews W9 ... 88 B1
Elphinstone St N5 ... 15 A4
Elrington Rd E8 ... 16 C2
Elsa St E1 ... 33 A4
Elsdale Ho [14] E9 ... 17 B2
Elsdale St E9 ... 17 B1
Elsden Mews E2 ... 25 B3
Elsenham St SW18, SW19 ... 70 B2
Elsfield NW5 ... 13 A3
Elsham Rd W14 ... 126 A3
Elsham Terr W14 ... 126 A3
Elsie Lane Ct W2 ... 100 A3
Elsiemaud Rd SE4 ... 66 B2
Elsie Rd SE22 ... 64 B3
Elsinore Gdns NW2 ... 1 A1
Elsinore Ho
[12] Camberwell SE5 ... 48 B1
Islington N1 ... 85 B3
Elsinore Way TW9 ... 55 A4
Elsley Rd SW11 ... 60 C4
Elsley Sch SW11 ... 60 C4
Elspeth Rd SW11 ... 60 B3
Elstead Ho [9] SW2 ... 74 B4
Elsted St SE17 ... 151 C3
Elstow Grange NW6 ... 9 C1
Elswick Rd SE13 ... 52 A1
Elswick St SW6 ... 166 C2
Elsworthy Rd NW3 ... 80 A4
Elsworthy Rise NW3 ... 12 A1
Elsworthy Terr NW3 ... 12 A1
Elsynge Rd SW18 ... 59 C2
Elsynge Road Mans SW18 ... 59 C2
Elthiron Rd SW6 ... 165 C3
Elthorne Rd N19 ... 4 C2
Elthruda Rd SE13 ... 67 C1
Elton Ho [3] E3 ... 26 B4
Elton Pl N16 ... 16 A3
Elton St [11] N16 ... 16 A3
Eltringham St SW18 ... 59 B3
Elvaston Mews SW7 ... 129 A2
Elvaston Pl SW7 ... 129 A1
Elveden Ho [17] SW9 ... 63 A3
Elver Gdns E2 ... 24 C2 99 C4
Elverson Rd SE8 ... 52 A1
Elverson Rd Sta SE8 ... 52 A1
Elverton St SW1 ... 147 B4
Elvin Ho [2] E9 ... 17 B2
Elvis Rd NW2 ... 9 B2
Elwin St E2 ... 24 C2 99 B4
Elwood Ho N5 ... 6 A1
Elwood St N4, N5 ... 6 A1
Elworth Ho SW8 ... 163 A1
Ely Cotts SW8 ... 162 C1
Ely Court Flats SW6 ... 164 A3
Ely Ct Holborn EC1 ... 107 C3
[3] Maida Vale NW6 ... 23 C3
Ely Ho [22] SE15 ... 49 C3
Ely Pl EC1 ... 107 C3
Elysium Gate SW6 ... 164 C2
Elysium Pl SW6 ... 164 C1
Elysium St SW6 ... 164 C1
Elystan Ct SW15 ... 57 A2
Elystan Pl SW3 ... 144 C2
Elystan St SW3 ... 144 B3
Elystan Wlk N1 ... 85 B3
Emanuel Ave W3 ... 28 B3
Emanuel Ct W3 ... 28 C3
Emanuel Sch SW11 ... 60 A2
Embankment SW15 ... 47 C1
Embankment Gdns SW3 ... 159 A4
Embankment Pier WC2 ... 120 B2
Embankment Pl WC2 ... 120 B2
Embankment Sta WC2 ... 120 B2
Embassy Ct NW8 ... 79 C1
Embassy Ho [2] NW6 ... 10 C1
Emba St SE16 ... 139 C3
Ember Ct [2] W12 ... 38 A3
Emberton SE5 ... 49 A4
Emberton Ct EC1 ... 96 A3
Embleton Rd SE13 ... 67 A3
Emden St SW6 ... 166 B4
Emerald Rd NW10 ... 20 C4
Emerald St WC1 ... 106 C4
Emerson Ho N16 ... 16 A3
Emerson St SE1 ... 122 C2
Emery Hill St SW1 ... 133 A1
Emery St SE1 ... 135 C2
Emily St [7] E16 ... 35 B3
Emirates Stad (Arsenal FC) N7 ... 14 C4
Emlyn Gdns [3] W12 ... 38 A3
Emlyn Rd W12 ... 38 B3
Emmanuel CE Prim Sch NW6 ... 10 C3
Emmanuel Ho
Dulwich SE21 ... 75 C1
Lambeth SE11 ... 149 B3
Emmanuel Rd SW12 ... 73 C3
Emma St E2 ... 25 A3
Emminster NW6 ... 78 A4
Emmott Cl E1 ... 26 A1
Emperor's Gate SW7 ... 142 C4
Empingham Ho [20] SE8 ... 40 C2
Empire Ho SW3 ... 130 A1
Empire Sq N19 ... 5 A1
Empire Wharf E3 ... 26 A4
Empire Wharf Rd E14 ... 42 C2
Empress Mews [36] SE5 ... 48 B1
Empress Pl SW5 ... 141 B1
Empress St SE17 ... 48 B4
Empson St E3 ... 27 A
Emsworth St SW2 ... 74 B
Emu Rd SW8 ... 170 A
Enard Ho [28] E3 ... 26 B
Enbrook St W10 ... 23 A
Enclave Ct EC1 ... 96 B
Endell St WC2 ... 106 A
Enderby St SE10 ... 43 A
Endlesham Ct [2] SW12 ... 72 C
Endlesham Rd SW12 ... 72 C
Endsleigh Gdns WC1 ... 93 B
Endsleigh Mans [4] SW16 ... 74 A
Endsleigh Pl WC1 ... 93 C
Endsleigh St WC1 ... 93 C
Endwell Rd SE4 ... 51 A
Endymion Rd
Harringay N4 ... 6 A
Tulse Hill SW2 ... 62 B

Energen Cl NW10 ... 8 A2
Enfield Cloisters N1 ... 24 A2 98 A4
Enfield Ho SW9 ... 172 B2
Enfield Rd
De Beauvoir Town E8, N1 ... 16 A1
South Acton W3 ... 37 A4
Enford St W1 ... 102 C4
Engadine St SW18 ... 70 C3
Engate St SE13 ... 67 B3
England's La NW3 ... 12 B2
Englefield NW1 ... 92 C3
Englefield Rd N1 ... 16 A1
Englewood Rd SW12 ... 61 B1
English Gardening Sch The SW3 ... 158 C4
English Grounds SE1 ... 124 A1
English Martyrs RC Prim Sch E1 ... 111 A1
English St E3 ... 26 B1
Enid St SE16 ... 139 A2
Enid Stacy Ho 11 N19 ... 4 C4
Enmore Ct SW14 ... 55 C2
Enmore Gdns SW14 ... 55 C2
Enmore Rd SW15 ... 57 B2
Ennerdale Ho 3 N4 ... 6 C4
Ennerdale Rd TW9 ... 44 B1
Ennersdale Rd SE13 ... 67 C2
Ennis Ho 16 E14 ... 34 A3
Ennismore Ave W4 ... 38 B2
Ennismore Gdns SW7 ... 130 A2
Ennismore Gdns Mews SW7 ... 130 A2
Ennismore Mews SW7 ... 130 A2
Ennismore St SW7 ... 130 A2
Ennis Rd N4 ... 5 C3
Ensbury Ho SW8 ... 162 C2
Ensign Ct E1 ... 125 C3
Ensign Ho 19 E14 ... 41 C4
Ensign St E1 ... 125 B4
Ensor Mews SW7 ... 143 B2
Enterprise Ho 36 E9 ... 17 B1
Enterprise Way
College Pk NW10 ... 21 C2
Wandsworth SW18 ... 58 C3
Enterprize Way SE8 ... 41 B2
Epirus Mews SW6 ... 155 B2
Epirus Rd SW6 ... 155 A2
Epping Cl E14 ... 41 C2
Epping Ho 8 E5 ... 7 C2
Epping Pl N1 ... 14 C2
Epple Rd SW6 ... 165 A4
Epstein Ct N1 ... 86 B3
Epworth St EC2 ... 97 C1
Equity Sq E2 ... 24 B2 99 A3
Erasmus St SW1 ... 147 C3
Erconwald St W12 ... 29 B3
Eresby Ho SW7 ... 130 B3
Eresby Pl NW6 ... 10 C1
Erica Ct SW4 ... 172 B3
Erica Ho SE4 ... 66 B4
Erica St W12 ... 29 C2
Ericcson Cl SW18 ... 58 C2
Eric Fletcher Ct 15 N1 ... 15 B1
Eric Macdonald Ho SW6 ... 165 C3
Eric Rd NW10 ... 8 B2
Ericson Ho
London SE13 ... 67 C3
Stamford Hill N16 ... 7 B3
Eric St E3 ... 26 B1
Eric Wilkins Ho SE1 ... 153 B1
Eridge Ho SE22 ... 64 B4
Eridge Rd W4 ... 37 C3
Erin Ct NW2 ... 9 B2
Erlanger Rd SE14 ... 50 C1
Ermine Rd SE13 ... 67 A3
Ernest Bevin Coll SW17 ... 72 A2
Ernest Gdns W4 ... 45 A4
Ernest Simmonds Ho SE14 ... 50 B1
Ernest St E1 ... 25 C1
Ernshaw Pl SW15 ... 58 A2
Eros (Shaftesbury Meml)* W1 ... 119 B3
Erpingham Rd SW15 ... 57 B4
Errington Rd W9 ... 23 B1
Errol St EC1 ... 97 A1
Erskine Ho SW1 ... 146 C1
Erskine Rd NW3 ... 12 B1
Escuan Lo N5 ... 15 B3
Esher Gdns SW19 ... 69 C2
Esher Ho SW8 ... 171 C2
Eskdale NW1 ... 82 C1
Esk Ho E3 ... 26 B1
Esme Ho SW15 ... 56 B3
Esmeralda Rd SE1 ... 153 C3
Esmond Ct W8 ... 128 B2
Esmond Gdns W4 ... 37 C2
Esmond Rd
Acton W4 ... 37 C3
Kilburn NW6 ... 23 B4
Esmond St SW15 ... 58 A3
Esparto St SW18 ... 71 A4
Espirit Ct E1 ... 110 C3
Espirit Ho 6 SW15 ... 58 A2
Essendine Mans W9 ... 23 C2
Essendine Prim Sch W9 ... 23 C2
Essendine Rd W9 ... 23 C2
Essex Ct
Barnes SW13 ... 46 B1
Hammersmith W6 ... 39 B3
Holborn EC4 ... 107 B1
Essex Ho 2 E14 ... 34 A3
Essex Park Mews W3 ... 29 A1
Essex Pl W4 ... 37 B2
Essex Place Sq 5 W4 ... 37 C2
Essex Rd Acton W3 ... 28 B2
Chiswick W4 ... 37 C2
Islington N1 ... 86 B4
Willesden NW10 ... 8 A1
Essex Road Sta N1 ... 15 B1
Essex St WC2 ... 121 B4
Essex Villas W8 ... 127 B3
Essian St E1 ... 33 A4
Essington SW15 ... 58 A1
Estcourt Rd SW6 ... 154 C2
Estella Ho 15 W11 ... 30 C2
Estelle Rd NW3 ... 12 B4
Esterbrooke St SW1 ... 147 B3
Este Rd SW11 ... 60 A4
Estoria Cl 22 SW2 ... 74 C4
Etal Ho N1 ... 15 A1
Etchingham Rd E15 ... 19 B4
Eternit Wlk SW6 ... 47 C2
Ethelbert Ho E9 ... 18 A4
Ethelbert St SW12 ... 73 A3
Ethelburga St SW11 ... 168 B4
Ethelburga Twr SW11 ... 168 B4
Ethelden Rd W12 ... 30 A1
Ethel Rankin Ct SW6 ... 164 C2
Ethel St SE17 ... 151 A3
Ethelworth Ct 4 SW2 ... 74 C3
Etherow St SE22 ... 76 C4
Ethnard Rd SE15 ... 50 A4
Eton Ave NW3 ... 12 A1
Eton Cl SW18 ... 71 A4
Eton College Rd NW3 ... 12 B2
Eton Ct NW3 ... 11 C1
Eton Garages 11 NW3 ... 12 A2
Eton Hall NW3 ... 12 B2
Eton Ho
Hackney E9 ... 18 B2
Highbury N5 ... 15 A4
Eton Pl NW1 ... 12 C1
Eton Rd NW3 ... 12 B2
Eton Rise NW3 ... 12 B2
Eton St TW10 ... 54 A2
Eton Villas NW3 ... 12 B2
Etta St SE8 ... 51 A4
Ettrick St E14 ... 34 B3
Eugene Cotter Ho SE17 ... 151 C3
Eugenia Rd SE16 ... 40 B2
Euro Cl NW10 ... 8 C2
Eurolink Bsns Ctr SW2 ... 62 C2
Europa Pl EC1 ... 96 C3
Eustace Bldg SW8 ... 160 A3
Eustace Ho SE11 ... 148 C4
Eustace Rd SW6 ... 155 B2
Euston Rd NW1 ... 93 A2
Euston Sq NW1 ... 93 B3
Euston Square Sta WC1 ... 93 A2
Euston St NW1 ... 93 A3
Euston Sta NW1 ... 93 B3
Euston Underpass NW1 ... 92 C2
Evandale Rd SW9 ... 173 C2
Evangelist Rd NW5 ... 13 A4
Evans Cl E8 ... 16 B2
Evans Ho
34 Shepherd's Bush W12 ... 30 A2
South Lambeth SW8 ... 161 C1
Evelina Mans 9 SE5 ... 48 C3
Evelina Rd SE15 ... 50 B1
Eveline Lowe Prim Sch SE1 ... 153 C1
Evelyn Ct
Marylebone W1 ... 102 C1
Evelyn Ct *continued*
Shacklewell E8 ... 16 C4
Shoreditch N1 ... 87 B1
Evelyn Denington Ct 2 N1 ... 15 A1
Evelyn Fox Ct W10 ... 30 B4
Evelyn Gdns
Richmond TW9 ... 54 A3
South Kensington SW7 ... 143 B1
Evelyn Ho
Bedford Pk W12 ... 38 B4
3 Brixton SW2 ... 62 B2
Spitalfields E1 ... 111 B3
Evelyn Rd
Acton W4 ... 37 C3
Richmond TW9 ... 54 A4
Evelyn St SE8 ... 41 A1
Evelyn Terr TW9 ... 54 A4
Evelyn Wlk N1 ... 87 B1
Evelyn Yd W1 ... 105 B2
Evenwood Cl SW15 ... 58 A2
Everard Ho E1 ... 111 C1
Everatt Cl SW18 ... 58 B2
Everdon Rd SW13 ... 46 C4
Everest Pl E14 ... 34 B4
Everett Ho
Islington N7 ... 14 C4
Walworth SE17 ... 151 B2
Evergreen Sq 3 E8 ... 16 B1
Everilda St N1 ... 85 A3
Evering Rd E5, N16 ... 7 C1
Everington St W6 ... 47 C4
Everitt Rd NW10 ... 20 C2
Everleigh St N4 ... 5 B3
Eversfield Rd TW9 ... 44 B1
Evershed Ho E1 ... 111 A2
Evershed Wlk W4 ... 37 C2
Eversholt St NW1 ... 93 B4
Evershot Rd N4 ... 5 B3
Eversleigh Rd SW11 ... 169 B1
Eversley Ho E2 ... 24 C2 99 B3
Everthorpe Rd SE15 ... 64 B4
Everton Bldgs NW1 ... 92 C3
Evesham Ct 2 TW10 ... 54 B1
Evesham Ho
1 Bethnal Green E2 ... 25 B3
Pimlico SW1 ... 146 B2
St John's Wood NW8 ... 78 C3
Evesham St W11 ... 30 C2
Evesham Way SW11 ... 60 C4
Evesham Wlk
Brixton SW9 ... 173 B2
Camberwell SE5 ... 48 C1
Ewald Rd SW6 ... 164 C1
Ewart Pl 13 E3 ... 26 B3
Ewe Cl N7 ... 14 A2
Ewen Cres SW2 ... 74 C4
Ewen Henderson Ct 10 SE14 ... 51 A3
Ewen Ho N1 ... 84 C3
Ewer St SE1 ... 122 C1
Ewhurst 18 SW15 ... 57 C1
Ewhurst Cl E1 ... 32 B4
Ewhurst Rd SE4 ... 66 B1
Exbury Ho
Hackney E9 ... 17 B2
4 London SW9 ... 62 B3
Excel Ct WC2 ... 119 C3
Excelsior Gdns SE13 ... 52 B1
Excelsior Ind Est SE16 ... 50 B4
Exchange Arc EC2 ... 110 B4
Exchange Ct WC2 ... 120 B3
Exchange Mans 2 NW11 ... 1 B4
Exchange Pl EC2 ... 110 A4
Exeter Ct NW6 ... 23 C3
Exeter Ho
Paddington W2 ... 100 C2
11 Peckham SE15 ... 49 C4
Putney SW15 ... 57 B1
Exeter Mans NW2 ... 10 A2
Exeter Mews
Fulham SW6 ... 155 B2
12 Hampstead NW6 ... 11 A2
Exeter Rd
Brondesbury NW2 ... 10 A2
Newham E16 ... 35 C4
Exeter St WC2 ... 120 C4
Exeter Way 2 SE14 ... 51 B3
Exford Ct SW11 ... 167 C4
Exhibition Cl W12 ... 30 B2
Exhibition Rd SW7 ... 129 C2
Exmoor Ho 25 E3 ... 26 A3
Exmoor St W10 ... 30 C4
Exmouth Ho
Clerkenwell EC1 ... 95 C2
6 Millwall E14 ... 42 A2
Exmouth Market EC1 ... 95 C2
Exmouth Mews NW1 ... 93 A3
Exmouth Pl E8 ... 17 A1
Exmouth St E1 ... 32 B3
Exonbury NW8 ... 78 B3
Exon St SE17 ... 152 A3
Explorers Ct 6 E14 ... 34 C2
Express Wharf 10 E14 ... 41 C4
Exton St SE1 ... 121 B1
Eynella Rd SE21 ... 76 B4
Eynham Rd W12 ... 30 B3
Eynsford Ho
Borough The SE1 ... 137 B4
12 Deptford SE15 ... 50 B4
Walworth SE17 ... 152 A3
Eyot Gdns W6 ... 38 B1
Eyot Gn W4 ... 38 B1
Eyre Ct NW8 ... 79 B2
Eyre St Hill EC1 ... 95 B1
Eythorne Rd SW9 ... 173 C3
Ezra St E2 ... 24 B2 99 A4

F

Fabian Rd SW6 ... 155 A2
Fabyc Ho TW9 ... 44 C3
Fairacres SW15 ... 56 C3
Fairbairn Gn 1 SW9 ... 48 A2
Fairbriar Residence SW7 ... 143 A4

Fairbridge Rd N19...4 C2
Fairburn Ct SW15..58 A2
Fairburn Ho
9 Stamford Hill N16...7 A3
West Kensington SW5...141 A1
Fairby Ho SE1...153 A4
Faircharm Trad Est SE8...52 A3
Fairchild Cl SW11 167 C1
Fairchild Ho
13 Hackney E9...17 B1
Pimlico SW1...147 A3
Shoreditch N1...24 A2 98 A4
Fairchild Pl EC2...24 A1 98 B1
Fairchild St EC2...24 A1 98 B1
Fairclough St E1...111 C1
Faircourt 14 NW3..12 B2
Faircroft N16...6 C3
Fairdale Gdns SW15...57 A3
Fairdene Ct N7...14 A3
Fairfax Ho
Brixton SW9...173 C1
6 Putney SW15...56 C2
Fairfax Mews SW15...57 B3
Fairfax Pl
Kensington W14...126 B1
South Hampstead NW6...11 B1
Fairfax Rd
Acton W4...38 A3
South Hampstead NW6...11 B1
Fairfield
Camden Town NW1...82 C3
4 Stepney E1...32 B4
Fairfield Ct
Harlesden NW10...21 C4
1 London SW18...59 A2
Fairfield Dr SW18..59 A2
Fairfield Rd E3...26 C3
Fairfield St SW18...59 A2
Fairfoot Rd E3...26 C1
Fairford Ho SE11. 149 C3
Fairhazel Gdns NW6...11 B1
Fairheathe SW15...57 C1
Fairholme Rd W14...140 B1
Fairholt Cl N16...7 A3
Fairholt Rd N16...6 C3
Fairholt St SW7...130 B2
Fairhurst 4 NW6...11 B2
Fairlawn Ave W4...37 B2
Fairlawn Ct 3 W4 .37 B2
Fairlawn Gr W4...37 B2
Fairlawn Mans SE14...50 C2
Fairlawns SW15...57 C2
Fairlead Ho 6 E14...41 C3
Fairley House Sch SW1...147 C2
Fairlie Ct
22 Bromley E3...27 A2
1 Tufnell Pk N7...13 C4
Fairlight Ave NW10...21 A3
Fairlight Ct 4 NW10...21 A3
Fairlop Pl NW8...89 C3
Fairmead Ho E9...18 A4
Fairmead Rd N7, N19...5 A1
Fairmont Ave E14..34 C1
Fairmont Ho 1 E3...26 C1
Fairmount Rd SW2...62 B1
Fair St SE1...138 C4
Fairstead Wlk N1...86 C4
Fairthorn Rd SE7, SE10...43 C1
Fairview Ho 14 SW2...74 B4
Fairview Pl SW2...74 B4
Fairwall Ho 9 SE5...49 A2
Fairway Cl NW11...2 B4
Fairway Ct 13 SE16...40 C4
Fairway The W3...29 A3
Fairweather Ho N7...14 A4
Faith Ct NW2...9 A2
Faithfull Ho N5...15 B3
Fakruddin St E1...24 C1 99 C1
Falconberg Ct W1...105 C2
Falconberg Mews W1...105 C2
Falconbrook Prim Sch SW11...59 C4
Falcon Cl
Chiswick W4...45 B4
Lambeth SE1...122 B2
Falcon Ct
9 Dulwich SE21...75 C2
Holborn EC4...107 B1
Islington N1...86 B1
Falconer Wlk 12 N7 .5 B2
Falcon Gr SW11...60 A4
Falcon Ho 11 SE15..49 B2
Falcon La SW11...60 A4
Falcon Lo
11 Paddington W9...31 C4
West Hampstead NW3...11 A4
Falcon Pk Ind Est NW10...8 A3
Falcon Point SE1. 122 B3
Falcon Rd SW11...60 A4
Falcon Terr SW11...60 A4
Falcon Way E14...42 A2
Falconwood Ct SE3...53 B1
Falkener Ct SW11 169 C3
Falkirk Ct 11 SE16..32 C1
Falkirk Ho W9...88 B4
Falkirk St N1...24 A3
Falkland Ho
Kensington W8...128 A1
West Kensington W14...140 C2
Falkland Pl 2 NW5...13 B3
Falkland Rd NW5...13 B3
Falkner House Sch SW7...143 A2
Fallodon Ho
London SW8...171 C2
Paddington W11...31 B4
Fallow Ct SE16...153 C1
Fallowfield N4...5 B2
Falmouth Ho
Bayswater W2...116 A4
Kennington SE11...149 C2
Falmouth Rd SE1 137 A1
Falmouth St E15...19 C3
Falstaff Ct SE11..150 A3
Falstaff Ho 18 N1...24 A3
Fane St W14...155 A4
Fann St EC1...97 A1
Fanshaw St N1...24 A2 98 A4
Fanthorpe St SW15...57 B4
Faraday Cl N7...14 B2
Faraday Ho
2 Balham SW12...73 A4
6 Gospel Oak NW5...13 A4
Kensal Town W10...31 A4
6 Poplar E14...33 B2
Faraday Lo SE10...43 B3
Faraday Rd
Acton W3...28 B2
Kensal Town W10...31 A4
Fareham Ho 13 SW15...68 C3
Fareham St W1..105 B2
Farjeon Ho NW6...11 C1
Farleigh Pl N16...16 B4
Farleigh Rd N16...16 B4
Farley Ct
Kensington W14...126 C2
Marylebone NW1...91 B1
Farlington Pl SW15...69 A4
Farlow Rd SW15...57 C4
Farlton Rd SW18...71 A4
Farm Ave NW2...1 B1
Farm Cl SW6...155 C2
Farmdale Rd SE10..43 C1
Farmer Ho 4 SE16...40 A3
Farmers Rd SE5...48 A3
Farmer St W8...31 C1 113 B2
Farm La SW6...155 C2
Farm Lane Trad Ctr SW6...155 C3
Farmleigh Ho SW9...63 A2
Farm Pl W8...31 C1 113 B2
Farm Rd NW10...20 C4
Farm St W1...118 A3
Farnaby Ho 2 W10...23 B2
Farnborough Ho 1 SW15...68 C3
Farncombe St SE16...139 C3
Farndale Ho NW6...78 A4
Farnell Mews SW5...142 A2
Farnell Pl W3...28 A2
Farnfield Ho 12 SW2...62 B2
Farnham Ct 2 N16..7 A3
Farnham Ho
Borough The SE1..122 C1
Marylebone NW1...90 B1
Farnham Pl SE1..122 B1
Farnham Royal SE11...149 A1
Farnhurst Ho SW11...169 B2
Farningham Ho 9 N4...6 C4
Farnley Ho SW8...171 B2
Farnsworth Ct SE10...43 B3
Farnworth Ho 5 E14...42 C2
Faroe Rd W14...39 C3
Farquhar Rd SW19...70 C1
Farrance St E14...33 C3
Farrant Ho 15 SW11...59 C4
Farrell Ho E1...32 B3
Farrer Ho SE8...51 C3
Farriers Mews SE15...65 B4
Farrier St NW1...13 B1
Farrier Wlk SW10 156 C4
Farringdon La EC1 95 C1
Farringdon Rd EC1...95 C1
Farringdon St EC4...108 A2
Farringdon Sta EC1...108 A4
Farrins Rents SE16...33 A1
Farrow La SE14...50 B3
Farrow Pl SE16...41 A3
Farthingale Wlk E15...19 C1
Farthing Alley SE1...139 B3
Farthing Fields 8 E1...32 A1
Fashion & Design Mus The★ SE1...138 A4
Fashion Retail Acad The W1...105 B2
Fashion St E1...111 A3
Fassett Rd E8...16 C2
Fassett Sq E8...16 C2
Fauconberg Ct W4...45 B4
Fauconberg Rd W4...45 B4
Faulkner Ho SW15 .47 B1
Faulkner's Alley EC1...108 A4
Faulkner St SE14...50 B2
Faunce Ho 1 SE17...48 A4
Faunce St SE17..150 A1
Favart Rd SW6...165 C4
Faversham Ho
Camden Town NW1...83 A3
Walworth SE17...152 A1
Fawcett Cl SW11. 167 C1
Fawcett Est E5...7 C3
Fawcett Ho SW9. 172 B2
Fawcett Rd NW10...8 B1
Fawcett St SW10. 156 C4
Fawe Park Rd SW15...58 B3
Fawe St E14...34 A4
Fawkham Ho SE1 153 A3
Fawley Ct SE27...75 A2
Fawley Lo 2 E14...42 C2
Fawley Rd NW6...11 A3
Fawnbrake Ave SE24...63 B2
Fayetville Ho 26 N19...4 C4
Faygate Rd SW2...74 B2
Fazerley Ct 49 W2..31 C4
Fearnley Ho SE5...49 A1
Fearon St SE10...43 C1
Feathers Pl SE10...52 C
Featherstone St EC1...97 B2
Featley Rd SW9...63 A
Felbridge Ho 21 SE22...64 A
Felday Rd SE13...67 A
Felden St SW6...164 C
Feldman Cl N16...7 C
Felgate Mews 4 W6...39 A
Felix St 19 E2...25 A
Felixstowe Rd NW10...22 A
Fellbrigg Rd SE22..64 B
Fellbrigg St 21 E1..25 A
Fell Ho 11 N19...4 B
Fellows Ct E2...24 B
Fellows Rd NW3...12 A
Fells Haugh 6 W3...28 B
Felltram Way SE7..43 C
Felmersham Cl 2 SW4...61 C
Felsberg Rd SW2...74 A
Felsham Ho SW15..57 C
Felsham Mews SW15...57 C
Felsham Rd SW15..57 C
Felstead St E9...18 B
Felstead Wharf E14...42 B
Felton Ho N1...87 C
Felton St N1...87 C
Fenchurch Ave EC3...110 A
Fenchurch Bldgs EC3...110 B
Fenchurch Pl EC3...124 B
Fenchurch St EC3...124 B
Fenchurch Street Sta EC3...124 B
Fen Ct EC3...124 A
Fendall St SE1...138 B
Fender Ct SW4...172 A
Fendt Cl 8 E16...35 B
Fenelon Pl W14..141 A
Fenham Rd SE15...50 A
Fenner Cl SE16...40 A
Fenner Ho 25 E1...32 A
Fenner Sq 10 SW11...59 C
Fenning St SE1...138 A
Fenn St E9...17 B
Fen St E16...35 B
Fenstanton 3 N4...5 B
Fenstanton Prim Sch SW2...74 C
Fentiman Rd SW8...162 C
Fenton Cl
Dalston E8...16 B
South Lambeth SW9...172 C
Fenton Ho SE14...51 A
Fenton House★ NW3...2 B
Fentons SE3...53 B
Fenton St E1...32 A
Fenwick Gr SE15...64 C
Fenwick Pl SW9...62 A
Fenwick Rd SE15...64 C
Ferdinand Ho 1 NW1...13 A
Ferdinand Pl NW1..12 C

Ferdinand St NW1 .. 12 C1
Ferguson Dr W3 ... 28 C3
Ferguson Ho SE10 .. 52 B2
Ferguson's Cl E14 .. 41 C2
Fergus Rd N5 ... 15 A3
Fermain Ct E N1 ... 24 A4
Fermain Ct N N1 ... 24 A4
Fermain Ct W N1 ... 24 A4
Fermoy Rd W9 ... 23 B1
Fernbank Mews SW12 ... 61 B1
Fern Cl 3 N1 ... 24 A3
Ferncliff Rd E8 ... 16 C3
Ferncroft Ave NW3 ... 10 C4
Fern Ct SE14 ... 50 C1
Ferndale Ct 3 SE3 ... 53 B3
Ferndale Ho N16 ... 6 C3
Ferndale Rd SW4, SW9 ... 62 B3
Ferndene Rd SE24 .. 63 B3
Ferndown Lo 17 E14 ... 42 B3
Fernhead Rd W9 ... 23 B2
Fernhill Ho E5 ... 7 C2
Fernholme Rd SE15 ... 65 C2
Fernhurst Rd SW6 ... 164 B4
Fernie Ho SE22 ... 64 B4
Fernlea Rd SW12 ... 73 A3
Fernleigh Cl W9 ... 23 B2
Fernsbury St WC1 . 95 B3
Fernshaw Mans SW10 ... 156 C3
Fernshaw Rd SW10 ... 156 C3
Fernside NW11 ... 1 C3
Fernside Rd SW12 .. 72 C4
Fern St E3 ... 26 C1
Ferntower Rd N5 ... 15 C3
Fern Wlk SE16 ... 153 C1
Fernwood SW19 ... 70 B3
Ferrey Mews SW9 ... 173 B1
Ferriby Cl N1 ... 14 C1
Ferrier Ind Est SW18 ... 59 A3
Ferrier Point 6 E16 ... 35 C4
Ferrier St SW18 ... 59 A3
Ferrings SE21 ... 76 A1
Ferris Rd SE22 ... 64 C3
Ferrybridge Ho SE11 ... 135 A1
Ferry La
Barnes SW13 ... 46 B4
Brentford TW8 ... 44 A4
Richmond TW9 ... 44 B4
Ferry Rd SW13 ... 46 C2
Ferry Sq 1 TW8 ... 44 A4
Ferry St E14 ... 42 B1
Festing Rd SW15 ... 57 C4
Festival Ct 5 E8 ... 16 B1
Festival Pier SE1 . 120 C2
Festival Pleasure Gdns SW11 ... 158 C1
Fetter La EC4 ... 107 C2
Fettes Ho NW8 ... 79 C1
Ffinch St SE8 ... 51 C3
Field Ct
Hampstead NW3 ... 11 B3
Holborn WC1 ... 107 A3
Lower Holloway N7 .. 14 A3
Wimbledon SW19 ... 70 C1
Fieldgate Mans E1 ... 111 C3
Fieldgate St E1 .. 111 C3
Field Ho NW10 ... 22 C2
Fieldhouse Rd SW12 ... 73 B3
Fielding Ho
Chiswick W4 ... 46 A4
6 Kilburn NW6 ... 23 C2
St John's Wood NW8 ... 78 C4
Fielding Mews SW13 ... 47 A4
Fielding Rd
Acton W4 ... 38 A3
Hammersmith W14 . 39 C3
Fielding St SE17 ... 48 B4
Field Lo NW10 ... 8 B2
Field Rd W6 ... 154 A4
Fields Est E8 ... 16 C1
Field St WC1 ... 94 C4
Fieldsway Ho N5 ... 14 C3
Fieldview SW17, SW18 ... 71 C3
Fieldview Ct 2 N5 ... 15 A3
Fieldway Cres N5, N7 ... 14 C3
Fieldwick Ho 14 E9 ... 17 C2
Fife Rd
Mortlake SW14 ... 55 B2
Newham E16 ... 35 C4
Fife Terr N1 ... 85 A2
Fifth Ave W10 ... 23 A2
Fig Tree Cl NW10 ... 21 A4
Filey Ave N16 ... 7 C3
Filey Ho SW18 ... 59 B3
Filigree Ct SE16 ... 33 B1
Filmer Ho SW6 ... 164 B4
Filmer Mews SW6 ... 164 B4
Filmer Rd SW6 ... 154 C1
Filton Ct 14 SE14 ... 50 B3
Finborough Rd SW10 ... 156 B4
Finchdean Ho SW15 ... 68 B4
Finch Ho 1 SE8 ... 52 A3
Finch La EC2, EC3 109 C1
Finchley Pl NW8 .. 79 B2
Finchley Rd
Hampstead NW3 ... 11 B2
St John's Wood NW8 ... 79 B2
Finchley Road & Frognal Sta NW3 ... 11 B3
Finchley Road Sta NW3 ... 11 B2
Finch Lo 15 W9 ... 31 C4
Finch Mews 3 SE15 ... 49 B2
Finch's Ct 10 E14 ... 34 A2
Findhorn St 8 E14 ... 34 B3
Findon Cl SW18 ... 58 C1
Findon Rd W12 ... 38 C4
Fineran Ct 16 SW11 ... 59 C3
Fingal St SE10 ... 43 B1
Fingest Ho NW8 ... 90 A2
Finland Rd SE4 ... 66 A4
Finland St SE16 ... 41 A3
Finlay St SW6 ... 47 C2
Finley Ct 21 SE5 ... 48 B3
Finmere Ho 1 N4 ... 6 B4
Finnemore Ho N1 . 86 C4
Finn Ho N1 ... 97 C4
Finnis St E2 ... 25 A1
FINSBURY ... 95 C4
Finsbury Ave EC2 109 C3
Finsbury Cir EC2 . 109 C3
Finsbury Coll N4 ... 5 C2
Finsbury Ct EC2 .. 109 B4
Finsbury Market EC2 ... 110 A4
Finsbury Mkt EC2 ... 24 A1 98 A1
FINSBURY PARK ... 5 C2
Finsbury Park Rd N4, N5 ... 6 A2
Finsbury Park Sta N4 ... 5 C2
Finsbury Pavement EC2 ... 109 C4
Finsbury Sq EC2 .. 109 C4
Finsbury St EC2 .. 109 B4
Finsen Rd SE5 ... 63 B4
Finstock Rd W10 ... 30 C3
Finton House Sch SW17 ... 72 B2
Finucane Ct TW9 ... 54 B4
Finwhale Ho E14 ... 42 A3
Fiona Ct 9 NW6 ... 23 B3
Firbank Rd SE15 ... 50 A1
Fircroft N1 ... 86 B4
Fircroft Prim Sch SW17 ... 72 B1
Fircroft Rd SW17 ... 72 B1
Fire Brigade Pier SE1 ... 148 B4
Firecrest Dr NW3 ... 2 A1
Firle Ho 7 W10 ... 30 B4
Fir Lo SW15 ... 57 A3
Firmston Ho 9 SW14 ... 55 C4
Firs Ave SW14 ... 55 B3
Firsby Rd N16 ... 7 C3
First Ave
East Acton W3 ... 29 B1
Mortlake SW14 ... 56 A4
West Kilburn W10 ... 23 B1
First St SW3 ... 144 B4
Firth Gdns SW6 .. 164 A3
Fir Tree Ho 11 SE14 ... 50 B3
Fir Trees Cl SE16 ... 33 A1
Fisher Ho
Islington N1 ... 85 B3
9 Shadwell E1 ... 32 B2
2 Tufnell Pk N19 ... 4 B1
Fishermans Dr SE16 ... 40 C4
Fisherman's Wlk E14 ... 33 C1
Fishers Cl SW16 ... 73 C1
Fishers Ct SE14 ... 50 C2
Fisher's La W4 ... 37 C2
Fisher St
Holborn WC1 ... 106 C3
Newham E16 ... 35 C4
Fisherton St NW8 . 89 C2
Fisherton Street Est NW8 ... 89 C1
Fishlock Ct SW4 .. 172 A2
Fish St Hill EC3 ... 123 C3
Fitch Ct SW2 ... 62 C2
Fitzalan St SE11 ... 149 B4
Fitzclarence Ho W11 ... 126 A4
Fitz-George Ave W14 ... 140 A3
Fitzgerald Ave SW14 ... 56 A4
Fitzgerald Ho
Brixton SW9 ... 173 B1
14 Poplar E14 ... 34 A3
Fitzgerald Rd SW14 ... 55 C4
Fitzhardinge Ho W1 ... 103 B2
Fitzhardinge St W1 ... 103 B2
Fitzherbert Ho 11 TW10 ... 54 B1
Fitzhugh Gr SW18 .. 59 C1
Fitzjames Ave W14 ... 140 B3
Fitzjohn's Ave NW3 ... 11 C3
Fitzjohns Mans NW3 ... 11 B2
Fitzjohns Prim Sch NW3 ... 11 C3
Fitzmaurice Ho 17 SE16 ... 40 A2
Fitzmaurice Pl W1 ... 118 B2
Fitzneal St W12 ... 29 B3
FITZROVIA ... 104 A4
Fitzroy Cl N6 ... 3 B3
Fitzroy Cres W4 ... 45 C3
Fitzroy Ct W1 ... 93 A1
Fitzroy Ho
Bermondsey SE1 .. 153 A2
12 Tower Hamlets E14 ... 33 B3
Fitzroy Mews W1 .. 92 C1
Fitzroy Pk N6 ... 3 B3
Fitzroy Rd NW1 ... 81 B4
Fitzroy Sq W1 ... 92 C1
Fitzroy St W1 ... 92 C1
Fitzroy Yd NW1 ... 81 B4
Fitzwarren Gdns N19 ... 4 B3
Fitzwilliam Ave TW9 ... 44 B1
Fitzwilliam Mews E16 ... 35 C1
Fitzwilliam Rd SW4 ... 61 B4
Fives Ct SE11 ... 136 A1
Fiveways Rd SW9 173 C1
Flamborough Ho 12 SE15 ... 49 C2
Flamborough St E14 ... 33 A3
Flamingo Ct 2 SE8 ... 51 C3
Flamsteed Ct 15 SE13 ... 52 A2
Flamsteed Ho* SE10 ... 52 C3
Flanchford Rd W12 ... 38 B3
Flanders Ho N16 ... 7 A1
Flanders Mans 1 W4 ... 38 B2
Flanders Rd W4 ... 38 A2
Flanders Way E9 ... 17 C2
Flank St E1 ... 125 B4
Flansham Ho 2 E14 ... 33 B3
Flask Cotts 4 NW3 ... 11 C4
Flask Wlk NW3 ... 11 C4
Flatiron Sq SE1 .. 123 A1
Flatiron Yd SE1 ... 123 A1
Flavell Mews SE10 .. 43 A1
Flaxman Ct W1 ... 105 B1
Flaxman Ho
10 Chiswick W4 ... 38 A1
Newington SE1 ... 136 B2
Flaxman Rd SE5 ... 48 A1
Flaxman Terr WC1 . 93 C3
Flecker Ho 6 SE5 ... 48 C3
Fleece Wlk N7 ... 14 A2
Fleet Ct 1 W12 ... 38 A3
Fleetfield WC1 ... 94 B4
Fleet Ho
6 Brixton SW2 ... 62 C2
4 Limehouse E14 ... 33 A2
Fleet Pl EC4 ... 108 A2
Fleet Prim Sch NW3 ... 12 B3
Fleet Rd NW3 ... 12 B3
Fleet Sq WC1 ... 95 A3
Fleet St EC4 ... 107 C1
Fleet Street Hill E1 ... 24 C1 99 B1
Fleetway WC1 ... 94 B4
Fleet Wood 6 N16 .. 7 B2
Fleetwood Rd NW10 ... 8 C3
Fleetwood St N16 ... 7 A2
Fleming Cl 4 W9 ... 23 C1
Fleming Ct W2 ... 101 B4
Fleming Ho
Bermondsey SE16 . 139 B3
Finsbury Pk N4 ... 6 B3
Fleming Rd SE17 ... 48 A4
Fletcher Bldgs WC2 ... 106 B1
Fletcher Ct 9 NW5 ... 13 A4
Fletcher Ho 16 N16 ... 16 A4
Fletcher Path 7 SE8 ... 51 C3
Fletcher Rd W4 ... 37 B3
Fletcher St E1 ... 125 C4
Fleur De Lis St E1 ... 24 B1 98 C1
Fleur Gates 7 SW19 ... 69 C4
Flinders Ho 28 E1 ... 32 A1
Flinton St SE17 ... 152 B2
Flint St SE17 ... 151 C3
Flitcroft St WC2 .. 105 C1
Flitton Ho 7 N1 ... 15 A1
Flock Mill Pl SW18 ... 71 A3
Flodden Rd SE5 ... 48 B2
Flood St SW3 ... 158 B4
Flood Wlk SW3 ... 158 B4
Flora Cl E14 ... 34 A3
Flora Gardens Prim Sch W6 ... 39 A2
Flora Gdns 2 W6 ... 39 A2
Floral St WC2 ... 120 A4
Florence Ct W9 ... 89 A3
Florence Gdns W4 ... 45 B4
Florence Ho
20 Bermondsey SE16 ... 40 A1
2 Brixton SW2 ... 62 B2
10 Shepherd's Bush W11 ... 30 C2
7 Wandsworth SW18 ... 59 C3
Florence Mans SW6 ... 164 C4
Florence Nightingale Ho 14 N1 ... 15 B2

Florence Nightingale Mus★ SE1 135 A3
Florence Rd
  Acton W4 37 C3
  Finsbury Pk N4 5 C4
  New Cross Gate SE14 51 B2
Florence St N1 15 A1
Florence Terr
  Kingston u T SW15 68 A1
  New Cross Gate SE14 51 B2
Florence Way SW12 72 B3
Flores Ho 13 E1 32 C4
Florfield Rd E8 17 A2
Florian SE5 49 A2
Florian Rd SW15 58 A3
Florida St E2 24 C2 99 C3
Florida State Univ WC1 105 C3
Florin Ct SE1 138 C3
Floris Pl 7 SW4 61 B4
Florys Ct 7 SW19 70 A3
Floss St SW15 47 B1
Flower & Dean Wlk E1 111 A3
Flowersmead SW17 72 C2
Flowers Mews 1 N19 4 B2
Flower Wlk The SW7 129 A4
Floyer Cl TW10 54 B2
Flynn Ct 19 E14 33 C2
Foley Ho 19 E1 32 B3
Foley St W1 104 C3
Folgate St E1 110 C4
Foliot Ho N1 84 C2
Foliot St W12 29 B3
Follett Ho SW10 157 B2
Follett St E14 34 B3
Folly Wall E14 42 B4
Fonda Ct 14 E14 33 C2
Fontarabia Rd SW11 60 C3
Fontenelle SE5 49 A2
Fontenoy Ho SE11 150 A3
Fontenoy Rd SW12, SW17 73 B2
Fonthill Ho
  Kensington W14 126 B2
  Pimlico SW1 146 B2
Fonthill Mews N4 5 B2
Fonthill Rd N4 5 C2
Fontley Way SW15 68 C4
Footpath The SW15 56 C2
Forber Ho 25 E2 25 B2
Forbes Ho 2 W4 36 C1
Forbes St E1 111 C1
Forburg Rd N16 7 C3
Ford Cl 12 E3 26 A3
Fordcombe 13 NW5 12 C2
Fordham Ho 11 SE14 51 A3
Fordham St E1 111 C2
Fordingley Rd W9 23 B2
Ford Rd E3 26 B3
Fords Park Rd E16 35 C3
Ford Sq E1 32 A4
Ford St Bow E3 26 A3
  Canning Town E16 35 B3
Fordwych Ct NW2 10 A2
Fordwych Rd NW2 10 A3
Fordyce Rd SE13 67 B2
Forecastle Ct E14 41 C4
Foreign, Commonwealth & Home Offices SW1 134 A4
Foreland Ho W11 31 A2 112 A4
Foreshore SE8 41 B2
Fore St EC2 109 A3
Forest Cl NW6 10 A1
Forester Rd SE15 65 A4
Forest Gr E8 16 B2
Forest Hill Rd SE22 65 A1
Forest Rd
  Dalston E8 16 B2
  Richmond TW9 44 C3
Fore Street Ave EC2 109 B3
Forest Way 9 N19 4 B2
Forfar Rd SW11 169 C4
Forge Pl NW1 12 C2
Forman Ho SE4 65 C3
Forman Pl N16 16 B4
Formby Ct 9 N7 14 C3
Formosa Ho 1 E1 26 A1
Formosa St W9 88 B1
Formunt Cl E16 35 B4
Forrest Ct N7 14 C2
Forrest Ho SW15 47 B1
Forset Ct W1 102 B2
Forset St W1 102 B2
Forster Rd SW2 74 A4
Forston St N1 87 A2
Forsyth Gdns SE17 48 A4
Forsyth Ho
  14 Hackney E9 17 B1
  Pimlico SW1 147 A3
Forsythia Ho SE4 66 A4
Fortescue Ave 1 E8 17 A1
Fortess Gr NW5 13 B3
Fortess Rd NW5 13 B4
Fortess Wlk NW5 13 A3
Forthbridge Rd SW11 60 C3
Forth Ho 30 E3 26 B3
Forties The 9 NW5 13 B3
Fortior Ct N6 4 B4
Fortnam Rd N19 4 C2
Fort Rd SE1 153 A3
Fortrose Cl E14 34 C3
Fortrose Gdns SW12, SW2 74 A3
Fort St E1 110 B3
Fortuna Cl N7 14 B2
Fortune Ct 6 E8 16 B1
Fortune Gate Rd NW10 21 A4
Fortune Green Rd NW6 10 C4
Fortune Ho
  Lambeth SE11 149 B3
  St Luke's EC1 97 A1
Fortune St EC1 97 A1
Fortune Way NW10 21 C2
Forty Acre La E16 35 C4
Forum Cl 7 E3 26 C4
Forward Bsns Ctr The 3 E16 27 C1
Fosbrooke Ho SW8 162 A1
Fosbury Ho 7 SW9 62 B3
Fosbury Mews W2 114 B3
Foscote Mews W9 31 C4
Foskett Rd SW6 165 A1
Fossil Rd SE13 66 C4
Foster Ct
  6 Camden Town NW1 13 B1
  Canning Town E16 35 B2
Foster Ho SE14 51 B2
Foster La EC2 108 C2
Foster Rd
  Acton W3 29 A2
  Chiswick W4 37 C1
Foubert's Pl W1 104 C1
Foulden Rd N16 16 B4
Foulden Terr N16 16 B4
Foulis Terr SW7 143 C2
Foulser Rd SW17 72 C1
Foundary Ho 6 E14 34 A4
Founders Ct EC2 109 B2
Founders Ho SW1 147 B2
Foundling Ct WC1 94 A2
Foundling Mus The★ WC1 94 B2
Foundry Cl SE16 33 A1
Foundry Mews NW1 93 A2
Foundry Pl
  Stepney E1 32 B4
  Wandsworth SW18 71 A4
Fountain Ct
  Belgravia SW1 146 A3
  14 Shepherd's Bush W11 39 C4
  Strand EC4 121 B4
Fountain Green Sq SE16 139 C3
Fountain Ho
  Bermondsey SE16 139 C3
  3 Brondesbury Pk NW6 10 A1
  Mayfair W1 117 B2
Fountain Mews
  1 Highbury N5 15 B4
  Maitland Pk NW3 12 B2
Fountain Pl SW9 173 C3
Fountayne Rd N16 7 C2
Fount St SW8 161 C1
Fournier St E1 111 A4
Fourscore Mans E8 16 C1
Four Seasons Cl E3 26 C3
Fourth Ave W10 23 A2
Fovant Ct SW8 170 C1
Fowey Cl E1 32 A1
Fowey Ho SE11 149 C2
Fowler Cl SW11 59 C4
Fowler Ho
  5 Camberwell SE5 49 A1
  Islington N1 86 B4
  South Lambeth SW8 171 C3
Fowler Rd N1 86 B4
Fownes St SW11 60 A4
Fox and Knot St EC1 108 B4
Foxberry Ct SE4 66 B3
Foxberry Rd SE4 66 A4
Foxborough Gdns SE4 66 C2
Foxbourne Rd SW17 72 C2
Fox Cl
  Bethnal Green E1 25 B1
  Newham E16 35 C4
Foxcombe Rd 6 SW15 68 C3
Foxcote SE5 152 B1
Foxcroft N1 85 A1
Foxfield NW1 82 B3
Foxglove St W12 29 B2
Foxham Rd N19 4 C1
Fox Ho 2 SW11 59 C3
Foxley Cl E8 16 C3
Foxley Ho 4 E3 27 A2
Foxley Rd SW9 48 A3
Foxley Sq 3 SW9 48 A2
Foxmore St SW11 168 C3
Fox Prim Sch W8 31 C1 113 B1
Fox Rd E16 35 B4
Fox's Yd E2 24 B1 99 A2
Foxwell Mews SE4 66 A4
Foxwell St SE4 66 A4
Foyle Rd SE3 53 B4
Fradel Lo N16 6 C3
Framfield Rd N5 15 A3
Frampton NW1 13 C1
Frampton Ct 3 W3 37 B4
Frampton Ho NW8 89 C1
Frampton Park Rd E9 17 B1
Frampton St NW8 89 C1
Francemary Rd SE4 66 C2
Franche Court Rd SW17 71 B1
Francis Chichester Way SW11 169 C3
Francis Cl 6 E14 42 C2
Francis Ct 12 SE14 50 C4
Francis Ho
  Harlesden NW10 21 B4
  11 Shoreditch N1 24 A4
  Walham Green SW10 156 B2
Francis Holland Sch
  Belgravia SW1 145 C3
  Marylebone NW1 90 C2
Francis Snary Lo 11 SW18 58 C2
Francis St SW1 147 A4
Francis Terr N19 4 B1
Francis Terrace Mews 16 N19 4 B1
Francis Wlk N1 84 C4
Franconia Rd SW4 61 C2
Frank Barnes Sch NW3 11 C1
Frank Beswick Ho SW6 155 A3
Frank Dixon Cl SE21 76 A3
Frank Dixon Way SE21 76 A3
Frankfurt Rd SE24 63 B2
Frankham Ho 8 SE8 51 C3
Frankham St SE8 51 C3
Frank Ho SW8 162 A2
Frankland Cl SE16 40 A2
Frankland Ho 4 SW12 73 A4
Frankland Rd SW7 129 B1
Franklin Bldg 5 E14 41 C4
Franklin Cl
  Greenwich SE13 52 A2
  West Norwood SE27 75 A1
Franklin Ho
  New Cross SE4 51 A1
  26 Wapping E1 32 A1
Franklin Pl SE13 52 A2
Franklin Sq SW5 141 A1
Franklin's Row SW3 145 A2
Franklin St 43 E3 27 A2
Franklyn Rd NW10 8 B2
Frank Soskice Ho SW6 155 A3
Frank Whymark Ho 4 SE16 40 B4
Frans Hals Ct E14 42 C3
Fraserburgh Ho 29 E3 26 B3
Fraser Ct SW11 168 A4
Fraser Ho
  Brentford TW8 36 B1
  Clapham SW8 171 B1
Fraser Regnart Ct 12 NW5 12 B3
Fraser St W4 38 A1
Frazier St SE1 135 B3
Frean St SE16 139 B2
Frearson Ho WC1 95 A4
Freda Corbett Cl 10 SE15 49 C3
Frederica St 4 N7 14 B1
Frederick Blg N1 16 A2
Frederick Charrington Ho 4 E1 25 B1
Frederick Cl W2 116 C4
Frederick Cres SW9 48 A3
Frederick Ct SW6 58 A4
Frederick's Pl EC2 109 B1
Frederick Sq 11 SE16 33 A2
Frederick's Row EC1 96 A4
Frederick St WC1 94 C3
Frederick Terr E8 16 B1
Frederic Mews SW1 131 B3
Freedom St SW11 169 A2
Freegrove Rd N7 14 A3
Freeling Ho NW8 79 B4
Freeling St 7 N1 14 B1
Freeman Ho 13 SW2 74 A4
Freemantle St SE17 152 A2
Freemens Hos 1 SW9 62 B3
Freke Rd SW11 60 C4
Fremantle Ho 14 E1 25 A1
Fremont St E9 25 B4
French Pl E1 24 A1 98 B2

Frendsbury Rd SE4 ... 66 A3
Frensham Ct N5 ... 15 B3
Frensham Dr SW15 ... 68 C2
Frensham St SE15 .. 49 C4
Frere St SW11 ... 168 B2
Freshfield Ave E8 .. 16 B1
Freshfield Cl SE13 .. 67 C3
Freshford St SW17, SW18 ... 71 B1
Freston Rd W10, W11 ... 30 C2
Freswick Ho [6] SE8 ... 41 A2
Freud Mus The★ NW3 ... 11 B2
Frewell Bldg EC1 . 107 B4
Frewin Rd SW18 ... 71 C3
Friar Mews SE27 ... 75 A1
Friars Ave SW15 ... 68 B1
Friars Cl SE1 ... 122 B1
Friars Gdns W3 ... 28 C3
Friars Mead E14 ... 42 B3
Friars Place La W3 ... 28 C2
Friars Prim Sch SE1 ... 136 B3
Friars Stile Pl [9] TW10 ... 54 A1
Friars Stile Rd TW10 ... 54 A1
Friar St EC4 ... 108 B1
Friars Way W3 ... 28 C3
Friary Park Ct [12] W3 ... 28 B3
Friary Rd
Acton W3 ... 28 C3
Peckham SE15 ... 49 C3
Friday Grove Mews [11] SW12 ... 73 B4
Friday St EC4 ... 122 C4
Frideswide Pl NW5 ... 13 B3
Friendly Pl [16] SE13 ... 52 A2
Friendly St SE8 ... 51 C2
Friendly Street Mews SE8 ... 51 C1
Friendship Way E15 ... 27 B4
Friend St EC1 ... 96 A4
Friern Rd SE22 ... 64 C1
Frigate Ho [7] E14 .. 42 B2
Frigate Mews SE8 .. 51 C4
Frimley Cl SW19 ... 70 A2
Frimley Way E1 ... 25 C1
Frinstead Ho [1] W10 ... 30 C2
Friston St SW6 ... 166 A1
Frith Ho
Bethnal Green E2 ... 24 C2 99 B3
Paddington NW8 ... 89 C1
Frith Rd E11 ... 19 C4
Frith St W1 ... 105 B1
Frithville Ct [2] W12 ... 30 B1
Frithville Gdns W12 ... 30 B1
Frobisher Ct
[1] Greenwich SE10 ... 52 C4
[3] Shepherd's Bush W12 ... 39 B4
Frobisher Ho [27] E1 ... 32 A1
Frobisher Pas E14 .. 33 C1
Frobisher Pl SE14 .. 50 B2
Frobisher St SE10 .. 53 A4
Frogley Rd SE22 ... 64 B3
Frogmore SW18 ... 58 C2
Frogmore Est NW10 ... 20 B2
Frogmore Ind Est N5 ... 15 B4
Frognal NW3 ... 11 B3
Frognal Cl NW3 ... 11 B3
Frognal Ct NW3 ... 11 B2
Frognal Gdns NW3 ... 11 B4
Frognal La NW3 ... 11 A3
Frognal Par NW3 ... 11 B2
Frognal Rise NW3 .. 11 B4
Frognal Way NW3 .. 11 B4
Frome Ho SE15 ... 65 B3
Frome St N1 ... 86 C2
Fromow's Cnr [14] W4 ... 37 B1
Frontenac NW10 ... 9 A1
Frostic Wlk E1 ... 111 A3
Froude St SW8 ... 170 B1
Frye Ct [5] E3 ... 26 B2
Frying Pan Alley E1 ... 110 C3
Fry Rd NW10 ... 21 B4
Fulbeck Ho N7 ... 14 B2
Fulbourne St E1 ... 32 A4
Fulbrook Rd N19 ... 13 B4
Fulcher Ct SE8 ... 51 B4
Fulcher Ho
[13] Deptford SE8 ... 41 B1
[10] Shoreditch N1 ... 24 A4
Fulford Mans [3] N19 ... 5 A1
Fulford St SE16 ... 40 A4
FULHAM ... 47 C1
Fulham Broadway SW6 ... 155 C1
Fulham Broadway Sh Ctr SW6 ... 155 C1
Fulham Broadway Sta SW6 ... 155 C2
Fulham Bsns Exchange SW6 .. 167 A3
Fulham Cross Sec Sch SW6 ... 154 A1
Fulham Ct SW6 .. 165 B4
Fulham High St SW6 ... 164 B1
Fulham Pal★ SW6 ... 164 A1
Fulham Palace Rd SW6, W6 ... 47 C4
Fulham Park Gdns SW6 ... 164 C2
Fulham Park Rd SW6 ... 164 C2
Fulham Prep Sch
Fulham SW6 ... 164 B1
Fulham W14 ... 154 B4
Fulham Prim Sch SW6 ... 155 B3
Fulham Rd
Chelsea SW10 ... 157 A4
Fulham SW6 ... 165 A4
Fuller Cl E2 .. 24 C1 99 B2
Fullers Ho [6] SW18 ... 58 C2
Fullerton Rd SW18 ... 59 B2
Fullwood's Mews N1 ... 97 C4
Fulmar Ct [6] SE21 .. 75 C2
Fulmar Ho
[12] Bermondsey SE16 ... 40 C2
Marylebone NW8 ... 90 B1
Fulmead St SW6 . 166 B3
Fulneck [1] E1 ... 32 B4
Fulthorp Rd SE3 ... 53 C1
Fulton Mews W2 114 C4
Fulwood Pl WC1 . 107 A3
Fulwood Wlk SW19 ... 70 A3
Furber St W6 ... 39 A3
Furley Ho [7] SE15 .. 49 C3
Furley Rd SE15 ... 49 C3
Furlong Rd N7 ... 14 C2
Furmage St SW18 .. 71 A4
Furness Ho SW1 . 146 A2
Furness Lo [4] SW14 ... 55 A3
Furness Prim Sch The NW10 ... 21 C3
Furness Rd
Harlesden NW10 ... 21 C3
Sands End SW6 ... 166 B2
Furnival St EC4 ... 107 B2
Furrow La E9 ... 17 B3
Fursecroft W1 ... 102 C2
Furze St E3 ... 33 C4
Fusion Ct SW15 ... 68 A1
Futters Ct [1] NW10 ... 21 A3
Fyfield N4 ... 5 C2
Fyfield Rd [5] SW9 .. 62 C4
Fynes St SW1 ... 147 B4

G

Gable Ho [12] W4 ... 38 A2
Gables Cl SE5 ... 49 A2
Gables The
[3] Clapham SW4 ... 61 B4
Hampstead NW3 ... 2 C2
Gabriel Ho SE11 .. 148 C4
Gabrielle Ct NW3 ... 11 C2
Gabriel Mews NW2 .. 1 B2
Gabriel's Wharf SE1 ... 121 B2
Gaddesden Ho EC1 ... 97 C3
Gadsden Ho
[6] Homerton E9 ... 17 C2
[8] Kensal Town W10 ... 23 A1
Gagarin Ho SW11 .. 59 C4
Gage Rd E16 ... 35 A4
Gage St WC1 ... 106 B4
Gainford Ho [18] E2 .. 25 A2
Gainford St N1 ... 85 B4
Gainsborough Ct
[6] Bermondsey SE16 ... 40 A1
Dulwich SE21 ... 76 A2
Shepherd's Bush W12 ... 39 B4
Gainsborough Gdns
Golders Green NW11 ... 1 B4
Hampstead NW3 ... 2 C1
Gainsborough Ho
Finsbury Pk N4 ... 5 B3
[3] Hampstead NW3 . 11 B4
[5] Limehouse E14 ... 33 A2
Westminster SW1 . 147 C3
Gainsborough Prim Sch E9 ... 18 C2
Gainsborough Rd
Bedford Pk W4 ... 38 B2
Richmond TW9 ... 54 B4
Gainsborough St [3] E9 ... 18 B2
Gainsborough Studios N1 ... 87 B3
Gainsford St SE1 . 139 A4
Gairloch Ho [2] NW1 ... 13 C1
Gairloch Rd SE5 ... 49 A1
Gaisford St NW5 ... 13 B2
Gaitskell Ct SW11 168 A2
Gaitskell Ho SE17 .. 48 C4
Gaitskell Way SE1 ... 136 C4
Galata Rd SW13 ... 46 C3
Galatea Sq SE15 ... 65 A4
Galaxy Bldg [6] E14 ... 41 C2
Galaxy Ho EC2 ... 97 C2
Galbraith St E14 ... 42 B3
Gale Ho [10] SW2 ... 62 B2
Galena Ho [5] W6 ... 39 A2
Galena Rd W6 ... 39 A2
Galen Pl WC1 ... 106 B3
Galesbury Rd SW18 ... 59 B1
Gales Gdns E2 ... 25 A2
Gale St E3 ... 33 C4
Galgate Cl [4] SW19 ... 70 A3
Galleon Cl SE16 ... 40 C4
Galleon Ho [8] E14 .. 42 B2
Gallery Ct SW10 .. 156 C3
Gallery Rd SE21 ... 75 C3
Galleywall Rd SE16 ... 40 A2
Galleywall Road Trad Est [12] SE16 ... 40 A2
Galleywood Ho [1] W10 ... 30 B4
Gallia Rd N5 ... 15 A3
Galloway Rd W12 .. 29 C1
Galsworthy Ave E14 ... 33 A4
Galsworthy Ct W3 .. 37 A3
Galsworthy Ho [4] W11 ... 31 A3
Galsworthy Rd NW2 ... 10 A4
Galton St W10 ... 23 A2
Galveston Ho [2] E1 ... 26 A1
Galveston Rd SW15 ... 58 B2
Galway Cl [28] SE16 .. 40 A1
Galway Ho
Finsbury EC1 ... 97 A3
[7] Stepney E1 ... 32 C4
Galway St EC1 ... 97 A3
Gambetta St SW8 170 B1
Gambia St SE1 ... 122 B1
Gambler Ho EC1 .. 97 A3
Gamlen Rd SW15 ... 57 C3
Gandolfi St [5] SE15 ... 49 A4
Ganley Ct [19] SW11 ... 59 C4
Gannet Ct [5] SE21 .. 75 C2
Gannet Ho SE15 ... 49 B2
Ganton St W1 ... 105 A1
Garand Ct [2] N7 ... 14 B3
Garbett Ho [2] SE17 ... 48 A4
Garbutt Pl W1 ... 103 C3
Garden Cl SW15 ... 69 A4
Garden Ct
[4] Richmond TW9 ... 44 B2
[12] South Acton W4 .. 37 B3
St John's Wood NW8 ... 89 B4
Strand EC4 ... 121 B4
Garden Flats SW16 ... 74 A1
Garden Ho SW9 .. 172 B2
Garden La SW2 ... 74 B3
Garden Mews W2 ... 31 C2 113 C3
Garden Pl [28] E2 ... 24 B4
Garden Rd
Richmond TW9 ... 54 C4
St John's Wood NW8 ... 89 A4
Garden Row SE1 . 136 A2
Garden Royal [16] SW15 ... 57 C1
Garden St E1 ... 32 C4
Gardens The
East Dulwich SE22 ... 64 C3
Stamford Hill N16 ... 7 B4
Garden Terr
Knightsbridge SW7 ... 130 B3
Pimlico SW1 ... 147 B2
Garden Wlk EC2 ... 24 A1 98 A2
Gardiner Ave NW2 ... 9 B3
Gardiner Ct NW10 .. 20 C4
Gardiner Ho SW11 ... 168 A4
Gardner Ct N5 ... 15 B4
Gardners La EC4 . 122 C4
Gardnor Mans [14] NW3 ... 11 B4
Gardnor Rd NW3 ... 11 C4
Gard St EC1 ... 96 B4
Gareth Ct SW16 ... 73 C1
Garfield Ho W2 .. 102 C1
Garfield Mews [7] SW11 ... 60 C4
Garfield Rd SW11 .. 60 C4
Garford St E14 ... 33 C2
Garland Ct [12] E14 ... 33 C2
Garland Ho N16 ... 6 C1
Garlands Ho NW8 . 78 B2
Garlick Hill EC4 .. 123 A4
Garlinge Ho SW9 . 173 B4
Garlinge Rd NW2 ... 10 B2
Garnault Mews EC1 ... 95 C3
Garnault Pl EC1 ... 95 C3
Garner St E2 ... 24 C3
Garnet Rd NW10 ... 8 A2
Garnet St E1 ... 32 B2
Garnett Ho [5] NW3 ... 12 B3
Garnett Rd NW3 ... 12 B3
Garnham Cl [2] N16 .. 7 B2
Garnham St [1] N16 .. 7 B2
Garnies Cl SE15 ... 49 B3
Garrad's Rd SW16 .. 73 C1
Garrard Wlk NW10 .. 8 A2
Garratt Ho [8] N16 ... 7 A3
Garratt La SW18 ... 71 A3
Garratt Park Sch SW18 ... 71 B1
Garraway Ct SW13 . 47 B3
Garraway Ho SE21 .. 76 B1
Garrett Cl W3 ... 28 C4
Garrett Ho [8] W12 ... 30 A3

Garrett St EC1 ... 97 A2
Garrick Cl SW18 ... 59 B3
Garrick Ho
Chiswick W4 ... 46 A4
Mayfair W1 ... 118 A1
Garrick Rd TW9 ... 44 C1
Garrick St WC2 ... 120 A4
Garrick Yd WC2 ... 120 A4
Garsdale Terr SW5 ... 141 A2
Garsington Mews SE4 ... 66 B4
Garson Ho W2 ... 115 B4
Garston Ho 6 N1 ... 15 A1
Garter Way SE16 ... 40 C4
Garth Ct W4 ... 45 C4
Garth Ho NW2 ... 1 B2
Garth Rd
Child's Hill NW2 ... 1 B2
8 Chiswick W4 ... 37 C1
Gartmoor Gdns SW19 ... 70 B3
Garton Ho 6 N6 ... 4 C4
Garton Pl SW18 ... 59 B1
Gartons Way SW11 ... 59 B4
Garway Rd W2 ... 100 A1
Gascoigne Pl E2 ... 24 B2 98 C3
Gascony Ave NW6 ... 10 C1
Gascoyne Ho 2 E9 ... 17 C1
Gascoyne Rd E9 ... 17 C1
Gaselee St E14 ... 34 B2
Gasholder Pl SE11 ... 149 A1
Gaskarth Rd SW12 ... 61 A1
Gaskell St SW4 ... 172 A2
Gaskin Ho N16 ... 6 C1
Gaskin St N1 ... 86 A4
Gaspar Cl SW7 ... 142 B4
Gaspar Mews SW5 ... 142 B4
Gasson Ho 24 SE14 ... 50 C4
Gastein Rd W6 ... 47 C4
Gastigny Ho EC1 ... 97 A3
Gaston Bell Cl TW9 ... 54 B4
Gaston Gate SW8 ... 172 C4
Gataker Ho 5 SE16 ... 40 A3
Gataker St 6 SE16 ... 40 A3
Gatcliff Cl SW1 ... 145 C1
Gatcombe Ho 20 SE22 ... 64 A4
Gatcombe Rd
8 Newham E16 ... 35 C1
Tufnell Pk N19 ... 4 C1
Gatefield Ct SE15 ... 64 C4
Gateforth St NW8 ... 90 A1
Gate Hill Ct W11 ... 31 B1 113 A2
Gatehouse Sch E2 ... 25 C3
Gatehouse Sq SE1 ... 123 A2
Gateley Ho 6 SE4 ... 65 C3
Gateley Rd SW9 ... 62 B4
Gate Mews SW7 ... 130 B3
Gatesborough St EC2 ... 24 A1 98 A2
Gates Ct SE17 ... 150 C2
Gatesden WC1 ... 94 B3
Gateside Rd SW17 ... 72 B1
Gate St WC2 ... 106 C2
Gateway SE17 ... 48 B4
Gateway Arc N1 ... 86 A2
Gateway Ho SW12 ... 61 A1
Gateway Mews 4 E8 ... 16 B3
Gateway Prim Sch NW8 ... 89 C2
Gateways The SW3 ... 144 B3
Gateway Trad Est NW10 ... 21 B2
Gathorne St 10 E2 ... 25 C3
Gatliff Rd SW1 ... 146 A1
Gatonby St SE15 ... 49 B2
Gatwick Ho 3 E14 ... 33 B3
Gatwick Rd SW18 ... 70 B4
Gauden Cl SW4 ... 61 C4
Gauden Rd SW4 ... 61 C4
Gaugin Ct 13 SE16 ... 40 A1
Gaunt St SE1 ... 136 C2
Gautrey Rd SE15 ... 50 B1
Gavel St SE17 ... 151 C4
Gaverick Mews 3 E14 ... 41 C2
Gaviller Pl 3 E5 ... 17 A4
Gawber St E2 ... 25 B2
Gawthorne Ct E3 ... 26 C3
Gay Cl NW2 ... 9 A3
Gaydon Ho W2 ... 100 A4
Gayfere St SW1 ... 134 A1
Gayford Rd W12 ... 38 B4
Gay Ho N16 ... 16 A3
Gayhurst SE17 ... 48 C4
Gayhurst Ho NW8 ... 90 B2
Gayhurst Prim Sch E8 ... 16 C1
Gayhurst Rd E8 ... 16 C1
Gaymead NW8 ... 78 B3
Gay Rd E15 ... 27 C3
Gaysley Ho SE11 ... 149 B3
Gay St SW15 ... 57 C4
Gayton Cres NW3 ... 11 C4
Gayton Ho E3 ... 26 C1
Gayton Rd NW3 ... 11 C4
Gayville Rd SW11 ... 60 B1
Gaywood Cl SW2 ... 74 C3
Gaywood St SE1 ... 136 B1
Gaza St SE17 ... 150 A1
Gaze Ho 11 E14 ... 34 C3
Gean Ct 3 E11 ... 19 C4
Geary Ho N7 ... 14 B3
Geary Rd NW10 ... 8 C3
Geary St N7 ... 14 B3
Gedling Ho SE22 ... 64 B4
Gedling Pl SE1 ... 139 A2
Gees Ct W1 ... 103 C1
Gee St EC1 ... 96 C2
Geffrye Ct N1 ... 24 A3
Geffrye Mus* E2 ... 24 B3
Geffrye St E2 ... 24 B3
Geldart Rd SE15 ... 50 A3
Geldeston Rd E5 ... 7 C2
Gellatly Rd SE14 ... 50 C1
Gemini Bsns Ctr E16 ... 27 C1
Gemini Ho 11 E3 ... 26 C4
General Wolfe Rd SE10 ... 52 C2
Genesis Bsns Pk NW10 ... 20 A3
Geneva Ct
1 Putney SW15 ... 57 C2
Stoke Newington N16 ... 6 C3
Geneva Dr SW9 ... 62 C3
Genoa Ave SW15 ... 57 B2
Genoa Ho 19 E1 ... 25 C1
Geoffrey Chaucer Tech Coll SE1 ... 137 C1
Geoffrey Cl SE5 ... 48 B1
Geoffrey Ct SE4 ... 66 B4
Geoffrey Ho SE1 ... 137 C2
Geoffrey Jones Ct NW10 ... 21 C4
Geoffrey Rd SE4 ... 66 B4
George Beard Rd 11 SE8 ... 41 B2
George Beare Lo 9 SW4 ... 61 B2
George Belt Ho 8 E2 ... 25 C2
George Ct WC2 ... 120 B3
George Downing Est N16 ... 7 B2
George Eliot Ho SW1 ... 147 A3
George Eliot Jun & Inf Schs NW8 ... 79 B4
George Elliot Ho SE17 ... 150 C2
George Elliston Ho SE1 ... 153 B1
George Eyre Ho NW8 ... 79 C1
George Green's Sec Sch E14 ... 42 B1
George Inn Yd SE1 ... 123 B1
George La SE13 ... 67 B1
George Lansbury Ho
7 Bow E3 ... 26 B2
3 Willesden NW10 ... 8 A1
George Lashwood Ct 12 SW9 ... 62 B3
George Leybourne Ho E1 ... 125 C4
George Lindgren Ho SW6 ... 155 A2
George Loveless Ho E2 ... 24 B2 99 A4
George Mathers Rd SE11 ... 150 A4
George Mews NW1 ... 92 C3
George Peabody Ct NW1 ... 102 A4
George Row SE16 ... 139 B3
George's Rd N7 ... 14 B3
George's Sq SW6 ... 155 A4
George St
6 Canning Town E16 ... 35 B3
Marylebone W1 ... 103 A2
George Tingle Ho SE1 ... 139 A2
Georgette Pl SE10 ... 52 B3
George Vale Ho 35 E2 ... 24 C3
George Walter Ho 11 SE16 ... 40 B2
George Wyver Cl SW18 ... 70 A4
George Yd
City of London EC3 ... 109 C1
Mayfair W1 ... 117 C4
Georgiana St NW1 ... 83 A4
Georgian Ct 12 E9 ... 25 B4
Georgina Gdns E2 ... 24 B2 99 A4
Geraldine Rd
Brentford W4 ... 44 C4
Wandsworth SW18 ... 59 B2
Geraldine St SE11 ... 136 A1
Gerald Mews SW1 ... 145 C4
Gerald Rd SW1 ... 145 C4
Gerard Ct NW2 ... 9 C3
Gerard Rd SW13 ... 46 B2
Gerards Cl SE16 ... 40 B1
Gernigan Ho SW18 ... 59 C1
Gernon Rd E3 ... 26 A3
Gerrard Ho 5 SE14 ... 50 C3
Gerrard Pl W1 ... 119 C4
Gerrard Rd N1 ... 86 B2
Gerrard St W1 ... 119 C4
Gerridge Ct SE1 ... 135 C2
Gerridge St SE1 ... 135 C2
Gerry Raffles Sq E15 ... 19 C2
Gertrude St SW10 ... 157 A3
Gervase St SE15 ... 50 A3
Getters Talmud Torah N16 ... 6 C4
Ghent Way E8 ... 16 B2
Giant Arches Rd SE24 ... 63 B1
Gibbings Ho SE1 ... 136 B3
Gibbins Rd E15 ... 19 B1
Gibbon Ho NW8 ... 89 C1
Gibbon Rd
Acton W3 ... 29 A2
Nunhead SE15 ... 50 B1
Gibbons Rd NW10 ... 8 A2
Gibbon's Rents SE1 ... 124 A1
Gibbon Wlk SW15 ... 56 C3
Gibbs Gn W14 ... 141 A2
Gibbs Green Rd W14 ... 140 C2
Gibbs Green Sch W14 ... 141 A2
Gibbs Ho 6 SW12 ... 73 A4
Gibraltar Ho NW10 ... 21 A3
Gibraltar Wlk E2 ... 24 B2 99 A3
Gibson Cl E1 ... 25 B1
Gibson Gdns N16 ... 7 B2
Gibson Rd SE11 ... 149 A3
Gibson Sq N1 ... 85 C4
Gibson St SE10 ... 43 A1
Gideon Rd SW11 ... 60 C4
Giesbach Rd N19 ... 4 C2
Giffen Square Mkt SE8 ... 51 C3
Giffin St SE8 ... 51 C3
Gifford Ho
5 Clapham SW4 ... 61 C3
Greenwich SE10 ... 42 C1
Pimlico SW1 ... 146 C1
Gifford St N1 ... 14 A1
Gilbert Ho
Barbican EC2 ... 109 A3
Deptford SE8 ... 51 C4
5 Globe Town E2 ... 25 C2
Pimlico SW1 ... 146 B1
South Lambeth SW8 ... 162 A2
Gilbert Pl WC1 ... 106 A3
Gilbert Rd SE11 ... 149 C4
Gilbert Sheldon Ho W2 ... 101 C4
Gilbertson Ho 11 E14 ... 41 C3
Gilbert St W1 ... 103 C1
Gilbeys Yd NW1 ... 12 C1
Gilby Ho 5 E9 ... 17 C2
Gilda Cres N16 ... 7 C3
Gildea St W1 ... 104 B3
Gilden Cres NW5 ... 12 C3
Giles Ho
Bermondsey SE16 ... 139 B2
Notting Hill W11 ... 31 C3
Gilesmead SE5 ... 48 C2
Gilkes Cres SE21 ... 64 A1
Gilkes Pl SE21 ... 64 A1
Gillam Ho 9 SE16 ... 40 B2
Gill Ave E16 ... 35 C3
Gillender St E3 ... 27 B1
Gillespie Prim Sch N5 ... 6 A1
Gillespie Rd N4, N5 ... 6 A1
Gillett Pl 27 E8 ... 16 A3
Gillett St E8, N16 ... 16 A3
Gillfoot NW1 ... 82 C1
Gillian St SE13 ... 67 A2
Gillies St NW5 ... 12 C3
Gilling Ct 5 NW3 ... 12 A2
Gillingham Ho SW1 ... 146 C4
Gillingham Mews SW1 ... 146 C4
Gillingham Rd NW2 ... 1 A1
Gillingham Row SW1 ... 146 C4
Gillingham St SW1 ... 146 C4
Gillison Wlk SE16 ... 139 C2
Gillman Ho 24 E2 ... 24 C3
Gillray Ho SW10 ... 157 B3
Gill St E14 ... 33 B2
Gilmore Ho SW4 ... 60 B3
Gilmore Rd SE13 ... 67 C3
Gilpin Ave SW14 ... 55 C3
Gilpin Cl W2 ... 101 A4
Gilpin Rd E5 ... 18 A4
Gilray Ho W2 ... 115 B4
Gilstead Rd SW6 ... 166 B2
Gilston Rd SW10 ... 143 A1
Giltspur St EC1 ... 108 B2
Gilwell Ct 7 E5 ... 17 A4
Gipsy Cnr W3 ... 28 C4
Gipsy La SW15 ... 57 A4
Gipsy Moth IV* SE10 ... 52 B4
Giraud St E14 ... 34 A3
Girdlers Rd W14 ... 39 C2
Girdlestone Wlk N19 ... 4 B2
Girdwood Rd SW18, SW19 ... 70 A4
Girling Ho 9 N1 ... 24 A4
Gironde Rd SW6 ... 155 A1
Girton Ho SW15 ... 57 C1
Girton Villas 6 W10 ... 30 C3
Gisburn Ho 23 SE15 ... 49 C3
Gissing Wlk N1 ... 14 C1
Glade The W12 ... 39 A4
Glading Terr N16 ... 7 B1
Gladsmuir Rd N19 ... 4 B3
Gladstone Ct
Westminster SW1 ... 147 C3
Willesden NW2 ... 9 A3
Gladstone Ho 16 E14 ... 33 C3
Gladstone Park Sch NW10 ... 9 A3
Gladstone Rd W4 ... 37 C3
Gladstone St SE1 ... 136 A3

Gladstone Terr SW8 170 B4
Gladwin Ho NW1 83 A1
Gladwyn Rd SW15 57 C4
Gladys Rd NW6 10 C1
Glaisher St SE8 52 A4
Glamis Ct W3 37 A4
Glamis Est [3] E1 32 C2
Glamis Pl E1 32 B2
Glamis Rd E1 32 B2
Glanville Ho [4] SW12 73 B4
Glanville Rd SW2 62 A2
Glasbury Ho [5] SW9 62 B3
Glaserton Rd N16 7 A4
Glasgow Ho W9 78 B1
Glasgow Terr SW1 146 C1
Glasshill St SE1 136 B4
Glasshouse Fields E1 32 C2
Glasshouse St W1 119 A3
Glasshouse The SE13 67 B3
Glasshouse Wlk SE11 148 C2
Glasshouse Yd EC1 96 C1
Glass St [4] E2 25 A1
Glastonbury Ct [12] SE14 50 B3
Glastonbury Ho SW1 146 A2
Glastonbury Pl [22] E1 32 B3
Glastonbury St NW6 10 B3
Glaucus St E3 34 A4
Glazbury Rd W14 140 B2
Glazebrook Cl SE21 75 C2
Glebe Cl [1] W4 38 A1
Glebe Ct [15] E3 27 A2
Glebe Ho [8] SE16 40 A3
Glebelands Cl SE5 64 A4
Glebe Pl SW3 158 A4
Glebe Rd
Barnes SW13 46 C1
Dalston E8 16 B1
Willesden NW10 8 C2
Glebe St W4 38 A1
Gledhow Gdns SW5 142 C3
Gledstanes Rd W14 140 B1
Glegg Pl [3] SW15 57 C3
Glenaffric Ave E14 42 C2
Glen Albyn Rd SW19 69 C2
Glenalmond Ho [2] SW15 57 C1
Glenarm Rd E5 17 C4
Glenbrook Prim Sch SW4 61 C1
Glenbrook Rd NW6 10 C3
Glenburnie Rd SW17 72 B1
Glencoe Mans SW9 163 B1
Glendall St SW9 62 B3
Glendarvon St SW15 57 C4
Glendower Gdns [10] SW14 55 C4
Glendower Pl SW7 143 B4
Glendower Prep Sch SW7 143 B4
Glendower Rd SW14 55 C4
Glendown Ho [2] E8 16 C3
Glendun Ct W3 29 A2
Glendun Rd W3 29 A2
Gleneagles Cl [21] SE16 40 A1
Glenelg Rd SW2 62 A2
Glenfield Rd SW12 73 B3
Glenfinlas Way SE5 48 A3
Glenforth St SE10 43 B1
Glengall Gr E14 42 B3
Glengall Pass [2] NW6 23 C4
Glengall Rd
Camberwell SE15 49 B4
Kilburn NW6 23 B4
Glengall Terr SE15 49 B4
Glengarnock Ave E14 42 B2
Glengarry Rd SE22 64 B2
Glenhurst Ave NW5 12 C4
Glenilla Rd NW3 12 A2
Glenister Rd SE10 43 B1
Glenkerry Ho [1] E14 34 B3
Glenloch Ct [2] NW3 12 A2
Glenloch Rd NW3 12 A3
Glenluce Rd SE3 53 C4
Glenmore SW15 57 C1
Glenmore Ho [6] TW10 54 A1
Glenmore Rd NW3 12 A2
Glennie Ct SE21 76 C3
Glennie Ho SE10 52 B2
Glennie Rd SE27, SW16 74 C1
Glenridding NW1 83 A1
Glenrosa St SW6 166 C2
Glenroy St W12 30 B3
Glensdale Rd SE4 66 B4
Glenshaw Mans SW9 163 B1
Glentanner Way SW17 71 C1
Glen Terr E14 42 B4
Glentham Gdns SW13 47 A4
Glentham Rd SW13 47 A4
Glenthorne Mews W6 39 A2
Glenthorne Rd W6 39 A2
Glenthorpe SW15 56 C3
Glentworth St NW1 91 A1
Glenville Gr SE8 51 B3
Glenville Mews SW18 70 C4
Glenworth Ave E14 42 C2
Gliddon Dr E5 17 A4
Gliddon Rd W14 140 A2
Globe Pond Rd SE16 33 A1
Globe Prim Sch E2 25 B2
Globe Rd E1, E2 25 B1
Globe St SE1 137 B3
Globe Terr [9] E2 25 B2
Globe Theatre The★ SE1 122 C3
GLOBE TOWN 25 C2
Globe View EC4 122 C4
Globe Yd W1 104 A1
Gloucester W14 141 A3
Gloucester Ave NW1 81 C4
Gloucester Cir SE10 52 B3
Gloucester Cres NW1 82 A4
Gloucester Ct
Borough The SE1 137 A2
City of London EC3 124 B3
Dulwich SE22 76 C3
Golders Green NW11 1 B4
Richmond TW9 44 C3
Gloucester Dr N4 6 A2
Gloucester Gate NW1 82 A2
Gloucester Gate Mews NW1 82 A2
Gloucester Gdns
Golders Green NW11 1 B4
Paddington W2 100 C2
Gloucester Ho
Kilburn NW6 23 C3
Richmond TW10 54 C2
Gloucester Mews W2 101 A1
Gloucester Mews W W2 101 A1
Gloucester Pk SW7 142 C4
Gloucester Pl W1 103 A4
Gloucester Pl Mews W1 103 A3
Gloucester Prim Sch SE15 49 A3
Gloucester Rd
Acton W3 37 B4
Richmond TW9 44 C3
South Kensington SW7 142 C4
Gloucester Road Sta SW7 142 C4
Gloucester Sq
[6] Hackney E2 24 C4
Paddington W2 102 A1
Gloucester St SW1 146 C2
Gloucester Terr W2 101 A1
Gloucester Way EC1 95 C3
Gloucester Wlk W8 127 C4
Glover Ho
London SE15 65 A3
[2] South Hampstead NW6 11 B1
Glycena Rd SW11 60 B4
Glyn Ct SE27 74 C1
Glynde Mews SW3 130 B1
Glynde Reach WC1 94 B3
Glynde St SE4 66 B1
Glynfield Rd NW10 8 A1
Glyn Mans W14 140 B4
Glyn Rd E5 17 C4
Glyn St SE11 148 C1
Goater's Alley SW6 155 A1
Goat Wharf TW8 44 A4
Godalming Rd E14 34 A4
Goddard Ho SW19 69 C2
Goddard Pl N19 4 B1
Godfrey Ho EC1 97 B3
Godfrey St
Chelsea SW3 144 B2
Mill Meads E15 27 B3
Goding St SE11 148 B1
Godley Rd SW18 71 C3
Godliman St EC4 122 C4
Godman Rd SE15 50 A1
Godolphin Ho
Primrose Hill NW3 12 A1
[7] Streatham SW2 74 C3
Godolphin & Latymer Sch W6 39 A2
Godolphin Pl W3 28 C2
Godolphin Rd W12 39 A4
Godson St N1 85 B2
Godstone Ct [1] N16 7 A3
Godstone Ho SE1 137 C2
Godwin Cl N1 87 A2
Godwin Ct NW1 83 A2
Godwin Ho
[2] Haggerston E2 24 B3
Kilburn NW6 78 A2
Goffers Ho SE3 53 A1
Goffers Rd SE3, SE13 53 A1
Goffton Ho SW9 173 A1
Golborne Gdns
[5] Kensal Town W10 23 A1
West Kilburn W10 23 B1
Golborne Mews [9] W10 31 A4
Golborne Rd W10 31 A4
Golden Cross Mews [2] W11 31 B3
Golden Hinde The★ SE1 123 B2
Golden Hind Pl [5] SE8 41 B2
Golden La EC1 97 A1
Golden Plover Cl E16 35 C3
Golden Sq W1 119 A4
Golders Ct NW11 1 B4
Golders Gdns NW11 1 B4
GOLDERS GREEN 1 C4
Golders Green Coll NW11 1 C3
Golders Green Cres NW11 1 C4
Golders Green Rd NW11 1 A4
Golders Green Sta NW11 1 C3
Golders Hill Sch NW11 1 C4
Golderslea NW11 1 C3
Golders Park Cl NW11 1 C3
Golders Way NW11 1 B4
Goldhawk Ind Est The W6 39 A3
Goldhawk Mews [2] W12 39 A4
Goldhawk Rd W12 38 C3
Goldhawk Road Sta W12 39 B4
Goldhurst Terr NW6 11 B1
Goldie Ho N19 4 C4
Golding St E1 111 C1
Goldington Cres NW1 83 B2
Goldington Ct NW1 83 B3
Goldington St NW1 83 B2
Goldman Cl E2 24 C1 99 B2
Goldney Rd W9 23 C1
Goldsboro Rd SW8 161 C1
Goldsborough Ho SW8 171 C3
Goldsmith Ave W3 28 C2
Goldsmith Ct WC1 106 B2
Goldsmith Ho W3 28 C2
Goldsmith Rd
Acton W3 28 C1
Peckham SE15 49 C2
Goldsmiths Bldgs W3 28 C1
Goldsmiths Cl W3 28 C1
Goldsmiths Coll, Univ of London SE14 51 A2
Goldsmith's Pl NW6 78 A3
Goldsmith's Row E2 24 C3
Goldsmith's Sq [17] E2 24 C3
Goldsmith St EC2 109 A2
Goldthorpe NW1 82 C3
Goldwell Ho SE22 64 A3
Goldwin Cl SE14 50 B2
Goldwing Cl E16 35 C3
Gomm Rd SE16 40 B3
Gondar Gdns NW6 10 B3
Gondar Mans NW6 10 B3
Gonson St SE8 52 A4
Gonston Cl SW19 70 A2
Gonville Ho [6] SW15 57 C1
Gonville St SW6 58 A4
Gooch Ho EC1 107 B4
Goodall Ho [10] SE4 65 C3
Goodenough Coll WC1 94 C2
Goodfaith Ho [18] E14 34 A2
Goodge Pl W1 105 A3
Goodge St W1 105 A3
Goodge Street Sta W1 105 B4
Goodhall St NW10 21 B2
Good Hart Pl E14 33 A2
Goodhope Ho [17] E14 34 A2
Goodinge Cl N7 14 A2
Goodinge Rd N7 14 A2
Goodman Cres SW2 73 C2

Goodman's Stile E1 111 B2
Goodman's Yd E1, EC3 124 C4
Goodrich Com Sch SE22 64 C1
Goodrich Ct 9 W10 30 C3
Goodrich Ho
20 Bethnal Green E2 25 B3
Stamford Hill N16 7 A4
Goodrich Rd SE22 64 C1
Good Shepherd RC Prim Sch The W12 38 B4
Goodson Rd NW10 8 A1
Goodspeed Ho 20 E14 34 A2
Goodsway NW1 84 A2
Goodway Gdns E14 34 C3
Goodwill Ho 22 E14 34 A2
Goodwin Cl SE16 139 A1
Goodwin Ho 2 SE15 65 A4
Goodwin Rd W12 38 C4
Goodwins Ct WC2 120 A4
Goodwin St N4 5 C2
Goodwood Ct W1 104 B4
Goodwood Ho 3 W4 37 B1
Goodwood Mans 3 SW9 62 C4
Goodwood Rd SE14 51 A3
Goose Green Prim Sch SE22 64 B3
Goose Green Trad Est SE22 64 C3
Gophir La EC4 123 B4
Gopsall St N1 87 C3
Gordon Ave SW14 56 A3
Gordonbrock Prim Sch SE4 66 C2
Gordonbrock Rd SE4 66 C2
Gordon Ct 5 W12 30 B3
Gordondale Rd SW18, SW19 70 C2
Gordon Gr SE5 48 A1
Gordon Ho 17 E1 32 B2
Gordon Hospl The SW1 147 B3
Gordon House Rd NW5 12 C4
Gordon Lo N16 6 C3
Gordon Mans WC1 93 B1
Gordon Pl W8 127 C4
Gordon Rd
Chiswick W4 45 A4
Leyton E15 19 B4
Peckham SE15 50 A1
Richmond TW9 44 B1
Gordon Sq WC1 93 C2
Gordon St WC1 93 B2
Gorefield Ho NW6 23 C3
Gorefield Pl NW6 23 C3
Gore Rd E9 25 B4
Gore St SW7 129 A2
Gorham Ho 12 SW4 61 B1
Gorham Pl W11 31 A2 112 A3
Goring St EC3 110 B2
Gorleston St W14 140 B4
Gorse Cl E16 35 C3
Gorsefield Ho 6 E14 33 C2
Gorst Rd
London SW11 60 B1
North Acton NW10 20 C1
Gorsuch Pl E2 24 B2 98 C4
Gorsuch St E2 24 B2 98 C4
Gosberton Rd SW12 72 C3
Gosfield St W1 104 C3
Gosford Ho 25 E3 26 B3
Goslett Yd WC2 105 C2
Gosling Ho 2 E1 32 B2
Gosling Way SW9 173 B4
Gospatric Home Ho SW14 56 A4
GOSPEL OAK 12 C4
Gospel Oak Prim Sch NW5 12 C4
Gospel Oak Sta NW5 12 C4
Gosport Ho 9 SW15 68 C3
Gosset St E2 24 C2 99 B4
Gosterwood St SE8 51 A4
Goswell Pl EC1 96 B3
Goswell Rd EC1 96 B4
Gothic Ct 17 SE5 48 B3
Gottfried Mews NW5 13 B4
Gough Ho N1 86 B4
Gough Sq EC4 107 C2
Gough St WC1 95 A1
Gough Wlk 14 E14 33 C3
Goulden Ho SW11 168 A2
Gouldman Ho 33 E1 25 B1
Gould Terr 26 E8 17 A3
Goulston St E1 110 C2
Goulton Rd E5 17 A4
Govan St E2 24 C4
Gover Ct SW4 172 B2
Gowan Ave SW6 164 A4
Gowan Ho E2 24 B2 99 A3
Gowan Rd NW10 9 A2
Gower Cl SW4 61 B1
Gower Ct WC1 93 B2
Gower Ho SE17 151 A2
Gower Mews WC1 105 C4
Gower Pl NW1, WC1 93 B2
Gower Sch The N7 14 A2
Gower St WC1 93 B1
Gower's Wlk E1 111 B1
Gowlett Rd SE15 64 C4
Gowrie Rd SW11 60 C4
Gracechurch St EC2, EC4 123 C4
Gracefield Gdns SW16 74 A1
Gracehill 2 E1 32 B4
Grace Ho SE11 163 A4
Grace Jones Cl E8 16 C2
Grace Pl E3 27 A2
Graces Mews NW8 79 A1
Grace's Mews SE5 49 A1
Grace's Rd SE5 49 A1
Grace St E3 27 A2
Graemesdyke Ave SW14 55 A3
Grafton Cres NW1 13 A2
Grafton Ct 10 E8 16 C3
Grafton Ho
16 Bow E3 26 C2
12 Deptford SE8 41 B1
Grafton Mans SW4 61 B3
Grafton Mews W1 92 C1
Grafton Pl NW1 93 C3
Grafton Prim Sch N7 5 A1
Grafton Rd
Acton W3 28 B2
Gospel Oak NW5 12 C3
Grafton Sq SW4 61 B4
Grafton St W1 118 B3
Grafton Terr NW5 12 C3
Grafton Way W1 93 A1
Grafton Yd NW5 13 A2
Graham Ct 5 SE14 50 C4
Graham Ho
5 Balham SW12 73 A4
6 Tufnell Pk N19 13 C4
Graham Mans 2 E8 17 A2
Graham Rd
Acton W4 37 C3
Dalston E8 16 C2
Graham St N1 86 B1
Graham Terr SW1 145 C3
Graham Twr W3 37 A3
Grainger Ct 22 SE5 48 B3
Grampian Gdns NW2 1 A3
Grampians The 10 W14 39 C4
Granard Ave SW15 57 A2
Granard Ho 20 E9 17 C2
Granard Prim Sch SW15 57 A1
Granard Rd SW11, SW12 72 B4
Granary Rd E1 25 A1
Granary Sq N1 14 C2
Granary St NW1 83 B3
Granary The SE8 51 C3
Granby Pl SE1 135 B3
Granby St
Bethnal Green E2 24 C1 99 B2
Shoreditch E2 24 B1 99 A2
Granby Terr NW1 82 C1
Grand Ave EC1 108 B4
Grandfield Ct W4 45 C4
Grandison Rd SW11 60 B2
Grand Junction Wharf N1 86 C1
Grand Par SW14 55 B3
Grand Union Cl W9 31 B4
Grand Union Cres E8 24 C4
Grand Union Ind Est NW10 20 A3
Grand Vitesse Ind Est SE1 122 B1
Granfield St SW11 167 C3
Grangecourt Rd N16 7 A3
Grange Ct
Peckham SE15 49 B1
Strand WC2 107 A1
1 Willesden NW10 8 A4
Grangefield NW1 14 A1
Grange Gdns NW3 2 A1
Grange Gr N1 15 B2
Grange Ho
Bermondsey SE1 138 C1
Willesden NW10 9 A1
Grange La SE21 76 B2
Grangemill 11 NW5 13 A4
GRANGE MILLS 73 B3
Grange Mills SW12 73 B3
Grange Pl NW6 10 C1
Grange Prim Sch SE1 138 A1
Grange Rd
Barnes SW13 46 C2
Bermondsey SE1 138 C1
Gunnersbury W4 37 A1
Willesden NW10 9 A2
Grange St N1 87 C3
Grange The
Bermondsey SE1 138 C1
7 Gunnersbury W4 37 A1
Hammersmith W12 39 A3
19 Maitland Pk NW3 12 B2
South Acton W3 37 A4
West Kensington W14 140 C3
Grangeway NW6 10 C1
Grange Wlk SE1 138 C1
Grange Yd SE1 138 C1
Granite Apts E15 19 C2
Grannary The 10 SE16 40 B4
Gransden Ave E8 17 A1
Gransden Ho 1 SE8 41 B1
Gransden Rd W12 38 B4
Grantbridge St N1 86 B2
Grantham Ct 9 SE16 40 C4
Grantham Ho 12 SE15 49 C4
Grantham Pl W1 118 A1
Grantham Rd
Chiswick W4 46 A3
South Lambeth SW9 172 B1
Grant Ho
Clapham SW8 171 B1
Clerkenwell EC1 108 B4
Grantley Ho
2 Deptford SE14 50 C4
5 Putney SW19 69 C3
Grantley St E1 25 C1
Grant Mus of Zoology & Comparative Anatomy★ WC1 93 B1
Grant Rd SW11 60 A4
Grant St N1 85 B2
Grantully Rd W9 88 A3
Granville Ct
8 Deptford SE14 51 A3
Shoreditch N1 87 C4
Granville Gr SE13 67 B
Granville Ho 18 E14 33 C
Granville Ind Est NW2 1 B
Granville Mans 8 W12 39 B
Granville Pk SE13 67 C
Granville Pl
Marylebone W1 103 B
Walham Green SW6 156 A
Granville Point NW2 1 B
Granville Rd
Child's Hill NW2 1 B
Kilburn NW6 23 C
Wandsworth SW18 70 B
Granville Sq
3 Camberwell SE15 49 A
Finsbury WC1 95 A
Granville St WC1 95 A
Grape St WC2 106 A
Grasgarth Cl W3 28 B
Grasmere NW1 92 B
Grasmere Ave W3 28 C
Grasmere Ct SW13 46 C
Grasmere Ho 20 N16 15 C
Grasmere Point 2 SE15 50 B
Grasmere Prim Sch N16 15 C
Grateley Ho 10 SW15 69 A
Gratton Rd W14 126 A
Graveley Ho 7 SE8 41 A
Gravel La E1 110 C
Gravesend Rd W12 29 C
Grayfriars Pas EC1 108 B
Gray Ho SE17 151 A
Grayland Ct WC1 94 C
Grayling Rd N16 6 C
Grayling Sq E2 24 C2 99 C
Grayshott Rd SW11 60 C
Gray's Inn★ WC1 107 A
Gray's Inn Pl WC1 107 A
Gray's Inn Rd WC1 95 A
Gray's Inn Sq WC1 107 B
Grayson Ho EC1 97 A
Gray St SE1 135 C
Grayswood Point 14 SW15 68 C
Gray's Yd W1 103 C
Grazebrook Prim Sch N16 7 A
Grazebrook Rd N16 6 C
Great Arthur Ho EC1 96 C
Great Bell Alley EC2 109 B
Great Castle St W1 104 C
Great Central St NW1 102 C
Great Chapel St W1 105 B
Great Chart St SW11 59 B

Great Chertsey Rd SW14, W4 .... 45 C2
Great Church La W6 .... 39 C1
Great College St SW1 .... 134 A2
Great Croft WC1 .... 94 B3
Great Cross Ave SE3 .... 53 A3
Great Cumberland Mews W1 .... 102 C1
Great Cumberland Pl W1 .... 103 A1
Great Dover St SE1 .... 137 B2
Great Eastern Bldgs 10 E8 .... 17 A2
Great Eastern Ent Ctr E14 .... 42 A4
Great Eastern Pier E14 .... 41 C1
Great Eastern Rd E15 .... 19 C2
Great Eastern St EC2 .... 24 A1 98 A2
Great Eastern Wharf SW11 .... 158 B1
Great Field 7 NW5 .... 13 B3
Greatfield Cl
London SE4 .... 66 C3
4 Tufnell Pk N19 .... 13 B4
Great George St SW1 .... 134 A3
Great Guildford Bsns Sq SE1 .... 122 C1
Great Guildford St SE1 .... 122 C1
Greatham Wlk 8 SW15 .... 68 C3
Great James St WC1 .... 106 C4
Great Marlborough St W1 .... 104 C1
Great Maze Pond SE1 .... 137 C4
Great Newport St WC2 .... 120 A4
Greatorex Ho E1 .... 111 B4
Greatorex St E1 .... 111 B4
Great Ormond St Hospl for Children WC1 .... 94 C1
Great Ormond St WC1 .... 94 C1
Great Percy St WC1 .... 95 B4
Great Peter St SW1 .... 133 C1
Great Portland St W1 .... 104 B4
Great Portland Street Sta W1 .... 92 B1
Great Pulteney St W1 .... 119 A4
Great Queen St WC2 .... 106 B2
Great Russell Mans WC1 .... 106 A3
Great Russell St WC1 .... 106 A3
Great St Helen's EC3 .... 110 A2
Great St Thomas Apostle EC4 .... 123 A4
Great Scotland Yd SW1, WC2 .... 120 A2
Great Smith St SW1 .... 133 C2
Great Spilmans SE22 .... 64 A2
Great Suffolk St SE1 .... 122 B1
Great Sutton St EC1 .... 96 B1
Great Swan Alley EC2 .... 109 B2
Great Titchfield St W1 .... 104 C3
Great Tower St EC3 .... 124 A4
Great Trinity La EC4 .... 123 A4
Great Turnstile WC2 .... 107 A3
Great Western Rd W2, W9 .... 31 B4
Great West Rd W4, W6 .... 45 C4
Great West Road Cedars Rd W4 .... 45 B4
Great West Road Hogarth La W4 .... 46 A4
Great Winchester St EC2 .... 109 C2
Great Windmill St W1 .... 119 B4
Great Yd SE1 .... 138 B4
Greaves Cotts 10 E14 .... 33 A4
Greaves Twr SW10 .... 157 A2
Grebe Ct 16 E14 .... 42 B4
Greek Ct W1 .... 105 C1
Greek St W1 .... 105 C1
Greenacre Ct E8 .... 16 C3
Greenacre Sq 26 SE16 .... 40 C4
Green Arbour Ct EC1 .... 108 A2
Greenaway Gdns NW3 .... 11 A4
Greenaway Ho
Finsbury WC1 .... 95 B3
St John's Wood NW8 .... 78 C4
Green Bank E1 .... 32 A1
Greenberry St NW8 .... 80 A1
Green Cl NW11 .... 2 B4
Greencoat Pl SW1 .... 147 A4
Greencoat Row SW1 .... 133 A1
Greencourt Ho 25 E1 .... 25 C1
Greencroft Gdns NW6 .... 11 B1
Green Ct 2 NW10 .... 8 A4
Green Dale SE22 .... 64 A2
Greendale Cl SE22 .... 64 A2
Green Dragon Ct SE1 .... 123 B1
Green Dragon Ho WC1 .... 106 B2
Green Dragon La TW8 .... 36 B1
Green Dragon Prim Sch TW8 .... 44 A4
Green Dragon Yd E1 .... 111 B3
Greene Ct 20 SE14 .... 50 C4
Greene Ho SE1 .... 137 B1
Greenend Rd W4 .... 38 A4
Greener Ho 3 SW4 .... 61 C4
Greenfell Mans SE8 .... 52 A4
Greenfield Gdns NW2 .... 1 A1
Greenfield Ho 28 SW19 .... 69 C3
Greenfield Rd E1 .... 111 C2
Greenham Cl SE1 .... 135 B3
Greenham Ho 5 E9 .... 25 B4
Greenheath Bsns Ctr 3 E2 .... 25 A1
Greenhill NW3 .... 11 C4
Greenhill Pk NW10 .... 21 A4
Greenhill Rd NW10 .... 21 A4
Greenhill's Rents EC1 .... 108 A4
Greenhills Terr 16 N1 .... 15 C2
Green Ho The 5 SW19 .... 70 A3
Green Hundred Rd SE15 .... 49 C4
Greening Ho SE13 .... 67 C3
Greenland Ho
Bermondsey SE8 .... 40 C1
4 Mile End E1 .... 26 A1
Greenland Mews SE8 .... 40 C1
Greenland Pl NW1 .... 82 B4
Greenland Quay SE16 .... 40 C2
Greenland Rd NW1 .... 82 C4
Greenland St NW1 .... 82 B4
Green Lanes N4, N8, N15 .... 6 A4
Greenleaf Cl 8 SW2 .... 74 C4
Green Link Wlk TW9 .... 45 A2
Greenman St N1 .... 86 C4
Greenmead Sch SW15 .... 57 A2
Greenock Rd 11 W3 .... 37 B3
Green Park★ SW1, W1 .... 132 B4
Green Park Sta W1 .... 118 C2
Greenroof Way SE10 .... 43 B3
Greens Ct W1 .... 119 B4
Green's Ct W11 .... 31 B1 112 C1
Greenside Prim Sch W12 .... 38 C4
Greenside Rd W12 .... 38 C4
Green St W1 .... 117 B4
Greenstead Gdns SW15 .... 57 A2
Greenstreet Hill SE4 .... 65 C4
Greensward Ho SW6 .... 166 C2
Green Terr EC1 .... 95 C3
Green The W3 .... 29 A3
Greenview Cl W3 .... 29 A1
Greenview Ct
East Dulwich SE22 .... 64 C3
Wandsworth SW18 .... 72 A4
Greenway Cl N4 .... 6 B2
Greenwell St W1 .... 92 B1
GREENWICH 43 C3
Greenwich Acad SE10 .... 52 A2
Greenwich Bsns Ctr SE10 .... 52 A3
Greenwich Bsns Pk SE10 .... 52 A3
Greenwich Church St SE10 .... 52 B4
Greenwich Coll SE10 .... 52 B3
Greenwich Ct 11 E1 .... 32 A3
Greenwich High Rd SE10 .... 52 A3
Greenwich Ho SE13 .... 67 C1
Greenwich Ind Est SE10 .... 52 A3
Greenwich Mkt SE10 .... 52 B4
Greenwich Mkt 2 SE10 .... 52 B4
Greenwich Park★ SE10 .... 53 A3
Greenwich Park St SE10 .... 52 C4
Greenwich Quay SE8 .... 52 A4
Greenwich South St SE10 .... 52 B2
Greenwich Sta SE10 .... 52 A3
Greenwich View Pl E14 .... 42 A3
Green Wlk SE1 .... 138 A1
Greenwood 8 SW19 .... 69 C4
Green Wood NW5 .... 13 B3
Greenwood Ho
Finsbury WC1 .... 95 B3
8 Nunhead SE4 .... 65 C3
Greenwood Pl NW5 .... 13 A3
Greenwood Rd E8 .... 16 C2
Greenwood Terr NW10 .... 20 C3
Green Yd WC1 .... 95 A2
Greet Ho SE1 .... 135 C3
Greet St SE1 .... 121 C1
Gregor Mews SE3 .... 53 C3
Gregory Pl W8 .... 128 A4
Greig Terr SE17 .... 48 A4
Grenada Ho 18 E14 .... 33 B2
Grenade St E14 .... 33 B2
Grena Gdns TW9 .... 54 B3
Grena Rd TW10, TW9 .... 54 B3
Grenard Cl SE15 .... 49 C3
Grendon Ho
29 Hackney E9 .... 17 B1
Pentonville N1 .... 84 C1
Grendon St NW8 .... 90 A2
Grenfell Ho SE5 .... 48 B3
Grenfell Rd W11 .... 30 C2
Grenfell Twr 5 W11 .... 30 C2
Grenfell Wlk 4 W11 .... 30 C2
Grenier Apartments 11 SE15 .... 50 A3
Grenville Ho
26 Bow E3 .... 26 A3
4 Deptford SE8 .... 51 C4
Grenville Lo N6 .... 4 B4
Grenville Mans WC1 .... 94 A2
Grenville Mews SW7 .... 142 C3
Grenville Pl SW7 .... 142 C4
Grenville Rd N19 .... 5 A3
Grenville St WC1 .... 94 B1
Gresham Almshouses 3 SW9 .... 62 B3
Gresham Coll EC1 .... 107 C3
Gresham Gdns NW11 .... 1 A3
Gresham Pl 2 N19 .... 4 C2
Gresham Rd SW9 .... 62 C4
Gresham St EC2 .... 109 A2
Gresham Way SW19 .... 70 C1
Gresham Way Est SW19 .... 71 A1
Gresley Ho SW8 .... 171 C4
Gresley Rd N19 .... 4 B4
Gressenhall Rd SW18 .... 70 B4
Gresse St W1 .... 105 B2
Greswell St SW6 .... 47 C2
Greta Ho SE3 .... 53 B4
Gretton Ho 2 E2 .... 25 B2
Greville Hall NW6 .... 78 B2
Greville Ho
Knightsbridge SW1 .... 131 B2
Putney SW15 .... 57 C4
Greville Lo W2 .... 100 A2
Greville Mews NW6 .... 78 A3
Greville Pl W9 .... 78 B2
Greville Rd
Kilburn NW6 .... 78 B2
Richmond TW10 .... 54 B1
Greville St EC1 .... 107 C4
Grey Coat Hospital Sch (St Michaels) The SW1 .... 147 B3
Grey Coat Hospital Sch The SW1 .... 133 B1
Greycoat Pl SW1 .... 133 B1
Greycoat St SW1 .... 133 B1
Grey Eagle St E1 .... 24 B1 99 A1
Greyfriars 16 SE26 .... 76 C1
Greyfriars Ho SE3 .... 53 B4
Grey Ho 27 W12 .... 30 A2
Greyhound Ct WC2 .... 121 B4
Greyhound Rd
College Pk NW10 .... 22 A2
Fulham W6 .... 154 A4
Greyladies Gdns SE10 .... 52 B1
Greystoke Ho SE15 .... 49 C4
Greystoke Pl EC4 .... 107 C2
Grey Turner Ho W12 .... 29 C3
Grice Ct N1 .... 15 B2
Grierson Rd SE23 .... 66 A1
Griffin Cl NW10 .... 9 A3
Griffin Ct
8 Brentford TW8 .... 44 A4
Chiswick W4 .... 38 B1
Shepherd's Bush W12 .... 30 A1
Griffin Gate SW15 .... 57 C4

Griffon Ho 3 SW11 ....60 A4
Grigg's Pl SE1 .... 138 B1
Grimaldi Ho N1 ... 84 C2
Grimsby St
Bethnal Green E2 ....24 C1 99 A2
Shoreditch E2 ....24 B1 99 A2
Grimsel Path SE5...48 A3
Grimshaw Cl N6.....3 C4
Grimston Rd SW6 164 C1
Grimthorpe Ho EC1 .... 96 A2
Grimwade Cl SE15..65 B4
Grindall Ho 26 E1 ...25 A1
Grindal St SE1 ... 135 B3
Grindley Ho 3 E3..33 B4
Grinling Gibbons Prim Sch SE8....51 B4
Grinling Pl SE8....51 C4
Grinstead Rd SE8...41 A1
Grisedale NW1.... 92 C4
Grittleton Rd W9...23 C1
Groombridge Rd E9....17 C1
Groom Cres SW18..71 C4
Groome Ho SE11 . 149 A3
Groom Pl SW1 ... 131 C2
Grosse Way SW15..57 A1
Grosvenor Ave
Canonbury N5.......15 B3
Mortlake SW14 .....56 A4
Richmond TW10.....54 A2
Grosvenor Bridge SW1 .... 160 B4
Grosvenor Cotts SW1 .... 145 B4
Grosvenor Court Mans W2 .... 102 C1
Grosvenor Cres SW1 .... 131 C3
Grosvenor Cres Mews SW1 .... 131 B3
Grosvenor Ct
Brondesbury Pk NW6....22 C4
Gunnersbury W4 ....37 A1
22 Poplar E14 ......33 B3
Putney SW15 ....58 A2
Grosvenor Gdns
Cricklewood NW2 ....9 B3
Mortlake SW14 .....56 A4
Westminster SW1 . 132 B1
Grosvenor Gdns Mews E SW1.... 132 B2
Grosvenor Gdns Mews N SW1.... 132 A1
Grosvenor Gdns Mews S SW1.... 132 B1
Grosvenor Hill W1 .... 118 A4
Grosvenor Hill Ct W1 .... 118 A4
Grosvenor Ho E5....7 C3
Grosvenor Park SE5 ....48 B3
Grosvenor Pier SW1 .... 161 B4
Grosvenor Pk SE5..48 B4
Grosvenor Pl SW1 .... 132 A3
Grosvenor Rd
Acton Green W4.....37 B1
Grosvenor Rd *continued*
Pimlico SW1...... 161 A4
Richmond TW10.....54 A2
Grosvenor Residences 1 W14 ....39 C3
Grosvenor Sq W1 117 C4
Grosvenor St W1 118 A4
Grosvenor Terr SE5 ....48 B4
Grosvenor The NW11 ....2 A4
Grosvernor Wharf Rd E14....42 C2
Grote's Bldgs SE3..53 A1
Grote's Pl SE3......53 A1
Groton Rd SW18....71 A2
Grotto Ct SE1 .... 136 C4
Grotto Pas W1 ... 103 B4
Grove Crescent Rd E15....19 C2
Grove Ct
Camberwell SE5.....49 A1
Clapham SW4.......61 B4
South Kensington SW10 .... 143 A1
St John's Wood NW8 .... 89 B4
Grovedale Rd N19...4 C2
Grove Dwellings E1....32 B4
Grove End NW5 ....13 A4
Grove End Gdns NW8 .... 79 A1
Grove End Ho NW8 .... 89 B3
Grove End Rd NW8 .... 89 B3
Grove Gdns NW8 .. 90 B3
Grove Hall Ct
Bow E3 ....26 C3
St John's Wood NW8 .... 89 A4
Grove Hill Rd SE5 ..64 A4
Grove Ho
Blackheath SE3 .....53 B1
Chelsea SW3 ..... 158 B4
Grove La SE5.......64 A4
Groveland Ct EC4 109 A1
Grovelands Cl SE5..49 A1
Grove Lane Terr SE5....48 C1
Groveley Ho 7 N4 ..6 B4
Grove Lo SW4......61 B3
Grove Mans
London SW4........60 B3
2 Shepherd's Bush W6 ....39 B4
3 Stamford Hill N16..7 C3
Grove Mews W6....39 B3
GROVE PARK 45 B2
Grove Park Bridge W4 ....45 B3
Grove Park Gdns W4 ....45 B3
Grove Park Mews W4 ....45 B3
Grove Park Prim Sch W4 ....45 B4
Grove Park Rd W4 ....45 A3
Grove Park Terr W4 ....45 A4
Grove Pk SE5 ......49 A1
Grove Pl Acton W3..28 B1
Balham SW12.......61 A1
Hampstead NW3 .....2 C1
Grover Ct SE13.....52 A1
Grove Rd Acton W3..28 B1
Barnes SW13.......46 B1
Bow E3 ....26 A3
Richmond TW10.....54 B1
Willesden NW2 ......9 B2
Grover Ho
4 London SW4.....61 B2
Vauxhall SE11..... 149 A1
Groveside Ct SW11 .... 167 B2
Grove St SE8.......41 B1
Grove Terr NW5 ....13 A4
Grove Terrace Mews NW5....4 A1
Grove The
Dulwich SE21.......76 C3
Hendon NW11 ....1 A4
Highgate N6.........3 C3
Stroud Green N4 .....5 B4
Grove Vale SE22....64 B3
Groveway SW9... 173 A3
Grovewood 9 TW9 ....44 C2
Grovewood Ho NW2....1 B2
Grummant Rd SE15....49 B2
Grundy St E14.....34 A3
Guardian Angels RC Prim Sch E3 ......26 A2
Guards Mus The★ SW1 .... 133 A3
Gubyon Ave SE24...63 A2
Guerin Sq E3.......26 B2
Guernsey Gr SE24 ..75 B4
Guernsey Ho 10 N1....15 B2
Guernsey Rd 11 N1....15 B2
Guildford Gr SE10 ..52 A2
Guildford Ho 23 SE5 ....48 B1
Guildford Rd SW8 .... 172 B4
Guild Hall★ EC2.. 109 A2
Guildhall Bldgs EC2.... 109 B2
Guildhall Ho EC2 . 109 B2
Guildhall Sch Music & Drama EC2...... 109 A4
Guildhall Yd EC2 . 109 A2
Guildhouse St SW1 .... 146 C3
Guilford Pl WC1... 94 C1
Guilford St WC1... 94 B1
Guillemot Ct 28 SE8....51 B4
Guilsborough Cl NW10....8 A1
Guinness Cl E9.....18 A1
Guinness Ct
Chelsea SW3 ..... 144 C3
Finsbury EC1 ...... 97 A3
Primrose Hill NW8.. 80 B3
Whitechapel E1 ... 111 A1
Guinness Sq SE1 . 152 A4
Guinness Trust Bldgs
Bermondsey SE1 .. 138 A4
7 Bethnal Green E2....24 C3
Chelsea SW3 ..... 144 C3
Hammersmith W6 ...39 B1
Kennington SE11 .. 150 A2
Guion Rd SW6 ... 165 A2
Gujarat Ho 1 N16...7 A1
Gulland Wlk 21 N1....15 B2
Gullane Ho 24 E3...26 B3
Gulliver St SE16....41 B3
Gulston Wlk SW3 145 A3
Gunmakers La E3 ..26 A4
GUNNERSBURY ...37 A2
Gunnersbury Avenue (North Circular Rd) W3 ....36 C3
Gunnersbury Cl 8 W4 ....37 A1
Gunnersbury Cres W3 ....36 C4
Gunnersbury Ct 8 W3 ....37 A4
Gunnersbury Dr W5 ....36 B4
Gunnersbury Gdns W3 ....36 C4
Gunnersbury La W3 ....36 C4
Gunnersbury Mews 6 W4 ....37 A1
Gunnersbury Park W3 ....36 C3
Gunnersbury Park Mus★ W3.........36 C3
Gunnersbury Sta W4 ....37 A1
Gunners Rd SW18..71 C2
Gunpowder Sq EC4.... 107 C2
Gun St E1........ 110 C3
Gunstor Rd N16 ....16 A4
Gunter Gr SW6... 156 C2
Gunterstone Rd W14 .... 140 B2
Gunthorpe St E1 . 111 A2
Gunwhale Cl SE16..32 C1
Gun Wharf
Old Ford E3........26 A4
Wapping E1 ....32 B1
Gurdon Ho 7 E14..33 C3
Gurdon Rd SE7.....43 C1
Gurney Ho
Bayswater W2 .... 100 A2
14 Bethnal Green E2....24 C3
Gurney Rd SW6 ....59 B4
Guthrie Ct SE1 ... 135 C3
Guthrie St SW3... 144 A2
Gutter La EC2.... 108 C2
Guyscliff Rd SE13 ..67 B2
Guy's Hospl SE1.. 137 C4
Guy's Hospl Sch SE1.... 123 C1
Guy St SE1....... 137 C4
Gwalior Rd SW15...57 C4
Gwendolen Ave SW15 ....57 C2
Gwendolen Cl SW15 ....57 C2
Gwendwr Rd W14 .... 140 B2
Gwent Ct 13 SE16 ..32 C1
Gwilym Maries Ho 11 E2....25 A2
Gwyn Cl SW6..... 156 C1
Gwynne Cl W4 .....46 B4
Gwynne Ho
Finsbury WC1...... 95 B3
6 Streatham SW2 ..74 B3
Whitechapel E1 .....32 A4
Gwynne Pl WC1... 95 A3
Gwynne Rd SW11 167 C2
Gye Ho 2 SW4.....62 A3
Gylcote Cl SE5 .....63 C3

H

Haarlem Rd 12 W14 ....39 C3
Haberdasher Pl N1.......24 A2 98 A4
Haberdashers' Aske's Hatcham Coll SE4....51 A1
Haberdasher St N1.... 97 C4
Hackford Rd SW9 173 A4
Hackford Wlk SW9 .... 173 B3
HACKNEY 17 A2
Hackney Central Sta E8....17 A2
Hackney Coll (Poplar Ctr) E3....27 A1
Hackney Com Coll N1......24 A2 98 B4
Hackney Downs Sta E8....17 A3
Hackney Free & Parochial CE Sec Sch E9....17 B2
Hackney Gr E8 .....17 A2
Hackney Hospl E9..18 A3
Hackney Rd E2.....24 C3
Hackney Stadium Mkt★ E15.........18 C2
HACKNEY WICK ...18 C2
Hackney Wick E9...18 B2
Hackney Wick Sta E9....18 C2
Hackworth Point 24 E3....27 A2
Hacon Sq 12 E8 ....17 A1
Haddo Ho
Gospel Oak NW5 ....13 A4
Greenwich SE10.....52 A4
Haddon Ct W3 .....29 B2
Haddo St SE10 .....52 B4
Haden Ct N4........5 C2
Hadfield Ho E1... 111 C1
Hadleigh Cl 17 E1 ..25 B1
Hadleigh Ho 16 E1....25 B1
Hadleigh St E2.....25 B2
Hadley Ct N16.......7 C3
Hadley Gdns W4 ...37 C1
Hadley St NW1 .....13 A2
Hadlow Ho SE17.. 152 B2
Hadrian Cl 5 E3 ...26 C4
Hadrian Ct SE4.....66 C4
Hadrian Est 33 E2 ..24 C3
Hadrian St SE10.....43 A1
Hadstock Ho NW1. 93 C4
Hadyn Park Ct 13 W12 ....38 C4
Hadyn Park Rd W12 ....38 C4
Hafer Rd SW11.....60 B3
HAGGERSTON 24 B3
Haggerston Rd E8..24 B4
Haggerston Sch E2....24 B3
Haggerston Studios 30 E8 ....24 B4
Hague Prim Sch E2....25 A1
Hague St E2 .24 C2 99 C3
Haig Ho 4 E2.....24 C3

Hailsham Ave SW2 74 B2
Hainford Cl SE4 65 C3
Haining Cl 3 W4 36 C1
Hainton Cl E1 32 A3
Halcomb St N1 24 A4
Halcrow St E1 32 A4
Halcyon Wharf E1 125 C2
Haldane Pl SW18 71 A3
Haldane Rd SW6 155 A3
Haldon Rd SW18 58 B1
Hale Ho SW1 147 C2
Hales Ho 3 SW12 73 A4
Hales Prior N1 84 C1
Hales St SE8 51 C3
Hale St E14 34 A2
Halesworth Rd SE13 67 A4
Half Moon Cres N1 85 A2
Half Moon Ct EC1 108 C3
Half Moon La SE24 63 B1
Halfmoon Pas E1 111 A1
Half Moon St W1 118 B1
Halford Ho 9 SW15 57 C2
Halford Rd
- Richmond TW10 54 A2
- West Brompton SW6 155 B3

Haliday Ho N1 15 C2
Haliday Wlk 4 N1 15 C2
Halidon Cl E9 17 B3
Haliwell Ho NW6 78 A3
Halkett Ho 1 E2 25 B4
Halkin Arc SW1 131 A2
Halkin Mews SW1 131 B2
Halkin Pl SW1 131 B2
Halkin St SW1 131 C3
Hallam Ct W1 104 B4
Hallam Ho
- London SW9 173 B4
- Pimlico SW1 147 A1

Hallam Mews W1 104 B4
Hallam Rd SW13 57 A4
Hallam St W1 104 B4
Halley Gdns SE13 67 C3
Halley Ho
- 16 Bethnal Green E2 24 C3
- 8 Cubitt Town SE10 43 B1

Halley Prim Sch E14 33 A4
Halley St E14 33 A4
Hallfield Jun & Inf Schs W2 100 B1
Hall Gate NW8 89 A4
Halliday Ho E1 111 C1
Halliford St N1 15 C1
Halling Ho SE1 137 C3
Hallings Wharf Studios 2 E15 27 C4
Halliwell Ct 4 SE22 64 C2
Halliwell Rd SW2 62 B1
Hall Oak Wlk NW6 10 B2
Hall Pl W2 89 B1
Hall Rd Leyton E15 19 C4
- St John's Wood NW8 89 A4

Hall Sch The NW3 11 C2
Hall Sch Wimbledon SW15 68 C1
Hall St EC1 96 B4
Hallsville Prim Sch E16 35 C3
Hallsville Rd E16 35 B3
Hall Twr W2 101 C4
Halpin Pl SE17 151 C3
Halsbury Ho 4 N7 14 B4
Halsbury Rd W12 30 A1
Halsey St SW3 144 C4
Halsmere Rd SE5 48 A2
Halstead Ct N1 87 C1
Halston Cl SW11 60 B1
Halstow 12 NW5 12 C2
Halstow Prim Sch SE10 43 C1
Halstow Rd
- Greenwich SE3, SE10 43 C1
- Kensal Green NW10 22 C2

Halton Cross St N1 86 B4
Haltone Ho SW4 171 C1
Halton Ho 22 N1 15 A1
Halton Mans N1 15 A1
Halton Pl N1 86 C4
Halton Rd N1 86 B4
Halyard Ho E14 42 B3
Hambalt Rd SW4 61 B2
Hambledon SE17 48 C4
Hambledon Chase N4 5 A4
Hambledon Ho E5 17 A4
Hambledon Pl SE21 76 B3
Hambledon Rd SW18 70 B4
Hamble St SW6 59 A4
Hambley Ho 5 SE16 40 A2
Hamblyn Ct N16 7 B4
Hambridge Way SW2 74 C4
Hambrook Ct 12 NW5 13 A4
Hamers Ho 19 SW2 74 C4
Hamilton Cl
- Rotherhithe SE16 41 A4
- St John's Wood NW8 89 B3

Hamilton Ct W9 88 C4
Hamilton Gdns NW8 89 A4
Hamilton Hall NW8 78 C1
Hamilton Ho
- 23 Bow E3 26 B2
- Chiswick W4 46 A4
- Kensington W8 128 A4
- 1 Poplar E14 33 B2
- Putney SW15 56 C2
- 10 Richmond TW9 44 C2
- St John's Wood NW8 89 B4

Hamilton La N5 15 A4
Hamilton Lo 37 E1 25 B1
Hamilton Mews W1 132 A4
Hamilton Pk N5 15 A4
Hamilton Pk W N5 15 A4
Hamilton Pl W1 117 C1
Hamilton Rd
- Acton W4 38 A4
- Hendon NW11 1 A4
- Willesden NW10 8 C3

Hamilton Sq SE1 137 C4
Hamilton St SE8 51 C4
Hamilton Terr NW8 89 A4
Hamlet Ct
- 1 Hammersmith W6 38 C2
- Kennington SE11 150 A2

Hamlet Gdns W6 38 C2
Hamlet Ind Est E9 18 C1
Hamlet Sq NW2 1 A1
Hamlets Way E3 26 B1
Hamlet The SE5 63 C4
Hamlet Way SE1 137 C4
Hammelton Gn 2 SW9 48 A2
Hammersley Ho 8 SE14 50 B3
HAMMERSMITH 39 B2
Hammersmith Bridge Rd W6, SW13 39 B1
Hammersmith Broadway
- Hammersmith W6 39 B1
- 5 Hammersmith W6 39 B2

Hammersmith Flyover W6 39 B1
Hammersmith Gr W6 39 B3
Hammersmith Hospl W12 30 A3
Hammersmith Rd
- Hammersmith W6 39 C2
- Kensington W14 140 B4

Hammersmith Sta W6 39 B2
Hammersmith Terr 6 W6 38 C1
Hammett St EC3 124 C4
Hammond Ho
- 10 Deptford SE14 50 B3
- Millwall E14 42 A3

Hammond Lo 6 W9 31 C4
Hammond St NW5 13 B2
Hamond Sq N1 24 A3
Hampden Cl NW1 83 C2
Hampden Gurney CE Prim Sch W1 102 B2
Hampden Gurney St W1 102 C1
Hampden Rd N19 4 C2
Hampshire Ct 6 SW13 46 B1
Hampshire Hog La
- 3 Hammersmith W6 39 A1
- 11 Hammersmith W6 39 A2

Hampshire Sch The SW7 130 A3
Hampshire St NW5 13 C2
Hampson Way SW8 172 C4
HAMPSTEAD 11 B2
Hampstead Coll of Fine Arts & Humanities NW3 12 A2
Hampstead Gate NW3 11 B3
Hampstead Gn NW3 12 A3
Hampstead Gr NW3 2 B1
Hampstead Heath★ NW3 2 C2
Hampstead Heath Sta NW3 12 A4
Hampstead High St NW3 11 C4
Hampstead Hill Gdns NW3 12 A4
Hampstead Hill Sch NW3 12 A3
Hampstead La N6 3 A4
Hampstead Parochial CE Prim Sch NW3 11 B4
Hampstead Rd NW1 92 C4
Hampstead Sch NW2 10 A4
Hampstead Sq 1 NW3 2 B1
Hampstead Sta NW3 11 B4
Hampstead West 4 NW6 10 C2
Hampstead Wlk 1 E3 26 B4
Hampton Cl NW6 23 C2
Hampton Ct
- 1 Islington N1 15 A2
- 19 Rotherhithe SE16 32 C1

Hampton St SE1 150 B3
Hamstead Gates 11 NW5 13 A2
Ham Yd W1 119 B4
Hana Mews E5 17 A4
Hanbury Ho
- Bethnal Green E1 111 B4
- South Lambeth SW8 162 B3

Hanbury Mews N1 87 A3
Hanbury Rd W3 37 A4
Hanbury St E1 111 A4
Hancock Nunn Ho 1 NW3 12 B1
Hancock Rd E3 27 B2
Handa Wlk 3 N1 15 B2
Hand Ct WC1 107 A3
Handel Mans
- Barnes SW13 47 B3
- Bloomsbury WC1 94 B2

Handel St WC1 94 B2
Handforth Rd SW9 163 B2
Handley Rd E9 25 B4
Hands Wlk E16 35 C3
Hanford Cl SW18 70 C3
Hankey Pl SE1 137 C3
Hanley Ct N4 5 B3
Hanley Gdns N4 5 B3
Hanley Rd N4, N19 5 A3
Hanmer Wlk N7 5 B2
Hannah Mary Way SE1 153 C3
Hannay La N8 4 C4
Hannay Wlk SW16 73 C2
Hannell Rd SW6 154 B2
Hannen Ho SE5 63 C4
Hannen Rd SE27 75 A1
Hannibal Rd E1 32 B4
Hannington Rd SW4 61 A4
Hanover Ave E16 35 C1
Hanover Cl TW9 44 C3
Hanover Ct
- Shepherd's Bush W12 29 C1

Hanover Ct *continued*
- Stamford Hill N16 7 B4

Hanover Gate Mans NW1 90 B2
Hanover Gdns SE11 163 B3
Hanover Ho NW8 80 A1
Hanover Mans 5 SW2 62 C2
Hanover Pk SE15 49 C2
Hanover Pl
- 16 Bow E3 26 B2
- St Giles WC2 106 B1

Hanover Prim Sch N1 86 C2
Hanover Rd NW10 22 B4
Hanover Sq W1 104 B1
Hanover St W1 104 B1
Hanover Stps W2 102 B1
Hanover Terr NW1 90 C3
Hanover Terrace Mews NW1 90 B3
Hanover West Ind Est NW10 20 C2
Hanover Yd N1 86 C2
Hansard Mews W14 39 C4
Hanscomb Mews SW4 61 B3
Hans Cres SW1 130 C2
Hansler Ct 14 SW19 70 A3
Hansler Rd SE22 64 B2
Hanson Cl
- Balham SW12 73 A4
- Mortlake SW14 55 B4

Hanson Ho E1 125 C4
Hanson St W1 104 C4
Hans Pl SW1 130 C2
Hans Rd SW3 130 C2
Hans St SW1 131 A1
Hanway Ho SW9 173 C4
Hanway Pl W1 105 B2
Hanway St W1 105 B2
Hanworth Ho SE5 48 A3
Harben Rd NW6 11 B1
Harberson Rd SW12 73 A3
Harberton Rd N19 4 B3
Harbet Rd W2 101 C3
Harbinger Prim Sch E14 42 A2
Harbinger Rd E14 42 A2
Harbin Ho 5 SW2 74 C3
Harbledown Ho SE1 137 B3
Harbledown Rd SW6 165 B4
Harbord Cl SE5 48 C1
Harbord Ho 5 SE16 40 C2
Harbord St SW6 47 C2
Harborough Sch N19 4 C2
Harbour Ave SW10 167 A3
Harbour Exchange Sq E14 42 A4
Harbour Rd SE5 63 B4
Harbridge Ave SW15 68 C4
Harbut Rd SW11 59 C3
Harcombe Rd N16 7 A1
Harcourt Ho
- Clapham SW8 171 B2

Harcourt Ho *continued*
Marylebone W1 ... 104 A2
[4] Willesden NW10 ... 9 B2
Harcourt Rd SE4 ... 66 B4
Harcourt St W1 ... 102 B3
Harcourt Terr SW10 ... 142 B1
Hardcastle Ho
[3] New Cross Gate SE14 ... 51 A2
[8] Peckham SE15 ... 49 C2
Hardel Rise SW2 ... 75 A3
Hardel Wlk SE24, SW2 ... 74 C4
Harden Ho SE5 ... 49 A1
Harders Rd SE15 ... 50 A1
Hardess St SE24 ... 63 B4
Hardham Ho [5] SW2 ... 62 C1
Harding Cl SE17 ... 48 B4
Hardinge Rd NW10 ... 22 B4
Hardinge St E1 ... 32 B3
Harding Ho SW13 ... 47 A4
Hardington [2] NW1 ... 12 C1
Hardwicke Ho [14] E3 ... 27 A2
Hardwicke Mews WC1 ... 95 A3
Hardwicke Rd W4 ... 37 C2
Hardwick Ho
London SW8 ... 171 B2
Marylebone NW8 ... 90 B2
Hardwick St EC1 ... 95 C3
Hardwick's Way SW18 ... 58 C2
Hardwidge St SE1 ... 138 A4
Hardy Ave [4] E16 ... 35 C1
Hardy Cl SE16 ... 40 C4
Hardy Cotts [2] SE10 ... 52 C4
Hardy Ct SE3 ... 53 B4
Hardy Rd SE3 ... 53 B4
Hare and Billet Rd SE3 ... 52 C1
Harecourt Rd N1 ... 15 B2
Hare Ct EC4 ... 107 B1
Haredale Ho SE16 ... 139 B3
Haredale Rd SE24 ... 63 B3
Harefield Mews SE4 ... 66 B4
Harefield Rd SE4 ... 66 B4
Hare Marsh E2 ... 24 C1 99 B2
Hare Pl EC4 ... 107 C1
Hare Row E2 ... 25 A3
Hare Wlk N1 ... 24 A3
Harewood Ave NW1 ... 90 B1
Harewood Pl W1 ... 104 B1
Harewood Row NW1 ... 102 B4
Harfield Gdns [1] SE5 ... 64 A4
Harfleur Ct SE11 ... 150 A3
Harford Ho
Camberwell SE5 ... 48 B4
Notting Hill W11 ... 31 B4
Harford Mews [6] N19 ... 4 C1
Harford St E1 ... 26 A1
Hargrave Mans [3] N19 ... 4 C2
Hargrave Park Prim Sch N19 ... 4 B2
Hargrave Pk N19 ... 4 B2
Hargrave Pl N7 ... 13 C3
Hargrave Rd N19 ... 4 B2
Hargraves Ho [14] W12 ... 30 A2
Hargwyne St SW9 ... 62 B4
Harkness Ho E1 ... 111 C1
Harlech Twr [5] W3 ... 37 B4
Harlescott Rd SE15 ... 65 C3
HARLESDEN ... 21 B4
Harlesden Gdns NW10 ... 21 B4
Harlesden Plaza [2] NW10 ... 21 B3
Harlesden Prim Sch NW10 ... 21 A3
Harlesden Rd NW10 ... 21 C4
Harlesden Sta NW10 ... 20 C3
Harleyford Ct SW8 ... 162 C4
Harleyford Manor [8] W3 ... 28 B1
Harleyford Rd SE11 ... 162 C4
Harleyford St SE11 ... 163 B3
Harley Gdns SW10 ... 143 A1
Harley Gr E3 ... 26 B2
Harley Ho NW1 ... 91 C1
Harley Pl W1 ... 104 A3
Harley Rd
Hampstead NW3 ... 11 C1
Harlesden NW10 ... 21 A3
Harley St W1 ... 104 A3
Harley Villas NW10 ... 21 A3
Harling Ct SW11 ... 168 C2
Harlowe Ho [13] E8 ... 24 B4
Harlynwood [19] SE5 ... 48 B3
Harman Cl
Bermondsey SE1 ... 153 B1
Cricklewood NW2 ... 1 A1
Harman Dr NW2 ... 10 A4
Harmon Ho [7] SE8 ... 41 B2
Harmood Gr NW1 ... 13 A1
Harmood Ho [2] NW1 ... 13 A1
Harmood St NW1 ... 13 A1
Harmsworth St SE17 ... 150 A1
Harnage Ho TW8 ... 36 A1
Harney Ct SE14 ... 51 A2
Harold Ct [14] SE16 ... 40 C4
Harold Est SE1 ... 138 B1
Harold Ho [16] E2 ... 25 C3
Harold Laski Ho EC1 ... 96 B3
Harold Maddison Ho SE17 ... 150 B2
Harold Rd NW10 ... 20 C2
Harold Wilson Ho SW6 ... 155 A3
Harp Alley EC4 ... 108 A2
Harpenden Rd SE27, SW16 ... 75 A2
Harpenmead Point NW2 ... 1 B2
Harper Ho [3] SW9 ... 63 A4
Harper Mews SW17 ... 71 B1
Harper Rd SE1 ... 137 A2
Harp La EC3 ... 124 A3
Harpley Sq E1 ... 25 C1
Harpsden St SW11 ... 169 B3
Harpur Mews WC1 ... 106 C4
Harpur St WC1 ... 106 C4
Harrier Ho [9] SW11 ... 60 A4
Harriet Cl E8 ... 24 C4
Harriet Ho SW6 ... 156 B1
Harriet St SW1 ... 131 A3
Harriet Tubman Cl [21] SW2 ... 74 C4
Harriet Wlk SW1 ... 131 A3
Harrington Ct
South Kensington SW7 ... 143 C4
[9] West Kilburn W9 ... 23 B2
Harrington Gdns SW7 ... 142 C3
Harrington Ho
Regent's Pk NW1 ... 92 C4
Westminster SW1 ... 147 C2
Harrington Rd SW7 ... 143 B4
Harrington Sq NW1 ... 82 C1
Harrington St NW1 ... 92 C4
Harriott Cl SE10 ... 43 B2
Harriott Ho [11] E1 ... 32 B3
Harris Girl's Acad SE15 ... 65 B2
Harris Ho
[11] Bow E3 ... 26 C2
[7] Brixton SW9 ... 62 C4
Harrison Ho SE17 ... 151 B2
Harrison Rd NW10 ... 20 C4
Harrisons Ct [1] SE14 ... 50 C4
Harrison St WC1 ... 94 B3
Harris St SE5 ... 48 C3
Harrodian Sch The SW13 ... 46 B3
Harrogate Ct [2] SE26 ... 76 C1
Harrold Ho [1] NW3 ... 11 B1
Harroway Rd SW11 ... 167 C2
Harrowby St W1 ... 102 B2
Harrowgate Ho [22] E9 ... 17 C2
Harrowgate Rd E9 ... 18 A1
Harrow La E14 ... 34 B2
Harrow Pl E1 ... 110 B2
Harrow Rd
Little Venice W2 ... 101 A3
Westbourne Green W2, W9 ... 23 C1
Harrow St NW1 ... 102 A4
Harry Gosling Prim Sch E1 ... 111 C1
Harry Hinkins Ho SE17 ... 151 A1
Harry Lambourn Ho [10] SE15 ... 50 A3
Hartfield Terr E3 ... 26 C3
Hartham Cl N7 ... 14 A3
Hartham Rd N7 ... 14 A3
Hart Ho SW2 ... 74 C3
Hartington Ct
Chiswick W4 ... 45 A3
South Lambeth SW8 ... 172 A4
Hartington Rd
Chiswick W4 ... 45 B2
South Lambeth SW8 ... 162 A1
Hartismere Rd SW6 ... 155 A2
Hartlake Rd E9 ... 18 A2
Hartland NW1 ... 83 A3
Hartland Rd
Camden Town NW1 ... 13 A1
Kilburn NW6 ... 23 B4
Hartley Ho
Bermondsey SE1 ... 153 A4
Putney SW15 ... 56 C2
Hartley St E2 ... 25 B2
Hartnoll Ho [4] N7 ... 14 C3
Hartnoll St N7 ... 14 B3
Harton Lodge [2] SE8 ... 51 C2
Harton St SE8 ... 51 C2
Hartopp Ct [20] N16 ... 7 A1
Hartopp Point SW6 ... 154 B2
Hartshorn Alley EC3 ... 110 B1
Hart's La SE14 ... 51 A2
Hart St EC3 ... 124 B4
Hartswood Ho [10] SW2 ... 74 A3
Hartswood Rd W12 ... 38 B3
Hartwell Ct SE22 ... 64 C3
Hartwell St E8 ... 16 B2
Harvard Ct NW6 ... 11 A3
Harvard Hill W4 ... 45 A4
Harvard Ho
[3] Camberwell SE17 ... 48 A4
Putney SW15 ... 57 C1
Harvard Mans [18] SW11 ... 59 C3
Harvard Rd
[11] Acton Green W4 ... 37 B1
Gunnersbury W4 ... 37 A1
Lewisham SE13 ... 67 B2
Harvey Ct SW11 ... 168 B4
Harvey Ho
[10] Bethnal Green E1 ... 25 A1
Brentford TW8 ... 36 A1
Pimlico SW1 ... 147 C1
Shoreditch N1 ... 87 C3
Harvey Lo [8] W9 ... 31 C4
Harvey Point [7] E16 ... 35 C4
Harvey Rd [15] SE5 ... 48 C2
Harvey St N1 ... 87 C3
Harvington Wlk E8 ... 16 C1
Harvist Rd NW6 ... 23 A3
Harwood Ct
Putney SW15 ... 57 B3
Shoreditch N1 ... 87 C3
Harwood Point SE16 ... 41 B4
Harwood Rd SW6 ... 156 A1
Harwood Terr SW6 ... 166 A4
Hascombe Ho [11] SW15 ... 69 A3
Hascombe Terr [2] SE5 ... 48 C1
Haselrigge Rd SW4 ... 61 C3
Hasker St SW3 ... 144 B4
Haslam Cl N1 ... 14 C1
Haslam Ho [12] N1 ... 15 B1
Haslam St SE15 ... 49 B2
Haslemere Ave SW18 ... 71 A2
Haslemere Ct [5] N16 ... 7 A3
Haslemere Ind Est SW18 ... 71 A2
Haslemere Rd N8 ... 5 A4
Hassard St E2 ... 24 B3
Hassett Rd E9 ... 18 A2
Hassop Rd NW2 ... 9 C4
Hastings Cl [17] SE15 ... 49 C3
Hastings Ho [18] W12 ... 30 A2
Hastings Hos WC1 ... 94 A3
Hastings St WC1 ... 94 A3
Hatcham Mews Bsns Ctr SE14 ... 50 C2
Hatcham Park Mews SE14 ... 50 C2
Hatcham Park Rd SE14 ... 50 C2
Hatcham Rd SE15 ... 50 B4
Hatchard Rd N19 ... 5 A2
Hatchers Mews SE1 ... 138 B3
Hatcliffe Almshouses [8] SE10 ... 43 A1
Hatcliffe St SE10 ... 43 B1
Hatfield Cl SE14 ... 50 C3
Hatfield Ct SE3 ... 53 C3
Hatfield Ho EC1 ... 96 C1
Hatfield Rd W4 ... 37 C4
Hatfields SE1 ... 121 C2
Hathaway Ho N1 ... 24 A2 98 A4
Hatherley Ct W2 ... 100 A2
Hatherley Gr W2 ... 100 A2
Hatherley Rd TW9 ... 44 B2
Hatherley St SW1 ... 147 A3
Hathersage Ct N1 ... 15 C3
Hathersley Ho [3] SW2 ... 74 C4
Hathorne Cl [3] SE15 ... 50 A1
Hathway Ho [3] SE15 ... 50 B1
Hathway St [4] SE15 ... 50 B1
Hatley Rd N4, N7 ... 5 B2
Hat & Mitre Ct EC1 ... 96 B1
Hatstone Ct NW3 ... 11 B3
Hatteraick St [6] SE16 ... 40 B4
Hatton Gdn EC1 ... 107 C4
Hatton Ho E1 ... 125 C4
Hatton Pl EC1 ... 107 C4
Hatton Row NW8 ... 89 C1
Hatton St NW8 ... 89 C1
Hatton Wall EC1 ... 107 C4
Haunch of Venison Yd W1 ... 104 A1
Hauteville Court Gdns [2] W6 ... 38 B3
Havana Rd SW18, SW19 ... 70 C2

Havannah St E14 41 C4
Havelock Cl 13 W12 30 A2
Havelock Ct 8 SE15 50 A3
Havelock St N1 84 B4
Havelock Terr SW8 160 B1
Haven Cl SW19 69 C1
Havenpool NW8 78 B3
Haven St 18 NW1 13 A1
Haven The TW9 54 C4
Havercourt 3 NW3 12 A2
Haverfield Gdns TW9 44 C3
Haverfield Rd E3 26 A2
Haverhill Rd SW12 73 B3
Havering 8 NW1 13 A1
Havering Ho N4 6 B4
Havering St E1 32 C3
Haversham Lo NW2 9 C3
Haversham Pl N6 3 B2
Haverstock Hill NW3 12 B2
Haverstock Rd NW5 12 C3
Haverstock Sch NW1 12 C2
Haverstock St N1 86 B1
Havil St SE5 49 A2
Havisham Ho SE16 139 B3
Hawarden Gr SE24 75 B4
Hawberry Lo N7 14 A2
Hawes St N1 15 A1
Hawgood St E3 33 C4
Hawke Ho 20 E1 25 C1
Hawke Pl 29 SE16 40 C4
Hawkesbury Rd SW15 57 A2
Hawkesworth Ho 5 SW4 61 B1
Hawke Twr 4 SE14 51 A4
Hawk Ho 7 SW11 60 A4
Hawkins Ho 3 SE8 51 C4
Hawkins Rd NW10 8 A1
Hawkley Gdns SE27 75 A2
Hawkridge 19 NW5 12 C2
Hawkshaw Cl 28 SW2 74 A4
Hawkshead NW1 92 C4
Hawkshead Rd
Acton W4 38 A4
Willesden NW10 8 B1
Hawkslade Rd SE15 65 C2
Hawksley Rd N16 7 A1
Hawks Mews 10 SE10 52 B3
Hawksmoor Mews E1 32 A2
Hawksmoor Pl E2 24 C1 99 B2
Hawksmoor St 5 W6 47 C4
Hawkstone Rd SE16 40 B2
Hawkwell Wlk N1 87 A4
Hawley Cres NW1 13 A1
Hawley Inf Sch NW1 13 A1
Hawley Mews 4 NW1 13 A1
Hawley Rd 3 NW1 13 A1
Hawley St NW1 13 A1
Haworth Ho 7 SW2 62 C1
Hawstead Rd SE6 67 A1
Hawthorn Ave E3 26 B4
Hawthorn Ct
Putney SW15 57 A4
Richmond TW9 45 A2
Hawthorne Cl N1 16 A2
Hawthorne Ho SW1 147 A1
Hawthorn Ho SE14 51 B2
Hawthorn Rd NW10 8 C1
Hawthorn Wlk W10 23 A1
Hawtrey Rd NW3 12 A1
Haycroft Gdns NW10 22 A4
Haycroft Mans NW10 21 C4
Haycroft Rd SW2 62 A2
Hay Currie St E14 34 A3
Hayday Rd E16 35 C4
Hayden Piper Ho SW3 158 C4
Hayden's Pl W11 31 B3
Haydon St E1, EC3 124 C4
Haydon Way SW11 59 C3
Haydon Wlk E1 111 A1
Hayes Ct
23 Camberwell SE5 48 B3
Streatham SW12 74 A3
Hayes Gr SE15, SE22 64 B3
Hayes Pl NW1 90 B1
Hayfield Pas E1 25 B1
Hayfield Yd 43 E1 25 B1
Hay Hill W1 118 B3
Hayhurst N1 86 B4
Hayles Bldgs SE11 150 B4
Hayles St SE11 150 A4
Hayling Cl 20 N16 16 A3
Haymans Point SE11 148 C2
Haymarket SW1 119 B3
Haymerle Ho 6 SE15 49 C3
Haymerle Rd SE15 49 C4
Haymerle Sch SE15 49 C4
Hayne Ho W11 31 A1 112 A2
Haynes Ho 3 E9 17 C2
Hayne St EC1 108 B4
Hay's Galleria* SE1 124 A2
Hay's La SE1 124 A2
Hay's Mews W1 118 A2
Hay St E2 24 C4
Hayter Ho W12 29 C2
Hayter Rd SW2 62 B2
Haythorn Ho SW11 167 C3
Hayton Cl 11 E8 16 B2
Hayward Ct SW4 172 B2
Hayward Gallery* SE1 121 A2
Hayward Gdns SW15 57 B1
Hayward Ho N1 85 B2
Haywards Pl EC1 96 A2
Hayward's Pl EC1 96 A2
Haywood Lo 23 N7 13 C3
Hazelbourne Rd SW12 61 A1
Hazel Cl
Peckham SE15 49 C1
Upper Holloway N19 4 B2
Hazel Ct 8 SE16 33 A1
Hazeldon Rd SE4 66 A2
Hazel Ho
London SE4 66 B4
12 Maitland Pk NW3 12 B2
Hazellville Rd N19 4 C3
Hazelmere Ct 10 SW2 74 B3
Hazelmere Rd NW6 23 B4
Hazel Rd NW10 22 B2
Hazel Way SE1 152 C4
Hazelwood Cl W5 36 A4
Hazelwood Ho 11 SE8 41 A2
Hazelwood Mans SW6 164 C4
Hazlebury Rd SW6 166 B2
Hazledene Rd W4 45 B4
Hazlewell Rd SW15 57 B2
Hazlewood Cres W10 23 A1
Hazlewood Twr W10 23 B1
Hazlitt Mews W14 126 A1
Hazlitt Rd W14 126 A1
Headbourne Ho SE1 137 C2
Headcorn 10 NW5 12 C2
Headfort Pl SW1 131 C3
Headington Rd SW18 71 B2
Headlam Rd SW4 73 C4
Headlam St E1 25 A1
Heads Mews W11 31 C3
Head St E1 32 C3
Heald St SE8, SE14 51 C2
Healey St NW1 13 A2
Healy Ho 2 E3 26 C1
Heanor Ct 4 E5 17 C4
Hearne Rd W4 44 C4
Hearn's Bldgs SE17 151 C3
Hearnshaw St 1 E14 33 A3
Hearn St EC2 24 A1 98 B1
Hearnville Rd SW12 72 C3
Heart Hospl The W1 103 C3
Heart Raido W11 30 C2
Heathbrook Prim Sch SW4 170 C1
Heath Brow NW3 2 B1
Heath Cl NW11 2 A4
Heathcote Point 25 E9 17 C2
Heathcote St WC1 94 C3
Heathcroft NW11 2 A3
Heath Ct
2 Hampstead NW3 11 B2
Heath Ct *continued*
Stoke Newington N16 6 C3
Heather Cl SW8 61 A4
Heather Ct SW4 172 B3
Heather Ho 11 E14 34 B3
Heatherley Ct N16 7 C1
Heatherley Sch of Fine Art SW10 157 A1
Heather Lo N16 7 A3
Heather Wlk W10 23 A1
Heathfield Ave SW18 71 C4
Heathfield Ct
3 Bow E3 26 C3
5 Chiswick W4 37 C1
Wandsworth SW18 71 C4
Heathfield Gdns
Acton Green W4 37 B1
Blackheath SE3 53 A1
Wandsworth SW18 59 C1
Heathfield Ho SE3 53 A1
Heathfield Pk NW2 9 B2
Heathfield Rd
South Acton W3 37 A4
Wandsworth SW18 59 C1
Heathfield Sq SW18 71 C4
Heathfield Terr W4 37 C1
Heathgate Pl NW3 12 B4
Heath Hurst Rd NW3 12 A4
Heath La SE3 52 C1
Heathland Rd N16 7 A3
Heath Mans
5 Hampstead NW3 11 B4
Putney SW15 57 C1
Heathman's Rd SW6 165 A3
Heath Mead SW19 69 C1
Heathmere Prim Sch SW15 68 C3
Heath Park Gdns NW3 2 A1
Heathpool Ct 8 E1 25 A1
Heath Rd SW8 170 B1
Heath Rise SW15 57 C1
Heath Royal SW15 57 C1
Heathshott 8 TW10 54 A1
Heathside NW3 11 C4
Heathside Prep Sch NW3 11 B4
Heath St NW3 2 B1
Heathstan Rd W12 29 C3
Heath View NW5 12 C4
Heathview Ct SW19 69 C2
Heathview Gdns SW15 69 B4
Heath Villas NW3 2 C1
Heathville Rd N4, N19 5 A4
Heathwall St SW11 60 B4
Heathway SE3 53 C3
Heathway Ct NW3 1 C2
Heathwood Ct SW12 73 B3
Heaton Ho
Chelsea SW10 157 A4
6 Peckham SE15 50 A1
Heaton Rd SE15 50 A1
Heaven Tree Cl N1 15 B3
Heaver Rd 24 SW11 59 C4
Hebden Ct 24 E2 24 B4
Hebdon Rd SW17 72 A1
Heber Prim Sch SE22 64 B1
Heber Rd
Cricklewood NW2 9 C4
East Dulwich SE22 64 B1
Hebron Rd W6 39 A3
Heckfield Pl SW6 155 B1
Heckford Ho E14 34 A3
Heckford St E1 32 C2
Hector Ct
London SW9 173 B4
Putney SW15 57 C2
Hector Ho 14 E2 25 A3
Heddington Gr N7 14 B3
Heddon St W1 118 C4
Hedger's Gr E9 18 A2
Hedger St SE11 150 A4
Hedingham Cl 6 N1 15 B1
Hedley Ct SW15 57 C1
Hedley Ho E14 42 B3
Hedley Row N5, N16 15 C3
Hedsor Ho E2 24 B1 98 C2
Heidegger Cres SW13 47 A3
Heights The NW3 11 B4
Heiron St SE17 48 A4
Helby Rd SW4 61 C1
Heldar Ct SE1 137 C3
Helena Pl 3 E9 25 B4
Helena Rd NW10 9 A3
Helena Sq 12 SE16 33 A2
Helen Gladstone Ho SE1 136 A4
Helen Ho 9 E2 25 A3
Helen Mackay Ho 10 E14 34 C3
Helen Peele Cotts 10 SE16 40 B3
Helenslea Ave NW11 1 C3
Helen's Pl E2 25 B2
Helen Taylor Ho SE16 153 B4
Heliport Est The SW11 167 B1
Helix Ct 17 W11 30 C1
Helix Gdns SW2 62 B1
Helix Rd SW2 62 B1
Helix The SW19 69 C2
Hellenic Coll of London SW1 130 C1
Hellings St E1 125 C1
Helmet Row EC1 97 A2
Helmsdale Ho NW6 78 A1
Helmsley Pl E8 17 A1
Helmsley St 7 E8 17 A1
Helperby Rd NW10 8 A1
Helsby Ct NW8 89 B2
Helsinki Sq SE16 41 A3
Helston NW1 83 A2
Helston Ho SE11 149 C2
Hemans Est SW8 161 C1
Hemans St SW8 161 C1

Hemberton Rd SW9 . . . 62 A4
Hemingford Rd N1 . . . 85 A4
Hemlock Rd W12 . . . 29 B2
Hemming St E1 . . . 24 C1 99 C1
Hemmingway Cl NW5 . . . 12 C4
Hemp Wlk SE17 . . 151 C4
Hemstal Rd NW6 . . . 10 C1
Hemsworth Ct N1 . . 24 A3
Hemsworth St N1 . . 24 A3
Hemus Pl SW3 . . . 144 B1
Henchman St W12 . 29 B3
Henderson Ct
8 Deptford SE14 . . . 50 C4
Hampstead NW3 . . . . 11 C3
Wandsworth SW18 . . 72 A4
Henderson Dr NW8 . . . 89 B2
Henderson Rd SW18 . . . 72 A4
Hendham Rd SW17 . . . 72 B2
Hendre Ho SE1 . . . 152 B3
Hendre Rd SE1 . . . 152 B3
Hendrick Ave SW12 . . . 72 B4
Heneage La EC3 . . 110 B1
Heneage Pl EC3 . . 110 B1
Heneage St E1 . . . 111 A4
Henfield Cl N19 . . . . . 4 B3
Henley Cl SE16 . . . . . 40 B4
Henley Ct
Brondesbury NW2 . . . . 9 C2
Peckham SE15 . . . . . 64 C4
Henley Dr SE1 . . . . 153 A4
Henley Ho E2 . . . 24 B1 99 A2
Henley Prior N1 . . . 84 C1
Henley Rd NW10 . . . 22 B4
Henley St SW11 . . . 169 C2
Henniker Mews SW3 . . . 157 B4
Henniker Rd E15 . . . 19 C3
Henning St SW11 168 A3
Henrietta Cl SE8 . . . 51 C4
Henrietta Ho 11 W6 . . . 39 B1
Henrietta Mews WC1 . . . 94 B2
Henrietta Pl W1 . . 104 A2
Henrietta St
Strand WC2 . . . . . . 120 B4
Stratford New Town E15 . . . 19 B3
Henriques St E1 . . 111 C1
Henry Cavendish Prim Sch SW12 . . . 73 B3
Henry Compton Sec Sch SW6 . . . 164 A4
Henry Dent Cl SE5 . . 63 C4
Henry Dickens Ct W11 . . . . . . 31 A1 112 A2
Henry Fawcett Prim Sch SE11 . . . 163 B4
Henry Ho
Lambeth SE1 . . . . . 121 C1
South Lambeth SW8 . . . 162 A2
St John's Wood NW8 . . . 80 A2
Henry Jackson Ho SW15 . . . 57 C4
Henry Jackson Rd SW15 . . . 57 C4
Henry Rd N4 . . . . . . 6 B3
Henryson Rd SE4 . . . 66 C2
Henry Wise Ho SW1 . . . 147 A3
Henshall Point 19 E3 . . . 27 A2
Henshall St N1 . . . . . 15 C2
Henshaw St SE17 . 151 B4
Hensley Point 28 E9 . . . 17 C2
Henslowe Rd SE22 . . . 64 C2
Henslow Ho 12 SE15 . . . 49 C3
Henson Ave NW2 . . . . 9 B3
Henson Ct 3 N5 . . . 15 B4
Henstridge Pl NW8 . . . 80 A3
Henty Cl SW11 . . . 168 B4
Henty Wlk SW15 . . . 57 A2
Hepburn Mews SW11 . . . 60 B2
Hepplestone Cl SW15 . . . 57 A1
Hepscott Rd E9 . . . . 18 C1
Hepworth Ct
Chelsea SW1 . . . . . 146 A1
Islington N1 . . . . 86 A4
Hera Ct 15 E14 . . . . 41 C2
Heralds Pl SE11 . . 150 A4
Herald St 5 E2 . . . . 25 A1
Herbal Hill EC1 . . . . 95 C1
Herbert Chapman Ct N5 . . . 15 A4
Herbert Cres SW1 . . . 131 A2
Herbert Gdns
Chiswick W4 . . . . 45 A4
Willesden Green NW10 . . . 22 A3
Herbert Ho E1 . . . 110 C2
Herbert Mews 15 SW2 . . . 62 C1
Herbert Morrison Ho SW6 . . . 154 C3
Herbert Morrison Prim Sch SW8 . . . 162 A1
Herbert St NW5 . . . . 12 C2
Herbrand Est WC1 . 94 A2
Herbrand St WC1 . . 94 A2
Hercules Ct 7 SE14 . . . 51 A4
Hercules Pl N7 . . . . . . 5 A1
Hercules Rd SE1 . 135 A1
Hercules St N7 . . . . . . 5 A1
Hereford Bldgs SW3 . . . 157 C4
Hereford Ho
5 Brixton SW2 . . . . . 62 C3
25 Camberwell SE5 . . 48 B1
Knightsbridge SW3 130 B2
Walham Green SW10 . . . 156 B2
Hereford Mans 10 W2 . . . 31 C3
Hereford Mews 11 W2 . . . 31 C3
Hereford Pl SE14 . . . 51 B3
Hereford Rd
Acton W3 . . . . 28 B2
Bayswater W2 . . . . . . 31 C2 113 C4
Hereford Retreat 5 SE15 . . . 49 C3
Hereford Sq SW7 143 A3
Hereford St E2 . . . . 24 C1 99 B2
Hereward House Sch NW3 . . . 11 C2
Heritage Cl SW9 . . . 63 A4
Heritage Ct SE8 . . . . 40 C1
Heritage Ho 22 SW19 . . . 69 C3
Hermes Cl 5 W9 . . . 23 C1
Hermes Ct SW9 . . 173 B4
Hermes St N1 . . . . . 85 B1
Hermitage Ct
2 Child's Hill NW2 . . . 1 C1
Wapping E1 . . . . . . 125 C1
Hermitage Gdns NW2 . . . 1 C1
Hermitage La NW2 . . 1 C1
Hermitage Prim Sch E1 . . . 125 C2
Hermitage Row 9 E8 . . . 16 C3
Hermitage St W2 . 101 B3
Hermitage The
Barnes SW13 . . . . 46 B2
Richmond TW10 . . . . . 54 A2
Hermitage Villas SW6 . . . 155 B4
Hermitage Wall E1 . . . 125 C1
Hermit Pl NW6 . . . . 78 A3
Hermit St EC1 . . . . . 96 A4
Herndon Rd SW18 . . 59 B2
HERNE HILL 63 B2
Herne Hill SE24 . . . . 63 B3
Herne Hill Ho SE24 . . . 63 A1
Herne Hill Mans SE24 . . . 63 B1
Herne Hill Rd SE24 . . . 63 B3
Herne Hill Sch SE24 . . . 63 B2
Herne Hill Sta SE24 . . . 63 A1
Herne Hill Stad SE24 . . . 63 C1
Herne Pl SE24 . . . . . 63 A2
Heron Cl NW10 . . . . . . 8 A2
Heron Ct
16 Cubitt Town E14 . . . 42 B3
7 Dulwich SE21 . . . . 75 C2
Herondale Ave SW18 . . . 72 A3
Heron Dr N4 . . . . 6 B2
Herongate N1 . . . . . 87 A4
Heron Ho
Battersea SW11 . . . 168 B4
Peckham SE15 . . . . . 49 B2
St John's Wood NW8 . . . 80 A1
Heron Ind Est E15 . . 27 A3
Heron Pl
Marylebone W1 . . . 103 C2
Rotherhithe SE16 . . . . 33 A1
Heron Quays E14 . . . . 33 C1
Heron Quays Sta E14 . . . 33 C1
Heron Rd SE24 . . . . . 63 B3
Heron Trad Est W3 . . . 28 A4
Herrick Ho
18 Camberwell SE5 . . . 48 C3
17 Canonbury N16 . . . 15 C4
Herrick Rd N5 . . . . 6 B1
Herrick St SW1 . . . 147 C3
Herries St W10 . . . . . 23 A3
Hersant Cl NW10 . . . 21 C4
Herschell's Mews SE5 . . . 63 B4
Hersham Cl SW15 . . 68 C4
Hershell Ct 1 SW14 . . . 55 A3
Hertford Ave SW14 . . . 56 A3
Hertford Ct 16 SW11 . . . 60 A4
Hertford Lo 10 SW19 . . . 70 A3
Hertford Pl W1 . . . . 93 A1
Hertford Rd N1 . . . . . 24 A4
Hertford St W1 . . . 118 A1
Hertmitage The 5 SE13 . . . 52 B1
Hertslet Rd N7 . . . . . . 5 B1
Hertsmere Rd E14 . . 33 C2
Hesewall Cl SW4 . 171 A1
Hesketh Pl W11 . . . . . . 31 A2 112 A3
Heslop Ct 1 SW12 . . . 72 C3
Heslop Rd SW12 . . . . 72 B3
Hesper Mews SW5 . . . 142 A3
Hesperus Cres E14 . . . 42 A2
Hessel St E1 . . . . 32 A3
Hestercombe Ave SW6 . . . 164 B3
Hester Rd SW11 . . 158 A1
Hester Terr TW9 . . . . 54 C4
Hestia Ho SE1 . . . . 138 A3
Heston Ho
Gunnersbury W4 . . . . 37 A1
5 St Johns SE8 . . . . . 51 C2
Heston St SE14 . . . . . 51 C2
Hetherington Rd SW2, SW4 . . . 62 A3
Hethpool Ho W2 . . 89 B1
Hetley Rd W12 . . . . . 39 A4
Hetty Rees Ct 6 N19 . . . 5 A4
Hevelius Cl SE10 . . . 43 B1
Hever Ho SE15 . . . . . 50 C4
Heversham Ho SE15 . . . 50 B4
Heward Ct SE13 . . . . 52 B1
Hewer Ho 6 SW4 . . . 61 B2
Hewer St W10 . . . . . . 30 C4
Hewett Ho SW15 . . . 47 B1
Hewett St EC2 . . . . 24 A1 98 B1
Hewison St E3 . . . . . 26 B3
Hewlett Rd E3 . . . . . 26 A3
Hewling Ho 1 N16 . . . 16 A3
Hexagon The N6 . . . . 3 B3
Hexham Rd SE27 . . . 75 B2
Hexton Ct N4 . . . . 6 B2
Heybridge 9 NW1 . . . 13 A2
Heydon Ho 3 SE14 . . . 50 B2
Heyford Ave SW8 . 162 B2
Heyford Terr SW8 . . . 162 B2
Heygate St SE17 . . 151 A4
Heylyn Sq E3 . . . . . . 26 B2
Heysham La NW3 . . . 2 A1
Heythorp St SW18 . . 70 B2
Heywood Ho
11 Deptford SE14 . . . 50 C4
6 Tulse Hill SW2 . . . . 62 C1
Heyworth Rd E5 . . . . 17 A4
Hibbert Ho 13 E14 . . 41 C3
Hibbert St SW11 . . . 59 C4
Hichisson Rd SE15 . 65 B2
Hickes Ho 6 NW6 . . 11 C1
Hickey's Almshouses 7 TW9 . . . 54 B3
Hickin St 2 E14 . . . . 42 B3
Hickleton NW1 . . . . 83 A3
Hickling Ho 10 SE16 . . . 40 A3
Hickmore Wlk SW4 . . . 61 B4
Hicks Cl SW11 . . . . . 60 A4
Hicks St SE8 . . . . 41 A1
Hide Pl SW1 . . . . . 147 B3
Hide Twr SW1 . . . . 147 B3
Hieover SE21 . . . . 75 B2
Higgins Ho 7 N1 . . 24 A4
Higginson Ho 2 NW3 . . . 12 B1
Higgs Ind Est 9 SE24 . . . 63 A4
Highbridge Ct 13 SE14 . . . 50 B3
High Bridge Wharf SE10 . . . 42 C1
Highburty Mans 24 N1 . . . 15 A1
HIGHBURY 15 A4
Highbury Cnr N5 . . . 15 A2
Highbury Corner N5 . . . 15 A2
Highbury Cres N5 . . 14 C3
Highbury Fields Sch N5 . . . 15 A3
Highbury Gr N5 . . . . 15 A3
Highbury Grange N5 . . . 15 B4
Highbury Grove Ct N5 . . . 15 A2
Highbury Grove Sch N5 . . . 15 B3
Highbury Hill N5 . . . 15 A4
Highbury & Islington Sta N1 . . . 15 A2
Highbury New Pk N5 . . . 15 B4
Highbury Pk N5 . . . . 15 A4
Highbury Pl N5 . . . . 15 A3
Highbury Quadrant N5 . . . 6 B1
Highbury Quadrant Prim Sch N5 . . . 15 B4
Highbury Station Rd N1 . . . 14 C2
Highbury Terr N5 . . . 15 A3
Highbury Terrace Mews N5 . . . 15 A3
Highcliffe Dr SW15 . . . 56 B1
Highcroft Rd N19 . . . . 5 A4
Highcross Way 4 SW15 . . . 68 C3
Highdown Rd SW15 . . . 57 A1
Highfield Ave NW11 . . . 1 A4
Highfield Cl SE13 . . . 67 C1
Highfield Mews NW6 . . . 11 A1
Highfield Rd W3 . . . 28 B4
Highfield Sch SW18 . . . 72 A4
Highfields Gr N6 . . . . 3 B3
HIGHGATE 3 C4

Highgate Archway N6 . . . 4 B3
Highgate Ave N6 . . . 4 A4
Highgate Cemetery★ N19 . . . 4 A2
Highgate Cl N6 . . . 3 C4
Highgate High St N6 . . . 4 A3
Highgate Hill N19 . . . 4 B3
Highgate Ho 11 SE26 . . . 76 C1
Highgate Rd NW5 . . 13 A4
Highgate Sch
Highgate N6 . . . 3 B4
Highgate N6 . . . 3 C4
Highgate West Hill N6 . . . 3 C2
Highgrove Point 2 NW3 . . . 11 B4
High Holborn WC1 . . . 106 C3
High Holborn Ho WC1 . . . 107 A3
Highlands Ave W3 . . 28 B2
Highlands Cl N4 . . . 5 A4
Highlands Heath SW15 . . . 69 B4
Highlever Rd W10 . . 30 B4
High London 5 N6 . . 4 C4
Highmore Rd SE3 . . 53 A3
High Mount 11 N4 . . . 5 A4
High Park Ave TW9 . . . 44 C2
High Park Rd TW9 . . 44 C2
High Par The SW16 . . . 74 A1
High Point N6 . . . 3 C4
High Rd NW10 . . . 8 C2
Highshore Rd SE15 . . . 49 B1
Highshore Sch SE15 . . . 49 B2
High St Acton W3 . . . 28 A1
Brentford TW8 . . . 44 A4
Stratford Marsh E15 . 27 B4
High Street Harlesden NW10 . . . 21 B3
High Street Kensington Sta W8 . . . 128 A3
High The SW16 . . . 74 A1
High Timber St EC4 . . . 122 C4
High Trees SW2 . . . 74 C3
Hightrees Ho SW12 . . . 60 C1
Highview N8 . . . 5 A4
Highview Ct 2 SW19 . . . 70 A3
High View Prim Sch SW11 . . . 59 C3
Highway Bsns Pk The 7 E1 . . . 32 C2
Highway The E1 . . . 32 B2
Highway Trad Ctr The 6 E1 . . . 32 C2
Highwood Cl SE22 . . 76 C3
Highwood Rd N19 . . . 5 A1
Highworth St NW1 . . . 102 B4
Hilary Cl SW6 . . . 156 A2
Hilary Rd W12 . . . 29 B2
Hilborough Ct 1 E8 . . . 24 B4
Hilborough Rd 1 E8 . . . 16 B1
Hilda Lockert Wlk SW9 . . . 48 A1
Hilda Terr SW9 . . . 173 C2
Hilditch Ho 7 TW10 . . . 54 B1
Hildred Ho SW1 . . 146 A4
Hildreth St SW12 . . . 73 A3
Hildreth Street Mews 2 SW12 . . . 73 A3
Hildyard Rd SW6 . 155 C4
Hiley Rd NW10 . . . 22 B2
Hilgrove Rd NW6 . . . 11 B1
Hillary Ct 13 W12 . . . 39 B4
Hillbeck Cl
Deptford SE15 . . . 50 B3
Deptford SE15 . . . 50 B4
Hillbrow 7 TW10 . . . 54 A1
Hillbury Rd SW17 . . . 73 A1
Hillcourt Rd SE22 . . 65 A1
Hillcrest
Camberwell SE24 . . . 63 C3
Highgate N6 . . . 3 C4
Notting Hill W11 . . . 31 B2 112 C3
Hillcrest Ct NW2 . . . 10 A3
Hillcrest Rd W3 . . . 28 A1
Hill Ct
Hampstead NW3 . . . 12 A4
Putney SW15 . . . 57 C2
Hilldrop Cres N7 . . . 13 C3
Hilldrop La N7 . . . 13 C3
Hilldrop Rd N7 . . . 13 C3
Hillersdon Ave SW13 . . . 46 C1
Hillersdon Ho SW1 . . . 146 A2
Hillery Cl SE17 . . . 151 C3
Hill Farm Rd W10 . . 30 C4
Hillfield Ct NW3 . . . 12 A3
Hillfield Ho N5 . . . 15 B3
Hillfield Mans NW3 . . . 12 A3
Hillfield Rd NW6 . . . 10 C3
Hillgate Pl
Balham SW12 . . . 73 A4
Kensington W8 . . . 31 C1 113 B2
Hillgate St W8 . . . 31 C1 113 B2
Hill House Sch SW1 . . . 131 A1
Hilliard Ho 15 E1 . . . 32 A1
Hilliard's Ct E1 . . . 32 B1
Hillier Ho 1 NW1 . . . 13 C1
Hillier Rd SW11 . . . 60 B1
Hillingdon St SE17 . . . 48 A4
Hill Lo SW11 . . . 59 C3
Hillman Dr 12 NW10 . . . 22 B1
Hillman St E8 . . . 17 A2
Hillmarton Rd N7 . . 14 A3
Hillmead Dr SW9 . . . 63 A3
Hill Mead Prim Sch SW9 . . . 63 A3
Hillmore Ct SE13 . . . 67 C4
Hill Rd NW8 . . . 79 A1
Hillrise Mans N19 . . . 5 A4
Hillrise Rd N19 . . . 5 A4
Hillsboro Rd SE22 . . 64 A2
Hillsborough Ct NW6 . . . 78 A3
Hillside
Greenwich SE10 . . . 52 C3
Stonebridge NW10 . . . 20 C4
Hillside Cl NW8 . . . 78 B2
Hillside Ct NW3 . . . 11 A3
Hillside Gdns SW2 . . 74 C2
Hillside Rd SW2 . . . 74 C2
Hillsleigh Rd W14 . . . 31 B1 113 A2
Hills Pl W1 . . . 104 C1
Hill St W1 . . . 118 A2
Hillstone Ct 5 E3 . . 27 A1
Hilltop Ct
12 London SW18 . . . 59 C3
South Hampstead NW8 . . . 11 B1
Hilltop Ho 7 N6 . . . 4 C4
Hilltop Rd NW6 . . . 10 C1
Hill View NW1 . . . 81 A4
Hillway N6 . . . 3 C2
Hill Wood Ho NW1 83 B1
Hillworth Rd SW2 . . 74 C4
Hillyard St SW9 . . . 173 B3
Hillyfield Cl E9 . . . 18 A3
Hilly Fields Cres SE4 . . . 66 C4
Hilsea Point 7 SW15 . . . 69 A3
Hilsea St E5 . . . 17 B4
Hilton Ho
Lower Holloway N7 . . . 14 A4
9 Nunhead SE4 . . . 65 C3
Hilversum Cres 10 SE22 . . . 64 A2
Hinckley Rd SE15 . . . 64 C3
Hind Ct EC4 . . . 107 C1
Hinde Mews W1 . 103 C2
Hinde St W1 . . . 103 C2
Hind Gr E14 . . . 33 C3
Hindhead Point 6 SW15 . . . 69 A3
Hind Ho
13 Deptford SE14 . . . 50 C4
Islington N7 . . . 14 C4
Hindle Ho E8 . . . 16 B3
Hindley Ho N7 . . . 5 B1
Hindlip Ho SW8 . . 171 B3
Hindmans Rd SE22 . . . 64 C2
Hindmarsh Cl E1 . 125 C4
Hindrey Rd E5 . . . 17 A3
Hinstock NW6 . . . 78 A4
Hinton Rd SE24 . . . 63 A4
Hippodrome Mews W11 . . . 31 A2 112 A3
Hippodrome Pl W11 . . . 31 A2 112 B3
Hirst Ct SW1 . . . 146 A1
Hitchin Sq E3 . . . 26 A3
Hithe Gr 15 SE16 . . . 40 B3
Hitherfield Prim Sch SW16 . . . 74 C2
Hitherfield Rd SW16, SW27 . . . 74 C1
Hither Green La SE13 . . . 67 C1
Hither Green Prim Sch SE13 . . . 67 C1
Hitherlands SW12 . . 73 A2
HM Prison Wormwood Scrubs W12 . . . 29 C3
HMS Belfast★ SE1 . . . 124 B2
Hoadly Rd SW16 . . . 73 C2
Hobart Pl SW1 . . . 132 A2
Hobbes Wlk SW15 . . 57 A2
Hobb's Ct SE1 . . . 139 A4
Hobbs' Pl N1 . . . 24 A4
Hobday St E14 . . . 34 A3
Hobhouse Ct SW1 . . . 119 C3
Hobsons Pl E1 . . . 111 B4
Hobury St SW10 . . . 157 B3
Hocker St E2 . . . 24 B2 98 C3
Hockett Cl SE8 . . . 41 B2
Hockley Ho 4 E9 . . 17 B2
Hockliffe Ho 5 W10 . . . 30 B4
Hockney Ct 1 SE16 . . . 40 A1
Hockworth Ho 7 N16 . . . 7 A3
Hocroft Ave NW2 . . . 1 B1
Hocroft Ct NW2 . . . 1 B1
Hocroft Rd NW2 . . . 1 B1
Hocroft Wlk NW2 . . . 1 B1
Hodford Lo NW11 . . . 1 C2
Hodford Rd NW11 . . . 1 B3
Hodister Cl 26 SE5 . 48 B3
Hoffman Sq N1 . . . 97 C4
Hofland Rd W14 . . 126 A2
Hogan Mews W2 . 101 B4
Hogan Way E5 . . . 7 C2
Hogarth Bsns Pk W4 . . . 46 A4
Hogarth Ct
8 Camden Town NW1 . . . 13 B1
City of London EC3 . 124 B4
Whitechapel E1 . . . 111 C1
Hogarth Ho SW1 . 147 C3
Hogarth Ind Est NW10 . . . 21 C1
Hogarth La W4 . . . 46 A4
Hogarth Pl SW5 . . 142 A3
Hogarth Rd SW5 . 142 A3
Hogarth Roundabout W4 . . . 46 A4
Hogarth's House★ W4 . . . 46 A4
Holbeach Mews 1 SW12 . . . 73 A3
Holbeck Row SE15 . . . 49 C3
Holbein Ho SW1 . . 145 B2
Holbein Mews SW1 . . . 145 B2
Holbein Pl SW1 . . 145 B3
Holberton Gdns NW10 . . . 22 A2
HOLBORN . . . 107 C3
Holborn EC1 . . . 107 C3
Holborn Cir EC1 . . 107 C3
Holborn Ho 1 W12 . . . 30 A3
Holborn Pl WC1 . . 106 C3
Holborn Sta WC1 106 C3
Holborn Viaduct EC1 . . . 108 A3
Holbrook Cl N19 . . . 4 A3
Holbrooke Ct N7 . . . 14 A4
Holbrook Ho
Acton W3 . . . 28 C4
5 Streatham SW2 . . 74 B3
Holcombe Ho SW9 . . . 62 A4
Holcombe Pl SE4 . . . 66 A4
Holcombe St W6 . . . 39 A2
Holcroft Ct W1 . . . 104 C4
Holcroft Ho
Battersea SW11 . . . 59 C4
Lewisham SE10 . . . 52 B2
Holcroft Rd E9 . . . 17 B1
Holdenby Rd SE4 . . . 66 A2
Holden Ho
12 Deptford SE8 . . . 51 C3
Islington N1 . . . 86 C3
Holden Point E15 . . 19 C2
Holden St SW11 . . 169 B1
Holdernesse Rd 6 SW17 . . . 72 C2
Holderness Ho SE5 . . . 64 A4
Holdsworth Ho 5 SW2 . . . 74 C4
Holford Ho
6 Bermondsey SE16 . . . 40 A2
Finsbury WC1 . . . 95 A4
Holford Pl WC1 . . . 95 A4
Holford Rd NW3 . . . 2 B1
Holford St WC1 . . . 95 B4
Holford Yd WC1 . . . 85 B1
Holgate Ave SW11 . . 59 C4
Holland Gdns
Brentford TW8 . . . 44 A4
Kensington W14 . . . 126 B2
Holland Gr SW9 . . 163 C1
Holland Park W11 . . . 31 B1 112 C1
Holland Park Ave W11 . . . 31 A1 112 B1
Holland Park Ct W14 . . . 126 B4
Holland Park Gdns W14 . . . 126 A4
Holland Park Mews W11 . . . 31 B1 112 C1
Holland Park Rd W14 . . . 127 A1
Holland Park Rdbt W12 . . . 39 C4
Holland Park Sch W8 . . . 127 A4
Holland Park Sta W11 . . . 31 B1 112 C1
Holland Pas N1 . . . 86 C4
Holland Pl W8 . . . 128 A4
Holland Rd
West Kensington W14 . . . 126 B2
Willesden Green NW10 . . . 22 A3
Holland Rise Ho SW9 . . . 163 A1
Holland St
Kensington W8 . . . 127 C4
Lambeth SE1 . . . 122 B2
Holland Villas Rd W14 . . . 126 A3
Holland Wlk
Kensington W14 . . . 127 A3
Upper Holloway N19 . . 4 C3
Hollar Rd N16 . . . 7 B1
Hollen St W1 . . . 105 B2
Holles Ho SW9 . . . 173 B2
Holles St W1 . . . 104 B2
Holley Rd W3 . . . 38 A4
Holliday Sq 7 SW11 . . . 59 C4
Hollies The SW12 . . . 73 B2
Hollies Way 1 SW12 . . . 72 C4
Hollingbourne Rd SE24 . . . 63 B2
Hollins Ho N7 . . . 14 A4
Hollisfield WC1 . . . 94 B3

Holloway Rd
Lower Holloway N7 14 B4
Upper Holloway N19 4 C2
Holloway Road Sta N7 14 B3
Holloway Sch N7 13 C3
Holly Berry La 8 NW3 11 B4
Hollybush Gdns E2 25 A2
Holly Bush Hill 4 NW3 11 B4
Hollybush Ho 23 E2 25 A2
Hollybush Pl E2 25 A2
Holly Bush Steps 6 NW3 11 B4
Holly Bush Vale 10 NW3 11 B4
Hollycroft Ave NW3 1 C1
Hollydale Prim Sch SE15 50 B1
Hollydale Rd SE15 50 B1
Hollydene
Hither Green SE13 67 C1
5 Peckham SE15 50 A2
Holly Gr SE15 49 C1
Hollyhedge Ho SE3 52 C1
Holly Hedge Terr SE13 67 C2
Holly Hill NW3 11 B4
Holly Lo W8 127 B4
Holly Lodge SE13 67 C3
Holly Lodge Gdns N6 3 C3
Holly Lodge Mans N6 3 C2
Holly Mews SW10 143 A1
Holly Mount NW3 11 B4
Hollymount Cl 9 SE10 52 B2
Holly Park Est N4 5 B4
Holly Pk N4 5 B4
Holly Pl NW3 11 B4
Holly Rd 6 W4 37 C2
Holly St E8 16 B1
Holly Terr N6 3 C3
Hollytree Cl SW19 69 C3
Holly Tree Ho SE4 66 B4
Holly Village N6 4 A2
Holly Wlk NW3 11 B4
Hollywood Lofts E1 24 B1 98 C1
Hollywood Mews SW10 156 C4
Hollywood Rd SW10 156 C4
Holman Ho 2 E2 25 C2
Holman Hunt Ho W14 140 A1
Holman Rd SW11 167 B1
Holmbrook NW1 83 A1
Holmbury Ct SW17 72 B1
Holmbury Ho SW9 63 A2
Holmbush Rd SW15 58 A1
Holmcote Gdns N5 15 B3
Holmdale Rd NW6 10 C3
Holmdene Ave SE24 63 B2
Holmead Rd SW6 156 B1
Holmefield Ct 4 NW3 12 A2
Holmefield Ho W10 23 A1
Holmes Cl SE22 64 C3
Holmes Ct
18 South Acton W4 37 B3
South Lambeth SW4 172 A2
Holmesdale Ave SW14 55 A3
Holmesdale Ho 12 NW6 23 C4
Holmesdale Rd
Highgate N6 4 A4
Richmond TW9 44 B2
Holmesley Rd SE23 66 A1
Holmes Pl SW10 157 A4
Holmes Rd NW5 13 A3
Holmes Terr SE1 135 B4
Holmewood Gdns SW2 74 B4
Holmewood Rd SW2 74 B4
Holmhurst SE13 67 C1
Holmleigh Prim Sch N16 7 A3
Holmleigh Rd N16 7 A3
Holm Oak Cl SW15 58 B1
Holmsbury Ho 6 N7 13 C3
Holmsdale Ho 24 E14 34 A2
Holmside Ct SW12 60 C1
Holmside Rd SW12 60 C1
Holmsley Ho SW15 68 B4
Holm Wlk SE3 53 C1
Holmwood Ct 3 N16 7 B4
Holocaust Meml Gdn★ W2 131 A4
Holroyd Rd SW15 57 B2
Holsgrove Ct W3 29 A1
Holst Mans SW13 47 B3
Holsworthy Ho 49 E3 27 A2
Holsworthy Sq WC1 95 A1
Holt Ct
Greenwich SE10 52 B4
Stratford New Town E15 19 B3
Holt Ho SW2 62 C1
Holton St E1 25 C1
Holwood Pl 7 SW4 61 C3
Holybourne Ave SW15 68 C4
Holy Cross RC Sch SW6 165 B4
Holy Family RC Prim Sch E14 33 C2
Holy Ghost RC Prim Sch SW12 72 C4
Holyhead Cl E3 26 C2
Holyoake Ct SE16 41 B4
Holyoak Rd SE11 150 B3
Holyport Rd SW6 47 C3
Holyrood Ho N4 6 B3
Holyrood Mews 10 E16 35 C1
Holyrood St SE1 124 A1
Holy Trinity CE Prim Sch
Belgravia SW1 145 B4
Dalston E8 16 B2
Hampstead NW3 11 B2
Richmond TW10 54 C3
Streatham SW2 74 B4
Holy Trinity & Saint Silas CE Prim Sch NW1 13 A1
Holywell Cl
35 Bermondsey SE16 40 A1
2 Greenwich SE3 53 C4
Holywell La EC2 24 A1 98 B2
Holywell Row EC2 24 A1 98 A1
Homan Ho 6 SW4 73 C4
Homecross Ho 7 W4 37 C2
Homefield Rd W4 38 B1
Homefield St 14 N1 24 A3
Homeleigh Ct 8 SW16 74 A1
Homeleigh Rd SE15 65 C2
Homemead SW12 73 A2
Home Office SW1 133 B3
Home Park Rd SW19 70 B1
Home Rd SW11 168 A2
Homer Dr E14 41 C2
Homer Rd E9 18 A2
Homer Row W1 102 B3
Homer St W1 102 B3
HOMERTON 17 C1
Homerton Coll of Technology E9 17 B3
Homerton Gr E9 17 C3
Homerton High St E9 17 C3
Homerton Rd E9 18 B3
Homerton Row E9 17 B3
Homerton Sta E9 17 C2
Homerton Terr E9 17 B2
Homerton University Hospl E9 17 C3
Homestall Rd SE22 65 B2
Homestead Rd SW6 155 A1
Homewoods 2 SW12 73 B4
Homildon Ho 10 SE26 76 C1
Honduras St EC1 96 C2
Honeybourne Rd NW6 11 A3
Honeybrook Rd SW12, SW4 73 B4
Honeyfield N4 5 C2
Honey La EC2 109 A1
Honey Lane Ho SW10 156 B4
Honeyman Cl NW6 9 C1
Honeywell Jun & Inf Schs SW11 60 B1
Honeywell Rd SW11 60 B1
Honeywood Ho 5 SE15 49 C2
Honeywood Rd NW10 21 B3
Honiton Gdns 1 SE15 50 B1
Honiton Ho 29 SE5 48 B1
Honiton Rd NW6 23 B3
HONOR OAK 65 B2
Honor Oak Park Sta SE23 65 C1
Honor Oak Pk SE23 65 C1
Honor Oak Rise SE23 65 B1
Honwell Ho 24 W2 31 C4
Hood Ave SW14 55 B2
Hood Ct N7 5 B1
Hood Ho 17 SE5 48 C3
Hooke Ct SE10 52 B2
Hooke Ho 32 E3 26 A3
Hookham Ct SW8 171 B4
Hooks Cl SE15 50 A2
Hooper Ho 9 SW18 58 B2
Hooper Rd E16 35 C3
Hooper's Ct SW1 130 C3
Hooper's Mews 4 W3 28 B1
Hooper St E1 111 B1
Hoop La NW11 1 C4
Hope Cl
2 Brentford TW8 36 A1
Canonbury N1 15 B2
Hopefield Ave NW6 23 A3
Hope Gdns 10 W3 37 A4
Hope St SW11 59 C4
Hopetown St E1 111 A3
Hopewell St SE5 48 C3
Hop Gdns WC2 120 A3
Hopgood St 5 W12 30 B1
Hopkins Ho 17 E14 33 C3
Hopkinson Ho SW11 169 B2
Hopkinson's Pl NW1 81 B4
Hopkins St W1 105 B1
Hopping La N1 15 A2
Hop St SE10 43 B2
Hopton Ho 5 SW9 48 A1
Hopton's Gdns SE1 122 B2
Hopton St SE1 122 B2
Hopwood Cl SW17 71 B1
Hopwood Rd SE17 48 C4
Hopwood Wlk E8 16 C1
Horatio Ho 13 E2 24 B3
Horatio Pl 9 E14 34 B1
Horatio St 11 E2 24 B3
Horbury Cres W11 31 C2 113 B3
Horbury Mews W11 31 B2 113 A3
Horder Rd SW6 164 B3
Hordle Prom E 15 SE15 49 B3
Hordle Prom N 4 SE15 49 B3
Hordle Prom S 7 SE15 49 B3
Horizon Bldg 22 E14 33 C2
Horizon Sch N16 16 A4
Horle Wlk SE5 48 A1
Hormead Rd W9 23 B1
Hornbeam Cl SE11 149 B4
Hornbeam Ho 2 NW3 12 B2
Hornbeam Sq 8 E3 26 B4
Hornblower Cl 2 SE16 41 A2
Hornby Cl NW3 11 C1
Hornby Ho SE11 163 C4
Horndean Cl 3 SW15 68 C3
Horner Hos 18 N1 24 A4
Horne Way SW15 47 B1
Horn La Acton W3 28 B3
Greenwich SE10 43 C2
Horn Link Way SE10 43 C2
Hornsby House Sch SW12 72 C3
Hornsey La N6 4 B4
Hornsey Lane Gdns N6 4 B4
Hornsey Rd N7, N19 5 B2
Hornsey Rise Gdns N19 5 A4
Hornsey St N7 14 B3
Hornshay St SE15 50 B4
Hornton Ct W8 127 C3
Hornton Pl W8 127 C3
Hornton St W8 127 C4
Horrocks Ho SW15 57 A2
Horse & Dolphin Yd W1 119 C4
Horseferry Pl SE10 52 B4
Horseferry Rd
Limehouse E14 33 A2
Westminster SW1 147 C4
Horseferry Rd Est SW1 133 B1
Horse Guards Ave SW1 120 A1
Horse Guards Par★ SW1 119 C1
Horse Guards Rd SW1 133 C4
Horsell Rd N5 14 C3
Horselydown La SE1 124 C1
Horselydown Mans SE1 138 C4
Horsemongers Mews SE1 137 A3
Horsendon Ho 11 N7 13 C3
Horseshoe Cl E14 42 B1
Horse Yd N1 86 B4
Horsfield Ho 13 N1 15 B1
Horsford Rd SW2 62 B2
Horsley Ct SW1 147 C3
Horsley Ho 11 SE4 65 C3
Horsley St 3 SE17 48 C4
Horsman Ho SE5 48 B4
Horsman St SE5 48 B4
Horsmonden Rd SE4 66 B1
Horston Ho N4 6 B4
Hortensia Ho SW10 156 C2
Hortensia Rd SW10 156 C2
Horticultural Pl 6 W4 37 C1

Horton Ave NW2 ...10 A4
Horton Ho
13 Deptford SE15 ...50 B4
South Lambeth SW8 ...162 C2
West Kensington W14 ...140 A1
Horton Rd E8 ...17 A2
Horton St SE13 ...67 A4
Horwood Ho
24 Bethnal Green E2 ...25 A2
Marylebone NW8 ...90 B2
Hosack Rd SW12, SW17 ...72 C2
Hosier La EC1 ...108 B3
Hoskins St SE10 ...42 C1
Hospl for Tropical Diseases
Fitzrovia WC1 ...93 A1
Somers Town NW1 ...83 C3
Hospl of St John & St Elizabeth NW8 ...79 B1
Hotham Prim Sch SW15 ...57 C3
Hotham Rd SW15 ...57 B4
Hothfield Pl SE16 ...40 B3
Hotspur St SE11 ...149 B2
Houblon Rd TW10 ...54 A2
Houghton Cl 10 E8 ...16 B2
Houghton Sq SW9 ...62 A4
Houghton St WC2 ...107 A1
Houndsditch EC3 ...110 B2
Houseman Way 20 SE5 ...48 C3
House of Detention★ EC1 ...95 C2
Houses of Parliament★ SW1 ...134 B2
Hoveden Rd NW2 ...10 A3
Howard Bldg SW8 ...160 A3
Howard Cl
Acton W3 ...28 A3
Cricklewood NW2 ...10 A4
Howard Ct
Lewisham SE10 ...52 B2
Peckham SE15 ...64 C4
Howard Ho
6 Brixton SW9 ...62 C4
14 Deptford SE8 ...51 B4
Fitzrovia W1 ...92 B1
Howard Mews N5 ...15 A4
Howard Rd
Canonbury N16 ...15 C4
Cricklewood NW2 ...9 C4
Howard's La SW15 ...57 B3
Howarth Ct E15 ...19 B3
Howbury Rd SE15 ...65 B4
Howcroft Ho 3 E3 ...26 B2
Howden St SE15 ...64 C4
Howell Ho 5 N7 ...13 C3
Howell Wlk SE1 ...150 B3
Howgate Rd SW14 ...55 C4
Howick Pl SW1 ...133 A1
Howie St SW11 ...158 A1
Howitt Cl
6 Maitland Pk NW3 ...12 A2
Stoke Newington N16 ...16 A4
Howitt Rd NW3 ...12 A2
Howland Ho 9 SW16 ...74 A1
Howland Mews E W1 ...105 A4
Howland St W1 ...105 A4
Howland Way SE16 ...41 A4
Howletts Rd SE24 ...63 B1
Howley Pl W2 ...101 A4
Howsman Rd SW13 ...46 C4
Howson Rd SE4 ...66 A3
Howson Terr TW10 ...54 A1
How's St E2 ...24 B3
HOXTON ...24 A3
Hoxton Mkt N1 ...24 A2 98 A3
Hoxton Point EC1 ...24 A2 98 A3
Hoxton Sq N1 ...24 A2 98 A3
Hoxton St N1 ...24 A3
Hoylake Rd W3 ...29 A3
Hoyland Cl 4 SE15 ...50 A3
Hoy St E16 ...35 B3
Hub Buildings The 4 SW12 ...73 A3
Huberd Ho SE1 ...137 C2
Hubert Gr SW9 ...62 A4
Hubert Ho NW8 ...90 A1
Hucknall Ct NW8 ...89 B2
Huddart St 6 E3 ...33 B4
Huddleston Cl E2 ...25 B3
Huddlestone Rd NW2 ...9 A2
Huddleston Rd N7 ...13 B4
Hudson Cl 15 W12 ...30 A2
Hudson Ct 1 E14 ...41 C1
Hudson Ho
Chelsea SW10 ...156 C2
5 Notting Hill W11 ...31 A3
Hudsons Ho N1 ...97 C3
Hudson's Pl SW1 ...146 C4
Huggin Ct EC4 ...123 A4
Huggin Hill EC4 ...123 A4
Huggins Ho 9 E3 ...26 C2
Huggins Pl SW2 ...74 B3
Hughan Rd E15 ...19 C3
Hugh Astor Ct SE1 ...136 B2
Hugh Dalton Ave SW6 ...154 C3
Hughenden Ho NW8 ...90 A2
Hughendon Terr E15 ...19 B4
Hughes Ho
26 Bethnal Green E2 ...25 B2
Camberwell SE5 ...48 B2
15 Deptford SE8 ...51 C4
Newington SE17 ...150 B3
Hughes Mans E1 ...24 C1 99 C1
Hughes Terr 6 E16 ...35 B4
Hugh Gaitskell Cl SW6 ...154 C3
Hugh Gaitskell Ho
Stoke Newington N16 ...7 B2
Willesden NW10 ...8 B1
Hugh Mews SW1 ...146 B3
Hugh Morgan Ho 5 SW4 ...61 C4
Hugh Myddelton Prim Sch EC1 ...95 C3
Hugh Platt Ho 29 E2 ...25 A3
Hugh St SW1 ...146 B3
Hugo Ho SW1 ...131 A2
Hugon Rd SW6 ...59 A4
Hugo Rd N19 ...13 B4
Huguenot Ct E1 ...111 B4
Huguenot Pl
London SW18 ...59 B2
Spitalfields E1 ...111 A4
Huguenot Sq SE15 ...65 A4
Hullbridge Mews N1 ...87 B4
Hull Cl SE16 ...32 C1
Hull Ct SE5 ...48 C1
Hull St EC1 ...96 C3
Hulme Pl SE1 ...137 A3
Humber Dr W10 ...22 C1
Humber Rd SE3 ...53 B4
Humberton Cl E9 ...18 A3
Humbolt Rd W6 ...154 A3
Hume Ct N1 ...15 A1
Hume Ho 14 W11 ...30 C1
Humphrey Ct SW11 ...167 C3
Humphrey St SE1 ...152 C2
Humphry Ho 10 SW15 ...57 C2
Hungerford Bridge WC2 ...120 C2
Hungerford Ho SW1 ...161 A4
Hungerford La WC2 ...120 B2
Hungerford Prim Sch N7 ...13 C2
Hungerford Rd
12 Camden Town N7 ...13 C2
Lower Holloway N7 ...14 A3
Hungerford St 21 E1 ...32 A3
Hunsdon Rd SE14 ...50 C3
Hunslett St 28 E2 ...25 B3
Hunstanton Ho NW1 ...102 B4
Hunt Cl W11 ...30 C1
Hunter Cl
Borough The SE1 ...137 C1
Upper Tooting SW12 ...72 C3
Huntercombe Roehampton Hospl The SW15 ...68 C4
Hunter Ct
8 London SE5 ...63 C3
27 Streatham SW2 ...74 C4
Hunter Ho
Bloomsbury WC1 ...94 B2
Lambeth SE1 ...136 B3
South Lambeth SW8 ...161 C1
1 Tufnell Pk N19 ...4 B1
West Brompton SW5 ...141 C1
Hunterian Mus★ WC2 ...107 A2
Hunter Lo 9 W9 ...31 C4
Hunter St WC1 ...94 B2
Huntingdon Ct SW14 ...55 B4
Huntingdon Gdns W4 ...45 B3
Huntingdon Ho SW5 ...141 C4
Huntingdon St
Canning Town E16 ...35 B3
Islington N1 ...14 B1
Huntingfield Rd SW15 ...56 C2
Huntingford Ho SW15 ...47 B1
Huntington Ho NW2 ...9 B2
Huntley St WC1 ...93 B1
Hunton St E1 ...111 B4
Hunts Cl SE3 ...53 C1
Hunt's Ct WC2 ...119 C3
Huntshaw Ho 37 E3 ...27 A2
Hunt's La E15 ...27 B3
Huntsman St SE17 ...152 A3
Huntspill St SW17 ...71 B1
Hunts Slip Rd SE21 ...76 A2
Huntsworth Mews NW1 ...90 C1
Hurdwick Ho NW1 ...82 C2
Hurdwick Pl NW1 ...82 C2
Hurleston Ho 11 SE8 ...41 B1
Hurley Cres SE16 ...40 C4
Hurley Ho
Lambeth SE11 ...149 C3
Shoreditch E2 ...24 B2 98 C3
Hurley Lo SE22 ...65 B1
Hurlingham Bsns Pk SW6 ...58 C4
Hurlingham & Chelsea Sec Sch SW6 ...58 C4
Hurlingham Court Mans SW6 ...165 B1
Hurlingham Ct SW6 ...58 B4
Hurlingham Gdns SW6 ...58 B4
Hurlingham Rd SW6 ...165 A1
Hurlingham Sch SW15 ...58 B3
Hurlingham Sq SW6 ...59 A4
Hurlock Ho 1 N5 ...6 A1
Hurlock St N5 ...6 A1
Huron Rd SW17 ...72 C1
Huron Univ WC1 ...106 A4
Hurstbourne Ho SW15 ...56 B1
Hurstdene Gdns N15 ...7 A4
Hurst Ho N1 ...85 A1
Hurst St SE24 ...63 A1
Hurstway Wlk 2 W11 ...30 C2
Husbourne Ho 8 SE8 ...41 A2
Huson Cl NW3 ...12 A1
Hutching's St E14 ...41 C4
Hutching's Wharf 11 E14 ...41 C4
Hutchins Cl E15 ...19 B1
Hutchins Ho 8 SW4 ...73 C4
Hutchinson Ho 9 SE14 ...50 B3
Hutton Ct 4 N4 ...5 B3
Hutton Ho E2 ...24 C2 99 B3
Hutton St EC4 ...107 C1
Huxbear St SE4 ...66 B2
Huxley Ho
London SW9 ...172 C2
Paddington NW8 ...89 C1
Huxley St W10 ...23 A2
Hyacinth Rd SW15 ...68 C3
Hyde Farm Mews SW12 ...73 C3
Hyde La SW11 ...168 A4
Hyde Park★ W2 ...116 C1
Hyde Park Cnr SW1 ...131 C4
Hyde Park Corner Sta SW1 ...131 C4
Hyde Park Cres W2 ...102 A1
Hyde Park Gate Mews SW7 ...129 A3
Hyde Park Gdns W2 ...115 C4
Hyde Park Gdns Mews W2 ...116 A4
Hyde Park Mans NW1 ...102 A3
Hyde Park Pl W2 ...116 B4
Hyde Park Sq W2 ...102 A1
Hyde Park Square Mews W2 ...102 A1
Hyde Park St W2 ...102 A1
Hyde Park Twrs W2 ...114 C3
Hyde Rd
Richmond TW10 ...54 B2
Shoreditch N1 ...24 A4
Hyde's Pl 12 N1 ...15 A1
Hyde St SE8 ...51 C4
Hydethorpe Rd SW12 ...73 B3
Hyde Vale SE10 ...52 B3
Hylda Ct NW5 ...3 C1
Hyndman Ho 4 N19 ...13 C4
Hyndman St SE15 ...50 A4
Hyperion Ho
27 Bow E3 ...26 A3
Streatham SW2 ...74 B4
Hyson Rd SE16 ...40 A1
Hythe Ho 14 SE16 ...40 B4
Hythe Rd NW10 ...21 C1
Hythe Road Ind Est NW10 ...21 C1

I

Ian Hamilton Ho NW1 ...93 B4
Ian Mikardo Sch E3 ...27 A2
Ibberton Ho
Kensington W14 ...126 B1
South Lambeth SW8 ...162 C2
Ibbotson Ave E16 ...35 B3
Ibbott St 22 E1 ...25 B1
Iberia Ho 17 N19 ...4 C4
Ibis Ct 16 SE8 ...51 B4
Ibis La W4 ...45 B2
Ibsley Gdns SW15 ...68 C3
Ibstock Place Sch SW15 ...56 A1
Icarus Ho 21 E3 ...26 B2

Iceland Rd E3 26 C4
Iceland Wharf SE16 41 A2
Iceni Ct 23 E3 26 B4
Ice Wharf NW1 84 B2
Idaho Bldg 7 SE13 52 A2
Ida St E14 34 B3
Idmiston Rd SE21, SE27 75 B2
Idol La EC3 124 A3
Idonia St SE8 51 C3
Iffley Ho E2 24 B2 98 C3
Iffley Rd W6 39 A3
Ifield Ho SE17 152 B2
Ifield Rd SW10 156 B4
Ifor Evans Pl E1 25 C1
Ightham Ho SE17 152 A3
Ikon Ho 21 E1 32 B2
Ikra Prim Sch N16 16 B4
Ilbert St W10 23 A2
Ilchester Gdns W2 114 A4
Ilchester Mans W8 127 B2
Ilchester Pl W14 127 A2
Ildersly Gr SE21 75 C2
Ilderton Prim Sch SE16 40 B1
Ilderton Rd SE15, SE16 50 B4
Ilex Rd NW10 8 B2
Ilford Ho 14 N1 15 C2
Ilfracombe Flats SE1 137 A4
Iliffe St SE17 150 B2
Iliffe Yd SE17 150 B2
Ilkeston Ct 7 E5 17 C4
Ilminster Gdns SW11 60 A3
Ilsley Ct SW8 170 C1
Imber St N1 87 B3
Imperial Ave 5 N16 16 A4
Imperial College Rd SW7 129 B2
Imperial Coll of Science, Technology & Medicine SW7 129 B2
Imperial Cres SW6 167 A1
Imperial Ct NW8 80 B2
Imperial Ho
1 Bow E3 26 A2
2 Poplar E14 33 B2
Strand WC2 106 C1
Imperial Rd SW6 166 B3
Imperial Sq SW6 166 B4
Imperial St E3 27 B2
Imperial Twrs 3 NW3 11 B2
Imperial War Mus* SE1, SE11 135 C1
Imperial Wharf Sta SW10 167 A3
Imre Cl W12 30 A1
Independent Pl E8 16 B3
Indescon Ct E14 42 A4
Indiana Bldg 7 SE8 51 C2
India St EC3 110 C1
India Way W12 30 A2
Indigo Mews N16 6 C1
Indus Ct 16 SE15 49 B3
Ingate Pl SW8 170 B3
Ingelow Ho W8 128 A4
Ingersoll Rd W12 30 A1
Ingestre Pl W1 105 A1
Ingestre Rd NW5 13 A4
Ingham Rd NW6 10 C4
Inglebert St EC1 95 B4
Ingleborough St SW9 173 B2
Ingleby Rd N7 5 A1
Inglefield Sq 12 E1 32 A1
Ingle Ho 3 SW12 73 C3
Inglesham Wlk E9 18 B2
Ingleside Gr SE3 53 B4
Inglethorpe Ho 6 E5 7 C2
Inglethorpe St SW6 47 C2
Ingleton St SW9 173 B2
Inglewood Cl E14 41 C2
Inglewood Mans 11 NW6 10 C3
Inglewood Rd NW6 10 C3
Inglis Ho 1 SW15 57 B2
Inglis St SE5 48 A2
Ingram Ave NW11 2 B4
Ingram Cl SE11 149 A4
Ingram Ho E3 26 A4
Ingram Lo 8 SW4 61 C1
Ingrave St SW11 60 A4
Ingrebourne Ho NW8 101 C4
Ingress St 4 W4 38 A1
Inigo Pl WC2 120 A4
Inkerman Rd NW5 13 A2
Inkerman Terr W8 127 C1
Inkster Ho 8 SW11 60 A4
Inman Rd
Harlesden NW10 21 A4
Wandsworth SW18 71 B4
Inner Circ NW1 91 B4
Inner Park Rd SW19 69 C2
Inner Temple* EC4 121 B4
Inner Temple La EC4 107 B1
Innes Gdns SW15 57 A1
Innisfree Ho NW2 9 C2
Innis Ho SE17 152 A2
Insley Ho 13 E3 27 A2
Inst for Child Health WC1 94 C1
Institute Pl E8 17 A3
Instituto Espanol Vicente Canada Blanch W10 31 A4
Inst of Neurology
Bloomsbury WC1 106 B4
St Pancras WC1 94 B1
Int Coll of Accountancy The SW17 72 B1
Interchange The NW5 13 A3
International House Language Sch WC2 106 B2
International Sch of London W3 36 C2
Inver Ct
Bayswater W2 100 B1
Inver Ct *continued*
4 Hammersmith W6 38 C3
Inverforth Cl NW3 2 B2
Inverforth Ho NW3 2 B2
Invergarry Ho NW6 78 A1
Invermead Cl W6 38 C2
Inverness Gdns W8 114 A1
Inverness Mews W2 114 B4
Inverness Pl W2 114 B4
Inverness St NW1 82 B4
Inverness Terr W2 114 B4
Inverton Rd SE15 65 C3
Invicta Cl 21 E3 33 C4
Invicta Plaza SE1 122 A2
Invicta Prim Sch SE3 53 C3
Invicta Rd SE3, SE7 53 C4
Inville Rd SE17 151 C1
Inwen Ct SE8 41 A1
Inwood Ct 12 NW1 13 B1
Inwood Ho 19 SE22 64 A4
Inworth St SW11 168 B2
Inworth Wlk N1 86 C4
Ion Ct 8 E2 24 C3
Ionian Bldg 19 E14 33 A2
Ionian Ho 22 E1 25 C1
Ipsden Bldgs SE1 135 C4
Ipswich Ho SE4 65 C2
Irby Ho SW2 62 C1
Ireland Yd EC4 108 B1
Irene Rd SW6 165 C3
Ireton Ho SW9 173 C1
Ireton St 12 E3 26 C1
Iris Ct 8 SE15 50 A1
Iroko Ho 7 NW3 11 A2
Iron Bridge Cl NW10 8 A3
Iron Bridge Ho NW3 12 B1
Irongate Ho EC3 110 B2
Iron Mill Pl SW18 59 A1
Iron Mill Rd SW18 59 A1
Ironmonger La EC2 109 B1
Ironmonger Pas EC1 97 A3
Ironmonger Row EC1 97 A3
Ironmonger's Pl 22 E14 41 C2
Ironside Cl SE16 40 C4
Ironside Ho E9 18 A4
Ironworks 1 E3 26 C4
Irvine Ct W1 93 A1
Irvine Ho N7 14 B2
Irving Gr SW9 172 C1
Irving Ho SE17 150 A1
Irving Mews N1 15 B2
Irving Rd W14 39 C3
Irving St WC2 119 C3
Irwell Est 31 SE16 40 B4
Irwin Gdns NW10 22 A4
Isabella Ct 8 TW10 54 B1
Isabella Ho
19 Hammersmith W6 39 B1
Kennington SE11 150 A2
Isabella Rd E9 17 B3
Isabella St SE1 122 A1
Isabel St SW9 173 A4
Isambard Mews E14 42 B3
Isambard Pl SE16 32 B1
Iseldon Ct N7 14 A4
Isel Way 4 SE22 64 A2
Isis Cl SW15 57 B3
Isis Ct W4 45 A3
Isis Ho NW8 89 C1
Isis St SW18 71 B2
Islamia Girls' High Sch NW6 23 A4
Islamia Prim Sch NW6 23 A4
Islamic Coll for Advanced Studies NW10 9 A2
Island Gardens Sta E14 42 B1
Island Ho E14 27 B2
Island Rd SE16 40 C2
Island Row E14 33 B3
Islay Wlk 17 N1 15 B2
Isleden Ho N1 86 C4
Isledon Rd N4, N7 5 C1
ISLE OF DOGS 42 B2
ISLINGTON 14 C2
Islington Arts & Media Sch N4 5 B3
Islington Bsns Ctr N1 87 A4
Islington Est N1 86 C4
Islington Gn N1 86 A3
Islington Green Sch N1 86 C3
Islington High St N1 86 A2
Islington Park Mews 1 N1 15 A1
Islington Park St N1 15 A1
Islington Sixth Form Ctr N7 14 C4
Islip St NW5 13 B3
Isokon Flats 3 NW3 12 B3
Issac Way SE1 137 A4
Italia Conti Acad of Theatre Arts EC1 96 C1
Ivanhoe Ho
11 Balham SW12 73 A4
34 Bow E3 26 A3
Ivanhoe Rd SE5 64 B4
Ivatt Pl W14 141 A1
Iveagh Cl E9 25 C4
Iveagh Ct EC3 110 C1
Iveagh Ho
2 Brixton SW9 48 A1
Chelsea SW10 157 A2
Ivebury Ct 9 W10 30 B3
Iveley Rd SW4 170 C1
Iver Ct N1 15 B2
Iverna Ct W8 127 C2
Iverna Gdns W8 127 C2
Iverson Rd NW6 10 C2
Ives Rd E16 35 A4
Ives St SW3 144 B4
Ivimey St E2 24 C2 99 C4
Ivinghoe Ho 14 N7 13 C3
Ivor Ct NW1 90 C2
Ivories The N1 15 B1
Ivor Mayor Lo SW12 60 C1
Ivor Pl NW1 90 C1
Ivor St NW1 13 B1
Ivory Ho
9 London SW11 59 B4
St George in t East E1 125 A2
Ivory Sq 15 SW18 59 B4
Ivybridge Ho 18 SE22 64 A4
Ivybridge La WC2 120 B3
Ivy Church La SE1, SE17 152 C2
Ivy Cres W4 37 B2
Ivy Ct SE16 153 C1
Ivydale Prim Sch SE15 65 C3
Ivydale Rd SE15 65 C3
Ivyday Gr SW16 74 B1
Ivy Lo W8 31 C1 113 B2
Ivymount Rd SE27 74 C1
Ivy Rd Brockley SE4 66 C3
Cricklewood NW2 9 B4
Newham E16 35 C3
Ivy St N1 24 A3
Ixworth Pl SW3 144 A3

J

Jacaranda Gr E8 16 B1
Jackman Ho 24 E1 32 A1
Jackman St E8 25 A4
Jackson Cl E9 17 C1
Jackson Ho 16 SW11 59 C4
Jackson Rd N7 14 B4
Jackson's La N6 4 A4
Jack Taylor Sch NW8 78 C4
Jack Tizard Sch W12 30 A1
Jack Walker Ct N5 15 A4
Jacobin Lo N7 14 A3
Jacob Mans 15 E1 32 A3
Jacobson Ct SW11 168 B3
Jacobson Ho E1 110 C2
Jacob St SE1 139 B4
Jacob's Well Mews W1 103 C2
Jacotts Ho W10 22 B1
Jacqueline Ho 8 E1 32 C4
Jaggard Way SW12 72 B4
Jagger Ho SW11 168 C4
Jago Wlk SE5 48 C3
Jamahirya Sch SW3 158 A4
Jamaica Rd
Bermondsey SE1 139 A3
Bermondsey SE16 40 A3
Jamaica St E1 32 B4
James Allen's Girls' Sch SE22 64 A2
James Allens Pre-Prep Sch SE21 63 C1
James Anderson Ct 28 E2 24 A3
James Ave NW2 9 B3
James Brine Ho E2 24 B2 99 A4
James Campbell Ho 2 E2 25 B3
James Collins Cl W9 23 B1

James Docherty Ho 4 E2 ... 25 B3
James Hammett Ho 9 E2 ... 24 B3
James Ho
Mile End E1 ... 26 A1
33 Rotherhithe SE16 ... 40 C4
James Joyce Wlk 7 SE24 ... 63 A3
James Leicester Hall of Residence N7 .. 14 A2
James Lind Ho 6 SE8 ... 41 B2
James Middleton Ho 20 E2 ... 25 A2
Jameson Ct 6 E2 .. 25 B3
Jameson Ho SE11 ... 148 C2
Jameson Pl 11 W3 ... 37 B4
Jameson St W8 ... 31 C1 113 C2
James's Cotts TW9 ... 44 C3
James St
Marylebone W1 ... 103 C1
Strand WC2 ... 120 B4
James Stewart Ho NW6 ... 10 B1
James Stroud Ho SE17 ... 151 A1
Jamestown Rd NW1 ... 82 A4
Jamestown Way E14 ... 34 C2
James Wolfe Prim Sch SE10 ... 52 B3
Jamuna Cl E14 ... 33 A4
Jane St E1 ... 32 A3
Janet St E14 ... 41 C3
Janeway Pl 2 SE16 ... 40 A4
Janeway St SE16 . 139 C3
Jansen Ho 5 SW15 ... 56 C2
Jansen Wlk SW11 .. 59 C3
Japan Cres N4 ... 5 B3
Jardine Rd E1 ... 32 C2
Jarman Ho
Bermondsey SE16 ... 40 C2
16 Stepney E1 ... 32 B4
Jarrett Cl SW2 ... 75 A3
Jarrow Rd SE16 ... 40 B1
Jarrow Way E9 ... 18 A4
Jarvis Ho 3 SE15 .. 49 C2
Jarvis Rd SE22 ... 64 A3
Jasmin SE1 ... 125 A1
Jasmine Sq 15 E3 .. 26 B4
Jasmin Ho SE4 ... 66 B4
Jasmin Lo 17 SE16 ... 40 A1
Jason Ct
London SW9 ... 173 B4
Marylebone W1 ... 103 C2
Jasper Wlk N1 ... 97 B4
Java Wharf SE1 .. 139 A4
Jay Ho SW15 ... 47 B1
Jay Mews SW7 ... 129 A3
Jean Darling Ho SW10 ... 157 B3
Jean Pardies Ho 23 E1 ... 32 B4
Jebb Ave SW2 ... 62 A1
Jebb St E3 ... 26 C3
Jedburgh St SW11 ... 60 C3
Jeddo Mews W12 .. 38 B4
Jeddo Rd W12 ... 38 B4
Jefferson Bldg 3 E14 ... 41 C4
Jeffrey's Ct SW4 . 172 A2
Jeffrey's Pl NW1 ... 13 B1
Jeffrey's Rd SW4 172 A2
Jeffrey's St NW1 ... 13 B1
Jeff Wooller Coll WC1 ... 106 B4
Jeger Ave E2 ... 24 B4
Jelf Rd SW2 ... 62 C2
Jellicoe Ho
5 Bethnal Green E2 ... 24 C3
Fitzrovia NW1 ... 92 B1
11 Putney SW15 ... 57 C2
Jemotts Ct 9 SE14 ... 50 C4
Jenkins Ho SW8 .. 171 B4
Jenkinson Ho 12 E2 ... 25 C2
Jenner Ave W3 ... 28 C4
Jenner Ho SE3 ... 53 A4
Jenner Pl SW13 ... 47 A4
Jenner Rd N16 ... 7 B1
Jennifer Ho SE11 149 C3
Jennings Ho SE10 .. 42 C1
Jennings Rd SE22 .. 64 B1
Jensen Ho 10 E3 ... 26 C1
Jephson Ct SW4 . 172 B1
Jephson Ho 6 SE17 ... 48 A4
Jephson St SE5 ... 48 C2
Jephtha Rd SW18 .. 58 C1
Jerdan Pl SW6 ... 155 B2
Jeremiah St 11 E14 ... 34 A3
Jeremy Bentham Ho E2 ... 24 C2 99 C3
Jermyn St SW1 ... 119 A2
Jerningham Ct SE14 ... 51 A2
Jerningham Rd SE14 ... 51 A2
Jerome Cres NW8 . 90 A2
Jerome Ho NW1 . 102 B4
Jerome St E1 ... 24 B1 98 C1
Jerome Twr 5 W3 ... 37 A4
Jerrard St SE13 ... 67 A4
Jerrold Lo SW15 ... 57 B4
Jerrold St 24 N1 ... 24 A3
Jersey Ho 15 N1 ... 15 B2
Jersey Rd N1 ... 15 B2
Jersey St E2 ... 25 A2
Jerusalem Pas EC1 ... 96 A1
Jervis Bay Ho 9 E14 ... 34 C3
Jervis Ct
2 Greenwich SE10 ... 52 B2
Marylebone W1 ... 104 B1
Jessel Ho
St Pancras WC1 ... 94 A3
Westminster SW1 . 147 C4
Jessica Rd SW18 ... 59 B2
Jessie Blythe La 4 N19 ... 5 A4
Jessie Duffett Ho 11 SE5 ... 48 B3
Jesson Ho SE17 .. 151 B3
Jessop Ct N1 ... 86 B1
Jessop Ho 9 W4 ... 37 C2
Jessop Prim Sch SE24 ... 63 B3
Jessop Sq E14 ... 33 C1
Jeston Ho 10 SE27 .. 75 A1
Jethou Ho 16 N1 ... 15 B2
Jevons Ho 9 NW8 ... 11 C1
Jewell Ho 3 SW12 ... 73 B4
Jewish Mus The★ NW1 ... 82 B3
Jewry St EC3 ... 110 C1
Jews Row SW18 ... 59 B3
Jeymer Ave NW2 ... 9 B3
Jeypore Rd SW18 .. 59 B1
Jim Griffiths Ho SW6 ... 155 A3
Joanna Ho 7 W6 .. 39 B1
Joan St SE1 ... 122 A1
Jocelin Ho N1 ... 85 A3
Jocelyn Rd TW9 ... 54 A4
Jocelyn St SE15 ... 49 C2
Jockey's Fields WC1 ... 107 A4
Jodane Rd SE8 ... 41 B2
Jodrell Rd E3 ... 18 B1
Johanna Prim Sch SE1 ... 135 B3
Johanna St SE1 .. 135 B3
John Adam St WC2 ... 120 B3
John Aird Ct W2 . 101 A4
John Archer Way SW18 ... 59 C1
John Ashby Cl SW2 ... 62 A1
John Ball Prim Sch SE3 ... 53 A1
John Barker Ct NW6 ... 10 A1
John Betts' Ho W12 ... 38 C3
John Betts Prim Sch W6 ... 39 A3
John Bond Ho 2 E3 ... 26 B3
John Brent Ho 8 SE8 ... 40 C2
John Buck Ho NW10 ... 21 B4
John Burns Prim Sch SW11 ... 169 C1
John Campbell Rd 26 N16 ... 16 A3
John Carpenter St EC4 ... 122 A4
John Cartwright Ho 7 E2 ... 25 A2
John Clynes Ct SW15 ... 57 A3
John Conwey Ho 23 SW2 ... 62 C1
John Dee Ho 3 SW14 ... 55 C4
John Donne Prim Sch SE15 ... 50 A2
John Dwight Ho SW6 ... 59 A4
John Fearon Wlk 5 W10 ... 23 A2
John Felton Rd SE16 ... 139 B3
John Fielden Ho 10 E2 ... 25 A2
John Fisher St E1 ... 125 B4
John F. Kennedy Specl Sch E15 ... 27 C4
John Harris Ho SE15 ... 64 C4
John Harrison Way SE10 ... 43 B3
John Islip St SW1 148 A3
John Keall Ho SW15 ... 57 C4
John Keble CE Prim Sch NW10 ... 21 B4
John Kennedy Ct 1 N1 ... 15 C2
John Kennedy Ho 1 SE16 ... 40 C2
John Kennedy Lo 2 N1 ... 15 C2
John King Ct 5 N19 ... 4 C2
John Kirk Ho
22 Battersea SW11 ... 59 C4
5 Streatham SW16 ... 74 A1
John Knight Lo SW6 ... 155 C2
John McDonald Ho 3 E14 ... 42 B3
John McKenna Wlk SE16 ... 139 C2
John & Mary Sch NW5 ... 13 C3
John Maurice Cl SE17 ... 151 B4
John Milton Prim Sch SW8 ... 160 C1
John Nettleford Ho 14 E2 ... 25 A2
John Orwell Sports Ctr E1 ... 32 A1
John Parker Sq 8 SW11 ... 59 C4
John Parry Ct 28 N1 ... 24 A3
John Paul II Sch SW19 ... 69 C4
John Penn Ho SE8 ... 51 B3
John Penn St SE13 ... 52 A2
John Perryn Prim Sch W3 ... 29 A3
John Prince's St W1 ... 104 B2
John Pritchard Ho E1 ... 24 C1 99 C1
John Ratcliffe Ho 8 NW6 ... 23 C2
John Rennie Wlk 1 E1 ... 32 B1
John Roan Sch The SE3 ... 53 A3
John Roll Way SE16 ... 139 C2
John Ruskin Prim Sch SE5 ... 48 B4
John Ruskin St SE5 ... 48 B4
John Scurr Ho 18 E14 ... 33 A3
John Scurr Prim Sch E1 ... 25 B1
John Silkin La SE8 ... 40 C1
John's Mews WC1 . 95 A1
John Smith Ave SW6 ... 154 C2
John Smith Mews E14 ... 34 C2
Johnson Cl E8 ... 24 C4
Johnson Ct 10 SW18 ... 59 C3
Johnson Ho
Belgravia SW1 ... 145 C3
Bethnal Green E2 ... 24 C2 99 C3
Somers Town NW1 .. 83 A1
South Lambeth SW8 ... 161 C1
Johnson Lo 12 W9 ... 31 C4
Johnson Rd NW10 .. 20 C4
Johnsons Ct EC4 . 107 C1
Johnson's Pl SW1 146 C1
Johnson St E1 ... 32 B3
Johnsons Way NW10 ... 20 A1
John Spencer Sq N1 ... 15 A2
John's Pl E1 ... 32 A3
John St WC1 ... 95 A1
John Stainer Com Prim Sch SE4 ... 66 A4
Johnston Cl SW9 173 A3
Johnstone Ho SE13 ... 67 C4
John Strachey Ho SW6 ... 155 A3
John Trundle Ct EC2 ... 108 C4
John Tucker Ho 3 E14 ... 41 C3
John Wesley's House & Mus★ EC1 ... 97 C2
John Wheatley Ho
14 London N19 ... 4 C4
West Brompton SW6 ... 155 A3
John Williams Cl SE14 ... 50 C4
Joiners Arms Yd 1 SE5 ... 48 C2
Joiner St SE1 ... 123 C1
Joiners Yd N1 ... 84 B1
Jolles Ho 9 E3 ... 27 A2
Jonathan Ct 9 W4 ... 38 A2
Jonathan St SE11 148 C2
Jones Ho
4 South Bromley E14 ... 34 C3
Stamford Hill N16 ... 7 A3
Jones St W1 ... 118 A3
Jones Wlk 6 TW10 ... 54 B1
Jonson Ho
Borough The SE1 .. 137 C1
16 Canonbury N16 ... 15 C4
Jordan Ct SW15 ... 57 C3
Jordan Ho
12 London SE4 ... 65 C3
Shoreditch N1 ... 87 C3
Jordans Ho NW8 .. 90 A1
Joscoyne Ho 5 E1 ... 32 A3
Joseph Ave W3 ... 28 C3
Joseph Conrad Ho SW1 ... 147 A3
Joseph Ct N16 ... 7 A4
Joseph Hardcastle Cl SE14 ... 50 C3

Josephine Ave SW2 ... 62 B2
Joseph Irwin Ho 11 E14 ... 33 B2
Joseph Lancaster Prim Sch SE1 ... 137 B1
Joseph Powell Cl 1 SW12 ... 61 B1
Joseph Priestley Ho 12 E2 ... 25 A2
Joseph St E3 ... 26 B1
Joseph Trotter Cl EC1 ... 95 C3
Joshua St E14 ... 34 B3
Joslings Cl W12 ... 29 C2
Josseline Ct 9 E3 ... 26 A3
Joubert Mans SW3 ... 144 B2
Joubert St SW11 ... 169 A2
Jowett Ho SW9 ... 172 B1
Jowett St SE15 ... 49 B3
Jubet Ho 9 N16 ... 15 C4
Jubilee Bldgs NW8 ... 79 B2
Jubilee Cl 4 NW10 ... 21 B3
Jubilee Cres E14 ... 42 B3
Jubilee Ct N1 ... 84 B4
Jubilee Ho SE11 ... 149 C3
Jubilee Hts NW2 ... 10 B2
Jubilee Mans 10 E1 ... 32 B3
Jubilee Mkt WC2 ... 120 B4
Jubilee Pl SW3 ... 144 B2
Jubilee Prim Sch
London SW2 ... 62 C1
Stamford Hill N16 ... 7 C3
Jubilee St E1 ... 32 B4
Jubilee The 2 SE10 ... 52 A3
Jubilee Yd SE1 ... 138 C4
Judd St WC1 ... 94 A3
Jude St E16 ... 35 B3
Judges' Wlk NW3 ... 2 B1
Juer St SW11 ... 158 B1
Julian Ave W3 ... 28 A2
Julian Ct SW13 ... 46 B2
Julian Pl E14 ... 42 A1
Julia St NW5 ... 12 C3
Juliet Ho 11 N1 ... 24 A3
Julius Ct TW8 ... 44 A3
Julius Ho 8 E14 ... 34 C3
Julius Nyerere Cl N1 ... 84 C3
Junction App
Battersea SW11 ... 60 A4
Lewisham SE13 ... 67 B4
Junction Mews W2 ... 102 A2
Junction Pl W2 ... 101 C2
Junction Rd N19 ... 4 B1
Juniper Cres NW1 ... 12 C1
Juniper Ct N16 ... 6 C2
Juniper Dr SW18 ... 59 B3
Juniper Ho
6 Peckham SE14, SE15 ... 50 B3
9 Richmond TW9 ... 45 A2
Juniper St 16 E1 ... 32 B2
Juno Ct SW9 ... 163 B1
Juno Ho 2 E3 ... 26 C4
Juno Way SE14 ... 50 C4
Juno Way Ind Est SE14 ... 50 C4
Jupiter Ct SW9 ... 163 B1
Jupiter Way N7 ... 14 B2
Jupp Rd E15 ... 19 C1
Jupp Rd W E15 ... 27 C4
Jura Ho SE16 ... 41 A2
Jurston Ct SE1 ... 135 C3
Justice Wlk SW3 ... 158 A3
Justines Pl E2 ... 25 C2
Jutland Cl N19 ... 5 A3
Jutland Ho 4 SE5 ... 48 B1
Juxon St SE11 ... 149 A4

K

Kambala Rd SW11 ... 59 C4
Kara Way NW2 ... 9 C4
Karen Ct
2 Camberwell SE5 ... 64 A4
Forest Hill SE23 ... 66 A1
Karen Ho 7 N16 ... 15 C4
Kasmin Ct NW10 ... 8 C1
Kassala Rd SW11 ... 169 A3
Katherine Cl 3 SE16 ... 32 C1
Katherine Ho 15 W10 ... 23 A1
Katherine Sq W11 ... 31 A1 112 A2
Kathleen Ave W3 ... 28 B4
Kathleen Rd SW11 ... 60 B4
Kay Rd SW9 ... 172 C1
Kay St E2 ... 24 C3
Kean Ho 5 SE17 ... 48 A4
Kean St WC2 ... 106 C1
Keates Est N16 ... 7 B2
Keats Cl
Bermondsey SE1 ... 152 C3
Hampstead NW3 ... 12 A4
Keats Gr NW3 ... 12 A4
Keats Ho
22 Bethnal Green E2 ... 25 B2
30 Camberwell SE5 ... 48 B3
Chelsea SW1 ... 161 A4
Keats House Mus* NW3 ... 12 A4
Keats Pl EC2 ... 109 B3
Keble Ho 4 SW15 ... 57 C1
Keble Pl SW13 ... 47 A4
Kedelston Ct E5 ... 18 A4
Kedge Ho 16 E14 ... 41 C3
Kedleston Wlk 21 E2 ... 25 A2
Keel Cl SE16 ... 32 C1
Keel Ct 8 E14 ... 34 C2
Keeley St WC2 ... 106 C1
Keeling Ho 4 E2 ... 25 A3
Keelson Ho 9 E14 ... 41 C3
Keen's Yd N1 ... 15 A2
Keeper Wharf E1 ... 32 C2
Keepier Wharf 15 E1 ... 32 C2
Keep The SE3 ... 53 C1
Keeton's Rd SE16 ... 40 A3
Keevil Dr SW19 ... 70 A4
Keighley Cl N7 ... 14 A4
Keildon Rd SW11 ... 60 B3
Keir Hardie Ho
Fulham W6 ... 47 C4
15 Upper Holloway N19 ... 4 C4
Willesden NW10 ... 8 B1
Keir Hardy Prim Sch E16 ... 35 C4
Keith Connor Cl 5 SW8 ... 61 A4
Keith Gr W12 ... 29 C1
Keith Ho NW6 ... 78 A1
Kelby Ho N7 ... 14 B2
Kelfield Ct 1 W10 ... 30 C3
Kelfield Gdns W10 ... 30 C3
Kelfield Mews W10 ... 30 C3
Kellett Ho N1 ... 87 C3
Kellett Rd SW2 ... 62 C3
Kellow Ho SE1 ... 137 B4
Kell St SE1 ... 136 B2
Kelly Ave SE15 ... 49 B2
Kelly Ct 18 E14 ... 33 C2
Kelly Mews 4 W9 ... 23 B1
Kelly St NW1 ... 13 A2
Kelman Cl SW4 ... 171 C1
Kelmore Gr SE22 ... 64 C3
Kelmscott Gdns W12 ... 38 C3
Kelmscott Rd SW11 ... 60 B2
Kelross Rd N5 ... 15 B4
Kelsall Mews TW9 ... 45 A2
Kelsey St E2 ... 24 C1 99 C2
Kelshall Ct N4 ... 6 B2
Kelson Ho E14 ... 42 B3
Kelso Pl W8 ... 128 B2
Kelvedon Ho SW8 ... 172 B4
Kelvedon Rd SW6 ... 155 A1
Kelvin Ct
Chiswick W4 ... 45 B3
Notting Hill W11 ... 31 C2 113 B3
Kelvington Rd SE15 ... 65 C2
Kelvin Rd N5 ... 15 B4
Kelyway Ho 20 SW2 ... 74 C4
Kember St N1 ... 14 B1
Kemble Ho SW9 ... 63 A4
Kemble St WC2 ... 106 C1
Kemerton Rd SE5 ... 63 B4
Kemey's St E9 ... 18 A3
Kemp Ct SW8 ... 162 A1
Kempe Ho SE1 ... 137 C1
Kempe Rd NW6 ... 22 C3
Kemp Ho
Finsbury EC1 ... 97 B3
1 Globe Town E2 ... 25 C3
Kempis Way 5 SE22 ... 64 A2
Kemplay Rd NW3 ... 11 C4
Kemp's Ct W1 ... 105 B1
Kemps Dr E14 ... 33 C2
Kempsford Gdns SW5 ... 141 C1
Kempsford Rd
Lambeth SE11 ... 149 C3
Newington SE11 ... 150 A3
Kemps Gdns SE13 ... 67 B2
Kempson Rd SW6 ... 155 C1
Kempthorne Rd SE8 ... 41 B2
Kempton Ct E1 ... 32 A4
Kempton Ho 13 N1 ... 24 A4
Kemsing Ho SE1 ... 137 C3
Kemsing Rd SE10 ... 43 C1
Kemsley SE13 ... 67 A2
Kenbrook Ho
Kensington W14 ... 127 A1
Kenbrook Ho *continued*
5 Kentish Town NW5 ... 13 B3
Kenbury Gdns 10 SE5 ... 48 B1
Kenbury Mans 18 SE5 ... 48 B1
Kenbury St SE5 ... 48 B1
Kenchester Cl SW8 ... 162 B1
Kendal NW1 ... 92 B4
Kendal Ave W3 ... 28 A4
Kendal Cl SE5 ... 48 A3
Kendal Ct NW2 ... 10 A3
Kendal Ho
32 Hackney E9 ... 17 B1
Islington N1 ... 85 A2
Kendall Ct 3 SE22 ... 64 C2
Kendall Pl W1 ... 103 B3
Kendal Pl SW15 ... 58 B2
Kendal Rd NW10 ... 8 C4
Kendal St W2 ... 102 B1
Kendal Stps W2 ... 102 B1
Kender Prim Sch SE14 ... 50 B2
Kender St SE14 ... 50 B2
Kendoa Rd 1 SW4 ... 61 C3
Kendon Ho E15 ... 19 C1
Kendrick Ct 12 SE15 ... 50 A2
Kendrick Mews SW7 ... 143 B3
Kendrick Pl SW7 ... 143 B3
Kenilford Rd SW12 ... 73 A4
Kenilworth Ct SW6 ... 58 A4
Kenilworth Rd
Bow E3 ... 26 A3
Kilburn NW6 ... 23 B4
Kenley Wlk W11 ... 31 A2 112 A3
Kenmont Gdns NW10 ... 22 A2
Kenmont Prim Sch NW10 ... 22 A2
Kenmore Cl TW9 ... 44 C3
Kenmore Ct NW6 ... 10 C1
Kenmure Rd E8 ... 17 A3
Kenmure Yd E8 ... 17 A3
Kennacraig Cl 6 E16 ... 35 C1
Kennard Ho SW11 ... 169 C3
Kennard Rd E15 ... 19 C1
Kennard St SW11 ... 169 B3
Kennedy Cox Ho 9 E16 ... 35 B4
Kennedy Ho SE11 ... 148 C2
Kennedy Wlk SE17 ... 151 C3
Kennet Cl SW11 ... 59 C3
Kennet Ct 47 W2 ... 31 C4
Kenneth Campbell Ho NW8 ... 89 C2
Kenneth Cres NW2 ... 9 A3
Kenneth Ct SE11 ... 149 C4
Kennet Ho NW8 ... 89 C1
Kenneth Younger Ho SW6 ... 155 A3
Kennet Rd W9 ... 23 B1
Kennet St E1 ... 125 C2
Kennett Wharf La EC4 ... 123 A4
Kenning Ho 6 N1 ... 24 A4
Kenning St 18 SE16 ... 40 B4
Kennings Way SE11 ... 149 C2
KENNINGTON ... 149 B1
Kennington Ent Ctr SE17 ... 150 A1
Kennington La SE11 ... 149 A1
Kennington Oval SE11 ... 163 A3
Kennington Palace Ct SE11 ... 149 B2
Kennington Park Gdns SE17 ... 48 A4
Kennington Park Ho SE11 ... 149 C1
Kennington Park Pl SE11 ... 48 A4
Kennington Park Rd SE11 ... 150 A2
Kennington Rd SE11 ... 149 B3
Kennington Sta SE17 ... 150 A2
Kennoldes SE21 ... 75 C2
Kenrick Pl W1 ... 103 B3
KENSAL GREEN ... 22 B2
Kensal Green Cemy (All Souls)* NW10 ... 22 B2
Kensal Green Sta NW10 ... 22 B2
Kensal Ho W10 ... 22 C1
Kensal Rd W10 ... 23 A1
KENSAL RISE ... 22 C3
Kensal Rise Prim Sch NW6 ... 22 C3
Kensal Rise Sta NW10 ... 22 C3
KENSAL TOWN ... 23 A1
KENSINGTON ... 127 C3
Kensington & Chelsea Coll
Chelsea SW10 ... 156 C2
Kensal Town W10 ... 31 A4
Kensington Church Ct W8 ... 128 A3
Kensington Church St W8 ... 31 C1 113 C1
Kensington Church Wlk W8 ... 128 A3
Kensington Court Mans W8 ... 128 B3
Kensington Court Mews W8 ... 128 B2
Kensington Court Pl W8 ... 128 B2
Kensington Ct W8 ... 128 B3
Kensington Ct Gdns W8 ... 128 B2
Kensington Gardens* W2 ... 115 A1
Kensington Gate W8 ... 128 C2
Kensington Gdns Sq W2 ... 100 A1
Kensington Gore SW7 ... 129 B3
Kensington Hall Gdns W14 ... 140 C2
Kensington High St W8 ... 127 C2
Kensington Ho 3 NW5 ... 13 B3

Kensington Hts W8 31 C1 113 B1
Kensington Mall W8 31 C1 113 C2
Kensington Mans SW5 141 C2
Kensington Olympia Sta W14 126 A2
Kensington Pal* W8 114 B1
Kensington Palace Gdns W8 114 A2
Kensington Park Gdns W11 31 B2 113 A3
Kensington Park Mews W11 31 B3
Kensington Park Rd W11 31 B2 113 A4
Kensington Pl W8 31 C1 113 B2
Kensington Prep Sch SW6 165 A4
Kensington Rd SW7 129 A3
Kensington Sports Ctr W11 31 A2 112 A4
Kensington Sq W8 128 A3
Kensington Village W14 141 A3
Kensington W W14 140 A4
Kensworth Ho EC1 97 C3
Kent Ct 3 E2 24 B3
Kent Ho
 Camberwell SE1 153 A1
 13 Chiswick W4 38 A1
 Marylebone W1 104 C2
 Pimlico SW1 147 B1
 Richmond TW10 54 C2
Kentish Bldgs SE1 123 B1
KENTISH TOWN 13 B2
Kentish Town CE Prim Sch NW5 13 B3
Kentish Town Rd NW1 13 A2
Kentish Town Sta NW5 13 B3
Kentish Town West Sta NW5 13 A2
Kent Lo 9 SW19 69 C3
Kentmere Ho SE15 50 B4
Kenton Ct W14 126 C1
Kenton Ho
 20 Globe Town E1 25 B1
 Highbury N5 5 C1
Kenton Rd E9 17 C2
Kenton St WC1 94 A2
Kent Pas NW1 90 C2
Kent Pk Ind Est SE15 50 A4
Kent Rd
 Richmond TW9 44 C3
 South Acton W4 37 B3
Kent St E2 24 B3
Kent Terr NW1 90 B3
Kentwell Cl SE4 66 A3
Kentwode Gn SW13 46 C3
Kent Yard SW7 130 B3
Kenway Rd SW5 142 A3
Ken Wilson Ho 19 E2 24 C3
Kenwood Cl NW3 2 C3
Kenwood Ho 15 SW9 63 A3
Kenwood Ho* NW3 3 A3
Kenworthy Rd E9 18 A2
Kenwrick Ho N1 85 A3
Kenwyn Rd SW4 61 C3
Kenyon Ho 31 SE5 48 B3
Kenyon St SW6 47 C2
Kepler Ho 9 SE10 43 B1
Kepler Rd SW2, SW4 62 A3
Keppel Ho
 Brompton SW3 144 A3
 5 Deptford SE8 41 B1
Keppel Row SE1 122 C1
Keppel St WC1 105 C4
Kerbela St E2 24 C1 99 B2
Kerbey St E14 34 A3
Kerfield Cres SE5 48 C2
Kerfield Pl SE5 48 C2
Kerridge Ct N1 16 A2
Kerrier Ho SW10 157 A1
Kerrington Ct 7 W12 39 B4
Kerrison Rd
 Battersea SW11 60 A4
 Mill Meads E15 27 C4
Kerry N7 14 A2
Kerry Ho 5 E1 32 B3
Kerry Path SE8 51 B4
Kerry Rd SE8 51 B4
Kerscott Ho 30 E3 27 A2
Kersfield Ho SW15 57 C1
Kersfield Rd SW15 57 C1
Kershaw Cl SW18 59 C1
Kershaw Ho 7 SE27 75 A1
Kersley Mews SW11 168 C3
Kersley Rd N16 7 A1
Kersley St SW11 168 C2
Kerwick Cl 1 N7 14 B1
Keslake Mans NW10 22 C3
Keslake Rd NW6 22 C3
Keston Ho SE17 152 B2
Keston Rd SE15 64 C4
Kestrel Ave SE24 63 B2
Kestrel Ho
 4 Battersea SW11 60 A4
 Finsbury EC1 96 C4
Kestrel Pl SE14 51 A4
Keswick Broadway 1 SW15 58 B2
Keswick Ct 2 SE22 64 C2
Keswick Ho 8 SE5 48 B2
Keswick Hts 9 SW15 58 A2
Keswick Lo E8 16 B2
Keswick Rd SW15 58 A2
Kett Gdns SW2 62 B2
Kettleby Ho SW9 63 A4
Ketton Ho 11 W10 22 B1
Kevan Ho SE5 48 B3
KEW 44 C4
Kew Bridge TW8 36 B1
Kew Bridge Ct 8 W4 36 C1
Kew Bridge Distribution Ctr TW8 36 B1
Kew Bridge Rd TW8 36 B1
Kew Bridge Sta TW8 36 B1
Kew Bridge Steam Mus* TW8 36 B1
Kew Coll TW9 44 C3
Kew Foot Rd TW9 54 A4
Kew Gardens Rd TW9 44 C2
Kew Gardens (Royal Botanic)* TW9 44 A2
Kew Gardens Sta TW9 44 C2
Kew Gn TW9 44 B4
Kew Green TW9 44 C4
Kew Green Prep Sch TW9 44 B4
Kew Lo 11 TW9 44 B2
Kew Montessori Sch TW9 44 C2
Kew Pal* TW9 44 A3
Kew Pier TW9 44 C4
Kew Rd TW9, W4 44 B2
Kew Ret Pk TW9 45 A2
Kew Riverside Prim Sch TW9 45 A1
Key Cl E1 25 A1
Keyes Ct SE22 64 C2
Keyes Rd NW2 9 C3
Keyham Ho 31 W2 31 C4
Key Ho SE11 163 B4
Keymer Rd SW2 74 B2
Keynsham Ho 2 N4 6 B4
Keyse Rd SE1 138 C1
Keystone Cres N1 84 B1
Keyworth Cl E5 18 A4
Keyworth Pl SE1 136 B2
Keyworth Prim Sch SE17 150 A2
Keyworth St SE1 136 B2
Kezia St SE8 41 A1
Khyber Rd SW11 168 A1
Kibworth St SW8 162 C1
Kidbrooke Gdns SE3 53 C2
Kidderpore Ave NW3 10 C4
Kidderpore Gdns NW3 10 C4
Kiffen St EC2 97 C2
Kilbrennan Ho 9 E14 34 B3
KILBURN 23 C4
Kilburn Bridge 14 NW6 23 C4
Kilburn Gate NW6 78 A2
Kilburn High Rd NW6 23 C4
Kilburn High Road Sta NW6 78 A3
Kilburn Ho 11 W9 23 B2
Kilburn La W10 23 A3
Kilburn Park Foundation Sch The NW6 23 B3
Kilburn Park Rd NW6 23 C2
Kilburn Park Sta NW6 23 C3
Kilburn Pl NW6 23 C4
Kilburn Priory NW6 78 A3
Kilburn Sq NW6 23 C4
Kilburn Sta NW2 10 B2
Kilburn Vale NW6 78 A3
Kilburn Vale Est 13 NW6 23 C4
Kilby Ct SE10 43 B3
Kildare Ct W2 31 C3
Kildare Gdns W2 31 C3
Kildare Rd E16 35 C4
Kildare Terr W2 31 C3
Kildare Wlk E14 33 C3
Kildoran Rd SW2 62 A2
Kilgour Rd SE23 66 A1
Kilkie St SW6 166 C1
Killarney Rd SW18 59 B1
Killick St N1 84 C1
Killieser Ave SW2 74 A2
Killip Cl E16 35 B3
Killoran Ho 9 E14 42 B3
Killowen Rd E9 17 C2
Killyon Rd SW8 171 B1
Kilmaine Rd SW6 154 B1
Kilmarsh Rd W6 39 B2
Kilmington Rd SW13 46 C4
Kilmore Ho 17 E14 34 A3
Kilmuir Ho SW1 145 C3
Kiln Ct E14 33 B2
Kilner Ho SE11 163 B4
Kilner St E14 33 C4
Kiln Pl NW5 12 C3
Kiloh Ct 1 SW11 60 A4
Kilpatrick Ct N16 7 B3
Kilpeck Ho 3 N4 6 B4
Kilravock St W10 23 A2
Kilronan 5 W3 28 C3
Kimbell Gdns SW6 164 A3
Kimber Ctr The SW18 70 C4
Kimberley Ave SE15 65 B4
Kimberley Ct NW6 23 A4
Kimberley Ho 7 E14 42 B3
Kimberley Rd
 Kilburn NW6 23 A4
 Stockwell SW9 62 A4
Kimber Rd SW18 71 A4
Kimble Ho
 Lisson Gr NW8 90 B2
 1 Lower Holloway N7 14 A3
Kimbolton Row SW3 144 A3
Kimpton Ct 12 SE5 48 C2
Kimpton Ho SW15 68 C4
Kimpton Rd SE5 48 C2
Kinburn St SE16 40 C4
Kincaid Rd SE15 50 A3
Kincardine Gdns W9 23 C1
Kindell Ho 4 SW14 55 C4
Kinder Ho N1 87 C2
Kindersley Ho E1 111 C1
Kinder St 10 E1 32 A3
Kinefold Ho N7 14 A2
Kinfauns Rd SW2 74 C2
King Alfred Sch NW11 2 A3
King Arthur Cl SE15 50 B3
King Charles Ct 16 SE17 48 A4
King Charles Ho SW6 156 B2
King Charles St SW1 134 A4
King Charles Terr 11 E1 32 A2
King Charles Wlk 6 SW19 70 A3
King David La E1 32 B2
Kingdon Ho 8 E14 42 B3
Kingdon Rd NW6 10 C2
Kingdown Cl W10 30 C3
King Edward Mans 12 E8 25 A4
King Edward Mews SW13 46 C2
King Edwards Mans SW6 155 B1
King Edward's Rd E9 25 B4
King Edward St EC1 108 C2
King Edward The Third Mews 11 SE16 40 A4
King Edward VII Hospl-Sister Agnes W1 103 C4
King Edward Wlk SE1 135 C2
King Fahed Acad W3 29 B2
Kingfield St E14 42 B2
Kingfisher Ct
 11 Battersea SW11 60 A4
 17 Cubitt Town E14 42 B4
 Putney SW19 70 A2
Kingfisher Ho
 16 Battersea SW18 59 B4
 Peckham SE15 49 B2
 West Kensington W14 126 C2
Kingfisher Mews SE13 67 A2
Kingfisher Sq 19 SE8 51 B4
King Frederick IX Twr SE16 41 B3
King George Sq TW10 54 B1
King George St SE10 52 B3
Kingham Cl
 3 Shepherd's Bush W11 39 C4
 Wandsworth SW18 71 B4
Kingham Ind Est NW10 20 C2
King Henry's Rd NW3 12 A1
King Henry's Reach W6 47 B4
King Henry St N16 16 A3
King Henry's Wlk N1 16 A2
King Henry's Yd 5 N16 16 A3
King Henry Terr 10 E1 32 A2
King Ho 5 W12 30 A3
Kinghorn St EC1 108 C3

King James St SE1 . . . 136 B3
King John Ct EC2 . . . 24 A1 98 B2
King John St E1 . . . 32 C4
Kinglake St SE17 . 152 B2
Kingly Ct W1 . . . 119 A4
Kingly St W1 . . . 118 C4
King & Queen St SE17 . . . 151 A2
King's Arms Ct E1 . . . 111 B3
King's Arms Yd EC2 . . . 109 B2
Kings Ave SW4 . . . 62 A1
Kings Avenue Sch SW4 . . . 62 A2
King's Bench St SE1 . . . 136 B4
King's Bench Wlk EC4 . . . 107 C1
Kingsbridge N16 . . . 6 C3
Kingsbridge Ave W3 . . . 36 B4
Kingsbridge Ct E14 . . . 41 C2
Kingsbridge Rd W10 . . . 30 B3
Kingsbury Rd N1 . . . 16 A2
Kingsbury Terr N1 . . . 16 A2
Kingsclere Cl SW15 . . . 68 C4
Kingscliffe Gdns SW19 . . . 70 B3
King's Coll
Dulwich Village SE24 . . . 63 C1
Strand WC2 . . . 121 A4
Kings College Ct NW3 . . . 12 A1
King's College Hospl SE5 . . . 48 C1
Kings College Rd NW3 . . . 11 C1
King's Coll London (Hampstead) NW3 . . . 10 C4
King's Coll Univ SE1 . . . 121 B1
Kingscote NW11 . . . 1 B3
Kingscote Rd W4 . . . 37 C3
Kingscote St EC4 122 A4
King's Court N SW3 . . . 144 A1
Kingscourt Rd SW16 . . . 74 A1
King's Court S SW3 . . . 144 A1
King's Cres N4, N5 . . . 6 B1
Kingscroft SW4 . . . 62 A1
Kingscroft Rd NW2 . . . 10 B2
KING'S CROSS . . . 84 C2
King's Cross WC1 . 94 B4
King's Cross Bridge WC1 . . . 94 B4
King's Cross Rd WC1 . . . 95 A3
King's Cross, St Pancras N1 . . . 94 A4
King's Cross Sta N1 . . . 84 B1
King's Cross (Thames Link) Sta WC1 . . . 94 B4
Kings Ct
6 Barnsbury N7 . . . 14 B1
Chiswick W6 . . . 38 C2
East Dulwich SE22 . . . 64 C3
Primrose Hill NW8 . . 80 C3
10 Putney SW15 . . . 68 C4
Kingsdale Gdns W11 . . . 30 C1
Kingsdale Sec Sch SE21 . . . 76 A1
Kingsdown Ave W3 . . . 29 A2
Kingsdown Cl
26 Deptford SE16 . . . 40 A1
8 Notting Hill W11 . . 31 A3
Kingsdown Ct SW11 . . . 60 A1
Kingsdown Ho 1 E8 . . . 16 C3
Kingsdown Rd 4 N19 . . . 5 A2
Kings Farm Ave TW10 . . . 54 C3
Kingsfield Ho 18 N16 . . . 7 A1
Kingsford St NW5 . . 12 B3
Kingsgate Est N1 . . . 16 A2
Kingsgate Ho SW9 . . . 173 C4
Kingsgate Par SW1 . . . 133 A1
Kingsgate Pl NW6 . . 10 C1
Kingsgate Prim Sch NW6 . . . 10 C1
Kingsgate Rd NW6 . . . 10 C1
King's Gdns 6 NW6 . . . 10 C1
King's Gr
Peckham SE15 . . . 50 A2
Peckham SE15 . . . 50 A3
Kingshall Mews SE13 . . . 67 B4
King's Head Yd SE1 . . . 123 B1
Kingshill SE17 . . . 151 A4
Kings Ho
19 Limehouse E14 . . . 33 B2
South Lambeth SW8 . . . 162 B2
Kingshold Rd E9 . . . 17 B1
King's House Sch TW10 . . . 54 B2
King's House Sch (Jun) TW10 . . . 54 B2
King's Keep 6 SW15 . . . 57 C2
KINGSLAND . . . 16 A2
Kingsland NW8 . . . 80 B3
Kingsland Gn 1 E8, N1 . . . 16 A2
Kingsland High St E8 . . . 16 B3
Kingsland Pas 2 E8 . . . 16 A2
Kingsland Rd E2 . . . 24 A3
Kingsland Sh Ctr 12 E8 . . . 16 B2
Kingslawn Cl SW15 . . . 57 A2
Kingsley Ct NW2 . . . 9 A2
Kingsley Flats SE1 . . . 152 B3
Kingsley Ho
Chelsea SW3 . . . 157 C3
Clapham SW4 . . . 171 C2
Kingsley Mews
Kensington W8 . . . 128 B1
15 St George in t East E1 . . . 32 A2
Kingsley Pl N6 . . . 3 C4
Kingsley Rd NW6 . . . 23 B4
Kingsley St SW11 . . . 60 B4
Kings Mall Sh Ctr W6 . . . 39 B2
King's Mans SW3 158 A3
Kingsmead TW10 . . . 54 B1
Kingsmead Ct N6 . . . 4 C4
Kingsmead Ho E9 . . 18 A4
Kingsmead Prim Sch E9 . . . 18 A4
Kingsmead Rd SW2 . . . 74 C2
King's Mead Way E5, E9 . . . 18 A4
Kingsmere Cl SW15 . . . 57 C4
Kingsmere Pl N16 . . . 6 C3
Kingsmere Rd SW19 . . . 69 C2
King's Mews
1 Clapham Pk SW4 . . . 62 A2
Gray's Inn WC1 . . . 95 A1
Kingsmill NW8 . . . 79 C2
Kingsmill Terr NW8 . . . 79 C2
Kingsnorth Ho 12 W10 . . . 30 C3
King's Par
3 Hammersmith W12 . . . 38 C3
Willesden NW10 . . . 22 B4
Kings Pl W4 . . . 37 B2
King's Pl SE1 . . . 136 C3
King Sq EC1 . . . 96 C3
King's Quay SW10 167 A4
Kings Rd
Richmond TW10, TW9 . . . 54 B2
Willesden NW10 . . . 9 A1
King's Rd
Chelsea SW3 . . . 144 B1
Chelsea SW10 . . . 157 B3
Mortlake SW14 . . . 55 C4
Kings Ride Gate TW10 . . . 54 C3
Kingsridge SW19 . . . 70 A2
King's Scholars' Pas SW1 . . . 146 C4
King St Acton W3 . . . 28 B1
Hammersmith W6 . . . 38 C2
St James SW1 . . . 119 A2
Strand WC2 . . . 120 A4
Whitechapel EC2 . . 109 A1
King Stairs Cl SE16 . . . 40 A4
King's Terr NW1 . . . 82 C3
Kingston Ho 4 NW6 . . . 10 A1
Kingston Ho E SW7 . . . 130 A3
Kingston Ho N SW7 . . . 130 A3
Kingston Ho S SW7 . . . 130 A3
Kingston Rd SW15, SW19 . . . 69 A3
Kingston Univ Roehampton Vale Campus SW15 . . . 68 B1
Kingston Vale SW15 . . . 68 A1
Kingstown St NW1 81 B4
King Street Cloisters 8 W6 . . . 39 A2
King Street Coll W12 . . . 39 B4
Kingswater Pl SW11 . . . 158 A1
Kingsway
Mortlake SW14, TW9 . . . 55 A4
St Giles WC2 . . . 106 C2
Kingsway Coll NW5 . . . 13 A2
Kingsway Mans WC1 . . . 106 C4
Kingsway Pl EC1 . . 96 A2
Kingswear Rd NW5 . . 4 A1
Kings Well 25 NW3 . . . 11 B4
Kings Wlk Sh Mall SW3 . . . 144 C2
Kingswood 31 E2 . . . 25 B3
Kingswood Ave NW6 . . . 23 A3
Kingswood Cl SW8 . . . 162 B1
Kingswood Ct
Hither Green SE13 . . . 67 C1
7 Richmond TW10 . . 54 B2
Kings Wood Ct 4 NW6 . . . 10 C1
Kingswood Rd
South Acton W4 . . . 37 B3
Streatham SW2 . . . 74 A4
Kingswood Terr W4 . . . 37 B3
Kings Yd E15 . . . 18 C2
Kington Ho NW6 . . 78 B3
Kingward Ho E1 . . 111 B4
Kingweston Cl NW2 . . . 1 A1
King William La 3 SE10 . . . 43 A1
King William St EC4 . . . 123 C4
King William Wlk SE10 . . . 52 B4
Kingwood Rd SW6 . . . 154 A1
Kinloch St N7 . . . 5 B1
Kinnaird Ave W4 . . . 45 B3
Kinnear Rd W12 . . . 38 B4
Kinnerton Pl N SW1 . . . 131 A3
Kinnerton Pl S SW1 . . . 131 A3
Kinnerton St SW1 . . . 131 B3
Kinnerton Yd SW1 . . . 131 B3
Kinnoull Mans 10 E5 . . . 17 A4
Kinnoul Rd W6 . . . 154 A4
Kinross Ho N1 . . . 84 C4
Kinsale Rd SE15 . . . 64 C4
Kinsham Ho E2 . . . 24 C1 99 C2
Kintore Way SE1 . . 152 C4
Kintyre Ct 17 SW2 . . 74 A4
Kintyre Ho 6 E14 . . 34 B1
Kinver Ho N4 . . . 6 C4
Kipling Ho 29 SE5 . . 48 B3
Kipling St SE1 . . . 137 C4
Kipling Twr 3 W3 . . 37 B3
Kirby Est SE16 . . . 40 A3
Kirby Gr SE1 . . . 138 A4
Kirby St EC1 . . . 107 C4
Kirkeby Bldg EC1 . 107 B4
Kirkland Wlk 4 E8 . . . 16 B2
Kirkley Ho N16 . . . 7 A3
Kirkman Ho W1 . . 105 B3
Kirkman Pl W1 . . . 105 B3
Kirkmichael Rd E14 . . . 34 B3
Kirkside Rd SE3 . . . 53 C4
Kirkstall Gdns SW2 . . . 74 A3
Kirkstall Ho SW1 . 146 A2
Kirkstall Rd SW2 . . . 74 A3
Kirkstead Ct E5 . . . 18 A4
Kirkstone NW1 . . . 92 C4
Kirkwall Pl E2 . . . 25 B2
Kirkwood Rd SE15 . . 50 A1
Kirtley Ho SW8 . . . 171 A4
Kirtling St SW8 . . . 160 C2
Kirton Cl W4 . . . 37 C2
Kirton Gdns E2 . . . 24 B2 99 A3
Kirwin Way SE5 . . . 48 A3
Kitcat Terr E3 . . . 26 C2
Kite Ho 5 SW11 . . . 60 A4
Kite Pl E2 . . . 24 C2 99 C4
Kitson Rd
Barnes SW13 . . . 46 C2
Camberwell SE5 . . . 48 B3
Kittiwake Ct 26 SE8 . . . 51 B4
Kitto Rd SE14 . . . 50 C1
Kiver Rd N19 . . . 5 A2
Klea Ave SW4 . . . 61 B1
Kleffens Ct 2 SE3 . . 53 B3
Kleine Wharf 30 N1 . . . 24 A4
Knapp Cl NW10 . . . 8 A2
Knapp Rd E3 . . . 26 C1
Knaresborough Dr SW18 . . . 71 A3
Knaresborough Ho 4 N4 . . . 6 B4
Knaresborough Pl SW5 . . . 142 A4
Knatchbull Rd
Brixton SE5 . . . 48 A2
Stonebridge NW10 . . . 20 C4
Knebworth Ho
South Lambeth SW8 . . . 171 C3
2 Stoke Newington N16 . . . 16 A4
Knebworth Rd 3 N16 . . . 16 A4
Kneller Ho SW8 . . 171 C2
Kneller Rd SE4 . . . 66 A3
Knighten St E1 . . . 32 A1
Knighthead Point 26 E14 . . . 41 C4
Knight Ho SE17 . . 152 A3
Knightleas Ct NW2 . . 9 B3
Knightrider Ct EC4 . . . 122 C
Knightrider St EC4 . . . 122 B4
Knights Arc SW1 . 130 C3
Knight's Ave W5 . . . 36 A4
KNIGHTSBRIDGE . . . 130 A3
Knightsbridge SW1, SW7 . . . 130 C
Knightsbridge Ct SW1 . . . 131 A
Knightsbridge Gn SW1 . . . 130 C

Knightsbridge Under Sch SW7 143 A3
Knights Cl E9 17 B3
Knights Ho
 Bermondsey SE1 138 C4
 South Lambeth SW8 162 B1
 West Kensington SW5 140 C2
Knight's Ho SW10 156 C2
Knights Rd E16 43 C4
Knight's Wlk SE11 150 A3
Knightswood Ct N6 4 C4
Knivet Rd SW6 155 B3
Knobs Hill Rd E15 27 A4
Knoll Ho NW8 78 C2
Knoll Rd SW18 59 B2
Knolly's Cl SE27, SW16 74 C1
Knolly's Rd SE27, SW16 74 C1
Knot Ho SE1 124 C1
Knottisford St E2 25 B2
Knowlden Ho 5 E1 32 B2
Knowle Cl SW9 62 C4
Knowledge Point Sch N7 14 B2
Knowles Hill Cres SE13 67 C2
Knowles Ho
 Wandsworth SW18 59 A1
 Willesden Green NW10 21 C4
Knowles Wlk SW4 61 B4
Knowlton Ho SW9 173 C4
Knowsley Rd SW11 168 C1
Knox Ct SW4 172 B2
Knox Ho SW15 47 B1
Knox St W1 102 C4
Knoyle Ho W14 126 B2
Knoyle St SE14 51 A4
Kobi Nazrul Prim Sch E1 111 C2
Kossuth St SE10 43 A1
Kotree Way SE1 153 C4
Kramer Mews SW5 142 A1
Kreedman Wlk 8 E8 16 C3
Kreisel Wlk TW9 44 B4
Kylemore Ct 4 W12 38 C4
Kylemore Rd NW6 10 C1
Kylestrome Ho SW1 145 C3
Kynance Mews SW7 128 B1
Kynance Pl SW7 128 C1
Kynaston Ho 7 SW2 74 B3
Kynaston Rd N16 7 A1
Kyrle Rd SW11 60 C1
Kyverdale Rd N16 7 B3

L

Laburnham Ct NW2 1 B2
Laburnum Cl 5 SE15 50 B3
Laburnum Ct 26 E2 24 B4
Laburnum Ho
 New Cross SE4 51 B1
 6 Stoke Newington N16 6 C2
Laburnum JMI Sch E2 24 B4
Laburnum St E2 24 B4
Lacey Ho 7 SE13 52 B1
Lacine Ct 12 SE16 40 C4
Lackington St EC2 109 C4
Lackland Ho SE1 153 A2
Lacland Ho SW10 157 B2
Lacon Rd SE22 64 C3
Lacy Rd SW15 57 C3
Ladbroke Cres W11 31 A3
Ladbroke Gdns W11 31 B2 112 C4
Ladbroke Gr
 Kensal Town W10 31 A4
 Notting Hill W11 31 B2 112 C4
Ladbroke Grove Ho W11 31 B2 112 C4
Ladbroke Grove Sta W10 31 A3
Ladbroke Ho E1 111 A3
Ladbroke Mews W11 31 A1 112 B1
Ladbroke Rd W11 31 B1 112 C2
Ladbroke Sq W11 31 B2 113 A3
Ladbroke Terr W11 31 B1 113 A2
Ladbroke Wlk W11 31 B1 113 A2
Ladlands SE22 76 C4
Ladybower Ct 6 E5 17 C4
Ladycroft Rd SE13 67 A4
Lady Elizabeth Ho SW14 55 B4
Ladyfern Ho 19 E3 33 C4
Lady Florence Ctyd 15 SE8 51 C3
Lady Margaret Rd NW5 13 B3
Lady Margaret Sch SW6 165 B3
Lady Somerset Rd NW5 13 A4
LADYWELL 66 C1
Ladywell Cl SE4 66 C3
Ladywell Hts SE4 66 B1
Ladywell Rd SE13 67 A2
Ladywell Sta SE13 67 A2
Ladywell Water Twr SE4 66 C2
Lafitte Ho 22 N19 4 C4
Lafone Ho 11 SW2 74 A4
Lafone St SE1 138 C4
Lagado Mews SE16 32 C1
Lagonda Ho 11 E3 26 C1
Lagonier Ho EC1 97 A3
Laindon Ho 6 N16 7 B3
Laing Ho SE5 48 B3
Lainson St SW18 70 C4
Lairdale Cl SE21 75 B4
Laird Ho SE5 48 B3
Lairs Cl N7 14 A2
Laitwood Rd SW12 73 A3
Lakanal 14 SE5 49 A2
Lake Ho SE1 136 C3
Laker Ct SW4 172 B2
Laker Pl SW15 58 A1
Lakeside Ct N4 6 B3
Lakeside Rd W14 39 C3
Lakeview 23 E3 25 C3
Lake View Ct SW1 132 B2
Lakis Cl NW3 11 B4
Laleham Ho E2 24 B1 98 C2
Lalor St SW6 164 B2
Lambard Ho 4 SE10 52 B3
Lamb Ct 16 E14 33 A2
Lamberhurst Ho 14 SE15 50 B4
Lambert Ave TW9 55 A4
Lambert Ho
 Brixton SW9 173 B1
 19 Crouch End N19 4 C4
Lambert Rd SW2 62 B2
Lambert St N1 14 C1
LAMBETH 134 C3
Lambeth Acad SW4 61 B2
Lambeth Coll (Brixton Ctr) SW2 62 B2
Lambeth Coll (Clapham Ctr) SW4 61 B2
Lambeth Coll (Tower Bridge Ctr) SE1 124 B1
Lambeth Coll (Vauxhall Ctr) SW8 171 B4
Lambeth Ct 8 SW18 58 C2
Lambeth High St SE1 148 C4
Lambeth Hill EC4 122 C4
Lambeth Hospl SW9 62 B4
Lambeth North Sta SE1 135 B2
Lambeth Pal* SE1 134 C1
Lambeth Palace Rd SE1 134 C2
Lambeth Pier SE1 134 B1
Lambeth Rd SE1 135 C1
Lambeth Twrs SE11 135 B1
Lambeth Wlk SE11 149 A4
Lambfold Ho N7 14 A2
Lamb Ho
 28 Camberwell SE5 48 B3
 11 Camberwell SE5 48 C2
 Greenwich SE10 52 B4
Lamb La E8 17 A1
Lamble St NW5 12 C4
Lambolle Pl NW3 12 A2
Lambolle Rd NW3 12 A2
Lambourn Cl 9 NW5 13 B4
Lambourne Gr SE16 40 C1
Lambourne Ho NW8 101 C4
Lambourn Rd SW4 61 A4
Lambrook Ho 13 SE15 49 C2
Lambrook Terr SW6 164 A4
Lamb's Bldgs EC1 97 B1
Lamb's Conduit Pas WC1 106 C4
Lamb's Conduit St WC1 94 C1
Lamb's Mews N1 86 A3
Lamb's Pas EC1 97 B1
Lamb St E1 110 C4
Lambton Ct 2 N19 5 A3
Lambton Mews 4 N19 5 A3
Lambton Pl W11 31 B2 113 A4
Lambton Rd N19 5 A3
Lamb Wlk SE1 138 A3
Lamerton Lo 10 TW9 44 B2
Lamerton St 8 SE8 51 C4
Lamington St 3 W6 39 A2
Lamlash St SE11 150 A4
Lamley Ho SE10 52 A3
Lammas Rd E9 17 C1
Lammermoor Rd SW12 73 A4
Lamont Rd SW10 157 B3
Lamont Rd Pas SW10 157 B3
Lampard Gr N16 7 B3
Lampern Sq E2 24 C2 99 C4
Lampeter Sq W6 154 A3
Lamplighter Cl 34 E1 25 B1
Lampson Ho 6 N19 13 B4
Lanark Ho SE1 153 B1
Lanark Mans
 Paddington W9 89 A2
 15 Shepherd's Bush W12 39 B4
Lanark Mews NW8 89 A3
Lanark Pl W9 89 A2
Lanark Rd W9 88 C3
Lanark Sq E14 42 A3
Lanbury Rd SE15 65 C3
Lancashire Ct W1 118 B4
Lancaster Ave SE21, SE27 75 B2
Lancaster Cl
 10 De Beauvoir Town N1 16 A1
 Kensington W2 114 A3
Lancaster Cotts 1 TW10 54 A1
Lancaster Ct
 Bayswater W2 115 A4
 Parsons Green SW6 155 A1
 West Norwood SE27 75 A2
Lancaster Dr
 Canary Wharf E14 34 B1
 Maitland Pk NW3 12 A2
Lancaster Gate W2 115 A4
Lancaster Gate Sta W2 115 B4
Lancaster Gr NW3 12 A2
Lancaster hall 14 E16 35 C1
Lancaster Ho SW15 47 B1
Lancaster Ho SW1 132 C4
Lancaster Ho SW18 71 A4
Lancaster Lo 2 W11 31 A3
Lancaster Mews
 Bayswater W2 115 A4
 2 Richmond TW10 54 A1
 3 Wandsworth SW18 59 A2
Lancaster Pk TW10 54 A2
Lancaster Pl WC2 120 C3
Lancaster Rd
 Dudden Hill NW10 8 C3
 Finsbury Pk N4 5 C4
 Notting Hill W11 31 A3
Lancaster St SE1 136 B3
Lancaster Stables 10 NW3 12 A2
Lancaster Terr W2 115 B4
Lancaster Wlk W2 115 A2
Lancefield Ho SE15 65 A4
Lancefield St W10 23 B2
Lancell St N16 7 A2
Lancelot Pl SW7 130 C3
Lancer Sq W8 128 A4
Lanchester Ct W2 102 C1
Lanchester Way SE14 50 C2
Lancing St NW1 93 B3
Lancresse Ct N1 24 A4
Landale Ct SE10 52 B2
Landale Ho 13 SE16 40 B3
Landcroft Rd SE22 64 B1
Landells Rd SE22 64 C1
Landford Rd SW15 57 B4
Landin Ho 1 E14 33 C3
Landleys Field 21 N7 13 C3
Landmann Ho 16 SE16 40 A2
Landmann Way SE14 40 C1
Landmark Hts E5 18 A4
Landon Pl SW1 130 C2
Landons Cl E14 34 B1
Landon Wlk 16 E14 34 A2
Landor Ct N16 16 A3
Landor Ho 7 SE5 48 C3
Landor Rd SW9 62 A4
Landor Wlk 11 W12 38 C4
Landrake NW1 83 A3
Landridge Rd SW6 164 C2
Landseer Ct 10 N19 5 A2
Landseer Ho
 Battersea SW11 169 C3
 Paddington NW8 89 C2
 Westminster SW1 147 C3
Landseer Rd N19 5 A2
Landulph Ho SE11 149 C2
Landward Ct W1 102 B2
Lane Ct SW11 72 B4
Lanercost Cl SW2 74 C2
Lanercost Rd SW2 74 C2
Lane The NW8 78 C1
Laneway SW15 57 A2

Laney Bldg EC1 107 B4
Lanfranc Rd E3 26 A3
Lanfrey Pl W14 140 C1
Langbourne Ave N6 3 C2
Langbourne Ho 7 SW2 62 C2
Langbourne Mans N6 3 C2
Langbourne Pl E14 42 A1
Langbourne Prim Sch SE21 76 A1
Langdale NW1 92 C4
Langdale Cl
Camberwell SE17 48 B4
Mortlake SW14 55 A3
Langdale Ho SW1 146 C1
Langdale Rd SE10 52 B3
Langdale St 25 E1 32 A3
Langdon Ct
Finsbury EC1 86 B1
Harlesden NW10 21 A4
Langdon Ho 3 E14 34 B3
Langdon Park Rd N6 4 B4
Langdon Park Sec Sch E14 34 B3
Langdon Pl SW14 55 B4
Langdon Way SE1 153 C3
Langford Cl
Shacklewell E8 16 C3
St John's Wood NW8 79 A2
Langford Ct NW8 79 A1
Langford Gn SE5 64 A4
Langford Ho 5 SE8 51 C4
Langford Pl NW8 79 A2
Langford Prim Sch SW6 166 B2
Langford Rd SW6 166 B2
Langham Ct 4 SW15 57 C2
Langham Ho SW4 61 B2
Langham Mans SW5 142 A1
Langham Pl
Chiswick W4 46 A4
Fitzrovia W1 104 B3
Langham St W1 104 B3
Lang Ho
South Lambeth SW8 162 A1
3 Tufnell Pk N19 4 B1
Langholm Cl SW12 73 C4
Langhorne Ct 10 NW8 11 C1
Langhurst Ho SW11 169 B2
Langland Gdns NW3 11 A3
Langland Ho 10 SE5 48 C3
Langland Mans NW3 11 A3
Langler Rd NW10 22 B3
Langley Ct
South Lambeth SW8 172 A4
Strand WC2 120 A4
Langley Dr W3 37 A4
Langley Ho
11 Lower Clapton E5 17 A3
36 Paddington W2 31 C4
Langley La SW8 162 B4
Langley Mans SW8 162 B4
Langley St WC2 106 A1
Langmead Ho 34 E3 27 A2
Langmore Ho E1 111 C1
Langport Ho 1 SW9 48 A1
Langridge 15 NW5 12 C2
Langroyd Rd SW17 72 B2
Langside Ave SW15 56 C3
Lang St E1 25 B1
Langston Hughes Cl 5 SE24 63 A3
Langthorn Ct EC2 109 C2
Langthorne Lo 30 SW2 74 C4
Langthorne St SW6 47 C3
Langton Cl WC1 95 A2
Langton Ct SW15 58 B1
Langton Ho SE11 149 A4
Langton Pl SW18 70 C3
Langton Rd SW9 48 A3
Langton St SW10 157 A3
Langton Way SE3 53 C3
Langtry Pl SW6 155 C4
Langtry Rd NW8 78 A3
Langtry Wlk NW8 78 C4
Lanhill Rd W9 23 C1
Lanier Rd SE13 67 C1
Lanner Ho 2 SW11 60 A4
Lannoy Point SW6 154 B2
Lanrick Rd E14 35 A3
Lansbury Gdns 1 E14 34 C3
Lansbury Lawrence Prim Sch E14 34 A3
Lanscombe Wlk SW8 162 A1
Lansdell Ho 9 SW2 62 C1
Lansdowne Coll W2 114 A3
Lansdowne Cres W11 31 A2 112 B3
Lansdowne Dr E8 16 C1
Lansdowne Gdns SW8 172 A4
Lansdowne Gr NW10 8 A4
Lansdowne Hill SE27 75 A1
Lansdowne Ho W11 31 B1 112 C2
Lansdowne Int Coll Ltd SW7 129 A1
Lansdowne Mews W11 31 B1 112 C2
Lansdowne Pl SE1 137 C2
Lansdowne Rd W11 31 A2 112 B3
Lansdowne Rise W11 31 A2 112 B3
Lansdowne Row W1 118 B2
Lansdowne Sch SW9 62 B4
Lansdowne Terr WC1 94 B1
Lansdowne Way SW4, SW8 172 B3
Lansdowne Wlk W11 31 B1 112 C2
Lansdowne Wood Cl 11 SE27 75 A1
Lansdown Ho 28 SE5 48 B1
Lantern Cl SW15 56 C3
Lantern Ho E14 41 C4
Lanterns Ct E14 41 C3
Lant Ho SE1 136 C3
Lantry Ct 1 W3 28 A1
Lant St SE1 137 A3
Lanvanor Rd SE15 50 B1
Lanyard Ho 4 SE8 41 B2
Lapford Cl W9 23 B1
Lapsang SE1 125 A1
Lapwing Twr 31 SE8 51 B4
Lapworth Ct W2 100 B4
Lara Cl SE13 67 B1
Larch Ave W3 29 A1
Larch Cl
Balham SW12 73 A2
15 Deptford SE8 51 B4
10 Upper Holloway N19 4 B2
Larch Ct 41 W2 31 C4
Larches Ave SW14 55 C3
Larchfield Ho 2 N5 15 B3
Larch Ho 23 SE16 40 B4
Larchmore Ct N19 5 A2
Larch Rd NW2 9 B4
Larcom St SE17 151 A3
Larden Rd W3 38 A4
La Retraite RC Girls Sch SW12 73 B4
Larissa St SE17 151 C3
Larix Ct NW10 21 C4
Larkfield Rd TW9 54 A3
Larkhall La SW4 172 A3
Larkhall Rise SW4 171 B1
Lark Row E2 25 B4
Larmenier & Sacred Heart RC Prim Sch W6 39 C2
Larnaca Ho SE1 138 C2
Larnach Rd W6 47 C4
Larpent Ave SW15 57 B2
La Saint Union RC Sec Sch NW5 3 C1
Lascelles Ho NW1 90 B1
Lassell St SE10 42 C1
Lasseter Pl SE3 53 B4
Latchmere Rd SW11 168 C1
Latchmere St SW11 168 C2
Latham Ho E1 32 C3
Latimer SE17 152 A1
Latimer Ho
11 Homerton E9 17 C2
Notting Hill W11 31 B2 113 A3
Latimer Ind Est 1 NW10 30 B3
Latimer Pl W10 30 B3
Latimer Rd W10 30 B3
Latimer Road Sta W10 30 C2
Latitude Ho NW1 82 A3
Latona Rd SE15 49 C4
Lattimer Pl W4 46 A4
Latvia Ct SE17 151 A1
Latymer Ct W6 39 C2
Latymer Upper Sch W6 38 C1
Lauderdale Mans W9 88 B3
Lauderdale Rd W9 88 B3
Lauderdale Twr EC2 108 C4
Laud St SE11 148 C2
Laughton Ho 11 SW2 62 C1
Launcelot St SE1 135 B3
Launceston Pl W8 128 C1
Launch St E14 42 B3
Laundress La N16 7 C1
Laundry La 7 N1 15 B1
Laundry Rd W6 154 A3
Laura Pl E5 17 B4
Laurel Bank Gdns SW6 165 A2
Laurel Cl 8 N19 4 B2
Laurel Ct
Dalston E8 16 B1
2 Putney SW15 57 C2
9 Rotherhithe SE16 33 A1
Laurel Ho
9 Deptford SE8 51 B4
5 Hamstead NW3 11 A2
Laurel Rd SW13 46 C1
Laurel St E8 16 B2
Laurence Mews 12 W12 38 C4
Laurence Pountney Hill EC4 123 B4
Laurence Pountney La EC4 123 C4
Laurie Gr SE14 51 A2
Laurie Ho
Newington SE1 136 B1
Notting Hill W8 31 C1 113 B1
Laurier Rd NW5 4 A1
Lauriston Ho 6 E9 17 C1
Lauriston Lo NW6 10 B2
Lauriston Rd E9 17 C1
Lauriston Sch E9 25 C4
Lausanne Rd SE15 50 B2
Lavell St N16 15 C4
Lavender Cl SW3 157 C3
Lavender Ct SW4 172 B3
Lavender Gdns SW11 60 B3
Lavender Gr E8 16 C1
Lavender Hill SW11 60 C4
Lavender Ho
8 Richmond TW9 45 A2
14 Rotherhithe SE16 32 C1
Lavender Rd
Battersea SW11 59 C4
Rotherhithe SE16 33 A1
Lavender Sweep SW11 60 B3
Lavender Terr 12 SW11 60 A4
Lavender Wlk SW11 60 B3
Lavendon Ho NW8 90 B2
Lavengro Rd SE27 75 B2
Lavenham Rd SW18 70 C3
Lavers Rd N16 7 A1
Laverstoke Gdns SW15 68 C4
Laverton Mews SW5 142 B3
Laverton Pl SW5 142 B3
Lavina Gr N1 84 C2
Lavington Cl E9 18 B2
Lavington St SE1 122 B1
Lawdale Jun Sch E2 24 C2 99 C4
Lawford Rd
Chiswick W4 45 B3
De Beauvoir Town N1 16 A1
Kentish Town NW5 13 B2
Lawfords Wharf 18 NW1 13 B1
Lawless Ho 5 E14 34 B2
Lawless St 12 E14 34 A2
Lawley St E5 17 B4
Lawman Ct 2 TW9 44 B2
Lawn Cres TW9 44 C1
Lawnfield Ct NW6 9 C1
Lawn House Cl E14 42 B4
Lawn La SW8 162 C4
Lawn Rd NW3 12 B3
Lawns The N16 16 A3
Lawrence Ave NW10 20 C4
Lawrence Bldgs 1 N16 7 B1
Lawrence Cl
Bow E3 26 C3
6 Shepherd's Bush W12 30 A2
Lawrence Ct
4 South Acton W3 37 B3
Stoke Newington N16 7 B1
Lawrence Ho
20 Camden Town NW1 13 A1
Westminster SW1 147 C3
Lawrence La EC2 109 A2
Lawrence Mans SW3 158 A3
Lawrence Pl N1 84 B4
Lawrence St
Canning Town E16 35 B4
Chelsea SW3 158 A3
Lawrence Trad Est SE10 43 A2
Lawrence Univ SW7 143 A3
Lawson Cl SW19 69 C1
Lawson Ct 1 N4 5 B3
Lawson Ho 17 W12 30 A2
Law St SE1 137 C2
Lawton Rd E3 26 A2
Laxfield Ct E8 24 C4
Laxley Cl SE5 48 A3
Laxton Path 1 SE4 65 C3
Laxton Pl NW1 92 B2
Layard Rd SE16 40 A2
Layard Sq SE16 40 A2
Laybourne Ho 18 E14 41 C4

Laycock Prim Sch N1 15 A2
Laycock St N1 14 C2
Layfield Ho 1 SE10 43 C1
Laystall Ct EC1 95 B1
Laystall St EC1 95 B1
Layton Pl TW9 44 C2
Lazar Wlk 2 N7 5 B2
Leabank Sq E9 18 C2
Leabourne Rd N16 7 C4
Leacroft Ave SW12 72 B4
Lea Ct 3 W12 38 A4
Leadenhall Mkt EC3 110 A1
Leadenhall Pl EC3 110 A1
Leadenhall St EC3 110 A1
Leadenham Ct 15 E3 26 C1
Lea Ho NW8 90 A1
Leahurst Rd SE13 67 C2
Lea Int E9 18 C3
Leake St
Lambeth SE1 135 B3
South Bank SE1 135 A4
Leamington Ct
4 Forest Hill SE26 76 C1
North Acton W3 28 C4
Leamington Ho 4 W11 31 B4
Leamington Pk W3 28 C4
Leamington Rd Villas W11 31 B4
Leamore St W6 39 B2
Leamouth Rd E14 34 C3
Leander Ct
27 Hackney E9 17 B1
St Johns SE8 51 C2
Leander Rd SW2 62 C1
Leary Ho SE11 149 A1
Lea Sq 22 E3 26 B4
Leatherdale St
32 Bethnal Green E1 25 B1
19 Globe Town E1 25 C2
Leatherhead Cl N16 7 B3
Leather La EC1 107 C4
Leathermarket Ct SE1 138 A3
Leathermarket St SE1 138 A3
Leather Rd SE16 40 C2
Leathwaite Rd SW11 60 B2
Leathwell Rd SE8 52 A1
Lebanon Gdns SW18 58 C1
Lebanon Rd SW18 58 C2
Lebus Ho NW8 80 A1
Lechmere Rd NW2 9 A2
Leckford Rd SW18 71 B3
Leckhampton Pl 23 SW2 74 C4
Lecky Ho NW2 9 A4
Lecky St SW7 143 B2
L'Ecole des Petits Sch SW6 166 A2
Leconfield Ave SW13, SW15 56 B4
Leconfield Ho SE5 64 A4
Leconfield Rd N5 15 C4
Lector Ct EC1 95 C1
Leda Ct SW9 163 B1
Ledam Bldg EC1 107 B4
Ledbury Ho 12 SE22 64 A4
Ledbury Mews N W11 31 C3
Ledbury Mews W W11 31 C2 113 B4
Ledbury Rd W11 31 C3
Ledbury St SE15 49 C3
Ledo Ho 1 N16 15 C4
Lee Conservancy Rd E9 18 B3
Lee Ct SE13 67 C3
Leeds Ct EC1 96 A2
Lee Ho 3 N19 13 C3
Leeke St WC1 94 C4
Leeland Way NW10 8 B4
Leerdam Dr E14 42 B3
Lees Ct W1 117 B4
Lees Ho SE17 151 C1
Leeson Rd 12 SE24 62 C3
Lees Pl W1 117 B4
Lee St E8 24 B4
Leet Ct N16 15 C4
Lee Valley Sp Ctr E10 19 A4
Leeve Ho 7 W9 23 B2
Leeward Ct E1 125 C2
Leeway SE8 41 B1
Lefevre Wlk E3 26 C4
Leffern Rd W12 38 C4
Leff Ho 9 NW6 10 A1
Lefroy Ho SE1 136 C3
Lefroy Rd W12 38 B4
Legard Rd N5 6 A1
Leggatt Rd E15 27 B3
Legge St SE13 67 B2
Leghorn Rd NW10 21 C3
Legion Cl N1 14 C1
Legion Terr E3 26 C4
Leicester Ct
46 Paddington W2 31 C4
St James WC2 119 C4
Leicester Ho
4 Brixton SW9 63 A4
5 Putney SW15 69 B4
Leicester Pl WC2 119 C4
Leicester Sq* WC2 119 C3
Leicester Square Sta WC2 119 C4
Leicester St WC2 119 C4
Leigham Ave SW16 74 A1
Leigham Hall 3 SW16 74 A1
Leigham Hall Par 2 SW16 74 A1
Leigham Vale SE27, SW16, SW2 74 C2
Leigh Ct 22 SW2 62 C1
Leighfield Ho 5 N4 6 B4
Leigh Gdns NW10 22 B3
Leigh Ho 9 SW15 56 C2
Leigh Orchard Cl SW16 74 B1
Leigh Pl EC1 107 B4
Leigh Rd N5 15 A4
Leigh St WC1 94 A3
Leighton Cres NW5 13 B3
Leighton Gdns NW10 22 B3
Leighton Gr NW5 13 B3
Leighton House (Art Gall & Mus)* W14 127 A2
Leighton Pl NW5 13 B3
Leighton Rd NW5 13 B3
Leinster Ave SW14 55 B3
Leinster Gdns W2 114 C4
Leinster Mews W2 114 C4
Leinster Pl W2 100 C1
Leinster Sq W2 100 A1
Leinster Terr W2 114 C4
Leitch Ho 8 NW8 11 C1
Leithcote Path SW16 74 B1
Leith Ho
7 Kentish Town N7 13 C3
13 Streatham SW2 74 B4
Leith Mans W9 88 A3
Leith Yd 3 NW6 23 C4
Lelitia Cl E8 24 C4
Leman St E1 111 B1
Lemmon Rd SE10 53 A4
Le Moal Ho 28 E1 32 B4
Lemsford Ct N4 6 B2
Lena Gardens Prim Sch W6 39 B3
Lena Gdns W6 39 B3
Lendal Terr 7 SW4 61 C4
Len Freeman Pl SW6 154 C3
Lenham 11 NW5 12 C2
Lenham Ho SE1 137 C3
Lennon Rd NW2 9 B2
Lennox Gdns
Knightsbridge SW1 130 C1
Willesden NW10 8 B4
Lennox Gdns Mews SW1 144 C4
Lennox Ho 10 E9 17 B2
Lennox Rd N4, N7 5 C2
Lenthall Ho SW1 147 A1
Lenthall Rd E8 16 C1
Lenthorp Rd SE10 43 B2
Lenton Rise TW9 54 A4
Len Williams Ct NW6 23 C3
Leonard Ct
Bloomsbury WC1 94 A2
Kensington W8 127 B2
Leonard Day Ho 3 NW5 13 A2
Leonard Pl 6 N16 16 A4
Leonard St EC2 97 C2
Leonora Ho W9 88 C2
Leontine Cl SE15 49 C3
Leopards Ct EC1 107 B4
Leopold Bldgs E2 24 B2 98 C4
Leopold Mews E9 25 B4
Leopold Prim Sch NW10 8 B1
Leopold Rd NW10 8 A1
Leopold St E3 33 B4
Leopold Wlk SE11 148 C1
Leo St SE15 50 A3
Leo Yd EC1 96 B1
Leppoc Rd SW4 61 C2
Leroy St SE1 152 A4
Lerry Cl W14 155 A4
Lerwick Ho SW18 59 B3
Lesley Ct SW1 133 B1
Leslie Prince Ct 8 SE5 48 C3
Leslie Rd E11 19 C4
Lessar Ave SW4 61 B1
Lessar Ct SW4 61 B1
Lester Ct 42 E3 27 A2
Leswin Pl N16 7 B1
Leswin Rd N16 7 B1
Letchford Gdns NW10 21 C2
Letchford Mews NW10 21 C2
Letchmore Ho 7 W10 22 B1
Lethaby Ho 15 SW4 62 B3
Lethbridge Cl SE13 52 B1
Letterstone Rd SW6 154 C1
Lettice St SW6 165 A3
Lett Rd E15 19 C1
Lettsom St SE5 49 A1
Levana Cl SW19 70 A3
Levant Ho 17 E1 25 C1
Levehurst Way SW4, SW9 172 B2
Leven Rd E14 34 C3
Lever Ct 15 E9 17 C2
Leverett St SW3 144 B4
Leverington Pl N1 97 C3
Lever St EC1 96 C3
Leverstock Ho SW3 144 B2
Leverton Pl NW5 13 B3
Leverton St NW5 13 B3
Levison Way 2 N19 4 C3
Levita Ho NW1 93 C4
Levyne Ct EC1 95 B2
Lewesdon Cl 13 SW19 69 C3
Lewes Ho
Bermondsey SE1 138 B4
Peckham SE15 49 C4
Leweston Pl N16 7 B4
Lewey Ho E3 26 B1
Lewin Rd SW14 55 C4
Lewis Ct 5 SE16 40 A1
Lewis Gr SE13 67 B4
LEWISHAM 67 B3
Lewisham Bridge Prim Sch SE13 67 A4
Lewisham Bsns Ctr SE14 50 C4
Lewisham Coll SE4 51 C1
Lewisham Ctr SE13 67 B4
Lewisham High St SE13 67 A2
Lewisham Hill SE13 52 B1
Lewisham Hospl SE13 67 A2
Lewisham Pk SE13 67 B1
Lewisham Rd SE13 52 B1
Lewisham St SW1 133 C3
Lewisham Sta SE13 67 B4
Lewisham Way SE4, SE14 51 B2
Lewis Pl E8 16 C3
Lewis Silkin Ho 9 SE15 50 B4
Lewis St NW1 13 A2
Lexden Rd W3 28 A1
Lexfield Ho N5 15 B4
Lexham Gardens Mews W8 128 B1
Lexham Gdns W8 142 A4
Lexham Mews W8 141 C4
Lexham Wlk W8 128 B1
Lexington St W1 119 A4
Lexton Gdns SW12 73 C3
Leyborne Pk TW9 44 C2
Leybourne Ho 20 SE15 50 B4
Leybourne Rd 17 NW1 13 A1
Leybourne St 5 NW1 13 A1
Leyden Mans 7 N19 5 A4
Leyden St E1 110 C3
Leydon Cl SE16 32 C1
Ley Ho SE1 136 C3
Leyland Ho 6 E14 34 A2
Leylands SW18 58 B1
Leylang Rd SE14 50 C3
Leys Ct SW9 173 B1
Leysdown 9 NW5 12 C2
Leysdown Ho SE17 152 B2
Leysfield Rd W12 38 C4
Leythe Rd W3 37 B4
LEYTON 19 C4
Leyton Mills E10 19 B4
Leyton Rd E15 19 C2
Liardet St SE14 51 A4
Liberia Rd N5 15 A2
Liberty Mews SW12 61 A1
Liberty St SW9 173 A4
Libra Rd 7 E3 26 B3
Library Mans 4 W12 39 B4
Library Par NW10 21 A4
Library Pl E1 32 A2
Library St SE1 136 B3
Lichfield Ct TW9 54 A3
Lichfield Gdns TW10, TW9 54 A2
Lichfield Ho 27 SE5 48 B1
Lichfield Rd
Mile End E3 26 A2
Richmond TW9 44 B2
West Hampstead NW2 10 A4
Lichfield Terr 1 TW9 54 A2
Lichport Ct N4 6 A3
Lickey Ho W14 155 A4
Lidcote Gdns SW9 173 A1
Liddell Gdns NW10 22 B3
Liddell Rd NW6 10 C2
Lidfield Rd N16 15 C4
Lidgate Rd 22 SE15 49 B3
Lidiard Rd SW18 71 B2
Lidlington Pl NW1 83 A1
Lidyard Rd N19 4 B3

Liffey Ct NW10 8 C1
Liffords Pl SW13 46 B1
Lifford St SW15 57 C3
Lighter Cl 16 SE16 41 A2
Lighterman Mews 15 E1 32 C3
Lighterman's Rd E14 42 A4
Lighterman's Wlk SW18 58 C3
Light Horse Ct SW1 145 B1
Ligonier St E2 24 B1 98 C2
Lilac Ho SE4 66 B4
Lilac Pl SE11 148 C3
Lilac St W12 29 C2
Lilestone Est NW8 89 C1
Lilestone Ho NW8 89 C2
Lilestone St NW8 90 A2
Lilford Ho 21 SE5 48 B1
Lilford Rd SE5 48 A1
Lilian Baylis Ho N1 15 B2
Lilian Baylis Tech Sch SE11 149 A1
Lilley Cl E1 125 C1
Lillian Ave W3 36 C4
Lillian Cl 14 N16 7 A1
Lillian Rd SW13 47 A4
Lillie Ho N5 14 C3
Lillie Rd SW6 154 C3
Lillie Road Mans SW6 154 B3
Lillieshall Rd SW4 61 B4
Lillie Yd SW6 155 B4
Lillingston Ho N7 14 C4
Lily Cl W14 39 C2
Lily Pl EC1 107 C4
Lilyville Rd SW6 164 C4
Limborough Ho 5 E14 33 C4
Limburg Rd SW11 60 A3
Limeburner La EC4 108 A2
Lime Cl E1 125 C2
Lime Ct SW15 57 A4
Lime Gr W12 39 B4
Limeharbour E14 42 A4
Lime Ho 7 TW9 45 A2
LIMEHOUSE 33 A2
Limehouse Cswy E14 33 B2
Limehouse Ct 5 E14 33 C3
Lime House Ct 23 E14 33 B3
Limehouse Cut 4 E14 34 A4
Limehouse Fields Est 14 E14 33 A4
Limehouse Link (Tunnel) E14 33 B2
Limehouse Sta E14 33 A3
Limekiln Wharf 21 E14 33 B2
Limerick Cl SW12 73 B4
Limerick Ct 1 SW12 73 B4
Limerston St SW10 157 A3
Lime St Pas EC3 124 A4
Limes Ave
Barnes SW13 46 B1
Limes Ave *continued*
Golders Green NW11 1 A4
Limes Ct NW6 9 C1
Limes Field Rd SW14 56 A4
Limesford Rd SE15 65 C3
Limes Gdns SW18 58 C1
Limes Gr SE13 67 B3
Lime St EC3 110 A1
Limes The
Camberwell SE5 64 A4
Kensington W2 31 C2 113 C3
Limes Wlk SE15 65 B3
Limetree Cl SW2 74 B3
Lime Tree Ct 14 E3 33 C4
Limpsfield Ave SW19 69 C2
Limscott Ho 35 E3 27 A2
Linacre Cl SE15 65 A4
Linacre Ct W6 39 C1
Linacre Rd NW2 9 A2
Linale Ho N1 87 B1
Linberry Wlk 3 SE8 41 B2
Lincoln Ave SW19 69 C1
Lincoln Ct N16 6 C4
Lincoln Ho
Bloomsbury WC1 107 A3
9 Dartmouth Pk NW5 4 B1
2 Islington N1 15 B1
Knightsbridge SW1 130 C3
10 Putney SW15 58 A2
Lincoln Mews NW6 23 B4
Lincoln's Inn★ WC2 107 A2
Lincoln's Inn Fields WC2 107 A2
Lincoln St SW3 144 C3
Lindale SW19 70 A2
Lindal Rd SE4 66 B2
Linden Ave NW10 22 C3
Linden Ct
8 Battersea SW18 59 C3
1 Shepherd's Bush W12 30 B1
Linden Gdns
Chiswick W4 37 C1
Notting Hill W2 31 C2 113 C3
Linden Gr SE15 65 B4
Linden Ho 10 SE8 51 B4
Linden Lodge Sch SW19 70 A3
Linden Mans N6 4 A3
Linden Mews
Kensington W2 31 C2 113 C3
Stoke Newington N1 15 C3
Lindens The W4 45 B2
Lindfield Gdns NW3 11 B3
Lindfield Hts NW3 11 B3
Lindfield St E14 33 C3
Lindford Christie Stadium The W12 30 A4
Lindisfarne Way E9 18 A4
Lindley Ho
13 Peckham SE15 49 C3
9 Stepney E1 32 B4
Lindley Pl TW9 44 C2
Lindley St E1 32 B4
Lindop Ho 8 E1 26 A1
Lindore Rd SW11 60 B3
Lindo St SE15 50 B1
Lindrop St SW6 166 C2
Lindsay Ct SW11 167 C3
Lindsay Sq SW1 147 C2
Lindsell St 6 SE10 52 B2
Lindsey Ho★ SW10 157 C2
Lindsey Mews 18 N1 15 B1
Lindsey St EC1 108 B4
Lind St SE8 52 A1
Linfield WC1 94 C3
Linford Ho 17 E2 24 C4
Linford St SW8 170 C3
Linford Street Bsns Est SW8 170 C4
Lingard Ho 11 E14 42 B3
Lingards Rd SE13 67 B3
Lingfield Ho
5 Acton Green W4 37 B1
Lambeth SE1 136 B3
Lingham St SW9 172 C1
Ling Rd E16 35 C4
Ling's Coppice SE21 75 C2
Lingwell Rd SW17 72 A1
Lingwood Rd E5 7 C4
Linhope St NW1 90 C1
Linkenholt Mans 3 W6 38 B2
Link St E9 17 B3
Links Yd
Spitalfields E1 111 B4
Spitalfields E1 111 A4
Link The W3 28 A3
Linkway N4 6 B4
Linkwood Wlk NW1 13 C1
Linnell Ho
Spitalfields E1 110 C4
St John's Wood NW8 78 C4
Linnell Rd SE5 49 A1
Linnet Mews SW12 72 C4
Linom Rd SW4 62 A3
Linscott Rd E5 17 B4
Linsey St
Bermondsey SE16 153 B4
Bermondsey SE16 139 C1
Linslade Ho
10 Hackney E2 24 C4
Marylebone NW8 90 B2
Linstead St 1 NW6 10 C1
Linstead Way SW18, SW19 70 A4
Lintaine Cl W6 154 B3
Linthorpe Rd N16 7 A4
Linton Ho
Lower Holloway N7 14 B4
2 Tower Hamlets E3 33 C4
Linton St N1 87 A3
Linver Rd SW6 165 B2
Linwood Cl SE5 49 B1
Lion Cl SE4 66 C1
Lionel Ho 5 W10 31 A4
Lionel Mans 14 W14 39 C3
Lionel Mews 13 W10 31 A4
Lionel Road N TW8 36 A2
Lionel Road Prim Sch TW8 36 A2
Lionel Road S TW8 36 B1
Lion Gate Gdns TW9 54 B4
Lion Gate Mews SW18 70 C4
Lion House Sch SW15 57 C3
Lion Mills 38 E2 24 C3
Lion Yd SW4 61 C3
Lipton Rd 9 E1 32 C3
Lisburne Rd NW3 12 B4
Lisford St SE15 49 B2
Lisgar Terr W14 140 C4
Liskeard Gdns SE3 53 C2
Liskeard Ho SE11 149 C2
Lisle Ct NW2 1 A1
Lisle St WC2 119 C4
Lismore Cir NW5 12 C3
Lismore Wlk 4 N1 15 B2
Lissenden Gdns NW5 12 C4
Lissenden Mans NW5 12 C4
Lisson Cotts NW1 102 B4
Lisson Gr NW1, NW8 90 A2
LISSON GROVE 90 B1
Lisson Ho NW1 102 A4
Lisson St NW1 102 A4
Lister Cl W3 28 C4
Lister Ct N16 7 A2
Lister Ho
Greenwich SE3 53 A4
Marylebone W1 104 A2
Spitalfields E1 111 C4
Lister Hospl SW1 146 A1
Lister Mews N7 14 B4
Liston Rd SW4 61 B4
Listowel Cl SW9 163 C2
Listria Lo N16 7 B2
Listria Pk N16 7 B2
Litcham Ho 23 E1 25 C2
Litchfield Gdns NW10 8 C2
Litchfield St WC2 119 C4
Lithos Rd NW3 11 B2
Little Albany St NW1 92 B2
Little Argyll St W1 104 C1
Little Boltons The SW10 142 B1
Little Britain EC1 108 C3
Littlebury Rd SW4 61 C4
Little Chelsea Ho SW10 157 A3
Little Chester St SW1 132 A2
Little Cloisters SW1 134 A2
Little College St SW1 134 A2
Little Combe Cl 13 SW15 57 C1
Littlecote Cl SW19 70 A4
Little Cottage Pl SE10 52 A3
Little Deans Yd SW1 134 A2
Little Dimocks SW12 73 A2
Little Dorrit Ct SE1 137 A4
Little Edward St NW1 92 B4
Little Essex St WC2 121 B4
Littlefield Cl N19 13 B4
Little George St SW1 134 A3
Little Green St NW5 13 A4
Little Marlborough St W1 104 C1
Little Newport St WC2 119 C4
Little New St EC4 107 C2
Little Portland St W1 104 C2
Little Russell St WC1 106 A3
Little St James's St SW1 118 C1
Little St Leonards SW14 55 B4
Little Sanctuary SW1 134 A3
Little Smith St SW1 133 C2
Little Somerset St E1 110 C1
Little Titchfield St W1 104 C3
Littleton St SW18 71 B2
Little Trinity La EC4 123 A4
Little Turnstile WC1 106 C3
LITTLE VENICE 101 A4
Little Venice★ W9 100 C4
Littlewood SE13 67 B1
Livermere Ct 3 E8 24 B4
Livermere Rd E8 24 B4
Liverpool Gr SE17 151 B1
Liverpool Ho N7 14 C2
Liverpool Rd
Islington N1 85 C3
Islington N1, N7 14 C1
Newham E16 35 A4
Liverpool St EC2 110 A3
Liverpool Street Sta EC2 110 A3
Livesey Mus★ SE15 50 A4
Livesey Pl SE15 49 C4
Livingstone Ho 16 SE5 48 B3
Livingstone Lo 13 W9 31 C4
Livingstone Pl E14 42 B1
Livingstone Rd
14 Battersea SW11 59 C4
Mill Meads E15 27 B4
Livity Sch The SW2 62 A2
Livonia St W1 105 A1
Lizard St EC1 97 A3
Llandovery Ho 1 E14 42 B4

Llanelly Rd NW2 .... 1 B2
Llanvanor Rd NW2 .. 1 B2
Llewellyn Ho 10 N19 .... 4 B1
Llewellyn St SE16 139 C3
Lloyd Baker St WC1 .... 95 B3
Lloyd Ct
Ladywell SE13 ...... 67 A2
6 West Norwood SE27 .... 75 A1
Lloyd Ho N16 .... 6 C1
Lloyd's Ave EC3 .. 110 B1
Lloyd's Bldg★ EC3 .... 110 A1
Lloyd's Pl SE3 ...... 53 A1
Lloyd Sq WC1 ..... 95 B4
Lloyd's Row EC1... 96 A3
Lloyd St WC1...... 95 B4
Lloyd Villas SE4 .... 51 C1
Loampit Hill SE13 .. 52 A1
Loampit Vale SE13 .... 67 B4
Loanda Cl 17 E8.... 24 B4
Loats Rd SW2...... 62 A1
Locarno Rd 6 W3.. 28 B1
Lochaline St W6 .. 47 B4
Lochbie 9 N4 ...... 5 A4
Lochinvar St SW12 .... 73 A4
Lochmore Ho SW1 .... 145 C3
Lochnagar St E14 .. 34 B4
Lockbridge Ct 3 W9 .... 31 C4
Locke Ho
Nine Elms SW8.... 170 C4
Stamford Hill N16..... 7 B3
Lockesfield Pl E14 .... 42 A1
Lockgate Cl E9..... 18 B3
Lockhart Cl N7..... 14 B2
Lockhart St E3..... 26 B1
Lockhurst St E5.... 17 C4
Lockington Rd SW8 .... 170 B4
Lockmead Rd SE13 .... 67 B4
Lock Mews 9 NW1 .... 13 C2
Lockside 17 E14.... 33 A2
Locksley St E14 .... 33 B4
Lock View Ct 9 E14 .... 33 A2
Lockwood Ho SE11 .... 163 B3
Lockwood Sq SE16 .... 40 A3
Lockyer Est SE1.. 137 C3
Lockyer Ho
7 Greenwich SE10 .... 43 B1
Putney SW15 .... 57 C4
South Lambeth SW8 .... 162 A2
Lockyer St SE1... 137 C3
Locton Gn 4 E3 .... 26 B4
Loddiges Ho 5 E9 .... 17 B1
Loddiges Rd E9 .... 17 B1
Loddon Ho NW8... 89 C1
Loder St SE15...... 50 B3
Lodge Ave SW14 ... 56 A4
Lodge Rd NW8 .... 90 A3
Lodge The 9 W4... 38 A3
Lodore St E14..... 34 B3
Lodsworth Ho SW11 .... 169 B3
Loftie St SE16.... 139 C3
Lofting Ho 8 N1... 14 C1
Lofting Rd N1...... 14 C1
Lofts on the Park 24 E9 .... 17 C2
Loftus Rd W12 ..... 30 A1
Loftus Rd (Queens Park Rangers FC) W12 .... 30 A1
Logan Mews W8 . 141 B4
Logan Pl W8..... 141 B4
Loggetts SE21...... 76 A2
Lohmann Ho SE11 .... 163 B4
Lolesworth Cl E1 111 A3
Lollard St SE11... 149 B3
Lollards Twr SE1.. 134 C1
Loman St SE1.... 136 B4
Lomas St E1 ..... 111 C4
Lombard Ct
14 Acton W3 .... 28 A1
City of London EC3 123 C4
Lombard La EC4.. 107 C1
Lombard Rd SW11 .... 167 B2
Lombard St EC3.. 109 C1
Lombardy Pl W2 . 114 B3
Lomley Ho 10 SW2 .... 62 C1
Lomond Gr SE5 .... 48 C3
Lomond Ho 10 SE5 .... 48 C2
Loncroft Rd SE5.... 49 A4
Londesborough Ho 1 N16 .... 16 A4
Londesborough Rd N16 .... 16 A4
London Acad of Computing & Electronics SW17.. 72 B1
London Aquarium★ SE1 .... 134 C3
London Bridge EC4, SE1 .... 123 C3
London Bridge City Pier SE1 .... 124 A2
London Bridge Hospl SE1 .... 123 C2
London Bridge St SE1 .... 123 C1
London Bridge Sta SE1 .... 123 C1
London Bridge Wlk SE1 .... 123 C2
London Britannia Coll N1 .... 97 B4
London Business Sch NW1 .... 90 C2
London Canal Mus★ N1 .... 84 B2
London Central Mosque★ NW8... 90 B3
London Chest Hospl E2 .... 25 B3
London Clinic NW1 .... 91 C1
London Coll of Advanced Studies SE1 .... 123 B1
London Coll of Beauty Therapy W1..... 105 A1
London Coll of Bsns & Computer Studies SW4 .... 61 C3
London Coll of Communication (Sch of Printing & Publishing) SE11 .... 136 B1
London Coll of Economics & Science NW10..... 20 B1
London Coll of Fashion
Broadgate EC2........ 24 A1 98 B2
Marylebone W1 ... 103 C1
Marylebone W1 ... 104 B2
Marylebone W1 ... 104 A1
St Luke's EC1 ...... 96 C1
London Coll of Fashion (Mare St) E8 .... 17 A1
London Coll of International Business Studies WC1 .... 106 B3
London Ct 3 SW18 .... 58 C2
London Docklands Visitor Ctr★ E14... 42 B4
London Dungeon The★ SE1....... 123 C2
London Electronics Coll SW5........ 142 A2
London Eye (Millennium Wheel)★ SE1 ... 134 C4
London Fields East Side E8 .... 17 A1
London Fields Prim Sch E8.......... 25 A4
London Fields Sta E8 .... 17 A1
London Fields West Side E8 .... 16 C1
London Fire Brigade Mus★ SE1 ...... 136 C4
London Gas Mus The★ E3, E16...... 27 C1
London Ho 13 W6 .. 38 C2
London Ho TW9.... 54 B4
London Ho NW8.... 80 B2
London Hospital Dental Inst E1..... 32 A4
London Independent Hospl The E1...... 32 C4
London Int Coll N7 .. 5 B1
London International Film Sch WC2... 106 A1
London La E8 ...... 17 A1
London Metropolitan Univ
Islington N7 .... 14 C3
Whitechapel E1 ... 110 C2
Whitechapel E1 ... 110 C1
Whitechapel EC3 .. 124 C4
London Metropolitan Univ (Central Ho) E1 .... 111 B2
London Metropolitan Univ (Commercial Rd) E1.......... 111 C2
London Metropolitan Univ (Ladbrook Ho) N5 .... 15 A3
London Metropolitan Univ (Moorgate) EC2 .... 109 C3
London Metropolitian Univ (Spring Ho) N7 .... 14 C2
London Mews W2 .... 101 C2
London Nautical Sch The SE1......... 121 C2
London Oratory Sch The SW6........ 155 C2
London Pavilion SW1 .... 119 B3
London Peace Pagoda★ SW3 .... 159 A2
London Rd SE1... 136 B2
London Sch of Economics & Political Science WC2 .... 107 A1
London St
City of London EC3 .... 124 B4
Paddington W2.... 101 B1
London Stile 5 W4 .... 36 C1
London Stock Exchange★ EC2 . 108 C2
London Terr 1 E2 .... 24 C3
London Transport Mus★ WC2...... 120 B4
London Wall EC2 109 C3
London Wall Bldgs EC2 .... 109 C3
London Wetland Ctr★ SW13 .... 47 A3
London Wetland Visitor Ctr★ SW13 .... 47 A2
London Wharf 4 E2 .... 25 A4
London Xtra Tuition Coll N4 .... 6 A2
London Zoo★ NW1 .... 81 B2
Long Acre WC2 .. 106 B1
Longbeach Rd SW11 .... 60 B4
Longberrys NW2 .... 1 B1
Longbridge Way SE13 .... 67 B2
Longcliffe Ho SW18 .... 59 A2
Long Dr W3........ 29 A3
Longfellow Way SE1 .... 153 A3
Longfield Dr SW14 .... 55 A2
Longfield Est SE1 153 A3
Longfield St SW18.. 70 C4
Longford Ct
1 Bedford Pk W12 .... 38 A4
2 Clapton Pk E5 .... 17 C4
Longford Ho 7 E1 .... 32 B3
Longford St NW1.. 92 B2
Longford Wlk 9 SW2 .... 74 C4
Longhope Cl SE15.. 49 B4
Longhurst Ho 8 W9 .... 23 B2
Long La
Bermondsey SE1 .. 137 C3
Holborn EC1...... 108 B4
Longland Ct
Bermondsey SE1 .. 153 B2
Longland Ct continued
Hackney E9......... 18 A3
Longlands Ct W11 ...... 31 B2 113 A4
Longleat Ho SW1. 147 B2
Longleigh Ho 8 SE5 .... 49 A2
Longlents Ho 3 NW10 .... 20 C4
Longley Ho 5 N19 .... 13 B4
Longley St SE1... 153 B4
Longman Ho
9 Globe Town E2 ... 25 C3
10 Shoreditch E8.... 24 B4
Long Meadow 20 N7 .... 13 C3
Longmoor Point 14 SW15 .... 69 A3
Longmore St SW1 .... 146 C3
Longnor Rd E1..... 25 C2
Long Pond Rd SE3 .... 53 A2
Long Rd SW4 ...... 61 B3
Longridge Ho SE1 .... 137 A1
Longridge Rd SW5 .... 141 C3
Longs Ct 2 TW9 ... 54 B3
Long's Ct W1 .... 119 C3
Longshore SE8..... 41 B2
Long St E2... 24 B2 98 C4
Longstaff Cres SW18 .... 70 C4
Longstaff Rd SW18 .... 58 C1
Longstone Ave NW10 .... 21 B4
Longthorne Ho 18 E3 .... 26 B2
Longthorpe Ct 9 W6 .... 38 C2
Longville Rd SE11 .... 150 B4
Long Wlk SE1.... 138 B2
Longwood Dr SW15 .... 56 C1
Long Yd WC1...... 94 C1
Lonsdale Ho
Fulham SW6........ 58 C4
6 Stoke Newington N4 .... 6 B4
Lonsdale Mews
Notting Hill W11..... 31 B3
4 Richmond TW9 ... 44 C2
Lonsdale Pl N1..... 14 C1
Lonsdale Rd
Barnes SW13....... 46 B3
Chiswick W4........ 38 B2
Kilburn NW6........ 23 B4
Notting Hill W11..... 31 B3
Lonsdale Sq
Islington N1 .... 14 C1
Islington N1 .... 85 C4
Lopez Ho 4 SW9... 62 A4
Loraine Rd
Chiswick W4........ 45 A4
Islington N7 .... 14 B4
Lord David Pitt Ho 8 SE24 .... 62 C3
Lorden Wlk E2.......... 24 C2 99 B3
Lord Hills Rd W2. 100 B4

Lord Holland La SW9 . . . 173 C2
Lord Napier Pl W6 . . . 38 C1
Lord North St SW1 . . . 134 A1
Lord Roberts Mews SW6 . . . 156 A1
Lords Cl SE21 . . . 75 B2
Lord's Cricket Mus★ NW8 . . . 89 C3
Lordship Gr N16 . . . 6 C2
Lordship Ho 3 N16 . 6 C2
Lordship La SE22 . . . 64 B1
Lordship Park Mews N16 . . . 6 B2
Lordship Pk N16 . . . 6 C2
Lordship Pl SW3 . 158 A3
Lordship Rd N16 . . . 6 C2
Lordship Terr N16 . . . 6 C2
Lord's Indoor Cricket Sch NW8 . . . 90 A4
Lord's (MCC & Middlesex Cty Cricket Ground)★ NW8 . . . 89 C4
Lord's View NW8 . . 89 C3
Loreburn Ho 2 N7 . . . 14 B4
Lorenzo St N1, WC1 . . . 94 C4
Loris Rd W6 . . . 39 B3
Lorn Ct SW9 . . . 173 B2
Lorne Cl NW8 . . . 90 B3
Lorne Ct SW15 . . . 57 C1
Lorne Gdns 5 W11 . . . 39 C4
Lorne Ho
Hornsey N4 . . . 5 B4
7 Tower Hamlets E1 . . . 33 A4
Lorne Rd
Finsbury Pk N4 . . . 5 B3
3 Richmond TW10 . . 54 B2
Lorn Rd SW9 . . . 173 B2
Lorraine Ct 10 NW1 . . . 13 A1
Lorrimore Rd SE17 . . . 48 A4
Lorrimore Sq SE17 . . . 48 A4
Lorton Ho 9 NW6 . . 23 C4
Lostock Ho SW8 . . 171 B2
Lothair Rd S N4 . . . 6 A4
Lothbury EC2 . . . 109 B2
Lothian Rd SW9 . . . 48 A2
Lothrop St W10 . . . 23 A2
Lots Rd SW10 . . . 157 A1
Loudoun Rd NW8 . 79 A3
Loughborough Ct 7 SW9 . . . 63 A4
Loughborough Junction Sta SW9 . . . 63 A4
Loughborough Pk SW9 . . . 63 A3
Loughborough Prim Sch SW9 . . . 48 A1
Loughborough Rd SE5, SW9 . . . 48 A1
Loughborough St SE11 . . . 149 A1
Lough Rd N7 . . . 14 B2
Louisa Cl E9 . . . 25 C4
Louisa Gdns E1 . . . 25 C1
Louisa Ho SW15 . . . 56 B3
Louisa St E1 . . . 25 C1
Louise Bennett Cl 9 SE24 . . . 63 A3
Louise De Marillac Ho 26 E1 . . . 32 B4
Louise White Ho 1 N19 . . . 4 C3
Louisville Rd SW17 . . . 72 C1
Louvaine Rd SW11 . . . 59 C3
Lovat La EC3 . . . 124 A3
Lovatt Ct SW12 . . . 73 A3
Loveday Ho 2 SW2 . . . 74 C3
Lovegrove St SE1 . . . 49 C4
Lovegrove Wlk E14 . . . 34 B1
Love La EC2 . . . 109 A2
Lovelace Ho 12 E8 . . 24 B4
Lovelace Rd SE21 . . 75 B3
Lovelinch Cl SE15 . . 50 B4
Lovell Ho E8 . . . 24 C4
Lovell Pl SE16 . . . 41 A3
Loveridge Mews NW6 . . . 10 B2
Loveridge Rd NW6 . . . 10 B2
Lover's Wlk W1 . . 117 B1
Lovette Ho 4 E3 . . . 26 C2
Lovetts Pl SW18 . . . 59 A3
Love Wlk SE5 . . . 48 C1
Lowden Rd SE24 . . . 63 B3
Lowder Ho 6 E1 . . . 32 A1
Lowe Ave E16 . . . 35 C4
Lowell Ho 10 SE5 . . . 48 B3
Lowell St E14 . . . 33 A3
Lower Addison Gdns W14 . . . 126 A3
Lower Belgrave St SW1 . . . 132 A1
LOWER CLAPTON . . . 17 B4
Lower Clapton Rd E5 . . . 17 B4
Lower Clarendon Wlk 9 W11 . . . 31 A3
Lower Comm S SW15 . . . 57 A4
Lower Grosvenor Pl SW1 . . . 132 B2
Lower Grove Rd TW10 . . . 54 B2
LOWER HOLLOWAY . . . 14 A3
Lower James St W1 . . . 119 A4
Lower John St W1 . . . 119 A4
Lower Lea Crossing E14, E16 . . . 35 A2
Lower Mall W6 . . . 39 A1
Lower Marsh SE1 135 B3
Lower Merton Rise NW3 . . . 12 A1
Lower Mortlake Rd TW9 . . . 54 B4
Lower Pk
Acton W3 . . . 20 B1
5 Putney SW15 . . . 57 C2
LOWER PLACE . . . 20 B3
Lower Place Bsns Ctr NW10 . . . 20 B3
Lower Rd SE16 . . . 40 B4
Lower Richmond Rd
Mortlake SW14, TW9 . . . 55 A4
Putney SW15 . . . 57 B4
Lower Robert St WC2 . . . 120 B3
Lower Sloane St SW1 . . . 145 B2
Lower Terr NW3 . . . 2 B1
Lower Thames St EC3 . . . 124 A3
Lowerwood Ct W11 . . . 31 A3
Loweswater Ho E3 . . . 26 B1
Lowfield Rd
Dagenham W3 . . . 28 B3
Hampstead NW6 . . . 10 C1
Lowlands NW3 . . . 12 A2
Lowman Rd N7 . . . 14 B4
Lowndes Cl SW1 . 131 C1
Lowndes Ct
Knightsbridge SW1 . . . 131 A2
Marylebone W1 . . . 104 C1
Lowndes Lo SW1 131 A2
Lowndes Pl SW1 . 131 B1
Lowndes Sq SW1 131 A3
Lowndes St SW1 . 131 B2
Lowood Ho 12 E1 . . 32 B2
Lowood St E1 . . . 32 A2
Lowry Ct 3 SE16 . . . 40 A1
Lowther Ho
Pimlico SW1 . . . 147 A1
11 Shoreditch E8 . . . 24 B4
Lowther Prim Sch SW13 . . . 46 C4
Lowther Rd
Barnes SW13 . . . 46 B2
Islington N7 . . . 14 C3
Lowth Rd SE5 . . . 48 B1
Loxford Ho SW1 . . 145 C3
Loxham St WC1 . . . 94 B3
Loxley Rd SW18 . . . 71 C3
LTC Coll London W1 . . . 104 C2
Lubavitch House Sch (Jun Boys) E5 . . . 7 B4
Lubbock Ho 21 E14 . . . 34 A2
Lubbock St SE14 . . . 50 B3
Lucan Ho N1 . . . 87 C3
Lucan Pl SW3 . . . 144 B3
Lucas Ct SW11 . . . 169 C3
Lucas Ho
Clapham SW8 . . . 171 A2
Walham Green SW10 . . . 156 B2
Lucas St SE4, SE8 . . . 51 C2
Lucas Vale Prim Sch SE8 . . . 51 C2
Lucerne Mews W8 . . . 31 C1 113 C2
Lucerne Rd N5 . . . 15 A4
Lucey Rd SE16 . . . 139 B1
Lucey Way SE16 . . 153 C4
Lucien Rd SW18 . . . 71 A2
Lucraft Ho 12 SW2 . . . 74 A4
Lucy Ashe Ho SE17 . . . 150 B3
Lucy Brown Ho SE1 . . . 123 A1
Lucy Cres W3 . . . 20 B1
Ludgate Broadway EC4 . . . 108 B1
Ludgate Cir EC4 . . 108 A1
Ludgate Hill EC4 . 108 B1
Ludgate Ho EC4 . . 108 A1
Ludgate Sq EC4 . . 108 B1
Ludham NW5 . . . 12 B3
Ludlow Ct W3 . . . 37 B4
Ludlow St EC1 . . . 96 C2
Ludovick Wlk SW15 . . . 56 A3
Ludwell Ho W14 . . 126 B2
Ludwick Mews SE14 . . . 51 A3
Lugard Ho 2 W12 . . 30 A1
Lugard Rd SE15 . . . 50 A2
Luke Ho 32 E1 . . . 32 A3
Luke St EC2 . . 24 A1 98 A2
Lukin St E1 . . . 32 B3
Lullingstone Ho 21 SE15 . . . 50 B4
Lullingstone La SE13 . . . 67 C1
Lulot Gdns N19 . . . 4 A2
Lulworth
Camden Town NW1 . . . 13 C1
Walworth SE17 . . . 151 B2
Lulworth Ho SW8 162 C1
Lulworth Rd SE15 . . 50 A1
Lumiere Ct 7 SW17 . . . 72 C2
Lumina Bldg 1 E14 . . . 34 B1
Lumley Ct WC2 . . . 120 B3
Lumley Flats SW1 . . . 145 B2
Lumley St W1 . . . 103 C1
Lumsdon NW8 . . . 78 B3
Lunan Ho 14 E3 . . . 26 B3
Lund Point E15 . . . 27 B4
Luntley Pl E1 . . . 111 B3
Lupin Cl SW2 . . . 75 A2
Lupino Ct SE11 . . . 149 A4
Lupin Point SE1 . . 139 A3
Lupton St NW5 . . . 13 B4
Lupus St SW1 . . . 147 A1
Luralda Gdns E14 . . 42 C1
Lurgan Ave W6 . . . 47 C4
Lurline Gdns SW11 . . . 169 C4
Luscombe Ho SW18 . . . 58 B2
Luscombe Way SW8 . . . 162 A2
Lusher Ho SW15 . . . 57 C1
Lushington Rd NW10 . . . 22 A3
Lushington Terr 11 E8 . . . 16 C3
Luton Pl SE10 . . . 52 B3
Luton St NW8 . . . 89 C1
Luttrell Ave SW15 . . 57 A2
Lutyens Ho SW1 . . 146 C1
Luxborough Ho W1 . . . 103 B4
Luxborough St W1 . . . 103 B4
Luxborough Twr W1 . . . 103 B4
Luxemburg Gdns W6 . . . 39 C2
Luxford St SE16 . . . 40 C2
Luxmore St SE4 . . . 51 B2
Luxor St SE5 . . . 63 B4
Lyall Mews SW1 . . 131 B1
Lyall Mews W SW1 . . . 131 B1
Lyall St SW1 . . . 131 B1
Lyal Rd E3 . . . 26 A3
Lyce e Francais Charles de Gaulle (French Univ Coll) SW7 . . . 143 B4
Lycee The SE11 . . . 149 C1
Lycett Ho 10 SW2 . . 74 A4
Lycett Pl 3 W12 . . . 38 C4
Lydden Gr SW18 . . . 71 A4
Lydden Rd SW18 . . . 71 A4
Lydford NW1 . . . 83 A3
Lydford Cl 22 N16 . . 16 A3
Lydford Rd
Brondesbury NW2 . . . 9 C2
Paddington W9 . . . 23 B1
Lydgate Ho 8 N16 . . . 16 A3
Lydhurst Ave SW2 . . 74 B2
Lydney Cl
Camberwell SE15 . . . 49 A3
Putney SW19 . . . 70 A2
Lydon Rd SW4 . . . 61 B4
Lydwell Ho SW8 . . 171 B1
Lyford Rd SW18 . . . 72 A3
Lygoe Ho 18 N6 . . . 4 C4
Lygon Ho E2 . . . 24 C2 99 B4
Lygon Pl SW1 . . . 132 A1
Lyham Cl SW2 . . . 62 A1
Lyham Rd SW2 . . . 62 A1
Lyle Pk SW15 . . . 57 C1
Lyly Ho SE1 . . . 137 C1
Lyme Gr E9 . . . 17 B1
Lyme Grove Ho 2 E9 . . . 17 B1
Lyme St NW1 . . . 82 C4
Lyminge Gdns SW17, SW18 . . . 72 A3
Lymington Mans NW6 . . . 11 A2
Lymington Rd NW6 . . . 11 A2
Lympstone Gdns SE15 . . . 49 C3
Lynbrook Gr SE15 . . 49 A3
Lynch Wlk 2 SE8 . . 51 B4
Lyncott Cres SW4 . . 61 A3
Lyncourt SE3 . . . 52 C1
Lyncroft Gdns NW6 . . . 10 C3
Lyncroft Mans 4 NW6 . . . 10 C3
Lyndale NW2 . . . 1 B1
Lyndale Ave NW2 . . . 1 B1
Lyndale Cl SE3 . . . 53 B4
Lynde Ho 2 SW4 . . . 61 C4
Lynden Gate SW15 . . . 69 A4
Lyndhurst Gdns NW3 . . . 11 C3
Lyndhurst Gr SE5, SE15 . . . 49 B1
Lyndhurst Ho 2 SW15 . . . 68 C4
Lyndhurst House Prep Sch NW3 . . . 11 C3
Lyndhurst Lo 3 E14 . . . 42 C2
Lyndhurst Rd NW3 . . . 11 C3
Lyndhurst Sch SE5 . . . 48 C1
Lyndhurst Sq SE15 . 49 B2
Lyndhurst Terr NW3 . . . 11 C3
Lyndhurst Way SE15 . . . 49 B1

Lyneham Wlk E5 ... 18 A3
Lynette Ave SW4 ... 61 B1
Lynford French Ho SE17 ... 150 C2
Lyngham Ct 10 N4 ... 5 A4
Lynhurst Ct NW8 ... 79 B3
Lyn Mews 12 E3 ... 26 B2
Lynmouth Rd N16 ... 7 B3
Lynne Ct NW6 ... 11 A1
Lynnett Ct E9 ... 18 A2
Lynn Ho SE15 ... 49 C4
Lynn Rd SW12 ... 73 A4
Lynton Cl NW10 ... 8 B3
Lynton Ct 9 W3 ... 28 B3
Lynton Est SE1 ... 153 B3
Lynton Ho W2 ... 100 B1
Lynton Lo N5 ... 15 A3
Lynton Mans SE1 ... 135 B2
Lynton Rd
Acton W3 ... 28 A2
Bermondsey SE1 ... 153 A3
Paddington NW6 ... 23 B3
Lynton Terr 4 W3 ... 28 B3
Lynx Terr SW19 ... 70 C1
Lyon Ho NW8 ... 90 A1
Lyons Pl NW8 ... 89 B1
Lyon St N1 ... 14 B1
Lyons Wlk W14 ... 140 A4
Lyric Rd SW13 ... 46 B2
Lysander Gr N19 ... 4 C3
Lysander Ho 10 E2 ... 25 A3
Lysia Ct SW6 ... 47 C3
Lysias Rd SW12 ... 61 A1
Lysia St SW6 ... 47 C3
Lysons Wlk SW15 ... 56 C2
Lytcott Gr SE22 ... 64 B2
Lytham St SE17 ... 151 B1
Lyttelton Cl NW3 ... 12 A1
Lytten Ct 6 W12 ... 38 C4
Lyttleton Ho 10 E9 ... 17 B1
Lytton Ct WC1 ... 106 B3
Lytton Gr SW15 ... 58 A1

M

Mabel Thornton Ho 12 N16 ... 15 C4
Mabledon Pl NW1, WC1 ... 93 C3
Mablethorpe Rd SW6 ... 154 A1
Mabley St E9 ... 18 A3
MacArthur Ho 4 SW2 ... 74 A4
Macartney Ho SE10 ... 52 C3
Macaulay CE Prim Sch SW4 ... 61 A3
MacAulay Ct SW4 ... 61 A4
MacAulay Ho
2 Kensal Town W10 ... 31 A4
10 Stoke Newington N16 ... 7 A1
MacAulay Rd SW4 ... 61 A4
MacAulay Sq SW4 ... 61 A3
McAuley Cl SE1 ... 135 B2
MacAuley Mews SE13 ... 52 B1
McAusland Ho 5 E3 ... 26 B3
Macbeth Ho 4 N1 ... 24 A3
Macbeth St W6 ... 39 A1
McBride Ho 6 E3 ... 26 B3
McCall Cl SW4 ... 172 A2
McCall Ho N7 ... 14 A4
Mccarthy Ct SW11 ... 168 B3
Macclesfield Rd EC1 ... 96 C4
Macclesfield St W1 ... 119 C4
McCoid Way SE1 ... 136 C3
McConnell Ho SW8 ... 171 B3
McCormick Ho 9 SW2 ... 74 C3
McCrone Mews 3 NW3 ... 11 C2
McCullum Rd E3 ... 26 B4
McDermott Cl SW11 ... 60 A4
McDermott Rd SE15 ... 64 C4
MacDonald Ho SW11 ... 169 B2
MacDonald Rd N19 ... 4 B2
McDougall Ct TW9 ... 44 C1
Mcdougall Ho E2 ... 24 C2 99 B3
McDowall Cl E16 ... 35 B4
McDowall Rd SE5 ... 48 B2
Macduff Rd SW11 ... 169 C4
Mace Cl E1 ... 32 A1
Mace St E2 ... 25 C3
McEwan Way E15 ... 27 C4
Macey Ho
Battersea SW11 ... 168 A3
10 Greenwich SE10 ... 52 B4
Macfarlane Rd W12 ... 30 B1
Macfarren Ho 7 W10 ... 23 A2
MacFarren Pl NW1 ... 91 C1
McGlashon Ho E1 ... 24 C1 99 B1
McGregor Ct N1 ... 24 A2 98 B4
MacGregor Ho 2 SW12 ... 73 C3
McGregor Rd W11 ... 31 B4
Machell Rd SE15 ... 65 B4
McIndoe Ct N1 ... 87 B4
McIntosh Ho 14 SE16 ... 40 B2
McIntyre Ct SW4 ... 172 B2
Mackay Ho 33 W12 ... 30 A2
Mackay Rd SW4 ... 61 A4
McKenna Ho 3 E3 ... 26 B3
Mackennal St NW8 ... 80 B2
Mackenzie Cl 7 W12 ... 30 A2
Mackenzie Rd N7 ... 14 B2
Mackenzie Wlk E14 ... 33 C1
McKerrell Rd SE15 ... 49 C2
Mackeson Rd NW3 ... 12 B4
Mackie Ho 18 SW2 ... 74 C4
Mackie Rd SW2 ... 74 C4
McKiernan Ct SW11 ... 168 A2
McKinnon Wood Ho E2 ... 24 C2 99 B3
Mackintosh La E9 ... 17 C3
Macklin St WC2 ... 106 B2
Mackonochie Ho EC1 ... 107 B4
Mackrow Wlk 11 E14 ... 34 B2
Macks Rd SE16 ... 153 C4
Mackworth Ho NW1 ... 92 C4
Mackworth St NW1 ... 92 C4
Mac Laren Mews SW15 ... 57 B3
Maclean Rd SE23 ... 66 A1
McLeod Ct SE21 ... 76 C3
McLeod's Mews SW7 ... 142 B4
MacLeod St SE17 ... 151 A1
Maclise Rd W14 ... 126 A1
McManus Ho 3 SW11 ... 59 C4
McMillan Ho SE4 ... 66 A4
Macmillan Ho
Cricklewood NW4 ... 9 A4
Lisson Gr NW8 ... 90 B3
McMillan St SE8 ... 51 C4
Mcmorran Ho 4 N7 ... 14 A4
Macnamara Ho SW10 ... 157 B2
McNeil Rd SE5 ... 49 A1
McNicol Dr NW10 ... 20 B3
Maconochies Rd 9 E14 ... 42 A1
Macquarie Way E14 ... 42 A2
Macready Ho W1 ... 102 B3
Macready Pl 2 N7 ... 14 A4
Macroom Ho W9 ... 23 B2
Macroom Rd W9 ... 23 B2
Mac's Pl EC4 ... 107 C2
Madame Tussaud's★ NW1 ... 91 B1
Maddams St E3 ... 27 A1
Maddocks Ho 3 E1 ... 32 A2
Maddock Way SE17 ... 48 A4
Maddox St W1 ... 118 B4
Madinah Rd E8 ... 16 C3
Madison Ho E3 ... 27 B2
Madras Pl N7 ... 14 C2
Madrid Rd SW13 ... 46 C3
Madron St SE17 ... 152 B2
Mafeking Ave TW8 ... 44 A4
Magdala Ave N19 ... 4 B2
Magdalene Cl 7 SE15 ... 50 A1
Magdalene Ho 7 SW15 ... 57 C1
Magdalen Pas E1 ... 125 A4
Magdalen Rd SW18 ... 71 C3
Magdalen St SE1 ... 124 A1
Magee St SE11 ... 163 B4
Magellan Ho 16 E1 ... 25 C1
Magellan Pl 25 E14 ... 41 C2
Magnin Cl 5 E8 ... 24 C4
Magnolia Ct
Richmond TW9 ... 45 A2
Wandsworth SW11 ... 60 B1
Magnolia Ho 13 SE8 ... 51 B4
Magnolia Pl SW4 ... 62 A2
Magnolia Rd W4 ... 45 A4
Magnolia Wharf W4 ... 45 A4
Magpie Ho 7 E3 ... 26 B4
Magpie Pl SE14 ... 51 A4
Magri Wlk 22 E1 ... 32 B4
Maguire St SE1 ... 139 A4
Mahatma Gandhi Ind Est 1 SE24 ... 63 A3
Mahogany Cl SE16 ... 33 A1
Mahoney Ho SE14 ... 51 B2
Maida Ave W2 ... 89 A1
MAIDA VALE ... 88 A4
Maida Vale W9 ... 88 C3
Maida Vale Sta W9 ... 88 B4
Maiden La
Borough The SE1 ... 123 A2
Camden Town NW1 ... 13 C1
Strand WC2 ... 120 B4
Maidenstone Hill SE10 ... 52 B2
Maidstone Bldgs SE1 ... 123 B1
Maidstone Ho 4 E14 ... 34 A3
Mail Coach Yd E2 ... 24 A2 98 B4
Main Yd E9 ... 18 C2
Maismore St SE15 ... 49 C4
Maitland Cl 3 SE10 ... 52 A3
Maitland Ct W2 ... 115 B4
Maitland Ho
Chelsea SW1 ... 160 C4
16 South Hackney E2 ... 25 B3
MAITLAND PARK ... 12 B2
Maitland Park Rd NW3 ... 12 B2
Maitland Park Villas NW3 ... 12 B2
Maitland Pl E5 ... 17 B4
Majestic Ct N4 ... 6 A3
Major Cl SW9 ... 63 A4
Majorie Mews 6 E1 ... 32 C3
Major Rd E15 ... 19 C3
Makepeace Ave N6 ... 3 C2
Makepeace Mans N6 ... 3 C2
Makins St SW3 ... 144 B3
Malabar Ct 20 W12 ... 30 A2
Malabar St E14 ... 41 C4
Malam Ct SE11 ... 149 B3
Malam Gdns 3 E14 ... 34 A2
Malay Ho 2 E1 ... 32 B1
Malbrook Rd SW15 ... 57 A3
Malcolm Ho 13 N1 ... 24 A3
Malcolm Pl E2 ... 25 B1
Malcolm Rd E1 ... 25 B1
Malcolmson Ho SW1 ... 147 C1
Malden Cres NW1 ... 12 C2
Malden Pl NW5 ... 12 C3
Malden Rd NW5 ... 12 C2
Maldon Cl
Camberwell SE5 ... 64 A4
Shoreditch N1 ... 87 A4
Maldon Cl *continued*
Stratford New Town E15 ... 19 C3
Maldon Rd W3 ... 28 B2
Malet Pl WC1 ... 93 B1
Malet St WC1 ... 105 C4
Maley Ave SE27 ... 75 A2
Malfort Rd SE5 ... 64 A4
Malins Ct SW12 ... 60 C1
Mallams Mews 1 SW9 ... 63 A4
Mallard Cl
1 Hackney E9 ... 18 B2
Kilburn NW6 ... 23 C4
Mallard Ho
8 Camberwell SE15 ... 49 B2
St John's Wood NW8 ... 80 A1
Mallard Point 6 E3 ... 26 C2
Mallet Ho 11 SW15 ... 56 C2
Mallet Rd SE13 ... 67 C1
Malling SE13 ... 67 A2
Mallinson Rd SW11 ... 60 B2
Mallon Gdns E1 ... 111 A3
Mallord St SW3 ... 157 C4
Mallory Bldgs EC1 ... 96 A1
Mallory Cl SE4 ... 66 A3
Mallory St NW8 ... 90 B2
Mallow Ct SE13 ... 52 B1
Mallow St EC1 ... 97 B2
Mall Rd W6 ... 39 A1
Mall Studios 9 NW3 ... 12 B3
Mall The
Mortlake SW14 ... 55 B2
St James SW1 ... 119 B1
Malmesbury 30 E2 ... 25 B3
Malmesbury Prim Sch E3 ... 26 B2
Malmesbury Rd
Bow E3 ... 26 B3
Newham E16 ... 35 A4
Malmesbury Terr E16 ... 35 B4
Malmsey Ho SE11 ... 149 A2
Malmsmead Ho E9 ... 18 A3
Malorees Jun & Inf Schs NW6 ... 9 C1
Malpas Rd
Hackney E8 ... 17 A2
New Cross SE4 ... 51 B1
Malta St EC1 ... 96 B2
Maltby St SE1 ... 138 C2
Malthouse Dr W4 ... 46 B4
Malthouse Pas SW13 ... 46 A1
Malting Ho E14 ... 33 B2
Maltings W4 ... 36 C1
Maltings Cl SW13 ... 46 A1
Maltings Lo W4 ... 46 A3
Maltings Pl
Bermondsey SE1 ... 138 B4
Parsons Green SW6 ... 166 B3
Malt Mill SE1 ... 124 C1
Malton Mews 1 W10 ... 31 A3
Malton Rd W10 ... 31 A3
Maltravers St WC2 ... 121 B4

Malt St SE1 ... 49 C4
Malva Cl SW18 ... 59 A2
Malvern Cl W10 ... 31 B4
Malvern Ct
15 Shepherd's Bush W12 ... 38 C4
South Kensington SW7 ... 143 C4
Malvern Gdns NW2 ... 1 A2
Malvern Ho
London N16 ... 7 B3
SE17 ... 151 A1
Malvern Mews NW6 ... 23 C2
Malvern Pl NW6 ... 23 B2
Malvern Rd
Dalston E8 ... 16 C1
Maida Vale NW6 ... 23 C2
Upper Holloway N19 ... 4 C3
Malvern Terr N1 ... 85 B4
Malwood Rd SW12 ... 61 A1
Malyons Rd SE13 ... 67 A2
Malyons Terr SE13 ... 67 A2
Managers St 8 E14 ... 34 B1
Manaton Cl SE15 ... 65 A4
Manbre Rd W6 ... 47 B4
Manchester Dr W10 ... 23 A1
Manchester Gr E14 ... 42 B1
Manchester Ho SE17 ... 151 A2
Manchester Mans N19 ... 4 C4
Manchester Mews W1 ... 103 B3
Manchester Rd E14 ... 42 B3
Manchester Sq W1 ... 103 C2
Manchester St W1 ... 103 B3
Manchuria Rd SW11 ... 60 C1
Manciple St SE1 ... 137 C2
Mandalay Ho 6 N16 ... 15 C4
Mandalay Rd SW4 ... 61 B2
Mandarin Ct 6 SE8 ... 51 C4
Mandela Cl 36 W12 ... 30 A2
Mandela Ho E2 ... 24 B2 98 C4
Mandela Rd E16 ... 35 C3
Mandela St
Camden Town NW1 ... 83 A4
Kennington SW9 ... 163 B1
Mandela Way SE1 ... 152 B4
Manderville Ho SE1 ... 153 A2
Mandeville Cl 5 SE3 ... 53 B3
Mandeville Ct NW3 ... 11 A3
Mandeville Ctyd SW11 ... 169 B3
Mandeville Ho 8 SW4 ... 61 B2
Mandeville Pl W1 ... 103 C2
Mandrake Rd SW17 ... 72 B1
Mandrell Rd SW2 ... 62 A2
Manette St W1 ... 105 C1
Manfred Ct 7 SW15 ... 58 B2
Manfred Rd SW15 ... 58 B2
Manger Rd N7 ... 14 A2
Manilla St E14 ... 41 C4
Manitoba Ct 29 SE16 ... 40 B4
Manley Ct N16 ... 7 B1
Manley Ho SE11 ... 149 B2
Manley St NW1 ... 81 B4
Manneby Prior N1 ... 85 A1
Mannering Ho 16 SW2 ... 62 B2
Manningford Cl EC1 ... 96 A4
Manning Ho 3 W11 ... 31 A3
Manning Pl TW10 ... 54 B1
Manningtree Cl SW19 ... 70 A3
Manningtree St E1 ... 111 B2
Manny Shinwell Ho SW6 ... 155 A3
Manor Ave SE4 ... 51 B1
Manor Circus TW9 ... 54 C4
Manor Ct
7 Brixton SW2 ... 62 B2
Camberwell SE15 ... 49 B2
Gunnersbury W3 ... 36 C2
Parsons Green SW6 ... 166 B3
Streatham SW16 ... 74 A1
Manorfield Cl 3 N19 ... 13 B4
Manorfield Prim Sch E14 ... 34 A4
Manor Gdns
8 Chiswick W4 ... 38 A1
Clapham SW4 ... 171 A1
Gunnersbury W3 ... 36 C2
Richmond TW10, TW9 ... 54 B3
Upper Holloway N7 ... 5 A1
Manor Gr
Deptford SE15 ... 50 B4
Richmond TW9 ... 54 C4
Manor Gt SW15 ... 58 A2
Manor Ho NW1 ... 102 B4
Manor House Ct W9 ... 88 C1
Manor House Dr NW6 ... 9 C1
Manor House Sta N4 ... 6 A3
Manor Lo NW2 ... 9 C2
Manor Mans
7 Hampstead NW3 ... 12 A2
Tufnell Pk N7 ... 5 A1
Manor Mews
New Cross SE4 ... 51 B1
Paddington NW6 ... 23 C3
Manor Oak Mans SE22 ... 65 A1
Manor Par N16 ... 7 B2
Manor Park Par SE13 ... 67 C3
Manor Park Rd NW10 ... 21 B4
Manor Pk TW9 ... 54 B3
Manor Pl SE17 ... 150 C2
Manor Rd
Richmond TW10, TW9 ... 54 B3
Stamford Hill N16 ... 7 A3
Manor Sch NW10 ... 22 B4
Manor Street Est SW3 ... 158 B4
Manor The W1 ... 118 A3
Manor Way W3 ... 36 C2
Manresa Rd SW3 ... 144 A1
Mansel Ct SW11 ... 168 B3
Mansell Ho SW8 ... 171 A4
Mansell Rd W3 ... 37 C4
Mansell St E1 ... 111 A1
Manse Rd N16 ... 7 B1
Mansfield Ct 27 E2 ... 24 B4
Mansfield Ho SW15 ... 57 C1
Mansfield Mews W1 ... 104 A3
Mansfield Pl 28 NW3 ... 11 B4
Mansfield Rd
Acton W3 ... 20 A1
Maitland Pk NW3 ... 12 B4
Mansfield St W1 ... 104 A3
Mansford St E2 ... 24 C3
Mansion Cl SW9 ... 173 C4
Mansion Gdns NW3 ... 2 A1
Mansion Ho★ EC4 ... 109 B1
Mansion House Pl EC3, EC4 ... 109 B1
Mansion House St EC2 ... 109 B1
Mansion House Sta EC4 ... 123 A4
Mansions The NW6 ... 10 B3
Manson Mews SW7 ... 143 B3
Manson Pl SW7 ... 143 B3
Manston NW1 ... 13 B1
Manstone Rd NW2 ... 10 A3
Manston Ho W14 ... 126 B1
Mantell Ho SW4 ... 61 B2
Mantle Rd SE4 ... 66 A4
Manton Ho N16 ... 6 C1
Mantua St 23 SW11 ... 59 C4
Mantus Cl
Bethnal Green E1 ... 25 B1
19 Stepney E1 ... 25 B1
Mantus Rd E1 ... 25 B1
Manville Gdns SW17 ... 73 A1
Manville Rd SW17 ... 73 A1
Manwood Rd SE4 ... 66 B1
Many Gates SW12 ... 73 A2
Mapesbury Ct NW2 ... 10 A3
Mapesbury Rd NW2 ... 10 A2
Mapeshill Pl NW2 ... 9 B2
Mapes Ho 7 NW6 ... 10 A1
Mape St E2 ... 25 A1
Maple Ave W3 ... 29 A1
Maple Cl SW4 ... 61 C1
Maple Ct 3 NW2 ... 9 C4
Mapledene Est E8 ... 16 C1
Mapledene Rd E8 ... 16 C1
Maple Ho
11 Maitland Pk NW3 ... 12 B2
Maple Ho *continued*
5 New Cross SE8 ... 51 B3
4 Richmond TW9 ... 45 A2
Maple Leaf Sq 27 SE16 ... 40 C4
Maple Lo SW15 ... 58 A1
Maple Mews NW6 ... 78 A2
Maple Pl W1 ... 93 A1
Maples Pl E1 ... 32 A4
Maple St
5 Bethnal Green E2 ... 25 A3
Fitzrovia W1 ... 93 A1
Maplestead Rd SW2 ... 74 B4
Mapleton Cres SW18 ... 59 A1
Mapleton Rd SW18 ... 59 A1
Maple Wlk W10 ... 22 C1
Maplin St E3 ... 26 B2
Marada Ho NW6 ... 10 A1
Marais W4 ... 45 B3
Marban Rd W9 ... 23 B2
Marble Arch★ W1 ... 117 A4
Marble Arch Sta W1 ... 103 A1
Marble Cl W3 ... 28 A1
Marbleford Ct 4 N6 ... 4 C4
Marble Ho W9 ... 23 B1
Marcella Rd SW9 ... 173 B1
Marchant Ho 13 SW2 ... 62 B2
Marchant St SE14 ... 51 A4
Marchbank Rd W14 ... 155 A4
March Ct SW15 ... 57 A3
Marchmont Rd TW10 ... 54 B2
Marchmont St WC1 ... 94 A2
Marchwood Cl 9 SE5 ... 49 A3
Marcia Rd SE1 ... 152 B3
Marcilly Rd SW18 ... 59 C2
Marcol Ho W1 ... 104 B2
Marcon Ct 23 E8 ... 17 A3
Marcon Pl E8 ... 17 A3
Marco Rd W6 ... 39 B3
Marcus Ct TW8 ... 44 A3
Marcus Garvey Mews SE22 ... 65 A2
Marcus Garvey Way 9 SE24 ... 62 C3
Marcus Ho 14 SE15 ... 49 B2
Marcus St SW18 ... 59 A1
Marcus Terr SW18 ... 59 A1
Marden Ho 6 E8 ... 17 A3
Marden Sq SE16 ... 40 A3
Mardyke Ho SE17 ... 151 C4
Maresfield Gdns NW3 ... 11 B2
Mare St E8 ... 17 A1
Margaret Bondfield Ho
5 Bow E3 ... 26 A3
22 Kentish Town N7 ... 13 C3
Margaret Ct W1 ... 104 C2
Margaret Herbison Ho SW6 ... 155 A3
Margaret Ho 16 W6 ... 39 B1
Margaret Ingram Cl SW6 ... 154 C3
Margaret Mcmillan Ho 10 N19 ... 4 C4
Margaret Rd N16 ... 7 B3
Margaret St W1 ... 104 C2
Margaretta Terr SW3 ... 158 B4
Margaret White Ho NW1 ... 93 B4
Margate Rd SW2 ... 62 A2
Margery Fry Ct N7 ... 5 A1
Margery St WC1 ... 95 B3
Margravine Gdns
Hammersmith W6 ... 39 C1
West Kensington W14 ... 140 A2
Margravine Rd W6 ... 154 A4
Marham Gdns SW17, SW18 ... 72 A3
Maria Cl SE1 ... 153 C4
Maria Fidelis Convent Sch (Lower) NW1 ... 93 A3
Maria Fidelis Convent Sch (Upper) NW1 ... 93 B4
Marian Ct E9 ... 17 B3
Marian Pl E2 ... 25 A3
Marian Sq E2 ... 25 A3
Marian St 2 E2 ... 25 A3
Marian Way NW10 ... 8 B1
Maria Terr E1 ... 25 C1
Maribor 13 SE10 ... 52 B3
Marie Curie SE5 ... 49 A2
Marie Lloyd Ct 13 SW9 ... 62 B3
Marie Lloyd Gdns 1 N19 ... 5 A4
Marie Lloyd Ho N1 ... 87 B1
Marie Stopes Ct 3 N19 ... 5 A4
Marigold St SE16 ... 40 A4
Marina Ct 12 E3 ... 26 C2
Marina Point 4 E14 ... 42 A3
Marinefield Rd SW6 ... 166 B2
Marinel Ho 25 SE5 ... 48 B3
Mariners Mews E14 ... 42 C2
Marine St SE16 ... 139 B2
Marine Twr 29 SE8 ... 51 B4
Marion Richardson Prim Sch E1 ... 32 C3
Marischal Rd SE13 ... 67 C4
Maritime Ho 5 SW4 ... 61 B4
Maritime Quay 5 E14 ... 41 C1
Maritime St E3 ... 26 B1
Marius Mans 3 SW17 ... 72 C2
Marius Rd SW17 ... 72 C2
Marjorie Gr SW11 ... 60 B3
Market Ct W1 ... 104 C2
Market La W12 ... 39 B4
Market Mews W1 ... 118 A1
Market Pl
3 Acton W3 ... 28 B1
1 Bermondsey SE16 ... 40 A2
Marylebone W1 ... 104 C2
Market Rd
Barnsbury N7 ... 14 A2

Market Rd *continued*
Richmond TW9 . . . . . . 54 C4
Market Sq E14 . . . . . 34 A3
Market St E1 . . . . . 110 C4
Market Studios 14
W12 . . . . 39 B4
Market Way E14 . . . . 34 A3
Market Yd Mews
SE1 . . . . 138 A2
Markham Pl SW3 144 C2
Markham Sq SW3 144 C2
Markham St SW3. 144 B2
Mark Ho 3 E2 . . . . . 25 C3
Mark La EC3 . . . . . 124 B4
Markland Ho W10 . . 30 C2
Mark Mans W12 . . . . 38 C4
Marksbury Ave
TW9 . . . . 54 C4
Mark Sq
EC2 . . . . 24 A1 98 A2
Mark St EC2 . . 24 A1 98 A2
Markstone Ho
SE1 . . . . 136 A3
Markyate Ho 6
W10 . . . . 22 B1
Marland Ho SW1 . 131 A2
Marlborough
11 Putney SW19 . . . . 69 C3
St John's Wood W9 . 88 C4
Marlborough Ave 3
E8 . . . . 24 C4
Marlborough Cl
SE17 . . . . 150 B3
Marlborough Cres
W4 . . . . 38 A3
Marlborough Ct
Kensington W8 . . . . 141 B4
Marylebone W1 . . . 104 C1
Marlborough Day
Hospl NW8 . . . . 78 C2
Marlborough Flats
SW3 . . . . 144 B4
Marlborough Gr
SE1 . . . . 153 B1
Marlborough Hill
NW8 . . . . 79 A3
Marlborough Ho
Marylebone NW1 . . . 92 B2
Richmond TW10 . . . . 54 C2
Stoke Newington N4 . . 6 B3
Marlborough Ho
SW1 . . . . 119 A1
Marlborough Ho
SW19 . . . . 69 C1
Marlborough Lo
36 Stepney E1 . . . . . . 25 B1
St John's Wood
NW8 . . . . 78 C1
Marlborough Mans 5
NW6 . . . . 10 C3
Marlborough Mews
18 SW2 . . . . 62 B3
Marlborough Pl
NW8 . . . . 79 A2
Marlborough Prim
Sch SW3 . . . . 144 B3
Marlborough Rd
Acton Green W4 . . . . . 37 B1
Richmond TW10 . . . . . 54 B1
St James SW1 . . . . 119 A1
Upper Holloway N19 . . 5 A2
Marlborough St
SW3 . . . . 144 B3
Marlborough Trad Est
TW9 . . . . 45 A2
Marlborough Yd
N19 . . . . 4 C2
Marlbury NW8 . . . . 78 B3
Marley Ho 14 W11 . . 30 C2
Marley Wlk NW2 . . . . 9 B3
Marlin Ho SW15 . . . . 58 A2
Marloes Rd W8 . . 128 A1
Marlow Ct NW6 . . . . . 9 C1
Marlowe Bsns Ctr 2
SE14 . . . . 51 A3
Marlowe Ct SW3 . 144 B3
Marlowe Ho 15
N16 . . . . 16 A4
Marlowes The
NW8 . . . . 79 B4
Marlow Ho
Bermondsey SE1 . . 138 C2
Kensington W2 . . . . 100 B1
Spitalfields
E2 . . . . 24 B2 98 C3
Marlow Studio
Workshops
E2 . . . . 24 B2 98 C3
Marlow Way SE16 . . 40 C4
Marl Rd SW18 . . . . . . 59 B3
Marlston NW1 . . . . . 92 B3
Marlton St SE10 . . . . 43 B1
Marmara Apts 4
E16 . . . . 35 C2
Marmion Ho 13
SW12 . . . . 73 A4
Marmion Mews 4
SW11 . . . . 60 C4
Marmion Rd
SW11 . . . . 60 C3
Marmont Rd SE15 . . 49 C3
Marmora Ho E1 . . . . 33 A4
Marmora Rd SE22 . . 65 B1
Marner Prim Sch
E3 . . . . 27 A1
Marne St W10 . . . . . . 23 A2
Marney Rd SW11 . . . 60 C3
Marnfield Cres
SW2 . . . . 74 B3
Marnham Ave
NW2 . . . . 10 A4
Marnock Ho SE17 151 B2
Marnock Rd SE4 . . . 66 B2
Maroon St E14 . . . . . 33 A4
Marquess Rd N1 . . . 15 C2
Marquess Rd N
N1 . . . . 15 C2
Marquess Rd S 22
N1 . . . . 15 B2
Marquis Ct N4 . . . . . . 5 B3
Marquis Rd
Finsbury Pk N4 . . . . 5 C3
Kentish Town NW1 . . . 13 C2
Marrick Cl SW15 . . . 56 C3
Marrick Ho NW6 . . . 78 B3
Marriott Rd N4 . . . . . . 5 B3
Marryat Ct 12 W6 . . 39 A2
Marryat Ho SW1 . 146 C1
Marryat Sq SW6 . . 164 A4
Marsala Rd SE13 . . . 67 A3
Marsalis Ho 3 E3 . . 26 C2
Marsden Rd SE15 . . 64 B4
Marsden St NW5 . . . 12 C2
Marshall Cl SW18 . . 59 B1
Marshall Ct SW4 . 172 B3
Marshall Ho
Paddington NW6 . . . . 23 B3
Shoreditch N1 . . . . . 87 C2
Walworth SE17 . . . . 151 B2
Marshall Rd E10 . . . . 19 A4
Marshall's Pl
SE16 . . . . 139 A1
Marshall St W1 . . 105 A1
Marshalsea Rd
SE1 . . . . 137 A4
Marsham Ct
19 Putney SW19 . . . . 69 C3
Westminster SW1 . 147 C4
Marsham St SW1 147 C4
Marsh Ct E8 . . . . 16 C2
Marshfield St E14 . . 42 B3
Marsh Gate Bsns Ctr
E15 . . . . 27 B3
Marshgate Ctr The
E15 . . . . 27 A4
Marshgate La E15 . . 19 A1
Marshgate Prim Sch
TW10 . . . . 54 B2
Marsh Hill E9 . . . . . . 18 A3
Marsh Ho
Nine Elms SW8 . . . . 171 A4
Pimlico SW1 . . . . . . 147 C1
Marsh St E14 . . . . 42 A2
Marsh Wall E14 . . . . 42 A4
Marshwood Ho 10
NW6 . . . . 23 C4
Marsland Cl SE17 . 150 B1
Marsom Ho N1 . . . . 87 B1
Marston SE17 . . . . 151 A4
Marston Cl NW6 . . . . 11 B1
Marston Ho SW9 . 173 C1
Marsworth Ho 8
E2 . . . . 24 C4
Martaban Rd N16 . . . 7 B2
Martello St E8 . . . . . 17 A1
Martello Terr E8 . . . . 17 A1
Martell Rd SE21 . . . . 75 C1
Martel Pl E8 . . . . 16 B2
Martha's Bldgs
EC1 . . . . 97 B2
Martha St E1 . . . . 32 B3
Martin Ct 15 E14 . . . 42 B4
Martindale SW14 . . . 55 B2
Martindale Ave 2
E16 . . . . 35 C2
Martindale Ho 23
E14 . . . . 34 A2
Martindale Rd
SW12 . . . . 73 A4
Martineau Ho
SW1 . . . . 146 C1
Martineau Mews
N5 . . . . 15 A4
Martineau Rd N5 . . . 15 A4
Martin Ho
Newington SE1 . . . . 137 A1
South Lambeth
SW8 . . . . 162 A2
Martin La EC4 . . . . 123 C4
Martlett Ct WC2 . . 106 B1
Martlett Lo NW3 . . . 11 A4
Martley Ho SW8 . . 171 A4
Martock Ct 10
SE15 . . . . 50 A2
Marton Rd 2 N16 . . . 7 A1
Marvel Ho 5 SE5 . . 48 C3
Marville Rd SW6 . 154 C1
Marvin St 3 E8 . . . . 17 A2
Marwell Ct SE3 . . . . . 52 C1
Mary Adelaide Cl
SW15 . . . . 68 A1
Mary Adelaide Ho
W2 . . . . 101 C4
Mary Ann Bldgs
SE8 . . . . 51 C4
Mary Datchelor Cl
SE5 . . . . 48 C2
Mary Dine Ct
SW8 . . . . 163 A1
Mary Gn NW8 . . . . . 78 B4
Mary Ho
8 Hammersmith
W6 . . . . 39 B1
Stockwell SW9 . . . . 172 C1
Mary James Ho 32
E2 . . . . 24 C3
Mary Jones Ho 20
E14 . . . . 33 C2
Maryland Rd
Paddington W9 . . . . . . 23 C1
Stratford New Town
E15 . . . . 19 C3
Marylands Rd W9 . 88 A1
Maryland Wlk N1 . 86 C4
Mary Lawrenson Pl 1
SE3 . . . . 53 C3
MARYLEBONE . . . 104 B2
Marylebone Flyover
NW1 . . . . 102 A3
Marylebone High St
W1 . . . . 103 C4
Marylebone La
W1 . . . . 103 C2
Marylebone Mews
W1 . . . . 104 A3
Marylebone Pas
W1 . . . . 105 A2
Marylebone Rd
NW1 . . . . 103 A4
Marylebone St
W1 . . . . 103 C3
Marylebone Sta
NW1 . . . . 90 C1
Marylee Way
SE11 . . . . 149 A3
Mary McArthur Ho 12
N19 . . . . 4 C4
Mary Macarthur Ho
15 Globe Town E2 . . . 25 C2
W14 . . . . 154 A4
Maryon Mews
NW3 . . . . 12 A4
Mary Pl
W11 . . . . . . 31 A2 112 A3
Mary's Ct NW8 . . . . 90 B2
Mary Secole Cl 21
E8 . . . . 24 B4
Mary Smith Ct
SW5 . . . . 141 C3
Mary St
5 Canning Town
E16 . . . . 35 B4
Shoreditch N1 . . . . . 87 A3
Mary Terr NW1 . . . . 82 C3
Mary Wharrie Ho 4
NW3 . . . . 12 B1
Masbro' Rd W14 . . . 39 C3
Mascotte Rd 2
SW15 . . . . 57 C3
Masefield Ct N5 . . . . 15 C3
Masefield Ho 4
NW6 . . . . 23 C2
Mashie Rd W3 . . . . . 29 A3
Maskall Cl SW2 . . . . 74 C3
Maskell Rd SW17 . . . 71 B1
Maskelyne Cl
SW11 . . . . 168 B4
Mason Cl
Bermondsey SE16 . 153 C2
Newham E16 . . . . 35 C2
Mason Ho
Bermondsey SE1 . . 153 C3
16 Hackney E9 . . . . . 17 B1
Mason's Arms Mews
W1 . . . . 118 B4
Mason's Ave EC2 . 109 B2
Mason's Pl EC1 . . . 96 C4
Mason St SE17 . . . 151 C4
Mason's Yd
Finsbury EC1 . . . . . . 96 B4
St James SW1 . . . . 119 A2
Massie Rd E8 . . . . . . 16 C2
Massinger St SE1,
SE17 . . . . 152 A3
Massingham St
E1 . . . . 25 C1
Mast Ct 17 SE16 . . . . 41 A2
Masterman Ho 1
SE5 . . . . 48 C3
Masters Dr SE16 . . . 40 A1
Masters Lo 24 E1 . . . 32 B3
Master's St 16 E1 . . 32 C4
Mast House Terr
E14 . . . . 41 C2
Mastin Ho SW18 . . . . 70 C3
Mastmaker Rd
E14 . . . . 41 C4
Matara Mews
SE17 . . . . 150 C1
Matching Ct 14 E3 . . 26 C2
Matham Gr SE22 . . . 64 B3
Matheson Lang Ho
SE1 . . . . 135 B3
Matheson Rd
W14 . . . . 140 C3
Mathews Yd WC2 106 A1
Mathieson Ct SE1 136 B3
Mathison Ho
SW10 . . . . 156 C2
Matilda Ho E1 . . . . 125 B2
Matilda St N1 . . . . . 85 A4
Matlock Cl SE24 . . . . 63 B3
Matlock Ct
7 Herne Hill SE5 . . . 63 C3
St John's Wood
NW8 . . . . 78 C2
Matlock St E14 . . . . . 33 A3
Maton Ho SW6 . . . 154 C2
Matson Ho
9 Bermondsey
SE16 . . . . 40 A3
16 Homerton E9 . . . . . 17 C2
Matthew Cl W10 . . . 22 C1
Matthew Parker St
SW1 . . . . 133 C3
Matthews Ct N5 . . . . 15 B4
Matthews Ho 3
E14 . . . . 33 C4
Matthews St
SW11 . . . . 168 C2
Matthias Ct 12
TW10 . . . . 54 A1
Matthias Ho 2
N16 . . . . 16 A3
Matthias Rd N16 . . . 16 A3
Mattingly Way 3
SE15 . . . . 49 B3
Maude Ho 3 E2 . . . 24 C3
Maude Rd SE5 . . . . . 49 A2
Maudlins Gn E1 . . 125 B2
Maudsley Ho TW8 . . 36 A1
Maudsley Hospl The
SE5 . . . . 48 C1
Maud St E16 . . . . 35 B4
Maud Wilkes Cl 10
NW5 . . . . 13 B3
Maugham Ct 5
W3 . . . . 37 B3
Mauleverer Rd
SW2 . . . . 62 A2
Maundeby Wlk
NW10 . . . . 8 A2

Maunsel St SW1 .. 147 B4
Maurer Ct 2 SE10 .. 43 B3
Mauretania Bldg 11 E1 ... 32 C2
Maurice Ct 4 E1 .. 26 A2
Maurice Ho SW9 . 172 C2
Maurice St W12 .... 30 A3
Mauritius Rd SE10 .. 43 A2
Maury Rd N16 .... 7 C1
Maverton Rd E3 .... 26 C4
Mavor Ho N1 ..... 85 A3
Mawbey Ho SE1 .. 153 A1
Mawbey Pl SE1 ... 153 A1
Mawbey Rd SE1 .. 153 A1
Mawbey St SW8 .. 162 A1
Mawdley Ho SE1 . 135 C3
Mawson Ct N1 .... 87 C3
Mawson Ho EC1 .. 107 B4
Mawson La W4 ..... 46 B4
Maxden Ct SE15 .... 64 C4
Maxted Rd SE15 .... 64 B4
Maxwell Ct SE21 ... 76 C3
Maxwell Rd SW6 . 156 B1
Maya Cl SE15 ...... 50 A1
Mayall Rd SE24 ..... 63 A2
Maybury Ct W1 .. 103 C3
Maybury Gdns NW10 ... 9 A2
Maybury Mews N6 .. 4 B4
Maydew Ho SE16 ... 40 B2
Maydwell Ho 6 E14 ... 33 C4
MAYFAIR 118 A3
Mayfair Pl W1 .... 118 B2
Mayfield Ave W4 ... 38 A2
Mayfield Cl
  Clapham Pk SW4 .... 61 C2
  Dalston E8 ..... 16 B2
Mayfield Ho
  31 Bethnal Green E2 ... 25 A3
  Stamford Hill N16 ..... 7 A4
Mayfield Mans SW15 ... 58 B2
Mayfield Rd
  Acton W3 ... 28 A2
  Bedford Pk W12 ..... 38 A4
  Dalston E8 ... 16 B1
Mayflower Cl SE16 ... 40 C2
Mayflower Prim Sch E14 ... 34 A3
Mayflower Rd SW9 ... 62 A4
Mayflower St 1 SE16 ... 40 B4
Mayford NW1 ..... 83 A2
Mayford Cl SW12 ... 72 B4
Mayford Rd SW12 .. 72 C4
Maygood Ho N1 ... 85 B2
Maygood St N1 ... 85 B2
Maygrove Rd NW6 .. 10 B2
Mayhew Ct 2 SE5 .. 63 C3
Maylands Ho SW3 ... 144 B3
Maylie Ho 4 SE16 .. 40 A4
Maynard Cl SW6 . 156 B1
Maynard Ho E1 .... 26 A2
Maynards Quay E1 ... 32 B2
Mayne Ct E8 ..... 16 C4
Mayo Ho 10 E1 ..... 32 B4
Mayola Rd E5 ..... 17 B4
Mayo Rd NW10 ..... 8 A2
May's Buildings Mews SE10 ... 52 C3
Mays Ct WC2 ..... 120 A3
May's Ct SE10 ..... 52 C3
Maysoule Rd SW11 ... 59 C3
May St W14 ..... 141 A1
Mayston Mews 3 SE10 ... 43 C1
Maythorne Cotts SE13 ... 67 C1
Mayton St N7 ..... 5 B1
May Tree Ho SE4 ... 66 B4
Maytree Wlk SW2 .. 74 C2
Mayward Ho 7 SE5 ... 49 A2
Maze Hill SE10, SE3 ... 53 A4
Maze Hill Lodge 7 SE10 ... 52 C4
Maze Hill Sta SE10 ... 53 A4
Mazenod Ave NW6 ... 10 C1
Maze Rd TW9 ... 44 C3
Mead Cl 3 NW1 ... 12 C1
Meadcroft Rd SE17 ... 48 A4
Meade Cl W4 ... 44 C4
Meader Ct SE14 ... 50 C3
Mead Ho W11 ... 31 B1 112 C2
Mead Lo W4 ... 37 C4
Meadowbank NW3 ... 12 B1
Meadow Bank 8 SW15 ... 58 B2
Meadowbank Cl SW6 ... 47 B3
Meadow Cl E9 ... 18 B3
Meadowcroft 9 W4 ... 36 C1
Meadowgate Sch SE4 ... 66 A4
Meadow Mews SW8 ... 162 C3
Meadow Pl
  Chiswick W4 ... 46 A3
  South Lambeth SW8 ... 162 B2
Meadow Rd SW8 162 C2
Meadow Row SE1 ... 136 C1
Mead Pl E9 ... 17 B2
Mead Row SE1 ... 135 B2
Meadway The SE3 .. 52 C1
Meakin Est SE1 .. 138 A2
Meakin Ho N7 ... 14 B3
Meard St W1 ... 105 B1
Meath Ho SE24 ... 63 A1
Meath St SW11 ... 170 A4
Mecklenburgh Pl WC1 ... 94 C2
Mecklenburgh Sq WC1 ... 94 C2
Mecklenburgh St WC1 ... 94 C2
Medburn St NW1 .. 83 B2
Medcroft Gdns SW14 ... 55 B3
Medfield St SW15 .. 69 A4
Medhurst Cl 19 E3 ... 26 A3
Median Rd E5 ... 17 B3
Medina Ct N7 ... 5 C1
Medina Gr N7 ... 5 C1
Medina Ho SE15 ... 65 B3
Medina Rd N7 ... 5 C1
Medlar St SE5 ... 48 B2
Medley Rd NW6 ... 10 C2
Medora Rd SW2 ... 74 B4
Medresco Ho NW3 ... 11 C3
Medusa Rd SE6, SE13 ... 67 A1
Medway Bldgs E3 .. 26 A3
Medway Ct WC1 ... 94 A3
Medway Ho
  Bermondsey SE1 .. 137 C3
  Paddington NW8 .. 102 A4
  Stoke Newington N16 ... 15 C4
Medway Mews 35 E3 ... 26 A3
Medway Rd E3 ... 26 A3
Medway St SW1 .. 133 C1
Medwin St SW4 ... 62 B3
Meecham Ct SW11 ... 168 A2
Meeson St E5 ... 18 A4
Meeting House Alley 7 E1 ... 32 A1
Meeting House La SE15 ... 50 A3
Mehetabel Rd E9 ... 17 B3
Melba Way SE13 ... 52 A2
Melbourne Ct
  Hackney E5 ... 18 A4
  Paddington W9 ... 89 A2
Melbourne Gr SE22 ... 64 B3
Melbourne Ho W8 ... 31 C1 113 B1
Melbourne Mews SW9 ... 173 B3
Melbourne Pl WC2 ... 107 A1
Melbourne Sq SW9 ... 173 B3
Melbray Mews SW6 ... 164 C1
Melbreak Ho 11 SE22 ... 64 A4
Melbury Ct W8 ... 127 A2
Melbury Dr SE5 ... 49 A3
Melbury Ho SW8 . 162 C2
Melbury Rd W14 . 127 A2
Melchester 5 W11 ... 31 B3
Melchester Ho 1 N19 ... 4 C1
Melcombe Ct NW1 ... 102 C4
Melcombe Ho SW8 ... 162 C1
Melcombe Pl NW1 ... 102 C4
Melcombe Prim Sch W6 ... 47 C4
Melcombe St NW1 91 A1
Meldon Cl SW6 ... 166 B4
Melford Ct
  Bermondsey SE1 .. 138 B2
  Dulwich SE22 ... 76 C4
Melford Rd SE21, SE22 ... 76 C3
Melgund Rd N5 ... 14 C3
Melina Ct
  Putney SW15 ... 56 C4
  St John's Wood NW8 ... 89 B3
Melina Pl NW8 ... 89 B3
Melina Rd W12 ... 39 A4
Melior Pl SE1 ... 138 A4
Melior St SE1 ... 138 A4
Melisa Ct N6 ... 4 C4
Mellington Ct 2 N16 ... 7 C1
Mellis Ave TW9 ... 45 A2
Mellish Ho 2 E1 ... 32 A3
Mellish St E14 ... 41 C3
Mellitus St W12 ... 29 B3
Mell St 6 SE10 ... 43 A1
Melody La N5 ... 15 B3
Melody Rd SW18 ... 59 B2
Melon Pl W8 ... 127 C4
Melon Rd SE15 ... 49 C2
Melrose Ave
  Cricklewood NW2 ... 9 B3
  Wimbledon SW19 ... 70 C1
Melrose Ct SW18 ... 58 B1
Melrose Gdns W6 .. 39 B3
Melrose Ho
  Maida Vale NW6 ... 23 C2
  Pimlico SW1 ... 146 B2
Melrose Rd
  1 Barnes SW13 ... 46 B1
  Wandsworth SW18 .. 58 B1
Melrose Terr W6 ... 39 B3
Melton Ct SW7 ... 143 C3
Melton Ho E5 ... 7 C2
Melton St NW1 ... 93 B3
Melville Court Flats 8 W12 ... 39 A4
Melville Ct
  4 Brentford W4 ... 36 C1
  Rotherhithe SE8 ... 41 A2
Melville Ho SE10 ... 52 B2
Melville Pl 4 N1 ... 15 B1
Melville Rd SW13 ... 46 C2
Melville Villas Rd W3 ... 28 C1
Melvin Ct 11 TW9 ... 44 C2
Melwood Ho 23 E1 ... 32 A3
Melyn Cl N7 ... 13 B4
Memel Ct EC1 ... 96 C1
Memel St EC1 ... 96 C1
Menai Pl 2 E3 ... 26 C3
Menard Ct EC1 ... 97 A3
Mendham Ho SE1 ... 138 A2
Mendip Ct
  12 Battersea SW11 ... 59 B4
  Deptford SE14 ... 50 B4
Mendip Dr NW2, NW11 ... 1 A2
Mendip Ho 2 N4 ... 6 C4
Mendip Hos 12 E2 .. 25 B2
Mendip Rd SW11 ... 59 B4
Mendora Rd SW6 154 C2
Menelik Rd NW2 ... 10 B4
Menorah Prim Sch NW11 ... 1 A4
Menotti St E2 ... 24 C1 99 C2
Menteath Ho 9 E14 ... 33 C3
Mentmore Terr E8 ... 17 A1
Mentone Ct SW8 . 172 B4
Meon Rd W3 ... 37 B4
Mepham St SE1 .. 121 B1
Merbury Cl SE13 ... 67 C2
Mercator Pl 4 E14 ... 41 C1
Mercator Rd SE13 .. 67 C3
Merceron Ho 3 E2 ... 25 B2
Merceron St E1 ... 25 A1
Mercers Cl SE10 ... 43 B2
Mercer's Cotts 8 E3 ... 33 A3
Mercers Mews N7 .. 13 C4
Mercers Pl W6 ... 39 C2
Mercers Rd N19 ... 4 C1
Mercer St WC2 ... 106 A1
Merchant Ct E1 ... 32 B1
Merchants Ho SE10 ... 42 C1
Merchant St E3 ... 26 B2
Merchant Taylors Hall★ EC3 ... 109 C1
Merchon Ho N7 ... 13 B4
Mercia Gr SE13 ... 67 B3
Mercia Ho 9 SE5 .. 48 B1
Mercie Ct SE22 ... 76 C3
Mercier Rd SW15 ... 58 A2
Mercury Ct
  Brixton SW9 ... 173 B4
  10 Millwall E14 ... 41 C2
Mercury Ho 6 E3 .. 26 C4
Mercury Way SE14 ... 50 C4
Mercy Terr SE13 ... 67 A2
Mere Cl SW15, SW19 ... 69 C4
Meredith Ave NW2 .. 9 B3
Meredith Ho 17 N16 ... 16 A3
Meredith Mews SE4 ... 66 B3
Meredith St EC1 ... 96 A3
Meredith Twr W3 ... 37 A3
Meredyth Rd SW13 ... 46 C1
Meretone Cl SE4 ... 66 A3
Mereton Mans 6 SE8 ... 51 C2
Mereworth Ho 3 SE15 ... 50 B4
Merganser Ct 17 SE8 ... 51 B4
Meridan Ct SE13 ... 67 C3
Meriden Ct SW3 .. 144 A1
Meriden Ho 25 N1 .. 24 A4
Meridian Building★ SE10 ... 52 C3
Meridian Ho SE10 .. 43 A2
Meridian Pl E14 ... 42 B4
Meridian Prim Sch SE10 ... 52 C4
Meridian Sq E15 ... 19 C1
Merivale Rd SW15 .. 58 A3
Merlin Ho
  7 Chiswick W4 ... 37 C1
  West Hampstead NW3 ... 11 A4
Merlin Sch SW15 ... 58 A2
Merlins Ct WC1 ... 95 B3
Merlin St EC1 ... 95 B3
Mermaid Ct
  Bermondsey SE1 .. 137 B4
  Rotherhithe SE16 ... 33 B1
Mermaid Ho 8 E14 ... 34 B2
Mermaid Twr 22 SE8 ... 51 B4
Meroe Ct N16 ... 7 A2
Merredene St SW2 ... 62 B1
Merriam Ave 2 E9 ... 18 B2
Merricks Ct 5 SW14 ... 55 A3
Merrick Sq SE1 .. 137 B2

Merrington Rd SW6 155 C4
Merritt Rd SE4 66 B2
Merrivale NW1 83 A3
Merrow St SE17 151 B1
Merrow Wlk SE17 151 C2
Merryfield SE3 53 B1
Merryweather Ct 13 N19 4 B1
Mersey Ho 10 N7 14 C3
Merstone Ho SW18 59 A1
Merthyr Terr SW13 47 A4
Merton Ave W4 38 B2
Merton Ho SW18 70 C3
Merton La N6 3 B2
Merton Rd SW18 70 C4
Merton Rise NW3 12 A1
Merton Road Ind Est SW18 70 C4
Merttins Rd SE15 65 C2
Meru Cl NW5 12 C3
Mervan Rd SW2 62 C3
Messaline Ave W3 28 B3
Messina Ave NW6 10 C1
Messiter Ho N1 85 A3
Metcalfe Ho SW8 171 B2
Meteor St SW11 60 C3
Methley Ho 8 N7 5 B2
Methley St SE11 149 C1
Methodist Central Hall★ SW1 133 C3
Methwold Rd W10 30 C4
Metropolis Apartments 5 SW12 73 A3
Metropolitan Benefit Societies Almshouses 3 N1 16 A2
Metropolitan Bsns Ctr 9 N1 16 A1
Metropolitan Cl 23 E14 33 C4
Mews St E1 125 B2
Mews The
Shoreditch N1 87 A4
5 Upper Holloway N19 5 A3
Mexborough NW1 82 C3
Mexfield Rd SW15 58 B2
Meyer Ho 1 SW12 73 A4
Meymott St SE1 122 A1
Meynell Cres E9 17 C1
Meynell Gdns E9 17 C1
Meynell Rd E9 17 C1
Meyrick Ho 8 E14 33 C4
Meyrick Rd
Battersea SW11 60 A4
Willesden NW10 8 C2
Miah Terr E1 125 C1
Micawber Ct N1 97 A4
Micawber Ho SE16 139 C3
Micawber St N1 97 A4
Michael Cliffe Ho EC1 95 C3
Michael Faraday Ho SE17 151 C1
Michael Faraday Sch SE17 151 C1
Michael Rd SW6 166 B4
Michael Tippet Sch SE27 75 B2
Michael Tippett Sch The SE11 149 C3
Michelangelo Ct 14 SE16 40 A1
Michelle Ct W3 28 C2
Michels Almshouses 11 TW10 54 A2
Michelsdale Dr 3 TW9 54 A3
Michelson Ho SE11 149 A3
Michel's Row 2 TW9 54 A3
Michigan Ho E14 41 C3
Mickledore NW1 83 A1
Micklethwaite Rd SW6 155 C3
Mickleton Ho 30 W2 31 C4
Middlefield NW8 79 B4
Middle Row W10 23 A1
Middle Row Prim Sch W10 23 A1
Middlesex Ct 5 W4 38 B2
Middlesex Ho W1 105 A4
Middlesex Pas EC1 108 B3
Middlesex Pl 13 E9 17 B2
Middlesex St E1 110 C2
Middle St EC1 108 C4
Middle Temple★ EC4 121 B4
Middle Temple La EC4 121 B4
Middleton Dr SE16 40 C4
Middleton Gr N7 14 A3
Middleton Ho
Dalston E8 16 B1
Newington SE1 137 B1
Middleton Mews N7 14 A3
Middleton Pl W1 104 C3
Middleton Rd
Dalston E8 16 B1
Golders Green NW11 1 C4
Middleton St E2 25 A2
Middleton Way SE13 67 C3
Midford Pl W1 93 A1
Midhope Ho WC1 94 B3
Midhope St WC1 94 B3
Midhurst Ct N8 5 A4
Midhurst Ho 6 E14 33 B3
Midhurst Way E5 16 C4
Midland Mainline Terminal NW1 83 C1
Midland Pl E14 42 B1
Midland Rd NW1 94 A4
Midland Terr NW10 21 A1
Midlothian Ho NW2 9 A4
Midlothian Rd E3 26 B1
Midmoor Rd SW12 73 B3
Midship Cl SE16 32 C1
Midship Point E14 41 C4
Midstrath Rd NW10 8 A4
Midway Ho EC1 96 B4
Milborne Gr SW10 143 A1
Milborne Ho 11 E9 17 B2
Milborne St E9 17 B2
Milbrook Ct NW3 2 B3
Milcote St SE1 136 B3
Mildmay Ave N1 15 C2
Mildmay Ct N1 15 C3
Mildmay Gr N N1 15 C3
Mildmay Gr S N1 15 C3
Mildmay Ho 6 SW15 57 B2
Mildmay Mission Hospl E2 24 B2 98 C3
Mildmay Pk N1 15 C3
Mildmay Rd N1 16 A3
Mildmay St N1 15 C2
MILE END 26 A1
Mile End Pl E1 25 C1
Mile End Rd E1, E3 25 C1
Mile End Sta E3 26 B2
Miles Bldgs NW1 102 A4
Miles Coverdale Prim Sch W12 39 B4
Miles Ct E1 32 A3
Miles Ho 5 SE10 43 A1
Miles Lo E15 19 C3
Miles Pl NW8 101 C4
Miles St SW8 162 B3
Milestone Green SW14 55 C3
Milfoil St W12 29 C2
Milford Ct 3 N16 7 A3
Milford La WC2 121 B4
Milford Mews SW16 74 B1
Milk St EC2 109 A2
Milkwell Yd 7 SE5 48 B2
Milkwood Rd SE24 63 A3
Milk Yd E1 32 B2
Millais Rd E11 19 C4
Milland Ho 11 SW15 68 C3
Millard Cl 21 N16 16 A3
Millbank SW1 148 A3
Millbank Prim Sch SW1 147 C3
Millbrooke Ct 7 SW15 58 A2
Millbrook Ho 4 SE15 49 C4
Millbrook Pl NW1 82 C2
Millbrook Rd SW9 63 A4
Millender Wlk SE16 40 B2
Millennium Bridge★ SE1, EC4 122 C3
Millennium City Acad W1 104 B3
Millennium Dr E14 42 C2
Millennium Harbour E14 41 C4
Millennium Pl 27 E2 25 A3
Millennium Prim Sch SE10 43 B3
Millennium Sq SE1 139 A4
Millennium Way SE10 43 A3
Miller Ho 9 SW2 74 A4
Miller's Ave E8, N16 16 B3
Miller's Ct 1 W4 38 B1
Miller's House Visitor Ctr★ 1 E3 27 B2
Miller St NW1 82 C2
Miller's Terr 1 E8 16 B3
Miller's Way W6 39 B4
Millers Wharf Ho E1 125 B1
Miller Wlk SE1 121 C1
Millfield N4 5 C2
Millfield La N6 3 B2
Millfield Pl N6 3 C2
Millfields Com Sch E5 17 B4
Millgrove St SW11 169 B2
Millharbour E14 42 A4
Mill Hill SW13 56 C4
Mill Hill Gr 11 W3 28 A1
Mill Hill Rd
Barnes SW13 46 C1
South Acton W3 37 A4
Mill Hill Terr 9 W3 28 A1
Mill Ho 4 SE13 67 B4
Milligan St E14 33 B2
Milliners Ho SW18 58 C3
Millington Ho N16 6 C1
Mill La NW6 10 B3
Millman Ct WC1 94 C1
Millman Mews WC1 94 C1
Millman Pl WC1 95 A1
Millman St WC1 94 C1
Millmark Gr SE14 51 A1
MILL MEADS 27 C3
Millner Ct SE4 51 B1
Mill Pl E14 33 A3
Mill Pond Cl SW8 161 C1
Millpond Est SE16 40 A4
Mill Row N1 24 A4
Mills Ct EC2 24 A2 98 A3
Mills Gr 1 E14 34 B4
Mills Ho SW8 171 A4
Millshott Cl SW6 47 B2
Mills Row W4 37 C2
Mill St
Bermondsey SE1 139 A4
Mayfair W1 118 C4
Millstream Ho 14 SE16 40 A4
Millstream Rd SE1 138 C3
Mill Trad Est The NW10 20 B2
MILLWALL 41 C3
Millwall Dock Rd E14 41 C3
Millwood St 10 W10 31 A4
Mill Yd E1 125 B4
Milman Rd NW6 23 A3
Milman's Ho SW10 157 B3
Milman's St SW10 157 B3
Milner Bldg N16 6 C1
Milner Ho 2 SW11 59 C4
Milner Pl N1 85 C4
Milner Sq N1 15 A1
Milner St SW3 144 C4
Milnthorpe Rd W4 45 C4
Milo Rd SE22 64 B1
Milrood Ho 5 E1 32 C4
Milroy Wlk SE1 122 A2
Milson Rd W14 126 A2
Milsted Ho 23 E5 17 A3
Milton Ave
Becontree NW10 20 C4
Crouch End N6 4 B4
Milton Cl SE1 152 C3
Milton Court Rd SE14 51 A4
Milton Ct
Fulham SW6 58 A4
St Luke's EC2 109 B4
9 Wandsworth SW18 58 C2
Milton Gr N16 16 A4
Milton Ho
19 Bethnal Green E2 25 B2
2 Camberwell SE5 48 C3
Milton House Mans E8 16 B4
Milton Pk N6 4 B4
Milton Pl 3 N7 14 C3
Milton Rd
Acton W3 28 C1
Crouch End N6 4 B4
Mortlake SW14 55 C4
Tulse Hill SE24 63 A2
Milton St EC1, EC2 109 B4
Milverton NW5 12 C3
Milverton Rd NW6 9 B1
Milverton St SE11 149 C1
Milward St E1 32 A4
Mimosa Ct SW4 172 B3
Mimosa St SW6 165 A3
Mina Rd SE17 152 B2
Minchin Ho 10 E14 33 C3
Mincing La EC3 124 A4
Minera Mews SW1 145 C4
Minerva Cl SW9 163 C2
Minerva Rd NW10 20 C2
Minerva St E2 25 A3
Minerva Wlk EC1 108 B2
Minet Ave NW10 21 A3
Minet Gdns NW10 21 A3
Minet Ho E1 111 B1
Minet Rd SE5, SW9 48 A1
Minford Gdns W14 39 C4
Mingard Wlk N7 5 B1
Ming St E14 33 C2
Minnow Wlk SE17 152 B3
Minories EC3 124 C4
Minshull St SW8 171 B3
Minson Rd E9 25 C4
Minstead Gdns SW15 68 B4
Minster Ct EC3 124 B4
Minster Rd NW2 10 A3
Mint Bsns Pk 12 E16 35 C4
Mintern St N1 87 C2
Minton Ho SE11 149 B4
Minton Mews 3 NW6 11 A2
Mint St SE1 137 A4
Mirabel Rd SW6 155 A2
Miranda Cl 19 E1 32 B4
Miranda Ho 17 N1 24 A3
Miranda Rd N19 4 B3
Missenden SE17 151 C1
Missenden Ho NW8 90 A2
Mission Pl SE15 49 C2
Mission Sq 13 TW8 44 A4

Mission The
13 Bermondsey SE16 . . . 40 A4
14 Poplar E14 . . . 33 B3
Misterton Ct SW11 . . . 167 C4
Mistral SE5 . . . 49 A2
Mitali Pas E1 . . . 111 B1
Mitcham Ho 9 SE5 . . . 48 B2
Mitchell Brook Prim Sch NW10 . . . 8 A2
Mitchell Ct SW14 . . . 56 A3
Mitchell Ho
Gunnersbury W4 . . . 37 A1
6 Islington N1 . . . 14 C1
31 Shepherd's Bush W12 . . . 30 A2
Mitchell's Pl SE21 . . . 76 A4
Mitchell St EC1 . . . 97 A2
Mitchison Rd N1 . . . 15 C2
Mitford Rd N19 . . . 5 A2
Mitre Bridge Ind Pk W10 . . . 22 A1
Mitre Rd SE1 . . . 135 C4
Mitre Sq EC3 . . . 110 B1
Mitre St EC3 . . . 110 B1
Mitre The 9 E14 . . . 33 B2
Mitre Way W10 . . . 30 A4
Mizzen Ct E14 . . . 41 C4
Moatfield NW6 . . . 10 A1
Moat Pl Acton W3 . . . 28 A3
Stockwell SW9 . . . 62 B4
Moat Sch The SW6 . . . 164 A2
Moberly Rd SW4 . . . 73 C4
Mobey Ct SW4 . . . 172 A3
Mocatta Ho 9 E1 . . . 25 A1
Modbury Gdns NW5 . . . 12 C2
Modder Pl SW15 . . . 57 C3
Model Cotts SW14 . . . 55 B4
Modling Ho 8 E2 . . . 25 C3
Moelwyn Hughes Ct N7 . . . 13 C3
Moffat Ho 24 SE5 . . . 48 B3
Mohawk Ho 33 E3 . . . 26 A3
Moira Ct SW17 . . . 72 C2
Moira Ho SW9 . . . 173 B4
Molasses Ho 1 SW11 . . . 59 B4
Molasses Row 2 SW11 . . . 59 B4
Mole Ct 2 W12 . . . 38 A4
Mole Ho NW8 . . . 89 C1
Molesey Ho E2 . . . 24 B1 98 C2
Molesford Rd SW6 . . . 165 B3
Molesworth Ho 9 SE17 . . . 48 A4
Molesworth St SE13 . . . 67 B4
Molly Huggins Cl SW12 . . . 73 B4
Molton Ho N1 . . . 85 A3
Molyneux Ho W1 . . . 102 B2
Molyneux St W1 . . . 102 B3
Mona Rd SE15 . . . 50 B1
Mona St E16 . . . 35 B4
Monck's Row SW18 . . . 58 B1
Monck St SW1 . . . 133 C1
Monckton Ct W14 . . . 126 C2
Monclar Rd SE5 . . . 63 C3
Moncorvo Cl SW7 . . . 130 A3
Moncrieff St SE15 . . . 49 C1
Mondragon Ho SW8 . . . 172 B4
Monet Ct 15 SE16 . . . 40 A1
Moneyer Ho N1 . . . 97 B4
Monica Shaw Ct NW1 . . . 83 C1
Monier Rd E3 . . . 18 C1
Monkbretton Ho E2 . . . 24 C2 99 B3
Monk Ct W12 . . . 29 C1
Monk Dr E16 . . . 35 C2
Monkridge 3 N8 . . . 4 C4
Monksfield N4 . . . 5 C2
Monkswell Ho E2 . . . 24 C2 99 B3
Monkton Ho
32 Bermondsey SE16 . . . 40 C4
22 Hackney E5 . . . 17 A3
Monkton St SE11 . . . 149 C4
Monkwell Sq EC2 . . . 109 A3
Monmouth Cl W4 . . . 37 C3
Monmouth Gr TW8 . . . 36 A2
Monmouth Ho
5 Camden Town NW5 . . . 13 A2
Wandsworth SW18 . . . 58 C1
Monmouth Pl W2 . . . 100 A1
Monmouth Rd W2 . . . 31 C3
Monmouth St WC2 . . . 106 A1
Monnery Rd N19 . . . 4 B1
Monnow Rd SE1 . . . 153 B3
Monroe Dr SW14 . . . 55 A2
Monroe Ho
10 Crouch End N19 . . . 4 C4
Lisson Gr NW8 . . . 90 B3
Monro Ho
16 Hampstead NW3 . . . 11 B4
Putney SW15 . . . 57 A2
Monro Way E5 . . . 16 C4
Monsal Ct E5 . . . 18 A4
Monsell Ct 4 N4 . . . 6 A1
Monsell Rd N4, N5 . . . 6 A1
Monson Prim Sch SE14 . . . 50 C3
Monson Rd
Deptford SE14 . . . 50 C3
Willesden Green NW10 . . . 22 A3
Montagu Ct W1 . . . 103 A3
Montague Ave SE4 . . . 66 C3
Montague Cl SE1 . . . 123 B2
Montague Pl WC1 . . . 105 C4
Montague Rd
Richmond TW10 . . . 54 A1
Shacklewell E8 . . . 16 C3
Montague Sq SE15 . . . 50 B3
Montague St
Bloomsbury WC1 . . . 106 A4
City of London EC1 . . . 108 C3
Montagu Mans W1 . . . 103 A3
Montagu Mews N W1 . . . 103 A3
Montagu Mews S W1 . . . 103 A2
Montagu Mews W W1 . . . 103 A2
Montagu Pl W1 . . . 103 A3
Montagu Row W1 . . . 103 A3
Montagu Sq W1 . . . 103 A2
Montagu St W1 . . . 103 A2
Montaigne Cl SW1 . . . 147 C3
Montana Bldg 4 SE13 . . . 52 A2
Montana Rd SW17 . . . 72 C1
Montcalm Ho E14 . . . 41 C3
Montclare St E2 . . . 24 B1 98 C2
Monteagle Ct 27 N1 . . . 24 A3
Monteagle Way
Nunhead SE15 . . . 65 A4
Shacklewell E5 . . . 7 C1
Montefiore Ct 2 N16 . . . 7 B3
Montefiore St SW8 . . . 170 B1
Montego Cl 10 SW2 . . . 62 C3
Montem Prim Sch N7 . . . 5 B1
Montem St N4 . . . 5 B3
Monteray Studios W10 . . . 23 A3
Montesquieu Terr 3 E16 . . . 35 B3
Montford Pl SE11 . . . 149 B1
Montfort Ho
4 Bethnal Green E2 . . . 25 B2
Cubitt Town E14 . . . 42 B3
Montfort Pl SW19 . . . 69 C3
Montgomery Ct W4 . . . 45 B4
Montgomery Ho 5 SW14 . . . 55 C4
Montgomery Lo 38 E1 . . . 25 B1
Montgomery Rd W4 . . . 37 B2
Montholme Rd SW11 . . . 60 B1
Monthope Rd E1 . . . 111 B3
Montolieu Gdns SW15 . . . 57 A2
Montpelier Gr NW5 . . . 13 B3
Montpelier Mews SW7 . . . 130 B2
Montpelier Pl
Knightsbridge SW7 . . . 130 B2
21 Stepney E1 . . . 32 B3
Montpelier Rd SE15 . . . 50 A2
Montpelier Rise NW11 . . . 1 A4
Montpelier Row SE3 . . . 53 B1
Montpelier Sq SW7 . . . 130 B3
Montpelier St SW7 . . . 130 B2
Montpelier Terr SW7 . . . 130 B3
Montpelier Vale SE3 . . . 53 B1
Montpelier Way NW11 . . . 1 A4
Montpelier Wlk SW7 . . . 130 B2
Montreal Pl WC2 . . . 120 C4
Montrell Rd SW2 . . . 74 A3
Montrose Ave NW6 . . . 23 A3
Montrose Ct SW7 . . . 129 C3
Montrose Ho
Belgravia SW1 . . . 131 C3
Millwall E14 . . . 41 C3
Montrose Pl SW1 . . . 131 C3
Montrose Villas 5 W6 . . . 38 C1
Montserrat Rd SW15 . . . 58 A3
Monument Gdns SE13 . . . 67 B2
Monument St EC3 . . . 123 C4
Monument Sta EC3 . . . 123 C4
Monument The* EC3 . . . 123 C4
Monza Bldg The E1 . . . 32 B2
Monza St E1 . . . 32 B2
Moodkee St SE16 . . . 40 B3
Moody Rd SE15 . . . 49 B2
Moody St E1 . . . 25 C2
Moon St N1 . . . 86 A4
Moorcroft Rd SW16 . . . 74 A1
Moore Cl SW14 . . . 55 B4
Moore Ct N1 . . . 86 A3
Moore Ho
16 Bethnal Green E2 . . . 25 B2
5 Greenwich SE10 . . . 43 B1
7 Shadwell E1 . . . 32 B2
Wandsworth SW17 . . . 71 C1
Moore Park Ct SW6 . . . 156 B2
Moore Park Rd SW6 . . . 156 A1
Moore St SW3 . . . 144 C4
Moorfields EC2 . . . 109 B3
Moorfields Eye Hospl EC1 . . . 97 B3
Moorfields Highwalk EC2 . . . 109 B3
Moorgate EC2 . . . 109 B3
Moorgate Pl EC2 . . . 109 B2
Moorgate Sta EC2 . . . 109 B3
Moorgreen Ho EC1 . . . 96 A4
Moorhouse Rd W2 . . . 31 C3
Moor La EC2 . . . 109 B3
Moorland Rd SW9 . . . 63 A3
Moor Pl EC2 . . . 109 B3
Moor St W1 . . . 105 C1
Morant Ho SW9 . . . 172 C2
Morant St E14 . . . 33 C2
Mora Prim Sch NW2 . . . 9 B4
Mora Rd NW2 . . . 9 B4
Mora St EC1 . . . 97 A3
Morat St SW9 . . . 173 A4
Moravian Cl SW3 . . . 157 C3
Moravian Pl SW10 . . . 157 C3
Moravian St 10 E2 . . . 25 B2
Moray Ho 9 E1 . . . 26 A1
Moray Mews N4, N7 . . . 5 B2
Moray Rd N4, N7 . . . 5 B2
Mordaunt Ho
4 Becontree NW10 . . . 20 C4
Clapham SW8 . . . 171 B1
Mordaunt Rd NW10 . . . 20 C4
Mordaunt St SW9 . . . 62 B4
Morden Hill SE13 . . . 52 B1
Morden Ho 19 SW2 . . . 62 C1
Morden La SE13 . . . 52 B2
Morden Mount Prim Sch SE13 . . . 52 A1
Morden Rd SE3 . . . 53 C1
Morden Road Mews SE3 . . . 53 C1
Morden St SE13 . . . 52 A2
Morden Wharf Rd SE10 . . . 43 A3
Mordern Ho NW1 . . . 90 B1
Morecambe Cl 3 E1 . . . 32 C4
Morecambe St SE17 . . . 151 A2
More Cl
Canning Town E16 . . . 35 B3
West Kensington W14 . . . 140 A3
Moredown Ho 3 E8 . . . 16 C3
More House Sch SW1 . . . 131 A1
Moreland Ct 3 NW2 . . . 1 C1
Moreland Prim Sch EC1 . . . 96 B3
Moreland St EC1 . . . 96 B4
Morella Rd SW11, SW12 . . . 72 B4
Morell Ho SW9 . . . 172 C1
Moresby Wlk SW8 . . . 170 B1
More's Gdn SW3 . . . 157 C3
Moreton Ho SE16 . . . 40 A3
Moreton Pl SW1 . . . 147 A2
Moreton St SW1 . . . 147 B2
Moreton Terr SW1 . . . 147 A2
Moreton Terr Mews N SW1 . . . 147 A2
Moreton Terr Mews S SW1 . . . 147 A2
Moreton Twr 3 W3 . . . 28 A1
Morgan Ct SW11 . . . 167 C2
Morgan Ho
Nine Elms SW8 . . . 171 A4
Pimlico SW1 . . . 147 A3
Morgan Rd
Islington N7 . . . 14 C3
Notting Hill W10 . . . 31 B4
Morgan St
Canning Town E16 . . . 35 B4
Globe Town E3 . . . 25 C2
Morgan's Wlk SW11 . . . 158 A1
Moriatry Cl N7 . . . 14 A4
Morie St SW18 . . . 59 A2
Morkyns Wlk SE21 . . . 76 A1
Morland Cl NW11 . . . 2 A3
Morland Ct W12 . . . 39 A4
Morland Est E8 . . . 16 C1
Morland Ho
Kilburn NW6 . . . 23 C4
Notting Hill W11 . . . 31 A3
Somers Town NW1 . . . 83 A1

Morland Ho *continued*
Westminster SW1 . 148 A4
Morland Mews N1 14 C1
Morley Coll SE1 135 C2
Morley Ct SE13 67 B3
Morley Ho
Stoke Newington N16 7 C2
Streatham SW2 74 A4
W1 104 B2
Morley Rd SE13 67 B3
Morley St SE1 135 C3
Morna Rd SE5 48 B1
Morning La E9 17 B2
Morningside Prim Sch E9 17 B2
Mornington Ave W14 140 C3
Mornington Avenue Mans W14 140 C3
Mornington Cres NW1 82 C2
Mornington Crescent Sta NW1 82 C2
Mornington Ct NW1 82 C2
Mornington Gr E3 26 C2
Mornington Mews 2 SE5 48 B2
Mornington Pl
4 New Cross SE8 51 B3
Regent's Pk NW1 82 C2
Mornington Rd SE14, SE8 51 B3
Mornington St NW1 82 B2
Mornington Terr NW1 82 B2
Morocco St SE1 138 A3
Morpeth Gr E9 25 C4
Morpeth Rd E9 25 C4
Morpeth Sec Sch E2 25 B2
Morpeth St E2 25 C2
Morpeth Terr SW1 146 C4
Morrel Ct 11 E2 24 C3
Morris Blitz Ct 2 N16 16 B4
Morris Ct 3 SE5 63 C3
Morris Gdns SW18 70 C4
Morris Ho
17 Bethnal Green E2 25 B2
Lisson Gr NW8 90 A1
1 Stockwell SW4 62 A3
10 Tufnell Pk N19 13 B4
Morrish Rd SW2 74 A4
Morrison Bldgs E1 111 B2
Morrison Ho SW2 74 C3
Morrison St SW11 60 C4
Morris Pl N4 5 C2
Morris Rd E14 34 A4
Morriss Ho 9 SE16 40 A4
Morris St E1 32 A3
Morshead Mans W9 23 C2
Morshead Rd W9 23 C2
Mortain Ho 9 SE16 40 A2
Morten Cl SW4 61 C1
Mortimer Cl
1 Child's Hill NW2 1 B1

Mortimer Cl *continued*
Streatham SW16 73 C2
Mortimer Cres NW6 78 B3
Mortimer Ct NW8 79 A1
Mortimer Est NW6 78 A3
Mortimer Ho
6 Shepherd's Bush W11 30 C1
West Kensington W14 140 B3
Mortimer Lo 11 SW19 70 A3
Mortimer Market WC1 93 A1
Mortimer Pl NW6 78 A3
Mortimer Rd
De Beauvoir Town N1 16 A1
Kensal Green NW10 22 B2
Mortimer Sq W11 30 C2
Mortimer St W1 105 A3
Mortimer Terr NW5 13 A4
MORTLAKE 55 B4
Mortlake High St SW14 55 C4
Mortlake Ho 7 W4 37 B2
Mortlake Rd SW14, TW9 44 C2
Mortlake Sta SW14 55 B4
Mortlake Terr TW9 44 C3
Mortlock Cl SE15 50 A2
Morton Cl E1 32 B3
Morton Ho SE17 48 A4
Morton Mews SW5 142 A3
Morton Pl SE1 135 B1
Morton Rd N1 15 B1
Morval Rd SW2 62 C2
Morven Rd SW17 72 B1
Morville Ho SW18 59 C1
Morville St E3 26 C3
Morwell St WC1 105 C3
Moscow Pl W2 114 A4
Moscow Rd W2 114 A4
Mosedale NW1 92 B3
Moseley Row SE10 43 B2
Mosque Tower E1 111 C3
Mossbourne Com Acad E8 16 C3
Mossbury Rd SW11 60 A4
Moss Cl E1 111 C4
Mossford St E3 26 B1
Mossington Gdns SE16 40 B2
Mossop St SW3 144 B4
Mostyn Gdns NW10 22 C3
Mostyn Gr E3 26 C3
Mostyn Lo N5 15 B4
Mostyn Rd SW9 173 C3
Motcomb St SW1 131 B2
Mothers Sq The 13 E5 17 A4
Motley Ave EC2 24 A1 98 A2
Motley St SW8 170 C2
Moules Ct SE5 48 B3
Moulins Rd E9 17 B1

Moulsford Ho
5 Lower Holloway N7 14 A3
32 Paddington W2 31 C4
Mounsey Ho 13 W10 23 A2
Mount Adon Pk SE21, SE22 76 C4
Mountague Pl 2 E14 34 B2
Mountain Ho SE11 148 C2
Mount Angelus Rd SW15 68 B4
Mount Ararat Rd TW10 54 A2
Mountbatten Ho N6 3 C4
Mountbatten Mews SW18 71 B3
Mount Carmel 3 N7 14 B3
Mount Carmel RC Tech Coll for Girls N19 4 C3
Mountearl Gdns SW16, SW2 74 B1
Mount Ephraim La SW16 73 C1
Mount Ephraim Rd SW16 73 C1
Mountfield NW2 1 B2
Mountfield Ct SE13 67 C1
Mount Ford St E1 111 B2
Mountfort Cres N1 14 C1
Mountfort Terr 1 N1 14 C1
Mountgrove Rd N5 6 B1
Mountjoy Ho EC2 108 C3
Mount Lodge SW4 61 C3
Mount Mills EC1 96 B3
Mount Nod Rd SW16, SW2 74 B1
Mount Pl 7 W3 28 A1
Mount Pleasant WC1 95 B1
Mount Pleasant Cres N4 5 B4
Mount Pleasant Rd
Lewisham SE13 67 B1
Willesden NW10 22 B4
Mount Pleasant Villas N4 5 B4
Mount Rd SW18, SW19 71 A2
Mount Row W1 118 A3
Mounts Pond Rd SE3, SE13 52 C1
Mount Sq The 3 NW3 2 B1
Mount St W1 117 C3
Mount Terr E1 32 A4
Mount The
Hampstead NW3 2 B1
Kensington W8 31 C1 113 B1
Mount Tyndal NW3 2 C3
Mount Vernon NW3 11 B4
Mountview 5 SW16 74 B1
Mountview Cl NW11 2 B3
Mount Villas SE27 75 A1

Mourne Ho NW3 11 B2
Mowatt Cl N19 4 C3
Mowbray Rd NW6 10 A1
Mowlem Prim Sch E2 25 B3
Mowlem St E2 25 A3
Mowll St SW9 163 B1
Moxon St W1 103 B3
Moye Cl 10 E2 24 C3
Moylan Rd W6 154 B3
Moyle Ho SW1 161 A4
Moyne Ho 16 SW9 63 A3
Mozart St W10 23 B2
Mudchute Sta E14 42 A2
Mudie Ho 8 SW2 74 A4
Mudlarks Blvd 3 SE10 43 B3
Muirdown Ave SW14 55 C3
Muir Dr SW18 60 A1
Muirfield W3 29 A3
Muirfield Cl 23 SE16 40 A1
Muirfield Cres E14 42 A3
Muir Rd E5 7 C1
Mulberry Bsns Ctr SE16 40 C4
Mulberry Cl
Chelsea SW3 157 C3
East Dulwich SE22 64 C1
Hampstead NW3 11 C4
Mulberry Ct
Finsbury EC1 96 B3
Islington N5 15 A3
1 Leyton E11 19 C4
10 Paddington W9 23 B2
Mulberry Ho
1 Bethnal Green E2 25 B2
8 Deptford SE8 51 B4
Mulberry House Sch The NW2 10 A3
Mulberry Mews SE14 51 B2
Mulberry Pl W6 38 C1
Mulberry Rd E8 16 B1
Mulberry Sch for Girls
Stepney E1 32 A3
St George in t East E1 32 A2
Mulberry St E1 111 B2
Mulberry Wlk SW3 157 C4
Mulgrave Rd
West Kensington W14 154 C4
Willesden NW10 8 B4
Mulkern Rd N19 4 C3
Mullard Ho WC1 105 B4
Mullens Ho 7 SW15 57 B2
Mullen Twr EC1 95 B1
Muller Rd SW4 61 C1
Mullet Gdns E2 24 C2 99 C4
Mulletsfield WC1 94 B3
Mull Ho 17 E3 26 B3
Mullins Path SW14 55 C4
Mulready St NW8 90 A1
Multi Way W3 38 A4
Multon Ho E9 17 B1
Multon Rd SW18 71 C4
Mulvaney Way SE1 137 C3

Mumford Rd SE24 63 A2
Muncaster Rd SW11 60 C2
Mundania Ct SE22 65 A1
Mundania Rd SE22 65 B1
Munday Ho SE1 137 B1
Munday Rd E16 35 C2
Munden Ho 5 E3 27 A2
Munden St W14 140 A4
Mund St W14 141 A1
Mundy Ho 6 W10 23 A2
Mundy St N1 24 A2 98 B4
Munro Ho
Bermondsey SE1 137 C3
Lambeth SE1 135 B3
Munro Mews W10 31 A4
Munster Ct SW6 164 C2
Munster Rd SW6 154 B2
Munster Residences SW6 164 B4
Munster Sq NW1 92 B2
Munton Rd SE1, SE17 151 A4
Murchison Ho 1 W10 31 A4
Murdoch Ho 4 SE16 40 B3
Murdock Cl E16 35 B3
Murdock St SE15 50 A4
Murfett Cl SW19 70 A2
Muriel St N1 85 A4
Murphy Ho SE1 136 B2
Murphy St SE1 135 B3
Murray Gr N1 87 B1
Murray Mews NW1 13 C1
Murray St NW1 13 C1
Murray Terr NW3 11 C4
Musard Rd W6 154 B4
Musbury St E1 32 B3
Muscal W6 154 A4
Muscatel Pl SE5 49 A2
Muschamp Rd SE15 64 B4
Muscott Ho 15 E2 24 C4
Muscovy St EC3 124 B4
Museum Ho 7 E2 25 B2
Museum in Docklands* E14 33 C2
Museum Mans WC1 106 A3
Museum of Brands* W11 31 B3
Museum St WC1 106 A2
Musgrave Cres SW6 165 C4
Musgrave Ct SW11 168 A4
Musgrove Ho 1 E9 17 C2
Musgrove Rd SE14 51 A2
Musical Mus The* TW8 44 A4
Musjid Rd SW11 167 C1
Mus of Childhood (V&A)* E2 25 B2
Mus of Culinary History & Alimentation* NW1 83 A2

Mus of Garden History★ SE1 134 C1
Mus of London★ EC2 108 C3
Mus of the Order of St John★ EC1 96 A1
Mustow Pl SW6 165 A2
Mutrix Rd NW6 23 C4
Mutton Pl NW1 12 C2
Myatt Garden Prim Sch SE4 51 B1
Myatt Ho SE5 48 A1
Myatt Rd SW9 48 A2
Myatts Field Ct SE5 48 B2
Mycenae Rd SE3 53 C4
Myddelton Pas EC1 95 C4
Myddelton Sq EC1 95 C4
Myddelton St EC1 95 C3
Myddleton Ave N4 6 B2
Myers Ho 5 SE5 48 B3
Myers La SE14 50 C4
Mylius Cl SE14 50 B2
Mylne Cl W6 38 C1
Mylne St EC1 85 B1
Mynterne Ct 16 SW19 69 C3
Myrdle Ct E1 111 C2
Myrdle St E1 111 C2
Myron Pl SE13 67 B4
Myrtle Ho SE14 50 C2
Myrtle Rd W3 28 B1
Myrtle Wlk 20 N1 24 A3
Mysore Rd SW11 60 B3
Myton Rd SE21 75 C1
Mytton Ho SW8 162 C1

N

N1 Shopping Ctr N1 85 C2
Nags Head N7 14 B4
Nags Head Ct EC1 97 A1
Nags Head Sh Ctr The N7 14 B4
Naima Jewish Prep Sch NW6 78 A2
Nainby Ho SE11 149 B3
Nairne Gr SE5, SE24 63 C3
Nairn St E14 34 B4
Naish Ct N1 84 B4
Naldera Gdns SE3 53 C4
Nalton Ho 4 NW6 11 B1
Nankin St E14 33 C3
Nansen Rd SW11 60 C4
Nant Ct NW2 1 B2
Nantes Cl SW18 59 B3
Nant Rd NW2 1 B2
Nant St E2 25 A2
Naoroji St WC1 95 B3
Napier Ave
Deptford E14 41 C1
Fulham SW6 58 B4
Napier Cl
New Cross SE14, SE8 51 B3
West Kensington W14 126 C2
Napier Ct
Fulham SW6 58 B4
Shoreditch N1 87 B2
Napier Gr N1 87 A2
Napier Ho SE17 48 A4
Napier Pl W14 126 C1
Napier Rd
College Pk NW10 22 A2
Kensington W14 126 C1
Napier Terr N1 15 A1
Narbonne Ave SW4 61 B2
Narborough St SW6 166 A1
Narcissus Rd NW6 10 C3
Narford Rd E5 7 C2
Narrow St
6 Acton W3 28 A1
Limehouse E14 33 A2
Nascot St W12 30 B3
Naseby Cl NW6 11 B1
Nashe Ho SE1 137 B1
Nash Ho
5 Millwall E14 41 C3
Pimlico SW1 146 B1
Nash Rd SE4 66 A2
Nash St NW1 92 B4
Nasmyth St W6 39 A3
Nassau Rd SW13 46 B2
Nassau St W1 104 C3
Nassington Rd NW3 12 B4
Nathan Ho SE11 149 C3
Nathaniel Cl E1 111 A3
National Army Mus★ SW3 159 A4
National Fan Mus★ SE10 52 B3
National Film Theatre★ SE1 121 A2
National Gallery★ W1 119 C3
National Hospl The WC1 94 B1
National Maritime Mus★ SE10 52 C4
National Portrait Gallery★ W1 119 C3
National Portrait Gallery (Annexe)★ SW1 119 C2
National Theatre★ SE1 121 A2
Natural History Mus★ SW7 129 B1
Nat West Twr★ EC2 110 A2
Nautilus Bldg The EC1 95 C4
Naval Row E14 34 B2
Navarino Gr E8 16 C2
Navarino Mans E8 16 C2
Navarino Rd E8 16 C2
Navarre St E2 24 B1 98 C2
Navenby Wlk 13 E3 26 C1
Navy St SW4 61 C4
Naxos Bldg 9 E14 41 C4
Naylor Bldg W E1 111 B2
Naylor Ho
Clapham SW8 171 B1
Walworth SE17 151 C2
5 West Kilburn W10 23 B2
Naylor Rd SE15 50 A3
Nayor Bldg E E1 111 B2
Nazareth Cl SE15 50 A1
Nazrul St E2 24 B2 98 C4
Nealden St SW9 62 B4
Neal St WC2 106 A1
Neal's Yd WC2 106 A1
Neasden Cl NW10 8 A3
Neasden Junc NW10 8 A4
Neasden La NW10 8 A3
Neasden Sta NW10 8 A3
Neate St SE5 49 B4
Neathouse Pl SW1 146 C4
Nebraska Bldg 11 SE13 52 A2
Nebraska St SE1 137 B3
Neckinger SE16 139 A2
Neckinger Est SE16 139 A2
Neckinger St SE1 139 A2
Nectarine Way SE13 52 A1
Nedahall Ct 4 NW11 1 B4
Needham Ho SE11 149 B3
Needham Rd W11 31 C3
Needleman St SE16 40 C4
Needwood Ho N4 6 B3
Neilson-Terry Ct 9 SW9 62 B3
Neil Wates Cres 17 SW2 74 C3
Nella Rd W6 47 C4
Nelldale Rd SE16 40 B2
Nell Gwynn Ho SW3 144 B3
Nelson Cl 2 NW6 23 C2
Nelson Ct SE16 33 B1
Nelson Dock Pier SE16 33 B1
Nelson Gdns E2 24 C2 99 C4
Nelson Pas EC1 97 A4
Nelson Pl N1 86 B1
Nelson Rd SE10 52 B4
Nelson's Monument★ WC2 120 A2
Nelson Sq SE1 136 A4
Nelsons Row SW4 61 C3
Nelson St
Canning Town E16 35 B2
Stepney E1 32 A3
Nelsons Yd NW1 82 C2
Nelson Terr N1 86 B1
Nemoure Rd W3 28 B2
Nepaul Rd 17 SW11 60 A4
Nepean St SW15 68 C4
Neptune Ct 13 E14 41 C2
Neptune Ho
2 Rotherhithe SE16 40 B3
14 Stoke Newington N16 16 A3
Neptune St SE16 40 B3
Nesham Ho 14 N1 24 A4
Nesham St E1 125 B2
Ness St SE16 139 B2
Nestor Ho 13 E2 25 A3
Netheravon Rd W4 38 B1
Netheravon Rd S W4 38 B1
Netherby Ho SW8 171 B1
Nethercombe Ho 1 SE3 53 C4
Nethercott Ho 27 E3 27 A2
Netherfield Rd SW17 72 C1
Netherford Rd SW4 171 A1
Netherhall Gdns NW3 11 B3
Netherhall Way NW3 11 B3
Netherleigh Cl N6 4 A3
Netherton Gr SW10 157 A3
Netherwood Rd W14 39 C4
Netherwood St NW6 10 C2
Netley 13 SE5 49 A2
Netley Prim Sch NW1 92 C3
Netley Rd TW8 44 A4
Netley St NW1 92 C3
Nettlecombe NW1 13 C1
Nettleden Ho SW3 144 B3
Nettlefold Pl SE27 75 A1
Nettleton Rd SE14 50 C2
Nevada St SE10 52 B4
Nevena Ct 3 SW2 62 C2
Nevern Mans SW5 141 B2
Nevern Pl SW5 141 C3
Nevern Rd SW5 141 B3
Nevern Sq SW5 141 C3
Nevil Ho 7 SW9 48 A1
Nevill Ct SW10 156 C2
Neville Cl
Acton W3 37 B4
Paddington NW6 23 B3
Peckham SE15 49 C2
Somers Town NW1 83 C1
Neville Ct 10 SW12 73 B4
Neville Gill Cl SW18 59 A1
Neville Rd NW6 23 B3
Neville St SW7 143 B2
Neville Terr SW7 143 B2
Nevill Rd N16 7 A1
Nevinson Cl SW18 59 C1
Nevis Rd SW17 72 C2
Nevitt Ho N1 87 C1
Newall Ho SE1 137 A2
Newark Cres NW10 20 C2
Newark Ho 3 SW9 48 A1
Newark St E1 32 A4
New Atlas Wharf E14 41 C3
New Bentham Ct 10 N1 15 B1
Newbery Ho N1 15 B1
Newbold Cotts 4 E1 32 B3
Newbolt Ho SE17 151 B2
New Bond St W1 118 B4
New Bridge St EC4 108 A1
New Broad St EC2 110 A3
New Bsns Ctr The NW10 21 B2
Newburgh Rd W3 28 B1
Newburgh St W1 105 A1
New Burlington Mews W1 118 C4
New Burlington Pl W1 118 C4
New Burlington St W1 118 C4
Newburn Ho SE11 149 A2
Newburn St SE11 149 A2
Newbury Ct E5 18 A3
Newbury Ho
Brixton SW9 48 A1
Kensington W2 100 B1
Newbury Mews NW5 12 C2
Newbury St EC1 108 C4
New Butt La SE8 51 C3
Newby NW1 92 C4
Newby Pl E14 34 B2
Newby St SW8 61 A4
New Caledonian Wharf SE16 41 B3
New Campden Ct 9 NW3 11 B4
Newcastle Cl EC4 108 A2
Newcastle Ct EC4 123 A4
Newcastle Ho W1 103 B4
Newcastle Pl W2 101 C4
Newcastle Row EC1 95 C1
New Cavendish St W1 104 A3
New Change EC4 108 C1
New Charles St EC1 96 B4
New Church Rd
32 Camberwell SE5 48 B3
Camberwell SE5 48 C4
New College Ct 6 NW3 11 B2
New College Mews 7 N1 14 C1
New College Par 1 NW3 11 C1
Newcombe Ho N5 15 B3
Newcombe St W8 31 C1 113 C2
Newcomen Ho 5 NW5 13 A4
Newcomen Rd SW11 59 C4
Newcomen St SE1 137 B4
New Compton St WC2 106 A1
New Concordia Wharf SE1 139 A4
Newcourt Ho 26 E2 25 A2
Newcourt St NW8 80 A1
New Covent Garden Flower Market SW8 162 A3
New Covent Garden Fruit & Vegetable Mkt SW8 161 B1
New Crane Pl E1 32 B1
New Crescent Yd 1 NW10 21 B3
NEW CROSS 51 B2
New Cross SE14 51 B3
NEW CROSS GATE 50 C2
New Cross Gate SE14 50 C2
New Cross Gate Sta SE14 51 A3

New Cross Hospl SE14 50 B3
New Cross Rd SE14 51 A2
New Cross Sta SE14 51 B3
New Ct
City of London EC4 107 B1
26 Hampstead NW3 11 B4
Stoke Newington N16 6 C3
New Den (Millwall FC) The SE16 40 B1
Newdigate Ho 5 E14 33 B3
Newell St E14 33 B3
New End NW3 2 B1
New End Prim Sch NW3 11 B4
New End Sq NW3 11 C4
Newent Cl SE15 49 A3
New Fetter La EC4 107 C2
Newfield Prim Sch NW10 8 B1
Newgate St EC1 108 B2
New Globe Wlk SE1 122 C2
New Goulston St E1 110 C2
Newham Sch of Nursing E3 27 A1
Newham Sixth Form Coll (Stratford Ctr) E15 19 C1
Newham's Row SE1 138 B3
Newhaven La 3 E16 35 C4
NEWINGTON 150 B4
Newington Barrow Way N7 5 B1
Newington Butts SE1, SE11 150 B3
Newington Cswy SE1 136 C2
Newington Gn N16 15 C3
Newington Green Mans N16 15 C3
Newington Green Prim Sch N16 15 C3
Newington Green Rd N1 15 C3
Newington Ind Est SE17 150 C3
New Inn Broadway EC2 24 A1 98 B2
New Inn Sq EC2 24 A1 98 B2
New Inn St EC2 24 A1 98 B2
New Inn Yd EC2 24 A1 98 B2
New James Ct SE15 65 A4
New Kent Rd SE1 151 A4
New King's Prim Sch SW6 165 A2
New King's Rd SW6 165 C3
New King St SE8 51 C4
Newland Ct EC1 97 B2
Newland Ho 17 SE14 50 C4
Newlands NW1 92 C4
Newlands Quay E1 32 B2
New London St EC3 124 B4
Newlyn NW1 83 A3
Newman Pas W1 105 A3
Newman's Ct EC3 109 C1
Newman's Row WC2 107 A3
Newman St W1 105 A3
Newmill Ho E3 27 B1
Newmount NW3 11 C3
New Mount St E15 19 C1
Newnes Path SW15 57 A3
Newnham Ho 9 SW15 57 C1
Newnham Terr SE1 135 B2
New North Com Sch The N1 15 C1
New North Pl EC2 24 A1 98 A2
New North Rd N1 87 B3
New North Road Bridge N1 87 B3
New North St WC1 106 C4
Newnton Cl N4 6 C4
New Oxford St WC1 106 A2
New Palace Yd SW1 134 A3
New Park Ct 26 SW2 74 A4
New Park Par 14 SW2 74 A4
New Park Rd SW2 74 A4
New Place Sq SE16 40 A3
Newport Ave E14 34 C2
Newport Ct WC2 119 C4
Newport Ho 2 E3 26 A2
Newport Pl WC2 119 C4
Newport Rd SW13 46 C2
Newport St SE11 149 A4
New Priory Ct 9 NW6 10 C1
New Providence Wharf E14 34 C1
Newquay Ho SE11 149 B2
New Quebec St W1 103 A1
New Rd E1 32 A4
New River Ct N5 15 C4
New River Way N4 6 C4
New Row WC2 120 A4
New St Sq EC4 107 C2
New Scotland Yard★ SW1 133 B2
New Shepherd's Bush Mkt★ 6 W12 39 B4
New Spring Gdns Wlk SE11 148 B1
New Sq WC2 107 A2
New Square Pas WC2 107 B2
New St EC2 110 B3
Newstead Ho N1 85 C2
Newton Ave W3 37 B4
Newton Gr W4 38 A2
Newton Ho
Clapham SW8 171 B2
Paddington NW8 78 B4
1 Stepney E1 32 A2
Newton Pl E14 41 C2
Newton Point 1 E16 35 B3
Newton Prep Sch SW8 170 B4
Newton Rd
Acton W3 37 B4
Kensington W2 100 A1
Stratford New Town E15 19 C3
Newton St WC2 106 B2
Newton's Yd 14 SW18 58 C2
New Tower Bldgs 21 E1 32 A1
Newtown Ct
Battersea SW11 170 A3
Clapham SW4 61 A2
New Union Cl E14 42 B3
New Union St EC2 109 B3
New Wharf Rd N1 84 B2
Niagara Cl N1 87 A2
Niagara Ct 6 SE16 40 B3
Nicholas Ct
Chiswick W4 46 A3
Golders Green NW11 1 C4
Nicholas Ho 2 SW15 56 C2
Nicholas La EC2, EC4 123 C4
Nicholas Pas EC3 123 C4
Nicholas Rd E1 25 B1
Nicholay Rd N19 4 C3
Nicholl Ho N4 6 B3
Nicholl St E2 24 C4
Nichols Cl N4 5 C3
Nichols Ct E2 24 B3
Nicholson Ho SE17 151 B2
Nicholson St SE1 122 A1
Nickleby Ho
Bermondsey SE1 139 B3
7 Shepherd's Bush W11 30 C1
Nickols Wlk SW18 59 A3
Nicoll Ct NW10 21 A4
Nicoll Rd NW10 21 A4
Nicosia Rd SW18 72 A4
Nigel Bldg EC1 107 B4
Nigel Playfair Ave W6 39 A1
Nigel Rd SE15 64 C4
Nightingale Cl W4 45 B4
Nightingale Ct
14 Cubitt Town E14 42 B3
Finsbury Pk N4 5 B2
Nightingale Gr SE13 67 C2
Nightingale Ho
21 Hoxton E1 24 A4
4 North Kensington W12 30 B3
St George in t East E1 125 B2
Nightingale La SW11, SW12 60 C1
Nightingale Lo 5 W9 31 C4
Nightingale Mans 4 SW12 60 C1
Nightingale Mews
1 Bow E3 26 A3
Newington SE11 150 A4
Nightingale Pl SW10 157 A4
Nightingale Prim Sch E5 16 C4
Nightingale Rd NW10 21 B3
Nightingale Sch SW17 72 A2
Nightingale Sq SW12 72 C4
Nightingale Wlk SW18, SW4 61 A1
Nile Cl N16 7 B1
Nile Ho N1 97 B4
Nile St N1 97 B4
Nile Terr SE1, SE15 153 A1
Nimegen Way 9 SE22 64 A2
Nimrod Pas 4 N1 16 A2
NINE ELMS 160 C2
Nine Elms La SW8 161 B3
Nisbet Ho E9 17 C3
Niton Rd TW9 54 C4
Niton St SW6 47 C3
No 2 Willow Rd★ NW3 12 A4
Nobel Ho 8 SE5 48 B1
Noble Ct E1 32 A2
Noble St EC2 108 C2
Noel Coward Ho SW1 147 A3
Noel Ho 3 NW3 11 C1
Noel Rd Acton W3 28 A3
Islington N1 86 B2
Noel St W1 105 A1
Noko NW10 22 C2
Nolan Way E5 16 C4
Noll Ho N7 5 B2
Norbiton Rd E14 33 B3
Norbroke St W12 29 B2
Norburn St W10 31 A4
Norcombe Ho 2 N19 4 C1
Norcott Rd N16 7 C1
Norcroft Gdns SE22 76 C4
Norden Ho 25 E2 25 A2
Nore Ct NW10 8 C1
Norfolk Cres W2 102 B2
Norfolk Ho
City of London EC4 122 C4
Greenwich SE3 53 A4
4 Putney SW15 69 B4
Richmond TW10 54 C2
Shacklewell E8 16 B4
St Johns SE8 51 C2
Westminster SW1 147 C4
Norfolk House Rd SW16 74 A1
Norfolk Mans
Battersea SW11 169 A3
10 Wandsworth SW18 58 C2
Norfolk Mews 12 W10 31 A4
Norfolk Pl W2 101 C2
Norfolk Rd
St John's Wood NW8 79 C3
Willesden NW10 8 A1
Norfolk Row SE1, SE11 148 C4
Norfolk Sq W2 101 C2
Norfolk Sq Mews W2 101 C1
Norgrove St SW12 72 C4
Norland Ho 13 W11 30 C1
Norland Pl W11 31 A1 112 B1
Norland Place Sch W11 31 A1 112 A1
Norland Rd 16 W11 30 C1
Norland Sq W11 31 A1 112 B1
Norley Vale SW15 68 C3
Norman Butler Ho 10 W10 23 A1
Normanby Cl SW15 58 B2
Normanby Rd NW10 8 B4
Norman Ct
Dulwich SE22 76 C4
Finsbury Pk N4 5 C4
Willesden NW10 8 C1
Normand Croft Com Sch W14 155 A4
Normand Mews W14 154 B4
Normand Rd W14 154 C4
Normandy Ho 8 E14 42 B4
Normandy Rd SW9 173 B3
Norman Gr E3 26 A3
Norman Ho SW8 162 A2
Normanhurst Rd SW2 74 B2
Norman Rd SE10 52 A3
Norman St EC1 97 A3
Normanton Ave SW18, SW19 70 C2
Normanton Ho 6 SW4 61 B1
Norman Way W3 28 A3
Norris Ho
12 Hoxton N1 24 A4
15 South Hackney E9 25 B4
Norris St SW1 119 B3
Norroy Rd SW15 57 C3
Norse Ho 13 SE5 48 B1
Norstead Pl SW15 68 C2
NORTH ACTON 20 C2
North Acton Rd NW10 20 C2
North Acton Sta W3 28 C4
Northampton Gr N1 15 C3
Northampton Pk N1 15 C2
Northampton Rd EC1 95 C2
Northampton Sq EC1 96 A3
Northampton St N1 15 B1
North Audley St W1 117 B4
North Ave 8 TW9 44 C2
Northaw Ho 4 W10 22 B1
North Bank NW8 90 A3
North Block 19 E1 32 B2

Northbourne Ho 21 E5 17 A3
Northbourne Rd SW4 61 C2
North Bridge House Sch NW3 11 B2
North Bridge House Senior Sch NW1 82 A3
Northburgh St EC1 96 B2
North Carriage Dr W2 116 B4
Northchurch SE17 151 C2
Northchurch Ho 19 E2 24 C4
Northchurch Rd N1 15 C1
Northchurch Terr N1 16 A1
North Circular Rd NW2, NW10 8 A3
North Colonnade The E14 34 A1
Northcote Lodge Sch SW11 60 B1
Northcote Rd
  Wandsworth SW11 60 B2
  Willesden NW10 8 A1
Northcourt W1 105 A4
North Cres
  Marylebone WC1 105 B4
  Newham E16 27 C1
Northcroft Ct 8 W12 38 C4
North Cross Rd SE22 64 C2
North Ct SW1 134 A1
Northdown St N1 84 C1
North Dulwich Sta SE21 63 C2
NORTH END 2 B2
North End NW3 2 B2
North End Ave NW3 2 B2
North End Cres W14 140 C3
North End Ho W14 140 B3
North End Par W14 140 B3
North End Rd
  Golders Green NW11 2 A3
  West Kensington W14 141 A1
North End Way NW3 2 B2
Northern Hts N8 4 C4
Northesk Ho 6 E1 25 A1
North Eyot Gdns 5 W6 38 B1
Northey St E14 33 A2
Northfield Hall N6 3 C4
Northfield Ho 3 SE15 49 C4
Northfield Rd N16 7 A4
Northfields SW18 58 C3
Northfields Prospect SW18 58 C3
Northfields Rd W3 28 B4
Northfleet Ho SE1 137 B4
North Flower Wlk W2 115 B3
North Gate NW8 80 A1
Northgate Ct 14 SW9 62 C4
North Gower St NW1 93 A3
North Gr N6 3 C4
North Greenwich Sta SE10 43 A4
North Hill Ct N6 3 C4
North Ho 3 SE8 41 B1
Northiam WC1 94 B3
Northiam St E9 25 A4
Northington St WC1 95 A1
NORTH KENSINGTON 30 C4
Northlands St SE5 48 B1
Northleigh Ho 36 E3 27 A2
North Lo SW4 61 A3
North Lodge Cl SW15 57 C2
North Mews WC1 95 A1
Northolme Rd N5 15 B4
North Pas SW18 58 C2
Northpoint Sq 8 NW1 13 C2
North Pole Rd W10 30 B4
Northport St N1 87 C3
North Rd
  Barnsbury N7 14 A2
  Brentford TW8 44 A4
  Highgate N6 3 C4
  Richmond TW9 44 C1
North Ride W2 116 A3
North Rise W2 102 B1
North Row W1 117 B4
NORTH SHEEN 44 C1
North Sheen Sta TW10 54 C3
North Side Wandsworth Comm SW18 59 C2
North St SW4 61 B4
Northstead Rd SW2 74 C2
North Tenter St E1 111 A1
North Terr SW3 130 A1
Northumberland Alley EC3 110 B1
Northumberland Ave WC2 120 A2
Northumberland Ho NW5 13 B2
Northumberland Mans E5 17 B4
Northumberland Pl W2 31 C3
Northumberland St WC2 120 A2
Northumbria Ct 10 TW9 54 A3
Northumbria St E14 33 C3
North Verbena Gdns 2 W6 38 C1
Northview 1 N7 5 A1
Northview Cres NW10 8 B4
Northview Prim Sch NW10 8 B4
North Villas NW1 13 C2
Northway Rd SE5 63 B4
Northways Par 2 NW3 11 C1
Northwest Pl N1 85 C2
North Wharf Rd W2 101 B3
Northwick Cl NW8 89 B2
Northwick Ho NW8 89 A2
Northwick Terr NW8 89 B2
North Wlk W2 114 C3
Northwold Prim Sch E5 7 C2
Northwold Rd E5, N16 7 C2
North Wood Lo NW3 11 A4
Northwood Rd N6 4 A4
North Worple Way SW14 55 C4
Norton Folgate E1 110 B4
Norton Ho
  14 Globe Town E2 25 C3
  30 Stepney E1 32 A3
  Stockwell SW9 173 A1
Norval Gn SW9 173 C2
Norvic Ho 5 SE5 48 B1
Norway Gate SE16 41 A3
Norway Pl E14 33 B3
Norway St SE10 52 A4
Norwich Ho 6 E14 34 A3
Norwich St EC4 107 B2
Norwood Cl NW2 1 A1
Norwood Ho 25 E14 34 A2
Norwood Rd SE24, SE27 75 A3
Notley St SE5 48 C3
Notre Dame RC Girls Sch SE1 136 B1
Notting Barn Rd W10 22 C1
Nottingdale Sq W11 31 A1 112 A2
Nottingham Ct WC2 106 A1
Nottingham Ho
  33 Camberwell SE5 48 B1
  Stoke Newington N4 6 B3
Nottingham Pl W1 103 B4
Nottingham Rd SW17 72 B3
Nottingham St W1 103 B4
Nottingham Terr NW1 91 B1
NOTTING HILL 112 C3
Notting Hill Gate W11 31 C1 113 B2
Notting Hill Gate Sta W11 31 C1 113 B2
Nottingwood Ho W11 31 A2 112 A4
Nova Bldg 1 E14 41 C2
Nova Ct E 3 E14 34 B1
Nova Ct W 2 E14 34 B1
Novello St SW6 165 B4
Nowell Rd SW13 46 C4
Noyna Rd SW17 72 B1
Nucleus NW10 20 B2
Nuding Cl SE13 66 C4
Nuffield Lo 14 W9 31 C4
Nugent Ct 3 N19 5 A3
Nugent Rd N19 5 A3
Nugent Terr NW8 79 A1
Nun Ct EC2 109 B2
NUNHEAD 65 B3
Nunhead Cres SE15 65 A4
Nunhead Gn SE15 65 A4
Nunhead Gr SE15 65 B4
Nunhead La SE15 65 A4
Nunhead Sta SE15 50 B1
Nursery Cl
  New Cross SE4 51 B1
  Putney SW15 57 C3
Nursery La
  North Kensington W10 30 B4
  Shoreditch E2 24 B4
Nursery Rd
  Hackney E9 17 B2
  Stockwell SW9 62 B3
Nursery Row SE17 151 B3
Nutbourne St W10 23 A2
Nutbrook St SE15 64 C4
Nutcroft Rd SE15 50 A3
Nutfield Rd
  East Dulwich SE22 64 B3
  Leyton E15 19 B4
Nutford Pl W1 102 C2
Nuthurst Ave SW2 74 B2
Nutley Terr NW3 11 C2
Nutmeg La E14 34 C3
Nuttall St N1 24 A3
Nutt St SE15 49 B3
NW London Jewish Day Sch NW6 10 A1
Nye Bevan Ho SW6 154 C2
Nye's Wharf SE1, SE15 49 C4
Nylands Ave TW9 44 C1
Nynehead St SE14 51 A3
Nyton Cl N19 5 A3

O

O2 Millennium Dome The★ SE10 35 A1
Oakbank Gr SE24 63 B3
Oakbury Rd SW6 166 B1
Oakcourt 17 SE15 49 B3
Oak Cres E16 35 A4
Oakcroft Ct SE3 53 C2
Oakcroft Rd SE13 52 C1
Oakdale Ct N19 5 A2
Oakdale Rd SE15 65 B4
Oakdene 3 SE15 50 A2
Oakdene Ho 11 N16 7 A3
Oakden St SE11 149 C4
Oake Ct SW15 58 A2
Oakeford Ho W14 126 B1
Oakend Ho 10 N4 6 C4
Oakeshott Ave N6 3 C2
Oakey La SE1 135 B2
Oakfield Ct
  Clapham Pk SW4 62 A1
  Finsbury Pk N8 5 A4
Oakfield Prep Sch SE21 75 C3
Oakfield Rd
  Finsbury Pk N4 5 C4
  Wimbledon SW19 69 C1
Oakfield St SW10 156 C4
Oakford Rd NW5 13 B4
Oak Gr NW2 10 A4
Oakham Ho 5 W10 22 B1
Oakhill Ave NW3 11 A4
Oakhill Ct
  Honor Oak SE23 65 B1
  Putney SW15 58 B2
Oak Hill Lo NW3 11 A4
Oak Hill Park Mews NW3 11 B4
Oak Hill Pk NW3 11 A4
Oakhill Pl SW15 58 C2
Oakhill Rd SW15 58 B2
Oak Hill Way NW3 11 B4
Oak Ho
  13 Cubitt Town E14 42 B4
  8 Maitland Pk NW3 12 B2
  2 Richmond TW9 45 A2
  9 Stoke Newington N16 6 C2
Oakhurst Gr SE22 64 C3
Oakington Rd W9 23 C1
Oakington Way N8 5 A4
Oak La E14 33 B2
Oaklands Ct
  Dagenham NW10 21 A4
  5 Shepherd's Bush W12 30 A1
Oaklands Gr W12 29 C1
Oaklands Ho SE4 66 B4
Oaklands Mews 1 NW2 9 C4
Oaklands Pas NW2 9 C4
Oaklands Pl 8 SW4 61 C3
Oaklands Rd
  Cricklewood NW2 9 C4
  Mortlake SW14 55 C4
Oaklands Sec Sch E2 25 A2
Oakley Cres EC1 86 B1
Oakley Dr SE13 67 C1
Oakley Gdns SW3 158 B4
Oakley Ho SW1 145 A4
Oakley Pl SE1 152 C1
Oakley Rd N1 15 C1
Oakley Sq NW1 83 A2
Oakley St SW3 158 A4
Oakley Wlk W6 47 C4
Oak Lodge 14 SE21 75 C2
Oak Lodge Sch SW12 72 C4
Oakman Ho 29 SW19 69 C3
Oakmead Rd SW12 73 A3
Oak Park Gdns SW19 69 C3
Oak Park Mews N16 7 B1
Oakshaw Rd SW18 71 A4
Oakshott Ct NW1 83 B1
Oaks Sh Ctr The W3 28 B1
Oaks The
  Brondesbury Pk NW6 9 C1
  Willesden NW10 9 A1
Oak Tree Ct
  Acton W3 28 A2
  8 Clapham Pk SW4 62 A2

Oak Tree Ho W9 ... 88 A2
Oak Tree Rd NW8 ... 90 A3
Oakview Lo NW11 ... 1 B4
Oak Village NW5 ... 12 C4
Oak Way W3 ... 29 A1
Oakwell Ho SW8 ... 171 B1
Oakwood Cl SE13 ... 67 C1
Oakwood Ct W14 ... 126 C2
Oakwood La W14 ... 126 C2
Oakworth Rd W10 ... 30 C4
Oast Ct 8 E14 ... 33 B2
Oast Lo W4 ... 46 A3
Oat La EC2 ... 109 A2
Oatlands Ct 3 SW19 ... 69 C3
Oatwell Ho SW3 ... 144 B3
Oban Ho E14 ... 34 C3
Oban St E14 ... 34 C3
Oberon Ho 5 N1 ... 24 A3
Oberstein Rd 15 SW11 ... 59 C3
Oborne Cl SE24 ... 63 A2
O'Brian Ho 10 E1 ... 25 C2
Observatory Gdns W8 ... 127 C4
Observatory Mews E14 ... 42 C2
Observatory Rd SW14 ... 55 B3
Occupation Rd SE17 ... 150 C2
Ocean St E1 ... 32 C4
Ocean Wharf E14 ... 41 C4
Ockbrook 3 E1 ... 32 B4
Ockendon Rd N1 ... 15 C2
Ockley Rd SW16 ... 74 A1
Octagon Arc EC2 ... 110 A3
Octagon The NW3 ... 10 C4
Octavia Ho W10 ... 23 A1
Octavia Mews 1 W9 ... 23 B1
Octavia St SW11 ... 168 B3
Octavius St SE8 ... 51 C3
Odell Wlk SE13 ... 67 B4
Odeon Ct
Dagenham NW10 ... 21 A4
1 Newham E16 ... 35 C4
Odessa Rd NW10 ... 21 C3
Odessa St SE16 ... 41 B3
Odette Duval Ho 29 E1 ... 32 B4
Odger St SW11 ... 169 A2
Odhams Wlk WC2 ... 106 B1
Odin Ho 6 SE5 ... 48 B1
O'Donnell Ct WC1 ... 94 B2
O'Driscoll Ho 4 W12 ... 30 A3
Offa's Mead E9 ... 18 A4
Offenbach Ho 12 E2 ... 25 C3
Offerton Rd SW4 ... 61 B4
Offham Ho SE17 ... 152 A3
Offley Ho 10 E9 ... 17 C2
Offley Rd SW9 ... 163 B2
Offord Rd N1 ... 14 B1
Offord St N1 ... 14 B1
Ogilvie Ho 12 E1 ... 32 C3
Oglander Rd SE15 ... 64 B4
Ogle St W1 ... 104 C4
O'Gorman Ho SW10 ... 157 A2
Ohio Bldg 13 SE13 ... 52 A2
Oil Mill La W6 ... 38 C1
Okehampton Rd NW10 ... 22 C4
Okeover Manor SW4 ... 61 A3
Olaf St W11 ... 30 C2
Old Bailey EC4 ... 108 B1
Old Barrack Yd SW1 ... 131 B3
Old Bellgate Wharf E14 ... 41 C3
Old Bethnal Green Rd E2 ... 25 A2
Old Billingsgate Wlk EC3 ... 124 A3
Old Bldgs WC2 ... 107 B2
Old Bond St W1 ... 118 C3
Old Brewery Mews NW3 ... 11 C4
Old Broad St EC2 ... 109 C2
Old Brompton Rd SW5, SW7 ... 143 A3
Old Burlington St W1 ... 118 C3
Oldbury Ct E9 ... 18 A3
Oldbury Pl W1 ... 103 C4
Old Castle St E1 ... 111 A2
Old Cavendish St W1 ... 104 A1
Old Change Ct EC4 ... 108 C1
Old Chiswick Yd W4 ... 46 A4
Old Church Rd E1 ... 32 C3
Old Church St SW3 ... 143 C1
Old Compton St W1 ... 105 B1
Old Court Ho W8 ... 128 A3
Old Court Pl W8 ... 128 A3
Old Covent Gdn★ WC2 ... 120 B4
Old Cty H★ SE1 ... 134 C4
Old Dairy Mews
5 Balham SW12 ... 72 C3
4 Camden Town NW5 ... 13 A2
Old Deer Park Gdns TW9 ... 54 A4
Old Devonshire Rd SW12 ... 73 A4
Old Dock Cl TW9 ... 44 C4
Oldfield Gr SE16 ... 40 C2
Oldfield Ho 14 W4 ... 38 A1
Oldfield Mews N6 ... 4 B4
Oldfield Rd
Bedford Pk W3, W12 ... 38 B4
Stoke Newington N16 ... 7 A1
Willesden NW10 ... 8 B1
Old Fish St Hill EC4 ... 122 C4
Old Fleet La EC4 ... 108 A2
OLD FORD ... 26 B4
Old Ford Prim Sch E3 ... 26 B3
Old Ford Rd E2, E3 ... 25 C3
Old Ford Trad Ctr 13 E3 ... 26 C4
Old Forge Mews W12 ... 39 A4
Old Forge Rd N19 ... 4 C2
Old Gloucester St WC1 ... 106 B4
Oldham Terr W3 ... 28 B1
Oldhill St N16 ... 7 C3
Old Hospital Cl SW12, SW17 ... 72 B3
Olding Ho 6 SW12 ... 73 B4
Old Jamaica Bsns Est SE16 ... 139 B1
Old Jamaica Rd SE16 ... 139 B2
Old James St SE15 ... 65 A4
Old Jewry EC2 ... 109 B1
Old Kent Rd
Deptford SE1, SE15 ... 50 A4
Walworth SE1 ... 152 B2
Old Laundry The 14 SW18 ... 59 C3
Old Manor Ct NW8 ... 79 A2
Old Manor Yd SW5 ... 142 A3
Old Market Sq E2 ... 24 B2 99 A4
Old Marylebone Rd NW1 ... 102 B3
Old Mitre Ct EC4 ... 107 C1
Old Montague St E1 ... 111 B3
Old Nichol St E2 ... 24 B1 98 C2
Old North St WC1 ... 106 C4
OLD OAK COMMON ... 21 B1
Old Oak Common La NW10 ... 21 A1
Old Oak La NW10 ... 21 B2
Old Oak Prim Sch W12 ... 29 B3
Old Oak Rd W3 ... 29 B2
Old Orch The NW3 ... 12 B4
Old Palace Prim Sch E3 ... 27 A2
Old Paradise St SE11 ... 148 C4
Old Park Ave SW12 ... 60 C1
Old Park La W1 ... 118 A1
Old Pye St SW1 ... 133 B2
Old Pye Street Est SW1 ... 133 B1
Old Quebec St W1 ... 103 A1
Old Queen St SW1 ... 133 C3
Oldridge Rd SW12 ... 73 A4
Old Royal Free Pl N1 ... 85 C3
Old Royal Free Sq N1 ... 85 C3
Old School Sq 12 E14 ... 33 C3
Old School The WC1 ... 107 A4
Old Seacoal La EC4 ... 108 A1
Old South Lambeth Rd SW8 ... 162 B2
Old Spitalfields Mkt E1 ... 111 A4
Old Sq WC2 ... 107 B2
Old St EC1 ... 97 C2
Old Stable Mews N5 ... 6 B1
Old Street Sta EC1 ... 97 C2
Old Sun Wharf E14 ... 33 A2
Old Swan Wharf SW11 ... 167 C4
Old Theatre Ct SE1 ... 123 A2
Old Town SW4 ... 61 B4
Old Vicarage Sch TW10 ... 54 A1
Old Woolwich Rd SE10 ... 42 C1
Old York Rd SW18 ... 59 A2
O'Leary Sq E1 ... 32 B4
Olga Prim Sch E3 ... 26 A3
Olga St 20 E3 ... 26 A3
Oliphant St W10 ... 23 A2
Olive Blythe Ho 14 W10 ... 23 A1
Oliver Bsns Pk NW10 ... 20 B3
Oliver Cl W4 ... 45 A4
Olive Rd NW2 ... 9 B4
Oliver Goldsmith Prim Sch SE5 ... 49 B2
Oliver Ho
Bermondsey SE16 ... 139 B3
Notting Hill W11 ... 31 A2 112 A3
South Lambeth SW8 ... 162 A2
Oliver House Prep Sch SW4 ... 61 A1
Oliver Mews SE15 ... 49 C1
Oliver's Yd EC1 ... 97 C2
Olive Tree Ho 7 SE15 ... 50 B4
Olive Tree Sch The SE13 ... 67 A1
Olivette St 1 SW15 ... 57 C3
Olive Waite Ho NW6 ... 11 A1
Ollerton Gn E3 ... 26 B4
Ollgar Cl W12 ... 29 B1
Olliffe St E14 ... 42 B3
Olmar St SE1 ... 49 C4
Olney Ho NW8 ... 90 B2
Olney Rd SE17 ... 48 B4
Olympia Ex Ctr★ W14 ... 126 B1
Olympian Ct 8 E14 ... 41 C2
Olympia Way W14 ... 126 B1
Olympia Yd W2 ... 114 B3
Olympic Ho 10 W10 ... 30 B3
Olympus Sq E5 ... 7 C1
Oman Ave NW2 ... 9 B4
Oman Ct NW4 ... 9 A4
Ombersley Ho N4 ... 6 B4
Omeara St SE1 ... 123 A1
Omega Cl E14 ... 42 A3
Omega Ho SW10 ... 157 A2
Omega Pl N1 ... 84 B1
Omega St SE14 ... 51 C2
Omega Works E3 ... 18 C1
Ommaney Rd SE14 ... 51 A2
Omnibus Bsns Ctr N7 ... 14 A3
Ondine Rd SE15 ... 64 B3
Onedin Point E1 ... 125 C3
Onega Gate SE16 ... 41 A3
O'Neill Ho NW8 ... 79 C1
One Tree Cl SE23 ... 65 B1
Ongar Ho 15 N1 ... 15 C2
Ongar Rd SW6 ... 155 C4
Onslow Ave TW10 ... 54 A2
Onslow Avenue Mans 10 TW10 ... 54 A2
Onslow Cl W9 ... 23 B2
Onslow Ct SW10 ... 143 A1
Onslow Gdns SW7 ... 143 B2
Onslow Lo 28 SW2 ... 74 C4
Onslow Mews E SW7 ... 143 B3
Onslow Mews W SW7 ... 143 B3
Onslow Rd TW10 ... 54 A1
Onslow Sq SW7 ... 143 C3
Onslow St EC1 ... 95 C1
Ontario St SE1 ... 136 B2
Ontario Way E14 ... 33 C2
Opal St SE11 ... 150 A2
Open Air Theatre, Regent's Pk★ NW1 ... 91 B3
Openview SW17, SW18 ... 71 C2
Opera Ct 7 N19 ... 4 C1
Operating Theatre Mus & Herb Garret★ SE1 ... 123 C1
Ophelia Gdns NW2 ... 1 A1
Ophir Terr SE15 ... 49 C2
Opie Ho NW8 ... 80 B2
Oppenheim Rd SE13 ... 52 B1
Oppidan Apartments NW6 ... 10 C2
Oppidans Rd NW3 ... 12 B1
Orange Pl SE16 ... 40 B3
Orangery Gallery The★ W8 ... 126 C3
Orange St WC2 ... 119 C3
Orange Yd WC2 ... 105 C1
Oransay Rd 25 N1 ... 15 B2
Oratory La SW3 ... 143 C2
Oratory RC Prim Sch SW3 ... 144 A2
Oratory The★ SW7 ... 130 A1
Orbain Rd SW6 ... 154 B1
Orbel St SW11 ... 168 A3
Orb St SE17 ... 151 B3
Orchard Cl
Honor Oak SE23 ... 65 B1
Islington N1 ... 15 B1
Kensal Town W10 ... 31 A4
Orchard Ct
Barnes SW13 ... 56 B4
Marylebone W1 ... 103 B2
Orchard Dr SE3 ... 53 A1
Orchard Hill SE13 ... 52 A2
Orchard Ho
Camberwell SE5 ... 48 B2
11 Rotherhithe SE16 ... 40 B3
Shepherd's Bush W12 ... 29 C1
Orchard Mead Ho NW11 ... 1 C2
Orchard Mews N1 ... 15 C1
Orchard Pl E14 ... 35 A2
Orchard Prim Sch E9 ... 17 B1
Orchard Rd
Highgate N6 ... 4 A4
Richmond TW9 ... 54 C4
Orchard Rise TW10 ... 55 A3
Orchardson Ho NW8 ... 89 C1
Orchardson St NW8 ... 89 C1

Orchard Sq W14 .. 140 C1
Orchard St W1 ... 103 C2
Orchard The
Acton Green W4 ..... 37 C2
Lewisham SE3 ...... 52 C1
Orchid St W12 ..... 29 C2
Orde Hall St WC1 106 C4
Orde Ho 10 N16 .... 15 C4
Ordell Ct 36 E3 .... 26 B3
Ordell Rd E3 .... 26 B3
Ordnance Cres SE10 .... 43 A4
Ordnance Hill NW8 .... 79 C3
Ordnance Mews NW8 .... 79 C2
Ordnance Rd E16 ... 35 B4
Oregano Dr E14 .... 34 C3
Oregon Bldg 5 SE13 .... 52 A2
Orestes Mews 1 NW6 .... 10 C3
Orford Ct SE27 ..... 75 A2
Oriana Ho 3 E14 .... 33 B2
Oriel Ct NW3 .... 11 B4
Oriel Dr SW13 ...... 47 B4
Oriel Rd
Hackney E9 .... 18 A2
Homerton E9 .... 17 C2
Orient St SE11 ... 150 A4
Orion Bsns Ctr SE14 .... 40 C1
Orion Ho 20 E1 ..... 25 A1
Orion Point 5 E14 .... 41 C2
Orkney Ho N1 ..... 84 C4
Orkney St SW11 .. 169 B2
Orlando Rd SW4 ... 61 B4
Orleston Mews N7 .... 14 C2
Orleston Rd N7 .... 14 C2
Orlop St SE10 ...... 43 A1
Orme Ct W2 ..... 114 A3
Orme Ct Mews W2 .... 114 B3
Orme Ho 8 E8 ..... 24 B4
Orme La W2 ..... 114 A3
Ormeley Rd SW12 .. 73 A3
Ormerod Ho 3 SW9 .... 62 A4
Orme Sq W2 ..... 114 A3
Ormiston Gr W12 ... 30 A1
Ormiston Rd SE10 .. 43 C1
Ormond Cl WC1 .. 106 B4
Ormonde Ct SW15 .. 57 B3
Ormonde Gate SW3 .... 145 A1
Ormonde Mans WC1 .... 106 B4
Ormonde Pl SW1 145 C3
Ormonde Rd SW14 .... 55 B4
Ormonde Terr NW8 .... 80 C3
Ormond Ho 7 N16 .. 6 C2
Ormond Mans WC1 .... 94 C1
Ormond Mews WC1 .... 94 B1
Ormond Rd N4, N19 .. 5 A3
Ormond Yd SW1 .. 119 A2
Ormrod Ct W11 .... 31 B3
Ormsby Lo 7 W4 .. 38 A3
Ormsby Pl N16 ...... 7 B1
Ormsby St E2 ...... 24 B3
Ormside St SE15 ... 50 B4
Ornan Rd NW3 ..... 12 A3
Orpen Ho SW5 ... 141 C3
Orpen Wlk N16 ...... 7 A1
Orpheus Ho 25 N19 .. 4 C4
Orpheus St SE5 .... 48 C2
Orsett Mews W2 . 100 C2
Orsett St SE11 .... 149 A2
Orsett Terr W2 ... 100 C2
Orsman Rd N1 ..... 24 A4
Orton St E1 ...... 125 B1
Orville Rd SW11 .. 167 C2
Orwell Ct
Hackney E8 .... 24 C4
Highbury N5 .... 15 B4
Orwell Ho W12 ..... 29 C2
Osbaldeston Rd N16 .... 7 C3
Osbert St SW1 ... 147 B3
Osborn Cl E8 .... 24 C4
Osborne Rd
Finsbury Pk N4 .... 5 C3
Hackney E9 .... 18 B2
South Acton W3 ..... 37 A4
Willesden NW2 .... 9 A2
Osborn St E1 ..... 111 A4
Osbourne Ho TW10 .... 54 C2
Oscar Faber Pl 8 N1 .... 16 A1
Oscar St SE8 .... 51 C1
Oseney Cres NW5 .. 13 C2
Osier Ct E1 .... 25 C1
Osier La SE10 ...... 43 B3
Osier Mews W4 .... 46 B4
Osiers Rd SW18 .... 58 C3
Osier St E1 .... 25 B1
Oslo Ct NW8 ...... 80 A1
Oslo Ho 2 SE5 ..... 48 B1
Oslo Sq SE16 .... 41 A3
Osmani Prim Sch E1 .... 111 C4
Osman Rd W6 ...... 39 B3
Osmington Ho SW8 .... 163 A1
Osmund St W12 .... 29 B4
Osnaburgh St NW1 .... 92 B2
Osnaburgh Terr NW1 .... 92 B2
Osprey Ct NW3 ..... 11 A3
Osprey Ho
Camberwell SE15 .... 49 B2
3 Limehouse E14 ... 33 A2
Ospringe Ho SE1 . 121 C1
Ospringe Rd NW5 .. 13 B4
Osram Ct W6 ...... 39 B3
Osric Path 8 N1 .... 24 A3
Ossian Mews N4 .... 5 B4
Ossian Rd N4 .... 5 B4
Ossington Bldgs W1 .... 103 B3
Ossington Cl W2 .... 31 C2 113 C3
Ossington St W2 . 114 A3
Ossory Rd SE1 ..... 49 C4
Ossulston St NW1 . 83 C2
Ostade Rd SW2 .... 74 B4
Osten Mews SW7 . 128 B1
Osterley Ho 5 E14 .... 34 A3
Osterley Rd N16 .... 16 A4
Oswald Bldg SW8 160 A3
Oswald's Mead E9 . 18 A4
Osward Rd SW12, SW17 .... 72 B2
Oswell Ho 9 E1 .... 32 A1
Oswin St SE11 .... 150 B4
Oswyth Rd SE5 ..... 49 A1
Otford Cres SE4 .... 66 B1
Otford Ho
Bermondsey SE1 .. 137 C3
6 Deptford SE15 ... 50 B4
Otha Ho SW9 ..... 172 B2
Othello Cl SE11 .. 150 A2
Otis St E3 .... 27 B2
Otley Ho N5 .... 6 A1
Ottaway Ct E5 .... 7 C1
Ottaway St E5 .... 7 C1
Otterburn Ho 12 SE5 .... 48 B3
Otter Cl E15 .... 27 B4
Otto St SE17 .... 48 A4
Our Lady of Dolours RC Prim Sch W2 100 A4
Our Lady of Lourdes RC Prim Sch SE13 .... 67 C4
Our Lady of Lourdes RC Sch NW10 ..... 20 B4
Our Lady of Victories RC Prim Sch
Putney SW15 .... 57 C3
South Kensington SW7 .... 143 A3
Our Lady Queen of Heaven RC Sch SW19 .... 69 C4
Our Lady RC Prim Sch
Camden Town NW1 .... 83 A4
Poplar E14 .... 33 B3
Our Lady & St Joseph RC Prim Sch N1 .. 16 A2
Our Lady's Convent RC High Sch N15 ... 7 A4
Ouseley Rd SW12 ... 72 B3
Outer Circ NW8 ... 81 A1
Outgate Rd NW10 ... 8 B1
Outram Pl N1 ..... 84 B4
Outwich St EC3 .. 110 B2
Outwood Ho 3 SW2 .... 74 B4
Oval Mans SE11 .. 163 A4
Oval Pl SW8 ...... 163 A2
Oval Rd NW1 ...... 82 A4
Oval Sta SE11 .... 163 B3
Oval The E2 .... 25 A3
Oval The (Surrey Cnty Crkt Gd) SE11 ... 163 A4
Oval Way SE11 ... 149 A1
Overbury Ho 3 E5 .... 17 C4
Overbury St E5 ..... 17 C4
Overcliff Rd SE13 ... 66 C4
Overhill Rd SE21, SE22 .... 76 C4
Overlea Rd E5 .... 7 C4
Oversley Ho 17 W2 .... 31 C4
Overstone Ho 19 E14 .... 33 C3
Overstone Rd W6 .. 39 B2
Overstrand Mans SW11 .... 169 B3
Overton Ho SW15 .. 68 B4
Overton Rd SW9 . 173 C1
Overy Ho SE1 .... 136 A3
Ovex Cl E14 .... 42 B4
Ovington Ct SW3 . 130 B1
Ovington Gdns SW3 .... 130 B1
Ovington Mews SW3 .... 130 B1
Ovington Sq SW3 . 130 B1
Ovington St SW3 . 144 B4
Owen Ho 11 N19 ... 13 B4
Owen's Ct EC1 .... 96 A4
Owen's Row EC1 .. 96 A4
Owen St EC1 ...... 86 A1
Owgan Cl SE5 ...... 48 C3
Oxberry Ave SW6 . 164 B2
Oxbridge Ct 4 W4 .... 37 A1
Oxendon St SW1, W1 .... 119 B3
Oxenford St SE15 ... 64 B4
Oxenham Ho 13 SE8 .... 51 C4
Oxenholme NW1 .. 83 A1
Oxestalls Rd SE8 ... 41 A1
Oxford & Cambridge Mans NW1 ...... 102 B3
Oxford Cir W1 .... 104 C1
Oxford Circus Ave W1 .... 104 C1
Oxford Circus Sta W1 .... 104 C1
Oxford Ct
City of London EC4 .... 123 B4
Gunnersbury W4 .... 37 A1
48 Paddington W2 ... 31 C4
Oxford Dr SE1 .... 124 A1
Oxford Gardens Prim Sch W10 .... 30 C3
Oxford Gate W6 .... 39 C2
Oxford Gdns
Brentford W4 .... 44 C4
North Kensington W10 .... 30 C3
Oxford Ho N4 .... 5 C3
Oxford Rd
Finsbury Pk N4 .... 5 C3
Paddington NW6 .... 23 C3
Putney SW15 .... 58 A3
Stratford E15 .... 19 C2
Oxford Rd N W4 .... 37 A1
Oxford Rd S W4 .... 37 A1
Oxford Sq W2 .... 102 B1
Oxford St W1 .... 104 B1
Oxley Cl SE1 ..... 153 A2
Oxonian St SE22 .... 64 B3
Oxo Tower Wharf SE1 .... 121 C3
Oxo Twr★ SE1 .... 121 C3
Oxted Ct N16 .... 7 A3
Oyster Row E1 ..... 32 B3
Ozolins Way E16 ... 35 C3

P

Pablo Neruda Cl 4 SE24 .... 63 A3
Pace Pl E1 .... 32 A3
Pacific Ho 15 E1 ... 25 C1
Pacific Rd E16 ..... 35 C3
Pacific Wharf SE16 .... 32 C1
Packenham Ho
24 Crouch End N19 ... 4 C4
Spitalfields E2 .... 24 B2 99 A4
Packington Sq N1 . 86 C4
Packington St N1 . 86 B3
Padbury SE17 .... 152 B1
Padbury Ct E2 .... 24 B2 99 A3
Padbury Ho NW8 .. 90 B2
Paddenswick Ct 2 W6 .... 39 A3
Paddenswick Rd W6 .... 38 C3
PADDINGTON ... 100 C3
Paddington Acad
Paddington W2 .... 101 B3
Paddington W9 ...... 23 C1
Paddington Com Hospl W9 .... 31 C4
Paddington Gn W2 .... 101 B4
Paddington Green Prim Sch NW8 ... 89 B1
Paddington St W1 .... 103 B4
Paddington Sta W2 .... 101 B2
Paddock Cl SE3 .... 53 C1
Paddock Sch SW15 .... 56 B3
Paddock Way 11 SW15 .... 69 B4
Padfield Rd SE5 .... 63 B4
Padstone Ho 50 E3 .... 27 A2
Padstow Ho 12 E14 .... 33 B2
Pagden St SW8 .. 170 B4
Pageant Cres SE16 .... 33 B1
Pageantmaster Ct EC4 .... 108 A1
Page Ho SE10 ...... 52 B4
Page St SW1 ..... 147 C4
Page's Wlk SE1 .. 138 B1
Page's Yd W4 ...... 46 A4
Paget Ho 15 E2 .... 25 B3
Paget Rd N16 .... 6 C3
Paget St EC1 ...... 96 A4
Pagham Ho 8 W10 .... 22 B1
Pagnell St SE14 .... 51 B3
Pagoda Ave TW9 ... 54 B4
Pagoda Gdns SE3 .. 52 C1
Pagoda Gr SE27 .... 75 B2
Paine Ct SE3 .... 53 B4
Painsthorpe Rd 3 N16 .... 7 A1
Painswick Ct 1 SE15 .... 49 B3
Painters Mews SE16 .... 153 C4
Pakeman Ho SE1 . 136 B4
Pakeman Prim Sch N7 .... 5 B1
Pakeman St N7 ..... 5 B1
Pakenham Cl SW12 .... 72 C3
Pakenham St WC1 . 95 A2
Palace Ave W8 ... 128 B4
Palace Ct
Hampstead NW3 .... 11 A3
Kensington W2 .... 114 A3
Streatham SW2 ..... 74 C2
Palace Garden Mews W8 .... 31 C1 113 C2
Palace Gate W8 .. 128 C3
Palace Gdns Mews W8 .... 114 B1
Palace Gn W8 .... 114 A1
Palace Mans W14 .... 140 B4
Palace Mews
Belgravia SW1 .... 145 C3
Fulham SW6 ...... 155 A2

Palace Pl SW1 132 C2
Palace Rd SE27, SW16, SW2 74 C2
Palace St SW1 132 C2
Palatine Ave N16 16 A4
Palatine Rd N16 16 A4
Palazzo Apartments 11 N1 16 A1
Palemead Cl SW6 47 C2
Palermo Rd NW10 21 C3
Palewell Common Dr SW14 55 C2
Palewell Pk SW14 55 C3
Palfrey Pl SW8 163 A2
Palgrave Gdns NW1 90 B2
Palgrave Ho
- 7 Camberwell SE5 48 B3
- 4 Maitland Pk NW3 12 B3
Palgrave Rd W12 38 B3
Palissy St E2 24 B2 98 C3
Pallant Ho SE1 137 C1
Pallester Ct NW11 1 A3
Palliser Ct W14 140 A1
Palliser Ho
- 3 Greenwich SE10 52 C4
- 21 Stepney E1 25 C1
Palliser Rd W14 140 A1
Pallister Terr SW15 68 B2
Pall Mall SW1 119 B1
Pall Mall E SW1 119 C2
Pall Mall Pl SW1 119 A1
Palm Ct
- 18 Camberwell SE15 49 B3
- Stoke Newington N16 6 C2
Palmer Ho
- 6 Deptford SE14 50 C3
- 8 Kentish Town NW5 13 B4
- 5 Tufnell Pk N19 4 B1
Palmer Pl N7 14 C3
Palmers Rd
- Globe Town E2 25 C3
- Mortlake SW14 55 B4
Palmer St SW1 133 B2
Palmerston Ct 22 E3 25 C3
Palmerston Ho
- Battersea SW11 169 C3
- Kensington W8 31 C1 113 B1
Palmerston Rd
- Acton Green W3 37 B3
- Brondesbury NW6 10 B1
- Hampstead NW6 10 C1
- Mortlake SW14 55 B3
Palmerston Way SW8 160 B1
Palm Gr W5 36 A3
Palm Tree Ho 2 SE14 50 C3
Pamela Ct NW10 8 C1
Pamela Ho 14 E8 24 B4
Pamlion Ct N4 5 A4
Panama Ho 6 E1 32 C4
Pancras La EC2 109 B1
Pancras Rd NW1 83 C2
Pandian Way 4 NW5 13 C2
Pandora Rd NW6 10 C2
Pangbourne NW1 92 C3
Pangbourne Ave W10 30 B4
Pangbourne Ho 4 N7 14 A3
Pankhurst Cl 7 SE14 50 C3
Pankhurst Ho 2 NW10 30 B3
Panmure Cl N5 15 A4
Pansy Gdns W12 29 C2
Panton St SW1 119 B3
Panyer Alley EC2 108 C2
Paper Mill Wharf E14 33 A2
Papworth Gdns N7 14 B3
Papworth Way SW2 74 C4
Parade Mans 19 SE5 48 B1
Parade Mews SE27, SW2 75 A2
Parade The SW11 159 A2
Paradise Pas N7 14 C3
Paradise Rd
- Richmond TW10 54 A2
- South Lambeth SW4 172 A2
Paradise Row E2 25 A2
Paradise St SE16 40 A4
Paradise Wlk SW3 159 A4
Paragon Cl E16 35 C3
Paragon Ho SE3 53 B1
Paragon Mews SE1 151 C4
Paragon Pl SE3 53 B1
Paragon Rd E9 17 B2
Paragon The
- Kidbrooke SE3 53 C1
- Walworth SE17 151 C4
Paramount Bldg EC1 96 A2
Paramount Ct WC1 93 A1
Parbury Rd SE23 66 A1
Pardoner St SE1 137 C2
Pardon St EC1 96 B2
Parfett St E1 111 C2
Parfitt Cl NW11 2 B3
Parfrey St W6 47 B4
Paris Gdn SE1 122 A2
Paris Ho 12 E2 25 A3
Park Ave
- Golders Green NW11 2 A3
- Mortlake SW14 55 C3
- Willesden NW2 9 B2
Park Ave N NW10 9 A3
Park Cl
- Kensington W14 127 A2
- Knightsbridge SW1 130 C3
- 13 South Hackney E9 25 B4
Park Cres W1 92 A1
Park Crescent Mews E W1 92 B1
Park Crescent Mews W W1 92 A1
Park Ct
- Battersea SW11 170 A4
- Clapham Pk SW4 61 C2
- Dulwich SE21 75 C1
- 12 Hammersmith W6 38 C2
- Upper Tooting SW12 72 C3
Park Dr Acton W3 36 C3
- Golders Green NW11 2 A3
- Mortlake SW14 55 C3
Park Dwellings 7 NW3 12 B3
Park End NW3 12 A4
Parker Ct
- Shoreditch N1 87 A4
- South Lambeth SW4 172 A3
Parke Rd SW13 46 C2
Parker Mews WC2 106 B2
Parkers Row SE16 139 B3
Parker's Row SE1 139 A3
Parker St WC2 106 B2
Parkfield Ave SW14 56 A3
Parkfield Ct SE14 51 B2
Parkfield Ind Est SW11 169 C2
Parkfield Rd
- New Cross SE14 51 B2
- Willesden NW10 9 A1
Parkfields SW15 57 B3
Parkfield St N1 85 C2
Park Flats N6 3 A4
Parkgate Gdns SW14 55 C2
Parkgate House Sch SW11 60 C3
Parkgate Mews N6 4 B4
Parkgate Rd SW11 158 B1
Park Hall SE10 52 C3
Park Hall Rd SE21 75 C1
Park Hall Road Trad Est SE21 75 C1
Parkham St SW11 168 A3
Park Heights Ct 21 E14 33 B3
Park Hill
- Clapham Pk SW4 61 C2
- Richmond TW10 54 B1
Park Hill Ct SW17 72 B1
Parkhill Rd NW3 12 B3
Park Hill Wlk 10 NW3 12 B3
Park Ho
- 8 Camberwell SE5 48 C2
- Finsbury Pk N4 6 A2
- 35 Hackney E9 17 B1
- Richmond TW10 54 A1
Parkholme Rd E8 16 C2
Parkhouse St SE5 48 C3
Parkhurst Ct N7 14 A4
Parkhurst Rd N7 14 A4
Parkinson Ct
- Finsbury N1 97 B3
- Shoreditch EC1 97 C4
Parkinson Ho 6 E9 17 B1
Park La
- Mayfair W1 117 B3
- Mill Meads E15 27 C4
Parkland Ct W14 126 A4
Parkland Gdns 12 SW19 69 C3
Parklands
- East Dulwich SE22 65 A2
- Highgate N6 4 A4
Parklands Cl SW14 55 B2
Park Lea Ct N16 7 A4
Park Lo
- 11 South Hampstead NW8 11 C1
- 10 Wapping E1 32 A1
- Willesden NW2 9 B4
Park Lofts 9 SW4 62 A2
Park Lorne NW8 90 B3
Park Mans
- Battersea SW11 168 C3
- Bedford Pk W6 38 B3
- Fulham SW6 164 B3
- Knightsbridge SW1 130 C3
- St John's Wood NW8 80 A1
- Vauxhall SW8 162 B4
Parkmead SW15 57 A1
Park Mews
- Greenwich SE10 43 B1
- Kensal Rise W10 23 A3
Park Par Acton W3 36 C3
- Dagenham NW10 21 B3
Park Pl
- Canary Wharf E14 33 C1
- Gunnersbury W3 36 C2
- Shoreditch N1 87 C4
- St James SW1 118 C2
Park Place Dr W3 36 C3
Park Place Ho 8 SE10 52 C4
Park Place Villas W2 101 A4
Park Rd
- Chiswick W4 45 C4
- Dagenham NW10 21 A4
- Lisson Gr NW1, NW8 90 B2
- Richmond TW10 54 B1
Park Rd E W3 37 B4
Park Rd N
- Chiswick W4 37 C1
- South Acton W3 37 A4
Park Road E 11 W3 37 A4
Park Row SE10 52 C4
PARK ROYAL 20 A2
Park Royal NW10 20 A4
Park Royal Bsns Ctr NW10 20 B1
Park Royal Metro Ctr NW10 20 A1
Park Royal Rd NW10, W3 20 B1
Park S SW11 169 B3
Park St James NW8 80 C3
Park Sheen 3 SW14 55 A3
Parkshot TW9 54 A3
Parkside
- East Acton W3 29 A1
- Greenwich SE3 53 B3
Park Side NW2 9 A4
Parkside Bsns Est SE8 51 A4
Parkside Cres N7 5 C1
Parkside Est E9 25 C4
Parkside (private) Hospl SW19 69 C1
Parkside St SW11 169 B3
Park Sq E NW1 92 B2
Park Square Mews NW1 92 A1
Park Sq W NW1 92 A1
Park St
- Borough The SE1 123 A2
- Mayfair W1 117 B3
Parkstead Rd SW15 57 A2
Parkstone Rd 5 SE15 49 C1
Park Stps W2 116 B4
Park The NW11 2 A3
Parkthorne Rd SW12 73 C4
Park Twrs W1 118 A1
Park View
- Dagenham W3 28 B4
- Highbury N5 15 B4
- Willesden NW2 9 B4
Parkview Ct SW6 164 B1
Park View Ct SW18 58 C1
Park View Ho SE24 63 A1
Park View Mans N4 6 A4
Park View Mews SW9 172 C2
Park View Rd NW10 8 B4
Park Village E NW1 82 B1
Park Village W NW1 82 A2
Parkville Rd SW6 154 C1
Park Vista SE10 52 C4
Park Walk Prim Sch SW10 157 B3
Parkway NW1 82 A3
Park Way W3 36 C2
Parkway Ho SW14 55 C3
Park West W2 102 B1
Park West Pl W1, W2 102 B2
Park Wlk
- Chelsea SW10 157 B4
- Highgate N6 3 C4
Parkwood NW8 80 C3
Parkwood Prim Sch N4 6 A2
Parliament Ct NW3 12 A4
Parliament Hill NW3 12 A4
Parliament Hill Mans NW5 12 C4
Parliament Hill Sch NW5 12 C4
Parliament Mews SW14 45 B1
Parliament Sq* SW1 134 A3
Parliament St SW1 134 A4
Parliament View Apartments SE11 148 C4
Parma Cres SW11 60 B3
Parminter Ind Est 24 E2 25 A3
Parmiter St E2 25 A3
Parmoor Ct EC1 96 C2
Parnell Cl W12 39 A3
Parnell Ho WC1 105 C2
Parnell Rd E3 26 B4
Parnham St E14 33 A3
Parolles Rd N19 4 B3
Parr Ct N1 87 B2
Parrington Ho 1 SW4 61 C1
Parr Pl W4 38 B2

Parr St N1 ... 87 B2
Parry Ho 32 E1 ... 32 A1
Parry Rd W10 ... 23 A2
Parry St SW8 ... 162 B4
Parsifal Coll NW3 ... 10 C4
Parsifal Ho NW3 ... 10 C4
Parsifal Rd NW6 ... 10 C3
Parsonage St E14 ... 42 B2
Parsons Gn SW6 ... 165 B3
PARSONS GREEN ... 165 B4
Parsons Green La SW6 ... 165 B4
Parsons Green Sta SW6 ... 165 B3
Parsons Ho
Paddington W2 ... 89 B1
21 Streatham SW12 ... 74 A4
Parsons Lo NW6 ... 11 A1
Parthenia Rd SW6 ... 165 C3
Partington Cl N19 ... 4 C3
Parton Lo 14 E8 ... 16 B2
Partridge Ct EC1 ... 96 A2
Partridge Ho 22 E3 ... 26 B3
Pascall Ho SE17 ... 48 B4
Pascal St SW8 ... 161 C2
Pascoe Rd SE13 ... 67 C2
Pasley Cl SE17 ... 150 C1
Passfield Dr E14 ... 34 A4
Passfields W14 ... 140 C1
Passing Alley EC1 ... 96 B1
Passmore St SW1 ... 145 B2
Pastor St SE1, SE11 ... 150 B4
Patcham Terr SW8 ... 170 B4
Patent Ho E14 ... 34 A4
Paternoster La EC4 ... 108 B2
Paternoster Row EC2, EC4 ... 108 C1
Paternoster Sq EC4 ... 108 B2
Pater St W8 ... 127 B1
Patience Rd SW11 ... 168 A1
Patience Villas SE13 ... 67 C4
Patio Cl SW4 ... 61 C1
Patmore Ho 9 N16 ... 16 A3
Patmore St SW8 ... 171 A4
Patmos Rd SW9 ... 48 A2
Paton Cl E3 ... 26 C2
Paton Ho SW9 ... 172 C2
Paton St EC1 ... 96 C3
Patrick Coman Ho EC1 ... 96 A3
Patrick Connolly Gdns 41 E3 ... 27 A2
Patriot Sq E2 ... 25 A3
Patrol Pl SE6 ... 67 A1
Pat Shaw Ho 2 E1 ... 25 C1
Patshull Pl NW5 ... 13 B2
Patshull Rd NW5 ... 13 B2
Patten Ho N4 ... 6 B3
Patten Rd SW18 ... 72 A4
Patterdale NW1 ... 92 B3
Patterdale Rd SE15 ... 50 B3
Pattina Wlk SE16 ... 33 A1
Pattinson Point 10 E16 ... 35 C4
Pattison Ho
Borough The SE1 ... 137 A4
1 Stepney E1 ... 32 C3
Pattison Rd NW2 ... 1 C1
Pat Williams Ho SE27 ... 75 B1
Paul Daisley Ct 2 NW6 ... 10 A1
Paulet Rd SE5 ... 48 A2
Paul Ho 13 W10 ... 23 A1
Pauline Ho E1 ... 111 C4
Paul Julius Cl E14 ... 34 C2
Paul St EC2 ... 24 A1 98 A2
Paultons Ho SW3 ... 157 C4
Paultons Sq SW3 ... 157 C4
Paultons St SW3 ... 157 C3
Pauntley Ho 6 N19 ... 4 B3
Pauntley St 4 N19 ... 4 B3
Pavan Ct 29 E2 ... 25 B2
Paveley Dr SW11 ... 158 A1
Paveley Ho N1 ... 84 C1
Paveley St NW8 ... 90 B2
Pavement The
Brentford W5 ... 36 A3
Clapham SW4 ... 61 B3
Pavilion Ct
7 Hampstead NW3 ... 11 B4
Hampstead NW3 ... 11 C3
3 Paddington NW6 ... 23 C2
Pavilion Mans 10 SW9 ... 62 B3
Pavilion Rd SW1 ... 131 A1
Pavilion Sq SW17 ... 72 B1
Pavilion St SW1 ... 131 A1
Pavilion Terr 8 W12 ... 30 B3
Pavillion Ct SW1 ... 160 A4
Pavitt Ct NW10 ... 8 C1
Paxton Cl TW9 ... 44 B1
Paxton Ho SE17 ... 151 A2
Paxton Rd W4 ... 46 A4
Paxton Terr SW1 ... 160 B4
Paymal Ho 33 E1 ... 32 B4
Payne Ho N1 ... 85 A3
Payne Rd E3 ... 27 A3
Paynesfield Ave SW14 ... 55 C4
Payne St SE8 ... 51 B4
Paynes Wlk W6 ... 154 A3
Peabody Ave SW1 ... 146 B1
Peabody Bldgs
6 Camberwell SE5 ... 48 C2
Walworth SE17 ... 151 B3
Peabody Cl SW1 ... 160 B4
Peabody Ct
9 Camberwell SE5 ... 48 C2
St Luke's EC1 ... 97 A1
Peabody Est
18 Bethnal Green E2 ... 25 A3
Borough The SE1 ... 122 C1
Fulham SW6 ... 155 A4
17 Hammersmith W6 ... 39 B1
Holborn EC1 ... 95 C1
Lambeth SE1 ... 121 C1
North Kensington W10 ... 30 B4
4 Ratcliff E1 ... 32 C2
St George in t East E1 ... 125 B4
Peabody Est *continued*
St Luke's EC1 ... 97 A1
Strand WC2 ... 106 C1
Streatham SE24 ... 75 B4
Westminster SW1 ... 147 A4
Peabody Hill SE21 ... 75 B3
Peabody Sq SE1 ... 136 A3
Peabody Twr EC1 ... 97 A1
Peabody Yd N1 ... 86 C4
Peach Rd W10 ... 23 A2
Peachum Rd SE3 ... 53 B4
Peach Walk Mews 24 E3 ... 25 C3
Peacock St SE17 ... 150 B3
Peacock Yd SE17 ... 150 B3
Peak Ho N4 ... 6 B3
Pearce Ho
Camden Town N19 ... 4 B1
7 Streatham SW2 ... 74 A4
Westminster SW1 ... 147 C3
Pear Cl SE14 ... 51 A3
Pear Ct 21 SE15 ... 49 B3
Peardon St SW8 ... 170 B1
Pearfield Ho 1 N5 ... 15 B3
Pearl St E1 ... 32 A1
Pearmain Ho 9 SE13 ... 52 B1
Pearman St SE1 ... 135 C3
Pear Pl SE1 ... 135 B4
Pearscroft Ct SW6 ... 166 B3
Pearscroft Rd SW6 ... 166 B3
Pearse St 3 SE15 ... 49 A4
Pearson Cl 4 SE5 ... 48 B2
Pearson Ho SW15 ... 47 B1
Pearson's Ave SE8, SE14 ... 51 C2
Pearson St E2 ... 24 B3
Peartree Ave SW17 ... 71 B1
Pear Tree Cl 23 E2 ... 24 B4
Pear Tree Ct
Holborn EC1 ... 95 C1
Putney SW15 ... 57 A3
Pear Tree Ho SE4 ... 66 B3
Peartree La E1 ... 32 B2
Peartree St EC1 ... 96 C2
Peartree Way SE10 ... 43 C2
Peary Pl E2 ... 25 B2
Peckarmans Wood SE21, SE26 ... 76 C1
Peckett Sq 3 N5 ... 15 A4
Peckford Pl SW9 ... 173 C1
PECKHAM ... 49 C2
Peckham Gr SE15 ... 49 A3
Peckham High St SE15 ... 49 C2
Peckham Hill St SE15 ... 49 C3
Peckham Park Prim Sch SE15 ... 49 C3
Peckham Park Rd SE15 ... 49 C3
Peckham Rd SE5 ... 49 A2
Peckham Rye
East Dulwich SE22 ... 64 C3
Peckham SE15, SE22 ... 65 A3
Peckham Rye Sta SE15 ... 49 C1
Peckwater Ho 2 NW5 ... 13 C2
Peckwater St NW5 ... 13 B3
Pedlars Wlk N7 ... 14 A3
Pedley St E1 ... 24 B1 99 A1
Pedro St E5 ... 17 C4
Pedworth Gdns 4 SE16 ... 40 B2
Peel Gr E2 ... 25 B3
Peel Pass W8 ... 31 C1 113 B1
Peel Prec NW6 ... 23 C3
Peel St W8 ... 31 C1 113 B1
Peerless St EC1 ... 97 B3
Pegasus Cl N16 ... 15 C4
Pegasus Ct
11 Acton W3 ... 28 B3
Brentford TW8 ... 36 B1
College Pk NW10 ... 22 A2
Pegasus Ho 9 E1 ... 25 C1
Pegwell Ho 10 E5 ... 17 A3
Pekin St E14 ... 33 C3
Pekoe SE1 ... 125 A1
Peldon Ct TW10 ... 54 B2
Pelham Cl SE5 ... 64 A4
Pelham Cres SW7 ... 144 A3
Pelham Ct SW3 ... 144 A3
Pelham Ho W14 ... 140 C3
Pelham Pl SW7 ... 144 A3
Pelham St SW7 ... 143 C4
Pelican Ho 8 SE8 ... 41 B2
Pelican Pas 3 E1 ... 25 B1
Pelier St SE17 ... 48 B4
Pella Ho SE11 ... 149 A2
Pellant Rd SW6 ... 154 B2
Pellatt Rd SE22 ... 64 B2
Pellerin Rd N16 ... 16 A3
Pellew Ho 15 E1 ... 25 A1
Pelling St E14 ... 33 C3
Pelter St E2 ... 24 B2 98 C4
Pelton Rd SE10 ... 43 A1
Pember Rd NW10 ... 22 C2
Pemberton Ct 18 E1 ... 25 C2
Pemberton Gdns N19 ... 4 B1
Pemberton Pl 2 E8 ... 17 A1
Pemberton Row EC4 ... 107 C2
Pemberton Terr N19 ... 4 B1
Pembridge Cres W11 ... 31 C2 113 B4
Pembridge Gdns W2 ... 31 C2 113 B3
Pembridge Hall Sch W2 ... 31 C2 113 C3
Pembridge Mews W11 ... 31 C2 113 B4
Pembridge Pl
Notting Hill W2 ... 31 C2 113 C4
1 Wandsworth SW15 ... 58 C2
Pembridge Rd W11 ... 31 C2 113 B3
Pembridge Sq W2 ... 31 C2 113 C3
Pembridge Villas W11 ... 31 C2 113 B4
Pembroke W14 ... 141 A3
Pembroke Ave N1 ... 84 B4
Pembroke Bldgs NW10 ... 21 C2
Pembroke Cl SW1 ... 131 C3
Pembroke Gdns W8 ... 141 A4
Pembroke Gdns Cl W8 ... 127 B1
Pembroke Ho
Acton W3 ... 37 B4
Chelsea SW1 ... 131 B1
5 Clapham Pk SW2 ... 62 A2
Kensington W2 ... 100 B1
Putney SW15 ... 56 C2
Pembroke Lo 2 SW16 ... 74 B1
Pembroke Mews
8 Bow E3 ... 26 A2
Kensington W8 ... 127 B1
Pembroke Pl W8 ... 127 B1
Pembroke Rd W8 ... 141 B4
Pembroke Sq W8 ... 127 B1
Pembroke St N1 ... 84 B4
Pembroke Studios W8 ... 127 A1
Pembroke Terr NW8 ... 79 B3
Pembroke Villas W8 ... 141 B4
Pembroke Wlk W8 ... 141 B4
Pembury Cl E5 ... 17 A3
Pembury Ho SE5 ... 49 A1
Pembury Pl 15 E5, E8 ... 17 A3
Pembury Rd E5 ... 17 A3
Pemell Cl 30 E1 ... 25 B1
Pemell Ho 31 E1 ... 25 B1
Penally Pl N1 ... 87 C4
Penang St E1 ... 32 A1
Penarth Ctr The SE15 ... 50 B4
Penarth St SE15 ... 50 B4
Pencombe Mews W11 ... 31 B2 113 A4
Pencraig Way SE15 ... 50 A4
Penda's Mead E9 ... 18 A4
Pendennis Ho 15 SE8 ... 41 A2
Penderyn Way N7 ... 13 C4
Pendle Ho 13 SE26 ... 76 C1
Pendley Ho 18 E2 ... 24 C4
Pendrell Ho WC2 ... 105 C1
Pendrell Rd SE4 ... 51 A1
Penelope Ho SW9 ... 173 B3
Penfield Lo 7 W9 ... 31 C4
Penfields Ho N7 ... 14 A2
Penfold Pl NW1 ... 102 A4
Penfold St NW8 ... 89 C1
Penford St SE5 ... 48 A1
Penhurst Mans SW6 ... 164 C4
Peninsula Ct E14 ... 42 A3
Peninsular Park Rd SE7 ... 43 C2
Penmayne Ho SE11 ... 149 C2
Pennack Rd SE15 ... 49 B4
Penn Almshouses 1 SE10 ... 52 B2
Pennant Mews W8 ... 142 A4
Pennard Mans 5 W12 ... 39 B4
Pennard Rd W12 ... 39 B4

Pennefather Ho N1 15 C2
Penner Cl SW19 70 A2
Pennethorne Cl E9 25 B4
Pennethorne Ho SW11 59 C4
Pennethorne Rd SE15 50 A3
Penn Ho NW8 90 A1
Pennine La NW2 1 A2
Pennine Mans NW2 1 A2
Pennine Par NW2 1 A2
Pennington Ct
4 Rotherhithe SE16 33 A1
St George in t East E1 125 C3
Pennington St E1 32 A2
Penn Rd N7 14 A4
Penn St N1 87 C3
Penny Ct SW10 157 A4
Pennyfields E14 33 C2
Pennyford Ct NW8 89 B2
Penny Mews SW12 73 A4
Pennymore Wlk W9 23 B1
Penny Rd NW10 20 A2
Penpoll Rd E8 17 A2
Penrhyn Cres SW14 55 B3
Penrith Cl SW15 58 A2
Penrith Pl SE27 75 A2
Penrose Gr SE17 150 C1
Penrose Ho SE17 150 C1
Penrose St SE17 150 C1
Penryn Ho SE11 150 A2
Penryn St NW1 83 B2
Penry St SE1 152 B3
Pensbury Pl SW8 171 A2
Pensbury St SW8 171 A2
Pensford Ave TW9 44 C1
Penshurst 2 NW5 12 C2
Penshurst Ho 1 SE15 50 B4
Penshurst Rd E9 17 C1
Pentland Cl NW11 1 A2
Pentland Gdns SW18 59 B1
Pentland Ho
17 Camden Town NW5 12 C2
7 Stamford Hill N16 7 B3
Pentland Rd 1 NW6 23 C2
Pentland St SW18 59 B1
Pentlow St SW15 57 B4
Pentney Rd SW12 73 B3
Penton Gr N1 85 B1
Penton Ho N1 85 B1
Penton Pl SE17 150 B2
Penton Rise WC1 95 A4
Penton St N1 85 B1
PENTONVILLE 85 A1
Pentonville Rd N1 84 C1
Pentridge St SE15 49 B3
Penwith Rd SW18 71 A2
Penwood Ho SW15 56 B1
Penywern Rd SW5 141 C2
Penzance Ho SE11 149 C2
Penzance Pl W11 31 A1 112 B2
Penzance St W11 31 A1 112 A2
Peony Gdns W12 29 C2
Peperfield WC1 94 C3
Pepler Ho 17 W10 23 A1
Pepler Mews SE1 152 C1
Peploe Rd NW6 22 C3
Peppermead Sq SE13 66 C2
Pepper St
Borough The SE1 136 C4
Millwall E14 42 A3
Peppie Cl N16 7 A2
Pepsi Trocadero* W1 119 B3
Pepys Cres 2 E16 35 C1
Pepys Ent Ctr 13 SE8 41 B2
Pepys Ho
14 Bethnal Green E2 25 B2
Clapham Pk SW4 61 C2
Pepys Rd SE14 50 C1
Pepys St EC3 124 B4
Perceval Ave NW3 12 A3
Percheron Ct 3 SW9 62 B4
Perch St E8 16 B4
Percival Rd SW14 55 B3
Percival St EC1 96 B3
Percy Cir WC1 95 A4
Percy Laurie Ho 6 SW15 57 C3
Percy Mews W1 105 B3
Percy Pas W1 105 B3
Percy Rd
Newham E16 35 A4
Shepherd's Bush W12 38 C4
Percy St W1 105 B3
Peregrine Ho
6 Battersea SW11 60 A4
Finsbury EC1 96 B4
Perham Rd W14 140 B1
Perifield SE21 75 B3
Perkins Ho 15 E14 33 B4
Perkins Rents SW1 133 B1
Perkins Sq SE1 123 A2
Perley Ho 9 E3 33 B4
Perotti Ho SW6 59 A4
Perran Rd SE24, SW2 75 A2
Perren St NW5 13 A2
Perrers Rd W6 39 A2
Perring Est E3 33 C4
Perrin's Ct 20 NW3 11 B4
Perrin's La NW3 11 B4
Perrin's Wlk NW3 11 B4
Perronet Ho SE1 136 B1
Perry Ave W3 28 C3
Perry Ct 6 E14 41 C1
Perry Ho 24 SW2 74 A4
Perrymead St SW6 166 A3
Perryn Ho W3 29 A2
Perryn Rd
Acton W3 28 C2
1 Bermondsey SE16 40 A3
Perry's Pl W1 105 B2
Perrywood Ho 17 E5 17 A3
Perseverance Works E2 24 A2 98 B4
Perth Ct 5 SE5 63 C3
Perth Ho N1 14 B1
Perth Rd N4 5 C3
Petchey Acad The E8 16 B3
Peter Ave NW10 9 A1
Peter Best Ho 1 E1 32 A3
Peterboat Cl SE10 43 A2
Peterborough Ct EC4 107 C1
Peterborough Mews SW6 165 B2
Peterborough Prim Sch SW6 165 C1
Peterborough Rd SW6 58 C4
Peterborough Villas SW6 166 A4
Peter Butler Ho SE1 139 B3
Peterchurch Ho SE15 50 A4
Petergate SW11 59 B3
Peter Heathfield Ho 4 E15 27 C4
Peter Hills Ho SE16 153 B4
Peter Hills with St Mary's & St Paul's CE Prim Sch SE16 32 C1
Peter Ho SW8 162 A2
Peter James Ent Ctr NW10 20 B2
Peterley Bsns Ctr 21 E2 25 A3
Peters Ct W2 100 B2
Peter's Ct SW4 62 A1
Petersfield Rd W3 37 B4
Petersfield Rise SW15 69 A3
Petersham Ho SW7 143 B4
Petersham La SW7 128 C2
Petersham Mews SW7 129 A1
Petersham Pl SW7 129 A2
Peter's La EC1 108 B4
Peter St W1 119 B4
Peterstow Cl SW19 70 A2
Petherton Ct NW10 22 C4
Petherton Ho N4 6 B3
Petherton Rd N5 15 B3
Petiver Cl 26 E9 17 B1
Petley Rd W6 47 C3
Peto Pl NW1 92 B2
Peto St N E16 35 B3
Petrel Ct 8 SE21 75 C2
Petrie Cl NW2 10 A2
Petrie Mus of Egyptian Archaeology* WC1 93 B1
Petros Gdns 1 NW3 11 B2
Petticoat Lane Mkt* EC2 110 C3
Petticoat Sq E1 110 C2
Petticoat Twr E1 110 C2
Pettiward Cl SW15 57 B3
Petty France SW1 133 B2
Petty Wales EC3 124 B3
Petworth Ho 16 SE22 64 A4
Petworth St SW11 168 B4
Petyt Pl SW3 158 A3
Petyward SW3 144 B3
Pevensey Ct
4 South Acton W3 37 A4
West Norwood SW16 74 C1
Pevensey Ho 5 E1 33 A4
Peveril Ho SE1 137 C1
Pewsham Ho N4 6 B3
Peyton Pl SE10 52 B3
Pharamond NW2 9 C2
Phelps Ho SW15 57 C4
Phelp St SE17 48 C4
Phene St SW3 158 B4
Philadelphia Ct SW10 157 A1
Philbeach Gdns SW5 141 B2
Phil Brown Pl 3 SW8 61 A4
Philchurch Pl E1 111 C1
Philia Ho 4 NW1 13 B1
Philip Blairman Ho E1 24 B1 98 C1
Philip Ct W2 101 B4
Philip Ho NW6 78 A3
Philip Turner Est 28 E9 17 B1
Philip Wlk SE15 64 C4
Phillimore Ct W8 127 C3
Phillimore Gardens Cl W8 127 B2
Phillimore Gdns
Kensington W8 127 B3
Willesden NW10 22 B4
Phillimore Pl W8 127 B3
Phillimore Terr W8 127 C2
Phillimore Wlk W8 127 C2
Phillip Ho E1 111 A3
Phillipp St N1 24 A4
Philpot La EC3 124 A4
Philpot Sq SW6 59 A4
Philpot St E1 32 A3
Philson Mans 13 E1 32 A3
Phipps Ho 16 W12 30 A2
Phipp St EC2 24 A1 98 A2
Phoebeth Rd SE4 66 C2
Phoenix Bsns Ctr 22 E3 33 C4
Phoenix Cl 18 E8 24 B4
Phoenix Ct
4 Brentford TW8 36 A1
2 Deptford SE14 51 A4
Millwall E14 41 C2
Phoenix High Sch W12 29 C2
Phoenix Ho SW1 145 B4
Phoenix Lodge Mans 1 W6 39 B2
Phoenix Pl WC1 95 A2
Phoenix Rd NW1 93 B4
Phoenix Sch E3 26 B2
Phoenix Sch The NW3 11 B2
Phoenix St WC2 105 C1
Phoenix Wharf Rd SE1 139 A3
Phyllis Hodges Ho NW1 83 B1
Physic Pl SW3 158 C4
Piccadilly W1 118 C2
Piccadilly Arc SW1 118 C2
Piccadilly Cir* W1 119 B3
Piccadilly Circus Sta SW1 119 B3
Piccadilly Ct 5 N7 14 B2
Piccadilly Pl W1 119 A3
Pickard St EC1 96 B4
Pickering Cl E9 17 C1
Pickering Ho
Kensington W2 100 B1
Stoke Newington N4 6 C4
Pickering Mews W2 100 B2
Pickering Pl SW1 119 A1
Pickering St N1 86 B4
Pickets St SW12 73 A4
Pickfords Wharf N1 86 C1
Pickwick Ho
Bermondsey SE16 139 B3
3 Shepherd's Bush W11 30 C1
Pickwick Rd SE21 76 A4
Pickwick St SE1 136 C3
Pickworth Cl SW8 162 B1
Picton Ho 1 SW4 74 A4
Picton Pl W1 103 C1
Picton St SE5 48 C3
Picture Ho 6 SW16 74 A2
Pied Bull Ct WC1 106 B3
Pied Bull Yd WC1 106 B3
Pier Head E1 32 A1
Pierhead Wharf 37 E1 32 A1
Pier Ho SW3 158 B3
Piermont Rd SE22 65 A2
Pierpoint Bldg 4 E14 41 C4
Pierrepoint Rd W3 28 A2
Pierrepoint Row N1 86 A2
Pier St E14 42 B2
Pier Terr SW18 59 B3
Piggott Ho 2 E2 25 C3
Pigott St E14 33 C3
Pilgrimage St SE1 137 B3
Pilgrim Ho SE1 137 C1
Pilgrims Cloisters 10 SE5 49 A3
Pilgrims Ct SE3 53 C2
Pilgrim's La NW3 11 C4
Pilgrims Mews 12 E14 34 C2
Pilgrim's Pl 6 NW3 11 C4
Pilgrim St EC4 108 A1
Pilgrims Way N19 4 C3
Pilgrims Way Prim Sch SE15 50 B4
Pilkington Rd 4 SE15 50 A1

Pilot Ind Ctr NW10 . . . . 21 A1
Pilsden Cl SW19 . . . . 69 C3
Pilton Pl SE17 . . . . 151 A2
Pimilico Sta SW1 . 147 B2
PIMLICO 146 C1
Pimlico Rd SW1 . . 145 C2
Pimlico Sch SW1 147 A1
Pimlico Wlk N1 . . . . 24 A2 98 A4
Pinchin St E1 . . . . 125 C4
Pincombe Ho SE17 . . . . 151 B2
Pincott Pl SE4 . . . . 65 C4
Pindar St EC2 . . . . 110 A4
Pindock Mews W9 88 B1
Pine Apple Ct SW1 . . . . 132 C2
Pine Ave E15 . . . . 19 C3
Pine Cl 11 N19 . . . . 4 B2
Pinedene 2 SE15 . . 50 A2
Pinefield Cl E14 . . . . 33 C2
Pine Gr N4, N19 . . . . 5 B2
Pine Ho Bow E3 . . . . 26 A4
21 Rotherhithe SE16 . . . . 40 B4
Pinehurst Ct 6 W11 . . . . 31 B3
Pinelands Cl 7 SE3 . . . . 53 B3
Pine Lo SW15 . . . . 58 A1
Pine Rd NW2 . . . . 9 C4
Pines Ct 14 SW19 . . . 69 C3
Pine St EC1 . . . . 95 B2
Pine Tree Ho SE14 . . . . 50 C3
Pinewood Ct SW4 . . 61 C1
Pinkham Mans W4 . . . . 36 C1
Pinnace Ho E14 . . . . 42 B3
Pinnacle Ho EC3 . 124 A3
Pinnacle The 7 N1 . . . . 15 C2
Pinner Ct NW8 . . . . 89 B2
Pinner Ho 30 SE5 . . . 48 B1
Pintail Ct 39 SE8 . . . 51 B4
Pinter Ho SW9 . . . . 172 B1
Pioneer Cl W12 . . . . 30 A3
Pioneer St SE15 . . . . 49 C2
Pioneer Way W12 . . 30 B3
Piper Cl N7 . . . . 14 B3
Pipers Ho SE10 . . . . 42 C1
Pippin Ho 17 W10 . . 30 C2
Pirbright Rd SW18 . . . . 70 C3
Pitcairn Ho 1 E9 . . . 17 B1
Pitfield Ho N5 . . . . 15 B3
Pitfield St N1 . . . . 24 A3
Pitman Ho 4 SE8 . . 51 C2
Pitman St SE5 . . . . 48 B3
Pitmaston Ho 2 SE13 . . . . 52 B1
Pitsea Pl E1 . . . . 32 C3
Pitsea St E1 . . . . 32 C3
Pitt Ho 4 SW11 . . . . 59 C3
Pitt's Head Mews W1 . . . . 117 C1
Pitt St W8 . . . . 127 C4
Pixley St E14 . . . . 33 B3
Planetree Ct W6 . . . 39 C2
Plane Tree Ho SE8 . . . . 51 A4
Plantain Pl SE1 . . . 137 B4
Plantation La EC3 124 A4
Plantation The SE3 . . . . 53 C1
Platehouse The 3 E14 . . . . 42 A1
Platina St EC2 . . . . 97 C2
Plato Pl SW6 . . . . 165 A2
Plato Rd SW2 . . . . 62 A3
Platt's La NW3 . . . . 1 C1
Platt St NW1 . . . . 83 B2
Plaxdale Ho SE17 152 A3
Playfair St W6 . . . . 39 B1
Playfield Cres SE22 . . . . 64 B2
Playford Rd Finsbury Pk N4 . . . . 5 B2
Finsbury Pk N4 . . . . 5 C2
Playhouse Yd EC4 . . . . 108 A1
Plaza Sh Ctr W1 . . 105 A2
Pleasance Rd SW15 . . . . 57 A2
Pleasance The SW15 . . . . 57 A3
Pleasant Pl N1 . . . . 15 A1
Pleasant Row NW1 . . . . 82 B3
Plender Ct NW1 . . . 83 A3
Plender St NW1 . . . 83 A3
Pleshey Rd N7 . . . . 13 C4
Plevna St E14 . . . . 42 B3
Pleydell Ave W6 . . . . 38 B2
Pleydell Ct EC4 . . . 107 C1
Pleydell St EC4 . . . 107 C1
Plimsoll Cl E14 . . . . 34 A3
Plimsoll Rd N4 . . . . 6 A1
Plough Ct EC3 . . . . 123 C4
Plough La SE22 . . . . 64 B1
Ploughmans Cl NW1 . . . . 83 B4
Plough Mews 19 SW11 . . . . 59 C3
Plough Pl EC4 . . . . 107 C2
Plough Rd SW11 . . . 59 C3
Plough St E1 . . . . 111 B2
Plough Terr SW11 . . 59 C3
Plough Way SE16 . . . 41 A2
Plough Yd EC2 . . . . 24 A1 98 B1
Plover Ho SW9 . . . . 163 B2
Plover Way SE16 . . . 41 A3
Plowman Ho SW19 . . . . 69 C2
Plumbers Row E1 . . . . 111 C2
Plumbridge St 7 SE10 . . . . 52 B2
Plume Ho SE10 . . . . 52 A4
Plummer Ct SE13 . . . 67 A1
Plummer Rd SW4 . . 73 C4
Plumtree Ct EC4 . 108 A2
Plymouth Ho 20 SE10 . . . . 52 A2
Plymouth Rd E16 . . . 35 C4
Plymouth Wharf E14 . . . . 42 C2
Plympton Ave NW6 . . . . 10 B1
Plympton Pl NW1 . 90 A1
Plympton Rd NW6 . . 10 B1
Plympton St NW8 . 90 A1
Pocklington Ct SW15 . . . . 68 C3
Pocklington Lo 6 W12 . . . . 38 C3
Pocock St SE1 . . . 136 B4
Podmore Rd SW18 . . . . 59 B3
Poets Cnr★ SW1 . 134 A2
Poet's Rd N5 . . . . 15 C3
Point Cl SE10 . . . . 52 B2
Pointer Sch The SE3 . . . . 53 C3
Pointers Cl E14 . . . . 42 A1
Point Hill SE10 . . . . 52 B2
Point Ho SE10 . . . . 52 B2
Point Pleasant SW18 . . . . 58 C3
Point Wharf La TW8 . . . . 44 A3
Poland Ho 3 E15 . . 27 C4
Poland St W1 . . . . 105 A1
Polesworth Ho 16 W2 . . . . 31 C4
Polish Inst & Sikorski Mus★ SW7 . . . . 129 C3
Polish Univ Abroad W6 . . . . 38 C2
Pollard Cl Islington N7 . . . . 14 B4
Newham E16 . . . . 35 C2
Pollard Ho N1 . . . . 84 C1
Pollard Row E2 . . . . 24 C2 99 C4
Pollard St E2 . . . . 24 C2 99 C4
Pollen St W1 . . . . 104 B1
Pollitt Dr NW8 . . . . 89 C2
Pollock Ho W10 . . . . 23 A1
Polperro Mans 3 NW6 . . . . 10 C3
Polperro Mews SE11 . . . . 150 A4
Polygon Rd NW1 . . 83 B1
Polygon The 1 Clapham SW4 . . . . 61 B3
St John's Wood NW8 . . . . 79 C4
Pomell Way E1 . . . 111 A2
Pomeroy Ct W11 . . . 31 A3
Pomeroy Ho 5 E2 . . . . 25 C3
Pomeroy St SE14 . . . 50 B2
Pomfret Rd SE5 . . . . 63 A4
Pomoja La N19 . . . . 5 A2
Pomona Ho 10 SE8 . . . . 41 A2
Pond Cl SE3 . . . . 53 C1
Pond Cotts SE21 . . . 76 A3
Ponder St 5 N7 . . . 14 B1
Pondfield Ho 4 N5 . . . . 15 B3
Pond Ho SW3 . . . . 144 A3
Pond Mead SE21 . . . 63 C1
Pond Pl SW3 . . . . 144 A3
Pond Rd SE3 . . . . 53 B1
Pond Sq N6 . . . . 3 C3
Pond St NW3 . . . . 12 A3
Ponler St E1 . . . . 32 A3
Ponsard Rd NW10 . . 22 A2
Ponsford St E9 . . . . 17 B2
Ponsonby Ho 13 E2 . . . . 25 B3
Ponsonby Pl SW1 147 C2
Ponsonby Rd SW15 . . . . 69 A4
Ponsonby Terr SW1 . . . . 147 C2
Ponton Ho SW2 . . . . 74 C3
Ponton Rd SW8 . . 161 C3
Pont St Mews SW1 . . . . 130 C1
Pont St SW1 . . . . 131 A1
Pontypool Pl SE1 136 A4
Poole Ct N1 . . . . 16 A1
Poole Ho SE11 . . . 135 A1
Poole Rd E9 . . . . 17 C2
Pooles Bldgs EC1 . 95 B1
Pooles La SW10 . . 156 C1
Pooles Park Prim Sch N4 . . . . 5 B2
Pooles Pk N4 . . . . 5 C2
Poole St N1 . . . . 87 B3
Pooley Ho E1 . . . . 25 C2
Pool Ho NW8 . . . . 101 C4
Poolmans St SE16 . . 40 C4
Poonah St E1 . . . . 32 B3
Pope Ho 7 Bermondsey SE16 . . . . 40 A2
3 Camberwell SE5 . . 48 C3
Pope John RC Prim Sch W12 . . . . 30 A2
Pope's Head Alley EC3 . . . . 109 C1
Pope's La W5 . . . . 36 A3
Pope's Rd SW9 . . . . 62 C4
Pope St SE1 . . . . 138 B3
Popham Ct N16 . . . . 7 A1
Popham Gdns TW9 . . . . 55 A4
Popham Rd N1 . . . . 86 C4
Popham St Islington N1 . . . . 86 B4
Shoreditch N1 . . . . 86 C4
POPLAR 33 C3
Poplar Bath St 11 E14 . . . . 34 A2
Poplar Bsns Pk E14 . . . . 34 B2
Poplar Cl E9 . . . . 18 B3
Poplar Ct 4 SW16 . 74 B1
Poplar Gr W6 . . . . 39 B4
Poplar High St E14 . . . . 34 A2
Poplar Ho Brockley SE4 . . . . 66 B3
19 Rotherhithe SE16 . . . . 40 C4
Poplar Mews 4 W12 . . . . 30 B1
Poplar Pl W2 . . . . 114 B4
Poplar Rd SE24 . . . . 63 B3
Poplar Sta E14 . . . . 34 A2
Poplars The NW5 . . . 13 B3
Poplar Wlk SE24 . . . 63 B3
Poppins Ct EC4 . . . 108 A1
Porchester Ct W2 . . . . 100 B1
Porchester Gate W2 . . . . 114 C3
Porchester Gdn Mews W2 . . . . 100 B1
Porchester Gdns W2 . . . . 114 B4
Porchester Ho 3 E1 . . . . 32 A3
Porchester Mews W2 . . . . 100 B2
Porchester Pl W2 . . . . 102 B1
Porchester Rd W2 . . . . 100 B2
Porchester Sq W2 . . . . 100 B2
Porchester Terr W2 . . . . 114 C4
Porchester Terr N W2 . . . . 100 B2
Porden Rd SW2 . . . . 62 B3
Porland Ct SE1 . . . 137 B2
Porlock Ho 5 SE26 . . . . 76 C1
Porlock St SE1 . . . 137 C4
Porson Ct SE13 . . . . 67 A4
Portal Cl SE27 . . . . 74 C1
Portal Way W3 . . . . 28 C4
Portbury Cl 17 SE15 . . . . 49 C2
Portchester Cl SE24 . . . . 63 C3
Portelet Ct 1 N1 . . . 24 A4
Portelet Rd E1 . . . . 25 C2
Porten Hos W14 . . 126 A1
Porten Rd W14 . . . 126 A1
Porter Sq N19 . . . . 5 A3
Porter St Borough The SE1 . . 123 A2
Marylebone W1 . . . 103 A4
Porteus Rd W2 . . . 101 A4
Portfleet Pl 34 N1 . . 24 A4
Portgate Cl W9 . . . . 23 B1
Port Ho 6 SW11 . . . 59 B4
Port House The 6 E14 . . . . 42 A1
Portia Way E3 . . . . 26 B1
Porticos The SW3 . . . . 157 B3
Portinscale Rd SW15 . . . . 58 B2
Portishead Ho 29 W2 . . . . 31 C4
Portland Ave N16 . . . 7 B4
Portland Ct 7 De Beauvoir Town N1 . . . . 16 A1
1 Deptford SE14 . . . 51 A4
Portland Gr SW8 . 172 C4
Portland Ho 19 SW2 . . . . 74 C3
Portland Hospl for Women & Children The W1 . . . . 92 B1
Portland Mews W1 . . . . 105 A1
Portland Pl W1 . . 104 B3
Portland Place Sch W1 . . . . 104 B3
Portland Place Schs W1 . . . . 104 B4
Portland Rd Notting Hill W11 . . . . 31 A1 112 B2
Notting Hill W11 . . . . 31 A2 112 A3
Portland Rise N4 . . . . 6 B3
Portland Sq 4 E1 . . 32 A1
Portland St SE17 . 151 B1
Portland Village W6 . . . . 39 B3
Portman Ave SW14 . . . . 55 C4
Portman Cl W1 . . 103 B2
Portman Gate NW1 . . . . 90 B1
Portman Hts 1 NW3 . . . . 1 C1
Portman Mews S W1 . . . . 103 B1
Portman Pl E2 . . . . 25 B2
Portman Sq W1 . . 103 B2
Portman St W1 . . 103 B1
Portman The NW11 . . 1 C4
Portman Twrs W1 . . . . 103 A2
Portnall Rd W9 . . . . 23 B2
Portobello Ct Est W11 . . . . 31 B3

Portobello Mews W11 ... 31 C2 113 B3
Portobello Rd W11 ... 31 B2 113 A4
Portobello Road Mkt★ W10 ... 31 A4
Portpool La EC1 ... 107 B4
Portree St E14 ... 34 C3
Port Royal Pl [3] N16 ... 16 A3
Portsea Hall W2 ... 102 B1
Portsea Ho [3] SW15 ... 69 A3
Portsea Mews W2 ... 102 B1
Portsea Pl W2 ... 102 B1
Portslade Rd SW8 ... 170 C2
Portsmouth Rd SW15 ... 69 B4
Portsmouth St WC2 ... 107 A1
Portsoken St E1, EC3 ... 124 C4
Portswood Pl SW15 ... 56 B1
Portugal St WC2 ... 107 A1
Poseidon Ct [9] E14 ... 41 C2
Postern The EC2 ... 109 A3
Post Office Way SW8 ... 161 B2
Potier St SE1 ... 137 C1
Potterne Cl [5] SW19 ... 69 C4
Potters Cl [5] SE15 ... 49 A3
Potters Fields SE1 ... 124 B1
Potters Lo E14 ... 42 B1
Potters Rd SW6 ... 166 C1
Pottery La W11 ... 31 A1 112 B2
Pottery Rd TW8 ... 44 A4
Pottery St SE16 ... 40 A4
Pott St E2 ... 25 A2
Poullett Ho SW2 ... 75 A3
Poulton Cl E8 ... 17 A2
Poultry EC2 ... 109 B1
Pound La NW10 ... 8 C2
Pountney Rd SW11 ... 60 C4
Povey Ho
Tulse Hill SW2 ... 62 C1
Walworth SE17 ... 152 A3
Powell's Wlk W4 ... 46 B4
Powergate Bsns Pk NW10 ... 20 C2
Power Ho [13] TW9 ... 44 C2
Power Ho The W4 ... 38 B2
Power Rd W4 ... 36 C2
Powerscroft Rd E5 ... 17 B4
Powis Gdns
Golders Green NW11 ... 1 B4
Notting Hill W11 ... 31 B3
Powis Ho WC2 ... 106 B2
Powis Mews W11 ... 31 B3
Powis Pl WC1 ... 94 B1
Powis Rd E3 ... 27 A2
Powis Sq W11 ... 31 B3
Powis Terr W11 ... 31 B3
Powlesland Ct [21] E14 ... 33 A3
Powlett Ho NW1 ... 13 A2
Powlett Pl NW1 ... 13 A1
Pownall Rd E8 ... 24 C4
Powrie Ho SW11 ... 167 C2
Poynder Ct [3] N7 ... 14 A3
Poynders Ct [9] SW4 ... 61 B1
Poynders Gdns SW12 ... 73 B4
Poynders Rd SW12, SW4 ... 73 C4
Poynings Rd N19 ... 4 B1
Poynter Ho
Paddington NW8 ... 89 B2
[10] Shepherd's Bush W11 ... 30 C1
Poyntz Rd SW11 ... 168 C1
Poyser St E2 ... 25 A3
Praed Mews W2 ... 101 C2
Praed St W2 ... 101 C2
Prague Pl SW2 ... 62 A2
Prah Rd N4 ... 5 C2
Prairie St SW8 ... 170 A1
Pratt Mews NW1 ... 82 C3
Pratt St NW1 ... 82 C4
Pratt Wlk SE1, SE11 ... 149 A4
Preachers Ct EC1 ... 96 B1
Prebend Gdns W4, W6 ... 38 B2
Prebend Mans [4] W4 ... 38 B2
Prebend St N1 ... 86 C4
Precinct The
Islington N1 ... 86 C3
Islington N5 ... 15 A3
Premier Corner NW6 ... 23 B3
Premier Ho [25] N1 ... 15 A1
Premier League Hall of Fame★ SE1 ... 134 C4
Premier Park Rd NW10 ... 20 A3
Premier Pk NW10 ... 20 A3
Premier Pl [17] E14 ... 33 C2
Prendergast Ho [7] SW4 ... 73 C4
Prendergast Sch SE4 ... 66 C3
Prescot St E1 ... 125 A4
Prescott Ho [13] SE17 ... 48 A4
Prescott Pl SW4 ... 61 C3
Presentation Mews SW2 ... 74 B3
President Dr E1 ... 32 A1
President Ho EC1 ... 96 B3
President St EC1 ... 96 C4
Prestage Way [13] E14 ... 34 B2
Prested Rd SW11 ... 60 A3
Preston Cl SE1 ... 152 A4
Preston Gdns NW10 ... 8 A2
Preston Ho
Bermondsey SE1 ... 138 C2
Walworth SE1 ... 152 A4
Preston Pl
Richmond TW10 ... 54 A2
Willesden NW2 ... 8 C2
Preston's Rd E14 ... 34 B1
Prestwich Terr SW4 ... 61 C2
Prestwood Ho [3] SE16 ... 40 A3
Prestwood St N1 ... 87 A1
Priam Ho [17] E2 ... 25 A3
Price Cl SW17 ... 72 B1
Price Ho N1 ... 86 C3
Prices Ct SW11 ... 59 C4
Price's St SE1 ... 122 B2
Price's Yd N1 ... 85 A3
Prichard Ct
Battersea SW11 ... 167 C3
Islington N7 ... 14 B3
Prideaux Ho WC1 ... 95 A4
Prideaux Pl
Acton W3 ... 28 C2
St Pancras WC1 ... 95 A4
Prideaux Rd SW9 ... 62 A4
Pride Ct N1 ... 85 C2
Priestley Cl N16 ... 7 B4
Priestley Ho
[2] Camden Town NW5 ... 13 A2
St Luke's EC1 ... 97 A2
Priestman Point [25] E3 ... 27 A2
Priests Bridge SW14 ... 56 A4
Priest's Ct EC2 ... 108 C2
Prima Rd SW9 ... 163 B2
Primrose Cl [6] E3 ... 26 C3
Primrose Ct
[2] Child's Hill NW2 ... 1 B1
Primrose Hill NW8 ... 80 C3
[11] Streatham SW12 ... 73 C4
Primrose Gdns NW3 ... 12 A2
PRIMROSE HILL ... 12 B1
Primrose Hill EC4 ... 107 C1
Primrose Hill Ct NW3 ... 12 B1
Primrose Hill Rd
Primrose Hill NW1, NW3 ... 12 B1
Primrose Hill NW1, NW3 ... 80 C4
Primrose Hill Sch NW1 ... 81 C4
Primrose Hill Studios NW1 ... 81 B4
Primrose Ho
[7] Peckham SE15 ... 49 C2
[1] Richmond TW9 ... 44 B2
Primrose Mans SW11 ... 169 B4
Primrose Mews [9] NW1 ... 12 B1
Primrose Sq E9 ... 25 B4
Primrose St EC2 ... 110 B4
Primrose Wlk [6] SE14 ... 51 A3
Primula St W12 ... 29 C3
Prince Albert Ct NW8 ... 80 C3
Prince Albert Rd NW8 ... 80 C3
Prince Arthur Ct [18] NW3 ... 11 B4
Prince Arthur Mews [17] NW3 ... 11 B4
Prince Arthur Rd NW3 ... 11 B3
Prince Charles Rd SE3 ... 53 B2
Prince Consort Ho SE1 ... 148 B2
Prince Consort Rd SW7 ... 129 B2
Princedale Rd W11 ... 31 A1 112 B2
Prince Edward Mans W2 ... 31 C2 113 C4
Prince Edward Rd E9 ... 18 B2
Prince George Rd N16 ... 16 A4
Princelet St E1 ... 111 A4
Prince of Orange La [3] SE10 ... 52 B3
Prince of Wales Dr SW11 ... 169 B4
Prince of Wales Mans
Battersea SW11 ... 169 C4
Clapham SW4 ... 61 A2
Prince of Wales Pas NW1 ... 92 C3
Prince of Wales Rd
Blackheath Vale SE3 ... 53 B2
Camden Town NW5 ... 12 C2
Prince of Wales Terr
Chiswick W4 ... 38 A1
Kensington W8 ... 128 B3
Prince Regent Ct [2] SE16 ... 33 A1
Prince Regent Mews NW1 ... 92 C3
Princes Arc SW1 ... 119 A2
Princes Ave W3 ... 36 C3
Princes Cir WC2 ... 106 A2
Princes Cl N4 ... 6 A3
Princes Coll WC1 ... 106 A2
Princes Court Bsns Ctr [14] E1 ... 32 A2
Princes Ct
Brondesbury NW2 ... 10 A3
Hampstead NW3 ... 11 C4
Stepney E1 ... 32 A2
Prince's Ct SE16 ... 41 B3
Princes Gate SW7 ... 129 C3
Prince's Gate SW7 ... 130 A3
Princes Gate Ct SW7 ... 129 C3
Princes Gate Mews SW7 ... 129 C2
Princes Gdns SW7 ... 129 C2
Princes Ho W11 ... 31 C2 113 B3
Prince's Mews
[1] Hammersmith W6 ... 39 A1
Kensington W2 ... 114 A4
Princes Pl
Notting Hill W11 ... 31 A1 112 A2
St James SW1 ... 119 A2
Princes Rd
Kew TW9 ... 44 B2
Richmond TW10 ... 54 B2
Prince's Rd SW14 ... 55 C4
Princes Rise SE13 ... 52 B1
Princes Riverside Rd [7] SE16 ... 32 C1
Princess Alexandra School of Nursing The E1 ... 32 A4
Princess Alice Ho [1] W10 ... 22 B1
Princess Beatrice Ho SW10 ... 142 A1
Princess Cres N4 ... 6 A2
Princess Ct
Hampstead NW6 ... 11 A1
Kensington W2 ... 114 B4
Princess Ct *continued*
Marylebone W1 ... 102 C3
Princess Frederica CE Prim Sch NW10 ... 22 B3
Princess Grace Hospl The W1 ... 91 B1
Princess Louise Cl W2 ... 101 C4
Princess Louise Hospl W10 ... 30 B4
Princess Mary Ho SW1 ... 147 C3
Princess May Prim Sch N16 ... 16 B4
Princess May Rd N16 ... 16 A4
Princess Mews NW3 ... 11 C2
Prince's Sq W2 ... 114 A4
Princess Rd
Camden Town NW1 ... 81 C4
Paddington NW6 ... 23 C3
Princess St SE1 ... 136 B1
Princes St W1 ... 104 B1
Prince's St
City of London EC2 ... 109 B1
Richmond TW10, TW9 ... 54 A2
Prince St SE8 ... 51 B4
Princes Way
Acton W3 ... 36 C3
Putney SW15, SW19 ... 70 A3
Princes Yd W11 ... 31 A1 112 B1
Princethorpe Ho W2 ... 100 A4
Princeton Ct SW15 ... 57 C4
Princeton Mans WC1 ... 106 C3
Princeton St WC1 ... 106 C4
Principal Sq E9 ... 17 C3
Printers Mews E3 ... 26 A4
Printer St EC4 ... 107 C2
Printing House Yd E2 ... 24 A2 98 B3
Printon Ho [16] E3 ... 33 B4
Print Village Ind Est SE15 ... 49 B1
Prior Bolton St N1 ... 15 A2
Prioress Ho [2] E3 ... 27 A2
Prioress Rd SE27 ... 75 A1
Prioress St SE1 ... 137 C1
Priors Lo [4] TW10 ... 54 A1
Prior St SE10 ... 52 B3
Prior Weston Prim Sch
Broadgate EC1 ... 97 B2
St Luke's EC1 ... 97 A1
Priory Ave W4 ... 38 A3
Priory Ct
City of London EC4 ... 108 B1
Homerton E9 ... 17 C3
Nunhead SE15 ... 65 B3
Roehampton SW15 ... 56 B3
South Lambeth SW8 ... 171 C4
Priory Gdns
Barnes SW13 ... 56 B4
[6] Chiswick W4 ... 38 A2

Priory Gn N1 84 C2
Priory Gr SW8 172 A3
Priory Ho
Clerkenwell EC1 96 A2
Pimlico SW1 147 B2
Spitalfields E1 110 C4
Priory Hospl The SW15 56 B3
Priory Htss N1 85 A2
Priory La SW15 56 B2
Priory Lo 7 W4 36 C1
Priory Mans
17 Maitland Pk NW3 12 B2
South Kensington SW10 143 A1
Priory Park Rd NW6 23 B4
Priory Rd
Bedford Pk W4 37 C3
Hampstead NW6 11 A1
Richmond TW9 44 C3
Priory St 16 E3 27 A2
Priory Terr NW6 78 A4
Priory The SE1 136 A3
Priory Wlk SW10 143 A1
Pritchard Ho 38 E2 24 C3
Pritchard's Rd E2 24 C3
Priter Rd SE16 139 C1
Priter Road Hostel SE16 139 C1
Probert Rd SW2 62 C2
Probyn Ho SW1 147 C4
Probyn Rd SW2 75 A2
Procter Ho 12 SE5 48 C3
Procter St WC1 106 C3
Proctor Ho SE1 153 B1
Prome Ho 3 N16 15 C4
Promenade Approach Rd W4 46 A3
Promenade The W4 46 A2
Prospect Cotts SW18 58 C3
Prospect Ho
1 Dalston E8 16 B2
Islington N1 85 B1
Newington SE1 136 B1
14 North Kensington W10 30 C3
Prospect House Sch SW15 69 C4
Prospect Pl
5 Child's Hill NW2 1 B1
2 Chiswick W4 37 C1
6 Deptford SE8 51 B4
12 Hampstead NW3 11 B4
7 Lower Holloway N7 14 A4
Wapping E1 32 B1
Prospect Quay SW18 58 C3
Prospect Rd NW2 1 C1
Prospect St SE16 40 A4
Prospect Wharf E1 32 B2
Prospero Rd N19 4 C3
Prothero Rd SW6 154 C2
Proud Ho 18 E1 32 A3
Prout Gr NW10 8 B4
Provence St N1 86 C2
Providence Cl E9 25 C4
Providence Ct
Islington N1 86 A3
Providence Ct *continued*
Mayfair W1 117 C4
Providence Pl N1 86 A3
Providence Row N1 84 C1
Providence Row Cl 30 E1 25 A2
Providence Sq SE1 139 B4
Providence Yd E2 24 C2 99 B4
Provost Ct NW3 12 B2
Provost Rd NW3 12 B1
Provost St N1 97 B4
Prowse Pl NW1 13 B1
Prudent Pas EC2 109 A1
Prusom's Island 8 E1 32 B1
Prusom St E1 32 A1
Pryors The NW3 2 C1
Public Record Office TW9 45 A3
Pudding La EC3 123 C4
Pudding Mill La E15 27 A4
Pudding Mill Lane Sta E15 27 A4
Puddle Dock EC4 122 B4
Pugin Ct N1 14 C1
Pulborough Rd SW18 70 B4
Pulham Ho SW8 162 C1
Pullman Ct SW2 74 B3
Pullman Gdns SW15 57 B1
Pulross Rd SW9 62 B4
Pulteney Cl 20 E3 26 B4
Pulteney Terr N1 85 A4
Pulton Ho SE4 66 A3
Pulton Pl SW6 155 B1
Puma Ct E1 110 C4
Pump Ct EC4 107 B1
Pump House Cl SE16 40 B4
Pumphouse Educational Mus The★ SE16 33 A1
Pumping Ho 3 E14 34 C2
Pumping Station Rd W4 46 A4
Pump La SE14 50 B3
Punderson's Gdns E2 25 A2
Purbeck Ho SW8 162 C1
Purbrook Est SE1 138 B3
Purbrook Ho 2 SW15 69 A3
Purbrook St SE1 138 B2
Purcell Cres SW6 154 A2
Purcell Ho SW10 157 B3
Purcell Mews 2 NW10 8 A1
Purcell St N1 24 A3
Purchese St NW1 83 C1
Purday Ho 4 W10 23 B2
Purdon Ho 11 SE15 49 C2
Purdy St E3 27 A1
Purley Ave NW2 1 A2
Purley Pl N1 15 A1
Purser Ho 3 SW2 62 C1
Pursers Cross Rd SW6 165 A4
Purves Rd NW10 22 B3
Pusey Ho 20 E14 33 C3
Puteaux Ho 6 E2 25 C3
PUTNEY 57 B2
Putney Bridge App SW6 58 A4
Putney Bridge Rd SW15 58 B3
Putney Bridge Sta SW6 58 B4
Putney Comm SW15 57 B4
Putney Exchange Shopping Ctr SW15 57 C3
PUTNEY HEATH 57 B1
Putney Heath SW15 57 B1
Putney Heath La SW15 57 C1
Putney High Sch SW15 57 C2
Putney High St SW15 58 A3
Putney Hill SW15 57 C2
Putney Park Ave SW15 56 C3
Putney Park La SW15 57 A2
Putney Park Sch SW15 57 A3
Putney Pier SW15 58 A4
Putney School of Art & Design SW15 58 A3
Putney Sta SW15 58 A3
PUTNEY VALE 68 C1
Putney Wharf Twr SW15 58 A4
Pykewell Lo 13 E8 16 C3
Pylon Trad Est E16 34 C4
Pymers Mead SE21 75 B3
Pynfolds SE16 40 A4
Pynnersmead SE24 63 B2
Pyrford Ho 12 SW9 63 A3
Pyrland Rd
Richmond TW10 54 B1
Stoke Newington N5 15 C3
Pyrmont Gr SE27 75 A1
Pyrmont Rd W4 44 C4
Pytchley Rd SE22 64 A4

Q

Quadrangle Cl SE1 152 A4
Quadrangle The
Chelsea SW10 167 A4
Fulham SW6 154 A1
Herne Hill SE24 63 B2
3 North Kensington W12 30 B3
Paddington W2 102 A2
Quadrant Arc W1 119 A3
Quadrant Bsns Ctr NW6 23 A4
Quadrant Gr NW5 12 B3
Quadrant The
4 Kensal Green W10 22 C2
Richmond TW9 54 A3
Quaker Ct EC1 97 A2
Quaker St E1 24 B1 98 C1
Quality Ct WC2 107 B2
Quantock Ho N16 7 B3
Quantock Mews 3 SE15 49 C1
Quarrendon St SW6 165 C2
Quarry Rd SW18 59 B1
Quarterdeck The E14 41 C4
Quartermile La E10, E15 19 A4
Quayside Ct 6 SE16 32 C1
Quebec & Crown Wharves E14 33 B3
Quebec Ind Est SE16 41 A3
Quebec Mews W1 103 A1
Quebec Way SE16 41 A4
Quebec Wharf 32 E8 24 A4
Quedgeley Ct 3 SE15 49 B4
Queen Alexandra Mans WC1 94 A3
Queen Anne Mews W1 104 B3
Queen Anne Rd E9 17 C2
Queen Anne's Gate SW1 133 B3
Queen Anne's Gdns
Bedford Pk W4 38 A3
Ealing W5 36 A4
Queen Anne's Gr
Bedford Pk W4 38 A3
Ealing W5 36 A4
Queen Anne St W1 104 A3
Queen Anne Terr 9 E1 32 A2
Queen Caroline St W6 39 B1
Queen Charlottes & Chelsea Hospl W12 29 C3
Queen Ct WC1 94 B1
Queen Elizabeth Ct 5 N1 15 C2
Queen Elizabeth Hall & Purcell Room★ SE1 121 A2
Queen Elizabeth Ho SW12 72 C4
Queen Elizabeth II Con Ctr SW1 133 C3
Queen Elizabeth II Jubilee Sch W9 23 B1
Queen Elizabeth II Pier SE10 35 B1
Queen Elizabeth's Cl N16 6 C2
Queen Elizabeth's Coll 15 SE10 52 B3
Queen Elizabeth St SE1 138 C4
Queen Elizabeth's Wlk N16 6 C2
Queen Elizabeth Wlk SW13 47 A2
Queenhithe EC4 123 A4
Queen Margaret Flats 22 E2 25 A2
Queen Margarets Ct N1 16 A3
Queen Margaret's Gr N1 16 A3
Queen Mary's Gdns★ NW1 91 B3
Queen Mary's Hospl NW3 2 B1
Queen Mary's Univ Hospl SW15 56 C1
Queen Mary, Univ of London E1 26 A1
Queen of Denmark Ct SE16 41 B3
Queen St Pl EC4 123 A4
Queensberry Mews W SW7 143 B4
Queensberry Pl SW7 143 B4
Queensberry Way SW7 143 B4
Queensborough Mews W2 114 C4
Queensborough Pas W2 114 C4
Queensborough Terr W2 114 B4
Queensbridge Ct 1 E2 24 B3
Queensbridge Inf Sch E8 16 B1
Queensbridge Rd
Dalston E8 16 B1
Shoreditch E2, E8 24 B4
Queensbury St N1 15 B1
Queen's CE Prim Sch The TW9 44 C3
Queen's Cir SW11 160 A1
Queen's Club Gdns W14 154 B4
Queen's Club The W14 140 B1
Queen's Coll W1 104 A3
Queens Cres TW10 54 B2
Queen's Cres NW5 12 C2
Queens Ct
Battersea SW11 170 A4
Camberwell SE5 49 A1
4 Limehouse E14 33 B2
Queen's Ct
Barnes SW13 56 C4
Kensington W2 114 B3
3 Richmond TW10 54 B1
St John's Wood NW8 79 B2
Queensdale W11 30 C1
Queensdale Cres W11 30 C1
Queensdale Pl W11 31 A1 112 A1
Queensdale Rd
Notting Hill W11 30 C1
Notting Hill W11 31 A1 112 A1
Queensdale Wlk W11 31 A1 112 A1
Queensdown Rd E5 17 A4
Queen's Dr N4 6 A2
Queen's Elm Par SW3 143 C2
Queen's Elm Sq SW3 143 C1
Queen's Gallery★ SW1 132 B3
Queen's Gate SW7 129 A1

Queensgate Gdns SW15 . . . 57 A3
Queen's Gate Gdns SW7 . . . 129 A1
Queensgate Ho 34 E3 . . . 26 B3
Queen's Gate Mews SW7 . . . 129 A2
Queensgate Pl 10 NW6 . . . 10 C1
Queen's Gate Pl SW7 . . . 129 A1
Queen's Gate Pl Mews SW7 . . . 129 A1
Queen's Gate Sch SW7 . . . 143 B4
Queen's Gate Terr SW7 . . . 129 A2
Queens Gate Villas E9 . . . 18 A1
Queen's Gdns W2 114 C4
Queen's Gr NW8 . . 79 C3
Queen's Head Pas EC2 . . . 108 C2
Queen's Head St N1 . . . 86 B3
Queen's Head Yd SE1 . . . 123 B1
Queens Ho 1 SE17 . . . 48 C4
Queen's House The★ SE10 . . . 52 C4
Queensland Rd N7 . . . 14 C4
Queens Manor Sch SW6 . . . 47 C3
Queens Mans NW6 . . . 11 A3
Queen's Mans W6 . . 39 C2
Queensmead NW8. 79 C4
Queensmere Cl SW19 . . . 69 C2
Queensmere Ct SW13 . . . 46 C4
Queensmere Rd SW19 . . . 69 C2
Queen's Mews W2 . . . 114 A4
Queensmill Rd SW6 . . . 47 C3
Queensmill Sch SW6 . . . 165 C1
Queens Par 3 NW2 . 9 B2
Queens Park Com Sch NW6 . . . 22 C4
Queens Park Ct 5 W10 . . . 22 C2
Queen's Park Prim Sch W10 . . . 23 A1
Queen's Park Sta NW6 . . . 23 B3
Queen Sq WC1 . . . 106 B4
Queen's Quay EC4 . . . 123 A4
Queen's Rd
Mortlake SW14 . . . 55 C4
New Cross Gate SE14, SE15 . . . 50 B2
Richmond TW10 . . . 54 B1
Queen's Ride SW13 . . . 57 A4
Queen's Rise TW10 . . . 54 B1
Queen's Road Sta SE15 . . . 50 B2
Queen's Row SE17 . 48 C4
Queen St
City of London EC4 . . . 123 A4
Mayfair W1 . . . 118 A2
Queens Terr NW8 . . 79 B2
Queenstown Mews SW8 . . . 170 A3
Queenstown Rd SW8 . . . 160 A2
Queenstown Road Sta SW8 . . . 170 B4
Queensville Rd SW12, SW4 . . . 73 C4
Queensway W2 . . 114 B4
Queensway Sta W2 . . . 114 B3
Queen's Wlk SW1 118 C1
Queenswood Ct 7 SW4 . . . 62 A2
Queens Yd E9 . . . 18 C2
Queen's Yd W1 . . . 93 A1
Queen Victoria Meml★ SW1 . . . 132 C4
Queen Victoria St EC4 . . . 122 C4
Queen Victoria Terr 12 E1 . . . 32 A2
Quelch Ho 2 N19 . . 13 C3
Quemerford Rd N7 . . . 14 B3
Quendon Ho 9 W10 . . . 22 B1
Quenington Ct 5 SE15 . . . 49 B4
Quenington Mans SW6 . . . 164 C4
Quennel Ho 7 SW12 . . . 73 B4
Querrin St SW6 . . 166 C1
Quested Ct 27 E8 . . 17 A3
Quex Mews NW6 . . . 23 C4
Quex Rd NW6 . . . 23 C4
Quick Rd W4 . . . 38 A1
Quick St N1 . . . 86 B1
Quick Street Mews N1 . . . 86 A1
Quickswood NW3 . . 12 A1
Quill La SW15 . . . 57 C3
Quill St N4 . . . 5 C1
Quilp St SE1 . . . 136 C4
Quilter St E2 . . . 24 C2 99 B4
Quilting Ct 23 SE16 . . . 40 C4
Quince Rd SE13 . . . 52 A1
Quintin Ct W4 . . . 45 B3
Quintin Kynaston Sch NW8 . . . 79 B3
Quintock Ho 2 TW9 . . . 44 C2
Quinton Ho SW8 . 162 A2
Quinton St SW18 . . . 71 B2
Quixley St 1 E14 . . . 34 C2
Quorn Rd SE22 . . . 64 A4

R

Rabbit Row W8 . . . 31 C1 113 C2
Raby St E14 . . . 33 A3
Racine 15 SE5 . . . 49 A2
Racton Rd SW6 . . 155 B3
Radbourne Cl E5 . . . 17 C4
Radbourne Rd SW12 . . . 73 C3
Radcliff Bldg EC1 107 B4
Radcliffe Ave NW10 . . . 21 C3
Radcliffe Coll
Marylebone W1 . . . 104 C1
Soho W1 . . . 105 B2
Radcliffe Ho 10 SE16 . . . 40 A2
Radcliffe Path SW8 . . . 170 B1
Radcliffe Rd SE1 . 138 B2
Radcliffe Sq SW15 . . 57 C1
Radcot St SE11 . . . 149 C1
Raddington Rd W10 . . . 31 A4
Radford Ho
7 Bow Comm E14 . . . 34 A4
Islington N7 . . . 14 B3
Radford Rd SE13 . . . 67 B1
Radipole Rd SW6 164 C4
Radland Rd E16 . . . 35 C3
Radlett Pl NW8 . . . 80 A4
Radley Ct 25 SE16 . . 40 C4
Radley Ho NW1 . . . 90 C2
Radley Lo 30 SW19 . . . 69 C3
Radley Mews W8 127 C1
Radley Terr 1 E16 . . . 35 B4
Radnor Lo W2 . . . 101 C1
Radnor Mews W2 101 C1
Radnor Pl W2 . . . 102 A1
Radnor Rd
Kensal Rise NW6 . . . 23 A4
Peckham SE15 . . . 49 C3
Radnor St EC1 . . . 97 A3
Radnor Terr W14 . 140 C4
Radnor Way NW10 . . . 20 A1
Radnor Wlk
Chelsea SW3 . . . 144 C1
21 Millwall E14 . . . 41 C2
Radstock St SW11 . . . 158 A1
Radway Ho 38 W2 . . 31 C4
Radwell Ho SW2 . . . 62 C2
Raebarn Ct 6 SW16 . . . 74 A1
Raeburn St SW2 . . . 62 A3
Ragged School Mus The★ E3 . . . 33 A4
Raglan Ct SW9 . . . 62 C4
Raglan St NW5 . . . 13 A2
Ragley Cl W3 . . . 37 B4
Rahere Ho EC1 . . . 96 C4
Railey Mews NW5 . . 13 B3
Railton Rd SE24 . . . 63 A2
Railway App SE1 . 123 C2
Railway Ave SE16 . . . 40 B4
Railway Cotts W6 . . 39 B4
Railway Gr SE14 . . . 51 B3
Railway Rise SE22 . . 64 A3
Railway Side SW13 . . . 56 A4
Railway St N1 . . . 84 B1
Railway Terr SE13 . . 67 A2
Rainbow Ave E14 . . . 42 A1
Rainbow Ct 3 SE14 . . . 51 A4
Rainbow Quay SE16 . . . 41 A3
Rainbow Sch The SW17 . . . 71 B2
Rainbow St SE5 . . . 49 A3
Raines Ct N16 . . . 7 B2
Raine's Foundation Lower Sch E2 . . . 25 A3
Raine's Foundation Sch E2 . . . 25 B3
Raine St E1 . . . 32 A1
Rainford Ho 9 N7 . . 5 B2
Rainham Cl SW11 . . 60 A1
Rainham Ho NW1 . 83 A3
Rainham Rd NW10 . 22 B2
Rainhill Way E3 . . . 26 C2
Rainsborough Ave SE8 . . . 41 A2
Rainsford Ct NW10 . . . 20 A3
Rainsford Ho 14 SW2 . . . 62 B2
Rainsford Rd NW10 . . . 20 A3
Rainsford St W2 . . 102 A2
Rainton Rd SE7 . . . 43 C1
Rainville Rd W6 . . . 47 B4
Raleigh Ct
7 Hammersmith W12 . . . 39 A4
2 Rotherhithe SE16 . . . 32 C1
Raleigh Gdns SW2 . . 62 B1
Raleigh Ho
Clapham SW8 . . . 171 B2
Isle of Dogs E14 . . . 42 A4
Raleigh Mews N1 . . 86 B3
Raleigh Rd TW9 . . . 54 B4
Raleigh St N1 . . . 86 B3
Ralph Ct W2 . . . 100 B2
Ralston St SW3 . . . 144 C1
Ramar Ho E1 . . . 111 B4
Ramilles Cl SW2 . . . 62 A1
Ramilles Ho W1 . . 105 A1
Ramillies Pl W1 . . 104 C1
Ramillies Rd W4 . . . 37 C3
Ramillies St W1 . . 104 C1
Rampart St E1 . . . 32 A3
Rampayne St SW1 . . . 147 B2
Ramsay Ho NW8 . . 80 A2
Ramsay Rd W3 . . . 37 B4
Ramsdean Ho 1 SW15 . . . 69 A3
Ramsden Rd SW12 . . . 72 C4
Ramsey Ct
Putney SW15 . . . 57 B1
6 Upper Holloway N19 . . . 4 C2
Ramsey Ho
5 Battersea SW11 . . . 59 C3
Kennington SW9 . . . 163 C1
Ramsey St E2 . . . 24 C1 99 C2
Ramsfort Ho 4 SE16 . . . 40 A2
Ramsgate St E8 . . . 16 B2
Ram St SW18 . . . 59 A2
Randal Cremer JMI Sch E2 . . . 24 B3
Randall Cl SW11 . . 168 A4
Randall Pl SE10 . . . 52 B3
Randall Rd SE11 . . 148 C3
Randall Row SE11 . . . 148 C3
Randell's Rd N1 . . . 84 B4
Randolf Ct
Paddington NW6 . . . 78 A1
St John's Wood NW8 . . . 78 C3
Randolph Ave W9 . 88 C3
Randolph Cres W9 88 C2
Randolph Gdns NW6 . . . 78 A1
Randolph Mews W9 . . . 89 A1
Randolph Rd W9 . . 89 A1
Randolph St NW1 . . 13 B1
Ranelagh Ave
Barnes SW13 . . . 46 C1
Fulham SW6 . . . 58 B4
Ranelagh Gardens Mans SW6 . . . 58 A4
Ranelagh Gardens (site of Chelsea Flower Show)★ SW1 . . . 145 C1
Ranelagh Gdns
3 Bedford Pk W6 . . . 38 B3
Chiswick W4 . . . 45 B3
Fulham SW6 . . . 58 B4
Ranelagh Gr SW1 145 C2
Ranelagh Ho SW3 . . . 144 C2
Ranelagh Mans SW6 . . . 165 A2
Ranelagh Rd
Dagenham NW10 . . . 21 B3
Pimlico SW1 . . . 147 A1
Rangdon St EC3 . . . 110 C1
Ranger's House (The Wernher Collection)★ SE10 . . . 52 C2
Rangers Sq SE10 . . . 52 C2
Rangoon Ho 5 N16 . . . 15 C4
Rankine Ho SE1 . . . 136 C1
Ranmere St SW12 . . 73 A3
Rann Ho 1 SW14 . . 55 C4
Rannoch Rd W6 . . . 47 C4
Ransomes Dock Bsns Ctr SW11 . . . 158 B1
Ransomes Mews SW11 . . . 158 B2
Ranston St NW1 . . 102 A4
Ranulf Rd NW2 . . . 10 B4
Ranwell Cl 18 E3 . . . 26 B4
Ranwell Ho 17 E3 . . 26 B4
Raphael Ct 9 SE16 . . . 40 A1
Raphael St SW7 . . 130 C3
Rapley Ho E2 . . . 24 C2 99 B3
Rashleigh Ct 8 SW8 . . . 61 A4
Rashleigh Ho WC1 94 A3
Rastell Ave SW12 . . . 73 C3
RATCLIFF . . . 32 C2
Ratcliffe Cross St E1 . . . 32 C3
Ratcliffe Ho 10 E14 . . . 33 A3
Ratcliffe La 16 E14 . . . 33 A3
Ratcliffe Orch 9 E1 . . . 32 C2
Rathbone Ho
5 Canning Town E16 . . . 35 B3
Kilburn NW6 . . . 23 C4
Rathbone Mkt 3 E16 . . . 35 B4
Rathbone Pl W1 . . 105 B2
Rathbone St
Canning Town E16 . . . 35 B3
Fitzrovia W1 . . . 105 A3

Rathgar Rd SW9 . . . 63 A4
Rathmell Dr SW4 . . . 61 C1
Rattray Rd SW2 . . . 62 C2
Raul Rd SE15 . . . 49 C2
Raveley St NW5 . . . 13 B4
Ravenet Ct
Battersea SW11 . . . 170 A3
Clapham SW4 . . . 61 A2
Ravenet St SW11 170 A3
Ravenfield Rd SW17 . . . 72 B1
Raven Ho [10] SE16 . . 40 C2
Ravenna Rd SW15 . . 57 C2
Raven Row E1 . . . 32 A4
Ravensbourne Ho NW8 . . . 102 A4
Ravensbourne Mans [9] SE8 . . . 51 C4
Ravensbourne Pl SE13 . . . 52 A1
Ravensbury Rd SW18 . . . 71 A2
Ravensbury Terr SW18 . . . 71 A2
Ravenscar NW1 . . . 82 C3
Ravenscourt [1] N16 . . . 7 C1
Ravenscourt Ave W6 . . . 38 C2
Ravenscourt Gdns W6 . . . 38 C2
Ravenscourt Ho [13] W6 . . . 39 A2
Ravenscourt Park Mans [1] W6 . . . 39 A3
Ravenscourt Park Prep Sch W6 . . . 38 C2
Ravenscourt Park Sta W6 . . . 39 A2
Ravenscourt Pk W6 . . . 38 C2
Ravenscourt Pl W6 . . . 39 A2
Ravenscourt Rd W6 . . . 39 A2
Ravenscourt Sq W6 . . . 38 C3
Ravenscourt Theatre Sch W6 . . . 39 A2
Ravenscroft Ave NW11 . . . 1 B4
Ravenscroft Cl [4] E16 . . . 35 C4
Ravenscroft Ct NW11 . . . 1 B4
Ravenscroft Point [26] E9 . . . 17 C2
Ravenscroft Rd
Acton W4 . . . 37 B2
Newham E16 . . . 35 C4
Ravenscroft St E2 . . . 24 B2 99 A4
Ravensdon St SE11 . . . 149 C1
Ravenshaw St NW6 . . . 10 B3
Ravenslea Rd SW11, SW12 . . . 72 B4
Ravensmede Way W4 . . . 38 B2
Ravenstone SE17 . 152 B1
Ravenstone Prim Sch SW12 . . . 72 C2
Ravenstone St SW12 . . . 72 C3
Ravenswood Rd SW12 . . . 73 A4
Ravensworth Ct SW6 . . . 155 B1
Ravensworth Rd NW10 . . . 22 A2
Raven Wharf SE1 138 C4
Ravey St EC2 . . . 24 A1 98 A2
Rav Pinter Cl N16 . . . 7 A4
Rawlings St SW3 144 C4
Rawlinson Ho SE13 . . . 67 C3
Rawlinson Point [8] E16 . . . 35 B4
Rawreth Wlk N1 . . 87 A4
Rawson Ct SW11 . 169 C3
Rawson St SW11 . 170 A3
Rawstorne Pl EC1 . 96 A4
Rawstorne St EC1 . 96 A4
Rayburne Ct W14 126 A2
Raydon St N19 . . . 4 A2
Ray Ho
[7] North Kensington W10 . . . 30 C3
Shoreditch N1 . . . 87 C3
Raymede Twr W10 . . . 30 C4
Raymond Bldgs WC1 . . . 107 A4
Raymouth Rd SE16 . . . 40 A2
Raynald Ho [15] SW16 . . . 74 A1
Rayne Ct SE1 . . . 138 C4
Rayne Ho
[1] Balham SW12 . . . 60 C1
Paddington W9 . . . 88 A2
Rayner Ct [10] W12 . . 39 B4
Rayner's Rd SW15 . . 58 A2
Raynes Ct NW2 . . . 10 A4
Raynham W2 . . . 102 A2
Raynham Ho [1] E1 . . . 25 C1
Raynham Rd W6 . . . 39 A2
Raynor Pl N1 . . . 87 A4
Ray St EC1 . . . 95 C1
Ray Wlk N7 . . . 5 B2
Reachview Cl [17] NW1 . . . 13 B1
Reade Ct [6] W3 . . . 37 B3
Reade Wlk [5] NW10 . . . 8 A1
Read Ho SE11 . . . 163 B4
Reading Ho
Paddington W2 . . . 100 C1
Peckham SE15 . . . 49 C4
Reading La E8 . . . 17 A2
Reapers Cl NW1 . . . 83 B4
Reardon Ho [5] E1 . . 32 A1
Reardon Path [31] E1 . . . 32 A1
Reardon St E1 . . . 32 A1
Reaston St SE14 . . . 50 C3
Reay Prim Sch SW9 . . . 163 A1
Reckitt Rd W4 . . . 38 A1
Record St SE16 . . . 50 B4
Rector St N1 . . . 86 C3
Rectory Gdns [6] SW4 . . . 61 B4
Rectory Gr SW4 . . . 61 B4
Rectory Rd
Barnes SW13 . . . 46 C1
[1] London W3 . . . 28 B1
Shacklewell N16 . . . 7 B1
Rectory Road Sta N16 . . . 7 B1
Rectory Sq E1 . . . 32 C4
Reculver Ho [2] SE15 . . . 50 B4
Reculver Rd SE16 . . 40 C1
Red Anchor Cl SW3 . . . 158 A3
Redan Pl W2 . . . 100 A1
Redan St W14 . . . 39 C3
Redan Terr SE5 . . . 48 A1
Redbourne Ho [7] E14 . . . 33 B3
Redbourn Ho [10] W10 . . . 22 B1
Redbridge Gdns SE5 . . . 49 A3
Redburn St SW3 . 158 C4
Redcar St SE5 . . . 48 B3
Redcastle Cl E1 . . . 32 B2
Redchurch St E2 . . . 24 B1 98 C2
Redcliffe Cl SW5 . 142 A1
Redcliffe Gdns
Chiswick W4 . . . 45 A3
Fulham SW10 . . . 156 B4
Redcliffe Mews SW10 . . . 142 B1
Redcliffe Pl SW10 . . . 156 C3
Redcliffe Rd SW10 . . . 157 A4
Redcliffe Sch SW10 . . . 156 C4
Redcliffe Sq SW10 . . . 142 B1
Redcliffe St SW10 . . . 156 B4
Redclyf Ho [13] E1 . . . 25 B1
Redcroft [5] NW6 . . . 10 C2
Red Cross Cotts SE1 . . . 137 A4
Redcross Way SE1 . . . 123 A1
Reddins Rd SE15 . . . 49 C4
Rede Pl W2 . . . 31 C2 113 C4
Redesdale St SW3 . . . 158 C4
Redfern Rd NW10 . . . 8 A1
Redfield La SW5 . 142 A4
Redfield Mews SW5 . . . 141 C4
Redfiff Est SE16 . . . 41 B3
Redford Wlk N1 . . . 86 C4
Redgate Terr SW15 . . . 57 C1
Redgrave Rd SW15 . . . 57 C4
Redhill Ct SW2 . . . 74 C2
Redhill St NW1 . . . 92 B4
Red House Sq [20] N1 . . . 15 B1
Redington Gdns NW3 . . . 11 A4
Redington Ho N1 . . 85 A2
Redington Rd NW3 . . . 11 A4
Redlands Prim Sch E1 . . . 32 B4
Redlands Way SW2 . . . 74 B4
Red Lion Cl [9] SE17 . . . 48 C4
Red Lion Ct EC4 . . 107 C1
Red Lion Row SE17 . . . 48 B4
Red Lion Sq WC1 106 C3
Red Lion St WC1 . 106 C3
Red Lion Yd W1 . . 117 C2
Redlynch Ct W14 . 126 B3
Redlynch Ho SW9 173 C4
Redman Bldg EC1 . . . 107 B4
Redman Ho SE1 . . 137 A3
Redman's Rd E1 . . . 32 B4
Redmayne Ho SW9 . . . 173 A2
Redmead La E1 . . 125 B1
Redmill Ho [24] E1 . . . 25 A1
Redmond Ho N1 . . 85 A3
Redmore Rd W6 . . . 39 A2
Red Pl W1 . . . 117 B4
Red Post Hill SE21, SE24 . . . 63 C2
Redriff Prim Sch SE16 . . . 41 A4
Redriff Rd SE16 . . . 41 A3
Red Rover SW13 . . . 56 C4
Redrup Ho [21] SE14 . . . 50 C4
Redruth Rd E9 . . . 25 B4
Red Sq The N16 . . . 6 C1
Redstart Cl SE14 . . . 51 A3
Redvers St E2 . . . 24 A2 98 B4
Redwald Rd E5 . . . 17 C4
Redwood Cl
[4] Bow E3 . . . 26 C3
Rotherhithe SE16 . . . 33 A1
Redwood Ct
Brondesbury NW6 . . . 10 A1
Crouch End N19 . . . 4 C4
Redwood Mews [2] SW4 . . . 61 A4
Redwoods SW15 . . . 68 C3
Reece Mews SW7 143 B4
Reed Cl E16 . . . 35 C4
Reedham St SE15 . . 64 C4
Reed Ho SW15 . . . 56 C1
Reedholm Villas N16 . . . 15 C4
Reed Pl SW4 . . . 61 C3
Reed's Pl NW1 . . . 13 B1
Reedworth St SE11 . . . 149 C3
Reef Ho E14 . . . 42 B3
Rees St N1 . . . 87 A3
Reeves Ho
Lambeth SE1 . . . 135 B3
Mayfair W1 . . . 117 B3
Reeves Mews W1 117 C3
Reeves Rd E3 . . . 27 A1
Reflection Ho E2 . . . 24 C1 99 B2
Reform St SW11 . . 169 A2
Regal Cl E1 . . . 111 C4
Regal La NW1 . . . 81 C3
Regal Pl
[8] Tower Hamlets E3 . . . 26 B2
Walham Green SW6 . . . 156 B1
Regan Way N1 . . . 24 A3
Regatta Point TW8 . . . 44 B4
Regency Ct
[9] Bow E3 . . . 26 B3
[14] South Hackney E9 . . . 25 B4
Regency Ho NW1 . . 92 B2
Regency Lo NW3 . . 11 C1
Regency Mews
Camberwell SW9 . . . 48 A3
Regency Mews *continued*
[1] Willesden NW10 . . . 8 C2
Regency Pl SW1 . . 147 C4
Regency St SW1 . . 147 C3
Regency Terr SW7 . . . 143 B2
Regency Wlk [8] TW10 . . . 54 A2
Regeneration Rd SE16 . . . 40 C1
Regent Ct
Lisson Gr NW8 . . . 90 A3
[1] Stamford Hill N16 . . 7 B4
Regent Ho W14 . . 140 A4
Regent Pl W1 . . . 119 A4
Regent Rd SE24 . . . 63 A2
Regents Bridge Gdns SW8 . . . 162 B2
Regents Canal Ho [19] E14 . . . 33 A3
Regent's Coll NW1 91 B2
Regents Ct E8 . . . 24 C4
Regents Gate Ho [20] E14 . . . 33 A2
Regents Lo [9] SW2 . . . 74 B3
Regents Mews NW8 . . . 79 A2
REGENT'S PARK . . 92 A4
Regent's Park★ NW1 . . . 81 B1
Regent's Park Barracks NW1 . . . 82 B1
Regent's Park Rd
Camden Town NW1 . . . 81 B4
Primrose Hill NW3 . . . 12 C1
Regent's Park Sta NW1 . . . 92 A1
Regent's Park Terr NW1 . . . 82 A4
Regent's Pl SE3 . . . 53 C1
Regents Plaza NW6 . . . 78 A2
Regent Sq
[23] Bromley E3 . . . 27 A2
St Pancras WC1 . . . 94 B3
Regent's Row E8 . . . 24 C4
Regent St
Brentford W4 . . . 36 C1
[7] Kensal Green NW10 . . . 22 C2
Mayfair W1 . . . 118 C4
Regents Wharf
[3] Hackney E2 . . . 25 A4
Islington N1 . . . 84 C2
Reginald Pl [6] SE8 . . . 51 C
Reginald Rd SE8 . . . 51 C
Reginald Sq SE8 . . . 51 C
Regina Point SE16 . . 40 B
Regina Rd N4 . . . 5 B
Regis Ct NW1 . . . 102 C
Regis Pl [17] SW2 . . . 62 B
Regis Rd NW5 . . . 13 A
Regnart Bldgs NW1 . . . 93 A
Reid Ct SW14 . . . 45 B
Reighton Rd E5 . . . 7 C
Reizel Cl N16 . . . 7 B
Relay Rd W12 . . . 30 B
Relf Rd SE15 . . . 64 C
Reliance Sq E2 . . . 24 A1 98 B
Relton Ct W3 . . . 36 C

Relton Mews SW7 ... 130 B2
Rembrandt Cl E14 .. 42 C3
Rembrandt Ct 10 SE16 ... 40 A1
Rembrant Cl SW1 145 B3
Remington St N1 .. 86 B1
Remnant St WC2 . 106 C2
Remsted Ho NW6 . 78 A3
Remus Rd E3 ... 18 C1
Renaissance Wlk 4 SE10 ... 43 B3
Renbold Ho 5 SE10 ... 52 B2
Rendlesham Ho 3 E5, N16 ... 7 C1
Rendlesham Rd E5 .. 7 C1
Renforth St SE16 ... 40 B4
Renfrew Ho NW6 .. 78 A1
Renfrew Rd SE11 150 A3
Rennell Ho 18 E9 ... 17 C2
Rennell St SE13 ... 67 B4
Rennie Cotts 29 E1 ... 25 B1
Rennie Ct SE1 ... 122 A2
Rennie Ho SE1 ... 136 C1
Rennie St SE1 ... 122 A2
Renoir Ct 7 SE16 .. 40 A1
Renton Cl SW2 ... 62 B1
Rephidim St SE1 . 138 A1
Replingham Rd SW18 ... 70 C3
Reporton Rd SW6 154 B1
Repton Ho SW1 .. 147 A3
Repton St E14 ... 33 A3
Reservoir Rd SE4 .. 51 A1
Reservoir Studios 14 E1 ... 32 C3
Resolution Way 14 SE8 ... 51 C3
Restell Cl SE3 ... 53 A4
Reston Pl SW7 ... 128 C3
Restoration Sq SW11 ... 167 C3
Retcar Pl N19 ... 4 A2
Retford St E2 ... 24 A3
Retreat Ho 5 E9 ... 17 B2
Retreat Pl E9 ... 17 B2
Retreat The SW14 .. 56 A4
Reunion Row E1 ... 32 A2
Reveley Sq SE16 ... 41 A4
Revelon Rd SE4 ... 66 A4
Revelstoke Rd SW18, SW19 ... 70 C2
Reverdy Rd SE1 .. 153 B3
Rewell St SW6 ... 156 C1
Rex Pl W1 ... 117 C2
Reynard Cl SE4 ... 66 A4
Reynard Pl SE14 ... 51 A4
Reynolds Cl NW11 ... 2 A4
Reynolds Ho
Finsbury Pk N4 ... 5 A3
18 South Hackney E2 ... 25 B3
St John's Wood NW8 ... 79 C1
Westminster SW1 . 147 C3
Reynolds Pl 12 TW10 ... 54 B1
Reynolds Rd
Acton Green W4 ... 37 B3
Nunhead SE15 ... 65 B3
Rheidol Mews N1 . 86 C2
Rheidol Terr N1 ... 86 C3
Rhoda St E2 .24 B1 99 A2
Rhodes Ho
Shepherd's Bush W12 ... 30 A1
Shoreditch N1 ... 97 B4
Rhodesia Rd SW9 172 B1
Rhodes St N7 ... 14 B3
Rhodeswell Rd E14 ... 33 B3
Rhondda Gr E3 ... 26 B2
Rhyl Prim Sch NW5 ... 12 C2
Rhyl St NW5 ... 12 C2
Ribblesdale Ho 11 NW6 ... 23 C4
Ribbon Dance Mews SE5 ... 48 C2
Ribstone Ho 12 E9 ... 17 C2
Ricardo St E14 ... 34 A3
Riceyman Ho WC1. 95 B3
Richard Anderson Ct 1 SE14 ... 50 C3
Richard Atkins Prim Sch SW2 ... 74 A4
Richard Burbidge Mans SW13 ... 47 B4
Richard Cloudesley Sch EC1 ... 96 C1
Richard Cobden Prim Sch NW1 ... 83 A3
Richard Fox Ho N4 .. 6 B1
Richard Ho 10 SE16 ... 40 B2
Richard Knight Ho SW6 ... 165 C4
Richard Neale Ho 2 E1 ... 32 A2
Richardson Cl 19 E8 ... 24 B4
Richardson Ct SW4 ... 172 B2
Richardson Ho 10 E14 ... 33 C4
Richardson's Mews W1 ... 92 C1
Richard's Pl SW3. 144 B4
Richard St 20 E1 ... 32 A3
Richbell WC1 ... 106 B4
Richbell Pl WC1 .. 106 C4
Richborne Terr SW8 ... 163 A2
Richborough Ho
10 Deptford SE15 ... 50 B4
14 Hackney E5 ... 17 A4
Richborough Rd NW2 ... 10 A4
Richbourne Ct W1 ... 102 B2
Richford Gate W6 .. 39 B3
Richford St W6 ... 39 B3
Rich La SW5 ... 142 A2
Richland Ho 4 SE15 ... 49 C2
Richman Ho 10 SE8 ... 41 B1
RICHMOND ... 54 B3
Richmond Ave
Islington N1 ... 85 A4
Willesden NW10 ... 9 B2
Richmond Bldgs W1 ... 105 B1
Richmond Circus TW9 ... 54 A3
Richmond Coll W8 ... 128 B2
Richmond Cres N1 ... 85 B4
Richmond Ct SW1 ... 131 A3
Richmond Gr N1 ... 15 A1
Richmond Healthcare Hamlet Hospl TW9 ... 54 A4
RICHMOND HILL .. 54 A1
Richmond Hill TW10 ... 54 A1
Richmond Hill Ct 5 TW10 ... 54 A1
Richmond Ho
12 Forest Hill SE26 ... 76 C1
Regent's Pk NW1 ... 82 B1
Walworth SE17 ... 151 B2
Richmond International Bsns Ctr 9 TW9 ... 54 B3
Richmond Mans
Earl's Ct SW5 ... 142 A2
Putney SW15 ... 58 A4
Richmond Mews W1 ... 105 B1
Richmond Park Rd SW14 ... 55 C3
Richmond Rd
Dalston E8 ... 16 C1
Ealing W5 ... 36 A4
Richmond Sta TW9 ... 54 A3
Richmond Terr SW1 ... 134 A4
Richmond Way W12, W14 ... 39 C4
Rich St E14 ... 33 B2
Rickard Cl SW2 ... 74 C3
Rickett St SW6 ... 155 C4
Rickman Ho 23 E2 .. 25 B1
Rickman St 24 E1 .. 25 B1
Rick Roberts Way E15 ... 27 C3
Rickthorne Rd 7 N19 ... 5 A2
Riddell Ct SE1 ... 152 C2
Ridgdale St E3 ... 27 A3
Ridge Hill NW11 ... 1 A3
Ridge Rd NW2 ... 1 B1
Ridgeway 11 TW10 ... 54 A1
Ridgeway Dr W3 ... 36 C3
Ridgeway Gdns N6 .. 4 B4
Ridgeway The
Acton W3 ... 36 C3
Golders Green NW11 .. 1 B3
Ridgewell Cl N1 ... 87 A4
Ridgmount Gdns WC1 ... 105 B4
Ridgmount Pl WC1 ... 105 B4
Ridgmount Rd SW18 ... 59 A2
Ridgmount St WC1 ... 105 B4
Ridgway Rd SW9 ... 63 A4
Riding House St W1 ... 104 C3
Ridings Cl N6 ... 4 B4
Riding The NW11 ... 1 B4
Ridley Ho 14 SW11 ... 60 A4
Ridley Rd
Dalston E8 ... 16 B3
Willesden Green NW10 ... 21 C3
Ridley Road Mkt E8 ... 16 B3
Riffel Rd NW2 ... 9 B3
Rifle Ct SE11 ... 163 C4
Rifle Pl W11 ... 30 C1
Rifle St E14 ... 34 A4
Riga Ho 12 E1 ... 32 C4
Rigault Rd SW6 .. 164 B1
Rigden St E14 ... 34 A3
Rigeley Rd NW10 ... 21 C2
Rigge Pl SW4 ... 61 C3
Rigg Ho 2 SW4 ... 74 A4
Rignold Ho 6 SE5 .. 49 A1
Riley Ho
9 Bow E3 ... 26 C1
Chelsea SW10 ... 157 B3
1 Streatham SW4 .. 73 C4
Riley Rd SE1 ... 138 C2
Riley St SW10 ... 157 B2
Rill Ho 16 SE5 ... 49 A3
Rimini Ct SW12 ... 72 B3
Rinaldo Rd SW12 ... 73 A4
Ringcroft St N7 ... 14 C3
Ringford Ho SW18 .. 58 B2
Ringford Rd SW18 .. 58 C1
Ring Ho 15 E1 ... 32 B2
Ringmer Ave SW6 ... 164 B3
Ringmer Gdns 3 N19 ... 5 A2
Ringmer Ho 15 SE22 ... 64 A4
Ring Rd W12 ... 30 B1
Ringsfield Ho SE17 ... 151 A1
Ringwood Gdns
17 Millwall E14 ... 41 C2
Roehampton SW15 .. 68 C3
Ripley Gdns SW14 .. 55 C4
Ripley Ho
Mortlake SW14 ... 56 A4
Nine Elms SW1 ... 160 C4
Riplington Ct SW15 ... 69 A4
Ripplevale Gr N1 ... 14 B1
Risborough SE17 150 C4
Risborough Ho NW8 ... 90 B2
Risborough St SE1 ... 136 B4
Risdon Ho 26 SE16 .40 B4
Risdon St 27 SE16 .. 40 B4
Riseholme Ct E9 ... 18 B2
Riseholme Ho 14 SE22 ... 64 A4
Riseldine Rd SE23 .. 66 A1
Risinghill St N1 ... 85 B2
Rising Sun Ct EC1 ... 108 B3
Risley Ho 7 E9 ... 17 C2
Rita Rd SW8 ... 162 C2
Ritchie Ho
Crouch End N19 ... 4 C4
8 Rotherhithe SE16 ... 40 B3
12 South Bromley E14 ... 34 C3
Ritchie St N1 ... 85 C2
Ritherdon Rd SW17 ... 73 A2
Ritson Ho N1 ... 84 C3
Ritson Rd E8 ... 16 C2
Rivaz Pl E9 ... 17 B2
Riven Ct W2 ... 100 B1
Riverains The SW11 ... 167 B3
River Barge Cl E14 ... 42 B4
Rivercourt Rd W6 .. 39 A1
River Ct SE1 ... 122 A3
Riverdale Dr SW18 ... 71 A3
Riverfleet WC1 ... 94 B4
Riverford Ho 28 W2 ... 31 C4
River Ho SW13 ... 46 A1
Rivermead Ct SW6 ... 58 B4
Rivermead Ho E9 .. 18 A3
River Pl N1 ... 15 B1
River Plate Ho EC2 ... 109 C3
Riversdale Prim Sch SW18 ... 70 C3
Riversdale Rd N5 ... 6 B1
Riversdene N5 ... 6 B1
Rivers Ho 11 TW8 .. 36 C1
Riverside
Battersea SW11 ... 158 B2
11 Rotherhithe SE16 ... 40 B4
St Pancras WC1 ... 94 B4
Riverside Bsns Ctr SW18 ... 71 A3
Riverside Ct SW8 161 C4
Riverside Dr W4 ... 46 A2
Riverside Gdns W6 ... 39 A1
Riverside Ho 14 N1 ... 15 B1
Riverside Mans 4 E1 ... 32 B1
Riverside Prim Sch SE16 ... 139 C3
Riverside Rd
Mill Meads E15 ... 27 B3
Wandsworth SW17, SW19 ... 71 B1
Riverside Workshops SE1 ... 123 A2
River St EC1 ... 95 B4
River Terr W6 ... 39 B1
Riverton Cl W9 ... 23 B2
Riverview Gdns SW13 ... 47 A4
Riverview Gr W4 ... 45 A4
Riverview Rd W4 ... 45 A4
River Way SE10 ... 43 B3
Rivet Ho SE1 ... 153 A2
Rivington Ct NW10 ... 21 C4
Rivington Pl EC2 ... 24 A2 98 B3
Rivington St EC2 ... 24 A2 98 A3
Rivington Wlk 4 E8 ... 24 C4
Rixon St N7 ... 5 C1
Roach Rd E3 ... 18 C1
Roads Pl N19 ... 5 A2
Roan St SE10 ... 52 B4
Robert Adam St W1 ... 103 B2
Roberta St E2 ... 24 C2 99 C3
Robert Bell Ho SE16 ... 153 B4
Robert Blair Prim Sch N7 ... 14 A2
Robert Browning Prim Sch SE17 .. 151 B2
Robert Cl W9 ... 89 A1
Robert Dashwood Way SE17 ... 150 C3

Robert Gentry Ho W14 140 B1
Robert Jones Ho SE16 153 B4
Robert Keen Cl 18 SE15 49 C2
Robert Lowe Cl SE14 50 C3
Robert Owen Ho
Fulham SW6 47 C2
Spitalfields E2 24 B2 99 A4
Robert Owen Lo 4 E5 17 A4
Roberts Ct
Islington N1 86 B3
Willesden NW10 8 A2
Roberts Ho 5 SE27 75 A1
Roberts Mews SW1 131 B1
Robertson Ho 11 SE10 52 B2
Robertson Rd E15 27 B4
Robertson St SW8 170 B1
Robert's Pl EC1 95 C2
Robert St
Regent's Pk NW1 92 B3
Strand WC2 120 B3
Robert Sutton Ho 20 E1 32 B3
Robeson St 7 E3 33 B4
Robin Ct 15 E14 42 B3
Robin Gr N6 3 C2
Robin Ho NW8 80 A1
Robin Hood SW15 68 A1
Robin Hood Gdns 12 E14 34 B2
Robin Hood La E14 34 B2
Robinscroft Mews 18 SE10 52 A2
Robins Ct TW10 54 A1
Robin's Ct SW4 62 A1
Robinsfield Inf Sch NW8 80 A2
Robinson Ct
Islington N1 86 B4
4 Richmond TW9 54 B3
Robinson Ho
4 North Kensington W10 30 C3
12 Tower Hamlets E14 33 C4
Robinson Rd E2 25 B3
Robinson St SW3 158 C4
Robsart St SW9 173 B2
Robson Ave NW10 8 C1
Robson Rd SE21, SE27 75 B1
Roby Ho EC1 96 C2
Rochdale Way 4 SE8 51 C3
Roche Ho 15 E14 33 B2
Rochelle Cl SW11 59 C3
Rochelle Ct 14 E1 32 B3
Rochelle St E2 24 B2 98 C3
Rochemont Wlk 2 E8 24 C4
Roche Sch The SW18 58 C2
Rochester Ct
1 Bethnal Green E2 25 A1
9 Camden Town NW1 13 B1
Rochester Ho
Bermondsey SE1 137 C3
18 Deptford SE15 50 B4
Rochester Mews NW1 13 B1
Rochester Pl NW1 13 B1
Rochester Rd NW1 13 B2
Rochester Row SW1 147 A4
Rochester Sq NW1 13 B1
Rochester St SW1 133 B1
Rochester Terr NW1 13 B2
Rochester Wlk SE1 123 B2
Rochford Wlk 3 E8 16 C1
Rochfort Ho 4 SE8 41 B1
Rock Ave 13 SW14 55 C4
Rockell's Pl SE22 65 A1
Rockfield Ho SE10 52 B4
Rock Grove Way SE16 153 C4
Rockhall Rd NW2 9 C4
Rockingham Cl SW15 56 B3
Rockingham St SE1 136 C1
Rockland Rd SW15 58 A3
Rockley Ct 9 W14 39 C4
Rockley Rd W14 39 C4
Rocks La SW13 56 C4
Rock St N4 5 C2
Rockstraw Ho 5 NW3 12 B1
Rockwood Ct N16 7 C4
Rocliffe St N1 86 B1
Rocque Ho SW6 154 C2
Rodborough Rd NW11 1 C3
Rodenhurst Ct SW4 61 C2
Rodenhurst Rd SW4 61 C1
Roden St N7 5 B1
Roderick Ho 3 SE16 40 B2
Roderick Rd NW3 12 B4
Rodgers Ho 4 SW4 73 C4
Rodin Ct N1 86 A3
Roding Ct 6 W12 38 A4
Roding Ho N1 85 B3
Roding Mews E1 125 C2
Roding Rd E5 18 A3
Rodmarton St W1 103 A3
Rodmell WC1 94 B3
Rodmere St SE10 43 A1
Rodmill La SW2 74 A4
Rodney Ct NW8 89 A2
Rodney Ho
4 Cubitt Town E14 42 A2
Islington N1 85 A1
Rodney Ho *continued*
Notting Hill W11 31 C2 113 B4
Rodney Pl SE17 151 A4
Rodney Rd SE17 151 B3
Rodney St N1 85 A1
Rodway Rd SW15 68 C4
Rodwell Rd SE22 64 B1
Roedean Cres SW15 56 A2
ROEHAMPTON 68 A4
Roehampton CE Prim Sch SW15 69 A4
Roehampton Cl SW15 56 C3
Roehampton Ct SW13 56 C4
Roehampton Gate SW15 56 A1
Roehampton High St SW15 68 C4
Roehampton La
Putney SW15 56 C1
Roehampton SW15 69 A3
Roehampton Univ (Digby Stuart Coll) SW15 56 C2
Roehampton Univ (Froebel Coll) SW15 56 B1
Roehampton Univ (Southlands Coll) SW15 56 C2
Roehampton Univ (Whitelands Coll) SW15 68 C4
Roehampton Vale SW15 68 B2
Roffey St E14 42 B4
Rogate Ho E5 7 C1
Roger Dowley Ct 8 E2 25 B3
Roger's Almshouses 2 SW9 62 B3
Rogers Ct 16 E14 33 C2
Rogers Est 28 E2 25 B2
Rogers Ho SW1 147 C4
Rogers Rd E16 35 B3
Roger St WC1 95 A1
Rokeby Ho
9 Balham SW12 73 A4
Bloomsbury WC1 94 C1
Rokeby Rd SE4 51 B1
Rokeby Sch E15 19 C1
Rokeland Ho SE4 66 A3
Roland Gdns SW7 143 A2
Roland Ho SW7 143 A2
Roland Mews 1 E1 32 C4
Roland Way
South Kensington SW7 143 A2
Walworth SE17 151 C1
Rollins St SE15 50 B4
Rollit Ho N7 14 C3
Rollit St N7 14 C3
Rollo Ct SW11 170 A3
Rolls Bldgs EC4 107 C2
Rollscourt Ave SE24 63 B2
Rolls Pas EC4 107 B2
Rolls Rd SE1 153 A2
Rolt St SE8 51 A4
Roman Cl W3 37 A4
Roman Ct 4 N7 14 B2
Romanfield Rd SW2 74 B4
Roman Rd
Chiswick W4 38 B2
Globe Town E2, E3 25 C3
25 Old Ford E3 26 B4
Roman Square Mkt 1 E3 26 B3
Roman Way
Barnsbury N7 14 B2
4 Deptford SE15 50 B3
Roma Read Cl SW15 69 A4
Romayne Ho SW4 61 C4
Romberg Rd SW17 72 C1
Romborough Gdns SE13 67 B2
Romborough Way SE13 67 B2
Romer Ho 9 SW2 62 B2
Romero Cl SW9 62 B4
Romeyn Rd SW16 74 B1
Romford Ho 17 N1 15 C2
Romford St E1 32 A4
Romilly Rd N4 6 A2
Romilly St W1 119 C4
Romily Ct SW6 164 B2
Romney Cl
7 Deptford SE14 50 B3
North End NW11 2 B3
Romney Ct
9 Hammersmith W12 39 B4
9 Hampstead NW3 12 A2
Romney Ho 2 E14 34 C2
Romney Mews W1 103 B4
Romney Rd SE10 52 C4
Romney St SW1 134 A1
Romola Rd SE24, SW2 75 A3
Ronald Ross Prim Sch SW19 70 A4
Ronaldshay N4 5 C3
Ronalds Rd N5 14 C3
Ronald St E1 32 B3
Rona Rd NW3 12 C4
Rona Wlk 20 N1 15 C2
Rondu Rd NW2 10 A3
Rood La EC3 124 A4
Rookery Rd SW4 61 B3
Rooke Way SE10 43 B1
Rookwood Rd N16 7 C4
Roosevelt Ct 15 SW19 70 A3
Rootes Dr W10 30 C4
Ropemaker Rd SE16 41 A3
Ropemaker's Fields 7 E14 33 B2
Ropemaker St EC2 109 B4
Roper La SE1 138 B3
Roper's Orch SW3 158 A3
Ropers Wlk 13 SE24 74 C4
Ropery St E3 26 B1
Rope St SE16 41 A3
Ropewalk Gdns E1 111 C2
Ropley St 6 E2 24 C3
Rosa Alba Mews N5 15 B4
Rosalind Ho 25 N1 24 A
Rosaline Rd SW6 154 B
Rosaline Terr SW6 154 B
Rosa Parks Ho SW9 172 C
Rosary Ct 17 E1 32 C
Rosary Gdns SW7 143 A
Rosary RC Prim Sch NW3 12 A
Rosaville Rd SW6 154 C
Rosbury SW15 58 A
Roscastle Rd SE4 66 A
Roscoe St EC1 97 A
Roscommon Ho 2 NW3 11 C
Rose Alley
Borough The SE1 123 A
Broadgate EC2 110 B
Rosebank
2 Dagenham W3 28 C
Fulham SW6 47 B
Rosebank Gdns
Bow E3 26 B
1 Dagenham W3 28 C
Rosebank Way W3 28 C
Rosebank Wlk NW1 13 C
Rosebay Ho 20 E3 33 C
Roseberry Pl E8 16 B
Roseberry St SE16 40 A
Rosebery Ave EC1 95 C
Rosebery Ct
Holborn EC1 95 B
Mayfair W1 118 A
Rosebery Ho 21 E2 25 B
Rosebery Rd SW2 62 A
Rosebery Sq EC1 95 B
Rosebury Rd SW6 166 B
Rose Bush Ct NW3 12 B
Rosecroft Ave NW3 1 C
Rose & Crown Ct EC2 108 C
Rose & Crown Yd SW1 119 A
Rose Ct
7 Dalston E8 16 B
Islington N1 86 A
Spitalfields E1 111 A
Rosedale Ct N5 15 A
Rosedale Ho N16 6 C
Rosedale Rd TW9 54 A
Rosedale Terr W6 39 A
Rosedene NW6 22 C
Rosedene Ave SW16 74 B
Rosedew Rd W6 47 C
Rosefield Gdns E14 33 C
Roseford Ct 16 W12 39 C
Rosegate Ho 32 E3 26 B
Rosehart Mews 8 W11 31 C
Rosehill Rd SW18 59 B
Roseland Ho SW6 58 A
Roseleigh Ave N5 15 A
Rosemary Branch Bridge N1 87 C

osemary Ct 35
E8 ... 51 B4
osemary Dr 16
14 ... 34 C3
osemary Gdns
W14 ... 55 B4
osemary Ho
horeditch N1 ... 87 C3
Villesden NW10 ... 22 A4
osemary La
W14 ... 55 B4
osemary Rd
Camberwell SE15 ... 49 B3
Wandsworth SW17 ... 71 B1
osemary St N1 ... 87 C4
osemary Works Sch
N1 ... 87 C3
osemead Prep Sch
E27 ... 75 B2
osemont Mans 11
W3 ... 11 A2
osemont Rd
Acton W3 ... 28 A2
Richmond TW10 ... 54 A1
South Hampstead
NW3 ... 11 B2
osemoor St
W3 ... 144 C3
osemount Ct 2
W3 ... 28 A1
osemount Lo
W3 ... 28 A2
osenau Cres
W11 ... 168 C3
osenau Rd
W11 ... 168 C4
osendale Prim Sch
E21 ... 75 B4
osendale Rd SE21,
E24 ... 75 B3
oseneath Rd
W11 ... 60 C1
osenthal Ho SE6 ... 67 A1
osenthal Rd SE6 ... 67 B1
osenthorpe Rd
E15 ... 65 C2
oserton St E14 ... 42 B4
ose Sq SW7 ... 143 C2
ose St
Holborn EC4 ... 108 B2
Strand WC2 ... 120 A4
osethorn Cl
W12 ... 73 C4
osetta Cl SW8 ... 162 B1
oseway SE21 ... 63 C1
osewood Ct 2
11 ... 19 C4
osewood Gdns
E13 ... 52 B1
osewood Ho 9
W3 ... 11 A2
osewood Sq
W12 ... 29 C3
osher Cl E15 ... 19 C1
osina St E9 ... 17 C2
oskell Rd SW15 ... 57 C4
oslin Ho 2 E1 ... 32 C2
oslin Rd W3 ... 37 A3
osmead Rd
W11 ... 31 A2 112 B4
osoman Pl EC1 ... 95 C2
osoman St EC1 ... 95 C3
oss Ct
1 Hackney E5 ... 17 A4
4 Putney SW15 ... 69 C4
ossdale Rd SW15 ... 57 B3
osse Gdns SE13 ... 67 C1

Rossendale Way
NW1 ... 83 A4
Rossetti Ct WC1 ... 105 B4
Rossetti Gdns Mans
SW3 ... 158 C4
Rossetti Ho SW1 ... 147 C3
Rossetti Mews
NW8 ... 79 C3
Rossetti Rd SE16 ... 40 A1
Rossetti Studios
SW3 ... 158 B4
Ross Ho 18 E1 ... 32 A1
Rossington St E5 ... 7 C2
Rossiter Rd SW12 ... 73 A3
Rosslyn Ave SW13 ... 56 B4
Rosslyn Ct NW3 ... 12 A3
Rosslyn Hill NW3 ... 11 C3
Rosslyn Ho 8
TW9 ... 44 B2
Rosslyn Mans
8 Hampstead
NW3 ... 11 B2
South Hampstead
NW6 ... 11 B2
Rosslyn Mews 7
NW3 ... 11 C4
Rosslyn Park Mews
NW3 ... 11 C3
Rossmore Ct NW1 ... 90 C2
Rossmore Rd NW1 ... 90 B2
Rostrevor Mans
SW6 ... 164 C4
Rostrevor Mews
SW6 ... 164 C3
Rostrevor Rd
SW6 ... 164 C4
Rotary Lo 12 SE27 ... 75 A1
Rotary St SE1 ... 136 B2
Rothay NW1 ... 92 B4
Rothbury Rd E9 ... 18 C1
Rotheley Ho 39 E9 ... 17 B1
Rotherfield Ct
De Beauvoir Town
N1 ... 15 C1
Shoreditch N1 ... 87 B4
Rotherfield Prim Sch
N1 ... 87 A4
Rotherfield St
Islington N1 ... 15 B1
Shoreditch N1 ... 87 A4
Rotherham Wlk
SE1 ... 122 A1
ROTHERHITHE ... 40 C3
Rotherhithe Bsns Est
6 SE16 ... 40 B2
Rotherhithe New Rd
SE16 ... 40 A1
Rotherhithe Old Rd
SE16 ... 40 C2
Rotherhithe Prim Sch
SE16 ... 40 C2
Rotherhithe St
SE16 ... 40 B4
Rotherhithe Sta
SE16 ... 40 B4
Rotherhithe Tunnel
SE16 ... 32 C1
Rother Ho SE15 ... 65 A3
Rotherwick Rd
NW11 ... 1 C4
Rotherwood Rd
SW15 ... 57 C4
Rothery St N1 ... 86 B4
Rothesay Ave SW14,
TW10 ... 55 A3
Rothesay Ct SE11 ... 163 B3
Rothley Ct NW8 ... 89 B2

Rothsay St SE1 ... 138 A1
Rothsay Wlk 19
E14 ... 41 C2
Rothschild Rd W4 ... 37 B3
Rothwell St
10 Hampstead
NW1 ... 12 B1
Primrose Hill NW1 ... 81 A4
Roth Wlk N7 ... 5 B2
Rotten Row SW1 ... 130 C4
Rotterdam Dr E14 ... 42 B3
Rouel Rd
Bermondsey SE16 ... 153 B4
Bermondsey SE16 ... 139 B1
Roundacre SW19 ... 69 C2
Roundel Cl SE4 ... 66 B3
Roundwood Rd
NW10 ... 8 B1
Rounton Rd E3 ... 26 C1
Roupell Rd SW2 ... 74 B3
Roupell St SE1 ... 121 C1
Rousden St NW1 ... 13 B1
Routh Rd SW18 ... 72 A4
Rover Ho 26 N1 ... 24 A4
Rowallan Rd SW6 ... 154 A1
Rowan Cl W5 ... 36 A4
Rowan Ct
19 Camberwell
SE15 ... 49 B3
Wandsworth SW11 ... 60 B1
Rowan Ho
9 Bow E3 ... 26 B4
Dagenham NW10 ... 21 A1
5 Maitland Pk
NW3 ... 12 B2
Rowan Rd W6 ... 39 C2
Rowan Terr W6 ... 39 C2
Rowan Wlk
7 Dartmouth Pk
N19 ... 4 B2
Kensal Town W10 ... 23 A1
Rowberry Cl SW6 ... 47 B3
Rowcross St SE1 ... 153 A2
Rowditch La
SW11 ... 169 B2
Rowdon Ave NW10 ... 9 A1
Rowe Ho E9 ... 17 B2
Rowe La E9 ... 17 B3
Rowena Cres
SW11 ... 168 B1
Rowfant Rd SW12,
SW17 ... 72 C2
Rowhill Mans 11
E5 ... 17 A4
Rowhill Rd E5 ... 17 A4
Rowington Cl W2 ... 100 A4
Rowland Hill Ho
SE1 ... 136 A4
Rowland Hill St
NW3 ... 12 A3
Rowley Gdns N4 ... 6 B4
Rowley Ho SE8 ... 51 C4
Rowley Ind Pk W3 ... 37 A3
Rowley Way NW8 ... 78 C4
Rowntree Cl NW6 ... 10 C2
Rowse Cl E15 ... 27 B4
Rowstock 1 NW5 ... 13 C2
Rowstock Gdns
N7 ... 13 C3
Roxby Pl SW6 ... 155 C4
Roxford Ho 2 E3 ... 27 A1
Roxley Rd SE13 ... 67 A1
Roxwell 10 NW1 ... 13 A2
Roxwell Rd W12 ... 38 C4
Royal Academy of
Dramatic Art★
WC1 ... 105 B4

Royal Acad of Arts★
W1 ... 118 C3
Royal Acad of Dance
SW11 ... 167 C3
Royal Acad of Music
NW1 ... 91 C1
Royal Albert Hall★
SW7 ... 129 B3
Royal Arc W1 ... 118 C3
Royal Armouries
The★ E1 ... 124 C3
Royal Ave SW3 ... 144 C2
Royal Avenue Ho
SW3 ... 144 C2
Royal Ballet Sch The
Hammersmith
W14 ... 39 C1
St Giles WC2 ... 106 B1
Royal Brompton
Hospl
Chelsea SW3 ... 143 B2
Chelsea SW3 ... 144 A2
Royal Cir SE27 ... 75 A1
Royal Cl
Deptford SE8 ... 51 B4
Putney SW19 ... 69 C2
Stamford Hill N16 ... 7 A3
Royal College of
Physicians Liby
NW1 ... 92 B2
Royal College St
NW1 ... 83 A4
Royal Coll of
Anaesthetists
WC1 ... 106 C3
Royal Coll of Art
SW7 ... 129 B3
Royal Coll of Art
Sculpture Sch
SW11 ... 158 A1
Royal Coll of
Midwives W1 ... 104 A3
Royal Coll of Music
SW7 ... 129 B2
Royal Coll of
Obstetricians &
Gynaecologists
NW1 ... 90 C2
Royal Coll of
Ophthalmologists
NW1 ... 91 B1
Royal Coll of
Paediatrics & Child
Health W1 ... 104 B4
Royal Coll of
Pathologists
SW1 ... 119 B1
Royal Coll of
Physicians NW1 ... 92 B2
Royal Coll of
Radiologists W1 ... 104 B4
Royal Coll of Science
SW7 ... 129 B2
Royal Coll of Speech
Language Therapists
SE1 ... 123 B1
Royal Coll of
Surgeons WC2 ... 107 A2
Royal Courts of
Justice WC2 ... 107 B1
Royal Cres
W11 ... 31 A1 112 A1
Royal Crescent Mews
W11 ... 30 C1

Royal Ct
City of London
EC3 ... 109 C1
Rotherhithe SE16 ... 41 B3
Royal Duchess Mews
SW12 ... 73 A4
Royal Exchange★
EC3 ... 109 C1
Royal Exchange Bldgs
EC3 ... 109 C1
Royal Festival Hall★
SE1 ... 121 A1
Royal Free Hospl
NW3 ... 12 A3
Royal Fusiliers Mus★
E1 ... 124 C3
Royal Geographical
Society SW7 ... 129 C3
Royal Hill SE10 ... 52 B3
Royal Hill Ct 2
SE10 ... 52 B3
Royal Horticultural
Society (Lawrence
Hall & Conf Ctr)
SW1 ... 133 B1
Royal Horticultural
Society (Lindley
Hall) SW1 ... 147 B4
Royal Hospital (Army
Pensioners)★
SW1 ... 145 B1
Royal Hospital Rd
SW3 ... 145 A1
Royal Hospl and
Home SW15 ... 58 A1
Royal Langford
Apartments NW6 ... 78 A2
Royal London Est The
NW10 ... 20 C3
Royal London
Homeopathic Hospl
The WC1 ... 106 B4
Royal London Hospl
Archives & Mus★
E1 ... 32 A4
Royal London Hospl
(Mile End) The
E2 ... 25 C2
Royal London Hospl
(St Clements) The
E3 ... 26 B2
Royal London Hospl
(Whitechapel) The
E1 ... 32 A4
Royal Marsden Hospl
SW3 ... 143 C2
Royal Mews The★
SW1 ... 132 B2
Royal Mint Pl E1 ... 125 B4
Royal Mint St E1 ... 125 A4
Royal National
Orthopaedic Hospl
W1 ... 92 B1
Royal National TNE
Hospl The WC1 ... 94 C4
Royal Naval Pl
SE14 ... 51 B3
Royal Oak Ct
N1 ... 24 A2 98 A4
Royal Oak Pl SE22 ... 65 A1
Royal Oak Rd 5
E8 ... 17 A2
Royal Oak Sta
W2 ... 100 B3
Royal Oak Yd SE1 ... 138 A3

Royal Obsy The★ SE10 52 C3
Royal Opera Arc SW1 119 B2
Royal Orchard Cl SW18 70 A4
Royal Par
Blackheath Vale SE3 53 B1
Fulham SW6 154 A2
12 Richmond TW9 44 C2
Royal Pl 11 SE10 52 B3
Royal Rd SE17 48 A4
Royal Sch Hampstead The NW3 11 C4
Royal St SE1 135 A2
Royalty Ho W1 105 B1
Royalty Mews W1 105 B1
Royalty Studios W11 31 A3
Royal United Services Mus★ SW1 120 A1
Royal Veterinary Coll NW1 83 B3
Royal Victoria Sta E16 35 C2
Royal Victor Pl E3 25 C3
Roycroft Cl SW2 74 C3
Roydon Cl SW11 168 C2
Roy Ridley Ho 6 SW4 61 C4
Roy Sq E14 33 A2
Royston Ct
New Cross SE4 51 B1
3 Richmond TW9 44 B2
Royston Ho 14 SE15 49 C4
Royston Rd TW10 54 A2
Royston St 24 E2 25 B3
Rozel Ct 3 N1 24 A4
Rozel Rd SW4 61 B4
Ruby St SE15 50 A4
Ruby Triangle SE15 50 A4
Rucklidge Ave NW10 21 C3
Rudall Cres NW3 11 C4
Rudbeck Ho 11 SE15 49 C3
Ruddlngton Cl E5 18 A4
Rudge Ho SE16 139 C2
Rudgwick Terr NW8 80 B3
Rudhall Ho 4 SW2 62 C1
Rudloe Rd SW12 73 B4
Rudolf Pl SW8 162 B3
Rudolph Rd NW6 23 C3
Rudstone Ho 10 E3 27 A2
Rudyard Ct SE1 137 C3
Rufford St N1 84 B4
Rufford Street Mews N1 14 A1
Rufford Twr 5 W3 28 A1
Rufus Bsns Ctr SW18 71 A2
Rufus Ho SE1 139 A2
Rufus St N1 24 A2 98 A3
Rugby Mans W14 140 B4
Rugby Rd W4 38 A4
Rugby St WC1 94 C1
Rugg St E14 33 C2
Rugless Ho 2 E14 42 B4
Rugmere 4 NW1 12 C1
Rumball Ho 14 SE5 49 A3
Rumbold Rd SW6 156 B1
Rum Cl E1 32 B2
Rumford Ho SE1 136 C1
Rumsey Rd SW9 62 B4
Runacres Ct SE17 150 C1
Runcorn Pl W11 31 A2 112 A4
Rundell Twr SW8 172 C4
Running Horse Yd 12 TW8 44 A4
Runnymede Ct SW15 68 C3
Runnymede Ho
Hackney E9 18 A4
Richmond TW10 54 C2
Rupack St 3 SE16 40 B4
Rupert Ct W1 119 B4
Rupert Gdns SW9 48 A1
Rupert Ho SE11 149 C3
8 Upper Holloway N19 4 C1
Rupert Rd
Bedford Pk W4 38 A3
Paddington NW6 23 B3
Upper Holloway N19 4 C2
Rupert St W1 119 B4
Rusbridge Cl E8 16 C3
Ruscoe Rd E16 35 B3
Rusham Rd SW12 72 B4
Rushbrook Ho SW8 171 B2
Rushby Ct SW4 172 A3
Rush Common Mews 18 SW2 74 B4
Rushcroft Rd SW2, SW9 62 C3
Rushcutters Ct 18 SE16 41 A2
Rushey Mead SE4 66 C2
Rushford Rd SE4 66 B1
Rush Hill Mews 3 SW11 60 C4
Rush Hill Rd SW11 60 C4
Rushlake Ho SW11 169 B2
Rushmead 5 E2 25 A2
Rushmere Ho 2 SW15 68 C3
Rushmore Cres 9 E5 17 C4
Rushmore Ho
9 Kentish Town N7 13 C3
W14 126 B1
Rushmore Prim Sch E5 17 C4
Rushmore Rd
Clapton Pk E5 17 C4
Hackney E5 18 A4
Rusholme Rd SW15 58 A1
Rushton Ho SW8 171 B1
Rushton St N1 87 C2
Rushworth St SE1 136 B3
Ruskin Ave TW9 44 C3
Ruskin Ct SE5 63 C4
Ruskin Ho SW1 147 C3
Ruskin Park Ho SE5 63 C4
Ruskin Wlk SE24 63 B2
Rusper Ct SW9 172 B1
Russell Cl W4 46 B4
Russell Ct
Battersea SW11 169 C3
Bloomsbury WC1 94 A1
5 Peckham SE15 50 A1
St James SW1 119 A1
Russell Gdns W14 126 A2
Russell Gdns Mews W14 126 A2
Russell Gr SW9 173 C4
Russell Ho
21 Poplar E14 33 C3
SW1 146 C2
Russell Kerr Cl W4 45 B3
Russell Lo SE1 137 B2
Russell Mans WC1 106 B4
Russell Pickering Ho 2 SW4 62 A4
Russell Pl
Hampstead NW3 12 A3
Rotherhithe SE16 41 A3
Russell Rd W14 126 B1
Russell Sq WC1 94 A1
Russell Square Ho WC1 94 A1
Russell Square Mans WC1 106 B4
Russell Square Sta WC1 94 A1
Russell St WC2 120 B4
Russell's Wharf 2 W9 23 B1
Russell Wlk 4 TW10 54 B1
Russet Cres N7 14 B3
Russett Way SE13 52 A1
Russia Dock Rd SE16 33 A1
Russia La E2 25 B3
Russia Row EC2 109 A1
Rusthall Ave W4 37 C3
Rusthall Mans 3 W4 37 C2
Ruston Mews W11 31 A3
Ruston St E3 26 B4
Rust Sq SE5 48 C3
Ruth Ct 16 E3 26 A3
Rutherford Ho 12 E1 25 A1
Rutherford St SW1 147 B4
Ruth Ho W10 23 A1
Ruthin Rd SE3 53 C4
Ruthven St E9 25 C4
Rutland Cl SW14 55 B4
Rutland Ct
Herne Hill SE5 63 C3
SW7 130 B3
Rutland Gate SW7 130 B3
Rutland Gate Mews SW7 130 A3
Rutland Gdns SW7 130 B3
Rutland Gdns Mews SW7 130 B3
Rutland Gr W6 39 A1
Rutland Ho
10 Putney SW15 69 B4
W8 128 A1
Rutland Mews E SW7 130 B2
Rutland Mews S SW7 130 A2
Rutland Mews W SW7 130 A2
Rutland Park Gdns 1 NW2 9 B2
Rutland Park Mans 2 NW2 9 B2
Rutland Pk NW2 9 B2
Rutland Pl EC1 108 B4
Rutland Rd E9 25 C4
Rutland St SW7 130 B2
Rutland Studios NW10 21 C2
Rutley Cl SE11 48 A4
Rutt's Terr SE14 50 C2
Ruvigny Gdns SW15 57 C4
Ruvigny Mans SW15 57 C4
Rycott Path SE22 76 C4
Ryculff Sq SE3 53 B1
Rydal Ho SW8 171 B1
Rydal Water NW1 92 C3
Ryde Ho 1 NW6 23 C4
Ryder Ct SW1 119 A2
Ryder Dr SE16 40 A1
Ryder Ho 18 E1 25 B1
Ryder St SW1 119 A2
Ryder's Terr NW8 78 C2
Ryder Yd SW1 119 A2
Ryde Vale Rd SW12 73 B2
Rydon St N1 87 A4
Rydston Cl 2 N7 14 B1
Ryecotes Mead SE21 76 A3
Ryecroft Rd SE13 67 B2
Ryecroft St SW6 166 A3
Ryedale SE22 65 A1
Ryefield Path 7 SW15 68 C3
Ryegates 2 SE15 50 A1
Rye Hill Pk SE15 65 B3
Rye Ho 17 SE16 40 B4
Rye La SE15 49 C1
Rye Lane Mkt SE15 49 C1
Rye Oak Sch SE15 65 A4
Rye Rd SE15 65 C3
Rye Wlk SW15 57 C2
Ryfold Rd SW19 70 C1
Ryland Rd NW5 13 A2
Rylett Cres W12 38 B3
Rylett Rd W12 38 B3
Rylston Rd SW6 154 C3
Rymer St SE24 63 A1
Rysbrack St SW1 130 C2

S

Saatchi Gallery Duke of York's HQ★ SW3 145 A2
Sabbarton St 9 E16 35 B3
Sabella Ct E3 26 B3
Sabine Rd SW11 60 C4
Sable St N1 15 A1
Sacketts Ho SW9 173 C4
Sackville Ho 16 SW16 74 A1
Sackville St W1 119 A3
Sacred Heart High Sch W6 39 B2
Sacred Heart Jun Sch W6 39
Sacred Heart Prim Sch, Battersea SW11 168
Sacred Heart RC Prim Sch
Islington N7 14
Putney SW15 56
Sacred Heart RC Sec Sch SE5 48
Saddlers Mews SW8 172
Sadler Ho
17 Bromley E3 27
EC1 96
Saffron Ave E14 34
Saffron Ct 10 N1 15
Saffron Hill EC1 107
Saffron Ho 6 TW9 45
Saffron St EC1 107
Saffron Wharf SE1 139
Sage Mews SE22 64
Sage St E1 32
Sage Way WC1 94
Sailacre Ho 10 SE10 43
Sail Ct 10 E14 34
Sailmakers Ct SW6 59
Sail St SE11 149
Sainfoin Rd SW17 72
St Agnes Cl E9 25
St Agnes Pl SE11 48
St Agnes RC Prim Sch E3 27
St Agnes RC Sch NW2 1
St Aidan's Prim Sch N4 5
St Aidan's Rd SE22 65
St Albans Ave W4 37
St Alban's CE Prim Sch EC1 107
St Alban's Cl NW11 1
St Alban's Gr W8 128
St Albans La NW11 1
St Albans Mans W8 128
St Alban's Pl N1 86
St Alban's Rd
Dagenham NW10 21
Dartmouth Pk NW5 4
St Alban's St SW1 119
St Albans Studios W8 128
St Albans Terr W6 154
St Alban's Villas NW5 3
St Alfege Pas SE10 52
St Alfege with St Peter's CE Prim Sch SE10 52
St Aloysius RC Coll N19 4
St Aloysius RC Inf Sch NW1 93
St Aloysius RC Jun Sch NW1 83
St Alphage Gdn EC2 109

St Alphage Highwalk EC2 .... 109 A3
St Alphonsus Rd SW4 .... 61 C3
St Andrew & St Francis CE Prim Sch NW2 .... 8 C2
St Andrew's (Barnsbury) CE Prim Sch N1 .... 85 A4
St Andrew's CE Prim Sch SW9 .... 172 B1
St Andrews Chambers W1 .... 105 A2
St Andrews Cl [25] SE16 .... 40 A1
St Andrews Ct W4 .. 45 B2
St Andrew's Ct [2] SW18 .... 71 B2
St Andrew's Gr N16 . 6 C3
St Andrew's Greek Sch NW1 .... 13 B2
St Andrew's Hill EC4 .... 108 B1
St Andrews Ho [11] SE16 .... 40 A3
St Andrew's Hospl E3 .... 27 A1
St Andrews Mans [9] E5 .... 17 A4
St Andrew's Mans W1 .... 103 B3
St Andrews Mews
Greenwich SE3 .... 53 C3
[4] Streatham SW12 .... 73 C3
St Andrew's Mews N16 .... 7 A3
St Andrew's Pl NW1 .... 92 B2
St Andrew's Rd
Dagenham W3 .... 29 A3
W14 .... 154 B4
Willesden NW2 .... 9 A2
St Andrew's Sq W11 .... 31 A3
St Andrew St EC4 107 C3
St Andrews Way E3 .... 27 A1
St Andrew's Wharf SE1 .... 139 A4
St Anne RC Prim Sch E1 .... 24 C1 99 B1
St Anne's CE Prim Sch SW18 .... 59 A2
St Anne's Cl N6 .... 3 C1
St Anne's Ct
Kensal Rise NW6 .... 23 A4
W1 .... 105 B1
St Anne's Flats NW1 .... 93 B4
St Anne's Pas E14 .. 33 B3
St Anne's RC Prim Sch SE11 .... 162 C4
St Anne's Row E14 .... 33 B3
St Anne St E14 .... 33 B3
St Anne's Trad Est [25] E14 .... 33 B3
St Ann's Cres SW18 .... 59 B1
St Ann's Gdns NW5 .... 12 C2
St Ann's Hill SW18 . 59 B1
St Ann's Ho WC1 .. 95 B3
St Ann's La SW1 .. 133 C1
St Ann's Park Rd SW18 .... 59 B1
St Anns Rd SW13 ... 46 B2
St Ann's Rd W11 ... 30 C2
St Ann's St SW1 .. 133 C2
St Ann's Terr NW8 . 79 C2
St Ann's Villas W11 .... 31 A1 112 A1
St Anselm's Pl W1 .... 118 A4
St Anselm's RC Prim Sch SW17 .... 72 C1
St Anthonys Cl SW17 .... 72 A2
St Anthony's Cl E1 .... 125 B2
St Anthony's Ct
[2] Balham SW12 .... 60 C1
Upper Tooting SW17 .... 72 C2
St Anthony's Flats NW1 .... 83 B1
St Anthony's RC Prim Sch SE22 .... 64 C1
St Asaph Ct SE4 .... 65 C4
St Asaph Rd SE4 ... 65 C4
St Aubins Ct N1 ... 87 C4
St Augustine's CE High Sch NW6 .... 23 C3
St Augustine's CE Prim Sch NW6 ... 78 A2
St Augustine's Ho NW1 .... 93 B4
St Augustine's RC Prim Sch W6 .... 154 B3
St Augustine's Rd NW1 .... 13 C1
St Austell Rd SE13 .. 52 C1
St Barnabas CE Prim Sch SW1 .... 145 C2
St Barnabas Cl [11] SE22 .... 64 A2
St Barnabas & St Philip's CE Prim Sch W8 .... 127 B1
St Barnabas St SW1 .... 145 C2
St Barnabas Terr E9 .... 17 C3
St Barnabas Villas SW8 .... 172 B4
St Bartholomew's Hospl EC1 .... 108 B3
St Bede's RC Inf Sch SW12 .... 73 C3
St Benets Cl SW17 .. 72 A2
St Benet's Pl EC3 123 C4
St Bernadette RC Jun Sch SW12 .... 73 B4
St Bernard Ho [6] E14 .... 42 B3
St Botolph St E1, EC3 .... 110 C2
St Brelades Ct N1 . 87 C4
St Bride's Ave EC4 .... 108 A1
St Bride's Pas EC4 .... 108 A1
St Bride St EC4 ... 108 A2
St Catherines Cl SW17 .... 72 A2
St Catherine's Ct [8] W4 .... 38 A3
St Catherine's Dr SE14 .... 50 C1
St Catherines Mews SW3 .... 144 C4
St Cecilia's CE Sch SW18 .... 70 B3
St Chad's Pl WC1 .. 94 C4
St Chad's St WC1 .. 94 B4
St Charles' Hospl W10 .... 30 C4
St Charles Pl W10 .. 31 A4
St Charles RC Prim Sch W10 .... 30 C4
St Charles RC Sixth Form Coll W10 .... 30 C4
St Charles Sq W10 .... 30 C4
St Christina's Sch NW8 .... 80 B2
St Christophers Ct [15] N19 .... 4 B1
St Christopher's Ho NW1 .... 83 B1
St Christopher's Pl W1 .... 103 C2
St Christopher's Sch NW3 .... 11 C3
St Clair Ho [17] E3 ... 26 B2
St Clare St EC3 ... 110 C1
St Clement Danes CE Prim Sch WC2 .. 106 C1
St Clement & St James CE Prim Sch W11 .... 31 A1 112 A2
St Clements Ct
Barnsbury N7 .... 14 B2
[7] SE14 .... 50 C4
[8] Shepherd's Bush W11 .... 30 C2
St Clement's Ct EC3 .... 123 C4
St Clements Ho E1 .... 110 C3
St Clement's La WC2 .... 107 A1
St Clements Mans [3] SW6 .... 47 C4
St Clements St N7 .. 14 C1
St Columb's Ho [11] W10 .... 31 A4
St Crispins Cl NW3 .... 12 A4
St Cross St EC1 ... 107 C4
St Cuthbert's Rd NW2 .... 10 B2
St Cuthbert with St Matthias Prim Sch SW5 .... 142 A2
St Davids Cl [27] SE16 .... 40 A1
St David's Sq E14 .. 42 A1
St Dionis Rd SW6 165 A2
St Dominic RC Prim Sch NW5 .... 12 B3
St Dominics RC Prim Sch E9 .... 18 A2
St Donatt's Rd SE14 .... 51 B2
St Dunstan's Alley EC3 .... 124 A3
St Dunstan's Ave W3 .... 28 C2
St Dunstan's Ct EC4 .... 107 C1
St Dunstan's Gdns W3 .... 28 C2
St Dunstan's Hill EC3 .... 124 A3
St Dunstan's La EC3 .... 124 A3
St Dunstan's Rd W6 .... 39 C1
St Edmund RC Sch E14 .... 41 C2
St Edmunds Cl SW17 .... 72 A2
St Edmund's Cl NW8 .... 80 C3
St Edmund's Ct NW8 .... 80 C3
St Edmund's Sq SW13 .... 47 B4
St Edmund's Terr NW8 .... 80 C3
St Edward's RC Prim Sch NW1 .... 90 B1
St Elizabeth RC Prim Sch E2 .... 25 B3
St Elizabeth's RC Prim Sch TW10 .... 54 B1
St Elmo Rd W12 .... 38 B4
St Elmos Rd SE16 .. 41 A4
St Ermin's Hill SW1 .... 133 B2
St Ervan's Rd W10 .. 31 B4
St Eugene de Mazenod Rc Prim Sch NW6 .... 10 C1
St Faith's CE Prim Sch SW18 .... 59 B2
St Faith's Rd SE24 .. 75 A3
St Francesca Cabrini Prim Sch SE23 .... 65 B1
St Francis' Ho NW1 .... 83 B1
St Francis of Assisi RC Prim Sch W11 .... 30 C2
St Francis Pl SW12 .... 61 A1
St Francis RC Prim Sch SE15 .... 49 C3
St Francis Rd SE22 .... 64 A3
St Francis Xavier Sixth Form Coll SW12 .... 61 A1
St Frideswides Mews [5] E14 .... 34 B3
St Gabriel's CE Prim Sch SW1 .... 146 C1
St Gabriels Cl [3] E14 .... 34 A4
St Gabriel's Rd NW2 .... 9 C3
St George Ho SW11 .... 169 C3
ST GEORGE IN THE EAST 32 A2
St George's Ave N7 .... 13 C4
St George's Battersea CE Prim Sch SW8 .... 161 A1
St George's Bldgs SE11 .... 136 B1
St George's Cath NW1 .... 92 B4
St George's Cath RC Jun & Inf Sch SE1 .... 136 A2
St George's CE Prim Sch SE5 .... 49 A3
St George's Circ SE1 .... 136 A2
St Georges Cl SW8 .... 171 A4
St Georges Coll N7 .. 5 C1
St Georges Ct SW15 .... 58 B3
St George's Ct
Brompton SW3 .... 144 A4
Kensington SW7 .... 128 C1
Newington SE1 .... 136 A1
St George's Dr SW1 .... 146 C2
St George's Field W2 .... 102 B1
St George's Gr SW17 .... 71 C1
St Georges Hanover Sq Sch W1 .... 117 C3
St George's Ho NW1 .... 83 A1
St George's La EC3 .... 124 A4
St Georges Mews [11] NW1 .... 12 B1
St George's Mews
[2] Rotherhithe SE8 .... 41 B2
SE1 .... 135 C2
St Georges Pl N7 ... 13 C4
St George's RC Cath SE1 .... 135 C2
St George's RC Sec Sch W9 .... 78 B1
St Georges Rd W4 .... 37 C4
St George's Rd
Newington SE1 .... 136 A1
Richmond TW9 .... 54 B4
St George's Residences [4] SW2 .... 62 C2
St Georges's Ct EC4 .... 108 A2
St Georges Sq [1] E14 .... 33 A2
St George's Sq
Rotherhithe SE8 .... 41 B2
SW1 .... 147 B1
St George's Square Mews SW1 .... 147 B1
St George St W1 . 118 B4
St Georges Terr
Hampstead NW1 .... 12 B1
NW1 .... 81 A4
St George's Way SE15 .... 49 A4
St George the Martyr CE Prim Sch WC1 95 A1
St George Wharf SW8 .... 162 A4
St Gerards Cl SW4 .. 61 B2
St German's Pl SE3 .... 53 C2
St Gildas' RC Jun Sch N8 .... 5 A4
ST GILES 106 A2
St Giles Cir WC1 . 105 C2
St Giles Coll WC1 106 B4
St Giles Ct WC2 .. 106 A2
St Giles High St WC2 .... 105 C2
St Giles Ho SW16 ... 74 A1
St Giles Hospl SE5 .. 49 A2
St Giles Pas WC2 105 C1
St Giles Rd SE5 .... 49 A2
St Giles Twr [3] SE5 .... 49 A2
St Gilles Ho [15] E2 .. 25 C3

St Helena Ho WC1 95 B3
St Helena Rd SE16 40 C2
St Helena St WC1 95 B3
St Helen's Gdns W10 30 C3
St Helen's Pl EC3 110 A2
St Helen's RC Sch SW9 62 C4
St Helier Ct 4 N1 24 A4
St Hildas Cl SW17 72 A2
St Hilda's Cl NW6 9 C1
St Hilda's Rd SW13 47 A4
St Hildas Wharf E1 32 B1
St Hubert's Ho 2 E14 41 C3
St Hughes Cl SW17 72 A2
St Ives Ct NW2 10 A2
ST JAMES 119 B2
St James Ct
Bethnal Green E2 24 C2 99 C3
10 Brentford W4 36 C1
St James' Ct
Bedford Pk W4 37 C3
SW1 133 A2
St James Ho N5 14 C3
St James Independent Schs W14 140 B4
St James Ind Mews SE1 153 C1
St James' Mans NW6 10 C1
St James Mews E14 42 B3
St James's SE14 51 A2
St James's App EC2 24 A1 98 A1
St James's Ave E2 25 B3
St James School Flats 5 N7 14 C3
St James's Cl NW8 80 C3
Upper Tooting SW17 72 B2
St James's Cloisters 2 SE22 64 B3
St James's Cres SW9 62 C4
St James's Dr
Balham SW12, SW17 72 B4
Upper Tooting SW17 72 B3
St James's Gdns W11 31 A1 112 A2
St James's Gr SW11 169 A2
St James's Hatcham CE Prim Sch SE14 51 A2
St James's Market SW1 119 B3
St James's Pal★ SW1 119 A1
St James's Park Sta SW1 133 B2
St James's Pas EC3 110 B1
St James's Pk★ SW1 133 B4
St James's Pl SW1 118 C1
St James's Rd
Bermondsey SE1, SE16 153 C4
Peckham SE1 49 C4
St James's & St Michael's CE Prim Sch W2 115 A4
St James's Sq SW1 119 A2
St James's St SW1 118 C2
St James St W6 39 B1
St James's Terr NW8 80 C4
2 Upper Tooting SW12 72 C3
St James's Terrace Mews NW8 80 C3
St James The Great RC Prim Sch SE15 49 B2
St James Wlk EC1 96 A2
St Joan of Arc RC Prim Sch N5 15 B4
St John Evangelist RC Prim Sch N1 86 A2
St John of Jerusalem CE Prim Sch E9 17 B1
ST JOHN'S 51 C1
St John & St James CE Prim Sch E9 17 B3
St John's Angell Town CE Prim Sch SW9 173 B1
St John's Ave
Dagenham NW10 21 B4
Putney SW15 57 C2
St John's CE Prim Sch
Fulham SW6 164 B4
SE17 151 A3
South Hackney E2 25 B3
St John's Church Rd E9 17 B3
St John's Cl SW6 155 B2
St Johns Concert Hall★ SW1 134 A1
St John's Cres SW9 62 C4
St Johns Ct 39 E1 32 A1
St John's Ct
Finsbury Pk N4 6 A2
Hammersmith W6 39 A2
Lewisham SE13 52 B1
5 South Hampstead NW3 11 B2
Saint John's Ct N5 15 A4
St John's Dr SW18 71 A3
St John's Est SE1 138 C3
St John's Gdns W11 31 B2 112 C3
St John's Gr
3 Barnes SW13 46 B1
1 Richmond TW9 54 A3
Upper Holloway N19 4 B2
St John's Highbury Vale CE Prim Sch N5 6 A1
St John's Hill SW11 59 C3
St John's Hill Gr SW11 59 C3
St Johns Ho 5 SE17 48 C4
St John's Ho 1 E14 42 B2
St John's La EC1 108 B4
St John's Lodge 8 SE8 51 C2
St John's Mans E5 17 B3
St John's Park Mans N19 4 B1
St John's Path EC1 96 A1
St John's Pk SE3 53 C3
St John's Pl EC1 96 A1
St John's RC Prim Sch SE16 41 A4
St John's Rd
Battersea SW11 60 A3
Canning Town E16 35 C3
Richmond TW9 54 A3
St John's & St Clements CE Prim Sch SE15 64 C4
St John's Sq EC1 96 A1
St Johns Sta SE8 51 C1
St John St EC1 96 A2
St John's Terr W10 22 C1
St John's Upper Holloway CE Prim Sch N19 4 C2
St John's Vale SE8 51 C1
St John's Villas
Upper Holloway N19 4 C2
W8 128 B1
St John's Way N19 4 C3
ST JOHN'S WOOD 79 B1
St John's Wood Ct NW8 89 C3
St John's Wood High St NW8 80 A1
St John's Wood Park NW8 79 B4
St John's Wood Pre-Prep Sch NW8 90 A4
St John's Wood Rd NW8 89 C3
St John's Wood Sta NW8 79 B2
St John's Wood Terr NW8 80 A2
St John the Baptist CE Prim Sch N1 87 C1
St John the Divine CE Jun & Inf Sch SE5 48 A3
St Joseph's Cl W10 31 A4
St Josephs Ct 3 NW10 21 B3
St Joseph's Flats NW1 93 B4
St Joseph's Ho W6 39 C2
St Joseph's Hospice E9, E8 25 A4
St Joseph's RC Inf & Jun Schs SE5 48 B3
St Joseph's RC Prim Sch
Chelsea SW3 144 C3
Deptford SE8 51 C3
Greenwich SE10 43 A1
Paddington W9 88 C3
Rotherhithe SE16 40 B3
St Giles WC2 106 B2
Upper Holloway N19 4 A3
Wandsworth SW18 58 C2
St Joseph's RC Prim Sch *continued*
Willesden NW10 8 A1
St Joseph's St SW8 170 B4
St Joseph's Vale SE3 67 C4
St Jude & St Paul's CE Prim Sch N1 16 A2
St Jude's CE Prim Sch SE24 63 A2
St Judes Ho 6 W10 23 B2
St Jude's Prim Sch SE1 136 A1
St Jude's Rd E2 25 A3
St Jude St N16 16 A3
St Julian's Rd NW6 23 C4
St Katharine's Ho N1 85 B2
St Katharine's Prec NW1 82 A2
St Katharine's Way E1 125 A2
St Katherine's Row EC3 110 B1
St Katherine's Wlk 1 W11 30 C1
St Kilda's Rd N16 7 A3
St Laurence's Cl NW6 22 C4
St Lawrence Ct N1 87 C4
St Lawrence Ho SE1 138 B2
St Lawrence St E14 34 B1
St Lawrence Terr W10 31 A4
St Lawrence Way SW9 173 C2
St Leonards Ct SW14 55 B4
St Leonard's Ct N1 97 C4
St Leonard's Hospl N1 24 A3
St Leonards Rd SW14 55 B4
St Leonard's Rd
Becontree NW10 20 C1
South Bromley E14 34 B4
St Leonard's Sq NW5 12 C2
St Leonard's St E3 27 A2
St Leonard's Terr SW3 145 A1
St Loo Ave SW3 158 B4
St Loo Ct SW3 158 C4
St Luke Prim Sch E16 35 B3
ST LUKE'S 97 A2
St Luke's Ave SW4 61 C3
St Luke's CE Prim Sch
Cubitt Town E14 42 C2
Paddington W9 23 B2
Shoreditch EC1 97 A3
St Luke's Cl EC1 97 A2
St Luke's Ct W11 31 B3
St Luke's Hospl W1 92 C1
St Luke's Mews W11 31 B3
St Luke's Rd W11 31 B4
St Luke's Sq E16 35 B3
St Luke's St SW3 144 B2
St Margaret's Cres SW15 57 A2
St Margaret's Ct
Putney SW15 57 A3
SE1 123 B1
St Margaret's La W8 128 A1
St Margarets Lo W3 37 A4
St Margaret's Rd
Brockley SE4 66 B3
Kensal Green NW10 22 B2
St Margaret's Sch NW3 11 A4
St Margaret St SW1 134 A3
St Mark's CE Prim Sch SE11 163 A4
St Marks Cl 5 SE10 52 B3
St Mark's Cres NW1 81 C4
St Marks Gate E9 18 B1
St Mark's Gr SW10 156 B2
St Marks Ho 6 SE17 48 C4
St Mark's Hospl EC1 96 B4
St Mark's Mans 14 N4 5 B2
St Mark's Pl W11 31 A3
St Mark's Prim Sch N19 5 A2
St Marks Rd 15 NW10 30 C3
St Mark's Rd
North Kensington W10 30 C4
Notting Hill W11 31 A3
St Mark's Rise E8 16 B3
St Mark's Sq NW1 81 B3
St Mark St E1 111 A1
St Martin-in-the-Fields High Sch for Girls SW2 74 C3
St Martin's Almshouses NW1 82 C4
St Martin's Cl NW1 82 C4
St Martins Ct N1 24 A4
St Martin's Ct
WC2 120 A4
West Norwood SE27 75 A2
St Martin's La WC2 120 A3
St Martin's Le Grand EC1 108 C2
St Martin's Pl WC2 120 A3
St Martin's Rd SW9 172 C2
St Martin's St WC2 119 C3
St Martin's Way SW17 71 B1
St Mary Abbots CE Prim Sch W8 128 A3
St Mary Abbot's Ct W14 126 C1
St Mary Abbot's Pl W8 127 A1
St Mary Abbots Terr W14 127 A1
St Mary at Hill EC3 124 A3
St Mary Axe EC3 110 B2

St Marychurch St SE16 40 B4
St Mary Graces Ct E1 125 A3
St Marylebone CE Sch The W1 103 C4
St Mary le Bow Church★ EC2 109 A1
St Mary- le-Park Ct SW11 158 B1
St Mary Magdalene CE Prim Sch
Islington N7 14 C2
Paddington W2 100 A4
Peckham SE15 50 A1
St Mary Magdalen's RC Prim Sch
Brockley SE4 66 A3
Mortlake SW14 55 C4
St Mary Magdelen's RC Jun Sch NW2 9 A2
St Mary Newington Cl SE17 152 B2
St Mary of the Angels RC Prim Sch W2 31 C3
St Mary RC Prim Sch W10 23 A1
St Mary & St Michael Prim Sch E1 32 B3
St Mary & St Pancras CE Prim Sch NW1 83 B1
St Mary's Bryanston Square CE Sch W1 102 C4
St Mary's CE Prim Sch
Islington N1 86 B4
Putney SW15 57 C4
Willesden NW10 8 A2
St Mary's Ct W6 38 B3
St Mary's Est 2 SE16 40 B4
St Mary's Flats NW1 93 B4
St Mary's Gate W8 128 A1
St Mary's Gdns SE11 149 C4
St Mary's Gr
Barnes SW13 57 A4
Chiswick W4 45 A4
Islington N1 15 A2
Richmond TW10, TW9 54 B3
St Mary's Ho N1 86 B4
St Mary's Hospl W2 101 C2
St Mary's Hospl Medical Sch W2 101 C2
St Mary's Kilburn CE Prim Sch NW6 23 C4
St Mary's Lewisham CE Prim Sch SE13 67 A2
St Mary's Mans
Dagenham NW10 21 A4
Paddington W2 101 B4
St Mary's Mews NW6 11 A1
St Mary's Path N1 86 B4
St Mary's Pl W8 128 A1
St Mary's RC Prim Sch
Chiswick W4 46 A4

St Mary's RC Prim Sch *continued*
Clapham Pk SW4 61 B2
Clapham SW8 170 B4
Hammersmith W14 39 C3
Paddington NW6 23 C3
St Mary's Rd
Dagenham NW10 21 A4
Golders Green NW11 1 A4
Nunhead SE15 50 B1
St Mary's Sch Hampstead NW3 11 C3
St Mary's Sq W2 101 B4
St Mary's Stoke Newington CE Prim Sch N16 7 A2
St Mary's Terr W2 101 B4
St Mary's Twr EC1 97 A1
St Mary's Wlk SE11 149 C4
St Matthews Ct SE1 136 C1
St Matthew's Ho 8 SE17 48 C4
St Matthew's Lo NW1 83 A2
St Matthew's Rd SW2 62 B2
St Matthew's Row E2 24 C1 99 B2
St Matthews Sch Westminster SW1 133 C2
St Matthew St SW1 133 B1
St Matthias CE Prim Sch E2 24 B1 99 A2
St Matthias's CE Prim Sch N16 16 A4
St Mauritius Ho SE13 67 B2
St Maur Rd SW6 165 A3
St Michael's Alley EC3 109 C1
St Michael's CE Prim Sch
Camden Town NW1 82 C4
Highgate N6 3 C4
Wandsworth SW18 70 B4
St Michaels Ct 2 E14 34 B4
St Michael's Ct NW11 1 B4
St Michael's Flats NW1 83 B1
St Michael's Gdns W10 31 A4
St Michael's Rd
Cricklewood NW2 9 B4
Stockwell SW9 172 C2
St Michael's St W2 102 A2
St Michael Steiner Sch The SW18 58 C2
St Mildred's Ct EC2 109 B1
St Monica's RC Prim Sch N1 24 A2 98 A4
St Nicholas' Flats NW1 83 B1
St Nicholas Ho SE8 51 C4
St Nicholas Mans SW17 72 B2

St Nicholas St SE8 51 C2
St Norbert Gn SE4 66 A3
St Norbert Rd SE4 66 A3
St Olaf's Rd SW6 154 B1
St Olaves Ct W2 114 A3
St Olave's Ct EC2 109 B1
St Olave's Est SE1 138 B4
St Olave's Gdns SE11 149 B4
St Olave's Mans SE11 149 B4
St Olav's Sq 32 SE16 40 B4
St Osmund's RC Prim Sch SW13 46 B2
St Oswald's Pl SE11 148 C1
St Oswulf St SW1 147 C3
St Owen Ho SE1 138 B2
ST PANCRAS 94 B4
St Pancras Almshouses 13 NW5 12 B3
St Pancras Commercial Ctr NW1 83 A4
St Pancras Hospl NW1 83 B3
St Pancras International Sta WC1 94 A4
St Pancras Way NW1 83 B4
St Patrick's Coll W1 105 B2
St Patrick's RC Prim Sch NW5 13 A3
St Paul's Ave
Rotherhithe SE16 32 C1
Willesden NW2 9 B2
St Paul's Cath★ EC4 108 C1
St Paul's Cath Sch EC4 108 C1
St Paul's CE Prim Sch
Hammersmith W6 39 B1
Hampstead NW3 12 B1
SE17 150 C2
St Paul's Church Yd EC4 108 C1
St Pauls Cl W5 36 B4
St Pauls Cres NW1 13 C1
St Paul's Ct
Clapham SW4 61 C3
6 Upper Holloway N19 5 A2
St Paul's Dr E15 19 C3
St Paul's Girls' Sch W6 39 C2
St Pauls Mews NW1 13 C1
St Paul's Pl N1 15 C2
St Pauls Rd TW9 54 B4
St Paul's Rd N1 15 B2
St Paul's Sch SW13 38 C1
St Paul's Sta EC2 108 C2
St Paul St N1 87 A3
St Paul's Terr SE17 48 A4
St Pauls View WC1 95 B3
St Paul's Way E3 33 C4

St Paul's Way Com Sch E3 33 C4
St Paul's with St Michael's Prim Sch E8 24 C4
St Paul with St Luke CE Prim Sch E3 33 B4
St Peter & St Paul RC Prim Sch EC1 96 B2
St Peter's Alley EC3 109 C1
St Peter's Ave 37 E2 24 C3
St Petersburgh Mews W2 114 A4
St Petersburgh Pl W2 114 A3
St Peter's CE Prim Sch
Chiswick W6 38 C1
Paddington W9 23 C1
SE17 151 B1
St Peter's Church Ct N1 86 B3
St Peters Cl SW17 72 A2
St Peter's Cl E2 24 C3
St Peters Ct
New Cross SE4 51 B1
28 Stepney E1 25 B1
St Peter's Eaton Square Prim Sch SW1 132 B1
St Peter's Gdns SE27 74 C1
St Peter's Gr W6 38 C2
St Peters Ho WC1 94 B3
St Peter's Ho
4 SE17 48 C4
Stamford Hill N16 7 A4
St Peter's London Docks CE Prim Sch E1 32 B1
St Peter's Pl W9 88 A1
St Peter's Rd W6 38 C1
St Peter's Sq
Chiswick W6 38 B1
Hackney E2 24 C3
St Peter's St N1 86 B3
St Peter's Street Mews N1 86 B2
St Peter's Terr SW6 154 B1
St Peter's Villas 5 W6 38 C2
St Peter's Way N1 16 A1
St Peter's Wharf 8 W6 38 C1
St Philip Ho WC1 95 B3
St Philip Sq SW8 170 A1
St Philip's Rd E8 16 C2
St Philip's Sch SW7 143 A3
St Philip St SW8 170 A1
St Philip's Way N1 87 A3
St Quentin Ho SW18 59 C1
St Quintin Ave W10 30 C4
St Quintin Gdns 21 W10 30 B4
St Regis Hts NW3 2 A1
St Richard's Ho NW1 93 B4
St Rule St SW8 170 C1
St Saviours SW4 61 A3

St Saviour's CE Prim Sch
Bow Comm E14 34 A4
Camberwell SE24 63 B4
Paddington W9 88 B1
St Saviours Ho SE1 139 B3
St Saviour's RC Prim Sch SE13 67 B3
St Saviour's Rd SW2 62 B2
St Saviours & St Olaves CE Sch SE1 137 C1
St Saviour's Wharf SE1 139 A4
St Scholastica's RC Prim Sch E5 7 C1
St Silas Pl NW5 12 C2
St Simon's Ave SW15 57 B2
St Stephen's Ave W12 39 A4
St Stephen's CE Prim Sch
Paddington W2 31 C4
Shepherd's Bush W12 39 B4
St Johns SE8 51 C1
SW8 162 C2
St Stephen's Cl
Maitland Pk NW5 12 B3
NW8 80 B3
St Stephen's Cres W2 31 C3
St Stephen's Gdns
Notting Hill W2 31 C3
4 Putney SW15 58 B2
St Stephen's Gr SE13 67 B4
St Stephens Ho 7 SE17 48 C4
St Stephen's Mews 34 W2 31 C4
St Stephen's Rd E3 26 B3
St Stephen's Row EC4 109 B1
St Stephen's Terr SW8 162 C1
St Stephen's Wlk SW7 142 C4
St Swithin's La EC4 123 B4
St Swithun's Rd SE13 67 C2
St Thomas' CE Prim Sch W10 23 A1
St Thomas Ct 14 NW1 13 B1
St Thomas Ho 2 E1 32 C3
St Thomas More Language Coll SW3 144 C3
St Thomas of Canterbury RC Prim Sch SW6 154 C2
St Thomas Rd E16 35 C3
St Thomas' Rd W4 45 B4
St Thomas's Gdns NW5 12 C2

St Thomas's Hospl SE1 ... 134 C2
St Thomas's Hospl Medical Sch SE1 134 C1
St Thomas's Pl [20] E9 ... 17 B1
St Thomas's Rd
Dagenham NW10 ... 21 A4
Highbury N4, N5 ... 5 C1
St Thomas's Sq E9 . 17 B1
St Thomas St SE1 123 C1
St Thomas's Way SW6 ... 155 A2
St Thomas the Apostle Coll The SE15 ... 50 B2
St Ursula's Convent Sch SE10 ... 52 C3
St Vincent De Paul Ho [24] E1 ... 32 B4
St Vincent De Paul RC Prim Sch SW1 ... 133 A2
St Vincent Ho SE1 ... 138 C2
St Vincent's RC Prim Sch
Acton W3 ... 28 A2
Marylebone W1 ... 103 C3
St Vincent St W1 . 103 C3
Salamanca Pl SE1 ... 148 C3
Salamanca St SE1, SE11 ... 148 C3
Salcombe Gdns SW4 ... 61 A3
Salcombe Lo NW5 .. 12 C4
Salcombe Rd [23] N16 ... 16 A3
Salcombe Villas [13] TW10 ... 54 A2
Salcot N4 ... 5 B2
Salcott Rd SW11 ... 60 B2
Salehurst Rd SE4 ... 66 B1
Salem Ho [13] E9 ... 17 C2
Salem Rd W2 ... 114 B4
Sale Pl W2 ... 102 A2
Salesian Coll SW11 ... 168 A3
Sale St E2 ... 24 C1 99 C2
Salford Ho [5] E14 .. 42 B2
Salford Rd SW12, SW2 ... 73 C3
Salisbury Cl SE17. 151 B4
Salisbury Ct
Bermondsey SE16 . 139 C1
Chiswick W4 ... 38 A2
EC4 ... 108 A1
Hackney E9 ... 18 A3
Salisbury Ho
[2] Islington N1 ... 15 A2
Islington N1 ... 86 A4
[3] Poplar E14 ... 34 A3
Westminster SW1 . 147 C2
Wimbledon SW19 ... 69 C1
Salisbury Mews SW6 ... 154 C1
Salisbury Pl
Camberwell SW9 ... 48 A3
Marylebone W1 ... 102 C4
Salisbury Rd TW9 .. 54 A3
Salisbury Sq EC4 . 107 C1
Salisbury St
[10] Acton W3 ... 37 B4
NW8 ... 90 A1
Salisbury Terr SE15 ... 65 B4
Salisbury Wlk N19 ... 4 B2
Salmon La E14 ... 33 A3
Salmon St [13] E14 .. 33 B3
Saltcoats Rd W4 ... 38 A4
Saltdene N4 ... 5 B3
Salter Rd SE16 ... 33 A1
Salters' Hall Ct EC4 ... 123 B4
Salters Rd W10 ... 22 C1
Salter St
College Pk NW10 ... 21 C2
[11] Poplar E14 ... 33 C2
Salterton Rd N7 ... 5 B1
Saltoun Rd SW2, SW9 ... 62 C3
Saltram Cres W9 ... 23 C2
Saltwell St E14 ... 33 C2
Saltwood Gr SE17 151 B1
Saltwood Ho [19] SE15 ... 50 B4
Salusbury Prim Sch NW6 ... 23 B4
Salusbury Rd NW6 ... 23 A4
Salutation Rd SE10 ... 43 A2
Salvin Rd SW15 ... 57 C4
Salway Rd E15 ... 19 C2
Salween Ho [2] N16 ... 15 C4
Samaritan Hospl for Women NW1 ... 102 C4
Sambrook Ho [25] E1 ... 32 B4
Samels Ct W6 ... 38 C1
Samford Ho N1 ... 85 B3
Samford St NW8 .. 90 A1
Sam Manners Ho [7] SE10 ... 43 A1
Sam March Ho [5] E14 ... 34 C3
Sampson St E1 ... 125 C1
Samuel Cl SE14 ... 50 C4
Shoreditch E8 ... 24 B4
Samuel Ct N1 ... 24 A2 98 A3
Samuel Ho [15] E8 ... 24 B4
Samuel Jones Ind Est [7] SE15 ... 49 A3
Samuel Lewis Bldgs N1 ... 14 C2
Samuel Lewis Trust Dwellings
[6] Camberwell SE5 ... 48 B2
Chelsea SW3 ... 144 A3
Walham Green SW6 ... 155 C2
West Kensington W14 ... 140 B4
Samuel Rhodes Sch N1 ... 85 B4
Samuel Richardson Ho W14 ... 140 C3
Samuel's Cl [2] W6 . 39 B2
Samuel St SE15 ... 49 B3
Sancroft Ct SW11 168 B4
Sancroft Ho SE11 149 A2
Sancroft St SE11 . 149 A2
Sanctuary Mews [15] E8 ... 16 B2
Sanctuary St SE1 137 A4
Sanctuary The
[35] Wapping E1 ... 32 A1
Sanctuary The *continued*
Westminster SW1 . 133 C2
Sandale Cl N16 ... 6 C1
Sandall Ho [7] E3 ... 26 A3
Sandall Rd NW5 ... 13 B2
Sandalwood Cl [11] E1 ... 26 A1
Sandalwood Ho [6] NW3 ... 11 A2
Sandbourne
[4] Kensington W11 ... 31 C3
Paddington NW8 ... 78 B4
Sandbourne Rd SE4 ... 51 A1
Sandbrook Rd N16 .. 7 A1
Sandby Ho
[11] Camberwell SE5 ... 49 A2
[6] Kilburn NW6 ... 23 C4
Sandell St SE1 ... 135 B4
Sanderling Ct [20] SE8 ... 51 B4
Sanders Ho WC1 .. 95 B4
Sanderson Cl NW5 ... 13 A4
Sanderson Ho [7] SE8 ... 41 B1
Sanderstead Ave NW2 ... 1 A2
Sanderstead Cl SW12 ... 73 B4
Sanders Way [3] N19 ... 4 C3
Sandfield WC1 ... 94 B3
Sandford Ct N16 ... 7 A3
Sandford Row SE17 ... 151 C2
Sandford St SW6 . 156 B1
Sandgate Ho [15] E5 ... 17 A4
Sandgate La SW17, SW18 ... 72 A3
Sandgate St SE15 .. 50 A4
Sandgate Trad Est SE15 ... 50 A4
Sandham Ct SW4 . 172 B3
Sandhills The SW10 ... 157 A4
Sandhurst Ct SW2 .. 62 A3
Sandhurst Ho [12] E1 ... 32 B4
Sandilands Rd SW6 ... 166 A3
Sandison St SE15 ... 64 C4
Sandland St WC1 107 A3
Sandlings Cl SE15 .. 50 A1
Sandmere Rd SW4 ... 62 A3
Sandon Ho [5] SW2 ... 74 A4
Sandown Ho [2] W4 ... 37 B1
Sandpiper Cl SE16 .. 41 B4
Sandpiper Ct
[13] Cubitt Town E14 ... 42 B3
[1] SE8 ... 51 C3
Sandridge St [3] N19 ... 4 B2
Sandringham Cl [1] SW19 ... 69 C3
Sandringham Ct
Marylebone W1 ... 105 A1
Putney SW15 ... 57 C1
Sandringham Ct *continued*
[18] Rotherhithe SE16 ... 32 C1
St John's Wood W9 . 89 A3
Sandringham Flats WC2 ... 119 C4
Sandringham Ho
Richmond TW10 ... 54 C2
W14 ... 140 A4
Sandringham Rd
Dalston E8 ... 16 B3
Golders Green NW11 .. 1 A4
Willesden NW2 ... 9 A2
Sandrock Rd SE13 .. 66 C4
SANDS END ... 59 B4
Sands End La SW6 ... 166 B4
Sandstone TW9 ... 44 C3
Sandstone Pl N19 ... 4 A2
Sandways [6] TW9 .. 44 C2
Sandwell Cres [2] NW6 ... 10 C2
Sandwell Mans [3] NW6 ... 10 C2
Sandwich Ho
[15] Rotherhithe SE16 ... 40 B4
WC1 ... 94 A3
Sandwich St WC1 . 94 A3
Sandycombe Ctr TW9 ... 54 C4
Sandycombe Rd TW9 ... 44 C1
Sandy Lo N6 ... 4 B4
Sandy Rd NW3 ... 2 A2
Sandy's Row E1 ... 110 B3
Sanford La [3] N16 ... 7 B2
Sanford St SE14, SE8 ... 51 A4
Sanford Terr N16 ... 7 B1
Sanford Wlk SE14 .. 51 A4
[4] Stoke Newington N16 ... 7 B2
Sangora Rd [17] SW11 ... 59 C3
San Ho [20] E9 ... 17 C2
Sankey Ho [22] E2 ... 25 B3
Sansom St
Camberwell SE5 ... 48 C2
SE5 ... 48 C3
Sans Wlk EC1 ... 96 A2
Santley Ho SE1 ... 135 C3
Santley St SW4 ... 62 B3
Santos Rd SW18 ... 58 C2
Sapcote Trad Ctr NW10 ... 8 B2
Saperton Wlk SE11 ... 149 A4
Sapperton Ct EC1 . 96 C2
Sapphire Ct E1 ... 125 B4
Sapphire Rd SE8 ... 41 A2
Saracen St E14 ... 33 C3
Sarah Ho
Roehampton SW15 .. 56 B3
[8] Stepney E1 ... 32 A3
Sarah Swift Ho SE1 ... 137 C4
Sara Lane Ct [31] N1 ... 24 A3
Saratoga Rd E5 ... 17 B4
Sardinia Ho WC2 106 C1
Sardinia St WC2 .. 106 C2
Sarjant Path SW19 ... 69 C2
Sark Ho [9] N1 ... 15 B2
Sarnersfield Ho SE15 ... 50 A4
Sarratt Ho [6] W10 .. 30 B4
Sarre Rd NW2 ... 10 B3
Sarsden Bldgs W1 ... 103 C1
Sarsfeld Rd SW12, SW17 ... 72 B3
Sartor Rd SE15 ... 65 C3
Sarum Hall Sch NW3 ... 12 A1
Sarum Ho W11 ... 31 B2 113 A3
Sassoon Ho SE15 ... 50 B1
Satchwell Rd E2 ... 24 C2 99 B3
Saturn Ho [4] E3 ... 26 C4
Saul Ct [4] SE15 ... 49 B4
Saunders Cl [14] E14 ... 33 B2
Saunders Ho [11] SW2 ... 74 C3
Saunders Ness Rd E14 ... 42 C2
Saunders St SE11 149 B4
Savage Gdns EC3. 124 B4
Savana N16 ... 7 A2
Savannah Cl [9] SE15 ... 49 B3
Savernake Ho N4 ... 6 C4
Savernake Rd NW3 ... 12 B4
Saville Rd W4 ... 37 C3
Saville Row W1 .. 118 C4
Savill Ho [2] SW4 ... 61 C1
Savona St SW8 ... 160 C1
Savoy Circus W3 ... 29 B2
Savoy Ct
Earl's Ct SW5 ... 141 C4
Strand WC2 ... 120 B3
Savoy Hill WC2 ... 120 C3
Savoy Mews SW9 ... 62 A4
Savoy Pier WC2 .. 120 C3
Savoy Pl WC2 ... 120 C3
Savoy Row WC2 .. 120 C4
Savoy St WC2 ... 120 C3
Savoy Stps WC2 .. 120 C3
Savoy Way WC2 ... 120 C3
Sawkins Cl SW19 ... 70 A2
Sawley Rd W12 ... 29 C1
Sawmill Yd E3 ... 26 A4
Sawyer St SE1 ... 136 C4
Saxby Rd SW2 ... 74 A4
Saxonbury Ct
[10] Kentish Town N7 ... 13 C3
[2] Lower Holloway N7 ... 14 A3
Saxoncroft Ho SW16 ... 73 C1
Saxon Dr W3 ... 28 A4
Saxonfield Cl SW2 .. 74 B4
Saxon Hall W2 ... 114 A3
Saxon Ho [4] SW4 .. 61 C3
Saxon Rd E3 ... 26 B3
Saxton Cl SE13 ... 67 C4
Sayer Ho SE4 ... 66 A3
Sayes Court St SE8 ... 51 B4
Sayes Ct SE8 ... 51 B4
Scafell NW1 ... 92 C4
Scala St W1 ... 105 A4
Scampston Mews [5] W10 ... 30 C3
Scandrett St [38] E1 ... 32 A1
Scarba Wlk N1 ... 15 C2

carborough Rd N4 ... 5 C3
carborough St E1 ... 111 A1
carlette Manor Wlk 10 SE24 ... 74 C4
carsbrook Ho 2 SW2 ... 62 C1
carsdale Pl W8 . 128 A2
carsdale Villas W8 ... 127 C1
carth Rd SW13 ... 56 B4
cawen Rd SE8 ... 41 A1
cawfell St E2 ... 24 B3
ceptre Ho 10 E1 ... 25 B1
ceptre Rd E2 ... 25 B2
chiller International Univ SE1 ... 121 B1
chofield Wlk SE3 .. 53 C3
ch of Pharmacy WC1 ... 94 B2
cholars Ct 5 N19 .. 4 C3
cholars Rd SW12 .. 73 B3
cholefield Rd N19 .. 4 C2
choley Ho SW11 .. 60 A4
chomberg Ho SW1 ... 147 C4
chonfeld Sq N16 ... 6 C3
chool App E2 ... 24 A2 98 B4
choolbank Rd SE10 ... 43 B2
chool Bell Cloisters 17 E3 ... 26 A3
choolbell Mews 18 E3 ... 26 A3
chool Flats SW8 172 A3
chool Ho SE1 ... 152 A4
choolhouse La E1 ... 32 C2
chool Rd NW10 ... 20 C1
chool Sq SE10 ... 43 B3
chooner Cl
Cubitt Town E14 ... 42 C3
1 Rotherhithe SE16 ... 40 C4
chubert Rd SW15 ... 58 B2
cience Mus* SW7 ... 129 B1
clater St E1 ... 24 B1 99 A2
coles Cres SW2 ... 74 C3
coresby St SE1 ... 122 A1
corton Ho 2 N1 .. 24 A3
cotch Ho SW1 .. 130 C3
coter Ct 23 SE8 ... 51 B4
cotia Bldg 10 E1 .. 32 C2
cotia Ct 3 SE16 ... 40 B3
cotia Rd 24 SW2 .. 74 C4
cotland Pl SW1 . 120 A1
cotney Ho E9 ... 17 B2
cotson Ho SE11 . 149 B3
cotswood St EC1 . 95 C2
cott Ct Acton W4 ... 37 C4
Clapham SW11 ... 170 B1
17 Stoke Newington N16 ... 7 A1
cott Ellis Gdns NW8 ... 89 B3
cott Ho
2 Barnsbury N7 ... 14 B2
Islington N1 ... 87 B4
Lisson Gr NW8 ... 90 A1
17 Millwall E14 ... 41 C4
cott Lidgett Cres SE16 ... 139 C3
Scotts Ct 6 W12 ... 39 A4
Scott's Rd W12 ... 39 A4
Scott's Sufferance Wharf SE1 ... 139 A3
Scott St E1 ... 25 A1
Scott's Yd EC4 ... 123 B4
Scoulding Ho 12 E14 ... 41 C3
Scoulding Rd E16 .. 35 C3
Scouler St E14 ... 34 C2
Scout App NW10 ... 8 A4
Scout La SW4 ... 61 B4
Scovell Cres SE1 . 136 C3
Scovell Rd SE1 ... 136 C3
Scriven Ct 2 E8 ... 24 B4
Scriven St E8 ... 24 B4
Scrooby St SE6 ... 67 A1
Scrope Bldg EC1 . 107 B4
Scrubs La NW10, W10, W12 ... 22 A1
Scrutton Cl SW12 .. 73 C4
Scrutton St EC2 ... 24 A1 98 A1
Scutari Rd SE22 ... 65 B2
Scylla Rd SE15 ... 65 A4
Seabright St 27 E2 ... 25 A2
Seacole Cl W3 ... 28 C4
Seacon Twr 8 E14 ... 41 C4
Seaford Ho 13 SE16 ... 40 B4
Seaford St WC1 ... 94 B3
Seaforth Cres N5 ... 15 B3
Seaforth Lo 2 SW13 ... 46 B1
Seaforth Pl SW1 . 133 A2
Seagrave Lo SW6 155 C4
Seagrave Rd SW6 155 C4
Seagrove Cl E1 ... 32 C4
Seagull La E16 ... 35 C2
Seal Ho SE1 ... 137 C2
Seal St E8 ... 16 B4
Searle Pl N4 ... 5 B3
Searles Cl SW11 .. 158 B1
Searles Rd SE1 ... 151 C4
Searson Ho SE17 . 150 B3
Sears St SE5 ... 48 C3
Seasalter Ho SW9 ... 173 B4
Seaton Cl SW15 ... 69 A4
Seaton Point E5 ... 16 C4
Seavington Ho 3 SE5 ... 64 A4
Sebastian Ho 22 N1 ... 24 A3
Sebastian St EC1 .. 96 B3
Sebbon St N1 ... 15 A1
Sebright Ho 22 E2 .. 24 C3
Sebright Pas 29 E2 ... 24 C3
Sebright Sch E2 ... 24 C3
Secker Ho SW9 ... 48 A1
Secker St SE1 ... 121 B1
Second Ave
East Acton W3 ... 29 B1
Kensal Town W10 ... 23 A1
Mortlake SW14 ... 56 A4
Sedan Way SE17 . 152 A2
Sedding St SW1 .. 145 B4
Seddon Ho EC2 .. 108 C4
Seddon St WC1 ... 95 A3
Sedgeford Rd W12 ... 29 B1
Sedgewick Ho SW19 ... 69 C2
Sedgley Ho N4 ... 5 B2
Sedgmoor Pl SE5 .. 49 A3
Sedgwick St E9 ... 17 C3
Sedleigh Rd SW18 .. 58 B1
Sedlescombe Rd SW6 ... 155 B4
Sedley Ho SE11 .. 149 A2
Sedley Pl W1 ... 104 A1
Seething La EC3 .. 124 B4
Sefton St SW15 ... 57 B4
Sekforde St EC1 ... 96 A2
Selbie Ave NW10 ... 8 B3
Selborne 2 SW11 .. 60 C4
Selborne Ho SE1 . 137 B3
Selborne Rd 1 SE5 ... 48 C1
Selby Ho 10 SW4 ... 61 B1
Selby Sq 1 W10 ... 23 A2
Selby St E1 .. 24 C1 99 C1
Selden Ho 2 SE15 ... 50 B1
Selden Rd SE15 ... 50 B1
Selden Wlk N7 ... 5 B2
Seldon Ho
Nine Elms SW8 ... 160 C1
Pimlico SW1 ... 146 C1
Selhurst Cl SW19 ... 69 C3
Selina Ho NW8 ... 89 C2
Selkirk Ho N1 ... 84 C4
4 Stoke Newington N16 ... 7 A1
Sellons Ave NW10 .. 21 B4
Selma Ho 7 W12 .. 30 A3
Selman Ho 8 E9 ... 18 A2
Selsdon Way E14 ... 42 A3
Selsea Pl N16 ... 16 A3
Selsey St E14 ... 33 C4
Selway Ho SW8 ... 172 B4
Selwood Ho 1 N4 ... 6 C4
Selwood Pl SW7 . 143 B2
Selwood Terr SW7 ... 143 B2
Selworthy Ho SW11 ... 167 C4
Selwyn Ave TW9 ... 54 B4
Selwyn Ct 8 TW10 ... 54 B2
Selwyn Ho 3 SW15 ... 57 C1
Selwyn Rd Bow E3 .. 26 B3
Willesden NW10 ... 8 A1
Semley Gate E9 ... 18 B2
Semley Ho SW1 .. 146 A3
Semley Pl SW1 ... 146 A3
Senate St SE15 ... 50 B1
Senators Lo 31 E3 .. 26 A3
Sendall Ct 13 SW11 ... 59 C4
Senior St W2 ... 100 A4
Senrab St E1 ... 32 C3
Seraph Ct EC1 ... 96 C4
Serenaders Rd SW9 ... 173 B1
Sergeant Ind Est The SW18 ... 59 A1
Serica Ct 14 SE10 ... 52 B3
Serjeants' Inn EC4 ... 107 C1
Serlby Ct W14 ... 126 C2
Serle St WC2 ... 107 A2
Sermon La EC4 ... 108 C1
Serpentine Ct 10 SE16 ... 40 C4
Serpentine Gallery* W2 ... 129 C4
Serpentine Rd W2 ... 116 C1
Serpentine The* W2 ... 116 B1
Service Route No 1 E15 ... 19 C1
Service Route No 2 1 E15 ... 19 C1
Service Route No 3 2 E15 ... 19 C1
Servite Ho SE13 ... 52 A2
Servite RC Prim Sch SW10 ... 156 C4
Setchell Rd SE1 .. 152 C4
Setchell Way SE1 152 C4
Seth St 25 SE16 ... 40 B4
Settlers Ct 11 E14 .. 34 C2
Settles St E1 ... 111 C2
Settrington Rd SW6 ... 166 A1
Seven Dials WC2 . 106 A1
Seven Mills Prim Sch E14 ... 41 C4
Sevenoaks Rd SE4 . 66 B1
Seven Sisters Rd
Finsbury Pk N4 ... 6 A2
Stoke Newington N4, N7, N15 ... 6 B4
Seven Stars Cnr W12 ... 38 C3
Seven Stars Yd E1 ... 111 A4
Severnake Cl E14 .. 41 C2
Severn Ave 2 W10 ... 23 A2
Severn Way NW10 ... 8 B3
Severus Rd SW11 ... 60 A3
Seville Ho E1 ... 125 C1
Seville Mews N1 ... 16 A1
Seville St SW1 ... 131 A3
Sevington St W9 .. 88 A1
Seward St EC1 ... 96 C3
Sewardstone Rd E2 ... 25 B3
Sewell Ho 7 N16 .. 16 A3
Sextant Ave E14 ... 42 C2
Sexton Ct 7 E14 ... 34 C2
Sexton's Ho 5 SE13 ... 52 B4
Seymour Ct
Putney SW15 ... 57 A3
Upper Clapton N16 ... 7 C3
Seymour Gdns SE4 ... 66 A4
Seymour Ho
Bloomsbury WC1 ... 94 A2
Clapham SW8 ... 171 A2
Somers Town NW1 .. 93 C3
Seymour Mews W1 ... 103 B2
Seymour Pl W1 .. 102 C2
Seymour Rd
Acton W4 ... 37 B2
Wandsworth SW18 .. 58 B1
Wimbledon SW19 ... 69 C1
Seymour St W1 .. 103 A1
Seymour Wlk SW10 ... 156 C4
Seyssel St E14 ... 42 B2
Shaa Rd W3 ... 28 C2
Shabana Ct 3 W12 ... 30 A1
Shackleton Ct
3 Dulwich SE21 ... 75 C2
2 Isle of Dogs E14 .. 41 C1
4 Shepherd's Bush W12 ... 39 A4
Shackleton Ho 5 E1 ... 32 B1
SHACKLEWELL ... 16 B4
Shacklewell Ho 3 E8 ... 16 B4
Shacklewell La E8 .. 16 B3
Shacklewell Prim Sch E8 ... 16 B4
Shacklewell Rd N16 ... 16 B4
Shacklewell Row E8 ... 16 B4
Shacklewell St E2 ... 24 B2 99 A3
Shad Thames SE1 ... 139 A4
SHADWELL ... 32 B2
Shadwell Gdns E1 .. 32 B2
Shadwell Pierhead E1 ... 32 B2
Shadwell Pl 1 E1 .. 32 B2
Shadwell Sta E1 ... 32 A2
Shaftesbury Ave W1 ... 119 C4
Shaftesbury Ct
Borough The SE1 .. 137 B2
1 Herne Hill SE5 ... 63 C3
Shoreditch N1 ... 87 B1
Streatham SW16 ... 73 C1
Shaftesbury Ctr NW10 ... 22 C1
Shaftesbury Gdns NW10 ... 21 A1
Shaftesbury Ho
11 Canning Town E16 ... 35 B3
13 Stoke Newington N16 ... 7 A1
W2 ... 114 B4
Shaftesbury Lo 9 E14 ... 34 A3
Shaftesbury Mews
2 Clapham Pk SW4 ... 61 B2
W8 ... 127 C1
Shaftesbury Park Chambers 1 SW11 ... 60 C4
Shaftesbury Rd
Finsbury Pk N4, N19 ... 5 A3
Richmond TW9 ... 54 A4
Shaftesbury St N1 . 87 B1
Shafteswood Ct SW17 ... 72 B1
Shafto Mews SW1 ... 131 A1
Shafton Rd E9 ... 25 C4
Shaftsbury Park Prim Sch SW11 ... 169 B1
Shafts Ct EC3 ... 110 A1
Shahjalal Ho 18 E2 ... 24 C3
Shakespeare Ave 7 NW10 ... 20 C4
Shakespeare Ho 3 E9 ... 17 B1
Shakespeare Rd
Acton W3 ... 28 B1
Brixton SE24 ... 63 A3
Shakespeare's Globe Theatre (site of)* SE1 ... 123 A2
Shakespeare Twr EC2 ... 109 A4
Shakspeare Mews 7 N16 ... 16 A4

Shakspeare Wlk N16 16 A4
Shalbourne Sq E9 18 B2
Shalcomb St SW10 157 A3
Shalden Ho SW15 56 B1
Shalfleet Dr W10 30 C2
Shalford NW10 21 C4
Shalford Ct N1 86 A2
Shalford Ho SE1 137 C2
Shalimar Gdns W3 28 B2
Shalimar Lo W3 28 B2
Shalimar Rd W3 28 B2
Shalstone Rd SW14, TW9 55 A4
Shamrock St SW4 61 C4
Shandon Ct SE4 51 A1
Shandon Rd SW4 61 B1
Shand St SE1 138 B4
Shandy St E1 25 C1
Shan Ho WC1 94 C1
Shannon Ct
11 Peckham SE15 49 B3
Stoke Newington N16 7 A1
Willesden NW10 8 C2
Shannon Gr SW9 62 B3
Shannon Pl NW8 80 B2
Shanti Ct SW18 70 C3
Shapla Prim Sch E1 125 C3
Shardcroft Ave SE24 63 A2
Shardeloes Rd SE14 51 B1
Shard's Sq SE15 49 C4
Sharebourne Ho SW2 62 C2
Sharman Ho 13 E14 34 B3
Sharnbrook Ho W6 155 B4
Sharon Gdns E9 25 B4
Sharon Rd W4 37 C1
Sharp Ho SW8 61 A4
Sharples Hall St 8 NW1 12 B1
Sharpness Ct 2 SE15 49 B3
Sharratt St SE15 50 B4
Sharsted St SE17 150 A1
Sharwood WC1 85 A1
Shaver's Pl SW1 119 B3
Shawbury Ct SE22 64 B2
Shawbury Rd SE22 64 B2
Shaw Cres 6 E14 33 A3
Shaw Ct
8 Acton Green W3 37 B3
12 Battersea SW11 59 C4
Upper Holloway N19 5 A2
Shawfield St SW3 144 B1
Shawford Ct 8 SW15 68 C4
Shaw Rd SE22 64 A3
Shearling Way N7 14 A2
Shearsmith Ho E1 125 C4
Shearwater Ct 24 SE8 51 B4
Sheba Pl E1 24 B1 99 A1
Sheen Common Dr SW14, TW10 54 C2
Sheen Court Rd TW10 54 C3
Sheen Ct TW10 54 C3
Sheendale Rd TW9 54 B3
Sheen Gate Gdns SW14 55 B3
Sheengate Mans SW14 55 C3
Sheen Gr N1 85 B4
Sheen La SW14 55 B3
Sheen Mount Prim Sch SW14 55 A2
Sheen Pk TW10, TW9 54 A3
Sheen Rd TW10, TW9 54 B3
Sheen Wood SW14 55 B2
Sheepcote La SW11 169 A1
Sheep La E8 25 A4
Sheffield Ho 15 SE15 49 B2
Sheffield Sq 2 E3 26 B2
Sheffield St WC2 106 C1
Sheffield Terr W8 31 C1 113 C1
Shelbourne Ho 20 N19 4 C4
Shelburne Ct SW15 57 C2
Shelburne Rd N7 14 B4
Shelbury Rd SE22 65 A2
Sheldon Ct SW8 162 A1
Sheldon Ho 9 E9 17 C2
Sheldon Pl E2 25 A3
Sheldon Rd NW2 9 C4
Sheldon Sq W2 101 A3
Sheldrake Ho 15 SE16 40 C2
Sheldrake Pl W8 127 B4
Shelduck Ct 37 SE8 51 B4
Shelford Pl N16 6 C1
Shelgate Rd SW11 60 B2
Shell Ctr SE1 121 A1
Shelley Cl SE15 50 A1
Shelley Ct
Finsbury Pk N4 5 B3
SW3 159 A4
Shelley Ho
21 Bethnal Green E2 25 B2
Chelsea SW1 160 C4
9 Stoke Newington N16 16 A4
Walworth SE17 151 A2
Shelley Rd NW10 20 C4
Shellgrove Rd N16 16 A3
Shellness Rd E5 17 A3
Shell Rd SE13 67 A4
Shellwood Rd SW11 168 C1
Shelmerdine Cl E3 33 C4
Shelton St WC2 106 A1
Shene Bldg EC1 107 B4
Shene Sch SW14 56 A3
Shenfield St N1 24 A3
Shenley Rd SE5 49 A2
Shepard Ho 18 SW11 59 C4
Sheperdess Pl N1 97 A4
Shepherd Cl W1 117 B4
Shepherdess Wlk N1 87 A1
Shepherd Ho
Barnsbury N7 14 A2
10 Poplar E14 34 A3
Shepherd Mkt W1 118 A1
SHEPHERD'S BUSH 30 A1
Shepherd's Bush (Central Line) Sta W12 39 C4
Shepherd's Bush Gn W12 39 B4
Shepherd's Bush (Hamm & City) Sta W12 30 B1
Shepherd's Bush Market W12 39 B4
Shepherd's Bush Pl W12 39 C4
Shepherd's Bush Rd W6 39 B3
Shepherds Ct 8 W12 39 C4
Shepherd's La E9 17 C2
Shepherds Pl W1 117 B4
Shepherd St W1 118 A1
Shepherd's Wlk NW3 11 C4
Sheppard Dr SE16 40 A1
Sheppard Ho
31 Hackney E2 24 C3
8 Streatham SW2 74 C3
Shepperton Rd N1 87 B4
Sheppey Ho 16 E5 17 A4
Shepton Ct SW11 167 C4
Shepton Hos 11 E2 25 B2
Sherard Ct N19 5 A1
Sherard Ho 24 E9 17 B1
Sheraton Ho SW1 160 B4
Sheraton St W1 105 B1
Sherborne Ho
Pimlico SW1 146 B2
South Lambeth SW8 162 C1
Sherborne La EC4 123 C4
Sherborne St N1 87 B4
Sherbourne Ct SW5 142 A4
Sherbrooke Ho 9 E2 25 B3
Sherbrooke Rd SW6 154 B1
Sherbrooke Terr SW6 154 B1
Shere Ho SE1 137 B2
Sherfield Gdns SW15 56 B1
Sheridan Bldgs WC2 106 B1
Sheridan Ct
Earl's Ct SW5 142 A3
South Hampstead NW6 11 B1
South Lambeth SW9 173 A3
Sheridan Ho SE11 149 C3
7 Stoke Newington N16 7 A1
Sheridan Pl SW13 56 B4
Sheridan St 34 E1 32 A3
Sheringdale Prim Sch SW18 70 B3
Sheringham NW8 79 C4
Sheringham Ho NW1 102 B4
Sheringham Mews 4 SW18 71 B2
Sheringham Rd N7 14 C2
Sherlock Ct NW8 79 B4
Sherlock Holmes Mus★ NW1 91 A1
Sherlock Mews W1 103 B4
Sherren Ho 35 E1 25 B1
Sherrick Green Rd NW10 9 A3
Sherriff Ct NW6 10 C2
Sherriff Rd NW6 10 C2
Sherrin Rd E10 19 A4
Sherston Ct
Finsbury WC1 95 B3
Newington SE1 150 B4
Sherwin Ho SE11 163 B4
Sherwin Rd SE14 50 C2
Sherwood NW6 10 A1
Sherwood Cl SW13 57 A4
Sherwood Ct
11 Battersea SW11 59 B4
St Johns SE13 52 A1
W1 102 C3
Sherwood Gdns
Bermondsey SE16 40 A1
Millwall E14 41 C2
Sherwood Ho N4 6 B4
Sherwood St W1 119 A4
Shetland Rd E3 26 B3
Shillaker Ct W3 29 B1
Shillibeer Pl W1 102 B3
Shillingford Ho 40 E3 27 A2
Shillingford St 23 N1 15 A1
Shillingstone Ho W14 126 B1
Shinfield St W12 30 B3
Shipka Rd SW12 73 A3
Ship La SW14 45 B1
Shiplake Ho E2 24 B2 98 C3
Shipley Ho SW8 171 B1
Ship & Mermaid Row SE1 138 A4
Ship St SE8 51 C2
Ship Tavern Pas EC3 124 A4
Shipton Ho
7 Camden Town NW5 12 C2
14 Haggerston E2 24 B3
Shipton St E2 24 B2 99 A4
Shipwright Rd SE16 41 A4
Shipwright Yd SE1 124 A1
Shirbutt St E14 34 A2
Shire Pl SW18 71 B4
Shirland Mews W9 23 B2
Shirland Rd W9 23 C1
Shirley Gr SW11 60 C4
Shirley Ho 13 SE5 48 C3
Shirley Rd W4 37 C4
Shirley St E16 35 B3
Shirlock Rd NW3 12 B4
Shoe La EC4 107 C2
Shooters Hill Rd SE3, SE10 53 A
Shoot-Up Hill NW2 10 A
Shopstop SW11 60 A
Shore Bsns Ctr 31 E9 17 B
SHOREDITCH 87 C
Shoreditch Ct 2 E8 16 B
Shoreditch High St E2 24 A1 98 B
Shoreditch Ho N1 97 C
Shoreham Cl SW18 59 A
Shore Ho SW8 61 A
Shore Mews 30 E9 17 B
Shore Pl E9 17 B
Shore Rd E9 17 B
Shorncliffe Rd SE1 152 C
Shorrolds Rd SW6 155 A
Shortcroft Mead Ct NW10 8 C
Shorter St EC3 125 A
Shortlands W6 39 C
Short Rd W4 46 A
Shorts Gdns WC2 106 A
Short St SE1 135 C
Shottendane Rd SW6 165 B
Shottfield Ave SW14 56 A
Shottsford 1 W11 31 C
Shoulder of Mutton Alley 10 E14 33 A
Shouldham St W1 102 B
Shreveport Ho 23 N19 4 C
Shrewsbury Ave SW14 55 C
Shrewsbury Ho
Chelsea SW3 158 A
Kennington SE11 163 A
Shrewsbury Mews 33 W2 31 C
Shrewsbury Rd W2 31 C
Shrewsbury St W10 22 B
Shropshire Ho WC1 93 A
Shroton St NW1 102 B
Shrubbery Cl N1 87 A
Shrubland Rd E8 24 C
Shrubs Ho SW1 147 C
Shurland Gdns SE15 49 B
Shuters Sq W14 140 C
Shuttle St E1 24 C1 99 B
Shuttleworth Rd SW11 168 A
Sibella Rd SW4 171 C
Sicilian Ave WC1 106 B
Sidbury St SW6 164 A
Siddons Ct WC2 106 C
Siddons Ho 8 NW3 12 B
Siddons La NW1 91 A
Sidford Ho SE1 135 A
Sidford Pl SE1 135 A
Sidgwick Ho SW9 172 B

Sidings Mews N7 ... 14 C4
Sidlaw Ho N16 ... 7 B3
Sidmouth Ho
  18 Camberwell SE15 ... 49 C3
  Marylebone W1 ... 102 B2
  26 Streatham SW2 ... 74 C4
Sidmouth Mews WC1 ... 94 C3
Sidmouth Par NW2 ... 9 B1
Sidmouth Rd NW2 ... 9 B1
Sidmouth St WC1 ... 94 C3
Sidney Boyd Ct NW6 ... 10 C1
Sidney Godley (VC) Ho 31 E2 ... 25 B2
Sidney Gr EC1 ... 86 A1
Sidney Ho 4 E2 ... 25 C3
Sidney Miller Ct 8 W3 ... 28 A1
Sidney Rd SW9 ... 173 A1
Sidney Sq E1 ... 32 B4
Sidney St E1 ... 32 B4
Sidworth St 6 E8 ... 17 A1
Siebert Rd SE3 ... 53 C4
Siege Ho 14 E1 ... 32 A3
Sigdon Rd E8 ... 16 C3
Signal Ho
  9 London E8 ... 17 A1
  SE1 ... 136 C3
Signmakers Yd NW1 ... 82 B3
Silbury Ho 9 SE26 ... 76 C1
Silbury St N1 ... 97 B4
Silchester Rd W10 ... 30 C3
Silesia Bldgs E8 ... 17 A1
Silex St SE1 ... 136 B3
Silk Mills Path SE13 ... 67 B4
Silk Mills Sq E9 ... 18 B2
Silk St EC2 ... 109 A4
Sillitoe Ho N1 ... 87 C3
Silsoe Ho NW1 ... 82 B1
Silverbirch Wlk 1 NW3 ... 12 C2
Silverburn Ho 4 SW9 ... 48 A2
Silver Cl SE14 ... 51 A3
Silver Cres W4 ... 37 A2
Silver Ct N19 ... 4 B1
Silverdale NW1 ... 92 C4
Silverdale Ct EC1 ... 96 B2
Silvermere Rd SE6 ... 67 A1
Silver Pl W1 ... 119 A4
Silver Rd
  Shepherd's Bush W12 ... 30 C2
  St Johns SE13 ... 67 A4
Silverthorn NW6 ... 78 B3
Silverthorne Rd SW8 ... 170 B1
Silverton Rd W6 ... 47 C4
Silvertown Way E16 ... 35 C1
Silver Wlk SE16 ... 33 B1
Silvester Ho
  27 Bethnal Green E2 ... 25 B2
  1 Notting Hill W11 ... 31 B3
  6 Stepney E1 ... 32 A3
Silvester Rd SE22 ... 64 B2
Silvester St SE1 ... 137 B3
Silwex Ho E1 ... 24 B1 98 C1
Silwood St SE16 ... 40 B1
Simla Ho SE1 ... 137 C3
Simmonds Ct SW5 ... 142 A3
Simmons Ho
  Bethnal Green E2 ... 24 C2 99 B3
  Finsbury Pk N7 ... 5 B2
Simms Ct SW6 ... 58 A4
Simms Rd SE1 ... 153 C3
Simon Cl W11 ... 31 B2 113 A4
Simon Ct W9 ... 23 C2
Simon Lo 31 SW19 ... 69 C3
Simon Marks Jewish Prim Sch N16 ... 7 B2
Simons Wlk E15 ... 19 C3
Simpson Dr W3 ... 28 C3
Simpson Ho
  Lisson Gr NW8 ... 90 A3
  Vauxhall SE11 ... 148 C1
Simpson's Rd E14 ... 34 A2
Simpson St SW11 ... 168 A1
Sinclair Ct N5 ... 15 B2
Sinclair Gdns W14 ... 39 C4
Sinclair Ho 1 SW12 ... 73 C3
Sinclair Mans 13 W12 ... 39 C4
Sinclair Pl SE4 ... 66 C1
Sinclair Rd W14 ... 126 A2
Sinclairs Ho 18 E3 ... 26 B3
Singer St EC2 ... 97 C3
Sion Ho SE13 ... 67 B3
Sion-Manning RC Sch for Girls
  Kensal Town W10 ... 31 A4
  North Kensington W10 ... 30 C4
Sir Abraham Dawes Cotts SW15 ... 58 A3
Sir Alexander Cl W3 ... 29 B1
Sir Alexander Rd W3 ... 29 B1
Sirdar Rd W11 ... 31 A2 112 A3
Sir Francis Drake Prim Sch SE8 ... 41 A1
Sirinham Point SW8 ... 163 A3
Sirius Bldg 13 E1 ... 32 C2
Sir James Barrie Prim Sch SW8 ... 171 A3
Sir John Cass Foundation & Redcoat CE Sec Sch E1 ... 32 C4
Sir John Cass's Foundation Prim Sch EC3 ... 110 B1
Sir John Kirk Cl 33 SE5 ... 48 B3
Sir John Lillie Prim Sch SW6 ... 154 B3
Sir Oswald Stoll Foundation The SW6 ... 156 A2
Sir Thomas Abney Sch N16 ... 6 C3
Sir Thomas More Est SW3 ... 157 C3
Sir William Burrough Prim Sch E14 ... 33 A3
Sir William Powell's Almshos SW6 ... 58 A4
Sise La EC4 ... 109 B1
Siskin Ho 14 SE16 ... 40 C2
Sispara Gdns SW18 ... 58 B1
Sissinghurst Ho 17 SE15 ... 50 B4
Sister Mabel's Way 15 SE15 ... 49 C3
Sisters Ave SW11 ... 60 B3
Sistova Rd SW12 ... 73 A3
Sisulu Pl SW9 ... 62 C4
Sitarey Ct 4 W12 ... 30 A1
Site of Changing of the Guard★ SW1 ... 132 C3
Sivill Ho E2 ... 24 B2 99 A4
Siward Rd SW17 ... 71 B1
Six Bridges Ind Est SE1 ... 153 C1
Sixth Ave W10 ... 23 A2
Skardu Rd NW2 ... 10 A3
Skeena Hill SW18, SW19 ... 70 A4
Skeggs Ho 5 E14 ... 42 B3
Skegness Ho 3 N7 ... 14 B1
Skelbrook St SW18 ... 71 B2
Skelgill Rd SW15 ... 58 B3
Skelton Cl 7 E8 ... 16 B2
Skelton Ho N16 ... 16 A3
Skelwith Rd W6 ... 47 B4
Skenfrith Ho SE15 ... 50 A4
Sketchley Gdns SE16 ... 40 C1
Skiffington Cl SW2 ... 74 C3
Skinner Pl SW1 ... 145 B3
Skinners Company Sch (Upper) N16 ... 7 B4
Skinners La EC4 ... 123 A4
Skinner St EC1 ... 95 C2
Skipsea Ho SW18 ... 59 C1
Skipton Ho SE4 ... 66 A3
Skipwith Bldg EC1 ... 107 B4
Skipworth Rd E9 ... 25 B4
Skua Ct 33 SE8 ... 51 B4
Skyline Ct SE1 ... 138 C1
Skyline Plaza Bldg E1 ... 111 C2
Skylines E14 ... 42 B4
Slade Ct NW2 ... 10 A3
Sladen Pl 12 E5 ... 17 A4
Slagrove Pl SE13 ... 67 A2
Slaidburn St SW10 ... 157 A3
Slaithwaite Rd SE13 ... 67 B3
Slaney Ct NW10 ... 9 B1
Slaney Pl 1 N7 ... 14 C3
Sleaford Ho 16 E3 ... 26 C1
Sleaford Ind Est SW8 ... 161 A1
Sleaford St SW8 ... 161 A1
Sleat Ho 11 E3 ... 26 B3
Slievemore Cl 8 SW4 ... 61 C4
Sligo Ho 8 E1 ... 25 C1
Slingsby Pl WC2 ... 120 A4
Slippers Pl SE16 ... 40 A3
Slipway Ho 1 E14 ... 42 A1
Sloane Ave SW3 ... 144 B3
Sloane Avenue Mans SW3 ... 144 C3
Sloane Ct E SW3 ... 145 B2
Sloane Ct W SW3 ... 145 B2
Sloane Gate Mans SW1 ... 145 B4
Sloane Gdns SW1 ... 145 B3
Sloane Ho 7 E9 ... 17 B1
Sloane Sq SW1 ... 145 A3
Sloane Square Sta SW1 ... 145 B3
Sloane St SW1 ... 131 A1
Sloane Terr SW1 ... 145 B4
Sloane Terr Mans SW1 ... 145 B4
Sly St 17 E1 ... 32 A3
Smallbrook Mews W2 ... 101 B1
Smalley Cl N16 ... 7 B1
Smart's Pl WC1, WC2 ... 106 B2
Smart St E2 ... 25 C2
Smeaton Ct SE1 ... 136 C1
Smeaton Rd SW18 ... 70 C4
Smeaton St E1 ... 32 A1
Smedley St SW4 ... 171 C2
Smeed Rd E3 ... 18 C1
Smiles Pl SE13 ... 52 B1
Smith Cl SE16 ... 32 C1
Smithfield Mkt EC1 ... 108 B3
Smithfield St EC1 ... 108 A3
Smithies Ct E15 ... 19 B3
Smith's Ct W1 ... 119 B4
Smith Sq SW1 ... 134 A1
Smith St SW3 ... 144 C1
Smith's Yd SW18 ... 71 B2
Smith Terr SW3 ... 144 C1
Smithwood Cl SW19 ... 70 A2
Smithy St E1 ... 32 B4
Smithy Street Sch E1 ... 32 B4
Smugglers Way SW18 ... 59 A3
Smyrk's Rd SE17 ... 152 B1
Smyrna Mans 8 NW6 ... 10 C1
Smyrna Rd NW6 ... 10 C1
Smythe St E14 ... 34 A2
Snarsgate St W10 ... 30 B4
Sneath Ave NW11 ... 1 B4
Sneyd Rd NW2 ... 9 B4
Snowberry Cl E11 ... 19 C4
Snowbury Rd SW6 ... 166 B1
Snowden St EC2 ... 24 A1 98 A1
Snowe Ho SE27 ... 75 A1
Snow Hill EC1 ... 108 A3
Snowman Ho NW6 ... 78 B4
Snowsfields SE1 ... 137 C4
Snowsfields Prim Sch SE1 ... 138 A4
Soames St SE15 ... 64 B4
Soane Ct 10 NW1 ... 13 B1
Soane Ho SE17 ... 151 C1
Soane Mus The★ WC2 ... 106 C2
Soaphouse La TW8 ... 44 A3
SOHO ... 105 B1
Soho★ W1 ... 105 B2
Soho Parish CE Prim Sch W1 ... 119 B4
Soho Sq W1 ... 105 B2
Soho St W1 ... 105 B2
Sojourner-Truth Cl 11 E8 ... 17 A2
Solander Gdns
  13 Shadwell E1 ... 32 B2
  Stepney E1 ... 32 A2
Soldene Ct N7 ... 14 B2
Solebay St E1 ... 26 A1
Solent Ho 6 E1 ... 33 A4
Solent Rd NW6 ... 10 C3
Soley Mews WC1 ... 95 B4
Solidarity Ho 5 NW10 ... 9 B2
Solna Ave SW15 ... 57 B2
Solomon's Pas SE15 ... 65 A3
Solon New Rd SW4 ... 62 A3
Solon Rd SW2 ... 62 A3
Solway Ho 12 E1 ... 25 C1
Solway Rd SE22 ... 64 C3
Somali Rd NW2 ... 10 B3
Somborne Ho 11 SW15 ... 68 C4
Sombrook Ho SE11 ... 149 B3
Somer Ct SW6 ... 155 B3
Somerfield Rd N4 ... 6 A2
Somerfield St SE16 ... 40 C1
Somerford Gr N16 ... 16 B4
Somerford Grove Est N16 ... 16 B4
Somerford St E1 ... 25 A1
Somerford Way SE16 ... 41 A4
Somerleyton Rd SW9 ... 62 C3
Somers Cl NW1 ... 83 B2
Somers Cres W2 ... 102 A1
Somerset Gdns
  Highgate N6 ... 3 C4
  St Johns SE13 ... 52 A1
Somerset Ho WC2 ... 121 A4
Somerset Ho SW19 ... 70 A1
Somerset Lo SW15 ... 57 A3
Somerset Rd
  Bedford Pk W4 ... 37 C3
  Wimbledon SW19 ... 70 A1
Somerset Sq W14 ... 126 C3
Somers Pl SW2 ... 74 B4
Somers Rd SW2 ... 62 B1
SOMERS TOWN ... 93 C4
Somers Town Est NW1 ... 83 A1
Somerton Ave TW9 ... 55 A4
Somerton Rd
  Cricklewood NW2 ... 1 A1
  Nunhead SE15 ... 65 A3
Somerville Ave SW13 ... 47 B4
Somerville Ho 10 SW15 ... 57 C1
Somerville Point SE16 ... 41 B4
Sonderburg Rd 13 N7 ... 5 B2
Sondes St SE17 ... 48 C4
Sonia Gdns NW10 ... 8 B4
Sonning Ho E2 ... 24 B2 98 C3
Sophia Cl N7 ... 14 B2
Sophia Ho 10 W6 ... 39 B1

Sophia Sq 14 SE16 . . 33 A2
Sopwith Way SW8 . . . 160 A2
Sorrel La 17 E14 . . . 34 C3
Sorrell Cl Brixton SW9 . . . 173 C2; SE14 . . . 51 A3
Soseki Mus★ SW4 . . 61 A4
Sotheby Rd N5 . . . 15 B4
Sotheran Cl E8 . . . 24 C4
Sotheron Pl SW6 . . 156 B1
Soudan Rd SW11 . . 168 C3
Souldern Rd 10 W14 . . . 39 C3
SOUTH ACTON . . . 37 A3
South Acton Sta W3, W4 . . . 37 B3
South Africa Rd W12 . . . 30 A2
Southall Pl SE1 . . . 137 B3
Southam Ho 9 W10 . . . 23 A1
Southampton Bldgs WC2 . . . 107 B3
Southampton Pl WC1 . . . 106 B3
Southampton Rd NW5 . . . 12 B3
Southampton Row WC1 . . . 106 B4
Southampton St WC2 . . . 120 B4
Southampton Way SE5 . . . 49 A3
Southam St W10 . . . 23 A1
South Audley St W1 . . . 117 C2
South Ave TW9 . . . 44 C1
SOUTH BANK . . . 120 C1
South Bank Bsns Ctr SW8 . . . 161 C3
Southbank International Sch NW3 . . . 11 B2
Southbank International Sch (Westminster Campus) W1 . . . 104 A4
Southbank Int Sch W11 . . . 31 C2 113 B3
South Bank Univ London SW8 . . . 171 C4; SE1 . . . 136 B2
South Bermondsey Sta SE16 . . . 40 B1
South Black Lion La 7 W6 . . . 38 C1
South Bldg SW1 . . 133 A2
South Block 20 E1 . . 32 B2
South Bolton Gdns SW10 . . . 142 B2
Southborough Ho SE17 . . . 152 B2
Southborough Rd E9 . . . 25 C4
SOUTH BROMLEY . . . 34 C4
South Building★ SE10 . . . 52 C3
Southbury NW8 . . . 79 A4
South Camden Com Sch NW1 . . . 83 B2
South Carriage Dr SW1, SW7 . . . 130 C4
South Chelsea Coll SW9 . . . 62 B3
South Colonnade The E14 . . . 34 A1
Southcombe St W14 . . . 140 A4
Southcote Rd N19 . . 13 B4
Southcott Ho 31 Bromley E3 . . . 27 A2; W9 . . . 89 A1
South Cres Newham E16 . . . 27 C1; WC1 . . . 105 B3
South Ct 17 SW15 . . 57 C1
Southdean Gdns SW19 . . . 70 B2
Southdown N7 . . . 14 A2
South Eastern Univ N7 . . . 5 B1
South Eaton Pl SW1 . . . 145 C4
South Edwardes Sq W8 . . . 127 B1
South End W8 . . . 128 B2
South End Cl NW3 . . 12 A4
South End Gn NW3 . . . 12 A4
South End Rd NW3 . . . 12 A4
South End Row W8 . . . 128 B2
Southerngate Way SE14 . . . 51 A3
Southern Gr E3 . . . 26 B1
Southern Row W10 . . . 23 A1
Southern St N1 . . . 84 C2
Southern Way SE10 . . . 43 B3
Southerton Rd W6 . . . 39 B2
Southey Ho SE17 151 A2
Southey Mews E16 . . . 35 C1
Southey Rd SW9 . 173 B4
Southfield Lo W4 . . 37 C4
Southfield Prim Sch W4 . . . 38 A4
Southfield Rd W4 . . 37 C4
SOUTHFIELDS . . . 71 A3
Southfields Com Coll SW18 . . . 70 C3
Southfields Rd SW18 . . . 58 C1
Southfields Sta SW18 . . . 70 B3
Southgate Ct N1 . . . 15 C1
Southgate Gr N1 . . . 15 C1
Southgate Rd N1 . . 87 C4
South Gr N6 . . . 3 C3
South Grove Ho N6 . . 3 C3
SOUTH HACKNEY . . . 25 B4
SOUTH HAMPSTEAD . . . 11 B1
South Hampstead High Sch NW3 . . . 11 C2
South Hampstead High Sch Jun Dept NW3 . . . 11 B2
South Hampstead Sta NW8 . . . 11 B1
South Hill Pk NW3 . . . 12 A4
South Hill Pk Gdns NW3 . . . 12 A4
Southill St E14 . . . 34 A3
South Island Pl SW9 . . . 163 B1
SOUTH KENSINGTON . . . 143 A3
South Kensington Sta SW7 . . . 143 C4
South Kensington Station Arc SW7 143 C4
SOUTH LAMBETH . . . 172 B3
South Lambeth Pl SW8 . . . 162 B4
South Lambeth Rd SW8 . . . 162 B2
Southlands Dr SW19 . . . 69 C2
South Lo NW8 . . . 89 B4
South London Montessori Sch SW11 . . . 168 A3
Southmead Prim Sch SW19 . . . 70 A3
Southmead Rd SW19 . . . 70 A3
South Molton La W1 . . . 104 A1
South Molton Rd E16 . . . 35 C3
South Molton St W1 . . . 104 A1
Southmoor Way E9 . . . 18 B3
Southolm St SW11 . . . 170 B3
South Par W4 . . . 37 C2
South Parade SW3 . . . 143 C2
South Park Mews SW6 . . . 59 A4
South Pl EC2 . . . 109 C3
South Pl Mews EC2 . . . 109 C3
South Quay Plaza E14 . . . 42 A4
South Quay Sta E14 . . . 42 A4
South Rise W2 . . . 116 B4
South Row SE3 . . . 53 B1
South Sea St SE16 . . 41 B3
Southside N7 . . . 13 C4
South Side W6 . . . 38 B3
Southside Ind Est SW8 . . . 170 C4
Southside Quarter SW11 . . . 168 C2
Southside Sh Ctr SW18 . . . 59 A1
South Sq WC1 . . . 107 B3
South St W1 . . . 117 C2
South Tenter St E1 . . . 111 A1
South Terr SW7 . . 144 A4
South Thames Coll (Battersea Ctr) SW11 . . . 169 A3
South Thames Coll (Putney Ctr) SW15 . . . 57 C2
South Thames Coll (Roehampton Ctr) SW15 . . . 56 C1
South Thames Coll (Wandsworth Ctr) SW18 . . . 59 A2
Southvale Rd SE3 . . 53 A1
Southview Ave NW10 . . . 8 B3
South Villas NW1 . . . 13 C2
Southville SW8 . . . 171 C3
SOUTHWARK . . . 40 B2
Southwark Bridge SE1, EC4 . . . 123 A3
Southwark Bridge Rd SE1 . . . 123 A1
Southwark Cath★ SE1 . . . 123 B2
Southwark Coll SE1 . . . 136 A4
Southwark Coll (Blackfriars Ctr) SE1 . . . 122 A1
Southwark Coll (Camberwell Ctr) SE5 . . . 49 A3
Southwark Coll (Grange Ctr) SE1 . . . 138 B1
Southwark Coll (Surrey Docks Ctr) SE16 . . . 40 A3
Southwark Park Est 11 SE16 . . . 40 A2
Southwark Park Prim Sch SE16 . . . 40 A3
Southwark Park Rd SE16 . . . 153 B4
Southwark St SE1 . . . 122 C1
Southwater Cl 8 E14 . . . 33 B3
Southway Cl 9 W12 . . . 39 A4
Southwell Gdns SW7 . . . 142 C3
Southwell Ho 8 Bermondsey SE16 . . . 40 A2; 13 Stoke Newington N16 . . . 16 A3
Southwell Rd SE5 . . 63 B4
South Wharf Rd W2 . . . 101 C2
Southwick Mews W2 . . . 101 C2
Southwick Pl W2 102 A1
Southwick St W2 102 A2
Southwick Yd W2 . . . 102 A1
Southwold Mans W9 . . . 23 C2
Southwood Ave N6 . . 4 A4
Southwood Ct EC1 96 A3
Southwood Ho W11 . . . 31 A2 112 A4
Southwood Hospl (Geriatric) N6 . . . 3 C4
Southwood Hts N6 . . 4 A4
Southwood La N6 . . . 3 C4
Southwood Lawn Rd N6 . . . 4 A4
Southwood Park N6 . . . 3 C4
Southwood Smith Ho 4 E2 . . . 25 A2
Southwood Smith St N1 . . . 86 A3
South Worple Ave SW14 . . . 56 A4
Southwyck Ho SW9 . . . 62 C3
South Yd EC1 . . . 109 B4
Sovereign Cl E1 . . . 32 A2
Sovereign Cres SE16 . . . 33 A2
Sovereign Ct 3 Richmond TW9 . . . 54 B3; 13 Stepney E1 . . . 32 A2
Sovereign Ho 23 E1 . . . 25 A1
Sovereign Mews 6 E2 . . . 24 B3
Sovereign Pk NW10 . . . 20 A1
Space Bsns Pk NW10 . . . 20 A2
Spa Ct SE16 . . . 139 B1
Spafield St EC1 . . . 95 B2
Spalding Ho SE4 . . . 66 A2
Spanby Rd E3 . . . 26 C1
Spaniards Cl NW11 . . 2 C3
Spaniards End NW3 . . . 2 C3
Spaniards Rd NW3 . . 2 B2
Spanish Pl W1 . . . 103 C2
Spanish Rd SW18 . . . 59 B2
Spa Rd SE16 . . . 139 A1
Sparke Terr 2 E16 . . . 35 B3
Sparkford Ho SW11 . . . 167 C4
Sparks Cl W3 . . . 28 C3
Sparsholt Rd N19 . . . 5 B3
Sparta St SE10 . . . 52 B2
Spa Sch SE1 . . . 153 B4
Spa View 6 SW16 . . 74 B1
Speakers' Corner★ W1 . . . 117 A4
Speakman Ho SE4 . . 66 A4
Spear Mews SW5 141 C3
Spears Rd N19 . . . 5 A3
Spectrum Ho NW5 . . . 12 C4
Spedan Cl NW3 . . . 2 B1
Speechly Mews E8 . . . 16 B3
Speed Ho EC2 . . . 109 B4
Speedwell St 5 SE8 . . . 51 C3
Speedy Pl WC1 . . . 94 A3
Speldhurst Rd Bedford Pk W4 . . . 37 C3; Homerton E9 . . . 17 C1
Spellbrook Wlk N1 . . . 87 A4
Spelman Ho E1 . . 111 B3
Spelman St E1 . . . 111 B4
Spence Cl SE16 . . . 41 B4
Spencer Gdns SW14 . . . 55 B2
Spencer Ho Clapham SW8 . . . 171 B1; 24 Putney SW19 . . . 69 C3; Vale of Health NW3 . . . 2 C1; Wimbledon SW19 . . . 69 C1
Spencer House Mus★ SW1 . . . 118 C1
Spencer Mews Fulham W6 . . . 154 A4; South Lambeth SW9 . . . 172 C3
Spencer Park Ct SW18 . . . 59 C2
Spencer Pk SW18 . . 59 C2
Spencer Pl 16 Islington N1 . . . 15 A1; SW1 . . . 133 A1
Spencer Rd Acton W3 . . . 28 B1; Chiswick W4 . . . 45 B3; Wandsworth SW18 . . 59 C2
Spencer Rise NW5 . . 4 A1

Spencer St EC1 ... 96 A3
Spencer Wlk
23 Hampstead NW3 ... 11 B4
Putney SW15 ... 57 C3
Spencer Yd SE3 ... 53 B1
Spenlow Ho SE16 139 C2
Spenser Gr N16 ... 16 A4
Spenser Mews SE21 ... 75 C3
Spenser Rd SE24 ... 63 A2
Spenser St SW1 ... 133 A2
Spens Ho WC1 ... 94 C1
Spensley Wlk N16 ... 6 C1
Spert St E14 ... 33 A2
Spey St E14 ... 34 B4
Spezia Rd NW10 ... 21 C3
Spice Ct
10 Battersea SW11 ... 59 B4
St George in t East E1 ... 125 C2
Spice Quay Htss SE1 ... 125 A1
Spicer Cl SE5, SW9 .. 48 A1
Spicer Ho E2 ... 24 C2 99 B3
Spindrift Ave E14 .. 42 A2
Spinnaker Ho 21 E14 ... 41 C4
Spinney The
Barnes SW13 ... 47 A4
Streatham SW16 ... 73 C1
Spire Ct 10 TW10 .. 54 A1
Spire Ho W2 ... 115 A4
Spirit Quay E1 ... 32 A1
SPITALFIELDS ... 111 A4
Spital Sq E1 ... 110 B4
Spital St E1 ... 111 B4
Spital Yd E1 ... 110 B4
Splendour Wlk SE16 ... 40 B1
Spode Ho SE11 ... 135 B1
Spode Wlk NW3 ... 11 A3
Sporle Ct 6 SW11 .. 59 C4
Sprewell SW15 ... 58 A1
Spriggs Ho 14 N1 .. 15 A1
Sprimont Pl SW3 144 C2
Springall St 9 SE15 ... 50 A3
Springalls Wharf SE16 ... 139 B4
Springbank Wlk NW1 ... 13 C1
Spring Cott 10 W12 ... 38 C4
Spring Ct NW2 ... 10 B2
Springdale Rd N16 ... 15 C4
Springett Ho 15 SW2 ... 62 B2
Springfield Ct
7 Dagenham W3 ... 28 B3
Hampstead NW3 ... 12 A1
Springfield Ho
Acton W3 ... 28 B1
1 Camberwell SE5 .. 49 A1
13 Dalston E8 ... 16 B2
Springfield Hospl SW17 ... 72 A1
Springfield La NW6 ... 78 A3
Springfield Rd NW8 ... 79 A3
Springfield Wlk NW6 ... 78 A3
Spring Gdns
Islington N5 ... 15 B3
SW1 ... 120 A2
Spring Gr W4 ... 44 C4
Spring Grove Rd TW10 ... 54 B2
Spring Hill E5 ... 7 C4
Springhill Cl SE5 ... 63 C4
Spring Ho WC1 ... 95 B3
Spring Mews W1 103 A4
Springpark Dr N4 ... 6 B3
Spring Pl NW5 ... 13 A3
Springrice Rd SE13 ... 67 C1
Spring St W2 ... 101 B1
Spring Terr TW10 ... 54 A2
Springtide Cl 10 SE15 ... 49 C2
Springvale Ave TW8 ... 36 A1
Springvale Terr 5 W14 ... 39 C3
Springwater WC1 106 C4
Springwell Ave NW10 ... 21 B4
Spring Wlk E1 ... 111 C4
Springwood Cl 8 E3 ... 26 C3
Spruce Ct W5 ... 36 A3
Spruce Ho 15 SE16 ... 40 C4
Sprules Rd SE4 ... 51 A1
Spurgeon St SE1 . 137 B2
Spurling Rd SE22 ... 64 B3
Spur Rd SE1 ... 135 B4
Spurstowe Rd E8 ... 17 A2
Spurstowe Terr E8 ... 17 A3
Square Rigger Row 7 SW11 ... 59 B4
Square The
Hammersmith W6 ... 39 B1
SW6 ... 165 B3
Squarey St SW17 ... 71 B1
Squire Gdns NW8 . 89 B3
Squires Ct SW4 .. 172 B3
Squire's Mount NW3 ... 2 C1
Squirrels The SE13 ... 67 C4
Squirries St E2 ... 24 C2 99 C3
Stable Ho 9 SE16 .. 40 B4
Stables Way SE11 149 B2
Stable Way W10 ... 30 B3
Stable Yd Rd SW1 ... 133 A4
Stacey St
Highbury N7 ... 5 C1
Soho WC2 ... 105 C1
Stack Ho SW1 ... 145 C3
Stackhouse St SW1 ... 130 C2
Stacy Path 13 SE5 .. 49 A3
Stadium St SW10 157 A1
Stafford Cl NW6 ... 23 C2
Stafford Cripps Ho
30 Bethnal Green E2 ... 25 B2
SW6 ... 155 A3
Stafford Ct
Kensington W8 ... 127 C2
South Lambeth SW8 ... 172 A4
Stafford Ho SE1 .. 153 A2
Stafford Mans
13 Hammersmith W14 ... 39 C3
14 Stockwell SW4 ... 62 A3
SW11 ... 158 C1
Stafford Pl SW1 .. 132 C2
Stafford Rd
Bow E3 ... 26 B3
Maida Vale NW6 ... 23 C2
Staffordshire St
Peckham SE15 ... 49 C2
Peckham SE15 ... 50 A2
Stafford St W1 ... 118 C2
Stafford Terr W8 . 127 B2
Stag La SW15 ... 68 B2
Stagshaw Ho 17 SE22 ... 64 A4
Stainer St SE1 ... 123 C1
Staining La EC2 .. 109 A2
Stainsbury St 25 E2 ... 25 B3
Stainsby Rd E14 ... 33 C3
Stalbridge Flats W1 ... 103 C1
Stalbridge Ho NW1 ... 82 C1
Stalbridge St NW1 ... 102 B4
Stalham St SE16 ... 40 A3
Stambourne Ho SW8 ... 172 B4
Stamford Bridge Stadium (Chelsea FC) SW6 ... 156 A2
Stamford Brook Ave W6 ... 38 B3
Stamford Brook Gdns 1 W6 ... 38 B3
Stamford Brook Mans 2 W6 ... 38 B2
Stamford Brook Rd W6 ... 38 B3
Stamford Brook Sta W6 ... 38 B2
Stamford Cl 2 NW3 ... 2 B1
Stamford Cotts SW10 ... 156 B2
Stamford Ct W6 ... 38 C2
Stamford Gr E 1 N16 ... 7 C3
Stamford Gr W 4 N16 ... 7 C3
STAMFORD HILL ... 7 A3
Stamford Hill N16 ... 7 B3
Stamford Hill Mans 1 N16 ... 7 B3
Stamford Hill Sta N16 ... 7 A4
Stamford Hospl W6 ... 38 C2
Stamford Lo 2 N16 ... 7 B4
Stamford Mans 2 N16 ... 7 C3
Stamford Rd N1 ... 16 A2
Stamford St SE1 ... 121 C2
Stamp Pl E2 .24 B2 99 A4
Stanard Cl N16 ... 7 A4
Stanborough Ho 4 E3 ... 27 A1
Stanborough Pas E8 ... 16 B2
Stanbridge Mans SW15 ... 57 B4
Stanbridge Rd SW15 ... 57 B4
Stanbrook Ct W1 118 C2
Stanbury Ct 16 NW3 ... 12 B2
Stanbury Rd
Nunhead SE15 ... 50 B1
Peckham SE15 ... 50 A1
Standard Pl EC2 ... 24 A2 98 B3
Standard Rd NW10 ... 20 C1
Standen Rd SW18 .. 70 C4
Standish Ho 6 W6 ... 38 C2
Standish Rd W6 ... 38 C2
Stanesgate Ho 20 SE15 ... 49 C3
Stanfield Ho NW8 . 89 C2
Stanfield Rd 14 E3 ... 26 A3
Stanford Ct
Kensington W8 ... 128 B1
Walham Green SW6 ... 166 B3
Stanford Pl SE1 .. 152 A3
Stanford Rd W8 .. 128 B2
Stanford St SW1 . 147 B3
Stangate SE1 ... 135 A2
Stanhope Cl 28 SE16 ... 40 C4
Stanhope Gate W1 ... 117 C2
Stanhope Gdns SW7 ... 143 A4
Stanhope Ho
4 Putney SW15 ... 57 B2
SE8 ... 51 B3
Stanhope Mews E SW7 ... 143 A4
Stanhope Mews S SW7 ... 143 A3
Stanhope Mews W SW7 ... 143 A4
Stanhope Par NW1 ... 92 C4
Stanhope Pl W2 .. 102 C1
Stanhope Rd N6 ... 4 B4
Stanhope Row W1 ... 118 A1
Stanhope St NW1 . 92 C3
Stanhope Terr W2 ... 115 C4
Stanier Cl SW5 ... 141 A1
Stanlake Mews 7 W12 ... 30 B1
Stanlake Rd W12 ... 30 B1
Stanlake Villas 8 W12 ... 30 B1
Stanley Bldgs NW1 ... 84 A1
Stanley Cl SW8 ... 162 C3
Stanley Cohen Ho EC1 ... 96 C1
Stanley Cres W11 ... 31 B2 112 C4
Stanley Gdns
Bedford Pk W3 ... 38 A4
Cricklewood NW2 ... 9 B3
W11 ... 31 B2 112 C4
Stanley Gr SW11 . 169 C1
Stanley Ho
Clapham SW8 ... 171 B1
22 Poplar E14 ... 33 C3
Stanley Holloway Ct E16 ... 35 C3
Stanley Mans SW10 ... 157 A4
Stanley Mans *continued*
Upper Tooting SW17 ... 72 B2
Stanley Rd
Acton Green W3 ... 37 B3
Mill Meads E15 ... 27 C4
Mortlake SW14 ... 55 A3
Stanley St SE14, SE8 ... 51 B3
Stanley Studios SW10 ... 157 A4
Stanley Terr 8 N19 ... 5 A2
Stanliff Ho 8 E14 .. 41 C3
Stanmer St SW11. 168 B2
Stanmore Gdns TW9 ... 54 B4
Stanmore Ho SW8 ... 171 C2
Stanmore Pl NW1 . 82 B4
Stanmore Rd TW9 .. 54 B4
Stanmore St N1 ... 84 C4
Stannard Cotts 27 E1 ... 25 B1
Stannard Mews E8 ... 16 C2
Stannard Rd E8 ... 16 C2
Stannary Pl SE11 149 C1
Stannary St SE11 149 C1
Stansbury Sq 3 W10 ... 23 A2
Stansfeld Ho SE1 153 A3
Stansfield Rd SW9 . 62 B4
Stanstead Ho E3 ... 27 B1
Stansted Express Terminal EC2 ... 110 A4
Stanswood Gdns SE5 ... 49 A3
Stanton Ct N16 ... 6 C4
Stanton Ho 9 SE10 ... 52 B4
Stanton Rd SW13 ... 46 B1
Stanway Ct 23 N1 .. 24 A3
Stanway St N1 ... 24 A3
Stanwick Rd W14 140 C3
Stanworth St SE1 139 A3
Staplefield Cl 3 SW2 ... 74 A3
Stapleford Cl SW19 ... 70 A4
Staplehurst Ct SW11 ... 60 B1
Staplehurst Ho 18 E5 ... 17 A3
Staple Inn WC2 ... 107 B3
Staple Inn Bldgs WC2 ... 107 B3
Staples Cl SE16 ... 33 A1
Staple St SE1 ... 137 C3
Stapleton Hall N4 ... 5 B4
Stapleton Hall Rd N4 ... 5 B4
Stapleton Ho 19 E2 ... 25 A2
Stapleton Rd SW17 ... 72 C1
Star Alley EC3 ... 124 B4
Starboard Way E14 ... 41 C3
Starcross St NW1 . 93 A3
Stardome* NW1 .. 91 B1
Starfield Rd W12 ... 38 C4
Star & Garter Mans SW15 ... 57 C4
Starliner Ct N7 ... 14 C2

Starling Ho NW8 80 A2
Star Pl E1 125 C3
Star Rd W14 140 C1
Star St W2 102 A2
Star Works NW10 21 C2
Star Yd WC2 107 B2
Statham Ct N7 5 A1
Statham Gr N16 6 C1
Statham Ho SW8 170 C4
Station App
Dagenham NW10 21 B2
Fulham SW6 58 A4
Richmond TW9 44 C2
Station Approach Rd W4 45 B3
Station Ave
5 Brixton SW9 63 A4
14 Richmond TW9 44 C2
Station Cres SE3 43 C1
Station Ct 5 SE15 50 B1
Stationers Hall Ct EC4 108 B1
Station Gdns W4 45 B3
Station Mews Terr 4 SE3 43 C1
Station Par
Cricklewood NW2 9 B2
Richmond TW9 44 C2
4 Upper Tooting SW12 72 C3
Station Pas SE15 50 B2
Station Pl N4 5 C2
Station Rd
Barnes SW13 46 B1
Camden Town N19 4 B1
Harlesden NW10 21 B3
Lewisham SE13 67 B4
Station Rise SE27 75 A2
Station St E15 19 C1
Station Terr
Camberwell SE5 48 B2
Kensal Rise NW10 22 C3
Staunton Ho SE17 152 A3
Staunton St SE8 51 B4
Staveley NW1 92 C4
Staveley Cl
Hackney E9 17 B3
Lower Holloway N7 14 A4
New Cross Gate SE15 50 B2
8 Peckham SE15 50 A2
Staveley Gdns W4 45 C2
Staveley Ho SE4 66 A2
Staveley Rd W4 45 C3
Stavers Ho 31 E3 26 B3
Staverton Rd NW2 9 B1
Stave Yard Rd SE16 33 A1
Stavordale Lo W14 127 A2
Stavordale Rd N5 15 A4
Stayner's Rd E1 25 C1
Steadman Ct EC1 97 A2
Stead St SE17 151 B3
Stean St E8 24 B4
Stebbing Ho 8 W11 30 C1
Stebondale St E14 42 B2
Stebon Prim Sch E14 33 C4
Stedham Pl WC1 106 A2
Steedman St SE17 150 C3
Steele Rd
Acton Green W4 37 B3
Becontree NW10 20 B3
Steele's Mews N NW3 12 B2
Steele's Mews S NW3 12 B2
Steele's Rd NW3 12 B2
Steel's La 23 E1 32 B3
Steen Way 7 SE22 64 A2
Steep Hill SW16 73 C1
Steeple Cl SW6 164 B1
Steeple Ct 19 E1 25 A1
Steeple Wlk N1 87 A4
Steerforth St SW18 71 B2
Steers Way SE16 41 A4
Stelfax Ho WC1 95 A4
Stellman Cl E5 7 C1
Stephan Cl E8 24 C4
Stephen Ct 18 SW19 69 C3
Stephendale Rd SW6 166 C2
Stephen Fox Ho 7 W4 38 A1
Stephen Hawking Sch E14 33 A3
Stephen Mews W1 105 B3
Stephen Pl SW4 61 B4
Stephen Saunders Ct SW11 60 A2
Stephens Ct SE4 66 A4
Stephenson Ho
2 Gospel Oak NW5 13 A4
6 Maitland Pk NW3 12 B3
Newington SE1 136 C2
Stephenson St
Dagenham NW10 21 B2
Newham E16 35 A4
Stephenson Way NW1 93 A2
Stephen St W1 105 B3
STEPNEY 32 C4
Stepney City E1 32 B4
Stepney Cswy E1 32 C3
Stepney Gn E1 32 C4
Stepney Greencoat CE Prim Sch The E14 33 B3
Stepney Green Ct 4 E1 32 C4
Stepney Green Sch E1 32 C4
Stepney Green Sta E1 25 C1
Stepney High St E1 32 C4
Stepney Way E1 32 B4
Sterling Cl NW10 8 C1
Sterling Gdns SE14 51 A4
Sterling Pl W5 36 A2
Sterling St SW7 130 B2
Sterndale Rd W14 39 C3
Sterne St W12 39 C4
Sternhall La SE15 64 C4
Sternhold Ave SW12, SW2 73 C2
Sterry St SE1 137 B3
Steve Biko Ct W10 22 C1
Steve Biko Rd N7 5 C1
Stevedore St 3 E1 32 A1
Stevenage Rd SW6 47 C2
Stevens Ave E9 17 B2
Stevenson Cres SE16 40 A1
Stevenson Ho
Battersea SW11 168 C1
6 Clapham Pk SW2 62 A2
NW8 78 C4
Stevens St SE1 138 B2
Steventon Rd W12 29 B2
Stewart Headlam Prim Sch E1 25 A1
Stewart Ho SE1 138 A1
Stewart Rd E15 19 C4
Stewart's Gr SW3 144 A2
Stewart's Rd SW8 170 C4
Stewart St E14 42 B4
Stew La EC4 122 C4
Steyne Ho
15 Acton W3 28 A1
11 Acton W3 28 B1
Steyne Rd W3 28 A1
Stifford Ho E1 32 B4
Stile Hall Gdns W4 36 C1
Stile Hall Par 6 W4 36 C1
Stileman Ho 4 E3 33 B4
Stillingfleet Rd SW13 46 C4
Stillington St SW1 147 A4
Stillness Jun & Inf Schs SE23 66 A1
Stillness Rd SE23 66 B1
Stirling Ct
Clerkenwell EC1 96 A2
Strand WC2 106 C1
Stirling Mans NW6 11 B2
Stirling Rd
South Acton W3 37 A3
Stockwell SW9 172 B1
Stoatley Ho 10 SW15 68 C3
Stockbeck NW1 83 A1
Stockfield Rd SW16 74 B1
Stockholm Ho E1 125 C4
Stockholm Rd SE16 40 B1
Stockholm Way E1 125 B2
Stockhurst Cl SW15 47 C1
Stockleigh Hall NW8 80 B2
Stock Orchard Cres N7 14 B3
Stock Orchard St N7 14 B3
Stocks Ct 5 E1 25 C1
Stocks Pl 16 E14 33 B2
Stockton Ho 16 E2 25 A2
STOCKWELL 62 A4
Stockwell Ave SW9 62 B4
Stockwell Gdns SW9 172 C3
Stockwell Gn SW9 172 C1
Stockwell La SW9 172 C1
Stockwell Park Cres SW9 173 A2
Stockwell Park Rd SW9 173 A3
Stockwell Park Sch SW9 172 C3
Stockwell Park Wlk SW9 62 C4
Stockwell Prim Sch SW9 62 B4
Stockwell St SE10 52 B4
Stockwell Sta SW4 172 B2
Stockwell Terr SW9 172 C3
Stoddart Ho SW8 163 A3
Stodmarsh Ho SW9 173 C4
Stoford Cl SW19 70 A4
Stokenchurch St SW6 166 A3
STOKE NEWINGTON 7 A2
Stoke Newington Church St N16 7 A2
Stoke Newington Comm N16 7 B2
Stoke Newington High St N16 7 B1
Stoke Newington Rd N16 16 B4
Stoke Newington Sch N16 6 C1
Stoke Newington Sta N16 7 B2
Stoke Pl NW10 21 B2
Stokesley St W12 29 B3
Stondon Pk SE23 66 A1
Stone Bldgs WC2 107 A3
STONEBRIDGE 20 B4
Stonebridge Ctr 6 NW10 20 C4
Stonebridge Sch The NW10 20 C4
Stone Cl SW4 171 A1
Stonecutter St EC4 108 A2
Stonefield N4 5 B2
Stonefield Mans N1 85 B3
Stonefield St N1 85 C4
Stonegate 8 NW5 12 C2
Stonehill Cl SW14 55 C2
Stonehill Rd
Brentford W4 36 C1
Mortlake SW14 55 C2
Stonehills Ct SE21 76 A1
Stonehill's Mans 3 SW16 74 A2
Stonehouse NW1 83 A3
Stonehouse Ct EC2 110 B2
Stonehouse Ho 27 W2 31 C4
Stoneleigh Lo 13 TW9 44 B2
Stoneleigh Mews 15 E3 26 A3
Stoneleigh Pl W11 30 C2
Stoneleigh St W11 30 C2
Stoneleigh Terr N19 4 A2
Stonell's Rd SW11 60 B2
Stonenest St N4 5 B3
Stones End St SE1 136 C3
Stoneyard La E14 34 A2
Stoney La E1 110 B2
Stoney St SE1 123 B2
Stonhouse St SW4 61 C3
Stonor Rd W14 140 C3
Stopes St SE15 49 B3
Stopford Rd SE17 150 B1
Stopher Ho SE1 136 B3
Storace Ho 6 SW4 62 A3
Storers Quay E14 42 C2
Store St
Bloomsbury WC1 105 B4
Stratford New Town E15 19 C3
Storey Ct NW8 89 B3
Storey Ho 18 E14 34 A2
Storey's Gate SW1 133 C3
Stories Rd SE5 64 A4
Storks Rd SE16 139 C1
Stormont House Sch E5 17 A4
Stormont Rd
Clapham SW11 60 C3
Highgate N6 3 B4
Storrington WC1 94 B3
Story St N1 14 B1
Stothard Ho 25 E1 25 B1
Stothard Pl E1 110 B4
Stothard St 12 E1 25 B1
Stott Cl SW18 59 C1
Stoughton Cl
Roehampton SW15 68 C3
SE11 149 A3
Stourcliffe Cl W1 102 C2
Stourcliffe St W1 102 C1
Stourhead Cl 6 SW19 69 C4
Stour Rd E3 18 C1
Stowage SE8 52 A4
Stowe Ho 11 N16 7 A1
Stowe Rd W12 39 A4
Stracey Rd NW10 20 C4
Stradbroke Rd N5 15 B4
Stradella Rd SE24 63 B1
Straffan Lo 8 NW3 12 A2
Strafford Ho 9 SE8 41 B1
Strafford Rd W3 37 B4
Strafford St E14 41 C4
Strahan Rd E3 26 A2
Straightsmouth SE10 52 B3
Straker's Rd SE15 65 A3
Strale Ho 17 N1 24 A4
STRAND 120 C4
Strand
Strand WC2 120 C4
Strand WC2 107 A1
Strand Dr TW9 45 A3
Strand La WC2 121 A4
STRAND ON THE GREEN 44 C4
Strand-on-the-Green W4 44 C4
Strand-on-the-Green Schs W4 44 C4
Strang Ho N1 86 C3
Strangways Terr W14 126 C1

Stranraer Way N1 . . 14 A1
Strasburg Rd SW11 . . . 170 A3
STRATFORD . . . 19 B2
Stratford Bus Sta E15 . . . 19 C1
Stratford Cir (Newham 6th Form Coll) E15 . . . 19 C2
Stratford Gr SW15 . . 57 C3
Stratford International Sta (under constr) E15 . . . 19 B2
STRATFORD MARSH . . . 27 A4
STRATFORD NEW TOWN . . . 19 B3
Stratford Pl W1 . . 104 A1
Stratford Rd W8 . . 127 C1
Stratford Sh Ctr E15 . . . 19 C1
Stratford Sta E15 . . 19 C1
Stratford Studios W8 . . . 128 A1
Stratford Villas NW1 . . . 13 C1
Stratford Workshops E15 . . . 27 C4
Strathan Cl SW18 . . 58 A1
Strathblaine Rd SW11 . . . 59 C3
Strathdon Dr SW17 . . . 71 C1
Strathearn Ho W2 . . . 116 A4
Strathearn Pl W2 116 A4
Stratheden Par SE3 . . . 53 C3
Stratheden Rd SE3 . . . 53 C3
Strathleven Rd SW2 . . . 62 A2
Strathmore Ct NW8 . . . 90 A4
Strathmore Gdns W8 . . . 31 C1 113 C2
Strathmore Rd SW19 . . . 70 C1
Strathnairn St SE1 . . . 153 C3
Strathray Gdns NW3 . . . 12 A2
Strath Terr SW11 . . . 60 A3
Strathville Rd SW18 . . . 71 A2
Stratton Ct [4] N1 . . 16 A1
Strattondale St E14 . . . 42 B3
Stratton St W1 . . . 118 B2
Strauss Rd W4 . . . 37 C4
Streamline Mews SE22 . . . 76 C3
Streatham Cl SW16 . . . 74 A2
Streatham & Clapham High Sch SW16 . . . 73 C1
Streatham Ct SW16 . . . 74 A1
STREATHAM HILL . . . 74 A3
Streatham Hill SW2 . . . 74 A3
Streatham Hill & Clapham High Sch SW2 . . . 74 B3
Streatham Hill Sta SW2 . . . 74 A2
Streatham Pl SW2 . . 74 A4
Streatham St WC1 . . . 106 A2
Streathbourne Rd SW17 . . . 72 C1
Streathem Wells Prim Sch SW2 . . . 74 C2
Streatleigh Par [4] SW16 . . . 74 A2
Streatley Pl
[27] Hampstead NW3 . . . 11 B4
Hampstead NW3 . . . 11 C4
Streatley Rd NW6 . . 10 B1
Streimer Rd E15 . . . 27 B3
Strelley Way W3 . . . 29 A2
Stretton Mans [16] SE8 . . . 51 C4
Strickland Ct SE15 . . . 64 C4
Strickland Ho E2 . . . 24 B2 99 A3
Strickland Row SW18 . . . 71 C4
Strickland St SE8 . . . 51 C2
Stringer Hos [19] N1 . . . 24 A4
Strode Ho [3] SW2 . . 74 C3
Strode Rd SW6 . . . 154 A2
Willesden NW10 . . . 8 C2
Strome Ho NW6 . . . 78 A1
Stronsa Rd W12 . . . 38 B4
Strood Ho SE1 . . . 137 C3
Stroud Cres SW15 . . 68 C1
Stroud Green Prim Sch N4 . . . 5 C3
Stroud Green Rd N4 . . . 5 C3
Stroudley Ho SW8 . . . 171 A4
Stroudley Wlk E3 . . . 27 A2
Stroud Rd SW19 . . . 70 C1
Strout's Pl E2 . . . 24 B2 98 C4
Strudwick Ct SW4 . . . 172 B3
Strutton Ground SW1 . . . 133 B1
Strype St E1 . . . 110 C3
Stuart Ave W5 . . . 36 B4
Stuart Ho
Hammersmith W6 . . . 39 B3
[1] Homerton E9 . . . 17 C1
[5] Stockwell SW4 . . . 62 A3
W14 . . . 140 A4
Stuart Mill Ho N1 . 84 C1
Stuart Rd
Acton W3 . . . 28 B1
Maida Vale NW6 . . . 23 C2
Nunhead SE15 . . . 65 B3
Wimbledon SW19 . . . 70 C1
Stubbs Dr SE16 . . . 40 A1
Stubbs Ho
Finsbury Pk N4 . . . 5 B3
[1] Globe Town E2 . . . 25 C2
Stucley Pl [19] NW1 . . 13 A1
Studdridge St SW6 . . . 165 C2
Studd St N1 . . . 86 A4
Studholme Ct NW3 . . . 10 C4
Studholme St SE15 . . . 50 A3
Studio Pl SW1 . . . 131 A3
Studios NW8 . . . 78 C2
Studios The
[4] Clapham SW4 . . . 61 B3
SW8 . . . 171 C3
Studland SE17 . . . 151 B2
Studland Ho E14 . . . 33 A3
Studland St W6 . . . 39 A2
Studley Cl E5 . . . 18 A3
Studley Ct [13] E14 . . 34 C2
Studley Rd SW4 . . 172 B2
Stukeley St WC2 . . 106 B2
Stunell Ho [23] SE14 . . . 50 C4
Sturdee Ho [2] E2 . . 24 C3
Sturdy Ho [28] E3 . . . 26 A3
Sturdy Rd SE15 . . . 50 A1
Sturgeon Rd SE17 . . . 150 C1
Sturge St SE1 . . . 136 C4
Sturmer Way N7 . . . 14 B3
Sturminster Ho SW8 . . . 163 A1
Sturry St E14 . . . 34 A3
Sturt St N1 . . . 87 A1
Stutfield St E1 . . . 111 C1
Stuttle Ho E1 . . . 24 C1 99 B1
Styles Gdns SW9 . . . 63 A4
Styles Ho SE1 . . . 122 A1
Stylus Apartments [25] E1 . . . 32 B3
Sudbourne Prim Sch SW2 . . . 62 B2
Sudbourne Rd SW2 . . . 62 B2
Sudbrooke Rd SW12 . . . 60 C1
Sudbury Ct SW8 . . 171 C4
Sudbury Ho SW18 . . 59 A2
Sudeley St N1 . . . 86 B1
Sudlow Rd SW18 . . . 58 C2
Sudrey St SE1 . . . 136 C3
Suffield Ho SE17 . 150 B2
Suffolk Ho [8] NW5 . . 4 B1
Suffolk La EC4 . . . 123 B4
Suffolk Pl SW1 . . . 119 C2
Suffolk Rd
Barnes SW13 . . . 46 C3
Willesden NW10 . . . 8 A1
Suffolk St SW1 . . . 119 C2
Sugar House La E15 . . . 27 B3
Sugar Loaf Wlk [6] E2 . . . 25 B2
Sugden Rd SW11 . . . 60 C3
Sulby Ho SE4 . . . 66 A3
Sulgrave Gdns [11] W6 . . . 39 B4
Sulgrave Rd W6 . . . 39 B3
Sulina Rd SW2 . . . 74 A4
Sulivan Ct SW6 . . . 165 B1
Sulivan Ent Ctr SW6 . . . 58 C4
Sulivan Prim Sch SW6 . . . 165 B1
Sulivan Rd SW6 . . . 58 C4
Sulkin Ho [11] E2 . . . 25 C2
Sullivan Cl SW11 . . . 60 A4
Sullivan Ct
Stamford Hill N16 . . . 7 B3
SW5 . . . 141 C4
Sullivan Ho
Chelsea SW1 . . . 160 B4
Vauxhall SE11 . . . 149 A3
Sullivan Rd SE11 . 149 C4
Sultan St SE5 . . . 48 B3
Sumatra Rd NW6 . . . 10 C2
Sumburgh Rd SW12 . . . 60 C1
Summercourt Rd E1 . . . 32 B3
Summerfield Ave NW6 . . . 23 A3
Summer Ho SE13 . . . 67 C3
Summerhouse Rd N16 . . . 7 A2
Summerlands Ave W3 . . . 28 B2
Summerley St SW18 . . . 71 A2
Summers St EC1 . . 95 B1
SUMMERSTOWN . . 71 B1
Summit Ct NW2 . . . 10 A3
Summit Est N16 . . . 7 C4
Sumner Ave SE15 . . 49 B2
Sumner Bldgs SE1 . . . 122 C2
Sumner Ct SW8 . . 172 A4
Sumner Ho [1] E3 . . 34 A4
Sumner Pl SW7 . . 143 C3
Sumner Place Mews SW7 . . . 143 C3
Sumner Rd SE15 . . . 49 B3
Sumner St SE1 . . . 122 C2
Sumpter Cl NW3 . . . 11 B2
Sun Alley [6] TW9 . . . 54 A3
Sun Alliance Ho WC2 . . . 107 B2
Sunbeam Cres W10 . . . 22 B1
Sunbeam Rd NW10 . . . 20 C1
Sunbury Ave SW14 . . . 55 C3
Sunbury Ct [3] SE14 . . . 50 C4
Sunbury Ho E2 . . . 24 B2 98 C3
Sunbury La SW11 167 C4
Sunbury Workshops E2 . . . 24 B2 98 C3
Sun Ct EC3 . . . 109 C1
Sunderland Ct SE22 . . . 76 C4
Sunderland Ho [26] W2 . . . 31 C4
Sunderland Terr W2 . . . 100 A2
Sundew Ave W12 . . . 29 C2
Sundra Wlk [26] E1 . . 25 C1
Sundridge Ho [4] E9 . . . 17 C1
Sunley Ho E1 . . . 111 A3
Sunlight Sq [29] E2 . . 25 A2
Sunningdale Ave W3 . . . 29 A2
Sunningdale Cl [22] SE16 . . . 40 A1
Sunningdale Gdns W8 . . . 127 C1
Sunninghill Ct [9] W3 . . . 37 B4
Sunninghill Rd SE13 . . . 52 A1
Sunnyhill Cl E5 . . . 18 A4
Sunnymead Rd SW15 . . . 57 A2
Sunnyside [4] NW2 . . 1 B1
Sunnyside Ho [3] NW2 . . . 1 B1
Sunnyside Rd N19 . . . 4 C4
Sun Pas SE16 . . . 139 B2
Sunray Ave SE5, SE24 . . . 63 C3
Sun Rd W14 . . . 140 C1
Sun St Pas EC2 . . . 110 A3
Sunset Rd SE5 . . . 63 C3
Sun St EC2 . . . 109 C4
Sunwell Cl SE15 . . . 50 A2
Surcot Ho SW4 . . . 171 C1
Surma Cl E1 . 24 C1 99 C1
Surrendale Pl W9 . . 23 C1
Surrey Canal Rd SE14, SE16, SE8 . . . 50 C4
Surrey Cres [1] W4 . . . 36 C1
Surrey Gr SE17 . . . 152 A1
Surrey Ho [8] SE16 . . 32 C1
Surrey La SW11 . . . 168 B3
Surrey Quays Rd SE16 . . . 40 C4
Surrey Quays Sh Ctr SE16 . . . 40 C3
Surrey Quays Sta SE16 . . . 40 C2
Surrey Rd SE15 . . . 65 C2
Surrey Row SE1 . . 136 B4
Surrey Sq SE17 . . . 152 B2
Surrey Square Inf Sch SE17 . . . 152 A2
Surrey Square Jun Sch SE17 . . . 152 A2
Surrey St WC2 . . . 121 A4
Surrey Terr SE17 . . . 152 B2
Surrey Water Rd SE16 . . . 32 C1
Surrey Wharf SE1 . . 49 C4
Surridge Ct SW9 . . . 172 B2
Surr St N7 . . . 14 A3
Susan Constant Ct [18] E14 . . . 34 C2
Susannah St E14 . . . 34 B3
Sussex Cl N19 . . . 5 A2
Sussex Ct
[4] Barnes SW13 . . . 46 B1
Greenwich SE10 . . . 52 B4
Paddington W2 . . . 101 B1
Sussex Gdns W2 . 101 C1
Sussex Ho
Hampstead NW3 . . . 12 A2
Richmond TW9 . . . 44 B1
Sussex House Sch SW3 . . . 144 C4
Sussex Lo W2 . . . 101 C1
Sussex Mans
South Kensington SW7 . . . 143 B3
Strand WC2 . . . 120 B4
Sussex Mews E W2 . . . 101 C1
Sussex Mews W W2 . . . 115 C4
Sussex Pl
[22] Hammersmith W6 . . . 39 B1
Lisson Gr NW1 . . . 90 C2
Paddington W2 . . . 101 C1
Sussex Sq W2 . . . 115 C4
Sussex St SW1 . . . 146 B2
Sussex Way
Upper Holloway N7 . . . 5 B1
Upper Holloway N7, N19 . . . 5 A2
Upper Holloway N19 . . 4 C3
Sutherland Ave W9 . . . 88 C2
Sutherland Ct
[3] Paddington W9 . . . 23 C1
Stoke Newington N16 . 6 C1

Sutherland Gdns SW14 .... 56 A4
Sutherland Gr SW18, SW19 .... 70 B4
Sutherland Ho
Kensington W8 .... 128 A1
7 Putney SW15 .... 69 B4
9 South Hampstead NW6 .... 11 B2
Sutherland Pl W2 .. 31 C3
Sutherland Rd W4 .... 46 A4
Sutherland Row SW1 .... 146 B2
Sutherland Sq SE17 .... 150 C1
Sutherland St SW1 .... 146 B2
Sutherland Wlk SE17 .... 151 A1
Sutterton St N7 .... 14 B2
Sutton Court Mans W4 .... 45 B4
Sutton Court Rd W4 .... 45 B4
Sutton Ct
Chiswick W4 .... 45 B4
8 Hackney E5 .... 17 A4
Sutton Est SW3 .. 144 B2
Sutton Est The 8 W10 .... 30 B4
Sutton House* E9 .... 17 B3
Sutton La EC1 .... 96 B1
Sutton La N W4 .... 37 B1
Sutton La S W4 .... 45 B4
Sutton Pl E9 .... 17 B3
Sutton Row W1 .. 105 C2
Sutton Sq E9 .... 17 B3
Sutton St E1 .... 32 B3
Suttons Way EC1 .. 97 A1
Sutton Way W10 ... 30 B4
Sutton Wlk SE1 .. 121 A1
Swaby Rd SW17, SW18 .... 71 B2
Swaffield Prim Sch SW18 .... 71 B4
Swaffield Rd SW18 .... 71 B4
Swain's La N6 .... 4 A2
Swainson Ho N7 ... 14 C4
Swainson Rd W3 ... 38 B4
Swain St NW8 .... 90 A2
Swallow Cl SE14 ... 50 C2
Swallow Ct 4 W9 .. 31 C4
Swallowfield NW1. 92 B3
Swallow Ho NW8 .. 80 A2
Swallow Pl
24 Poplar E14 .... 33 B3
W1 .... 104 B1
Swallow St W1 ... 119 A3
Swanage Ct 5 N1 .. 16 A1
Swanage Ho SW8 162 C1
Swanage Rd SW18 . 59 B1
Swanbourne SE17 .... 150 C3
Swanbourne Ho NW8 .... 90 A2
Swan Bsns Ctr 8 W4 .... 37 C2
Swan Ct
Chelsea SW3 .... 144 B1
Parsons Green SW6 .... 155 B1
Poplar E14 .... 33 B3
Swan Ctr SW17 .... 71 B1
Swandon Way SW18 .... 59 A3
Swanfield St E2 .... 24 B2 99 A3
Swan Ho N1 .... 15 C1
Swan La EC4 .... 123 C3
Swan Lane Pier EC4 .... 123 B3
Swanlea Sec Sch E1 .... 25 A1
Swanley Ho SE17. 152 B2
Swan Mead SE1 .. 138 A1
Swan Mews
Stockwell SW9 .... 172 C2
SW6 .... 165 B4
Swanmore Ct SW18 .... 59 B1
Swanne Ho 12 SE10 .... 52 B3
Swan Pas E1 .... 125 B3
Swan Pl SW13 .... 46 B1
Swan Rd SE16 .... 40 B4
Swanscombe Ho 11 W11 .... 30 C1
Swanscombe Point 7 E16 .... 35 B4
Swanscombe Rd
5 Chiswick W4 .... 38 A1
Shepherd's Bush W11 .... 30 C1
Swan St SE1 .... 137 A3
Swanton Gdns SW19 .... 69 C3
Swanwick Cl SW15 .... 68 B4
Swan Wlk SW3 ... 158 C4
Swan Yd N1 .... 15 A2
Swaton Rd E3 .... 26 C1
Swaythling Ho SW15 .... 56 B1
Swedenborg Gdns E1 .... 32 A2
Sweden Gate SE16 .... 41 A2
Swedish Quays SE16 .... 41 A3
Swedish Sch The SW13 .... 46 C4
Sweeney Cres SE1 .... 139 A3
Sweyn Pl SE3 .... 53 C1
Swift Ho
16 Stepney E1 .... 32 B3
15 Stoke Newington N16 .... 7 A1
SW9 .... 163 C2
Swift St SW6 .... 164 C4
Swinbrook Rd W10 .... 31 A4
Swinburne Ct 4 SE5 .... 63 C3
Swinburne Ho 15 E2 .... 25 B2
Swinburne Rd SW15 .... 56 C3
Swindon St W12 ... 30 B1
Swinford Gdns SW9 .... 63 A4
Swingfield Ho 4 E9 .... 25 B4
Swinley Ho NW1 .. 92 B4
Swinnerton St E9 .. 18 A3
Swinton Ho E2 .... 24 C2 99 B3
Swinton Pl WC1 ... 94 C4
Swinton St WC1 ... 94 C4
Swiss Cottage NW3 .... 11 C1
Swiss Cottage Sch
South Hampstead NW3 .... 11 C1
St John's Wood NW8 .... 79 C4
Swiss Cottage Sta NW3 .... 11 C1
Swiss Re Building* EC2 .... 110 B2
Swiss Terr 7 NW3 .... 11 C1
Switch Ho 4 E14 .. 34 C2
Sybil Phoenix Cl SE8 .... 40 C1
Sybil Thorndike Casson Ho SW5 . 141 C1
Sybil Thorndike Ho 12 N1 .... 15 B2
Sycamore Ave E3 .. 26 B4
Sycamore Cl W3 ... 29 A1
Sycamore Ct
Kilburn NW6 .... 23 C4
Tufnell Pk N19 .... 4 C1
Sycamore Gdns W6, W12 .... 39 A3
Sycamore Gr SE6 ... 67 B1
Sycamore Ho
10 Maitland Pk NW3 .... 12 B2
17 Rotherhithe SE16 .... 40 C4
3 Shepherd's Bush W6 .... 39 A4
2 Stoke Newington N16 .... 6 C2
Sycamore Lo SW15 .... 57 A4
Sycamore Mews 4 SW4 .... 61 B4
Sycamore St EC1 .. 96 C1
Sycamore Wlk 1 W10 .... 23 A1
Sydcote SE21 .... 75 B3
Sydenham Hill SE21, SE22, SE23, SE26, SE19 .... 76 C1
Sydenham Hill Sta SE21 .... 76 B1
Sydner Mews N16 .. 16 B4
Sydner Rd N16 .... 16 B4
Sydney Cl SW3 ... 143 C3
Sydney Ho 4 W4 .. 38 A2
Sydney Mews SW3 .... 143 C3
Sydney Pl SW7 ... 144 A3
Sydney Rd TW10, TW9 .... 54 A3
Sydney St SW3 ... 144 A2
Sylva Cotts 3 SE8 .. 51 C2
Sylva Ct 3 SW15 ... 69 C4
Sylvan Ct NW6 .... 78 A4
Sylvan Gr
Hampstead NW2 .... 9 C4
SE15 .... 50 A4
Sylvester Ho 7 E8 .... 17 A2
Sylvester Path 8 E8 .... 17 A2
Sylvester Rd E8 .... 17 A2
Sylvia Ct N1 .... 87 B1
Sylvia Pankhurst Ho 14 E2 .... 25 C2
Sylvia Young Theatre Sch NW1 .... 90 B1
Symes Mews NW1. 82 C2
Symington Ho SE1 .... 137 B1
Symington Mews E9 .... 17 C3
Symister Mews N1 .... 24 A2 98 A3
Symons St SW3 .. 145 A3
Symphony Mews 15 W10 .... 23 A2
Syringa Ho SE4 .... 66 B4

T

Tabard Ct 6 E14 ... 34 B3
Tabard Ho SE1 ... 137 C2
Tabard St SE1 .... 137 B2
Tabernacle St EC2. 97 C2
Tableer Ave SW4 ... 61 C2
Tabley Rd N7 .... 14 A4
Tabor Rd W6 .... 39 A3
Tachbrook Est SW1 .... 147 C1
Tachbrook Mews SW1 .... 146 C4
Tachbrook St SW1 .... 147 A3
Tack Mews SE4 .... 66 C4
Tadema Ho NW8 .. 89 C1
Tadema Rd SW10 157 A1
Tadmor St W12 .... 30 C1
Tadworth Ho SE1 136 A3
Taeping St E14 .... 42 A2
Taffrail Ho 2 E14 .. 42 A1
Taft Way 44 E3 .... 27 A2
Tailworth St E1 .. 111 B3
Tait Ct
16 Old Ford E3 .... 26 B4
SW8 .... 171 C4
Tait Ho SE1 .... 121 C1
2 Tufnell Pk N19 .... 13 B4
Takhar Mews SW11 .... 168 B1
Talacre Rd NW5 .... 12 C2
Talbot Ct EC3 .... 123 C4
Talbot Grove Ho 10 W11 .... 31 A3
Talbot Ho
Highbury N7 .... 5 C1
Poplar E14 .... 34 A3
Talbot Pl SE3 .... 53 A1
Talbot Rd
Camberwell SE22 .... 64 A3
Notting Hill W2 .... 31 C3
Notting Hill W11 .... 31 B3
Talbot Sq W2 .... 101 B1
Talbot Wlk
Notting Hill W11 .... 31 A3
Willesden NW10 .... 8 A2
Talbot Yd SE1 .... 123 B1
Talcott Path 12 SW2 .... 74 C3
Talfourd Pl SE15 .... 49 B2
Talfourd Rd SE15 ... 49 B2
Talgarth Rd
Hammersmith W6 ... 39 B1
W14 .... 140 B2
Talia Ho E14 .... 42 B3
Talina Ctr SW6 ... 166 C3
Talleyrand Ho SE5 .. 48 B1
Tallis St EC4 .... 121 C4
Talma Rd SW2 .... 62 C3
Talmud Torah Chaim Meirim Sch N16 .... 7 B3
Talmud Torah Machzikei Hadass Sch E5 .... 7 C4
Talmud-Torah Yetev-Lev N16 .... 7 C3
Talwin St E3 .... 27 A2
Tamar Cl 24 E3 .... 26 B4
Tamar Ho
10 Cubitt Town E14 .... 42 B4
SE11 .... 149 C2
Tamarind Ct 8 W3 .... 28 B3
Tamarind Ho 4 SE15 .... 49 C3
Tamarind Yd E1 .. 125 C2
Tamarisk Sq W12 ... 29 B2
Tamworth N7 .... 14 A2
Tamworth St SW6 .... 155 B3
Tangier Rd TW10 ... 55 A4
Tangley Gr SW15 ... 68 B4
Tangmere WC1 .... 94 C3
Tanhurst Ho 27 SW2 .... 74 A4
Tankerton St WC1 . 94 B3
Tanner Ho SE1 ... 138 B3
Tanner's Hill SE8 ... 51 C2
Tanners Mews SE8 .... 51 B2
Tanner St SE1 .... 138 B3
Tanners Yd 33 E2 ... 25 A3
Tannery Ho E1 ... 111 B4
Tannington Terr N5 .... 5 C1
Tansley Cl N7 .... 13 C3
Tanswell St SE1 .. 135 B3
Tantallon Rd SW12 .... 72 C3
Tant Ave E16 .... 35 B3
Tanza Rd NW3 .... 12 B4
Tapley Ho SE1 .... 139 B3
Taplow NW3 .... 11 C1
Taplow Ho E2 .... 24 B2 98 C3
Taplow St N1 .... 87 A1
Tappesfield Rd SE15 .... 65 B4
Tapp St E1 .... 25 A1
Taranto Ho 14 E1 ... 32 C4
Tarbert Rd SE22 .... 64 A2
Tarbert Wlk E1 .... 32 B2
Tarling Rd E16 .... 35 B3
Tarling St E1 .... 32 B3
Tarnbrook Ct SW1 .... 145 B3
Tarn St SE1 .... 136 C1
Tarns The NW1 .... 92 C4
Tarplett Ho 22 SE14 .... 50 C4
Tarragon Cl SE14 ... 51 A3
Tarranbrae NW6 .... 10 A1
Tarrant Ho E2 .... 25 B2
Tarrant Pl W1 .... 102 C3
Tarrantt Ho W14 . 126 A2
Tarriff Cres SE8 .... 41 B2
Tarrington Cl SW16 .... 73 C1
Tartan Ho 12 E14 ... 34 B3
Tarver Rd SE17 ... 150 B2
Tarves Way SE10 ... 52 A3
Tasker Ho 17 E14 ... 33 B4
Tasker Lo W8 .... 127 B4
Tasker Rd NW3 .... 12 B3
Tasman Ct 9 E14 .. 42 A2
Tasman Ho 17 E1 ... 32 A1
Tasman Rd SW9 .... 62 A4

Tasso Rd W6 154 A4
Tasso Yd W6 154 A3
Tatchbury Ho SW15 56 B1
Tate Britain★ SW1 148 A3
Tate Ho 13 E2 25 C3
Tate Modern★ EC4 122 B2
Tatham Pl NW8 79 C2
Tatnell Rd SE23 66 A1
Tatton Cres E5, N16 7 B4
Tatum St SE17 151 C3
Tauheed Cl N4 6 B2
Taunton Ho W2 100 C1
Taunton Mews NW1 90 C1
Taunton Pl NW1 90 C2
Tavern Ct SE1 137 A1
Taverner Ho N16 6 C1
Taverners Cl W11 31 A1 112 A1
Taverner Sq 4 N5 15 B4
Tavern La SW9 173 C2
Tavistock Cl N16 16 A3
Tavistock Cres W11 31 B4
Tavistock Ct WC1 93 C2
Tavistock Ho 3 W11 31 B4
Tavistock Mews 3 W11 31 B3
Tavistock Pl WC1 94 A2
Tavistock Rd
Dagenham NW10 21 B3
Notting Hill W11 31 B4
Tavistock Sq WC1 93 C2
Tavistock St WC2 120 B4
Tavistock Terr N19 4 C1
Tavistock Twr SE16 41 A3
Taviton St WC1 93 B2
Tavy Cl SE11 149 C2
Tawny Way SE16 40 C2
Taybridge Rd SW11 60 C3
Tayburn Cl E14 34 B3
Tay Ho 10 E3 26 B3
Tayler Ct NW8 79 B4
Taylor Ave TW9 45 A1
Taylor Cl SE8 51 B4
Taylor Ct E15 19 B3
Taylor Ho 10 SW2 74 C3
Taylor's Gn W3 29 A3
Taylor's La NW10 8 A1
Tayport Cl N1 14 A1
Tayside Ct 6 SE5 63 C3
Teak Cl SE16 33 A1
Tealby Ct N7 14 B2
Teal Ct 30 SE8 51 B4
Teale St E2 24 C3
Teal St 1 SE10 43 B3
Teather St 12 SE5 49 A3
Tebbs Ho 14 SW2 74 C4
Tedman Ct SE13 67 B3
Ted Roberts Ho 25 E2 25 A3
Tedworth Gdns SW3 144 C1
Tedworth Sq SW3 144 C1
Teesdale Cl E2 25 A3
Teesdale St E2 25 A3
Teesdale Yd 34 E2 25 A3
Tee The W3 29 A3
Teignmouth Cl 6 SW4 61 C3
Teignmouth Rd NW2 9 C2
Telegraph Hill NW3 2 A1
Telegraph Pl E14 42 A2
Telegraph Rd SW15 69 B4
Telegraph St EC2 109 B2
Telephone Pl SW6 155 A4
Telfer Cl 4 W3 37 B4
Telfer Ho EC1 96 B3
Telferscot Prim Sch SW12 73 C3
Telferscot Rd SW12 73 C3
Telford Ave SW12, SW2 74 A3
Telford Avenue Mans 7 SW2 74 A3
Telford Ho
8 Kensal Town W10 31 A4
SE1 136 C2
Telford Parade Mans 8 SW2 74 A3
Telford Rd W10 31 A4
Telford Terr SW1 160 C4
Telford Way W3 29 A4
Tell Gr SE22 64 B3
Telscombe Ho SW11 169 B3
Temair Ho 1 SE10 52 B3
Temeraire Pl TW8 36 B1
Temeraire St SE16 40 B4
Temperley Rd SW12 72 C4
Templar Ho NW2 10 B2
Templars Ho E15 19 A3
Templar St SE5 48 A1
Temple Ave EC4 121 C4
Templecombe Rd E9 25 B4
Temple Ct
Stepney E1 32 C4
SW8 162 A1
Temple Dwellings 7 E2 25 A3
Temple Ho
13 Battersea SW11 60 A4
4 Tufnell Pk N7 4 B1
Temple La EC4 107 C1
Templemead Cl W3 29 A3
Templemead Ho E9 18 A4
Temple Mill La E10, E15 19 B4
TEMPLE MILLS 19 A3
Temple Mills Rd E9 18 C4
Temple Pl WC2 121 A4
Temple Rd
Acton Green W4 37 B3
Richmond TW9 54 B4
Temple Sheen SW14 55 B2
Temple Sheen Rd SW14 55 B3
Temple St E2 25 A3
Temple Sta WC2 121 B4
Templeton Cl 25 N16 16 A3
Templeton Pl SW5 141 C3
Temple West Mews SE11 136 A1
Templewood Ave NW3 2 A1
Templewood Gdns NW3 2 A1
Templewood Point NW2 1 B2
Tenbury Ct SW12 73 C3
Tenby Ho
Islington N7 14 C4
W2 100 C1
Tench St E1 32 A1
Tenda Rd SE16 40 A2
Tendring Ho SW2 62 C1
Tenham Ave SW2 73 C2
Tenison Ct W1 118 C4
Tenison Way SE1 121 B1
Tenniel Cl W2 114 B4
Tennis St SE1 137 B4
Tennyson Ho SE17 151 A2
Tennyson Rd NW6 23 B4
Tennyson St SW8 170 A1
Tensing Ho N1 15 A2
Tenterden Ho SE17 152 B2
Tenterden St W1 104 B1
Tenter Ground E1 110 C3
Tent St E1 25 A1
Tequila Wharf E14 33 A3
Terborch Way 6 SE22 64 A2
Tercelet Terr NW3 11 B4
Teredo St SE16 40 C3
Terling Ho 9 W10 30 B4
Terling Wlk N1 86 C4
Terminus Pl SW1 132 B1
Tern Ho 9 SE15 49 B2
Terrace Gdns SW13 46 B1
Terrace La TW10 54 A1
Terrace Rd E9 17 B1
Terrace The
Barnes SW13, SW14 46 A1
EC4 107 C1
Kilburn NW6 23 C4
10 Rotherhithe SE8 41 B2
Terrano Ho 1 TW9 45 A2
Terrapin Ct SW17 73 A1
Terrapin Rd SW17 73 A1
Terrick St W12 30 A3
Territorial Ho SE11 149 C3
Terry Ho SW2 74 C3
Tersha St TW9 54 B3
Tessa Sanderson Pl 6 SW8 61 A4
Testerton Wlk 3 W11 30 C2
Tetcott Rd SW10 156 C1
Teversham La SW8 172 B4
Teviot St E14 34 B4
Teyham Ct SW11 60 B1
Thackeray Ct
Chelsea SW3 144 C2
West Kensington W14 126 A1
Thackeray Ho
College Pk NW10 21 C2
WC1 94 A2
Thackeray Mews E8 16 C2
Thackeray Rd SW8 170 B1
Thackeray's Almshouses SE6 67 A1
Thackeray St W8 128 B2
Thalia Cl SE10 52 C4
Thame Rd SE16 40 C4
Thames Ave SW10 167 A4
Thames Bank SW14 45 B1
Thames Christian Coll SW11 59 C4
Thames Circ E14 41 C2
Thames Cres W4 46 A3
Thames Ct 10 SE15 49 B3
Thames Hts SE1 138 C4
Thameside Ctr TW8 44 B4
Thames Link Ho 7 TW9 54 A3
Thames Pl SW15 57 C4
Thames Quay
Millwall E14 42 A4
SW10 167 A3
Thames Rd W4 45 A4
Thames Reach W6 47 B4
Thames Row TW9 44 B4
Thames St SE10 52 A4
Thames Village W4 45 B2
Thames Wlk SW11 158 A2
Thane Mans N7 5 B1
Thanet Ho WC1 94 A3
1 West Norwood SE27 75 A1
Thanet Lo NW2 10 A2
Thanet St WC1 94 A3
Thane Villas N7 5 B1
Thane Works N7 5 B1
Thavies Inn EC4 107 C2
Thaxted Ct N1 87 C1
Thaxted Ho SE16 40 B2
Thaxton Rd W14 155 A4
Thayer St W1 103 C2
Theatre Mus★ WC2 120 B4
Theatre Sq E15 19 C2
Theatre St SW11 60 B4
Theberton St N1 86 A4
Theed St SE1 121 C1
Thelbridge Ho 28 E3 27 A2
Theobalds Ct N4 6 B2
Theobald's Rd WC1 106 C4
Theobald St SE1 137 B1
Theodore Ct SE13 67 C1
Theodore Ho 1 SW15 56 C2
Theodore Rd SE13 67 C1
Therapia Rd SE22 65 B1
Theresa Rd W6 38 C2
Therfield Ct N4 6 B2
Thermopylae Gate E14 42 A2
Theseus Ho
2 South Bromley E14 34 C3
Theseus Ho *continued*
2 E14 34 C3
Theseus Wlk N1 86 B1
Thessaly Ho SW8 160 C1
Thessaly Rd SW8 171 A4
Thetford Ho SE1 138 C2
Thetis Terr TW9 44 C4
Third Ave
East Acton W3 29 B1
West Kilburn W10 23 A2
Thirleby Rd SW1 133 A1
Thirlmere NW1 92 B4
Thirlmere Ho 19 N16 15 C4
Thirsk Rd SW11 60 C3
Thistle Gr SW7 143 A1
Thistle Ho 10 E14 34 B3
Thistlewood Cl 3 N7 5 B2
Thistly Ct SE8 52 A4
Thomas Baines Rd SW11 59 C4
Thomas Burt Ho 9 E2 25 A2
Thomas Buxton Jun & Inf Sch E1 24 C1 99 C1
Thomas Crowell Ct 29 N1 16 A3
Thomas Doyle St SE1 136 B2
Thomas Fairchild Com Sch N1 87 A2
Thomas Ho
3 Hackney E9 17 B2
4 Stockwell SW4 62 A3
Thomas Hollywood Ho 3 E2 25 B3
Thomas Jones Prim Sch W11 31 A3
Thomas Milner Ho 8 SE15 49 C3
Thomas More Ho EC2 108 C3
Thomas More Sq E1 125 B3
Thomas More St E1 125 B2
Thomas North Terr 4 E16 35 B4
Thomas Pl W8 128 A1
Thomas Rd E14 33 C4
Thomas Road Ind Est 2 E14 33 C3
Thomas's London Day Schs SW11 167 C3
Thomas's Prep Sch Clapham SW11 60 B2
Thompson Ave
Richmond TW9 54 C4
6 SE5 48 B3
Thompson Ho
11 Kensal Town W10 23 A1
SE14 50 C4
Thompson Rd SE22 64 B1
Thomson Ct 4 E8 16 C2
Thomson Ho
Pimlico SW1 147 C1
Walworth SE17 152 A3
Thorburn Ho SW1 131 B3
Thorburn Sq SE1 153 B3
Thoresby Ho N16 6 C1
Thoresby St N1 97 A4

Thornaby Ho [15] E2 25 A2
Thornbill Ho [1] SE15 49 C3
Thornbury Cl N16 16 A3
Thornbury Ct W11 31 C2 113 B4
Thornbury Ho N6 4 B3
Thornbury Rd SW2 62 A1
Thornbury Sq N6 4 B3
Thorncliffe Ct SW2 62 A1
Thorncliffe Rd SW2 62 A1
Thorncombe Rd SE22 64 A2
Thorncroft St SW8 162 A1
Thorndale Ho [10] N16 7 A3
Thorndean St SW18 71 B2
Thorndike Cl SW10 156 C2
Thorndike Ho SW1 147 B2
Thorndike Rd [21] N1 15 C2
Thorndike St SW1 147 B3
Thorne Cl E16 35 C3
Thorne Ho
[34] Bethnal Green E2 25 B2
[4] Cubitt Town E14 42 B3
Thorne Pas [7] SW13 46 B1
Thorne Rd SW8 162 B1
Thorness Ct SW18 59 B1
Thorne St SW13, SW14 56 A4
Thornewill Ho [8] E1 32 B2
Thorney Cres SW11 157 C1
Thorneycroft Ho [11] W4 38 A1
Thorney Ct W8 128 C3
Thorney Hedge Rd W4 37 A2
Thorney St SW1 148 A4
Thornfield Ho [5] E14 33 C2
Thornfield Rd W12 39 A4
Thornford Rd SE13 67 B2
Thorngate Rd W9 23 C1
Thornham Gr E15 19 C3
Thorn Ham Ho SE1 137 C2
Thornham St SE10 52 A4
Thornhaugh St WC1 93 C1
Thornhill Bridge Wharf N1 84 C3
Thornhill Cres N1 14 B1
Thornhill Gr N1 14 C1
Thornhill Ho
[12] Chiswick W4 38 A1
Islington N1 14 C1
Thornhill Mews SW15 58 B3
Thornhill Prim Sch N1 14 C1
Thornhill Rd N1 85 B4
Thornhill Sq N1 14 B1
Thornicroft Ho SW9 173 A1
Thornley Pl [2] SE10 43 A1
Thornsett Rd SW18 71 A3
Thornton Ave
Chiswick W4 38 A2
Streatham SW2 73 C3
Thornton Ct N7 14 A3
Thornton Gdns SW12 73 C3
Thornton Ho SE17 152 A3
Thornton Pl W1 103 A4
Thornton Rd
Mortlake SW14 55 C4
Streatham SW12, SW2 73 C3
Thornton St SW9 173 B2
Thornville St SE8 51 C2
Thornwood Gdns W8 127 B4
Thornwood Lo W8 127 B4
Thornycroft Ct TW9 44 B1
Thorold Ho SE1 136 C4
[6] Streatham SW2 74 A4
Thorparch Rd SW8 161 C1
Thorpebank Rd W12 29 C1
Thorpe Cl W10 31 A3
Thorpedale Rd N4 5 B3
Thorpe Ho N1 85 A3
Thorverton Rd NW2 1 A1
Thoydon Rd E3 26 A3
Thrale St SE1 123 A1
Thrasher Cl [20] E8 24 B4
Thrawl St E1 111 A3
Thrayle Ho [2] SW9 62 B4
Threadgold Ho [8] N1 15 C2
Threadneedle St EC2, EC3 109 C1
Three Colts La E2 25 A1
Three Colt St E14 33 B2
Three Cups Yd WC1 107 A3
Three Kings Yd W1 118 A4
Three Mill La E3 27 B2
Three Mills Studios E14 27 B2
Three Nun Ct EC2 109 A2
Three Oak La SE1 138 C4
Threshers Pl W11 31 A2 112 A4
Thring Ho SW9 172 C2
Throgmorton Ave EC2 109 C2
Throgmorton St EC2 109 C2
Thrush St SE17 150 C2
Thurland Ho [3] SE16 40 A2
Thurland Rd SE16 139 B2
Thurleigh Ave SW12 60 C1
Thurleigh Ct SW12 60 C1
Thurleigh Rd SW12 60 C1
Thurloe Cl SW7 144 A4
Thurloe Ct SW3 144 A3
Thurloe Pl SW7 143 C4
Thurloe Place Mews SW7 143 C4
Thurloe Sq SW7 144 A4
Thurloe St SW7 143 C4
Thurlow Hill SE21 75 B2
Thurlow Ho [17] SW16 74 A1
Thurlow Park Rd SE21, SE24 75 B2
Thurlow Rd NW3 11 C3
Thurlow St SE17 152 A1
Thurlow Terr NW5 12 C3
Thurlow Twrs SE27 74 C1
Thurlow Wlk SE17 152 A1
Thurnscoe NW1 82 C3
Thursley Gdns SW19 69 C2
Thursley Ho [10] SW2 74 B4
Thurso Ho NW6 78 A1
Thurston Ind Est SE13 67 A4
Thurston Rd SE8, SE13 52 A1
Thurtle Rd E2 24 B3
Tibbatt's Rd E3 27 A1
Tibberton Sq N1 86 C4
Tibbets Cl SW19 69 C3
Tibbet's Corner SW19 69 C4
Tibbet's Ride SW19 69 C4
Tiber Cl [10] E3 26 C4
Tiber Gdns N1 84 B3
Tickford Ho NW8 90 A3
Tidal Basin Rd E16 35 B2
Tidbury Ct SW8 160 C1
Tidemill Prim Sch SE8 51 C3
Tideswell [10] NW5 13 A4
Tideswell Rd SW15 57 B3
Tideway Ct [9] SE16 32 C1
Tideway Ho E14 41 C4
Tideway Ind Est SW8 161 A3
Tideway Wharf SW13 46 A1
Tideway Yd SW13 46 A1
Tidey St E3 33 C4
Tidworth Ho [13] SE22 64 A4
Tidworth Rd E3 26 C1
Tierney Rd SW2 74 A3
Tierney Terr SW2 74 A3
Tiger Ho WC1 93 C3
Tiger Way E5 17 A4
Tignel Ct W3 36 C4
Tilbury Cl [14] SE15 49 B3
Tilbury Ho [4] SE14 50 C4
Tildesley Rd SW15 57 B1
Tilehurst NW1 92 B3
Tilehurst Rd SW17, SW18 71 C3
Tile Kiln La N6 4 B3
Tileyard Rd N7 14 A1
Tilford Gdns SW19 69 C3
Tilford Ho [8] SW2 74 B4
Tilia Rd E5 17 A4
Tilia Wlk [21] SW9 63 A3
Tiller Ho [28] N1 24 A4
Tiller Rd E14 41 C3
Tillet Sq SE16 41 A4
Tillet Way E2 24 C2 99 B4
Tilling Ho [1] SE15 65 A4
Tillman Ho [8] SW2 74 B3
Tillman St E1 32 A3
Tilloch St [9] N1 14 B1
Tillotson Ct SW8 161 C1
Tilney Ct EC1 97 A2
Tilney Gdns [12] N1 15 C2
Tilney St W1 117 C2
Tilson Cl [2] SE15 49 A3
Tilson Gdns SW2, SW4 74 A4
Tilson Ho SW2 74 A4
Tilton St SW6 154 B3
Tiltwood The W3 28 B2
Timberland Cl [16] SE15 49 C3
Timberland Rd E1 32 A3
Timber Mill Way SW4 61 C4
Timber Pond Rd SE16 40 C4
Timber St EC1 96 C2
Time Sq E8 16 B3
Timothy Cl [1] SW4 61 B2
Timsbury Wlk [5] SW15 68 C3
Tina Ct SW16 74 C1
Tindal St SW9 48 A2
Tinniswood Cl N5 14 C3
Tinsley Rd E1 32 B4
Tintagel Cres SE22 64 B3
Tintagel Ct EC1 96 A2
Tintern Cl SW15 58 A2
Tintern Ho
Belgravia SW1 146 A3
Regent's Pk NW1 82 B1
Tintern St SW4 62 A3
Tinworth St SE11 148 B2
Tipthorpe Rd SW11 60 C4
Tiptree [7] NW1 13 A1
Tisbury Ct W1 119 B4
Tisdall Pl SE17 151 C3
Tissington Ct [4] SE16 40 C2
Titan Bsns Est [3] SE8 51 C3
Titan Ct TW8 36 B1
Titchborne Row W2 102 B1
Titchfield Rd NW8 80 C4
Titchwell Rd SW18 71 C3
Tite St SW3 158 C4
Titmuss St W12 39 B4
Tiverton Rd NW6, NW10 22 C4
Tiverton St SE1 136 C2
Tivoli Ct SE16 33 B1
Tobago St [12] E14 41 C4
Tobin Cl NW3 12 A1
Toby La E1 26 A1
Todber Ho W14 126 A2
Todds Wlk N7 5 B2
Tokenhouse Yd EC2 109 B2
Toland Sq SW15 56 C2
Tolchurch [2] W11 31 C3
Toldos Yakov Yosef sch N16 7 A3
Tolhurst Dr [4] W10 23 A2
Tollbridge Cl W10 23 A1
Tollet St E1 25 C1
Tollgate Dr SE21 76 A2
Tollgate Ho NW6 78 A2
Tollhouse Way N19 4 B2
Tollington Ct N4 5 B2
Tollington Ho [4] N19 5 A1
Tollington Pk N4 5 B2
Tollington Pl N4 5 B2
Tollington Rd N7 14 B4
Tollington Way N7 5 A1
Tolmers Sq NW1 93 A2
Tolpaide Ho SE11 149 B3
Tolpuddle St N1 85 B2
Tolsford Rd E5 17 A3
Tom Groves Cl E15 19 C3
Tom Hood Cl E15 19 C3
Tom Jenkinson Rd [5] E16 35 C1
Tomkyns Ho SE11 149 B3
Tomline Ho SE1 122 C1
Tomlin's Gr E3 26 C2
Tomlinson Cl
[5] Gunnersbury W4 37 A1
Spitalfields E2 24 B2 99 A3
Tomlin's Terr E14 33 A3
Tomlins Wlk [4] N7 5 B2
Tompion Ho EC1 96 B2
Tompion St EC1 96 B3
Tom Smith Cl SE10 53 A4
Tomson Ho SE1 138 C2
Tom Williams Ho SW6 154 C3
Tonbridge Hos WC1 94 A3
Tonbridge St WC1 94 A3
Toneborough NW8 78 B3
Tonsley Hill SW18 59 A2
Tonsley Pl SW18 59 A2
Tonsley Rd SW18 59 A2
Tonsley St SW18 59 A2
Took's Ct EC4 107 B2
Tooley St SE1 124 A1
Tooting Bec Sta SW17 72 C1
Topham Ho [8] SE10 52 B3
Topham St EC1 95 B2
Topiary Sq TW9 54 B4
Topmast Point [23] E14 41 C4
Torbay Ct [13] NW1 13 A1
Torbay Mans NW6 23 B4
Torbay Rd NW6 10 B1
Torbay St [15] NW1 13 A1
Tor Ct W8 127 C4
Tor Gdns W8 127 B4
Tornay Ho
Hackney E9 17 B1
N1 84 C2
Torquay St W2 100 A3

Torrence Ho 6 N19 ... 4 B2
Torrens Ct SE5 ... 63 C4
Torrens Rd SW2 ... 62 B2
Torrens St EC1 ... 86 A1
Torres Sq E14 ... 41 C1
Torriano Ave NW5 ... 13 C3
Torriano Cotts NW5 ... 13 B3
Torriano Jun & Inf Schs NW5 ... 13 C3
Torriano Mews NW5 ... 13 B3
Torridge Gdns SE15 ... 65 B3
Torridon Ho NW6 ... 78 A1
Torrington Pl
Bloomsbury WC1 ... 105 B4
St George in t East E1 ... 125 C2
Torrington Sq WC1 ... 93 C1
Tortington Ho 1 SE15 ... 50 A3
Torwood Rd SW15 ... 56 C2
Tothill Ho SW1 ... 147 C4
Tothill St SW1 ... 133 C3
Totland Ho SW18 ... 59 A1
Tottan Terr E1 ... 32 C3
Tottenhall 5 NW1 ... 12 C1
Tottenham Court Rd W1 ... 105 A4
Tottenham Court Road Sta W1 ... 105 C2
Tottenham Mews W1 ... 105 A4
Tottenham Rd N1 ... 16 A2
Tottenham St W1 ... 105 A4
Totteridge Ho SW11 ... 167 C2
Touchard Ho N1 ... 97 C3
Toulmin St SE1 ... 136 C3
Toulon St SE5 ... 48 B3
Toulouse Ct 2 SE16 ... 40 A1
Tounson Ct SW1 ... 147 C3
Tournay Rd SW6 ... 155 A2
Toussaint Wlk SE16 ... 139 C2
Tovy Ho SE1 ... 153 B1
Towcester Rd E3 ... 27 B1
Tower 42★ EC2 ... 110 A2
Tower Bldgs 22 E1 ... 32 A1
Tower Br App E1, EC3 ... 124 C3
Tower Bridge★ E1, EC3, SE1 ... 124 C2
Tower Bridge Bsns Complex SE16 ... 40 A3
Tower Bridge Bsns Sq SE16 ... 40 A2
Tower Bridge Piazza SE1 ... 124 C1
Tower Bridge Prim Sch SE1 ... 138 C4
Tower Bridge Rd SE1 ... 138 A3
Tower Bridge Sq SE1 ... 138 C4
Tower Cl NW3 ... 11 C3
Tower Ct
Brockley SE4 ... 66 A3
Stamford Hill E5 ... 7 B4
St Giles WC2 ... 106 A1
Tower Ct *continued*
St John's Wood NW8 ... 80 B2
Towergate SE1 ... 152 A4
Towergate Ho 35 E3 ... 26 B3
Tower Gateway Sta EC3 ... 124 C4
TOWER HAMLETS ... 33 B4
Tower Hamlets Coll
Poplar E14 ... 34 A2
Poplar E14 ... 34 A3
Stepney E1 ... 32 C3
Tower Hill EC3 ... 125 A3
Tower Hill Sta EC3 ... 124 C4
Tower Mans SE1 ... 138 C1
Tower Mews E5 ... 18 A3
Tower Millennium Pier EC3 ... 124 B2
Tower Mill Rd 1 SE15 ... 49 A3
Tower Pl E EC3 ... 124 B3
Tower Pl W EC3 ... 124 B3
Tower Rd NW10 ... 8 C1
Tower Rise TW9 ... 54 A4
Tower Royal EC4 ... 123 B4
Towers Pl TW10 ... 54 A2
Tower St WC2 ... 106 A1
Towers The
Dartmouth Pk NW5 ... 4 A1
1 Richmond TW9 ... 54 B3
Tower Terr SE4 ... 66 A3
Tower The★ EC3 ... 124 C3
Towerview SE13 ... 66 C2
Tower Wharf SE1 ... 138 C4
Tower Wlk SE1 ... 152 A4
Towncourt Path N4 ... 6 B3
Townhall Ave 3 W4 ... 37 C1
Town Hall Rd SW11 ... 60 B4
Town Hos EC1 ... 96 B1
Townley Rd SE22 ... 64 A2
Townley St SE17 ... 151 B2
Townmead Bsns Ctr SW6 ... 59 B4
Townmead Rd
Richmond TW9 ... 45 A1
Sands End SW6 ... 166 C1
Townsend Ho SE1 ... 153 C3
Townsend Ind Est NW10 ... 20 B3
Townsend Mews 3 SW18 ... 71 B2
Townsend Prim Sch SE17 ... 152 A4
Townsend St SE1, SE17 ... 152 A4
Townsend Yd N6 ... 4 A3
Townshend Ct NW8 ... 80 B2
Townshend Est NW8 ... 80 A2
Townshend Rd
Primrose Hill NW8 ... 80 A3
Richmond TW9 ... 54 B3
Townshend Terr TW9 ... 54 B3
Towns Ho 4 SW4 ... 61 C4
Towpath Wlk E9 ... 18 B3
Towton Rd SE27 ... 75 B2
Toxteth Ho N4 ... 6 B4
Toynbee St E1 ... 110 C3
Tracey Ave NW2 ... 9 B3
Tracy Ho 15 E3 ... 26 B2
Tradescant Ho 15 E9 ... 17 B1
Tradescant Rd SW8 ... 162 B1
Trade Twr 8 SW11 ... 59 B4
Trade Winds Ct E1 ... 125 C2
Trading Estate Rd NW10 ... 20 B1
Traemore Ct SW16 ... 74 C1
Trafalgar Ave SE15 ... 49 B4
Trafalgar Cl 1 SE16 ... 41 A2
Trafalgar Gdns
Stepney E1 ... 32 C4
W8 ... 128 B2
Trafalgar Gr SE10 ... 52 C4
Trafalgar Ho SE17 ... 151 A2
Trafalgar Mews E9 ... 18 B2
Trafalgar Point 2 N1 ... 15 C1
Trafalgar Rd SE10 ... 43 A1
Trafalgar Sq★ SW1 ... 119 C2
Trafalgar St SE17 ... 151 C2
Trafalgar Way E14 ... 34 B1
Trafford Cl E15 ... 19 A3
Trafford Ho N1 ... 87 C2
Tragail SW15 ... 58 A2
Trahorn Cl E1 ... 25 A1
Traitors Gate★ EC3 ... 124 C2
Tralee Ct 31 SE16 ... 40 A1
Tramway Ave E15 ... 19 C1
Trance Way W3 ... 36 C3
Tranmere Ho 7 N7 ... 14 C3
Tranmere Rd SW17, SW18 ... 71 B2
Tranquil Pas SE3 ... 53 B1
Tranquil Vale SE3 ... 53 A1
Transept St NW1 ... 102 B3
Transom Cl SE16 ... 41 A2
Transom Sq E14 ... 42 A1
Tranton Rd SE16 ... 40 A3
Trappes Ho 2 SE16 ... 40 A2
Travers Ho 6 SE10 ... 52 C4
Travers Rd N7 ... 5 C1
Travis Ho SE10 ... 52 B2
Treadgold Ho 7 W11 ... 30 C2
Treadgold St W11 ... 30 C2
Treadway St E2 ... 25 A3
Treasury Bldgs SW1 ... 134 A4
Treaty St N1 ... 84 C3
Trebeck St W1 ... 118 A1
Treborough Ho W1 ... 103 B4
Trebovir Rd SW5 ... 141 C3
Treby St E3 ... 26 B1
Trecastle Way 2 N7 ... 13 C4
Tredegar Mews 10 E3 ... 26 B2
Tredegar Rd E3 ... 26 B3
Tredegar Sq E3 ... 26 B2
Tredegar Terr E3 ... 26 B2
Trederwen Rd E8 ... 24 C4
Treen Ave SW13 ... 56 B4
Trees The N16 ... 6 C4
Trefil Wlk N7 ... 14 A4
Trefoil Rd SW18 ... 59 B2
Tregarvon Rd SW11 ... 60 C3
Trego Rd E9 ... 18 C1
Tregothnan Rd SW9 ... 62 A4
Tregunter Rd SW10 ... 142 C1
Treherne Ct SW9 ... 48 A2
Trehern Rd 12 SW14 ... 55 C4
Trehurst St E5 ... 18 A3
Trelawney Est E9 ... 17 B2
Trelawney Ho SE1 ... 136 C4
Trelawn Rd SW2 ... 62 C2
Trellis Sq 1 E3 ... 26 B2
Tremadoc Rd SW4 ... 61 C3
Tremaine Cl SE4 ... 51 C1
Trematon Ho SE11 ... 149 C2
Tremlett Gr N19 ... 4 B1
Tremlett Mews N19 ... 4 B1
Trenchard St SE10 ... 42 C1
Trenchold St SW8 ... 162 A3
Trendell Ho 8 E14 ... 33 C3
Trenmar Gdns NW10 ... 22 A2
Trentham Ct W3 ... 28 C4
Trentham St SW18 ... 70 C3
Trent Ho SE15 ... 65 B3
Trent Rd SW2 ... 62 B2
Treport St SW18 ... 71 A4
Tresco Ho SE11 ... 149 B2
Tresco Rd SE15 ... 65 A3
Tresham Cres NW8 ... 90 A2
Tresham Wlk E9 ... 17 B3
Tresidder Ho 10 SW4 ... 73 C4
Tressel Cl 20 N1 ... 15 A1
Tressillian Cres SE4 ... 66 C4
Tressillian Rd SE4 ... 66 C4
Trevanion Rd W14 ... 140 B2
Trevelyan Gdns NW10 ... 22 B4
Trevelyan Ho
16 Globe Town E2 ... 25 C2
SE5 ... 48 A3
Treveris St SE1 ... 122 B1
Treverton St W10 ... 22 C1
Treverton Twr W10 ... 30 C4
Treves Ho E1 ... 24 C1 99 C1
Treville St SW15 ... 69 A4
Trevithick Ho
13 Bermondsey SE16 ... 40 A2
3 Gospel Oak NW5 ... 13 A4
SW8 ... 171 B4
Trevithick St SE8 ... 51 C4
Trevor Pl SW7 ... 130 B3
Trevor Roberts Tutorial Coll NW8 ... 11 C1
Trevor Sq SW7 ... 130 B3
Trevor St SW7 ... 130 B3
Trevose Ho SE11 ... 149 A2
Trewint St SW18 ... 71 B2
Triangle Ct SE1 ... 123 A1
Triangle Est The SE11 ... 149 B1
Triangle Ho SE1 ... 138 C4
Triangle Pl SW4 ... 61 C3
Triangle Rd 7 E8 ... 25 A4
Triangle The
Crouch End N19 ... 4 C4
EC1 ... 96 B2
Hackney E8 ... 25 A4
Trident Ho 14 E14 ... 34 B3
Trident St SE16 ... 40 C2
Trieste Ct SW12 ... 72 B3
Trig La EC4 ... 122 C4
Trigon Rd SW8 ... 163 A2
Trillington Ho W12 ... 29 C1
Trimdon NW1 ... 83 A3
Trimmer Wlk 11 TW8 ... 44 A4
Trim St SE8 ... 51 B4
Trinder Gdns N19 ... 5 A3
Trinder Rd N4, N19 ... 5 A3
Trinidad Ho 17 E14 ... 33 B2
Trinidad St E14 ... 33 B2
Trinity Church Rd SW13 ... 47 A4
Trinity Church Sq SE1 ... 137 A2
Trinity Cl
3 Clapham SW4 ... 61 B3
Lewisham SE13 ... 67 C3
Trinity Cotts TW9 ... 54 B4
Trinity Cres SW17 ... 72 C2
Trinity Ct
Finsbury WC1 ... 94 C2
2 Hoxton N1 ... 24 A4
Rotherhithe SE16 ... 41 A4
Willesden NW2 ... 9 B3
Trinity Gdns E16 ... 35 B4
Stockwell SW2, SW9 ... 62 B3
Trinity Gn E1 ... 32 B4
Trinity Gr 8 SE10 ... 52 B2
Trinity Ho SE1 ... 137 A2
Trinity Homes 14 SW2 ... 62 B3
Trinity Mews SW18 ... 70 C3
Trinity Pl EC3 ... 124 C3
Trinity Rd
Richmond TW9 ... 54 B4
Wandsworth SW17, SW18 ... 72 A4
Trinity Rise SE24, SW2 ... 75 A4
Trinity St Mary's CE Prim Sch SW12 ... 72 C3
Trinity Sq EC3 ... 124 B4
Trinity St
9 Newham E16 ... 35 C4
SE1 ... 137 B2
Trinity Way W3 ... 29 B2
Trio Pl SE1 ... 137 A3
Tristan Ct 34 SE8 ... 51 B4
Triton Ct EC2 ... 97 C1
Triton Ho 2 E14 ... 42 A2
Triton Sq NW1 ... 92 C2
Tritton Rd SE21, SE27 ... 75 C1

Trocette Mans SE1 . . . 138 B2
Trojan Ct NW6 . . . 10 A1
Trojan Ind Est NW10 . . . 8 B2
Troon Cl 34 SE16 . . . 40 A1
Troon Ho 9 E14 . . . 33 A3
Troon St E1 . . . 33 A3
Tropical Ct 2 W10 . . . 22 C2
Trossachs Rd SE22 . . . 64 A2
Trothy Rd SE1 . . . 153 C3
Trotman Ho 1 SE14 . . . 50 B2
Trott St SW11 . . . 168 A3
Trotwood Ho 3 SE16 . . . 40 A4
Troubridge Ct 12 W4 . . . 37 B1
Troutbeck NW1 . . . 92 B3
Troutbeck Rd SE14 . . . 51 A2
Trouville Rd SW4 . . . 61 B1
Trowbridge Rd E9 . . . 18 B2
Trower Ho 5 E9 . . . 18 A2
Troy Ct W8 . . . 127 B2
Troyes Ho NW3 . . . 12 B3
Troy Town SE15 . . . 64 C4
Troy Town Flats SE15 . . . 64 C4
Truman's Rd 24 N16 . . . 16 A3
Trump St EC2 . . . 109 A1
Trundle St SE1 . . . 136 C4
Trundleys Rd SE8 . . . 51 A4
Trundley's Rd SE8 . . . 40 C1
Trundley's Terr SE8 . . . 40 C2
Truro Ho 25 W2 . . . 31 C4
Truro St NW5 . . . 12 C2
Trussley Rd W6 . . . 39 B3
Trust Wlk SE21 . . . 75 A3
Tryon Cres E9 . . . 25 B4
Tryon St SW3 . . . 144 C2
Tubbs Rd NW10 . . . 21 B3
Tudor Cl
Crouch End N6 . . . 4 B4
Hampstead NW3 . . . 12 A2
Tulse Hill SW2 . . . 62 B1
Tudor Coll WC1 . . . 94 A3
Tudor Ct
Kingsland N1 . . . 16 A2
5 Rotherhithe SE16 . . . 32 C1
South Acton W5 . . . 36 C4
Tudor Est NW10 . . . 20 A3
Tudor Gdns SW14 . . . 56 A4
Tudor Gr E9 . . . 17 B1
Tudor Ho
Brook Green W14 . . . 39 C2
34 Hackney E9 . . . 17 B1
Tudor Mews 2 NW10 . . . 8 C2
Tudor Rd E9 . . . 25 A4
Tudor St EC4 . . . 121 C4
Tudor Way W3 . . . 36 C4
Tufnell Ct 19 E3 . . . 26 B4
Tufnell Mans 7 N7 . . . 13 C4
TUFNELL PARK . . . 13 C4
Tufnell Park Mans 2 N7 . . . 5 A1
Tufnell Park Prim Sch N7 . . . 13 C4
Tufnell Park Rd N19, N7 . . . 13 C4
Tufnell Park Sta N19 . . . 13 B4
Tufton Ct SW1 . . . 134 A1
Tufton St SW1 . . . 134 A1
Tuke Sch SE15 . . . 50 A2
Tullis Ho 12 E9 . . . 17 B1
TULSE HILL . . . 75 A4
Tulse Hill
Tulse Hill SW2 . . . 74 C4
Tulse Hill SW27 . . . 75 A2
Tulse Hill Sta SE27 . . . 75 A2
Tulse Ho SW2 . . . 62 C1
Tulsemere Rd SE21, SE27 . . . 75 B2
Tunbridge Ct 1 SE26 . . . 76 C1
Tunbridge Ho EC1 . . . 96 A4
Tunis Rd W12 . . . 30 A1
Tunley Gn 12 E14 . . . 33 B4
Tunley Rd
Dagenham NW10 . . . 21 A4
Upper Tooting SW12, SW17 . . . 72 C2
Tunnel Avenue Trad Est SE10 . . . 42 C4
Tunnel Rd SE16 . . . 40 B4
Tunstall Ct 14 TW9 . . . 44 B2
Tunstall Rd SW9 . . . 62 B3
Tunstall Wlk 10 TW8 . . . 44 A4
Tunworth Cres SW15 . . . 56 B1
Tun Yd SW8 . . . 61 A4
Tupman Ho SE16 . 139 B3
Turberville Ho 1 SW9 . . . 62 B4
Turenne Cl SW18 . . . 59 B3
Turin St E2 . . . 24 C2 99 B3
Turk's Head Yd EC1 . . . 108 A4
Turks Row SW3 . . . 145 A2
Turle Rd N4 . . . 5 B2
Turlewray Cl N4 . . . 5 B3
Turnagain La EC4 108 A2
Turnberry Cl 24 SE16 . . . 40 A1
Turnberry Quay 1 E14 . . . 42 A3
Turnbull Ho N1 . . . 86 B4
Turnchapel Mews 1 SW4 . . . 61 A4
Turner Cl 7 SW9 . . . 48 A2
Turner Ct
9 Herne Hill SE5 . . . 63 C3
24 Rotherhithe SE16 . . . 40 B4
Turner Ho
Finsbury Pk N4 . . . 5 B3
24 Millwall E14 . . . 41 C4
St John's Wood NW8 . . . 80 A2
Strand WC2 . . . 120 B3
Westminster SW1 . 147 C3
Turner Lo 10 SW19 . . . 69 C3
Turner Pl SW11 . . . 60 A2
Turners Ct E15 . . . 19 B4
Turner's Rd E3 . . . 33 B4
Turner St
Canning Town E16 . . . 35 B3
Stepney E1 . . . 32 A4
Turneville Rd W14 . . . 154 C4
Turney Prim & Sec Specl Sch SE21 . . . 75 B4
Turney Rd SE21 . . . 75 C4
Turnham Green Sta W4 . . . 38 A2
Turnham Green Terr W4 . . . 38 A2
Turnham Ho SE4 . . . 66 A3
Turnham Prim Sch SE4 . . . 66 A3
Turnham Rd SE4 . . . 66 A3
Turnmill Ho 8 SW2 . . . 62 C2
Turnmill St EC1 . . . 108 A4
Turnour Ho 31 E1 . . . 32 A3
Turnpike Cl SE8 . . . 51 B3
Turnpike Ho EC1 . . . 96 B3
Turnpin La 3 SE10 . . . 52 B4
Turpentine La SW1 . . . 146 B1
Turpin Ho SW11 . . . 170 A4
Turpin Way N19 . . . 4 C3
Turquand St SE17 151 A3
Turret Gr SW4 . . . 61 B4
Turville Ho NW8 . . . 90 A2
Turville St E2 . . . 24 B1 98 C2
Tuscan Ho 36 E2 . . . 25 B2
Tuskar St SE10 . . . 43 A1
Tuttle Ho SW1 . . . 147 C1
Tweedale Ct E15 . . . 19 B3
Tweed Ho E14 . . . 27 B1
Tweezer's Alley WC2 . . . 121 B4
Twelvetrees Bsns Pk E16 . . . 27 C1
Twelvetrees Cres E3 . . . 27 B1
Twice Times Montessori Sch SW6 . . . 165 C1
Twig Folly Cl 21 E2 . . . 25 C3
Twilley St SW18 . . . 71 A4
Twine Ct E1 . . . 32 B2
Twisden Rd NW5 . . . 13 A4
Twyford CE High Sch W3 . . . 28 A1
Twyford Ho N5 . . . 6 A1
Twyford St N1 . . . 84 C4
Twynholm Mans SW6 . . . 154 A2
Tyburn Tree (site of)★ W2 . . . 116 C4
Tyburn Way W1 . . . 117 A4
Tyer's Est SE1 . . . 138 A4
Tyers Gate SE1 . . . 138 A3
Tyers St SE11 . . . 148 C2
Tyers Terr SE11 . . . 149 A1
Tyler Cl E2 . . . 24 B3
Tyler Ho SE3 . . . 52 C1
Tyler St
Greenwich SE10 . . . 43 A1
SE10 . . . 53 A4
Tylney Ho 10 E1 . . . 32 A3
Tymperley Ct SW19 . . . 70 A3
Tyndale La N1 . . . 15 A1
Tyndale Mans N1 . . . 15 A1
Tyndale Terr 13 N1 . . . 15 A1
Tyneham Cl 10 SW11 . . . 60 C4
Tyneham Rd SW11 . . . 60 C4
Tynemouth St SW6 . . . 166 C2
Tyne St E1 . . . 111 A2
Tynsdale Rd NW10 . . . 8 A2
Tynte Ct E9 . . . 18 A3
Tynwald Ho 14 SE26 . . . 76 C1
Type St E2 . . . 25 C3
Tyrawley Rd SW6 166 A4
Tyrells Ct 3 SE15 . . . 65 A4
Tyrrell Ho SW1 . . . 161 A4
Tyrrell Rd SE22 . . . 64 C3
Tyrwhitt Rd SE4 . . . 66 C4
Tysoe St EC1 . . . 95 C3
Tyssen Com Prim Sch N16 . . . 7 C3
Tyssen Rd N16 . . . 7 B1
Tyssen St
Dalston E8 . . . 16 B2
Hoxton N1 . . . 24 A3
Tysson Ho E9 . . . 18 A1
Tytherton 28 E2 . . . 25 B3
Tytherton Rd N19 . . . 4 C1

U

Uamvar St E14 . . . 34 A4
Udall St SW1 . . . 147 A3
Udimore Ho 11 W10 . . . 30 B4
Uffington Rd NW10 . . . 22 A4
Ufford St SE1 . . . 135 C4
Ufton Gr N1 . . . 15 C1
Ufton Rd N1 . . . 16 A1
Uhura Sq 19 N16 . . . 7 A1
Ujima Ct N19 . . . 5 A3
Ullin St E14 . . . 34 B4
Ullswater SW15 . . . 57 C1
Ullswater Ho SE15 . . 50 B4
Ullswater Rd
Barnes SW13 . . . 46 C3
West Norwood SE27, SW16 . . . 75 A2
Ulster Pl NW1 . . . 92 A1
Ulster Terr NW1 . . . 92 A2
Ulundi Rd SE3 . . . 53 A4
Ulva Rd SW15 . . . 57 C3
Ulverscroft Rd SE22 . . . 64 C2
Ulverstone Rd SE27 . . . 75 A2
Ulysses Rd NW6 . . . 10 B3
Umberston St E1 . . . 32 A3
Umbria St SW15 . . . 56 C1
Una Ho 7 NW5 . . . 13 A2
Undercliff SE10 . . . 52 B2
Undercliff Rd SE13 . . . 67 A4
Underhill Ho 7 E14 . . . 33 C4
Underhill Pas NW1 . . . 82 B4
Underhill St NW1 . . 82 B3
Undershaft EC3 . . 110 A1
Underwood Ho W6 . . . 39 A3
Underwood Rd E1 . . . 24 C1 99 C1
Underwood Row N1 . . . 97 A4
Underwood St N1 . 97 A4
Undine Rd E14 . . . 42 A2
Unicorn Bldg 14 E1 . . . 32 C2
Unicorn Sch TW9 . . 44 B2
Union Cl E11 . . . 19 C4
Union Ct
45 Paddington W2 . . . 31 C4
2 Richmond TW10 . . 54 A2
South Lambeth SW4 . . . 172 A1
Union Dr E1 . . . 26 A1
Union Gr SW8 . . . 171 C2
Union Mews SW9 172 A1
Union Pk 11 SE10 . . . 43 B1
Union Rd SW8 . . . 171 C1
Union Sq N1 . . . 87 A3
Union St
Mill Meads E15 . . . 27 C4
SE1 . . . 122 C1
Union Wharf N1 . . . 87 A2
Union Wlk E2 . . . 24 A2 98 B4
Union Yd W1 . . . 104 B1
Unity Cl NW10 . . . 8 C2
Unity Mews NW1 . . 83 B2
Univ Coll Jun Sch NW3 . . . 11 B4
Univ Coll London
Bloomsbury WC1 . . . 93 B2
Bloomsbury WC1 . . . 94 B2
Univ Coll London (Windeyer Inst) W1 . . . 105 A4
Univ Coll London (Wolfson Ho) NW1 . . . 93 A3
University Coll Hospl WC1 . . . 93 A2
University Coll Sch NW3 . . . 11 B3
University Mans SW15 . . . 57 C4
University St WC1 . 93 A1
Univ of California WC1 . . . 105 C3
Univ of East London (Duncan Ho) E15 . . 27 C4
Univ of Greenwich SE10 . . . 52 C4
Univ of Greenwich Rachel Mcmillan Campus SE8 . . . 51 C4
Univ of London WC1 . . . 93 C1
Univ of London (King's Coll Hall) SE5 . . . 63 C4
Univ of London (Queen Mary & Westfield Coll) E1 . . . 26 A1
Univ of Westminster NW1 . . . 92 C2
Univ of Westminster (Cavendish Campus) W1 . . . 104 C4
Univ of Westminster (Marylebone Campus) W1 . . . 103 B4
Univ of Westminster (Regent Campus) W1 . . . 104 C3
Univ of Westminster (Regent Campus, Univ HQ) W1 . . . 104 B2
Unwin Cl SE15 . . . 49 C4
Unwin Rd SW7 . . . 129 C2
Upbrook Mews W2 . . . 101 A1
Upcerne Rd SW10 . . . 157 A1

Upcott Ho
33 Bromley E3 27 A2
4 Hackney E9 17 B1
Upgrove Manor Way 12 SE24 74 C4
Upham Park Rd W4 38 A2
Upland Rd SE22 64 C1
Uplands Cl SW14 55 A2
Upnall Ho 16 SE15 50 B4
Upnor Way SE17 152 B2
Upper Addison Gdns W14 126 A4
Upper Bank St E14 34 A1
Upper Bardsey Wlk 7 N1 15 B2
Upper Belgrave St SW1 131 C2
Upper Berkeley St W1 103 A1
Upper Brockley Rd SE4 51 B1
Upper Brook St W1 117 B4
Upper Caldy Wlk 18 N1 15 B2
Upper Camelford Wlk 14 W10 31 A3
Upper Cheyne Row SW3 158 A4
Upper Clarendon Wlk 12 W11 31 A3
Upper Dengie Wlk N1 86 C4
Upper Grosvenor St W1 117 B3
Upper Ground SE1 121 B2
Upper Gulland Wlk 23 N1 15 B2
Upper Hampstead Wlk 29 NW3 11 B4
Upper Handa Wlk 2 N1 15 B2
Upper Harley St NW1 91 C1
Upper Hawkwell Wlk N1 87 A4
UPPER HOLLOWAY 4 C2
Upper Holloway Sta N19 4 C2
Upper James St W1 119 A4
Upper John St W1 119 A4
Upper Lismore Wlk 8 N1 15 B2
Upper Mall W6 39 A1
Upper Marsh SE1 135 A2
Upper Montague St W1 102 C3
Upper North St E3, E14 33 C4
Upper Park Rd NW3 12 B3
Upper Phillimore Gdns W8 127 B3
Upper Ramsey Wlk 19 N1 15 C2
Upper Rawreth Wlk N1 87 A4
Upper Richmond Rd SW15 57 B3
Upper Richmond Rd W TW10, SW14, SW15 55 B3
Upper St Martin's La WC2 120 A4
Upper St N1 86 A3
Upper Tachbrook St SW1 147 A4
Upper Talbot Wlk 7 W10 31 A3
Upper Terr NW3 2 B1
Upper Thames St EC4 123 A4
Upper Tollington Pk N4 5 C3
UPPER TOOTING 72 B1
Upper Tooting Park Mans 1 SW17 72 C2
Upper Tooting Pk SW17 72 B2
Upper Tooting Rd SW17 72 B1
Upper Tulse Hill SW2 74 B3
Upper Wimpole St W1 103 C4
Upper Woburn Pl NW1, WC1 93 C3
Upstall St SE5 48 A2
Upton Cl NW2 1 A1
Urban Mews N4 6 A4
Urlwin St SE5 48 B4
Urlwin Wlk SW9 48 A2
Urmston Dr SW19 70 A3
Urmston Ho 4 E14 42 B2
Ursula Mews N4 6 B3
Ursula St SW11 168 A3
Urswick Rd E5, E9 17 B3
Usborne Mews SW8 163 A2
Usher Rd E3 26 B3
Usk Rd SW11 59 B3
Usk St E2 25 C2
Utah Bldg 3 SE13 52 A2
Utopia Ho 3 NW2 8 C2
Utopia Village NW1 81 B4
Uverdale Rd SW10 157 A1
Uxbridge Rd W12 30 A1
Uxbridge St W8 31 C1 113 B2

V

Vadnie Bish Ho NW5 13 B2
Vaine Ho 4 E9 18 A2
Vale Cl W9 88 C3
Vale Ct
East Acton W3 29 B1
St John's Wood W9 88 C3
Vale End SE22 64 B3
Vale Est The W3 29 A1
Vale Gr Acton W3 28 C1
Stoke Newington N4 6 B4
Valens Ho 1 SW2 74 C3
Valentia Pl SW9 62 C3
Valentine Ho
11 Clapham Pk SW4 61 B1
26 Old Ford E3 26 B4
Valentine Pl SE1 136 A4
Valentine Rd E9 17 C2
Valentine Row SE1 136 A3
VALE OF HEALTH 2 C1
Vale of Health NW3 2 C1
Vale Rd N4 6 B4
Vale Rise NW11 1 B3
Vale Row N5 6 A1
Vale Royal N7 14 A1
Vale Sch The SW7 128 C1
Vale The
Cricklewood NW11 1 A2
East Acton W3 29 A1
SW3 157 C4
Valetta Rd W3 38 B4
Valette Ho E9 17 B2
Valette St E8 17 A2
Valiant Ho
9 Cubitt Town E14 42 B4
SW11 167 C3
Vallance Rd E1 24 C1 99 C1
Valliere Rd NW10 21 C2
Val McKenzie Ave N7 5 C1
Valmar Rd SE5 48 B2
Valmar Trad Est SE5 48 B2
Valois Ho SE1 138 C2
Valonia Gdns SW18 58 B1
Vanbern Ho NW5 12 C2
Vanbrugh Ct SE11 149 C3
Vanbrugh Fields SE3 53 B3
Vanbrugh Hill SE10, SE3 53 B4
Vanbrugh Ho 8 E9 17 B1
Vanbrugh Park Rd SE3 53 B3
Vanbrugh Park Rd W SE3 53 B3
Vanbrugh Pk SE3 53 B3
Vanbrugh Rd W4 37 C3
Vanbrugh Terr SE3 53 B2
Vanburgh Ho E1 110 C4
Vancover Ho 33 E1 32 A1
Vanderbilt Rd SW18 71 B3
Vanderbilt Villas 1 W12 39 C4
Vandon Ct SW1 133 A2
Vandon Pas SW1 133 A2
Vandon St SW1 133 A2
Vandyke Cl SW15 57 C1
Vandy St EC2 24 A1 98 A1
Vane Cl NW3 11 C4
Vane St SW1 147 A4
Vange Ho 12 W10 30 B4
Van Gogh Ct E14 42 C3
Vanguard Bldg 6 E14 41 C4
Vanguard Ho 11 E8 17 A1
Vanguard St SE8 51 C2
Vanguard Trad Ctr E15 27 B4
Vanneck Sq SW15 56 C2
Vanner Point 27 E9 17 C2
Vansittart St 7 SE14 51 A3
Vanston Pl SW6 155 C2
Vantage Mews 7 E14 34 B1
Vantage Pl W8 127 C1
Vantrey Ho SE11 149 B3
Varcoe Rd SE16 40 B1
Vardens Rd SW11 59 C3
Varden St E1 32 A3
Vardon Cl W3 28 C3
Vardon Ho SE10 52 B2
Varey Ho E1 26 A2
Varley Ho 5 NW6 23 C4
Varma Ct SE3 53 C2
Varna Rd SW6 154 C1
Varndell St NW1 92 C4
Varsity Row SW14 45 B1
Vascroft Est NW10 20 A1
Vassall Ho 8 E3 26 A2
Vassall Rd SW9 163 C1
Vat Ho SW8 162 B2
Vauban Est SE16 139 A1
Vauban St SE16 139 A1
Vaudeville Ct N4 5 C2
Vaughan Ave W6 38 B2
Vaughan Est E2 24 B2 98 C4
Vaughan Ho SE1 136 A4
Vaughan Rd SE5 63 B4
Vaughan St SE16 41 B4
Vaughan Way E1 125 C2
Vaughan Williams Cl SE8 51 C3
VAUXHALL 148 B1
Vauxhall Bridge Rd SW1 147 A3
Vauxhall Cross SE1, SW8 148 B1
Vauxhall Gr SW8 162 C4
Vauxhall Prim Sch SE11 149 A2
Vauxhall St SE11 149 A2
Vauxhall Sta SE11 148 B1
Vauxhall Wlk SE11 148 C2
Vawdrey Cl E1 25 B1
Vaynor Ho N7 14 A4
Vectis Ct SW18 59 A1
Veda Rd SE13 66 C3
Velde Way 1 SE22 64 A2
Vellacott Ho 3 W12 30 A3
Velletri Ho 17 E2 25 C3
Venables St NW8 101 C4
Vencourt Pl W6 38 C2
Venetian Rd SE5 48 B1
Venice Ct 14 SE5 48 B3
Venn Ho N1 85 A3
Venn St SW4 61 B3
Ventnor Rd SE14 50 C3
Ventura Ho 12 SW2 62 A3
Venue St E14 34 B4
Venus Ho
7 Millwall E14 41 C2
8 Old Ford E3 26 C4
Vera Ct W2 100 A2
Vera Rd SW6 164 B4
Verbena Gdns 4 W6 38 C1
Verdi Cres W10 23 A3
Verdun Rd SW13 46 C3
Vere Bank SW19 70 B3
Vereker Rd W14 140 B1
Vere St W1 104 A1
Verity Cl W11 31 A3
Verity Ho 20 E3 26 B2
Vermeer Ct E14 42 C3
Vermont Rd SW18 59 A1
Verne Ct 9 W3 37 B3
Verneer Gdns SE15 65 B3
Verney Ho
Lisson Gr NW8 90 A2
South Kensington SW10 156 C4
Verney Rd SE16 40 A1
Verney Way SE16 40 A1
Vernon Ct NW2 1 B1
Vernon Ho SE11 149 A1
Vernon Mews W14 140 B3
Vernon Pl WC1 106 B3
Vernon Rd Bow E3 26 B3
Mortlake SW14 55 C4
Vernon Rise WC1 95 A4
Vernon Sq WC1 95 A4
Vernon St W14 140 B3
Vernon Yd W11 31 B2 112 C4
Verona Ct
Chiswick W4 38 A1
10 SE14 50 C4
Veronica Ho
Brockley SE4 66 B4
46 Bromley E3 27 A2
Veronica Rd SW17 73 A2
Verran Rd SW12 73 A4
Verulam Bldgs WC1 107 A4
Verulam Ho 1 W6 39 B4
Verulam St EC1 107 B4
Vervain Ho 2 SE15 49 C3
Verwood Ho SW8 163 A1
Verwood Lo 1 E14 42 C2
Vesage Ct EC1 107 C3
Vesey Path 15 E14 34 A3
Vespan Rd W12 38 C4
Vesta Ct SE1 138 A3
Vesta Ho 9 E3 26 C4
Vesta Rd SE4, SE14 51 A1
Vestry Mews 12 SE5 49 A2
Vestry Rd SE5 49 A2
Vestry St N1 97 B4
Viaduct Pl 28 E2 25 A2
Viaduct St E2 25 A2
Vian St SE13 67 A4
Vibart Gdns SW2 74 B4
Vibart Wlk N1 84 B4
Vicarage Ave SE3 53 C3
Vicarage Cres SW11 167 B3
Vicarage Ct
7 Putney SW15 68 C4
W8 128 A4
Vicarage Dr SW14 55 C2
Vicarage Gate W8 114 A1
Vicarage Gdns
Mortlake SW14 55 C2
W8 31 C1 113 C1
Vicarage Gr SE5 48 C2
Vicarage Rd SW14 55 C2

Vicarage Wlk SW11 167 C4
Vicar's Cl E9 25 B4
Vicars Hill SE13 67 A3
Vicar's Rd NW5 12 C3
Viceroy Ct NW8 80 B2
Viceroy Rd SW8 172 A4
Vic Johnson Ho 21 E3 26 B4
Vickery Ct EC1 97 A2
Vickery Ho 13 SW4 62 A3
Vickery's Wharf 3 E14 33 C3
Victor Cazalet Ho N1 86 A4
Victoria & Albert Mus* SW7 129 C1
Victoria Arc SW1 132 B1
Victoria Ave EC2 110 B3
Victoria Bldgs 13 E8 25 A4
Victoria Chambers EC2 24 A1 98 A2
Victoria Coach Sta SW1 146 A3
Victoria Coll WC2 107 B2
Victoria Cotts
7 Richmond TW9 44 C2
Spitalfields E1 111 B4
Victoria Ct
5 Clapham Pk SW4 61 C1
South Acton W3 36 C4
St George in t East E1 125 B3
Victoria Dr SW19 69 C3
Victoria Emb WC2 121 B3
Victoria Gdns W11 31 C1 113 B2
Victoria Gr W8 128 C2
Victoria Gr Mews W2 114 A3
Victoria Hall 15 E16 35 C1
Victoria Ho
6 Clapham Pk SW4 61 C1
2 Shepherd's Bush W12 38 C4
SW1 146 A2
Victoria Ind Est W3 29 A4
Victoria Mans
8 Islington N7 14 C3
Willesden NW10 9 A1
Victoria Mews
Kilburn NW6 23 C4
Wandsworth SW18 71 B3
Victoria Mills 1 E15 27 C4
Victorian Gr N16 7 A1
Victorian Rd N16 7 B1
Victoria Park Ct 11 E9 17 B1
Victoria Park Ind Ctr E9 18 B1
Victoria Park Lofts E9 25 C4
Victoria Park Rd E9 17 C1
Victoria Park Sq E2 25 B2
Victoria Pas NW8 89 B2
Victoria Place Sh Ctr SW1 146 B4
Victoria Rd
Finsbury Pk N4 5 B3
Kensington W8 128 C2
Kilburn NW6 23 B4
Mortlake SW14 55 C4
North Acton NW10 21 A1
Victoria Rise SW4 61 A4
Victoria Sq SW1 132 B2
Victoria St SW1 133 A1
Victoria Sta SW1 146 B4
Victoria Terr
Dagenham NW10 21 A1
Finsbury Pk N4 5 C3
Victoria (Underground) SW1 132 B1
Victoria Villas TW9 54 B3
Victoria Wharf E14 33 A2
Victoria Yd E1 111 C1
Victor Rd NW10 22 A2
Victory Pl
6 Limehouse E14 33 A2
SE17 151 B4
Victory Sch SE17 151 A4
Victory Way SE16 41 A4
Victory Wlk SE8 51 C2
Video Ct N4 5 A4
View Cl N6 3 B4
Viewfield Rd SW18 58 B1
Viewpoint 3 N5 15 A3
Vigo St W1 118 C3
Viking Cl 13 E3 26 A3
Viking Ho 3 SE5 48 B1
Village Cl NW3 11 C3
Village Mount 19 NW3 11 B4
Village Sch The NW3 12 B2
Village The SW11 60 B4
Village Way SE21 63 C1
Villa Rd SW9 62 C4
Villas On The Heath NW3 2 B1
Villa St SE17 151 C1
Villiers Ct SW11 168 B4
Villiers Rd NW2 8 C2
Villiers St WC2 120 B2
Vince Ct N1 97 C3
Vincent Ct
Finsbury Pk N4 5 A3
Marylebone W1 102 C2
South Lambeth SW9 173 A3
Vincent Mews 1 E3 26 C3
Vincent Rd W3 37 B3
Vincents Cl SE16 41 A4
Vincent Sq SW1 147 B4
Vincent St
Canning Town E16 35 B4
Westminster SW1 147 C4
Vincent Terr N1 86 B2
Vince St EC1 97 C3
Vine Ct E1 111 C3
Vinegar St E1 32 A1
Vinegar Yd SE1 138 A4
Vine Hill EC1 95 B1
Vine La SE1 124 B1
Vine Rd SW13 56 B4
Vine St Bridge EC1 95 C1
Vine Sq W14 141 A1
Vines Sch The SW11 60 C3
Vine St W1 119 A3
Whitechapel EC3 110 C1
Vineyard Path SW14 55 C4
Vineyard Sch The TW10 54 A1
Vineyard The TW10 54 A2
Vineyard Wlk EC1 95 B2
Viney Ct 9 SW4 61 C1
Vine Yd SE1 137 A4
Viney Rd SE13 67 A4
Vining St SW2, SW9 62 C3
Vinson Ho N1 87 C1
Vintners Ct EC4 123 A4
Viola Sq W12 29 B2
Violet Cl 32 SE8 51 B4
Violet Hill NW8 78 C1
Violet Hill Ho NW8 78 C1
Violet Rd E3 27 A1
Violet St E2 25 A1
Virgil Pl W1 102 C3
Virgil St SE1 135 A2
Virginia Ct 7 SE16 40 C4
Virginia Ho 3 E14 34 B2
Virginia Prim Sch E2 24 B2 98 C3
Virginia Rd E2 24 B2 98 C3
Virginia St E1 125 C3
Virginia Wlk SW2 62 B1
Viscount Ct 9 W11 31 C3
Viscount St EC1 108 C4
Vista Bldgs 19 E3 26 B2
Vitae Apartments 7 W6 38 C3
Vittoria Ho N1 85 A3
Vittoria Prim Sch N1 85 B2
Vivian Comma Cl 3 N4 6 A1
Vivian Ct NW6 78 A2
Vivian Ho N4 6 C4
Vivian Rd E3 26 A3
Vivian Sq SE15 65 A4
Vogans Mill SE1 139 A4
Vogler Ho 3 E1 32 B2
Vollasky Ho E1 111 B4
Voltaire
2 Camberwell SE5 49 B2
15 Richmond TW9 44 B2
Voltaire Ct SW11 169 C2
Voltaire Rd SW4 61 C4
Volt Ave NW10 21 A2
Vorley Rd N19 4 B2
Voss St E2 24 C2 99 C3
Voyager Bsns Est SE16 139 B2
Vulcan Rd SE4 51 B1
Vulcan Sq E14 41 C2
Vulcan Terr SE4 51 B1
Vulcan Way N7 14 B2
Vyner Ct E5 7 C2
Vyner Rd W3 28 C2
Vyner St E2 25 A4

W

Wadcroft Ct SE4 66 B4
Wadding St SE17 151 B3
Waddington Rd E15 19 C2
Waddington St E15 19 C2
Wade Ho SE1 139 B3
Wadeson St E2 25 A3
Wade's Pl E14 34 A2
Wadham Gdns NW3 80 A4
Wadham Rd SW15 58 A3
Wadhurst Rd W4 37 C3
Wager St E3 26 B1
Waghorn St SE15 64 C4
Wagner St SE15 50 B3
Wainford Cl SW19 69 C3
Wainwright Ho 3 E1 32 B1
Waite St SE15 49 B4
Waithman St EC4 108 A1
Wakefield Ho 6 SE15 49 C2
Wakefield Mews WC1 94 B3
Wakefield St WC1 94 B3
Wakeford Cl SW4 61 B2
Wakeham St 9 N1 15 C2
Wakehurst Rd SW11 60 B2
Wakeling Ho 8 SE27 75 A1
Wakeling St 11 E14 33 A3
Wakelin Ho 19 N1 15 A1
Wakeman Rd NW10 22 C2
Wakley St EC1 96 A4
Walberswick St SW8 162 B1
Walbrook EC4 123 B4
Walbrook Ct 32 N1 24 A3
Walbrook Wharf EC4 123 B4
Walburgh St E1 32 A3
Walcorde Ave SE17 151 A3
Walcot Gdns SE11 149 B4
Walcot Ho 9 SE22 64 A4
Walcot Sq SE11 149 C4
Walcott St SW1 147 A4
Waldeck Gr SE27 75 A1
Waldeck Rd
Brentford W4 44 C4
Mortlake SW14 55 B4
Waldeck Terr SW14 55 B4
Waldegrave Ho 5 SW15 57 B2
Waldemar Ave SW6 164 B2
Waldemar Avenue Mans SW6 164 A3
Walden Ct SW8 171 C4
Walden Ho
Clapham SW11 169 B2
SW1 145 C3
Walden St E1 32 A3
Waldo Cl SW4 61 B2
Waldo Rd NW10 22 A2
Waldron Ho 17 SW2 62 B2
Waldron Mews SW3 157 C4
Waldron Rd SW18 71 B1
Walerand Rd SE13 52 B1
Waleran Flats SE1 152 A4
Wales Cl SE15 50 A4
Wales Farm Rd W3 28 C4
Waley St 1 E1 33 A4
Walford Ho 28 E1 32 A3
Walford Rd N16 16 A4
Walham Ct 15 NW3 12 B2
Walham Gr SW6 155 B2
WALHAM GREEN 156 A1
Walham Green Arc SW6 155 C2
Walham Yd SW6 155 B2
Walker Ho NW1 83 B1
Walker Mews 9 SW2 62 C2
Walkerscroft Mead SE21 75 B3
Walker's Ct W1 119 B4
Walkers Lo 18 E14 42 B4
Walker's Pl SW15 58 A3
Walkinshaw Ct 9 N1 15 B1
Walkynscroft 1 SE15 50 A1
Wallace Collection* W1 103 B2
Wallace Ct NW1 102 B3
Wallace Ho N7 14 B2
Wallace Lo N4 5 C3
Wallace Rd N1, N5 15 B2
Wallbutton Rd SE4 51 A1
Wall Ct N4 5 B3
Waller Rd SE14 50 C1
Wallett Ct 11 NW1 13 B1
Wallflower St W12 29 B2
Wallgrave Rd SW5 142 A3
Wallingford Ave W10 30 C3
Wallis Alley SE1 137 A4
Wallis Cl SW11 59 C4
Wallis Ho 5 SE14 51 A2
Wallis Rd E9 18 C2
Wallorton Gdns SW14 55 C3
Wallside EC2 109 A3
Wall St N1 15 C2
Wallwood St E14 33 B4
Walmer Ho 8 W10 30 C3
Walmer Pl W1 102 C4
Walmer Rd
North Kensington W10 30 B3
W11 31 A2 112 A3
Walm La NW2 9 B2
Walney Wlk 6 N1 15 B2
Walnut Cl SE8 51 B4
Walnut Ho 11 E3 26 B4
Walnut Tree Cl SW13 46 B2
Walnut Tree Ho SW10 156 B4
Walnut Tree Rd
Brentford TW8 44 A4

Walnut Tree Rd
continued
Greenwich SE10 ... 43 A1
Walnut Tree Walk Prim Sch SE11 ... 149 B4
Walnut Tree Wlk SE11 ... 149 B4
Walpole Ave TW9 ... 44 B1
Walpole Ct
7 Hammersmith W14 ... 39 C3
South Hampstead NW6 ... 11 B1
Walpole Gdns W4 ... 37 B1
Walpole Mews NW8 ... 79 B3
Walpole St SW3 ... 145 A2
Walsham Cl N16 ... 7 C3
Walsham Ho
New Cross Gate SE14 ... 50 C1
SE17 ... 151 B2
Walsham Rd SE14 ... 50 C1
Walsingham NW8 ... 79 C4
Walsingham Lo SW13 ... 46 C2
Walsingham Mans SW6 ... 156 B2
Walsingham Pl SW4, SW11 ... 60 C1
Walsingham Rd E5 ... 7 C1
Walter Besant Ho 20 E1 ... 25 C2
Walter Ct 3 W3 ... 28 B3
Walter Green Ho SE15 ... 50 B2
Walter Ho SW10 ... 157 B2
Walter Northcott Ho 2 NW6 ... 10 C3
Walters Cl SE17 ... 151 A3
Walters Ho
3 Camberwell SE5 ... 49 A1
Islington N1 ... 86 B4
10 Kennington SE17 ... 48 A4
Walter Sickert Hall N1 ... 86 C1
Walter St E2 ... 25 C2
Walters Way SE23 ... 65 C1
Walter Taylor Ct SE4 ... 66 B3
Walter Terr E1 ... 32 C3
Walterton Rd W9 ... 23 C1
Waltham Green Ct SW6 ... 156 A1
Waltham Ho NW8 ... 78 C4
Stockwell SW9 ... 173 A1
Walton Cl SW8 ... 162 B2
Walton Gdns W3 ... 28 A4
Walton Ho
E2 ... 24 B1 99 A2
Upper Holloway N7 ... 5 B1
Wandsworth SW18 ... 58 C1
Walton Pl SW3 ... 130 C2
Walton St SW3 ... 130 B1
Walton Way W3 ... 28 A4
Walt Whitman Cl 6 SE24 ... 63 A3
WALWORTH ... 151 C2
Walworth Pl SE17 ... 151 A1
Walworth Rd SE17 ... 151 A2
Walworth Sch SE17 ... 152 B1
Wanborough Dr SW15 ... 69 A3
Wandle Ct 4 W12 ... 38 A4
Wandle Ho NW8 ... 102 A4
Wandsworth SW18 ... 71 A4
Wandle Rd SW17 ... 72 A2
Wandle Way SW18 ... 71 A3
Wandon Rd SW6 ... 156 B1
WANDSWORTH ... 58 C1
Wandsworth Bridge Rd SW6 ... 166 A3
Wandsworth Common Sta SW12 ... 72 B4
Wandsworth Common West Side SW18 ... 59 B2
Wandsworth Gyratory SW18 ... 59 A2
Wandsworth High St SW18 ... 59 A2
Wandsworth Mus* SW18 ... 59 A2
Wandsworth Plain SW18 ... 59 A2
Wandsworth Rd SW8 ... 162 A1
Wandsworth Road Sta SW4 ... 171 A1
Wandsworth Town Sta SW18 ... 59 A3
Wangford Ho 13 SW9 ... 63 A3
Wanless Rd SE24 ... 63 B4
Wanley Rd SE5 ... 63 C3
Wansbeck Rd E3, E9 ... 18 B1
Wansdown Pl SW6 ... 156 A2
Wansey St SE17 ... 151 A3
WAPPING ... 32 A1
Wapping Dock St 19 E1 ... 32 A1
Wapping High St E1 ... 32 A1
Wapping La E1 ... 32 A1
Wapping Sta E1 ... 32 B1
Wapping Wall E1 ... 32 B1
Warbeck Rd W12 ... 39 A4
Warburg Ho E2 ... 24 C2 99 B3
Warburton Cl 6 N1 ... 16 A2
Warburton Ct SE15 ... 64 C4
Warburton Ho 5 E8 ... 25 A4
Warburton Rd 8 E8 ... 25 A4
Warburton St 6 E8 ... 25 A4
Wardalls Ho 12 SE8 ... 51 B4
Wardell Ho 7 SE10 ... 52 B4
Warden Rd NW5 ... 12 C2
Wardens Gr SE1 ... 122 C1
Wardle St E9 ... 17 C3
Wardley St SW18 ... 71 A4
Wardlow 8 NW5 ... 13 A4
Wardo Ave SW6 ... 164 A4
Wardour Mews W1 ... 105 A1
Wardour St W1 ... 105 B1
Ward Point SE11 ... 149 B3
Ward Rd
Camden Town N19 ... 4 B1
Mill Meads E15 ... 27 C4
Wardrobe Pl EC4 ... 108 B1
Wardrobe Terr EC4 ... 122 B4
Wareham Ct 2 N1 ... 16 A1
Wareham Ho SW8 ... 162 C2
Warfield Rd NW10 ... 22 C2
Warfield Yd 6 NW10 ... 22 C2
Wargrave Ho E2 ... 24 B2 98 C3
Warham St SE5 ... 48 A3
Waring Ho E2 ... 24 C2 99 C3
Warley Ho N1 ... 15 C2
Warley St E2 ... 25 C2
Warlock Rd W9 ... 23 C1
Warlters Cl N7 ... 14 A4
Warlters Rd N7 ... 14 A4
Warltersville Mans N19 ... 5 A4
Warltersville Rd N4, N8, N19 ... 5 A4
War Meml Homes W4 ... 45 C3
Warmington Rd SE24 ... 63 B1
Warmsworth NW1 ... 82 C4
Warndon St SE16 ... 40 B2
Warneford St E9 ... 25 A4
Warner Ho
4 Homerton E9 ... 17 C2
Lewisham SE13 ... 52 A1
NW8 ... 88 C4
Warner Pl E2 ... 24 C2 99 C4
Warner Rd SE5 ... 48 B2
Warner St EC1 ... 95 B1
Warner Yd EC1 ... 95 B1
Warnford Ho SW15 ... 56 A1
Warnham WC1 ... 94 C3
Warnham Ho 6 SW2 ... 74 B4
Warple Mews W3 ... 38 A4
Warple Way W3, W12 ... 38 A4
Warren Ave SW14, TW10 ... 55 A3
Warren Cl SE21 ... 75 B4
Warren Ct N1 ... 85 B2
Warrender Rd N19 ... 13 B4
Warren Gdns E15 ... 19 C3
Warren Ho 21 E3 ... 27 A2
Warren Mews W1 ... 92 C1
Warren St W1 ... 92 C1
Warren Street Sta NW1 ... 93 A2
Warriner Gdns SW11 ... 169 B3
Warrington Cres W9 ... 88 C2
Warrington Gdns W9 ... 88 C1
Warspite Ho 3 E14 ... 42 A2
Warton Rd E15 ... 27 B4
Warwick W14 ... 141 A3
Warwick Ave W9 ... 88 C1
Warwick Avenue Sta W9 ... 88 C1
Warwick Bldg SW8 ... 160 A3
Warwick Chambers W8 ... 127 B2
Warwick Cres W2 ... 100 C4
Warwick Ct WC1 ... 107 A3
Warwick Dr SW15 ... 57 A4
Warwick Gdns W14 ... 141 A4
Warwick Ho
Brixton SW9 ... 173 B1
6 Putney SW15 ... 69 B4
Stoke Newington N4 ... 6 B3
Warwick House St SW1 ... 119 C2
Warwick La EC4 ... 108 B1
Warwick Lo NW2 ... 10 A3
Warwick Mans SW5 ... 141 B4
Warwick Pas EC4 ... 108 B2
Warwick Pl W9 ... 100 C4
Warwick Pl N SW1 ... 146 C3
Warwick Rd W14, SW5 ... 141 A4
Warwick Row SW1 ... 132 B2
Warwickshire Path SE8 ... 51 B3
Warwick Sq
Holborn EC4 ... 108 B2
Pimlico SW1 ... 146 C2
Warwick Sq Mews SW1 ... 146 C3
Warwick St W1 ... 119 A4
Warwick Way SW1 ... 146 B4
Warwick Yd EC1 ... 97 A1
Wasdale NW1 ... 92 B3
Washbrook Ho SW2 ... 62 C1
Washington Bldg 1 SE13 ... 52 A2
Washington Cl 45 E3 ... 27 A2
Washington Ho SW1 ... 130 C3
Washington Rd SW13 ... 46 C3
Watchfield Ct 7 W4 ... 37 B1
Watcombe Cotts TW9 ... 44 C4
Watercress Pl N1 ... 16 A1
Waterden Cres E9 ... 18 C3
Waterden Rd E15 ... 18 C2
Waterford Rd SW6 ... 156 A1
Waterford Way NW10 ... 8 C3
Water Gardens The W2 ... 102 B2
Watergate EC4 ... 122 A4
Watergate St SE8 ... 51 C4
Watergate Wlk WC2 ... 120 B2
Waterhead NW1 ... 92 C4
Waterhouse Cl
Hammersmith W6 ... 39 C1
Hampstead NW3 ... 11 C3
Wateridge Cl E14 ... 41 C3
Water La
16 Camden Town NW1 ... 13 A1
SE14 ... 50 B3
Waterloo Bridge SE1, WC2 ... 121 A3
Waterloo Cl E9 ... 17 B3
Waterloo East Sta SE1 ... 121 C1
Waterloo Gdns
26 Islington N1 ... 15 A1
South Hackney E2 ... 25 B3
Waterloo Int Sta SE1 ... 135 A4
Waterloo Pier SE1 ... 134 C4
Waterloo Pl
Kew TW9 ... 44 C4
9 Richmond TW9 ... 54 A3
SW1 ... 119 B2
Waterloo Rd SE1 ... 135 C4
Waterloo Sta SE1 ... 135 B4
Waterloo Terr N1 ... 15 A1
Waterlow Ct NW11 ... 2 A4
Waterlow Rd N19 ... 4 B3
Waterman Bldg 2 E14 ... 41 C4
Watermans Ct 2 TW8 ... 44 A4
Waterman St SW15 ... 57 C4
Waterman Way E1 ... 32 A1
Watermead Ho E9 ... 18 B3
Watermeadow La SW6 ... 166 C1
Water Mews SE15 ... 65 B3
Watermill Ct SE13 ... 67 A4
Watermint Quay N16 ... 7 C4
Water's Edge SW6 ... 47 B2
Waterside N1 ... 86 C1
Waterside Cl
Bermondsey SE16 ... 139 C3
Old Ford E3 ... 26 B4
Waterside Ct SE13 ... 67 C3
Waterside Pl NW1 ... 81 C4
Waterside Point SW11 ... 158 B2
Waterson St E2 ... 24 B2 98 C4
Waters Pl SW15 ... 47 B1
Water St WC2 ... 121 B4
Waterview Ho 13 E14 ... 33 A4
Waterworks Rd SW2 ... 62 B1
Watford Cl SW11 ... 168 B4
Watford Rd E16 ... 35 C4
Watkins Ho 11 E14 ... 42 B4
Watkinson Rd N7 ... 14 B2
Watling Ct EC4 ... 109 A1
Watling Gdns NW2 ... 10 A2
Watling St
4 Camberwell SE15 ... 49 A4
City of London EC4 ... 109 A1
Watney Cotts SW14 ... 55 B4
Watney Mkt* E1 ... 32 A3
Watney Rd SW14 ... 55 B4
Watney St E1 ... 32 A3
Watson Cl N16 ... 15 C3
Watson Ho 3 SW2 ... 74 A4
Watsons Mews W1 ... 102 B3
Watson's St SE8 ... 51 C3
Watts Gr E3 ... 34 A4
Watts Ho 6 W10 ... 31 A4
Watts St SE15 ... 49 B2
Wapping E1 ... 32 A1

Wat Tyler Rd SE10 52 C2
Wavel Ct
7 Streatham SW16 74 A1
7 Wapping E1 32 B1
Wavel Mews NW6 11 A1
Wavendon Ave W4 37 C1
Waveney Ave SE15 65 A3
Waveney Cl E1 125 C2
Waveney Ho SE15 65 A3
Waverley Ct
5 Brondesbury NW6 10 A1
W1 103 C4
Waverley Pl
Finsbury Pk N4 6 A3
St John's Wood NW8 79 B2
Waverley Rd N8 5 A4
Waverly Ct NW3 12 B2
Waverton Ho 2 E3 26 B4
Waverton Rd SW18 71 B4
Waverton St W1 118 A2
Wavertree Ct 9 SW2 74 A3
Wavertree Rd SW2 74 B3
Waxham NW5 12 B3
Waxlow Rd NW10 20 C3
Wayford St SW11 168 B1
Wayland Ave E8 16 C3
Wayland Ho SW9 173 B2
Waylett Ho SE11 149 B1
Waylett Pl SE27 75 A1
Wayman Ct E8 17 A2
Waynflete Sq
18 North Kensington W10 30 C3
16 Shepherd's Bush W10 30 C2
Waynflete St SW18 71 B2
Wayside
Golders Green NW11 1 A3
Mortlake SW14 55 B2
Weald Cl 16 SE16 40 A1
Weardale Ho N4 6 B4
Weardale Rd SE13 67 C3
Wearmouth Ho 1 E3 33 B4
Wear Pl 13 E2 25 A2
Wearside Rd SE13 67 A3
Weatherbury 6 W2 31 C3
Weatherbury Ho 3 N19 4 C1
Weatherley Cl E3 33 B4
Weaver Ct 2 E2 25 A1
Weaver Ho E1 24 C1 99 B1
Weaver's La SE1 124 B1
Weaver St E1 24 C1 99 B1
Weavers Way
6 Camden Town NW1 13 C1
NW1 83 B4
Webb Cl NW10 22 B1
Webb Ct W3 37 A4
Webber Row SE1 136 A3
Webber St SE1 136 A3
Webb Est E5 7 C4
Webb Ho SW8 161 C1
Webb Pl NW10 21 B2
Webb Rd SE3 53 B4
Webb's Rd SW11 60 B2
Webb St SE1 138 A1
Webheath 6 NW6 10 B1
Webster Ho 16 N16 16 A3
Webster Rd SE16 139 C1
Weddell Ho 23 E1 25 C1
Wedderburn Rd NW3 11 C3
Wedgewood Ho SW1 146 C1
Wedgewood Mews W1 105 C1
Wedgewood Wlk NW3 11 A3
Wedgwood Ho
17 Globe Town E2 25 C2
SE11 135 B1
Wedlake St W10 23 A1
Wedmore Gdns N19 4 C2
Wedmore St N19 4 C1
Weech Rd NW6 10 C4
Weedington Rd NW5 12 C3
Weedon Ho W12 29 C3
Weekley Sq SW11 59 C4
Weighhouse St W1 103 C1
Weimar St SW15 58 A4
Weir Ho 8 SW12 73 B4
Weir Rd
Streatham SW12 73 B4
Wimbledon SW18, SW19 71 A1
Weir's Pas NW1 93 C4
Weiss Rd SW15 57 C4
Welbeck Ct W14 140 C4
Welbeck Mans 10 NW6 10 C3
Welbeck St W1 104 A2
Welbeck Way W1 104 A2
Welbury Ct E8 16 A1
Welby Ho N19 4 C4
Welby St SE5 48 A2
Weldon Ct SE8 51 C1
Welford Ct
12 Camden Town NW1 13 A1
Clapham SW8 170 C1
Welland Ho SE15 65 B3
Welland Mews E1 125 C2
Welland St SE10 52 B4
Wellclose Sq E1 125 C4
Wellclose St E1 125 C3
Well Ct EC4 109 A1
Wellday Ho 2 E9 18 A2
Welldon Ct 1 SE21 75 C2
Weller Ho SE16 139 B3
Weller St SE1 136 C4
Welles Ct 15 E14 33 C2
Wellesley Ave W6 39 A3
Wellesley Ct W9 88 C4
Wellesley Ho NW1 93 B3
Wellesley Pl
Camden Town NW5 12 C3
NW1 93 B3
Wellesley Rd
Gospel Oak NW5 12 C3
Wellesley Rd *continued*
Gunnersbury W4 37 A1
Wellesley St E1 32 C4
Wellesley Terr N1 97 A4
Wellfit St 6 SE24 63 A4
Wellgarth Rd NW11 2 A3
Wellington Arch★ SW1 131 C4
Wellington Bldgs
15 Bow E3 26 C2
SW1 145 C1
Wellington Cl
Kensington W11 31 C3
New Cross Gate SE14 50 C2
Wellington Ct
Knightsbridge SW1 130 C3
St John's Wood NW8 79 C1
Strand WC2 120 A4
Wandsworth SW18 60 A2
Wellington Gr SE10 52 C3
Wellington Ho 18 NW3 12 B2
Wellington Hospl The NW8 79 C1
Wellington Mans N16 16 B4
Wellington Mews
East Dulwich SE22 64 C3
3 Islington N7 14 B2
Streatham SW16 73 C1
Wellington Mus (Apsley Ho)★ SW1 131 C4
Wellington Pl NW8 89 C4
Wellington Prim Sch E3 26 C2
Wellington Rd
Kensal Green NW10 22 C2
St John's Wood NW8 79 C1
Wimbledon SW19 70 C2
Wellington Row E2 24 C2 99 B4
Wellington Sq SW3 144 C2
Wellington St WC2 120 C4
Wellington Terr 2 E1 32 A1
Wellington Way E3 26 C2
Well La SW14 55 B2
Well Rd NW3 2 C1
Wells Ct
21 Hampstead NW3 11 B4
1 Paddington NW6 23 C3
Stoke Newington N1 16 A3
Wells Ho
Finsbury EC1 96 A4
12 Kensal Town W10 23 A1
New Cross Gate SE4 51 A1
9 Rotherhithe SE16 40 B3
Wells Ho The 2 NW3 11 C4
Wells House Rd NW10 29 A4
Wellside Gdns SW14 55 B2
Wells Mews W1 105 A2
Wells Pl SW18 71 B4
Wells Rd W12 39 B4
Wells Rise NW8 80 C3
Wells Sq WC1 95 A3
Wells St W1 105 A2
Well St E9 17 B1
Wells Terr N4 5 C2
Wells Way
Brompton SW7 129 B2
Camberwell SE5 49 A4
Well Wlk NW3 2 C1
Wellwood Ct SW15 57 B3
Welmar Works SW4 61 C3
Welsford St SE1 153 B3
Welsh Ho 14 E1 32 A1
Welshpool Ho 22 E8 24 C4
Welshpool St 1 E8 25 A4
Welstead Ho 20 E1 32 A3
Welstead Way W4 38 B2
Weltje Rd W6 38 C1
Welton Ct SE5 49 A2
Welton Ho E1 32 C4
Welwyn St E2 25 B2
Wembury Mews N6 4 B4
Wembury Rd N6 4 A4
Wemyss Rd SE3 53 B1
Wendell Park Prim Sch W12 38 B4
Wendell Rd W12 38 B4
Wendle Ct SW8 162 A3
Wendling NW5 12 B3
Wendon St E3 26 B4
Wendover SE17 152 A1
Wendover Ct
Acton W3 20 A1
Becontree W3 20 B1
4 Child's Hill NW2 1 C1
W1 103 B3
Wendover Ho W1 103 B3
Wendover Rd NW10 21 B3
Wengham Ho W12 29 C2
Wenham Ho SW8 160 C1
Wenlake Ho EC1 96 C2
Wenlock Ct N1 87 C1
Wenlock Rd N1 87 A1
Wenlock St N1 87 B1
Wennington Rd E3 25 C3
Wensdale Ho E5 7 C2
Wensleydale Ho 8 N4 6 B4
Wentworth Cres SE15 49 C3
Wentworth Ct
W6 154 A3
Wandsworth SW18 59 A1
Wentworth Dwellings E1 110 C2
Wentworth Ho 4 SE3 53 C3
Wentworth Mews E3 26 B2
Wentworth St E1 111 A3
Werrington St NW1 83 A1
Werter Rd SW15 58 A3
Wesleyan Pl NW5 13 A4
Wesley Ave NW10 20 C2
Wesley Cl
Finsbury Pk N7 5 B2
SE17 150 B3
Wesley Ct W1 103 C3
Wesley Ho SE24 63 C1
Wesley Rd NW10 20 B4
Wesley Sq W11 31 A3
Wesley St W1 103 C3
Wessex Ct SW15 57 C2
Wessex Gardens Prim Sch NW11 1 A3
Wessex Gdns NW11 1 A3
Wessex Ho SE1 153 A1
4 Tufnell Pk N19 4 C1
Wessex St E2 25 B2
Wessex Way NW11 1 A3
West 12 Sh Ctr W12 39 C4
Westacott Cl N19 4 C3
West Acton Prim Sch W3 28 A3
West Arbour St E1 32 C3
West Bank N16 7 A4
Westbere Rd NW2 10 A3
West Block 18 E1 32 B2
Westbourne Ave W3 28 C3
Westbourne Cres W2 115 B4
Westbourne Ct W2 100 C
Westbourne Gdns W2 100 A
Westbourne Gr
Notting Hill W2, W11 31 C
W11 31 B2 113 A
WESTBOURNE GREEN 88 A
Westbourne Gr Mews
7 W11 31 C
Westbourne Gr Terr W2 100 A
Westbourne Ho SW1 146 A
Westbourne Park Rd
Notting Hill W2 31 C
Notting Hill W11 31 B
Westbourne Park Sta W11 31 B
Westbourne Park Villas W2 100 A
Westbourne Rd N7 14 B
Westbourne St W2 115 B
Westbourne Terr W2 101 A
Westbourne Terrace Mews W2 100 C
Westbourne Terrace Rd W2 100 C
Westbridge Cl W12 29 C
Westbridge Prim Sch SW11 168 A
Westbridge Rd SW11 168 A
WEST BROMPTON 156 A
West Brompton Sta SW5 141 C
Westbrook Ho
5 Bethnal Green E2 25

Westbrook Ho *continued*
5 Clapham Pk SW4 . . . . 61 B2
Westbury Ct SW4 . . . 61 A1
Westbury Ho 6 NW10 . . . . 8 A1
Westbush Ct 1 W12 . . . . 39 A4
West Carriage Dr W2 . . . . 116 A2
West Central St WC1 . . . . 106 A2
Westchester Ho W2 . . . . 102 C1
Westcliff Ho 13 N1 . . . . 15 C2
Westcombe Ct 1 SE3 . . . . 53 B3
Westcombe Hill SE3, SE10 . . . . 53 C4
Westcombe Park Rd SE3 . . . . 53 B3
Westcombe Park Sta SE3 . . . . 43 C1
Westcott Ho 1 E14 . . . . 34 A2
Westcott Rd SE17 . . 48 A4
West Cotts NW6 . . . . 10 C3
Westcroft Cl NW2 . . 10 A4
Westcroft Ct 3 W6 . . . . 38 C2
Westcroft Sq W6 . . . 38 C2
Westcroft Way NW2 . . . . 10 A4
West Cromwell Rd W14 . . . . 141 A2
West Cross Route W10, W11 . . . . 30 C2
Westdean Cl SW18 . . . . 59 A1
Westdown Rd E15 . . 19 B4
WEST DULWICH . . . 75 B2
West Dulwich Sta SE21 . . . . 75 C3
West Eaton Pl SW1 . . . . 145 B4
West Eaton Pl Mews SW1 . . . . 145 B4
West Ella Rd NW10 . . 8 A1
West End Ct NW6 . . 11 A1
West End La NW6 . . 11 A2
Westerdale Ct N5 . . 15 A4
Westerdale Rd 2 SE10 . . . . 43 C1
Westerham NW1 . . 82 C3
Westerham Ho SE1 . . . . 137 C2
Western Ave W3 . . . 28 C3
Western Avenue Bsns Pk W3 . . . . 20 A1
Western Beach Apts E16 . . . . 35 C1
Western Ct
4 Dagenham W3 . . . 28 C3
3 Kilburn W9 . . . . 23 B3
Western Eye Hospl The NW1 . . . . 102 C4
Western Gateway E16 . . . . 35 C2
Western Ho 3 W9 . . . . 23 B1
Western La SW12 . . . 72 C4
Western Mews W9 . . . . 23 B1
Western Pl 19 SE16 . . . . 40 B4
Western Rd
Becontree NW10 . . . . 20 B1
Brixton SW9 . . . . 62 C4
Western Terr 3 W6 . . . . 38 C1
Western Wharf 2 SE15 . . . . 49 C4
Westferry Cir E14 . . 33 C1
Westferry Rd E14 . . . 41 C3
Westferry Sta E14 . . 33 C2
Westfield NW3 . . . . 10 C4
Westfield Cl SW10 . . . . 156 C1
Westfield Ct 1 W10 . . . . 22 C2
Westfield Ho 6 SE16 . . . . 40 C2
Westfields SW13 . . . 56 B4
Westfields Ave SW13 . . . . 56 A4
Westfields Rd W3 . . 28 A4
Westfield Way E1 . . 26 A1
West Garden Pl W2 . . . . 102 B1
Westgate Bsns Ctr
2 Kensal Town W10 . . . . 23 A1
North Kensington W10 . . . . 22 C1
Westgate Ct 15 SW9 . . . . 62 C4
Westgate St E8 . . . . 25 A4
Westgate Terr SW10 . . . . 156 B4
West Gdns E1 . . . . 32 A2
West Gr SE10 . . . . 52 C2
Westgrove La SE10 . . . . 52 B2
West Halkin St SW1 . . . . 131 B2
West Hall Rd TW9 . . 45 A2
WEST HAMPSTEAD 10 C4
West Hampstead Mews NW6 . . . . 11 A2
West Hampstead Sta NW6 . . . . 10 C2
West Hampstead Thameslink Sta NW6 . . . . 10 C2
West Harding St EC4 . . . . 107 C2
Westhay Gdns SW14 . . . . 55 A2
West Heath Ave NW11 . . . . 1 C3
West Heath Cl NW3 . 1 C1
West Heath Ct NW11 . . . . 1 C3
West Heath Dr NW11 . . . . 1 C3
West Heath Gdns NW3 . . . . 1 C1
West Heath Rd NW3 . . . . 2 A1
WEST HILL 58 B1
West Hill
Highgate N6 . . . . 3 C3
Putney SW15 . . . . 58 A1
Westhill Ct W11 . . . . 31 B2 113 A4
West Hill Ct N6 . . . . 3 C1
Westhill Pk
Dartmouth Pk N6 . . . . 3 C2
Highgate N6 . . . . 3 B2
West Hill Prim Sch SW18 . . . . 58 C2
West Hill Rd SW18 . . 58 B1
West Ho 9 SW12 . . . 73 B4
Westhope Ho E2 . . . . 24 C2 99 C3
Westhorpe Rd SW15 . . . . 57 B4
West House Cl SW19 . . . . 70 A3
West India Ave E14 . . . . 33 C1
West India Dock Rd E14 . . . . 33 C2
West India Ho 1 E14 . . . . 33 C2
West India Quay Sta E14 . . . . 33 C2
WEST KENSINGTON 140 B3
West Kensington Ct W14 . . . . 140 C2
West Kensington Mans W14 . . . . 140 C1
West Kensington Sta W14 . . . . 140 C2
WEST KILBURN . . . 23 A2
West La SE16 . . . . 40 A4
Westlake 12 SE16 . . . 40 B2
Westland Pl N1 . . . 97 B4
Westlands Terr 3 SW12 . . . . 61 B1
Westleigh Ave SW15 . . . . 57 B2
West London Stad The W12 . . . . 30 A4
Westly Ct NW2 . . . . 9 C2
Westmacott Ho NW8 . . . . 89 C1
West Mall W11 . . . . 31 C1 113 C2
Westmark Point 13 SW15 . . . . 69 A3
Westmead SW15 . . . 57 A1
West Mews SW1 . 146 C3
Westmill Ct N4 . . . . 6 B2
WESTMINSTER . 133 A1
Westminster Abbey* SW1 . . . . 134 A2
Westminster Abbey Choir Sch SW1 . . 133 C2
Westminster Acad NW1 . . . . 102 A4
Westminster Acad (Sch of English) W1 . . . . 105 A2
Westminster Boating Base SW1 . . . . 161 B4
Westminster Bridge SE1, SW1 . . . . 134 B3
Westminster Bridge Rd SE1 . . . . 134 C3
Westminster Cath* SW1 . . . . 132 C1
Westminster Cath Choir Sch SW1 . . 147 A4
Westminster Cath RC Prim Sch SW1 . . . 147 C2
Westminster City Hall SW1 . . . . 133 A2
Westminster City Sch SW1 . . . . 133 A2
Westminster Ct
22 Rotherhithe SE16 . . . . 32 C1
5 Wandsworth SW18 . . . . 58 C2
Westminster Gdns SW1 . . . . 148 A4
Westminster Kingsway Coll
Battersea SW11 . . . 169 C4
St Pancras WC1 . . . . 94 C3
Westminster Kingsway Coll (Regent's Park Ctr) NW1 . . . . 92 C2
Westminster Pier SW1 . . . . 134 B3
Westminster Sch SW1 . . . . 134 A2
Westminster Sta SW1 . . . . 134 B3
Westminster Under Sch SW1 . . . . 147 B3
Westmore Ct SW15 . . . . 58 A2
Westmoreland Ho NW10 . . . . 21 C2
Westmoreland Pl SW1 . . . . 146 B1
Westmoreland Rd
Barnes SW13 . . . . 46 C2
Camberwell SE17 . . . . 48 C4
Westmoreland St W1 . . . . 103 C3
Westmoreland Terr SW1 . . . . 146 B1
WEST NORWOOD 75 B1
West Norwood Sta SE27 . . . . 75 A1
Westonbirt Ct 6 SE15 . . . . 49 B4
Weston Ct N4 . . . . 6 B1
Weston Ed Ctr The SE5 . . . . 48 B1
West One Ho W1 104 C3
West One Sh Ctr W1 . . . . 104 A1
Weston Ho
6 Brondesbury NW6 . . . . 10 A1
8 South Hackney E9 . . . . 25 B4
Weston Rd W4 . . . . 37 B3
Weston Rise N1, WC1 . . . . 95 A4
Weston St SE1 . . . 137 C4
Weston Wlk 3 E8, E9 . . . . 17 A1
Westover Hill NW3 . . 1 C2
Westover Rd SW18 . . . . 59 B1
West Park Ave TW9 . . . . 45 A2
West Park Rd TW9 . . . . 44 C2
West Parkside
Greenwich SE10 . . . . 43 B3
Greenwich SE10 . . . . 43 C2
West Plaza E14 . . . . 34 A1
Westpoint SW15 . . . . 57 C1
West Point SE1 . . . . 153 B2
Westpoint Trad Est W3 . . . . 28 A4
Westport St E1 . . . . 32 C3
West Poultry Ave EC1 . . . . 108 A3
West Quarters W12 . . . . 29 C3
West Rd
Chelsea SW3 . . . . 159 A4
Clapham Pk SW4 . . . . 61 C2
Westrow SW15 . . . . 57 B1
West Row W10 . . . . 23 A1
West Sheen Vale TW9 . . . . 54 B3
Westside 11 W6 . . . . 38 C2
Westside Ct 1 W9 . . . . 23 C1
West Silvertown Sta E16 . . . . 35 C1
West Smithfield EC1 . . . . 108 B3
West Sq SE11 . . . . 136 A1
West St
30 Bethnal Green E2 . . . . 25 A3
Soho WC2 . . . . 105 C1
West Temple Sheen SW14 . . . . 55 A2
West Tenter St E1 . . . . 111 A1
Westvale Mews W3 . . . . 38 A4
Westview Cl
North Kensington W10 . . . . 30 B3
Willesden NW10 . . . . 8 B3
Westville Rd W12 . . 38 C4
West Warwick Pl SW1 . . . . 146 C3
Westway W10, W12 . . . . 29 C2
Westway (Elevated Rd) W10 . . . . 31 B4
Westway Lo 35 W2 . . . . 31 C4
Westwell 4 NW5 . . . 12 C2
Westwick Gdns W14 . . . . 39 C4
Westwood Bsns Ctr NW10 . . . . 21 A1
Westwood Gdns SW13 . . . . 56 B4
Westwood Ho
6 Shepherd's Bush W12 . . . . 30 B1
5 Stoke Newington N4 . . . . 6 C4
Westwood Park Trad Est W3 . . . . 20 A1
Westwood Rd SW13 . . . . 56 B4
Wetherby Gdns SW5 . . . . 142 C3
Wetherby Mans SW5 . . . . 142 A2
Wetherby Mews SW5 . . . . 142 B2
Wetherby Pl SW7 143 A3
Wetherell Rd E9 . . . 25 C4
Wevco Wharf SE15 . . . . 50 A4
Wexford Ho 11 E1 . . 32 B4
Wexford Rd SW12 . . 72 B4
Weybourne St SW18 . . . . 71 B2
Weybridge Ct 19 SE16 . . . . 40 A1
Weybridge Ho N4 . . . 6 B4
Weybridge Point SW11 . . . . 169 A2
Weydown Cl SW19 . . . . 70 A3
Weyhill Ho 28 SE5 . . 48 B1
Weyhill Rd E1 . . . . 111 C2
Wey Ho NW8 . . . . 89 C1

Weymouth Ct
[5] Haggerston E2 ... 24 B3
[15] Streatham SW2 ... 74 B4
Weymouth Ho
Fitzrovia W1 ... 104 B4
South Lambeth SW8 ... 162 C1
Weymouth Mews W1 ... 104 A4
Weymouth St W1 104 A4
Weymouth Terr E2 ... 24 B3
Whadcoat St N4 ... 5 C2
Whaddon Ho
[10] Camberwell SE5 ... 64 A4
SW1 ... 131 A3
Wharfdale Rd N1 .. 84 B2
Wharfedale Ct [5] E5 ... 17 C4
Wharfedale St SW10 ... 142 A1
Wharf La [19] E14 ... 33 B3
Wharf Pl E2 ... 25 A4
Wharf Rd
King's Cross NW1 .. 83 C3
Shoreditch N1 ... 86 C1
Wharf Road NW1 .. 84 A2
Wharfside Rd E16 .. 35 A4
Wharf St E16 ... 35 A4
Wharf View Ct [15] E14 ... 34 B3
Wharncliffe Ho [3] SW15 ... 57 B2
Wharton Cl NW10 ... 8 A2
Wharton Ho SE1 . 138 C2
Wharton St WC1 .. 95 A3
Whateley Rd SE22 .. 64 B2
Whatman Ho [10] E14 ... 33 B3
Wheatland Ho [7] SE22 ... 64 A4
Wheatlands Rd SW17 ... 72 C1
Wheatley Ho
Gospel Oak NW5 ... 13 A4
[3] Putney SW15 ... 68 C4
Wheatley St W1 .. 103 C3
Wheat Sheaf Cl E14 ... 42 A2
Wheatsheaf La
Fulham SW6 ... 47 B3
SW8 ... 162 B2
Wheatsheaf Terr SW6 ... 155 A1
Wheatstone Ho [7] W10 ... 31 A4
Wheatstone Rd W10 ... 31 A4
Wheeler Ct [5] SW11 ... 59 C4
Wheeler Gdns N1 . 84 B4
Wheeler La E1 ... 110 C4
Wheelhouse The [4] E14 ... 42 A1
Wheelwright St N7 ... 14 B1
Wheldon Ct SE1 .. 138 C4
Wheler Ho E1 ... 24 B1 98 C1
Wheler St E1 ... 24 B1 98 C1
Whellock Rd W4 ... 38 A3
Whetstone Park WC2 ... 106 C2
Whewell Rd N19 ... 5 A2
Whichcote St SE1 ... 121 B1
Whidborne Bldgs WC1 ... 94 A3
Whidborne Cl SE8 .. 51 C1
Whidborne St WC1 ... 94 B3
Whippingham Ho [22] E3 ... 26 B2
Whiskin St EC1 ... 96 A3
Whistler Mews [23] SE15 ... 49 B3
Whistlers Ave SW11 ... 157 C1
Whistler St N5 ... 15 A3
Whistler Twr SW10 ... 156 C1
Whistler Wlk SW10 ... 157 A2
Whiston Ho [18] N1 .. 15 A1
Whiston Rd E2 ... 24 C4
Whitbread Ctr EC1 97 B1
Whitbread Rd SE4 .. 66 B3
Whitburn Rd SE13 .. 67 B3
Whitby Ave NW10 .. 20 A2
Whitby Ct [6] N7 ... 14 A4
Whitby Ho NW8 ... 78 C3
Whitby St E1 ... 24 B1 98 C2
Whitcher Cl SE14 ... 51 A4
Whitcher Pl NW1 ... 13 B2
Whitchurch Ho [16] W10 ... 30 C3
Whitchurch Rd W11 ... 30 C2
Whitcomb Ct W1 119 C3
Whitcomb St WC2 ... 119 C3
Whitcome Mews TW9 ... 45 A2
Whiteacre Mews SE11 ... 149 C1
Whiteadder Way E14 ... 42 A2
Whitear Wlk E15 ... 19 C2
Whitebeam Cl SW9 ... 163 A1
Whitebeam Ho [3] NW3 ... 12 B2
White Bear Pl [1] NW3 ... 11 C4
White Bear Yd EC1 ... 95 B1
WHITECHAPEL .. 110 C1
Whitechapel High St E1 ... 111 A2
Whitechapel Mkt E1 ... 111 C3
Whitechapel Rd E1 ... 32 A4
Whitechapel Sta E1 ... 32 A4
Whitechurch La E1 ... 111 B2
Whitechurch Pas E1 ... 111 B2
White City W10 ... 30 B3
White City Cl W12 .. 30 B2
White City Est W12 ... 30 A2
White City Rd W12 ... 30 B2
White City Sta W12 ... 30 B2
Whitecliff Ho SW18 ... 59 A1
White Conduit St N1 ... 85 C2
Whitecross Pl EC2 ... 109 C4
Whitecross St EC1. 97 A1
White Cube The, Art Gallery★ N1 ... 24 A2 98 A3
Whitefield Cl SW15 ... 58 A1
Whitefriars St EC4 ... 107 C1
Whitehall SW1 ... 134 A4
Whitehall Ct SW1 120 B1
Whitehall Gdns
Chiswick W4 ... 45 A4
SW1 ... 120 A1
Whitehall Mans [3] N19 ... 4 B3
Whitehall Park Rd W4 ... 45 A4
Whitehall Pk N19 ... 4 B3
Whitehall Pl WC2, SW1 ... 120 A1
White Hart La
Mortlake SW13 ... 56 A4
Willesden NW10 ... 8 B2
White Hart St
Holborn EC4 ... 108 B2
Kennington SE11 .. 149 C2
White Hart Yd SE1 ... 123 B1
Whitehaven St NW8 ... 90 A1
Whitehead Cl SW18 ... 71 B4
Whitehead Ho [8] SW15 ... 57 C2
Whitehead's Gr SW3 ... 144 B3
White Ho
Battersea SW11 ... 167 C2
[3] Streatham SW4 .. 73 C4
Whitehorn Ho [6] E1 ... 32 B1
White Horse La E1 ... 32 C4
Whitehorse Mews SE1 ... 136 A2
Whitehorse Rd E1 .. 33 A4
White Horse Rd E1 ... 33 A3
White Horse St W1 ... 118 B1
White Horse Yd EC2 ... 109 B2
White Ho The NW1 ... 92 B2
White Kennett St E1 ... 110 B2
Whitelands Cres SW18 ... 70 A4
Whitelands Ho SW3 ... 145 A2
Whiteley Ho [9] SW4 ... 73 C4
Whiteleys Ctr W2 100 B1
White Lion Ct EC3 ... 110 A1
White Lion Hill EC4 ... 122 B4
White Lion St N1 .. 85 C1
White Lo NW11 ... 1 B3
Whitelock Ho [21] E9 ... 17 C2
White Lyon Ct EC2 ... 108 C4
Whiteness Ho SW9 ... 173 B4
White Post La E9 .. 18 C2
White Post St SE14, SE15 ... 50 B3
White's Grounds SE1 ... 138 B4
White's Grounds Est SE1 ... 138 B4
White's Row E1 .. 110 C3
White's Sq SW4 ... 61 C3
Whitestone La NW3 . 2 B1
Whitestone Wlk NW3 ... 2 B1
Whitethorn St E3 .. 33 C4
Whitfield Ct SW4 172 A3
Whitfield Gdns W1 ... 105 A4
Whitfield Ho NW8 . 90 A1
Whitfield Pl W1 ... 93 A1
Whitfield St W1 ... 105 A4
Whitgift Ho
Battersea SW11 ... 168 A4
Lambeth SE11 ... 148 C4
Whitgift St SE11 .. 148 C4
Whitington Ave EC3 ... 110 A1
Whitley Ho SW1 .. 161 A4
Whitlock Dr SW19 .. 70 A3
Whitman Ho [20] E2 ... 25 B2
Whitman Rd E3 ... 26 A1
Whitmore Gdns NW10 ... 22 B3
Whitmore Ho [20] E1 ... 24 A4
Whitmore Prim Sch N1 ... 87 C3
Whitmore Rd N1 ... 24 A4
Whitnell Ct [7] SW15 ... 57 C2
Whitnell Way SW15 ... 57 C2
Whitney Ho [6] SE22 ... 64 A4
Whitstable Ho [11] W10 ... 30 C3
Whitsters Ho SE1 138 C4
Whittaker Ct SW4 ... 172 B3
Whittaker St SW1 145 B3
Whittaker Way SE1 ... 153 C4
Whittingham Ct W4 ... 46 A3
Whittingstall Mans SW6 ... 165 A3
Whittingstall Rd SW6 ... 165 A3
Whittington Hospl The N19 ... 4 B2
Whittlebury Ho N4 .. 6 B4
Whittlesey St SE1 121 C1
Whitton NW3 ... 12 B1
Whitton Wlk E3 ... 26 C2
Whitworth Ho SE1 ... 137 A1
Whitworth St SE10 ... 43 A1
Whorlton Rd SE15 .. 65 A4
Whytlaw Ho [10] E3 .. 33 B4
Wicker St [24] E1 ... 32 A3
Wickfield Ho SE16 ... 139 C3
Wickford Ho [5] E1 ... 25 B1
Wickford St E1 ... 25 B1
Wickham Cl E1 ... 32 B4
Wickham Gdns SE4 ... 66 B4
Wickham Ho SW15 ... 57 C1
Wickham Mews SE4 ... 51 B1
Wickham Rd SE4 ... 66 B4
Wickham St SE11 148 C2
Wick La
Hackney E3 ... 18 B1
Stratford Marsh E3 .. 26 C4
Wicklow Ho N16 ... 7 B3
Wicklow St WC1 .. 94 C4
Wick Rd
Hackney E9 ... 17 C2
Hackney E9 ... 18 A2
Wickstead Ho TW8 ... 36 B1
Wicksteed Ho SE1 ... 137 A1
Wickway Ct [7] SE15 ... 49 B4
Wickwood St SE5 .. 48 A1
Widdenham Rd N7 ... 14 B4
Widecombe Ho [32] SE5 ... 48 B1
Widegate St E1 .. 110 B3
Widford [8] NW1 ... 13 A2
Widford Ho N1 ... 86 A1
Widley Rd W9 ... 23 C1
Widnes Ho [6] N7 ... 14 C3
Wigmore Hall★ W1 ... 104 A2
Wigmore Pl W1 ... 104 A2
Wigmore St W1 .. 103 C2
Wigram Ct SW11 . 168 A4
Wigram Ho [7] E14 ... 34 A2
Wigton Pl SE11 ... 149 C1
Wilberforce Ho [4] SW11 ... 59 C4
Wilberforce Mews [9] SW4 ... 61 C3
Wilberforce Prim Sch W10 ... 23 A2
Wilberforce Rd
Finsbury Pk N4 ... 6 A2
Highbury N4, N5 ... 6 B1
Wilbraham Ho SW8 ... 162 A1
Wilbraham Pl SW1 ... 145 B4
Wilby Mews W11 ... 31 B1 113 A2
Wilcox Cl SW8 ... 162 B2
Wilcox Ho [5] E3 ... 33 B4
Wilcox Pl SW1 ... 133 A1
Wilcox Rd SW8 ... 162 A2
Wildcroft Manor SW15 ... 69 B4
Wildcroft Rd SW15 ... 69 B4
Wild Ct WC2 ... 106 C2
Wilde Cl E8 ... 24 C4
Wilde Pl SW18 ... 71 C4
Wilderness Mews SW4 ... 61 A3
Wilderton Rd N16 ... 7 A4
Wild Goose Dr SE14 ... 50 B2
Wilding Ho [17] E9 ... 17 C2
Wild's Rents SE1 . 138 A2
Wild St WC2 ... 106 C1
Wildwood Gr NW3 ... 2 B3
Wildwood Rd NW11 . 2 B4

Wildwood Rise NW11 2 B3
Wildwood Terr NW3 2 B3
Wilfred Fienburgh Ho N7 13 C4
Wilfred St SW1 132 C2
Wilfrid Gdns W3 28 B4
Wilkes Rd 3 TW8 44 A4
Wilkes St E1 111 A4
Wilkie Ho SW1 147 C2
Wilkins Ho SW1 160 C4
Wilkinson Ho N1 87 C1
Wilkinson St SW8 162 C1
Wilkinson Way W4 37 C4
Wilkin St NW5 13 A2
Wilks Pl N1 24 A3
Willan Wall E16 35 B2
Willard St SW8 61 A4
Willbury Ho 4 N7 13 C3
Willcott Rd W3 28 A1
Willenfield Rd NW10 20 B3
WILLESDEN 8 B1
Willesden Community Hospl The NW10 8 C1
WILLESDEN GREEN 22 A4
Willesden Green Sta NW2 9 B2
Willesden Junction Sta NW10 21 B2
Willesden La NW2, NW6 9 C2
Willes Rd NW5 13 A2
Willett Ho SW9 62 A4
William Banfield Ho SW6 164 C2
William Blake Ho 2 SE15 49 C1
William Bonney Est 10 SW4 61 C3
William Booth Meml Training Coll SE5 48 C1
William Brown Ct SE27 75 A2
William Caslon Ho 23 E2 25 A3
William Channing Ho 6 E2 25 A2
William Cl SE13 67 B4
William Davis Prim Sch E2 24 C1 99 B2
William Dromey Ct NW6 10 B1
William Dunbar Ho NW6 23 B3
William Ellis Sch NW5 3 C1
William Ellis Way SE16 139 C1
William Evans Ho 9 SE8 40 C2
William Gdns SW15 57 A2
William Guy Gdns 17 E3 27 A2
William Harvey Ho 1 SW19 70 A3
William Hogarth Prim Sch The W4 38 A1
William Hunt Mans SW13 47 B4
William IV St WC2 120 A3
William Margrie Cl 1 SE15 49 C1
William Mews SW1 131 A3
William Morris Acad W6 39 C1
William Morris Ho W6 47 C4
William Morris Way SW6 166 C1
William Patten Prim Sch N16 7 B2
William Pl 37 E3 26 B3
William Rathbone Ho 3 E2 25 A2
William Rd NW1 92 C3
William Rushbrooke Ho SE16 153 B4
William Saville Ho 2 NW6 23 B3
William's Bldgs 1 E2 25 B1
Williams Cl SW6 154 B2
Williams Coll EC1 107 C3
Williams Ho
10 Bow E3 26 C2
9 Hackney E9 25 A4
14 Streatham SW2 74 C3
Williams La SW14 45 B1
Williamson Cl SE10 43 B1
Williamson Ct SE17 150 C1
Williamson St N7 14 A4
William Sq 15 SE16 33 A2
William St SW1 131 A3
William Tyndale Prim Sch N1 15 A1
William Winter Ct 29 SW2 74 C4
Willingham Cl 4 NW5 13 B3
Willingham Terr NW5 13 B3
Willington Rd SW9 62 A4
Willis Ho 8 E14 34 A2
Willis St E14 34 A3
Willoughby Ho
EC2 109 B3
34 Wapping E1 32 A1
Willoughby Rd NW3 11 C4
Willoughby St WC1 106 A3
Willoughbys The SW14 56 A3
Willow Ave SW13 46 B1
Willowbank SW6 58 A4
Willowbank Rd SE15 49 B4
Willow Bridge Rd N1 15 B2
Willow Cotts TW9 44 C4
Willow Ct
Brixton SW9 173 B3
Chiswick W4 46 A3
EC2 24 A1 98 A2
Islington N7 14 B3
40 Paddington W2 31 C4
3 Streatham SW16 74 B1
Willowdene
Highgate N6 3 B4
1 Peckham SE15 50 A2
5 SE15 50 A3
Willow Farm La SW15 57 A4
Willow Hall NW3 11 C4
Willow Ho
9 Maitland Pk NW3 12 B2
North Kensington W10 22 C1
Willow Lo
Fulham SW6 47 C2
Putney SW15 57 A4
Willow Lodge 10 SW8 61 A4
Willowmere SE13 67 A2
Willow Pl SW1 147 A4
Willow Rd
Ealing W5 36 A4
Hampstead NW3 11 C4
Willow St EC2 24 A1 98 A2
Willows Terr NW10 21 B3
Willow Tree Cl
14 Old Ford E3 26 B4
Wandsworth SW18 71 A3
Willow Vale W12 29 C1
Willow Way 9 W11 30 C2
Willow Wlk SE1 152 C4
Willsbridge Ct 1 SE15 49 B4
Wilman Gr E8 16 C1
Wilmcote Ho W2 100 A4
Wilmer Gdns 22 N1 24 A4
Wilmer Ho 6 E3 26 A3
Wilmer Lea Cl E15 19 C1
Wilmer Pl N16 7 B2
Wilmers Ct 5 NW10 20 C4
Wilmington Ave W4 45 C3
Wilmington Sq WC1 95 B3
Wilmington St WC1 95 B3
Wilmot Cl SE15 49 C3
Wilmot Pl NW1 13 B1
Wilmot St E2 25 A1
Wilna Rd SW18 71 B4
Wilsham St W11 31 A1 112 A2
Wilshaw Ho 10 SE8 51 C3
Wilshaw St SE14 51 C2
Wilson Gr SE16 40 A4
Wilson Ho
Clapham SW8 171 B1
South Hampstead NW6 11 B1
Wilson Rd SE5 49 A2
Wilson's Pl E14 33 B3
Wilson's Rd W6 39 C1
Wilson St EC2 109 C4
Wiltern Ct NW2 10 A2
Wilton Ave W4 38 A1
Wilton Cres SW1 131 B3
Wilton Ct
4 Richmond TW10 54 A2
7 Stepney E1 32 A3
Wilton Est E8 16 C2
Wilton Ho 8 SE22 64 A4
Wilton Mews SW1 131 C2
Wilton Pl SW1 131 B3
Wilton Rd SW1 146 C4
Wilton Row SW1 131 B3
Wilton Sq N1 87 B4
Wilton St SW1 132 A2
Wilton Terr SW1 131 B2
Wilton Villas N1 87 B3
Wilton Way E8 16 C2
Wiltshire Cl SW3 144 C3
Wiltshire Ct 2 N4 5 B3
Wiltshire Rd SW9 62 C4
Wiltshire Row N1 87 C3
Wimbart Rd SW2 74 B4
Wimbledon Lawn Tennis Mus★ SW19 70 A1
Wimbledon Park Ct SW19 70 B3
Wimbledon Park Montessori Sch SW18 70 C2
Wimbledon Park Prim Sch SW19 71 A2
Wimbledon Park Rd SW18, SW19 70 B3
Wimbledon Park Side SW19 69 C3
Wimbledon Park Sta SW19 70 C1
Wimbledon Stadium Bsns Ctr SW17 71 A1
Wimbledon Windmill Mus★ SW19 69 B1
Wimbolt St E2 24 C2 99 B4
Wimborne Ho
Canning Town E16 35 B2
Marylebone NW1 90 B1
South Lambeth SW8 163 A1
Upper Tooting SW12 73 B1
Wimbourne Ct N1 87 B2
Wimbourne St N1 87 B2
Wimpole Mews W1 104 A3
Wimpole St W1 104 A2
Winans Wlk SW9 173 B1
Winant Ho 19 E14 34 A2
Wincanton Rd SW18 70 B4
Winchelsea Cl SW15 57 C2
Winchelsea Ho 16 SE16 40 B4
Winchelsea Rd NW10 20 C4
Winchendon Rd SW6 165 A4
Winchester Ave NW6 10 A1
Winchester Cl SE17 150 B3
Winchester Ct
Richmond TW9 54 B4
W8 128 A4
Winchester Ho
Bayswater W2 100 C1
Chelsea SW3 157 C3
24 Tower Hamlets E3 26 B2
Winchester Pal★ SE1 123 B2
Winchester Pl
6 Dalston E8 16 B3
Highgate N6 4 A3
Winchester Rd
Highgate N6 4 A3
Winchester Rd *continued*
South Hampstead NW3 11 C1
Winchester Sq SE1 123 B2
Winchester St
Acton W3 37 B4
SW1 146 B2
Winchester Wlk SE1 123 B2
Winchfield Ho SW15 56 B1
Winch Ho
Isle of Dogs E14 42 A3
SW10 157 A2
Winchilsea Ho NW8 89 C3
Wincott St SE11 149 C3
Windermere NW1 92 B4
12 Putney SW15 57 C1
Windermere Ave NW6 23 A4
Windermere Ct SW13 46 B4
Windermere Ho E3 26 B1
Windermere Point 3 SE15 50 B3
Windermere Rd N19 4 B2
Winders Rd SW11 168 A2
Windham Rd TW9 54 B4
Windlass Pl SE8 41 A2
Windlesham Gr SW19 69 C3
Windmill WC1 106 C4
Windmill Alley 7 W4 38 A2
Windmill Cl
Bermondsey SE1 153 C4
4 Lewisham SE13 52 B1
Windmill Ct NW2 10 A2
Windmill Dr
Clapham SW4 61 A2
Cricklewood NW2 1 A1
Windmill Gdns SW2 62 B1
Windmill Hill
Hampstead NW3 2 B1
1 Hampstead NW3 11 B4
Windmill Ho
4 Millwall E14 41 C2
SE1 121 C1
Windmill La E15 19 C2
Windmill Pas 10 W4 38 A2
Windmill Rd
Chiswick W4 38 A2
Roehampton SW19 69 A1
Wandsworth SW18 59 C1
Windmill Row SE11 149 B1
Windmill St W1 105 B3
Windmill Wlk SE1 135 C4
Windrose Cl SE16 40 C4
Windrush Cl
Battersea SW11 59 C3
Chiswick W4 45 B3
Windrush Ho NW8 101 C4
Windrush Rd NW10 20 C4

Windsock Cl 1 SE16 . . . 41 B2
Windsor Ct
Battersea SW11 . . . 167 C2
Bayswater W2 . . . 114 A4
Chelsea SW3 . . . 144 B2
2 Clapham SW4 . . . 61 B3
Fulham SW6 . . . 58 A4
20 Rotherhithe SE16 . . . 32 C1
4 Wandsworth SW18 . . . 58 C2
West Hampstead NW3 . . . 10 C4
Windsor Gdns W9 . . 23 C1
Windsor Ho
4 Acton Green W4 . . . 37 B1
Brondesbury NW2 . . . 10 A2
4 Globe Town E2 . . . 25 C2
Regent's Pk NW1 . . . 92 B4
Shoreditch N1 . . . 87 A2
Stoke Newington N4 . . 6 B3
Windsor Pl SW1 . . 147 A4
Windsor Rd
Richmond TW9 . . . 44 B1
Upper Holloway N7 . . . 5 A1
Willesden NW2 . . . 9 A2
Windsor St N1 . . . 86 B4
Windsor Terr N1 . . . 97 A4
Windsor Way W14 . . . 140 A4
Windsor Wharf E9 . 18 B3
Windsor Wlk SE5 . . . 48 C1
Windspoint Dr SE15 . . . 50 A4
Windus Rd N16 . . . 7 B3
Windus Wlk N16 . . . 7 B3
Wine Cl E1 . . . 32 B2
Wine Office Ct EC4 . . . 107 C2
Winfield Ho SW11 . . . 167 C2
Winford Ct 16 SE15 . . . 49 C2
Winford Ho E3 . . . 18 B1
Winforton St SE10 . . 52 B2
Winfrith Rd SW18 . . 71 B3
Wingate Ho
26 Bromley E3 . . . 27 A2
8 Stoke Newington N16 . . . 15 C4
Wingate Rd W6 . . . 39 A3
Wingfield Ct 5 E14 . . . 34 C2
Wingfield Ho
Paddington NW6 . . . 78 A2
Spitalfields E2 . . . 24 B2 98 C3
Wingfield Mews SE15 . . . 64 C4
Wingfield St SE15 . . 64 C4
Wingford Rd SW2 . . 62 A1
Wingham 3 NW5 . . 12 C2
Wingmore Rd SE24 . . . 63 B4
Wingrad Ho 18 E1 . . 32 B4
Wingrave SE17 . . . 151 B3
Wingrave Rd W6 . . . 47 B4
Wingreen NW8 . . . 78 B4
Winicotte Ho W2 101 C4
Winifrede Paul Ho 7 NW5 . . . 13 A4
Winkley St 6 E2 . . . 25 A3
Winkworth Cotts 14 E1 . . . 25 B1
Winnett St W1 . . . 119 B4
Winnington Ho
19 Kensal Town W10 . . . 23 A1
8 SE5 . . . 48 B3
Winscombe St N19 . . 4 A2
Winsham Gr SW11 . . . 60 C2
Winsham Ho NW1 . 93 C4
Winslade Rd SW2 . . 62 A2
Winsland Mews W2 . . . 101 B2
Winsland St W2 . . 101 B2
Winsley St W1 . . . 105 A2
Winslow SE17 . . . 152 A1
Winslow Rd W6 . . . 47 B4
Winstanley Rd SW11 . . . 59 C4
Winston Ho WC1 . . . 93 C2
Winston Rd N16 . . . 15 C4
Winston Wlk 2 W4 . . . 37 C2
Winterbourne Ho W11 . . . 31 A2 112 A3
Winter Box Wlk TW10 . . . 54 B2
Winterbrook Rd SE24 . . . 63 B1
Winterfold Cl SW19 . . . 70 A2
Winterleys 7 NW6 . . . 23 B3
Winter Lo SE16 . . . 153 C1
Winterslow Ho 20 SE5 . . . 48 B1
Winterton Ho 15 E1 . . . 32 B3
Winterton Pl SW10 . . . 157 A4
Winterwell Rd SW2 . . . 62 A2
Winthorpe Rd SW15 . . . 58 A3
Winthrop Ho 10 W12 . . . 30 A2
Winthrop St E1 . . . 32 A4
Winton Prim Sch N1 . . . 84 C1
Wirrall Ho 15 SE26 . . . 76 C1
Wisbech 5 N4 . . . 5 B3
Wisden Ho SW8 . . 163 A3
Wise Rd E15 . . . 27 C4
Wiseton Rd SW17 . . 72 B3
Wisley Ho SW1 . . . 147 B2
Wisley Rd SW11 . . . 60 C2
Wisteria Ho SE4 . . . 66 A4
Wisteria Rd SE13 . . . 67 C3
Wistow Ho 14 E2 . . . 24 C4
Witanhurst La N6 . . . 3 C3
Witan St E2 . . . 25 A2
Witchwood Ho 10 SW9 . . . 62 C4
Witcombe Point 14 SE15 . . . 49 C2
Witham Ct SW17 . . . 72 B1
Witham Ho 34 SE5 . . 48 B1
Witherington Rd N5 . . . 14 C3
Withers Pl EC1 . . . 97 A2
Withycombe Rd SW19 . . . 69 C4
Withy Ho 4 E1 . . . 25 C1
Witley Ct WC1 . . . 94 A1
Witley Ho 2 SW2 . . 74 B4
Witley Point 8 SW15 . . . 69 A3
Witley Rd N19 . . . 4 B2
Wittering Ho SW11 . . . 169 A2
Wivenhoe Cl SE15 . . 65 A4
Wix Prim Sch SW4 . . . 61 A3
Wix's La SW4 . . . 61 A3
Woburn Ct
32 Bermondsey SE16 . . . 40 A1
Richmond TW9 . . . 54 B4
Woburn Pl WC1 . . . 94 A1
Woburn Sq WC1 . . . 93 C1
Woburn Wlk WC1 . 93 C3
Wodeham Gdns 1 E1 . . . 32 A4
Wodehouse Ave SE15 . . . 49 B2
Wodehouse Ct 10 W3 . . . 37 B3
Woking Cl SW15 . . . 56 B3
Wolcot Ho NW1 . . . 83 A1
Wolfe Cres 34 SE16 . . . 40 C4
Wolfe Ho 10 W12 . . . 30 A2
Wolfson Ct
Golders Green NW11 . . . 1 A4
SE1 . . . 139 A4
Wolftencroft Cl SW11 . . . 59 C4
Wollaston Cl SE1 150 C4
Wollotan Ho N1 . . . 85 C2
Wolseley Ave SW18, SW19 . . . 70 C2
Wolseley Gdns W4 . . . 45 A4
Wolseley Rd W4 . . . 37 B2
Wolseley St SE1 . . 139 A3
Wolsey Ct NW6 . . . 11 B1
Wolsey Ho 3 NW5 . . . 13 C2
Wolsey Mews NW5 . . . 13 B2
Wolsey Rd N1 . . . 15 C3
Wolsey St E1 . . . 32 B4
Wolverley St E2 . . . 25 A2
Wolverton SE17 . . 152 A2
Wolverton Gdns W6 . . . 39 C2
Wontner Cl 5 N1 . . 15 B1
Wontner Rd SW12, SW17 . . . 72 B2
Woodall Cl 15 E14 . . 34 A2
Woodberry Down N4 . . . 6 B4
Woodberry Down Com Prim Sch N4 . . 6 B4
Woodberry Gr N4 . . . 6 B4
Woodbine Terr E9 . . 17 B2
Woodborough Rd SW15 . . . 57 A3
Woodbourne Ave SW16 . . . 73 C1
Woodbourne Cl SW16 . . . 74 A1
Woodbridge Cl 10 N7 . . . 5 B2
Woodbridge Ct N16 . . . 6 C1
Woodbridge St EC1 . . . 96 A2
Woodchester Sq W2 . . . 100 A4
Woodchurch Ho SW9 . . . 173 B4
Woodchurch Rd NW6 . . . 11 A1
Wood Cl E2 . . 24 C1 99 B2
Woodcock Ho 4 E14 . . . 33 C4
Woodcote Ho 4 SE8 . . . 51 B4
Woodcott Ho 1 SW15 . . . 68 C4
Woodcroft Mews SE8 . . . 41 A2
Wood Dene 6 SE15 . . . 50 A2
Woodfall Rd N4 . . . 5 C2
Woodfall St SW3 . 144 C1
Woodfarrs SE5 . . . 63 C3
Wood Field NW3 . . . 12 B3
Woodfield Ave SW16 . . . 73 C1
Woodfield Ct SW16 . . . 73 C1
Woodfield Gr SW16 . . . 73 C1
Woodfield Pl W9 . . . 23 B1
Woodfield Rd W9 . . 31 B4
Woodford Ct 15 W12 . . . 39 C4
Woodger Rd W12 . . 39 B4
Woodhall NW1 . . . 92 C3
Woodhall Ave SE21 . . . 76 B1
Woodhall Dr SE21 . . 76 B1
Woodhall Ho SW18 . . . 59 C1
Woodheyes Rd NW10 . . . 8 A3
Wood Ho
Clapham SW4 . . . 171 C2
6 Paddington NW6 . . 23 B3
Woodhurst Rd W3 . . 28 B2
Woodison St E3 . . . 26 A1
Wood La W12 . . . 30 B2
Woodland Cres
18 Rotherhithe SE16 . . . 40 C4
SE10 . . . 53 A4
Woodland Gr SE10 . . . 43 A1
Woodland Hts SE3 . . . 53 A4
Woodland Mews SW16 . . . 74 A1
Woodlands SW4 . . . 61 A3
Woodlands Ave W3 . . . 28 A1
Woodlands Ct NW10 . . . 22 C4
Woodlands Gt SW15 . . . 58 B2
Woodlands Park Rd SE10 . . . 53 A4
Woodlands Rd SW13 . . . 56 B4
Woodland St 2 E8 . . . 16 B2
Woodlands The
Highbury N5 . . . 15 B4
12 Hornsey N8 . . . 5 A4
Woodlands Way SW15 . . . 58 B2
Woodland Wlk
9 Greenwich SE10 . . . 43 A1
Hampstead NW3 . . . 12 A3
Wood Lane High Sch W12 . . . 30 A3
Woodlawn Cl SW15 . . . 58 B2
Woodlawn Rd SW6 . . . 47 C2
Woodlea Rd N16 . . . 7 A1
Woodleigh Gdns SW16 . . . 74 A1
Woodman Mews TW9 . . . 45 A2
Woodmans Gr NW10 . . . 8 B3
Woodmans Mews W12 . . . 30 A4
Woodmere Cl 11 SW11 . . . 60 C4
Woodpecker Mews SE13 . . . 67 C3
Woodpecker Rd 6 SE14 . . . 51 A4
Wood Point 8 E16 . . . 35 C4
Woodquest Ave SE24 . . . 63 B2
Woodruff Ho 12 SW2 . . . 62 C1
Woodrush Cl 4 SE14 . . . 51 A3
Woodseer St E1 . . . 111 B4
Woodsford SE17 . . . 151 B1
Woodsford Sq W14 . . . 126 B4
Woods Ho SW8 . . . 170 C4
Wood's Mews W1 117 B4
Woodsome Rd NW5 . . . 4 A1
Wood's Pl SE1 . . . 138 B1
Woodspring Rd SW19 . . . 70 A2
Wood's Rd SE15 . . . 50 A2
Wood St
Chiswick W4 . . . 38 A1
City of London EC2 109 A2
Woodstar Ho 3 SE15 . . . 49 C3
Woodstock Ave NW11 . . . 1 A4
Woodstock Ct SE11 . . . 149 A2
Woodstock Gr W12 . . . 39 C4
Woodstock Ho 2 N5 . . . 15 B4
Woodstock Mews W1 . . . 103 C3
Woodstock Rd
Bedford Pk W4 . . . 38 A3
Finsbury Pk N4 . . . 5 C3
Golders Green NW11 . . 1 B3
Woodstock St W1 . . . 104 A1
Woodstock Studios 17 W12 . . . 39 C4
Woodstock Terr E14 . . . 34 A2
Woodthorpe Rd SW15 . . . 57 A3
Woodview Cl N4 . . . 6 A4
Woodville Ct 3 SE10 . . . 52 B2
Woodville Ho SE1 138 C2
Woodville Rd
Golders Green NW11 . . . 1 A4
Paddington NW6 . . . 23 B3

Woodville Rd *continued*
Stoke Newington N16 ... 16 A3
Woodwarde Rd SE22 ... 64 A1
Woodwell St SW18 ... 59 B2
Wood Wharf SE10 ... 52 B4
Woodyard Cl NW5 ... 12 C3
Woodyard La SE21 ... 76 A4
Woolcombes Ct 4 SE16 ... 32 C1
Wooler St SE17 ... 151 C2
Woolf Ct 7 W3 ... 37 B3
Woolf Mews WC1 ... 94 A2
Woolley Ho SW9 ... 63 A4
Woollon Ho 1 E1 ... 32 B3
Woolmore Prim Sch E14 ... 34 B2
Woolmore St E14 ... 34 B2
Woolneigh St SW6 ... 166 A1
Woolpack Ho 1 E9 ... 17 B2
Woolridge Way E9 ... 17 B1
Woolstaplers Way SE16 ... 153 B4
Woolstone Ho 7 E2 ... 24 C4
Woolven Ho SE3 ... 53 B4
Wooster Gdns E14 ... 34 C3
Wooster Pl SE1 ... 151 C4
Wootton St SE1 ... 121 C1
Worcester Ct 44 W2 ... 31 C4
Worcester Dr W4 ... 38 A4
Worcester Gdns SW11 ... 60 B2
Worcester Ho
Bayswater W2 ... 100 C1
3 Islington N1 ... 15 B1
Lambeth SE11 ... 135 B1
9 Putney SW15 ... 69 B4
Worcester Mews 2 NW6 ... 11 A2
Wordsworth Ho NW6 ... 23 C2
Wordsworth Pl 11 NW5 ... 12 B3
Wordsworth Rd
Bermondsey SE1 ... 153 A3
Stoke Newington N16 ... 16 A4
Worfield St SW11 ... 158 B1
Worgan St
Rotherhithe SE16 ... 40 C2
SE11 ... 148 C2
Working Men's Coll The NW1 ... 83 A2
World's End Pas SW10 ... 157 B2
World's End Pl SW10 ... 157 A2
World Trade Ctr London E14 ... 42 A4
Worlidge St W6 ... 39 B1
Worlingham Rd SE22 ... 64 B3
Wormholt Park Prim Sch W12 ... 29 C2
Wormholt Rd W12 ... 29 C1
Wormwood St EC2 ... 110 A2
Wornington Rd W10 ... 31 A4
Woronzow Rd NW8 ... 80 A3
Worple St SW14 ... 55 C4
Worple Way TW10 ... 54 A3
Worship St EC2 ... 24 A1 98 A1
Worsley Gr E5 ... 16 C4
Worsopp Dr SW4 ... 61 B2
Worth Gr SE17 ... 151 B1
Worthington Ho EC1 ... 95 C4
16 Streatham SW2 ... 74 C4
Wotton Ct 14 E14 ... 34 C2
Wotton Rd 18 SE8 ... 51 B4
Wouldham Rd E16 ... 35 B3
Wrayburn Ho SE16 ... 139 C3
Wray Cres N4 ... 5 B2
Wray Ct N4 ... 5 B2
Wray Ho 11 SW2 ... 74 A3
Wren Ave NW2 ... 9 B4
Wren Cl E16 ... 35 B3
Wren Ho
29 Bow E3 ... 26 A3
SW1 ... 147 B1
Wren Landing E14 ... 33 C1
Wrenn Ho SW13 ... 47 B4
Wren Rd SE5 ... 48 C2
Wren St WC1 ... 95 A2
Wrentham Ave NW10 ... 22 C3
Wren View N6 ... 4 B3
Wrestlers Ct EC3 ... 110 A2
Wrexham Rd E3 ... 26 C3
Wrigglesworth St SE14 ... 50 C3
Wright Cl SE13 ... 67 C3
Wright Ho SW15 ... 57 A2
Wright's Gn SW4 ... 61 C3
Wright's La W8 ... 128 A2
Wright's Rd E3 ... 26 B3
Wrights Wlk SW14 ... 55 C4
Wrotham Ho SE1 ... 137 C2
Wrotham Rd 13 NW1 ... 13 B1
Wrottesley Rd NW10 ... 21 C3
Wroughton Rd SW11 ... 60 B1
Wroxton Rd SE15 ... 50 B1
Wr Twr Pl N1 ... 86 A3
Wulfstan St W12 ... 29 B3
Wyatt Cl SE16 ... 41 B4
Wyatt Dr SW13 ... 47 A3
Wyatt Ho
Blackheath Vale SE3 ... 53 B1
NW8 ... 89 C1
Wyatt Park Mans 1 SW2 ... 74 A2
Wyatt Park Rd SW2 ... 74 B2
Wyatt Rd N5 ... 6 B1
Wybert St NW1 ... 92 C2
Wycherley Cl SE3 ... 53 B3
Wychwood End N6 ... 4 B4
Wychwood Ho N4 ... 6 B4
Wyclif Ct EC1 ... 96 A3
Wycliffe Ho 13 N16 ... 16 A4
Wyclif St EC1 ... 96 A3
Wycombe Ct SE3 ... 53 C3
Wycombe Gdns NW11 ... 1 C2
Wycombe Ho NW8 ... 90 A2
Wycombe Pl SW18 ... 59 B1
Wycombe Sq W8 ... 31 C1 113 B1
Wyersdale Ho N4 ... 6 B4
Wye St SW11 ... 167 C1
Wyfold Rd SW6 ... 154 A1
Wyke Rd E3 ... 18 C1
Wyldes Cl NW11 ... 2 B3
Wyllen Cl E1 ... 25 B1
Wymering Mans 9 W9 ... 23 C2
Wymering Rd W9 ... 23 C2
Wymondham Ct NW8 ... 79 C4
Wymond St SW15 ... 57 B4
Wynan Rd E14 ... 42 A1
Wyndham Cres N19 ... 4 B1
Wyndham Deedes Ho 30 E2 ... 24 C3
Wyndham Ho SW1 ... 145 B3
Wyndham Mews W1 ... 102 C3
Wyndham Pl W1 ... 102 C3
Wyndham Rd SE5 ... 48 B3
Wyndhams Ct 4 E8 ... 16 B1
Wyndham St W1 ... 102 C4
Wyndham Yd W1 ... 102 C3
Wyneham Rd SE24 ... 63 C2
Wynford Rd N1 ... 85 A2
Wynne Ho SE14 ... 50 C2
Wynne Rd SW9 ... 173 B1
Wynnstay Gdns W8 ... 127 C2
Wynter Ho SW9 ... 173 A1
Wynter St SW11 ... 59 B3
Wynton Pl W3 ... 28 A3
Wynyard Ho SE11 ... 149 A2
Wynyard Terr SE11 ... 149 A2
Wynyatt Ho EC1 ... 96 A4
Wynyatt St EC1 ... 96 A4
Wytham Ho NW8 ... 89 C1
Wythburn Ct W1 ... 102 C2
Wythburn Pl W1 ... 102 C2
Wyvil Prim Sch SW8 ... 162 B2
Wyvil Rd SW8 ... 162 A2
Wyvis St E14 ... 34 A4

Y

Yabsley St E14 ... 34 B1
Yaldam Ho SE1 ... 152 A3
Yalding Ho 20 E5 ... 17 A3
Yalding Rd SE16 ... 153 B4
Yale Ct NW6 ... 11 A3
Yardley St WC1 ... 95 B3
Yard The N1 ... 84 B1
Yarmouth Pl W1 ... 118 A1
Yarnfield Sq 15 SE15 ... 49 C2
Yarrow Ho
12 Cubitt Town E14 ... 42 B3
16 North Kensington W10 ... 30 B4
Yatesbury Ct E5 ... 18 A3
Yates Ct NW2 ... 9 C2
Yates Ho E2 ... 24 C2 99 C4
Yatton Ho 15 W10 ... 30 B4
Yeadon Ho 14 W10 ... 30 B4
Yearby Ho W10 ... 22 B1
Yeate St N1 ... 15 C1
Yeats Cl NW10 ... 8 A2
Yeldham Ho W6 ... 39 C1
Yeldham Rd W6 ... 39 C1
Yelverton Rd SW11 ... 167 C1
Yeoman Cl SE27 ... 75 A1
Yeoman's Row SW3 ... 130 B1
Yeoman St SE8 ... 41 A2
Yeoman's Yd E1 ... 125 A4
Yeo St E3 ... 34 A4
Yeovil Ho
Finsbury Pk N7 ... 5 B2
North Kensington W10 ... 22 B1
Yerbury Prim Sch N19 ... 4 C1
Yerbury Rd N19 ... 4 C1
Yeshivo Horomo Tadmudical Coll N16 ... 6 C3
Yesodey Hatorah Sch N16 ... 7 B4
Yet Lev Ct E5 ... 7 C3
Yewfield Rd NW10 ... 8 B2
Yew Gr NW2 ... 9 C4
Yew Ho SE14 ... 51 B1
Yew Tree Cl 3 SE13 ... 67 B4
Yew Tree Ct 8 N16 ... 6 C2
Yew Tree Rd W12 ... 29 B2
Yoakley Rd N16 ... 7 A2
Yoke Cl N7 ... 14 A2
Yonge Pk N4, N7 ... 5 C1
York Ave
Mortlake SW14 ... 55 B2
Walworth SE17 ... 151 A2
York Bldgs WC2 ... 120 B3
York Bridge NW1 ... 91 B2
York Cl 17 SE5 ... 48 B1
York Gate NW1 ... 91 C1
York Gr SE15 ... 50 B2
York Hill SE27, SW16 ... 75 A1
York Ho Acton W3 ... 28 B2
Chelsea SW3 ... 145 A2
Islington N5 ... 14 C3
Kensington W8 ... 128 A4
11 Kentish Town N7 ... 13 C2
Kew TW9 ... 44 C2
Lambeth SE1 ... 135 A1
Marylebone W1 ... 102 C4
Pentonville N1 ... 84 C1
Richmond TW10 ... 54 C2
York House Pl W8 ... 128 A4
Yorkley Ho 3 W10 ... 22 B1
York Mans
Battersea SW11 ... 169 C4
Marylebone W1 ... 103 B4
Walworth SE17 ... 151 A2
York Mews NW5 ... 13 A3
York Pl
Battersea SW11 ... 59 C4
WC2 ... 120 B3
York Place Mans NW1 ... 103 A4
York Rd
Battersea SW11, SW18 ... 59 C4
Dagenham W3 ... 28 C3
4 Richmond TW10 ... 54 B2
SE1 ... 135 A4
York Rise NW5 ... 4 A1
York Road Bsns Ctr SW11 ... 167 B1
York St Chambers W1 ... 102 C4
Yorkshire Cl N16 ... 7 A1
Yorkshire Grey Pl 13 NW3 ... 11 B4
Yorkshire Grey Yd WC1 ... 106 C3
Yorkshire Rd E14 ... 33 A3
York Sq 12 E14 ... 33 A3
York St W1 ... 103 A4
York Terr E NW1 ... 91 C1
York Terr W NW1 ... 91 B1
Yorkton St E2 ... 24 C3
York Way
Barnsbury N1, N7, NW1 ... 14 A1
N1 ... 84 B3
York Way Ct
Islington N1 ... 84 C3
Islington N1 ... 84 B3
Young's Bldgs EC1 ... 97 A2
Youngs Brewery Visitor Ctr* SW18 ... 59 A2
Youngs Ct SW11 ... 169 C3
Young St W8 ... 128 A3
Yoxall Ho 2 W10 ... 22 B1
Yukon Rd SW12 ... 73 A4

Z

Zampa Rd SE16 ... 40 B1
Zander Ct E2 ... 24 C2 99 C4
Zangwill Ho NW6 ... 23 B3
Zealand Ho 11 SE5 ... 48 B1
Zealand Rd E3 ... 26 A3
Zennor Rd SW12 ... 73 B3
Zenoria St SE22 ... 64 B3
Zetland Ho W8 ... 128 A2
Zetland St E14 ... 34 B4
Zeus Ho N1 ... 97 B3
Zion Ho 6 E1 ... 32 B3
Zoar St SE1 ... 122 C2
Zodiac Ho 3 E3 ... 26 C1
Zoffany St N19 ... 4 C2

List of numbered locations

This atlas shows thousands more place names than any other London street atlas. In some busy areas it is impossible to fit the name of every place.

Where not all names will fit, some smaller places are shown by a number. If you wish to find out the name associated with a number, use this listing.

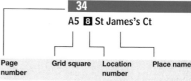

34
A5 8 St James's Ct
Page number — Grid square — Location number — Place name

1

B1 1 Mortimer Cl
2 Primrose Ct
3 Sunnyside Ho
4 Sunnyside
5 Prospect Pl
B4 1 Berkeley Ct
2 Exchange Mans
3 Beechcroft Ct
4 Nedahall Ct
C1 1 Portman Hts
2 Hermitage Ct
3 Moreland Ct
4 Wendover Ct

2

B1 1 Hampstead Sq
2 Stamford Cl
3 Mount Sq The

4

B1 1 Hunter Ho
2 Fisher Ho
3 Lang Ho
4 Temple Ho
5 Palmer Ho
6 Carlisle Ho
7 Durham Ho
8 Suffolk Ho
9 Lincoln Ho
10 Llewellyn Ho
11 Fell Ho
12 Aveling Ho
13 Merryweather Ct
14 Brennands Ct
15 St Christophers Ct
16 Francis Terrace Mews
B2 1 Flowers Mews
2 Archway Cl
3 Sandridge St
4 Bovingdon Cl
5 Cavell Ct
6 Torrence Ho
7 Rowan Wlk
8 Laurel Cl
9 Forest Way
10 Larch Cl
11 Pine Cl
12 Alder Mews
13 Aspen Cl
B3 1 Calvert Ct
2 Academy The
3 Whitehall Mans
4 Pauntley St
5 Archway Hts
6 Pauntley Ho
C1 1 Melchester Ho
2 Norcombe Ho
3 Weatherbury Ho
4 Wessex Ho
5 Archway Bsns Ctr
6 Harford Mews
7 Opera Ct
8 Rupert Ho
9 All Saints Church
C2 1 Bowerman Ct
2 Gresham Pl
3 Hargrave Mans
4 Church Garth
5 John King Ct
6 Ramsey Ct
C3 1 Louise White Ho
2 Levison Way
3 Sanders Way
4 Birbeck Ho
5 Scholars Ct
C4 1 Eleanor Rathbone Ho
2 Christopher Lo
3 Monkridge
4 Marbleford Ct
5 High London
6 Garton Ho
7 Hilltop Ho
8 Caroline Martyn Ho
9 Arthur Henderson Ho
10 Margaret Mcmillan Ho
11 Enid Stacy Ho
12 Mary McArthur Ho
13 Bruce Glasier Ho
14 John Wheatley Ho
15 Keir Hardie Ho
16 Monroe Ho
17 Iberia Ho
18 Lygoe Ho
19 Lambert Ho
20 Shelbourne Ho
21 Arkansas Ho
22 Lafitte Ho
23 Shreveport Ho
24 Packenham Ho
25 Orpheus Ho
26 Fayetville Ho
27 Bayon Ho

5

A1 1 Northview
2 Tufnell Park Mans
3 Fulford Mans
4 Tollington Ho
A2 1 Bracey Mews
2 Christie Ct
3 Ringmer Gdns
4 Kingsdown Rd
5 Cottenham Ho
6 St Paul's Ct
7 Rickthorne Rd
8 Stanley Terr
9 Arundel Lo
10 Landseer Ct
A3 1 Beeches The
2 Lambton Ct
3 Nugent Ct
4 Lambton Mews
5 Mews The
A4 1 Marie Lloyd Gdns
2 Edith Cavell Cl
3 Marie Stopes Ct
4 Jessie Blythe La
5 Barbara Rudolph Ct
6 Hetty Rees Ct
7 Leyden Mans
8 Brambledown
9 Lochbie
10 Lyngham Ct
11 High Mount
12 Woodlands The
B2 1 Berkeley Wlk
2 Lazar Wlk
3 Thistlewood Cl
4 Tomlins Wlk
5 Andover Ho
6 Barmouth Ho
7 Chard Ho
8 Methley Ho
9 Rainford Ho
10 Woodbridge Cl
11 Allerton Wlk
12 Falconer Wlk
13 Sonderburg Rd
14 St Mark's Mans
15 Athol Ct
B3 1 Lawson Ct
2 Wiltshire Ct
3 Fenstanton
4 Hutton Ct
5 Wisbech
C2 1 Brookfield
2 Churnfield

6

A1 1 Hurlock Ho
2 Blackstock Ho
3 Vivian Comma Cl
4 Monsell Ct
B4 1 Finmere Ho
2 Keynsham Ho
3 Kilpeck Ho
4 Knaresborough Ho
5 Leighfield Ho
6 Lonsdale Ho
7 Groveley Ho
8 Wensleydale Ho
9 Badminton Ct
C2 1 Chestnut Cl
2 Sycamore Ho
3 Lordship Ho
4 Clissold Ho
5 Beech Ho
6 Laburnum Ho
7 Ormond Ho
8 Yew Tree Ct
9 Oak Ho
C4 1 Selwood Ho
2 Mendip Ho
3 Ennerdale Ho
4 Delamere Ho
5 Westwood Ho
6 Bernwood Ho
7 Allerdale Ho
8 Chattenden Ho
9 Farningham Ho
10 Oakend Ho

7

A1 1 Gujarat Ho
2 Marton Rd
3 Painsthorpe Rd
4 Selkirk Ho
5 Defoe Ho
6 Edward Friend Ho
7 Sheridan Ho
8 Barrie Ho
9 Arnold Ho
10 MacAulay Ho
11 Stowe Ho
12 Carlyle Ho
13 Shaftesbury Ho
14 Lillian Cl
15 Swift Ho
16 Dryden Ho
17 Scott Ct
18 Kingsfield Ho
19 Uhura Sq
20 Hartopp Ct
A3 1 Godstone Ct
2 Farnham Ct
3 Milford Ct
4 Cranleigh Ct
5 Haslemere Ct
6 Belmont Ct
7 Hockworth Ho
8 Garratt Ho
9 Fairburn Ho
10 Thorndale Ho
11 Oakdene Ho
12 Briardale Ho
B1 1 Lawrence Bldgs
2 Cottage Wlk
3 Batley Pl
B2 1 Garnham St
2 Garnham Cl
3 Sanford La
4 Sanford Wlk
5 Abney Gdns
6 Fleet Wood
B3 1 Stamford Hill Mans
2 Montefiore Ct
3 Berwyn Ho
4 Clent Ho
5 Chiltern Ho
6 Laindon Ho
7 Pentland Ho
B4 1 Regent Ct
2 Stamford Lo
3 Holmwood Ct
C1 1 Ravenscourt
2 Mellington Ct
3 Rendlesham Ho
4 Carroll Ct
C2 1 Cazenove Mans
2 Chedworth Ho
3 Aldergrove Ho
4 Abbotstone Ho
5 Briggeford Cl
6 Inglethorpe Ho
7 Ashdown Ho

8 Epping Ho
9 Cypress Cl
C3 1 Stamford Gr E
2 Stamford Mans
3 Grove Mans
4 Stamford Gr W

8

A1 1 Beveridge Rd
2 Purcell Mews
3 George Lansbury Ho
4 Charles Hobson Ho
5 Reade Wlk
6 Westbury Ho
7 Bridge Ct
A4 1 Grange Ct
2 Green Ct
C2 1 Regency Mews
2 Tudor Mews
3 Utopia Ho
4 Bell Flats
5 Angel Ct

9

B2 1 Rutland Park Gdns
2 Rutland Park Mans
3 Queens Par
4 Harcourt Ho
5 Solidarity Ho
6 Electra Ct
7 Cassandra Ct
8 Carlton Ct
C4 1 Oaklands Mews
2 Acer Ct
3 Maple Ct
4 Argyle Mans

10

A1 1 Christ Church Ct
2 Paul Daisley Ct
3 Fountain Ho
4 Kingston Ho
5 Waverley Ct
6 Weston Ho
7 Mapes Ho
8 Athelstan Gdns
9 Leff Ho
B1 1 Alma Birk Ho
2 Brooklands Ct
3 Brooklands Court Apartments
4 Cleveland Mans
5 Buckley Ct
6 Webheath
C1 1 Linstead St
2 Embassy Ho
3 Acol Ct
4 Kings Wood Ct
5 Douglas Ct
6 King's Gdns
7 Carlton Mans
8 Smyrna Mans
9 New Priory Ct
10 Queensgate Pl
11 Brondesbury Mews
C2 1 Dene Mans
2 Sandwell Cres
3 Sandwell Mans
4 Hampstead West
5 Redcroft
C3 1 Orestes Mews
2 Walter Northcott Ho
3 Polperro Mans
4 Lyncroft Mans
5 Marlborough Mans
6 Alexandra Mans
7 Cumberland Mans
8 Cavendish Mans
9 Ambassador Ct
10 Welbeck Mans
11 Inglewood Mans
12 Dennington Park Mansions

11

A2 1 Beswick Mews
2 Worcester Mews
3 Minton Mews
4 Doulton Mews
5 Laurel Ho
6 Sandalwood Ho
7 Iroko Ho
8 Banyan Ho
9 Rosewood Ho
10 Ebony Ho
11 Rosemont Mans
12 Exeter Mews
B1 1 Harrold Ho
2 Glover Ho
3 Byron Ct
4 Nalton Ho
B2 1 Petros Gdns
2 Heath Ct
3 Imperial Twrs
4 Fairhurst
5 St John's Ct
6 New College Ct
7 Chalford
8 Rosslyn Mans
9 Sutherland Ho
B4 1 Windmill Hill
2 Highgrove Point
3 Gainsborough Ho
4 Holly Bush Hill
5 Heath Mans
6 Holly Bush Steps
7 Pavilion Ct
8 Holly Berry La
9 New Campden Ct
10 Holly Bush Vale
11 Benham's Pl
12 Prospect Pl
13 Yorkshire Grey Pl
14 Gardnor Mans
15 Ellerdale Cl
16 Monro Ho
17 Prince Arthur Mews
18 Prince Arthur Ct
19 Village Mount
20 Perrin's Ct
21 Wells Ct
22 Bakers Pas
23 Spencer Wlk
24 Bird In Hand Yd
25 Kings Well
26 New Ct
27 Streatley Pl
28 Mansfield Pl
29 Upper Hampstead Wlk
C1 1 New College Par
2 Northways Par
3 Noel Ho
4 Campden Ho
5 Centre Hts
6 Hickes Ho
7 Swiss Terr
8 Leitch Ho
9 Jevons Ho
10 Langhorne Ct
11 Park Lo
12 Avenue Lo
C2 1 Belsize Park Mews
2 Baynes Mews
3 McCrone Mews
C3 1 Belsize Court Garages
2 Roscommon Ho
3 Akenside Ct
C4 1 White Bear Pl
2 Wells Ho The
3 Boades Mews
4 Flask Cotts
5 Coach House Yd
6 Pilgrim's Pl
7 Rosslyn Mews

12

A2 1 Banff Ho
2 Glenloch Ct
3 Havercourt
4 Holmefield Ct
5 Gilling Ct
6 Howitt Cl
7 Manor Mans
8 Straffan Lo
9 Romney Ct
10 Lancaster Stables
11 Eton Garages
B1 1 Hancock Nunn Ho
2 Higginson Ho
3 Duncan Ho
4 Mary Wharrie Ho
5 Rockstraw Ho
6 Cleaver Ho
7 Chamberlain St
8 Sharples Hall St
9 Primrose Mews
10 Rothwell St
11 St Georges Mews
B2 1 Alder Ho
2 Hornbeam Ho
3 Whitebeam Ho
4 Aspen Ho
5 Rowan Ho
6 Beech Ho
7 Chestnut Ho
8 Oak Ho
9 Willow Ho
10 Sycamore Ho
11 Maple Ho
12 Hazel Ho
13 Elaine Ct
14 Faircourt
15 Walham Ct
16 Stanbury Ct
17 Priory Mans
18 Wellington Ho
19 Grange The
B3 1 Cayford Ho
2 Du Maurier Ho
3 Isokon Flats
4 Palgrave Ho
5 Garnett Ho
6 Stephenson Ho
7 Park Dwellings
8 Siddons Ho
9 Mall Studios
10 Park Hill Wlk
11 Wordsworth Pl
12 Fraser Regnart Ct
13 St Pancras Almshouses
C1 1 Bridge Ho
2 Hardington
3 Mead Cl
4 Rugmere
5 Tottenhall
6 Beauvale
7 Broomfield
C2 1 Silverbirch Wlk
2 Penshurst
3 Wingham
4 Westwell
5 Chislet
6 Burmarsh
7 Shipton Ho
8 Stonegate
9 Leysdown
10 Headcorn
11 Lenham
12 Halstow
13 Fordcombe
14 Cannington
15 Langridge
16 Athlone Ho
17 Pentland Ho
18 Beckington
19 Hawkridge
20 Edington

13

A1 1 Ferdinand Ho
2 Harmood Ho
3 Hawley Rd
4 Hawley Mews
5 Leybourne St
6 Barling
7 Tiptree
8 Havering
9 Candida Ct
10 Lorraine Ct
11 Donnington Ct
12 Welford Ct
13 Torbay Ct
14 Bradfield Ct
15 Torbay St
16 Water La
17 Leybourne Rd
18 Haven St
19 Stucley Pl
20 Lawrence Ho
A2 1 Ashington
2 Priestley Ho
3 Leonard Day Ho
4 Old Dairy Mews
5 Monmouth Ho
6 Alpha Ct
7 Una Ho
8 Widford
9 Heybridge
10 Roxwell
11 Hamstead Gates
A4 1 Denyer Ho
2 Stephenson Ho
3 Trevithick Ho
4 Brunel Ho
5 Newcomen Ho
6 Faraday Ho
7 Winifrede Paul Ho
8 Wardlow
9 Fletcher Ct
10 Tideswell
11 Grangemill
12 Hambrook Ct
13 Calver
B1 1 Cherry Tree Ct
2 Chichester Ct
3 Durdans Ho
4 Philia Ho
5 Bernard Shaw Ct
6 Foster Ct
7 Bessemer Ct
8 Hogarth Ct
9 Rochester Ct
10 Soane Ct
11 Wallett Ct
12 Inwood Ct
13 Wrotham Rd
14 St Thomas Ct
15 Caulfield Ct
16 Bruges Pl
17 Reachview Cl
18 Lawfords Wharf
B3 1 Eleanor Ho
2 Falkland Pl
3 Kensington Ho
4 Willingham Cl
5 Kenbrook Ho
6 Aborfield
7 Great Field
8 Appleford
9 Forties The
10 Maud Wilkes Cl
11 Dunne Mews
12 Dowdeny Cl
B4 1 Benson Ct
2 Tait Ho
3 Manorfield Cl
4 Greatfield Cl
5 Longley Ho
6 Lampson Ho
7 Davidson Ho
8 Palmer Ho
9 Lambourn Cl
10 Morris Ho
11 Owen Ho
C1 1 Hillier Ho
2 Gairloch Ho
3 Cobham Mews
4 Bergholt Mews
5 Blakeney Cl
6 Weavers Way
7 Allensbury Pl
C2 1 Rowstock
2 Peckwater Ho
3 Wolsey Ho
4 Pandian Way
5 Busby Mews
6 Caledonian Sq
7 Canal Bvd
8 Northpoint Sq
9 Lock Mews
10 Carters Cl
11 York Ho
12 Hungerford Rd
13 Cliff Road Studios
14 Cliff Ct
15 Camelot Ho
16 Church Studios
17 Camden Terr
C3 1 Blake Ho
2 Quelch Ho
3 Lee Ho
4 Willbury Ho
5 Howell Ho
6 Holmsbury Ho
7 Leith Ho
8 Betchworth Ho
9 Rushmore Ho
10 Dugdale Ho
11 Horsendon Ho
12 Colley Ho
13 Coombe Ho
14 Ivinghoe Ho
15 Buckhurst Ho
16 Saxonbury Ct
17 Charlton Ct
18 Apollo Studios

19 Barn Cl
20 Long Meadow
21 Landleys Field
22 Margaret Bondfield Ho
23 Haywood Lo
C4 1 Fairlie Ct
2 Trecastle Way
3 Dalmeny Avenue Est
4 Hyndman Ho
5 Carpenter Ho
6 Graham Ho
7 Tufnell Mans

14

A3 1 Kimble Ho
2 Saxonbury Ct
3 Poynder Ct
4 Pangbourne Ho
5 Moulsford Ho
A4 1 Arcade The
2 Macready Pl
3 Cardwell Rd
4 Mcmorran Ho
5 Crayford Ho
6 Whitby Ct
7 Prospect Pl
B1 1 Kerwick Cl
2 Rydston Cl
3 Skegness Ho
4 Frederica St
5 Ponder St
6 Kings Ct
7 Freeling St
8 Coatbridge Ho
9 Tilloch St
B2 1 Burns Ho
2 Scott Ho
3 Wellington Mews
4 Roman Ct
5 Piccadilly Ct
B3 1 Culverin Ct
2 Garand Ct
3 Mount Carmel
B4 1 Buckmaster Ho
2 Loreburn Ho
3 Cairns Ho
4 Halsbury Ho
5 Chelmsford Ho
6 Cranworth Ho
C1 1 Mountfort Terr
2 Avon Ho
3 Buckland Ho
4 Dovey Lo
5 Carfree Cl
6 Mitchell Ho
7 New College Mews
8 Lofting Ho
9 Brooksby Ho
10 Cara Ho
C3 1 Slaney Pl
2 Eastwood Cl
3 Milton Pl
4 Hartnoll Ho
5 St James School Flats
6 Widnes Ho
7 Tranmere Ho
8 Victoria Mans
9 Formby Ct
10 Mersey Ho
11 Birkenhead Ho
12 Drayton Park Mews

15

A1 1 Islington Park Mews
2 Evelyn Denington Ct
3 Bassingbourn Ho
4 Cadmore Ho
5 Adstock Ho
6 Garston Ho
7 Flitton Ho
8 Datchworth Ho
9 Battishill St
10 Almeida St
11 Edward's Cotts
12 Hyde's Pl
13 Tyndale Terr
14 Spriggs Ho
15 Barratt Ho
16 Spencer Pl
17 Chadston Ho
18 Whiston Ho
19 Wakelin Ho
20 Tressel Cl
21 Canonbury Ct
22 Halton Ho
23 Shillingford St
24 Highbury Mans
25 Premier Ho
26 Waterloo Gdns
A2 1 Hampton Ct
2 Salisbury Ho
A3 1 De Barowe Mews
2 Fieldview Ct
3 Viewpoint
4 Ashurst Lo
A4 1 Chestnuts The
2 Bowen Ct
3 Peckett Sq
B1 1 Astey's Row
2 Lincoln Ho
3 Worcester Ho
4 Melville Pl
5 Wontner Cl
6 Hedingham Cl
7 Laundry La
8 Base Apartments
9 Walkinshaw Ct
10 New Bentham Ct
11 Bentham Ct
12 Haslam Ho
13 Horsfield Ho
14 Riverside Ho
15 Eric Fletcher Ct
16 Annette Cres
17 Ashby Ho
18 Lindsey Mews
19 Cardigan Wlk
20 Red House Sq
B2 1 Crowline Wlk
2 Upper Handa Wlk
3 Handa Wlk
4 Lismore Wlk
5 Bardsey Wlk
6 Walney Wlk
7 Upper Bardsey Wlk
8 Upper Lismore Wlk
9 Sark Ho
10 Guernsey Ho
11 Guernsey Rd
12 Sybil Thorndike Ho
13 Clephane Rd
14 Florence Nightingale Ho
15 Jersey Ho
16 Jethou Ho
17 Islay Wlk
18 Upper Caldy Wlk
19 Caldy Wlk
20 Alderney Ho
21 Gulland Wlk
22 Marquess Rd S
23 Upper Gulland Wlk
24 Church Rd
25 Oransay Rd
B3 1 Pearfield Ho
2 Larchfield Ho
3 Beresford Terr
4 Pondfield Ho
5 Ashfield Ho
6 Elmfield Ho
B4 1 Fountain Mews
2 Woodstock Ho
3 Henson Ct
4 Taverner Sq
C1 1 Downham Ct
2 Trafalgar Point
C2 1 John Kennedy Ct
2 John Kennedy Lo
3 Ball's Pond Pl
4 Haliday Wlk
5 Queen Elizabeth Ct
6 Canonbury Hts
7 Pinnacle The
8 Threadgold Ho
9 Wakeham St
10 Saffron Ct
11 Callaby Terr
12 Tilney Gdns
13 Westcliff Ho
14 Ilford Ho
15 Ongar Ho
16 Greenhills Terr
17 Romford Ho
18 Bute Wlk
19 Upper Ramsey Wlk
20 Rona Wlk
21 Thorndike Rd
C4 1 Ledo Ho
2 Salween Ho
3 Prome Ho
4 Arakan Ho
5 Rangoon Ho
6 Mandalay Ho
7 Karen Ho
8 Wingate Ho
9 Jubet Ho
10 Orde Ho
11 Chindit Ho
12 Mabel Thornton Ho
13 Crawshay Ho
14 Avon Ho
15 Connaught Mans
16 Jonson Ho
17 Herrick Ho
18 Donne Ho
19 Thirlmere Ho
20 Grasmere Ho

16

A1 1 Dorchester Ct
2 Wareham Ct
3 Dorset Ct
4 Stratton Ct
5 Swanage Ct
6 Blandford Ct
7 Portland Ct
8 Oscar Faber Pl
9 Metropolitan Bsns Ctr
10 Lancaster Cl
11 Palazzo Apartments
A2 1 Kingsland Gn
2 Kingsland Pas
3 Metropolitan Benefit Societies Almshouses
4 Nimrod Pas
5 De Beauvoir Pl
6 Warburton Cl
7 Buckingham Mews
8 Aztec Ct
A3 1 Hewling Ho
2 Matthias Ho
3 Port Royal Pl
4 Cressington Cl
5 King Henry's Yd
6 Bronte Ho
7 Sewell Ho
8 Lydgate Ho
9 Patmore Ho
10 Congreve Ho
11 Elton St
12 Conrad Ho
13 Southwell Ho
14 Neptune Ho
15 Campion Ho
16 Webster Ho
17 Meredith Ho
18 Beckford Ho
19 Ashley Ct
20 Hayling Cl
21 Millard Cl
22 Lydford Cl
23 Salcombe Rd
24 Truman's Rd
25 Templeton Cl
26 John Campbell Rd
27 Gillett Pl
28 Bradbury St
29 Thomas Crowell Ct
A4 1 Londesborough Ho
2 Knebworth Ho
3 Knebworth Rd
4 Bransby Ct
5 Imperial Ave
6 Leonard Pl
7 Shakspeare Mews
8 Binyon Ho
9 Shelley Ho
10 Browning Ho
11 Burns Ho
12 Andrew Marvell Ho
13 Wycliffe Ho
14 Blake Ho
15 Marlowe Ho
16 Fletcher Ho
17 Chaucer Ct
B1 1 Hilborough Rd
2 Shoreditch Ct
3 Evergreen Sq
4 Wyndhams Ct
5 Festival Ct
6 Fortune Ct
7 Rose Ct
8 Ability Plaza
B2 1 Prospect Ho
2 Woodland St
3 Crosby Wlk
4 Kirkland Wlk
5 Bowness Cl
6 Carlisle Wlk
7 Skelton Cl
8 Camerton Cl
9 Buttermere Wlk
10 Houghton Cl
11 Hayton Cl
12 Kingsland Sh Ctr
13 Springfield Ho
14 Parton Lo
15 Sanctuary Mews
B3 1 Miller's Terr
2 Chow Sq
3 Drysdale Flats
4 Gateway Mews
5 Birkbeck Mews
6 Winchester Pl
B4 1 Coronation Ave
2 Morris Blitz Ct
3 Shacklewell Ho
4 Alexandra Ct
C1 1 Aldington Ct
2 Bayton Ct
3 Rochford Wlk
C2 3 Burdon Ct
4 Thomson Ct
5 Bruno Ct
C3 1 Kingsdown Ho
2 Glendown Ho
3 Moredown Ho
4 Blakeney Cl
5 Beeston Cl
6 Benabo Ct
7 David Devine Ho
8 Kreedman Wlk
9 Hermitage Row
10 Grafton Ct
11 Lushington Terr
12 Aspen Ct
13 Pykewell Lo
14 Albion Works Studios

17

A1 1 Fortescue Ave
2 Pemberton Pl
3 Weston Wlk
4 Bayford St Ind Ctr
5 Bayford St
6 Sidworth St
7 Helmsley St
8 Cyntra Pl
9 Signal Ho
10 All Nations Ho
11 Vanguard Ho
12 Hacon Sq
A2 1 Bohemia Pl
2 Graham Mans
3 Marvin St
4 Boscobel Ho
5 Royal Oak Rd
6 Colonnades The
7 Sylvester Ho
8 Sylvester Path
9 Doctor Spurstowe Almshouses
10 Great Eastern Bldgs
11 Sojourner-Truth Cl
A3 1 Birchington Ho
2 Bicknor Ho
3 Boxley Ho
4 Adisham Ho
5 Cranbrook Ho
6 Marden Ho
7 Broome Ho
8 Crandale Ho
9 Cheriton Ho
10 Ditton Ho
11 Langley Ho
12 Dymchurch Ho
13 Elham Ho
14 Davina Ho
15 Pembury Pl
16 Downs Ct
17 Perrywood Ho
18 Staplehurst Ho
19 Pegwell Ho

20 Yalding Ho
21 Northbourne Ho
22 Monkton Ho
23 Milsted Ho
24 Athlone Cl
25 Clarence Pl
26 Gould Terr
27 Quested Ct
28 Brett Pas
29 Marcon Ct
30 Appleton Ct
A4 1 Ross Ct
2 Downs La
3 Gaviller Pl
4 Robert Owen Lo
5 Apprentice Way
6 Arrowe Ct
7 Gilwell Ct
8 Sutton Ct
9 St Andrews Mans
10 Kinnoull Mans
11 Rowhill Mans
12 Sladen Pl
13 Mothers Sq The
14 Richborough Ho
15 Sandgate Ho
16 Sheppey Ho
B1 1 Pitcairn Ho
2 Lyme Grove Ho
3 Shakespeare Ho
4 Upcott Ho
5 Loddiges Ho
6 Parkinson Ho
7 Sloane Ho
8 Vanbrugh Ho
9 Cambridge Pas
10 Lyttleton Ho
11 Victoria Park Ct
12 Tullis Ho
13 Fairchild Ho
14 Forsyth Ho
15 Tradescant Ho
16 Mason Ho
17 Capel Ho
18 Cordwainers Ct
19 Bridgeman Ho
20 St Thomas's Pl
21 Barclay Ho
22 Clayton Ho
23 Danby Ho
24 Sherard Ho
25 Catesby Ho
26 Petiver Cl
27 Leander Ct
28 Philip Turner Est
29 Grendon Ho
30 Shore Mews
31 Shore Bsns Ctr
32 Kendal Ho
33 Classic Mans
34 Tudor Ho
35 Park Ho
36 Enterprise Ho
37 Alpine Gr
38 Clarendon Cl
39 Rotheley Ho
40 Bernie Grant Ho
2 1 Woolpack Ho
2 Elvin Ho
3 Thomas Ho
4 Hockley Ho
5 Retreat Ho
6 Butfield Ho
7 Brooksbank Ho
8 Cresset Ho
9 Brooksbank St
10 Lennox Ho

11 Milborne Ho
12 Collent Ho
13 Middlesex Pl
14 Elsdale Ho
15 Devonshire Hall
16 Brent Ho
C1 1 Stuart Ho
2 Gascoyne Ho
3 Chelsfield Point
4 Sundridge Ho
5 Banbury Ho
6 Lauriston Ho
C2 1 Musgrove Ho
2 Cheyney Ho
3 Haynes Ho
4 Warner Ho
5 Gilby Ho
6 Gadsden Ho
7 Risley Ho
8 Baycliffe Ho
9 Sheldon Ho
10 Offley Ho
11 Latimer Ho
12 Ribstone Ho
13 Salem Ho
14 Fieldwick Ho
15 Lever Ct
16 Matson Ho
17 Wilding Ho
18 Rennell Ho
19 Dycer Ho
20 Granard Ho
21 Whitelock Ho
22 Harrowgate Ho
23 Cass Ho
24 Lofts on the Park
25 Heathcote Point
26 Ravenscroft Point
27 Vanner Point
28 Hensley Point
29 San Ho
C4 1 Cromford Path
2 Longford Ct
3 Overbury Ho
4 Heanor Ct
5 Wharfedale Ct
6 Ladybower Ct
7 Ilkeston Ct
8 Derby Ct
9 Rushmore Cres
10 Blackwell Cl
11 Belper Ct

18

A2 1 Chigwell Ct
2 Wellday Ho
3 Selman Ho
4 Vaine Ho
5 Trower Ho
B2 1 Mallard Cl
2 Merriam Ave
3 Gainsborough St

19

C1 1 Service Route No 2
2 Service Route No 3
C4 1 Mulberry Ct
2 Rosewood Ct
3 Gean Ct
4 Blackthorn Ct
5 Cypress Ct

20

1 Carlyle Rd
2 Bernard Shaw Ho
3 Longlents Ho
4 Mordaunt Ho

5 Wilmers Ct
6 Stonebridge Ctr
7 Shakespeare Ave

21

A3 1 Futters Ct
2 Barrett Ct
3 Elms The
4 Fairlight Ct
B3 1 New Crescent Yd
2 Harlesden Plaza
3 St Josephs Ct
4 Jubilee Cl
5 Ellery Cl

22

B1 1 Princess Alice Ho
2 Yoxall Ho
3 Yorkley Ho
4 Northaw Ho
5 Oakham Ho
6 Markyate Ho
7 Letchmore Ho
8 Pagham Ho
9 Quendon Ho
10 Redbourn Ho
11 Ketton Ho
12 Hillman Dr
C2 1 Westfield Ct
2 Tropical Ct
3 Chamberlayne Mans
4 Quadrant The
5 Queens Park Ct
6 Warfield Yd
7 Regent St
8 Cherrytree Ho
9 Artisan Mews
10 Artisan Quarter

23

A1 1 Sycamore Wlk
2 Westgate Bsns Ctr
3 Buspace Studios
4 Bosworth Ho
5 Golborne Gdns
6 Appleford Ho
7 Adair Twr
8 Gadsden Ho
9 Southam Ho
10 Norman Butler Ho
11 Thompson Ho
12 Wells Ho
13 Paul Ho
14 Olive Blythe Ho
15 Katherine Ho
16 Breakwell Ct
17 Pepler Ho
18 Edward Kennedy Ho
19 Winnington Ho
A2 1 Selby Sq
2 Severn Ave
3 Stansbury Sq
4 Tolhurst Dr
5 John Fearon Wlk
6 Mundy Ho
7 Macfarren Ho
8 Bantock Ho
9 Banister Ho
10 Batten Ho
11 Croft Ho
12 Courtville Ho
13 Mounsey Ho
14 Bliss Mews
15 Symphony Mews
B1 1 Octavia Mews

2 Russell's Wharf
3 Western Ho
4 Kelly Mews
B2 1 Boyce Ho
2 Farnaby Ho
3 Danby Ho
4 Purday Ho
5 Naylor Ho
6 St Judes Ho
7 Leeve Ho
8 Longhurst Ho
9 Harrington Ct
10 Mulberry Ct
11 Kilburn Ho
B3 1 Claremont Ct
2 William Saville Ho
3 Western Ct
4 Bond Ho
5 Crone Ct
6 Wood Ho
7 Winterleys
8 Carlton Ho
9 Fiona Ct
C1 1 Westside Ct
2 Byron Mews
3 Sutherland Ct
4 Fleming Cl
5 Hermes Cl
C2 1 Pentland Rd
2 Nelson Cl
3 Pavilion Ct
4 Masefield Ho
5 Austen Ho
6 Fielding Ho
7 Argo Bsns Ctr
8 John Ratcliffe Ho
9 Wymering Mans
C3 1 Wells Ct
2 Cambridge Ct
3 Ely Ct
4 Durham Ct
C4 1 Ryde Ho
2 Glengall Pass
3 Leith Yd
4 Daynor Ho
5 Varley Ho
6 Sandby Ho
7 Colas Mews
8 Bishopsdale Ho
9 Lorton Ho
10 Marshwood Ho
11 Ribblesdale Ho
12 Holmesdale Ho
13 Kilburn Vale Est
14 Kilburn Bridge

24

A3 1 Bracer Ho
2 Scorton Ho
3 Fern Cl
4 Macbeth Ho
5 Oberon Ho
6 Buckland Ct
7 Crondall Ct
8 Osric Path
9 Caliban Twr
10 Celia Ho
11 Juliet Ho
12 Bacchus Wlk
13 Malcolm Ho
14 Homefield St
15 Crondall Pl
16 Blanca Ho
17 Miranda Ho
18 Falstaff Ho
19 Charmian Ho
20 Myrtle Wlk

21 Arden Ho
22 Sebastian Ho
23 Stanway Ct
24 Jerrold St
25 Rosalind Ho
26 Cordelia Ho
27 Monteagle Ct
28 John Parry Ct
29 James Anderson Ct
30 Ben Jonson Ct
31 Sara Lane Ct
32 Walbrook Ct
A4 1 Portelet Ct
2 Trinity Ct
3 Rozel Ct
4 St Helier Ct
5 Corbiere Ho
6 Kenning Ho
7 Higgins Ho
8 Cavell Ho
9 Girling Ho
10 Fulcher Ho
11 Francis Ho
12 Norris Ho
13 Kempton Ho
14 Nesham Ho
15 Crossbow Ho
16 Catherine Ho
17 Strale Ho
18 Horner Hos
19 Stringer Hos
20 Whitmore Ho
21 Nightingale Ho
22 Wilmer Gdns
23 Arrow Ho
24 Archer Ho
25 Meriden Ho
26 Rover Ho
27 Bowyer Ho
28 Tiller Ho
29 Canalside Studios
30 Kleine Wharf
31 Benyon Wharf
32 Quebec Wharf
33 Belvedere Ct
34 Portfleet Pl
B3 1 Queensbridge Ct
2 Godwin Ho
3 Kent Ct
4 Brunswick Ho
5 Weymouth Ct
6 Sovereign Mews
7 Dunloe Ct
8 Cremer Bsns Ctr
9 James Hammett Ho
10 Allgood St
11 Horatio St
12 Cadell Ho
13 Horatio Ho
14 Shipton Ho
B4 1 Hilborough Ct
2 Scriven Ct
3 Livermere Ct
4 Angrave Ct
5 Angrave Pas
6 Benfleet Ct
7 Belford Ho
8 Orme Ho
9 Clemson Ho
10 Longman Ho
11 Lowther Ho
12 Lovelace Ho
13 Harlowe Ho

14 Pamela Ho
15 Samuel Ho
16 Acton Ho
17 Loanda Cl
18 Phoenix Cl
19 Richardson Cl
20 Thrasher Cl
21 Mary Secole Cl
22 Canal Path
23 Pear Tree Cl
24 Hebden Ct
25 Charlton Ct
26 Laburnum Ct
27 Mansfield Ct
28 Garden Pl
29 Amber Wharf
30 Haggerston Studios
C3 1 London Terr
2 Sturdee Ho
3 Maude Ho
4 Haig Ho
5 Jellicoe Ho
6 Ropley St
7 Guinness Trust Bldgs
8 Ion Ct
9 Columbia Rd
10 Moye Cl
11 Morrel Ct
12 Courtauld Ho
13 Drummond Ho
14 Gurney Ho
15 Atkinson Ho
16 Halley Ho
17 Goldsmith's Sq
18 Shahjalal Ho
19 Ken Wilson Ho
20 April Ct
21 Crofts Ho
22 Sebright Ho
23 Beechwood Ho
24 Gillman Ho
25 Cheverell Ho
26 Besford Ho
27 Dinmont Ho
28 Elizabeth Mews
29 Sebright Pas
30 Wyndham Deedes Ho
31 Sheppard Ho
32 Mary James Ho
33 Hadrian Est
34 Blythendale Ho
35 George Vale Ho
36 Lion Mills
37 St Peter's Ave
38 Pritchard Ho
C4 1 Broke Wlk
2 Rochemont Wlk
3 Marlborough Ave
4 Rivington Wlk
5 Magnin Cl
6 Gloucester Sq
7 Woolstone Ho
8 Marsworth Ho
9 Cheddington Ho
10 Linslade Ho
11 Cosgrove Ho
12 Blisworth Ho
13 Eleanor Ct
14 Wistow Ho
15 Muscott Ho
16 Boxmoor Ho
17 Linford Ho
18 Pendley Ho
19 Northchurch Ho
20 Debdale Ho
21 Broadway Market Mews
22 Welshpool Ho
23 Ada Ho

25

A1 1 Rochester Ct
2 Weaver Ct
3 Greenheath Bsns Ctr
4 Glass St
5 Herald St
6 Northesk Ho
7 Codrington Ho
8 Heathpool Ct
9 Mocatta Ho
10 Harvey Ho
11 Blackwood Ho
12 Rutherford Ho
13 Bullen Ho
14 Fremantle Ho
15 Pellew Ho
16 Ashington Ho
17 Dinnington Ho
18 Bartholomew Sq
19 Steeple Ct
20 Orion Ho
21 Fellbrigg St
22 Eagle Ho
23 Sovereign Ho
24 Redmill Ho
25 Berry Ho
26 Grindall Ho
27 Collingwood Ho
A2 1 Charles Dickens Ho
2 Adrian Bolt Ho
3 William Rathbone Ho
4 Southwood Smith Ho
5 Rushmead
6 William Channing Ho
7 John Cartwright Ho
8 Charles Darwin Ho
9 Thomas Burt Ho
10 John Fielden Ho
11 Gwilym Maries Ho
12 Joseph Priestley Ho
13 Wear Pl
14 John Nettleford Ho
15 Thornaby Ho
16 Stockton Ho
17 Barnard Ho
18 Gainford Ho
19 Stapleton Ho
20 James Middleton Ho
21 Kedleston Wlk
22 Queen Margaret Flats
23 Hollybush Ho
24 Horwood Ho
25 Norden Ho
26 Newcourt Ho
27 Seabright St
28 Viaduct Pl
29 Sunlight Sq
30 Providence Row Cl
A3 1 Dinmont St
2 Marian St
3 Claredale Ho
4 Keeling Ho
5 Maple St
6 Winkley St
7 Temple Dwellings
8 Argos Ho
9 Helen Ho
10 Lysander Ho
11 Antenor Ho
12 Paris Ho
13 Nestor Ho
14 Hector Ho
15 Ajax Ho
16 Achilles Ho
17 Priam Ho
18 Peabody Est
19 Felix St
20 Cambridge Cres
21 Peterley Bsns Ctr
22 Beckwith Ho
23 Brookfield Ho
24 Parminter Ind Est
25 Ted Roberts Ho
26 Cambridge Ct
27 Millennium Pl
28 William Caslon Ho
29 Hugh Platt Ho
30 West St
31 Mayfield Ho
32 Apollo Ho
33 Tanners Yd
34 Teesdale Yd
A4 1 Welshpool St
2 Broadway Ho
3 Regents Wharf
4 London Wharf
5 Warburton Ho
6 Warburton St
7 Triangle Rd
8 Warburton Rd
9 Williams Ho
10 Booth Cl
11 Albert Cl
12 King Edward Mans
13 Victoria Bldgs
14 Andrews Wharf
B1 1 William's Bldgs
2 Donegal Ho
3 Pelican Pas
4 Frederick Char-rington Ho
5 Wickford Ho
6 Braintree Ho
7 Doveton Ho
8 Doveton St
9 Cephas Ho
10 Sceptre Ho
11 Bancroft Ho
12 Stothard St
13 Redclyf Ho
14 Winkworth Cotts
15 Amiel St
16 Hadleigh Ho
17 Hadleigh Cl
18 Ryder Ho
19 Mantus Cl
20 Kenton Ho
21 Colebert Ho
22 Ibbott St
23 Rickman Ho
24 Rickman St
25 Stothard Ho
26 Barbanel Ho
27 Stannard Cotts
28 St Peters Ct
29 Rennie Cotts
30 Pemell Cl
31 Pemell Ho
32 Leatherdale St
33 Gouldman Ho
34 Lamplighter Cl
35 Sherren Ho
36 Marlborough Lo
37 Hamilton Lo
38 Montgomery Lo
39 Cleveland Gr
40 Cromwell Lo
41 Bardsey Pl
42 Charrington Ho
43 Hayfield Yd
44 Allport Mews
45 Colin Winter Ho
B2 1 Mulberry Ho
2 Gretton Ho
3 Merceron Ho
4 Montfort Ho
5 Westbrook Ho
6 Sugar Loaf Wlk
7 Museum Ho
8 Burnham Est
9 Globe Terr
10 Moravian St
11 Shepton Hos
12 Mendip Hos
13 Academy Ct
14 Pepys Ho
15 Swinburne Ho
16 Moore Ho
17 Morris Ho
18 Burns Ho
19 Milton Ho
20 Whitman Ho
21 Shelley Ho
22 Keats Ho
23 Dawson Ho
24 Bradbeer Ho
25 Forber Ho
26 Hughes Ho
27 Silvester Ho
28 Rogers Est
29 Pavan Ct
30 Stafford Cripps Ho
31 Sidney Godley (VC) Ho
32 Butler Ho
33 Butler St
34 Thorne Ho
35 Bevin Ho
36 Tuscan Ho
B3 1 Evesham Ho
2 James Campbell Ho
3 Thomas Hollywood Ho
4 James Docherty Ho
5 Ebenezer Mussel Ho
6 Jameson Ct
7 Edinburgh Cl
8 Roger Dowley Ct
9 Sherbrooke Ho
10 Calcraft Ho
11 Burrard Ho
12 Dundas Ho
13 Ponsonby Ho
14 Barnes Ho
15 Paget Ho
16 Maitland Ho
17 Chesil Ct
18 Reynolds Ho
19 Cleland Ho
20 Goodrich Ho
21 Rosebery Ho
22 Sankey Ho
23 Cyprus Pl
24 Royston St
25 Stainsbury St
26 Hunslett St
27 Baildon
28 Brockweir
29 Tytherton
30 Malmesbury
31 Kingswood
32 Colville Ho
B4 1 Halkett Ho
2 Christchurch Sq
3 Helena Pl
4 Swingfield Ho
5 Greenham Ho
6 Dinmore Ho
7 Anstey Ho
8 Weston Ho
9 Carbroke Ho
10 Bluebell Cl
11 Cherry Tree Cl
12 Georgian Ct
13 Park Cl
14 Regency Ct
15 Norris Ho
C1 1 Raynham Ho
2 Pat Shaw Ho
3 Colmar Cl
4 Withy Ho
5 Stocks Ct
6 Downey Ho
7 Bay Ct
8 Sligo Ho
9 Pegasus Ho
10 Barents Ho
11 Biscay Ho
12 Solway Ho
13 Bantry Ho
14 Aral Ho
15 Pacific Ho
16 Magellan Ho
17 Levant Ho
18 Adriatic Ho
19 Genoa Ho
20 Hawke Ho
21 Palliser Ho
22 Ionian Ho
23 Weddell Ho
24 Carlyle Mews
25 Greencourt Ho
26 Sundra Wlk
C2 1 Stubbs Ho
2 Holman Ho
3 Clynes Ho
4 Windsor Ho
5 Gilbert Ho
6 Chater Ho
7 Ellen Wilkinson Ho
8 George Belt Ho
9 Ayrton Gould Ho
10 O'Brian Ho
11 Sulkin Ho
12 Jenkinson Ho
13 Bullards Pl
14 Sylvia Pankhurst Ho
15 Mary Macarthur Ho
16 Trevelyan Ho
17 Wedgwood Ho
18 Pemberton Ct
19 Leatherdale St
20 Walter Besant Ho
21 Barber Beaumont Ho
22 Brancaster Ho
23 Litcham Ho
C3 1 Kemp Ho
2 Piggott Ho
3 Mark Ho

4 Sidney Ho
5 Pomeroy Ho
6 Puteaux Ho
7 Doric Ho
8 Modling Ho
9 Longman Ho
10 Ames Ho
11 Alzette Ho
12 Offenbach Ho
13 Tate Ho
14 Norton Ho
15 St Gilles Ho
16 Harold Ho
17 Velletri Ho
18 Bridge Wharf
19 Gathorne St
20 Bow Brook The
21 Twig Folly Cl
22 Palmerston Ct
23 Lakeview
24 Peach Walk Mews
25 Caesar Ct

26

A1 1 Formosa Ho
2 Galveston Ho
3 Arabian Ho
4 Greenland Ho
5 Coral Ho
6 Anson Ho
7 Cambay Ho
8 Lindop Ho
9 Moray Ho
10 Azov Ho
11 Sandalwood Cl
12 Broadford Ho
A2 1 Imperial Ho
2 Newport Ho
3 Vassall Ho
4 Maurice Ct
5 Creed Ct
6 Christopher France Ho
7 Beaumont Ct
8 Pembroke Mews
A3 1 Nightingale Mews
2 Bunsen Ho
3 Bunsen St
4 Beatrice Webb Ho
5 Margaret Bondfield Ho
6 Wilmer Ho
7 Sandall Ho
8 Butley Ct
9 Josseline Ct
10 Dalton Ho
11 Brine Ho
12 Ford Cl
13 Viking Cl
14 Stanfield Rd
15 Stoneleigh Mews
16 Ruth Ct
17 School Bell Cloisters
18 Schoolbell Mews
19 Medhurst Cl
20 Olga St
21 Conyer St
22 Diamond Ho
23 Daring Ho
24 Crane Ho
25 Exmoor Ho
26 Grenville Ho
27 Hyperion Ho
28 Sturdy Ho
29 Wren Ho
30 Ardent Ho
31 Senators Lo
32 Hooke Ho
33 Mohawk Ho
34 Ivanhoe Ho
35 Medway Mews
B2 1 Trellis Sq
2 Sheffield Sq
3 Howcroft Ho
4 Astra Ho
5 Frye Ct
6 Byas Ho
7 George Lansbury Ho
8 Regal Pl
9 Coborn Mews
10 Tredegar Mews
11 Cavendish Terr
12 Lyn Mews
13 Buttermere Ho
14 Coniston Ho
15 Tracy Ho
16 Hanover Pl
17 St Clair Ho
18 Longthorne Ho
19 Vista Bldgs
20 Verity Ho
21 Icarus Ho
22 Whippingham Ho
23 Hamilton Ho
24 Winchester Ho
B3 1 Roman Square Mkt
2 John Bond Ho
3 McKenna Ho
4 Dennis Ho
5 McAusland Ho
6 McBride Ho
7 Libra Rd
8 Dave Adams Ho
9 Regency Ct
10 Tay Ho
11 Sleat Ho
12 Brodick Ho
13 Ewart Pl
14 Lunan Ho
15 Cruden Ho
16 Anglo Rd
17 Mull Ho
18 Sinclairs Ho
19 Driftway Ho
20 Clayhall Ct
21 Berebinder Ho
22 Partridge Ho
23 Barford Ho
24 Gullane Ho
25 Gosford Ho
26 Dornoch Ho
27 Dunnet Ho
28 Enard Ho
29 Fraserburgh Ho
30 Forth Ho
31 Stavers Ho
32 Rosegate Ho
33 Crowngate Ho
34 Queensgate Ho
35 Towergate Ho
36 Ordell Ct
37 William Pl
B4 1 Hampstead Wlk
2 Waverton Ho
3 Elton Ho
4 Locton Gn
5 Birtwhistle Ho
6 Clare Ho
7 Magpie Ho
8 Hornbeam Sq
9 Rowan Ho
10 Barge La
11 Walnut Ho
12 Birdsfield La
13 Atkins Ct
14 Willow Tree Cl
15 Jasmine Sq
16 Tait Ct
17 Ranwell Ho
18 Ranwell Cl
19 Tufnell Ct
20 Pulteney Cl
21 Vic Johnson Ho
22 Lea Sq
23 Iceni Ct
24 Tamar Cl
25 Roman Rd
26 Valentine Ho
C1 1 Fairmont Ho
2 Healy Ho
3 Zodiac Ho
4 Buick Ho
5 Consul Ho
6 Bentley Ho
7 Cresta Ho
8 Daimler Ho
9 Riley Ho
10 Jensen Ho
11 Lagonda Ho
12 Ireton St
13 Navenby Wlk
14 Burwell Wlk
15 Leadenham Ct
16 Sleaford Ho
17 Bow Triangle Bsns Ctr
C2 1 Bow Ho
2 Denmark Pl
3 Marsalis Ho
4 Lovette Ho
5 Drapers Almhouses
6 Mallard Point
7 Creswick Wlk
8 Bevin Ho
9 Huggins Ho
10 Williams Ho
11 Harris Ho
12 Marina Ct
13 Electric Ho
14 Matching Ct
15 Wellington Bldgs
16 Grafton Ho
17 Berkeley Ho
18 Columbia Ho
C3 1 Vincent Mews
2 Menai Pl
3 Heathfield Ct
4 Redwood Cl
5 Acorn Ct
6 Primrose Cl
7 Briar Ct
8 Springwood Cl
C4 1 Ironworks
2 Juno Ho
3 Chariot Cl
4 Saturn Ho
5 Hadrian Cl
6 Mercury Ho
7 Forum Cl
8 Venus Ho
9 Vesta Ho
10 Tiber Cl
11 Gemini Ho
12 Crown Close Bsns Ctr
13 Old Ford Trad Ctr

27

A1 1 Broxbourne Ho
2 Roxford Ho
3 Biscott Ho
4 Stanborough Ho
5 Hillstone Ct
A2 1 Bradley Ho
2 Prioress Ho
3 Alton Ho
4 Foxley Ho
5 Munden Ho
6 Canterbury Ho
7 Corbin Ho
8 Barton Ho
9 Jolles Ho
10 Rudstone Ho
11 Baxter Ho
12 Baker Ho
13 Insley Ho
14 Hardwicke Ho
15 Glebe Ct
16 Priory St
17 Sadler Ho
18 Ballinger Point
19 Henshall Point
20 Dorrington Point
21 Warren Ho
22 Fairlie Ct
23 Regent Sq
24 Hackworth Point
25 Priestman Point
26 Wingate Ho
27 Nethercott Ho
28 Thelbridge Ho
29 Bowden Ho
30 Kerscott Ho
31 Southcott Ho
32 Birchdown Ho
33 Upcott Ho
34 Langmead Ho
35 Limscott Ho
36 Northleigh Ho
37 Huntshaw Ho
38 Chagford Ho
39 Ashcombe Ho
40 Shillingford Ho
41 Patrick Connolly Gdns
42 Lester Ct
43 Franklin St
44 Taft Way
45 Washington Cl
46 Veronica Ho
47 William Guy Gdns
48 Denbury Ho
49 Holsworthy Ho
50 Padstone Ho
B2 1 Miller's House Visitor Ctr
C1 1 Crescent Court Bsns Ctr
2 Ashmead Bsns Ctr
3 Forward Bsns Ctr The
C4 1 Victoria Mills
2 Hallings Wharf Studios
3 Poland Ho
4 Peter Heathfield Ho
5 Burford Rd

28

A1 1 Lantry Ct
2 Rosemount Ct
3 Moreton Twr
4 Acton Central Ind Est
5 Rufford Twr
6 Narrow St
7 Mount Pl
8 Sidney Miller Ct
9 Mill Hill Terr
10 Cheltenham Pl
11 Mill Hill Gr
12 Benjamin Ho
13 Arlington Ct
14 Lombard Ct
15 Steyne Ho
B1 1 Rectory Rd
2 Derwentwater Mans
3 Market Pl
4 Hooper's Mews
5 Cromwell Pl
6 Locarno Rd
7 Edgecote Cl
8 Harleyford Manor
9 Coopers Ct
10 Avingdor Ct
11 Steyne Ho
B3 1 Avon Ct
2 Bromley Lo
3 Walter Ct
4 Lynton Terr
5 Acton Ho
6 Fells Haugh
7 Springfield Ct
8 Tamarind Ct
9 Lynton Ct
10 Aspen Ct
11 Pegasus Ct
12 Friary Park Ct
C3 1 Rosebank Gdns
2 Rosebank
3 Edinburgh Ho
4 Western Ct
5 Kilronan

30

A1 1 Arlington Ho
2 Lugard Ho
3 Shabana Ct
4 Sitarey Ct
5 Oaklands Ct
6 Davenport Mews
A2 1 Abercrombie Ho
2 Bathurst Ho
3 Brisbane Ho
4 Bentinck Ho
5 Ellenborough Ho
6 Lawrence Cl
7 Mackenzie Cl
8 Carteret Ho
9 Calvert Ho
10 Winthrop Ho
11 Auckland Ho
12 Blaxland Ho
13 Havelock Cl
14 Hargraves Ho
15 Hudson Cl
16 Phipps Ho
17 Lawson Ho
18 Hastings Ho
19 Wolfe Ho
20 Malabar Ct
21 Commonwealth Ave
22 Charnock Ho
23 Canning Ho
24 Cornwallis Ho
25 Commonwealth Ave
26 Champlain Ho

30 A2

27 Grey Ho
28 Durban Ho
29 Baird Ho
30 Campbell Ho
31 Mitchell Ho
32 Denham Ho
33 Mackay Ho
34 Evans Ho
35 Davis Ho
36 Mandela Cl
A3 1 Holborn Ho
2 Clement Danes Ho
3 Vellacott Ho
4 O'Driscoll Ho
5 King Ho
6 Daley Ho
7 Selma Ho
8 Garrett Ho
B1 1 Linden Ct
2 Frithville Ct
3 Blomfield Mans
4 Poplar Mews
5 Hopgood St
6 Westwood Ho
7 Stanlake Mews
8 Stanlake Villas
9 Alexandra Mans
B3 1 Latimer Ind Est
2 Pankhurst Ho
3 Quadrangle The
4 Nightingale Ho
5 Gordon Ct
6 Ducane Cl
7 Browning Ho
8 Pavilion Terr
9 Ivebury Ct
10 Olympic Ho
B4 1 Galleywood Ho
2 Edgcott Ho
3 Cuffley Ho
4 Addlestone Ho
5 Hockliffe Ho
6 Sarratt Ho
7 Firle Ho
8 Sutton Est The
9 Terling Ho
10 Danes Ho
11 Udimore Ho
12 Vange Ho
13 Binbrook Ho
14 Yeadon Ho
15 Yatton Ho
16 Yarrow Ho
17 Clement Ho
18 Danebury
19 Coronation Ct
20 Calderon Pl
21 St Quintin Gdns
C1 1 St Katherine's Wlk
2 Dorrit Ho
3 Pickwick Ho
4 Dombey Ho
5 Caranday Villas
6 Mortimer Ho
7 Nickleby Ho
8 Stebbing Ho
9 Boxmoor Ho
10 Poynter Ho
11 Swanscombe Ho
12 Darnley Terr
13 Norland Ho
14 Hume Ho
15 Boundary Ho
16 Norland Rd
17 Helix Ct
C2 1 Frinstead Ho
2 Hurstway Wlk
3 Testerton Wlk
4 Grenfell Wlk
5 Grenfell Twr
6 Barandon Wlk
7 Treadgold Ho
8 St Clements Ct
9 Willow Way
10 Florence Ho
11 Dora Ho
12 Carton Ho
13 Agnes Ho
14 Marley Ho
15 Estella Ho
16 Waynflete Sq
17 Pippin Ho
18 Baseline Business Studios
C3 1 Kelfield Ct
2 Downing Ho
3 Crosfield Ct
4 Robinson Ho
5 Scampston Mews
6 Girton Villas
7 Ray Ho
8 Walmer Ho
9 Goodrich Ct
10 Arthur Ct
11 Whitstable Ho
12 Kingsnorth Ho
13 Bridge Cl
14 Prospect Ho
15 St Marks Rd
16 Whitchurch Ho
17 Blechynden Ho
18 Waynflete Sq
19 Bramley Ho
20 Dixon Ho

31

A3 1 Malton Mews
2 Lancaster Lo
3 Manning Ho
4 Galsworthy Ho
5 Hudson Ho
6 Cambourne Mews
7 Upper Talbot Wlk
8 Kingsdown Cl
9 Lower Clarendon Wlk
10 Talbot Grove Ho
11 Clarendon Wlk
12 Upper Clarendon Wlk
13 Camelford Wlk
14 Upper Camelford Wlk
15 Camelford Ct
A4 1 Murchison Ho
2 MacAulay Ho
3 Chesterton Ho
4 Chiltern Ho
5 Lionel Ho
6 Watts Ho
7 Wheatstone Ho
8 Telford Ho
9 Golborne Mews
10 Millwood St
11 St Columb's Ho
12 Norfolk Mews
13 Lionel Mews
B3 1 Silvester Ho
2 Golden Cross Mews
3 Tavistock Mews
4 Clydesdale Ho
5 Melchester
6 Pinehurst Ct
7 Denbigh Ho
B4 1 Blagrove Rd
2 All Saints Ho
3 Tavistock Ho
4 Leamington Ho
C3 1 Shottsford
2 Tolchurch
3 Casterbridge
4 Sandbourne
5 Anglebury
6 Weatherbury
7 Westbourne Gr Mews
8 Rosehart Mews
9 Viscount Ct
10 Hereford Mans
11 Hereford Mews
C4 1 Ascot Ho
2 Ashgrove Ct
3 Lockbridge Ct
4 Swallow Ct
5 Nightingale Lo
6 Hammond Lo
7 Penfield Lo
8 Harvey Lo
9 Hunter Lo
10 Barnard Lo
11 Falcon Lo
12 Johnson Lo
13 Livingstone Lo
14 Nuffield Lo
15 Finch Lo
16 Polesworth Ho
17 Oversley Ho
18 Derrycombe Ho
19 Buckshead Ho
20 Combe Ho
21 Culham Ho
22 Dainton Ho
23 Devonport Ho
24 Honwell Ho
25 Truro Ho
26 Sunderland Ho
27 Stonehouse Ho
28 Riverford Ho
29 Portishead Ho
30 Mickleton Ho
31 Keyham Ho
32 Moulsford Ho
33 Shrewsbury Mews
34 St Stephen's Mews
35 Westway Lo
36 Langley Ho
37 Brindley Ho
38 Radway Ho
39 Astley Ho
40 Willow Ct
41 Larch Ct
42 Elm Ct
43 Beech Ct
44 Worcester Ct
45 Union Ct
46 Leicester Ct
47 Kennet Ct
48 Oxford Ct
49 Fazerley Ct

32

A1 1 China Ct
2 Wellington Terr
3 Stevedore St
4 Portland Sq
5 Reardon Ho
6 Lowder Ho
7 Meeting House Alley
8 Farthing Fields
9 Oswell Ho
10 Park Lo
11 Doughty Ct
12 Inglefield Sq
13 Chopin's Ct
14 Welsh Ho
15 Hilliard Ho
16 Clegg St
17 Tasman Ho
18 Ross Ho
19 Wapping Dock St
20 Bridewell Pl
21 New Tower Bldgs
22 Tower Bldgs
23 Chimney Ct
24 Jackman Ho
25 Fenner Ho
26 Franklin Ho
27 Frobisher Ho
28 Flinders Ho
29 Chancellor Ho
30 Beechey Ho
31 Reardon Path
32 Parry Ho
33 Vancover Ho
34 Willoughby Ho
35 Sanctuary The
36 Dundee Ct
37 Pierhead Wharf
38 Scandrett St
39 St Johns Ct
A2 1 Newton Ho
2 Richard Neale Ho
3 Maddocks Ho
4 Cornwall St
5 Brockmer Ho
6 Dellow Ho
7 Bewley Ho
8 Artichoke Hill
9 Queen Anne Terr
10 King Henry Terr
11 King Charles Terr
12 Queen Victoria Terr
13 Sovereign Ct
14 Princes Court Bsns Ctr
15 Kingsley Mews
A3 1 Peter Best Ho
2 Mellish Ho
3 Porchester Ho
4 Dickson Ho
5 Joscoyne Ho
6 Silvester Ho
7 Wilton Ct
8 Sarah Ho
9 Bridgen Ho
10 Tylney Ho
11 Greenwich Ct
12 Damien Ct
13 Philson Mans
14 Siege Ho
15 Jacob Mans
16 Proud Ho
17 Sly St
18 Barnett St
19 Kinder St
20 Richard St
21 Hungerford St
22 Colstead Ho
23 Melwood Ho
24 Wicker St
25 Langdale St
26 Chapman Ho
27 Burwell Cl
28 Walford Ho
29 Welstead Ho
30 Norton Ho
31 Turnour Ho
32 Luke Ho
33 Dunch St
34 Sheridan St
35 Brinsley St
A4 1 Wodeham Gdns
2 Castlemaine St
3 Court St
B1 1 John Rennie Wlk
2 Malay Ho
3 Wainwright Ho
4 Riverside Mans
5 Shackleton Ho
6 Whitehorn Ho
7 Wavel Ct
8 Prusom's Island
B2 1 Shadwell Pl
2 Gosling Ho
3 Vogler Ho
4 Donovan Ho
5 Knowlden Ho
6 Chamberlain Ho
7 Moore Ho
8 Thornewill Ho
9 Fisher Ho
10 All Saints Ct
11 Coburg Dwellings
12 Lowood Ho
13 Solander Gdns
14 Chancery Bldgs
15 Ring Ho
16 Juniper St
17 Gordon Ho
18 West Block
19 North Block
20 South Block
21 Ikon Ho
B3 1 Woollon Ho
2 Dundalk Ho
3 Anne Goodman Ho
4 Newbold Cotts
5 Kerry Ho
6 Zion Ho
7 Longford Ho
8 Bromehead St
9 Athlone Ho
10 Jubilee Mans
11 Harriott Ho
12 Brayford Sq
13 Clearbrook Way
14 Rochelle Ct
15 Winterton Ho
16 Swift Ho
17 Brinsley Ho
18 Dean Ho
19 Foley Ho
20 Robert Sutton Ho
21 Montpelier Pl
22 Glastonbury Pl
23 Steel's La
24 Masters Lo
25 Stylus Apartments
26 Arta Ho
B4 1 Fulneck
2 Gracehill
3 Ockbrook
4 Fairfield
5 Dunstan Hos
6 Cressy Ct
7 Cressy Hos
8 Callahan Cotts
9 Lindley Ho
10 Mayo Ho
11 Wexford Ho

12 Sandhurst Ho
13 Addis Ho
14 Colverson Ho
15 Beckett Ho
16 Jarman Ho
17 Armsby Ho
18 Wingrad Ho
19 Miranda Cl
20 Drake Ho
21 Ashfield Yd
22 Magri Wlk
23 Jean Pardies Ho
24 St Vincent De Paul Ho
25 Sambrook Ho
26 Louise De Marillac Ho
27 Dagobert Ho
28 Le Moal Ho
29 Odette Duval Ho
30 Charles Auffray Ho
31 Boisseau Ho
32 Clichy Ho
33 Paymal Ho
C1 1 Clarence Mews
2 Raleigh Ct
3 Katherine Cl
4 Woolcombes Ct
5 Tudor Ct
6 Quayside Ct
7 Princes Riverside Rd
8 Surrey Ho
9 Tideway Ct
10 Edinburgh Ct
11 Falkirk Ct
12 Byelands Cl
13 Gwent Ct
14 Lavender Ho
15 Abbotshade Rd
16 Bellamy's Ct
17 Blenheim Ct
18 Sandringham Ct
19 Hampton Ct
20 Windsor Ct
21 Balmoral Ct
22 Westminster Ct
23 Beatson Wlk
C2 1 Barnardo Gdns
2 Roslin Ho
3 Glamis Est
4 Peabody Est
5 East Block
6 Highway Trad Ctr The
7 Highway Bsns Pk The
8 Cranford Cotts
9 Ratcliffe Orch
10 Scotia Bldg
11 Mauretania Bldg
12 Compania Bldg
13 Sirius Bldg
14 Unicorn Bldg
15 Keepier Wharf
C3 1 Pattison Ho
2 St Thomas Ho
3 Arbour Ho
4 Bladen Ho
5 Antill Terr
6 Majorie Mews
7 Billing Ho
8 Dowson Ho
9 Lipton Rd
10 Chalkwell Ho
11 Corringham Ho
12 Ogilvie Ho
13 Edward Mann Cl
14 Reservoir Studios
15 Lighterman Mews
C4 1 Roland Mews
2 Beatrice Ho
3 Morecambe Cl
4 Stepney Green Ct
5 Milrood Ho
6 Panama Ho
7 Galway Ho
8 Jacqueline Ho
9 Crown Mews
10 Caspian Ho
11 Darien Ho
12 Riga Ho
13 Flores Ho
14 Taranto Ho
15 Aden Ho
16 Master's St
17 Rosary Ct

33

A1 1 Edward Sq
2 Prince Regent Ct
3 Codrington Ct
4 Pennington Ct
5 Cherry Ct
6 Ash Ct
7 Beech Ct
8 Hazel Ct
9 Laurel Ct
A2 1 St Georges Sq
2 Drake Ho
3 Osprey Ho
4 Fleet Ho
5 Gainsborough Ho
6 Victory Pl
7 Challenger Ho
8 Conrad Ho
9 Lock View Ct
10 Shoulder of Mutton Alley
11 Frederick Sq
12 Helena Sq
13 Elizabeth Sq
14 Sophia Sq
15 William Sq
16 Lamb Ct
17 Lockside
18 Adriatic Bldg
19 Ionian Bldg
20 Regents Gate Ho
A3 1 Hearnshaw St
2 Berry Cotts
3 Causton Cotts
4 Elizabeth Blount Ct
5 Carr St
6 Shaw Cres
7 Darnley Ho
8 Mercer's Cotts
9 Troon Ho
10 Ratcliffe Ho
11 Wakeling St
12 York Sq
13 Anglia Ho
14 Cambria Ho
15 Caledonia Ho
16 Ratcliffe La
17 Bekesbourne St
18 John Scurr Ho
19 Regents Canal Ho
20 Basin App
21 Powlesland Ct
A4 1 Waley St
2 Edith Ramsay Ho
3 Andaman Ho
4 Atlantic Ho
5 Pevensey Ho
6 Solent Ho
7 Lorne Ho
8 Cromarty Ho
9 Dakin Pl
10 Greaves Cotts
11 Donaghue Cotts
12 Ames Cotts
13 Waterview Ho
14 Limehouse Fields Est
B2 1 Hamilton Ho
2 Imperial Ho
3 Oriana Ho
4 Queens Ct
5 Brightlingsea Pl
6 Faraday Ho
7 Ropemaker's Fields
8 Oast Ct
9 Mitre The
10 Bate St
11 Joseph Irwin Ho
12 Padstow Ho
13 Bethlehem Ho
14 Saunders Cl
15 Roche Ho
16 Stocks Pl
17 Trinidad Ho
18 Grenada Ho
19 Kings Ho
20 Dunbar Wharf
21 Limekiln Wharf
22 Belgrave Ct
23 Eaton Ho
B3 1 Dora Ho
2 Flansham Ho
3 Gatwick Ho
4 Ashpark Ho
5 Newdigate Ho
6 Midhurst Ho
7 Redbourne Ho
8 Southwater Cl
9 Andersens Wharf
10 Whatman Ho
11 Butler Ho
12 Fitzroy Ho
13 Salmon St
14 Mission The
15 Aithan Ho
16 Britley Ho
17 Cheadle Ho
18 Elland Ho
19 Wharf La
20 Docklands Ct
21 Park Heights Ct
22 Grosvenor Ct
23 Lime House Ct
24 Swallow Pl
25 St Anne's Trad Est
B4 1 Wearmouth Ho
2 Elmslie Point
3 Grindley Ho
4 Stileman Ho
5 Wilcox Ho
6 Huddart St
7 Robeson St
8 Couzens Ho
9 Perley Ho
10 Whytlaw Ho
11 Booker Cl
12 Tunley Gn
13 Callingham Cl
14 Bowry Ho
15 Perkins Ho
16 Printon Ho
17 Tasker Ho
C2 1 West India Ho
2 Berber Pl
3 Birchfield Ho
4 Elderfield Ho
5 Thornfield Ho
6 Gorsefield Ho
7 Arborfield Ho
8 Colborne Ho
9 East India Bldgs
10 Compass Point
11 Salter St
12 Garland Ct
13 Bogart Ct
14 Fonda Ct
15 Welles Ct
16 Rogers Ct
17 Premier Pl
18 Kelly Ct
19 Flynn Ct
20 Mary Jones Ho
21 Cannon Dr
22 Horizon Bldg
C3 1 Landin Ho
2 Thomas Road Ind Est
3 Vickery's Wharf
4 Abbotts Wharf
5 Limehouse Ct
6 Charlesworth Ho
7 Gurdon Ho
8 Trendell Ho
9 Menteath Ho
10 Minchin Ho
11 Donne Ho
12 Old School Sq
13 Anglesey Ho
14 Gough Wlk
15 Baring Ho
16 Gladstone Ho
17 Hopkins Ho
18 Granville Ho
19 Overstone Ho
20 Pusey Ho
21 Russell Ho
22 Stanley Ho
C4 1 Bredel Ho
2 Linton Ho
3 Matthews Ho
4 Woodcock Ho
5 Limborough Ho
6 Maydwell Ho
7 Underhill Ho
8 Meyrick Ho
9 Ambrose Ho
10 Richardson Ho
11 Carpenter Ho
12 Robinson Ho
13 Bellmaker Ct
14 Lime Tree Ct
15 Bracken Ho
16 Bramble Ho
17 Berberis Ho
18 Bilberry Ho
19 Ladyfern Ho
20 Rosebay Ho
21 Invicta Cl
22 Phoenix Bsns Ctr
23 Metropolitan Cl
24 Busbridge Ho

34

A2 1 Westcott Ho
2 Corry Ho
3 Malam Gdns
4 Blomfield Ho
5 Devitt Ho
6 Leyland Ho
7 Wigram Ho
8 Willis Ho
9 Balsam Ho
10 Finch's Ct
11 Poplar Bath St
12 Lawless St
13 Storey Ho
14 Abbot Ho
15 Woodall Cl
16 Landon Wlk
17 Goodhope Ho
18 Goodfaith Ho
19 Winant Ho
20 Goodspeed Ho
21 Lubbock Ho
22 Goodwill Ho
23 Martindale Ho
24 Holmsdale Ho
25 Norwood Ho
26 Constant Ho
A3 1 Colebrook Ho
2 Essex Ho
3 Salisbury Ho
4 Maidstone Ho
5 Osterley Ho
6 Norwich Ho
7 Clarissa Ho
8 Elgin Ho
9 Shaftesbury Lo
10 Shepherd Ho
11 Jeremiah St
12 Elizabeth Cl
13 Chilcot Cl
14 Fitzgerald Ho
15 Vesey Path
16 Ennis Ho
17 Kilmore Ho
18 Cygnet House N
19 Cygnet House S
A4 1 Sumner Ho
2 David Hewitt Ho
3 St Gabriels Cl
4 Limehouse Cut
5 Colmans Wharf
6 Foundary Ho
7 Radford Ho
B1 1 Lumina Bldg
2 Nova Ct W
3 Nova Ct E
4 Aurora Bldg
5 Arran Ho
6 Kintyre Ho
7 Vantage Mews
8 Managers St
9 Horatio Pl
10 Concordia Wharf
B2 1 Discovery Ho
2 Mountague Pl
3 Virginia Ho
4 Collins Ho
5 Lawless Ho
6 Carmichael Ho
7 Commodore Ho
8 Mermaid Ho
9 Bullivant St
10 Anderson Ho
11 Mackrow Wlk
12 Robin Hood Gdns
13 Prestage Way
B3 1 Glenkerry Ho
2 Carradale Ho
3 Langdon Ho
4 Balfron Twr
5 St Frideswides Mews

6 Tabard Ct
7 Delta Bldg
8 Findhorn St
9 Kilbrennan Ho
10 Thistle Ho
11 Heather Ho
12 Tartan Ho
13 Sharman Ho
14 Trident Ho
15 Wharf View Ct
B4 1 Mills Gr
2 St Michaels Ct
3 Duncan Ct
C2 1 Quixley St
2 Romney Ho
3 Pumping Ho
4 Switch Ho
5 Wingfield Ct
6 Explorers Ct
7 Sexton Ct
8 Keel Ct
9 Bridge Ct
10 Sail Ct
11 Settlers Ct
12 Pilgrims Mews
13 Studley Ct
14 Wotton Ct
15 Cape Henry Ct
16 Bartholomew Ct
17 Adventurers Ct
18 Susan Constant Ct
19 Atlantic Ct
C3 1 Lansbury Gdns
2 Theseus Ho
3 Adams Ho
4 Jones Ho
5 Sam March Ho
6 Arapiles Ho
7 Athenia Ho
8 Julius Ho
9 Jervis Bay Ho
10 Helen Mackay Ho
11 Gaze Ho
12 Ritchie Ho
13 Blairgowrie Ct
14 Circle Ho
15 Dunkeld Ho
16 Rosemary Dr
17 Sorrel La
18 East India Dock Road Tunnel

35

B3 1 Newton Point
2 Sparke Terr
3 Montesquieu Terr
4 Crawford Point
5 Rathbone Ho
6 George St
7 Emily St
8 Fendt Cl
9 Sabbarton St
10 Briary Ct
11 Shaftesbury Ho
B4 1 Radley Terr
2 Bernard Cassidy St
3 Rathbone Mkt
4 Thomas North Terr
5 Mary St
6 Hughes Terr
7 Swanscombe Point
8 Rawlinson Point
9 Kennedy Cox Ho
10 Cooper St

C1 1 Capulet Mews
2 Pepys Cres
3 De Quincey Mews
4 Hardy Ave
5 Tom Jenkinson Rd
6 Kennacraig Cl
7 Charles Flemwell Mews
8 Gatcombe Rd
9 Badminton Mews
10 Holyrood Mews
11 Britannia Gate
12 Dalemain Mews
13 Bowes-Lyon Hall
14 Lancaster hall
15 Victoria Hall
C2 1 Clements Ave
2 Martindale Ave
3 Balearic Apts
4 Marmara Apts
5 Baltic Apts
6 Coral Apts
7 Aegean Apts
8 Capital East Apts
C4 1 Odeon Ct
2 Edward Ct
3 Newhaven La
4 Ravenscroft Cl
5 Douglas Rd
6 Ferrier Point
7 Harvey Point
8 Wood Point
9 Trinity St
10 Pattinson Point
11 Clinch Ct
12 Mint Bsns Pk

36

A1 1 Burford Ho
2 Hope Cl
3 Centaur Ct
4 Phoenix Ct
C1 1 Surrey Cres
2 Forbes Ho
3 Haining Cl
4 Melville Ct
5 London Stile
6 Stile Hall Par
7 Priory Lo
8 Kew Bridge Ct
9 Meadowcroft
10 St James Ct
11 Rivers Ho

37

A1 1 Churchdale Ct
2 Cromwell Cl
3 Cambridge Rd S
4 Oxbridge Ct
5 Tomlinson Cl
6 Gunnersbury Mews
7 Grange The
8 Gunnersbury Cl
9 Bellgrave Lo
A4 1 Cheltenham Pl
2 Beaumaris Twr
3 Arundel Ho
4 Pevensey Ct
5 Jerome Twr
6 Anstey Ct
7 Bennett Ct
8 Gunnersbury Ct
9 Barrington Ct
10 Hope Gdns
11 Park Road E
B1 1 Arlington Park Mans

2 Sandown Ho
3 Goodwood Ho
4 Windsor Ho
5 Lingfield Ho
6 Ascot Ho
7 Watchfield Ct
8 Belgrave Ct
9 Beverley Ct
10 Beaumont Ct
11 Harvard Rd
12 Troubridge Ct
13 Branden Lo
14 Fromow's Cnr
B2 1 Chiswick Green Studios
2 Bell Ind Est
3 Fairlawn Ct
4 Dukes Gate
5 Dewsbury Ct
6 Chiswick Terr
7 Mortlake Ho
B3 1 Blackmore Twr
2 Bollo Ct
3 Kipling Twr
4 Lawrence Ct
5 Maugham Ct
6 Reade Ct
7 Woolf Ct
8 Shaw Ct
9 Verne Ct
10 Wodehouse Ct
11 Greenock Rd
12 Garden Ct
13 Barons Gate
14 Cleveland Rd
15 Carver Cl
16 Chapter Cl
17 Beauchamp Cl
18 Holmes Ct
19 Copper Mews
B4 1 Belgrave Cl
2 Buckland Wlk
3 Frampton Ct
4 Telfer Cl
5 Harlech Twr
6 Corfe Twr
7 Barwick Ho
8 Charles Hocking Ho
9 Sunninghill Ct
10 Salisbury St
11 Jameson Pl
12 Castle Cl
C1 1 Chatsworth Lo
2 Prospect Pl
3 Townhall Ave
4 Devonhurst Pl
5 Heathfield Ct
6 Horticultural Pl
7 Merlin Ho
8 Garth Rd
9 Autumn Rise
C2 1 Disraeli Cl
2 Winston Wlk
3 Rusthall Mans
4 Bedford Park Mans
5 Essex Place Sq
6 Holly Rd
7 Homecross Ho
8 Swan Bsns Ctr
9 Jessop Ho

38

A1 1 Glebe Cl
2 Devonshire Mews
3 Binns Terr
4 Ingress St
5 Swanscombe Rd

6 Brackley Terr
7 Stephen Fox Ho
8 Manor Gdns
9 Coram Ho
10 Flaxman Ho
11 Thorneycroft Ho
12 Thornhill Ho
13 Kent Ho
14 Oldfield Ho
A2 1 Chestnut Ho
2 Bedford Ho
3 Bedford Cnr
4 Sydney Ho
5 Bedford Park Cnr
6 Priory Gdns
7 Windmill Alley
8 Castle Pl
9 Jonathan Ct
10 Windmill Pas
11 Chardin Rd
12 Gable Ho
A3 1 Fleet Ct
2 Ember Ct
3 Emlyn Gdns
4 Clone Ct
5 Brent Ct
6 Abbey Ct
7 Ormsby Lo
8 St Catherine's Ct
9 Lodge The
A4 1 Longford Ct
2 Mole Ct
3 Lea Ct
4 Wandle Ct
5 Beverley Ct
6 Roding Ct
7 Crane Ct
B1 1 Miller's Ct
2 British Grove Pas
3 British Grove S
4 Berestede Rd
5 North Eyot Gdns
B2 1 Flanders Mans
2 Stamford Brook Mans
3 Linkenholt Mans
4 Prebend Mans
5 Middlesex Ct
B3 1 Stamford Brook Gdns
2 Hauteville Court Gdns
3 Ranelagh Gdns
C1 1 Chisholm Ct
2 North Verbena Gdns
3 Western Terr
4 Verbena Gdns
5 Montrose Villas
6 Hammersmith Terr
7 South Black Lion La
8 St Peter's Wharf
C2 1 Hamlet Ct
2 Derwent Ct
3 Westcroft Ct
4 Black Lion Mews
5 St Peter's Villas
6 Standish Ho
7 Chambon Pl
8 Court Mans
9 Longthorpe Ct
10 Charlotte Ct
11 Westside
12 Park Ct
13 London Ho
C3 1 Elizabeth Finn Ho
2 Ashchurch Ct

3 King's Par
4 Inver Ct
5 Ariel Ct
6 Pocklington Lo
7 Vitae Apartments
C4 1 Becklow Gdns
2 Victoria Ho
3 Lycett Pl
4 Kylemore Ct
5 Alexandra Ct
6 Lytten Ct
7 Becklow Mews
8 Northcroft Ct
9 Bailey Ct
10 Spring Cott
11 Landor Wlk
12 Laurence Mews
13 Hadyn Park Ct
14 Askew Mans
15 Malvern Ct

39

A1 1 Prince's Mews
2 Aspen Gdns
3 Hampshire Hog La
4 Blades Ct
A2 1 Albion Gdns
2 Flora Gdns
3 Lamington St
4 Felgate Mews
5 Galena Ho
6 Albion Mews
7 Albion Ct
8 King Street Cloisters
9 Dimes Pl
10 Clarence Ct
11 Hampshire Hog La
12 Marryat Ct
13 Ravenscourt Ho
A3 1 Ravenscourt Park Mans
2 Paddenswick Ct
3 Ashbridge Ct
A4 1 Westbush Ct
2 Goldhawk Mews
3 Sycamore Ho
4 Shackleton Ct
5 Drake Ct
6 Scotts Ct
7 Raleigh Ct
8 Melville Court Flats
9 Southway Cl
B1 1 Bridge Avenue Mans
2 Bridgeview
3 College Ct
4 Beatrice Ho
5 Amelia Ho
6 Edith Ho
7 Joanna Ho
8 Mary Ho
9 Adela Ho
10 Sophia Ho
11 Henrietta Ho
12 Charlotte Ho
13 Alexandra Ho
14 Bath Pl
15 Elizabeth Ho
16 Margaret Ho
17 Peabody Est
18 Eleanor Ho
19 Isabella Ho
20 Caroline Ho
21 Chancellors Wharf
22 Sussex Pl

B2 1 Phoenix Lodge Mans
2 Samuel's Cl
3 Broadway Arc
4 Brook Ho
5 Hammersmith Broadway
6 Broadway Ctr The
7 Cambridge Ct
8 Ashcroft Sq
B4 1 Verulam Ho
2 Grove Mans
3 Frobisher Ct
4 Library Mans
5 Pennard Mans
6 New Shepherd's Bush Mkt
7 Kerrington Ct
8 Granville Mans
9 Romney Ct
10 Rayner Ct
11 Sulgrave Gdns
12 Bamborough Gdns
13 Hillary Ct
14 Market Studios
15 Lanark Mans
C3 1 Grosvenor Residences
2 Blythe Mews
3 Burnand Ho
4 Bradford Ho
5 Springvale Terr
6 Ceylon Rd
7 Walpole Ct
8 Bronte Ct
9 Boswell Ct
10 Souldern Rd
11 Brook Green Flats
12 Haarlem Rd
13 Stafford Mans
14 Lionel Mans
15 Barradell Ho
C4 1 Vanderbilt Villas
2 Bodington Ct
3 Kingham Cl
4 Clearwater Terr
5 Lorne Gdns
6 Cameret Ct
7 Bush Ct
8 Shepherds Ct
9 Rockley Ct
10 Grampians The
11 Charcroft Ct
12 Addison Park Mans
13 Sinclair Mans
14 Fountain Ct
15 Woodford Ct
16 Roseford Ct
17 Woodstock Studios

40

A1 1 Hockney Ct
2 Toulouse Ct
3 Lowry Ct
4 Barry Ho
5 Lewis Ct
6 Gainsborough Ct
7 Renoir Ct
8 Blake Ct
9 Raphael Ct
10 Rembrandt Ct
11 Constable Ct
12 Da Vinci Ct
13 Gaugin Ct
14 Michelangelo Ct
15 Monet Ct
16 Weald Cl
17 Jasmin Lo
18 Birchmere Lo
19 Weybridge Ct
20 Florence Ho
21 Gleneagles Cl
22 Sunningdale Cl
23 Muirfield Cl
24 Turnberry Cl
25 St Andrews Cl
26 Kingsdown Cl
27 St Davids Cl
28 Galway Cl
29 Edenbridge Cl
30 Birkdale Cl
31 Tralee Ct
32 Woburn Ct
33 Belfry Cl
34 Troon Cl
35 Holywell Cl
A2 1 Market Pl
2 Trappes Ho
3 Thurland Ho
4 Ramsfort Ho
5 Hambley Ho
6 Holford Ho
7 Pope Ho
8 Southwell Ho
9 Mortain Ho
10 Radcliffe Ho
11 Southwark Park Est
12 Galleywall Road Trad Est
13 Trevithick Ho
14 Barlow Ho
15 Donkin Ho
16 Landmann Ho
17 Fitzmaurice Ho
18 Dodd Ho
A3 1 Perryn Rd
2 Chalfont Ho
3 Prestwood Ho
4 Farmer Ho
5 Gataker Ho
6 Gataker St
7 Cornick Ho
8 Glebe Ho
9 Matson Ho
10 Hickling Ho
11 St Andrews Ho
A4 1 Butterfield Cl
2 Janeway Pl
3 Trotwood Ho
4 Maylie Ho
5 Cranbourn Pas
6 Cranbourn Ho
7 Cherry Garden Ho
8 Burton Ho
9 Morriss Ho
10 Dixon's Alley
11 King Edward The Third Mews
12 Cathay St
13 Mission The
14 Millstream Ho
B2 1 Damory Ho
2 Antony Ho
3 Roderick Ho
4 Pedworth Gdns
5 Banner Ct
6 Rotherhithe Bsns Est
7 Beamish Ho
8 Corbetts Pas
9 Gillam Ho
10 Richard Ho
11 George Walter Ho
12 Westlake
13 Adron Ho
14 McIntosh Ho
B3 1 Blick Ho
2 Neptune Ho
3 Scotia Ct
4 Murdoch Ho
5 Edmonton Ct
6 Niagara Ct
7 Columbia Point
8 Ritchie Ho
9 Wells Ho
10 Helen Peele Cotts
11 Orchard Ho
12 Dock Offices
13 Landale Ho
14 Courthope Ho
15 Hithe Gr
16 China Hall Mews
B4 1 Mayflower St
2 St Mary's Est
3 Rupack St
4 Frank Whymark Ho
5 Adams Gardens Est
6 Hatteraick St
7 East India Ct
8 Bombay Ct
9 Stable Ho
10 Grannary The
11 Riverside
12 Cumberland Wharf
13 Seaford Ho
14 Hythe Ho
15 Sandwich Ho
16 Winchelsea Ho
17 Rye Ho
18 Kenning St
19 Western Pl
20 Ainsty St
21 Pine Ho
22 Beech Ho
23 Larch Ho
24 Turner Ct
25 Seth St
26 Risdon Ho
27 Risdon St
28 Aylton Est
29 Manitoba Ct
30 Calgary Ct
31 Irwell Est
32 St Olav's Sq
33 City Bsns Ctr
C2 1 John Kennedy Ho
2 Brydale Ho
3 Balman Ho
4 Tissington Ct
5 Harbord Ho
6 Westfield Ho
7 Albert Starr Ho
8 John Brent Ho
9 William Evans Ho
10 Raven Ho
11 Egret Ho
12 Fulmar Ho
13 Dunlin Ho
14 Siskin Ho
15 Sheldrake Ho
16 Buchanan Ct
17 Burrage Ct
18 Biddenham Ho
19 Ayston Ho
20 Empingham Ho
21 Deanshanger Ho
22 Codicote Ho
23 Buryfield Ct
C4 1 Schooner Cl
2 Dolphin Cl
3 Clipper Cl
4 Deauville Ct
5 Colette Ct
6 Coniston Ct
7 Virginia Ct
8 Derwent Ct
9 Grantham Ct
10 Serpentine Ct
11 Career Ct
12 Lacine Ct
13 Fairway Ct
14 Harold Ct
15 Spruce Ho
16 Cedar Ho
17 Sycamore Ho
18 Woodland Cres
19 Poplar Ho
20 Adelphi Ct
21 Basque Ct
22 Aberdale Ct
23 Quilting Ct
24 Chargrove Cl
25 Radley Ct
26 Greenacre Sq
27 Maple Leaf Sq
28 Stanhope Cl
29 Hawke Pl
30 Drake Cl
31 Brass Talley Alley
32 Monkton Ho
33 James Ho
34 Wolfe Cres

41

A2 1 Trafalgar Cl
2 Hornblower Cl
3 Cunard Wlk
4 Caronia Ct
5 Carinthia Ct
6 Freswick Ho
7 Graveley Ho
8 Husbourne Ho
9 Crofters Ct
10 Pomona Ho
11 Hazelwood Ho
12 Cannon Wharf Bsns Ctr
13 Bence Ho
14 Clement Ho
15 Pendennis Ho
16 Lighter Cl
17 Mast Ct
18 Rushcutters Ct
19 Boat Lifter Way
B1 1 Gransden Ho
2 Daubeney Twr
3 North Ho
4 Rochfort Ho
5 Keppel Ho
6 Camden Ho
7 Sanderson Ho
8 Berkeley Ho
9 Strafford Ho
10 Richman Ho
11 Hurleston Ho
12 Grafton Ho
13 Fulcher Ho
14 Citrus Ho
B2 1 Windsock Cl
2 St George's Mews
3 Linberry Wlk
4 Lanyard Ho
5 Golden Hind Pl
6 James Lind Ho
7 Harmon Ho
8 Pelican Ho
9 Bembridge Ho
10 Terrace The
11 George Beard Rd
12 Colonnade The
13 Pepys Ent Ctr
C1 1 Hudson Ct
2 Shackleton Ct
3 De Gama Pl
4 Mercator Pl
5 Maritime Quay
6 Perry Ct
7 Amundsen Ct
C2 1 Nova Bldg
2 Apollo Bldg
3 Gaverick Mews
4 Windmill Ho
5 Orion Point
6 Galaxy Bldg
7 Venus Ho
8 Olympian Ct
9 Poseidon Ct
10 Mercury Ct
11 Aphrodite Ct
12 Cyclops Mews
13 Neptune Ct
14 Artemis Ct
15 Hera Ct
16 Ares Ct
17 Ringwood Gdns
18 Dartmoor Wlk
19 Rothsay Wlk
20 Ashdown Wlk
21 Radnor Wlk
22 Ironmonger's Pl
23 Britannia Rd
24 Deptford Ferry Rd
25 Magellan Pl
26 Dockers Tanner Rd
C3 1 Bowsprit Point
2 St Hubert's Ho
3 John Tucker Ho
4 Broadway Wlk
5 Nash Ho
6 Fairlead Ho
7 Crosstrees Ho
8 Stanliff Ho
9 Keelson Ho
10 Clara Grant Ho
11 Gilbertson Ho
12 Scoulding Ho
13 Hibbert Ho
14 Cressall Ho
15 Alexander Ho
16 Kedge Ho
C4 1 Anchorage Point
2 Waterman Bldg
3 Jefferson Bldg
4 Pierpoint Bldg
5 Franklin Bldg
6 Vanguard Bldg
7 Edison Bldg
8 Seacon Twr
9 Naxos Bldg
10 Express Wharf
11 Hutching's Wharf
12 Tobago St
13 Bellamy Cl
14 Dowlen Ct
15 Cochrane Ho
16 Beatty Ho
17 Scott Ho
18 Laybourne Ho
19 Ensign Ho
20 Beaufort Ho
21 Spinnaker Ho
22 Bosun Cl

23 Topmast Point
24 Turner Ho
25 Constable Ho
26 Knighthead Point

42

A1 1 Slipway Ho
2 Taffrail Ho
3 Platehouse The
4 Wheelhouse The
5 Chart House The
6 Port House The
7 Beacon Ho
8 Blasker Wlk
9 Maconochies Rd
A2 1 Brassey Ho
2 Triton Ho
3 Warspite Ho
4 Rodney Ho
5 Conway Ho
6 Exmouth Ho
7 Akbar Ho
8 Arethusa Ho
9 Tasman Ct
10 Cutty Sark Ho
A3 1 Turnberry Quay
2 Balmoral Ho
3 Aegon Ho
4 Marina Point
B2 1 St John's Ho
2 Betty May Gray Ho
3 Castleton Ho
4 Urmston Ho
5 Salford Ho
6 Capstan Ho
7 Frigate Ho
8 Galleon Ho
9 Barons Lo
B3 1 Cardale St
2 Hickin St
3 John McDonald Ho
4 Thorne Ho
5 Skeggs Ho
6 St Bernard Ho
7 Kimberley Ho
8 Kingdon Ho
9 Killoran Ho
10 Alastor Ho
11 Lingard Ho
12 Yarrow Ho
13 Sandpiper Ct
14 Nightingale Ct
15 Robin Ct
16 Heron Ct
17 Ferndown Lo
18 Crosby Ho
B4 1 Llandovery Ho
2 Rugless Ho
3 Ash Ho
4 Elm Ho
5 Cedar Ho
6 Castalia Sq
7 Aspect Ho
8 Normandy Ho
9 Valiant Ho
10 Tamar Ho
11 Watkins Ho
12 Alice Shepherd Ho
13 Oak Ho
14 Ballin Ct
15 Martin Ct
16 Grebe Ct
17 Kingfisher Ct
18 Walkers Lo
19 Antilles Bay
C2 1 Verwood Lo
2 Fawley Lo
3 Lyndhurst Lo
4 Blyth Cl
5 Farnworth Ho
6 Francis Cl

43

A1 1 Bellot Gdns
2 Thornley Pl
3 King William La
4 Bolton Ho
5 Miles Ho
6 Mell St
7 Sam Manners Ho
8 Hatcliffe Almshouses
9 Woodland Wlk
10 Earlswood Cl
B1 1 Baldrey Ho
2 Christie Ho
3 Dyson Ho
4 Cliffe Ho
5 Moore Ho
6 Collins Ho
7 Lockyer Ho
8 Halley Ho
9 Kepler Ho
10 Sailacre Ho
11 Union Pk
B3 1 Teal St
2 Maurer Ct
3 Mudlarks Blvd
4 Renaissance Wlk
5 Alamaro Lo
C1 1 Layfield Ho
2 Westerdale Rd
3 Mayston Mews
4 Station Mews Terr

44

A4 1 Ferry Sq
2 Watermans Ct
3 Wilkes Rd
4 Albany Par
5 Charlton Ho
6 Albany Ho
7 Alma Ho
8 Griffin Ct
9 Cressage Ho
10 Tunstall Wlk
11 Trimmer Wlk
12 Running Horse Yd
13 Mission Sq
14 Distillery Wlk
B2 1 Primrose Ho
2 Lawman Ct
3 Royston Ct
4 Garden Ct
5 Capel Lo
6 Devonshire Ct
7 Celia Ct
8 Rosslyn Ho
9 Branstone Ct
10 Lamerton Lo
11 Kew Lo
12 Dunraven Ho
13 Stoneleigh Lo
14 Tunstall Ct
15 Voltaire
C2 1 Clarendon Ct
2 Quintock Ho
3 Broome Ct
4 Lonsdale Mews
5 Elizabeth Cotts
6 Sandways
7 Victoria Cotts
8 North Ave
9 Grovewood
10 Hamilton Ho
11 Melvin Ct
12 Royal Par
13 Power Ho
14 Station Ave
15 Blake Mews

45

A2 1 Terrano Ho
2 Oak Ho
3 Aura Ho
4 Maple Ho
5 Cedar Ho
6 Saffron Ho
7 Lime Ho
8 Lavender Ho
9 Juniper Ho

46

B1 1 Melrose Rd
2 Seaforth Lo
3 St John's Gr
4 Sussex Ct
5 Carmichael Ct
6 Hampshire Ct
7 Thorne Pas
8 Brunel Ct
9 Beverley Path

47

C4 1 Cobb's Hall
2 Dorset Mans
3 St Clements Mans
4 Bothwell St
5 Hawksmoor St

48

A1 1 Langport Ho
2 Iveagh Ho
3 Newark Ho
4 Edgehill Ho
5 Hopton Ho
6 Ashby Ho
7 Nevil Ho
A2 1 Fairbairn Gn
2 Hammelton Gn
3 Foxley Sq
4 Silverburn Ho
5 Butler Ho
6 Dalkeith Ho
7 Turner Cl
8 Bathgate Ho
9 Black Roof Ho
A4 1 Faunce Ho
2 Garbett Ho
3 Harvard Ho
4 Doddington Pl
5 Kean Ho
6 Jephson Ho
7 Cornish Ho
8 Bateman Ho
9 Molesworth Ho
10 Walters Ho
11 Cruden Ho
12 Brawne Ho
13 Prescott Ho
14 Chalmer's Wlk
15 Copley Cl
16 King Charles Ct
B1 1 Bergen Ho
2 Oslo Ho
3 Viking Ho
4 Jutland Ho
5 Norvic Ho
6 Odin Ho
7 Baltic Ho
8 Nobel Ho
9 Mercia Ho
10 Kenbury Gdns
11 Zealand Ho
12 Elsinore Ho
13 Norse Ho
14 Denmark Mans
15 Dane Ho
16 Canterbury Cl
17 York Cl
18 Kenbury Mans
19 Parade Mans
20 Winterslow Ho
21 Lilford Ho
22 Bartholomew Ho
23 Guildford Ho
24 Boston Ho
25 Hereford Ho
26 Weyhill Ho
27 Lichfield Ho
28 Lansdown Ho
29 Honiton Ho
30 Pinner Ho
31 Baldock Ho
32 Widecombe Ho
33 Nottingham Ho
34 Witham Ho
35 Barnet Ho
36 Empress Mews
B2 1 Bertha Neubergh Ho
2 Mornington Mews
3 Badsworth Rd
4 Pearson Cl
5 Elm Tree Ct
6 Samuel Lewis Trust Dwellings
7 Milkwell Yd
8 Keswick Ho
9 Mitcham Ho
B3 1 Boundary Ho
2 Day Ho
3 Burgess Ho
4 Carlyle Ho
5 Myers Ho
6 Thompson Ave
7 Palgrave Ho
8 Winnington Ho
9 Brantwood Ho
10 Lowell Ho
11 Jessie Duffett Ho
12 Otterburn Ho
13 Crossmount Ho
14 Venice Ct
15 Bowyer St
16 Livingstone Ho
17 Gothic Ct
18 Coniston Ho
19 Harlynwood
20 Carey Ct
21 Finley Ct
22 Grainger Ct
23 Hayes Ct
24 Moffat Ho
25 Marinel Ho
26 Hodister Cl
27 Arnot Ho
28 Lamb Ho
29 Kipling Ho
30 Keats Ho
31 Kenyon Ho
32 New Church Rd
33 Sir John Kirk Cl
C1 1 Selborne Rd
2 Hascombe Terr
C2 1 Joiners Arms Yd
2 Butterfly Wlk
3 Cuthill Wlk
4 Colonades The
5 Artichoke Mews
6 Peabody Bldgs
7 Brighton Ho
8 Park Ho
9 Peabody Ct
10 Lomond Ho
11 Lamb Ho
12 Kimpton Ct
13 Belham Wlk
14 Datchelor Pl
15 Harvey Rd
C3 1 Masterman Ho
2 Milton Ho
3 Pope Ho
4 Chester Ct
5 Marvel Ho
6 Flecker Ho
7 Landor Ho
8 Leslie Prince Ct
9 Evelina Mans
10 Langland Ho
11 Drinkwater Ho
12 Procter Ho
13 Shirley Ho
14 Drayton Ho
15 Bridges Ho
16 Cunningham Ho
17 Hood Ho
18 Herrick Ho
19 Dekker Ho
20 Houseman Way
21 Coleby Path
C4 1 Queens Ho
2 Arnside Ho
3 Horsley St
4 St Peter's Ho
5 St Johns Ho
6 St Marks Ho
7 St Stephens Ho
8 St Matthew's Ho
9 Red Lion Cl
10 Boyson Rd
11 Bradenham

49

A1 1 Springfield Ho
2 Craston Ho
3 Walters Ho
4 Edgecombe Ho
5 Fowler Ho
6 Rignold Ho
7 Chatham Ho
A2 1 Barnwell Ho
2 Brunswick Villas
3 St Giles Twr
4 Bentley Ho
5 Dawson Ho
6 Dryden Ho
7 Mayward Ho
8 Longleigh Ho
9 Fairwall Ho
10 Bodeney Ho
11 Sandby Ho
12 Vestry Mews
13 Netley
14 Lakanal
15 Racine
A3 1 Tower Mill Rd
2 Tilson Cl
3 Granville Sq
4 Edgar Wallace Cl
5 Potters Cl
6 Dorton Cl

7 Samuel Jones Ind Est
8 Dibden Ho
9 Marchwood Cl
10 Pilgrims Cloisters
11 Beacon Ho
12 Teather St
13 Stacy Path
14 Rumball Ho
15 Ballow Cl
16 Rill Ho
A4 1 Downend Ct
2 Andoversford Ct
3 Pearse St
4 Watling St
5 Gandolfi St
B2 1 Colbert
2 Voltaire
3 Finch Mews
4 Charles Coveney Rd
5 Bamber Rd
6 Crane St
7 Curlew Ho
8 Mallard Ho
9 Tern Ho
10 Crane Ho
11 Falcon Ho
12 Bryanston Ho
13 Basing Ct
14 Marcus Ho
15 Sheffield Ho
B3 1 Painswick Ct
2 Sharpness Ct
3 Mattingly Way
4 Hordle Prom N
5 Burcher Gale Gr
6 Calypso Cres
7 Hordle Prom S
8 Cinnamon Cl
9 Savannah Cl
10 Thames Ct
11 Shannon Ct
12 Amstel Ct
13 Danube Ct
14 Tilbury Cl
15 Hordle Prom E
16 Indus Ct
17 Oakcourt
18 Palm Ct
19 Rowan Ct
20 Blackthorn Ct
21 Pear Ct
22 Lidgate Rd
23 Whistler Mews
24 Boathouse Wlk
B4 1 Willsbridge Ct
2 Cam Ct
3 Quedgeley Ct
4 Saul Ct
5 Quenington Ct
6 Westonbirt Ct
7 Wickway Ct
C1 1 William Margrie Cl
2 William Blake Ho
3 Quantock Mews
4 Choumert Sq
5 Parkstone Rd
6 Atwell Rd
C2 1 Canal Head Public Sq
2 Angelina Ho
3 Jarvis Ho
4 Richland Ho
5 Honeywood Ho
6 Wakefield Ho
7 Primrose Ho
8 Hardcastle Ho
9 Dunstall Ho
10 Springtide Cl
11 Purdon Ho
12 Flamborough Ho
13 Lambrook Ho
14 Witcombe Point
15 Yarnfield Sq
16 Winford Ct
17 Portbury Cl
18 Robert Keen Cl
C3 1 Thornbill Ho
2 Vervain Ho
3 Woodstar Ho
4 Tamarind Ho
5 Hereford Retreat
6 Haymerle Ho
7 Furley Ho
8 Thomas Milner Ho
9 Applegarth Ho
10 Freda Corbett Cl
11 Rudbeck Ho
12 Henslow Ho
13 Lindley Ho
14 Collinson Ho
15 Sister Mabel's Way
16 Timberland Cl
17 Hastings Cl
18 Sidmouth Ho
19 Budleigh Ho
20 Stanesgate Ho
21 Breamore Ho
22 Ely Ho
23 Gisburn Ho
C4 1 Bowles Rd
2 Western Wharf
3 Northfield Ho
4 Millbrook Ho
5 Denstone Ho
6 Deerhurst Ho
7 Caversham Ho
8 Battle Ho
9 Cardiff Ho
10 Bridgnorth Ho
11 Exeter Ho
12 Grantham Ho
13 Aylesbury Ho
14 Royston Ho

50

A1 1 Walkynscroft
2 Ryegates
3 Hathorne Cl
4 Pilkington Rd
5 Russell Ct
6 Heaton Ho
7 Magdalene Cl
8 Iris Ct
A2 1 Willowdene
2 Pinedene
3 Oakdene
4 Beechdene
5 Hollydene
6 Wood Dene
7 Staveley Cl
9 Carnicot Ho
10 Martock Ct
11 Cherry Tree Ct
12 Kendrick Ct
A3 1 Tortington Ho
2 Credenhill Ho
3 Bromyard Ho
4 Hoyland Cl
5 Willowdene
6 Ashdene
7 Acorn Par
8 Havelock Ct
9 Springall St
10 Harry Lambourn Ho
11 Grenier Apartments
B1 1 Honiton Gdns
2 Selden Ho
3 Hathway Ho
4 Hathway St
5 Station Ct
B2 1 Trotman Ho
2 Boddington Ho
3 Heydon Ho
4 Boulter Ho
5 Astbury Bsns Pk
B3 1 Ambleside Point
2 Grasmere Point
3 Windermere Point
4 Roman Way
5 Laburnum Cl
6 Juniper Ho
7 Romney Cl
8 Hammersley Ho
9 Hutchinson Ho
10 Hammond Ho
11 Fir Tree Ho
12 Glastonbury Ct
13 Highbridge Ct
14 Filton Ct
15 Chiltern Ct
16 Cheviot Ct
B4 1 Penshurst Ho
2 Reculver Ho
3 Mereworth Ho
4 Camber Ho
5 Chiham Ho
6 Otford Ho
7 Olive Tree Ho
8 Aspen Ho
9 Lewis Silkin Ho
10 Richborough Ho
11 Dover Ho
12 Eynsford Ho
13 Horton Ho
14 Lamberhurst Ho
15 Canterbury Ind Pk
16 Upnall Ho
17 Sissinghurst Ho
18 Rochester Ho
19 Saltwood Ho
20 Leybourne Ho
21 Lullingstone Ho
C3 1 Richard Anderson Ct
2 Palm Tree Ho
3 Edward Robinson Ho
4 Antony Ho
5 Gerrard Ho
6 Palmer Ho
7 Pankhurst Cl
C4 1 Harrisons Ct
2 Grantley Ho
3 Sunbury Ct
4 Tilbury Ho
5 Graham Ct
6 Connell Ct
7 St Clements Ct
8 Henderson Ct
9 Jemotts Ct
10 Verona Ct
11 Heywood Ho
12 Francis Ct
13 Hind Ho
14 Donne Ho
15 Carew Ct
16 Burbage Ho
17 Newland Ho
18 Dobson Ho
19 Dalton Ho
20 Greene Ct
21 Redrup Ho
22 Tarplett Ho
23 Stunell Ho
24 Gasson Ho
25 Bryce Ho
26 Barnes Ho
27 Barkwith Ho
28 Bannister Ho
29 Apollo Ind Bsns Ctr

51

A2 1 Archer Ho
2 Browning Ho
3 Hardcastle Ho
4 Brooke Ho
5 Wallis Ho
A3 1 Batavia Ho
2 Marlowe Bsns Ctr
3 Batavia Mews
4 Woodrush Cl
5 Alexandra St
6 Primrose Wlk
7 Vansittart St
8 Granville Ct
9 Cottesbrook St
10 Ewen Henderson Ct
11 Fordham Ho
A4 1 Portland Ct
2 Phoenix Ct
3 Rainbow Ct
4 Hawke Twr
5 Chubworthy St
6 Woodpecker Rd
7 Hercules Ct
B3 1 Austin Ho
2 Exeter Way
3 Crossleigh Ct
4 Mornington Pl
5 Maple Ho
B4 1 Chester Ho
2 Lynch Wlk
3 Arlington Ho
4 Woodcote Ho
5 Cornbury Ho
6 Prospect Pl
7 Akintaro Ho
8 Mulberry Ho
9 Laurel Ho
10 Linden Ho
11 Ashford Ho
12 Wardalls Ho
13 Magnolia Ho
14 Howard Ho
15 Larch Cl
16 Ibis Ct
17 Merganser Ct
18 Wotton Rd
19 Kingfisher Sq
20 Sanderling Ct
21 Dolphin Twr
22 Mermaid Twr
23 Scoter Ct
24 Shearwater Ct
25 Brambling Ct
26 Kittiwake Ct
27 Diana Cl
28 Guillemot Ct
29 Marine Twr
30 Teal Ct
31 Lapwing Twr
32 Violet Cl
33 Skua Ct
34 Tristan Ct
35 Rosemary Ct
36 Cormorant Ct
37 Shelduck Ct
38 Eider Ct
39 Pintail Ct
C2 1 Admiralty Cl
2 Harton Lodge
3 Sylva Cotts
4 Pitman Ho
5 Heston Ho
6 Mereton Mans
7 Indiana Bldg
8 St John's Lodge
C3 1 Sandpiper Ct
2 Flamingo Ct
3 Titan Bsns Est
4 Rochdale Way
5 Speedwell St
6 Reginald Pl
7 Fletcher Path
8 Frankham Ho
9 Cremer Ho
10 Wilshaw Ho
11 Castell Ho
12 Holden Ho
13 Browne Ho
14 Resolution Way
15 Lady Florence Ctyd
16 Covell Ct
17 Albion Ho
C4 1 Dryfield Wlk
2 Blake Ho
3 Hawkins Ho
4 Grenville Ho
5 Langford Ho
6 Mandarin Ct
7 Bittern Ct
8 Lamerton St
9 Ravensbourne Mans
10 Armada St
11 Armada Ct
12 Benbow Ho
13 Oxenham Ho
14 Caravel Mews
15 Hughes Ho
16 Stretton Mans

52

A2 1 Washington Bldg
2 California Bldg
3 Utah Bldg
4 Montana Bldg
5 Oregon Bldg
6 Dakota bldg
7 Idaho Bldg
8 Atlanta Bldg
9 Colorado Bldg
10 Arizona Bldg
11 Nebraska Bldg
12 Alaska Bldg
13 Ohio Bldg
14 Charter Bldgs
15 Flamsteed Ct
16 Friendly Pl
17 Dover Ct
18 Robinscroft Mews
19 Doleman Ho
20 Plymouth Ho
A3 1 Finch Ho
2 Jubilee The
3 Maitland Cl
4 Ashburnham Retreat
B1 1 Ellison Ho
2 Pitmaston Ho
3 Aster Ho

52 B1
4 Windmill Cl
5 Hertmitage The
6 Burnett Ho
7 Lacey Ho
8 Darwin Ho
9 Pearmain Ho
B2 1 Penn Almshouses
2 Jervis Ct
3 Woodville Ct
4 Darnall Ho
5 Renbold Ho
6 Lindsell St
7 Plumbridge St
8 Trinity Gr
9 Hollymount Cl
10 Cade Tyler Ho
11 Robertson Ho
B3 1 Temair Ho
2 Royal Hill Ct
3 Prince of Orange La
4 Lambard Ho
5 St Marks Cl
6 Ada Kennedy Ct
7 Arlington Pl
8 Topham Ho
9 Darnell Ho
10 Hawks Mews
11 Royal Pl
12 Swanne Ho
13 Maribor
14 Serica Ct
15 Queen Elizabeth's Coll
B4 1 Crescent Arc
2 Greenwich Mkt
3 Turnpin La
4 Durnford St
5 Sexton's Ho
6 Bardsley Ho
7 Wardell Ho
8 Clavell St
9 Stanton Ho
10 Macey Ho
11 Boreman Ho
12 Clipper Appts
C4 1 Frobisher Ct
2 Hardy Cotts
3 Palliser Ho
4 Bernard Angell Ho
5 Corvette Sq
6 Travers Ho
7 Maze Hill Lodge
8 Park Place Ho

53
B3 1 Westcombe Ct
2 Kleffens Ct
3 Ferndale Ct
4 Combe Mews
5 Mandeville Cl
6 Pinelands Cl
C3 1 Mary Lawrenson Pl
2 Bradbury Ct
3 Dunstable Ct
4 Wentworth Ho
C4 1 Nethercombe Ho
2 Holywell Cl

54
A1 1 Lancaster Cotts
2 Lancaster Mews
3 Bromwich Ho
4 Priors Lo
5 Richmond Hill Ct
6 Glenmore Ho
7 Hillbrow
8 Heathshott
9 Friars Stile Pl
10 Spire Ct
11 Ridgeway
12 Matthias Ct
A2 1 Lichfield Terr
2 Union Ct
3 Carrington Lo
4 Wilton Ct
5 Egerton Ct
6 Beverley Lo
7 Bishop Duppa's Almshouses
8 Regency Wlk
9 Clear Water Ho
10 Onslow Avenue Mans
11 Michels Almshouses
12 Albany Pas
13 Salcombe Villas
A3 1 St John's Gr
2 Michel's Row
3 Michelsdale Dr
4 Blue Anchor Alley
5 Clarence St
6 Sun Alley
7 Thames Link Ho
8 Benns Wlk
9 Waterloo Pl
10 Northumbria Ct
B1 1 Chester Cl
2 Evesham Ct
3 Queen's Ct
4 Russell Wlk
5 Charlotte Sq
6 Jones Wlk
7 Hilditch Ho
8 Isabella Ct
9 Damer Ho
10 Eliot Ho
11 Fitzherbert Ho
12 Reynolds Pl
13 Chisholm Rd
B2 1 Alberta Ct
2 Beatrice Rd
3 Lorne Rd
4 York Rd
5 Connaught Rd
6 Albany Terr
7 Kingswood Ct
8 Selwyn Ct
9 Broadhurst Cl
B3 1 Towers The
2 Longs Ct
3 Sovereign Ct
4 Robinson Ct
5 Calvert Ct
6 Bedford Ct
7 Hickey's Almshouses
8 Church Estate Almshouses
9 Richmond International Bsns Ctr
10 Abercorn Mews

55
A3 1 Hershell Ct
2 Deanhill Ct
3 Park Sheen
4 Furness Lo
5 Merricks Ct
C4 1 Rann Ho
2 Craven Ho
3 John Dee Ho
4 Kindell Ho
5 Montgomery Ho
6 Avondale Ho
7 Addington Ct
8 Dovecote Gdns
9 Firmston Ho
10 Glendower Gdns
11 Chestnut Ave
12 Trehern Rd
13 Rock Ave

56
C2 1 Theodore Ho
2 Nicholas Ho
3 Bonner Ho
4 Downing Ho
5 Jansen Ho
6 Fairfax Ho
7 Devereux Ho
8 David Ho
9 Leigh Ho
10 Clipstone Ho
11 Mallet Ho
12 Arton Wilson Ho

57
B2 1 Inglis Ho
2 Ducie Ho
3 Wharncliffe Ho
4 Stanhope Ho
5 Waldegrave Ho
6 Mildmay Ho
7 Mullens Ho
C1 1 Balmoral Cl
2 Glenalmond Ho
3 Selwyn Ho
4 Keble Ho
5 Bede Ho
6 Gonville Ho
7 Magdalene Ho
8 Armstrong Ho
9 Newnham Ho
10 Somerville Ho
11 Balliol Ho
12 Windermere
13 Little Combe Cl
14 Classinghall Ho
15 Chalford Ct
16 Garden Royal
17 South Ct
18 Anne Kerr Ct
19 Ewhurst
C2 1 Geneva Ct
2 Laurel Ct
3 Cambalt Ho
4 Langham Ct
5 Lower Pk
6 King's Keep
7 Whitnell Ct
8 Whitehead Ho
9 Halford Ho
10 Humphry Ho
11 Jellicoe Ho
C3 1 Olivette St
2 Mascotte Rd
3 Glegg Pl
4 Crown Ct
5 Charlwood Terr
6 Percy Laurie Ho

58
A2 1 Claremont
2 Downside
3 Cavendish Cl
4 Ashcombe Ct
5 Carltons The
6 Espirit Ho
7 Millbrooke Ct
8 Coysh Ct
9 Keswick Hts
10 Lincoln Ho
11 Avon Ct
B2 1 Keswick Broadway
2 Burlington Mews
3 Cambria Lo
4 St Stephen's Gdns
5 Atlantic Ho
6 Burton Lo
7 Manfred Ct
8 Meadow Bank
9 Hooper Ho
10 Aspire Bld
C2 1 Pembridge Pl
2 Adelaide Rd
3 London Ct
4 Windsor Ct
5 Westminster Ct
6 Fullers Ho
7 Bridge Pk
8 Lambeth Ct
9 Milton Ct
10 Norfolk Mans
11 Francis Snary Lo
12 Bush Cotts
13 Downbury Mews
14 Newton's Yd

59
A2 1 Fairfield Ct
2 Blackmore Ho
3 Lancaster Mews
4 Cricketers Mews
5 College Mews
6 Arndale Wlk
B4 1 Molasses Ho
2 Molasses Row
3 Cinnamon Row
4 Calico Ho
5 Calico Row
6 Port Ho
7 Square Rigger Row
8 Trade Twr
9 Ivory Ho
10 Spice Ct
11 Sherwood Ct
12 Mendip Ct
13 Chalmers Ho
14 Coral Row
15 Ivory Sq
16 Kingfisher Ho
C3 1 Burke Ho
2 Fox Ho
3 Buxton Ho
4 Pitt Ho
5 Ramsey Ho
6 Beverley Cl
7 Florence Ho
8 Linden Ct
9 Dorcas Ct
10 Johnson Ct
11 Agnes Ct
12 Hilltop Ct
13 Courtyard The
14 Old Laundry The
15 Oberstein Rd
16 Fineran Ct
17 Sangora Rd
18 Harvard Mans
19 Plough Mews
C4 1 Benham Cl
2 Milner Ho
3 McManus Ho
4 Wilberforce Ho
5 Wheeler Ct
6 Sporle Ct
7 Holliday Sq
8 John Parker Sq
9 Carmichael Cl
10 Fenner Sq
11 Clark Lawrence Ct
12 Shaw Ct
13 Sendall Ct
14 Livingstone Rd
15 Farrant Ho
16 Jackson Ho
17 Darien Ho
18 Shepard Ho
19 Ganley Ct
20 Arthur Newton Ho
21 Chesterton Ho
22 John Kirk Ho
23 Mantua St
24 Heaver Rd
25 Candlemakers

60
A4 1 Kiloh Ct
2 Lanner Ho
3 Griffon Ho
4 Kestrel Ho
5 Kite Ho
6 Peregrine Ho
7 Hawk Ho
8 Inkster Ho
9 Harrier Ho
10 Eagle Hts
11 Kingfisher Ct
12 Lavender Terr
13 Temple Ho
14 Ridley Ho
15 Eden Ho
16 Hertford Ct
17 Nepaul Rd
C1 1 Rayne Ho
2 St Anthony's Ct
3 Earlsthorpe Mews
4 Nightingale Mans
C4 1 Shaftesbury Park Chambers
2 Selborne
3 Rush Hill Mews
4 Marmion Mews
5 Crosland Pl
6 Craven Mews
7 Garfield Mews
8 Audley Cl
9 Basnett Rd
10 Tyneham Cl
11 Woodmere Cl

61
A4 1 Turnchapel Mews
2 Redwood Mews
3 Phil Brown Pl
4 Bev Callender Cl
5 Keith Connor Cl
6 Tessa Sanderson Pl
7 Daley Thompson Way
8 Rashleigh Ct
9 Abberley Mews
10 Willow Lodge
11 Beaufoy Rd
B1 1 Joseph Powell Cl
2 Cavendish Mans
3 Westlands Terr
4 Cubitt Ho
5 Hawkesworth Ho
6 Normanton Ho

7 Eastman Ho
8 Couchman Ho
9 Poynders Ct
10 Selby Ho
11 Valentine Ho
12 Gorham Ho
13 Deauville Mans
14 Deauville Ct
B2 1 Timothy Cl
2 Shaftesbury Mews
3 Brook Ho
4 Grover Ho
5 Westbrook Ho
6 Hewer Ho
7 Batten Ho
8 Mandeville Ho
9 George Beare Lo
B3 1 Polygon The
2 Windsor Ct
3 Trinity Cl
4 Studios The
5 Bourne Ho
B4 1 Clapham Manor Ct
2 Clarke Ho
3 Gables The
4 Sycamore Mews
5 Maritime Ho
6 Rectory Gdns
7 Floris Pl
C1 1 Parrington Ho
2 Savill Ho
3 Blackwell Ho
4 Bruce Ho
5 Victoria Ct
6 Victoria Ho
7 Belvedere Ct
8 Ingram Lo
9 Viney Ct
10 Bloomsbury Ho
11 Belgravia Ho
12 Barnsbury Ho
C3 1 Kendoa Rd
2 Felmersham Cl
3 Abbeville Mews
4 Saxon Ho
5 Gifford Ho
6 Teignmouth Cl
7 Holwood Pl
8 Oaklands Pl
9 Wilberforce Mews
10 William Bonney Est
C4 1 Chelsham Ho
2 Lynde Ho
3 Greener Ho
4 Towns Ho
5 Hugh Morgan Ho
6 Roy Ridley Ho
7 Lendal Terr
8 Slievemore Cl
9 Cadmus Cl
10 Clapham North Bsns Ctr

62

A2 1 King's Mews
2 Clapham Court Terr
3 Clapham Ct
4 Clapham Park Terr
5 Pembroke Ho
6 Stevenson Ho
7 Queenswood Ct
8 Oak Tree Ct
9 Park Lofts
10 Ashby Mews
A3 1 Morris Ho
2 Gye Ho
3 Clowes Ho
4 Thomas Ho
5 Stuart Ho
6 Storace Ho
7 Bedford Ho
8 Ascot Ct
9 Ascot Par
10 Ashmere Ho
11 Ashmere Gr
12 Ventura Ho
13 Vickery Ho
14 Stafford Mans
15 Beresford Ho
A4 1 Callingham Ho
2 Russell Pickering Ho
3 Ormerod Ho
4 Lopez Ho
5 Coachmaker Mews
B2 1 Beatrice Ho
2 Florence Ho
3 Evelyn Ho
4 Diana Ho
5 Brixton Hill Ct
6 Austin Ho
7 Manor Ct
8 Camsey Ho
9 Romer Ho
10 Gale Ho
11 Byrne Ho
12 Farnfield Ho
13 Marchant Ho
14 Rainsford Ho
15 Springett Ho
16 Mannering Ho
17 Waldron Ho
B3 1 Freemens Hos
2 Roger's Almshouses
3 Gresham Almshouses
4 Exbury Ho
5 Glasbury Ho
6 Dalbury Ho
7 Fosbury Ho
8 Chalbury Ho
9 Neilson-Terry Ct
10 Pavilion Mans
11 Daisy Dormer Ct
12 George Lashwood Ct
13 Marie Lloyd Ct
14 Trinity Homes
15 Lethaby Ho
16 Edmundsbury Ct Est
17 Regis Pl
18 Marlborough Mews
19 Alpha Ho
20 Beta Pl
21 Cedars Ho
B4 1 Turberville Ho
2 Thrayle Ho
3 Percheron Ct
4 Draymans Ct
C1 1 Eccleston Ho
2 Scarsbrook Ho
3 Purser Ho
4 Rudhall Ho
5 Hardham Ho
6 Heywood Ho
7 Haworth Ho
8 Birch Ho
9 Lansdell Ho
10 Lomley Ho
11 Laughton Ho
12 Woodruff Ho
13 Bascome St
14 Dudley Mews
15 Herbert Mews
16 Blades Lo
17 Dick Shepherd Ct
18 Charman Ho
19 Morden Ho
20 Bishop Ct
21 Blackburn Ct
22 Leigh Ct
23 John Conwey Ho
24 Bristowe Cl
C2 1 Crownstone Ct
2 Brockwell Ct
3 Nevena Ct
4 St George's Residences
5 Hanover Mans
6 Fleet Ho
7 Langbourne Ho
8 Turnmill Ho
9 Walker Mews
10 Cossar Mews
11 Carter Ho
C3 1 Electric Mans
2 Electric La
3 Connaught Mans
4 Clifton Mans
5 Hereford Ho
6 Chaplin Ho
7 Brixton Oval
8 Lord David Pitt Ho
9 Marcus Garvey Way
10 Montego Cl
11 Bob Marley Way
12 Leeson Rd
C4 1 Buckmaster Cl
2 Albemarle Ho
3 Goodwood Mans
4 Angell Park Gdns
5 Fyfield Rd
6 Howard Ho
7 Harris Ho
8 Broadoak Ct
9 Burgate Ct
10 Witchwood Ho
11 Blacktree Mews
12 Chartham Ct
13 Chilham Ct
14 Northgate Ct
15 Westgate Ct
16 Dover Mans

63

A3 1 Mahatma Gandhi Ind Est
2 Dylan Rd
3 Bessemer Park Ind Est
4 Pablo Neruda Cl
5 Langston Hughes Cl
6 Walt Whitman Cl
7 James Joyce Wlk
8 Alice Walker Cl
9 Louise Bennett Cl
10 Chadacre Ho
11 Burwood Ho
12 Pyrford Ho
13 Wangford Ho
14 Ashford Ho
15 Kenwood Ho
16 Moyne Ho
17 Elveden Ho
18 Carrara Cl
19 Broughton Dr
20 Angela Davis Ind Est
21 Tilia Wlk
22 County Ho
A4 1 Mallams Mews
2 Amberley Ct
3 Harper Ho
4 Leicester Ho
5 Station Ave
6 Wellfit St
7 Loughborough Ct
8 Belinda Rd
9 Higgs Ind Est
C3 1 Shaftesbury Ct
2 Mayhew Ct
3 Morris Ct
4 Swinburne Ct
5 Perth Ct
6 Tayside Ct
7 Matlock Ct
8 Hunter Ct
9 Turner Ct

64

A2 1 Velde Way
2 Delft Way
3 Arnhem Way
4 Isel Way
5 Kempis Way
6 Terborch Way
7 Steen Way
8 Deventer Cres
9 Nimegen Way
10 Hilversum Cres
11 St Barnabas Cl
A4 1 Harfield Gdns
2 Karen Ct
3 Seavington Ho
4 Appleshaw Ho
5 Birdsall Ho
6 Whitney Ho
7 Wheatland Ho
8 Wilton Ho
9 Walcot Ho
10 Whaddon Ho
11 Melbreak Ho
12 Ledbury Ho
13 Tidworth Ho
14 Riseholme Ho
15 Ringmer Ho
16 Petworth Ho
17 Stagshaw Ho
18 Ivybridge Ho
19 Inwood Ho
20 Gatcombe Ho
21 Felbridge Ho
22 Cowdray Ho
B3 1 Dulwich Mews
2 St James's Cloisters
C2 1 Dorothy Charrington Ho
2 Keswick Ct
3 Kendall Ct
4 Halliwell Ct

65

A4 1 Tilling Ho
2 Goodwin Ho
3 Tyrells Ct
4 Citron Terr
5 Basswood Cl
6 Cheam St
C3 1 Laxton Path
2 Barlings Ho
3 Bayfield Ho
4 Coston Wlk
5 Coverham Ho
6 Gateley Ho
7 Dereham Ho
8 Greenwood Ho
9 Hilton Ho
10 Goodall Ho
11 Horsley Ho
12 Jordan Ho

67

B4 1 Bankside Ave
2 Elder Wlk
3 Yew Tree Cl
4 Mill Ho

68

C3 1 Farnborough Ho
2 Rushmere Ho
3 Horndean Cl
4 Highcross Way
5 Timsbury Wlk
6 Foxcombe Rd
7 Ryefield Path
8 Greatham Wlk
9 Gosport Ho
10 Stoatley Ho
11 Milland Ho
12 Clanfield Ho
13 Fareham Ho
14 Grayswood Point
C4 1 Woodcott Ho
2 Lyndhurst Ho
3 Wheatley Ho
4 Allbrook Ho
5 Bordon Wlk
6 Chilcombe Ho
7 Vicarage Ct
8 Shawford Ct
9 Eastleigh Wlk
10 Kings Ct
11 Somborne Ho

69

A3 1 Ramsdean Ho
2 Purbrook Ho
3 Portsea Ho
4 Blendworth Point
5 Eashing Point
6 Hindhead Point
7 Hilsea Point
8 Witley Point
9 Buriton Ho
10 Grateley Ho
11 Hascombe Ho
12 Dunhill Point
13 Westmark Point
14 Longmoor Point
15 Cadnam Point
B4 1 Cumberland Ho
2 Devonshire Ho
3 Cornwall Ho
4 Norfolk Ho
5 Leicester Ho
6 Warwick Ho
7 Sutherland Ho
8 Carmarthen Ho
9 Worcester Ho
10 Rutland Ho
11 Paddock Way
C3 1 Sandringham Cl
2 Eastwick Ct
3 Oatlands Ct
4 Banning Ho
5 Grantley Ho
6 Caryl Ho
7 Duncombe Ho

8 Chilworth Ct
9 Kent Lo
10 Turner Lo
11 Marlborough
12 Parkland Gdns
13 Lewesdon Cl
14 Pines Ct
15 Ashtead Ct
16 Mynterne Ct
17 Arden
18 Stephen Ct
19 Marsham Ct
20 Doradus Ct
21 Acorns The
22 Heritage Ho
23 Conifer Ct
24 Spencer Ho
25 Chartwell
26 Blenheim
27 Chivelston
28 Greenfield Ho
29 Oakman Ho
30 Radley Lo
31 Simon Lo
32 Admirals Ct
C4 1 Brett Ho
2 Brett House Cl
3 Sylva Ct
4 Ross Ct
5 Potterne Cl
6 Stourhead Cl
7 Fleur Gates
8 Greenwood

70

A3 1 William Harvey Ho
2 Highview Ct
3 Cameron Ct
4 Galgate Cl
5 Green Ho The
6 King Charles Wlk
7 Florys Ct
8 Augustus Ct
9 Albert Ct
10 Hertford Lo
11 Mortimer Lo
12 Allenswood
13 Ambleside
14 Hansler Ct
15 Roosevelt Ct

71

B2 1 Beemans Row
2 St Andrew's Ct
3 Townsend Mews
4 Sheringham Mews

72

C2 1 Upper Tooting Park Mans
2 Cecil Mans
3 Marius Mans
4 Boulevard The
5 Elmfield Mans
6 Holdernesse Rd
7 Lumiere Ct
C3 1 Heslop Ct
2 St James's Terr
3 Boundaries Mans
4 Station Par
5 Old Dairy Mews
C4 1 Hollies Way
2 Endlesham Ct

73

A3 1 Holbeach Mews
2 Hildreth Street Mews
3 Coalbrook Mans
4 Hub Buildings The
5 Metropolis Apartments
A4 1 Meyer Ho
2 Faraday Ho
3 Hales Ho
4 Frankland Ho
5 Graham Ho
6 Gibbs Ho
7 Dalton Ho
8 Ainslie Wlk
9 Rokeby Ho
10 Caistor Ho
11 Ivanhoe Ho
12 Catherine Baird Ct
13 Marmion Ho
14 Devonshire Ct
15 Blueprint Apartments
B4 1 Limerick Ct
2 Homewoods
3 Jewell Ho
4 Glanville Ho
5 Dan Bryant Ho
6 Olding Ho
7 Quennel Ho
8 Weir Ho
9 West Ho
10 Neville Ct
11 Friday Grove Mews
C3 1 Sinclair Ho
2 MacGregor Ho
3 Ingle Ho
4 St Andrews Mews
C4 1 Riley Ho
2 Bennett Ho
3 White Ho
4 Rodgers Ho
5 Dumphreys Ho
6 Homan Ho
7 Prendergast Ho
8 Hutchins Ho
9 Whiteley Ho
10 Tresidder Ho
11 Primrose Ct
12 Angus Ho
13 Currie Ho

74

A1 1 De Montfort Ct
2 Leigham Hall Par
3 Leigham Hall
4 Endsleigh Mans
5 John Kirk Ho
6 Raebarn Ct
7 Wavel Ct
8 Homeleigh Ct
9 Howland Ho
10 Beauclerk Ho
11 Bertrand Ho
12 Drew Ho
13 Dowes Ho
14 Dunton Ho
15 Raynald Ho
16 Sackville Ho
17 Thurlow Ho
18 Astoria Mans
A2 1 Wyatt Park Mans
2 Broadlands Mans
3 Stonehill's Mans
4 Streatleigh Par
5 Dorchester Ct
6 Picture Ho
A3 1 Beaumont Ho
2 Christchurch Ho
3 Staplefield Cl
4 Chipstead Ho
5 Coulsdon Ho
6 Conway Ho
7 Telford Avenue Mans
8 Telford Parade Mans
9 Wavertree Ct
10 Hartswood Ho
11 Wray Ho
A4 1 Picton Ho
2 Rigg Ho
3 Watson Ho
4 MacArthur Ho
5 Sandon Ho
6 Thorold Ho
7 Pearce Ho
8 Mudie Ho
9 Miller Ho
10 Lycett Ho
11 Lafone Ho
12 Lucraft Ho
13 Freeman Ho
14 New Park Par
15 Argyll Ct
16 Dumbarton Ct
17 Kintyre Ct
18 Cotton Ho
19 Crossman Hos
20 Cameford Ct
21 Parsons Ho
22 Brindley Ho
23 Arkwright Ho
24 Perry Ho
25 Brunel Ho
26 New Park Ct
27 Tanhurst Ho
28 Hawkshaw Cl
B1 1 Carisbrooke Ct
2 Pembroke Lo
3 Willow Ct
4 Poplar Ct
5 Mountview
6 Spa View
B3 1 Charlwood Ho
2 Earlswood Ho
3 Balcombe Ho
4 Claremont Cl
5 Holbrook Ho
6 Gwynne Ho
7 Kynaston Ho
8 Tillman Ho
9 Regents Lo
10 Hazelmere Ct
11 Dykes Ct
B4 1 Archbishop's Pl
2 Witley Ho
3 Outwood Ho
4 Dunsfold Ho
5 Deepdene Lo
6 Warnham Ho
7 Albury Lo
8 Tilford Ho
9 Elstead Ho
10 Thursley Ho
11 Brockham Ho
12 Capel Lo
13 Leith Ho
14 Fairview Ho
15 Weymouth Ct
16 Ascalon Ct
17 China Mews
18 Rush Common Mews
C3 1 Valens Ho
2 Loveday Ho
3 Strode Ho
4 Ethelworth Ct
5 Harbin Ho
6 Brooks Ho
7 Godolphin Ho
8 Sheppard Ho
9 McCormick Ho
10 Taylor Ho
11 Saunders Ho
12 Talcott Path
13 Derrick Ho
14 Williams Ho
15 Baldwin Ho
16 Churston Cl
17 Neil Wates Cres
18 Burnell Ho
19 Portland Ho
C4 1 Ellacombe Ho
2 Booth Ho
3 Hathersley Ho
4 Brereton Ho
5 Holdsworth Ho
6 Dearmer Ho
7 Cherry Cl
8 Greenleaf Cl
9 Longford Wlk
10 Scarlette Manor Wlk
11 Chandlers Way
12 Upgrove Manor Way
13 Ropers Wlk
14 Tebbs Ho
15 Bell Ho
16 Worthington Ho
17 Courier Ho
18 Mackie Ho
19 Hamers Ho
20 Kelyway Ho
21 Harriet Tubman Cl
22 Estoria Cl
23 Leckhampton Pl
24 Scotia Rd
25 Charles Haller St
26 Sidmouth Ho
27 Hunter Ct
28 Onslow Lo
29 William Winter Ct
30 Langthorne Lo

75

A1 1 Thanet Ho
2 Chapman Ho
3 Beaufoy Ho
4 Easton Ho
5 Roberts Ho
6 Lloyd Ct
7 Kershaw Ho
8 Wakeling Ho
9 Edridge Ho
10 Jeston Ho
11 Lansdowne Wood Cl
12 Rotary Lo
C2 1 Welldon Ct
2 Coppedhall
3 Shackleton Ct
4 Bullfinch Ct
5 Gannet Ct
6 Fulmar Ct
7 Heron Ct
8 Petrel Ct
9 Falcon Ct
10 Eagle Ct
11 Dunnock Ct
12 Dunlin Ct
13 Cormorant Ct
14 Oak Lodge
15 Corfe Lodge

76

C1 1 Tunbridge Ct
2 Harrogate Ct
3 Bath Ct
4 Leamington Ct
5 Porlock Ho
6 Cissbury Ho
7 Eddisbury Ho
8 Dundry Ho
9 Silbury Ho
10 Homildon Ho
11 Highgate Ho
12 Richmond Ho
13 Pendle Ho
14 Tynwald Ho
15 Wirrall Ho
16 Greyfriars

www.philips-maps.co.uk

First published 2001 by

Philip's, a division of
Octopus Publishing Group Ltd
www.octopusbooks.co.uk
2–4 Heron Quays
London E14 4JP
An Hachette Livre UK Company
www.hachettelivre.co.uk

Third edition 2007
Third impression 2008

LONCB

Spiral-bound
ISBN 978-0-540-09044-0

Perfect-bound
ISBN 978-0-540-09045-7

Hardback (navy)
ISBN 978-0-540-09107-2

Hardback (pink)
ISBN 978-0-540-09108-9

Hardback (red)
ISBN 978-0-540-09110-2

Hardback (grey)
ISBN 978-0-540 09111-9

Hardback (green)
ISBN 978-0-540-09113-3

Hardback (brown)
ISBN 978-0-540-09115-7

Hardback (leopardskin pattern)
ISBN 978-0-540-09443-1

Printed and bound in Dubai by Oriental

NOTES

NOTES

NOTES

NOTES

NOTES

NOTES

NOTES

NOTES

NOTES

NOTES

Theatres and cinemas

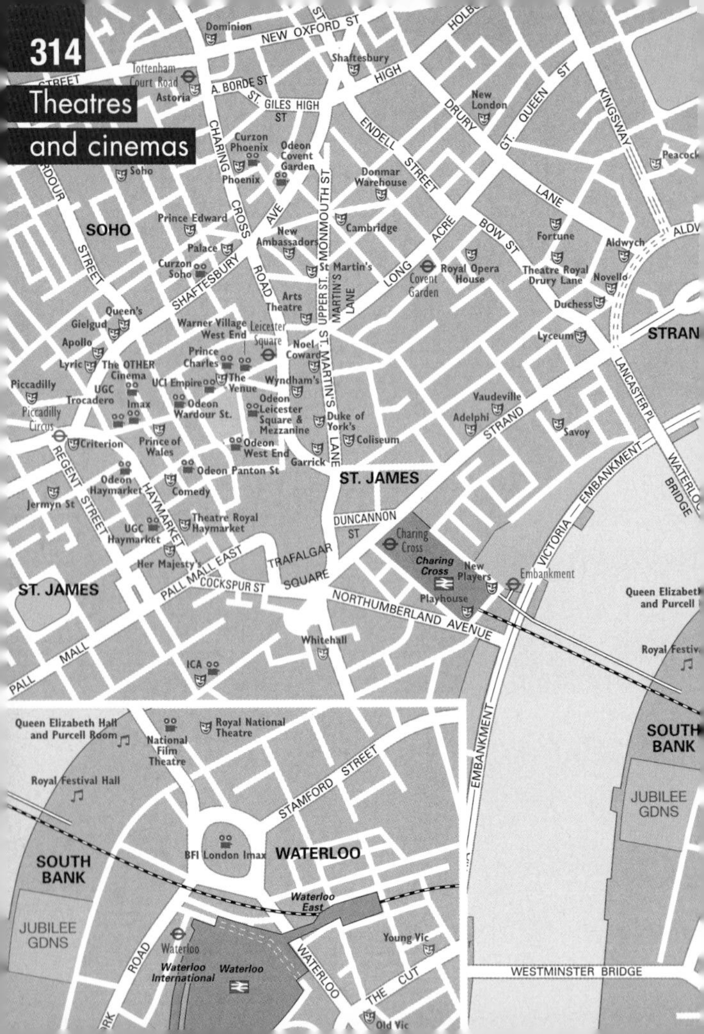
Dominion
NEW OXFORD ST
Shaftesbury
HOLBO
Tottenham Court Road
Astoria
A. BORDE ST
ST. GILES HIGH ST
HIGH
New London
DRURY
GT. QUEEN ST
KINGSWAY
ENDELL STREET
CHARING CROSS ROAD
Curzon Phoenix
Odeon Covent Garden
Phoenix
Soho
Peacock
Donmar Warehouse
MONMOUTH ST
SOHO
Prince Edward
AVE
Cambridge
LANE
New Ambassadors
Fortune
BOW ST
ALDW
Palace
Aldwych
Curzon Soho
SHAFTESBURY
St Martin's
LONG ACRE
Covent Garden
Royal Opera House
Theatre Royal Drury Lane
Novello
STREET
UPPER ST. MARTIN'S LANE
Arts Theatre
Duchess
Queen's
Gielgud
Warner Village West End
Leicester Square
STRAN
Apollo
Prince Charles
Noel Coward
Lyceum
Lyric
The OTHER Cinema
ST. MARTIN'S LANE
UCI Empire
The Venue
Wyndham's
LANCASTER PL
Piccadilly
UGC Trocadero
Imax
Odeon Wardour St.
Odeon Leicester Square & Mezzanine
Vaudeville
Piccadilly Circus
Duke of York's
Adelphi
Savoy
STRAND
Criterion
Prince of Wales
Odeon West End
Coliseum
REGENT STREET
Garrick
EMBANKMENT
WATERLOO BRIDGE
Odeon Panton St
ST. JAMES
Odeon Haymarket
HAYMARKET
Comedy
Jermyn St
Theatre Royal Haymarket
DUNCANNON ST
VICTORIA
UGC Haymarket
Charing Cross
Her Majesty's
TRAFALGAR SQUARE
PALL MALL EAST
Charing Cross
New Players
Embankment
ST. JAMES
COCKSPUR ST
Queen Elizabeth Hall and Purcell
Playhouse
NORTHUMBERLAND AVENUE
Whitehall
Royal Festiva
PALL MALL
ICA
Queen Elizabeth Hall and Purcell Room
National Film Theatre
Royal National Theatre
SOUTH BANK
EMBANKMENT
Royal Festival Hall
STAMFORD STREET
JUBILEE GDNS
SOUTH BANK
BFI London Imax
WATERLOO
Waterloo East
JUBILEE GDNS
Young Vic
Waterloo
ROAD
WATERLOO
Waterloo International
Waterloo
THE CUT
WESTMINSTER BRIDGE
Old Vic

Reg. user No. 08/1101/LS

MAYOR OF LONDON

Website
tfl.gov.uk

24 hour travel informati
020 7222 12